American Government

Power and Purpose

EIGHTH EDITION

FOR OUR FAMILIES:

Angele, Anna, and Jason Lowi
Sandy, Cindy, and Alex Ginsberg
Rise, Nilsa, and Seth Shepsle

American Government

Power and Purpose

EIGHTH
EDITION

Theodore J. Lowi
Cornell University

Benjamin Ginsberg
The Johns Hopkins University

and

Kenneth A. Shepsle
Harvard University

W • W • NORTON & COMPANY  NEW YORK • LONDON

W. W. Norton & Company has been independent since its founding in 1923, when William Warder Norton and Mary D. Herter Norton first published lectures delivered at the People's Institute, the adult education division of New York City's Cooper Union. The Nortons soon expanded their program beyond the Institute, publishing books by celebrated academics from America and abroad. By mid-century, the two major pillars of Norton's publishing program—trade books and college texts—were firmly established. In the 1950s, the Norton family transferred control of the company to its employees, and today—with a staff of four hundred and a comparable number of trade, college, and professional titles published each year—W. W. Norton & Company stands as the largest and oldest publishing house owned wholly by its employees.

The text of this book is composed in Berling Roman
with the display set in Bawdy.
Composition by TSI Graphics
Manufacturing by Quebecor World Versailles
Book designer: Sandra Watanabe
Production manager: Diane O'Connor
Editor: Stephen P. Dunn
Manuscript editor: Carol Flechner
Managing editor, college: Marian Johnson
Editorial assistant: Susan Cronin
Graphic artist: John McAusland

Library of Congress Cataloging-in-Publication Data

Lowi, Theodore J.
    American government: power and purpose / Theodore J. Lowi, Benjamin Ginsberg, and Kenneth A. Shepsle.—8th ed.
        p. cm.
    Includes bibliographical references and index.
    ISBN 0-393-92482-3
    1. United States—Politics and government. I. Ginsberg, Benjamin. II. Shepsle, Kenneth
A. III. Title.

    JK276.L69 2004b
    320.473—dc22

                                                                          2003070218

W. W. Norton & Company, Inc.,
500 Fifth Avenue, New York, NY 10110
www.wwnorton.com
W. W. Norton & Company Ltd.,
Castle House, 75/76 Wells Street, London W1T 3QT
1 2 3 4 5 6 7 8 9 0

Contents

PART 3   POLITICS   363

Preface

Someone once asked if it is difficult for scholars to "write down" to introductory students. No. It is difficult to "write up" to them. Introductory students, of whatever age or reading level, need more, require more, and expect more of a book. A good teaching book, like a good novel or play, is written on two levels. One is the level of the narrative, the story line, the characters in action. The second is the level of character development, of the argument of the book or play. We would not be the first to assert that theater is an aspect of politics, but our book may be unusual to the extent that we took that assertion as a guide. We have packed it full of narrative—with characters and with the facts about the complex situations in which they find themselves. We have at the same time been determined not to lose sight of the second level, yet we have tried to avoid making the second level so prominent as to define us as preachers rather than teachers.

Our collective one-hundred-plus years of teaching has taught us not to underestimate students. Their raw intelligence is not satisfied until a second level provides a logic linking the disparate parts of what we were asserting was a single system of government. And these linkages had to be made in ordinary language. We hope we brought this to the book.

We hope also that we brought over from our teaching experience a full measure of sympathy for all who teach the introductory course, most particularly those who are obliged to teach the course from departmental necessity rather than voluntarily as a desired part of their career. And we hope our book will help them appreciate the course as we do—as an opportunity to make sense of a whole political system, one's own, and one of the largest, most durable, and most consequential ever. Much can be learned about the system from a re-examination of the innumerable familiar facts under the still more challenging condition that the facts be somehow interesting, significant, and, above all, linked.

All Americans are to a great extent familiar with the politics and government of their own country. No fact is intrinsically difficult to grasp, and in such an open society, facts abound. In America, many facts are commonplace that are suppressed elsewhere. The ubiquity of political commonplaces is a problem, but it can be turned into a virtue. These very commonplaces give us a vocabulary that is widely shared, and such a vocabulary enables us to communicate effectively at the first level of the book, avoiding abstract concepts and professional language (jargon). Reaching beyond the commonplaces to the second level also identifies what is to us the single most important task of the teacher of political science—to confront the million commonplaces and to choose from among them the small number of really significant concepts. Students give us proportion; we must in turn give the students priorities. Virtually everything we need to know about the institutions and processes of government and politics is readily at hand. But to choose a few commonplaces from the millions—there's the rub.

THE APPROACH OF THE BOOK

This book was written for faculty and students who are looking for a little more than just "nuts and bolts" and who are drawn to an analytical perspective. Although we don't specifically address political-science methodology, the book serves as an integration of the historical-institutional and rational-choice perspectives and as a set of tools (the "Five Principles of Politics") that students can use to think analytically about politics. The feedback we have received thus far from students and fellow professors gives us confidence that the most appealing feature of the book is the analytical framework based on the "five principles of politics." With this new eighth edition, we hope to broaden our appeal among political scientists and their students by incorporating new applications of the "five principles of politics in action" and new pedagogy that keeps students focused on the main points of each chapter. The book is based on the idea that the best way to teach students is to expose them to repeated applications of a small number of the core ideas of the discipline in a presentation devoid of the usual clutter. We hope that students will get from this book more than just a bunch of facts about American government; we hope that they will develop a way of thinking about and analyzing politics.

The book's analytical approach is incorporated in the following ways:

Emphasis on five fundamental, underlying principles of politics provides students with the "tools" for analysis. Politics is messy, complex, and contentious. How do we make sense of what seems too large and impossible to explain? In explaining these questions throughout the chapter, we repeatedly draw on five fundamental principles of politics:

- All political behavior has a purpose.
- All politics is collective action.
- Institutions matter.
- Political outcomes are the products of individual preferences and institutional procedures.
- History matters.

The application of the five principles to each chapter's topic is first introduced in a **"Previewing the Principles" box** at the beginning of every chapter. Each time one of these principles is used in the analysis, a marginal icon will appear, reminding students of the core principle. These principles are also summarized in a **"Principles of Politics in Review" box** toward the conclusion of every chapter. Our goal is to equip students with the tools to evaluate the political world that they observe around them.

Four new applications of the "Five Principles of Politics." Merely knowing a principle is different from understanding it. For students to analyze politics, they need a framework (the five principles) and models of how to use the framework. Students also need to be prompted to use the framework on their own. In this eighth edition, we've added four new applications that show students how to apply the framework and then actively use it on their own in in-class simulations and Web-based exercises.

1. **"Applying the Five Principles of Politics" boxed case studies** (one per chapter). These case studies go beyond the text and apply one or more of the five principles to a central, topical question such as "Why Can't Congress Get Anything Done?" or "Was It Rational to Vote for Ralph Nader?"
2. **"Politics in the News: Reading between the Lines"** (one per chapter). These two-page spreads show students how to use the five principles to better understand current politics reported in the news, such as Bush's latest tax cut or the 2004 presidential election. This feature includes an excerpt from a *New York Times* article, a bulleted summary of the article's central issues, and a bulleted "political analysis" showing how to use the five principles to analyze the story.
3. **"Playing Politics" game-theory-based simulations workbook** (authored by Tobin Grant, Southern Illinois University—Carbondale). Active involvement by students is an essential part of effective learning. These role-playing simulations will allow students to put themselves in the shoes of strategic political actors and how they respond to a wide scenario of political situations. The simulations are designed to take from 30 to 45 minutes in class and include an out-of-class written analysis by students. They are a perfect supplement to use in discussion sections.
4. **Web-site exercise based on "Applying the Five Principles of Politics" and "Politics in the News: Reading between the Lines."** Another component of "active learning," these exercises help students build their analytical skills, while demonstrating that the five principles of politics can be used to interpret current political events. By repeated practice of "analyzing politics," students internalize the five core principles and, as citizens, are able to draw on them for the rest of their lives. To preview these exercises, go to www.wwnorton.com/lowi8.

An "analytic narrative" ties the five principles together. As teachers and scholars, we believe that is is easiest to understand the system of American government by looking at political institutions (Principle 3). In every chapter, we look at an institution's source and its historical development (Principle 5). Along the way, we offer historical accounts of important events and analysis of the individual decisions and choices by political actors (Principle 1). Throughout, we analyze political conflict and compromise (Principle 2) and the outcomes of these conflicts and compromises (Principle 4). History gives each chapter a narrative flow, making the book more engaging to read. The focus on individual decisions and choices and the conflicts between them explains not only political outcomes such as policy, but also how and why institutions develop and change. For example, in discussing the presidency, we evaluate how presidents have used the threat of a veto and "going public" as a means of building power vis-à-vis Congress. By the time students get to the end of this chapter, they will understand why some policies get adopted while others don't. But students will also have a richer sense of why today's institutions function as they do and how they interact with each other.

THE ORGANIZATION OF THE BOOK

The book is divided into three parts, reflecting the historical process by which Americans have used governmental power. Part 1, "Foundations," comprises the chapters concerned with the bases of political analysis and the writing of the rules of the "game." The founding of 1787–1789 put it all together, but that was actually a second effort after a first failure. The original contract, the Articles of Confederation, did not achieve an acceptable balance—too much freedom and not enough power. The second founding, the Constitution ratified in 1789, was itself an imperfect effort to establish the rules, and within two years new terms were added—the first ten amendments, called the Bill of Rights. And for the next century and a half following their ratification in 1791, the courts played umpire and translator in the struggle to interpret those terms. Chapter 1 introduces our five analytical principles of politics. Chapter 2 concentrates on the founding itself. Chapters 3 and 4 chronicle the long struggle to establish what was meant by the three great principles of limited government: federalism, separation of powers, and individual liberties and rights.

Part 2, "Institutions," includes the chapters sometimes referred to as the "nuts and bolts." But none of these particles of government means anything except in the larger context of the goals governments must meet and the limits, especially of procedure, that have been imposed upon them. Chapter 5 is an introduction to the fundamental problem of representative government as this has been institutionalized in Congress. Congress, with all its problems, is the most creative legislative body in the world. But how well does Congress provide a meeting ground between consent and governing? How are society's demands taken into account in debates on the floor of Congress and deliberations by its committees? What interests turn out to be most effectively "represented" in Congress? What is the modern Congress's constituency?

Chapter 6 explores the same questions for the presidency. Although Article II of the Constitution provides that the president should see that the laws made by Congress are "faithfully executed," the presidency was always part of our theory of representative government, and the modern presidency has increasingly become a law *maker* rather than merely a law implementer. What, then, does the strong presidency do to the conduct and the consequences of representative government? Chapter 7 treats the executive branch as an entity separate from the presidency, but ultimately it has to be brought back into the general process of representative government. That, indeed, is the overwhelming problem of what we call "bureaucracy in a democracy." After spelling out the organization and workings of "the bureaucracy" in detail, we then turn to an evaluation of the role of Congress and the president in imposing some political accountability on an executive branch composed of roughly 5 million civilian and military personnel.

Chapter 8 on the judiciary should not be lost in the shuffle. Referred to by Hamilton as "the least dangerous branch," the judiciary truly has become a co-equal branch to such an extent that if Hamilton were alive today, he would probably eat his words.

Part 3 we entitle simply "Politics" because politics encompasses all the efforts by any and all individuals and groups inside as well as outside the government to determine what government will do and on whose behalf it will be done. Our chapters take the order of our conception of how politics developed since the Age of Revolution and how politics works today: Chapter 9, "Public Opinion"; Chapter 10, "Elections"; Chapter 11, "Political Parties"; Chapter 12, "Groups and Interests"; and Chapter 13, "The Media."

Part 4 is entitled "Governance." These are chapters primarily about public policies, which are the most deliberate and goal-oriented aspects of the still-larger phenomenon of "government in action." We begin Chapter 14, "Government in Action: Public Policy and the Economy," by looking at policies that are concerned with the conduct of business, the obligations of employers, the rights and limits of workers to organize, and the general ability of the economy to operate without flying apart. Chapter 15, "Government and Society," looks at policies that affect society at large, outside and beyond the economic marketplace. Since ours is a commercial society, many policies aimed at the society have direct economic consequences. For example, many aspects of what we call the welfare system are social policies, but they have a profound effect on the economy because welfare, as we put it, changes the rules governing who shall be poor. Chapter 16, "Foreign Policy and Democracy," turns to the international realm and America's place in it. Our concern here is to understand American foreign policies and why we have adopted them. Given the traditional American fear of "the state" and the genuine danger of international involvements to domestic democracy, a chapter on foreign policies is essential to a book on American government and also reveals a great deal about America as a culture.

ACKNOWLEDGMENTS

Our students at Cornell, Johns Hopkins, and Harvard have already been identified as an essential factor in the writing of this book. They have been our most immediate intellectual community, a hospitable one indeed. Another part of our community, perhaps a large suburb, is the discipline of political science itself. Our debt to the scholarship of our colleagues is scientifically measurable, probably to several decimal points, in the footnotes of each chapter. Despite many complaints that the field is too scientific or not scientific enough, political science is alive and well in the United States. It is an aspect of democracy itself, and it has grown and changed in response to the developments in government and politics that we have chronicled in our book. If we did a "time line" on the history of political science, as we have done in each chapter of the book, it would show a close association with developments in "the American state." Sometimes the discipline has been out of phase and critical; at other times, it has been in phase and perhaps apologetic. But political science has never been at a loss for relevant literature, and without it, our job would have been impossible.

There have, of course, been individuals on whom we have relied in particular. Of all writers, living and dead, we find ourselves most in debt to the writing of two—James Madison and Alexis de Tocqueville. Many other great authors have shaped us as they have shaped all political scientists. But Madison and Tocqueville have stood for us not only as the bridge to all timeless political problems; they represent the ideal of political science itself—that political science must be steadfastly scientific in the search for what is, yet must keep alive a strong sense of what ought to be, recognizing that democracy is neither natural nor invariably good, and must be fiercely dedicated to constant critical analysis of all political institutions in order to contribute to the maintenance of a favorable balance between individual freedom and public power.

We are pleased to acknowledge our debt to the many colleagues who had a direct and active role in criticism and preparation of the manuscript. The first edition was read and reviewed by Gary Bryner, Brigham Young University; James F. Herndon, Virginia Polytechnic Institute and State University; James W. Riddlesperger, Jr., Texas Christian University; John Schwarz, University of Arizona; Toni-Michelle Travis, George Mason University; and Lois Vietri, University of Maryland. We also want to reiterate our thanks to the four colleagues who allowed us the privilege of testing a trial edition of our book by using it as the major text in their introductory American Government courses. Their reactions, and those of their students, played an important role in our first edition. We are grateful to Gary Bryner, Brigham Young University; Allan J. Cigler, University of Kansas; Burnet V. Davis, Albion College; and Erwin A. Jaffe, California State University—Stanislaus.

For subsequent editions, we relied heavily on the thoughtful manuscript reviews we received from David Canon, University of Wisconsin; Russell Hanson, Indiana University; William Keech, Carnegie Mellon University; Donald Kettl, University of Wisconsin; Anne Khademian, University of Wisconsin; William McLauchlan, Purdue University; J. Roger Baker, Wittenburg University; James Lennertz, Lafayette College; Allan McBride, Grambling State University; Joseph Peek, Jr., Georgia State University; Grant Neeley, Texas Tech

University; Mark Graber, University of Maryland; John Gilmour, College of William and Mary; Victoria Farrar-Myers, University of Texas at Arlington; Timothy Boylan, Winthrop University; Robert Huckfeldt, University of California—Davis; Mark Joslyn, University of Kansas; Beth Leech, Rutgers University; Charles Noble, California State University, Long Beach; For the eighth edition, we benefited from the comments of Scott Ainsworth, University of Georgia; Thomas Brunell, Northern Arizona University; Daniel Carpenter, Harvard University; Brad Gomez, University of South Carolina; Paul Gronke, Reed College; Marc Hetherington, Bowdoin College; Gregory Huber, Yale University; Robert Lowry, Iowa State University; and Anthony Nownes, University of Tennessee; Scott Adler, University of Colorado—Boulder; John Coleman, University of Wisconsin—Madison; Richard Conley, University of Florida; Keith Dougherty, University of Georgia; John Ferejohn, Stanford University; Douglas Harris, Loyola College; Brian Humes, University of Nebraska—Lincoln; Jeffrey Jenkins, Northwestern University; Paul Johnson, University of Kansas; Andrew Polsky, Hunter College—CUNY; Mark Richards, Grand Valley State University; Charles Shipan, University of Iowa; Craig Volden, Ohio State University; and Garry Young, George Washington University.

We are also extremely grateful to a number of colleagues who were kind enough to lend us their classrooms. During the past eight years, we had the opportunity to lecture at a number of colleges and universities around the country and to benefit from discussing our book with those who know it best—colleagues and students who used it. We appreciate the gracious welcome we received at Austin Community College, California State University—Fullerton, University of Central Oklahoma, Emory University, Gainesville College, Georgia Southern University, Georgia State University, Golden West College, Grambling State University, University of Houston—University Park, University of Illinois—Chicago, University of Illinois—Urbana-Champaign, University of Maryland—College Park, University of Massachusetts—Amherst, Morgan State University, University of North Carolina—Chapel Hill, University of North Texas, University of Oklahoma, Oklahoma State University, Pasadena City College, University of Richmond, Sam Houston State University, San Bernadino Valley College, Santa Barbara City College, Santa Monica College, University of Southern California, Temple University, University of Texas—Austin, Texas Tech University, Virginia Commonwealth University, and University of Wisconsin–Madison.

We owe a debt to Greg Wawro of Columbia University, who served as an intellectual bridge between the sixth and seventh editions, and helped us set our sights for future editions of the book. We owe a special debt to Paul Gronke of Reed College for authoring the new "Applying the Five Principles of Politics" and "Politics in the News—Reading between the Lines" features. We also are grateful for the talents and hard work of several research assistants, whose contribution can never be adequately compensated: Mingus Mapps, Douglas Dow, John Forren, Michael Harvey, Doug Harris, Brenda Holzinger, Steve McGovern, Melody Butler, Nancy Johnson, Noah Silverman, Rebecca Fisher, David Lytell, Dennis

Merryfield, Rachel Reiss, Nandini Sathe, Rob Speel, Jennifer Waterston, and Daniel Wirls. For the seventh edition, Israel Waismel-Manor devoted a great deal of time and energy and original ideas.

Jacqueline Discenza not only typed several drafts of the manuscript, but also helped to hold the project together. We thank her for her hard work and dedication.

Theodore Lowi would like to express his gratitude to the French-American Foundation and the Gannett Foundation, whose timely invitations helped him prepare for his part of this enterprise.

Perhaps above all, we wish to thank those who kept the production and all the loose ends of the book coherent and in focus. Steve Dunn has been an extremely talented editor, continuing to offer numerous suggestions for each new edition. Carol Flechner has been a superb manuscript editor, following in the great tradition of her predecessors. Diane O'Connor has been an efficient production manager. Denise Shanks brought a vision to the Web site and spent countless hours making it a reality. For their work on previous editions of the book, we want to thank Jan Hoeper, Kathy Talalay, Scott McCord, Margaret Farley, Traci Nagle, Margie Brassil, Stephanie Larson, Sarah Caldwell, Nancy Yanchus, Jean Yelovich, Sandra Smith, Sandy Lifland, Amy Cherry, Roby Harrington, and especially Ruth Dworkin.

We are more than happy, however, to absolve all these contributors from any flaws, errors, and misjudgments that will inevitably be discovered. We wish the book could be free of all production errors, grammatical errors, misspellings, misquotes, missed citations, etc. From that standpoint, a book ought to try to be perfect. But substantively we have not tried to write a flawless book; we have not tried to write a book to please everyone. We have again tried to write an effective book, a book that cannot be taken lightly. Our goal was not to make every reader a political scientist. Our goal was to restore politics as a subject matter of vigorous and enjoyable discourse, recapturing it from the bondage of the thirty-second sound bite and the thirty-page technical briefing. Every person can be knowledgeable because everything about politics is accessible. One does not have to be a television anchorperson to profit from political events. One does not have to be a philosopher to argue about the requisites of democracy, a lawyer to dispute constitutional interpretations, an economist to debate a public policy. We would be very proud if our book contributes in a small way to the restoration of the ancient art of political controversy.

Theodore J. Lowi
Benjamin Ginsberg
Kenneth A. Shepsle
December 2003

American Government

Power and Purpose

EIGHTH EDITION

CHAPTER

1

Five Principles of Politics

Americans often complain about "government interference" with their personal affairs and private property. In fact, when polled about where they thought the biggest domestic threat to the country would come from, most Americans answered "big government" (see Table 1.1). At the same time, however, Americans have come to expect a great deal of service from every level of government. After September 11, 2001, most Americans forgot their qualms about "big government." They were willing to accept unprecedented levels of government surveillance in their lives in order to stop terrorist activity.

One example of just how much we demand from our government and the dilemmas and complexities these expectations can create is the creation of the Department of Homeland Security (DHS). Within days of September 11, 2001, President George W. Bush created by executive order a White House Office of Homeland Security, to advise the president and to be responsible for identifying and coordinating over fifty agencies of the national government plus thousands of state and local governmental bodies, in a defense against terrorism. President Bush summoned the governor of Pennsylvania, Tom Ridge, to accept the president's assignment: "To develop and coordinate the implementation of a comprehensive national strategy to secure the United States from terrorist attacks or threats." Ridge soon discovered that coordinating even two or three agencies at a time was harder than herding cats because "no Cabinet Secretary I have ever seen

TABLE 1.1

Poll: Which of the Following Will Be the Biggest Threat to the Country?

YEAR OF POLL	BIG GOVERNMENT	BIG BUSINESS	BIG LABOR
2000	65%	22%	7%
2002	47	38	10

SOURCES for both years: Gallup Organization, www.lexis-nexis.com.

wants to give up a part of his department."[1] Thus, by June 2002, President Bush reversed his decision to have an advisory office and called on Congress to create an all-new Department of Homeland Security that would have the authority to draw twenty-two agencies and formal operations from eight existing cabinet departments and independent agencies (see Table 1.2). In November 2002, Congress authorized the president's request. As the newly appointed DHS secretary, Ridge became the manager of 22 agencies, 170,000 employees, and "2,800 power plants, 800,000 bridges, 463 skyscrapers, 190,000 miles of natural-gas pipelines and 20,000 miles of border and counting."[2] As shown on Table 1.2, these agencies and operations are not merely small and insignificant ciphers in the vast bureaucracy, eager to

[1]Tom Ridge, as quoted in Eric Pianin and Bill Miller, "For Ridge, Ambition and Realities Clash," *Washington Post*, 23 January 2002, p. A1.
[2]Mark Liebowitz, "The Image of Security—As America Plays a Waiting Game, Tom Ridge Sells Reassurance," *Washington Post National Weekly Edition*, 26 May–1 June 2003, p. 12.

CHAPTER OUTLINE

What Is Government, and Why Is It Necessary?

- Forms of Government
- Foundations of Government
- Why Is Government Necessary?
- Influencing the Government: Politics

Why Do Governments Do What They Do?

- Principle 1: All Political Behavior Has a Purpose
- Principle 2: All Politics Is Collective Action
- Principle 3: Institutions Matter
- Principle 4: Political Outcomes Are the Products of Individual Preferences and Institutional Procedures
- Principle 5: History Matters

The Paradoxes of American Democracy

- Delegating Authority in a Representative Democracy
- The Trade-off between Freedom and Order
- The Instability of Majority Rule

TABLE 1.2

A Single Roof for the Department of Homeland Security

COMPONENT	MISSION	OPERATIONS ABSORBED	MOVED FROM
Border and transportation security	Bring the major border security and transportation operations under one roof.	Immigration and Naturalization Service .... Justice Customs Service (part) .... Treasury Animal and Plant Health Inspection Service (part) .... Agriculture Coast Guard .... Transportation Federal Protective Service .... GSA Transportation Security Administration .... Transportation	
Emergency preparedness and response	Oversee domestic disaster-preparedness training and coordinate government disaster response.	Federal Emergency Management Agency .... (independent) Chemical, biological, radiological and nuclear response assets .... HHS Domestic emergency support team .... (interagency) Nuclear incident response .... Energy Domestic emergency support teams .... Justice National Domestic Preparedness Office .... FBI Federal Law Enforcement Training Center .... Treasury	
Science and technology	Lead federal government's efforts to prepare for and respond to terrorist threats involving weapons of mass destruction, including agroterrorism.	Civilian biodefense research programs .... HHS Lawrence Livermore National Laboratory (part) .... Energy BW Defense Analysis Center .... Defense Plum Island Animal Disease Center .... Agriculture	
Information analysis and infrastructure protection	Analyze homeland intelligence from other agencies involving threats to homeland security. Evaluate vulnerabilities of the nation's infrastructure.	Critical Infrastructure Assurance Office .... Commerce Federal Computer Incident Response Center .... GSA National Communications System .... Defense National Infrastructure Protection Center .... FBI National Infrastructure Simulation and Analysis Center .... Energy	
Secret Service	The Secret Service would report directly to the secretary of homeland security. It would remain intact, and its primary mission remains the protection of the president and other government leaders.		Treasury
Coast Guard	The Coast Guard would report directly to the secretary of homeland security. It would remain intact, and its primary mission would remain securing the nation's waters and ports.		Transportation

SOURCES: White House, House Select Committee on Homeland Security; *Washington Post*, 14 November 2002, p. A12.

please by shedding current responsibilities for the new and exciting, post-9/11 ones. These are professional agencies with their own "brand," their own esprit de corps, and their own supportive interest groups and clientele. For example, the Coast Guard is as old as the Republic; so is the Customs Service. More recent agencies such as the Immigration and Naturalization Service (including the Border Patrol), the Federal Emergency Management Agency (FEMA), parts of the FBI and the Drug Enforcement Agency have long histories of professional independence; and all were more or less comfortably lodged within other departments. Also shown on Table 1.2 is the organization plan, comprised of components (or divisions), each with its new mission defined by the White House and Congress.

During its first year of life, the Department of Homeland Security, operating with an annual budget of about $35 billion, could only lay one claim of performance as a cabinet department: the color-coded scheme of threat levels. After two or three moves by the secretary up and back down the spectrum, it had become something of a laughing stock. Of the twenty-two agencies to be brought over to DHS from elsewhere, virtually none had been moved—geographically speaking—from their previous home to a new DHS headquarters. These agencies were continuing to carry out the missions that had been set for them long ago. Only time, and a good bit of it, will tell whether more effective and efficient coordination against terrorism has been achieved.

The case of the DHS helps to point out four very important facts about American government. The first of these is the sheer scope of government involvement in American life. In 1789, 1889, and even in 1929, America's national government was limited in size, scope, and influence, and most of the important functions of government were provided by the states. By 1933, however, the influence of the government expanded to meet the crises created by the stock-market crash of 1929, the Great Depression, and the run on banks of 1933. Congress passed legislation that brought the government into the business of home mortgages, farm mortgages, credit, and relief of personal distress. Whereas in 1933 people tried to withdraw their money from the banks only to find that their savings had been wiped out, seventy years later most are confident that although many savings and loan institutions may be insolvent, their money is still safe because it is guaranteed by the government. Today, the national government is an enormous institution with programs and policies reaching into every corner of American life. It oversees the nation's economy; it is the nation's largest employer; it provides citizens with a host of services; it controls a formidable military establishment; and it protects the country from external and internal threat. America's founders never dreamed that the government could take on such obligations; today we can hardly dream of a time when the government was not such a large part of our lives.

The second important point illustrated by the DHS case is that Americans of all political stripes are ready to turn to the national government to solve their problems or deal with issues beyond the reach or jurisdiction of state and local governments. Indeed, there seems to be a consensus nowadays in favor of a large

TABLE 1.3

2002 Poll: Which Federal Government Program Do You Feel Should Be Expanded, Kept about the Same Level, or Cut?

PROGRAM	EXPAND	SAME LEVEL	CUT
Aid to education	75%	21%	4%
Social Security	64	30	3
Health care	77	19	4
Crime control	70	24	5
Homeland security	65	27	5
Defense spending	44	38	15

SOURCE: Harris Interactive, Worldviews 2002 Survey, www.lexis-nexis.com.

and active national government. Even self-styled "conservatives" differ more with their "liberal" counterparts over the proper character of government than over its ultimate desirability. In his 1981 inaugural address, Ronald Reagan, our most conservative president in more than half a century, pledged to curb the growth of the federal establishment but at the same time declared, "Now so there will be no misunderstanding, it is not my intention to do away with government. It is, rather, to make it work."[3] Reagan repeated this sentiment in his 1985 inaugural address. In 1992, in his speech accepting the Democratic presidential nomination, Bill Clinton correctly noted that "the Republicans have campaigned against big government for a generation. . . . But have you noticed? They've run this big government for a generation and they haven't changed a thing."[4]

According to the polls, Americans want to keep the political and economic benefits that they believe they derive from government. A 2002 survey, for example, revealed that around 75 percent of all Americans favored more government spending on education and health care. About two-thirds favored increased spending on Social Security, crime control, and homeland security (see Table 1.3). It is safe to conclude that many Americans want the government not only to continue its present involvement but actually to do more in a variety of areas. According to another poll, over half of all voters believe that it is important for the

---

[3]"President Reagan's Inaugural Address," *New York Times*, 21 January 1981, p. B1.
[4]E. J. Dionne, "Beneath the Rhetoric, an Old Question," *Washington Post*, 31 August 1992, p. 1.

government to provide more services, even if it requires more spending and even if the benefits are indirect.[5]

A third point illustrated by the DHS case is that perfection in government, its institutions, and its policies cannot be achieved. Americans are inveterate believers in the perfectibility of institutions. We believe that there must be one best way that will satisfy all people of good intentions. However, what if those people of good intentions have genuine and legitimate differences of outlook and interest? Administration officials, many members of Congress, and many Americans believed that bringing a number of agencies together within a single department would improve communication and intelligence sharing among agencies and enhance the effectiveness of the government's efforts to prevent future acts of terrorism. At the same time, a number of civil libertarians were concerned that the concentration of power within the DHS, coupled with other aggressive antiterrorism policies developed by the Bush administration, posed a threat to the liberties of all Americans. Still another set of political forces, consisting mainly of the leaders of public employee unions and their congressional supporters, feared that the new department would weaken the hard-won rights of unionized federal employees. All these points of view should be seen as valid and legitimate. The question is how we resolve issues in which many sides have legitimate but competing claims. As we shall see, the answer to this question is not a simple one. Political life often requires cooperation and compromise among those with competing goals. Such trade-offs, in which all of the involved parties are forced to accept something less than their idea, are a normal part of politics.

Finally, the fourth point brought to the fore by the DHS example is the complexity of government politics and policy. The creation of DHS involved the reorganization of twenty-two existing agencies, promulgation of new rules governing the activities of tens of thousands of federal employees, and the imposition of new management systems to account for billions of dollars in equipment and budgets. Congress was forced to plan for the reorganization of its committee system to ensure legislative oversight of the new agency. Federal employee unions had to consider the impact of the reorganization plan for their work rules and seniority systems. State and local officials drafted plans to deal with new federal partners. In due course, the courts will certainly be asked to rule on the structure and activities of the new agency. And, after all this, it remains to be seen whether we have increased the security of our homeland or merely created another bureaucratic monster along the Potomac River.

What we blithely call "the government" is actually a complex arrangement of institutions and processes that are frequently disjointed and often work at cross-purposes. We hope that by the time you have completed this book, you will have a healthy respect for the complexity of government and political life as well as a command of some principles that will allow you to bring some order to this chaos.

---

[5]1998 American National Election Study conducted by the Center for Political Studies at the University of Michigan. Data are provided by the Inter-University Consortium for Political and Social Research in Ann Arbor, Michigan.

WHAT IS GOVERNMENT, AND WHY IS IT NECESSARY?

government
Institutions and procedures through which a land and its people are ruled.

autocracy A form of government in which a single individual—a king, queen, or dictator—rules.

oligarchy A form of government in which a small group of landowners, military officers, or wealthy merchants controls most of the governing decisions.

democracy A system of rule that permits citizens to play a significant part in the governmental process, usually through the selection of key public officials.

constitutional government A system of rule in which formal and effective limits are placed on the powers of the government.

authoritarian government A system of rule in which the government recognizes no formal limits but may nevertheless be restrained by the power of other social institutions.

totalitarian government A system of rule in which the government recognizes no formal limits on its power and seeks to absorb or eliminate other social institutions that might challenge it.

Government is the term generally used to describe the formal institutions through which a land and its people are ruled. To govern is to rule. *Government is composed of institutions and processes that rulers establish to strengthen and perpetuate their power or control over a land and its inhabitants.* A government may be as simple as a tribal council that meets occasionally to advise the chief, or as complex as our own vast establishment with its forms, rules, and bureaucracies. This more complex government is sometimes referred to as "the state," an abstract concept referring to the source of all public authority.

Forms of Government

Governments vary in their institutional structure, in their size, and in their modes of operation. Two questions are of special importance in determining how governments differ from each other: Who governs? How much government control is permitted?

In some nations, governing is done by a single individual—a king or dictator, for example. This state of affairs is called ***autocracy.*** Where a small group of landowners, military officers, or wealthy merchants controls most of the governing decisions, that government is said to be an ***oligarchy.*** If more people participate and if the populace is deemed to have some influence over decision making, that government is tending toward ***democracy.***

Governments also vary considerably in terms of how they govern. In the United States and a small number of other nations, governments are severely limited as to *what* they are permitted to control (substantive limits), as well as *how* they go about it (procedural limits). Governments that are so limited are called ***constitutional,*** or liberal, governments. In other nations, including many in Europe as well as in South America, Asia, and Africa, though the law imposes few real limits, a government is nevertheless kept in check by other political and social institutions that the government is unable to control but must come to terms with—such as autonomous territories, an organized church, organized business groups, or organized labor unions. Such governments are generally called ***authoritarian.*** In a third group of nations, including the Soviet Union under Joseph Stalin, Nazi Germany, and perhaps pre–World War II Japan and Italy, governments not only are free of legal limits but seek to eliminate those organized social groupings that might challenge or limit their authority. These governments typically attempt to dominate or control every sphere of political, economic, and social life and, as a result, are called ***totalitarian.***

Foundations of Government

Whatever their makeup, governments historically have included two basic components: a means of coercion, such as an army or police force, and a means of collecting revenue. These two components have been the essential foundations

TABLE 1.4

The Means of Coercion

FORMS	INSTANCES	LEVEL OF GOVERNMENT
Arrests	11,231,000	Federal, state, and local (1998)
Prison inmates	1,194,581	Federal and state (1997)
Jail inmates	605,943	County and municipal (1999)
Executions	98	State (1999)

SOURCE: U.S. Bureau of the Census, *Statistical Abstract of the United States: 2000* (Washington, D.C.: U.S. Department of Commerce, 2000).

of government—the building blocks that all individuals and groups who ever sought to rule have been compelled to construct if they were to secure and maintain a measure of control over their territory and its people. Groups aspire to govern for a variety of reasons. Some have the most high-minded aims, while others are little more than ambitious robbers. But whatever their motives and character, those who aspire to rule must be able to secure obedience and fend off rivals as well as collect the revenues needed to accomplish these tasks.[6] Some governments, including many of those in the less developed nations today, have consisted of little more than an army and a tax-collecting agency. Other governments, especially those in the developed nations, have attempted to provide services as well as to collect taxes in order to secure popular consent and control. For some, power is an end in itself. For most, power is necessary for the maintenance of public order. For all, power is needed to permit governments to provide the collective goods and services that citizens want and need but cannot provide for themselves.

The Means of Coercion Government must have the power to order people around, to get people to obey its laws, and to punish them if they do not. Coercion takes many different forms, and each year millions of Americans are subject to one form of government coercion or another. Table 1.4 is an outline of the uses of coercion by federal and state governments in America.

---

[6]For an excellent discussion, see Charles Tilly, "Reflections on the History of European State-Making," in *The Formation of National States in Western Europe,* ed. Charles Tilly (Princeton: Princeton University Press, 1975), pp. 3–83. See also Charles Tilly, "War Making and State Making as Organized Crime," in *Bringing the State Back In,* ed. Peter B. Evans, Dietrich Rueschemeyer, and Theda Skocpol (New York: Cambridge University Press, 1985), pp. 169–91.

conscription
Compulsory military service, usually for a prescribed period or for the duration of a war; "the draft."

One aspect of coercion is ***conscription,*** whereby government requires certain involuntary services of citizens. The best-known example of conscription is military conscription, which is called "the draft." Although there has been no draft since 1974, there were drafts during the Civil War, World War I, World War II, and the wars in Korea and Vietnam. With these drafts, our government compelled millions of men to serve in the armed forces; half a million of these soldiers made the ultimate contribution by giving their lives in their nation's service. If the need arose, military conscription would undoubtedly be reinstituted. All eighteen-year-old males are required to register today, just in case.

Military conscription, however, is not the only form of involuntary service that government can compel Americans to perform. We can, by law, be compelled to serve on juries, to appear before legal tribunals when summoned, to file a great variety of official reports, including income tax returns, and to attend school or to send our children to school.

The Means of Collecting Revenue Each year American governments collect enormous sums from their citizens to support their institutions and programs. Taxation has grown steadily over the years. In 2001, the national government alone collected $972 billion in individual income taxes, $195 billion in corporate income taxes, $682 billion in social insurance taxes, $77 billion in excise taxes, $21 billion in custom duties, and another $40 billion in miscellaneous revenue. The grand total amounted to more than $2 trillion, or almost $7,000 from every living soul in the United States. And of course, while some groups receive more in benefits from the government than they pay in taxes, others get less for their tax dollar. One of the perennial issues in American politics is the distribution of tax burdens versus the distribution of program benefits. Every group would like more of the benefits while passing more of the burdens of taxation onto others.

Why Is Government Necessary?

As we have just seen, control is the basis for government. But what forms of government control are justifiable? To answer this question, we begin by examining the ways in which government makes it possible for people to live together in harmony.

To Maintain Order Human beings usually do not venture out of their caves (or the modern counterpart) unless there is a reasonable probability that they can return safely. But in order for people to live together peacefully, law and order are required, the institutionalization of which is called government. From the standpoint of this definition, the primary purpose of government is to maintain order. But order can only come about by controlling a territory and its people. This may sound like a threat to freedom until you ponder the absence of government, or anarchy—the absence of rule. According to Thomas Hobbes (1588–1679), author of the first great masterpiece of political philosophy in the

English language, anarchy is even worse than the potential tyranny of government because anarchy, or life outside "the state," is one of "continual fear, and danger of violent death [where life is] solitary, poor, nasty, brutish and short."[7] Governmental power can be a threat to freedom, yet we need government to maintain order so that we can enjoy our freedom.

To Protect Property   After safety of persons comes security of a person's labor, which we call property, or private property. Protection of property is almost universally recognized as a justifiable function of government. John Locke (1632–1704), the worthy successor to Thomas Hobbes, was first to assert clearly that whatever we have removed from nature and also mixed our labor with, is considered our property:

> For this "labour" being the unquestionable property of the laborer, no man but [the laborer] can have a right to what that [labour is joined to]. . . .

But even Locke recognized that although the right to the ownership of what we have produced by our own labor is absolute, it means nothing if someone with greater power than ours decides to take it or trespass on it. As Locke puts it,

> If man . . . be absolute Lord of his own person and possessions . . . why will he part with his freedom . . . ? To which, it is obvious to answer, that the enjoyment of it is very uncertain. . . . This makes him willing to quit this condition, which, however free, is full of fears and continual danger; and it is not without reason that he seeks out and is willing to join in society with others . . . for the mutual preservation of their lives, liberties, and estates.[8]

So, something we call our own *is only ours as long as the laws against trespass* improve the probability that we can enjoy it, use it, consume it, trade it, and sell it. In reality, then, property can be defined as *all the laws against trespass* that not only permit us to call something our own but also to make sure that our claim sticks. In other words, property—that is, private property—is virtually meaningless without a government of laws and policies that makes trespass prohibitive.

To Provide Public Goods   David Hume (1711–1776), another worthy successor to Thomas Hobbes, observed that although two neighbors may agree voluntarily to cooperate in draining a swampy meadow, the more neighbors there are, the more difficult it will be to cooperate in order to get the task done. A few neighbors might clear the swamp because they understand the benefits each of them

---

[7]Thomas Hobbes, *Leviathan* (New York: Macmillan, 1947), p. 82.
[8]This quote and the previous one are from John Locke's masterpiece, *Two Treatises of Government* (London: Everyman, 1993), pp. 178 and 180.

will receive. But as you expand the number of neighbors who benefit from clearing the swamp, many neighbors will realize that all of them can get the same benefit if only a few clear the swamp and the rest do nothing. This is an example of *free riding*. A *public* (or collective) *good* is, therefore, a benefit that neighbors or members of a group cannot be kept from enjoying once any individual or small minority of members have provided the benefit for themselves—the clearing of the swamp, for example, or national defense, for another example. National defense is one of the most important public goods—especially when the nation is threatened by war or terrorism. Without government's coercive powers through a policy (backed by taxation) to build a bridge, produce an army, provide a swamp-free meadow, "legal tender," or uniform standards of weights and measures, there is no incentive—in fact, very often there is a *dis*incentive—for even the richest, most concerned members to provide the benefit.[9]

Although public order, the protection of property, and the provision of public goods are justifications for government, they are not justifications for all its actions. A government's actions can only be justified by the people being governed. This is why government would be intolerable without politics. With politics, we have at least a faint hope that a government's actions can be influenced in some way.

Influencing the Government: Politics

In its broadest sense, the term *politics* refers to conflicts over the character, membership, and policies of any organization to which people belong. As Harold Lasswell, a famous political scientist, once put it, politics is the struggle over "who gets what, when, how."[10] Although politics is a phenomenon that can be found in any organization, our concern in this book is more narrow. Here, politics will be used to refer only to conflicts and struggles over the leadership, structure, and policies of *governments*. The goal of politics, as we define it, is to have a share or a say in the composition of the government's leadership, how the government is organized, or what its policies are going to be. Having a share is called *power* or *influence*. Most people are eager to have some "say" in matters affecting them; witness the willingness of so many individuals over the past two centuries to risk their lives for voting rights and representation. In recent years, Americans have become more skeptical about their actual "say" in government, and many do not bother to vote. This increased skepticism, however, does not mean that Americans no longer want to have a share in the governmental process. Rising levels of skepticism mean, rather, that many Americans doubt the capacity of the political system to provide them with influence.

---

[9]The most instructive treatment of the phenomenon of public goods and the "free rider" is Mancur Olson, *The Logic of Collective Action: Public Goods and the Theory of Groups* (Cambridge: Harvard University Press, 1965 and 1971), pp. 33–43, esp. n. 53.

[10]Harold D. Lasswell, *Politics: Who Gets What, When, How* (New York: Meridian Books, 1958).

---

free riding
Enjoying the benefits of some good or action and letting others bear the costs.

public good A good that (1) may be enjoyed by anyone if it is provided and that (2) may not be denied to anyone once it has been provided.

WHY DO GOVERNMENTS DO WHAT THEY DO?

Choosing between cheese pizza and pepperoni pizza may not seem like a political decision, but American government has made it one. The Food and Drug Administration (FDA) regulates the safety of cheese pizza, while pepperoni pizza is the responsibility of the U.S. Department of Agriculture (USDA).[11] All totaled, the federal government's efforts to maintain a safe food supply—from meat, poultry, and seafood to fresh produce, frozen foods, and the use of pesticides—are guided by more than thirty-five laws and divided among twelve federal government agencies.[12] In the early 1900s, shocking disclosures in the meatpacking industry spurred political actions that quickly brought the federal government into a novel commitment to try to regulate food safety. In the ensuing decades, new federal laws were adopted in response both to new risks and to new efforts to set standards for different foods.[13] Some of the laws were housed in the FDA, but others were housed in new agencies and different departments. There was never a clear blueprint for any of this; politics imposed its influence on government in a haphazard way. Today, the USDA focuses on meat and poultry, employing more than seven thousand inspectors who examine every carcass in the nation's slaughterhouses. The USDA is supervised by the House and Senate Agriculture Committees. The FDA, which was once part of the USDA and now (since 1988) is in the Department of Health and Human Services, is responsible for most other food products, including produce and seafood. It is overseen by the House Committee on Energy and Commerce and the Senate Health, Education, Labor, and Pensions committees. Ten other agencies are involved in one aspect or another of food safety.

Many have argued that government regulation of food safety should be handled by just one agency rather than the current twelve. Yet, without the emergency of a war or the threat of another September 11, proposals of this sort, while rational, are considered "dead on arrival" when submitted as bills in the House or Senate. As with the twenty-two agencies of the DHS, each of the twelve agencies is linked to different congressional committee jurisdictions and each is tied to different interests or interest groups—from dairy farmers to restaurant associations to the meat industry to consumer groups. These groups, and members of Congress with a stake in one or another of these agencies, are reluctant to risk losing influence by moving everything into one new agency; thus, battles over jurisdiction become "turf wars."[14] Consequently, all of the

[11]Allan Freedman, "Battles over Jurisdiction Likely to Keep Congress from Merging Food Agencies," *Congressional Quarterly Weekly*, 30 May 1998.

[12]Allan Freedman, "Unsafe Foods Spark Outbreaks of Concern, Little Action," *Congressional Quarterly Weekly*, 30 May 1998.

[13]"Milestones in U.S. Food and Drug Law History," FDA Backgrounder, FDA Web site (http://www.fda.gov/opacom/backgrounders/miles.html).

[14]Freedman, "Battles over Jurisdiction . . . ." For a more general treatment of this subject, see David C. King, *Turf Wars: How Congressional Committees Claim Jurisdiction* (Chicago: University of Chicago Press, 1997).

interested groups and members of Congress continue to disagree with each other on a number of things. One thing they do agree about, however, is to prevent the merger.

The difficulty in getting interested parties to agree on political goals and to act together to accomplish them, the accumulation of rules, laws, and official bodies, the layering of related policies and precedents, and the sheer weight of history and public expectations—these are the aspects of political life on which we draw to understand and explain the complex politics of something as diffuse as homeland security or as seemingly trivial as pizza regulation. Our two case studies of homeland security and food safety provide a basis for deriving five principles that will help us in our effort to understand why government does what it does:

Principle 1: All political behavior has a purpose.
Principle 2: All politics is collective action.
Principle 3: Institutions matter.
Principle 4: Political outcomes are the products of individual preferences and institutional procedures.
Principle 5: History matters.

Principle 1: All Political Behavior Has a Purpose

Rationality Principle

All political behavior has a purpose.

One compelling reason why governments do what they do is that all people have goals and they work to achieve those goals through their political behavior. For many citizens, political behavior is as simple as reading a headline or editorial in the newspaper while drinking their morning coffee or discussing the latest local political controversy with a neighbor over the back fence. Though political, these actions are basically routines of everyday life. Beyond these almost perfunctory acts, citizen political behavior broadens to include still relatively modest activities like watching a political debate on television, arguing about politics with a coworker, signing a petition, or attending a city council meeting. These are understood to be explicitly political activities that require some forethought and advanced reflection—these are discretionary *choices* rather than mechanical *acts* like accidentally catching a political headline in the newspaper on your way to the sports section, the comics, or the movie listings. Political behavior requiring even more "premeditation"—even calculation—includes going to the polls and casting a vote in the November election (having first registered in a timely manner), writing one's legislative representatives about a political issue, contributing time or money to a political campaign, or even running for local office.

Some of these acts require effort, time, financial resources, and courage, while others place small, even insignificant, demands on a person. Nevertheless, all of these acts are done for specific reasons. They are not random; they are not entirely automatic or mechanical, even the smallest of them. Sometimes they are engaged in for the sake of entertainment (reading the front page in the morning) or just to be sociable (chatting about politics with a neighbor, coworker, or family member). At other times, they take on considerable personal importance explicitly because of their political content—because an individual cares about, and wants to influence, an issue, a candidate, a party, or a cause. We will treat all of this political activity as *purposeful*, as having a point. Indeed, our attempts to discern the point of various political activities will help us to understand them better.

We've just noted that many political activities of ordinary citizens are hard to distinguish from conventional everyday behavior—reading newspapers, watching television news, discussing politics, and so on. For the professional politician, on the other hand—legislator, executive, judge, party leader, bureau chief, or agency head—nearly everything he or she does is political. The legislator's decision to introduce a particular piece of legislation, to give a speech in the legislative chamber, to move an amendment to a pending bill, to vote for or against that bill, or to accept a contribution from a PAC[15] requires the politician's careful attention. There are pitfalls and dangers, however, and the slightest miscalculation can have huge consequences. Introduce a bill that appears to be too pro-labor in the eyes of your constituents, for example, and before you know it you're charged with being in bed with the unions during the next election campaign. Give a speech against job quotas for minorities, and you set yourself up to have your words turned against you by an electoral opponent, risking your standing with the minority communities in your state or district. Accept campaign contributions from local businesspeople, and environmentalists think you are no friend of the earth. Nearly every move a legislator makes is fraught with risks. And because of these risks, legislators think about their moves before they make them—sometimes carefully, sometimes not; sometimes correctly, sometimes not. But whatever actions they take, or decide against taking, they do so with forethought, with deliberation, with calculation. Their actions are not knee-jerk, but are, in a word, ***instrumental.*** Individuals think through the benefits and the costs of a decision, speculate about future effects, and weigh the risks of their decision. Making decisions is all about weighing probabilities of various events and determining the personal value of various outcomes.

instrumental To do something with purpose, sometimes requiring forethought and even calculation.

Principle 2: All Politics Is Collective Action

The second factor that helps explain why governments do what they do is that political action is collective, involving the building, combining, mixing, and amalgamating of the individual goals of people. They join together in order to achieve these goals. But, as we shall see, collective action can be very difficult to orchestrate since the individuals involved in the decision-making process often have somewhat different goals and preferences. The result is mixed motives for cooperation. Conflict is inevitable; the question is how it can be resolved. The

 Collective Action Principle All politics is collective action.

[15]A PAC (political action committee) is a group established by an interest group, labor union, or some other political organization to collect donations and distribute them as campaign contributions to candidates and political parties.

most typical and widespread means is bargaining, involving a small number of individuals. But when the number of parties involved is too large to engage in face-to-face bargaining, incentives must be provided to get everyone to act collectively.

Informal Bargaining   Political bargaining is a process that may be highly formal or entirely informal. Relations among neighbors, for example, are usually based on informal give-and-take. To give a personal example, one of this book's authors has a neighbor with whom he shares a privet hedge on the property line. First one takes responsibility for trimming the hedge and then the other, alternating from year to year. This arrangement is merely an "understanding," not a legally binding agreement, and it was reached amicably and without much fuss or fanfare after a brief conversation. No organizational effort was required—like hiring lawyers, drafting an agreement, having it signed, witnessed, notarized, filed at the county courthouse, and so on.

Bargaining in politics can also be informal and unstructured. Whether called horse trading, back-scratching, logrolling, or wheeling and dealing, it has much the same flavor as the casual, over-the-fence negotiations among neighbors just described. Deals will be struck depending upon the preferences and beliefs of the participants. If preferences are too incompatible or beliefs too inconsistent with one another, then a deal simply may not be in the cards. On the other hand, if preferences and beliefs are not too far out of line, then there will be a range of possible bargaining outcomes, some of which slightly advantage one party, others of which advantage other parties. But all deals in this range are at least acceptable to all the parties involved.

In fact, much of politics *is* informal, unstructured bargaining. First, many disputes subjected to bargaining are of sufficiently low impact that it is just not worth establishing elaborate formal machinery for dealing with them. Rules of thumb often develop as a benchmark—such as "split the difference" or "take turns" (the outcome of the hedge-trimming example given earlier). Second, there is repetition. If a small group engages in bargaining today over one matter and tomorrow over another—as neighbors bargain over draining a meadow one day, fixing a fence another, and trimming a hedge on still another occasion—then patterns develop. If one party constantly tries to extract maximal advantage, then the other parties will undoubtedly cease doing business with her. If, on the other hand, each party "gives a little" in order to "get a little," reciprocating kindness at one point with kindness at another, then a pattern of cooperation develops over time. It is the repetition of mixed-motive occasions that allows this pattern to emerge without formal trappings. Many political circumstances are either amenable to rules of thumb like those mentioned above or are repeated with sufficient frequency so as to allow cooperative patterns to emerge.

Formal Bargaining   Formal bargaining entails interactions among bargainers that are governed by rules. The rules describe such things as who gets to make the first offer, how long the recipient parties have to consider it, whether recipient parties must "take it or leave it" or can make counteroffers, the method by which they convey their assent or rejection, what happens when all (or some decisive subset) of the others accept or reject, what transpires next if the proposal is rejected, and so on. One could not imagine two neighbors deciding how to trim their common hedge under procedures as explicit and formal as these. One could, however, imagine a bargaining session over wages and working conditions between labor and management at the local manufacturing plant proceeding in just this manner. This suggests that some parties are more appropriately suited to formal proceedings, whereas others get on well enough without them. The same may be said about situations. A husband and wife are likely to divide household chores by informal bargaining, but this same couple would employ a formal procedure if it were household assets they were dividing (in a divorce settlement).

Formal bargaining is often associated with events that take place in official institutions—legislatures, courts, party conventions, administrative and regulatory agencies. These are settings in which mixed-motive situations arise over and over again. Year in and year out, legislatures pass statutes, approve executive budgets, and oversee the administrative branch of government. Courts administer justice, determine guilt or innocence, impose sentences, resolve differences between disputants, and render interpretive opinions about the meaning of the law. Party conventions nominate candidates and approve the platforms on which they base their campaigns. Administrative and regulatory agencies implement policy and make rulings about its applicability. All of these are instances of mixed-motive circumstances where gains from cooperation are possible, but bargaining failures are also a definite possibility. Consequently, the formal bargaining that takes place under the aegis of institutions is governed by rules that regularize proceedings both to maximize the prospects of reaching agreement and to guarantee that procedural "wheels" don't have to be reinvented each time a similar bargaining problem arises.

Collective Action   The idea of political bargaining suggests an "intimate" kind of politics, involving face-to-face relations, negotiation, compromise, give-and-take, and so on. Such bargaining results from the combination of mixed motives and small numbers. When the numbers become large, bargaining may no longer be practical. If one hundred people own property bordering a swampy meadow, or if a privet hedge runs the length of Main Street in a small town, insulating hundreds of households from the street, then how do these communities solve the swamp's mosquito problem or resolve to trim the hedge to a common height? How do these communities secure the dividends that arise from cooperation?

These are clearly mixed-motive situations. Everyone shares some common values—eliminating the mosquito habitat or giving the hedge the look of uniformity—but they may disagree on other matters. Some may want to use pesticides in the meadow, while others are concerned about the environmental impact. Some may want the privet hedge cut very short, allowing it to be maintained easily by each household; others may want it kept tall to shield homes from street noise. And in both situations there are bound to be disagreements over how to pay for the project. The collective-action problem arises, as in these examples, when there is something to be gained if the group can cooperate and assure group members that some do not get away with bearing less than their fair share of the effort. Face-to-face bargaining, however, is compromised by sheer numbers. The issue, then, is how to accomplish some common objective when explicit bargaining is not an option.

collective action The pooling of resources and coordination of effort and activity by a group of people (often a large one) to achieve common goals.

Groups of individuals intent upon ***collective action*** will ordinarily establish some decision-making procedures—relatively formal arrangements by which to resolve differences, coordinate the group around a course of action, and sanction slackers, if necessary. Most groups will also require a structure of leadership, which is necessary even if all the members of the group are in agreement about how to proceed. This is due to a phenomenon that we saw in the swamp-draining example above: free riding. Each owner of land bordering the swamp wants the area cleared. But if one or a few owners were to clear the swamp alone, their actions would benefit all the other owners as well, without any efforts on the part of those other owners. Those owners would be free riders. It is this prospect of free riding that risks undermining collective action. A leadership structure will have to be in place to threaten and, if necessary, inflict punishments to discourage individuals from reneging on the individual contributions required to enable the group to pursue its common goals.

by-product theory The idea that groups provide members with private benefits to attract membership; the possibility for group collective action emerges as a consequence.

Various solutions to the collective action problem have been proposed. The most famous is Mancur Olson's ***by-product theory***.[16] Briefly, Olson's idea is this: the nub of free riding derives from the fact that most individuals in a large group don't make much difference to the final result, and they know it. This is why they may comfortably abstain from participation—they know that in following their inclination to avoid the costs of participation, they do not damage their prospects (or anyone else's) for receiving benefits. The problem is that while no one person's free riding does much harm, if enough people free ride, then the purpose of the collective action will be compromised. What if, however, something of value were at stake that would be lost if the person abstained from participation? What if participants were given something special that nonparticipants were denied? That is, what if some benefits were contingent on contributing to the group effort? Many organizations use this tactic, giving dues-paying or effort-contributing members special insurance or education benefits, reduced-fare travel, free or subsidized subscriptions to magazines and newsletters, bowling and golf tournaments, soccer leagues, access to members-only social events, and so on. Olson argued that if members were prepared to "pay their dues" to join an organization partially (or even mainly) for these special benefits of which they would otherwise be deprived—what Olson called ***selective benefits***—then the collective cooperation would end up being provided as well, *as a*

selective benefits Benefits that do not go to everyone, but rather are distributed selectively—only to those who contribute to the group enterprise.

[16]On the general subject of collective action, the interested reader should consult Kenneth A. Shepsle and Mark S. Bonchek, *Analyzing Politics: Rationality, Behavior, and Institutions* (New York: W. W. Norton, 1997), ch. 9, where Olson's work, among others, is taken up.

by-product, with whatever surplus the dues structure generated. A member's inclination to free ride would be alleviated, not because of feelings of obligation to his or her fellow members, not because of a moral imperative to participate, not even because of a desire for the collective benefit supplied by the group, but rather because of naked self-interest—the desire for selective benefits! Clearly this is an extreme version of the argument; the main point here is that the selective benefits available only to participants and contributors—and denied to nonparticipants and noncontributors—are the key to successful collective action. A group that appeals to its members *only* on the basis of its common collective purposes is a group that will have trouble achieving those purposes.[17]

Individuals try to accomplish things not only as individuals but also as members of larger collectivities—families, friendship groups, clubs and associations, political parties, and in larger categories like economic class, ethnicity, and nationality. Principle 1 covers individual initiative. Principle 2 describes the paradoxes encountered, the obstacles that must be overcome, and the incentives necessary for individuals to combine with like-minded others in order to coordinate their energies, accomplish collective purposes, and secure the dividends of cooperation. Much of politics is about doing this or failing to do this. The next principle takes this argument to its logical conclusion, focusing on collective activities that are regularized because they are both important and frequently occurring. Institutions do the public's business while relieving communities of having to reinvent collective action each time it is required. Here we provide a rationale for government.

Principle 3: Institutions Matter

In the last section, we looked at the conditions in which people engage in bargaining, cooperation, and collective action in order to solve some political problem. As people, especially elected leaders and other government officials, repeatedly are required to confront recurring problems, they develop routines and standard ways of dealing with things. In a word, responses to regularly recurring problems are *institutionalized*. Collective action results because standard procedures and rules are established that provide people with appropriate incentives to take the action necessary to solve the problems. Routinized, structured relations are what we call ***institutions***. What interests students of politics most is how institutions discourage conflict, enable bargaining, and thus facilitate decision making, cooperation, and collective action.

Institution Principle
Institutions matter.

institutions
Rules and procedures that provide incentives for political behavior, thereby shaping politics.

[17]Getting such an organizational effort up and running, however, is no mean feat. Olson's argument appreciates what is necessary to keep a group going but underestimates what it takes to organize collective action in the first place. Put differently, a prior collective-action problem needs to be solved—an organizational problem. The solution is leadership, and the individuals imaginative enough to see this need are referred to as *political entrepreneurs*. That is, there must be a selective benefit available to those who bear organizational burdens, thereby facilitating the collective action; the selective benefits of leadership include perquisites of office, financial reward, honor and status, and so forth.

Institutions are part script and part scorecard. As scripts, they choreograph political activity. As scorecards, they list the players, their positions, what they want, what they can do, and when they can do it. While the Constitution sets the broad framework, much adaptation and innovation takes place as the institutions themselves are bent to the various political purposes of strategic political actors who want to win for their side and defeat the other side. Our focus here will be on the authority that institutions provide politicians for the pursuit of public policies. The discussion is divided into four broad subjects: jurisdiction, decisiveness, agenda and veto power, and delegation and transaction costs.

Jurisdiction   A critical feature of an institution is the designation of who has the authority to apply the rules or make the decisions; members recognize the jurisdiction of the main players and are quick to impose limits on these players if they feel jurisdictional authority has been exceeded. Political institutions are full of specialized jurisdictions. One of the most unusual features of the U.S. Congress is the existence of the "standing committee," whose jurisdictions are carefully defined in law. Some members of Congress are generalists, but most members become specialists in all aspects of the jurisdiction of their committees—and they often seek committee assignments based on the subject in which they want to specialize. Committee members are granted specific authority within their jurisdiction to set the agenda of the larger parent chamber. Thus, the legislative institution in the United States is affected by the way its jurisdiction-specific committees are structured.

Decisiveness   Another crucial feature of an institution is its rules for making decisions. It might sound like a straightforward task to lay out what the rules for deciding are, but it really isn't so easy to do without a raft of conditions and qualifications. Every institutionalized organization has procedural rules, and the more an organization values participation by the broadest range of its members, the more it actually needs these rules: the requirement of participation must be balanced with the need to bring discussion and activity to a close at some point so that an actual decision can be made! This is why one of the most privileged motions that can be made on the floor of a legislature is "to move the previous question," a motion to close the debate and to move immediately to a vote.[18] It is no accident that *Deschler's Procedures*, a book of rules and interpretations about procedure in the House of Representatives, runs to more than six hundred pages! Its companion for the U.S. Senate, *Jefferson's Manual*, is shorter but no less

---

[18]For a general discussion of motions to close debate and get on with the decision, see Henry M. Robert, *Robert's Rules of Order* (1876), items III, #21, and VI, #38. *Robert's* has achieved the status of an icon and now exists in an enormous variety of forms and shapes, but the basic principles remain. See, for example, *Robert's Rules of Order*, rev. ed., Darwin Patnod (Uhrichsville, Ohio: Barbour & Company, n.d.).

intricate.[19] Institutions are complicated, as are descriptions of what constitutes a decision and the conditions under which it can be made.

Even juries have rules for decisiveness; if discussion goes on too long among the members, the judge may in fact declare a *hung jury*, leading to a new trial and another round of discussion. In most organizations, including corporations, the decision to close discussion is left in the hands of the presiding officer, who might simply ask for a motion to vote on the issue in question. But even such a ruling by the chair can be appealed if the participants decide that they have not discussed the matter enough to decide.

Agenda Power and Veto Power   If decisiveness characterizes what it takes to win, then **agenda power** describes who determines what will be taken up for consideration in the first place. Those who exercise some form of agenda power are said to engage in *gatekeeping*. They determine what alternatives may pass through the gate onto the agenda and which ones have the gate slammed in their face. Gatekeeping, in other words, consists of the power to make proposals and the power to block proposals from being made. The ability to keep something off an institution's agenda should not be confused with **veto power.** The latter is the ability to defeat something, *even if it does become part of the agenda*. In the legislative process, for example, the president has (limited) veto power. Congress cannot be prevented from taking up a particular bill—the president does not have agenda power in Congress. They cannot be prevented from passing such a measure—the president has no power to block in Congress. But a presidential veto can prevent the measure from becoming the law of the land.[20]

> **agenda power**
> Control over what the group will consider for discussion.

> **veto power**   The ability to defeat something, even if it has made it onto the agenda of an institution.

Delegation and Transaction Costs   Representative democracy is the quintessential instance of **delegation** in which citizens, through voting, delegate the authority to make decisions on their behalf to representatives—chiefly legislators and executives—rather than exercising political authority directly.[21] We think of our

> **delegation**
> Transmitting authority to some other official or body for the latter's use (though often with the right of review and revision).

[19]Lewis Deschler was the long-time Parliamentarian of the House of Representatives who, for many years, kept track of House rules, precedents, and interpretations on little slips of paper stored in his desk in the Capitol. Finally, in the 1970s, he was prevailed upon to codify these. Thomas Jefferson, of course, was the third president of the United States. Before that, while he was vice president under President John Adams, he presided over the U.S. Senate (one of the few duties specified in the Constitution). This, apparently, was not an arduous task for Jefferson, for he had the time to study rules of procedure and write down a body of rules for the Senate that has survived mostly intact for more than two centuries.

[20]Article I, Section 7, of the Constitution specifies that a bill becomes a law in either of two ways: (1) a majority of the House and Senate approve it, and it is signed by the president, or (2) a majority of each chamber approves a measure, the president *vetoes* it, and then, upon congressional reconsideration, at least two-thirds of each chamber approves the measure.

[21]A surviving vestige of the direct exercise of political authority is the New England town meeting. This institution still exists in one form or another throughout states in the Northeast. Increasingly, however, town meetings occur only occasionally, with day-to-day governance delegated to an advisory committee and to an elected board of selectmen.

political representatives as our *agents*, just as we think of professionals and crafts-men whose services we retain—doctors, lawyers, accountants, plumbers, me-chanics, and so on—as agents whom we hire to act on our behalf. Now, why would those with authority, whom we will call *principals*, delegate some of their authority to agents? In effect, we are asking about the virtues of decentralization and of a division and specialization of labor. The answer is that both principals and agents benefit from it. Principals benefit because they are able to off-load tasks that they themselves are far less capable of performing to experts and spe-cialists. Ordinary citizens, for example, are not as well versed in the tasks of gov-ernance and other forms of collective action as are professional politicians. Thus, by delegating, citizens do not have to be specialists and can focus their energies on other things. This is the rationale for representative democracy.

This same rationale applies to the division and specialization of labor we often observe in specific political institutions. Legislators generally benefit from a decentralized arrangement in which they focus on those aspects of public pol-icy for which they are best equipped—issue areas of special interest to their con-stituents or on which their prior occupational and life experiences give them familiarity and perspective. In exchange, they are freed from having to be policy generalists, avoiding areas of little interest or relevance to them. The legislative committee system accomplishes this by partitioning policy into different juris-dictions and allowing legislators to gravitate to those committees that most suit their purposes.

The delegation principle, in which a principal delegates authority to an agent, seems almost too good to be true. And it is! Even though both principals and agents benefit, there is a dark side to this relationship too which we gener-ally refer to as ***principal-agent problems.*** As the eighteenth-century economist Adam Smith noted in his classic, *The Wealth of Nations*, economic agents are not motivated by the welfare of their customers to grow vegetables, make shoes, or weave cloth; rather, they do these things out of their own self-interest. Thus, a principal must take care when delegating to agents that these agents are properly motivated to serve the principal's interests, either by sharing the principal's in-terests or by deriving something of value (reputation, compensation, etc.) for acting to advance those interests. Alternatively, the principal will need to have some instruments by which to monitor and validate what his or her agent is doing and then reward or punish the agent accordingly. Nevertheless, a principal will not bother to eliminate *entirely* the agent's prospective deviations from the principal's interests. The reason is ***transaction costs.*** The organizational effort necessary to negotiate and then police every aspect of a principal-agent relation-ship becomes, at some point, more costly than it is worth. In sum, the upside of delegation consists of the assignment of activities to precisely those agents who possess a comparative advantage in performing them. (A corollary is that those who are poorly prepared to conduct these activities are relieved of performing them.) The downside is the prospective misalignment of agent goals with the goals of principals, and thus the possibility of agents marching to the beat of their own drummer.

principal-agent problems The tension that may exist between a prin-cipal and his or her agent caused by the fact that each is moti-vated by self-interest, yet their interests may not be well aligned.

transaction costs The cost of clarifying each aspect of a principal-agent relationship and monitoring it to make sure arrangements are complied with.

Characterizing institutions in terms of jurisdiction, decisiveness, agenda and veto power, and delegation and transaction cost, covers an immense amount of ground. Our purpose here has been to introduce the reader to the multiplicity of ways collectivities arrange their business and routinize it, thereby facilitating the recurring political requirements of bargaining and collective action. A second purpose has been to impress upon the reader the potential diversity in institutional arrangements—there are so many ways to do things collectively—for this underscores the amazing sophistication and intelligence of the framers of the U.S. Constitution in the institutional choices they made more than two centuries ago. Finally, we want to make clear that institutions not only comprise rules for governing, but they also describe strategic opportunities for various political interests—opportunities to influence the agenda, to engineer political action, or to block it. As George Washington Plunkitt, the savvy and candid political boss of Tammany Hall, said of the institutional situations in which he found himself, "I seen my opportunities, and I took 'em."[22]

Principle 4: Political Outcomes Are the Products of Individual Preferences and Institutional Procedures

Policy Principle

Political outcomes are the products of individual preferences and institutional procedures.

At the end of the day, politics leads to collective decisions that emerge from the political process and the consequences of these decisions for individuals. A Nebraska farmer is not much interested in the various facets of institutions we've just described, even those concerning the House Agriculture Committee. What he does care about is how public laws and rulings affect his welfare and that of his family, friends, and neighbors. He cares about how export policies affect the prices his crops and livestock products earn in international markets; how monetary policy influences inflation and, as a result, the cost of purchasing fuel, feed, seed, and fertilizer; research and development efforts, both public and private, and their impact on the quality and reliability of scientific information he obtains; the affordability of the state university where he hopes to educate his children; and he cares, eventually, about inheritance laws and their effect on his ability to pass his farm on to his kids without Uncle Sam taking a huge chunk of it in estate taxes. As students of American politics, we need to consider the link between institutional arrangements and policy outcomes. Do the organizational features of institutions leave their marks on policy? What biases, predilections, and tendencies manifest themselves in policies?

The linchpin connecting institutions to policy is the motivations of political actors. As we saw earlier in our discussion of Principle 1, their ambitions—ideological, personal, electoral, and institutional—provide politicians with the incentives to craft policies in particular ways. In fact, most policies make sense only as reflections of individual politicians' interests, goals, and beliefs. Examples include

[22]In the nineteenth century and well into the twentieth, Tammany Hall was the club that ran New York City's Democratic party like a machine.

Personal interests—Congressman Xcitement is an enthusiastic supporter of subsidizing home heating oil (but opposes regulation to keep its price down) because some of his friends own heating-oil distributorships.[23]

Electoral ambitions—Senator Yougottabekidding, a well-known political moderate, has lately been introducing very conservative amendments to bills dealing with the economy in order to appeal to more conservative financial donors who might then contribute to her budding presidential campaign.

Institutional ambitions—Representative Zeal has promised his vote and given a rousing speech on the House floor supporting a particular amendment because he knows it is near and dear to the Speaker's heart. He hopes his support will earn him the Speaker's endorsement next year for an assignment to the prestigious Appropriations Committee.

These examples illustrate how policies are politically crafted according to institutional procedures and individual aspirations. The procedures, as we have seen in a previous discussion, are a series of chutes and ladders that shape, channel, filter, and prune the alternatives from which ultimate policy choices are made. The politicians that populate these institutions, as we have just noted, are driven both by private objectives and public purposes, pursuing their own private interests while working on behalf of their conception of the public interest.

Since the institutional features of the American political system are complex and policy change requires success at every step, change is often impossibly difficult, meaning the status quo usually prevails. A long list of players must be satisfied with the change, or it won't happen. Most of these politicians will need some form of "compensation" to provide their endorsement and support.

Majorities are usually built by drafting bills so as to spread the benefits to enough members of the legislature to get the requisite number of votes for that particular bill. Derisively, this is called "pork-barrel legislation." It can be better understood by remembering that the overwhelming proportion of "pork-barrel projects" that are distributed to build policy majorities are justified to voters as valuable additions to the "public good" of the various districts. What may be "pork" to the critic are actual bridges, roads, and post offices.

Elaborate institutional arrangements, complicated policy processes, and intricate political motivations make for a highly combustible mixture. The policies that emerge are inevitably lacking in the neatness that citizens desire. But policies in the United States today are sloppy and slapdash for clear reason—it is the tendency to spread the benefits broadly that results when political ambition comes up against a decentralized political system.

---

[23]These friends would benefit from people having the financial means to buy home heating oil but would not want the price they charge for the oil restricted.

Principle 5: History Matters

There is one more aspect of our analysis that is important: we must ask how we have gotten to where we are. By what series of steps? When by choice, and when by accident? To what extent was the history of Congress, the parties, and the presidency a fulfillment of constitutional principle, and when were the developments a series of dogged responses to economic necessity? Are the parties a product of democracy, or is democracy a product of the parties? Every question and problem we confront has a history. History will not tell the same story for every institution. Nevertheless, without history, there is neither a sense of causation nor a sense of how institutions are related to each other. In explaining the answer to why governments do what they do, we must turn to history to see what choices were available to political actors at a given time and what consequences resulted from these choices.

Imagine a tree growing from the bottom of the page. Its trunk grows upward from some root ball at the bottom, dividing into branches that continue to grow upward, further dividing into smaller branches. Imagine a "path" through this tree, from its very roots at the bottom of the page to the end of one of the highest branches at the top of the page. There are many such paths, beginning from the one point at the bottom to many possible points at the top. If instead of a tree, this were a "time diagram," then the root ball at the bottom would represent some specific beginning point and all of the top-branch endings would represent some terminal time. Each path is now a *history*, the delineation of movement from some specific beginning to some concluding time. Alternative histories, like paths through trees, entail *irreversibilities*. Once one starts down a historical path (or up a tree), one cannot always retrace one's steps.[24] Once things happen, they cannot always "un-happen." One need not subscribe uncompromisingly to historical determinism in order to take the position that some futures are foreclosed by the choices people have already made, or if not literally foreclosed, then made extremely unlikely.

It is in this sense that we explain a current situation at least in part by alluding to the historical path by which we arrived at it. We say that the situation is *path-dependent*, that various features of the current situation are what they are in part because of the path by which the situation occurred, and, had a different path been taken, the features might well be different, too. Today's events and situations are a storehouse of the historical past. History provides contemporaries with an interpretive framework and a context in which to update beliefs. The principle of *path dependency* underscores the contingent nature of things: a particular unfolding of history precludes some things from happening. The historical record combines with the choices of contemporaries and the institutional arrangements they invent to produce final results or outcomes.

History Principle
History matters.

path dependency
The idea that certain possibilities are made more or less likely because of the historical path taken.

---

[24]Clearly, with tree climbing this is not literally true, or once we started climbing a tree we would never get down! So the tree analogy is not perfect here.

New Wine in Old Bottles? Bureaucratic Inertia and the Department of Homeland Security

On March 1, 2003, twenty-two federal agencies with responsibilities for combating international terrorism in the United States were transferred to the Department of Homeland Security. By all accounts, this event marked the most dramatic reform of the federal bureaucracy since the establishment of the Department of Defense in 1947. However, that earlier transformation took forty years to be fully realized, a time frame that is unacceptable in the midst of a "hot" war on terrorism. The principles of politics help us understand the events that led to the creation of a new cabinet level department. The principles also help us identify the likely hurdles that the department's leadership has faced and will continue to face. It is likely going to be a long time—if it occurs at all—before these disparate agencies are working as an efficient bureaucratic unit.

Political forces coalesced soon after the catastrophic events of September 11, 2001. Both Republicans and Democrats realized that the public was going to demand some ongoing response to the terrorist threat (beyond the immediate military response in Afghanistan). Politicians on both sides of the aisle, then, were in agreement of their primary political goal—do *something* about the terrorist threat. This agreement made it almost certain that significant political change would occur.[25]

But why did we end up with the particular solution—a new cabinet level agency? Democrats were quick to call for the creation of a new Department of Homeland Security. Yet, with Republicans—a party traditionally averse to large-scale bureaucratic solutions—in control of the White House and Congress, one would have expected at most a call for beefing up the intelligence and defense budgets, along with an attempt to shift blame to the previous administration. A congressional investigation, however, quickly revealed that serious security lapses and a lack of coordination among the various agencies with responsibility for domestic and foreign intelligence had occurred under *both* Clinton's and Bush's watch. Both parties could be blamed if the government did not respond aggressively enough to the terrorist threat.

Furthermore, the major alternative solution—the creation of a Homeland Security "czar"—proved inadequate. Tom Ridge, ex-governor of Pennsylvania, did not have the power to hire and fire his subordinates. He did not have budgetary authority. He had little beyond his title. In this case, the *lack* of rules and procedures meant that Ridge had no power to shape bureaucratic outcomes, and, according to the same principles of politics, the government needed to institutionalize rules and procedures to make Ridge's leadership effective. In the end, no alternative seemed available to the president and members of Congress on both sides of the aisle. The path to a cabinet-level agency was clear.

Eventually, the Department of Homeland Security (DHS) was authorized by Congress. Did that mean that the coordination problems faced by Ridge withered away? The last time the federal government attempted such a significant reorganization was in 1947, when the National Security Act merged the Departments of Navy and War to create the

Department of Defense. Today, more than five decades after the passage of the act, Secretary of Defense Donald Rumsfeld compares the Defense Department bureaucracy to Soviet central planning.[26]

According to Principle 2, coordination becomes more difficult as the number of people and the diversity of goals or preferences grows. In the case of DHS, the number of agencies that have to be brought under one umbrella are tremendously diverse (see the description in the text). Principle 5 reminds us that each of these agencies has gone down a particular path. Some of these bureaus had developed a bureaucratic culture and esprit de corps over more than two centuries (for example, the Customs Service or the Coast Guard), while others had grown aggressively in response to new threats (the Drug Enforcement Agency). It will be very difficult to set these agencies on a new course.

To take just one example, the most visible change for most Americans is the army of new screeners who have appeared at airports around the country. But just as the DHS is encountering great difficulties in merging and coordinating twenty-two separate agencies, the new Transportation Security Administration (TSA) has discovered that its immediate goal—assuring security at thousands of American airports—conflicts directly with the goal of a traveling population used to convenience and protective of its privacy. The TSA's new rules and procedures ran roughshod over an economically distressed airline industry accustomed to managing its own gates and monitoring its own security.

TSA officials found that dozens of their screeners had criminal histories. Many of their supervisory staff have resigned in frustration. And airlines continue to bicker with the agency over speed and convenience. Originally, the TSA projected that it could hire and train 55,000 airport screeners and establish new security protocols for $5.1 billion. Already by June 2003, the agency had spent $9 billion and was still counting. And this is just a small part of the new, sprawling DHS.

Other political outcomes have been limited thus far. The Immigration and Naturalization Service (whose new name is the Bureau of Citizenship and Immigration Services) has undergone a high-profile housecleaning due to some well-publicized snafus (for example, delivering visas to dead terrorists). The department issues "color-coded" warning alerts that seem to be mostly ignored by the general population. In January 2003, the Government Accounting Office listed the DHS as one of the departments most vulnerable to waste, fraud, and mismanagement.[27] At least, by July 22, 2003, the new department announced its official seal. But it will surely be a long time before the seal—an eagle with twenty-two arrows—reflects a fully institutionalized agency.

---

[25] John W. Kingdon calls events that limit and focus our political options "windows of political opportunity." See John W. Kingdon, *Agendas, Alternatives, and Public Policies* (Boston: Little, Brown, 1984).

[26] Cited in the "CATO Handbook for the 108th Congress," p. 63; available at www.cato.com.

[27] Government Accounting Office, "Major Management Challenges and Program Risks" (January 2003); GAO-03-95 (available at www.gao.gov).

Rationality Principle	Collective Action Principle	Institution Principle	Policy Principle	History Principle
All political behavior has a purpose.	All politics is collective action.	Institutions matter.	Political outcomes are the products of individual preferences and institutional procedures.	History matters.

Finally, without history we cannot appreciate change. We are not concerned with history for its own sake. But history does allow us the ability to analyze the consequences of institutional change in government, both intended and unintended. For example, the construction of democratic electoral institutions and popular representative bodies in the United States and other Western societies has had historic consequences that influence how government operates and what it does.

THE PARADOXES OF AMERICAN DEMOCRACY

The growth of democracy in the United States has led to wider participation, which in turn has fulfilled the democratic ideals of popular sovereignty and majority rule. Thus, democratization creates the possibility that citizens can use government for their own benefit. But given the opportunity, how do citizens create an "ideal" democracy? What are the trade-offs involved in doing so? Are there unintended consequences of too much democracy?[28] The answers to these questions are complex. Despite over two hundred years of development, American democracy has still not worked out the inconsistencies and contradictions woven in its very fiber by the framers of the Constitution. Similarly, despite all that political scientists and political historians know about American government and politics, some of which wisdom we hope we have captured in the

---

[28]For a review and analysis of the detrimental consequences of the "opening up" of American democracy since the 1960s, see Morris P. Fiorina, "Parties, Participation, and Representation in America: Old Theories Face New Realities," in *Political Science: State of the Discipline*, ed. Ira Katznelson and Helen V. Milner (New York: W. W. Norton, 2002). For a more general and provocative analysis of the detrimental effects of too much democracy, see Fareed Zakaria, *The Future of Freedom: Illiberal Democracy at Home and Abroad* (New York: W. W. Norton, 2003).

pages to follow, puzzles and anomalies reflective of the contradictions within American democracy remain for which we don't have fully satisfactory answers. We conclude this chapter by examining three of them.

Delegating Authority in a Representative Democracy

For over two centuries, we have expanded popular sovereignty to the point where a citizen, from the time he or she is roughly the age of a college freshman to the time that final breath is taken, can engage in political activity at various levels of government. Yet citizens often find it pragmatic and convenient to delegate many of these activities, sometimes (as when we don't pay attention, or vote, or even register to vote) conceding the field entirely to highly motivated individuals and groups ("special interests"). Popular sovereignty is power *if exercised*. We don't always understand why citizens participate or abstain; this is a puzzle.

Citizens delegate governance to representatives: executives, legislators, regulators, judges—politicians, in a word. Ours is a *representative* democracy for very pragmatic reasons. Most citizens have lives to live and private concerns to attend to, and, therefore, acquiesce in an arrangement enabling them to economize on the effort they must devote to their own governance. This leaves their governance agents on a fairly long leash (or, to continue the metaphor, a leash on which the hands of the more intensely active have considerable pull). This means that citizens don't always get what they want, despite popular sovereignty, because, inadvertently or not, they allow agents to pursue their own purposes or to be influenced unduly by those who care more or who have more at stake. Thus, popular sovereignty is qualified (some would say undermined) by the freedom *not* to exercise it and by our willingness to off-load governance responsibilities onto professional agents.

The Trade-off between Freedom and Order

If the imperfect fit between popular sovereignty and delegation of governance to a "political class" constitutes one anomaly, a second involves the trade-off between liberty and coercion. We have taken pains to suggest that governments are necessary to maintain order, to protect property, and to provide public goods. All these activities require a degree of coercion. Laws, regulations, and rulings constrain behavior and restrict the uses of property. Taxes include claims on labor income, on gains in the value of capital, and on the transmission of estates from one generation to another. In short, all of these things constitute limits on liberty. The anomaly here is that liberty is one of the very purposes for which the coercion is necessary in the first place. So, a pinch of coercion is one of the ingredients in the stew of liberty. But where to draw the line? And, even if we had an answer to this question, there is another: how to arrange our political life to ensure just the right amount of coercion and no more. As the history of experiments in democratic self-government reveals, and to which the American experience constitutes a significant exception, coercion is a slippery slope. Especially after the events of September 11, it is clear that a strong desire for public goods like security from terrorism lulls us into accepting extensive limitations on citizens' liberties.

The Instability of Majority Rule

A third anomaly involves the multitude of purposes pursued by different citizens. It is not always easy to add them up into a collective choice without doing damage to the interest of some. Majority rule, as we shall see in subsequent chapters, especially as manifested in the real institutions of constitutional democracies, is vulnerable to the powers of agenda setters, veto players, financial fat cats, and groups leaders (political bosses, union heads, corporate CEOs, religious leaders). All democracies struggle with the fact that outcomes, because they entail disproportionate influence by some, are not always fair. In our American democracy, we put a great deal of faith in frequent elections, checks and balances among government institutions, and multiple levels of government. But again we may ask where to draw the line: Elections how frequent? How powerful the checks? How many governmental levels? At what point is something "broke enough" to need fixing? American political history is filled with instances of decisions, followed by reactions, followed by a revisiting of those decisions, followed by further reactions. The disproportionate influence of some would appear inescapable, despite our efforts to control it. We revisit decisions. We reform institutions. We alter political practices. But still perfection eludes us.

In all these puzzles and anomalies, normative principles sometimes clash. Popular sovereignty, individual liberty, delegation, and multiple purposes constitute the circle that cannot quite be squared. The great success of American democracy, we believe, is that at the end of the day our citizens are pragmatic, tolerant, and appear to avoid letting the best be the enemy of the good.

SUMMARY

The enormous scope of national programs in the last century has required the construction of a large and elaborate state apparatus and the transfer of considerable decision-making power from political bodies like Congress to administrative agencies. As a consequence, the development and implementation of today's public policies are increasingly dominated by complicated bureaucratic institutions, rules, and procedures that are not easily affected by the citizen's preferences expressed in the voting booth. Can citizens use the power of the institutions we have created, or are we doomed simply to become their subjects?

In addition, as government has grown in size and power, the need for citizen action has diminished. Unlike their predecessors, many governments today have administrative, military, and police agencies that *can* curb disorder, collect taxes, and keep their foes in check without necessarily depending on popular involvement or approval. Will governments continue to bow to the will of the people even though public opinion may not be as crucial as it once was? Likewise, will citizens participate in the political process when few incentives are provided to do so? And by what means will citizens band together to accomplish their shared goals?

Our five principles of politics provide a focus and a means for answering these and other questions. Understanding the complexities of government might seem an overwhelming task, but these basic principles are where we need to begin. Throughout this book, we will refer to the five principles introduced in this chapter. When we do, an icon will appear in the margin to indicate which principle is involved and how that principle applies to the discussion. Try to keep these principles in mind beyond the reading of this book. They are not only the basis of political science as an academic enterprise; they are also important tools for citizens to employ as participants in America's democratic process.

FOR FURTHER READING

Bianco, William T. *American Politics: Strategy and Choice.* New York: W. W. Norton, 2001.

Dahl, Robert A. *Who Governs? Democracy and Power in an American City.* New Haven: Yale University Press, 1961.

Downs, Anthony. *An Economic Theory of Democracy.* New York: Harper & Row, 1957.

Lupia, Arthur, and Mathew D. McCubbins. *The Democratic Dilemma: Can Citizens Learn What They Need to Know?* New York: Cambridge University Press, 1998.

Olson, Mancur, Jr. *The Logic of Collective Action: Public Goods and the Theory of Groups.* Cambridge: Harvard University Press, 1965.

Putnam, Robert D. *Making Democracy Work: Civic Traditions in Modern Italy.* Princeton: Princeton University Press, 1993.

Riker, William H. *Liberalism against Populism: A Confrontation between the Theory of Democracy and the Theory of Social Choice.* San Francisco: Freeman, 1982.

Skocpol, Theda. *States and Social Revolutions: A Comparative Analysis of France, Russia, and China.* New York: Cambridge University Press, 1979.

Threats and Responses:
The President:
Signing Homeland Security Bill,
Bush Appoints Ridge as Secretary

By RICHARD W. STEVENSON

President Bush signed legislation today creating a Department of Homeland Security and named Tom Ridge, the former Pennsylvania governor who has been the White House's domestic security coordinator, to run it.

Mr. Bush's signature on the bill, which won final Congressional approval last week after a bitter political fight, set in motion a vast bureaucratic reorganization that the president said would "focus the full resources of the American government on the safety of the American people." . . .

In announcing that he would nominate Mr. Ridge as the first secretary of homeland security, Mr. Bush was entrusting him not just to oversee what is sure to be a difficult merger of disparate government agencies but also to elevate defense of Americans at home to a new level in the face of what officials say are ever-evolving terrorist threats. . . .

The birth of the department flowed from a bipartisan consensus after last year's terrorist attacks that the nation needed to do more to protect its citizens at home. It will require the largest reshuffling of governmental responsibilities since the founding of the Defense Department after World War II, a process sure to encompass turf battles and culture clashes even as the country parries a steady stream of terrorist threats and girds for possible war with Iraq.

It will bring together nearly 170,000 workers from 22 agencies with widely varying histories and missions, like the Coast Guard, the Secret Service, the federal security guards in airports and the Customs Service. The goal is to improve security along and within the

New York Times, 25 November 2002, p. A1.

nation's borders, strengthen the ability of federal, state and local authorities to respond to an attack, better focus research into nuclear, chemical and biological threats and more rigorously assess intelligence about terrorists. . . .

"Dozens of agencies charged with homeland security will now be located within one cabinet department with the mandate and legal authority to protect our people," he [President Bush] said as he prepared to sign the bill in the East Room. . . .

But Mr. Bush also injected a note of caution, saying, "No department of government can completely guarantee our safety against ruthless killers, who move and plot in shadows." . . .

With many agencies struggling to deal with deeply entrenched problems, experts said improvements to domestic security would not take place with the stroke of Mr. Bush's pen today or even the submission of the reorganization plan. They said it could be years before the department could be expected to operate at full effectiveness.

"The first challenge is to lower expectations," said Paul C. Light, who studies government organization at the Brookings Institution. . . . "People should think they will be safer, but remember we have a long way to go."

Some Democrats also suggested that there were risks that the reorganization could be a distraction to some of the agencies most directly involved in domestic security, especially since government employee unions are already concerned that Mr. Bush wants to scale back Civil Service protections for workers in the new department.

Moreover, some Democrats said, the administration is not providing the department with the money it will need to do its job effectively. . . .

The bill came to Mr. Bush's desk only after generating deep partisan dif-

ESSENCE OF THE STORY

- President Bush signed into law a bill creating a new cabinet level Department of Homeland Security.

- The department was created in response to the terrorist threat and will bring under one umbrella twenty-two separate agencies responsible for homeland security.

- Some disagree on whether the department is sufficiently funded; others note the complexities involved in merging so many agencies.

POLITICAL ANALYSIS

- Rules and procedures matter: the reporter notes that the initial proposed solution, a White House office, was deemed ineffective, and a cabinet agency was proposed instead.

- Cooperation and coordination among twenty-two agencies that have developed distinct missions and bureaucratic cultures will be very difficult.

- Even when many agree on a primary political goal, differences on subsidiary goals will spark political conflict.

ferences through much of the year. The idea of a cabinet-level department was first pushed more than a year ago by Mr. Lieberman and other Democrats on the Senate Governmental Affairs Committee. Mr. Bush said at the time that the job could be better done, at least initially, by an office within the White House rather than by creating a new bureaucracy.

Mr. Bush endorsed the idea in June, after pressure grew in both parties to address weaknesses in the government's performance in battling terrorism. But the two parties in Congress then became enmeshed in an argument over whether to grant the president broad powers to hire and fire federal workers and move them among jobs. . . .

CHAPTER

2

Constructing a Government: The Founding and the Constitution

"No taxation without representation" were words that stirred a generation of Americans long before they even dreamed of calling themselves Americans rather than Englishmen. Reacting to new English attempts to extract tax revenues to pay for the troops that were being sent to defend the colonial frontier, protests erupted throughout the colonies against the infamous Stamp Act of 1765. This act required that all printed and legal documents, including newspapers, pamphlets, advertisements, notes and bonds, leases, deeds, and licenses be printed on official paper stamped and sold by English officials. To show their displeasure with the act, the colonists conducted mass meetings, parades, bonfires, and other demonstrations throughout the spring and summer of 1765. In Boston, for example, a stamp agent was hanged and burned in effigy. Later, the home of the lieutenant governor was sacked, leading to his resignation and that of all of his colonial commission and stamp agents. By November 1765, business proceeded and newspapers were published without the stamp; in March 1766, Parliament repealed the detested law. Through their protest, the nonimportation agreements that the colonists subsequently adopted, and the Stamp Act Congress that met in October 1765, the colonists took the first steps that ultimately would lead to war and a new nation.

The people of every nation tend to glorify their own history and especially their nation's creation. Generally, through such devices as public-school texts and national holidays, governments encourage a heroic view of the nation's past as a way of promoting national pride and unity in the present. Great myths are part of the process of nation building and citizenship training in every nation, and America is no exception. To most contemporary Americans, the revolutionary period represents a brave struggle by a determined and united group of colonists against British oppression. The Boston Tea Party, the battles of Lexington and Concord, the winter at Valley Forge—these are the events that we emphasize in our history. Similarly, the American Constitution—the document establishing the system of government that ultimately emerged from this struggle—is often seen as an inspired, if not divine, work, expressing timeless principles of democratic government. These views are by no means false. During the founding era, Americans did struggle against misrule. Moreover, the American Constitution did establish the foundations for over two hundred years of democratic government.

To really understand the character of the American founding and the meaning of the American Constitution, however, it is essential to look beyond the myths and rhetoric.

The men and women who became revolutionaries were guided by principles, to be sure, but they also had interests. Most of them were not political theorists, but were hard-headed and pragmatic in their commitments and activities. Although their interests were

CHAPTER OUTLINE

The First Founding: Interests and Conflicts

- British Taxes and Colonial Interests

- Political Strife and the Radicalizing of the Colonists

- The Declaration of Independence

- The Articles of Confederation

The Second Founding: From Compromise to Constitution

- International Standing and Balance of Power

- The Annapolis Convention

- Shays's Rebellion

- The Constitutional Convention

The Constitution

- The Legislative Branch

- The Executive Branch

- The Judicial Branch

- National Unity and Power

- Amending the Constitution

- Ratifying the Constitution

- Constitutional Limits on the National

- Government's Power

The Fight for Ratification: Federalists versus Antifederalists

- Representation

- The Threats Posed by the Majority

- Governmental Power

Changing the Institutional Framework: Constitutional Amendment

- Amendments: Many Are Called, Few Are Chosen

- The Twenty-seven Amendments

Reflections on the Founding: Principles or Interests?

not identical, they did agree that a relationship of political and economic dependence on a colonial power, one that did not treat them as full-fledged citizens of the empire, was intolerable. In the end, the decision to break away and, over the succeeding decade, to fashion institutions of self-governance was the consequence.

Many of those most active in the initial days of the Revolution felt pushed into a corner, their hands forced. For years, the imperial center in London, preoccupied by a war with France that spread across several continents, had left the colonists to their own devices. These were years in which colonists enjoyed an immense amount of local control and home rule. But suddenly, as the war with France drew to a close in the 1760s, the British presence became more onerous and intrusive. This historical experience incited the initial reactions to taxes. Nearly a century of relatively light-handed colonial administration by London had produced a set of expectations in the colonists that later British actions unmistakably violated.

PREVIEWING THE PRINCIPLES

All five principles of politics come into play in this chapter. The framers of the Constitution, in addition to being guided by underlying values, also had conflicting interests that were ultimately settled in the rules and procedures set forth in the Constitution. The Constitution not only provides a framework for government, but often acts as a brake on the policy process—even to this day.

History Principle

The American colonists, used to years of self-governance, believed that the Stamp Act of 1765 threatened their autonomy.

This is where we begin our story in the present chapter. We will first assess the political backdrop of the American Revolution. Then we will examine the Constitution that ultimately emerged— after a rather bumpy experience in self-government just after the Revolution—as the basis for America's government. We will conclude with a reflection upon the founding period by emphasizing a lesson to be learned from the founding that continues to be important throughout American history. This lesson is that politics, as James Madison said in *The Federalist*, generally involves struggles among conflicting interests. In 1776, the conflict was between pro- and anti-revolutionary forces. In 1787, the struggle was between the Federalists and the Antifederalists. Today, the struggle is between the Democrats and the Republicans, each representing competing economic, social, and sectional interests. Often, political principles are the weapons developed by competing interests to further their own causes. The New England merchants who cried "no taxation without representation" cared more about lower taxes than expanded representation. Yet, today, representation is one of the foundations of American democracy.

What were the great principles that emerged from the conflicts during the founding period? How do these principles continue to shape our lives long after the Constitution's framers completed their work? These are the important questions that will be addressed in this chapter.

THE FIRST FOUNDING:
INTERESTS AND CONFLICTS

Competing ideals and principles often reflect competing interests, and so it was in revolutionary America. The American Revolution and the American Constitution were outgrowths and expressions of a struggle among economic and political forces within the colonies. Five sectors of society had interests that were important in colonial politics: (1) the New England merchants; (2) the southern planters; (3) the "royalists"—holders of royal lands, offices, and patents (licenses to engage in a profession or business activity); (4) shopkeepers, artisans, and laborers; and (5) small farmers. Throughout the eighteenth century, these groups were in conflict over issues of taxation, trade, and commerce. For the most part, however, the southern planters, the New England merchants, and the royal office and patent holders—groups that together made up the colonial elite—were able to maintain a political alliance that held in check the more radical forces representing shopkeepers, laborers, and small farmers. After 1750, however, by seriously threatening the interests of New England merchants and southern planters, British tax and trade policies split the colonial elite, permitting radical forces to expand their political influence, and set into motion a chain of events that culminated in the American Revolution.[1]

British Taxes and Colonial Interests

Beginning in the 1750s, the debts and other financial problems faced by the British government forced it to search for new revenue sources. This search rather quickly led to the Crown's North American colonies, which, on the whole, paid remarkably little in taxes to the mother country. The British government reasoned that a sizable fraction of its debt was, in fact, attributable to the expenses it had incurred in defense of the colonies during the recent French and Indian wars, as well as to the continuing protection that British forces were giving the colonists from Indian attacks and that the British navy was providing for colonial shipping. Thus, during the 1760s, England sought to impose new, though relatively modest, taxes upon the colonists.

Like most governments of the period, the British regime had at its disposal only limited ways to collect revenues. The income tax, which in the twentieth century has become the single most important source of governmental revenue, had not yet been developed. For the most part, in the mid-eighteenth century, governments relied on tariffs, duties, and other taxes on commerce, and it was to such taxes, including the Stamp Act, that the British turned during the 1760s.

---

[1]The social makeup of colonial America and some of the social conflicts that divided colonial society are discussed in Jackson Turner Main, *The Social Structure of Revolutionary America* (Princeton: Princeton University Press, 1965).

The Stamp Act and other taxes on commerce, such as the Sugar Act of 1764, which taxed sugar, molasses, and other commodities, most heavily affected the two groups in colonial society whose commercial interests and activities were most extensive—the New England merchants and southern planters. Under the famous slogan "no taxation without representation," the merchants and planters together sought to organize opposition to the new taxes. In the course of the struggle against British tax measures, the planters and merchants broke with their royalist allies and turned to their former adversaries—the shopkeepers, small farmers, laborers, and artisans—for help. With the assistance of these groups, the merchants and planters organized demonstrations and a boycott of British goods that ultimately forced the Crown to rescind most of its new taxes. It was in the context of this unrest that a confrontation between colonists and British soldiers in front of the Boston customshouse on the night of March 5, 1770, resulted in what came to be known as the Boston Massacre. Nervous British soldiers opened fire on the mob surrounding them, killing five colonists and wounding eight others. News of this event quickly spread throughout the colonies and was used by radicals to fan anti-British sentiment.

From the perspective of the merchants and planters, however, the British government's decision to eliminate most of the hated taxes represented a victorious end to their struggle with the mother country. They were anxious to end the unrest they had helped to arouse, and they supported the British government's efforts to restore order. Indeed, most respectable Bostonians supported the actions of the British soldiers involved in the Boston Massacre. In their subsequent trial, the soldiers were defended by John Adams, a pillar of Boston society and a future president of the United States. Adams asserted that the soldiers' actions were entirely justified, provoked by a "motley rabble of saucy boys, negroes and mulattoes, Irish teagues and outlandish Jack tars." All but two of the soldiers were acquitted.[2]

Despite the efforts of the British government and the better-to-do strata of colonial society, it proved difficult to bring an end to the political strife. The more radical forces representing shopkeepers, artisans, laborers, and small farmers, who had been mobilized and energized by the struggle over taxes, continued to agitate for political and social change within the colonies. These radicals, led by individuals like Samuel Adams, cousin of John Adams, asserted that British power supported an unjust political and social structure within the colonies, and they began to advocate an end to British rule.[3]

Organizing resistance to the British authorities, however, required widespread support. Collective action, as we saw in the previous chapter, may emerge

---

[2]George B. Tindall and David E. Shi, *America: A Narrative History*, 5th ed. (New York: W. W. Norton, 1999), p. 218.

[3]For a discussion of events leading up to the Revolution, see Charles M. Andrews, *The Colonial Background of the American Revolution: Four Essays in American Colonial History* (New Haven: Yale University Press, 1924).

spontaneously in certain circumstances, but the colonists' campaign against the British imperial power in late eighteenth-century America was a series of encounters, maneuvers, and, ultimately, confrontations that required planning, coalition building, bargaining, compromising, and coordinating, all elements of the give-and-take of politics. Conflicts among the colonists had to be solved by bargaining, persuasion, and even force. Cooperation needed cultivation and encouragement. Leadership was clearly a necessary ingredient.

Collective Action Principle
The colonists required strong leaders to resolve differences and to organize resistance to British authority.

Political Strife and the Radicalizing of the Colonists

The political strife within the colonies was the background for the events of 1773–1774. In 1773, the British government granted the politically powerful East India Company a monopoly on the export of tea from Britain, eliminating a lucrative form of trade for colonial merchants. To add to the injury, the East India Company sought to sell the tea directly in the colonies instead of working through the colonial merchants. Tea was an extremely important commodity in the 1770s, and these British actions posed a mortal threat to the New England merchants. The merchants once again called upon their radical adversaries for support. The most dramatic result was the Boston Tea Party of 1773, led by Samuel Adams.

This event was of decisive importance in American history. The merchants had hoped to force the British government to rescind the Tea Act, but they did not support any demands beyond this one. They certainly did not seek independence from Britain. Samuel Adams and the other radicals, however, hoped to provoke the British government to take actions that would alienate its colonial supporters and pave the way for a rebellion. This was precisely the purpose of the Boston Tea Party, and it succeeded. By dumping the East India Company's tea into Boston Harbor, Adams and his followers goaded the British into enacting a number of harsh reprisals. Within five months after the incident in Boston, the House of Commons passed a series of acts that closed the port of Boston to commerce, changed the provincial government of Massachusetts, provided for the removal of accused persons to England for trial, and, most important, restricted movement to the West—further alienating the southern planters who depended upon access to new western lands. These acts of retaliation confirmed the worst criticisms of England and helped radicalize Americans.

The choice of this course of action by English politicians looks puzzling in retrospect, but at the time it appeared reasonable to those who prevailed in Parliament that a show of force was required. The toleration of lawlessness and the making of concessions, they felt, would only egg on the more radical elements in the colonies to take further liberties and demand further concessions. The English, in effect, drew a line in the sand. Their repressive reactions served as a clear point around which dissatisfied colonists could rally. Radicals like Samuel Adams had been agitating for more violent measures to deal with England. But ultimately they needed Britain's political repression to create widespread support for independence.

Thus, the Boston Tea Party set into motion a cycle of provocation and retaliation that in 1774 resulted in the convening of the First Continental Congress—an assembly consisting of delegates from all parts of the country—that called for a total boycott of British goods and, under the prodding of the radicals, began to consider the possibility of independence from British rule. The eventual result was the Declaration of Independence.

The Declaration of Independence

In 1776, the Second Continental Congress appointed a committee consisting of Thomas Jefferson of Virginia, Benjamin Franklin of Pennsylvania, Roger Sherman of Connecticut, John Adams of Massachusetts, and Robert Livingston of New York to draft a statement of American independence from British rule. The Declaration of Independence, written by Jefferson and adopted by the Second Continental Congress, was an extraordinary document both in philosophical and political terms. Philosophically, the Declaration was remarkable for its assertion that certain rights, called "unalienable rights"—including life, liberty, and the pursuit of happiness—could not be abridged by governments. In the world of 1776, a world in which some kings still claimed to rule by divine right, this was a dramatic statement. Politically, the Declaration was remarkable because, despite the differences of interest that divided the colonists along economic, regional, and philosophical lines, the Declaration identified and focused on problems, grievances, aspirations, and principles that might unify the various colonial groups. The Declaration was an attempt to identify and articulate a history and set of principles that might help to forge national unity.[4]

The Articles of Confederation

Articles of Confederation and Perpetual Union America's first written constitution. Adopted by the Continental Congress in 1777, the Articles of Confederation and Perpetual Union was the formal basis for America's national government until 1789, when it was supplanted by the Constitution.

Having declared their independence, the colonies needed to establish a governmental structure. In November of 1777, the Continental Congress adopted the *Articles of Confederation and Perpetual Union*—the United States' first written constitution. Although it was not ratified by all the states until 1781, it was the country's operative constitution for almost twelve years, until March 1789.

The Articles of Confederation was a constitution concerned primarily with limiting the powers of the central government. The central government, first of all, was based entirely in Congress. Since it was not intended to be a powerful government, it was given no executive branch. Execution of its laws was to be left to the individual states. Second, Congress had little power. Its members were not much more than delegates or messengers from the state legislatures. They were chosen by the state legislatures, their salaries were paid out of the state

---

[4]See Carl L. Becker, *The Declaration of Independence: A Study in the History of Political Ideas* (New York: Vintage, 1942).

treasuries, and they were subject to immediate recall by state authorities. In addition, each state, regardless of its size, had only a single vote.

Congress was given the power to declare war and make peace, to make treaties and alliances, to coin or borrow money, and to regulate trade with the Native Americans. It could also appoint the senior officers of the United States Army. But it could not levy taxes or regulate commerce among the states. Moreover, the army officers it appointed had no army to serve in because the nation's armed forces were composed of the state militias. Probably the most unfortunate part of the Articles of Confederation was that the central government could not prevent one state from discriminating against other states in the quest for foreign commerce.

In brief, the relationship between Congress and the states under the Articles of Confederation was much like the contemporary relationship between the United Nations and its member states, a relationship in which virtually all governmental powers are retained by the states. It was properly called a "confederation" because, as provided under Article II, "each state retains its sovereignty, freedom, and independence, and every power, jurisdiction, and right, which is not by this Confederation expressly delegated to the United States, in Congress assembled." Not only was there no executive, there was also no judicial authority and no other means of enforcing Congress's will. If there was to be any enforcement at all, it would be done for Congress by the states.[5]

THE SECOND FOUNDING: FROM COMPROMISE TO CONSTITUTION

The Declaration of Independence and the Articles of Confederation were not sufficient to hold the nation together as an independent and effective nation-state. From almost the moment of armistice with the British in 1783, moves were afoot to reform and strengthen the Articles of Confederation.

International Standing and Balance of Power

There was a special concern for the country's international position. Competition among the states for foreign commerce allowed the European powers to play the states against each other, which created confusion on both sides of the Atlantic. At one point during the winter of 1786–1787, John Adams of Massachusetts, a leader in the independence struggle, was sent to negotiate a new treaty with the British, one that would cover disputes left over from the war. The British government responded that, since the United States under the Articles of Confederation was unable to enforce existing treaties, it would negotiate with each of the thirteen states separately.

[5]See Merrill Jensen, *The Articles of Confederation* (Madison: University of Wisconsin Press, 1963).

At the same time, well-to-do Americans—in particular the New England merchants and southern planters—were troubled by the influence that "radical" forces exercised in the Continental Congress and in the governments of several of the states. The colonists' victory in the Revolutionary War had not only meant the end of British rule, but it also significantly changed the balance of political power within the new states. As a result of the Revolution, one key segment of the colonial elite—the royal land, office, and patent holders—was stripped of its economic and political privileges. In fact, many of these individuals, along with tens of thousands of other colonists who considered themselves loyal British subjects, left for Canada after the British surrender. And while the pre-revolutionary elite was weakened, the pre-revolutionary radicals were now better organized than ever before and were the controlling forces in such states as Pennsylvania and Rhode Island, where they pursued economic and political policies that struck terror into the hearts of the pre-revolutionary political establishment. In Rhode Island, for example, between 1783 and 1785, a legislature dominated by representatives of small farmers, artisans, and shopkeepers had instituted economic policies, including drastic currency inflation, that frightened businessmen and property owners throughout the country. Of course, the central government under the Articles of Confederation was powerless to intervene.

Institution Principle

Institutional arrangements matter, but there is no guarantee that they will be perfect, as the Articles of Confederation make apparent.

The Annapolis Convention

The continuation of international weakness and domestic economic turmoil led many Americans to consider whether their newly adopted form of government might not already require revision. Institutional arrangements are experiments in governance, and they don't always work out. Nearly a decade under the Articles had made amply clear the flaws it contained. In the fall of 1786, many state leaders accepted an invitation from the Virginia legislature for a conference of representatives of all the states. Delegates from five states actually attended. This conference, held in Annapolis, Maryland, was the first step toward the second founding. The one positive thing that came out of the Annapolis Convention was a carefully worded resolution calling on Congress to send commissioners to Philadelphia at a later time "to devise such further provisions as shall appear to them necessary to render the Constitution of the Federal Government adequate to the exigencies of the Union."[6] This resolution was drafted by Alexander Hamilton, a thirty-four-year-old New York lawyer who had played a significant role in the Revolution as George Washington's secretary and who would play a still more significant role in framing the Constitution and forming the new government in the 1790s. But the resolution did not necessarily imply any desire to do more than improve and reform the Articles of Confederation.

[6]Reported in Samuel Eliot Morrison, Henry Steele Commager, and William E. Leuchtenburg, *The Growth of the American Republic*, 6th ed., vol. 1 (New York: Oxford University Press, 1969), p. 244.

Shays's Rebellion

It is possible that the Constitutional Convention of 1787 in Philadelphia would never have taken place at all except for a single event that occurred during the winter following the Annapolis Convention: Shays's Rebellion. Like the Boston Tea Party, this was a focal event. It concentrated attention, coordinated beliefs, produced widespread fear and apprehension, and thus convinced waverers that "something was broke and needed fixing." In short, it provided politicians who had long been convinced that the Articles were flawed and insufficient with just the ammunition they needed to persuade a much broader public of these facts.[7]

Daniel Shays, a former army captain, led a mob of farmers in a rebellion against the government of Massachusetts. The purpose of the rebellion was to prevent foreclosures on their debt-ridden land by keeping the county courts of western Massachusetts from sitting until after the next election. The state militia dispersed the mob, but for several days, Shays and his followers terrified the state government by attempting to capture the federal arsenal at Springfield, provoking an appeal to Congress to help restore order. Within a few days, the state government regained control and captured fourteen of the rebels (all were eventually pardoned). In 1787, a newly elected Massachusetts legislature granted some of the farmers' demands.

Although the incident ended peacefully, its effects lingered and spread. Washington summed it up: "I am mortified beyond expression that in the moment of our acknowledged independence we should by our conduct verify the predictions of our transatlantic foe, and render ourselves ridiculous and contemptible in the eyes of all Europe."[8]

Congress under the Confederation had been unable to act decisively in a time of crisis. This provided critics of the Articles of Confederation with precisely the evidence they needed to push Hamilton's Annapolis resolution through the Congress. Thus, the states were asked to send representatives to Philadelphia to discuss constitutional revision. Delegates were eventually sent by every state except Rhode Island.

History Principle

Shays's Rebellion focused attention on the flaws of the Articles of Confederation, leading to the Constitutional Convention.

The Constitutional Convention

Twenty-nine of a total of 73 delegates selected by the state governments convened in Philadelphia in May 1787, with political strife, international embarrassment, national weakness, and local rebellion fixed in their minds. Recognizing that these issues were symptoms of fundamental flaws in the Articles of Confederation, the delegates soon abandoned the plan to revise the Articles and committed themselves to a second founding—a second, and ultimately successful, attempt to create a legitimate and effective national system. This effort occupied the convention for the next five months.

[7]For an easy-to-read argument that supports this view, see Keith L. Dougherty, *Collective Action under the Articles of Confederation* (New York: Cambridge University Press, 2001).
[8]Morrison et al., *The Growth of the American Republic*, p. 242.

A Marriage of Interest and Principle   For years, scholars have disagreed about the motives of the founders in Philadelphia. Among the most controversial views of the framers' motives is the "economic" interpretation put forward by historian Charles Beard and his disciples.[9] According to Beard's account, America's founders were a collection of securities speculators and property owners whose only aim was personal enrichment. From this perspective, the Constitution's lofty principles were little more than sophisticated masks behind which the most venal interests sought to enrich themselves.

Contrary to Beard's approach is the view that the framers of the Constitution *were* concerned with philosophical and ethical principles. Indeed, the framers sought to devise a system of government consistent with the dominant philosophical and moral principles of the day. But, in fact, these two views belong together; the founders' interests were reinforced by their principles. The convention that drafted the American Constitution was chiefly organized by the New England merchants and southern planters. Though the delegates representing these groups did not all hope to profit personally from an increase in the value of their securities, as Beard would have it, they did hope to benefit in the broadest political and economic sense by breaking the power of their radical foes and establishing a system of government more compatible with their long-term economic and political interests. Thus, the framers sought to create a new government capable of promoting commerce and protecting property from radical state legislatures. They also sought to liberate the national government from the power of individual states and their sometimes venal and corrupt local politicians. At the same time, they hoped to fashion a government less susceptible than the existing state and national regimes to populist forces hostile to the interests of the commercial and propertied classes.

The Great Compromise   The proponents of a new government fired their opening shot on May 29, 1787, when Edmund Randolph of Virginia offered a resolution that proposed corrections and enlargements in the Articles of Confederation. The proposal, which showed the strong influence of James Madison, was not a simple motion. It provided for virtually every aspect of a new government. Randolph later admitted it was intended to be an alternative draft constitution, and it did in fact serve as the framework for what ultimately became the Constitution. (There is no verbatim record of the debates, but Madison was present during virtually all of the deliberations and kept full notes on them.)[10]

This proposal, known as the "Virginia Plan," provided for a system of representation in the national legislature based on the population of each state or the

---

[9]Charles A. Beard, *An Economic Interpretation of the Constitution of the United States* (New York: Macmillan, 1913).

[10]Madison's notes along with the somewhat less complete records kept by several other participants in the convention are available in a four-volume set. See Max Farrand, ed., *The Records of the Federal Convention of 1787*, rev. ed., 4 vols. (New Haven: Yale University Press, 1966).

proportion of each state's revenue contribution, or both. (Randolph also proposed a second branch of the legislature, but it was to be elected by the members of the first branch.) Since the states varied enormously in size and wealth, the Virginia Plan was thought to be heavily biased in favor of the large states.

While the convention was debating the Virginia Plan, additional delegates were arriving in Philadelphia and were beginning to mount opposition to it. Their resolution, introduced by William Paterson of New Jersey and known as the "New Jersey Plan," did not oppose the Virginia Plan point for point. Instead, it concentrated on specific weaknesses in the Articles of Confederation, in the spirit of revision rather than radical replacement of that document. Supporters of the New Jersey Plan did not seriously question the convention's commitment to replacing the Articles. But their opposition to the Virginia Plan's scheme of representation was sufficient to send its proposals back to committee for reworking into a common document. In particular, delegates from the less populous states, which included Delaware, New Jersey, Connecticut, and New York, asserted that the more populous states, such as Virginia, Pennsylvania, North Carolina, Massachusetts, and Georgia, would dominate the new government if representation were to be determined by population. The smaller states argued that each state should be equally represented in the new regime regardless of its population.

The issue of representation was one that threatened to wreck the entire constitutional enterprise. Delegates conferred, factions maneuvered, and tempers flared. James Wilson of Pennsylvania told the small-state delegates that if they wanted to disrupt the union they should go ahead. The separation could, he said, "never happen on better grounds." Small-state delegates were equally blunt. Gunning Bedford of Delaware declared that the small states might look elsewhere for friends if they were forced. "The large states," he said, "dare not dissolve the confederation. If they do the small ones will find some foreign ally of more honor and good faith, who will take them by the hand and do them justice." These sentiments were widely shared. The union, as Oliver Ellsworth of Connecticut put it, was "on the verge of dissolution, scarcely held together by the strength of a hair."

The outcome of this debate was the Connecticut Compromise, also known as the *Great Compromise.* Under the terms of this compromise, in the first branch of Congress—the House of Representatives—the representatives would be apportioned according to the number of inhabitants in each state. This, of course, was what delegates from the large states had sought. But in the second branch—the Senate—each state would have an equal vote regardless of its size; this was to deal with the concerns of the small states. This compromise was not immediately satisfactory to all the delegates. Indeed, two of the most vocal members of the small-state faction, John Lansing and Robert Yates of New York, were so incensed by the concession that their colleagues had made to the large-state forces that they stormed out of the convention. In the end, however, both sets of forces preferred compromise to the breakup of the union, and the plan was accepted.

Great Compromise
Agreement reached at the Constitutional Convention of 1787 that gave each state an equal number of senators regardless of its population, but linked representation in the House of Representatives to population.

The Question of Slavery: The Three-fifths Compromise   The story so far is too neat, too easy, and too anticlimactic. If it were left here, it would only contribute to American mythology. After all, the notion of a bicameral (two-chambered) legislature was very much in the air in 1787. Some of the states had had this for years. The Philadelphia delegates might well have gone straight to the adoption of two chambers based on two different principles of representation even without the dramatic interplay of conflict and compromise. But a far more fundamental issue had to be confronted before the Great Compromise could take place: the issue of slavery.

Many of the conflicts that emerged during the Constitutional Convention were reflections of the fundamental differences between the slave and the nonslave states—differences that pitted the southern planters and New England merchants against one another. This was the first premonition of a conflict that was almost to destroy the Republic in later years. In the midst of debate over large versus small states, Madison observed:

> The great danger to our general government is the great southern and northern interests of the continent, being opposed to each other. Look to the votes in Congress, and most of them stand divided by the geography of the country, not according to the size of the states.[11]

Over 90 percent of all slaves resided in five states—Georgia, Maryland, North Carolina, South Carolina, and Virginia—where they accounted for 30 percent of the total population. In some places, slaves outnumbered nonslaves by as much as 10 to 1. If the Constitution were to embody any principle of national supremacy, some basic decisions would have to be made about the place of slavery in the general scheme. Madison hit on this point on several occasions as different aspects of the Constitution were being discussed. For example, he observed:

> It seemed now to be pretty well understood that the real difference of interests lay, not between the large and small but between the northern and southern states. The institution of slavery and its consequences formed the line of discrimination. There were five states on the South, eight on the northern side of this line. Should a proportional representation take place it was true, the northern side would still outnumber the other: but not in the same degree, at this time; and every day would tend towards an equilibrium.[12]

Three-fifths Compromise
Agreement reached at the Constitutional Convention of 1787 that stipulated that for purposes of the apportionment of congressional seats, every slave would be counted as three-fifths of a person.

Northerners and southerners eventually reached agreement through the ***Three-fifths Compromise.*** The seats in the House of Representatives would be apportioned according to a "population" in which five slaves would count as three persons. The slaves would not be allowed to vote, of course, but the num-

[11]Ibid., I, p. 476.
[12]Ibid., II, p. 10.

ber of representatives would be apportioned accordingly. This arrangement was supported by the slave states, which obviously included some of the biggest and some of the smallest states at that time. It was also accepted by many delegates from nonslave states who strongly supported the principle of property representation, whether that property was expressed in slaves or in land, money, or stocks. The concern exhibited by most delegates was over how much slaves would count toward a state's representation rather than whether the institution of slavery would continue. The Three-fifths Compromise, in the words of political scientist Donald Robinson, "gave Constitutional sanction to the fact that the United States was composed of some persons who were 'free' and others who were not, and it established the principle, new in republican theory, that a man who lives among slaves had a greater share in the election of representatives than the man who did not. Although the Three-fifths Compromise acknowledged slavery and rewarded slave owners, nonetheless, it probably kept the South from unanimously rejecting the Constitution."[13]

The issue of slavery was the most difficult one faced by the framers, and it nearly destroyed the Union. Although some delegates believed slavery to be morally wrong, an evil and oppressive institution that made a mockery of the ideals and values espoused in the Constitution, morality was not the issue that caused the framers to support or oppose the Three-fifths Compromise. Whatever they thought of the institution of slavery, most delegates from the northern states opposed counting slaves in the distribution of congressional seats. Wilson of Pennsylvania, for example, argued that if slaves were citizens they should be treated and counted like other citizens. If on the other hand, they were property, then why should not other forms of property be counted toward the apportionment of Congress? But southern delegates made it clear that if the northerners refused to give in, they would never agree to the new government. William R. Davie of North Carolina heatedly said that it was time "to speak out." He asserted that the people of North Carolina would never enter the Union if slaves were not counted as part of the basis for representation. Without such agreement, he asserted ominously, "the business was at an end." Even southerners like Edmund Randolph of Virginia, who conceded that slavery was immoral, insisted upon including slaves in the allocation of congressional seats. This conflict between the southern and northern delegates was so divisive that many came to question the possibility of creating and maintaining a union of the two. Pierce Butler of South Carolina declared that the North and South were as different as Russia and Turkey. Eventually, the North and South compromised on the issue of slavery and representation. Indeed, northerners even agreed to permit a continuation of the odious slave trade to keep the South in the union. But, in due course, Butler proved to be correct, and a bloody war was fought when the disparate interests of the North and South could no longer be reconciled.

Collective Action Principle

The framers preferred compromise to the breakup of the union, and thus accepted the Great Compromise and the Three-fifths Compromise.

[13]Donald L. Robinson, *Slavery in the Structure of American Politics, 1765–1820* (New York: Harcourt Brace Jovanovich, 1971), p. 201.

Were the Framers Rational Actors?

How can we use the five principles of politics to interpret events that occurred centuries ago? The strategic decision making at the American Constitutional Convention has been a fertile area of study.

Many of the basic ingredients for a strategic politics analysis are present. The historical record is detailed and seemingly very accurate. The entire Constitutional Convention took place in secret, and the delegates took pains to ensure that the media and mass public were not aware of the decisions being made, the alternatives that were rejected, or the process that was being utilized.

In line with Principle 2, keeping the group small and homogeneous increased the chance of successful collective action. Participation was restricted to those delegates who were directly appointed by the state legislatures. By keeping the proceedings closed, it reduced the likelihood that outside parties could influence the discussion or that new issues could be introduced that would complicate the process.

At the same time, the convention allowed for extensive internal discussion. Most participants knew the preferences of the other participants. In the language of rational choice, the setting was close to "full information." In situations where every player knows the goals and options of every other player, it is far easier to predict everyone's behavior.[14]

In a famous article and book, historian Charles Beard advocated the view of the founders as strategic actors by making the provocative argument that the Constitution is a document written by wealthy elites to preserve their own economic and political power.[15] Beard focused on the secretive and elite-centered nature of the convention and the limited franchise found throughout the process. In Beard's analysis, the Constitution is not the grand design of political philosophers, but instead the product of hard-nosed political bargaining and self-interests. An infamous example of this is the "three-fifths" rule for counting slaves. This was the result of a bargain between pro-slavery, anti-tariff southerners and northerners who were opposed to slavery yet wanted to retain protective tariffs.

William Riker similarly shows how delegates, such as Gouverneur Morris, delegate from Pennsylvania, manipulated the procedures at the convention in order to obtain his desired outcome. According to Riker, Morris and a few other Pennsylvanians were the only opposition to the "Virginia Plan," whereby the executive would be elected by the national legislature (the two houses of Congress). If adopted, the Virginia Plan would have rendered states wholly subservient to the national government because the plan also allowed the national legislature to abrogate state laws.[16] In essence, Morris was able to change the order in which various provisions of the Virginia Plan were considered such that it became apparent that endorsing the Virginia Plan was tantamount to endorsing a lifetime presidency.[17] As Principle 3 indicates, rules and procedures—particularly agenda control—matter.

Still, this approach to the founding remains controversial. Americans revere the founders as angels and brilliant philosophers. Many object to this self-interested interpretation. Historian Robert Brown disputes Beard's account of the convention.[18] What Beard fails to appreciate, Brown argues, is that American society as a whole was in favor of the democratic changes enshrined in the Constitution. Americans did not perceive the Constitution as an elite vehicle being foisted upon them. Brown argues that agrarian, commercial, and mercantile interests felt that they were well represented by the delegates.

Regardless if you believe that the founders "truly" were strategic or not, rational choice can help you understand how the convention proceeded the way it did. Keep the group small (Principle 2), keep control of rules and procedures (Principle 3), and you can readily control the outcome. Even when actors are motivated by altruistic concerns, institutional rules and procedures can be used to obtain a preferred outcome.

[14]These types of situations are rare in everyday life. Substantial research in political science and economics has focused on how individuals make do with "limited" information.

[15]Charles A. Beard, *An Economic Interpretation of the Constitution of the United States* (New York: Macmillan, 1913).

[16]This was precisely the goal of the supporters of the Virginia Plan. They believed that state legislatures were incompetent and that states should be governed by a national elite.

[17]The specifics are laid out in more detail in Chapter 4 of William H. Riker's *The Art of Political Manipulation* (New Haven: Yale University Press, 1986).

[18]Robert E. Brown, *Charles Beard and the Constitution: A Critical Analysis of "An Economic Interpretation of the Constitution"* (New York: W. W. Norton, 1965).

THE CONSTITUTION

The political significance of the Great Compromise and Three-fifths Compromise was to reinforce the unity of the mercantile and planter forces that sought to create a new government. The Great Compromise reassured those who feared that the importance of their own local or regional influence would be reduced by the new governmental framework. The Three-fifths Compromise temporarily defused the rivalry between the merchants and planters. Their unity secured, members of the alliance supporting the establishment of a new government moved to fashion a constitutional framework consistent with their economic and political interests.

In particular, the framers sought a new government that, first, would be strong enough to promote commerce and protect property from radical state legislatures such as Rhode Island's. This became the constitutional basis for national control over commerce and finance, as well as the establishment of national judicial supremacy and the effort to construct a strong presidency. Second, the framers sought to prevent what they saw as the threat posed by the "excessive democracy" of the state and national governments under the Articles of

bicameralism
Having a legislative
assembly composed
of two chambers or
houses.

Confederation. This led to such constitutional principles as **bicameralism** (division of the Congress into two chambers), checks and balances, staggered terms in office, and indirect election (selection of the president by an electoral college rather than by voters directly). Third, the framers, lacking the power to force the states or the public at large to accept the new form of government, sought to identify principles that would help to secure support. This became the basis of the constitutional provision for direct popular election of representatives and, subsequently, for the addition of the Bill of Rights to the Constitution. Finally, the framers wanted to be certain that the government they created did not use its power to pose even more of a threat to its citizens' liberties and property rights than did the radical state legislatures they feared and despised. To prevent the new government from abusing its power, the framers incorporated principles such as the separation of powers and federalism into the Constitution.

The framers provided us with a grand lesson in instrumental behavior. They came to Philadelphia united by a common distaste for government under the Articles and animated by the agitation following Shays's Rebellion. They didn't always agree on what it was they disliked about the Articles. They certainly didn't agree on how to proceed—hence the necessity for the historic compromises we have just described. But they did believe that the fostering of commerce and the protection of property could better be served by an alternative set of institutional arrangements than that of the Articles. They agreed that the institutional arrangements of government mattered for their lives and those of their fellow citizens. They believed that both too much democracy and too much governmental power were threats to the common good, and they felt compelled to find instruments and principles that weighed against these. Let us assess the major provisions of the Constitution's seven articles to see how each relates to these objectives.

Rationality Principle
The framers of the Constitution were guided by principles, but they also had interests.

Institution Principle
The constitutional framework promoted commerce, protected property, prevented "excessive democracy," and limited the power of the national government.

The Legislative Branch

The first seven sections of Article I of the Constitution provided for a Congress consisting of two chambers—a House of Representatives and a Senate. Members of the House of Representatives were given two-year terms in office and were to be elected directly by the people. Members of the Senate were to be appointed by the state legislatures (this was changed in 1913 by the Seventeenth Amendment, which instituted direct election of senators) for six-year terms. These terms, moreover, were staggered so that the appointments of one-third of the senators would expire every two years. The Constitution assigned somewhat different tasks to the House and Senate. Though the approval of each body was required for the enactment of a law, the Senate alone was given the power to ratify treaties and approve presidential appointments. The House, on the other hand, was given the sole power to originate revenue bills.

The character of the legislative branch was directly related to the framers' major goals. The House of Representatives was designed to be directly responsible to the people in order to encourage popular consent for the new Constitution and to help enhance the power of the new government. At the same time, to guard against "excessive democracy," the power of the House of Representatives was checked by the Senate, whose members were to be appointed for long terms rather than be elected directly by the people. The purpose of this provision, according to Alexander Hamilton, was to avoid "an unqualified complaisance to every sudden breeze of passion, or to every transient impulse which the people may receive."[19] Staggered terms of service in the Senate, moreover, were intended to make that body even more resistant to popular pressure. Since only one-third of the senators would be selected at any given time, the composition of the institution would be protected from changes in popular preferences transmitted by the state legislatures. This would prevent what James Madison called "mutability in the public councils arising from a rapid succession of new members."[20] Thus, the structure of the legislative branch was designed to contribute to governmental power, to promote popular consent for the new government, and at the same time to place limits on the popular political currents that many of the framers saw as a radical threat to the economic and social order.

The issues of power and consent were important throughout the Constitution. Section 8 of Article I specifically listed the powers of Congress, which include the authority to collect taxes, to borrow money, to regulate commerce, to declare war, and to maintain an army and navy. By granting it these powers, the framers indicated very clearly that they intended the new government to be far more influential than its predecessor. At the same time, by defining the new government's most important powers as belonging to Congress, the framers sought to promote popular acceptance of this critical change by reassuring citizens that their views would be fully represented whenever the government exercised its new powers.

As a further guarantee to the people that the new government would pose no threat to them, the Constitution implied that any powers not listed were not granted at all. This is the doctrine of **expressed power.** The Constitution grants only those powers specifically *expressed* in its text. But the framers intended to create an active and powerful government, and so they included the **necessary and proper clause,** sometimes known as the elastic clause, which signified that the enumerated powers were meant to be a source of strength to the national government, not a limitation on it. Each power could be used with the utmost vigor, but no new powers could be seized upon by the national government without a constitutional amendment. In the absence of such an amendment, any power not enumerated was conceived to be "reserved" to the states (or the people).

The Executive Branch

The Constitution provided for the establishment of the presidency in Article II. As Alexander Hamilton commented, the presidential article aimed toward "energy in the Executive." It did so in an effort to overcome the natural stalemate

expressed power
The notion that the Constitution grants to the federal government only those powers specifically named in its text.

necessary and proper clause
Article I, Section 8, of the Constitution, which enumerates the powers of Congress and provides Congress with the authority to make all laws "necessary and proper" to carry them out; also referred to as the "elastic clause."

[19]E. M. Earle, ed., *The Federalist* (New York: Modern Library, 1937), No. 71.
[20]Ibid., No. 62.

that was built into the bicameral legislature as well as into the separation of powers among the legislative, executive, and judicial branches. The Constitution afforded the president a measure of independence from the people and from the other branches of government—particularly the Congress.

In line with the framers' goal of increased power to the national government, the president was granted the unconditional power to accept ambassadors from other countries; this amounted to the power to "recognize" other countries. He was also given the power to negotiate treaties, although their acceptance required the approval of the Senate. The president was given the unconditional right to grant reprieves and pardons, except in cases of impeachment. And he was provided with the power to appoint major departmental personnel, to convene Congress in special session, and to veto congressional enactments. (The veto power is formidable, but it is not absolute since Congress can override it by a two-thirds vote.)

The framers hoped to create a presidency that would make the federal government rather than the states the agency capable of timely and decisive action to deal with public issues and problems. This was the meaning of the "energy" that Hamilton hoped to impart to the executive branch.[21] At the same time, however, the framers sought to help the president withstand (excessively) democratic pressures by making him subject to indirect rather than direct election (through his selection by a separate electoral college). The extent to which the framers' hopes were actually realized will be the topic of Chapter 6.

The Judicial Branch

In establishing the judicial branch in Article III, the Constitution reflected the framers' preoccupations with nationalizing governmental power and checking radical democratic impulses, while guarding against potential interference with liberty and property from the new national government itself.

Under the provisions of Article III, the framers created a court that was to be literally a supreme court of the United States and not merely the highest court of the national government. The most important expression of this intention was granting the Supreme Court the power to resolve any conflicts that might emerge between federal and state laws. In particular, the Supreme Court was given the right to determine whether a power was exclusive to the federal government, concurrent with the states, or exclusive to the states. The significance of this was noted by Justice Oliver Wendell Holmes, who observed:

> I do not think the United States would come to an end if we lost our power to declare an act of Congress void. I do think the union would be imperilled if we could not make that declaration as to the laws of the several states.[22]

[21]Ibid., No. 70.
[22]Oliver Wendell Holmes, *Collected Legal Papers* (New York: Harcourt Brace, 1920), pp. 295–96.

In addition, the Supreme Court was assigned jurisdiction over controversies between citizens of different states. The long-term significance of this was that as the country developed a national economy, it came to rely increasingly on the federal judiciary, rather than on the state courts, for resolution of disputes.

Judges were given lifetime appointments in order to protect them from popular politics and from interference by the other branches. This, however, did not mean that the judiciary would actually remain totally impartial to political considerations or to the other branches, for the president was to appoint the judges and the Senate to approve the appointments. Congress would also have the power to create inferior (lower) courts, to change the jurisdiction of the federal courts, to add or subtract federal judges, even to change the size of the Supreme Court.

No direct mention is made in the Constitution of *judicial review*—the power of the courts to render the final decision when there is a conflict of interpretation of the Constitution or of laws between the courts and Congress, the courts and the executive branch, or the courts and the states. Scholars generally feel that judicial review is implicit in the very existence of a written Constitution and in the power given directly to the federal courts over "all Cases . . . arising under this Constitution, the Laws of the United States, and Treaties made, or which shall be made, under their Authority" (Article III, Section 2). The Supreme Court eventually assumed the power of judicial review. Its assumption of this power, as we shall see in Chapter 8, was not based on the Constitution itself but on the politics of later decades and the membership of the Court.

judicial review
Power of the courts to declare actions of the legislative and executive branches invalid or unconstitutional. The Supreme Court asserted this power in *Marbury v. Madison*.

National Unity and Power

Various provisions in the Constitution addressed the framers' concern with national unity and power, including Article IV's provisions for comity (reciprocity) among states and among citizens of all states.

Each state was prohibited from discriminating against the citizens of other states in favor of its own citizens, with the Supreme Court charged with deciding in each case whether a state had discriminated against goods or people from another state. The Constitution restricted the power of the states in favor of ensuring enough power to the national government to give the country a free-flowing national economy.

The framers' concern with national supremacy was also expressed in Article VI, in the *supremacy clause,* which provided that national laws and treaties "shall be the supreme Law of the Land." This meant that all laws made under the "Authority of the United States" would be superior to all laws adopted by any state or any other subdivision, and the states would be expected to respect all treaties made under that authority. This was a direct effort to keep the states from dealing separately with foreign nations or businesses. The supremacy clause also bound the officials of all state and local as well as federal governments to take an oath of office to support the national Constitution. This meant that every action taken by the United States Congress would have to be applied within each state as though the action were in fact state law.

supremacy clause
Article VI of the Constitution, which states that all laws passed by the national government and all treaties are the supreme laws of the land and superior to all laws adopted by any state or any subdivision.

Amending the Constitution

The Constitution established procedures for its own revision in Article V. Its provisions are so difficult that Americans have availed themselves of the amending process only seventeen times since 1791, when the first ten amendments were adopted. Many other amendments have been proposed in Congress, but fewer than forty of them have even come close to fulfilling the Constitution's requirement of a two-thirds vote in Congress, and only a fraction have gotten anywhere near adoption by three-fourths of the states. The Constitution could also be amended by a constitutional convention. Occasionally, proponents of particular measures, such as a balanced-budget amendment, have called for a constitutional convention to consider their proposals. Whatever the purpose for which it was called, however, such a convention would presumably have the authority to revise America's entire system of government.

It should be noted that any body of rules, including a national constitution, must balance the need to respond flexibly to changes, on the one hand, with the caution not to be too flexible, on the other. An inflexible body of rules is one that cannot accommodate major change. It risks being rebelled against, a circumstance in which the slate is wiped clean and new rules designed, or ignored altogether. Too much flexibility, however, is disastrous. It invites those who lose in normal everyday politics to replay battles at the constitutional level. If institutional change is too easy to accomplish, the stability of the political system becomes threatened.

Ratifying the Constitution

The rules for ratification of the Constitution of 1787 were set forth in Article VII of the Constitution. This provision actually violated the amendment provisions of the Articles of Confederation. For one thing, it adopted a nine-state rule in place of the unanimity required by the Articles of Confederation. For another, it provided that ratification would occur in special state conventions called for that purpose rather than in the state legislatures. All the states except Rhode Island eventually did set up state conventions to ratify the Constitution.

Constitutional Limits on the National Government's Power

As we have indicated, although the framers sought to create a powerful national government, they also wanted to guard against possible misuse of that power. To that end, the framers incorporated two key principles into the Constitution—the *separation of powers* and *federalism* (see Chapter 3). A third set of limitations, in the form of the ***Bill of Rights,*** was added to the Constitution to help secure its ratification when opponents of the document charged that it paid insufficient attention to citizens' rights.

The Separation of Powers   No principle of politics was more widely shared at the time of the 1787 founding than the principle that power must be used to balance power. The French political theorist Baron de Montesquieu (1689–1755)

separation of powers The division of governmental power among several institutions that must cooperate in decision making.

federalism System of government in which power is divided by a constitution between a central government and regional governments.

Bill of Rights The first ten amendments to the U.S. Constitution, ratified in 1791. They ensure certain rights and liberties to the people.

FIGURE 2.1

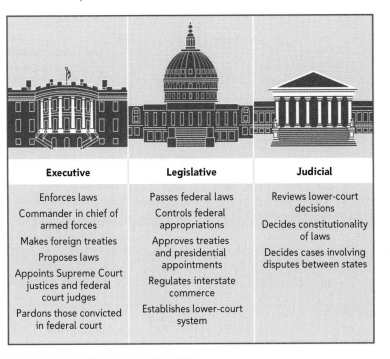

The Separation of Powers

Executive	Legislative	Judicial
Enforces laws	Passes federal laws	Reviews lower-court decisions
Commander in chief of armed forces	Controls federal appropriations	Decides constitutionality of laws
Makes foreign treaties	Approves treaties and presidential appointments	Decides cases involving disputes between states
Proposes laws	Regulates interstate commerce	
Appoints Supreme Court justices and federal court judges	Establishes lower-court system	
Pardons those convicted in federal court		

believed that this balance was an indispensable defense against tyranny, and his writings, especially his major work, *The Spirit of the Laws,* "were taken as political gospel" at the Philadelphia convention.[23] The principle of the separation of powers is nowhere to be found explicitly in the Constitution, but it is clearly built on Articles I, II, and III, which provide for the following:

1. Three separate and distinct branches of government (see Figure 2.1).
2. Different methods of selecting the top personnel, so that each branch is responsible to a different constituency. This is supposed to produce a "mixed regime," in which the personnel of each department will develop very different interests and outlooks on how to govern, and different groups in society will be assured some access to governmental decision making.

[23]Max Farrand, *The Framing of the Constitution of the United States* (New Haven: Yale University Press, 1962), p. 49.

FIGURE 2.2

Checks and Balances

LEGISLATIVE

Executive over Legislative
Can veto acts of Congress
Can call Congress into a special session
Carries out, and thereby interprets, laws passed by Congress
Vice president casts tie-breaking vote in the Senate

Legislative over Judicial
Can change size of federal court system and the number of Supreme Court justices
Can propose constitutional amendments
Can reject Supreme Court nominees
Can impeach and remove federal judges

Legislative over Executive
Can override presidential veto
Can impeach and remove president
Can reject president's appointments and refuse to ratify treaties
Can conduct investigations into president's actions
Can refuse to pass laws or to provide funding that president requests

Judicial over Legislative
Can declare laws unconstitutional
Chief justice presides over Senate during hearing to impeach the president

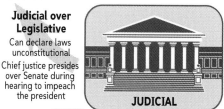

JUDICIAL

Executive over Judicial
Nominates Supreme Court justices
Nominates federal judges
Can pardon those convicted in federal court
Can refuse to enforce Court decisions

Judicial over Executive
Can declare executive actions unconstitutional
Power to issue warrants
Chief justice presides over impeachment of president

EXECUTIVE

checks and balances
Mechanisms through which each branch of government is able to participate in and influence the activities of the other branches. Major examples include the presidential veto power over congressional legislation, the power of the Senate to approve presidential appointments, and judicial review of congressional enactments.

3. *Checks and balances*—a system under which each of the branches is given some power over the others. Familiar examples are the presidential veto power over legislation, the power of the Senate to approve presidential appointments, and judicial review of acts of Congress (see Figure 2.2).

One clever formulation of the separation of powers is that of a system not of separated powers but of "separated institutions sharing power,"[24] and thus diminishing the chance that power will be misused.

[24]Richard E. Neustadt, *Presidential Power: The Politics of Leadership* (New York: Wiley, 1960), p. 33.

Federalism   Compared to the confederation principle of the Articles of Confederation, federalism was a step toward greater centralization of power. The delegates agreed that they needed to place more power at the national level, without completely undermining the power of the state governments. Thus, they devised a system of two sovereigns—the states and the nation—with the hope that competition between the two would be an effective limitation on the power of both.

The Bill of Rights   Late in the Philadelphia convention, a motion was made to include a bill of rights in the Constitution. After a brief debate in which hardly a word was said in its favor and only one speech was made against it, the motion to include it was almost unanimously turned down. Most delegates sincerely believed that since the federal government was already limited to its expressed powers, further protection of citizens was not needed. The delegates argued that the states should adopt bills of rights because their greater powers needed greater limitations. But almost immediately after the Constitution was ratified, there was a movement to adopt a national bill of rights. This is why the Bill of Rights, adopted in 1791, comprises the first ten amendments to the Constitution rather than being part of the body of it. We will have a good deal more to say about the Bill of Rights in Chapter 4.

THE FIGHT FOR RATIFICATION: FEDERALISTS VERSUS ANTIFEDERALISTS

The first hurdle faced by the new Constitution was ratification by state conventions of delegates elected by the people of each state. This struggle for ratification was carried out in thirteen separate campaigns. Each involved different men, moved at a different pace, and was influenced by local as well as national considerations. Two sides faced off throughout all the states, however, calling themselves Federalists and Antifederalists (see Table 2.1)[25]. The Federalists (who more accurately should have called themselves "Nationalists," but who took their name to appear to follow in the revolutionary tradition) supported the Constitution and preferred a strong national government. The Antifederalists opposed the Constitution and preferred a federal system of government that was decentralized; they took on their name by default, in reaction to their better-organized

---

[25]An excellent analysis of these ratification campaigns, based on a quantitative assessment of the campaigners' own words as found in campaign documents, pamphlets, tracts, public letters, and the eighteenth-century equivalent of op-ed pieces (like the individual essays that comprise the *Federalist Papers*) is William H. Riker, *The Strategy of Rhetoric: Campaigning for the American Constitution* (New Haven: Yale University Press, 1996).

TABLE 2.1

Federalists versus Antifederalists

	FEDERALISTS	ANTIFEDERALISTS
Who were they?	Property owners, creditors, merchants	Small farmers, frontiersmen, debtors, shopkeepers
What did they believe?	Believed that elites were best fit to govern; feared "excessive democracy"	Believed that government should be closer to the people; feared concentration of power in hands of the elites
What system of government did they favor?	Favored strong national government; believed in "filtration" so that only elites would obtain governmental power	Favored retention of power by state governments and protection of individual rights
Who were their leaders?	Alexander Hamilton James Madison George Washington	Patrick Henry George Mason Elbridge Gerry George Clinton

opponents. The Federalists were united in their support of the Constitution, while the Antifederalists were divided as to what they believed the alternative to the Constitution should be.

During the struggle over ratification of the proposed Constitution, Americans argued about great political issues and principles. How much power should the national government be given? What safeguards were most likely to prevent the abuse of power? What institutional arrangements could best ensure adequate representation for all Americans? Was tyranny to be feared more from the many or from the few?

In political life, of course, principles—even great principles—are seldom completely divorced from some set of interests. In 1787, Americans were divided along economic, regional, and political lines. These divisions inevitably influenced their attitudes toward the profound political questions of the day.

Rationality Principle

The debate over ratification revealed the conflicting interests of the Federalists and Antifederalists.

Many well-to-do merchants and planters, as we saw earlier, favored the creation of a stronger central government that would have the capacity to protect property, promote commerce, and keep some of the more radical state legislatures in check. At the same time, many powerful state leaders, like Governor George Clinton of New York, feared that strengthening the national government would reduce their own influence and status. Each of these interests, of course, justified its position with an appeal to principle.

Principles are often important weapons in political warfare, and seeing how and by whom they are wielded can illuminate their otherwise obscure implications. In our own time, dry academic discussions of topics such as "free trade" become easier to grasp once it is noted that free trade and open markets are generally favored by low-cost producers, while protectionism is the goal of firms whose costs of production are higher than the international norm.

Even if a principle is invented and initially brandished to serve an interest, however, once it has been articulated it can take on a life of its own and prove to have implications that transcend the narrow interests it was created to serve. Some opponents of the Constitution, for example, who criticized the absence of a bill of rights in the initial document did so simply with the hope of blocking the document's ratification. Yet, the Bill of Rights that was later added to the Constitution has proven for two centuries to be a bulwark of civil liberty in the United States.

Similarly, closer to our own time, support for the extension of voting rights and for massive legislative redistricting under the rubric of "one man, one vote" during the 1960s came mainly from liberal Democrats who were hoping to strengthen their own political base since the groups that would benefit most from these initiatives were overwhelmingly Democratic. The principles of equal access to the ballot and one man, one vote, however, have a moral and political validity that is independent of the political interests that propelled these ideas into the political arena.

These examples show us that truly great political principles surmount the interests that initially set them forth. The first step in understanding a political principle is understanding why and by whom it is espoused. The second step is understanding the full implications of the principle itself—implications that may go far beyond the interests that launched it. Thus, even though the great political principles about which Americans argued in 1787 *did* reflect competing interests, they also represented views of society, government, and politics that surmount interest and so must be understood in their own terms. Whatever the underlying clash of interests that may have guided them, the Federalists and Antifederalists presented important alternative visions of America.

During the ratification struggle, thousands of essays, speeches, pamphlets, and letters were presented in support of and in opposition to the proposed Constitution. The best-known pieces supporting ratification of the Constitution were the eighty-five essays written, under the name of "Publius," by Alexander Hamilton, James Madison, and John Jay between the fall of 1787 and the spring of 1788. These *Federalist Papers*, as they are collectively known today, defended the principles of the Constitution and sought to dispel fears of a national authority. The Antifederalists published essays of their own, arguing that the new Constitution betrayed the Revolution and was a step toward monarchy. Among the best of the Antifederalist works were the essays, usually attributed to New York Supreme Court justice Robert Yates, that were written under the name of "Brutus" and published in the *New York Journal* at the same time the *Federalist Papers* appeared. The Antifederalist view was also ably presented in the pamphlets and letters written by a former delegate to the Continental Congress and future U.S. senator, Richard Henry Lee of Virginia, using the pen name "the Federal Farmer." These essays highlight the major differences of opinion between Federalists and Antifederalists. Federalists appealed to basic principles of government in support of their nationalist vision. Antifederalists cited equally fundamental precepts to support their vision of a looser confederacy of small republics.

The two sides engaged in what was almost certainly the very first nationwide political campaign in the history of the world. Though each side was itself only loosely organized, a rudimentary form of coordination and cooperation was manifest—especially in the division of labor between Hamilton, Madison, and Jay as they alternately wrote under the "Publius" pseudonym on different aspects of the newly drafted Constitution in an effort to affect its ratification in the state of New York.

Representation

One major area of contention between the two sides was the question of representation. The Antifederalists asserted that representatives must be "a true picture of the people, . . . [possessing] the knowledge of their circumstances and their wants."[26] This could only be achieved, argued the Antifederalists, in small, relatively homogeneous republics such as the existing states. In their view, the size and extent of the entire nation precluded the construction of a truly representative form of government.

The absence of true representation, moreover, would mean that the people would lack confidence in and attachment to the national government and would refuse to obey its laws voluntarily. As a result, according to the Antifederalists, the national government described by the Constitution would be compelled to resort to force to secure popular compliance. The Federal Farmer averred that laws of the remote federal government could be "in many cases disregarded, unless a multitude of officers and military force be continually kept in view, and employed to enforce the execution of the laws, and to make the government feared and respected."[27]

[26]Melancton Smith, quoted in Herbert J. Storing, *What the Anti-Federalists Were For: The Political Thought of the Opponents of the Constitution* (Chicago: University of Chicago Press, 1981), p. 17.

[27]"Letters from the Federal Farmer," No. 2, in *The Complete Anti-Federalist*, ed. Herbert J. Storing, 7 vols. (Chicago: University of Chicago Press, 1981).

Federalists, for their part, did not long for pure democracy and saw no reason that representatives should be precisely like those they represented. In their view, government must be representative *of* the people, but must also have a measure of autonomy *from* the people. Their ideal government was to be so constructed as to be capable of serving the long-term public interest even if this conflicted with the public's current preference.

Federalists also dismissed the Antifederalist claim that the distance between representatives and constituents in the proposed national government would lead to popular disaffection and compel the government to use force to secure obedience. Federalists replied that the system of representation they proposed was more likely to produce effective government. In Hamilton's words, there would be "a probability that the general government will be better administered than the particular governments."[28] Competent government, in turn, should inspire popular trust and confidence more effectively than simple social proximity between rulers and ruled.

The Threats Posed by the Majority

A second important issue dividing Federalists and Antifederalists was the threat of **tyranny**—unjust rule by the group in power. Both opponents and defenders of the Constitution frequently affirmed their fear of tyrannical rule. Each side, however, had a different view of the most likely source of tyranny and, hence, of the way in which the threat was to be forestalled.

tyranny
Oppressive government that employs the cruel and unjust use of power and authority.

From the Antifederalist perspective, the great danger was the tendency of all governments—including republican governments—to become gradually more and more "aristocratic" in character, where the small number of individuals in positions of authority would use their stations to gain more and more power over the general citizenry. In essence, the few would use their power to tyrannize the many. For this reason, Antifederalists were sharply critical of those features of the Constitution that divorced governmental institutions from direct responsibility to the people—institutions such as the Senate, the executive, and the federal judiciary. The latter, appointed for life, presented a particular threat: "I wonder if the world ever saw . . . a court of justice invested with such immense powers, and yet placed in a situation so little responsible," protested Brutus.[29]

The Federalists, too, recognized the threat of tyranny. They were not naive about the motives and purposes of individuals and took them to be no less opportunistic and self-interested than the Antifederalists did. But the Federalists believed that the danger particularly associated with republican governments was not aristocracy, but instead, majority tyranny. The Federalists were concerned that a popular majority, "united and actuated by some common impulse of passion, or of interest, adverse to the rights of other citizens," would endeavor

---

[28]*The Federalist*, No. 27.
[29]"Essays of Brutus," No. 15, in *The Complete Anti-Federalist*.

to "trample on the rules of justice."[30] From the Federalist perspective, it was precisely those features of the Constitution attacked as potential sources of tyranny by the Antifederalists that actually offered the best hope of averting the threat of oppression. The size and extent of the nation, for instance, was for the Federalists a bulwark against tyranny. In Madison's famous formulation,

> The smaller the society, the fewer probably will be the distinct parties and interests . . . the more frequently will a majority be found of the same party; and the smaller the number of individuals composing a majority, and the smaller the compass within which they are placed, the more easily will they concert and execute their plans of oppression. Extend the sphere, and you take in a greater variety of parties and interests; you make it less probable that a majority of the whole will have a common motive to invade the rights of other citizens; or if such a common motive exists, it will be more difficult for all who feel it to discover their own strength, and to act in unison with each other.[31]

The Federalists understood that, in a democracy, temporary majorities could abuse their power. The Federalists' misgivings about majority rule were reflected in the constitutional structure. The indirect election of senators, the indirect election of the president, the judicial branch's insulation from the people, the separation of powers, the president's veto power, the bicameral design of Congress, and the federal system were all means to curb majority tyranny. These design features in the Constitution suggest an awareness on the part of the framers of the problems of majority rule and the need for institutional safeguards. Except for the indirect election of senators (which was changed in 1913), these aspects of the constitutional structure remain in place today.[32]

Governmental Power

A third major difference between Federalists and Antifederalists, and the one most central to this book, was the issue of governmental power. Both the opponents and proponents of the Constitution agreed on the principle of limited government. They differed, however, on the fundamentally important question of how to place limits on governmental action. Antifederalists favored limiting and enumerating the powers granted to the national government in relation both to the states and to the people at large. To them, the powers given the national gov-

---

[30]*The Federalist*, No. 10.

[31]Ibid.

[32]A classic development of this theme is found in James M. Buchanan and Gordon Tullock, *The Calculus of Consent: Logical Foundations of Constitutional Democracy* (Ann Arbor: University of Michigan Press, 1962). For a review of the voting paradox and a case study of how it applies today, see Kenneth A. Shepsle and Mark S. Bonchek, *Analyzing Politics: Rationality, Behavior, and Institutions* (New York: W. W. Norton, 1997), pp. 49–81.

ernment ought to be "confined to certain defined national objects."[33] Otherwise, the national government would "swallow up all the power of the state governments."[34] Antifederalists bitterly attacked the supremacy clause and the necessary and proper clause of the Constitution as unlimited and dangerous grants of power to the national government.[35]

Antifederalists also demanded that a bill of rights be added to the Constitution to place limits upon the government's exercise of power over the citizenry. "There are certain things," wrote Brutus, "which rulers should be absolutely prohibited from doing, because if they should do them, they would work an injury, not a benefit to the people."[36] Similarly, the Federal Farmer maintained that "there are certain unalienable and fundamental rights, which in forming the social compact . . . ought to be explicitly ascertained and fixed."[37]

Federalists favored the construction of a government with broad powers. They wanted a government that had the capacity to defend the nation against foreign foes, guard against domestic strife and insurrection, promote commerce, and expand the nation's economy. Antifederalists shared some of these goals but still feared governmental power. Hamilton pointed out, however, that these goals could not be achieved without allowing the government to exercise the necessary power. Federalists acknowledged, of course, that every power could be abused but argued that the way to prevent misuse of power was not by depriving the government of the powers needed to achieve national goals. Instead, they argued that the threat of abuse of power would be mitigated by the Constitution's internal checks and controls. As Madison put it, "the power surrendered by the people is first divided between two distinct governments, and then the portion allotted to each subdivided among distinct and separate departments. Hence a double security arises to the rights of the people. The different governments will control each other, at the same time that each will be controlled by itself."[38] The Federalists' concern with avoiding unwarranted limits on governmental power led them to oppose a bill of rights, which they saw as nothing more than a set of unnecessary restrictions on the government.

The Federalists acknowledged that abuse of power remained a possibility, but felt that the risk had to be taken because of the goals to be achieved. "The very idea of power included a possibility of doing harm," said the Federalist John Rutledge during the South Carolina ratification debates. "If the gentleman would show the power that could do no harm," Rutledge continued, "he would at once discover it to be a power that could do no good."[39]

[33]"Essays of Brutus," No. 7.
[34]"Essays of Brutus," No. 6.
[35]Storing, *What the Antifederalists Were For*, p. 28.
[36]"Essays of Brutus," No. 9.
[37]"Letters from the Federal Farmer," No. 2.
[38]*The Federalist*, No. 51.
[39]Quoted in Storing, *What the Antifederalists Were For*, p. 30.

CHANGING THE INSTITUTIONAL FRAMEWORK: CONSTITUTIONAL AMENDMENT

The Constitution has endured for two centuries as the framework of government. But it has not endured without change. Without change, the Constitution might have become merely a sacred relic, stored under glass.

Amendments: Many Are Called, Few Are Chosen

The need for change was recognized by the framers of the Constitution, and the provisions for amendment incorporated into Article V were thought to be "an easy, regular and Constitutional way" to make changes, which would occasionally be necessary because members of Congress "may abuse their power and refuse their consent on the very account . . . to admit to amendments to correct the source of the abuse."[40] Madison made a more balanced defense of the amendment procedure in Article V: "It guards equally against that extreme facility, which would render the Constitution too mutable; and that extreme difficulty, which might perpetuate its discovered faults."[41]

Experience since 1789 raises questions even about Madison's more modest claims. The Constitution has proven to be extremely difficult to amend. In the history of efforts to amend the Constitution, the most appropriate characterization is "many are called, few are chosen." Between 1789 and 1993, 9,746 amendments were formally offered in Congress. Of these, Congress officially proposed only 29, and 27 of these were eventually ratified by the states. But the record is even more severe than that. Since 1791, when the first 10 amendments, the Bill of Rights, were added, only 17 amendments have been adopted. And two of them—Prohibition and its repeal—cancel each other out, so that for all practical purposes, only 15 amendments have been added to the Constitution since 1791. Despite vast changes in American society and its economy, only 12 amendments have been adopted since the Civil War amendments in 1868.

Four methods of amendment are provided for in Article V:

1. Passage in House and Senate by two-thirds vote; then ratification by majority vote of the legislatures of three-fourths (thirty-eight) of the states.
2. Passage in House and Senate by two-thirds vote; then ratification by conventions called for the purpose in three-fourths of the states.
3. Passage in a national convention called by Congress in response to petitions by two-thirds of the states; ratification by majority vote of the legislatures of three-fourths of the states.

Institution Principle

The procedures for amending the Constitution are difficult. As a result, the amendment route to political change is extremely limited.

[40]Observation by Colonel George Mason, delegate from Virginia, early during the convention period. Quoted in Farrand, *The Records of the Federal Convention of 1787*, I, pp. 202–3.
[41]Clinton Rossiter, ed., *The Federalist Papers* (New York: New American Library, 1961), No. 43, p. 278.

FIGURE 2.3

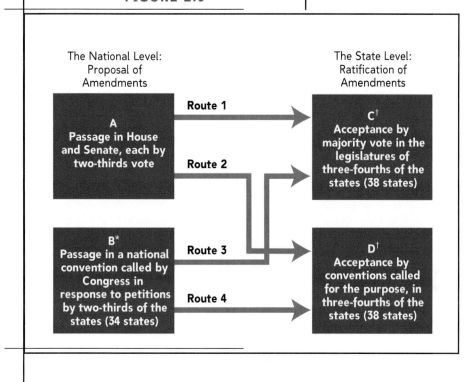

The National Level:
Proposal of
Amendments

The State Level:
Ratification of
Amendments

A
Passage in House and Senate, each by two-thirds vote

Route 1

Route 2

C†
Acceptance by majority vote in the legislatures of three-fourths of the states (38 states)

B*
Passage in a national convention called by Congress in response to petitions by two-thirds of the states (34 states)

Route 3

Route 4

D†
Acceptance by conventions called for the purpose, in three-fourths of the states (38 states)

4. Passage in a national convention, as in method 3; then ratification by conventions called for the purpose in three-fourths of the states.

(Figure 2.3 illustrates each of these possible methods.) Since no amendment has ever been proposed by national convention, however, methods 3 and 4 have never been employed. And method 2 has only been employed once (the Twenty-first Amendment, which repealed the Eighteenth, or Prohibition, Amendment). Thus, method 1 has been used for all the others.

Now we should be better able to explain why it has been so difficult to amend the Constitution. The main reason is the requirement of a two-thirds vote in the House and the Senate, which means that any proposal for an amendment in Congress can be killed by only 34 senators *or* 146 members of the House. What is more, if the necessary two-thirds vote is obtained, the amendment can still be killed by the refusal or inability of only thirteen state legislatures to ratify it. Since each state has an equal vote regardless of its population, the thirteen holdout states may represent a very small fraction of the total American population.

The Twenty-seven Amendments

Despite difficulties of the process, the Constitution has been amended twenty-seven times since the framers completed their work. The first ten of these amendments, known as the Bill of Rights, were added to the Constitution shortly after its ratification. As we saw, Federalists feared that a bill of rights would weaken the new government, but they were forced to commit themselves to the principle of an enumeration of rights when the Antifederalists charged that the proposed Constitution was a threat to liberty.

Most of the Constitution's twenty-seven amendments share a common characteristic: all but two are concerned with the structure or composition of government. This is consistent with the dictionary, which defines *constitution* as the makeup or composition of a thing, anything. And it is consistent with the concept of a constitution as "higher law," because the whole point and purpose of a higher law is to establish *a framework within which government and the process of making ordinary law can take place.* Even those who would have preferred more changes in the Constitution would have to agree that there is great wisdom in this principle. A constitution ought to enable legislation and public policies to take place, but it should not determine what that legislation or those public policies ought to be.

The purpose of the ten amendments in the Bill of Rights was basically structural, *to give each of the three branches clearer and more restricted boundaries.* The First Amendment clarified the jurisdiction of Congress. Although the powers of Congress under Article I, Section 8, would not have justified laws regulating religion, speech, and the like, the First Amendment made this limitation explicit: "Congress shall make no law. . . ." The Second, Third, and Fourth Amendments similarly spelled out specific limits on the executive branch. This was seen as a necessity given the abuses of executive power Americans had endured under British rule.

The Fifth, Sixth, Seventh, and Eighth Amendments contain some of the most important safeguards for individual citizens against the arbitrary exercise of government power. And these amendments sought to accomplish their goal by defining the judicial branch more concretely and clearly than had been done in Article III of the Constitution. Table 2.2 analyzes the ten amendments included in the Bill of Rights.

Five of the seventeen amendments adopted since 1791 are directly concerned with expansion of the electorate (see Table 2.3). These occasional efforts to expand the electorate were made necessary by the fact that the founders were unable to establish a national electorate with uniform voting qualifications. Stalemated on that issue, the delegates decided to evade it by providing in the final draft of Article I, Section 2, that eligibility to vote in a national election would be the same as "the Qualifications requisite for Electors of the most numerous Branch of the State Legislature." Article I, Section 4, added that Congress could alter state regulations as to the "Times, Places and Manner of holding Elections for Senators and Representatives." Nevertheless, this meant that any

TABLE 2.2

The Bill of Rights: Analysis of Its Provisions

AMENDMENT	PURPOSE
I	*Limits on Congress:* Congress is not to make any law establishing a religion or abridging the freedom of speech, press, assembly, or the right to petition freedoms.
II, III, IV	*Limits on Executive:* The executive branch is not to infringe on the right of people to keep arms (II), is not to arbitrarily take houses for a militia (III), and is not to engage in the search or seizure of evidence without a court warrant swearing to belief in the probable existence of a crime (IV).
V, VI, VII, VIII	*Limits on Courts:* The courts are not to hold trials for serious offenses without provision for a grand jury (V), a petit (trial) jury (VII), a speedy trial (VI), presentation of charges, confrontation of hostile witnesses (VI), immunity from testimony against oneself (V), and immunity from trial more than once for the same offense (V). Neither bail nor punishment can be excessive (VIII), and no property can be taken without just compensation (V).
IX, X	*Limits on National Government:* All rights not enumerated are reserved to the states or the people.

important *expansion* of the American electorate would almost certainly require a constitutional amendment.

Six more amendments are also electoral in nature, although not concerned directly with voting rights and the expansion of the electorate (see Table 2.4). These six amendments are concerned with the elective offices themselves (the Twentieth, Twenty-second, and Twenty-fifth) or with the relationship between elective offices and the electorate (the Twelfth, Fourteenth, and Seventeenth).

Another five amendments have sought to expand or to delimit the powers of the national and state governments (see Table 2.5).[42] The Eleventh Amendment

[42]The Fourteenth Amendment is included in this table as well as in Tables 2.2 and 2.3 because it seeks not only to define citizenship but *seems* to intend also that this definition of citizenship included, along with the right to vote, all the rights of the Bill of Rights, regardless of the state in which the citizen resided. A great deal more will be said about this in Chapter 4.

TABLE 2.3

Amending the Constitution to Expand the Electorate

AMENDMENT	PURPOSE	YEAR PROPOSED	YEAR ADOPTED
XIV	Section I provided national definition of citizenship*	1866	1868
XV	Extended voting rights to all races	1869	1870
XIX	Extended voting rights to women	1919	1920
XXIII	Extended voting rights to residents of the District of Columbia	1960	1961
XXIV	Extended voting rights to all classes by abolition of poll taxes	1962	1964
XXVI	Extended voting rights to citizens aged 18 and over	1971	1971

*In defining *citizenship*, the Fourteenth Amendment actually provided the constitutional basis for expanding the electorate to include all races, women, and residents of the District of Columbia. Only the "eighteen-year-olds' amendment" should have been necessary since it changed the definition of citizenship. The fact that additional amendments were required following the Fourteenth suggests that voting is not considered an inherent right of U.S. citizenship. Instead it is viewed as a privilege.

protected the states from suits by private individuals and took away from the federal courts any power to take suits by private individuals of one state (or a foreign country) against another state. The other three amendments in Table 2.5 are obviously designed to reduce state power (Thirteenth), to reduce state power and expand national power (Fourteenth), and to expand national power (Sixteenth). The Twenty-seventh put a limit on Congress's ability to raise its own salary.

The two missing amendments underscore the meaning of the rest: the Eighteenth, or Prohibition, Amendment and the Twenty-first, its repeal. This is the only instance in which the country tried to *legislate* by constitutional amendment. In other words, the Eighteenth is the only amendment that was designed to deal directly with some substantive social problem. And it was the only amendment ever to have been repealed. Two other amendments—the Thirteenth, which abolished slavery, and the Sixteenth, which established the power to levy an income tax—can be said to have had the effect of legislation. But the purpose of the Thirteenth was to restrict the power of the states by forever for-

TABLE 2.4

Amending the Constitution to
Change the Relationship between
Elected Offices and the Electorate

AMENDMENT	PURPOSE	YEAR PROPOSED	YEAR ADOPTED
XII	Provided separate ballot for vice president in the electoral college	1803	1804
XIV	Section 2 eliminated counting of slaves as "three-fifths" citizens for apportionment of House seats	1866	1868
XVII	Provided direct election of senators	1912	1913
XX	Eliminated "lame duck" session of Congress	1932	1933
XXII	Limited presidential term	1947	1951
XXV	Provided presidential succession in case of disability	1965	1967

bidding them to treat any human being as property. As for the Sixteenth, it is certainly true that income-tax legislation followed immediately; nevertheless, the amendment concerns itself strictly with establishing the power of Congress to enact such legislation. The legislation came later; and if down the line a majority in Congress had wanted to abolish the income tax, they could also have done this by legislation rather than through the arduous path of a constitutional amendment repealing the income tax.

For those whose hopes for change center on the Constitution, it must be emphasized that the amendment route to social change is, and always will be, extremely limited. Through a constitution it is possible to establish a working structure of government; and through a constitution it is possible to establish basic rights of citizens by placing limitations and obligations on the powers of that government. Once these things have been accomplished, the real problem is how to extend rights to those people who do not already enjoy them. Of course, the Constitution cannot enforce itself. But it can and does have a real influence on everyday life because a right or an obligation set forth in the Constitution can become a *cause of action* in the hands of an otherwise powerless person.

TABLE 2.5

	Amending the Constitution to Expand or Limit the Power of Government		
AMENDMENT	**PURPOSE**	**YEAR PROPOSED**	**YEAR ADOPTED**
XI	Limited jurisdiction of federal courts over suits involving the states	1794	1798
XIII	Eliminated slavery and eliminated the rights of states to allow property in persons	1865*	1865
XIV	(Part 2) Applied due process of Bill of Rights to the states	1866	1868
XVI	Established national power to tax incomes	1909	1913
XXVII	Limited Congress's power to raise its own salary	1789	1992

*The Thirteenth Amendment was proposed January 31, 1865, and adopted less than a year later, on December 18, 1865.

Private property is an excellent example. Property is one of the most fundamental and well-established rights in the United States; but it is well established not because it is recognized in so many words in the Constitution, but because legislatures and courts have made it a crime for anyone, including the government, to trespass or to take away property without compensation.

REFLECTIONS ON THE FOUNDING: PRINCIPLES OR INTERESTS?

The final product of the Constitutional Convention would have to be considered an extraordinary victory for the groups that had most forcefully called for the creation of a new system of government to replace the Articles of Confederation. Antifederalist criticisms forced the Constitution's proponents to accept the addition of a bill of rights designed to limit the powers of the national government. In general, however, it was the Federalist vision of America that triumphed. The Constitution adopted in 1789 created the framework for a powerful national government that for more than two hundred years has defended the nation's interests, promoted its commerce, and maintained national unity. In one notable instance, the national government fought and won a bloody war to prevent the nation from breaking apart.

Though the Constitution was the product of a particular set of political forces, the principles of government it established have a significance that goes far beyond the interests of its authors. As we have observed, political principles often take on lives of their own. The great political principles incorporated into the Constitution continue, more than two centuries later, to shape our political lives in ways that the Constitution's framers may not always have anticipated. For example, when they empowered the Congress of the United States to regulate commerce among the states in Article I, Section 8, of the Constitution, the framers could hardly have anticipated that this would become the basis for many of the federal government's regulatory activities in areas as diverse as the environment and civil rights.

Two great constitutional principles, federalism and civil liberties, will be discussed in Chapters 3 and 4. A third important constitutional principle that has affected America's government for the past two hundred years is the principle of *checks and balances*. As we saw earlier, the framers gave each of the three branches of government a means of intervening in and blocking the actions of the others. Often, checks and balances have seemed to prevent the government from getting much done. During the 1960s, for example, liberals were often infuriated as they watched Congress stall presidential initiatives in the area of civil rights. More recently, conservatives were outraged when President Clinton thwarted congressional efforts to enact legislation promised in the Republican "Contract with America." At various times, all sides have vilified the judiciary for invalidating legislation enacted by Congress and signed by the president.

Over time, checks and balances have acted as brakes on the governmental process. Groups hoping to bring about changes in policy or governmental institutions seldom have been able to bring about decisive and dramatic transformations in a short period of time. Instead, checks and balances have slowed the pace of change and increased the need for compromise and accommodation.

Groups able to take control of the White House, for example, must bargain with their rivals who remain entrenched on Capitol Hill. New forces in Congress must reckon with the influence of other forces in the executive branch and in the courts. Checks and balances inevitably frustrate those who desire change, but they also function as a safeguard against rash action. During the 1950s, for example, Congress was caught up in a quasi-hysterical effort to unmask subversive activities in the United States, which might have led to a serious erosion of American liberties if not for the checks and balances provided by the executive and the courts. Thus, a governmental principle that serves as a frustrating limitation one day may become a vitally important safeguard the next.

As we close our discussion of the founding, it is also worth reflecting on the Antifederalists. Although they were defeated in 1789, the Antifederalists present us with an important picture of a road not taken and of an America that might have been. Would we have been worse off as a people if we had been governed by a confederacy of small republics linked by a national administration with severely limited powers? Were the Antifederalists correct in predicting that a government given great power in the hope that it might do good would, through "insensible progress," inevitably turn to evil purposes? Two hundred plus years of

Policy Principle

The constitutional framework, such as the principle of checks and balances, can act as a brake on the policy process.

Rationality Principle	Collective Action Principle	Institution Principle	Policy Principle	History Principle
The framers of the Constitution were guided by principles, but they also had interests.	The colonists required strong leaders to resolve differences and to organize resistance to British authority.	Institutional arrangements, such as the Articles of Confederation, can be flawed.	The constitutional framework, such as the principle of checks and balances, can act as a brake on the policy process.	The American colonists, used to years of self-governance, believed that the Stamp Act of 1765 threatened their autonomy.
The debate over ratification revealed the conflicting interests of the Federalists and Antifederalists.	The framers preferred compromise to the breakup of the union, and thus accepted the Great Compromise and the Three-fifths Compromise.	The constitutional framework promoted commerce, protected property, prevented "excessive democracy," and limited the power of the national government.		Shays's Rebellion focused attention on the flaws of the Articles of Confederation, leading to the Constitutional Convention.
		The procedures for amending the Constitution are difficult. As a result, the amendment route to political change is extremely limited.		

government under the federal Constitution are not necessarily enough to definitively answer these questions. Only time will tell.

SUMMARY

Political conflicts between the colonies and England, and among competing groups within the colonies, led to the first founding as expressed by the Declaration of Independence. The first constitution, the Articles of Confederation, was adopted one year later (1777). Under this document, the states retained their sovereignty. The central government, composed solely of Congress, had few powers and no means of enforcing its will. The national government's weakness soon led to the Constitution of 1787, the second founding.

In this second founding the framers sought, first, to fashion a new government sufficiently powerful to promote commerce and protect property from radical state legislatures. Second, the framers sought to bring an end to the "excessive democracy" of the state and national governments under the Articles of

Confederation. Third, the framers introduced mechanisms that helped secure popular consent for the new government. Finally, the framers made certain that their new government would not itself pose a threat to liberty and property.

The Constitution consists of seven articles. In part, Article I provides for a Congress of two chambers (Sections 1–7), defines the powers of the national government (Section 8), and interprets the national government's powers as a source of strength rather than a limitation (necessary and proper clause). Article II describes the presidency and establishes it as a separate branch of government. Article III is the judiciary article. While there is no direct mention of judicial review in this article, the Supreme Court eventually assumed that power. Article IV addresses reciprocity among states and their citizens. Article V describes the procedures for amending the Constitution. Thousands of amendments have been offered, but only twenty-seven have been adopted. With the exception of the two Prohibition amendments, all amendments were oriented toward some change in the framework or structure of government. Article VI establishes that national laws and treaties are "the supreme Law of the Land." And finally, Article VII specifies the procedure for ratifying the Constitution of 1787.

The struggle for the ratification of the Constitution pitted the Antifederalists against the Federalists. The Antifederalists thought the proposed new government would be too powerful, and they fought against the ratification of the Constitution. The Federalists supported the Constitution and were able to secure its ratification after a nationwide political debate.

FOR FURTHER READING

Bailyn, Bernard. *The Ideological Origins of the American Revolution.* Cambridge: Harvard University Press, 1967.

Beard, Charles A. *An Economic Interpretation of the Constitution of the United States.* New York: Macmillan, 1913.

Farrand, Max, ed. *The Records of the Federal Convention of 1787.* Rev. ed. 4 vols. New Haven: Yale University Press, 1966.

Hamilton, Alexander, James Madison, and John Jay. *The Federalist Papers.* Edited by Isaac Kramnick. New York: Viking Press, 1987.

Lipset, Seymour M. *The First New Nation: The United States in Historical and Comparative Perspective.* New York: Basic Books, 1963.

Main, Jackson Turner. *The Social Structure of Revolutionary America.* Princeton: Princeton University Press, 1965.

Riker, William H. *The Strategy of Rhetoric: Campaigning for the American Constitution.* New Haven: Yale University Press, 1996.

Storing, Herbert J., ed. *The Complete Anti-Federalist.* 7 vols. Chicago: University of Chicago Press, 1981.

Wood, Gordon S. *The Creation of the American Republic, 1776–1787.* New York: W. W. Norton, 1982.

Politics in the News— Reading between the Lines

Burning the Flag and the Constitution

Given New Legs, an Old Idea Is Back

By SHERYL GAY STOLBERG

Anyone who doubts the appeal of the American flag need only wander through the basement corridors of the Capitol. There, thousands of boxed flags that have flown over the building await pickup by members of Congress, who send them to constituents by request. Last year alone, nearly 124,000 were sent, up from 97,401 the year before.

The Republican-controlled House understands that these are good times for Old Glory, as Americans respond to the threat of terrorism and the war in Iraq. So today, when the House considered a perennial legislative favorite—a constitutional amendment that would give Congress the power to bar desecration of the American flag—it came as no surprise that the measure passed handily, 300 to 125.

This was the fifth time the House had passed the measure. But it has always died in the Senate, where opponents, mainly Democrats, argue that it would infringe on the First Amend-ment. Now the question is whether the surge of patriotism will overcome those objections and carry the measure to passage.

The White House backs the bill, and proponents say it has support from the legislatures of all 50 states. If ever there were a chance to outlaw burning the flag, they say, this is it.

But with the Senate majority leader, Bill Frist, focused on pressing matters like a Medicare prescription drug bene-fit, the amendment may not come up for a Senate vote until next year. So its backers were unwilling to make any predictions today.

"It's always an uphill battle," said the amendment's Senate sponsor, Orrin G. Hatch of Utah, the Judiciary Com-mittee chairman. "But we're hoping we can get it done this year. Well, maybe not this year, but probably next year."

Much has changed in the Senate since the last time the bill was consid-ered there, in March 2000. There are 10 new senators, 8 of them Republicans.

New York Times, 4 June 2003, p. A28.

Some, like John Cornyn of Texas, Norm Coleman of Minnesota and Saxby Chambliss of Georgia, said today that they would support the amendment. Others, like Lamar Alexander of Tennessee, were more circumspect. "What flag amendment?" Mr. Alexander said. "I haven't seen one yet."

The measure, which requires a two-thirds majority in each house and ratification by three-fourths of the states, is intended to circumvent two Supreme Court rulings. In 1989, the court struck down a Texas law prohibiting flag burning. Congress responded with federal legislation. But in 1990, by a 5-to-4 vote, the justices overturned that measure, too.

The amendment's chief sponsor, Representative Randy Cunningham, Republican of California, complained today that the court had reversed "200 years of tradition." He added, "I'm not proposing this, but in the Civil War it was a penalty of death to desecrate the flag."

The House debate today was marked by fiery exchanges over whether there should be limits on freedom of speech, and whether opposition to the amendment was unpatriotic. One opponent, Representative Alcee L. Hastings, Democrat of Florida, thundered, "All of us are superpatriots in the sense that we provide service for our country, each in our way!"

Lawmakers fought as well over whether it would be wise to alter the Constitution for a problem that, after all, is virtually nonexistent.

"We're amending the Constitution for a noncrisis," said Representative Ron Paul of Texas, one of 11 Republicans voting against the bill. . . .

Still, there have been just 100 cases or so of flag burning in the United States since the 1960's, according to David White, executive director of the National Flag Foundation, a Pittsburgh-based group that takes no position on

ESSENCE OF THE STORY

- The surge of patriotism after the terrorist attacks of September 11, 2001, encouraged the Republican-led House of Representatives to attempt to pass a constitutional amendment banning desecration of the flag.

- An amendment has passed the House five times but has always died in the Senate. Recent Court decisions and turnover in the Senate has also emboldened the supporters.

- There is disagreement over whether flag burning is serious enough to merit a constitutional amendment.

POLITICAL ANALYSIS

- Some suggest that voting for the flag amendment in the House is a strategic no-brainer, even for someone who opposes amending the Constitution in this way. A member can wear the patriotic mantle while being assured that the amendment will fail in the Senate.

- The different procedures of the House and Senate mean that politically popular but controversial legislation such as the flag amendment often passes the House, only to be stopped by a filibuster in the Senate.

- Some believe that the amendment procedure is too cumbersome, making it too hard to change the Constitution on matters such as flag burning. Others believe that the Constitution represents our most basic laws and should be amended only in the most weighty circumstances.

the amendment, instead promoting education as a way to counter desecration of the flag.

For all the battling, there is one instance in which flag burning is accepted by all. If a flag is old and tattered, Mr. White noted, the proper way to dispose of it is to burn it, "in a dignified manner." The rules are detailed, he said, in the Flag Code, guidelines for flag etiquette that were adopted by many patriotic organizations in 1923 and passed by Congress in 1942.

"Isn't that ironic?" Mr. White asked.

CHAPTER

3

The Constitutional Framework: Federalism and the Separation of Powers

Replacement of the Articles of Confederation by the Constitution is a classic case study of political realism. As an instrument of government, the Articles of Confederation had many virtues. Many considered it the second greatest constitution ever drafted. But as a confederation, it left too much power to the states, whose restrictions and boundaries interfered with national and international markets being sought by new economic interests. The Articles of Confederation had to be replaced, and a stronger national power had to be provided for, if the barriers to economic progress were to be lowered.[1]

To a point, political realists are correct. Everything in politics revolves around interests; a constitution must satisfy those interests or it will not last long as a governing instrument. But just as pure force is an inadequate foundation for government, so is pure interest, despite its immediate importance. Interests must be

[1]For two important realist interpretations of the rejection of the Articles in favor of the Constitution, see John P. Roche, "The Founding Fathers: A Reform Caucus in Action," *American Political Science Review* 55 (December 1961): 799–816, and the discussion of Charles Beard's economic interpretation in the text.

translated into higher principles, and there will be no loyalty or support for any government unless most of the powerful as well as the powerless accept the principles as *legitimate*.

A government can be considered legitimate when its actions appear to be consistent with the highest principles that people already hold. The American approach to legitimacy is based on *contract*. A contract is an exchange, a deal. The contract we call the American Constitution was simply this: *the people would give their consent to a strong national government if that government would in turn accept certain strict limitations on its powers*. In other words, power in return for limits, or **constitutionalism.**

constitutionalism
A system of rule in which formal and effective limits are placed on the powers of the government.

sovereignty
Supreme and independent political authority.

Three fundamental limitations were the basis of the contract between the American people and the framers of the Constitution: *federalism*, the *separation of powers*, and *individual rights*. Nowhere in the Constitution were these mentioned by name, but we know from the debates and writings that they were the primary framework of the Constitution. We can call them the *framework* because they were to be the structure, the channel through which governmental power would flow.

Federalism sought to limit government by dividing it into two levels—national and state—each with sufficient independence, or **sovereignty,** to compete with the other, thereby restraining the power of both.[2]

The *separation of powers* sought to limit the power of the national government by dividing government against itself—by giving the legislative, executive, and judicial branches separate functions, thus forcing them to share power.

Individual rights as embodied in the Bill of Rights sought to limit government by defining the people as separate from it—granting to each individual an identity in opposition to the government

CHAPTER OUTLINE

Federalism and the Separation of Powers as Political Institutions

Who Does What? The Changing Federal Framework

- Federalism in the Constitution

- The Slow Growth of the National Government's Power

- Cooperative Federalism and Grants-in-Aid

- Regulated Federalism and the National Standards

- New Federalism and the National-State Tug-of-War

The Separation of Powers

- Checks and Balances

- Legislative Supremacy

- The Role of the Supreme Court

Altering the Balance of Power: What are the Consequences?

---

[2]The notion that federalism requires separate spheres or jurisdictions in which lower and higher levels of government are uniquely decisive is developed fully in William H. Riker, *Federalism: Origin, Operation, Significance* (Boston: Little, Brown, 1964). This American version of federalism is applied to the emerging federal arrangements in the People's Republic of China during the 1990s in a paper by Barry R. Weingast, "The Economic Role of Political Institutions: Market-Preserving Federalism and Economic Development," *Journal of Law, Economics & Organization* 11 (1995): 1–32.

Although this chapter refers to all five principles of politics, the most salient principle is that institutions matter—that is, rules and procedures shape politics. As we learned in Chapter 1, institutions are part "script" and part "scorecard." Throughout American political history, the institutional script has determined whether states or the national government would exercise influence in a given policy area. Similarly, at the national level, the separation-of-powers system that delineates the role and authority of members of Congress, the president, and the courts provides the scorecard that allows political actors to predict who will be influential on a given political issue. And, in that they are consequential, these institutional structures channel and constrain the actions of political actors as they pursue their different goals.

itself. Individuals are given rights, which are claims to identity, to property, and to personal satisfaction or "the pursuit of happiness," that cannot be denied except by extraordinary procedures that demonstrate beyond doubt that the need of the government or the "public interest" is more compelling than the claim of the citizen.

This chapter will be concerned with federalism and the separation of powers. The purpose here is to look at the evolution of each in order to understand how we got to where we are and what the significance of each in operation is. Together federalism and the separation of powers constitute a script and a scorecard for the exercise of governmental power. They characterize the way the different fragments of governmental machinery mesh together into a whole, and they provide a list and a description of the players in the game of politics. We will conclude by reviewing the question "How do federalism and the separation of powers limit the power of the national government?" Individual rights will be the topic of the next chapter. But all of this is for introductory purposes only. All three elements form the background and the context for every chapter in this book.

FEDERALISM AND THE SEPARATION OF POWERS AS POLITICAL INSTITUTIONS

The great achievement of American politics is the fashioning of an effective constitutional structure of political institutions. Although it is an imperfect and continuously evolving "work in progress," this structure of law and political practice has served its people well for more than two centuries by managing conflict, providing inducements for bargaining and cooperation, and facilitating collective action. There has been one enormous failure—the cruel practice of slavery, which ended only after a destructive civil war. But the basic configuration of institutions first formulated in Philadelphia in 1787 survived these debacles, though severely scarred by them, and has otherwise stood the test of time.

As we noted earlier, institutional arrangements like federalism and the separation of powers are part *script* and part *scorecard*. As two of the most important features of the constitutional structure, federalism and the separation of powers serve to channel and constrain political agents, first by limiting their jurisdictional authority and second by pitting them against one another as political competitors.

One of the ingenious features of the constitutional design adopted by the framers is the principle of dividing and separating. Leaving political authority unobstructed and undivided, it was thought, would invite intense competition of a winner-take-all variety. The winners would then be in a position to tyrannize, while the losers would either submit or, with nothing else to lose, be tempted to violent opposition. By adopting the divide-and-separate principle—implemented as federalism and the separation of powers, and consisting of checks and balances—the framers of the Constitution created *jurisdictional arrangements*. The Constitution reflects this in two distinct ways. First, it encourages diversity in the political actors occupying the various institutions of government by requiring that they be selected at different times, from different constituencies, by different modes of selection (chiefly various forms of election and appointment). This, it was believed, would prevent a small clique or narrow slice of the political elite from dominating all the institutions of government at the same time. Second, the Constitution allocates the consideration of different aspects of policy to different institutional arenas. Some explicitly mentioned activities, like the coinage of money or the declaration of war, were assigned to Congress. Matters relating to the execution and implementation of the law were delegated to the president and the executive bureaucracy. Other activities, like adjudicating disputes between states, were made the preserve of the judicial branch. Those activities not explicitly mentioned in the Constitution were reserved to the states. In short, through a jurisdictional arrangement, the Constitution sought a balance in which there was the capacity for action, but in which power was not so concentrated as to make tyranny likely.

The amazing thing about these American political institutions is that they are not carved in granite (even if the official buildings that house them are!). While the Constitution initially set a broad framework for the division of authority between the national government and the states, and the division of labor among the branches of the national government, much adaptation and innovation took place as these institutions themselves were bent to the purposes of various political players. Politicians, remember, are goal-oriented and are constantly exploring the possibilities provided them by their institutional positions and political situations. Another political player that has helped shape the current jurisdictional arrangements and sharing of power is worth remembering as well. This is the United States Supreme Court. As former Supreme Court Justice Charles Evans Hughes once remarked, "We are under a Constitution, but the Constitution is what the judges say it is."[3] As we shall see in this chapter, the Court has been a

Institution Principle

The Constitution created jurisdictional arrangements by encouraging diversity in the elected leaders occupying office and allocating the consideration of different aspects of policy to different institutional arenas.

Rationality Principle

As political institutions, federalism and the separation of powers have adapted to the purposes of various political players.

History Principle

Since the time of the founding, federalism has been shaped strongly by the Supreme Court.

[3]Charles Evans Hughes, speech at Elmira, New York, 3 May 1907.

central player in settling the ongoing debate over how power should be divided between the national government and the states and between Congress and the president.

WHO DOES WHAT? THE CHANGING FEDERAL FRAMEWORK

federalism
System of government in which power is divided by a constitution between a central government and regional governments.

Federalism can be defined with misleading ease and simplicity as the division of powers and functions between the national government and the state governments.

Federalism sought to limit national and state power by creating two sovereigns—the national government and the state governments, each to a large extent independent of the other. As we saw in Chapter 2, the states had already existed as former colonies before independence, and for nearly thirteen years they were virtually autonomous units under the Articles of Confederation. In effect, the states had retained too much power under the Articles, a problem that led directly to the Annapolis Convention in 1786 and to the Constitutional Convention in 1787. Under the Articles, disorder within states was beyond the reach of the national government (see Shays's Rebellion, Chapter 2), and conflicts of interest between states were not manageable. For example, states were making their own trade agreements with foreign countries and companies that might then play one state against another for special advantages. Some states adopted special trade tariffs and further barriers to foreign commerce that were contrary to the interest of another state.[4] Tax and other barriers were also being erected between the states.[5] But even after the ratification of the Constitution, the states continued to be more important than the national government. For nearly a century and a half, virtually all of the fundamental policies governing the lives of Americans were made by the state legislatures, not by Congress.

Federalism in the Constitution

The United States was the first nation to adopt federalism as its governing framework. With federalism, the framers sought to limit the national government by creating a second layer of state governments. American federalism recognized two sovereigns in the original Constitution and reinforced the principle in the Bill of Rights by granting a few *"expressed powers"* to the national government and reserving all the rest to the states.

expressed powers Specific powers granted to Congress under Article 1, Section 8, of the Constitution.

The Powers of the National Government As we saw in Chapter 2, the "expressed powers" granted to the national government are found in Article I, Sec-

---

[4]For good treatment of these conflicts of interests between states, see Forrest McDonald, *E Pluribus Unum: The Formation of the American Republic, 1776–1790* (Boston: Houghton Mifflin, 1965), Chapter 7, especially pp. 319–38.

[5]See David M. O'Brien, *Constitutional Law and Politics*, 3rd ed., 2 vols. (New York: W. W. Norton, 1997), I, pp. 602–3.

tion 8, of the Constitution. These seventeen powers include the power to collect taxes, to coin money, to declare war, and to regulate commerce (which, as we will see, became a very important power for the national government). Article I, Section 8, also contains another important source of power for the national government: the ***implied powers*** that enable Congress "to make all Laws which shall be necessary and proper for carrying into Execution the foregoing Powers." Not until several decades after the founding did the Supreme Court allow Congress to exercise the power granted in this ***necessary and proper clause,*** but, as we shall see later in this chapter, this doctrine allowed the national government to expand considerably the scope of its authority, although the process was a slow one. In addition to these expressed and implied powers, the Constitution affirmed the power of the national government in the supremacy clause (Article VI), which made all national laws and treaties "the supreme Law of the Land."

implied powers
Powers derived from the necessary and proper clause of Article I, Section 8, of the Constitution. Such powers are not specifically expressed but are implied through the expansive interpretation of delegated powers.

necessary and proper clause
From Article I, Section 8, of the Constitution, it provides Congress with the authority to make all laws "necessary and proper" to carry out its expressed powers.

The Powers of State Government   One way in which the framers sought to preserve a strong role for the states was through the Tenth Amendment to the Constitution. The Tenth Amendment states that the powers that the Constitution does not delegate to the national government or prohibit to the states are "reserved to the States respectively, or to the people." The Antifederalists, who feared that a strong central government would encroach on individual liberty, repeatedly pressed for such an amendment as a way of limiting national power. Federalists agreed to the amendment because they did not think it would do much harm, given the powers of the Constitution already granted to the national government. The Tenth Amendment is also called the ***reserved powers*** amendment because it aims to reserve powers to the states.

reserved powers
Powers, derived from the Tenth Amendment to the Constitution, that are not specifically delegated to the national government or denied to the states.

The most fundamental power that is retained by the states is that of coercion—the power to develop and enforce criminal codes, to administer health and safety rules, to regulate the family via marriage and divorce laws. The states have the power to regulate individuals' livelihoods; if you're a doctor or a lawyer or a plumber or a barber, you must be licensed by the state. Even more fundamentally, the states had the power to define private property—private property exists because state laws against trespass define who is and is not entitled to use a piece of property. If you own a car, your ownership isn't worth much unless the state is willing to enforce your right to possession by making it a crime for anyone else to drive your car. These are fundamental matters, and the powers of the states regarding these domestic issues are much greater than the powers of the national government, even today.

A state's authority to regulate these fundamental matters is commonly referred to as the ***police power*** of the state and encompasses the state's power to regulate the health, safety, welfare, and morals of its citizens. Policing is what states do—they coerce you in the name of the community in order to maintain public order. And this was exactly the type of power that the founders intended the states to exercise.

police power
Power reserved to the government to regulate the health, safety, and morals of its citizens.

concurrent powers
Authority possessed by *both* state and national governments, such as the power to levy taxes.

In some areas, the states share ***concurrent powers*** with the national government, wherein they retain and share some power to regulate commerce and to affect the currency—for example, by being able to charter banks, grant or deny corporate charters, grant or deny licenses to engage in a business or practice a trade, and regulate the quality of products or the conditions of labor. This issue of concurrent versus exclusive power has come up from time to time in our history, but wherever there is a direct conflict of laws between the federal and the state levels, the issue will most likely be resolved in favor of national supremacy.

State Obligations to One Another   The Constitution also creates obligations among the states. These obligations, spelled out in Article IV, were intended to promote national unity. By requiring the states to recognize actions and decisions taken in other states as legal and proper, the framers aimed to make the states less like independent countries and more like parts of a single nation.

Article IV, Section I, calls for "Full Faith and Credit" among states, meaning that each state is normally expected to honor the "public Acts, Records, and judicial Proceedings" that take place in any other state. So, for example, if a couple is married in Texas—marriage being regulated by state law—Missouri must also recognize that marriage, even though they were not married under Missouri state law.

full faith and credit clause
Provision from Article IV, Section 1, of the Constitution requiring that the states normally honor the public acts and judicial decisions that take place in another state.

This *full faith and credit clause* has recently become embroiled in the controversy over gay and lesbian marriage. In 1993, the Hawaii Supreme Court prohibited discrimination against gay and lesbian marriage except in very limited circumstances. Many observers believed that Hawaii would eventually fully legalize gay marriage. In fact, after a long political battle, Hawaii passed a constitutional amendment in 1998 outlawing gay marriage. However, in December 1999, the Vermont Supreme Court ruled that gay and lesbian couples should have the same rights as heterosexuals. The Vermont legislature responded with a new law that allowed gays and lesbians to form "civil unions." Although not legally considered marriages, such unions allow gay and lesbian couples most of the benefits of marriage, such as eligibility for the partner's health insurance, inheritance rights, and the right to transfer property. The Vermont statute could have broad implications for other states. More than thirty states have passed "defense of marriage acts" that define marriage as a union between men and women only. Anxious to show its disapproval of gay marriage, Congress passed the Defense of Marriage Act in 1996, which declared that states will *not* have to recognize a same-sex marriage, even if it is legal in one state. The act also said that the federal government will not recognize gay marriage—even if it is legal under state law—and that gay marriage partners will not be eligible for the federal benefits, such as Medicare and Social Security, normally available to spouses.[6]

Because of this controversy, the extent and meaning of the full faith and credit clause is sure to be considered by the Supreme Court. In fact, it is not clear that the clause requires states to recognize gay marriage because the

[6]Ken I. Kersch, "Full Faith and Credit for Same-Sex Marriages?" *Political Science Quarterly* 112 (Spring 1997): 117–36; Joan Biskupic, "Once Unthinkable, Now under Debate," *Washington Post*, 3 September 1996, p. A1.

Court's past interpretation of the clause has provided exceptions for "public policy" reasons: if states have strong objections to a law, they do not have to honor it. In 1997 the Court took up a case involving the full faith and credit clause. The case concerned a Michigan court order that prevented a former engineer for General Motors from testifying against the company. The engineer, who left the company on bad terms, later testified in a Missouri court about a car accident in which a woman died when her Chevrolet Blazer caught fire. General Motors challenged his right to testify, arguing that Missouri should give "full faith and credit" to the Michigan ruling. The Supreme Court ruled that the engineer could testify and that the court system in one state cannot hinder other state courts in their "search for the truth."[7]

Article IV, Section 2, known as the "comity clause," also seeks to promote national unity. It provides that citizens enjoying the ***"Privileges and Immunities"*** of one state should be entitled to similar treatment in other states. What this has come to mean is that a state cannot discriminate against someone from another state or give special privileges to its own residents. For example, in the 1970s, when Alaska passed a law that gave residents preference over nonresidents in obtaining work on the state's oil and gas pipelines, the Supreme Court ruled the law illegal because it discriminated against citizens of other states.[8] This clause also regulates criminal justice among the states by requiring states to return fugitives to the states from which they have fled. Thus, in 1952, when an inmate escaped from an Alabama prison and sought to avoid being returned to Alabama on the grounds that he was being subjected to "cruel and unusual punishment" there, the Supreme Court ruled that he must be returned according to Article IV, Section 2.[9] This example highlights the difference between the obligations among states and those among different countries. Recently, France refused to return an American fugitive because he might be subject to the death penalty, which does not exist in France.[10] The Constitution clearly forbids states from doing something similar.

States' relationships to one another are also governed by the interstate compact clause (Article I, Section 10), which states that "No State shall, without the Consent of Congress . . . enter into any Agreement or Compact with another State." The Court has interpreted the clause to mean that states may enter into agreements with one another, subject to congressional approval. Compacts are a way for two or more states to reach a legally binding agreement about how to solve a problem that crosses state lines. In the early years of the Republic, states turned to compacts primarily to settle border disputes. Today they are used for a wide range of issues but are especially important in regulating the distribution of

privileges and immunities clause Provision from Article IV, Section 2, of the Constitution that a state cannot discriminate against someone from another state or give its own residents special privileges.

[7]Linda Greenhouse, "Supreme Court Weaves Legal Principles from a Tangle of Legislation," *New York Times*, 30 June 1988, p. A20.

[8]Hicklin v. Orbeck, 437 U.S. 518 (1978).

[9]Sweeny v. Woodall, 344 U.S. 86 (1953).

[10]Marlise Simons, "France Won't Extradite American Convicted of Murder," *New York Times*, 5 December 1997, p. A9.

river water, addressing environmental concerns, and operating transportation systems that cross state lines.[11]

Local Government and the Constitution   Local government occupies a peculiar but very important place in the American system. In fact, the status of American local government is probably unique in world experience. First, it must be pointed out that local government has no status in the American Constitution. *State* legislatures created local governments, and *state* constitutions and laws permit local governments to take on some of the responsibilities of the state governments. Most states amended their own constitutions to give their larger cities *home rule*—a guarantee of noninterference in various areas of local affairs. But local governments enjoy no such recognition in the Constitution. Local governments have always been mere conveniences of the states.[12]

Local governments became administratively important in the early years of the Republic because the states possessed little administrative capability. They relied on local governments—cities and counties—to implement the laws of the state. Local government was an alternative to a statewide bureaucracy.

The Slow Growth of the National Government's Power

As we have noted, the Constitution created two layers of government: the national government and the state governments. This two-layer system can be called ***dual federalism.*** The consequences of dual federalism are fundamental to the American system of government in theory and in practice. They have meant that states have done most of the fundamental governing. Table 3.1 is a listing of the major types of public policies by which Americans were governed for the first century and a half under the Constitution. We call it the "traditional system" because it prevailed for three-quarters of our history and because it closely approximates the intentions of the framers of the Constitution. The contrast between national and state policies, as shown by the table, demonstrates the difference in the power vested in each. The list of items in column 2 could actually have been made much longer. Moreover, each item on the list is only a category made up of laws that fill many volumes of statutes and court decisions for each state.

Questions about how to divide responsibilities between the states and the national government first arose more than two hundred years ago, when the framers wrote the Constitution to create a stronger union. But they did not solve the issue of who should do what. There is no "right" answer to that question;

home rule   Power delegated by the state to a local unit of government to manage its own affairs.

dual federalism   The system of government that prevailed in the United States from 1789 to 1937 in which most fundamental governmental powers were shared between the federal and state governments.

 Institution Principle

In answering "Who does what?" federalism determines the flow of government functions and through that, the political development of the country.

[11]Patricia S. Florestano, "Past and Present Utilization of Interstate Compacts in the United States," *Publius* 24 (Fall 1994): 13–26.

[12]A good discussion of the constitutional position of local governments is in York Y. Willbern, *The Withering Away of the City* (Bloomington: Indiana University Press, 1971). For more on the structure and theory of federalism, see Thomas R. Dye, *American Federalism: Competition among Governments* (Lexington, Mass.: Lexington Books, 1990), Chapter 1; and Martha Derthick, "Up-to-Date in Kansas City: Reflections on American Federalism" (the 1992 John Gaus Lecture), *PS: Political Science & Politics* 25 (December 1992): 671–75.

TABLE 3.1

The Federal System: Specialization of Governmental Functions in the Traditional System (1789–1937)

NATIONAL GOVERNMENT POLICIES (DOMESTIC)	STATE GOVERNMENT POLICIES	LOCAL GOVERNMENT POLICIES
Internal improvements	Property laws (including slavery)	Adaptation of state laws to local conditions ("variances")
Subsidies	Estate and inheritance laws	Public works
Tariffs	Commerce laws	Contracts for public works
Public lands disposal	Banking and credit laws	Licensing of public accommodations
Patents	Corporate laws	Assessable improvements
Currency	Insurance laws	Basic public services
	Family laws	
	Morality laws	
	Public health laws	
	Education laws	
	General penal laws	
	Eminent domain laws	
	Construction codes	
	Land-use laws	
	Water and mineral laws	
	Criminal procedure laws	
	Electoral and political parties laws	
	Local government laws	
	Civil service laws	
	Occupations and professions laws	

each generation of Americans has provided its own answer. In recent years, Americans have grown distrustful of the federal government and have supported giving more responsibility to the states.[13] Even so, they still want the federal government to set standards and promote equality.

Political debates about the division of responsibility often take sides: some people argue for a strong federal role to set national standards, while others say the states should do more. These two goals are not necessarily at odds. The key is to find the right balance. During the first 150 years of American history, that balance favored state power. But the balance began to shift toward Washington in the 1930s. Since the mid-1990s, there have been efforts to shift the balance back toward the states.

Having created the national government, and recognizing the potential for abuse of power, the states sought through federalism to constrain the national government. The "traditional system" of weak national government prevailed for over a century despite economic forces favoring its expansion and despite Supreme Court cases giving a pro-national interpretation to Article I, Section 8, of the Constitution.

That article delegates to Congress the power "to regulate commerce with foreign nations, and among the several States and with the Indian tribes." This *commerce clause* was consistently interpreted *in favor* of national power by the Supreme Court for most of the nineteenth century. The first and most important case favoring national power over the economy was *McCulloch v. Maryland*.[14] The case involved the Bank of the United States and the question of whether Congress had the power to charter a bank since such an explicit grant of power was nowhere to be found in Article I, Section 8. Chief Justice John Marshall answered that the power could be "implied" from other powers that were expressly delegated to Congress, such as the "powers to lay and collect taxes; to borrow money; to regulate commerce; and to declare and conduct a war." The constitutional authority for the implied powers doctrine is a clause in Article I, Section 8, which enables Congress "to make all Laws which shall be necessary and proper for carrying into Execution the foregoing Powers." By allowing Congress to use the "necessary and proper" clause to interpret its delegated powers, the Supreme Court created the potential for an unprecedented increase in national government power.

A second historic question posed by *McCulloch* was whether a state had the power to tax the Baltimore branch of the U.S. Bank since it was a national agency. Here Marshall again took the side of national supremacy, arguing that an agency created by a legislature representing all the people (Congress) could not be put out of business by a state legislature (Maryland) representing only a small portion of the people (since "the power to tax is the power to destroy"). Marshall

Institution Principle

The national-state tug-of-war is an institutional feature of the federal system.

commerce clause
Article I, Section 8, of the Constitution, which delegates to Congress the power "to regulate Commerce with foreign Nations, and among the several States, and with the Indian Tribes." This clause was interpreted by the Supreme Court in favor of national power over the economy.

---

[13]See the poll reported in Guy Gugliotta, "Scaling Down the American Dream," *Washington Post*, 19 April 1995, p. A21.
[14]McCulloch v. Maryland, 4 Wheaton 316 (1819).

concluded that whenever a state law conflicted with a federal law, the state law would be deemed invalid since "the laws of the United States . . . 'shall be the supreme law of the land.'" Both parts of this historic case were "pro-national," yet Congress did not immediately attempt to expand the policies of the national government.

This nationalistic interpretation of the Constitution was reinforced by another major case, that of *Gibbons v. Ogden* in 1824. The important but relatively narrow issue was whether the state of New York could grant a monopoly to Robert Fulton's steamboat company to operate an exclusive service between New York and New Jersey. Ogden had secured his license from Fulton's company, while Gibbons, a former partner, secured a competing license from the U.S. government. Chief Justice Marshall argued that Gibbons could not be kept from competing because the state of New York did not have the power to grant this particular monopoly. In order to reach this decision, it was necessary for Chief Justice Marshall to define what Article I, Section 8, meant by "Commerce . . . among the several States." Marshall insisted that the definition was "comprehensive," extending to "every species of commercial intercourse." He did say that this comprehensiveness was limited "to that commerce which concerns more states than one," giving rise to what later came to be called "interstate commerce." *Gibbons* is important because it established the supremacy of the national government in all matters affecting interstate commerce.[15] What would remain uncertain during several decades of constitutional discourse was the precise meaning of interstate commerce, notwithstanding John Marshall's expansive reading of "commerce among the several states."

Article I, Section 8, backed by the "implied powers" decision in *McCulloch* and by the broad definition of "interstate commerce" in *Gibbons*, was a source of power for the national government as long as Congress sought to improve commerce through subsidies, services, and land grants. But later in the nineteenth century, when the national government sought to use those powers to *regulate* the economy rather than merely to promote economic development, the concept of interstate commerce began to operate as a restraint on rather than as a source of national power. Any effort of the federal government to regulate commerce in such areas as fraud, the production of impure goods, the use of child labor, or the existence of dangerous working conditions or long hours was declared unconstitutional by the Supreme Court as a violation of the concept of interstate commerce. Such legislation meant that the federal government was entering the factory and workplace, and these areas were considered inherently local because the goods produced there had not yet passed into commerce. Any effort to enter these local workplaces was an exercise of police power—the power reserved to the states for the protection of the health, safety, and morals of their citizens. No one questioned the power of the national government to regulate certain kinds of businesses, such as railroads, gas pipelines, and waterway

[15]Gibbons v. Ogden, 9 Wheaton 1 (1824).

transportation, because they intrinsically involved interstate commerce.[16] But well into the twentieth century, most other efforts by the national government to regulate commerce were blocked by the Supreme Court's interpretation of federalism, which used the concept of interstate commerce as a barrier against most efforts by Congress to expand the national government's power.

After 1937, the Supreme Court threw out the old distinction between interstate and intrastate commerce, converting the commerce clause from a source of limitations to a source of power. The Court began to refuse to review appeals challenging acts of Congress protecting the rights of employees to organize and engage in collective bargaining, regulating the amount of farmland in cultivation, extending low-interest credit to small businesses and farmers, and restricting the activities of corporations dealing in the stock market, and many other laws that contributed to the construction of the "welfare state."

History Principle

In 1937, the Supreme Court converted the commerce clause from a source of limitations to a source of power for the national government.

Cooperative Federalism and Grants-in-Aid

cooperative federalism A type of federalism existing since the New Deal era in which grants-in-aid have been used strategically to encourage states and localities (without commanding them) to pursue nationally defined goals. Also known as intergovernmental cooperation.

grants-in-aid
A general term for funds given by Congress to state and local governments.

If the traditional system of two sovereigns performing highly different functions could be called dual federalism, the system since the 1930s could be called *cooperative federalism*—which generally refers to supportive relations, sometimes partnerships, between national government and the state and local governments. It comes in the form of federal subsidization of special state and local activities; these subsidies are called *grants-in-aid.* But make no mistake about it: although many of these state and local programs would not exist without the federal grant-in-aid, the grant-in-aid is also an important form of federal influence. (Another form of federal influence, the mandate, will be covered in the next section.)

A grant-in-aid is really a kind of bribe, or "carrot," whereby Congress appropriates money for state and local governments with the condition that the money be spent for a particular purpose as defined by Congress. Congress uses grants-in-aid because it does not have the political or constitutional power to command cities to do its bidding. When you can't command, a monetary inducement becomes a viable alternative. Grants-in-aid are also mechanisms that help to coordinate the separate activities of all those state and local governments around a common set of standards or policy principles in circumstances when a multiplicity of these things would undermine the purposes of the policy.

Collective Action Principle

Grants-in-aid allow the national government to coordinate state and local policies around a common set of national standards.

The principle of the grant-in-aid goes back to the nineteenth-century land grants to states for the improvement of agriculture and farm-related education. Since farms were not in "interstate commerce," it was unclear whether the Constitution would permit the national government to provide direct assistance to agriculture. Grants-in-aid to the states, earmarked to go to farmers, presented a way of avoiding the constitutional problem while pursuing what was recognized in Congress as a national goal.

---

[16]In Wabash, St. Louis, and Pacific Railway Company v. Illinois, 118 U.S. 557 (1886), the Supreme Court struck down a state law prohibiting rate discrimination by a railroad; in response, Congress passed the Interstate Commerce Act of 1887 creating the Interstate Commerce Commission (ICC), which was the first federal administrative agency.

FIGURE 3.1

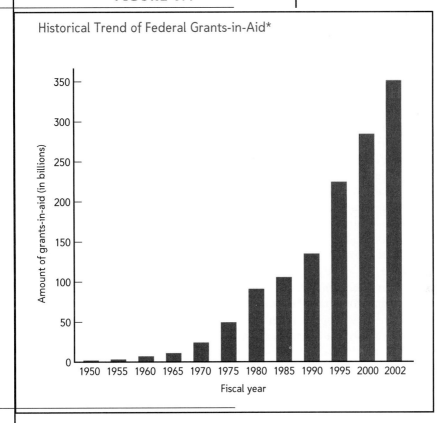

Historical Trend of Federal Grants-in-Aid*

*Excludes outlays for national defense, international affairs, and net interest.

SOURCE: Office of Management and Budget, *Budget of the United States Government, Fiscal Year 2004, Analytical Perspectives* (Washington, D.C.: Government Printing Office, 2003), Table 10-2, p. 255.

Beginning in the late 1930s, this same approach was applied to cities. Congress set national goals such as public housing and assistance to the unemployed and provided grants-in-aid to meet these goals. World War II temporarily stopped the distribution of these grants. But after the war, Congress resumed providing grants for urban development and lunches in the schools. The value of such ***categorical grants-in-aid*** increased from $2.3 billion in 1950 to $350 billion in 2002 (see Figure 3.1). Sometimes Congress requires the state or local government to match the national contribution dollar for dollar, but for some programs, such as the interstate highway system, the congressional grant-in-aid provides 90 percent of the cost of the program. The nationwide speed limit of 55 mph was not imposed on individual drivers by an act of Congress. Instead,

categorical grants-in-aid
Funds given by Congress to states and localities, earmarked by law for specific categories such as education or crime prevention.

Congress bribed the state legislatures by threatening to withdraw the federal highway grants-in-aid if the states did not set a 55 mph speed limit. In the early 1990s, Congress began to ease up on the states, permitting them, under certain conditions, to go back to the 65 mph speed limit (or higher) without losing their highway grants.

For the most part, the categorical grants created before the 1960s simply helped the states perform their traditional functions such as education and policing.[17] In the 1960s, however, the national role expanded, and the number of categorical grants increased dramatically. For example, during the Eighty-ninth Congress (1965–1966) alone, the number of categorical grant-in-aid programs grew from 221 to 379.[18] The grants authorized during the 1960s announced national purposes much more strongly than did earlier grants. Central to that national purpose was the need to provide opportunities to the poor.

Many of the categorical grants enacted during the 1960s were *project grants,* which require state and local governments to submit proposals to federal agencies. In contrast to the older *formula grants,* which used a formula (composed of such elements as need and state and local capacities) to distribute funds, the new project grants made funding available on a competitive basis. Federal agencies would give grants to the proposals they judged to be the best. In this way, the national government acquired substantial control over which state and local governments got money, how much they got, and how they spent it.

The most important student of the history of federalism, Morton Grodzins, characterized the shift to post–New Deal cooperative federalism as a move from "layer cake federalism" to "marble cake federalism,"[19] in which intergovernmental cooperation and sharing have blurred the distinguishing line, making it difficult to say where the national government ends and the state and local governments begin (see Figure 3.2). Figure 3.3 demonstrates the financial basis of the marble cake idea. At the high point of grant-in-aid policies in the late 1970s federal aid contributed about 25–30 percent of the operating budgets of all the state and local governments in the country. The numbers in Table 3.2 present some of the more extreme examples from 1977 and the severe drop since that time.

Regulated Federalism and National Standards

Developments from the 1960s to the present have moved well beyond cooperative federalism to what might be called "regulated federalism."[20] In some areas

---

[17]Kenneth T. Palmer, "The Evolution of Grant Policies," in Lawrence D. Brown, James W. Fossett, and Kenneth T. Palmer, *The Changing Politics of Federal Grants,* (Washington, D.C.: Brookings Institution, 1984), p. 15.

[18]Ibid., p. 6.

[19]Morton Grodzins, "The Federal System," in *Goals for Americans* (Englewood Cliffs, N.J.: Prentice-Hall, 1960), p. 265. In a marble cake, the white cake is distinguishable from the chocolate cake, but the two are streaked rather than in distinct layers.

[20]The concept and the best discussion of this modern phenomenon will be found in Donald F. Kettl, *The Regulation of American Federalism* (Baltimore: Johns Hopkins University Press, 1983 and 1987), especially pp. 33–41.

FIGURE 3.2

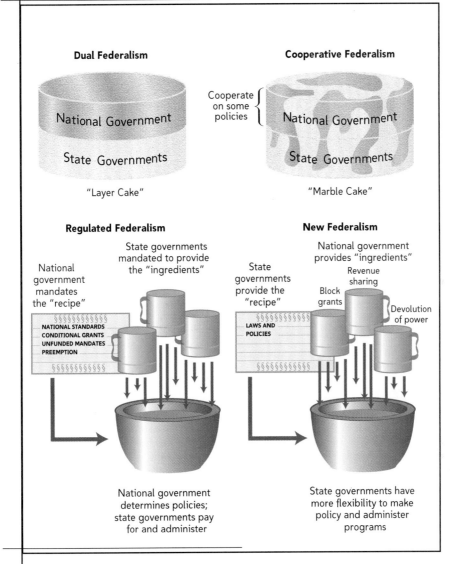

Dual Federalism

National Government

State Governments

"Layer Cake"

Cooperative Federalism

Cooperate on some policies

National Government

State Governments

"Marble Cake"

Regulated Federalism

National government mandates the "recipe"

State governments mandated to provide the "ingredients"

NATIONAL STANDARDS
CONDITIONAL GRANTS
UNFUNDED MANDATES
PREEMPTION

National government determines policies; state governments pay for and administer

New Federalism

National government provides "ingredients"

State governments provide the "recipe"

Revenue sharing

Block grants

Devolution of power

LAWS AND POLICIES

State governments have more flexibility to make policy and administer programs

FIGURE 3.3

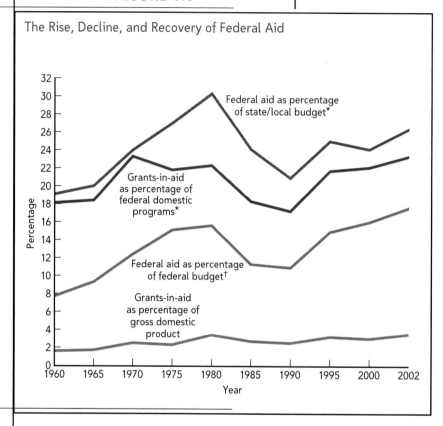

The Rise, Decline, and Recovery of Federal Aid

*Federal aid as a percentage of state/local expenditures after transfers.
†Federal aid as a percentage of federal expenditures from own funds.
‡Excludes outlays for national defense, international affairs, and net interest.

SOURCE: Office of Management and Budget, *Budget of the United States Government, Fiscal Year 2004, Analytical Perspectives* (Washington, D.C.: Government Printing Office, 2003), Table 10-2, p. 255.

the national government actually regulates the states by threatening to withhold grant money unless state and local governments conform to national standards. The most notable instances of this regulation are in the areas of civil rights, poverty programs, and environmental protection. This reflects a general shift in federal regulation away from the oversight and control of strictly economic activities toward "social regulation"—interventions on behalf of individual rights and liberties, environmental protection, workplace safety, and so on. In these instances, the national government provides grant-in-aid financing but sets condi-

TABLE 3.2

	Federal Aid as a Percentage of General Annual Expenditure					
CITY	**1977**	**1999**	**CITY**	**1977**	**1999**
Chicago	20	8	Houston	13	6
Cleveland	29	8	Indianapolis	21	3
Denver	14	2	Los Angeles	22	7
Detroit	31	9	San Antonio	28	2
Honolulu	30	9	Seattle	23	4

SOURCE: Department of Commerce, *Statistical Abstract of the United States, 2002* (Washington, D.C.: Government Printing Office, 2002), Tables 437 and 438.

tions the states must meet in order to keep the grants. The national government refers to these policies as "setting national standards." Important examples include the Asbestos Hazard Emergency Act of 1986, which requires school districts to inspect for asbestos hazards and to remove them from school buildings when necessary, and the Americans with Disabilities Act of 1990, which requires all state and local governments to promote access for the handicapped to all government buildings. The net effect of these national standards is that state and local policies are more uniform from coast to coast. As we noted earlier about grants-in-aid, national regulations and standards provide coordination across states and localities and solve collective action problems. However, there are a number of other programs in which the national government engages in regulated federalism by imposing national standards on the states *without providing any funding at all.* These have come to be called ***unfunded mandates.*** States complained that mandates took up so much of their budgets that they were not able to set their own priorities.[21]

These burdens became a major part of the rallying cry that produced the famous Republican Congress elected in 1994, with its Contract with America.

unfunded mandates Regulations or conditions for receiving grants that impose costs on state and local governments for which they are not reimbursed by the federal government.

[21]John J. DiIulio and Donald F. Kettl report that in 1980 there were thirty-six laws that could be categorized as unfunded mandates. And despite the concerted opposition of the Reagan and Bush administrations, another twenty-seven laws qualifying as unfunded mandates were adopted between 1982 and 1991. See John DiIulio, Jr., and Donald F. Kettl, *Fine Print: The Contract with America, Devolution, and the Administrative Realities of American Federalism* (Washington, D.C.: Brookings Institution, 1995), p. 41.

One of the first measures adopted by the 104th Republican Congress was an act to limit unfunded mandates—the Unfunded Mandates Reform Act (UMRA). This was considered a triumph of lobbying efforts by state and local governments, and it was "hailed as both symbol and substance of a renewed congressional commitment to federalism."[22] Under this law, any mandate with an uncompensated state and local cost estimated at greater than $50 million a year, as determined by the Congressional Budget Office (CBO), can be stopped by a point of order raised on the House or Senate floor. This was called a "stop, look and listen" requirement, forcing Congress to take positive action to own up to the mandate and its potential costs. During 1996, its first full year of operation, only eleven bills included mandates that exceeded the $50 million threshold—from a total of sixty-nine estimates of actions in which mandates were included. Examples included minimum wage increase, parity for mental health and health insurance, mandated use of Social Security numbers on driver's licenses, and extension of Federal Occupation Safety and Health to state and local employees. Most of them were modified in the House, to reduce their costs. However, as one expert put it, "The primary impact of UMRA came not from the affirmative blockage of [mandate] legislation, but rather from its effect as a deterrent to mandates in the drafting and early consideration of legislation."[23]

As indicated by the first year of its operation, the effect of UMRA will not be revolutionary. UMRA does not prevent congressional members from passing unfunded mandates; it only makes them think twice before they do. Moreover, the act exempts several areas from coverage by UMRA. And states must still enforce antidiscrimination laws and meet other requirements to receive federal assistance. But, on the other hand, UMRA does represent a serious effort to move the national/state relationship a bit further toward the state side.

New Federalism and the National-State Tug-of-War

Federalism in the United States can best be understood today as a tug-of-war between those seeking more uniform national standards and those seeking more room for variability from state to state. This is a struggle over federalism's script and scorecard—over who does what and how the various activities are structured and sequenced. Presidents Nixon and Reagan called their efforts to reverse the trend toward national standards and reestablish traditional policy making and implementation the "new federalism." They helped to craft national policies whose purpose was to return more discretion to the states. Examples of these policies include Nixon's revenue sharing and Reagan's **block grants,** which consolidated a number of categorical grants into one larger category, leaving the state (or local) government more discretion to decide how to use the money.

block grants
Federal funds given to state governments to pay for goods, services, or programs, with relatively few restrictions on how the funds may be spent.

[22]Paul Posner, "Unfunded Mandate Reform: How Is It Working?" *Rockefeller Institute Bulletin* (Albany: Nelson A. Rockefeller Institute of Government, 1998): 35.
[23]Ibid., 36.

Presidents Nixon and Reagan, as well as former president Bush, were sincere in wanting to return somewhat to a traditional notion of freedom of action for the states. They called it new federalism, but their concepts and their goals were really much closer to the older, traditional federalism that predated the 1930s.

In effect, President Clinton adopted the "new federalism" of Nixon and Reagan even while expanding federal grant activity: he signed the Unfunded Mandates Reform Act of 1995 as well as the Personal Responsibility and Work Opportunity Reconciliation Act of 1996, which goes further than any other act of Congress in the past sixty years to relieve the states from national mandates, funded or unfunded. This new law replaces the sixty-one-year-old program of Aid to Families with Dependent Children (AFDC) and its education, work, and training program, with block grants to states for Temporary Assistance to Needy Families (TANF). Although some national standards remain, the place of the states in the national welfare system has been virtually revolutionized through ***devolution,*** the strategy of delegating to the states more and more authority over a range of policies that had up until then been under national government authority, plus providing the states with a substantial portion of the cost of these programs. Since the mid-1990s, devolution has been quite consequential for the national-state tug-of-war.

By changing welfare from a combined federal-state program into a block grant to the states, Congress gave the states more responsibility for programs that serve the poor. One argument in favor of devolution is that states can act as "laboratories of democracy" by experimenting with many different approaches to find one that best meets the needs of their citizens.[24] As states have altered their welfare programs in the wake of the new law, they have indeed designed diverse approaches. For example, Minnesota has adopted an incentive-based approach that offers extra assistance to families that take low-wage jobs. Other states, such as California, have more "sticks" than "carrots" in their new welfare programs.[25]

President George W. Bush, though sometimes compared to Ronald Reagan, has not proven to be an unwavering supporter of new federalism and states' rights. On certain matters dear to his heart, Bush has been closer to the spirit of "regulated federalism." The most visible example of Bush's occasional preference for national standards is the education program known as No Child Left Behind. This program sets standards of accomplishment in reading and math that are to be applied nationally and backed by federal grants that are to be withheld if the standards are not met. The program gives the states "full freedom" to use the federal money, but states are to be held accountable for results, as measured by national standards of performance. Failure to meet the standard will be punished

devolution
A policy to remove a program from one level of government by deregulating it or passing it down to a lower level of government, such as from the national government to the state and local governments.

Collective Action Principle
States compete with one another not only for new business, but also in terms of being less attractive to welfare recipients.

Policy Principle
Devolution has had an important influence on policy outcomes, particularly welfare.

[24]The phrase "laboratories of democracy" was coined by Supreme Court Justice Louis Brandeis in his dissenting opinion in New State Ice Co. v. Liebman, 285 U.S. 262 (1932).

[25]For assessments of the use of welfare grants to the states for increased regulation as a condition for welfare benefits, see Frances Fox Piven, "Welfare and Work," and Dorothy Roberts, "Welfare's Ban on Poor Motherhood," in *Whose Welfare?* ed. Gwendolyn Mink (Ithaca, N.Y.: Cornell University Press, 1999), pp. 83–99 and 152–167.

The End of Big Government?
Federalism in the Last Quarter Century

Beginning with Roosevelt's New Deal, the federal government grew into areas tradition-ally reserved for the states or private organizations. The dominance of the federal govern-ment was once so strong that Republican president Dwight Eisenhower supported massive federal programs for building highways and expanding educational opportuni-ties. Lyndon Johnson's Great Society, begun after the watershed election of 1964, was ar-guably the apex of the twentieth century American welfare state. By the late 1960s, President Richard Nixon created the Environmental Protection Agency, instituted wage price freeze, and once proposed a minimum income for every citizen.

By the 1990s, support for new federal programs had withered away. Over the last thirty years, programs to expand the scope of the central government have stalled or been eliminated. Presidents Reagan and George H. W. Bush came to office promising to curb federal power and shrink the size and scope of the government. President Bill Clin-ton's proposal for national health insurance was an embarrassing early defeat for the ad-ministration, and eventually Clinton proposed the "end of welfare as we know it."

The principles of politics can help us understand the conditions that led to this rapid growth in federal authority as well as trace its eventual decline. During the Depression, our collective decision-making institutions—state governments and Congress—seemed unable to formulate public policies that would address the economic crisis. Institutional rules in Congress, particularly the hammerlock of seniority and the resulting control of policy making by a small group of conservative southern senators, short-circuited propos-als for a major federal response.[26]

FDR was able to get Congress to pass much of the New Deal legislation (and, by threatening the autonomy of the Supreme Court with his "court packing" plan, convince the Court not to declare it unconstitutional). By the end of World War II, federal leader-ship action in many areas of politics—areas that would have been unthinkable just a quar-ter century before—were well accepted. Thus, during the 1950s and 1960s, grants-in-aid and regulated federalism were well-accepted solutions to cooperation and coordination problems. The future of the United States, it seemed, was firmly on the path of federal dominance, with less and less policy authority residing in the states. State legislators, na-tional political leaders, and the courts went along.

Starting in the 1970s, however, support for new federal programs began to decline (in large part because many of these programs seemed to stall or decline in effectiveness). A series of presidents, beginning with Richard Nixon, tried to change our historical path. Changes in the Republican party, beginning in 1964, meant that "Rockefeller" and "Main Street" Republicans who were more positively inclined toward federal intervention were increasingly replaced in Congress by westerners and southerners who were hostile (al-though for different reasons) to federal authority. The election of Ronald Reagan (a west-erner) and the resulting conservative shift meant that strategic political actors in all three branches of government were looking for ways to reduce federal authority. Block grants, revenue sharing, devolution, and other ways of shifting power from national to state and local actors were proposed.

Still, many laws and procedures remain in place that keep policy-making authority with the federal government yet require taxation and spending by the states. Politically, this is an easy choice for strategic politicians at the federal level: they get to take credit for cutting taxes but can still promise a social safety net (paid for by the states).

There may be advantages to this newly dispersed system of authority. We may be returning to an era when state governments become the main tax collectors and service providers. This has led to some political oddities, such as conservative Republican governors in Alabama and Idaho proposing tax increases in order to maintain services, while a liberal Democratic governor in Oregon refuses to consider new revenues.

States are likely to become policy "laboratories" where innovative new policies are developed, some successful, some a failure. While the same principles of politics apply to state as well as to the federal government, this will undoubtedly make the American political system more varied and more complex.

[26]See Robert A. Caro's compelling portrayal of southern dominance in the twentieth-century Senate in *Master of the Senate: The Life and Times of Lyndon Baines Johnson* (New York: Knopf, 2002). William E. Leuchtenberg, in *Franklin D. Roosevelt and the New Deal, 1932–1940* (New York: Harper & Row, 1963), argues that the political conditions of the 1920s and 1930s, particularly ineptness in Congress and in the states, required forceful and creative leadership by FDR.

by withholding federal funds. This is especially significant considering that education is the most local of all activities. On certain other matters, historical circumstance has made Bush a proponent of nationalization. Homeland security policies are the prime example. President Bush has sought billions of dollars to pull cities and states into assuming more of their own security measures. He has even supported some "unfunded mandates" on the larger and more vulnerable cities, leaving himself open to attack from such liberal Democratic senators as Charles Schumer and Hillary Clinton of New York, who are demanding a lot more federal reimbursement for federally generated local safety measures. Another circumstance that has pushed more responsibility back on the national government is the spate of recent state budget crises. Since many states are constitutionally prohibited from running budget deficits, the national government has been forced to fill in the gaps.

As these examples from the last decade show, assessments about "the right way" to divide responsibility in the federal system change over time. The case of speed limits provides another example. Speed limits have traditionally been a state and local responsibility. But in 1973, at the height of the oil shortage, Congress passed legislation to withhold federal highway funds from states that did not adopt a maximum speed limit of 55 mph. The lower speed limit, it was argued, would reduce energy consumption by cars. Although Congress had not formally taken over the authority to set speed limits, the power of its purse was so important that every state adopted the new speed limit. As the energy crisis faded, the national speed limit lost much of its support, even though it was found to have reduced the number of traffic deaths. In 1995, Congress repealed the penalties for higher speed limits, and states once again became free to set their own speed limits. Many states with large rural areas raised their maximum to 75 mph; Montana set unlimited speeds in the rural areas during daylight hours. Early research indicates that numbers of highway deaths have indeed risen in the states that increased the limits.[27] As new evidence becomes available, it will surely provide fuel for the ongoing debate about what are properly the states' responsibilities and what the federal government should do.

The Supreme Court as Referee For much of the nineteenth century, federal power remained limited. The Tenth Amendment was used to bolster arguments about *states' rights,* which in their extreme version claimed that the states did not have to submit to national laws when they believed the national government had exceeded its authority. These arguments in favor of states' rights were voiced less often after the Civil War. But the Supreme Court continued to use the Tenth Amendment to strike down laws that it thought exceeded national power, including the Civil Rights Act passed in 1875.

In the early twentieth century, however, the Tenth Amendment appeared to lose its force. Reformers began to press for national regulations to limit the power of large corporations and to preserve the health and welfare of citizens. The Supreme Court approved of some of these laws, but it struck others down, including a law combating child labor. The Court stated that the law violated the Tenth Amendment because only states should have the power to regulate conditions of employment. By the late 1930s, however, the Supreme Court had approved such an expansion of federal power that the Tenth Amendment appeared irrelevant. In fact, in 1941, Justice Harlan Fiske Stone declared that the Tenth Amendment was simply a "truism," that it had no real meaning.[28]

Recent years have seen a revival of interest in the Tenth Amendment and important Supreme Court decisions limiting federal power. Much of the interest in the Tenth Amendment stems from conservatives who believe that a strong federal government encroaches on individual liberties. They believe such freedoms are better protected by returning more power to the states through the process of devolution. In 1996, Republican presidential candidate Bob Dole carried a copy of the Tenth Amendment in his pocket as he campaigned, pulling it out to

states' rights
The principle that states should oppose increasing authority of the national government. This view was most popular before the Civil War.

---

[27]"Motor Vehicle Fatalities in 1996 Were 12 Percent Higher on Interstates, Freeways in 12 States That Raised Speed Limits," press release of the Insurance Institute for Highway Safety, 10 October 1997.
[28]United States v. Darby Lumber Co., 312 U.S. 100 (1941).

read at rallies.[29] Around the same time, the Eleventh Amendment concept of *state sovereign immunity* was revived by the Court. This legal doctrine holds that states are immune from lawsuits by private persons or groups claiming that the state violated a statute enacted by Congress.

The Supreme Court's ruling in *United States v. Lopez* in 1995 fueled further interest in the Tenth Amendment. In that case, the Court, stating that Congress had exceeded its authority under the commerce clause, struck down a federal law that barred handguns near schools. This was the first time since the New Deal that the Court had limited congressional powers in this way. The Court further limited the power of the federal government over the states in a 1996 ruling based on the Eleventh Amendment that prevented Native Americans from the Seminole tribe from suing the state of Florida in federal court. A 1988 law had given Indian tribes the right to sue a state in federal court if the state did not negotiate in good faith over issues related to gambling casinos on tribal land. The Supreme Court's ruling appeared to signal a much broader limitation on national power by raising new questions about whether individuals can sue a state if it fails to uphold federal law.[30]

Another significant decision involving the relationship between the federal government and state governments was the 1997 case *Printz v. United States* (joined with *Mack v. United States*), in which the Court struck down a key provision of the Brady Bill, enacted by Congress in 1993 to regulate gun sales. Under the terms of the act, state and local law enforcement officers were required to conduct background checks on prospective gun purchasers. The Court held that the federal government cannot require states to administer or enforce federal regulatory programs. Since the states bear administrative responsibility for a variety of other federal programs, this decision could have far-reaching consequences. Finally, in another major ruling from the 1996–1997 term, in *City of Boerne v. Flores*, the Court ruled that Congress had gone too far in restricting the power of the states to enact regulations they deemed necessary for the protection of public health, safety, or welfare. These rulings signal a move toward a much more restricted federal government.

In 1999, the Court's ruling on another Eleventh Amendment case further strengthened the doctrine of state sovereign immunity, finding that "the federal system established by our Constitution preserves the sovereign status of the States. . . . The generation that designed and adopted our federal system considered immunity from private suits central to sovereign dignity."[31] In 2000 in *United States v. Morrison*,[32] the Supreme Court invalidated an important provision of the 1994 Violence against Women Act, which permitted women to bring private damage suits if their victimization was "gender-motivated." Although the

state sovereign immunity
Legal doctrine that holds that states cannot be sued for violating an act of Congress.

---

[29]W. John Moore, "Pleading the 10th," *National Journal*, 29 July 1995, p. 1940.
[30]Seminole Indian Tribe v. Florida, 116 S. Ct. 1114 (1996).
[31]Alden v. Maine.
[32]United States v. Morrison, 529 U.S. 598 (2000).

1994 act did not add any new national laws imposing liability or obligations on the states, the Supreme Court still held the act to be "an unconstitutional exercise" of Congress's power. And, although *Morrison* is a quite narrow federalism decision, when it is coupled with *United States v. Lopez* (1995)—the first modern holding against national authority to use commerce power to reach into the states—there is a definite trend toward strict scrutiny of the federal intervention aspects of all national civil rights, social, labor, and gender laws.

This puts federalism and the Court directly in the line of fire. With an aging and ailing Court, President Bush will likely have at least one Supreme Court justice appointment to make, and this will determine the future of federalism (and many other key issues) for the next quarter century. However, for an appointment to go through, the president must obtain the Senate's "advice and consent"; Senate debate over these appointments promises to be heated, since the makeup of the Supreme Court impacts the future of the federal government's authority to impose on the states national standards in many areas of social policy.[33]

There has clearly been a historical ebb and flow to the federal relationship: the national government's authority grew relative to that of the states during the middle decades of the twentieth century but moderated as the century drew to a close. For the moment, the balance seems to be tipped toward the states, although the tug-of-war between the states and national government will certainly continue. As a result of this ongoing struggle for power, federalism remains a vital part of the American system of government. States and cities may clamor (and lobby) for a larger share of the national budget, and state and local leaders have shown a willingness to cooperate with the national standards embodied in environmental protection laws and civil rights laws. But states, with the help of the Supreme Court, continue to hold on jealously to the maximum freedom of action that is embodied in the historic concept of federalism.

THE SEPARATION OF POWERS

In his discussion of the separation of powers, James Madison quotes the originator of the principle, the French political thinker Baron de Montesquieu:

> There can be no liberty where the legislative and executive powers are united in the same person . . . [or] if the power of judging be not separated from the legislative and executive powers.[34]

Using this same reasoning, many of Madison's contemporaries argued that there was not *enough* separation among the three branches, and Madison had to backtrack to insist that the principle did not require complete separation:

---

[33]For a superb account of the case United States v. Morrison, see Linda Greenhouse, "Battle on Federalism," *New York Times*, 17 May 2000, p. 18. See also Cass Sunstein, "The Returns of States' Rights," *American Prospect*, 20 November 2000, p. 30.

[34]Clinton Rossiter, ed., *The Federalist Papers* (New York: New American Library, 1961), No. 47, p. 302.

> . . . unless these departments [branches] be so far connected and blended as to give to each a constitutional control over the others, the degree of separation which the maxim requires, as essential to a free government, can never in practice be duly maintained.[35]

This is the secret of how we have made the separation of powers effective: we made the principle self-enforcing by giving each branch of government the means to participate in, and partially or temporarily to obstruct, the workings of the other branches.

Institution Principle

Checks and balances is a system of "separated institutions sharing power."

Checks and Balances

The means by which each branch of government interacts is known informally as *checks and balances.* The best-known examples are the presidential power to veto legislation passed by Congress; the power of Congress to override the veto by a two-thirds majority vote, to impeach the president, and (of the Senate) to approve presidential appointments; the power of the president to appoint the members of the Supreme Court and the other federal judges with Senate approval; and the power of the Supreme Court to engage in judicial review (to be discussed below). These and other examples are shown in Table 3.3. The framers sought to guarantee that the three branches would in fact use the checks and balances as weapons against each other by giving each branch a different political constituency: direct, popular election of the members of the House; indirect election of senators (until the Seventeenth Amendment, adopted in 1913); indirect election of the president (which still exists, at least formally, today); and appointment of federal judges for life. All things considered, the best characterization of the separation of powers principle in action is, as we said in Chapter 2, "separated institutions sharing power."[36]

checks and balances
Mechanisms through which each branch of government participates in and influences the activities of the other branches. Major examples include the presidential veto power over congressional legislation, the power of the Senate to approve presidential appointments, and judicial review of congressional enactments.

Legislative Supremacy

Although each branch was to be given adequate means to compete with the other branches, it is also clear that within the system of separated powers the framers provided for *legislative supremacy* by making Congress the preeminent branch. Legislative supremacy made the provision of checks and balances in the other two branches all the more important.

The most important indication of the intention of legislative supremacy was made by the framers when they decided to place the provisions for national powers in Article I, the legislative article, and to treat the powers of the national government as powers of Congress. In a system based on the "rule of law," the power to make the laws is the supreme power. Section 8 provides in part that "*Congress* shall

legislative supremacy The preeminent position assigned to the Congress by the Constitution.

Institution Principle

The framers provided for legislative supremacy by making Congress the preeminent branch.

[35]Ibid., No. 48, p. 308.
[36]Richard E. Neustadt, *Presidential Power and the Modern Presidents: The Politics of Leadership from Roosevelt to Reagan*, rev. ed. (New York: Free Press, 1990; orig. published 1960), p. 33.

TABLE 3.3

Checks and Balances

	LEGISLATIVE BRANCH CAN BE CHECKED BY:	EXECUTIVE BRANCH CAN BE CHECKED BY:	JUDICIAL BRANCH CAN BE CHECKED BY:
Legislative branch can check:	NA*	Can overrule veto (two-thirds vote) Controls appropriations Controls by statute Impeachment of president Senate approval of appointments and treaties Committee oversight	Controls appropriations Can create inferior courts Can add new judges Senate approval of appointments Impeachment of judges
Executive branch can check:	Can veto legislation Can convene special session Can adjourn Congress when chambers disagree Vice president presides over Senate and votes to break ties	NA*	President appoints judges
Judicial branch can check:	Judicial review of legislation Chief justice presides over Senate during proceedings to impeach president	Judicial review over presidential actions Power to issue warrants Chief justice presides over impeachment of president	NA*

*NA = Not applicable.

have Power . . . To lay and collect Taxes . . . To borrow Money . . . To regulate Commerce . . ." [emphasis added]. The founders also provided for legislative supremacy in their decision to give Congress the sole power over appropriations and to give the House of Representatives the power to initiate all revenue bills. Madison recognized legislative supremacy as part and parcel of the separation of powers:

> . . . It is not possible to give to each department an equal power of self-defense. In republican government, the legislative authority necessarily predominates. The remedy for this inconveniency is to divide the legislature into different branches; and to render them, by different modes of election and different principles of action, as little connected with each other as the nature of their common functions and their common dependence on the society will admit.[37]

In other words, Congress was so likely to dominate the other branches that it would have to be divided against itself, into House and Senate. One could say that the Constitution provided for four branches, not three.

Although "presidential government" seemed to supplant legislative supremacy after 1937, the relative power position of the executive and legislative branches since that time has not been static. The degree of conflict between the president and Congress has varied with the rise and fall of political parties, and it has been especially tense during periods of *divided government,* when one party controls the White House and another controls the Congress, as has been the case almost solidly since 1969 (see Table 3.4).

divided government The condition in American government wherein the presidency is controlled by one party while the opposing party controls one or both houses of Congress.

The Role of the Supreme Court

The role of the judicial branch in the separation of powers has depended upon the power of judicial review (see also Chapter 8), a power not provided for in the Constitution but asserted by Chief Justice Marshall in 1803:

> If a law be in opposition to the Constitution; if both the law and the Constitution apply to a particular case, so that the Court must either decide that case conformable to the law, disregarding the Constitution, or conformable to the Constitution, disregarding the law; the Court must determine which of these conflicting rules governs the case: This is of the very essence of judicial duty.[38]

Review of the constitutionality of acts of the president or Congress is relatively rare.[39]

---

[37]*The Federalist Papers*, No. 51, p. 322.
[38]Marbury v. Madison, 1 Cranch 137 (1803).
[39]C. Herman Pritchett, *The American Constitution* (New York: McGraw-Hill, 1959), pp. 180–86.

TABLE 3.4

The Record of Divided Government

DATE	PARTY CONTROLLING: PRESIDENT	CONGRESS	GOVERNMENT: YEARS DIVIDED
1946–1948	Truman, Democratic	Republican	Divided 2
1948–1952	Truman, Democratic	Democratic	
1952–1954	Eisenhower, Republican	Republican	
1954–1960	Eisenhower, Republican	Democratic	Divided 6
1960–1964	Kennedy/Johnson, Democratic	Democratic	
1964–1968	Johnson, Democratic	Democratic	
1968–1972	Nixon, Republican	Democratic	Divided 4
1972–1976	Nixon/Ford, Republican	Democratic	Divided 4
1976–1980	Carter, Democratic	Democratic	
1980–1986	Reagan, Republican	Republican Senate Democratic House	Divided/mixed 6
1986–1988	Reagan, Republican	Democratic	Divided 2
1988–1992	Bush, Republican	Democratic	Divided 4
1992–1994	Clinton, Democratic	Democratic	
1994–2000	Clinton, Democratic	Republican	Divided 6
2000–2002	Bush, Republican	Republican House Democratic Senate	Divided/Mixed 2
2002–2004	Bush, Republican	Republican	
	TOTAL YEARS 58	TOTAL YEARS DIVIDED 36	

For example, there were no Supreme Court reviews of congressional acts in the fifty plus years between *Marbury v. Madison* (1803) and *Dred Scott* (1857). In the century or so between the Civil War and 1970, eighty-four acts of Congress were held unconstitutional (in whole or in part), but this includes long periods of complete Supreme Court deference to the Congress, punctuated by flurries of judicial review during periods of social upheaval. The most significant of these was 1935–1936, when twelve acts of Congress were invalidated, blocking virtually the entire New Deal program.[40] Then, after 1937, when the Court made its great reversals, no significant acts were voided until 1983, when the Court declared unconstitutional the legislative veto.[41] Another, in 1986, struck down the Gramm-Rudman Act mandating a balanced budget, which, the Court held, delegated too much power to the comptroller general to direct the president to reduce the budget.[42] The Supreme Court became much more activist (i.e., less deferential to Congress) after the elevation of Justice William H. Rehnquist to chief justice (1986), and "a new program of judicial activism"[43] seemed to be in place; but this could be a conservative one against Congress comparable to the liberal activism against the states during the Warren Court of the 1960s and 1970s. All of the cases in Table 3.5 altered some aspect of federalism by declaring unconstitutional all or an important portion of an act of Congress, and the end of this episode of judicial activism against Congress is not over. Between 1995 and 2002, at least twenty-six acts or parts of acts of Congress were struck down on constitutional grounds.[44]

Since the New Deal period, the Court has been far more deferential toward the president, with only four significant confrontations. One was the so-called *Steel Seizure* case of 1952, in which the Court refused to permit President Truman to use "emergency powers" to force workers back into the steel mills during the Korean War.[45] A second case was *United States v. Nixon*, in which the Court declared unconstitutional President Nixon's refusal to respond to a subpoena to make available the infamous White House tapes as evidence in a criminal prosecution. The Court argued that although ***executive privilege*** did protect confidentiality of communications to and from the president, this did not extend to data in presidential files or tapes varying upon criminal prosecutions.[46] During the heat of the Clinton scandal, the Supreme Court rejected the claim that the pressures and obligations of the office of president was so demanding that all litigation "but the most exceptional cases" should be deferred until his term ends.[47] Most recently, and of far greater importance, the Supreme Court

executive privilege The claim that confidential communications between a president and close advisers should not be revealed without the consent of the president.

---

[40]In response to New Deal legislation, the Supreme Court struck down eight out of ten New Deal statutes. For example, in Panama Refining Co. v. Ryan, 293 U.S. 388 (1935), the Court ruled that a section of the National Industrial Recovery Act was an invalid delegation of legislative power to the executive branch. And in Schechter Poultry Co. v. United States, 295 U.S. 495 (1935), the Court found the National Industrial Recovery Act itself to be invalid for the same reason. But since 1935, the Supreme Court has rarely confronted the president or Congress on constitutional questions.

[41]Immigration and Naturalization Service v. Chadha, 462 U.S. 919 (1983).

[42]Bowsher v. Synar, 478 U.S. 714 (1986).

[43]Cass R. Sunstein, "Taking Over the Courts," *New York Times*, 9 November 2002, p. A19.

[44]Ibid.

[45]Youngstown Sheet & Tube Co. v. Sawyer, 343 U.S. 579 (1952).

[46]United States v. Nixon, 418 U.S. 683 (1974).

[47]Clinton v. Jones, 117 S.Ct. 1636 (1997).

TABLE 3.5

A NEW FEDERAL SYSTEM?
The Recent Case Record

CASE	DATE	COURT HOLDING
United States v. Lopez, 514 U.S. 549	1995	Voids federal law barring handguns near schools. Beyond Congress's power to regulate commerce.
Seminole Indian Tribe v. Florida, 517 U.S. 44	1996	Voids federal law giving tribes the right to sue a state in federal court. "Sovereign immunity" requires state permission to be sued.
Printz v. United States (and *Mack v. United States*), 117 S.Ct. 2365	1997	Voids key provision of Brady Law requiring states to make background checks on gun purchases. As "unfunded mandate," it violates state sovereignty under Tenth Amendment.
City of Boerne v. Flores, 521 U.S. 507	1997	Restricts Congress's power to regulate city zoning, health and welfare policies to "remedy" rights but not expand rights, under Fourteenth Amendment.
Alden v. Maine, 119 S.Ct. 2240	1999	State also "immune" from suits by their *own* employees for overtime pay under federal Fair Labor Standards Act. (See also *Seminole* case.)
United States v. Morrison, 529 U.S. 598	2000	Extends *Seminole* case by invalidating Violence against Women Act, holding that states are immune to suits by individuals to enforce federal laws.

struck down the Line-Item Veto Act of 1996 on the grounds that it violated Article I, Section 7, which prescribed procedures for congressional enactment and presidential acceptance or veto of statutes. Any such change in the procedures of adopting laws would have to be made by amendment to the Constitution, not by legislation.[48]

ALTERING THE BALANCE OF POWER: WHAT ARE THE CONSEQUENCES?

Federalism and the separation of powers are two of the three most important constitutional principles upon which the United States' system of limited government is based (the third is the principle of individual rights). As we have seen, federalism limits the power of the national government in numerous ways. By its very existence, federalism recognizes the principle of two sovereigns, the national government and the state government (hence the term *dual federalism*). In addition, the Constitution specifically restrained the power of the national government to regulate the economy. As a result, the states were free to do most of the fundamental governing for the first century and a half of American government. This began to change during and following the New Deal, as the national government began to exert more influence over the states through grants-in-aid and mandates. In the last decade, however, we have noticed a countertrend to the growth of national power as Congress has opted to devolve some of its powers to the states. The most recent notable instance of devolution was the welfare reform plan of 1996.

But the problem that arises with devolution is that programs that were once uniform across the country (because they were the national government's responsibility) can become highly variable, with some states providing benefits not available in other states. To a point, variation can be considered one of the virtues of federalism. But there are dangers inherent in large variations and inequalities in the provision of services and benefits in a democracy. For example, since the Food and Drug Administration has been under attack in recent years, could the problem be solved by devolving its regulatory tasks to the states? Would people care if drugs would require "caution" labels in some states and not in others? Would Americans want each state to set its own air and water pollution control policies without regard to the fact that pollution flows across state boundaries? Devolution, as attractive as it may be, is not an approach that can be applied across the board without analyzing carefully the nature of the program and of the problems it is designed to solve. Even the capacity of states to handle "devolved" programs will vary. According to the Washington research organization the Brookings Institution, the level of state and local government employment varies from state to state—from a low of 400 per 10,000 residents in some states

History Principle

The legacy of cooperative federalism and national standards has raised some doubts about devolution.

[48]Clinton v. City of New York, 524 U.S. 417 (1998).

to a high of 700 per 10,000 in others. "Such administrative diversity is bound to mediate the course and consequences of any substantial devolution of federal responsibility; no one-size-fits-all devolution [from federal to state and local government] can work."[49]

Moreover, the temptation is ever present for federal politicians to limit state discretion in order to achieve their own policy objectives. Indeed, the "devolution revolution" promised by congressional Republicans created much more rhetoric than action. Despite the complaints of Republican governors, Congress has continued to use its power to preempt state action and impose mandates on states.

The second principle of limited government, separation of powers, is manifested in our system of checks and balances, whereby separate institutions of government share power with each other. Even though the Constitution clearly provided for legislative supremacy, checks and balances have functioned well. Some would say they have worked too well. The last fifty years have witnessed long periods of divided government, when one party has controlled the White House and the other party controlled Congress. During these periods, the level of conflict between the executive and legislative branches has been particularly divisive, resulting in what some analysts derisively call gridlock. Nevertheless, this is a genuine separation of powers, not so far removed from the intent of the framers. With the rise of political parties, Americans developed a parliamentary theory that "responsible party government" requires that the same party control both branches, including both chambers of the legislature. But that kind of parliamentary/party government is a "fusion of powers," not a separation of powers. Although it may not make for good government, having an opposition party in majority control of the legislature reinforces the separation and the competition that was built into the Constitution. We can complain at length about the inability of divided government to make decisions, and we can criticize it as stalemate or gridlock,[50] but even that is in accord with the theory of the framers of the Constitution that public policy is supposed to be difficult to make.

SUMMARY

In this chapter we have traced the development of two of the three basic principles of the U.S. Constitution—federalism and the separation of powers. Federalism involves a division between two layers of government: national and state. The separation of powers involves the division of the national government into

---

[49]Eliza Newlin Carney, "Power Grab," *National Journal*, 11 April 1998, p. 798.

[50]Not everybody will agree that divided government is all that less productive than government in which both branches are controlled by the same party. See David R. Mayhew, *Divided We Govern: Party Control, Lawmaking, and Investigations, 1946–1990* (New Haven: Yale University Press, 1991). For another good evaluation of divided government, see Charles O. Jones, *Separate but Equal Branches: Congress and the Presidency* (Chatham, N.J.: Chatham House, 1995).

Rationality Principle	Collective Action Principle	Institution Principle	Policy Principle	History Principle
As political institutions, federalism and the separation of powers have adapted to the purposes of various political players.	States compete with one another not only for new businesses, but also in terms of being less attractive to welfare recipients.	Federalism and the separation of powers are two of the most important principles on which the U.S. system of limited government is based.	Devolution has had an important influence on policy outcomes, particularly welfare.	Since the time of the founding, federalism has been shaped strongly by the Supreme Court.
	Grants-in-aid allow the national government to coordinate state and local policies around a common set of national standards.	In answering "Who does what?" federalism determines the flow of government functions and, through that, the political development of the country.		In 1937, the Supreme Court converted the commerce clause from a source of limitations to a source of power for the national government.
		The national-state tug-of war is an institutional feature of the federal system.		The legacy of cooperative federalism and national standards has raised some doubts about devolution.
		Checks and balances is a system of "separated institutions sharing power."		
		The framers provided for legislative supremacy by making Congress the preeminent branch.		
		The Constitution created jurisdictional arrangements by encouraging diversity in the elected leaders occupying office and allocating the consideration of different aspects of policy to different institutional arenas.		

three branches. These principles are limitations on the powers of government; Americans made these compromises as a condition for giving their consent to be governed. And these principles became the framework within which the government operates. The persistence of local government and the reliance of the national government on grants-in-aid to coerce local governments into following national goals were used as case studies to demonstrate the continuing vitality of the federal framework. Examples were also given of the intense competition among the president, Congress, and the courts to dramatize the continuing vitality of the separation of powers.

The purpose of a constitution is to organize the makeup or the composition of the government, the *framework within which* government and politics, including actual legislation, can take place. A country does not require federalism and the separation of powers to have a real constitutional government. And the country does not have to approach individual rights in the same manner as the American Constitution. But to be a true constitutional government, a government must have a few limits so that it cannot be manipulated by people in power merely for their own convenience. This is the essence of constitutionalism—limits on power that are above the reach of everyday legislatures, executives, bureaucrats, and politicians, yet are not so far above their reach that they cannot be adapted to changing times.

FOR FURTHER READING

Bensel, Richard F. *Sectionalism and American Political Development: 1880–1980.* Madison: University of Wisconsin Press, 1984.

Bernstein, Richard B., with Jerome Agel. *Amending America—If We Love the Constitution So Much, Why Do We Keep Trying to Change It?* (Lawrence: University Press of Kansas, 1993).

Black, Charles L., Jr. *Impeachment: A Handbook.* New Haven: Yale University Press, 1974, 1998.

Caraley, Demetrios. "Dismantling the Federal Safety Net: Fictions versus Realities." *Political Science Quarterly,* 8, no. 2 (Summer 1996): 225–58.

Corwin, Edward, and J. W. Peltason. *Corwin & Peltason's Understanding the Constitution.* 13th ed. Fort Worth: Harcourt Brace, 1994.

Crovitz, L. Gordon, and Jeremy A. Rabkin, eds. *The Fettered Presidency: Legal Constraints on the Executive Branch.* Washington, D.C.: American Enterprise Institute, 1989.

Dye, Thomas R. *American Federalism: Competition among Governments.* Lexington, Mass.: Lexington Books, 1990.

Elazar, Daniel J. *American Federalism: A View from the States.* 3rd ed. New York: Harper & Row, 1984.

Ferejohn, John A., and Barry R. Weingast, eds. *The New Federalism: Can the States Be Trusted?* Stanford, Calif.: Hoover Institution Press, 1997.

Grodzins, Morton. *The American System: A New View of Government in the United States.* Chicago: Rand McNally, 1974.

Kahn, Ronald. *The Supreme Court and Constitutional Theory, 1953–1993.* Lawrence: University Kansas Press, 1994.

Kettl, Donald F. *The Regulation of American Federalism.* Baltimore: Johns Hopkins University Press, 1987.

Noonan, John T. *Narrowing the Nation's Power: The Supreme Court Sides with the States.* Berkeley: University of California Press, 2002.

Peterson, Paul E. *The Price of Federalism.* Washington, D.C.: Brookings Institution, 1995.

Smith, Rogers M. *Civic Ideals: Conflicting Visions of Citizenship in U.S. History.* New Haven: Yale University Press, 1997.

Politics in the News—
Reading between the Lines

Fiscal Federalism in the Twenty-First Century

Drip, Drip, Drip

By MATT BAI

For [Governor] Jim Doyle, it's a day like any other. . . .

. . . His state is in financial free fall— it's short about $3.2 billion—and no one in Washington seems to care. . . .

. . . 49 other state governors . . . are going through some version of the same ordeal. . . .

Amid all the political rhetoric about saving taxpayers money, we seem to have forgotten how governments actually function. . . . For a lot of Americans, the president's tax cut won't end up being a tax cut at all; it's really just a tax shift.

Here's how it works. The tax cut will choke off revenue to the federal government, which is precisely what conservatives want it to do. Their thinking is that the less money Washington has, the less it will waste. This means Congress can't increase financing for the mandates it's been heaping onto the states for 40 years. . . .

Unlike the president, who can run up deficits at will, governors are legally bound to pass balanced budgets. . . . So in order to finance programs like special education and Medicaid . . . governors must pull money from universities, parks and highways. . . .

. . . Desperate governors are slashing the aid that flows from each state to the cities and towns where people actually live. . . . This is the hidden effect of the Bush tax agenda. . . . If Bush and Congress cut taxes, and your governor doesn't raise them, then the buck ultimately stops with your mayor. . . .

There is a legitimate conservative theory at work here. . . . Conservatives believe that it's simply fairer to have people taxed by their local governments than by Washington. This way, the people who pay for the services are the ones using them. . . .

That said, you won't see Bush campaigning in 2004 on the notion that he shifted taxes to the local level and thus made government more accountable. . . . Bush will insist that he cut your taxes more than any president in history. . . . This is, at best, disingenuous. At worst, it helps create a cynical society where people believe they shouldn't have to pay for anything and their elected officials are too afraid to tell them they should.

New York Times Magazine, 8 June 2003, p. 78.

Influential Republicans aren't merely indifferent to the crises facing governors; they are openly hostile. Conservatives like Moore and Grover Norquist . . . say it would be insane for Washington to help states that won't help themselves. What governors really need, they argue, is the spine to cut back sprawling government programs.

This is not the ideological fringe talking. It is, in fact, the center of power in the Republican Party . . . these same Republican activists now declaring war on the state bureaucracies that deliver those services. . . .

That's fine, except taxpayers . . . have come to demand a certain threshold of services. . . . The nation's governors find that they are not only governors in the traditional sense, but advocates. . . . Under an ever-darkening economic sky, they're forced to play the role of civics teachers, trying to make people in their communities . . . understand that you can't get everything for nothing.

I recently talked with Dirk Kempthorne, the Republican governor of Idaho and a staunch supporter of the Bush agenda. . . . This year, with income-tax revenues off by $35 million, Kempthorne persuaded his Republican-dominated Legislature to temporarily raise the sales tax and add a tax on cigarettes. For this, he has been vilified by conservatives in Washington, who vow that no governor who raises taxes or asks for more aid will have a future in the party.

"I did what was unpopular, but in my mind and heart it was the right thing to do. And I think the measures that I've taken that are being criticized by my brethren conservatives, well. . . ." He sighed. "They're not standing in my shoes."

ESSENCE OF THE STORY

- The Bush administration and the Republican leadership pushed a major tax cut in 2003, on the heels of a tax cut in 2001. However, the federal government is not reducing the *mandates* that it places on state governments.

- The result is that the tax cut is more properly described as a tax shift—from the federal government to the state governments. Because the economic downturn has reduced revenues and because most state governments are required to balance their budgets, many state governments, both Republican and Democratic, have had to raise taxes.

- Republican governors disagree with Republican members of Congress and with anti-tax advocates about how and when taxes should be raised.

POLITICAL ANALYSIS

- Institutional rules are central to understanding the relationship between the federal and state governments. The Supreme Court decided long ago that the federal government is preeminent. The federal government has tended to pass mandates onto the state governments without paying for them.

- Constitutional provisions that require a balanced budget reduce the flexibility of many states.

- Reducing taxes at the federal level is politically popular; keeping mandates for political programs is also popular. The combination of these preferences at the federal level and the *lack* of rules that hold Congress financially responsible for these mandates created this situation.

- Political activists are now organizing at the state and local levels. We may predict that cooperation to change government ought to be easier because states and localities are smaller. On the other hand, coordinating activities over many different settings makes it harder to cooperate successfully. The next ten years will show us which prediction is correct.

CHAPTER

4

The Constitutional Framework and the Individual: Civil Liberties and Civil Rights

When the First Congress under the new Constitution met in late April of 1789 (having been delayed since March 4 by lack of a quorum because of bad winter roads), the most important item of business was consideration of a proposal to add a bill of rights to the Constitution. Such a proposal by Virginia delegate George Mason had been turned down with little debate in the waning days of the Philadelphia Constitutional Convention in September 1787, not because the delegates were too tired or too hot or against rights, but because of arguments by Hamilton and other Federalists that a bill of rights was irrelevant in a constitution providing the national government with only delegated powers. How could the national government abuse powers not given to it in the first place? But when the Constitution was submitted to the states for ratification, Antifederalists, most of whom had *not* been delegates in Philadelphia, picked up on the argument of Thomas Jefferson (who also had not been a delegate) that the omission of a bill of rights was a major imperfection of the new Constitution. Whatever the merits of Hamilton's or Jefferson's positions, in order to gain ratification, the Federalists in Massachusetts, South Carolina, New Hampshire, Virginia, and New York made an "unwritten but unequivocal pledge" to add a bill of rights and a promise to confirm (in what became the Tenth Amendment) the understanding that all powers not delegated to the national government or explicitly prohibited to the states were reserved to the states.[1]

James Madison, who had been a delegate at the Philadelphia convention and later became a member of Congress, may still have agreed privately that a bill of rights was not needed. But in 1789, recognizing the urgency of obtaining the support of the Antifederalists for the Constitution and the new government, he fought for the bill of rights, arguing that the principle it embodied would acquire "the character of fundamental maxims of free Government, and as they become incorporated with the national sentiment, counteract the impulses of interest and passion."[2] Madison and his fellow Virginian delegates were, if nothing else, practical men. While they may have conceded on principle Hamilton's argument against the need for a bill of rights, *principle* was not what the debate was all about. They felt that, as a practical political matter, it was essential to put to rest the arguably unnecessary and exaggerated fears of the less-than-enthusiastic supporters of the new Constitution. It was also thought prudent to take off the table, so to speak, a possible issue—the absence of explicit protections a bill of rights would provide—that could be brandished by opponents of the new regime the first time a crisis occurred. Prudence, foresight, and practicality were behind Madison's support for these changes in the new Constitution.

"After much discussion and manipulation . . . at the delicate prompting of Washington and under the masterful prodding of Madison," the House adopted seventeen amendments; the Senate adopted twelve of these. Ten of the amendments

Collective Action Principle

The Federalists supported a bill of rights because it would gain the support of the Antifederalists for the Constitution.

Rationality Principle

Madison believed a bill of rights would remove a potential source of opposition to the new government.

[1] Clinton L. Rossiter, *1787: The Grand Convention,* Norton Library Edition (New York: W. W. Norton, 1987), p. 302.

[2] Quoted in Milton Konvitz, "The Bill of Rights: Amendments I–X," in *An American Primer,* ed. Daniel J. Boorstin (Chicago: University of Chicago Press, 1966), p. 159.

were ratified by the states on December 15, 1791—from the start, these ten were called the Bill of Rights.[3]

The Bill of Rights—its history and the controversy of interpretation surrounding it—can be usefully subdivided into two categories: civil liberties and civil rights. This chapter will be divided accordingly. **Civil liberties** are defined as *protections of citizens from improper government action*. When adopted in 1791, the Bill of Rights was seen as guaranteeing a private sphere of personal liberty free of governmental restrictions.[4] As Jefferson had put it, a bill of rights "is what people are entitled to *against every government on earth.* . . ." Note the emphasis—citizen *against* government. In this sense, we could call the Bill of Rights a "bill of liberties" because the amendments focus on what government must *not* do. For example (with emphasis added),

1. "Congress shall make *no* law . . ." (I)
2. "The right . . . to . . . bear Arms, shall *not* be infringed" (II)
3. "*No* Soldier shall . . . be quartered . . ." (III)
4. "*No* Warrants shall issue, but upon probable cause . . ." (IV)
5. "*No* person shall be held to answer . . . unless on a presentment or indictment of a Grand Jury . . ." (V)
6. "Excessive bail shall *not* be required . . . *nor* cruel and unusual punishments inflicted." (VIII)

Thus, the Bill of Rights is a series of "thou shalt nots"—restraints addressed to governments. Some of these restraints are *substantive*, putting limits on *what* the government shall and shall not have power to do—such as establishing a religion, quartering troops in private homes without consent, or seizing private property without just compensation. Other restraints are *procedural*, dealing with *how* the government is supposed to act. For example, even though the government has the substantive power to declare certain acts to be crimes and to arrest and imprison persons who violate its criminal laws, it may not do so except by fairly meticulous observation of procedures designed to protect the accused person. The best-known procedural rule is that "a person is presumed innocent until proven guilty." This rule does not question the government's power to punish someone for committing a crime; it questions only the way the government determines *who* committed the crime. Substantive and procedural restraints together identify the realm of civil liberties.

We define **civil rights** as obligations imposed on government to guarantee equal citizenship and to protect citizens from discrimination by other private cit-

civil liberties
Protections of citizens from improper government action.

civil rights Legal or moral claims that citizens are entitled to make upon the government.

[3]Rossiter, *1787: The Grand Convention*, p. 303, where he also reports that "in 1941 the States of Connecticut, Massachusetts, and Georgia celebrated the sesquicentennial of the Bill of Rights by giving their hitherto withheld and unneeded assent."

[4]Lest there be confusion in our interchangeable use of the words *liberty* and *freedom*, treat them as synonyms. *Freedom* is from the German *Freiheit*. *Liberty* is from the French *liberté*. Both have to do with the absence of restraints on individual choices of action.

izens and other government agencies. Civil rights did not become part of the Constitution until 1868 with the adoption of the Fourteenth Amendment, which addressed the issue of who was a citizen and provided for each citizen "the equal protection of the laws." From that point on, we can see more clearly the distinction between civil liberties and civil rights, because civil liberties issues arise under the "due process of law" clause, and civil rights issues arise under the "equal protection of the laws" clause.

We turn first to civil liberties and to the long history of the effort to make personal liberty a reality for every citizen in America. The struggle for freedom against arbitrary and discriminatory actions by governments has continued to this day. And inevitably it is tied to the continuing struggle for civil rights, to persuade those same governments to take positive actions. We shall deal with that in the second section of this chapter, but we should not lose sight of the connection in the real world between civil liberties and civil rights. We should also not lose sight of the connection to the constitutional framework established in Chapter 3. Although individual liberties and rights were identified in Chapter 3 as comprising the third of the three most important bases in the Constitution, the third cannot be understood except in the context of the other two, especially federalism.

PREVIEWING THE PRINCIPLES

We can conceive of both civil liberties and civil rights as the "rules" that govern government action and the responsibilities the government has to protect citizens from one another. History matters as well. The rules and procedures that are adopted in one era live on and shape the political reasoning, goals, and actions of political actors in subsequent eras. In many ways, debates over civil liberties and rights today are shaped by the historical development of these concepts and their interpretations by key political actors, most notably the members of the Supreme Court.

CIVIL LIBERTIES: NATIONALIZING THE BILL OF RIGHTS

The First Amendment provides that "Congress shall make no law respecting an establishment of religion . . . or abridging the freedom of speech, or of the press; or the right of [assembly and petition]." But this is the only amendment in the Bill of Rights that addresses itself exclusively to the national government. For example, the Second Amendment provides that "the right of the people to keep and bear Arms, shall not be infringed." The Fifth Amendment says, among other things, that *no person* "shall . . . be twice put in jeopardy of life or limb" for the same crime; that *no person* "shall be compelled in any criminal case to be a witness against himself"; that *no person* shall "be deprived of life, liberty, or property, without due process of law"; and that private property cannot be taken "without just compensation."[5] Since the First Amendment is the only part of the Bill of Rights that is explicit in its intention to put limits on the national government, a fundamental question inevitably arises: *Do the remaining amendments of the Bill of Rights put limits on state governments or only on the national government?*

Dual Citizenship

The question concerning whether the Bill of Rights also limits state governments was settled in 1833 in a way that seems odd to Americans today. The 1833 case was *Barron v. Baltimore*, and the facts were simple. In paving its streets, the city of Baltimore had disposed of so much sand and gravel in the water near Barron's wharf that the value of the wharf for commercial purposes was virtually destroyed. Barron brought the city into court on the grounds that it had, under the Fifth Amendment, unconstitutionally deprived him of his property. Barron had to take his case all the way to the Supreme Court, despite the fact that the argument made by his attorney seemed airtight. The following is Chief Justice Marshall's characterization of Barron's argument:

> The plaintiff [Barron] . . . contends that it comes within that clause in the Fifth Amendment of the Constitution which inhibits the taking of private property for public use without just compensation. He insists that this amendment, being in favor of the liberty of the citizen, ought to be so construed as to restrain the legislative power of a state, as well as that of the United States.[6]

Then Marshall, in one of the most significant Supreme Court decisions ever handed down, disagreed:

> The Constitution was ordained and established by the people of the United States for themselves, for their own government, and not for the government of individual States. Each State established a constitution for itself, and in that constitution provided such limitations and restrictions on the powers of its particular government as its judgment dictated. . . . If these propositions be correct, *the fifth amendment must be understood as restraining the power of the General Government, not as applicable to the States.*[7]

In other words, if an agency of the *national* government had deprived Barron of his property, there would have been little doubt about Barron's winning his case. But if the constitution of the state of Maryland contained no such provision pro-

[5]It would be useful at this point to review all the provisions of the Bill of Rights (in the Appendix) to confirm this distinction between the wording of the First Amendment and the rest. Emphasis in the example quotations was not in the original. For a spirited and enlightening essay on the extent to which the entire Bill of Rights was about equality, see Martha Minow, "Equality and the Bill of Rights," in Michael J. Meyer and William A. Parent, eds., *The Constitution of Rights: Human Dignity and American Values* (Ithaca, N.Y.: Cornell University Press, 1992), pp. 118–28.
[6]Barron v. Baltimore, 7 Peters 243 (1833).
[7]Ibid [emphasis added].

tecting citizens of Maryland from such action, then Barron had no legal leg to stand on against Baltimore, an agency of the state of Maryland.

Barron v. Baltimore confirmed "dual citizenship"—that is, that each American was a citizen of the national government and *separately* a citizen of one of the states. This meant that the Bill of Rights did not apply to decisions or to procedures of state (or local) governments. Even slavery could continue, because the Bill of Rights could not protect anyone from state laws treating people as property. In fact, the Bill of Rights did not become a vital instrument for the extension of civil liberties for anyone until after a bloody Civil War and a revolutionary Fourteenth Amendment intervened. And even so, as we shall see, nearly another century would pass before the Bill of Rights would truly come into its own.

Institution Principle

Dual citizenship meant that the Bill of Rights did not apply to decisions or to procedures of state governments.

The Fourteenth Amendment

From a constitutional standpoint, the defeat of the South in the Civil War settled one question and raised another. It probably settled forever the question of whether secession was an option for any state. After 1865 there was to be more "united" than "states" to the United States. But this left unanswered just how much the states were obliged to obey the Constitution and, in particular, the Bill of Rights. Just reading the words of the Fourteenth Amendment, anyone might think it was almost perfectly designed to impose the Bill of Rights on the states and thereby to reverse *Barron v. Baltimore*. The very first words of the Fourteenth Amendment point in that direction:

> All persons born or naturalized in the United States, and subject to the jurisdiction thereof, are citizens of the United States and of the State wherein they reside.

This provides for a *single national citizenship*, and at a minimum that means that civil liberties should not vary drastically from state to state. That would seem to be the spirit of the Fourteenth Amendment: *to nationalize the Bill of Rights by nationalizing the definition of citizenship.*

This interpretation of the Fourteenth Amendment is reinforced by the next clause of the Amendment:

> *No State* shall make or enforce any law which shall abridge the privileges or immunities of citizens of the United States; nor shall any State deprive any person of life, liberty, or property, without due process of law. [Emphasis added.]

All of this sounds like an effort to extend the Bill of Rights in its *entirety* to citizens *wherever* they might reside.[8] But this was not to be the Supreme Court's

---

[8]The Fourteenth Amendment also seems designed to introduce civil rights. The final clause of the all-important Section 1 provides that no state can "deny to any person within its jurisdiction the equal protection of the laws." It is not unreasonable to conclude that the purpose of this provision was to obligate the state governments as well as the national government to take *positive* actions to protect citizens from arbitrary and discriminatory actions, at least those based on race. This will be explored in the second half of this chapter.

**History
Principle**

Dual citizenship was
upheld by the
Supreme Court for
nearly one hundred
years after *Barron v.
Baltimore* (1833).

interpretation for nearly a hundred years. Within five years of ratification of the Fourteenth Amendment, the Court was making decisions as though it had never been adopted. The shadow of *Barron* grew longer and longer. In an important 1873 decision known as the *Slaughter-House Cases*, the Supreme Court determined that the federal government was under no obligation to protect the "privileges and immunities" of citizens of a particular state against arbitrary actions by that state's government. The case had its origins in 1867, when a corrupt Louisiana legislature conferred upon a single corporation a monopoly of all the slaughterhouse business in the city of New Orleans. The other slaughterhouses, facing bankruptcy, all brought suits claiming, like Mr. Barron, that this was a taking of their property in violation of Fifth Amendment rights. But unlike Mr. Barron, they believed that they were protected now because, they argued, the Fourteenth Amendment incorporated the Fifth Amendment, applying it to the states. The suits were all rejected. The Supreme Court argued, first, that the primary purpose of the Fourteenth Amendment was to protect "Negroes as a class." Second, and more to the point here, the Court argued, without trying to prove it, that the framers of the Fourteenth Amendment could not have intended to incorporate the entire Bill of Rights.[9] Yet, when the Civil Rights Act of 1875 attempted to protect blacks from discriminatory treatment by proprietors of hotels, theaters, and other public accommodations, the Supreme Court disregarded its own primary argument in the previous case and held the act unconstitutional, declaring that the Fourteenth Amendment applied only to discriminatory actions by state officials, "operating under cover of law," and not to discrimination against blacks by private individuals, even though these private individuals were companies offering services to the public.[10] Such narrow interpretations raised the inevitable question of whether the Fourteenth Amendment had incorporated *any* of the Bill of Rights. The Fourteenth Amendment remained shadowy until the mid-twentieth century. The shadow was *Barron v. Baltimore* and the Court's unwillingness to "nationalize" civil liberties—that is, to interpret the civil liberties expressed in the Bill of Rights as imposing limitations not only on the federal government but also on the states.

It was not until the very end of the nineteenth century that the Supreme Court began to nationalize the Bill of Rights by incorporating its civil liberties provisions into the Fourteenth Amendment. Table 4.1 outlines the major steps in this process. The only change in civil liberties during the first sixty years following the adoption of the Fourteenth Amendment came in 1897, when the Supreme Court held that the due process clause of the Fourteenth Amendment did in fact prohibit states from taking property for a public use without just compensation.[11] This effectively overruled *Barron* because it meant that the citizen of Maryland or any state was henceforth protected from a "public taking" of

---

[9]The Slaughter-House Cases, 16 Wallace 36 (1873).
[10]The Civil Rights Cases, 109 U.S. 3 (1883).
[11]Chicago, Burlington, and Quincy Railroad Company v. Chicago, 166 U.S. 226 (1897).

TABLE 4.1

Incorporation of the Bill of Rights into the
Fourteenth Amendment

SELECTED PROVISIONS AND AMENDMENTS	NOT "INCORPORATED" UNTIL	KEY CASE
Eminent domain (V)	1897	Chicago, Burlington, and Quincy R.R. v. Chicago
Freedom of speech (I)	1925	Gitlow v. New York
Freedom of press (I)	1931	Near v. Minnesota
Freedom of assembly (I)	1939	Hague v. CIO
Freedom from warrantless search and seizure (IV) ("exclusionary rule")	1961	Mapp v. Ohio
Right to counsel in any criminal trial (VI)	1963	Gideon v. Wainwright
Right against self-incrimination and forced confessions (V)	1964	Malloy v. Hogan Escobedo v. Illinois
Right to counsel and to remain silent (VI)	1966	Miranda v. Arizona
Right against double jeopardy (V)	1969	Benton v. Maryland
Right to privacy (III, IV, & V)	1973	Roe v. Wade Doe v. Bolton

property (eminent domain) even if the state constitution did not provide such protection. However, in a broader sense, *Barron* still cast a shadow because the Supreme Court had "incorporated" into the Fourteenth Amendment only the property protection provision of the Fifth Amendment and no other clause, let alone the other amendments of the Bill of Rights. In other words, although "due process" applied to the taking of life and liberty as well as property, only property was incorporated into the Fourteenth Amendment as a limitation on state power.

No further expansion of civil liberties through incorporation occurred until 1925, when the Supreme Court held that freedom of speech is "among the fundamental personal rights and 'liberties' protected by the due process clause of the Fourteenth Amendment from impairment by the states."[12] In 1931, the Court added freedom of the press to that short list of civil rights protected by the Bill of Rights from state action; in 1939, it added freedom of assembly.[13] But that was as far as the Court was willing to go. As late as 1937, the Supreme Court was still loathe to nationalize civil liberties beyond the First Amendment. In fact, the Court in that year took one of its most extreme turns backward toward *Barron v. Baltimore*. The state of Connecticut had indicted a man named Palko for first-degree murder, but a lower court had found him guilty of only second-degree murder and sentenced him to life in prison. Unhappy with the verdict, the state of Connecticut appealed the conviction to its highest court, won the appeal, got a new trial, and then succeeded in getting Palko convicted of first-degree murder. Palko appealed to the Supreme Court on what seemed an open and shut case of **double jeopardy**—being tried twice for the same crime. Yet, though the majority of the Court agreed that this could indeed be considered a case of double jeopardy, they decided that double jeopardy was *not* one of the provisions of the Bill of Rights incorporated in the Fourteenth Amendment as a restriction on the powers of the states. Justice Benjamin Cardozo, considered one of the most able Supreme Court justices of the twentieth century, rejected the argument made by Palko's lawyer that "whatever is forbidden by the Fifth Amendment is forbidden by the Fourteenth also." Cardozo responded tersely, "There is no such general rule." As far as Cardozo and the majority were concerned, the only rights from the Bill of Rights that ought to be incorporated into the Fourteenth Amendment as applying to the states as well as to the national government were those that were "implicit in the concept of ordered liberty." He asked the questions: Does double jeopardy subject Palko to a "hardship so acute and shocking that our polity will not endure it? Does it violate those 'fundamental principles of liberty and justice which lie at the base of all our civil and political institutions?' . . . The answer must surely be 'no.'"[14] Palko was eventually executed for the crime, because he lived in the state of Connecticut rather than in some state whose constitution included a guarantee against double jeopardy.

Cases like *Palko* extended the shadow of *Barron* into its second century, despite adoption of the Fourteenth Amendment. The Constitution, as interpreted by the Supreme Court, left standing the framework in which the states had the power to determine their own law on a number of fundamental issues. It left states with the power to pass laws segregating the races—and thirteen southern states chose to exercise that power. The constitutional framework also left states with the power to engage in searches and seizures without a warrant, to indict

double jeopardy
Trial more than once for the same crime. The Constitution guarantees that no one shall be subjected to double jeopardy.

[12]Gitlow v. New York, 268 U.S. 652 (1925).
[13]Near v. Minnesota, 283 U.S. 697 (1931); Hague v. CIO, 307 U.S. 496 (1939).
[14]Palko v. Connecticut, 302 U.S. 319 (1937).

accused persons without benefit of a grand jury, to deprive persons of trial by jury, to force persons to testify against themselves, to deprive accused persons of their right to confront adverse witnesses, and, as we have seen, to prosecute accused persons more than once for the same crime.[15] Few states chose the option to use that kind of power, but some states did, and the power to do so was there for any state whose legislative majority so chose.

The Constitutional Revolution in Civil Liberties

For nearly thirty years following the *Palko* case,[16] the nineteenth-century framework was sustained, but signs of change came after 1954, in *Brown v. Board of Education*, when the Supreme Court overturned the infamous *Plessy v. Ferguson*.[17] *Plessy* was a civil rights case involving the "equal protection" clause of the Fourteenth Amendment and was not an issue of applying the Bill of Rights to the states. (It will be dealt with in the next section.) Nevertheless, even though *Brown* was not a civil liberties case, it indicated clearly that the Supreme Court was going to be expansive about civil liberties because with *Brown* the Court had effectively promised that it was *actively* going to subject the states and all actions affecting civil rights and civil liberties to *strict scrutiny*. In retrospect, one could say that this constitutional revolution was given a "jump start" by the *Brown* decision,[18] even though the results were not apparent until after 1961, when the number of civil liberties incorporated increased (see Table 4.1).

Nationalizing the Bill of Rights   As with the federalism revolution, the constitutional revolution in civil liberties was a movement toward nationalization. But the two revolutions required opposite motions on the part of the Supreme Court. In the area of commerce (the first revolution), the Court had to decide to assume a *passive* role by not interfering as Congress expanded the meaning of the commerce clause of Article I, Section 8. This expansion has been so extensive that the national government can now constitutionally reach a single farmer growing twenty acres of wheat or a small neighborhood restaurant selling barbecues to local "whites only" without being anywhere near interstate commerce routes. In the second revolution—involving the Bill of Rights through the Fourteenth Amendment rather than the commerce clause—the Court had to assume an *active* role, which required close review not of Congress but of the laws of state legislatures and decisions of state courts, in order to apply a single national Fourteenth Amendment standard to the rights and liberties of all citizens.

---

[15]All of these were implicitly identified in the *Palko* case as "not incorporated" into the Fourteenth Amendment as limitations on the powers of the states.

[16]*Palko* was explicitly reversed in Benton v. Maryland, 395 U.S. 784 (1969), in which the Court said that double jeopardy was in fact incorporated in the Fourteenth Amendment as a restriction on the states.

[17]Plessy v. Ferguson, 163 U.S. 537 (1896).

[18]The First Constitutional Revolution began with NLRB v. Jones & Laughlin Steel Corp. (1937).

Table 4.1 shows that until 1961, only the First Amendment had been fully and clearly incorporated into the Fourteenth Amendment.[19] After 1961, several other important provisions of the Bill of Rights were incorporated. Of the cases that expanded the Fourteenth Amendment's reach, the most famous was *Gideon v. Wainwright*, which established the right to counsel in a criminal trial, because it became the subject of a best-selling book and a popular movie.[20] In *Mapp v. Ohio*, the Court held that evidence obtained in violation of the Fourth Amendment ban on unreasonable searches and seizures would be excluded from trial.[21] This "exclusionary rule" was particularly irksome to the police and prosecutors because it meant that patently guilty defendants sometimes got to go free because the evidence that clearly damned them could not be used. In *Miranda*,[22] the Court's ruling required that arrested persons be informed of the right to remain silent and to have counsel present during interrogation. This is the basis of the **Miranda rule** of reading persons their rights, which has been made famous by TV police shows. By 1969, in *Benton v. Maryland*, the Supreme Court had come full circle regarding the rights of the criminally accused, explicitly reversing the *Palko* ruling and thereby incorporating double jeopardy.

During the 1960s and early 1970s, the Court also expanded another important area of civil liberties: rights to privacy. When the Court began to take a more activist role in the mid-1950s and 1960s, the idea of a "right to privacy" was revived. In 1958, the Supreme Court recognized "privacy in one's association" in its decision to prevent the state of Alabama from using the membership list of the National Association for the Advancement of Colored People in the state's investigations.[23]

The sphere of privacy was drawn in earnest in 1965, when the Court ruled that a Connecticut statute forbidding the use of contraceptives violated the right of marital privacy. Estelle Griswold, the executive director of the Planned Parenthood League of Connecticut, was arrested by the state of Connecticut for providing information, instruction, and medical advice about contraception to married couples. She and her associates were found guilty as accessories to the crime and fined $100 each. The Supreme Court reversed the lower court decisions and declared the Connecticut law unconstitutional because it violated "a right of privacy older than the Bill of Rights—older than our political parties, older than our school system."[24] Justice William O. Douglas, author of the ma-

Miranda rule
Principles developed by the Supreme Court in the 1966 case of *Miranda v. Arizona* requiring that persons under arrest be informed of their legal rights, including their right to counsel, prior to police interrogation.

Institution Principle

Most of the important provisions of the Bill of Rights were nationalized by the Supreme Court during the 1960s.

---

[19]The one exception was the right to public trial (the Sixth Amendment), but the 1948 case did not actually mention the right to public trial as such; it was cited in a 1968 case as a case establishing the right to public trial as part of the Fourteenth Amendment. The 1948 case was in re Oliver, 33 U.S. 257, where the issue was put more generally as "due process" and public trial itself was not actually mentioned. Later opinions, such as Duncan v. Louisiana, 391 U.S. 145 (1968), cited the *Oliver* case as the precedent for incorporating public trials as part of the Fourteenth Amendment.

[20]Gideon v. Wainwright, 372 U.S. 335 (1963); Anthony Lewis, *Gideon's Trumpet* (New York: Random House, 1964).

[21]Mapp v. Ohio, 367 U.S. 643 (1961).

[22]Miranda v. Arizona, 384 U.S. 436 (1966).

[23]NAACP v. Alabama ex rel. Patterson, 357 U.S. 449 (1958).

[24]Griswold v. Connecticut, 381 U.S. 479 (1965).

jority decision in the *Griswold* case, argued that this right of privacy is also grounded in the Constitution because it fits into a "zone of privacy" created by a combination of the Third, Fourth, and Fifth Amendments. A concurring opinion, written by Justice Arthur Goldberg, attempted to strengthen Douglas's argument by adding that "the concept of liberty . . . embraces the right of marital privacy though that right is not mentioned explicitly in the Constitution [and] is supported by numerous decisions of this Court . . . and *by the language and history of the Ninth Amendment* [emphasis added]."[25]

The right to privacy was confirmed—and extended—in 1973 in the most important of all privacy decisions, and one of the most important Supreme Court decisions in American history: *Roe v. Wade.*[26] This decision established a woman's right to have an abortion and prohibited states from making abortion a criminal act. The basis for the Supreme Court's decision in *Roe* was the evolving right to privacy. But it is important to realize that the preference for privacy rights and for their extension to include the rights of women to control their own bodies was not something invented by the Supreme Court in a political vacuum. Most states did not begin to regulate abortions in any fashion until the 1840s (by 1839 only six of the twenty-six existing states had any regulations governing abortion). In addition, many states began to ease their abortion restrictions well before the 1973 Supreme Court decision. In recent years, however, a number of states have reinstated restrictions on abortion, testing the limits of *Roe*.

 History Principle

Roe v. Wade was not decided in a political vacuum. Many states had already eased their restrictions on abortion prior to 1973.

Like any important principle, once privacy was established as an aspect of civil liberties protected by the Bill of Rights through the Fourteenth Amendment, it took on a life all its own. In a number of important decisions, the Supreme Court and the lower federal courts sought to protect rights that could not be found in the text of the Constitution but could be discovered through the study of the philosophic sources of fundamental rights. Through this line of reasoning, the federal courts sought to protect sexual autonomy, lifestyle choices, sexual preferences, procreational choice, and various forms of intimate association.

Criticism mounted with every extension of this line of reasoning. The federal courts were accused of creating an uncontrollable expansion of rights demands. The Supreme Court, the critics argued, had displaced the judgments of legislatures and state courts with its own judgment of what is reasonable, without regard to local popular majorities and without regard to specific constitutional provisions. This is virtually the definition of what came to be called "judicial activism" in the 1980s, and it was the basis for a more strongly critical label, "the imperial judiciary."[27]

 Institution Principle

As a political institution, the Bill of Rights has not been carved in stone. Through subsequent amendments, on the one hand, and constant updating of the original ten through judicial review, on the other, the balance between freedom and power has been transformed.

The history of civil liberties in the United States is evidence that, as a political institution, the Bill of Rights has not been carved in stone. Through subsequent

---

[25]Griswold v. Connecticut, concurring opinion. In 1972, the Court extended the privacy right to unmarried women: Eisenstadt v. Baird, 405 U.S. 438 (1972).

[26]Roe v. Wade, 410 U.S. 113 (1973).

[27]A good discussion will be found in Paul Brest and Sanford Levinson, *Processes of Constitutional Decision-Making: Cases and Materials*, 2nd ed. (Boston: Little, Brown, 1983), p. 660. See also Chapter 8.

amendments, on the one hand, and the interpretations of the Supreme Court, on the other, the balance between freedom and power has been transformed. Indeed, the framers of the Constitution would be unlikely to recognize their original handiwork. But, as we shall see next, what the Supreme Court gives, the Supreme Court can also take away.

Rehnquist: A De-nationalizing Trend?

While constitutional developments may be represented as the history of doctrinal disputes and the general evolution of interpretation—and, as the last few pages have made clear, there is nothing linear and straightforward about these developments—it must be recognized that these events are as much *political* as *philosophical*. Judges and justices are, after all, *politicians*. And courts are *political institutions*. The backdrop, therefore, for debates over legal doctrine and constitutional meaning consists of the preferences of politicians, on the one hand, and the tug and pull of maneuvering between the courts and other (separate) institutions of government, on the other.

Rationality Principle

The preferences of individual Supreme Court justices have been consequential for the development of civil liberties.

The preferences of individual Supreme Court justices have certainly been consequential during the first two centuries of our republic, with John Marshall probably casting the longest shadow. Likewise, conflicts between the judiciary, legislature, and executive have ebbed and flowed. Throughout, controversy over judicial power has not diminished. In fact, it is intensifying under Chief Justice William Rehnquist. Although it is difficult to determine just how much influence Rehnquist has had as chief justice, the Court has in fact been moving in a more conservative, de-nationalizing direction.

Rationality Principle

The preference of the members of the Rehnquist Court has been to accept fewer cases for review.

A good measure of the Court's growing conservatism is the following comparison made by constitutional scholar David M. O'Brien: between 1961 and 1969, more than 76 percent of the Warren Court's rulings from term to term tended to be liberal—that is, tending toward nationalizing the Bill of Rights to protect individuals and minorities mainly against the actions of state government. During the Burger years, 1969–1986, the liberal tendency dropped on the average below 50 percent. During the first four years of the Rehnquist Court (the extent of O'Brien's research), the average liberal "score" dropped to less than 35 percent.[28]

The Supreme Court has moved in a conservative direction, for example, regarding the First Amendment's "establishment clause," which established a "wall of separation" between church and state. In the 1995 case of *Rosenberger v. University of Virginia*, the Court seemed to open a new breach in the wall between church and state when it ruled that the university had violated the free speech rights of a Christian student group by refusing to provide student activity funds to the group's magazine, although other student groups had been given funds

[28]David M. O'Brien, *Supreme Court Watch—1991*, Annual Supplement to *Constitutional Law and Politics* (New York: W. W. Norton, 1991), p. 6 and Chapter 4.

for their publications. In the 1997 case of *Agostini v. Felton*, the Court again breached the wall between church and state, ruling that states could pay public school teachers to offer remedial courses at religious schools.[29]

The civil liberties decisions of the Rehnquist Court during the 1990s reveal the conservative preferences of a majority of its justices.

Policy Principle

The conservative trend has also extended to the burning question of abortion rights. In *Webster v. Reproductive Health Services*, the Court narrowly upheld by a 5-to-4 majority the constitutionality of restrictions on the use of public medical facilities for abortion.[30] And in 1992, in the most recent major decision on abortion, *Planned Parenthood v. Casey*, another 5-to-4 majority of the Court barely upheld *Roe* but narrowed its scope, refusing to invalidate a Pennsylvania law that significantly restricts freedom of choice. The decision defined the right to an abortion as a "limited or qualified" right subject to regulation by the states as long as the regulation does not impose an "undue burden."[31]

Will the Supreme Court, with a majority of conservatives, reverse the nationalization of the Bill of Rights? Possibly, but not necessarily. First of all, the Rehnquist Court has not actually reversed any of the decisions made during the 1960s by the Warren or Burger Courts nationalizing most of the clauses of the Bill of Rights. As we have seen, the Rehnquist Court has given narrower and more restrictive interpretations of the earlier decisions, but it has not reversed any, not even *Roe v. Wade*. Second, President Clinton's appointments to the Court, Ruth Bader Ginsburg and Stephen Breyer, have helped form a centrist majority that seems unwilling, for the time being at least, to sanction any major steps to turn back the nationalization of the Bill of Rights. But with a Republican president whose nominations to the Court will have to be approved by a Democrat-controlled Senate, the question of the contraction of the Bill of Rights and the Fourteenth Amendment is certain to be in the forefront of political debate for a long time to come.

Thus, we end about where we began. *Barron v. Baltimore* has not been entirely put to rest; its spirit still hovers, casting a shadow over the Bill of Rights. A Court with the power to expand the Bill of Rights also has the power to contract it.[32]

---

[29]Rosenberger v. University of Virginia, 94-329 (1995); Agostini v. Felton, 96-522 (1997).

[30]In Webster v. Reproductive Health Services, 109 S.Ct. 3040 (1989), Chief Justice Rehnquist's decision upheld a Missouri law that restricted the use of public medical facilities for abortion. The decision opened the way for other states to limit the availability of abortion. The first to act was the Pennsylvania legislature, which adopted in late 1989 a law banning all abortions after pregnancy had passed twenty-four weeks, except to save the life of the pregnant woman or to prevent irreversible impairment of her health. In 1990, the pace of state legislative action increased, with new statutes passed in South Carolina, Ohio, Minnesota, and Guam. In 1991, the Louisiana legislature adopted, over the governor's veto, the strictest law yet. The Louisiana law prohibits all abortions except when the mother's life is threatened or when rape or incest victims report these crimes immediately.

[31]Planned Parenthood of Southeastern Pennsylvania v. Casey, 112 S.Ct. 2791 (1992).

[32]For a lively and readable treatment of the possibilities of restricting provisions of the Bill of Rights, without actually reversing Warren Court decisions, see David G. Savage, *Turning Right: The Making of the Rehnquist Supreme Court* (New York: Wiley, 1992).

CIVIL RIGHTS

With the adoption of the Fourteenth Amendment in 1868, civil rights became part of the Constitution, guaranteed to each citizen through "equal protection of the laws." These words launched a century of political movements and legal efforts to press for racial equality. The African American quest for civil rights, in turn, inspired many other groups, including members of other racial and ethnic groups, women, the disabled, and gays and lesbians, to seek new laws and constitutional guarantees of their civil rights.

Congress passed the Fourteenth Amendment, and the states ratified it in the aftermath of the Civil War. Together with the Thirteenth Amendment, which abolished slavery, and the Fifteenth Amendment, which guaranteed voting rights for black men, it seemed to provide a guarantee of civil rights for the newly freed black slaves. But the general language of the Fourteenth Amendment meant that its support for civil rights could be far-reaching. The very simplicity of the ***equal protection clause*** of the Fourteenth Amendment left it open to interpretation:

equal protection clause Provision of the Fourteenth Amendment guaranteeing citizens "the equal protection of the laws." This clause has served as the basis for the civil rights of African Americans, women, and other groups.

> No State shall make or enforce any law which shall . . . deny to any person within its jurisdiction the equal protection of the laws.

Plessy v. Ferguson: "Separate but Equal"

The Supreme Court was no more ready to enforce the civil rights aspects of the Fourteenth Amendment than it was to enforce the civil liberties provisions. The Court declared the Civil Rights Act of 1875 unconstitutional on the ground that the act sought to protect blacks against discrimination by *private* businesses, while the Fourteenth Amendment, according to the Court's interpretation, was intended to protect individuals from discrimination only against actions by *public* officials of state and local governments.

In 1896, the Court went still further, in the infamous case of *Plessy v. Ferguson*, by upholding a Louisiana statute that *required* segregation of the races on trolleys and other public carriers (and, by implication, in all public facilities, including schools). Homer Plessy, a man defined as "one-eighth black," had violated a Louisiana law that provided for "equal but separate accommodations" on trains and a $25 fine for any white passenger who sat in a car reserved for blacks or any black passenger who sat in a car reserved for whites. The Supreme Court held that the Fourteenth Amendment's "equal protection of the laws" was not violated by racial distinction as long as the facilities were equal. People generally pretended they were equal as long as some accommodation existed. The Court said that although "the object of the [Fourteenth] Amendment was undoubtedly to enforce the absolute equality of the two races before the law, . . . it could not have intended to abolish distinctions based on color, or to enforce social, as distinguished from political, equality, or a commingling of the two races upon terms unsatisfactory to either."[33] What the Court was saying in effect was that the use of race as a criterion of exclusion in public matters was not unreasonable. This was the origin of the *"separate but equal" rule,* which was not reversed until 1954.

"separate but equal" rule
Doctrine that public accommodations could be segregated by race but still be equal.

Racial Discrimination after World War II

The Supreme Court had begun to change its position on racial discrimination before World War II by being stricter about the criterion of equal facilities in the "separate but equal" rule. In 1938, the Court rejected Missouri's policy of paying the tuition of qualified blacks to out-of-state law schools rather than admitting them to the University of Missouri Law School.[34]

After the war, modest progress resumed. In 1950, the Court rejected Texas's claim that its new "law school for Negroes" afforded education equal to that of the all-white University of Texas Law School; without confronting the "separate but equal" principle itself, the Court's decision anticipated *Brown v. Board of Education* by opening the question of whether *any* segregated facility could be truly equal.[35] The same was true in 1944, when the Supreme Court struck down the southern practice of "white primaries," which legally excluded blacks from participation in the nominating process. Here the Court simply recognized that primaries could no longer be regarded as the private affairs of the parties but were an integral aspect of the electoral process. This made parties "an agency of the State," and, therefore, any practice of discrimination against blacks was "state action within the meaning of the Fifteenth Amendment."[36] The most important pre-1954 decision was probably *Shelley v. Kraemer,*[37] in which the Court ruled against the widespread practice of "restrictive covenants," whereby the seller of a home added a clause to the sales contract requiring the buyers to agree not to sell their home to any non-Caucasian, non-Christian, etc. The Court ruled that although private persons could sign such restrictive covenants, they could not be judicially enforced since the Fourteenth Amendment prohibits any organ of the state, including the courts, from denying equal protection of its laws.

However, none of these pre-1954 cases had yet confronted head-on the principle of "separate but equal" as such and its legal and constitutional support for racial discrimination. Each victory by the Legal Defense Fund of the National Association for the Advancement of Colored People (NAACP) was celebrated for itself and was seen, hopefully, as a trend; but each was still a small victory, not a leading case. The massive effort by the southern states to resist direct desegregation, and to prevent further legal actions against it by making a show of

[33]Plessy v. Ferguson, 163 U.S. 537 (1896).
[34]Missouri ex rel. Gaines v. Canada, 305 U.S. 337 (1938).
[35]Sweatt v. Painter, 339 U.S. 629 (1950).
[36]Smith v. Allwright, 321 U.S. 649 (1944).
[37]Shelley v. Kraemer, 334 U.S. 1 (1948).

equalizing the quality of white and black schools, kept the NAACP pessimistic about the readiness of the Supreme Court for a full confrontation with the constitutional principle sustaining segregation. But the continued unwillingness of Congress after 1948 to consider fair employment legislation seemed to have convinced the NAACP that the courts were their only hope. Thus, by 1951, the NAACP finally decided to attack the principle of segregation itself as unconstitutional and, in 1952, instituted cases in South Carolina, Virginia, Kansas, Delaware, and the District of Columbia. The obvious strategy was that by simultaneously filing suits in different federal districts, inconsistent results between any two states would more quickly lead to Supreme Court acceptance of at least one appeal.[38] Of these, the Kansas case became the chosen one. It seemed to be ahead of the pack in its district court, and it had the special advantage of being located in a state outside the Deep South.[39]

Oliver Brown, the father of three girls, lived "across the tracks" in a low-income, racially mixed Topeka neighborhood. Every school-day morning, Linda Brown took the school bus to the Monroe School for black children about a mile away. In September 1950, Oliver Brown took Linda to the all-white Sumner School, which was actually closer to home, to enter her into the third grade in defiance of state law and local segregation rules. When they were refused, Brown took his case to the NAACP, and soon thereafter *Brown v. Board of Education* was born. In mid-1953, the Court announced that the several cases on their way up would be re-argued within a set of questions having to do with the intent of the Fourteenth Amendment. Almost exactly a year later, the Court responded to those questions in one of the most important decisions in its history.

In deciding the case, the Court, to the surprise of many, basically rejected as inconclusive all the learned arguments about the intent and the history of the Fourteenth Amendment and committed itself to considering only the consequences of segregation:

> Does segregation of children in public schools solely on the basis of race, even though the physical facilities and other "tangible" factors may be equal, deprive the children of the minority group of equal educational opportunities? We believe that it does. . . . We conclude that, in the field of public education, the doctrine of "separate but equal" has no place. Separate educational facilities are inherently unequal.[40]

[38]The best reviews of strategies, tactics, and goals is found in John Hope Franklin, *From Slavery to Freedom: A History of Negro Americans*, 4th ed. (New York: Knopf, 1974), Chapter 22; and Richard Kluger, *Simple Justice: The History of Brown v. Board of Education and Black America's Struggle for Equality* (New York: Vintage, 1977), Chapters 21 and 22.

[39]The District of Columbia case came up too, but since the District of Columbia is not a state, this case did not directly involve the Fourteenth Amendment and its "equal protection" clause. It confronted the Court on the same grounds, however—that segregation is inherently unequal. Its victory in effect was "incorporation in reverse," with equal protection moving from the Fourteenth Amendment to become part of the Bill of Rights. See Bolling v. Sharpe, 347 U.S. 497 (1954).

[40]Brown v. Board of Education of Topeka, Kansas, 347 U.S. 483 (1954).

The *Brown* decision altered the constitutional framework in two fundamental respects. First, after *Brown*, the states would no longer have the power to use race as a criterion of discrimination in law. Second, the national government would from then on have the constitutional basis for extending its power (hitherto in doubt, as we saw earlier) to intervene with strict regulatory policies against the discriminatory actions of state or local governments, school boards, employers, and many others in the private sector.

Civil Rights after *Brown v. Board of Education*

Although *Brown v. Board of Education* withdrew all constitutional authority to use race as a criterion of exclusion, this historic decision was merely a small opening move. First, most states refused to cooperate until sued, and many ingenious schemes were employed to delay obedience (such as paying the tuition for white students to attend newly created "private" academies). Second, even as southern school boards began to cooperate by eliminating their legally enforced *(de jure)* school segregation, there remained extensive actual *(de facto)* school segregation in the North as well as in the South as a consequence of racially segregated housing that could not be reached by the 1954–1955 *Brown* principles. Third, discrimination in employment, public accommodations, juries, voting, and other areas of social and economic activity were not directly touched by *Brown*.

A decade of frustration following *Brown* made it fairly obvious to all that adjudication alone would not succeed. The goal of "equal protection" required positive, or affirmative, action by Congress and by administrative agencies. And given massive southern resistance and a generally negative national public opinion toward racial integration, progress would not be made through courts, Congress, *or* agencies without intense, well-organized support. Table 4.2 shows the increase in civil rights demonstrations for voting rights and public accommodations during the fourteen years following *Brown*.

It shows that organized civil rights demonstrations began to mount slowly but surely after *Brown v. Board of Education*. By the 1960s, the many organizations that made up the civil rights movement had accumulated experience and built networks capable of launching massive direct-action campaigns against southern segregationists. The Southern Christian Leadership Conference, the Student Nonviolent Coordinating Committee, and many other organizations had built a movement that stretched across the South. The movement used the media to attract nationwide attention and support. In the massive March on Washington in 1963, the Reverend Martin Luther King, Jr., staked out the movement's moral claims in his famous "I Have a Dream" speech. The image of protesters being beaten, attacked by police dogs, and set upon with fire hoses did much to win broad sympathy for the cause of black civil rights and to discredit state and local governments in the South. In this way, the movement created intense pressure for reluctant federal government to take more assertive steps to defend black civil rights.

Institution Principle

The *Brown* decision altered the constitutional framework by giving the national government the power to intervene against the discriminatory actions of state and local governments and some aspects of the private sector.

History Principle

The *Brown* decision was the basis of the modern civil rights movement.

***de jure* segregation**
Racial segregation that is a direct result of law or official policy.

***de facto* segregation**
Racial segregation that is not a direct result of law or government policy but is, instead, a reflection of residential patterns, income distributions, or other social factors.

Collective Action Principle

Given the massive resistance to the *Brown* decision, the civil rights movement required large, well-organized protests.

TABLE 4.2

Peaceful Civil Rights Demonstrations, 1954–1968*

YEAR	TOTAL	FOR PUBLIC ACCOMMODATIONS	FOR VOTING
1954	0	0	0
1955	0	0	0
1956	18	6	0
1957	44	9	0
1958	19	8	0
1959	7	11	0
1960	173	127	0
1961	198	122	0
1962	77	44	0
1963	272	140	1
1964	271	93	12
1965	387	21	128
1966	171	15	32
1967	93	3	3
1968	97	2	0

*This table is drawn from a search of the *New York Times Index* for all references to civil rights demonstrations during the years the table covers. The table should be taken simply as indicative, for the data—news stories in a single paper—are very crude. The classification of the incident as peaceful or violent and the subject area of the demonstration are inferred from the entry in the *Index*, usually the headline from the story. The two subcategories reported here—public accommodations and voting—do not sum to the total because demonstrations dealing with a variety of other issues (e.g., education, employment, police brutality) are included in the total.

SOURCE: Jonathan D. Casper, *The Politics of Civil Liberties* (New York: Harper & Row, 1972), p. 90.

One of the tenets of our five principles of politics from Chapter 1 is that individuals have little incentive to participate in mass action politics. After all, what possible difference could one person make by taking part in a civil rights protest? Participation was costly in terms of time; and, in the case of civil rights marchers, even health or one's life were endangered. The risks outweighed the potential benefits, yet hundreds of thousands of people *did* participate. Why?

Even though little scholarly attention has been paid by those who apply this perspective to the civil rights movements,[41] a general answer is available. Most rational analysis takes behavior to be *instrumental*—to be motivated by and directed toward some purpose or objective. But behavior may also be *experiential*. People do things, on this account, because they like doing them—they feel good inside, they feel free of guilt, they take pleasure in the activity for its own sake. We maintain that this second view of behavior is entirely compatible with rational accounts. Instrumental behavior may be thought of as *investment activity*, whereas experiential behavior may be thought of as *consumption activity*. It is the behavior itself that generates utility, rather than the consequences produced by the behavior. To take a specific illustration of collective action, many people certainly attended the 1964 march on Washington because they cared about civil rights. But it is unlikely that many deluded themselves into thinking their individual participation made a large difference to the fate of the civil rights legislation in support of which the march was organized. Rather, they attended because they wanted to be a part of a social movement, to hear Martin Luther King speak, and to identify with the hundreds of thousands of others who felt the same way. Also—and this should not be minimized—they participated because they anticipated that the march would be fun, an adventure of sorts.

So, experiential behavior is consumption-oriented activity predicated on the belief that the activity in question is fulfilling, apart from its consequences. Individuals, complicated things that they are, are bound to be animated both by the consumption value of a particular behavior that we just described *and* its instrumental value, the rational (investment) explanation that we have used throughout this book. To insist on only one of these complementary forms of rationality, and to exclude the other, is to provide but a partial explanation.

School Desegregation, Phase One   Although the District of Columbia and some of the school districts in the border states began to respond almost immediately to court-ordered desegregation, the states of the Deep South responded with a carefully planned delaying tactic called "massive resistance." Southern politicians stood shoulder to shoulder to declare that the Supreme Court's decisions and orders were without effect. The legislatures in these states enacted statutes ordering school districts to maintain segregated schools and state superintendents to terminate state funding wherever there was racial mixing in the classroom. Some southern states violated their own long traditions of local school

Collective Action Principle

People participated in the civil rights movement for experiential as well as instrumental purposes.

[41]One notable exception is Dennis Chong, *Collective Action and the Civil Rights Movement* (Chicago: University of Chicago Press, 1991).

autonomy by centralizing public school authority under the governor or the state board of education and by giving states the power to close the schools and to provide alternative private schooling wherever local school boards might be tending to obey the Supreme Court.

Most of these plans of "massive resistance" were tested in the federal courts and were struck down as unconstitutional.[42] But southern resistance was not confined to legislation. For example, in Arkansas in 1957, Governor Orval Faubus mobilized the National Guard to intercede against enforcement of a federal court order to integrate Little Rock's Central High School, and President Eisenhower was forced to deploy U.S. troops and literally place the city under martial law. The Supreme Court considered the Little Rock confrontation so historically important that the opinion it rendered in that case was not only agreed

[42]The two most important cases were Cooper v. Aaron, 358 U.S. 1 (1958), which required Little Rock, Arkansas, to desegregate; and Griffin v. Prince Edward County School Board, 377 U.S. 218 (1964), which forced all the schools of that Virginia county to reopen after five years of closing to avoid desegregation.

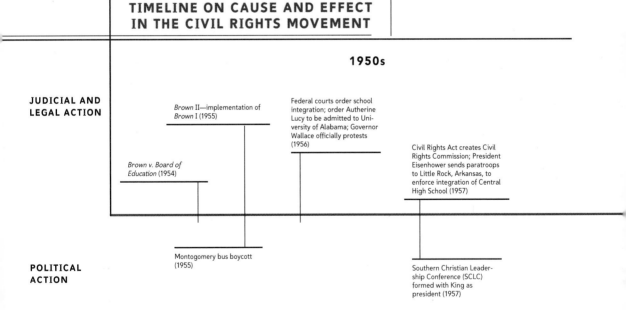

TIMELINE ON CAUSE AND EFFECT IN THE CIVIL RIGHTS MOVEMENT

1950s

JUDICIAL AND LEGAL ACTION

Brown v. *Board of Education* (1954)

Brown II—implementation of *Brown* I (1955)

Federal courts order school integration; order Autherine Lucy to be admitted to University of Alabama; Governor Wallace officially protests (1956)

Civil Rights Act creates Civil Rights Commission; President Eisenhower sends paratroops to Little Rock, Arkansas, to enforce integration of Central High School (1957)

Montogomery bus boycott (1955)

POLITICAL ACTION

Southern Christian Leadership Conference (SCLC) formed with King as president (1957)

to unanimously but was, unprecedentedly, signed personally by each and every one of the justices.[43] The end of massive resistance, however, became simply the beginning of still another southern strategy, "pupil placement" laws, which authorized school districts to place each pupil in a school according to a whole variety of academic, personal, and psychological considerations, never mentioning race at all. This put the burden of transferring to an all-white school on the nonwhite children and their parents, making it almost impossible for a single court order to cover a whole district, let alone a whole state. This delayed desegregation a while longer.[44]

[43]In *Cooper*, the Supreme Court ordered immediate compliance with the lower court's desegregation order and went beyond that with a stern warning that it is "emphatically the province and duty of the judicial department to say what the law is."

[44]Shuttlesworth v. Birmingham Board of Education, 358 U.S. 101 (1958), upheld a "pupil placement" plan purporting to assign pupils on various bases, with no mention of race. This case interpreted *Brown* to mean that school districts must stop explicit racial discrimination but were under no obligation to take positive steps to desegregate. For a while black parents were doomed to case-by-case approaches.

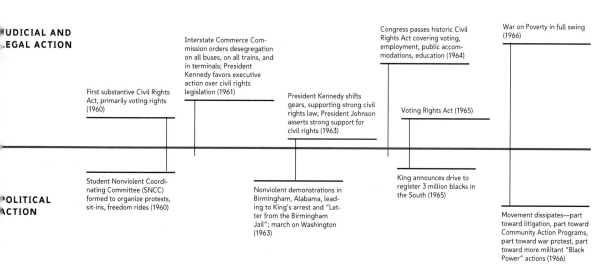

1960s

JUDICIAL AND LEGAL ACTION

First substantive Civil Rights Act, primarily voting rights (1960)

Interstate Commerce Commission orders desegregation on all buses, on all trains, and in terminals; President Kennedy favors executive action over civil rights legislation (1961)

President Kennedy shifts gears, supporting strong civil rights law; President Johnson asserts strong support for civil rights (1963)

Congress passes historic Civil Rights Act covering voting, employment, public accommodations, education (1964)

Voting Rights Act (1965)

War on Poverty in full swing (1966)

POLITICAL ACTION

Student Nonviolent Coordinating Committee (SNCC) formed to organize protests, sit-ins, freedom rides (1960)

Nonviolent demonstrations in Birmingham, Alabama, leading to King's arrest and "Letter from the Birmingham Jail"; march on Washington (1963)

King announces drive to register 3 million blacks in the South (1965)

Movement dissipates—part toward litigation, part toward Community Action Programs, part toward war protest, part toward more militant "Black Power" actions (1966)

**Collective
Action
Principle**

Enforcement of civil
rights law required
courts and legisla-
tures to work
together.

As new devices were invented by the southern states to avoid desegregation, the federal courts followed with cases and decisions quashing them. Ten years after *Brown*, less than 1 percent of black school-age children in the Deep South were attending schools with whites.[45] It had become unmistakably clear well before that time that the federal courts could not do the job alone. The first modern effort to legislate in the field of civil rights was made in 1957, but the law contained only a federal guarantee of voting rights, without any powers of enforcement, although it did create the Civil Rights Commission to study abuses. Much more important legislation for civil rights followed, especially the Civil Rights Act of 1964. It is important to observe here the mutual dependence of the courts and legislatures—not only do the legislatures need constitutional authority to act, but the courts need legislative and political assistance, through the power of the purse and the power to organize administrative agencies to implement court orders, and through the focusing of political support. Consequently, even as the U.S. Congress finally moved into the field of school desegregation (and other areas of "equal protection"), the courts continued to exercise their powers, not only by placing court orders against recalcitrant school districts, but also by extending and reinterpreting aspects of the "equal protection" clause to support legislative and administrative actions.

School Desegregation: Busing and Beyond   The most important judicial extension of civil rights in education after 1954 was probably the *Swann* decision (1971), which held that state-imposed desegregation could be brought about by busing children across school districts even where relatively long distances were involved. But the decision went beyond that, adding that under certain limited circumstances even racial quotas could be used as the "starting point in shaping a remedy to correct past constitutional violations," and that pairing or grouping of schools and reorganizing school attendance zones would also be acceptable.[46]

Three years later, however, the *Swann* case was severely restricted when the Supreme Court determined that only cities found guilty of deliberate and *de jure* racial segregation (segregation in law) would have to desegregate their schools.[47] This decision was handed down in the 1974 case of *Milliken v. Bradley* involving the city of Detroit and its suburbs. The *Milliken* ruling had the effect of exempting most northern states and cities from busing because school segregation in northern cities is generally *de facto* segregation (segregation in fact) that follows from segregated housing and from thousands of acts of private discrimination against blacks and other minorities.

---

[45]For good treatments of that long stretch of the struggle of the federal courts to integrate the schools, see Brest and Levinson, *Process of Constitutional Decision-Making*, pp. 471–80; and Alfred Kelly, Winfred A. Harbison, and Herman Beltz, *The American Constitution: Its Origins and Development*, 7th ed. (New York: W. W. Norton, 1991), pp. 610–16.

[46]Swann v. Charlotte-Mecklenburg Board of Education, 402 U.S. 1 (1971).

[47]Milliken v. Bradley, 418 U.S. 717 (1974).

Additional progress in the desegregation of schools is likely to be extremely slow unless the Supreme Court decides to permit federal action against *de facto* segregation and against the varieties of private schools and academies that have sprung up for the purpose of avoiding integration. The prospects for further school integration diminished with a series of Supreme Court decisions handed down in the 1990s. For example, in 1995 in *Missouri v. Jenkins*, the Court signaled to the lower courts that they should "disengage from desegregation efforts."[48] This is a direct and explicit threat to the main basis of the holding in the original 1954 *Brown v. Board*.

The Rise of the Politics of Rights

Outlawing Discrimination in Employment   Despite the agonizingly slow progress of school desegregation, there was some progress in other areas of civil rights during the 1960s and 1970s. Voting rights were established and fairly quickly began to revolutionize southern politics. Service on juries was no longer denied to minorities. But progress in the right to participate in politics and government dramatized the relative lack of progress in the economic domain, and it was in this area that battles over civil rights were increasingly fought.

The federal courts and the Justice Department entered this area through Title VII of the Civil Rights Act of 1964, which outlawed job discrimination by all private and public employers, including governmental agencies (such as fire and police departments), that employed more than fifteen workers. We have already seen that the Supreme Court gave "interstate commerce" such a broad definition that Congress had the constitutional authority to cover discrimination by virtually any local employers.[49] Title VII makes it unlawful to discriminate in employment on the basis of color, religion, sex, or national origin as well as race.

The first problem with Title VII was that the complaining party had to show that deliberate discrimination was the cause of the failure to get a job or a training opportunity. Rarely does an employer explicitly admit discrimination on the basis of race, sex, or any other illegal reason. Recognizing the rarity of such an admission, the courts have allowed aggrieved parties (the plaintiffs) to make their

[48]Missouri v. Jenkins, 115 S.Ct. 2038 (1995). The quote is from O'Brien, *Supreme Court Watch—1996*, p. 220.

[49]See especially Katzenbach v. McClung, 379 U.S. 294 (1964). Almost immediately after passage of the Civil Rights Act of 1964, a case challenged the validity of Title II, which covered discrimination in public accommodations. Ollie's Barbecue was a neighborhood restaurant in Birmingham, Alabama. It was located eleven blocks from an interstate highway and even farther from railroad and bus stations. Its table service was for whites only; there was only a takeout service for blacks. The Supreme Court agreed that Ollie's was strictly an intrastate restaurant, but since a substantial proportion of its food and other supplies were bought from companies outside Alabama, there was a sufficient connection to interstate commerce; therefore, racial discrimination at such restaurants would "impose commercial burdens of national magnitude upon interstate commerce." Although this case involved Title II, it had direct bearing on the constitutionality of Title VII.

case if they can show that an employer's hiring practices had the *effect* of exclusion. A leading case in 1971 involved a "class action" by several black employees in North Carolina attempting to show with statistical evidence that blacks had been relegated to only one department in the Duke Power Company, which involved the least desirable, manual-labor jobs, and that they had been kept out of contention for the better jobs because the employer had added high school education and the passing of specially prepared aptitude tests as qualifications for higher jobs. The Supreme Court held that although the statistical evidence did not prove intentional discrimination, and although the requirements were race-neutral in appearance, their effects were sufficient to shift the burden of justification to the employer to show that the requirements were a "business necessity" that bore "a demonstrable relationship to successful performance."[50] The ruling in this case was subsequently applied to other hiring, promotion, and training programs.[51]

Gender Discrimination   Even before equal employment laws began to have a positive effect on the economic situation of blacks, something far more dramatic began happening—the universalization of civil rights. The right not to be discriminated against was being successfully claimed by the other groups listed in Title VII—those defined by sex, religion, or national origin—and eventually by still other groups defined by age or sexual preference. This universalization of civil rights has become the new frontier of the civil rights struggle, and women have emerged with the greatest prominence in this new struggle. The effort to define and end gender discrimination in employment has led to the historic joining of women's rights to the civil rights cause.

Despite its interest in fighting discrimination, the Supreme Court during the 1950s and 1960s paid little attention to gender discrimination. Ironically, it was left to the more conservative Burger Court (1969–1986) to establish gender discrimination as a major and highly visible civil rights issue. Although the Burger Court refused to treat gender discrimination as the equivalent of racial discrimination,[52] it did make it easier for plaintiffs to file and win suits on the basis of gender discrimination by applying an "intermediate" level of review to these cases.[53] This intermediate level of scrutiny is midway between traditional rules of evidence, which put the burden of proof on the plaintiff, and the doctrine of "strict scrutiny," which requires the defendant to show not only that a particular classification is reasonable but also that there is a need or compelling interest for it. "Intermediate" scrutiny, therefore, shifts the burden of proof partially onto the defendant, rather than leaving it entirely on the plaintiff.

---

[50]Griggs v. Duke Power Company, 401 U.S. 24 (1971). See also Allan P. Sindler, *Bakke, DeFunis, and Minority Admissions: The Quest for Equal Opportunity* (New York: Longman, 1978), pp. 180–89.

[51]For a good treatment of these issues, see Charles O. Gregory and Harold A. Katz, *Labor and the Law*, 3rd ed. (New York: W. W. Norton, 1979), Chapter 17.

[52]See Frontiero v. Richardson, 411 U.S. 677 (1973).

[53]See Craig v. Boren, 423 U.S. 1047 (1976).

One major step was taken in 1992, when the Court decided in *Franklin v. Gwinnett County Public Schools* that violations of Title IX of the 1972 Education Act could be remedied with monetary damages.[54] Title IX forbade gender discrimination in education, but it initially sparked little litigation because of its weak enforcement provisions. The Court's 1992 ruling that monetary damages could be awarded for gender discrimination opened the door for more legal action in the area of education. The greatest impact has been in the areas of sexual harassment—the subject of the *Franklin* case—and in equal treatment of women's athletic programs. The potential for monetary damages has made universities and public schools take the problem of sexual harassment more seriously. Colleges and universities have also started to pay more attention to women's athletic programs. In the two years after the *Franklin* case, complaints to the Education Department's Office for Civil Rights about unequal treatment of women's athletic programs nearly tripled. In several high-profile legal cases, some prominent universities have been ordered to create more women's sports programs; many other colleges and universities have begun to add more women's programs in order to avoid potential litigation.[55] In 1997, the Supreme Court refused to hear a petition by Brown University challenging a lower-court ruling that the university establish strict sex equity in its athletic programs. The Court's decision meant that in colleges and universities across the country, varsity athletic positions for men and women must now reflect their overall enrollment numbers.[56]

In 1996, the Supreme Court made another important decision about gender and education by putting an end to all-male schools supported by public funds. It ruled that the policy of the Virginia Military Institute not to admit women was unconstitutional.[57] Along with the Citadel, another all-male military college in South Carolina, VMI had never admitted women in its 157-year history. VMI argued that the unique educational experience it offered—including intense physical training and the harsh treatment of freshmen—would be destroyed if women students were admitted. The Court, however, ruled that the male-only policy denied "substantial equality" to women. Two days after the Court's ruling, the Citadel announced that it would accept women. VMI considered becoming a private institution in order to remain all-male, but in September 1996, the school board finally voted to admit women. The legal decisions may have removed formal barriers to entry, but the experience of the new female cadets at these schools has not been easy. The first female cadet at the Citadel, Shannon Faulkner, won admission in 1995 under a federal court order but quit after four days. Although four women were admitted to the Citadel after the Supreme

[54]Franklin v. Gwinnett County Public Schools, 503 U.S. 60 (1992).
[55]Jennifer Halperin, "Women Step Up to Bat," *Illinois Issues* 21 (September 1995): 11–14.
[56]Joan Biskupic and David Nakamura, "Court Won't Review Sports Equity Ruling," *Washington Post*, 22 April 1997, p. A1.
[57]United States v. Virginia, 116 S.Ct. 2264 (1996).

Court decision, two of the four quit several months later. They charged harassment from male students, including attempts to set the female cadets on fire.[58]

Ever since sexual harassment was first declared a form of employment discrimination, employers and many employees have worried about the ambiguity of the issue. When can an employee bring charges, and when is the employer liable? In 1998, the Court clarified these questions in an important ruling. It said that if a company has an effective antiharassment policy in place, which the employee fails to use, the company cannot be held liable for sexual harassment. If no policy is in place, the company may be held legally responsible for harassment. In addition, the Court ruled that to pursue a suit on the grounds of sexual harassment, the employee does not have to show that she or he suffered a tangible loss, such as loss of promotion. Most important is whether an effective policy is in place and available to employees.[59]

The development of gender discrimination as an important part of the civil rights struggle has coincided with the rise of women's politics as a discrete movement in American politics. As with the struggle for racial equality, the relationship between changes in government policies and political action suggests a two-way pattern of causation, where changes in government policies can produce political action and vice versa. Today, the existence of a powerful women's movement derives in large measure from the enactment of Title VII of the Civil Rights Act of 1964 and from the Burger Court's vital steps in applying that law to protect women. The recognition of women's civil rights has become an issue that in many ways transcends the usual distinctions of American political debate. In the heavily partisan debate over the federal crime bill enacted in 1994, for instance, the section of the bill that enjoyed the widest support was the Violence against Women Act, whose most important feature was that it defined gender-biased violent crimes as a matter of civil rights and created a civil rights remedy for women who had been the victims of such crimes. But since the act was ruled unconstitutional by the Supreme Court in 2000, the struggle for women's rights will likely remain part of the political debate.

Discrimination against Other Groups   As gender discrimination began to be seen as an important civil rights issue, other groups arose demanding recognition and active protection of their civil rights. Under Title VII of the 1964 Civil Rights Act, any group or individual can try—and in fact is encouraged to try—to convert goals and grievances into questions of rights and the deprivation of those rights. A plaintiff must only establish that his or her membership in a group is an

---

[58]Judith Havemann, "Two Women Quit Citadel over Alleged Harassment," *Washington Post*, 13 January 1997, p. A1.

[59]Burlington Industries v. Ellerth, 118 S.Ct. 2257 (1998); Faragher v. City of Boca Raton, 118 S.Ct. 2275 (1998).

unreasonable basis for discrimination unless it can be proven to be a "job-related" or otherwise clearly reasonable and relevant decision. In America today, the list of individuals and groups claiming illegal discrimination is lengthy. The disabled, for instance, increasingly press their claim to equal treatment as a civil rights matter, a stance encouraged by the Americans with Disabilities Act of 1990.[60] Deaf Americans increasingly demand social and legal recognition of deafness as a separate culture, not simply as a disability.[61] One of the most familiar of these groups has been the gay and lesbian movement, which in less than thirty years has emerged from invisibility to become one of the largest civil rights movements in contemporary America. Beginning with street protests in the 1960s, the movement has grown into a well-financed and sophisticated lobby. The Human Rights Campaign Fund is the primary national political action committee (PAC) focused on gay rights; it provides campaign financing and volunteers to work for candidates endorsed by the group. The movement has also formed legal rights organizations, including the Lambda Legal Defense and Education Fund.

Gay and lesbian rights drew national attention in 1993, when President Bill Clinton confronted the question of whether gays should be allowed to serve in the military. As a candidate, Clinton had said he favored lifting the ban on homosexuals in the military. The issue set off a huge controversy in the first months of Clinton's presidency. After nearly a year of deliberation, the administration enunciated a compromise: their "Don't ask, don't tell" policy. This policy allows gays and lesbians to serve in the military as long as they do not openly proclaim their sexual orientation or engage in homosexual activity. The administration maintained that the ruling would protect gays and lesbians against witch-hunting investigations, but many gay and lesbian advocates expressed disappointment, charging the president with reneging on his campaign promise.

But until 1996, there was no Supreme Court ruling or national legislation explicitly protecting gays and lesbians from discrimination. The first gay rights case that the Court decided, *Bowers v. Hardwick*, ruled against a right to privacy that would protect consensual homosexual activity.[62] After the *Bowers* decision, the gay and lesbian rights movement sought suitable legal cases to test the constitutionality of discrimination against gays and lesbians, much as the black civil rights movement did in the late 1940s and 1950s. As one advocate put it, "Lesbians and gay men are looking for their *Brown v. Board of Education*."[63] Among the cases tested were those stemming from local ordinances restricting gay rights

---

[60]In 1994, for instance, after pressure from the Justice Department under the terms of the Americans with Disabilities Act, one of the nation's largest rental-car companies agreed to make special hand controls available to any customer requesting them. See "Avis Agrees to Equip Cars for Disabled," *Los Angeles Times*, 2 September 1994, p. D1.

[61]Thus a distinction has come to be made between "deaf," the pathology, and "Deaf," the culture. See Andrew Solomon, "Defiantly Deaf," *New York Times Magazine*, 28 August 1994, pp. 40ff.

[62]Bowers v. Hardwick, 478 U.S. 186 (1986).

[63]Quoted in Joan Biskupic, "Gay Rights Activists Seek a Supreme Court Test Case," *Washington Post*, 19 December 1993, p. A1.

(including the right to marry), job discrimination, and family law issues such as adoption and parental rights. In 1996, the Supreme Court, in *Romer v. Evans*, explicitly extended fundamental civil rights protections to gays and lesbians by declaring unconstitutional a 1992 amendment to the Colorado state constitution that prohibited local governments from passing ordinances to protect gay rights.[64] The decision's forceful language highlighted the connection between gay rights and civil rights as it declared discrimination against gay people unconstitutional.

In *Lawrence v. Texas* (2003), the Court then overturned *Bowers* and struck down a Texas statute criminalizing certain intimate sexual conduct between consenting partners of the same sex.[65] Drawing from the tradition of negative liberty, the Court maintained: "In our tradition the State is not omnipresent in the home. And there are other spheres of our lives and existence outside the home, where the State should not be a dominant presence." Explicitly encompassing lesbians and gay men within the umbrella of privacy, the Court concluded that the "petitioners are entitled to respect for their private lives. The State cannot demean their existence or control their destiny by making their private sexual conduct a crime."

A victory for lesbians and gays every bit as significant as *Roe v. Wade* was for women, *Lawrence v. Texas* extends at least one aspect of civil liberties to sexual minorities: the right to privacy. However, this decision by itself does not undo the various exclusions that deprive lesbians and gays full civil rights, including the right to marry.

Affirmative Action

affirmative action A policy or program designed to redress historic injustices committed against specific groups by making special efforts to provide members of these groups with access to educational and employment opportunities.

The politics of rights not only spread to increasing numbers of groups in the society, it also expanded its goal. The relatively narrow goal of equalizing opportunity by eliminating discriminatory barriers had been developing toward the far broader goal of *affirmative action*—compensatory action to overcome the consequences of past discrimination and to encourage greater diversity. An affirmative action policy tends to involve two novel approaches: (1) positive or benign discrimination in which race or some other status is actually taken into account, but for compensatory action rather than mistreatment; and (2) compensatory action to favor members of the disadvantaged group who themselves may never have been the victims of discrimination. Quotas may be, but are not necessarily, involved in affirmative action policies.

In 1965, President Johnson attempted to inaugurate affirmative action by executive orders directing agency heads and personnel officers to pursue vigorously

[64]Romer v. Evans, 116 S.Ct. 1620 (1996).
[65]Lawrence v. Texas, 123 S.Ct. 2472 (2003).

a policy of minority employment in the federal civil service and in companies doing business with the national government. But affirmative action did not become a prominent goal until the 1970s.

The Supreme Court and the Burden of Proof   As this movement spread, it also began to divide civil rights activists and their supporters. The whole issue of qualification versus minority preference was addressed in the case of Allan Bakke. Bakke, a white male with no minority affiliation, brought suit against the University of California at Davis Medical School on the grounds that in denying him admission the school had discriminated against him on the basis of his race (that year the school had reserved 16 of 100 available slots for minority applicants). He argued that his grades and test scores had ranked him well above many students who had been accepted at the school and that the only possible explanation for his rejection was that those others accepted were black or Hispanic while he was white. In 1978, Bakke won his case before the Supreme Court and was admitted to the medical school, but he did not succeed in getting affirmative action declared unconstitutional. The Court rejected the procedures at the University of California because its medical school had used both a quota *and* a separate admissions system for minorities. The Court agreed with Bakke's argument that racial categorizations are suspect categories that place a severe burden of proof on those using them to show a "compelling public purpose." The Court went on to say that achieving "a diverse student body" was such a public purpose, but the method of a rigid quota of student slots assigned on the basis of race was incompatible with the equal protection clause. Thus, the Court permitted universities (and other schools, training programs, and hiring authorities) to continue to take minority status into consideration, but limited severely the use of quotas to situations in which (1) previous discrimination had been shown, and (2) in which quotas were used more as a *guideline* for social diversity than as a mathematically defined ratio.[66]

For nearly a decade after *Bakke*, the Supreme Court was tentative and permissive about efforts by corporations and governments to experiment with affirmative action programs in employment.[67] But in 1989, the Court returned to the *Bakke* position that any "rigid numerical quota" is suspect. In *Wards Cove v. Atonio*, the Court further weakened affirmative action by easing the way for employers to prefer white males, holding that the burden of proof of unlawful discrimination should be shifted from the defendant (the employer) to the plaintiff (the person claiming to be the victim of discrimination).[68] This decision virtu-

---

[66]Regents of the University of California v. Bakke, 438 U.S. 265 (1978).
[67]United Steelworkers v. Weber, 443 U.S. 193 (1979); and Fullilove v. Klutznick, 100 S.Ct. 2758 (1980).
[68]Wards Cove v. Atonio, 109 S.Ct. 2115 (1989).

ally overruled the Court's prior holding.[69] That same year, the Court ruled that any affirmative action program already approved by federal courts could be subsequently challenged by white males who alleged that the program discriminated against them.[70]

In 1991, after a lengthy battle with the White House, Congress enacted a piece of legislation designed to undo the effects of these decisions. Under the terms of the Civil Rights Acts of 1991, the burden of proof in employment discrimination cases was shifted back to employers, overturning the *Wards Cove* decision. In addition, the act made it more difficult to mount later challenges to consent decrees in affirmative action cases, reversing the *Martin v. Wilks* decision. Despite Congress's actions, however, the federal judiciary will have the last word when cases under the new law reach the courts. In a 5-to-4 decision in 1993, the Court ruled that employees had to prove that their employers intended discrimination, thus again placing the burden of proof on employees.[71]

In 1995, the Supreme Court's ruling in *Adarand Constructors, Inc. v. Pena* further weakened affirmative action. This decision stated that race-based policies, such as preferences given by the government to minority contractors, must survive strict scrutiny, placing the burden on the government to show that such affirmative action programs serve a compelling government interest and are narrowly tailored to address identifiable past discrimination.[72] President Clinton responded to the *Adarand* decision by ordering a review of all government affirmative action policies and practices. Although many observers suspected that the president would use the review as an opportunity to back away from affirmative action, the conclusions of the task force largely defended existing policies. Reflecting the influence of the Supreme Court's decision in *Adarand*, President Clinton acknowledged that some government policies would need to change. But on the whole, the review found that most affirmative action policies were fair and did not "unduly burden nonbeneficiaries."[73]

Although Clinton sought to "mend, not end" affirmative action, developments in the courts and the states continued to restrict affirmative action in important ways. One of the most significant was the *Hopwood* case, in which white students challenged admissions practices in the University of Texas Law School, charging that the school's affirmative action program discriminated against whites. In 1996, a federal court (the U.S. Court of Appeals for the Fifth Circuit)

---

[69]Griggs v. Duke Power Company, 401 U.S. 24 (1971).

[70]Martin v. Wilks, 109 S.Ct. 2180 (1989). In this case, some white firefighters in Birmingham challenged a consent decree mandating goals for hiring and promoting blacks. This was an affirmative action plan that had been worked out between the employer and aggrieved black employees and had been accepted by a federal court. Such agreements become "consent decrees" and are subject to enforcement. Chief Justice Rehnquist held that the white firefighters could challenge the legality of such programs even though they had not been parties to the original litigation.

[71]St. Mary's Honor Center v. Hicks, 113 S.Ct. 2742 (1993).

[72]Adarand Constructors, Inc. v. Pena, 115 S.Ct. 2097 (1995).

[73]Ann Devroy, "Clinton Study Backs Affirmative Action," *Washington Post*, 19 July 1995, p. A1.

ruling on the case stated that race could never be considered in granting admissions and scholarships at state colleges and universities.[74] This decision effectively rolled back the use of affirmative action permitted by the 1978 *Bakke* case. In *Bakke*, as discussed earlier, the Supreme Court had outlawed quotas but said that race could be used as one factor among many in admissions decisions. Many universities and colleges have since justified affirmative action as a way of promoting racial diversity among their student bodies. What was new in the *Hopwood* decision was the ruling that race could *never* be used as a factor in admissions decisions, even to promote diversity.

In 1996, the Supreme Court refused to hear a challenge to the *Hopwood* case. This meant that its ruling remains in effect in the states covered by the Fifth Circuit—Texas, Louisiana, and Mississippi—but does not apply to the rest of the country. The impact of the *Hopwood* ruling is greatest in Texas because Louisiana and Mississippi are under conflicting court orders to desegregate their universities. In Texas, in the year after the *Hopwood* case, minority applications to Texas universities declined. Concerned about the ability of Texas public universities to serve the state's minority students, the Texas legislature quickly passed a new law granting students who graduate in the top 10 percent of their classes automatic admission to the state's public universities. State officials hoped that this measure would ensure a racially diverse student body.[75]

The weakening of affirmative action in the courts was underscored in a case the Supreme Court agreed to hear in 1998. A white schoolteacher in New Jersey who had lost her job had sued her school district, charging that her layoff was racially motivated: a black colleague hired on the same day was not laid off. Under former President George Bush, the Justice Department had filed a brief on her behalf in 1989, but in 1994 the Clinton administration formally reversed course in a new brief supporting the school district's right to make distinctions based on race as long as it did not involve the use of quotas. Three years later, the administration, worried that the case was weak and could result in a broad decision against affirmative action, reversed course again. It filed a brief with the Court urging a narrow ruling in favor of the dismissed worker. Because the school board had justified its actions on the grounds of preserving diversity, the administration feared that a broad ruling by the Supreme Court could totally prohibit the use of race in employment decisions, even as one factor among many designed to achieve diversity. But before the Court could issue a ruling, a coalition of civil rights groups brokered and arranged to pay for a settlement. This unusual move reflected the widespread fear of a sweeping negative decision. Cases involving dismissals, as the New Jersey case did, are generally viewed as much more difficult to defend than cases that concern hiring. In addition, the

---

[74]Hopwood v. State of Texas, 78 F3d 932 (Fifth Circuit, 1996).

[75]See Lydia Lum, "Applications by Minorities down Sharply," *Houston Chronicle*, 8 April 1997, p. A1; R. G. Ratcliffe, "Senate Approves Bill Designed to Boost Minority Enrollments," *Houston Chronicle*, 8 May 1997, p. A1.

particular facts of the New Jersey case—two equally qualified teachers hired on the same day—were seen as unusual and unfavorable to affirmative action.[76]

This betwixt and between status of affirmative action was how things stood in 2003, when the Supreme Court took two cases against the University of Michigan that were virtually certain to clarify, if not put closure on, affirmative action. The first suit, *Gratz v. Bollinger* (the university president), was against the University of Michigan's undergraduate admissions policy and practices, alleging that by using a point-based ranking system that automatically awarded 20 points (out of 150) to African American, Latino, and Native American applicants, the university discriminated unconstitutionally against white students of otherwise equal or superior academic qualifications. The Supreme Court agreed, 6 to 3, arguing that something tantamount to a quota was involved because undergraduate admissions lacked the necessary "individualized consideration," employing instead a "mechanical one," based too much on the favorable minority points.[77] The Court's ruling in *Gratz v. Bollinger* was not surprising, given *Bakke's* (1978) holding against quotas and given recent decisions calling for strict scrutiny of all racial classifications, even those that are intended to remedy past discrimination or promote future equality.

The second case, *Grutter v. Bollinger*, broke new ground. Grutter sued the Law School on the grounds that it had discriminated in a race-conscious way against white applicants with equal or superior grades and law boards. A precarious majority of 5 to 4 aligned the majority of the Supreme Court with Justice Powell's lone plurality opinion in *Bakke* for the first time. In *Bakke*, Powell argued that (1) diversity in education is a compelling state interest and (2) race could be constitutionally considered as a plus factor in admissions decisions. In *Grutter*, the Court reiterated Powell's holding and, applying strict scrutiny to the Law School's policy, found that the Law School's admissions process is narrowly tailored to the school's compelling state interest in diversity because it gives a "highly individualized, holistic review of each applicant's file" in which race counts but is not used in a "mechanical way."[78]

Throughout the 1990s, federal courts, including the Supreme Court, had subjected public affirmative action programs to strict scrutiny in order to invalidate them. *Adarand Constructors, Inc. v. Pena* (1995) definitively established the Supreme Court's view that constitutionally permissible use of race must serve a compelling state interest. Since *Korematsu v. United States* (1944) and until *Grutter*, no consideration of race had survived strict scrutiny. Such affirmative action plans as had survived constitutional review did so before 1995 under a lower standard of review reserved for policies intended to remedy racial injus-

---

[76]Linda Greenhouse, "Settlement Ends High Court Case on Preferences," *New York Times*, 22 November 1997, p. A1; Barry Bearak, "Rights Groups Ducked a Fight, Opponents Say," *New York Times*, 22 November 1997, p. A1.

[77]Gratz v. Bollinger 123 S.Ct. 2411 (2003).

[78]Grutter v. Bollinger 123 S.Ct. 2325 (2003).

tice. For affirmative action to survive under the post-1995 judicial paradigm, the Court needed to find that sometimes racial categories can be deployed to serve a compelling state interest. That the Court found exactly this in *Grutter* puts affirmative action on stronger ground—at least if its specific procedures pass the Supreme Court's muster, and until the Court's majority changes.

Referendums on Affirmative Action   The courts have not been the only center of action: challenges to affirmative action have also emerged in state and local politics. One of the most significant state actions was the passage of the California Civil Rights Initiative, also known as Proposition 209, in 1996. Proposition 209 outlawed affirmative action programs in the state and local governments of California, thus prohibiting state and local governments from using race or gender preferences in their decisions about hiring, contracting, or university admissions. The political battle over Proposition 209 was heated, and supporters and defenders took to the streets as well as the airwaves to make their cases. When the referendum was held, the measure passed with 54 percent of the vote, including 27 percent of the black vote, 30 percent of the Latino vote, and 45 percent of the Asian American vote.[79] In 1997, the Supreme Court refused to hear a challenge to the new law.

> **Policy Principle**
>
> Individual challenges in the courts as well as several state and local referenda have weakened affirmative action.

Many observers predicted that the success of California's ban on affirmative action would provoke similar movements in states and localities across the country. But the political factors that contributed to the success of Proposition 209 in California may not exist in many other states. Winning a controversial state referendum takes leadership and lots of money. Popular California Republican governor Pete Wilson led with a strong anti–affirmative action stand (favoring Proposition 209), and his campaign had a lot of money for advertising. But those conditions did not exist elsewhere. Few prominent Republican leaders in other states were willing to come forward to lead the anti–affirmative action campaign. Moreover, the outcome of any referendum, especially a complicated and controversial one, depends greatly on how the issue is drafted and placed on the ballot for the voters. California's Proposition 209 was framed as a civil rights initiative: "the state shall not discriminate against, or grant preferential treatment to, any individual or group on the basis of race, sex, color, ethnicity, or national origin." Different wording can produce quite different outcomes, as a 1997 vote on affirmative action in Houston revealed. There, the ballot initiative asked voters whether they wanted to ban affirmative action in city contracting and hiring, not whether they wanted to end preferential treatment. Fifty-five percent of Houston voters decided in favor of affirmative action.[80]

[79]Michael A. Fletcher, "Opponents of Affirmative Action Heartened by Court Decision," *Washington Post*, 13 April 1997, p. A21.

[80]See Sam Howe Verhovek, "Houston Vote Underlined Complexity of Rights Issue," *New York Times*, 6 November 1997, p. A1.

The Politics of Affirmative Action

In the 1950s, the public was still substantially split on the principle of racial equality.[81] Congress remained deeply divided on civil rights. State governments in the South were also firmly opposed. The rules and procedures of Congress—the committee system and seniority—allowed a small group of conservative southern members to block any civil rights legislation. The political outcome was the status quo. In this case, the third principle of politics illustrates ways that institutions can be barriers to rather than tools of change.

These barriers encouraged the NAACP and their chief counsel, Thurgood Marshall (who later served on the Court as its first black member), to choose a different and ultimately successful political strategy: the Courts. The Supreme Court took a big political risk in reviewing and deciding *Brown v. Board of Education* in 1954. While the Court has the power of suasion, it has no actual way to implement its rulings—these powers are left to other institutions of government. History looks favorably on the actions of Presidents Eisenhower, Kennedy, and Johnson, who made sure that the decisions of the Court were actually implemented, using that most powerful of political institutions—the power of the armed forces—when they were necessary.

The sweeping civil rights laws enacted in the 1960s officially ended state-sanctioned segregation. Today, there is little conflict over basic civil rights. While the Supreme Court led the mass public, even the Court is fundamentally a political institution. Principle 4 reminds us that it would have been difficult for the Court to maintain its political legitimacy if public preferences did not eventually follow. This change in American public opinion on race over the past half century has been truly remarkable.[82]

The civil rights laws did not end racism or erase stark inequities between the races in such areas as employment and education. As a consequence, affirmative action policies were enacted to ensure equality between the races.

However, unlike equal access to facilities, employment, and voting, affirmative action has remained contentious. In part, this is a historical legacy of the way affirmative action was created—not from a set of public demands, but from governmental action. Unlike civil and voting rights laws, which were passed in response to a well-organized and disciplined collective-action movement, affirmative action began as an executive order issued by President Lyndon Johnson in 1965.[83] This illustrates an important feature of collective action: often, political entrepreneurs or other forms of leadership—including government—are necessary to stimulate the formation and continuation of group activities. Today, most civil rights organizations argue fervently in favor of affirmative action, even though the policy was created by government.

Affirmative action continues to divide the nation, by race and by ideology. Many believe it is because affirmative action places into conflict two of the fundamental aspects of the American political culture: equality and freedom. Affirmative action is an attempt to remove continuing disparities in access to education and occupational advancement by minorities, especially African Americans, as well as women. In doing so, though, some argue that affirmative action limits the freedom of others, primarily white men, to gain admission to school, pursue employment, and advance in their jobs.[84]

The conflict is clearly illustrated in the "Michigan affirmative action" case. In 2003, the Court heard a series of arguments about admission policies and affirmative action in public universities (for undergraduates and at the law school). According to the University of Michigan, the defendant in the case, racial diversity has an important educational value. Furthermore, history matters: the legacy of racial divisions in this country means that, without affirmative action policies, virtually no minority students would be admitted to the law school, and the number in the undergraduate body would plummet.[85] According to the opponents, however, history does not matter. Past racial discrimination is no excuse for current discrimination.

The eventual split decision also mirrored the split in public attitudes about race. The Court ruled, by a 6-to-3 vote, that the university's policy of giving "points"" to minority applicants to the college was a quota and, thus, unconstitutional. But the same Court upheld the constitutionality of preferential admissions policies at the law school (by a 5-to-4 vote). As a political institution reliant on public support for its legitimacy and power, the Court straddled the issue adroitly.

Interestingly, for all the controversy, empirical studies show that colleges and universities, because they control the rules of admission, may not even need "affirmative action" as a way to promote diversity. By de-emphasizing those aspects of the admissions policy that have race differentials (such as standardized tests) and emphasizing other measures of academic achievement, colleges and universities have been able to reach their desired goal—a diverse student body—even without affirmative action.[86] These institutions understand Principles 3 and 4: control of the rules equals control over the outcomes.

Affirmative action will continue to spark political controversy. In California, opponents to affirmative action took another route, attempting to pass a referendum that banned the state government from collecting data on the racial characteristics of individuals. This rule would have ended affirmative action because the data would not exist![87]

[81]For the history of public opinion on race, see Howard Schuman, Charlotte Steeh, and Lawrence Bobo. *Racial Attitudes in America: Trends and Interpretations* (Cambridge, Mass.: Harvard University Press, 1985).

[82]Ibid.

[83]The actual phrase "affirmative action" first appeared in Executive Order 11246, which required federal contractors to "take affirmative action to ensure that applicants are employed, and that employees are treated during employment, without regard to their race, creed, color, or national origin." The executive order is available online at http://www.dol.gov/esa/regs/fedreg/final/97033352.htm.

[84]The political divisions are not as simple as you might believe. According to Paul Sniderman, conservatives are opposed to affirmative action. It is among liberals that affirmative action causes problems; many liberals cannot reconcile their desire for racial justice with a desire for equal treatment. See Paul M. Sniderman and Edward G. Carmines, *Reaching beyond Race* (Cambridge, Mass.: Harvard University Press, 1997).

[85]The University of Michigan's official position on the case is available at their Web site: http://www.umich.edu/-urel/admissions.

[86]See Jimmy Chan and Erik Eyster, "Does Banning Affirmative Action Lower College Student Quality?" (19 March 2002), available online at http://www.nuff.ox.ac.uk/Users/Eyster/papers/euroafac.pdf.

[87]The referendum, measure 54, was defeated in the October 7, 2003, California election, the same election that saw Gray Davis recalled and Arnold Schwarzenegger elected as California's next governor.

SUMMARY

Civil liberties and *civil rights* are two different phenomena and have to be treated legally and constitutionally in two different ways. We have defined *civil liberties* as that sphere of individual freedom of choice created by restraints on governmental power. When the Constitution was ratified, it was already seen as inadequate in the provision of protections of individual freedom and required the addition of the Bill of Rights. The Bill of Rights explicitly placed a whole series of restraints on government. Some of these were *substantive*, regarding *what* government could do; and some of these restraints were *procedural*, regarding *how* the government was permitted to act. We call the rights in the Bill of Rights civil liberties because they are rights to be free from arbitrary government interference.

But *which* government? This was settled in the *Barron* case in 1833 when the Supreme Court held that the restraints in the Bill of Rights were applicable only to the national government and not to the states. The Court was recognizing "dual citizenship." At the time of its adoption in 1868, the Fourteenth Amendment was considered by many a deliberate effort to reverse *Barron*, to put an end to dual citizenship, and to nationalize the Bill of Rights, applying its restrictions to state governments as well as to the national government. But the post–Civil War Supreme Court interpreted the Fourteenth Amendment otherwise. Dual citizenship remained almost as it had been before the Civil War, and the shadow of *Barron* extended across the rest of the nineteenth century and well into the twentieth century. The slow process of nationalizing the Bill of Rights began in the 1920s, when the Supreme Court recognized that at least the restraints of the First Amendment had been "incorporated" into the Fourteenth Amendment as restraints on the state governments. But it was not until the 1960s that most of the civil liberties in the Bill of Rights were incorporated into the Fourteenth Amendment. Almost exactly a century after the adoption of the Fourteenth Amendment, the Bill of Rights was nationalized. Citizens now enjoy close to the same civil liberties regardless of the state in which they reside.

As for the second aspect of protection of the individual, *civil rights*, stress has been put upon the expansion of governmental power rather than restraints upon it. If the constitutional base of civil liberties is the "due process" clause of the Fourteenth Amendment, the constitutional base of civil rights is the "equal protection" clause. This clause imposes a positive obligation on government to advance civil rights, and its original motivation seems to have been to eliminate the gross injustices suffered by "the newly emancipated negroes . . . as a class." But as with civil liberties, there was little advancement in the interpretation or application of the "equal protection" clause until after World War II. The major breakthrough came in 1954 with *Brown v. Board of Education*, and advancements came in fits and starts during the succeeding ten years.

After 1964, Congress finally supported the federal courts with effective civil rights legislation that outlawed a number of discriminatory practices in

Rationality Principle	Collective Action Principle	Institution Principle	Policy Principle	History Principle
Madison believed that passage of a bill of rights was a practical political matter because it would remove a potential source of opposition to the new government.	The Federalists supported the addition of a bill of rights because it would help gain the support of the Antifederalists for the Constitution as a whole.	Dual citizenship meant that the Bill of Rights did not apply to decisions or to procedures of state governments.	The civil liberties decisions of the Rehnquist Court during the 1990s reveal the conservative preferences of a majority of its justices.	Dual citizenship was upheld by the Supreme Court for nearly one hundred years after *Barron v. Baltimore* (1833)
The preferences of individual Supreme Court justices have been consequential for the development of civil liberties.	Given the massive resistance to the *Brown* decision, the civil rights movement required large, well-organized protests.	Most of the important provisions of the Bill of Rights were nationalized by the Supreme Court during the 1960s.	Individual challenges in the courts as well as several state and local referenda have weakened affirmative action.	*Roe v. Wade* was not decided in a political vacuum. Many states had already eased their restrictions on abortion prior to 1973.
The preference of the members of the Rehnquist Court has been to accept fewer cases for review.	Enforcement of civil rights law required courts and legislatures to work together.	As a political institution, the Bill of Rights has not been carved in stone. Through subsequent amendments, on the one hand, and constant updating of the original ten through judicial review, on the other, the balance between freedom and power has been transformed.		The *Brown* decision was the basis of the modern civil rights movement.
	People participated in the civil rights movement for experiential as well as by giving the national instrumental purposes.			The civil rights and women's rights movements both government policies can produce political action and vice versa.
		The *Brown* decision altered the constitutional framework by giving the national government the power to intervene against the discriminatory actions of state and local governments and some aspects of the private sector.		

the private sector and provided for the withholding of federal grants-in-aid to any local government, school, or private employer as a sanction to help enforce the civil rights laws. From that point, civil rights developed in two ways. First, the definition of civil rights was expanded to include victims of discrimination other than African Americans. Second, the definition of civil rights became increasingly positive; affirmative action has become an official term. Judicial decisions, congressional statutes, and administrative agency actions all have moved beyond the original goal of eliminating discrimination and toward creating new opportunities for minorities and, in some areas, compensating today's minorities for the consequences of discriminatory actions not directly against them but against members of their group in the past. Because compensatory civil rights action has sometimes relied upon quotas, there has been intense debate over the constitutionality as well as the desirability of affirmative action.

The story has not ended and is not likely to end. The politics of rights will remain an important part of American political discourse.

FOR FURTHER READING

Abraham, Henry J., and Barbara A. Perry. *Freedom and the Court: Civil Rights and Liberties in the United States.* 6th ed. New York: Oxford University Press, 1994.

Baer, Judith A. *Equality under the Constitution: Reclaiming the Fourteenth Amendment.* Ithaca, N.Y.: Cornell University Press, 1983.

Drake, W. Avon, and Robert D. Holsworth. *Affirmative Action and the Stalled Quest for Black Progress.* Urbana: University of Illinois Press, 1996.

Garrow, David J. *Bearing the Cross: Martin Luther King, Jr., and the Southern Christian Leadership Conference: A Personal Portrait.* New York: William Morrow, 1986.

Glendon, Mary Ann. *Rights Talk: The Impoverishment of Political Discourse.* New York: Free Press, 1991.

Greenberg, Jack. *Crusaders in the Courts: How a Dedicated Band of Lawyers Fought for the Civil Rights Revolution.* New York: Basic Books, 1994.

Kelly, Alfred, Winfred A. Harbison, and Herman Beltz. *The American Constitution: Its Origins and Development.* 7th ed. New York: W. W. Norton, 1991.

Levy, Leonard W. *Freedom of Speech and Press in Early America: Legacy of Suppression.* New York: Harper & Row, 1963.

Lewis, Anthony. *Gideon's Trumpet.* New York: Random House, 1964.

Minow, Martha. *Making All the Difference—Inclusion, Exclusion, and American Law.* Ithaca, N.Y.: Cornell University Press, 1990.

Nava, Michael, and Robert Dawidoff. *Created Equal: Why Gay Rights Matter to America.* New York: St. Martin's Press, 1994.

Rosenberg, Gerald N. *The Hollow Hope: Can Courts Bring About Social Change?* Chicago: University of Chicago Press, 1991.

Silverstein, Mark. *Constitutional Faiths: Felix Frankfurter, Hugo Black, and the Process of Judicial Decision Making.* Ithaca, N.Y.: Cornell University Press, 1984.

Thernstrom, Abigail M. *Whose Votes Count? Affirmative Action and Minority Voting Rights.* Cambridge, Mass.: Harvard University Press, 1987.

Politics in the News—
Reading between the Lines

The Affirmative Action Debate in Social and Historical Context

By LINDA GREENHOUSE

As they approached the University of Michigan affirmative action cases, Justice Sandra Day O'Connor and Justice Clarence Thomas appeared to be responding to completely different cues.

For Justice O'Connor, the broad societal consensus in favor of affirmative action in higher education . . . was clearly critical to her conclusion that the law school's "holistic" and "individualized" consideration of race was not only acceptable but also, at least for the next 25 years, necessary to achieve a more equal society.

Justice Thomas . . . took as his text not the briefs but his own life story.

"I must contest the notion that the law school's discrimination benefits those admitted as a result of it," he said at the start of a remarkable series of paragraphs, most without footnotes, statistics or outside references, about the pain and stigma suffered by recipients of affirmative action.

Justice O'Connor observed in her opinion that "context matters when reviewing race-based governmental action under the Equal Protection Clause." The context provided by the briefs from Fortune 500 companies, senior military officers, and colleges and universities . . . quite clearly won the day for Michigan.

Context always matters at the court, though it is not always acknowledged by justices who, unlike Justice O'Connor, prefer to deal in absolutes. What the rulings demonstrated was not simply the power of context but the importance of the different contexts from which the justices view the cases that bring them face to face with society's most profound disputes.

For Justices O'Connor and Thomas, their opposite starting points as well as their opposite conclusions make the law school case . . . a useful window into the styles of two of the court's most distinctive members.

In her new book . . . Justice O'Connor wrote that "courts, in particular, are mainly reactive institutions." Noting that "change comes principally from attitudinal shifts in the population at large," she said that "rare indeed is the legal victory—in court or legislature—

Linda Greenhouse, "The Supreme Court: The Justices; Context and the Court," *New York Times*, 25 June 2003, p. A1.

that is not a careful byproduct of an emerging social consensus."

The challenge facing the University of Michigan and its defenders was to demonstrate such a consensus on behalf of affirmative action, and they met the challenge brilliantly. The briefs . . . provided the context for concluding that affirmative action's benefits "are not theoretical but real, as major American businesses have made clear."

Another part of the context for Justice O'Connor was the 25-year-old opinion in the Bakke case by an admired mentor, Justice Lewis F. Powell Jr. Justice Powell's solitary opinion establishing diversity as a "compelling state interest" justifying affirmative action in admissions had been on shaky ground before five justices embraced it on Monday.

At the heart of Justice Thomas's dissenting opinion was a highly personal critique of affirmative action, which he called the "cruel farce of racial discrimination."

"The law school tantalizes unprepared students with the promise of a . . . degree and all of the opportunities that it offers," he said, adding, "These overmatched students take the bait, only to find that they cannot succeed in the cauldron of competition."

Justice Thomas, himself a beneficiary of affirmative action at Yale Law School, compiled a respectable record at . . . the country's most elite law school. So his opinion reflected not objective failure so much as a lifelong struggle with the ambiguous position in which beneficiaries of affirmative action . . . often found themselves as elite institutions felt their way, sometimes clumsily, toward a more inclusive identity.

Asking, "Who can differentiate between those who belong and those who do not?" he continued: "The majority of blacks are admitted to the law school because of discrimination, and because of this policy all are tarred as undeserv-

ESSENCE OF THE STORY

- The Supreme Court ruled that the University of Michigan Law School could continue to consider racial criteria in admissions.

- For Justice Sandra Day O'Connor, private and public institutions demonstrated the benefits of affirmative action.

- For Justice Clarence Thomas, his own life history and experiences speak to the problems of affirmative action.

POLITICAL ANALYSIS

- The debate over affirmative action poses the benefits of a collective policy against the costs to particular individuals. This is a fundamental tension in political action, especially well revealed by affirmative action.

- Because the Supreme Court is such a small institution, interpreting its ruling often turns on the membership at any particular historical moment.

- Members of the Court may interpret the same body of evidence in very different ways, based on their legal training, judicial temperament, and even personal life experiences.

ing. . . . When blacks take positions in the highest places of government, industry or academia, it is an open question today whether their skin color played a part in their advancement."

He added, "The question itself is the stigma—because either racial discrimination did play a role, in which case the person may be deemed 'otherwise unqualified,' or it did not, in which case asking the question itself unfairly marks those blacks who would succeed without discrimination." . . .

"In this opinion is the entire panoply of the contradictions this country has about race," said Goodwin Liu, a lawyer here whose article in support of affirmative action was cited by Justice Ruth Bader Ginsburg. . . .

two

Institutions

CHAPTER

5

Congress: The First Branch

The U.S. Congress is the "first branch" of government under Article I of our Constitution and is also among the world's most important representative bodies.

Congress is also the only national representative assembly that can actually be said to govern. Many of the world's representative bodies only represent—that is, their governmental functions consist mainly of affirming and legitimating the national leadership's decisions.

Although many of the world's representative bodies possess only the right to say "yes," a second, smaller group of representative institutions—most notably Western European parliaments—also have the power to say "no" to the proposals of executive agencies. Such institutions as the British Parliament have the power to reject programs and laws sought by the government, although the use of this power is constrained by the fact that the rejection of an important governmental proposal can lead to Parliament's dissolution and the need for new elections. While they can and sometimes do say "no," Western European parliaments generally do not have the power to modify governmental proposals or, more important, to initiate major programs. The only national representative body that actually possesses such powers is the U.S. Congress. For example, while the U.S. Congress never accedes to the president's budget proposals without making major changes, both the British House of Commons and the Japanese Diet always accept the budget exactly as proposed by the government.

In this chapter, we shall try to understand how the U.S. Congress is able to serve simultaneously as a representative assembly and a powerful agency of government. Unlike most of its counterparts around the world, Congress controls a formidable battery of powers that it uses to shape policies and, when necessary, defend its prerogatives against the executive branch.

Congress has vast authority over the two most important powers given to any government: the power of force (control over the nation's military forces) and the power over money. Specifically, in Article I, Section 8, Congress can "lay and collect Taxes," deal with indebtedness and bankruptcy, impose duties, borrow and coin money, and generally control the nation's purse strings. It also may "provide for the common Defense and general welfare," regulate interstate commerce, undertake public works, acquire and control federal lands, promote science and "useful Arts" (pertaining mostly to patents and copyrights), and regulate the militia.

In the realm of foreign policy, Congress has the power to declare war, deal with piracy, regulate foreign commerce, and raise and regulate the armed forces and military installations. These powers over war and the military are supreme— even the president, as commander in chief of the military, must obey the laws and orders of Congress *if* Congress chooses to assert its constitutional authority. (In the past century, Congress

CHAPTER OUTLINE

Representation

- House and Senate: Differences in Representation
- The Electoral System

The Organization of Congress

- Cooperation in Congress
- Other Underlying Problems
- Party Leadership in the House and the Senate
- The Committee System: The Core of Congress
- The Staff System: Staffers and Agencies
- Informal Organization: The Caucuses

Rules of Lawmaking: How a Bill Becomes a Law

- Committee Deliberation
- Debate
- Conference Committee: Reconciling House and Senate Versions of a Bill
- Presidential Action
- The Distributive Tendency in Congress

How Congress Decides

- Constituency
- Interest Groups
- Party Discipline
- Weighing Diverse Influences

Beyond Legislation: Additional Congressional Powers

- Advice and Consent: Special Senate Powers
- Impeachment

Power and Representation

has usually surrendered this authority to the president.) Further, the Senate has the power to approve treaties (by a two-thirds vote) and to approve the appointment of ambassadors. Capping these powers, Congress is charged to make laws "which shall be necessary and proper for carrying into Execution the foregoing Powers, and all other Powers vested by this Constitution in the Government of the United States, or in any Department or Officer thereof."

If it seems to the reader that many of these powers belong to the president, from war power to spending power, that is because modern presidents do exercise great authority in these areas. The modern presidency is a more powerful institution than it was two hundred years ago, and much of that power has come from Congress, either because Congress has delegated the power to the president by law or because Congress has simply allowed, or even urged, presidents to be more active in these areas. This also helps explain why the executive branch seems like a more important branch of government today than Congress. Still, the constitutional powers of Congress remain intact in the document. This takes us to Congress's pivotal role as a representative institution.

As we shall see congressional power cannot be separated from congressional representation. Indeed, there is a reciprocal relationship between the two. Without its array of powers, Congress could do little to represent effectively the views and interests of its constituents. Power is necessary for effective congressional representation. At the same time, the power of Congress is ultimately a function of its capacity to represent important groups and forces in American society effectively.

Questions of power and representation are also closely tied to the issue of congressional reform. Critics of Congress want it to be both more representative and more effective. On the one hand, Congress is frequently criticized for falling victim to "gridlock" and failing to reach decisions on important issues like Social Security reform. This was one reason why, in 1995, the Republican House leadership reduced the number of committees and subcommittees in the lower chamber. Having fewer committees and subcommittees generally means greater centralization of power and more expeditious decision making. On the other hand, critics demand that Congress become more representative of the changing makeup and values of the American populace. In recent years, for example, some reformers have demanded limits on the number of terms that any member of Congress can serve. Term limits are seen as a device for producing a more rapid turnover of members and, hence, a better chance for new political and social forces to be represented in Congress. The problem, however, is that while reforms such as term limits and greater internal diffusion of power may make Congress more representative, they may also make it less efficient and effective. By the same token, reforms that may make Congress better able to act, such as strong central leadership, reduction of the number of committees and subcommittees, and retention of members with seniority and experience, may make Congress less representative.

Congressional power cannot be separated either from the bases of congressional representation or from the precise form taken by its decision-making institutions. We begin our discussion with a brief consideration of representation. Then we examine the institutional structure of the contemporary Congress, and the manner in which congressional powers are organized and employed. Throughout, we will point out the connections between these two aspects—the ways in which representation affects congressional operations (especially through "the electoral connection") and the ways in which congressional institutions enhance or diminish representation (especially Congress's division- and specialization-of-labor committee system).

REPRESENTATION

Congress is the most important representative institution in American government. Each member's primary responsibility is to the district, to his or her **constituency,** not to the congressional leadership, a party, or even Congress itself. Yet the task of representation is not a simple one. Views about what constitutes fair and effective representation differ, and constituents can make very different kinds of demands on their representatives. Members of Congress must consider these diverse views and demands as they represent their districts (see Process Box 5.1). A representative claims to act or speak for some other person or group. But how can one person be trusted to speak for another? How do we know that those who call themselves our representatives are actually speaking on our behalf, rather than simply pursuing their own interests?

Legislators generally vary in the weight given to personal priorities and the things desired by campaign contributors and past supporters. Some see themselves as perfect agents of others; they have been elected to do the bidding of those that sent them to the legislature, and they act as **delegates.** Other legislators see themselves as being selected by their fellow citizens to do what the legislator thinks is "right," and they act as **trustees.** Most legislators are mixes of these two types.

PREVIEWING THE PRINCIPLES

All five principles of politics are important to our understanding of Congress. Members of Congress, like all politicians, are ambitious and are, thus, eager to serve the interests of constituents in order to improve their own chances of re-election. In many ways, Congress works because its system of representation harnesses individual legislators' goals and puts them to use. Because the policy goals of members of Congress are many and varied, cooperation among members can be difficult to achieve. The internal organization of Congress seeks to remedy the problems of collective action by regularizing patterns of cooperation and creating a division of labor among members. Similarly, the legislative process tries to provide coordination to a diverse institution, and in the legislative process it is clear that rules matter. The legislative process also reveals that political outcomes result from preferences and procedures. Finally, in the discussion of the evolution of the committee system and the influence of political parties in Congress, we see that history matters. In fact, the ebb and flow of Congress's power in the political system can only be evaluated in historical context.

constituency The district comprising the area from which an official is elected.

delegate A representative who votes according to the preferences of his or her constituency.

trustee A representative who votes based on what he or she thinks is best for his or her constituency.

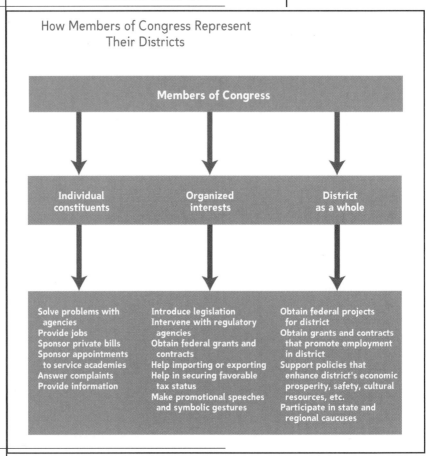

How Members of Congress Represent
Their Districts

Members of Congress

Individual constituents	Organized interests	District as a whole
Solve problems with agencies Provide jobs Sponsor private bills Sponsor appointments to service academies Answer complaints Provide information	Introduce legislation Intervene with regulatory agencies Obtain federal grants and contracts Help importing or exporting Help in securing favorable tax status Make promotional speeches and symbolic gestures	Obtain federal projects for district Obtain grants and contracts that promote employment in district Support policies that enhance district's economic prosperity, safety, cultural resources, etc. Participate in state and regional caucuses

agency representation
The type of representation by which representatives are held accountable to their constituents if they fail to represent them properly; that is, constituents have the power to hire and fire their representatives. This is the incentive for good representation when the personal backgrounds, views, and interests of the representatives differ from their constituents'.

As we discussed in Chapter 1, one person might be trusted to speak for another if the two are formally bound together so that the representative is in some way accountable to those he or she purports to represent. If representatives can somehow be punished or held to account for failing to speak properly for their constituents, then we know they have an incentive to provide good representation even if their own personal backgrounds, views, and interests differ from those they represent. This principle is called *agency representation*—the sort of representation that takes place when constituents have the power to hire and fire their representatives. Frequent competitive elections constitute an important means by which constituents hold their representatives in account and keep them responsive to constituency views and preferences. The idea of representative as agent is similar to the relationship of lawyer and client. True, the relationship between the member of Congress and as many as 630,000 "clients" in the district, or the senator and millions of clients in the state, is very different from that of the lawyer and client. But the criteria of performance are comparable.

One expects at the very least that each representative will constantly be seeking to discover the interests of the constituency and will be speaking for those interests in Congress and in other centers of government.[1] We expect this because we believe that members of Congress, like politicians everywhere, are ambitious. For many, this ambition is satisfied simply by maintaining a hold on their present office and advancing up the rungs of power in that legislative body. Some may be looking ahead to the next level—to higher legislative office, as when a representative seeks a Senate seat, or to an executive office, as when a legislator returns home to run for his or her state's governorship, or, at the highest level, when a legislator seeks the presidency.[2] We will return to this topic shortly in a discussion of elections. But we can say here that in each of these cases, the legislator is eager to serve the interests of constituents, either to enhance his or her prospects of contract renewal at the next election or to improve the chances of moving to another level. In short, the agency conception of representation works in proportion to the ambition of politicians (as "agents") and the capacity of constituents (as "principals") to reward or punish on the basis of their legislator's performance and reputation. This latter capacity depends on, among other things, the quality of political competition, which, in turn, is a product of the electoral and campaign finance systems.

Institution Principle

According to the principle of agency representation, elections induce a member of Congress to act according to the preferences of his or her constituency.

Rationality Principle

Members of Congress, like all politicians, are ambitious and, thus, eager to serve the interests of constituents in order to improve their own chances of re-election.

House and Senate: Differences in Representation

The framers of the Constitution provided for a ***bicameral legislature***—that is, a legislative body consisting of two chambers. As we saw in Chapter 2, the framers intended each of these chambers, the House and Senate, to represent a different constituency. Members of the Senate, appointed by state legislatures for six-year terms, were to represent the elite members of society and to be more attuned to the interests of property than of population. Today, members of the House and Senate are elected directly by the people. The 435 members of the House are elected from districts apportioned according to population; the 100 members of the Senate are elected by state, with two senators from each. Senators continue to have much longer terms in office and usually represent much larger and more diverse constituencies than do their counterparts in the House of Representatives (see Table 5.1).

bicameral legislature A legislative assembly composed of two chambers or houses.

---

[1] For some interesting empirical evidence, see Angus Campbell, Philip Converse, Warren Miller, and Donald Stokes, *Elections and the Political Order* (New York: Wiley, 1966), Chapter 11. See also Richard F. Fenno, Jr., *Home Style: House Members in Their Districts* (Boston: Little, Brown, 1978).

[2] For more on "progressive ambition," see Joseph A. Schlesinger, *Ambition and Politics: Political Careers in the United States* (Chicago: Rand McNally, 1966).

TABLE 5.1

Differences between the House and the Senate

	HOUSE	**SENATE**
Minimum age of member	25 years	30 years
U.S. citizenship	at least 7 years	at least 9 years
Length of term	2 years	6 years
Number per state	Depends on population: 1 per 30,000 in 1789; now 1 per 630,000	2 per state
Constituency	Tends to be local	Both local and national

The House and Senate play different roles in the legislative process. In essence, the Senate is the more deliberative of the two bodies—the forum in which any and all ideas can receive a thorough public airing. The House is the more centralized and organized of the two bodies—better equipped to play a routine role in the governmental process. In part, this difference stems from the different rules governing the two bodies. These rules give House leaders more control over the legislative process and provide for House members to specialize in certain legislative areas. The rules of the much-smaller Senate give its leadership relatively little power and discourage specialization.

Both formal and informal factors contribute to differences between the two chambers of Congress. Differences in the length of terms and requirements for holding office specified by the Constitution in turn generate differences in how members of each body develop their constituencies and exercise their powers of office. The result is that members of the House most effectively and frequently serve as the agents of well-organized local interests with specific legislative agendas—for instance, used-car dealers seeking relief from regulation, labor unions seeking more favorable legislation, or farmers looking for higher subsidies. The small size and relative homogeneity of their constituencies and the frequency with which they must seek re-election make House members more attuned to the legislative needs of local interest groups. This is what the framers intended when they drafted the Constitution—namely, that the House of Representatives would be "the people's house" and that its members would reflect and represent public opinion in a timely manner.

Senators, on the other hand, serve larger and more heterogeneous constituencies. As a result, they are somewhat better able than members of the House to serve as the agents for groups and interests organized on a statewide or national basis. Moreover, with longer terms in office, senators have the luxury of considering "new ideas" or seeking to bring together new coalitions of interests, rather than simply serving existing ones. This, too, was the intent of the Constitution's drafters—that the Senate should provide a balance to the more responsive House with its narrower and more homogenous constituencies. The Senate was said to be "the saucer that cools the tea," bringing deliberation, debate, inclusiveness, calm, and caution to policy formulation.

In recent years, the House has exhibited considerably more intense partisanship and ideological division than the Senate. Because of their diverse constituencies, senators are more inclined to seek compromise positions that will offend as few voters and interest groups as possible. Members of the House, in contrast, typically represent more homogeneous districts in which their own party is dominant. This situation has tended to make House members less inclined to seek compromises and more willing to stick to their partisan and ideological guns than their counterparts in the Senate during the past several decades. For instance, the House divided almost exactly along partisan lines on the 1998 vote to impeach President Clinton. In the Senate, by contrast, ten Republicans joined Democrats to acquit Clinton of obstruction of justice charges, and, in a separate vote, five Republicans joined Democrats to acquit Clinton of perjury.[3] Also, in October 2001, the Senate passed an airport security bill unanimously. The House, however, divided votes along partisan lines over whether new security personnel should be federal employees or private contractors.

The Electoral System

In light of their role as agents for various constituencies in their states and districts, and the importance of elections as a mechanism by which principals (constituents) reward and punish their agents, representatives are very much influenced by electoral considerations. Three factors related to the U.S. electoral system affect who gets elected and what he or she does once in office. The first set of issues concerns who decides to run for office and which candidates have an edge over others. The second issue is that of incumbency advantage. Finally, the way congressional district lines are drawn can greatly affect the outcome of an election. Let us examine more closely the impact that these considerations have on who serves in Congress.

Running for Office   Voters' choices are restricted from the start by who decides to run for office. In the past, decisions about who would run for a particular elected office were made by local party officials. A person who had a record of

History Principle

The historical intentions of the founders for the House to represent current passions and the Senate to balance it by serving a more deliberative function are still manifest in these legislative bodies more than two centuries later.

---

[3]Eric Pianin and Guy Gugliotta, "The Bipartisan Challenge: Senate's Search for Accord Marks Contrast to House," *Washington Post*, 8 January 1999, p. 1.

service to the party, or who was owed a favor, or whose "turn" had come up might be nominated by party leaders for an office. Today, few party organizations have the power to slate candidates in that way. Instead, the decision to run for Congress is a more personal choice. One of the most important factors determining who runs for office is a candidate's individual ambition.[4] A potential candidate may also assess whether he or she can attract enough money to mount a credible campaign. The ability to raise money depends on connections with other politicians, interest groups, and national party organizations. Wealthy individuals may finance their own races. In 2000, for example, New Jersey Democrat and former investment banker Jon Corzine spent more than $60 million of his own money to win a U.S. Senate seat.

In the past, the difficulty of raising campaign funds posed a disadvantage to female candidates. Since the 1980s, however, a number of political action committees (PACs) and other organizations have emerged to recruit women and fund their campaigns. The largest of them, EMILY's List, has become one of the most powerful fund-raisers in the nation. Recent research shows that money is no longer the barrier it once was to women running for office.[5]

Features distinctive to each congressional district also affect the field of candidates. Among them are the range of other political opportunities that may lure potential candidates away. In addition, the way the congressional district overlaps with state legislative boundaries may affect a candidate's decision to run. A state-level representative or senator who is considering running for the U.S. Congress is more likely to assess his or her prospects favorably if his or her state district coincides with the congressional district (because the voters will already know him or her). For similar reasons, U.S. representatives from small states, whose congressional districts overlap with a large portion of their state, are far more likely to run for statewide office than members of Congress from large states. And for any candidate, decisions about running must be made early because once money has been committed to already declared candidates, it is harder for new candidates to break into a race. Thus, the outcome of a November election is partially determined many months earlier, when decisions to run are finalized.

Incumbency   *Incumbency* plays a very important role in the American electoral system and in the kind of representation citizens get in Washington. Once in office, members of Congress typically are eager to remain in office and make politics a career. Throughout the twentieth century, Congress developed into a *professional legislature,* a legislature with members that serve full time for mul-

Rationality Principle
One of the most important factors determining who runs for office is each candidate's individual ambition.

incumbency
Holding a political office for which one is running.

professional legislature   A legislature with members that serve full time for multiple terms.

---

[4]See Linda L. Fowler and Robert D. McClure, *Political Ambition: Who Decides to Run for Congress* (New Haven: Yale University Press, 1989); and Alan Ehrenhalt, *The United States of Ambition: Politicians, Power, and the Pursuit of Office* (New York: Times Books, 1991).

[5]See Barbara C. Burrell, *A Woman's Place Is in the House: Campaigning for Congress in the Feminist Era* (Ann Arbor: University of Michigan Press, 1994), Chapter 6; and the essays in Elizabeth Adell Cook, Sue Thomas, and Clyde Wilcox, eds., *The Year of the Woman: Myths and Realities* (Boulder, Col.: Westview, 1994).

FIGURE 5.1

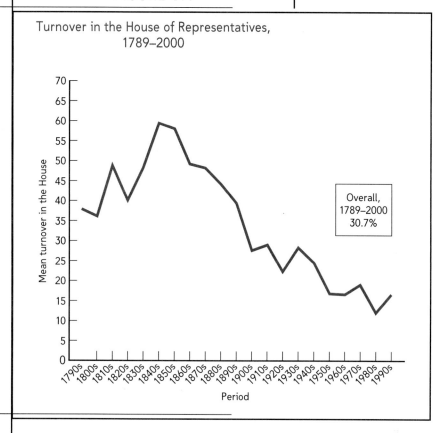

Turnover in the House of Representatives, 1789–2000

SOURCE: Revised from John Swain, Stephen A. Borelli, Brian C. Reed, and Sean F. Evans, "A New Look at Turnover in the U.S. House of Representatives, 1789–1998," *American Politics Quarterly* 28 (2000): 435–57.

tiple terms (See Figure 5.1).[6] The career ambitions of members of Congress are helped by an array of tools that they can use to stack the deck in favor of their re-election. Through effective use of this arsenal of weapons, an incumbent establishes a reputation for competence, imagination, and responsiveness—the attributes most principals look for in an agent. One well-known tool of incumbency is the franking privilege. Under a law enacted by the first U.S. Congress in 1789, members of Congress may send mail to their constituents free of charge to keep them informed of government business and public affairs. Under

[6]Nelson W. Polsby, "The Institutionalization of the U.S. House of Representatives," *American Political Science Review* 63 (1968): 144–68.

current law, members receive an average of about $100,000 in free postage for mailings to their constituents. Members may not use these funds to send mail outside their own districts or to send out mass mailings within ninety days of a primary or general election. Despite these restrictions, the franking privilege provides incumbents with a valuable resource for publicizing their activities and making themselves visible to voters.

A particularly important tool is the incumbent's reputation for constituency service: taking care of the problems and requests of individual voters. Through such services and their advertisement by word of mouth, the incumbent seeks to establish an attractive political reputation and a "personal" relationship with his or her constituents. Well over a quarter of the representatives' time and nearly two-thirds of the time of their staff members is devoted to constituency service (termed *"casework"*). This service is not merely a matter of writing and mailing letters. It includes talking to constituents, providing them with minor services, presenting special bills for them, and attempting to influence decisions by regulatory commissions on their behalf. Indeed, one might think of the member's legislative staff and office operation as a "congressional enterprise," much like a firm, with the member him- or herself as the CEO.[7]

One very direct way in which incumbent members of Congress serve as the agents of their constituencies is through the venerable institution of *patronage.* Patronage refers to a variety of forms of direct services and benefits that members provide for their districts. One of the most important forms of patronage is *pork-barrel legislation.* Through pork-barrel legislation, representatives seek to capture federal projects and federal funds for their own districts (or states in the case of senators), and thus to "bring home the pork" for their constituents. Many observers of Congress argue that pork-barrel bills are the only ones that some members are serious about moving toward actual passage because they are seen as important to members' re-election bids.

A common form of pork barreling is the "earmark," the practice through which members of Congress insert into otherwise pork-free bills language that provides special benefits for their own constituents.[8] For instance, the massive transportation bill enacted in 1998 contained billions of dollars in earmarks. One senator, Ted Kennedy (D-Mass.), claimed that he was able to obtain nearly $200 million in earmarks. In addition to $100 million for highway construction in Boston, these included a myriad of small items such as $1.6 million for the Longfellow National Historic Site and $3.17 million for the Silvio Conte National Fish and Wildlife Refuge.[9]

casework An effort by members of Congress to gain the trust and support of constituents by providing them with personal service. One important type of casework consists of helping constituents obtain favorable treatment from the federal bureaucracy.

patronage The resources available to higher officials, usually opportunities to make partisan appointments to offices and to confer grants, licenses, or special favors to supporters.

pork-barrel legislation Appropriations made by legislative bodies for local projects that are often not needed but that are created so that local representatives can carry their home district in the next election.

---

[7]For more on the congressional office as an "enterprise" that processes the casework demands of constituents, see Robert H. Salisbury and Kenneth A. Shepsle, "Congressman as Enterprise," *Legislative Studies Quarterly* 6 (1981): 559–76.

[8]For an excellent study of academic earmarking, see James D. Savage, *Funding Science in America: Congress, Universities, and the Politics of the Academic Pork Barrel* (New York: Cambridge University Press, 1999).

[9]*Congressional Quarterly Weekly Report*, 17 October 1998, p. 2792.

The pork-barrel tradition in Congress is so strong that some members insist on providing their districts with special benefits whether their constituents want them or not. In 1994, for example, members of the House Public Works Committee managed to channel millions of dollars in federal highway funds to their own states and districts. California, which has eight representatives on the Public Works Committee, received fifty-one special federal highway projects worth nearly $300 million. The problem is that under federal law, these special funds are charged against the state's annual grant from the Highway Trust Fund. States rely heavily upon their Highway Trust Fund grants to fund high-priority road work. One exasperated state official declared, "For years our members have tried to explain that to the members of Congress . . . 'No, you did not bring me any new money. All you did was reprogram money from here to there.'"[10]

So why do legislators continue this exasperating practice? One answer is that each individual legislator can credibly and visibly claim personal responsibility, and thus take personal credit, for earmarked programs and special highway projects. This enhances the legislator's reputation back home as a Washington mover and shaker, while also enhancing his or her re-election prospects. If the same money came to the states or districts through an existing program, like the Highway Trust Fund, the individual legislator would get little credit for being personally responsible.

The incumbency advantage is evident in the high rates of re-election for congressional incumbents: over 95 percent for House members and nearly 90 percent for members of the Senate in recent years (see Figure 5.2).[11] In the 2002 national elections, incumbency had a powerful effect, with nearly 98 percent of House incumbents re-elected and 89 percent of incumbent candidates re-elected to the Senate. It is also evident in what is called sophomore surge—the tendency for candidates to win a higher percentage of the vote when seeking future terms in office. Once in office, members of Congress find it much easier to raise campaign funds and are thus able to outspend their challengers (see Figure 5.3).[12] Members of the majority party in the House and Senate are particularly attractive to donors who want access to those in power.[13]

Incumbency can help a candidate by scaring off potential challengers. In many races, potential candidates may decide not to run because they fear that the

Policy Principle

Pork-barrel legislation exists because it allows members of Congress to claim credit for federally granted resources, thus improving their chances for re-election.

[10]Jon Healey, "The Unspoken Expense of the Highway Bill," *Congressional Quarterly Weekly Report*, 28 May 1994, p. 1375.

[11]Norman J. Ornstein, Thomas E. Mann, and Michael J. Malbin, *Vital Statistics on Congress, 1995–1996* (Washington, D.C.: Congressional Quarterly Press, 1996), pp. 60–61; Robert S. Erickson and Gerald C. Wright, "Voters, Candidates, and Issues in Congressional Elections," in *Congress Reconsidered*, ed. Lawrence C. Dodd and Bruce I. Oppenheimer, 5th ed. (Washington, D.C.: Congressional Quarterly Press, 1993), p. 99; John R. Alford and David W. Brady, "Personal and Partisan Advantage in U.S. Congressional Elections, 1846–1990," in *Congress Reconsidered*, pp. 141–57.

[12]Stephen Ansolabehere and James Snyder, "Campaign War Chests and Congressional Elections," *Business and Politics* 2 (2000): 9–34.

[13]Gary W. Cox and Eric Magar, "How Much Is Majority Status in the U.S. Congress Worth?" *American Political Science Review* 93 (1999): 299–309.

FIGURE 5.2

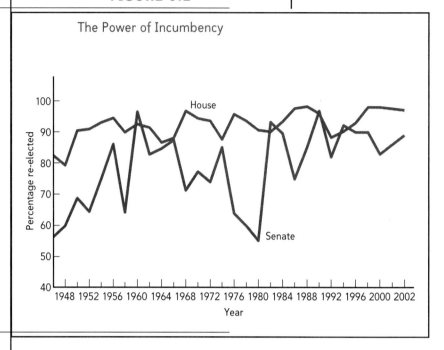

The Power of Incumbency

SOURCE: Norman J. Ornstein, Thomas E. Mann, and Michael J. Malbin, eds., *Vital Statistics on Congress, 1995–1996* (Washington, D.C.: Congressional Quarterly Press, 1996), pp. 60–61 and authors' update.

incumbent simply has brought benefits to the district, has too much money, or is too well liked or too well known.[14] Potentially strong challengers may also decide that a district's partisan leanings are too unfavorable. The experience of Republican representative Dan Miller in Florida is instructive. When Miller first ran in 1992, he faced five opponents in the Republican primary and a bruising campaign against his Democratic opponent in the general election. In the 1994 election, by contrast, Miller faced only nominal opposition in the Republican primary, winning 81 percent of the vote. In the general election, the strongest potential challenger from the Democratic party decided not to run; the combination of the incumbency advantage coupled with the strongly Republican leanings of the district gave the Democrats little chance of winning. Miller was re-elected without a challenge.[15]

[14]Kenneth Bickers and Robert Stein, "The Electoral Dynamics of the Federal Pork Barrel," *American Journal of Political Science* 40 (November 1996): 1300–26.

[15]Kevin Merida, "The 2nd Time Is Easy; Many House Freshmen Have Secured Seats," *Washington Post*, 18 October 1994, p. A1.

FIGURE 5.3

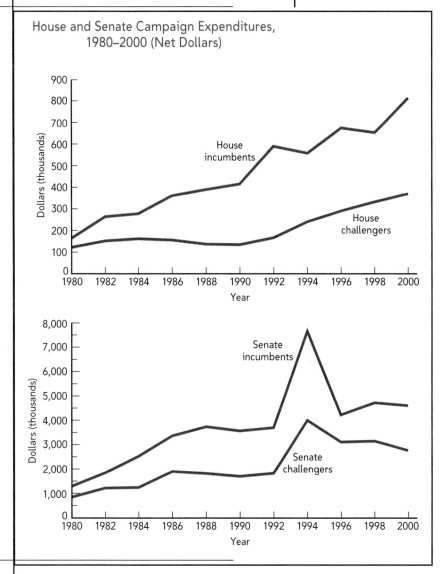

House and Senate Campaign Expenditures, 1980–2000 (Net Dollars)

SOURCE: Norman J. Ornstein, Thomas E. Mann, and Michael J. Malbin, eds., *Vital Statistics on Congress, 2001–2002* (Washington, D.C.: American Enterprise Institute, 2002), pp. 87, 93.

The advantage of incumbency thus tends to preserve the status quo in Congress by discouraging potentially strong challengers from running. When incumbents do face strong challengers, they are often defeated.[16] For example, in 1998, New York Republican senator Al D'Amato was trounced by former representative Charles Schumer, a strong candidate who was able to raise nearly as much money as D'Amato. The role of incumbency has implications for the social composition of Congress. For example, incumbency advantage makes it harder for women to increase their numbers in Congress because most incumbents are men. Women who run for open seats (for which there are no incumbents) are just as likely to win as male candidates.[17] Supporters of term limits argue that such limits are the only way to get new faces into Congress. They believe that incumbency advantage and the tendency of many legislators to view politics as a career mean that very little turnover will occur in Congress unless limits are imposed on the number of terms a legislator can serve.

But the tendency toward the status quo is not absolute. In recent years, political observers have suggested that the incumbency advantage may be declining. In the 1992 and 1994 elections, for example, voters expressed considerable anger and dissatisfaction with incumbents, producing a 25 percent turnover in the House in 1992 and a 20 percent turnover in 1994. Yet the defeat of incumbents was not the main factor at work in either of these elections; 88.3 percent of House incumbents were re-elected in 1992, and 90.2 percent won re-election in 1994. In 1992, an exceptionally high retirement rate (20 percent, as opposed to the norm of 10 percent) among members of Congress created more open seats, which brought new faces into Congress. In 1994, a large number of open seats combined with an unprecedented mobilization of Republican voters to shift control of Congress to the Republican party.

Congressional Districts   The final factor that affects who wins a seat in Congress is the way congressional districts are drawn. Every ten years, state legislatures must redraw congressional districts to reflect population changes. In 1929, Congress enacted a law fixing the total number of congressional seats at 435. As a result, when states with growing populations gain districts they do so at the expense of states whose populations have remained stagnant or declined. In recent decades, this has meant that the nation's growth areas in the South and West have gained congressional seats at the expense of the Northeast and Midwest (see Figure 5.4). After the 2000 Census, for example, Arizona, Texas, Florida, and Georgia each gained two seats while New York and Pennsylvania each lost two seats (see Figure 5.5). Redrawing congressional districts is a highly political process: districts are shaped to create an advantage for the majority party in the state legislature, which controls the redistricting process. In this complex process, those charged with drawing districts use sophisticated computer tech-

[16]Gary C. Jacobson, *The Politics of Congressional Elections*, 4th ed. (New York: Longman, 1997).

[17]See Burrell, *A Woman's Place Is in the House;* and David Broder, "Key to Women's Political Parity: Running," *Washington Post*, 8 September 1994, p. A17.

FIGURE 5.4

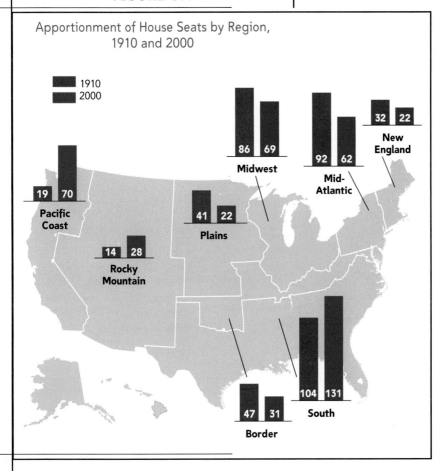

Apportionment of House Seats by Region, 1910 and 2000

■ 1910
▨ 2000

Pacific Coast **19** **70**

Rocky Mountain **14** **28**

Plains **41** **22**

Midwest **86** **69**

Mid-Atlantic **92** **62**

New England **32** **22**

Border **47** **31**

South **104** **131**

SOURCE: Norman J. Ornstein, Thomas E. Mann, and Michael J. Malbin, eds., *Vital Statistics on Congress, 2001–2002* (Washington, D.C.: American Enterprise Institute, 2002), p. 59.

nologies to come up with the most favorable district boundaries. Redistricting can create open seats and may pit incumbents of the same party against one another, ensuring that one of them will lose. Redistricting can also give an advantage to one party by clustering voters with some ideological or sociological characteristics in a single district, or by separating those voters into two or more districts. *Gerrymandering* can have a major impact upon the outcomes of congressional elections. For example, prior to 1980, California House seats had been almost evenly divided between the two parties. After the 1980 census, a redistricting effort controlled by the Democrats, who held both houses of the state

gerrymandering
Apportionment of voters in districts in such a way as to give unfair advantage to one political party.

FIGURE 5.5

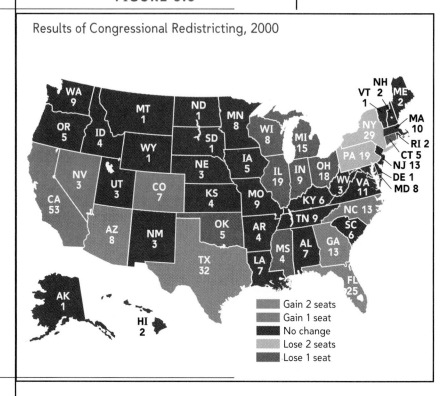

Results of Congressional Redistricting, 2000

legislature as well as the governorship, resulted in Democrats taking control of two-thirds of the state's seats in the U.S. House of Representatives.[18] Examples like this explain why the two parties invest substantial resources in state legislative and gubernatorial contests during the electoral cycle prior to the year that congressional district boundaries will be redrawn.

As we shall see in Chapter 10, since the passage of the 1982 amendments to the 1965 Voting Rights Act, race has become a major—and controversial—consideration in drawing voting districts. These amendments, which encouraged the creation of districts in which members of racial minorities have decisive majorities, have greatly increased the number of minority representatives in Con-

[18]David Butler and Bruce Cain, *Congressional Redistricting: Comparative and Theoretical Perspectives* (New York: Macmillan, 1992).

gress. After the 1991–1992 redistricting, the number of predominantly minority districts doubled, rising from twenty-six to fifty-two. Among the most fervent supporters of the new minority districts were white Republicans, who used the opportunity to create more districts dominated by white Republican voters.[19] These developments raise thorny questions about representation. Some analysts argue that the system may grant minorities greater sociological representation, but it has made it more difficult for minorities to win substantive policy goals.[20]

In 1995, the Supreme Court limited racial redistricting in *Miller v. Johnson*, in which the Court stated that race could not be the predominant factor in creating electoral districts. Yet concerns about redistricting and representation have not disappeared. The distinction between race being a "predominant" factor and its being one factor among many is very hazy. Because the drawing of district boundaries affects incumbents as well as the field of candidates who decide to run for office, it continues to be a key battleground on which political parties fight about the meaning of representation.

THE ORGANIZATION OF CONGRESS

The United States Congress is not only a representative assembly. It is also a legislative body. For Americans, representation and legislation go hand in hand. As we saw earlier, however, many parliamentary bodies are representative without the power to legislate. It is no small achievement that the U.S. Congress both represents *and* governs.

It is extraordinarily difficult for a large, representative assembly to formulate, enact, and implement laws. The internal complexities of conducting business within Congress—the legislative process—alone are daunting. In addition, there are many individuals and institutions that have the capacity to influence the legislative process. Since successful legislation requires the confluence of so many distinct factors, it is little wonder that most of the thousands of bills considered by Congress each year are defeated long before they reach the president.

Before an idea or proposal can become a law, it must pass through a complex set of organizations and procedures in Congress. Collectively, these are called the policy-making process, or the legislative process. Understanding this process is central to understanding why some ideas and proposals eventually become law while most do not. Although the supporters of legislative proposals often feel that the formal rules of the congressional process are deliberately designed to prevent their own deserving proposals from ever seeing the light of day, these rules allow Congress to play an important role in lawmaking. If it wants to be more than simply a rubber stamp for the executive branch, like so many other

---

[19]David Lublin, *The Paradox of Representation: Racial Gerrymandering and Minority Interests in Congress* (Princeton, N.J.: Princeton University Press, 1997).

[20]Lani Guinier, *The Tyranny of the Majority: Fundamental Fairness in Representative Democracy* (New York: Free Press, 1995).

representative assemblies around the world, a national legislature like the Congress must develop a division of labor, set an agenda, maintain order through rules and procedures, and place limits on discussion. If it wants to accomplish these things in a representative setting in which a veritable diversity of political preferences exists, then it must find the ways and means to enable cooperation despite the variety of interests and coalitions, and compromises despite conflicts. We will first take up the general issues that face any legislature or decision-making group possessing diverse preferences—the problems of cooperation, coalitions, and compromises.

Cooperation in Congress

A popularly elected legislative assembly—the Boston city council, the Massachusetts legislature, the U.S. Congress, the French National Assembly, or the European Parliament—consists of politicians who harbor a variety of political objectives. Since they got where they are by winning an election, and many hope to stay where they are or possibly advance their political careers, these politicians are intimately aware of whom they must please to do so:

- Because campaigns are expensive propositions, most politicians are eager to please those who can supply resources for the next campaign—financial "fat cats," political action committees, important endorsers, small contributors, party officials, volunteer activists.
- The most recent campaign—one that the politician won—provides her with information about just why the victory was secured. It is sometimes quite difficult to sort out the myriad factors, but at the very least the politician has a good sense of what categories of voters supported her and may be prepared to support her again, if performance is adequate.
- Many politicians aim to please not only campaign contributors and voters; they also have an agenda of their own. Whether for virtuous reasons or evil ones, for private gain or public good, politicians come to the legislature with policy goals of personal importance.

Congress therefore consists of a motley crew of legislators, each motivated by a combination of desires—wanting to please those who control his or her political future and wanting to achieve personal policy goals.

Rationality Principle

The political opinions and policy goals of members of Congress are many and varied.

In a representative democracy the specific public policies that representatives want to pursue are many and varied. We mean this in two respects. First, owing to their different constituencies, legislators will give priority to different realms of public policy. A Cape Cod congressman will be interested in shipping, fishing, coastal preservation, harbor development, tourism, and shipbuilding. A Philadelphia congresswoman may not care much at all about any of those issues, focusing her attention instead on welfare reform, civil rights policy, aid to inner-city school systems, and job retraining programs. Montana's sole member of Congress is probably not interested in coastal preservation, nor in inner-city schools, but rather in issues of ranching, agriculture, mining, and public land use. Congress contains a mélange of legislative priorities.

Congress is also varied in the opinions its members hold on any given issue. While some may care passionately about the issue in question, and others not a whit, there is bound to be conflict, both at the broad philosophical or ideological level and at the practical level, on how to proceed. Thus, while interest in environmental protection ranges from high priority among those who count many Sierra Club members among their constituents to low priority among those who have other fish to fry, once environmental protection is on the agenda there is a broad range of preferences over specific environmental initiatives. Some want pollution discharges carefully monitored and regulated by a relatively powerful environmental watchdog agency. Others believe that more decentralized and less intrusive means, such as marketable pollution permits, are the way to go. Still others think the entire issue is overblown, that any proposed cure is worse than the disease, and that the republic would best be served by leaving well enough alone. The distribution of individual preferences reflects a range of ideal policies.

As a result, diversity in priorities and preferences among legislators is sufficiently abundant that the view of no group of legislators predominates. Legislative consensus must be built—this is what legislative politics is all about. Each legislator clamors to get her priority issue the attention she believes it deserves, or to make sure that her position on a given issue prevails. But neither effort is likely to succeed on its own merits. Support must be assembled, deals consummated, and promises and threats utilized. In short, legislators intent upon achieving their objectives must cooperate, coalesce, and compromise.

Cooperation may be assembled separately on each occasion. But one-shot efforts at cooperating often run into insurmountable difficulties. Cooperating parties are often suspicious, for one thing, and thus guard against being taken advantage of. At the very same time, they contemplate the pros and cons of taking advantage of others. Finally, they loathe having to waste resources on securing compliance each and every time.

Cooperation, especially on recurring matters like congressional votes, is facilitated by *institutionalization*. Indeed, we shall claim that many institutional practices in Congress reflect the requirements of facilitating cooperation. This leads to work being divided and specialized, procedures regularized, specific forms of agenda power and other distinctive advantages delegated, and the interactions fostered by these arrangements monitored to assure compliance with cooperative objectives. All of these organizational features of Congress arise as part of a cooperative governance structure.

Collective Action Principle

Cooperation on recurring matters like congressional votes is facilitated by the institutionalization of legislative structures and procedures.

Other Underlying Problems

Before we can understand why Congress selects particular ways to institutionalize its practices, we need a finer appreciation of other underlying problems with which legislators must grapple.

Matching Influence and Interest Legislatures are highly egalitarian institutions. Each legislator has one vote on any issue coming before the body. Unlike a consumer, who has a cash budget that she may allocate in any way she wishes over categories of consumer goods, a legislator is not given a vote budget in quite the same sense. Instead, his budget of votes is "earmarked"—one vote for each motion before the assembly. He is a bit like a consumer who is given a series of $1 bills, each designated for a different consumer-good category; he cannot aggregate the votes in his possession and cast them all, or some large fraction of them, for a motion on a subject near and dear to his heart (or those of his constituents). This is a source of frustration since, as we have noted, the premise of instrumental behavior means that legislators would, if they could, concentrate whatever resources they commanded on those subjects of highest priority to them.

Information The refrain of many urban legislators in the early twenty-first century, like our Philadelphia congresswoman above, is "more jobs at a living wage." This is a response both to the disappearance of many jobs from most American cities (they gravitate to lower-wage regions of the country or out of the country altogether to lower-wage regions of the world) and to the often unattractive wages, benefits, and career prospects attached to those jobs that remain. Many legislative solutions to this serious problem have been proposed. Some urge a higher minimum wage; some mandate better fringe benefits—health-care coverage, day-care subsidies, pension benefits, parental-leave policies, and so on; some underwrite training programs to improve the productivity of workers; some advocate all these things and more. What works? These are very complicated matters; even those legislators for whom the problems are most pressing are often unsure how to answer this question.

If legislators voted directly for social outcomes, then this wouldn't be a problem at all. The Philadelphia legislator could simply offer a bill "mandating" more jobs at a better wage in urban areas and, if it passed, then—*abracadabra!*—the mandated effects would become a reality. Alas, legislators do not vote for outcomes directly, but rather for *instruments* (or policies) whose effects produce outcomes. Thus legislators, in order to vote intelligently, must know the connection between the instruments they vote for and the effects they desire. In short, they must have information and knowledge about how the world works.

Few legislators—indeed, few people in general—know how the world works in very many policy domains except in the most superficial of ways. Nearly everyone in the legislature would benefit from the production of valuable information—at the very least information that would allow legislators to eliminate policy instruments that make very little difference in solving social problems, or even make matters worse. Producing such information, however, is not a trivial matter. Simply to digest the knowledge that is being produced outside the legislature by knowledge-industry specialists (academics, scientists, journalists, interest groups) is a taxing task. Clearly, institutional arrangements that provide incentives to some legislators to produce, evaluate, and disseminate this knowledge for others will permit public resources to be utilized more effectively.

Compliance   The legislature is not the only game in town. The promulgation of public policies is a joint undertaking in which courts, executives, bureaucrats, and others participate alongside legislators. If the legislature develops no means to monitor what happens after a bill becomes law, then it risks public policies implemented in ways other than those intended when the law was passed. Cooperation does not end with the successful passage of a law. If legislators wish to have an impact on the world around them, especially on those matters to which their constituents give priority, then it is necessary to attend to policy *implementation* as well as policy *formulation*. But it is just not practical for all 435 representatives and all 100 senators to march down to this or that agency at the other end of Pennsylvania Avenue to ensure appropriate implementation by the executive bureaucracy. Compliance will not "just happen," and, like the production and dissemination of reliable information at the policy-formulation stage, the need for oversight of the executive bureaucracy is but an extension of the cooperation that produced legislation in the first place. It, too, must be institutionalized.

What we have tried to suggest in this abstract discussion about legislative institutions and practices is that, first and foremost, Congress is a place in which very different kinds of representatives congregate and try to accomplish things so that they may reap the support of their respective constituents back home. This very diversity is problematic—it requires cooperation, coalitions, and compromise. In addition, there is a mismatch between influence and interest (owing to one person, one vote), information about the effectiveness of alternative policies is in short supply, and the legislature must worry about how its product—public laws—gets treated by other branches of government. These are the problems for which legislatures, of which the U.S. Congress is the preeminent example, devise institutional arrangements to mitigate, if not solve altogether.

We will now examine the organization of Congress and the legislative process, particularly the basic building blocks of congressional organization: political parties, the committee system, congressional staff, the caucuses, and the parliamentary rules of the House and Senate. Each of these factors plays a key role in the organization of Congress and in the process through which Congress formulates and enacts laws. We will also look at other powers Congress has in addition to lawmaking and explore the future role of Congress in relation to the powers of the executive.

Party Leadership in the House and the Senate

One significant aspect of legislative life is not part of the *official* organization at all: political parties. The legislative parties—primarily Democratic and Republican in modern times, but numerous others over the course of American history—are exemplars of organizations that foster cooperation, coalitions, and compromise. They are the vehicles of collective action, both for legislators sharing common policy objectives inside the legislature and for those very same legislators as candidates in periodic election contests back home.[21] In short, political parties in Congress are the fundamental building blocks from which policy coalitions are fashioned to pass legislation and monitor its implementation, thereby providing a track record on which members build electoral support back home.

Every two years, at the beginning of a new Congress, the members of each party gather to elect their House leaders. This gathering is traditionally called the *party caucus,* or conference (by the Republicans). The elected leader of the majority party is later proposed to the whole House and is automatically elected to the position of *Speaker of the House,* with voting along straight party lines. The House majority caucus (or conference) then also elects a *majority leader.* The minority party goes through the same process and selects the *minority leader.* Both parties also elect whips to line up party members on important votes and relay voting information to the leaders.

In December 2002, prior to the opening of the 108th Congress, Democrats and Republicans chose their leaders. House Republicans, who increased their slim majority in the chamber, retained J. Dennis Hastert of Illinois as Speaker. Tom DeLay of Texas, formerly majority whip, moved up to the position of majority leader to replace Dick Armey, who did not run for reelection. Roy Blunt of Missouri was named majority whip to replace DeLay. On the Democratic side, Nancy Pelossi of California became the first woman to lead a major party in Congress when she was elected to replace Dick Gephardt, who left Congress to devote all his attention to a 2004 presidential bid. Steny Hoyer of Maryland was named Democratic whip to replace David Bonior, who left Congress to run (unsuccessfully) for governor of Michigan.

Next in order of importance come the caucus (Democrats) or conference (Republicans) chairs, followed by the Committee on Committees (called the Steering and Policy Committee by the Democrats), whose tasks are to assign new legislators to committees and to deal with the requests of incumbent members for transfers from one committee to another. The Speaker serves as chair of the Republican Committee on Committees, while the minority leader chairs the Democratic Steering and Policy Committee. (The Republicans have a separate Policy Committee.) At one time, party leaders strictly controlled committee assignments, using them to enforce party discipline. Today, representatives expect to receive the assignments they want and resent leadership efforts to control committee assignments. For example, during the 104th Congress (1995–1996) the then-chairman of the powerful Appropriations Committee, Robert Livingston (R-La.), sought to remove freshman Mark Neumann (R-Wisc.) from the

party caucus
A normally closed meeting of a political or legislative group to select candidates, plan strategy, or make decisions regarding legislative matters.

Speaker of the House The chief presiding officer of the House of Representatives. The Speaker is elected at the beginning of every Congress on a straight party vote. The Speaker is the most important party and House leader, and can influence the legislative agenda, the fate of individual pieces of legislation, and members' positions within the House.

majority leader
The elected leader of the party holding a majority of the seats in the House of Representatives or in the Senate. In the House, the majority leader is subordinate in the party hierarchy to the Speaker.

minority leader
The elected leader of the party holding less than a majority of the seats in the House or Senate.

---

[21]For a historically grounded analysis of the development of political parties as well as a treatment of their general contemporary significance, see John H. Aldrich, *Why Parties? The Origin and Transformation of Political Parties in America* (Chicago: University of Chicago Press, 1995). For an analysis of the parties in the legislative process, see Gary W. Cox and Mathew D. McCubbins, *Legislative Leviathan: Party Government in the House* (Berkeley: University of California Press, 1993).

committee because of his lack of party loyalty. The entire Republican freshman class angrily opposed this move and forced the leadership to back down. Not only did Neumann keep his seat on the Appropriations Committee, but he was given a seat on the Budget Committee as well to placate the freshmen.[22] The leadership's best opportunities to use committee assignments as rewards and punishments come when a seat on the same committee is sought by more than one member.

Generally, representatives seek assignments that will allow them to influence decisions of special importance to their districts. Representatives from farm districts, for example, may request seats on the Agriculture Committee.[23] This is one method by which the egalitarian allocation of power in the legislature is overcome. Even though each legislator has just one vote in the full chamber on each and every issue, he or she, by serving on the right committees, is nevertheless able to acquire more influence in areas important to constituents. Seats on powerful committees such as Ways and Means, which is responsible for tax legislation, and Appropriations are especially popular.

Within the Senate, the president pro tempore exercises mainly ceremonial leadership. Usually, the majority party designates the member with the greatest seniority to serve in this capacity. Real power is in the hands of the majority leader and minority leader, each elected by party caucus. The majority and minority leaders, together, control the Senate's calendar, or agenda for legislation. In addition, the senators from each party elect a whip. Each party also selects a Policy Committee, which advises the leadership on legislative priorities. The structure of majority party leadership in the House and Senate is shown in Figures 5.6 and 5.7.

The 2002 elections gave the Republican party a one-seat majority in the Senate. Republicans elected Trent Lott of Mississippi majority leader, while Democrats elected Tom Daschle of South Dakota minority leader. On December 20, however, Lott was forced to step down as majority leader after making comments that many deemed racially insensitive. At a birthday party for Senator Strom Thurmond, Lott suggested that the nation would have been better off if Thurmond's 1948 "Dixiecrat" presidential campaign had been successful. Lott denied any racist intent but could not calm the firestorm of protest. In the wake of Lott's resignation, Republicans elected Tennessee senator Bill Frist to the majority leader's post. Frist is the only physician in the Senate and is a close ally of President George W. Bush.

Combined with the near toss-up in the 2000 presidential election, all the elected national institutions were controlled by the Republicans, but only just. With only a few votes separating the two sides, the majority's control has been

 Rationality Principle

Generally, members of Congress seek committee assignments that allow them to acquire more influence in areas important to their constituents.

---

[22]Linda Killian, *The Freshmen: What Happened to the Republican Revolution?* (Boulder, Col.: Westview, 1998).

[23]Fenno, Jr., *Home Style.* For an extensive discussion of the committee assignment process in the U.S. House, see Kenneth A. Shepsle, *The Giant Jigsaw Puzzle: Democratic Committee Assignments in the Modern House* (Chicago: University of Chicago Press, 1978).

FIGURE 5.6

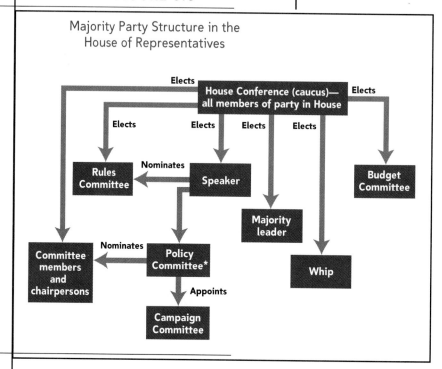

Majority Party Structure in the House of Representatives

Elects
House Conference (caucus)— all members of party in House
Elects

Elects   Elects   Elects   Elects

Rules Committee — Nominates — Speaker

Budget Committee

Majority leader

Committee members and chairpersons — Nominates — Policy Committee*

Whip

Appoints

Campaign Committee

*Includes Speaker (chair), majority leader, chief and deputy whips, caucus chair, four members appointed by the Speaker, and twelve members elected by regional caucuses.

fragile. The possibility of idiosyncratic factors affecting legislative participation—a senator is ill, a winter storm delays a House member's return to the Capitol from her district—necessitates a much greater emphasis on partisan organization in *both* chambers as each party struggles for advantage on nearly every matter coming before these bodies.

In recent years, party leaders have sought to augment their formal powers by reaching outside Congress for resources that might enhance their influence within Congress. One aspect of this external strategy is the increased use of national communications media, including televised speeches and talk-show appearances by party leaders. Former Republican House Speaker Newt Gingrich, for example, used television extensively to generate support for his programs among Republican loyalists.[24] As long as it lasted, Gingrich's support among the

[24]Douglas Harris, "The Public Speaker" (Ph.D. diss., Johns Hopkins University, 1998).

FIGURE 5.7

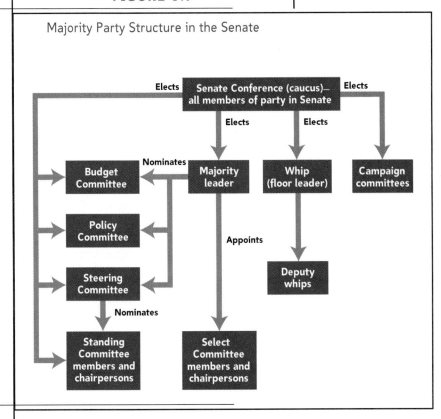

Majority Party Structure in the Senate

Republican rank and file gave him an added measure of influence over Republican members of Congress.

A second external strategy involves fund-raising. In recent years, congressional leaders have frequently established their own political action committees. Interest groups are usually eager to contribute to these "leadership PACs" to curry favor with powerful members of Congress. The leaders, in turn, use these funds to support the various campaigns of their party's candidates in order to create a sense of obligation. For example, in the 1998 congressional election, House majority leader Dick Armey, who was running unopposed, raised more than $6 million, which he distributed to less well-heeled Republican candidates.

Armey's generosity served him well in the leadership struggle that erupted after the election.

In addition to the tasks of organizing Congress, congressional party leaders may also seek to set the legislative agenda. Since the New Deal, presidents have taken the lead in creating legislative agendas (this trend will be discussed in the next chapter). But in recent years congressional leaders, especially when facing a White House controlled by the opposing party, have attempted to devise their own agendas. Democratic leaders of Congress sought to create a common Democratic perspective in 1981 when Ronald Reagan became president. The Republican Congress elected in 1994 expanded on this idea with its "Contract with America." In both cases, the majority party leadership has sought to create a consensus among its congressional members around an overall vision to guide legislative activity and to make individual pieces of legislation part of a bigger picture that is distinct from the agenda of the president. Not only do party leaders have considerable sway over Congress's agenda "in the large," but also they regulate the fine-grained deliberation over specific items on the agenda. This aspect of agenda setting is multifaceted. For example, at the outset, when a bill is initially "dropped in the hopper" as a legislative proposal, the Speaker of the House determines which committee has jurisdiction over the proposal. Indeed, since the mid-1970s, the Speaker has been given additional bill-assignment powers, known as *multiple referral*, permitting him to assign different parts of a bill to different committees or to assign the same parts sequentially or simultaneously to several committees.[25] We have hinted at the steering and agenda setting by party leaders. They work, however, within an institutional framework consisting of structures and procedures. Let's now turn to this "backbone" of Congress, the committee system, and the party leadership's role in guiding it.

Institution Principle

Party leaders have considerable agenda-setting powers.

The Committee System: The Core of Congress

History Principle

The committee system evolved during the early nineteenth century as a means of allowing individual legislators disproportionate influence in areas of policy most important to them.

If the system of leadership in each party and chamber constitutes the first set of organizational arrangements in the U.S. Congress, then the committee system provides it with a second set of organizational structures. But these are more a division- and specialization-of-labor system rather than the hierarchy-of-power system that determines leadership arrangements.

Congress began as a relatively unspecialized assembly, with each legislator participating equally in each and every step of the legislative process in all realms of policy. By the time of the War of 1812, if not earlier, Congress began employing a system of specialists, the committee system, as members with different interests

---

[25]For a now-classic treatment of the ebbs and flows of parties and their leaders in the modern era, see David W. Rohde, *Parties and Leaders in the Postreform House* (Chicago: University of Chicago Press, 1991). For a historical look, see David W. Rohde and Kenneth A. Shepsle, "Leaders and Followers in the House of Representatives: Reflections on Woodrow Wilson's *Congressional Government*," *Congress and the Presidency* 14 (1987): 111–33.

and talents wished to play disproportionate roles in some areas of policy making while ceding influence in other areas in which they were less interested.[26]

The congressional committee system consists of a set of standing committees, each with its own jurisdiction, membership, and authority to act. Each ***standing committee*** is given a permanent status by the official rules, with a fixed membership, officers, rules, staff, offices, and, above all, a jurisdiction that is recognized by all other committees and usually the leadership as well (see Table 5.2). The jurisdiction of each standing committee is defined by the subject matter of legislation. Except for the House Rules Committee, all the important committees receive proposals for legislation and process them into official bills. The House Rules Committee decides the order in which bills come up for a vote and determines the specific rules that govern the length of debate and opportunity for amendments. Standing committees' jurisdictions usually parallel those of the major departments or agencies in the executive branch. There are important exceptions—Appropriations (House and Senate) and Rules (House), for example—but by and large, the division of labor is self-consciously designed to parallel executive-branch organization.

Jurisdiction   Congress is organized into specialized jurisdictions. The world of policy is partitioned into policy jurisdictions, which become the responsibility of committees. The members of the Committee on Armed Services, for example, become specialists in all aspects of military affairs, the subject matter defining their committee's jurisdiction. Committee members tend to have disproportionate influence in their respective jurisdictions, not only because they have become the most knowledgeable members of the legislature in that area of policy, but also because they are given the opportunity to exercise various forms of agenda power—a subject we will develop further in the next section.

Dividing up institutional activities among jurisdictions, thus encouraging participants to specialize, has its advantages. But it has costs, too. If the Armed Services Committee of the House of Representatives had no restraints, its members would undoubtedly shower their own districts with military facilities and contracts. In short, the delegation of authority and resources to specialist subunits exploits the advantages of the division and specialization of labor, but risks jeopardizing collective objectives of the group as a whole.

The monitoring of subunit activities, thus, goes hand in hand with delegation. A political majority either of the full chamber or of the majority party in a chamber can control the assignment of members to committees, the assignment of policy areas to a committee's jurisdiction, and the final disposition of any legislation the committee approves, thereby keeping committees from pursuing a private agenda at the expense of the larger institution.

standing committee   A permanent legislative committee that considers legislation within its designated subject area; the basic unit of deliberation in the House and Senate.

Institution Principle

The committee system is a means of dividing labor and allowing members of Congress to specialize in certain policy areas.

[26]The story of the evolution of the standing committee system in the House and Senate in the early part of the nineteenth century is told in Gerald Gamm and Kenneth A. Shepsle, "Emergence of Legislative Institutions: Standing Committees in the House and Senate, 1810–1825," *Legislative Studies Quarterly* 14 (1989): 39–66.

TABLE 5.2

Standing Committees of Congress

HOUSE COMMITTEES

Agriculture	Judiciary
Appropriations	Resources
Armed Services	Rules
Budget	Science
Education and the Workforce	Small Business
Energy and Commerce	Standards of Official Conduct
Financial Services	Transportation and Infrastructure
Government Reform	Veterans' Affairs
House Administration	Ways and Means
International Relations	

SENATE COMMITTEES

Agriculture, Nutrition, and Forestry	Finance
Appropriations	Foreign Relations
Armed Services	Governmental Affairs
Banking, Housing, and Urban Affairs	Health, Education, Labor, and Pensions
Budget	Judiciary
Commerce, Science, and Transportation	Rules and Administration
Energy and Natural Resources	Small Business
Environment and Public Works	Veterans' Affairs

Sometimes, however, new issues arise that often fit neatly into no jurisdiction. Some, like the issue of energy supplies that emerged during the 1970s, are so multifaceted that bits and pieces of them are spread across many committee jurisdictions. Thus, the Energy and Commerce Committee of the U.S. House of

Representatives had jurisdiction over the regulation of energy prices, the Armed Services Committee dealt with military implications, the Ways and Means Committee dealt with tax-related energy aspects, the Science and Technology Committee claimed jurisdiction over energy research, the Agriculture Committee dealt with grain-to-energy conversion matters, and several other committees picked off still other pieces of this hydra-headed issue. Other issues, like that of regulating tobacco products, fall in the gray area claimed by several different committees—in this case the Energy and Commerce Committee, with its traditional claim over health-related issues, fought with the Agriculture Committee, whose traditional domain includes crops like tobacco, for jurisdiction over this issue. Turf battles between committees of the U.S. Congress are notorious.[27] These battles, often extending over many years, involve committee chairs, the Parliamentarian's Office, the political leadership of the chamber, and, from time to time, select committees appointed to realign committee jurisdictions. All in all, jurisdictional conflict is the raw stuff of politics since, as we shall see, committees with jurisdiction over issues have significant leverage over their resolution.

Authority Committees may be thought of as *agents* of the parent body to whom jurisdiction-specific authority is provisionally delegated. Of what does this delegation consist? In this section, we describe committee authority in terms of gatekeeping and after-the-fact authority.

Normally, any member of the legislature can submit a bill calling for changes in some policy area. Almost automatically, this bill is assigned to the committee of jurisdiction and, very nearly always, there it languishes. In a typical session in the House of Representatives, about 8,000 bills are submitted, fewer than 1,000 of which are acted on by the appropriate committee of jurisdiction. In effect, then, while any member is entitled to make proposals, committees get to decide whether or not to open the gates and allow the bill to be voted on by the full chamber. Related to **gatekeeping authority** is a committee's **proposal power.** After a bill is referred to a committee, the committee may amend the legislation in any way or even write its own legislation before bringing the bill to a vote on the floor. Committees, then, are lords of their jurisdictional domains, setting the table, so to speak, for their parent chamber.[28]

gatekeeping authority The right and power to decide if a change in policy will be considered.

proposal power The capacity to bring a proposal to the full legislature.

---

[27]An outstanding description and analysis of these battles is found in David C. King, "The Nature of Congressional Committee Jurisdictions," *American Political Science Review* 88 (1994): 48-63. See also his *Turf Wars: How Congressional Committees Claim Jurisdiction* (Chicago: University of Chicago Press, 1997).

[28]This clearly gives committee members extraordinary power in their respective jurisdictions, allowing them to push policy into line with their own preferences. But only up to a point. If the abuse of their agenda power becomes excessive, the parent body has structural and procedural remedies available to counteract this—like stacking the committee with more compliant members, deposing a particularly obstreperous committee chair, or removing policies from a committee's jurisdiction. These are the "clubs behind the door" that only rarely have to be employed; their mere presence suffices to keep committees from the more outrageous forms of advantage taking.

after-the-fact authority The authority to follow up on the fate of a proposal once it has been approved by the full chamber.

 Institution Principle
Among the powers delegated to committees are gatekeeping authority, bargaining with the other chamber, and oversight.

conference committee A joint committee created to work out a compromise for House and Senate versions of a piece of legislation.

oversight The effort by Congress, through hearings, investigations, and other techniques, to exercise control over the activities of executive agencies.

A committee also has responsibilities for bargaining with the other chamber and for conducting oversight or **after-the-fact authority.** Because many legislatures are bicameral—the U.S. Congress, for instance, has a House and a Senate—once one chamber passes a bill, it must be transmitted for consideration to the other chamber. If the other chamber passes a bill different from the one passed in the first chamber, and the first chamber refuses to accept the changes made, then the two chambers ordinarily meet in a **conference committee** in which representatives from each chamber hammer out a compromise. In the wide majority of cases, conferees are drawn from the committees that had original jurisdiction over the bill. For example, in a sample of Congresses in the 1980s, of the 1,388 House members who served as conferees for various bills during a three-year period, only 7 were not on the committee of original jurisdiction; similarly, in the Senate on only 7 of 1,180 occasions were conferees not drawn from the "right" committee.[29] The committee's effective authority to represent its chamber in conference-committee proceedings constitutes after-the-fact power that complements its before-the-fact gatekeeping and proposal powers.

A second manifestation of after-the-fact committee authority consists of the committee's primacy in legislative **oversight** of policy implementation by the executive bureaucracy. Even after a bill becomes a law, it is not always (indeed, it is rarely) self-implementing. Executive agents—bureaucrats in the career civil service, commissioners in regulatory agencies, political appointees in the executive branch—march to their own drummers. Unless legislative actors hold their feet to the fire, they may not do precisely what the law requires (especially in light of the fact that statutes are often vague and ambiguous). Given this possibility, the Legislative Reorganization Act of 1946, a law that reformed and redefined how the House and Senate have conducted their business through most of the postwar period, instructed congressional committees to be "continuously watchful" of the manner in which legislation is implemented and administered. Committees of jurisdiction play this after-the-fact role by allocating committee staff and resources to keep track of what the executive branch is doing and, from time to time, holding oversight hearings in which particular policies and programs are given intense scrutiny. Anticipating this surveillance, and knowing what grief a congressional committee can cause an executive-branch agent found deviating from what legislators want, these officials are very keen to keep their congressional "masters" content. This, in turn, gives congressional committees an additional source of leverage over policy in their jurisdictions.

Subcommittees Committees, in effect, are legislatures writ small; they have the corresponding motive to divide business and specialize labor. Thus, the roughly twenty standing committees of the U.S. House are, in turn, divided into about a hundred, even more specialized *subcommittees*. With so many of the Montana

[29]See Kenneth A. Shepsle and Barry R. Weingast, "The Institutional Foundations of Committee Power," *American Political Science Review* 81 (1987), pp. 85–104.

congressman's constituents involved in growing wheat, for example, he could best serve them—and best position himself to secure their votes in the next election—if he were not only a member of the Agriculture Committee, but also on its Subcommittee on Feedgrains. These subcommittees serve their full committees in precisely the same manner the full committees serve the parent chamber. Thus, in their narrow jurisdictions, they have gatekeeping, proposal, interchamber bargaining, and oversight powers. In order for a bill on wheat to be taken up by the full Agriculture Committee, it first has to clear the Feedgrains Subcommittee. All of the issues involving assignments, jurisdictions, amendment control, and monitoring that we discussed earlier regarding full committees apply at the subcommittee level as well.

Hierarchy   At the committee level, the mantle of leadership falls on the committee chair. He or she determines, together with party leaders, the committee's agenda and then orchestrates the proceedings of the committee's staff, investigatory resources, and subcommittee structure.[30] This includes scheduling hearings, marking up bills—that is, transforming legislative drafts into final versions—and scripting the process by which a bill goes from introduction to final passage. For many years, the Congress followed a rigid *seniority* rule for the selection of these chairs. Accordingly, a person was elevated to the chair if he or she was the majority-party member with the longest continuous service on the committee. The benefits of this rule are twofold. First, the chair will be occupied by someone knowledgeable in the committee's jurisdiction, familiar with interest group and executive-branch players, and politically experienced. Second, the larger institution will be spared divisive leadership contests that often reduce the legislative process to efforts in vote grubbing by contenders. There are costs, however. Senior individuals may well be knowledgeable, familiar, and experienced, as suggested above; but they also may be unenergetic, out of touch, even senile. Even when these liabilities do not appear, senior members may nevertheless be out of step with their committee and the parent chamber. Despite the fact that, from the time of the 1965 Voting Rights Act to the Republican Revolution of 1994, old-fashioned southern conservatives have been a declining force within the Democratic party, those that remained benefited from a seniority system that elevated them to chairmanships. It was, thus, not at all unusual for a committee consisting chiefly of northern and "New South" Democrats to be run by a southerner who had been around for thirty years.

Different legislatures make the trade-off differently between seniority-rule automatic elevation, with its profile of benefits and costs, and leadership election, the main alternative to seniority. The U.S. House operated according to a strict seniority principle from about 1910 until the mid-1970s, when most members felt that the burdens of this arrangement were beginning to outweigh

seniority   Priority or status ranking given to an individual on the basis of length of continuous service on a congressional committee.

---

[30]Since subcommittee chairs do essentially the same things in their narrower jurisdictions, we won't provide a separate discussion of them.

its advantages.[31] Committee chairs are now elected by the majority-party members of the full legislature, though there remains a presumption (which may be rebutted) that the most senior committee member will normally assume the chair.

Monitoring Committees   If unchecked, committees could easily take advantage of their authority. Indeed, what prevents committees from exploiting their before-the-fact proposal power and their after-the-fact bargaining and oversight authority? As we saw in Chapter 1 in our discussion of the principal-agent problem, principals must be certain that agents are *properly motivated* to serve the principal's interests, either by actually sharing the principal's interest themselves or by deriving something of value (reputation, compensation, etc.) for acting to advance that interest. Alternatively, the principal will need to have some instruments by which to monitor and validate what his or her agent is doing, rewarding or punishing the agent accordingly.

Consider again the example of congressional committees. The House or Senate delegates responsibility to its Committee on Agriculture to recommend legislative policy in the field of agriculture. Not surprisingly, legislators from farm districts are most eager to get onto this committee, and, for the most part, their wishes are accommodated. The Committee on Agriculture, consequently, is composed mainly of these farm legislators. And non-farm legislators are relieved at not having to spend their time on issues of little material interest to themselves or their constituents. In effecting this delegation, however, the parent legislature is putting itself in the hands of its farm colleagues, benefiting from their expertise on farm-related matters, to be sure, but laying itself open to the danger of planting the fox squarely in the henhouse. The Committee on Agriculture will have become not only a collection of specialists, but also a collection of *advocates* for farm interests. How can the parent body know for certain that a recommendation from that committee is not more a reflection of its advocacy than of its expertise? This is the risk inherent in principal-agent relationships.

And it is for this reason that the parent legislature maintains a variety of tools and instruments to protect itself from being exploited by its agents. First, it does not allow committees to make final decisions on agriculture policy, but only *recommendations*, which the parent legislature retains the authority to accept, amend, or reject. A committee has agenda power, but it is not by itself decisive. Second, the parent body relies on the committee's concern for its own reputation. Making a recommendation on a piece of legislation is not a one-shot action; the committee knows it will return to the parent body time and time again with legislative recommendations, and it will not want to tarnish its repu-

---

[31]In 1972, the Democratic caucus approved caucus-wide election of committee chairs even though it was assumed at the time that no incumbent, previously elevated to a chair because of seniority, would lose his or her chairmanship. This in fact occurred, though John L. McMillan (D-S.C.), chair of the District of Columbia Committee, attracted considerable opposition. After the 1974 elections, on the other hand, three committee chairs were defeated (and a fourth resigned to avoid defeat).

tation for expertise by too much advocacy. Third, the parent body relies on *competing* agents—interest groups, expert members not on the committee, legislative specialists in the other chamber of the legislature, executive-branch specialists, and even academics—to keep its own agents honest. In sum, a principal—in this case, the House or Senate—will balance the benefits of delegation against the risks, utilizing specialized agents and delegating authority to them, but doing so prudently.

Institution Principle

The House and Senate have methods of keeping committees in check.

Nevertheless, a principal will not bother to eliminate *entirely* these prospective deviations from his or her interests by agents who have interests of their own. A principal will suffer some **agency loss** from having delegated authority to a "hired hand"; therefore, nearly all principal-agent relationships will be imperfect in some respects from the principal's perspective. Agents will be in a position to extract some advantage from the privileged relationship they have with their principal—not too much or it will undermine the relationship altogether, but enough to diminish the benefits of the relationship a bit from the principal's point of view. The Committee on Agriculture, for example, cannot get away with spending huge proportions of the federal budget on agricultural subsidies to farmers. But they can insert small things into agriculture bills from time to time—an experimental grain-to-fuel conversion project in an important legislator's state or district, for example, or special funds to the U.S. trade representative to give priority to agriculture trade issues.

agency loss The difference between what a principal would like an agent to do and the agent's actual performance.

While the parent body, as we suggested, will find it worth its while to keep an eye on the Agriculture Committee in order to guard against egregious behavior, it won't be worth its while to take action on every single instance of indulgence by the committee. The reason is *transaction costs* (see Chapter 1). If the cure for agency loss is worse than the disease, then some agency loss will be tolerated. The great advantage to legislators of delegating authority for making recommendations on agriculture policy to specialist legislators interested in this subject is the freedom the delegating legislators win to pursue their own interests. They certainly don't want to spend much of their newly found time and freed-up resources watching over the shoulders of their experts. The cost of doing that—the transaction cost of monitoring and oversight—gets excessive if perfection is the objective. Imperfect principal-agent relationships survive and prosper from a pragmatic willingness that "the best not be the enemy of the good."

Committee Reform Over the years, Congress has reformed its organizational structure and operating procedures. Most changes have been made to improve efficiency, but some reforms have also represented a response to political considerations. In the 1970s, for example, a series of reforms substantially altered the organization of power in Congress. Among the most important changes put into place at that time were an increase in the number of subcommittees; greater autonomy for subcommittee chairs; the opening of most committee deliberations to the public; and a system of multiple referral of bills that allowed several committees to consider one bill at the same time. One of the driving impulses behind these reforms was an effort to reduce the power of committee chairs. In the past, committee chairs exercised considerable power; they determined hearing schedules, selected subcommittee members, and appointed committee staff. Some chairs used their power to block consideration of bills they opposed. Because of the seniority system, many of the key committees, as we saw earlier, were chaired by conservative southern Democrats who stymied liberal legislation throughout the 1960s and early 1970s. By enhancing subcommittee power and allowing more members to chair subcommittees and appoint subcommittee staff, the reforms undercut the power of committee chairs.

Yet the reforms of the 1970s created unintended consequences for Congress. One of these reforms, the opening of most committee hearings to the public—sometimes called a "sunshine" rule—is frequently criticized by members of Congress. Most members believe that "sunshine" makes deliberation difficult—because members "grandstand" for the TV camera—and renders compromise impossible because rival constituency groups often view any compromise as a betrayal of principle.[32] As a consequence of the reforms, power became more fragmented, making it harder to reach agreement on legislation. With power dissipated over a large number of committees and subcommittees, members spent more time in unproductive "turf battles."[33] In addition, as committees expanded in size, members found they had so many committee meetings that they had to run from meeting to meeting. Thus their ability to specialize in a particular policy area diminished as their responsibilities increased.[34] The Republican leadership of the 104th Congress sought to reverse the fragmentation of congressional power and concentrate more authority in the party leadership. One of the ways the House achieved this was by abandoning the principle of seniority in the selection of a number of committee chairs, appointing them instead according to their loyalty to the party. This move tied committee chairs more closely to the leadership. In addition, the Republican leadership eliminated 25 of the House's 115 subcommittees and gave committee chairs more power over their subcommittees. The result was an unusually cohesive congressional majority, which pushed forward a common agenda. In 1995, House Republicans also agreed to impose a three-term limit on committee and subcommittee heads. As a result, all the chairmen were replaced in 2001 when the 107th Congress convened. In many instances, chairmen were replaced by the most senior Republican committee member, but the net result was some redistribution of power in the House of Representatives.

[32]See, for example, Dale Bumpers, "How the Sunshine Harmed Congress," *New York Times*, 3 January 1999, p. 9.

[33]See King, *Turf Wars*.

[34]See Thomas E. Mann and Norman J. Ornstein, *Renewing Congress: A First Report of the Renewing Congress Project* (Washington, D.C.: American Enterprise Institute and Brookings Institution, 1992). See also the essays in Roger H. Davidson, ed., *The Postreform Congress* (New York: St. Martin's, 1992).

The Staff System: Staffers and Agencies

A congressional institution second in importance only to the committee system is the staff system. Every member of Congress employs a large number of staff members, whose tasks include handling constituency requests and, to a large and growing extent, dealing with legislative details and the activities of administrative agencies. Increasingly, staffers bear the primary responsibility for formulating and drafting proposals, organizing hearings, dealing with administrative agencies, and negotiating with lobbyists. Indeed, legislators typically deal with one another through staff, rather than through direct, personal contact. Representatives and senators together employ nearly eleven thousand staffers in their Washington and home offices. Today, staffers even develop policy ideas, draft legislation, and, in some instances, have a good deal of influence over the legislative process.

In addition to the personal staffs of individual senators and representatives, Congress also employs roughly two thousand committee staffers. These individuals comprise the permanent staff, who stay regardless of turnover in Congress and are attached to every House and Senate committee. They are responsible for organizing and administering the committee's work, including research, scheduling, organizing hearings, and drafting legislation. Congressional staffers can come to play key roles in the legislative process. One example of the importance of congressional staffers is the so-called Gephardt health-care reform bill, named for the then-House majority leader Richard Gephardt of Missouri, and introduced in August 1994. Though the bill bore Gephardt's name, it was actually crafted by a small group of staff members of the House Ways and Means Committee. These aides, under the direction of David Abernathy, the staff's leading health-care specialist, debated methods of cost control, service delivery, the role of the insurance industry, and the needs of patients, and listened to hundreds of lobbyists before drafting the complex Gephardt bill.[35]

The number of congressional staff members grew rapidly during the 1960s and 1970s, leveled off in the 1980s, and decreased dramatically in 1995. This sudden drop fulfilled the Republican congressional candidates' 1994 campaign promise to reduce the size of committee staffs.

Not only does Congress employ personal and committee staff, but it has also established three ***staff agencies*** designed to provide the legislative branch with resources and expertise independent of the executive branch. These agencies enhance Congress's capacity to oversee administrative agencies and to evaluate presidential programs and proposals. They are the Congressional Research Service, which performs research for legislators who wish to know the facts and competing arguments relevant to policy proposals or other legislative business; the General Accounting Office, through which Congress can investigate the financial and administrative affairs of any government agency or program; and the

staff agency An agency responsible for providing Congress with independent expertise, administration, and oversight capability.

---

[35]Robert Pear, "With Long Hours and Little Fanfare, Staff Members Crafted a Health Bill," *New York Times*, 6 August 1994, p. 7.

Congressional Budget Office, which assesses the economic implications and likely costs of proposed federal programs, such as health care reform proposals.

Informal Organization: The Caucuses

In addition to the official organization of Congress, there also exists an unofficial organizational structure—the caucuses, formally known as legislative service organizations (LSOs). **Caucuses** are groups of senators or representatives who share certain opinions, interests, or social characteristics. They include ideological caucuses such as the liberal Democratic Study Group, the conservative Democratic Forum (popularly known as the "boll weevils"), and the moderate Republican Wednesday Group. At the same time, there are a large number of caucuses composed of legislators representing particular economic or policy interests, such as the Travel and Tourism Caucus, the Steel Caucus, the Mushroom Caucus, and the Concerned Senators for the Arts. Legislators who share common backgrounds or social characteristics have organized caucuses such as the Congressional Black Caucus, the Congressional Caucus for Women's Issues, and the Hispanic Caucus. All these caucuses seek to advance the interests of the groups they represent by promoting legislation, encouraging Congress to hold hearings, and pressing administrative agencies for favorable treatment. The Congressional Black Caucus, for example, which included forty representatives and one senator in 1996, has played an active role in Congress since 1970.

caucus An association of members of Congress based on party, interest, or social group such as gender or race.

RULES OF LAWMAKING: HOW A BILL BECOMES A LAW

The institutional structure of Congress is one key factor that helps to shape the legislative process. A second and equally important set of factors are the rules of congressional procedures. These rules govern everything from the introduction of a bill through its submission to the president for signing. Not only do these regulations influence the fate of each and every bill, they also help to determine the distribution of power in the Congress.

Committee Deliberation

Even if a member of Congress, the White House, or a federal agency has spent months developing and drafting a piece of legislation, it does not become a bill until it is submitted officially by a senator or representative to the clerk of the House or Senate and referred to the appropriate committee for deliberation. No floor action on any bill can take place until the committee with jurisdiction over it has taken all the time it needs to deliberate. During the course of its deliberations, the committee typically refers the bill to one of its subcommittees, which may hold hearings, listen to expert testimony, and amend the proposed legislation before referring it to the full committee for its consideration. The full committee may accept the recommendation of the subcommittee or hold its own hearings and prepare its own amendments. Or, even more frequently, the committee and subcommittee may do little or nothing with a bill that has been submitted to them. Many bills are simply allowed to "die in committee" with little or no serious consideration given to them. Often, members of Congress introduce legislation that they neither expect nor desire to see enacted into law, merely to please a constituency group. This is what the political scientist David R. Mayhew refers to as "position taking."[36] These bills die a quick and painless death. Other pieces of legislation have ardent supporters and die in committee only after a long battle. But, in either case, most bills are never reported out of the committees to which they are assigned. In a typical congressional session, 85 to 90 percent of the roughly eight thousand bills introduced die in committee— an indication of the power of the congressional committee system.

Once the bill's assigned committee or committees in the House of Representatives have acted affirmatively, the whole bill or various parts of it are transmitted to the Rules Committee, which determines the specific rules under which the legislation will be considered by the full House. Here the Speaker influences when debate will be scheduled, for how long, what amendments will be in order, and in what order they will be considered. The Speaker also rules on all procedural points of order and points of information raised during the debate. A bill's supporters generally prefer what is called a **_closed rule,_** which puts severe limits on floor debate and amendments. Opponents of a bill usually prefer an **_open rule,_** which permits potentially damaging floor debate and makes it easier to add amendments that may cripple the bill or weaken its chances for passage. Thus, the outcome of the Rules Committee's deliberations can be extremely important, and the committee's hearings can be an occasion for sharp conflicts.

Debate

Party control of the agenda is reinforced by the rule giving the Speaker of the House and the majority leader of the Senate the power of recognition during debate on a bill. Usually the chair knows the purpose for which a member intends to speak well in advance of the occasion. Spontaneous efforts to gain recognition are often foiled. For example, the Speaker may ask, "For what purpose does the member rise?" before deciding whether to grant recognition. In general, the party leadership in the House has total control over debate. In the Senate, each member has substantial power to block the close of debate. A House majority can override opposition, while it takes an *extraordinary* majority (a three-fifths vote) to close debate in the Senate; thus, the Senate tends to be far more tolerant in debate, far more accommodating of various views, and far less partisan.

In the House, virtually all of the time allotted by the Rules Committee for debate on a given bill is controlled by the bill's sponsor and by its leading opponent.

[36]David R. Mayhew, *Congress: The Electoral Connection* (New Haven: Yale University Press, 1974).

 Institution Principle

The Rules Committee's decision about whether to adopt a closed or open rule for floor debate greatly influences a bill's chances for passage.

closed rule Provision by the House Rules Committee prohibiting the introduction of amendments during debate.

open rule Provision by the House Rules Committee that permits floor debate and the addition of new amendments to a bill.

In almost every case, these two people are the committee chair and the ranking minority member of the committee that processed the bill—or those they designate. These two participants are, by rule and tradition, granted the power to allocate most of the debate time in small amounts to members who are seeking to speak for or against the measure. Preference in the allocation of time goes to the members of the committee whose jurisdiction covers the bill.

In the Senate, other than the power of recognition, the leadership has much less control over floor debate. Indeed, the Senate is unique among the world's legislative bodies for its commitment to unlimited debate. Once given the floor, a senator may speak as long as he or she wishes. On a number of memorable occasions, senators have used this right to prevent action on legislation that they opposed. Through this tactic, called the ***filibuster***, small minorities or even one individual in the Senate can force the majority to give in to their demands. During the 1950s and 1960s, for example, opponents of civil rights legislation often sought to block its passage by adopting the tactic of filibuster. The votes of three-fifths of the Senate, or sixty votes, are needed to end a filibuster. This procedure is called ***cloture***.

Although it is the best known, the filibuster is not the only technique used to block Senate debate. Under Senate rules, members have a virtually unlimited ability to propose amendments to a pending bill. Each amendment must be voted on before the bill can come to a final vote. The introduction of new amendments can only be stopped by unanimous consent. This, in effect, can permit a determined minority to filibuster-by-amendment, indefinitely delaying the passage of a bill.

Senators can also place "holds," or stalling devices, on bills to delay debate. Senators place holds on bills when they fear that openly opposing them will be unpopular. Because holds are kept secret, the senators placing the holds do not have to take public responsibility for their actions.

Once a bill is debated on the floor of the House and the Senate, the leaders schedule it for a vote on the floor of each chamber. By this time, congressional leaders know what the vote will be; leaders do not bring legislation to the floor unless they are fairly certain it is going to pass. As a consequence, it is unusual for the leadership to lose a bill on the floor. On rare occasions, the last moments of the floor vote can be very dramatic, as each party's leadership puts its whip organization into action to make sure that wavering members vote with the party.

Conference Committee: Reconciling House and Senate Versions of a Bill

Getting a bill out of committee and through one of the houses of Congress is no guarantee that a bill will be enacted into law. Frequently, bills that began with similar provisions in both chambers emerge with little resemblance to each other. Alternatively, a bill may be passed by one chamber but undergo substantial revision in the other chamber. In such cases, a conference committee composed of the senior members of the committees or subcommittees that initiated

filibuster A tactic used by members of the Senate to prevent action on legislation they oppose by continuously holding the floor and speaking until the majority backs down. Once given the floor, senators have unlimited time to speak, and it requires a cloture vote of three-fifths of the Senate to end the filibuster.

cloture A rule allowing a majority of two-thirds or three-fifths of the members in a legislative body to set a time limit on debate over a given bill.

the bills may be required to iron out differences between the two pieces of legislation. Sometimes members or leaders will let objectionable provisions pass on the floor with the idea that they will get the change they want in conference. Usually, conference committees meet behind closed doors. Agreement requires a majority of each of the two delegations. Legislation that emerges successfully from a conference committee is more often a compromise than a clear victory of one set of forces over another.

When a bill comes out of conference, it faces one more hurdle. Before a bill can be sent to the president for signing, the House-Senate conference report must be approved on the floor of each chamber. Usually such approval is given quickly. Occasionally, however, a bill's opponents use the conference report as one last opportunity to defeat a piece of legislation.

Collective Action Principle
If a bill passes both the House and Senate, the differences need to be ironed out in a conference committee.

Presidential Action

Once adopted by the House and Senate, a bill goes to the president, who may choose to sign the bill into law or **veto** it (see Process Box 5.2). The veto is the president's constitutional power to reject a piece of legislation. To veto a bill, the president returns it within ten days to the house of Congress in which it originated, along with his objections to the bill. If Congress adjourns during the ten-day period and the president has taken no action, the bill is also considered to be vetoed. This latter method is known as the **pocket veto.** The possibility of a presidential veto affects how willing members of Congress are to push for different pieces of legislation at different times. If they think a proposal is likely to be vetoed, they might shelve it for a later time. Alternatively, the sponsors of a popular bill opposed by the president might push for passage in order to force the president to pay the political costs of vetoing it.[37] For example, in 1996 and 1997, Republicans passed bills outlawing partial-birth abortions even though they knew President Clinton would veto them. The GOP calculated that Clinton would be hurt politically by vetoing legislation that most Americans favored.

A presidential veto may be overridden by a two-thirds vote in both the House and Senate. A veto override says much about the support that a president can expect from Congress, and it can deliver a stinging blow to the executive branch. Presidents will often back down from a veto threat if they believe that Congress will override the veto.

veto The president's constitutional power to turn down acts of Congress. A presidential veto may be overridden by a two-thirds vote of each house of Congress.

pocket veto A method by which the president vetoes a bill by taking no action on it when Congress has adjourned.

The Distributive Tendency in Congress

In order to pass a policy, it is necessary to *authorize* the policy—that is, to provide statutory authority to a government agency to implement the legislation—and then to provide *appropriations* to fund the implementation. It is not too much of

[37]John B. Gilmour, *Strategic Disagreement: Stalemate in American Politics* (Pittsburgh: University of Pittsburgh Press, 1995).

How a Bill Becomes a Law

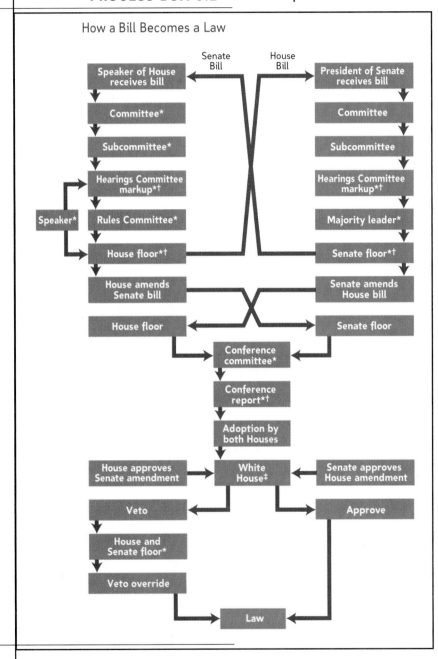

*Points at which bill can be amended.
†Points at which bill can die.
‡If the president neither signs nor vetoes the bill within ten days, it automatically becomes law.

an exaggeration to suggest the following list of political actors whose support is necessary in order to get a measure through Congress and signed into law:

- a majority of the authorizing subcommittees in House and Senate (probably including the subcommittee chairs)
- a majority of the full authorizing committees in House and Senate (probably including committee chairs)
- a majority of the appropriations subcommittees in House and Senate (probably including the subcommittee chairs)
- a majority of the full appropriations committees in House and Senate (probably including committee chairs)
- a majority of the House Rules Committee (including its chair)
- a majority of the full House
- a majority—possibly as many as sixty votes, if needed to shut off a filibuster—of the Senate
- the Speaker and majority leader in the House
- the majority leader in the Senate
- the president

This list constitutes an extraordinarily large number of public officials. Some of them may go along without requiring much for their states or districts in the bill on the assumption that their turn will come on another bill. But most of these politicians will need some form of "compensation" to provide their endorsement and support.

With so many hurdles to clear for a legislative initiative to become a public law, the benefits must be spread broadly. It is as though a bill must travel on a toll road past a number of tollbooths, each one containing a collector with his or her hand out for payment. On rare occasions, the required toll is in the form of a personal bribe—a contract to a firm run by a congressman's brother, a job for a senator's son, a boondoggle "military inspection" trip to some exotic Pacific isle for a legislator and spouse. Occasionally, there is a "wink and a nod" understanding, usually given by the majority leader or committee chair, that support from a legislator today will result in reciprocal support for legislation of interest to him or her down the road. Most frequently, features of the bill are drafted initially or revised so as to be more inclusive, spreading the benefits widely among beneficiaries. This is the ***distributive tendency.***

The distributive tendency is part of the American system of representative democracy. It is as American as apple pie! Legislators, in advocating the interests of their constituents, are eager to advertise their ability to deliver for their state or district. They maneuver to put themselves in a position to claim credit for good things that happen there and to duck blame for bad things. This is the way they earn trust back home, deter strong challengers in upcoming elections, and defeat those who do run against them. This means that legislators must take advantage of every opportunity that presents itself. In some instances, the results may seem bizarre. For example, in April 2003, Senator Thad Cochran (R-Miss.)

distributive tendency The tendency of Congress to spread the benefits of a policy over a wide range of members' districts.

Why Congress Cannot Get Things Done

If you want to know how to get something done, you need to know who can stop you. In the language of institutional analysis, "veto points" are wielded by individuals (but they may also be groups, committees, courts, etc.) who must approve any change to the status quo.[38] If a change from the status quo is a form of *collective action,* then it is possible to set rules that make change easier or harder. To take an extreme example, dictatorships have a distinct advantage over democracies: they can get things done quickly. A huge "electronic democracy," in comparison, could be highly egalitarian and participatory, but it's unlikely that in today's complex society, New England meetings on a grand scale could agree on anything.

In American democracy, we err on the side of making it hard to get things done. Our democracy privileges individual and minority rights. The Federalists were suspicious of governmental power and especially worried about legislative power, so they created a set of *rules and procedures* that would make it difficult to change the status quo.[39]

Our bicameral legislature promotes stability yet is problematic when major policy needs to be enacted. The slowing of the legislative process can prevent initially popular but potentially destructive policies and precedents from being enacted. Examples of this include Franklin Roosevelt's court-packing plan, the controversy following Harry Truman's dismissal of Douglas MacArthur, and Thomas Jefferson's attempt to impeach Justice Samuel Chase. The prerogative for unlimited debate can also turn the Senate into a graveyard for important bills. The most famous example might be the ability of southern Senators to halt the passage of major civil rights legislation for nearly one hundred years. Originally, there was no procedural way to end debate, but since 1917 the Senate has adopted a cloture rule. Invoking cloture limits debate and can force a vote. However, cloture requires 60 votes, not a simple majority. This means that the operational majority required to pass legislation in the Senate is 60, not 51, votes.

In the language of *institutional analysis,* the United States Congress has many more veto points than other advanced industrial democracies. Any piece of legislation, for example, must obtain a majority in both the House, whose members are elected from relatively homogeneous and small (half million) districts, and the Senate, whose members vary from those elected from California, Texas, and Florida to those who ran in districts contiguous to House districts (Delaware, Wyoming, South Dakota). Why was the Congress designed in this way? The Senate was designed to give disproportionate representation to minority interests. House seats are allotted in proportion to states' populations, but each state gets two senators, no more and no less.

The House was designed to be the "people's branch" of government, representing the will of the majority. Power is highly concentrated in the ruling party. Bills can be enacted quickly, and the majority can ride roughshod over the minority. This often leads to complaints from the minority that they are being ignored. After the Republicans took over the House in 1994, they promised to end perceived abuses of majority power. But they have not followed through on many of these promises. The tools of procedural control are too important to getting things done.

In contrast, the Senate is a bastion of minority power, but it can also be frustratingly devoted to its own institutional prerogatives. Over time, the Senate has never developed the elaborate rules and procedures of the House. There is no Senate equivalent to the House's Rules Committee. The Senate has a long tradition of unlimited debate. As illustrated in popular lore, such as the famous movie *Mr. Smith Goes to Washington,* this means that a heroic individual senator can stand up for truth, justice, and the American way. The modern filibuster, however, bears little resemblance to Jimmy Stewart speaking in the well of the Senate. Instead, senators propose an endless series of dilatory motions to stall the progress of the institution.

Some celebrate the U.S. legislative system. The American political system is heavily tilted toward the status quo. The government is unlikely to change in response to superficial changes in public sentiments. But this also creates the impression of gridlock. Another advantage of our system is greater representation of minority interests. But the accompanying disadvantage is the potential to frustrate the will of the majority. Conflict between the two chambers is exacerbated by the different sets of rules that they employ. The differences between the rules of the House and Senate reflect the different purposes of each.[40]

[38]George Tsebelis, *Veto Players: How Political Institutions Work* (Princeton, N.J.: Princeton University Press, 2002).

[39]See Clinton Rossiler, ed., *The Federalist Papers* (New York: New American Library, 1961), especially Nos. 10 and 51.

[40]For further comparisons, see Ross K. Baker, *House and Senate,* 3rd ed. (New York: W. W. Norton, 2002).

---

was able to insert language into the bill funding the war in Iraq that provided $250 million for "disaster relief" for southern catfish farmers.[41] Most Americans would never have guessed that driving Saddam Hussein from power would have an effect upon catfish farmers in Mississippi.

This system, which is practiced in Washington and most state capitals, means that political pork gets spread around; it is not controlled by a small clique of politicians or concentrated in a small number of states or districts. But it also means that public authority and appropriations are not targeted where they are most needed. The most impoverished cities do not get as much money as is appropriate because some of the money must be diverted elsewhere to buy political support. The most needy individuals often do not get tax relief, health care,

Policy Principle

The distributive tendency in Congress results from the need for a broad base of support in order for a bill to be passed.

[41]Dan Morgan, "War Funding Bill's Extra Riders," *Washington Post,* 8 April 2003, p. A4.

or occupational subsidies for reasons unrelated to philosophy or policy grounds. It is the distributive tendency at work. It is one of the unintended consequences of the separation of powers and the multiple veto.

HOW CONGRESS DECIDES

What determines the kinds of legislation that Congress ultimately produces? According to the simplest theories of representation, members of Congress respond to the views of their constituents. In fact, the process of creating a legislative agenda, drawing up a list of possible measures, and deciding among them is very complex, one in which a variety of influences from inside and outside government play important roles. External influences include a legislator's constituency and various interest groups. Influences from inside government include party leadership, congressional colleagues, and the president. Let us examine each of these influences individually and then consider how they interact to produce congressional policy decisions.

Policy Principle

Multiple factors influence how a member of Congress votes on legislation. These include constituency, interest groups, party leaders, congressional colleagues, and the president.

Constituency

Because members of Congress, for the most part, want to be re-elected, we would expect the views of their constituents to have a key influence on the decisions that legislators make. Yet constituency influence is not so straightforward as we might think. In fact, most constituents do not even know what policies their representatives support. The number of citizens who *do* pay attention to such matters—the attentive public—is usually very small. Nonetheless, members of Congress spend a lot of time worrying about what their constituents think because these representatives realize that the choices they make may be scrutinized in a future election and used as ammunition by an opposing candidate. Because of this possibility, members of Congress will try to anticipate their constituents' policy views.[42] Legislators are more likely to act in accordance with those views if they think that voters will take them into account during elections. In this way, constituents may affect congressional policy choices even when there is little direct evidence of their influence.

Interest Groups

Collective Action Principle

Interest groups with the ability to mobilize followers in many congressional districts are especially influential in Congress.

Interest groups are another important external influence on the policies that Congress produces. When members of Congress are making voting decisions, those interest groups that have some connection to constituents in particular members' districts are most likely to be influential. For this reason, interest groups with the ability to mobilize followers in many congressional districts may

[42]See John W. Kingdon, *Congressmen's Voting Decisions* (New York: Harper & Row, 1973). Chapter 3; and R. Douglas Arnold. *The Logic of Congressional Action* (New Haven: Yale University Press, 1990).

be especially influential in Congress. The small-business lobby, for example, played an important role in defeating President Clinton's proposal for comprehensive health-care reform in 1993–1994. The mobilization of networks of small businesses across the country meant that virtually every member of Congress had to take their views into account.

In the 2000 electoral cycle, many millions of dollars in campaign contributions were given by interest groups and political action committees (PACs) to incumbent legislators and challengers. What does this money buy? A popular conception is that campaign contributions buy votes. In this view, legislators vote for whichever proposal favors the bulk of their contributors. Although the vote-buying hypothesis makes for good campaign rhetoric, it has little factual support. Empirical studies by political scientists show little evidence that contributions from large PACs influence legislative voting patterns.[43]

If contributions don't buy votes, then what do they buy? Our claim is that campaign contributions influence legislative behavior in ways that are difficult for the public to observe and for political scientists to measure. The institutional structure of Congress provides opportunities for interest groups to influence legislation outside the public eye.

Committee proposal power enables legislators, if they are on the relevant committee, to introduce legislation that favors contributing groups. Gatekeeping power enables committee members to block legislation that harms contributing groups. The fact that certain provisions are *excluded* from a bill is as much an indicator of PAC influence as the fact that certain provisions are *included*. The difference is that it is hard to measure what you don't see. Committee oversight powers enable members to intervene in bureaucratic decision making on behalf of contributing groups.

The point here is that voting on the floor, the alleged object of campaign contributions according to the vote-buying hypothesis, is a highly visible, highly public act, one that could get a legislator in trouble with his or her broader electoral constituency. The committee system, on the other hand, provides loads of opportunities for legislators to deliver "services" to PAC contributors and other donors that are more subtle and disguised from broader public view. Thus, we suggest that the most appropriate places to look for traces of campaign contribution influence on the legislative process are in the manner in which committees deliberate, mark up proposals, and block legislation from the floor; outside public view, these are the primary arenas for interest-group influence.

Party Discipline

In both the House and Senate, party leaders have a good deal of influence over the behavior of their party members. This influence, sometimes called "party discipline," was once so powerful that it dominated the lawmaking process. At the

---

[43]See Janet M. Grenke, "PACs and the Congressional Supermarket: The Currency Is Complex," *American Journal of Political Science* 33 (1989): 1–24.

turn of the twentieth century, party leaders could often command the allegiance of more than 90 percent of their members. A vote on which 50 percent or more of the members of one party take one position while at least 50 percent of the members of the other party take the opposing position is called a *party vote.* At the beginning of the twentieth century, most *roll-call votes* in the House of Representatives were party votes. Today, this type of party-line voting is less common in Congress. In the fifteen Congresses between 1887 and 1917, there were twelve Congresses in which over 1 in 5 votes had 90 percent of Republicans voting against 90 percent of Democrats. In only one Congress from 1917 to 1969 has this level of partisanship been met—the first two years of Franklin Roosevelt's New Deal. Indeed, after 1950, the level of 90 percent versus 90 percent party voting never reached 10 percent.[44]

Typically, party unity is greater in the House than in the Senate. House rules grant greater procedural control to the majority party leaders, which gives them more influence over House members. In the Senate, however, the leadership has few sanctions over its members. Senate Majority Leader Tom Daschle once observed that a Senate leader seeking to influence other senators has as incentives "a bushel full of carrots and a few twigs."[45]

Party unity increased somewhat in recent decades as a result of the intense partisan struggles that began during the Reagan and Bush years (see Figure 5.8). Straight party-line voting was seen briefly in the 103rd Congress (1993–1994) following Bill Clinton's election in 1992. The situation, however, soon gave way to the many long-term factors working against party discipline in Congress (see Figure 5.8).[46]

In 2001, newly elected president George W. Bush called for an end to partisan squabbling in Congress. During the 2000 campaign, Bush claimed that as governor of Texas he had been able to build effective bipartisan coalitions, which, he said, should serve as a model for the conduct of the nation's business, as well. September 11, 2001, prompted almost every member of Congress to rally behind President Bush's military response. But, as we read earlier, Democrats and Republicans in the House divided sharply over the issue of airport security. Over the next several years, partisan differences emerged on a variety of issues, including taxation and foreign policy. On the issue of taxation, President Bush had sought to slash federal taxes by as much as $700 billion over a period of several years. Many Democrats, on the other hand, opposed most or all of Bush's tax-cut proposals and called for increased federal spending on social programs, especially health care. On issues of foreign policy, many Democrats were

party vote A roll-call vote in the House or Senate in which at least 50 percent of the members of one party take a particular position and are opposed by at least 50 percent of the members of the other party. Party votes are rare today, although they were fairly common in the nineteenth century.

roll-call vote A vote in which each legislator's yes or no vote is recorded.

[44]See Joseph Cooper, David W. Brady, and Patricia Hurley, "The Electoral Basis of Party Voting: Patterns and Trends in the U.S. House of Representatives, 1887–1969," in *The Impact of the Electoral Process,* ed. Louis Maisel and Joseph Cooper (Beverly Hills, Calif.: Sage, 1977), pp. 133–65.

[45]Holly Idelson, "Signs Point to Greater Loyalty on Both Sides of the Aisle," *Congressional Quarterly Weekly Report,* 19 December 1992, p. 3849.

[46]David Broder, "Hill Democrats Vote as One: New Era of Unity or Short-Term Honeymoon?" *Washington Post,* 14 March 1993, p. A1. See also Adam Clymer, "All Aboard: Clinton's Plan Gets Moving," *New York Times,* 21 March 1993, sec. 4, p. 1.

FIGURE 5.8

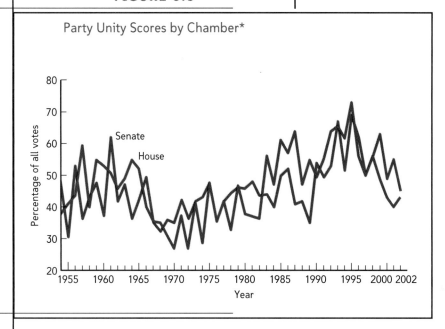

Party Unity Scores by Chamber*

*The percentage of times that members voted with the majority of their party, based on recorded votes on which a majority of one party voted against the majority of the other party.

SOURCE: *Congressional Quarterly Weekly Report*, 14 December 2002, p. 3240.

deeply troubled by the president's willingness to use military force on a unilateral basis when he deemed it necessary to do so. Prior to the 2003 Iraq war, Democratic leaders argued for giving UN weapons inspectors and diplomacy more time. Even after the quick conclusion of the war, some Democrats accused the president of undermining America's relations with its allies.

To some extent, party divisions are based on ideology and background. Republican members of Congress are more likely than Democrats to be drawn from rural or suburban areas. Democrats are likely to be more liberal on economic and social questions than their Republican colleagues. This ideological gap has been especially pronounced since 1980 (see Figure 5.9). Ideological differences certainly help to explain roll-call divisions between the two parties.[47] Ideology and background, however, are only part of the explanation of party unity. The other part has to do with party organization and leadership. Although party

[47]Keith T. Poole and Howard Rosenthal, *Congress: A Political-Economic History of Roll Call Voting* (New York: Oxford University Press, 1997).

FIGURE 5.9

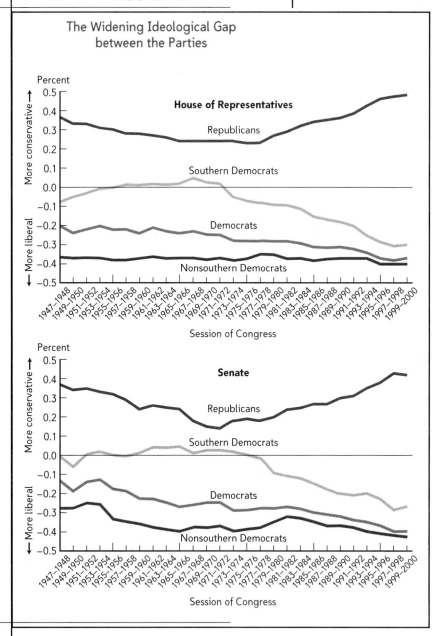

The Widening Ideological Gap
between the Parties

House of Representatives

Republicans

Southern Democrats

Democrats

Nonsouthern Democrats

Session of Congress

Senate

Republicans

Southern Democrats

Democrats

Nonsouthern Democrats

Session of Congress

SOURCES: Data from Keith T. Poole and Howard Rosenthal, computed by Gary Jacobson, and reprinted in Poole and Rosenthal's *Congress: A Political-Economic History of Roll Call Voting* (New York: Oxford University Press, 1997); updates by Keith T. Poole.

organization has weakened since the beginning of the twentieth century, today's party leaders still have some resources at their disposal: (1) committee assignments, (2) access to the floor, (3) the whip system, (4) logrolling, and (5) the presidency. These resources are regularly used and are often effective in securing the support of party members. [48]

Committee Assignments Leaders can create debts among members by helping them get favorable committee assignments. These assignments are made early in the congressional careers of most members and cannot be taken from them if they later balk at party discipline. Nevertheless, if the leadership goes out of its way to get the right assignment for a member, this effort is likely to create a bond of obligation that can be called upon without any other payments or favors.

Access to the Floor The most important everyday resource available to the parties is control over access to the floor. With thousands of bills awaiting passage and most members clamoring for access in order to influence a bill or to publicize themselves, floor time is precious. In the Senate, the leadership allows ranking committee members to influence the allocation of floor time—who will speak for how long; in the House, the Speaker, as head of the majority party (in consultation with the minority leader), allocates large blocks of floor time. Thus, floor time is allocated in both houses of Congress by the majority and minority leaders. More importantly, the Speaker of the House and the majority leader in the Senate possess the power of recognition. Although this power may not appear to be substantial, it is a formidable authority and can be used to stymie a piece of legislation completely or to frustrate a member's attempts to speak on a particular issue. Because the power is significant, members of Congress usually attempt to stay on good terms with the Speaker and the majority leader in order to ensure that they will continue to be recognized.

---

[48]Legislative leaders may behave in ways that embellish their reputation for being willing to punish party members who stray from the party line. The problem for leaders of developing such credible reputations is analyzed in Randall Calvert, "Reputation and Legislative Leadership," *Public Choice* 55 (1987): 81–120, and is summarized in Kenneth A. Shepsle and Mark S. Boncheck, *Analyzing Politics: Rationality, Behavior, Institutions* (New York: W. W. Norton, 1997), pp. 397–403. The classic example of such punishment occurred after the 1964 election, in which two prominent House Democrats, John Bell Williams of Mississippi and Albert Watson of South Carolina, were disciplined for having supported the Republican presidential nominee, Barry Goldwater. The party leaders pushed for, and the Democratic caucus supported, a punishment in which each was demoted to the bottom of the seniority roster on the committees of which they were members. In Williams's case, the punishment was serious because he was the second highest ranking Democrat on the House Commerce Committee. Each resigned from the House in the wake of this punishment, and ran for elective office (both successfully) as Republicans. The message was clear: there are some partisan lines that party members cross at their peril! Put slightly differently, the famous mid-twentieth-century House Speaker, Sam Rayburn (D-Tex.), is known to have believed that deviation from the party position would be tolerated for "reasons of conscience or constituency." Of one wayward Democrat he is alleged to have said that the departure from the party line "better be a matter of conscience, because it damn sight isn't because of his constituency." In short, there would be hell to pay!

whip system
Primarily a communications network in each house of Congress, whips take polls of the membership in order to learn their intentions on specific legislative issues and to assist the majority and minority leaders in various tasks.

Collective Action Principle

The whip system helps maintain party unity in Congress.

logrolling A legislative practice wherein reciprocal agreements are made between legislators, usually in voting for or against a bill. In contrast to bargaining, logrolling unites parties that have nothing in common but their desire to exchange support.

Collective Action Principle

Logrolling is an informal means of facilitating cooperation in Congress.

The Whip System   Some influence accrues to party leaders through the ***whip system,*** which is primarily a communications network. Between twelve and twenty assistant and regional whips are selected by zones to operate at the direction of the majority or minority leader and the whip. They take polls of all the members in order to learn their intentions on specific bills. This enables the leaders to know if they have enough support to allow a vote as well as whether the vote is so close that they need to put pressure on a few swing votes. Leaders also use the whip system to convey their wishes and plans to the members, but only in very close votes do they actually exert pressure on a member. In those instances, the Speaker or a lieutenant will go to a few party members who have indicated they will switch if their vote is essential. The whip system helps the leaders limit pressuring members to a few times per session.

The whip system helps maintain party unity in both houses of Congress, but it is particularly critical in the House of Representatives because of the large number of legislators whose positions and votes must always be accounted for. The majority and minority whips and their assistants must be adept at inducing compromise among legislators who hold widely differing viewpoints. The whips' personal styles and their perception of their function significantly affect the development of legislative coalitions and influence the compromises that emerge.

Logrolling   An agreement between two or more members of Congress who have nothing in common except the need for support is called ***logrolling.*** The agreement states, in effect, "You support me on bill X and I'll support you on another bill of your choice." Since party leaders are the center of the communications networks in the two chambers, they can help members create large logrolling coalitions. Hundreds of logrolling deals are made each year, and while there are no official record-keeping books, it would be a poor party leader whose whips did not know who owed what to whom.[49] In some instances, logrolling produces strange alliances. A seemingly unlikely alliance emerged in Congress in June 1994, when 119 mainly conservative senators and representatives from oil-producing states met with President Clinton to suggest that they might be willing to support the president's health-care proposals in exchange for his support for a number of tax breaks for the oil industry. Senator J. Bennett Johnston of Louisiana, a leader of the oil-state representatives, contended that the issues of health care and oil production were closely related since both "affected the

---

[49]For an analysis of the formal problems that logrolling (or vote trading) both solves and creates, see Shepsle and Bonchek, *Analyzing Politics*, pp. 317–19. They argue that logrolling cannot be the entire solution to the problem of assembling majority coalitions out of the diverse preferences found in any political party. The reason is that, while party leaders can try to keep track of who owes what to whom, this is imperfect and highly complex bookkeeping at best. Nevertheless, if anyone is positioned to orchestrate a system of logrolls, it is the party leaders. And, of all those who have tried to facilitate such "cooperation," Robert Byrd of West Virginia, who served both as majority whip and majority leader in the Senate, has been the acknowledged master.

longterm economic security of the nation." Ironically, the oil-producing groups that promoted this alliance are generally among the most conservative forces in the nation. When asked what he personally thought of the president's health-care proposal, George Alcorn, a leading industry lobbyist involved in the logrolling effort, dismissed Clinton's plan as "socialized medicine." Another logrolling alliance of strange bedfellows was the 1994 "corn for porn" logroll, in which liberal urbanites supported farm programs in exchange for rural support for National Endowment for the Arts funding. Good logrolling, it would seem, is not hampered by minor ideological concerns.[50]

The Presidency   Of all the influences that maintain the clarity of party lines in Congress, the influence of the presidency is probably the most important. Indeed, it is a touchstone of party discipline in Congress. Since the late 1940s, under President Truman, presidents each year have identified a number of bills to be considered part of their administration's program. By the mid-1950s, both parties in Congress began to look to the president for these proposals, which became the most significant part of Congress's agenda. The president's support is a criterion for party loyalty, and party leaders are able to use it to rally some members.

Weighing Diverse Influences

Clearly, many different factors affect congressional decisions. But at various points in the decision-making process, some factors are likely to be more influential than others. For example, interest groups may be more effective at the committee stage, when their expertise is especially valued and their visibility is less obvious. Because committees play a key role in deciding what legislation actually reaches the floor of the House or Senate, interest groups can often put a halt to bills they dislike, or they can ensure that the options that do reach the floor are those that the group's members support.

Once legislation reaches the floor and members of Congress are deciding among alternatives, constituent opinion will become more important. Legislators are also influenced very much by other legislators: many of their assessments about the substance and politics of legislation come from fellow members of Congress.

The influence of the external and internal forces described in the preceding section also varies according to the kind of issue being considered. On policies of great importance to powerful interest groups—farm subsidies, for example—those groups are likely to have considerable influence. On other issues, members of Congress may be less attentive to narrow interest groups and more willing to consider what they see as the general interest.

[50]Allen R. Meyerson, "Oil-Patch Congressmen Seek Deal with Clinton," *New York Times*, 14 June 1994, p. D2.

Finally, the mix of influences varies according to the historical moment. The 1994 electoral victory of Republicans allowed their party to control both houses of Congress for the first time in forty years. The fact, combined with an unusually assertive Republican leadership, meant that party leaders became especially important in decision making. The willingness of moderate Republicans to support measures they had once opposed indicated the unusual importance of party leadership in this period. As House Minority Leader Richard Gephardt put it, "When you've been in the desert forty years, your instinct is to help Moses."[51]

BEYOND LEGISLATION: ADDITIONAL CONGRESSIONAL POWERS

In addition to the power to make the law, Congress has at its disposal an array of other instruments through which to influence the process of government.

Advice and Consent: Special Senate Powers

The Constitution has given the Senate a special power, one that is not based on lawmaking. The president has the power to make treaties and to appoint top executive officers, ambassadors, and federal judges—but only "with the Advice and Consent of the Senate" (Article II, Section 2). For treaties, two-thirds of those present must concur; for appointments, a majority is required.

The power to approve or reject presidential requests also involves the power to set conditions. The Senate only occasionally exercises its power to reject treaties and appointments. Only nine Supreme Court nominees have been rejected by the Senate during the past century, while hundreds have been approved.

More common than Senate rejection of presidential appointees is a senatorial "hold" on an appointment. By Senate tradition, any member may place an indefinite hold on the confirmation of a mid- or lower-level presidential appointment. The hold is typically used by senators trying to wring concessions from the White House on matters having nothing to do with the appointment in question.

Most presidents make every effort to take potential Senate opposition into account in treaty negotiations and will frequently resort to *executive agreements* with foreign powers instead of treaties. The Supreme Court has held that such agreements are equivalent to treaties, but they do not need Senate approval.[52] In the past, presidents sometimes concluded secret agreements without informing Congress of the agreements' contents or even their existence. For

executive agreement An agreement between the president and another country that has the force of a treaty but does not require the Senate's "advice and consent."

[51]David Broder, "At 6 Months, House GOP Juggernaut Still Cohesive," *Washington Post*, 17 July 1995, p. A1.

[52]United States v. Pink, 315 U.S. 203 (1942). For a good discussion of the problem, see James W. Davis, *The American Presidency: A New Perspective* (New York: Harper & Row, 1987), Chapter 8.

example, American involvement in the Vietnam War grew in part out of a series of secret arrangements made between American presidents and the South Vietnamese during the 1950s and 1960s. Congress did not even learn of the existence of these agreements until 1969. In 1972, Congress passed the Case Act, which requires that the president inform Congress of any executive agreement within sixty days of its having been reached. This provides Congress with the opportunity to cancel agreements that it opposes. In addition, Congress can limit the president's ability to conduct foreign policy through executive agreement by refusing to appropriate the funds needed to implement an agreement. In this way, for example, executive agreements to provide American economic or military assistance to foreign governments can be modified or even canceled by Congress.

Impeachment

The Constitution also grants Congress the power of *impeachment* over the president, vice president, and other executive officials. Impeachment means to charge a government official (president or otherwise) with "Treason, Bribery, or other high Crimes and Misdemeanors" and bring him or her before Congress to determine guilt. Impeachment is thus like a criminal indictment in which the House of Representatives acts like a grand jury, voting (by simple majority) on whether the accused ought to be impeached. If a majority of the House votes to impeach, the impeachment trial moves to the Senate, which acts like a trial jury by voting whether to convict and forcibly remove the person from office (this vote requires a two-thirds majority of the Senate).

impeachment
To charge a governmental official (president or otherwise) with "Treason, Bribery, or other high Crimes and Misdemeanors" and bring him or her before Congress to determine guilt.

Controversy over Congress's impeachment power has arisen over the grounds for impeachment, especially the meaning of "high Crimes and Misdemeanors." A strict reading of the Constitution suggests that the only impeachable offense is an actual crime. But a more commonly agreed upon definition is that "an impeachable offense is whatever the majority of the House of Representatives considers it to be at a given moment in history."[53] In other words, impeachment, especially impeachment of a president, is a political decision.

The closest that the United States has come to impeaching and convicting a president came in 1867. President Andrew Johnson, a southern Democrat who had battled a congressional Republican majority over Reconstruction, was impeached by the House but saved from conviction by one vote in the Senate. At the height of the Watergate scandal in 1974, the House started impeachment proceedings against President Richard M. Nixon, but Nixon resigned before the House could proceed. The possibility of impeachment arose again in 1998, when President Clinton was accused of lying under oath and obstructing justice in the investigation into his sexual affair with White House intern Monica

[53]Carroll J. Doherty, "Impeachment: How It Would Work," *Congressional Quarterly Weekly Report*, 31 January 1998, p. 222.

Lewinsky. In October 1998, the House voted to open an impeachment inquiry against President Clinton. At the conclusion of the Senate trial in 1999, Democrats, joined by a handful of Republicans, acquitted the president of both charges.

The impeachment power is a considerable one; its very existence in the hands of Congress is a highly effective safeguard against the executive tyranny so greatly feared by the framers of the Constitution.

POWER AND REPRESENTATION

Because they feared both executive and legislative tyranny, the framers of the Constitution pitted Congress and the president against one another. But for more than one hundred years, the contest was unequal. During the first century of American government, Congress was the dominant institution. American foreign and domestic policy was formulated and implemented by Congress; and, generally, the most powerful figures in American government were the Speaker of the House and the leaders of the Senate—not the president. During the nineteenth century, Congress—not the president—dominated press coverage on "the affairs of government."[54] The War of 1812 was planned and fought by Congress. The great sectional compromises prior to the Civil War were formulated in Congress, without much intervention from the executive branch. Even during the Civil War, a period of extraordinary presidential leadership, a joint congressional committee on the conduct of the war played a role in formulating war plans and campaign tactics, and even had a hand in the promotion of officers. After the Civil War, when President Andrew Johnson sought to interfere with congressional plans for Reconstruction, he was summarily impeached, saved from conviction by only one vote. Subsequent presidents understood the moral and did not attempt to thwart Congress.

This congressional preeminence began to diminish after the turn of the twentieth century, so that by the 1960s, the executive had become, at least temporarily, the dominant branch of American government. The major domestic policy initiatives of the twentieth century—Franklin Roosevelt's "New Deal," Harry Truman's "Fair Deal," John F. Kennedy's "New Frontier," and Lyndon Johnson's "Great Society"—all included some congressional involvement but were essentially developed, introduced, and implemented by the executive. In the area of foreign policy, although Congress continued to be influential during the twentieth century, the focus of decision-making power clearly moved into the executive branch. The War of 1812 may have been a congressional war, but in the twentieth century, American entry into World War I, World War II, Korea, Vietnam, and a host of lesser conflicts was essentially a presidential—not a congressional—decision. In the last thirty-five years, there has been a good deal of

---

[54]Samuel Kernell and Gary C. Jacobson, "Congress and the Presidency as News in the Nineteenth Century," *Journal of Politics* 49 (1987): 1016–35.

resurgence of congressional power vis-à-vis the executive. This has occurred mainly because Congress has sought to represent many important political forces, such as the civil rights, feminist, environmental, consumer, and peace movements, which in turn became constituencies for congressional power. During the mid-1990s, Congress became more receptive to a variety of new conservative political forces, including groups on the social and religious right as well as more traditional economic conservatives. After Republicans won control of both houses in the 1994 elections, Congress took the lead in developing programs and policies supported by these groups. These efforts won Congress the support of conservative forces in its battles for power against a Democratic White House.

To herald the new accessibility of Congress, Republican leaders instituted a number of reforms designed to eliminate many of the practices that they had criticized as examples of Democratic arrogance during their long years in opposition. Republican leaders reduced the number of committees and subcommittees, eliminated funding of the various unofficial caucuses, imposed term limits on committee chairmen, eliminated the practice of proxy voting, reduced committee staffs by one-third, ended Congress's exemption from the labor health and civil rights laws that it imposed on the rest of the nation, and prohibited members from receiving most gifts. With these reforms, Republicans hoped to make Congress both more effective and more representative. Term limits and gift bans were seen as increasing the responsiveness of Congress to new political forces and to the American people more generally. Simplification of the committee structure was seen as making Congress more efficient and, thus, potentially more effective and powerful. To some extent, unfortunately, the various reforms worked at cross-purposes. Simplification of the committee structure and elimination of funding for the caucuses increased the power of the leadership but reduced the representation of a variety of groups in the legislative process. For example, the Congressional Black Caucus, one of the major groups to lose its funding, had come to play an important role in representing African Americans. For their part, when term limits for committee and subcommittee chairmen were finally imposed in 2001, the result was confusion as experienced chairmen were forced to step down. This is the dilemma of congressional reform. Efficiency and representation are often competing principles in our system of government, and we must be wary of gaining one at the expense of the other.

At the same time, the constant struggle between Congress and the president can hinder stable, effective governance. Over the past three decades, in particular, presidents and Congresses have often seemed to be more interested in undermining one another than in promoting the larger public interest. On issues of social policy, economic policy, and foreign policy, Congress and the president have been at each other's throats while the nation suffered.

For example, during the first two years of the Bush administration Democrats fought vigorously to block many of the president's appointments to the

History Principle

During the first century of American government, Congress was the dominant institution. In recent decades, members of Congress have sought to restore that dominance.

federal court of appeals. Even though several of the judicial nominees had excellent records, Senate Democrats found them ideologically unpalatable. And even though Republicans held a slim Senate majority, Democratic procedural maneuvers, including the use of the filibuster, thwarted the president's efforts.

Thus, we face a fundamental dilemma: a representative system that can undermine the government's power. Indeed, it can undermine the government's very capacity to govern. In the next chapter, we will turn to the second branch of American government, the presidency, to view this dilemma from a somewhat different angle.

SUMMARY

The U.S. Congress is one of the few national representative assemblies that actually govern. Members of Congress take their representative function seriously. They devote a significant portion of their time to constituent contact and service. Representation and power go hand in hand in congressional history.

The legislative process must provide the order necessary for legislation to take place amid competing interests. It is dependent on a hierarchical organizational structure within Congress. Six basic dimensions of Congress affect the legislative process: (1) the parties, (2) the committees, (3) the staff, (4) the caucuses (or conferences), (5) the rules, and (6) the presidency.

Since the Constitution provides only for a presiding officer in each house, some method had to be devised for conducting business. Parties quickly assumed the responsibility for this. In the House, the majority party elects a leader every two years. This individual becomes Speaker. In addition, a majority leader and a minority leader (from the minority party) and party whips are elected. Each party has a committee whose job it is to make committee assignments.

The committee system surpasses the party system in its importance in Congress. In the early nineteenth century, standing committees became a fundamental aspect of Congress. They have, for the most part, evolved to correspond to executive-branch departments or programs and thus reflect and maintain the separation of powers.

The Senate has a tradition of unlimited debate, on which the various cloture rules it has passed have had little effect. Filibusters still occur. The rules of the House, on the other hand, restrict talk and support committees; deliberation is recognized as committee business. The House Rules Committee has the power to control debate and floor amendments. The rules prescribe the formal procedure through which bills become law. Generally, the parties control scheduling and agenda, but the committees determine action on the floor. Committees, seniority, and rules all limit the ability of members to represent their constituents. Yet, these factors enable Congress to maintain its role as a major participant in government.

While voting along party lines remains strong, party discipline has declined. Still, parties do have several means of maintaining discipline:

PRINCIPLES OF POLITICS IN REVIEW

Rationality Principle	Collective Action Principle	Institution Principle	Policy Principle	History Principle
Members of Congress, like all politicians, are ambitious and, thus, eager to serve the interests of constituents in order to improve their own chances of re-election.	Cooperation on recurring matters like congressional votes is facilitated by the institutionalization of legislative structures and procedures.	According to the principle of agency representation, elections induce a member of Congress to act according to the preferences of his or her constituency.	Pork-barrel legislation exists because it allows members of Congress to claim credit for federally granted resources, thus improving their chances for re-election.	The historical intentions of the founders for the House to represent current passions and the Senate to balance it by serving a more deliberative function are still manifest in these legislative bodies more than two centuries later.
One of the most important factors determining who runs for office is each candidate's individual ambition.	If a bill passes both the House and Senate, the differences need to be ironed out in a conference committee.	Party leaders have considerable agenda-setting powers.	The distributive tendency in Congress results from the need for a broad base of support in order for a bill to be passed.	The committee system evolved during the early nineteenth century as a means of allowing individual legislators disproportionate influence in areas of policy most important to them.
The political opinions and policy goals of members of Congress are many and varied.	Interest groups with the ability to mobilize followers in many congressional districts are especially influential in Congress.	The committee system is a means of dividing labor and allowing members of Congress to specialize in certain policy areas.	Multiple factors influence how a member of Congress votes on legislation. These include constituency, interest groups, party leaders, congressional colleagues, and the president.	
Generally, members of Congress seek committee assignments that allow them to acquire more influence in areas important to their constituents.	The whip system helps maintain party unity in Congress.	Among the powers delegated to committees are gatekeeping authority, bargaining with the other chamber, and oversight.		During the first century of American government, Congress was the dominant institution. In recent decades, members of Congress have sought to restore that dominance.
	Logrolling is an informal means of facilitating cooperation in Congress.	The House and Senate have methods of keeping committees in check.		
		The Rules Committee's decision about whether to adopt a closed or open rule for floor debate greatly influences a bill's chances for passage.		

1. Favorable committee assignments create obligations.
2. Floor time in the debate on one bill can be allocated in exchange for a specific vote on another.
3. The whip system allows party leaders to assess support for a bill and convey their wishes to members.
4. Party leaders can help members create large logrolling coalitions.
5. The president, by identifying pieces of legislation as his own, can muster support along party lines.

In most cases, party leaders accept constituency obligations as a valid reason for voting against the party position.

The power of the post–New Deal presidency does not necessarily signify the decline of Congress and representative government. During the 1970s, Congress again became the "first branch" of government. During the early years of the Reagan administration, some of the congressional gains of the previous decade were diminished, but in the last two years of Reagan's second term, and in former president Bush's term, Congress reasserted its role. At the start of the Clinton administration, congressional leaders promised to cooperate with the White House rather than confront it. But only two years later, confrontation was once again the order of the day.

FOR FURTHER READING

Arnold, R. Douglas. *The Logic of Congressional Action*. New Haven: Yale University Press, 1990.

Baker, Ross K. *House and Senate*. 3rd ed. New York: W. W. Norton, 2001.

Dodd, Lawrence C., and Bruce I. Oppenheimer, eds. *Congress Reconsidered*. 7th ed. Washington, D.C.: Congressional Quarterly Press, 2001.

Fenno, Richard F., Jr. *Home Style: House Members in Their Districts*. Boston: Little, Brown, 1978.

Fiorina, Morris P. *Congress: Keystone of the Washington Establishment*. 2nd ed. New Haven: Yale University Press, 1989.

Fowler, Linda L., and Robert D. McClure. *Political Ambition: Who Decides to Run for Congress*. New Haven: Yale University Press, 1989.

Mayhew, David R. *Congress: The Electoral Connection*. New Haven: Yale University Press, 1974.

Rieselbach, Leroy N. *Congressional Reform*. Washington, D.C.: Congressional Quarterly Press, 1986.

Rohde, David W. *Parties and Leaders in the Postreform House*. Chicago: University of Chicago Press, 1991.

Sinclair, Barbara. *The Transformation of the U.S. Senate*. Baltimore: Johns Hopkins University Press, 1989.

Smith, Steven S., and Christopher J. Deering. *Committees in Congress.* 3rd ed. Washington, D.C.: Congressional Quarterly Press, 1997.

Sundquist, James L. *The Decline and Resurgence of Congress.* Washington, D.C.: Brookings Institution, 1981.

Politics in the News—
Reading between the Lines

Differences between the House and Senate

2 Chambers That Don't Understand Each Other

By CARL HULSE

WASHINGTON, May 11—Forget Republicans and Democrats. The lawmakers who seem least to understand each other are senators and representatives— no matter the party. . . .

Even with one-party control, the vast differences in the way the House and the Senate operate make policy blowups inevitable. Throughout history, the House and the Senate have clashed. But lately those clashes have been frequent—and loud.

The House is insisting on oil drilling in Alaska; the Senate has rejected the idea. The Senate blocked a Bush administration proposal to give public money to religious groups, compelling the House to go along. The House is ready to advance a Medicare overhaul; the Senate is taking it slower. And the latest dispute was on Friday. House Republicans pushed through a tax-cut package substantially at odds in size and content with the measure emerging in the Senate, setting up a nasty negotiation to reconcile the two.

"We expedite, they obstruct," a top House Republican aide said.

While differences in policy goals certainly exist, the problem can often be found in the very nature of the institutions. House rules severely restrain the power of the opposition, giving Mr. Hastert and Mr. DeLay iron-fisted control so they can—and do—rapidly ram through almost anything they want.

In the Senate, every member wields tremendous power through the ability to put blind "holds" on legislation, raise procedural obstacles on the floor and generally gum things up. That makes the Senate a place where the majority does not always rule.

The House leadership uses a Rules Committee to limit debate; the Senate routinely engages in interminable debates without limits. . . .

The power of the individual in the Senate was on vivid display again last week as Senator Olympia J. Snowe, Republican of Maine, single-handedly forced the Finance Committee to com-

New York Times, 12 May 2003, p. A18.

promise on a tax-cutting plan that raised some taxes to pay for tax cuts elsewhere. That idea did not go down well in the House.

"I think the Capitol Police better check to see if someone's slipped something into the water over there," said Representative Mark Foley, Republican of Florida, adding that the Senate tax-writers were "not acting like Republicans."

Indeed. They were acting like senators. . . .

The framers of the Constitution envisioned the Senate as a legislative bulwark against the more populist House, and Washington famously and perhaps apocryphally described it to Jefferson as the saucer to "cool" the passions of the House members. . . .

In the early years of the nation, the House was where the action was, with the Senate a sleepy chamber caught up in confirmations. The Senate historian Richard A. Baker said that balance of power changed with the rising emphasis on slavery issues in the 19th century. With the Senate split between slave states and free states, politicians quickly realized that one lawmaker in the Senate could wield significant power.

"That is where the political talent of the nation went, where a single member could make a difference if only to stand up and say no," Mr. Baker said. . . .

Because Senators represent entire states, they often are less ideological and unyielding than House members, who are often elected from safe partisan districts and can afford to be less willing to compromise.

Things could well get worse before they get better in the current Congress, with coming negotiations over the tax bill, drug coverage under Medicare, energy policy and the usual list of spending measures. . . .

ESSENCE OF THE STORY

- For the first time since 1953, the Republicans had unified control of the House, Senate, and presidency after the 2002 election. Republicans want to promote their agenda.

- House members have made progress on a series of issues important to the White House, including drilling in the Arctic National Wildlife Refuge, a tax cut, and Medicare reform.

- The Senate has moved much more slowly on these issues, prompting complaints from their colleagues in the House.

- Individual members celebrate their own institution and complain about the other.

POLITICAL ANALYSIS

- Collective action (passage of a bill) is affected by both rules and member preferences. Member preferences, furthermore, are shaped by another set of rules (the electoral game).

- Structured rules for debate and participation in the House means that Republican House leaders can push forward their legislation even if Democrats object. House leaders are less concerned with cross-party coalitions.

- In the Senate, individual members can slow down progress even though the Republicans are ostensibly in control. Senate leaders must build cross-party coalitions.

- Difference in the electoral calendar and the makeup of their constituencies exacerbate these differences. House members have to point to accomplishments in just two years. Partisans in their districts demand results. Senators can afford to move more slowly. Because states tend to be more heterogeneous and because Senate races are more competitive, senators have to be more attentive to a wider variety of demands.

- The relative influence of the two chambers has ebbed and flowed throughout our history, mainly in response to real-world events such as the growth of our nation, increasing economic and governmental complexity, and foreign conflicts.

CHAPTER

6

The President: From Chief Clerk to Chief Executive

Although the first domestic impact of war is inevitably on civil liberties, war has ramifications throughout all governmental and political institutions as well as public policies. For example, President Abraham Lincoln's 1862 declaration of martial law and Congress's 1863 legislation giving the president the power to make arrests and imprisonments through military tribunals amounted to a "constitutional dictatorship," which lasted through the war and Lincoln's re-election in 1864. But these measures were viewed as emergency powers that could be taken back once the crisis of union was resolved. In less than a year after Lincoln's death, Congress had reasserted its power, leaving the presidency in many respects the same as, if not weaker than, it had been before.

War also transformed the presidency of Woodrow Wilson. In 1917, one of Congress's rare declarations of war provided America with another "constitutional dictatorship." In addition to restrictions on civil liberties, Congress gave the president a number of significant powers: to censor not only all international communications but also to take over and operate the railroads and all other common carriers; to seize and operate all telephone and telegraph lines; to regulate at his discretion the manufacture and distribution of all foods and related commodities; to fix prices on all such commodities and on stock exchanges; and to take over all aspects of mines and factories. As one leading constitutional-history treatise puts it, "Legislative delegation [to the president] on this scale was unprecedented and little short of revolutionary. . . . [However,] if Wilson was in any sense a dictator, it was because Congress in certain spheres came close to a virtual delegation of its entire legislative power to the president *for the duration of the war*" [emphasis added]. The setting of a precise time limit on the duration of emergency powers later came to be called a "sunset" provision. In hindsight, some of the strengthening of the presidency did last beyond Wilson and the sunset provision. Fortunately for America, civil liberties not only survived the war restrictions, but First Amendment rights actually flourished afterward.

During World War II, Franklin D. Roosevelt, like Lincoln, did not bother to wait for Congress but took executive action first and expected Congress to follow. Roosevelt brought the United States into an undeclared naval war against Germany a year before Pearl Harbor, and he ordered the unauthorized use of wiretaps and other surveillance as well as the investigation of suspicious persons for reasons not clearly specified. The most egregious (and revealing) of these was his segregation and eventual confinement of 120,000 individuals of Japanese descent, many of whom were American citizens. Even worse, the Supreme Court validated Roosevelt's treatment of the Japanese, on the flimsy grounds of military necessity. One dissenter on the Court called the president's assumption of emergency powers "a loaded weapon ready for the hand of any authority that can bring forward a plausible claim of an urgent need."

The "loaded weapon" was seized again on September 14, 2001, when Congress defined the World Trade Center and Pentagon attacks as an act of war and proceeded to adopt a joint resolution authorizing the president to use "all necessary and appropriate force against those nations, organizations or persons he determines planned, authorized, committed or aided the terrorist

CHAPTER OUTLINE

The Constitutional Basis of the Presidency

- The President as Head of State

- The Domestic Presidency: The President as Head of Government

The Rise of Presidential Government

- The Legislative Epoch, 1800–1933

- The New Deal and the Presidency

Presidential Government

- What Are the Formal Resources of Presidential Power?

- What Are the Informal Resources of Presidential Power?

Is a Parliamentary System Better?

- Governmental Arrangements

- The Government Formation Process

attacks that occurred on September 11, 2001, or harbored such organizations or persons. . . ." Congress did attach a "sunset provision" to the authorization resolution and planned for congressional oversight during the war.

September 11 and its aftermath immensely accentuated the president's role and place in foreign policy. By 2002, foreign policy was the centerpiece of the Bush administration's agenda. In a June 1 speech at West Point, the "Bush Doctrine" of preemptive war was announced. Bush argued that "our security will require all Americans . . . to be ready for preemptive action when necessary to defend our liberty and to defend our lives." Bush's statement was clearly intended to justify his administration's plans to invade Iraq, but it had much wider implications, including the increasing power of the American president in guiding foreign policy.

National emergencies provide presidents a source of power, and the way presidents exercise these powers has profound consequences for the country. As we have seen, civil liberties are particularly threatened by what presidents do during times of war. In this chapter, we will go beyond this and look at the long-term consequences of national emergencies on presidential power. What circumstances explain why some emergencies produced new and long-lasting powers for the president, while others did not? In the instances in which new powers were institutionalized, what was the long-term impact? The central task of this chapter is to explain why the American system of government could be described as presidential government and how it got to be that way. In doing so, we will see that it's the office that wields great power, not necessarily the person.

The power of the office has gradually developed over time. The framers, wanting "energy in the Executive," provided for a single-headed office with an electoral base independent of Congress. But by giving the presidency no explicit powers independent of Congress, each president would have to provide that energy by asserting the inherent powers of the office.

A tug-of-war between formal constitutional provisions for a president who is little more than chief clerk and a theory of necessity favoring a real chief executive has persisted for over two centuries. President Jefferson's acquisition of the Louisiana Territory in virtual defiance of the Constitution seemed to establish the chief-executive presidency; yet he was followed by three chief clerks, James Madison, James Monroe, and John Quincy Adams. Presidents Andrew Jackson and Abraham Lincoln believed in and acted on the theory of the strong president with power transcending the formal Constitution, but neither of them institutionalized the role, and both were followed by a series of chief clerks. Theodore Roosevelt and Woodrow Wilson were also considered genuine chief executives. But it was not until Franklin Roosevelt's election in 1932 that the tug-of-war seems to have been won for the chief-executive presidency, because after FDR, as we shall see, every president has been strong, whether he was committed to the strong presidency or not.

Thus, a strong executive, a genuine chief executive, was institutionalized in the twentieth century. But it continues to operate in a schizoid environment: as the power of the presidency has increased, popular expectations of presidential performance have increased at an even faster rate, requiring more leadership than was ever exercised by any but the greatest presidents in the past.

Our focus in this chapter will be on the development of the institutional character of the presidency, the power of the presidency, and the relationship between the two. The chapter is divided into four sections. First, we shall review the constitutional origins of the presidency. In particular, this will involve an examination of the constitutional basis for the president's foreign and domestic roles. Second, we shall review the history of the American presidency to see how the office has evolved from its original status under the Constitution. We will look particularly at the ways in which Congress has augmented the president's constitutional powers by deliberately delegating to the presidency many of Congress's own responsibilities. Third, we shall assess both the formal and informal means by which presidents can enhance their own ability to govern. We will conclude by analyzing an alternative to the U.S. presidential system: parliamentary democracy.

PREVIEWING THE PRINCIPLES

All presidents have goals and want to be influential, but presidential power is constrained by the constitutional and structural contours of the institution of the presidency. The Constitution endows the president with only a small number of expressed powers, so the presidency is an office whose powers are primarily delegated to it by Congress. Presidents have sought to broaden their inherent powers by their successful execution of the law. Presidential power can be enhanced through strategic interactions that a president has with other political actors and a president's ability to build and sustain popular support. Historical events requiring bold action and leadership from the president, such as the Great Depression, can also contribute to the president's power. The institution of the presidency has accumulated more and more power over time, but a president's ultimate success is based on the skillful use of those powers.

THE CONSTITUTIONAL BASIS OF THE PRESIDENCY

Article II of the Constitution, which establishes the presidency and defines a small number of **expressed powers** of the office, is the basis for the dual nature of the presidency. Although Article II has been called "the most loosely drawn chapter of the Constitution,"[1] the framers were neither indecisive nor confused. They held profoundly conflicting views of the executive branch, and Article II was probably the best compromise they could make. The formulation that the framers agreed upon is magnificent in its ambiguity: "The executive Power shall

expressed powers The notion that the Constitution grants to the federal government only those powers specifically named in its text.

---

[1]E. S. Corwin, *The President, Office and Powers, 1787–1957: History and Analysis of Practice and Opinion,* 4th rev. ed. (New York: New York University Press, 1957), p. 2.

be vested in a President of the United States of America" (Article II, Section 1, first sentence). The meaning of "executive power," however, is not defined except indirectly in the very last sentence of Section 3, which provides that the president "shall take Care that the Laws be faithfully executed."[2]

One very important conclusion can be drawn from these two provisions: the office of the president was to be an office of ***delegated powers.*** Since, as we have already seen, all of the powers of the national government are defined as powers of Congress and are incorporated into Article I, Section 8, then the "executive Power" of Article II, Section 3, must be understood to be defined as the power to execute faithfully the laws *as they are adopted* by Congress. This does not doom the presidency to weakness. Presumably, Congress can pass laws delegating almost any of its powers to the president. But presidents are not free to discover sources of executive power completely independent of the laws as passed by Congress. In the 1890 case of *In re Neagle*, the Supreme Court did hold that the president could be bold and expansive in the inferences he drew from the Constitution as to "the rights, duties and obligations" of the presidency; but the ***inherent powers*** of the president would have to be inferred from that Constitution and laws, not from some independent or absolute idea of executive power.[3]

Immediately following the first sentence of Section 1, Article II defines the manner in which the president is to be chosen. This is a very odd sequence, but it does say something about the struggle that the delegates were having over how to provide great power of action or energy to the executive and, at the same time, how to balance that power with limitations. The struggle was between those delegates who wanted the president to be selected by, and thus responsible to, Congress and those delegates who preferred that the president be elected directly by the people. Direct popular election would create a more independent and more powerful presidency. With the adoption of a scheme of indirect election through an electoral college in which the electors would be selected by the state legislatures (and close elections would be resolved in the House of Representatives), the framers hoped to achieve a "republican" solution: a strong president responsible to state and national legislators rather than directly to the electorate.

The heart of presidential power as defined by the Constitution, however, is found in Sections 2 and 3, where the several clauses define the presidency in two dimensions: the president as head of state and the president as head of government. Although these will be given separate treatment here, the presidency can be understood only by the combination of the two.

delegated powers Constitutional powers assigned to one governmental agency that are exercised by another agency with the express permission of the first.

 Institution Principle
The Constitution established the presidency as an office of delegated powers.

inherent powers Powers claimed by a president that are not expressed in the Constitution but are inferred from it.

---

[2]Article II, Section 3. There is a Section 4, but all it does is define impeachment.

[3]In re Neagle, 135 U.S. 1 (1890). Neagle, a deputy U.S. marshal, had been authorized by the president to protect a Supreme Court justice whose life had been threatened by an angry litigant. When the litigant attempted to carry out his threat, Neagle shot and killed him. Neagle was then arrested by the local authorities and tried for murder. His defense was that his act was "done in pursuance of a law of the United States." Although the law was not an act of Congress, the Supreme Court declared that it was an executive order of the president, and the protection of a federal judge was a reasonable extension of the president's power to "take Care that the Laws be faithfully executed."

The President as Head of State

The constitutional position of the president as head of state is defined by three constitutional provisions, which are the source of some of the most important powers on which presidents can draw. The areas can be classified as follows:

1. *Military.* Article II, Section 2, provides for the power as "Commander in Chief of the Army and Navy of the United States, and of the Militia of the several States, when called in to the actual Service of the United States."
2. *Judicial.* Article II, Section 2, also provides the power to "grant Reprieves and Pardons for Offenses against the United States, except in Cases of Impeachment."
3. *Diplomatic.* Article II, Section 3, provides the power to "receive Ambassadors and other public Ministers."

Military First, the position of commander in chief makes the president the highest military authority in the United States, with control of the entire defense establishment. But final authority over military matters rests with Congress, which may direct the commander in chief as it chooses. In the nineteenth century, Congress normally directed the president's military actions and decisions. In the twentieth century, however, presidents engaged the country in many military campaigns abroad without congressional approval. In most of these cases, Congress chose not to assert its authority, which caused many to believe that the president was better suited to make military decisions.[4]

The president is also the head of the secret intelligence hierarchy, which includes not only the Central Intelligence Agency (CIA) but also the National Security Council (NSC), the National Security Agency (NSA), the Federal Bureau of Investigation (FBI), and a host of less well-known but very powerful international and domestic security agencies. But care must be taken not to conclude too much from this—as some presidents have done. Although Article II, Section 1, does state that all the executive power is vested in the president, and Section 2 does provide that the president shall be commander in chief of all armed forces, including state militias, these impressive provisions must be read in the context of Article I, wherein seven of the eighteen clauses of Section 8 provide particular military and foreign policy powers to Congress, including the power to declare wars that presidents are responsible for. Presidents have tried to evade this at their peril. They may seek formal congressional authorization, as in 1965, when President Lyndon Johnson convinced Congress to adopt the Gulf of Tonkin Resolution, authorizing him to expand the American military presence in Vietnam. Johnson interpreted the resolution as a delegation of discretion to use any and all national resources according to his own judgment. Others may not

---

[4]Louis Fisher, *Presidential War Power* (Lawrence, Kans.: University Press of Kansas, 1995); Robert J. Spitzer, *President and Congress: Executive Hegemony at the Crossroads of American Government* (New York: McGraw-Hill, 1993), Chapter 5.

even bother with the authorization but merely assume it, as President Nixon did when he claimed to need no congressional authorization at all to continue or to expand the Vietnam War.

These presidential claims and actions led to a congressional reaction, however. In 1973, Congress passed the War Powers Resolution over President Nixon's veto. This resolution asserted that the president could send American troops into action abroad only in the event of a declaration of war or other statutory authorization by Congress, or if American troops were attacked or directly endangered. This was an obvious effort to revive the principle that the presidency is an office of *delegated* powers—that is, powers granted by Congress—and that there is no blanket prerogative—that is, no inherent presidential power. In full awareness of the woe visited upon President Lyndon Johnson for evading and misleading Congress at the outset of the Vietnam War, former president George H. W. Bush sought congressional authorization for the Gulf War in January 1991. President George W. Bush followed in his father's footsteps by seeking congressional authorization for the war against the Taliban regime in Afghanistan; it was granted in a joint resolution adopted in the Senate by a vote of 98 to 0 and in the House by a vote of 420 to 1. In June 2002, President Bush declared that since Saddam Hussein's regime in Iraq was the biggest single threat in the war against worldwide terrorism, the United States's only recourse was to "change the regime." Later that summer, Bush sought a resolution from Congress authorizing him to use any means he determined appropriate, including military force. After weeks of debate in the House and Senate, Congress overwhelmingly approved, by 296 to 133 in the House and 77 to 23 in the Senate, a resolution authorizing Bush to use the armed forces "as he determines to be necessary and appropriate" and to enforce "all relevant" United Nations Security Council resolutions on Iraq. The resolution was far less broad than the initial request put forward by Bush, which would have also allowed military action outside of Iraq. It also urged Bush to work first through the United Nations before opting to invade Iraq unilaterally and required that the president report to Congress within forty-eight hours of any military action. Throughout the debate, Bush said his powers as commander in chief permitted him to act in defense of the nation. He sought congressional approval, however, so he could argue to the United Nations that the American people supported his position.

Judicial   The presidential power to grant reprieves, pardons, and amnesties involves the power of life and death over all individuals who may be a threat to the security of the United States. Presidents may use this power on behalf of a particular individual, as did Gerald Ford when he pardoned Richard Nixon in 1974 "for all offenses against the United States which he . . . has committed or may have committed." Or they may use it on a large scale, as did President Andrew Johnson in 1868, when he gave full amnesty to all Southerners who had participated in the "Late Rebellion," and President Carter in 1977, when he declared an amnesty for all the draft evaders of the Vietnam War. This power of life and death over others helped elevate the president to the level of earlier conquerors and kings by establishing him as the person before whom supplicants might come to make their pleas for mercy.

Diplomatic   The ultimate status of the president as head of state is the power to make treaties for the United States (with the advice and consent of the Senate). When President Washington received Edmond Genet ("Citizen Genet") as the formal emissary of the revolutionary government of France in 1793 and had his cabinet officers and Congress back his decision, he established a greatly expanded interpretation of the power to "receive Ambassadors and other public Ministers," extending it to the power to "recognize" other countries. That power gives the president the almost unconditional authority to review the claims of any new ruling groups to determine if they indeed control the territory and population of their country, so that they can commit it to treaties and other agreements.

In order to circumvent the Senate's constitutionally prescribed role, presidents can also use executive agreements to conduct foreign policy.[5] An ***executive agreement*** is like a treaty because it is a contract between two countries; but an executive agreement does not require a two-thirds vote of approval by the Senate. Ordinarily, executive agreements are used to carry out commitments already made in treaties or to arrange for matters well below the level of policy. But when presidents have found it expedient to use an executive agreement in place of a treaty, Congress and the Supreme Court have gone along.

executive agreement   An agreement between the president and another country, which has the force of a treaty but does not require the Senate's "advice and consent."

The Domestic Presidency: The President as Head of Government

The constitutional basis of the domestic presidency also has three parts. And here, again, although real power grows out of the combination of the parts, the analysis is greatly aided by examining the parts separately:

1. *Executive.* The "executive Power" is vested in the president by Article II, Section 1, to see that all the laws are faithfully executed (Section 3), and to appoint, remove, and supervise all executive officers and to appoint all federal judges (Article II, Section 2).
2. *Military.* This power is derived from Article IV, Section 4, which stipulates that the president has the power to protect every state "against Invasion; and . . . against domestic Violence."
3. *Legislative.* The president is given the power under various provisions to participate effectively and authoritatively in the legislative process.

---

[5]In United States v. Pink, 315 U.S. 203 (1942), the Supreme Court confirmed that an executive agreement is the legal equivalent of a treaty, despite the absence of Senate approval. This case approved the executive agreement that was used to establish diplomatic relations with the Soviet Union in 1933. An executive agreement, not a treaty, was used in 1940 to exchange "fifty over-age destroyers" for ninety-nine-year leases on some important military bases.

Another component of the president's power as chief executive is **executive privilege**. Executive privilege is the claim that confidential communications between a president and close advisers should not be revealed without the consent of the president. Presidents have made this claim ever since George Washington refused a request from the House of Representatives to deliver documents concerning negotiations of an important treaty. Washington refused (successfully) on the grounds that, first, the House was not constitutionally part of the treaty-making process and, second, that diplomatic negotiations required secrecy.

Executive privilege became a popular part of the "checks and balances" counterpoint between president and Congress, and presidents have usually had the upper hand when invoking it. The expansion of executive privilege into a claim of "uncontrolled discretion" to refuse Congress's request for information came when President Nixon was beginning to get into political trouble over the Vietnam War in 1971.[6] It was President Nixon's claim to an almost absolute immunity to congressional inquiry that led to a Supreme Court rejection of the doctrine as a constitutional feature of the presidency in *United States v. Nixon* (418 U.S. 683, 1974). Although the doctrine continued to be invoked by succeeding presidents, the occasions were usually when presidents had something to hide that was of questionable legality (Iran-Contra) or potentially scandalous (Clinton's various scrapes). The exercise of presidential power through the executive-privilege doctrine has been all the more frequent in the past twenty years, when we have been living nearly 90 percent of the time under conditions of "divided government," where the party not in control of the White House is in control of one or both of the chambers of Congress.

Executive Power   The most important basis of the president's power as chief executive is to be found in Article II, Section 3, which stipulates that the president must see that all the laws are faithfully executed, and Section 2, which provides that the president will appoint, remove, and supervise all executive officers, and appoint all federal judges (with Senate approval). The *Neagle* case has already demonstrated the degree to which Article II, Section 1, is a source of executive power. Further powers do indeed come from this appointing power, although at first this may not seem to be very impressive. But the power to appoint the "principal executive officers" and to require each of them to report to the president on subjects relating to the duties of their departments makes the president the true chief executive officer (CEO) of the nation. In this manner, the Constitution focuses executive power and legal responsibility upon the president. The famous sign on President Truman's desk, "The buck stops here," was not merely an assertion of Truman's personal sense of responsibility but was in fact recognition by him of the legal and constitutional responsibility of the president. The president is subject to some limitations because the appointment of all such officers, including ambassadors, ministers, and federal judges, is subject

---

[6]Raoul Berger, *Executive Privilege: A Constitutional Myth* (Cambridge, Mass.: Harvard University Press, 1974), pp. 1–14.

to a majority approval by the Senate. But these appointments are at the discretion of the president, and the loyalty and the responsibility of each appointment are presumed to be directed toward the president. Although the Constitution is silent on the power of the president to remove such officers, the federal courts have filled this silence with a series of decisions that grant the president this power.[7] Although the United States has no cabinet in the parliamentary sense of a collective decision-making body or board of directors with collective responsibilities (discussed later in this chapter), the Constitution nevertheless recognizes departments with department heads, and that recognition establishes the lines of legal responsibility up and down the executive hierarchy, culminating in the presidency (see Figure 6.1).

Military Sources of Domestic Presidential Power   Although Article IV, Section 4, provides that the "United States shall [protect] every State . . . against Invasion . . . and . . . domestic Violence," Congress has made this an explicit presidential power through statutes directing the president as commander in chief to discharge these obligations.[8] The Constitution restrains the president's use of domestic force by providing that a state legislature (or governor, when the legislature is not in session) must request federal troops before the president can send them into the state to provide public order. Yet this proviso is not absolute. First, presidents are not obligated to deploy national troops merely because the state legislature or governor makes such a request. And, more important, the president may deploy troops in a state or city without a specific request from the state legislature or governor if he considers it necessary in order to maintain an essential national service, in order to enforce a federal judicial order, or in order to protect federally guaranteed civil rights.

One historic example of the unilateral use of presidential power to protect the states against domestic disorder, even when the states don't request it, was the decision by President Eisenhower in 1957 to send troops into Little Rock, Arkansas, against the wishes of the state of Arkansas, to enforce court orders to integrate Little Rock's Central High School (see Chapter 4). Arkansas Governor Orval Faubus had actually posted the Arkansas National Guard at the entrance of the Central High School to prevent the court-ordered admission of nine black students. After an effort to negotiate with Governor Faubus failed, President

---

[7]The Supreme Court defined the president's removal power very broadly in Myers v. United States, 272 U.S. 52 (1926). Later, in Humphrey's Executor v. United States, 295 U.S. 62 (1935), the Court accepted Congress's effort to restrict presidential removal powers as they applied to heads of independent regulatory commissions. In those instances, the president can remove officers only "for cause." Two later cases restricted presidential power a bit further by providing that he could not remove at his pleasure certain other officers whose tasks require independence from the executive. See Wiener v. United States, 357 U.S. 349 (1958); and Bowsher v. Synar, 478 U.S. 714 (1986). In another, more tricky case, the Court held that the attorney general, not the president, could remove a special prosecutor because of the power and obligation of the prosecutor to investigate the president. See Morrison v. Olson, 108 S.Ct. 2597 (1988).

[8]These statutes are contained mainly in Title 10 of the United States Code, Sections 331, 332, and 333.

FIGURE 6.1

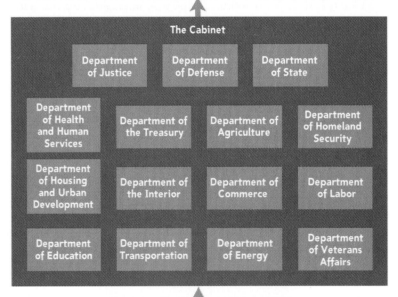

The Institutional Presidency*

The President

The White House Staff

Executive Office of the President

White House Office
Office of Management and Budget
Council of Economic Advisers
National Security Council
Office of National Drug Control Policy

Office of the U.S. Trade Representative
Council on Environmental Quality
Office of Science and Technology Policy
Office of Policy Development
Office of Administration
Vice President

The Cabinet

| Department of Justice | Department of Defense | Department of State |

| Department of Health and Human Services | Department of the Treasury | Department of Agriculture | Department of Homeland Security |

| Department of Housing and Urban Development | Department of the Interior | Department of Commerce | Department of Labor |

| Department of Education | Department of Transportation | Department of Energy | Department of Veterans Affairs |

Independent Establishments and Government Corporations

*NOTE: Arrows are used to indicate lines of legal responsibility.
SOURCE: Office of the Federal Register, National Archive and Records Administration, *The United States Government Manual*, 1995–1996 (Washington, D.C.: U.S. Government Printing Office, 1995), p. 22.

Eisenhower reluctantly sent a thousand paratroopers to Little Rock, who stood watch while the black students took their places in the all-white classrooms. This case makes clear that the president does not have to wait for a request by a state legislature or governor before acting as a domestic commander in chief.[9]

However, in most instances of domestic disorder—whether from human or from natural causes—presidents tend to exercise unilateral power by declaring a "state of emergency," thereby making available federal grants, insurance, and direct assistance. In 1992, in the aftermath of the devastating riots in Los Angeles and the hurricanes in Florida, American troops were very much in evidence, sent in by the president, but in the role more of Good Samaritans than of military police.

The President's Legislative Power The president plays a role not only in the administration of government but also in the legislative process. Two constitutional provisions are the primary sources of the president's power in the legislative arena. The first of these is the provision in Article II, Section 3, providing that the president "shall from time to time give to the Congress Information of the State of the Union, and recommend to their Consideration such Measures as he shall judge necessary and expedient." The second of the president's legislative powers is, of course, the "veto power" assigned by Article I, Section 7.[10]

Institution Principle

The president can be an important agenda setter for congressional action.

The first of these powers does not at first appear to be of any great import. It is a mere obligation on the part of the president to make recommendations for Congress's consideration. But as political and social conditions began to favor an increasingly prominent role for presidents, each president, especially since Franklin Delano Roosevelt, began to rely upon this provision to become the primary initiator of proposals for legislative action in Congress and the principal source for public awareness of national issues as well as the most important single individual participant in legislative decisions. This is an instance of agenda power (see Chapter 1). Few today doubt that the president and the executive branch together are the primary agenda setters for many important congressional actions.[11]

[9] The best study covering all aspects of the domestic use of the military is that of Adam Yarmolinsky, *The Military Establishment: Its Impact on American Society* (New York: Harper & Row, 1971).

[10] There is a third source of presidential power implied from the provision for faithful execution of the laws. This is the president's power to impound funds—that is, to refuse to spend money Congress has appropriated for certain purposes. One author referred to this as a "retroactive veto power" (Robert E. Goosetree, "The Power of the President to Impound Appropriated Funds," *American University Law Review* [January 1962]). This impoundment power was used freely and to considerable effect by many modern presidents, and Congress occasionally delegated such power to the president by statute. But in reaction to the Watergate scandal, Congress adopted the Budget and Impoundment Control Act of 1974 and designed this act to circumscribe the president's ability to impound funds by requiring the president to spend all appropriated funds unless both houses of Congress consent to an impoundment within forty-five days of a presidential request. Therefore, since 1974, the use of impoundment has declined significantly. Presidents have had either to bite their tongues and accept unwanted appropriations or to revert to the older and more dependable but politically limited method of vetoing the entire bill.

[11] For a different perspective, see William F. Grover, *The President as Prisoner: A Structural Critique of the Carter and Reagan Years* (Albany: State University of New York Press, 1989).

veto The president's constitutional power to turn down acts of Congress. A presidential veto may be overridden by a two-thirds vote of each house of Congress.

pocket veto A method by which the president vetoes a bill by taking no action on it when Congress has adjourned.

The **veto** power is the president's constitutional power to turn down acts of Congress. This power alone makes the president the most important single legislative leader.[12] No bill vetoed by the president can become law unless both the House and Senate override the veto by a two-thirds vote. In the case of a **pocket veto,** Congress does not even have the option of overriding the veto but must reintroduce the bill in the next session. A pocket veto can occur when the president is presented with a bill during the last ten days of a legislative session. Usually, if a president does not sign a bill within ten days, it automatically becomes law. But this is true only while Congress is in session. If a president chooses not to sign a bill within the last ten days that Congress is in session, then the ten-day limit does not expire until Congress is out of session, and instead of becoming law, the bill is vetoed. Process Box 6.1 illustrates the president's veto options. In 1996, a new power was added—the line-item veto—giving the president power to strike specific spending items from appropriations bills passed by Congress, unless re-enacted by a two-thirds vote of both House and Senate. In 1997, President Clinton used this power eleven times to strike eighty-two items from the federal budget. But in 1998, the Supreme Court ruled that the Constitution does not authorize the line-item veto power. Only a constitutional amendment would restore this power to the president.

Institution Principle

The veto power makes the president the most important single legislative leader.

Collective Action Principle

Vetoes are usually part of an intricate bargaining process between the president and Congress.

The Games Presidents Play: The Veto   Use of the veto varies according to the political situation that each president confronts. During Bill Clinton's first two years in office, when Democrats controlled both houses of Congress, he vetoed no bills. Following the congressional elections of 1994, however, Clinton confronted a Republican-controlled Congress with a definite agenda, and he began to use his veto power more vigorously. In general, presidents have used the veto to equalize or perhaps upset the balance of power with Congress. While the simple power to reject or accept legislation in its entirety might seem like a crude tool for making sure that legislation adheres to a president's preferences, the politics surrounding the veto are complicated, and it is rare that vetoes are used simply as bullets to kill legislation. Instead, vetoes are usually part of an intricate bargaining process between the president and Congress, involving threats of vetoes, vetoes, repassing legislation, and re-vetoes.[13]

---

[12]Although the veto power is the most important legislative resource in the hands of the president, it can often end in frustration, especially when the presidency and Congress are held by opposing parties. George H. W. Bush vetoed forty-six congressional enactments during his four years, and only one was overridden. Ronald Reagan vetoed thirty-nine in his eight years, and nine were overridden. This compares to thirty-one during Jimmy Carter's four years, with two overridden. In 1994, Bill Clinton did not veto a single bill, a record unmatched since the days of President Millard Fillmore in 1853; both, of course, were working with Congresses controlled by their own political party. For more on the veto, see Chapter 5 and Robert J. Spitzer, *The Presidential Veto: Touchstone of the American Presidency* (Albany: State University of New York Press, 1988).

[13]Charles M. Cameron, *Veto Bargaining: Presidents and the Politics of Negative Power* (New York: Cambridge University Press, 2000).

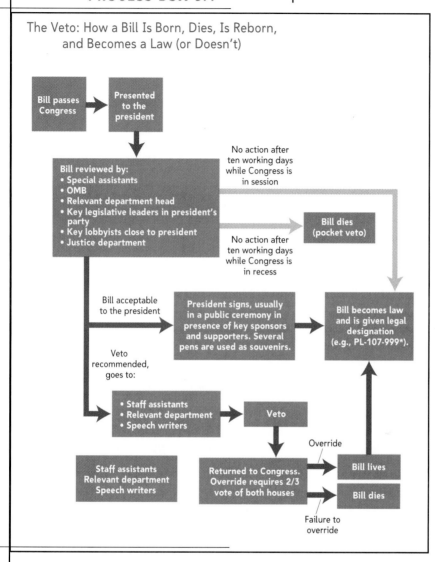

The Veto: How a Bill Is Born, Dies, Is Reborn, and Becomes a Law (or Doesn't)

*PL = Public Law; 107 = number of Congress (107th is 2000–2001); 999 = the number of the actual law.

Although presidents rarely veto legislation, this does not mean vetoes and veto bargaining have an insignificant influence over the policy process. The fact that presidents vetoed only 434 of the 17,000 public bills that Congress sent to them between 1945 and 1992 belies the centrality of the veto to presidential power. Many of these bills were insignificant and not worth the veto effort. Thus, it is important to separate "significant" legislation, for which vetoes frequently occur, from insignificant legislation.[14] Vetoes can also be effective—even though they are rarely employed—because of a concept known as "the second face of power," that is, individuals will condition their actions based on how they think others will respond.[15] With respect to vetoes, this means that members of Congress will alter the content of a bill to make it more to a president's liking in order to preempt a veto. Thus, the veto power can be influential even when the veto pen rests in its inkwell. The concept of "the second face of power" works to influence the content of legislation.

⚖ **Policy Principle**
Because of the president's veto power, Congress will alter the content of a bill to make it more to a president's liking.

Rhetoric and reputation take on particular importance when vetoes become part of a bargaining process. The key to veto bargaining is uncertainty. Members of Congress are often unsure about the president's policy preferences and, therefore, don't know which bills the president would be willing to sign. When the policy preferences of the president and Congress diverge, as they typically do under divided government, the president tries to convince Congress that his preferences are more extreme than they really are in order to get Congress to enact something that is closer to what he really wants. If members of Congress knew the president's preferences ahead of time, they would pass a bill that was closest to what *they* wanted, minimally satisfying the president. Through strategic use of the veto and veto threats, a president tries to shape Congress's beliefs about his policy preferences to gain greater concessions from Congress. Reputation is central to presidential effectiveness.[16] By influencing congressional beliefs, the president is building a policy reputation that will affect future congressional behavior.

The back-and-forth negotiating between the president and Congress was no more evident than in the events surrounding the creation of a cabinet-level Department of Homeland Security in 2002-2003. As part of his decisive leadership in the wake of the terrorist attacks of September 11, 2001, President Bush established a Department of Homeland Security in the Executive Office of the President (this office will be discussed below). The president believed that his "terrorism czar," Tom Ridge, had ample authority to coordinate national policy in the fight against terrorism. Capitol Hill critics felt that a cabinet-level department should be created, partly because they felt that Ridge lacked the necessary resources and authority to do the job, but also because it would permit the House and Senate a more explicit role (through the appropriations process). Ultimately, President Bush relented, but the conflict between president and Congress did not end there as the executive and legislature negotiated, threatened, promised, and eventually settled on the details of this department. President Bush had veto power as his "club behind the door," while Senate Democrats

[14]David R. Mayhew, *Divided We Govern: Party Control, Lawmaking, and Investigations, 1946–1990* (New Haven: Yale University Press, 1991).

[15]Jack H. Nagel, *The Descriptive Analysis of Power* (New Haven: Yale University Press, 1975).

[16]Richard E. Neustadt, *Presidential Power: The Politics of Leadership* (New York: Wiley, 1960).

(Bush's main opponents), even though in the minority, could threaten delay through dilatory tactics and the filibuster (see Chapter 5). Both sides "went public" in an effort to sway public opinion and brandished "blame" in attempts to weaken the credibility of the other side. This kind of public, high-visibility squabbling is unusual, but on matters of salient national policy that pits the two parties against one another, it occasionally emerges, giving us a picture of the full array of powers possessed by executive and legislature.

What about the relationship between mass public support for the president and the use of the veto? At least for the modern presidency, a crucial resource for the president in negotiating with Congress has been his public approval as measured by opinion polls.[17] In some situations, members of Congress pass a bill, not because they want to change policy but because they want to force the president to veto a popular bill that he disagrees with in order to hurt his approval ratings.[18] The key is that the public, uncertain of the president's policy preferences, uses information conveyed by vetoes to reassess what they know about his preferences. As a result, vetoes may come at a price to the president. A president must weigh the advantages of vetoing or threatening to do so—to gain concessions from Congress—against the hit he may take in his popularity. The president may be reluctant to use the veto or the threat of a veto to gain concessions from Congress if such vetoes will hurt him in the polls. But in some cases, the president will take a hit in his approval ratings if the bill is drastically inconsistent with his policies.

 Rationality Principle
A president must weigh the advantages of vetoing legislation against the possible drop in his public approval.

Legislative Initiative   Although not explicitly stated, the Constitution provides the president with the power of legislative initiative. *To initiate* means "to originate," and in government that can mean power. The framers of the Constitution clearly saw legislative initiative as one of the keys to executive power. Initiative obviously implies the ability to formulate proposals for important policies, and the president, as an individual with a great deal of staff assistance, is able to initiate decisive action more frequently than Congress, with its large assemblies that have to deliberate and debate before taking action. With some important exceptions, Congress banks on the president to set the agenda of public policy. And clearly, there is power in initiative; there is power in being able to set the terms of discourse in the making of public policy.

For example, during the weeks immediately following September 11, Bush took many presidential initiatives to Congress, and each was given almost unanimous support—from commitments to pursue al-Qaeda to the removal of the Taliban, the reconstitution of the Afghanistan regime, all the way to almost unlimited approval for mobilization of both military power and power over the regulation of American civil liberties. Following the 2002 elections, in which the

[17]Theodore J. Lowi, *The Personal President: Power Invested, Promise Unfulfilled* (Ithaca, N.Y.: Cornell University Press, 1985).

[18]Timothy Groseclose and Nolan McCarty, "Presidential Vetoes: Bargaining, Blame-Game, and Gridlock," *American Journal of Political Science* 45 (2001): 100–19.

Republicans retook the Senate and maintained their House majority, major domestic initiatives began to flow from the White House. Bush's second big tax cut was the first item to arrive, and he got it through Congress even though he had to accept a reduction by almost half of its value—from an estimated request of $750 billion to one of approximately $350 billion (spread over seven years). Other domestic White House initiatives included a comprehensive energy bill; an education bill covering individuals with disabilities; the controversial "partial birth" abortion bill; an authorization of $15 billion to combat AIDS; raising the $6.4 trillion debt limit by nearly $1 trillion; a new clean-air act using the market to reduce industrial air pollution; a bill to tighten requirements in the 1996 welfare law; and the highly complex Medicare bill to add prescription drug coverage. Not all of these were "done deals" through Congress by the end of the 2003 session, but they dominated the congressional agenda and can be called "the president's program."

The president's initiative does not end with policy making involving Congress and the making of laws in the ordinary sense of the term. The president has still another legislative role (in all but name) within the executive branch. This is designated as the power to issue **executive orders.** The executive order is, first and foremost, simply a normal tool of management, a power possessed by virtually any CEO to make "company policy" rules setting procedures, etiquette, chains of command, functional responsibilities, etc. But evolving out of this normal management practice is a recognized presidential power to promulgate rules that have the effect and the formal status of legislation.[19] Most of the executive orders of the president provide for the reorganization of structures and procedures or otherwise direct the affairs of the executive branch—either to be applied across the board to all agencies or applied in some important respect to a single agency or department.

As the size and scope of the executive branch grew throughout the twentieth century, so did the president's use of executive orders (see Figure 6.2). Presidential executive orders give the president the capacity to make policy on his own, but they do not abrogate the legislature's authority to legislate. So there are limits. In some Latin American democracies, on the other hand, presidents have the power of *executive decree*, effectively allowing them to govern without any participation of the legislature and essentially without constitutional limit. American presidential authority does not run this far. Nevertheless, the power to issue executive orders does illustrate that, although reputation and persuasion are typically required in presidential policy making, the practice of executive order, within limits, allows a president to govern without the necessity to persuade.[20]

executive order
A rule or regulation issued by the president that has the effect and formal status of legislation.

---

[19]Kenneth R. Mayer, *With the Stroke of a Pen: Executive Orders and Presidential Power* (Princeton, N.J.: Princeton University Press, 2001).

[20]This point is developed both by Kenneth R. Mayer and in William G. Howell, *Power without Persuasion: The Politics of Direct Presidential Action* (Princeton, N.J.: Princeton University Press, 2003).

FIGURE 6.2

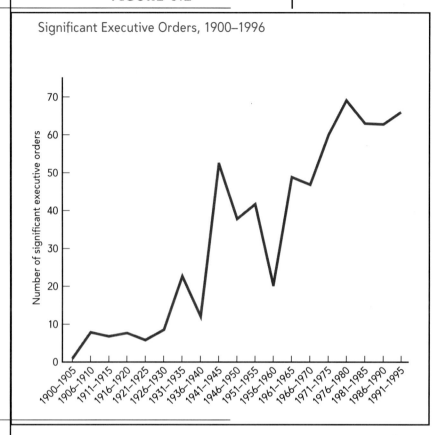

Significant Executive Orders, 1900–1996

SOURCE: William Howell, "The President's Powers of Unilateral Action: The Strategic Advantages of Acting Alone" (Ph.D. diss., Stanford University, 1999).

One of the most important examples is Executive Order No. 8248, September 8, 1939, establishing the divisions of the Executive Office of the President. Another one of equal importance is President Nixon's executive order establishing the Environmental Protection Agency in 1970–1971, which included establishment of the Environmental Impact Statement. President Reagan's Executive Order No. 12291 of 1981 provided for a regulatory reform process that was responsible for more genuine deregulation in the past twenty years than was accomplished by any acts of congressional legislation. President Clinton's most important policy toward gays and gay rights in the military took the form of an executive order referred to as "Don't ask, don't tell." And within two weeks after the terrorist attacks of September 11, President Bush issued an executive order to create the Office of Homeland Security.

This legislative or policy leadership role of the presidency is an institutionalized feature of the office that exists independent of the occupant of the office. That is to say, any duly elected president would possess these powers regardless of his or her individual energy or leadership.

When these two sources of power—agenda power from the president's constitutional duty to address Congress on the state of the union and the president's power to veto legislation—are taken together, it is remarkable that it took so long—well over a century—for these constitutional powers to be fully realized. Let us see how this happened as well as why it took so long.

THE RISE OF PRESIDENTIAL GOVERNMENT

Most of the real influence of the modern presidency derives from the powers granted by the Constitution and the laws made by Congress. Thus, any person properly elected and sworn in as president will possess almost all of the power held by the strongest presidents in American history. Even when they are "lame ducks," presidents still possess all the power of the office. For example, in the weeks following the election of 2000, lame-duck President Clinton took the opportunity to become the first U.S. president to visit a united Vietnam and to continue major diplomatic efforts to bring peace to the Middle East.

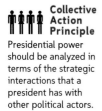
Collective Action Principle

Presidential power should be analyzed in terms of the strategic interactions that a president has with other political actors.

This case illustrates an extremely important fact about the presidency: *the popular base of the presidency is important less because it gives the president power than because it gives him consent to use all the powers already vested by the Constitution in the office.* Anyone installed in the office could exercise most of its powers. But what variables account for a president's success in exercising these powers? Why are some presidents considered to be great successes and others colossal failures? This relates broadly to the very concept of presidential power. Is it a reflection of the attributes of the person or is it more characteristic of the political situations that a president encounters? The personal view of presidential power dominated political scientists' view for several decades,[21] but recent scholars have argued that presidential power should be analyzed in terms of the strategic interactions that a president has with other political actors. The veto, which we reviewed in the last section, is one example of this sort of strategic interaction, but there are many other "games" that presidents play: the Supreme-Court-nomination and treaty-ratification games with the Senate, the executive-order game, the agency-supervision-and-management game with the executive branch. As the political scientist Charles M. Cameron has argued, *"Understand-*

---

[21]Neustadt, *Presidential Power.*

ing the presidency means understanding these games."[22] Success in these "games" translates into presidential power.

We must not forget, however, the tremendous resources that a president can rely on in his strategic interactions with others. Remember that the presidency is a democratic institution with a national constituency. Its broad popular base is a strategic presidential resource that can be deployed in the various bargaining games just discussed; a president's success depends on the qualities of the person in office and the situations that arise. For example, political scientist Samuel Kernell suggests that presidents may rally public opinion and put pressure on Congress by "going public."[23] With the occasional exception, however, it took more than a century, perhaps as much as a century and a half, before presidents came to be seen as consequential players in these strategic encounters. A bit of historical review will be helpful in understanding how the presidency has risen to its current level of influence.

Collective Action Principle

The president can use public approval as a strategic resource.

The Legislative Epoch, 1800–1933

In 1885, a then-obscure political-science professor named Woodrow Wilson entitled his general textbook *Congressional Government* because American government was just that, "congressional government." There is ample evidence that Wilson's description of the national government was not only consistent with nineteenth-century reality but also with the intentions of the framers. Within the system of three separate and competing powers, the clear intent of the Constitution was for *legislative supremacy.*

The strongest evidence of original intent is the fact that the powers of the national government were not placed in a separate article of the Constitution, but were instead listed in Article I, the legislative article. Madison had laid it out explicitly in *The Federalist,* No. 51: "In republican government, the legislative authority necessarily predominates." President Washington echoed this in his first inaugural address in 1789:

> By the article establishing the Executive Department, it is made the duty of the President "to recommend to your consideration, such measures as he shall judge necessary and expedient." The circumstances under which I now meet you, will acquit me from entering into that subject, farther than to refer to the Great Constitutional Charter . . . which, in defining your powers, designates the objects to which your attention is to be given. It will be more consistent with those circumstances . . . to substitute, in place of a recommendation of particular measures, the tribute that is due . . . the characters selected to devise and adopt them.

[22]Charles M. Cameron, "Bargaining and Presidential Power," in Robert Y. Shapiro, Martha Joynt Kumar, and Lawrence R. Jacobs, eds., *Presidential Power: Forging the Presidency for the Twenty-first Century* (New York: Columbia University Press, 2000), p. 47. [Emphasis in original.]

[23]Samuel Kernell, *Going Public: New Strategies of Presidential Leadership,* 3rd ed. (Washington, D.C.: Congressional Quarterly Press, 1998).

The first decade was, of course, unique precisely because it was first; everything was precedent-making, and nothing was secure. It was a state-building decade in which relations between the president and Congress were more cooperative than they would be at any time thereafter. The First Congress of 1789–1791 accomplished an incredible amount. In seven short months following Washington's inauguration, Congress provided for the organization of the executive and judicial branches, established a system of national revenue, and worked through the first seventeen amendments proposed to the Constitution, ten of which were to be ratified to become the Bill of Rights.[24]

One of the last actions of the First Congress, First Session, was to authorize the secretary of the treasury, Alexander Hamilton, to develop a policy to establish a system for national credit. In January 1790, during the Second Session, Hamilton submitted to Congress such a proposal; his *Report on Public Credit* is one of the great state papers in the history of American public policy. In 1791, Hamilton presented the second of the reports ordered by Congress, the *Report on Manufactures*, probably of even greater significance than the first because its proposals for internal improvements and industrial policies influenced Congress's agenda for years to come. Thus, it was Congress that ordered that a policy agenda be prepared by the president or his agent. In creating the executive departments, however, Congress (in particular the House) was so fearful of the powers to be lodged in the Treasury Department that it came close to adopting a three-man board, which many Antifederalists favored. The compromise tried to make the Treasury Department an agent of Congress rather than simply a member of the independent executive branch.[25] This kind of cooperation resembles the British parliamentary system, but it was not to last.

Before the Republic was a decade old, Congress began to develop a strong organization, including its own elected leadership, the first standing committees, and the party hierarchies. By President Jefferson's second term (1805), the executive branch was beginning to play the secondary role anticipated by the Constitution. The quality of presidential performance and then of presidential personality and character declined accordingly. The president during this era was seen by some observers as little more than America's "chief clerk." It was said of President James Madison, who had been principal author of the Constitution, that he knew everything about government except how to govern. Indeed, after Jefferson and until the beginning of this century, most historians agree that Presidents Jackson and Lincoln were the only exceptions to what had been a dreary succession of weak presidents. And those two exceptions can be explained. Jackson was a war hero and founder of the Democratic party. Lincoln was also a founder of his party, the Republican party, and although not a war hero, he was a wartime president who exercised the extraordinary powers that are available to any president during

---

[24]See Richard Buel, Jr., *Securing the Revolution: Ideology in American Politics, 1789–1815* (Ithaca, N.Y.: Cornell University Press, 1972), Part I.

[25]See, for example, Forrest McDonald, *The Presidency of George Washington* (Lawrence: University Press of Kansas, 1974), pp. 36–42.

war because during war the Constitution is put on hold. Both Jackson and Lincoln are considered great presidents because they used their great power wisely. But it is important in the history of the presidency that neither of these great presidents left their own powers as a new institutional legacy to their successors. That is to say, once Jackson and Lincoln left office, the presidency went back to the subordinate role that it played during the nineteenth century.

One of the reasons that so few great men became presidents in the nineteenth century is that there was only occasional room for greatness in such a weak office.[26] As Chapter 3 indicated, the national government of that period was not a particularly powerful entity. Moreover, most of the policies adopted by the national government were designed mainly to promote the expansion of commerce. These could be directed and administered by the congressional committees and political parties without much reliance on an executive bureaucracy.

Another reason for the weak presidency of the nineteenth century is that during this period the presidency was not closely linked to major national political and social forces. Indeed, there were few important *national* political or social forces to which presidents could have linked themselves even if they had wanted to. Federalism had taken very good care of this by fragmenting political interests and diverting the energies of interest groups toward the state and local levels of government, where most key decisions were being made.

The presidency was strengthened somewhat in the 1830s with the introduction of the national convention system of nominating presidential candidates. Until then, presidential candidates had been nominated by their party's congressional delegates. This was the *caucus* system of nominating candidates, and it was derisively called "King Caucus" because any candidate for president had to be beholden to the party's leaders in Congress in order to get the party's nomination and the support of the party's congressional delegation in the election. The national nominating convention arose outside Congress in order to provide some representation for a party's voters who lived in districts where they weren't numerous enough to elect a member of Congress. The political party in each state made its own provisions for selecting delegates to attend the presidential nominating convention, and in virtually all states the selection was dominated by the party leaders (called "bosses" by the opposition party). It is only in recent decades that state laws have intervened to regularize the selection process and to provide (in all but a few instances) for open election of delegates. The convention system quickly became the most popular method of nominating candidates for all elective offices and remained so until well into the twentieth century, when it succumbed to the criticism that it was a nondemocratic method dominated by a few leaders in a "smoke-filled room." But in the nineteenth century, it was seen as a victory for democracy against the congressional elite. And the national convention gave the presidency a base of power independent of Congress.

[26]For related appraisals, see Jeffrey Tulis, *The Rhetorical Presidency* (Princeton, N.J.: Princeton University Press, 1987); Stephen Skowronek, *The Politics Presidents Make: Leadership from John Adams to George Bush* (Cambridge: Harvard University Press, 1993); and Spitzer, *President and Congress*.

History Principle

The presidency was strengthened somewhat in the 1830s with the introduction of a national-convention system of nominating presidential candidates.

This additional independence did not immediately transform the presidency into the office we recognize today because the parties disappeared back into their states and Congress once the national election was over. But the national convention did begin to open the presidency to larger social forces and newly organized interests in society. In other words, it gave the presidency a constituency base that would eventually support and demand increased presidential power. Improvements in telephone, telegraph, and other forms of mass communication allowed individuals to share their complaints and allowed national leaders—especially presidents and presidential candidates—to reach out directly to people to ally themselves with, and even sometimes to create, popular groups and forces. Eventually, though more slowly, the presidential selection process began to be further democratized, with the adoption of primary elections through which millions of ordinary citizens were given an opportunity to take part in the presidential nominating process by popular selection of convention delegates.

Despite political and social conditions favoring the enhancement of presidential power, however, the development of presidential government as we know it today did not mature until the middle of our own century. For a long period, even as the national government began to grow, Congress was careful to keep tight rein on the president's power. For example, when Congress began to make its first efforts to exert power over the economy (beginning in 1887 with the adoption of the Interstate Commerce Act and in 1890 with the adoption of the Sherman Antitrust Act), it sought to keep this power away from the president and the executive branch by placing these new regulatory policies in "independent regulatory commissions" responsible to Congress rather than to the president (see also Chapter 7).

The real turning point in the history of American national government came during the administration of Franklin Delano Roosevelt. The New Deal was a response to political forces that had been gathering national strength and focus for fifty years. What is remarkable is not that they gathered but that they were so long gaining influence in Washington—and even then it took the Great Depression, a popular new president, and substantial working majorities for his party in both chambers of Congress to bring about a new shape to the national government. The New Deal combined the personal brilliance and persuasiveness of a new president, economic conditions that generated an agenda of political action and unified partisan government, and a bargaining circumstance that put a premium on coordination among kindred spirits in the Capitol and White House. Roosevelt seized the opportunity, and the shape of American government has never been the same since.

The New Deal and the Presidency

The "First Hundred Days" of the Roosevelt administration in 1933 had no parallel in U.S. history. But this period was only the beginning. The policies proposed by President Roosevelt and adopted by Congress during the first thousand days of his administration so changed the size and character of the national government that they constitute a moment in American history equivalent to the founding or to the Civil War. The president's constitutional obligation to see "that the laws be faithfully executed" became, during Roosevelt's presidency, virtually a responsibility to shape the laws before executing them.

New Programs Expand the Role of National Government Many of the New Deal programs were extensions of the traditional national-government approach, which was described already in Chapter 3 (see especially Table 3.1). But the New Deal went well beyond the traditional approach, adopting types of policies never before tried on a large scale by the national government; it began intervening into economic life in ways that had hitherto been reserved to the states. In other words, the national government discovered that it, too, had "police power" and could directly regulate individuals as well as provide roads and other services.

The new programs were such dramatic departures from the traditional policies of the national government that their constitutionality was in doubt. The Supreme Court in fact declared several of them unconstitutional, mainly on the grounds that in regulating the conduct of individuals or their employers, the national government was reaching beyond "*inter*state" into "*intra*state," essentially local, matters. Most of the New Deal remained in constitutional limbo until 1937, five years after Roosevelt was first elected and one year after his landslide 1936 re-election.

The turning point came with *National Labor Relations Board v. Jones & Laughlin Steel Corporation*. At issue was the National Labor Relations Act, or Wagner Act, which prohibited corporations from interfering with the efforts of employees to organize into unions, to bargain collectively over wages and working conditions, and, under certain conditions, to go on strike and engage in picketing. The newly formed National Labor Relations Board (NLRB) had ordered Jones & Laughlin to reinstate workers fired because of their union activities. The appeal reached the Supreme Court because Jones & Laughlin had made a constitutional issue over the fact that its manufacturing activities were local and, therefore, beyond the national government's reach. The Supreme Court rejected this argument with the response that a big company with subsidiaries and suppliers in many states was innately in interstate commerce:

> When industries organize themselves on a national scale, making their relation to interstate commerce the dominant factor in their activities, how can it be maintained that their industrial labor relations constitute a forbidden field into which Congress may not enter when it is necessary to protect interstate commerce from the paralyzing consequences of industrial war?[27]

[27]National Labor Relations Board v. Jones & Laughlin Steel Corporation, 301 U.S. 1 (1937). Congress had attempted to regulate the economy before 1933, as with the Interstate Commerce Act and Sherman Antitrust Act of the late nineteenth century and with the Federal Trade Act and the Federal Reserve in the Wilson period. But these were rare attempts, and each was restricted very carefully to a narrow and acceptable definition of "interstate commerce." The big break did not come until after 1933.

Since the end of the New Deal, the Supreme Court has never again seriously questioned the constitutionality of an important act of Congress broadly authorizing the executive branch to intervene into the economy or society.[28]

Delegation of Power   The most important constitutional effect of Congress's actions and the Supreme Court's approval of those actions during the New Deal was the enhancement of *presidential power.* Most major acts of Congress in this period involved significant exercises of control over the economy. But few programs specified the actual controls to be used. Instead, Congress authorized the president or, in some cases, a new agency to determine what the controls would be. Some of the new agencies were independent commissions responsible to Congress. But most of the new agencies and programs of the New Deal were placed in the executive branch directly under presidential authority.

Technically, this form of congressional act is called the "delegation of power." In theory, the delegation of power works as follows: (1) Congress recognizes a problem; (2) Congress acknowledges that it has neither the time nor expertise to deal with the problem; and (3) Congress, therefore, sets the basic policies and then delegates to an agency the power to "fill in the details." But, in practice, Congress was delegating not merely the power to "fill in the details," but actual and real *policy-making powers*—that is, real legislative powers—to the executive branch. For example, in order to keep prices up and surpluses down, the president, through the secretary of agriculture, was authorized by the 1938 Agricultural Adjustment Act to determine the amount of acreage each and every farmer could devote to crops that had been determined to be surplus commodities. This new authority extended from growers of thousands of acres of wheat for market to farmers cultivating twenty-five acres of feed for their own livestock.[29]

This authority continues today in virtually the same form, covering many commodities and millions of acres. Lest this is thought to be a power delegated to the president only during emergencies like the 1930s, take the example of environmental protection laws passed by Congress in the 1960s and 1970s. Under the president, the Environmental Protection Agency was given the authority to "monitor the conditions of the environment," "establish quantitative base lines

---

[28]Some will argue that there are exceptions to this statement. One was the 1976 case declaring unconstitutional Congress's effort to supply national minimum wage standards to state and local government employees (National League of Cities v. Usery, 426 U.S. 833 [1976]). But the Court reversed itself nine years later, in 1985 (Garcia v. San Antonio Metropolitan Transit Authority, 469 U.S. 528 [1985]). Another was the 1986 case declaring unconstitutional the part of the Gramm-Rudman law authorizing the comptroller general to make "across the board" budget cuts when total appropriations exceeded legally established ceilings (Bowsher v. Synar, 478 U.S. 714 [1986]). In 1999, executive authority was compromised somewhat by the Court's decision to question the Federal Communication Commission's authority to supervise telephone deregulation under the Telecommunications Act of 1996. But cases such as these are few and far between, and they only touch on part of a law, not the constitutionality of an entire program.

[29]See Wickard v. Filburn, 317 U.S. 111 (1942).

for pollution levels," and "set and enforce standards of air and water quality and for individual pollutants."[30]

History Principle

The New Deal's expanded role for the national government enhanced presidential power.

No modern government can avoid the delegation of significant legislative powers to the executive branch. But the fact remains that this delegation produced a fundamental shift in the American constitutional framework. During the 1930s, the growth of the national government through acts delegating legislative power tilted the American national structure away from a Congress-centered government toward a president-centered government.[31] Make no mistake, Congress continues to be the constitutional source of policy. Legislative supremacy remains a constitutional fact of life, even at the beginning of the twenty-first century, because delegations are *contingent*. And not all delegations are the same. A Democratic Congress, for example, is unwilling to empower a Republican president and vice versa; unified governments are more likely to engage in broad delegation than divided governments are.[32] In short, Congress can rescind these delegations of power, restrict them with later amendments, and oversee the exercise of delegated power through congressional hearings, oversight agencies, budget controls, and other administrative tools. However, it is fair to say that presidential government has become an administrative fact of life as government-by-delegation has expanded greatly over the past hundred years. The world of Woodrow Wilson's *Congressional Government* is forever changed. But Congress has many "clubs behind its door" with which to influence the manner in which the executive branch exercises its newly won power to delegate authority.

PRESIDENTIAL GOVERNMENT

The locus of policy decision making shifted to the executive branch because, as we just noted, Congress made delegations of authority to the president. But this should not be construed as Congress having abdicated its constitutional position in policy making. Delegation is not abdication, and Congress retained many strings by which to oversee and regulate the executive's use of delegated

Rationality Principle

Congress delegates more power to the president as more demands are made on its agenda.

[30]Environmental Reorganization Plan of 9 July 1970, reprinted in *Congressional Quarterly Almanac*, 1970, pp. 119a–120a. Other examples of broad delegations of power to the president will be found in Theodore J. Lowi, *The End of Liberalism: The Second Republic of the United States*, 2nd ed. (New York: W. W. Norton, 1979), Chapter 5. See also Sotirios A. Barber, *The Constitution and the Delegation of Congressional Power* (Chicago: University of Chicago Press, 1975).

[31]The Supreme Court did in fact *dis*approve broad delegations of legislative power by declaring the National Industrial Recovery Act of 1933 unconstitutional on the grounds that Congress did not accompany the broad delegations with sufficient standards or guidelines for presidential discretion (Panama Refining Co. v. Ryan, 293 U.S. 388 [1935], and Schechter Poultry Corp. v. United States, 295 U.S. 495 [1935]). The Supreme Court has never reversed those two decisions, but it has also never really followed them. Thus, broad delegations of legislative power from Congress to the executive branch can be presumed to be constitutional.

[32]David Epstein and Sharyn O'Halloran, *Delegating Powers: A Transaction Cost Politics Approach to Policy Making under Separate Powers* (New York: Cambridge University Press, 1999).

Institution Principle

Congress delegates authority to the president but also maintains the means to influence how the executive branch exercises this power.

authority.[33] Congress delegated to the executive for instrumental reasons, much as a principal delegates to an agent. An expanded agenda of political demands, necessitated first by economic crisis—the Great Depression—but also by an accumulation of the effects of nearly a century's worth of industrialization, urbanization, and greater integration into the world economy, confronted the national government, forcing Congress's hand. The legislature itself was limited in its ability to expand its own capacity to undertake these growing responsibilities, so delegation proved a natural administrative strategy. If you can't do it yourself, then hire agents to do it! The president, executive-branch bureaus, and the independent regulatory commissions constituted precisely this army of agents. They were (at least in part) *congressional* agents, however, since it was delegation with a catch—oversight, regulation, amendment, budgetary control, etc., from the legislative branch. Nevertheless, these delegations certainly gave a far greater role to the president, empowering this "agent" to initiate in his own right.

In the case of Franklin D. Roosevelt, it is especially appropriate to refer to his New Deal as launching an era of "presidential government." Congress certainly retained many "clubs behind its door" with which to threaten, cajole, encourage, and persuade its executive agent to do its bidding. But presidents in general, and Roosevelt in particular, are not *only* agents of the Congress, and not *only* dependent upon Congress for resources and authority. They are also agents of national constituencies before whom they are eager to demonstrate their capacity for leadership in executing constituency policy agendas.[34] Likewise, congressional delegations of power are not the only resources available to a president.

Presidents have at their disposal a variety of other formal and informal resources that have important implications for their ability to govern. Indeed, without these other resources, presidents would lack the ability—the tools of management and public mobilization—to make much use of the power and responsibility given to them by Congress. Let us first consider the president's formal or official resources and then, in the section following, turn to the more informal resources that affect a president's capacity to govern, in particular the president's base of popular support.

What Are the Formal Resources of Presidential Power?

patronage The resources available to higher officials, usually opportunities to make partisan appointments to offices and to confer grants, licenses, or special favors to supporters.

Patronage   The first tool of management available to most presidents is a form of *patronage*—the choice of high-level political appointees. Political appointments should be thought of as *strategic* resources for presidents—as productive

---

[33]D. Roderick Kiewiet and Mathew D. McCubbins, *The Logic of Delegation: Congressional Parties and the Appropriations Process* (Chicago: University of Chicago Press, 1991).

[34]As the political scientist Terry Moe writes, "This is the rational basis for the institutional presidency. Throughout [the twentieth] century, presidents have struggled to provide themselves with a structural capacity for leadership by building institutions of their own." See Terry Moe, "Presidents, Institutions, and Theory," in George C. Edwards III, John H. Kessel, and Bert A. Rockman, eds., *Researching the Presidency: Vital Questions, New Approaches* (Pittsburgh: University of Pittsburgh Press, 1993), p. 367.

factors or instruments that may be deployed to achieve presidential objectives. These appointments allow the president to fill top management positions with individuals who will attempt to carry out his agenda. But he must appoint individuals who have experience and interest in the programs that they are to administer and who share the president's goals with respect to these programs. At the same time, presidents use the appointment process to build links to powerful political and economic constituencies by giving representation to important state political party organizations, the business community, organized labor, the scientific and university communities, organized agriculture, and certain large and well-organized religious groups. Of course, most high-level appointments to the bureaucracy and the courts must be confirmed by the Senate. This means that appointees must be acceptable to a Senate majority, but such appointments also constitute opportunities for a president to repay senators for previous favors or to obligate senators for favors down the road.

The Cabinet   In the American system of government, the *cabinet* is the traditional but informal designation for the heads of all the major federal government departments. The cabinet has no constitutional status. Unlike in England and many other parliamentary countries, where the cabinet *is* the government, the American cabinet is not a collective body. It meets but makes no decisions as a group. Each appointment must be approved by the Senate, but cabinet members are not responsible to the Senate or to Congress at large. Cabinet appointments help build party and popular support, but the cabinet is not a party organ. The cabinet is made up of directors, but is not a board of directors.

cabinet The secretaries, or chief administrators, of the major departments of the federal government. Cabinet secretaries are appointed by the president with the consent of the Senate.

Aware of this fact, the president tends to develop a burning impatience with and a mild distrust of cabinet members; to make the cabinet a rubber stamp for actions already decided on; and to demand results, or the appearance of results, more immediately and more frequently than most department heads can provide. Since cabinet appointees generally have not shared political careers with the president or with each other, and since they may meet literally for the first time after their selection, the formation of an effective governing group out of this motley collection of appointments is unlikely.

Some presidents have relied more heavily on an "inner cabinet," the National Security Council (NSC). The NSC, established by law in 1947, is composed of the president, the vice president, the secretaries of state, defense, and the treasury, the attorney general, and other officials invited by the president. It has its own staff of foreign-policy specialists run by the special assistant to the president for national security affairs. For these highest appointments, presidents turn to people from outside Washington, usually long-time associates. George W. Bush's "inner cabinet" is composed largely of former and proven senior staffers and cabinet members of former Republican administrations, most particularly Vice President Cheney, Defense Secretary Rumsfeld, and Secretary of State Powell.

Presidents have obviously been uneven and unpredictable in their reliance on the NSC and other subcabinet bodies because executive management is inherently a personal matter. Despite all the personal variations, however, one generalization can be made: presidents have increasingly preferred the White House staff instead of the cabinet as their means of managing the gigantic executive branch.

The White House Staff[35]   The White House staff is composed mainly of analysts and advisers. Although many of the top White House staffers are given the title "special assistant" for a particular task or sector, the types of judgments they are expected to make and the kinds of advice they are supposed to give are a good deal broader and more generally political than those that come from the Executive Office of the President or from the cabinet departments.

From an informal group of fewer than a dozen people (at one time popularly called the **Kitchen Cabinet**), and no more than four dozen at the height of the domestic Roosevelt presidency in 1937, the White House staff has grown substantially (see Figure 6.3).[36] President Clinton promised during the 1992 campaign to reduce the White House staff by 25 percent, and by 1996 had trimmed it by about 15 percent. Nevertheless, a large White House staff has become essential.

The Executive Office of the President   The development of the White House staff can be appreciated only in its relation to the still larger Executive Office of the President (EOP). Created in 1939, the EOP is what is often called the "institutional presidency"—the permanent agencies that perform defined management tasks for the president. The most important and the largest EOP agency is the Office of Management and Budget (OMB). Its roles in preparing the national budget, designing the president's program, reporting on agency activities, and overseeing regulatory proposals make OMB personnel part of virtually every conceivable presidential responsibility. The status and power of the OMB has grown in importance with each successive president. The process of budgeting at one time was a "bottom up" procedure, with expenditure and program requests passing from the lowest bureaus through the departments to "clearance" in OMB and hence to Congress, where each agency could be called in to reveal what its "original request" had been before OMB revised it. Now the budgeting process is "top down"; OMB sets the terms of discourse for agencies as well as for Congress. The director of OMB is now one of the most powerful officials in Washington. The staff of the Council of Economic Advisers (CEA) constantly analyzes the economy and economic trends, and attempts to give the president the ability to anticipate events rather than to wait and react to events. The Council on Environmental Quality was designed to do the same for environmental issues as the CEA does for economic issues. The National Security Council (NSC) is composed of designated cabinet officials who meet regularly with the presi-

Kitchen Cabinet
An informal group of advisers to whom the president turns for counsel and guidance. Members of the official cabinet may or may not also be members of the Kitchen Cabinet.

---

[35]A substantial portion of this section is taken from Lowi, *The Personal President*, pp. 141–50.

[36]All the figures since 1967, and probably 1957, are understated because additional White House staff members were on "detailed" service from the military and other departments (some secretly assigned) and are not counted here because they were not on the White House payroll.

FIGURE 6.3

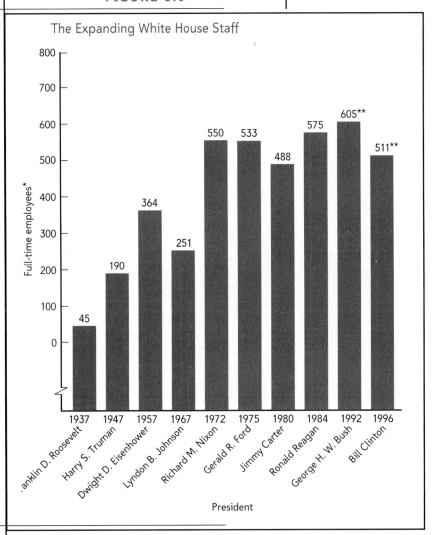

The Expanding White House Staff

*The vice president employs over 20 staffers, and there are at least 100 on the staff of the National Security Council. These people work in and around the White House and Executive Office but are not included in the above totals.

**These figures include the staffs of the Office of the President, the Executive Residence, and the Office of the Vice President. None of the figures includes the employees temporarily detailed to the White House from outside agencies (approximately 50 to 75 in 1992 and 1996). While not precisely comparable, these figures convey a sense of scale.

SOURCE: Thomas E. Cronin, "The Swelling of the Presidency: Can Anyone Reverse the Tide?" in *American Government: Readings and Cases,* ed. Peter Woll, 8th ed. (Boston: Little Brown, 1984), p. 347. Copyright © 1984 by Thomas E. Cronin. Appearing with the permission of the author. Figures for 1992 and 1996 provided by the Office of Management and Budget and the White House.

dent to advise him on the large national security picture. The staff of the NSC both assimilates and analyzes data from all intelligence-gathering agencies (the CIA etc.). Other EOP agencies perform more specialized tasks for the president.

Somewhere between 1,500 and 2,000 highly specialized people work for the EOP agencies.[37] Figure 6.4 shows the official numbers of employees in each agency of the EOP. However, these numbers do not include a substantial but variable number of key specialists detailed to EOP agencies from outside agencies, especially from the Pentagon to the staff of the NSC. The importance of each agency in the EOP varies according to the personal orientations of each president. For example, the NSC staff was of immense importance under President Nixon especially because it served essentially as the personal staff of presidential assistant Henry Kissinger. But it was of less importance to former president Bush, who looked outside the EOP altogether for military policy matters, much more to the Joint Chiefs of Staff and its chair at the time, General Colin Powell.

The Vice Presidency   The vice presidency is a constitutional anomaly even though the office was created along with the presidency by the Constitution. The vice president exists for two purposes only: to succeed the president in case of death, resignation, or incapacitation and to preside over the Senate, casting the tie-breaking vote when necessary.[38]

The main value of the vice presidency as a political resource for the president is electoral. Traditionally, a presidential candidate's most important rule for the choice of a running mate is that he or she bring the support of at least one state (preferably a large one) not otherwise likely to support the ticket. Another rule holds that the vice-presidential nominee should provide some regional balance and, wherever possible, some balance among various ideological or ethnic subsections of the party. It is very doubtful that John Kennedy would have won in 1960 without his vice-presidential candidate, Lyndon Johnson, and the contribution Johnson made by carrying Texas. The emphasis, however, has recently shifted away from geographical to ideological balance. George W. Bush's choice of Dick Cheney in 2000 was completely devoid of direct electoral value since Cheney came from one of our least populous states (Wyoming, which casts only 3 electoral votes). But given Cheney's stalwart right-wing record both in Congress and as President Bush's secretary of defense, coupled with his even more prominently right-wing wife, Lynne Cheney, his inclusion on the Republican ticket was clearly an effort to consolidate the support of the restive right wing of his party. Al Gore's choice of Joe Lieberman was also remote from electoral consideration. Lieberman's home state, Connecticut, contributes only 8 electoral votes and was already certain to go Democratic. And as the first Jewish vice-

[37]The actual number is difficult to estimate because, as with White House staff, some EOP personnel, especially in national security work, are detailed to the EOP from outside agencies.
[38]Article I, Section 3, provides that "The Vice President . . . shall be President of the Senate, but shall have no Vote, unless they be equally divided." This is the only vote the vice president is allowed.

FIGURE 6.4

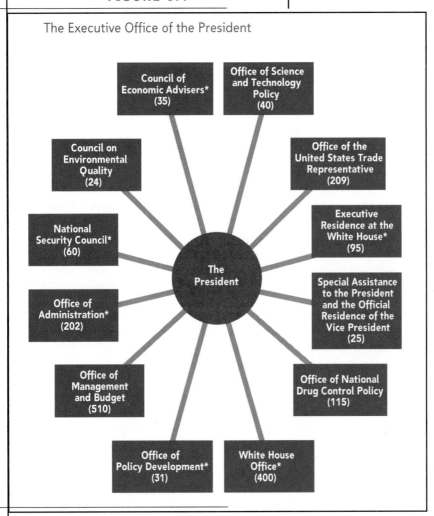

The Executive Office of the President

Council of Economic Advisers* (35)

Office of Science and Technology Policy (40)

Council on Environmental Quality (24)

Office of the United States Trade Representative (209)

National Security Council* (60)

Executive Residence at the White House* (95)

The President

Office of Administration* (202)

Special Assistance to the President and the Official Residence of the Vice President (25)

Office of Management and Budget (510)

Office of National Drug Control Policy (115)

Office of Policy Development* (31)

White House Office* (400)

NOTE: Figures in parentheses refer to number of staff. Figures are estimates for 2003.
*These have all been consolidated into one appropriation called "the White House."
SOURCE: Office of Management and Budget, *Budget of the United States Government, Fiscal Year 2004* (Washington, D.C.: Government Printing Office, 2003), pp. 881–87.

presidential nominee, Lieberman could add only marginally to the national Democratic vote because 80 percent of the Jewish vote was already Democratic. However, as a devoutly religious man and the first and only Democrat in the Senate to denounce President Clinton's behavior in the Lewinsky affair—and as

The Politics of Presidential Appointments

In the TV show *The West Wing,* viewers seldom see the cabinet officers—political opera-tives run everything. Sam, the deputy communications director, and Josh, the deputy chief of staff, seem to have more influence on foreign policy than the secretaries of de-fense and state. Luckily, these young and attractive staff members always seem to make the right choices.

Although Hollywood is not reality, it does reflect important institutional changes in the twentieth-century presidency. The growth of the Executive Office of the President and the appearance of cabinet officials who have little independent political influence other than personal loyalty to the president are two very important developments.[39] The presi-dential transition is about a lot more than just missing *W*s from keyboards.[40] Transitions and new appointments can be a clue to understanding administration success and failure.

Article II, Section 2, of the Constitution gives the president the power to appoint "Judges of the Supreme Court" and "Officers of the United States," subject to Senate ap-proval, but this does not fully explain how the appointment system really works. Not sur-prisingly, politics comes into play. Are loyal ideological warriors appointed? How many presidents use a Kitchen Cabinet of longtime friends and advisers? Are appointments pri-marily payback for support, or are they based solely on expertise and qualifications? And does our answer change if the position requires Senate approval or not?

As the discussion on pages 246 ff. notes, political appointments are strategic instru-ments for presidents to use to achieve presidential objectives. Throughout American his-tory, presidents have used the appointment power to further their own goals (Principle 1 reminds us that all political behavior has a purpose). The "spoils system" of appointments characterized the process through much of the nineteenth century. Beginning with Presi-dent Andrew Jackson, each administration brought in a completely new group of staffers and bureaucrats, often providing jobs to party loyalists. Cabinet officials consisted of in-fluential politicians who often had significant political standing in their own right.

Opposition to the excesses of the spoils system helped fuel the Progressive move-ment, which enacted civil service reforms in the late nineteenth and early twentieth cen-turies. These reforms made many low-level jobs outside the purview of the president. This path of historical development in the United States has meant that many governmental jobs are now not controlled directly by the president. In addition to protecting individuals from political retribution, it has also significantly reduced the ability of the president to control the bureaucracy and implement his political program.

In many cases, rules and procedures matter, too, as Principle 3 tells us. For appoint-ments that require Senate approval (federal judges and top officials in the executive branch), presidents have come to prize political viability. Concern over the political viabil-ity of nominees is an acknowledgment of the power of the Senate over confirmation. Com-mittee chairs can kill a nomination by refusing to allow a hearing to occur, thus preventing the nomination from ever coming up for a vote on the Senate floor. In addition, individual senators can have an enormous sway over the nomination process by placing a "hold" (a threat to filibuster) on a nomination. The invasive and occasionally grueling investigations that nominees undergo can at times be prohibitive. The Senate rarely rejects a nominee, but these tactics often lead the president to withdraw a nomination. And, as Principles 1 and 2 predict, presidents sometimes anticipate Senate opposition and do not nominate their top preference for an appointment.

In light of these constraints on the president's appointment power, strategic presidents can go outside of the formal process prescribed by the Constitution and rely on a Kitchen Cabinet of longtime friends and like-minded advisers who can avoid the strictures of rules and procedures that bind regular appointees. Presidents have also created and increasingly relied on their own institutions of power in the form of the White House staff and Executive Office of the President. These developments, in turn, have led to calls for a more vigorous role for the Senate in the appointments process.

[39]Compare today's cabinet to that of Abraham Lincoln, who appointed two of his rivals for the 1860 Republican nomination (William Seward and Salmon Chase) to key cabinet posts. Or consider Henry Clay, who served as senator, House member and Speaker of the House, secretary of state and senator (in that order). This is a political career that would be unheard of today.

[40]After the 2000 presidential transition from Clinton to Bush, it came out that Clinton staffers had, among other pranks, apparently removed all of the *W* keys from computer keyboards; http://www.cnn.com/2001/ALLPOLITICS/stories/01/27/w.h.pranks.

a conservative Democrat—Lieberman's presence was a message to the nation that Gore was not a "Clinton clone" and was solidly mainstream in all the policy initiatives he had promised to take as president.

Presidents have constantly promised to give their vice presidents more responsibility, but they almost always break their promises, indicating that they are unable to utilize the vice presidency as a management or political resource after the election. No one can explain exactly why. Perhaps it is just too much trouble to share responsibility. Perhaps the president as head of state feels unable to share any part of that status. Perhaps, like many adult Americans who do not draw up their wills, presidents may simply dread contemplating their own death. But management style is certainly a factor. George H. W. Bush, as vice president, was "kept within the loop" of decision making because President Reagan delegated so much power. A copy of virtually everything made for Reagan was made for Bush, especially during the first term, when Bush's close friend James Baker was chief of staff. Former President Bush did not take such pains to keep Dan Quayle "in the loop," but President Clinton relied greatly on his vice president, Al Gore, and Gore emerged as one of the most trusted and effective figures in the Clinton White House. Gore's most important task was to oversee the National Performance Review (NPR), an ambitious program to "reinvent" the way the federal government conducts its affairs. The presidency of George W. Bush has resulted in unprecedented power and responsibility for his vice president, Dick Cheney.

What Are the Informal Resources of Presidential Power?

Elections   Any ordinary citizen placed legitimately in the presidency would be very powerful, regardless of any other consideration because the Constitution and Congress have delegated to that office the legal powers and resources—in money and personnel—to carry out the duties of that office. But, as we also saw, presidential power comes from resources other than the formal, legal ones; success often results from strategic interactions with others and reliance on the democratic base of the presidency. Obviously, presidents vary in their real power according to the size of their electoral victory. With a landslide (decisive) national victory in an issues-oriented electoral campaign, a president may claim a ***mandate***, which is interpreted to mean that the electorate approved the victorious candidate's promised programs and that Congress must, therefore, go along.[41] A decisive election increases the effectiveness of presidential leadership in Congress. Presidents Johnson and Reagan were much more effective in Congress during the "honeymoon" year following their landslide elections of 1964 and 1980, respectively, than were Kennedy after 1960, Nixon after 1968, and Carter after 1976. All three were hampered by their narrow victory margins.

> **mandate**   A claim by a victorious candidate that the electorate has given him or her special authority to carry out promises made during the campaign.

President Clinton, an action-oriented president, was nevertheless seriously hampered by having been elected in 1992 by a minority of the popular vote, a mere 43 percent. Clinton was re-elected in 1996 with 49 percent of the vote, a larger percentage of the electorate, but still a minority. His appeals to bipartisanship in 1997 reflected his lack of a mandate from the electorate.

The outcome of the 2000 presidential election indicated a popular-vote deadlock of 48 percent to 48 percent, reflecting a difference of a mere 500,000 votes out of approximately 103 million cast. Given the closeness of the election—as well as the close partisan balance in Congress, initially it mattered little that George W. Bush won since any president possessing such a narrow margin of victory would have little claim to mandate. September 11, however, changed everything and gave Bush the mandate that the election failed to provide.

But the electoral base of presidential power goes deeper than the size of the margin during an election. Presidential power also comes from the selection process prior to the election. In the United States this is called the nominating process. Nomination means to name, and naming is what each party does when its members select the person they want to support as their candidate for a particular elective office. We will deal with this in detail in Chapter 11, but it is important to place the nominating process in the context of the presidency.

---

[41]Patricia Heidotting Conley, *Presidential Mandates: How Elections Shape the National Agenda* (Chicago: University of Chicago Press, 2001).

As we mentioned earlier, the original method for nominating presidential candidates was called "King Caucus"—the selection of a party's candidate for president by members of Congress who were declared affiliates of that party. But King Caucus was actually undermining both the independence of the presidency and the viability of the separation of powers by making all candidates for president, including the one eventually elected, beholden to Congress. America was becoming a parliamentary, "fusion of powers" system. The rise of the national presidential nominating convention in the 1830s gave the presidency a popular power base, which allowed enough independence from Congress to restore the separation of powers. Although the national-convention method fell into disrepute during the twentieth century for being too much under the control of party bosses in "smoke-filled rooms," it was, relative to King Caucus, an extremely significant democratizing force in the nineteenth century: the method broadened the base of the parties by permitting all districts in the country to send delegates to a national convention for president, even if that district was not represented in Congress by a member of its party. Thus, the national convention provided a channel for popular loyalty to the president that was separate from any loyalty that individuals might hold for their member of Congress.

Nomination by primary elections has become the more popular method, but primaries did not destroy the national-convention system, because primaries *elect* the delegates who go to the national conventions (rather than letting the state bosses appoint their own personal choices). It has now become an absolute prerequisite that presidential candidates prove themselves by having a significant number of delegates pledge their support in the primaries. This has made presidential candidacies much more expensive, but has also given the victor a far wider public base. The evolution of presidential selection, from caucus to convention to primary, is an example of the "democratization" of the presidency.

Initiative   *To initiate* means "to originate," and in government that can mean power.[42] The framers of the Constitution clearly saw this as one of the keys to executive power. The president as an individual is able to initiate decisive action, while Congress, as a relatively large assembly, must deliberate and debate before it can act. Initiative also means the ability to formulate proposals for important policies. There is power in this, too.

Presidents often send proposals to Congress. Congress, in turn, takes these proposals up by referring them to the relevant committee of jurisdiction. Sometimes these proposals are said to be "dead on arrival," an indication that presidential preferences are at loggerheads with those in the House or Senate. This is especially common during periods of divided government in which the president and at least one chamber majority are loyal to different parties. In such circumstances, presidents and legislators engage in *bargaining*, although at the end of the day the status quo may prevail. Presidents are typically in a weak position in

[42]Paul Pierson, "Not Just What, but *When:* Timing and Sequence in Political Processes," *Studies in American Political Development* 14 (2000): 72–92.

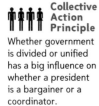

Collective Action Principle

Whether government is divided or unified has a big influence on whether a president is a bargainer or a coordinator.

this circumstance, especially if they have grand plans to change the status quo.[43] During periods of unified government, the president has fellow co-partisans in charge of each chamber; in these cases, the president may, indeed, seize the initiative, seeking to *coordinate* policy initiatives from the White House. Political scientist Charles M. Cameron suggests that the distinction between unified and divided government is quite consequential for presidential "style": it makes the chief executive either bargainer in chief or coordinator in chief.[44]

Over the years, Congress has sometimes deliberately and sometimes inadvertently enhanced the president's power to seize the initiative. Curiously, the most important congressional gift to the president seems the most mundane—namely, the Office of Management and Budget, known until 1974 as the Bureau of the Budget.

In 1921, Congress provided for an "executive budget" and turned over to a new Bureau of the Budget in the executive branch the responsibility for maintaining the nation's accounts. In 1939, this bureau was moved from the Treasury Department to the newly created Executive Office of the President. The purpose of this move was to permit the president to make use of the budgeting process as a management tool. Through the new budgeting process, the president could keep better track of what was going on among all of the executive branch's hundreds of agencies and hundreds of thousands of civil servants. In this respect, the budget is simply a good investigative and informational tool for management. But in addition to that, Congress provided for a process called *legislative clearance,* defined as the power given to the president to require all agencies of the executive branch to submit through the budget director all requests for new legislation along with estimates of their budgetary needs. Thus, heads of agencies must submit budget requests to the White House so that the requests of all the competing agencies can be balanced. Although there are many violations of this rule, it is usually observed.

legislative clearance The power given to the president to require all agencies of the executive branch to submit through the budget director all requests for new legislation along with estimates of their budgetary needs.

At first, legislative clearance was a defensive weapon, used mainly to allow the president to avoid the embarrassment of having to oppose or veto legislation originating in his own administration. But, eventually, legislative clearance became far more important. It became the starting point for the development of comprehensive presidential programs.[45] As noted earlier, recent presidents have also used the budget process as a method of gaining tighter "top down" management control.

Presidential proposals fill the congressional agenda and tend to dominate congressional hearings and floor debates, not to speak of the newspapers. Everyone recognizes this, but few appreciate how much of this ability to maintain the

---

[43]Kiewiet and McCubbins, *The Logic of Delegation.*

[44]Cameron, "Bargaining and Presidential Power."

[45]Although dated in some respects, the best description and evaluations of budgeting as a management tool and as a tool of program planning is still found in Richard E. Neustadt's two classic articles, "Presidency and Legislation: Planning the President's Program" and "Presidency and Legislation: The Growth of Central Clearance," in *American Political Science Review* (September 1954 and December 1955, respectively).

initiative is directly and formally attributable to legislative clearance. Through this seemingly routine process, the president is able to review the activities of his administrators, to obtain a comprehensive view of all legislative proposals, and to identify those that are in accord with his own preferences and priorities. This is why the whole process of choice has come to be called "planning the president's program." Professed anti-government Republicans, such as Reagan and Bush, as well as allegedly pro-government Democrats, such as Clinton, are alike in their commitment to central management, control, and program planning. This is precisely why all three presidents have given the budget director cabinet status.

The Media   The president is able to take full advantage of access to the communications media mainly because virtually all newspapers and television networks habitually look to the White House as the chief source of news about public policy. They tend to assign one of their most skillful reporters to the White House "beat." And since news is money, they need the president as much as he needs them in order to meet their mutual need to make news. In this manner, the formal and the informal aspects of initiative tend to reinforce each other: the formal resources put the president at the center of policy formulation; this becomes the center of gravity for all buyers and sellers of news, which in turn requires the president to provide easy access to this news. Members of Congress, especially senators, are also key sources of news. But Congress is an anarchy of sources. The White House has more control over what and when. That's what initiative is all about.

Different presidents have used the media in different ways. For example, the press conference as an institution probably got its start in the 1930s, when Franklin Roosevelt gave several a month. But his press conferences were not recorded or broadcast "live"; direct quotes were not permitted. The model we know today got its start with Eisenhower and was put into final form by Kennedy. Since 1961, the presidential press conference has been a distinctive institution, available whenever the president wants to dominate the news

In addition to the presidential press conference there are other routes from the White House to news prominence.[46] For example, President Nixon preferred direct television addresses, and President Carter tried to make the initiatives more homey with a television adaptation of President Roosevelt's "fireside chats." President Reagan made unusually good use of primetime television addresses and also instituted more informal but regular Saturday afternoon radio broadcasts, a tradition that President Clinton continued. Clinton also added various kinds of impromptu press conferences and town meetings.

Walter Mondale, while vice president in 1980, may have summed up the entire media matter with his observation that if he had to choose between the

---

[46]See George C. Edwards III, *At the Margins: Presidential Leadership of Congress* (New Haven: Yale University Press, 1989), Chapter 7; and Robert Locander, "The President and the News Media," in *Dimensions of the Modern Presidency*, ed. Edward N. Kearney (St. Louis, Mo.: Forum Press, 1981), pp. 49–52.

FIGURE 6.5

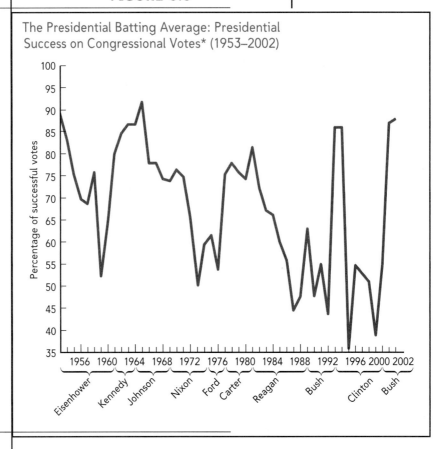

The Presidential Batting Average: Presidential Success on Congressional Votes* (1953–2002)

*Percentages based on votes on which presidents took a position.
SOURCE: *Congressional Quarterly Weekly Report*, 14 December 2002, p. 3275.

power to get on the nightly news and veto power, he would keep the former and jettison the latter.[47] Modern presidents have learned that they can use the media to mobilize popular support for their programs and to attempt to force Congress to follow their lead.

Party   Although on the decline, the president's party is far from insignificant as a political resource (see also Chapter 11). Figure 6.5 dramatically demonstrates

[47]Reported in Timothy E. Cook, *Governing with the News: The News Media as a Political Institution* (Chicago: University of Chicago Press, 1998), p. 133.

the point with a forty-seven-year history of the "presidential batting average" in Congress—the percentage of winning roll-call votes in Congress on bills publicly supported by the president.

Bill Clinton, in his first two years in office, enjoyed very high legislative success rates—86 percent in both 1993 and 1994. But these dropped drastically to 35.1 percent in 1995 and hovered around 50 percent in the years after (except for 1999, when success rates dropped to 39 percent). Clinton's pattern of congressional success demonstrates the *importance of the political party as a presidential resource.* Democratic control of Congress was a regular pattern between 1954 and 1994, and, therefore, presidential batting averages were very high, with a Democratic president and a Democratic House and Senate. President Eisenhower's averages were also very high for his first two years, when his own party controlled Congress; but they quickly dropped when Republicans lost control of Congress, as did President Clinton's success rate when Republicans took over Congress in 1995.

At the same time, party has its limitations as a resource. The more unified the president's party is behind his legislative requests, the more unified the opposition party is also likely to be. Unless the president's party majority is very large, he must also appeal to the opposition to make up for the inevitable defectors within the ranks of his own party. Consequently, the president often poses as being above partisanship in order to win "bipartisan" support in Congress. But to the extent he pursues a bipartisan strategy, he cannot throw himself fully into building the party loyalty and party discipline that would maximize the value of his own party's support in Congress. This is a dilemma for every president, particularly those faced with an opposition-controlled Congress.

The role of the filibuster in the Senate should not be underestimated in this context. Even a president with a large House majority and a good working Senate majority may not have the 60 votes needed to shut down debate in the Senate. Put differently, those in a position to threaten filibuster, though often constituting only a minority, can nevertheless extract concessions from a president who "thinks" he has the initiative! This is especially apparent in the case of presidential appointments, where individual senators can place a "hold" on the nomination, putting everyone on notice that if the president pursues this particular candidate, it will trigger a filibuster.[48]

Groups   The classic case in modern times of groups as a resource for the presidency is the Roosevelt or New Deal coalition.[49] The New Deal coalition was composed of an inconsistent, indeed contradictory, set of interests. Some of these

> **Collective Action Principle**
> The more unified the president's party is in Congress, the more unified the opposition is likely to be.

---

[48]A powerful argument that invokes this logic is that of Keith Krehbiel in *Pivotal Politics: A Theory of U.S. Lawmaking* (Chicago: University of Chicago Press, 1998).

[49]A wider range of group phenomena will be covered in Chapter 12. In that chapter the focus is on the influence of groups *upon* the government and its policy-making processes. Here our concern is more with the relationship of groups to the presidency and the extent to which groups and coalitions of groups become a dependable resource for presidential government.

interests were not organized interest groups, but were regional interests, such as southern whites, or residents of large cities in the industrial Northeast and Midwest, or blacks who later succeeded in organizing as an interest group. In addition to these sectional interests that were drawn to the New Deal, there were several large, self-consciously organized interest groups. The most important in the New Deal coalition were organized labor, agriculture, and the financial community.[50] All of the parts were held together by a judicious use of patronage—not merely patronage in jobs but patronage in policies. Many of the groups were permitted virtually to write their own legislation. In exchange, the groups supported President Roosevelt and his successors in their battles with opposing politicians.

Republican presidents have had their group coalition base also. The most important segments of organized business, especially the large, "labor intensive" industries that deal with unions affiliated with the CIO, have tended to support Republican presidents. Organized business has been joined by upper-income interests, not set up as a single upper-class group but usually organized around their respective areas of wealth. Republicans also have their share of ethnic groups, including staunch Republican organizations whose members hail from Eastern European countries. An important and recent sectionally based ethnic group is the white South. Once a solid-Democratic South, whites in most of the southern states have become virtually a solid-Republican group; and not far behind in importance within the Republican coalition is the so-called Sun Belt. Except for the white South, most of these groups have been Republicans for a long time. A newer presence within the white South is the Christian Right; although heavily southern, its membership extends far beyond the South. The two best organized groups within the Christian Right—the Christian Coalition and the Focus on the Family—have a strong and effective presence in many states in the West, the Northwest, and the border states.

The interest bases of the two parties have remained largely unchanged since 1980, when the GOP completed its absorption of most white southerners and religious conservatives. But whether these coalitions will last remains to be seen.

Public Opinion and Mass Popularity: Resource or Liability?   As presidential government grew, a presidency developed whose power is directly linked to the people. Successful presidents have to be able to mobilize mass opinion. Recent presidents, particularly Bill Clinton, have "gone public" by reaching out directly to the American public to gain its approval. If successful, presidents can use this approval as a weapon against Congress.[51] President Clinton's high public profile,

---

[50]For a more detailed review of the New Deal coalition in comparison with later coalitions, see Thomas Ferguson and Joel Rogers, *Right Turn: The Decline of the Democrats and the Future of American Politics* (New York: Hill & Wang, 1986), Chapter 2. For updates on the group basis of presidential politics, see Thomas Ferguson, "Money and Politics," in *The United States*, Handbooks to the Modern World, 3 vols. ed. Godfrey Hodgson (New York: Facts on File, 1992), II, pp. 1060–84; and Lucius J. Barker, ed., "Black Electoral Politics," *National Political Science Review* 2 (New Brunswick, N.J.: Transaction Publishers, 1990).

[51]Kernell, *Going Public*

FIGURE 6.6

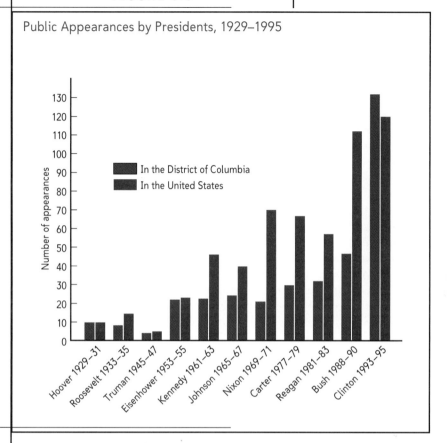

Public Appearances by Presidents, 1929–1995

Legend:
- In the District of Columbia
- In the United States

Y-axis: Number of appearances

X-axis categories: Hoover 1929–31, Roosevelt 1933–35, Truman 1945–47, Eisenhower 1953–55, Kennedy 1961–63, Johnson 1965–67, Nixon 1969–71, Carter 1977–79, Reagan 1981–83, Bush 1988–90, Clinton 1993–95

SOURCE: Samuel Kernell, *Going Public: New Strategies of Presidential Leadership*, 3rd ed. (Washington, D.C.: Congressional Quarterly Press, 1997), p. 118.

as is indicated by the number of public appearances he made (see Figure 6.6), was a dramatic expression of the presidency as a ***permanent campaign*** for re-election. A study by political scientist Charles O. Jones shows that President Clinton engaged in campaignlike activity throughout his presidency and proved to be the most-traveled American president in history. In his first twenty months in office, he made 203 appearances outside of Washington, compared with 178 for George H. W. Bush and 58 for Ronald Reagan. Clinton's tendency to go around rather than through party organizations is reflected in the fact that while Presidents Bush and Reagan devoted about 25 percent of their appearances to

permanent campaign A description of presidential politics in which all presidential actions are taken with re-election in mind.

Collective Action Principle

Presidents now engage in a permanent campaign for public support.

party functions, Clinton's comparable figure was only 8 percent.[52] President George W. Bush, in only his first one-hundred days in office, made public appearances in twenty-six states. This is the essence of the permanent campaign.

Even with the help of all other institutional and political resources, successful presidents have to be able to mobilize mass opinion in their favor in order to keep Congress in line. But, as we shall see, each president tends to *use up* mass resources. Virtually everyone is aware that presidents are constantly making appeals to the public over the heads of Congress and the Washington community. But the mass public is not made up of fools. The American people react to presidential actions rather than to mere speeches or other image-making devices.

The public's sensitivity to presidential actions can be seen in the tendency of all presidents to lose popular support. As shown in Figure 6.7, the percentage of positive responses to "Do you approve of the way the president is doing his job?" starts out at a level significantly higher than the percentage of votes the president got in the previous national election and then declines over the next four years. Though the shape of the line differs, the destination is the same. This downward tendency is to be expected if American voters are rational, inasmuch as almost any action taken by the president can be divisive. Public disapproval of specific actions has a cumulative effect on the president's overall performance rating. Thus, all presidents face the problem of boosting their approval ratings. And the public generally reacts favorably to presidential actions in foreign policy or, more precisely, to international events associated with the president. For example, President George W. Bush's approval ratings surpassed the 90-percent level as the Taliban fell from power in Afghanistan. Bush also enjoyed a substantial boost in popularity following the Iraqi war in March 2003. Analysts call this the *rallying effect.* Nevertheless, the rallying effect is only a momentary reversal of the more general tendency of presidents to lose popular support. In fact, following the successful conclusion to the war in Iraq, Bush's performance rating showed a steady decline, resulting from the tepid economy and the slow pace and high cost of establishing a new Iraqi government. The rise and fall of presidential performance ratings are evidence that with power goes vulnerability.

rallying effect
The generally favorable reaction of the public to presidential actions taken in foreign policy or, more precisely, to decisions made during international crises.

IS A PARLIAMENTARY SYSTEM BETTER?

Institution Principle
A parliamentary system is a fusion of powers, rather than a separation of powers.

Americans often get depressed over the phenomenon referred to as *divided government*. It is alleged by inside-the-beltway pundits that this is a formula for gridlock as partisan majorities in the different branches of government prevent anything from happening. Such pundits often cast a wistful look across the

---

[52]Study cited in Ann Devroy, "Despite Panetta Pep Talk, White House Aides See Daunting Task," *Washington Post*, 8 January 1995, p. A4.

FIGURE 6.7

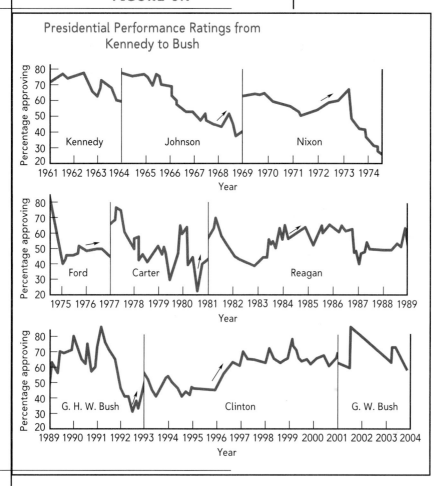

Presidential Performance Ratings from Kennedy to Bush

*NOTE: Arrows indicate pre-election upswings.
SOURCE: Courtesy of the Gallup Organization and Louis Harris &Associates.

Atlantic, touting the advantages of parliamentary government. Parliamentary democracy is organized according to a principle that emphasizes the coordination and concentration of power. The textbooks refer to this as a "fusion of powers" in contrast to the American-style "separation of powers." The centerpieces of this arrangement are the supremacy of parliament and the accountability of the political executive to it.

Governmental Arrangements

In parliamentary regimes, there is a division and specialization of labor. The House of Commons does not run British politics. Nor does the Dutch Tweede Kamer, the German Bundestag, the Japanese Diet, or the Norwegian Storting run the politics of the Netherlands, Germany, Japan, or Norway, respectively. Rather, each parliament "elects" a *government* to serve as the executive arm of the regime. We, thus, need to describe exactly what a "government" is, on the one hand, and how a country's parliament "elects" one, on the other.

The political executive in a parliamentary democracy is, with a few exceptions that we won't stop to consider here, chosen by parliament. This executive is called the *government;* it is also known as the *cabinet* or *council of ministers.* It is a collection of senior politicians, each of whom is the head of a department or ministry of state. In nearly every parliamentary regime, there is a finance minister, foreign minister, interior minister, defense minister, justice minister, education minister, environment minister, and so on.

Thus, there is a division and specialization of labor at two different levels. The first distinguishes between legislature and executive. The legislature selects the executive in the first place; keeps it in place or replaces it with a different one; and considers various pieces of legislation, the most important of which is the annual budget.[53] We will discuss these features momentarily. The second level of division and specialization of labor is in the government itself. In a manner parallel to the arrangements involving committees in the U.S. Congress, each ministry of state has jurisdiction over specified dimensions of public policy, called a *ministerial portfolio.* In this domain, the minister and his or her senior civil servants have considerable discretion to interpret statutory authority and implement public policy.

Another way to think about this arrangement is as a chain of principal-agent relationships. Parliament, as principal, delegates executive authority to a collective agent, the cabinet. The cabinet, as principal, in turn, delegates discretionary authority in various policy jurisdictions to its agents—namely, particular cabinet ministers. To control its agents and coordinate their activities, the cabinet employs various before-the-fact and after-the-fact mechanisms; usually one member of the cabinet plays the role of policeman and maestro—the *prime minister.* Likewise, to control *its* agent, parliament, too, exercises before-the-fact and after-the-fact authority. We refer to this authority as "making and breaking governments" since parliament votes a cabinet into office in the first place and, if it is unhappy with cabinet performance after the fact, may vote it out of office and replace it with an alternative cabinet.[54]

---

[53]It should be noted that legislatures in parliamentary regimes are not the hyperactive lawmaking engines we encounter in the American setting. Typically, parliaments vote a few broad delegations of statutory authority, which are then implemented by the government. In America, on the other hand, Congress and the various state legislatures legislate with much greater frequency and in a much more fine-grained fashion.

[54]These details are developed in Michael Laver and Kenneth A. Shepsle, *Making and Breaking Governments: Cabinets and Legislatures in Parliamentary Democracies* (New York: Cambridge University Press, 1996).

TABLE 6.1

Government Parties in Parliament*

		MAJORITY	MINORITY
EXECUTIVE	**SINGLE PARTY**	Unified (0.134)	Single-party minority (0.238)
	COALITION	Multiparty majority (0.500)	Multiparty minority (0.128)

*Cell entries give the proportion of each type as determined by Strom for a sample of Western parliamentary democracies, 1945–1982.
SOURCE: Kaare Strom, *Minority Government and Majority Rule* (New York: Cambridge University Press, 1990), p. 61.

The Government Formation Process

A typical sequence of events in one cycle of parliamentary democracy begins with a triggering event like an election. When the new parliament convenes, a number of parties may be represented, no one of which commands a majority of votes on its own. Each party has an *endowment* of a certain number of seats under its control and a set of policy priorities and positions on which it has just conducted its electoral campaign. Also at this time there will be a government in place—the cabinet that was running the country just before the election. The first order of business facing the new parliament is whether to retain the status quo cabinet or replace it with a new cabinet. If the political fortunes of the various parties have changed as a result of the election, it is highly likely that a new cabinet will be selected to better reflect the balance of political forces in the new parliament. But since no one party is a majority in its own right, the new government will have to reflect the preferences of a *coalition* of political parties. Government formation requires coalition building. This process produces governments of a variety of sizes and shapes (Table 6.1).

The number of parties represented at the cabinet table can be one or many—in which case the executive is a single party or a coalition, respectively. The number of seats in parliament controlled by the government parties can constitute either a majority or a minority. Thus, there are four different types of government. Their relative frequencies in Europe since 1945 are given parenthetically in Table 6.1.

Unified governments, which arise in slightly more than one of every eight governments in the period of study, are formed by parties that win outright parliamentary majorities. This is a relatively rare event, occurring frequently in Great Britain but only occasionally anywhere else in Europe. In this case the majority party votes itself all of the cabinet portfolios. The only serious threat to these "juggernauts" is intraparty factionalism. One faction of the majority party, if sufficiently numerous, can bring the government down by deserting it on a key vote.

Much more common, occurring about half the time in the postwar era, is a cabinet composed of several parties that jointly control a parliamentary majority. These *multiparty majority* governments need to control their rank and file in order to continue in office, but the ordinary tools of party discipline are typically sufficient for this task. A member of parliament that threatens to break ranks with the majority may find that his or her parliamentary career prospects suddenly become bleak, not to speak of the fact that the party organization will refuse to back him or her at the next election.

A more serious threat to these governments is that, during their incumbency, one or more of the governing parties will become dissatisfied and resign, essentially uniting with the opposition to bring down the government. Short of pulling out of a sitting government in order to defeat it, a governing party may insist on a reallocation of portfolios. If, for example, recent poll results suggested that one of the minor government parties were rising in popularity at the expense of one of the major government parties, the former could insist on a *cabinet reshuffle* in which it received more portfolios, or more important portfolios.

A *single-party minority* government sounds strange to American ears (although we shall suggest shortly that the reader has more familiarity with it than he or she realizes). It is a government in which one party receives all cabinet portfolios but has less than a majority of parliamentary seats. It governs at the sufferance of an opposition that, in combination, controls a majority of parliamentary seats. How can this be? It is able to retain office, as we shall shortly demonstrate, because the opposition, even though a majority, cannot agree on an alternative that it prefers. Imagine a large social democratic party—slightly left of center—controlling, say, 40 percent of parliamentary seats, that faces a radical left-wing party, an extremist right-wing party, and a religious party, controlling roughly 20 percent of the seats each. It is quite likely that anything preferred to a social democratic minority government by the left-wingers is strongly opposed by the right-wingers and religious partisans, whereas anything preferred to the social democrats by the two more conservative parties is opposed by the left-wingers. The opposition majority simply cannot get its act together, allowing the social democrats to survive in office even though they comprise but a minority of the whole parliament. This is not at all an unusual scenario, and, as the evidence in Table 6.1 suggests, something like it occurs nearly one-quarter of the time in Western parliamentary democracies.

To complete the picture, about one in every eight governments in the postwar Western experience is a coalition government whose partners control less than a parliamentary majority. Typically, they will be center-left or center-right coalitions that, like the single-party minority governments described in the previous paragraph, split the opposition.

So while some might wish that an alternative institutional arrangement might solve the alleged problems of divided government, the data of Table 6.1 suggest that parliamentary regimes are also highly prone to divided government. Multi-party majority coalition governments are those that control a parliamentary majority, but divided government occurs *within* the executive. Single-party minority governments have a unified executive but, lacking a majority in parliament, are divided in exactly the same way American governments often are—an executive whose party lacks a legislative majority. (Thus, despite sounding strange to American ears, single-party minority governments are structurally identical to the divided governments with which Americans have had frequent experience.) Minority coalition governments are divided both within the executive and between executive and legislature. Indeed, European parliamentary experience suggests that governments are divided about seven-eighths of the time, a proportion roughly equal to the postwar American experience. Parliamentary government, in short, is no cure for divided government.

SUMMARY

The foundations for presidential government were laid in the Constitution by providing for a unitary executive who is head of state as well as head of government. The first section of the chapter reviewed the powers of each: the head of state with its military, judicial, and diplomatic powers; and the head of government with its executive, military, and legislative powers. But this section noted that the presidency was subordinated to congressional government during the nineteenth century and part of the twentieth, when the national government was relatively uninvolved in domestic functions and inactive or sporadic in foreign affairs.

The second section of the chapter traced out the rise of modern presidential government after the much longer period of congressional dominance. There is no mystery in the shift to government centered on the presidency. Congress built the modern presidency by delegating to it not only the power to implement the vast new programs of the 1930s but also by delegating its own legislative power to make the policies themselves. The cabinet, the other top appointments, the White House staff, and the Executive Office of the President are some of the impressive formal resources of presidential power.

The chapter then focused on the president's informal resources, in particular his political party, the supportive group coalitions, and his access to the media and, through that, his access to the millions of Americans who make up the general public. But it was noted that these resources are not cost- or risk-free. The president's direct relation with the mass public is his most potent modern resource but also the most problematic. The chapter concluded with a description of the parliamentary system, a common form of government in many of today's powerful democracies; while the parliamentary and presidential systems differ in setup, they both often end up in gridlock.

Rationality Principle	Collective Action Principle	Institution Principle	Policy Principle	History Principle
Presidents can and have advanced their own priorities, and those of their office, by claiming inherent powers through the faithful execution of the law.	Vetoes are usually part of an intricate bargaining process between the president and Congress.	The Constitution established the presidency as an office of delegated powers.	Because of the president's veto power, Congress will alter the content of a bill to make it more to a president's liking.	The presidency was strengthened somewhat in the 1830s with the introduction of a national-convention system of nominating presidential candidates.
A president must weigh the advantages of vetoing legislation against the possible drop in his public approval.	Presidential power should be analyzed in terms of the strategic interactions that a president has with other political actors.	The president can be an important agenda setter for congressional action.	Public policy is used by presidents as a means to build and maintain political support.	The New Deal's expanded role for the national government enhanced presidential power.
Congress delegates more power to the president as more demands are made on its agenda.	The president can use public approval as a strategic resource.	The veto power makes the president the most important single legislative leader.	A parliamentary system is no cure for divided government.	
Presidential appointments are strategic resources that help a president achieve political objectives.	Whether government is divided or unified has a big influence on whether a president is a bargainer or a coordinator.	Congress delegates authority to the president but also maintains the means to influence how the executive branch exercises this power.		
	The more unified the president's party is in Congress, the more unified the opposition is likely to be.			
	Presidents now engage in a permanent campaign for public support.	A parliamentary system is a fusion of powers, rather than a separation of powers.		

FOR FURTHER READING

Brace, Paul, and Barbara Hinckley. *Follow the Leader: Opinion Polls and the Modern Presidents*. New York: Basic Books, 1992.

Cameron, Charles M. *Veto Bargaining: Presidents and the Politics of Negative Power*. New York: Cambridge University Press, 2000.

Drew, Elizabeth. *On the Edge: The Clinton Presidency*. New York: Simon & Schuster, 1994.

Kernell, Samuel. *Going Public: New Strategies of Presidential Leadership*. 3rd ed. Washington, D.C.: Congressional Quarterly Press, 1997.

Lowi, Theodore J. *The Personal President: Power Invested, Promise Unfulfilled*. Ithaca, N.Y.: Cornell University Press, 1985.

Milkis, Sidney M. *The President and the Parties: The Transformation of the American Party System since the New Deal*. New York: Oxford University Press, 1993.

Nelson, Michael, ed. *The Presidency and the Political System*. 7th ed. Washington, D.C.: Congressional Quarterly Press, 2003.

Neustadt, Richard E. *Presidential Power and the Modern Presidents: The Politics of Leadership from Roosevelt to Reagan*. New York: Free Press, 1990.

Pfiffner, James P. *The Modern Presidency*. New York: St. Martin's Press, 1994.

Polsby, Nelson W., and Aaron Wildavsky. *Presidential Elections: Contemporary Strategies of American Electoral Politics*. 8th ed. New York: Free Press, 1991.

Skowronek, Stephen. *The Politics Presidents Make: Leadership from John Adams to Bill Clinton*. Cambridge: Harvard University Press, 1997.

Spitzer, Robert J. *The Presidential Veto: Touchstone of the American Presidency*. Albany: State University of New York Press, 1988.

Tulis, Jeffrey. *The Rhetorical Presidency*. Princeton, N.J.: Princeton University Press, 1987.

Politics in the News—
Reading between the Lines

The President's Use of Executive Orders

Bush Orders Faster Track for Approval of Projects

By CHRISTOPHER MARQUIS

President Bush ordered federal agencies today to speed environmental reviews for major transportation projects, arguing that excessive red tape had impeded the construction of airports and highways.

Environmental groups immediately denounced the action, which was released this evening as an executive order. They said the order was part of an effort to restrict public debate and undermine environmental protections in place for three decades.

The president's order calls on the secretary of transportation to draw up a list of high-priority projects like roads, bridges, tunnels and airports that should receive expedited reviews and permits. It sets up an interagency task force to "identify and promote policies that can effectively streamline the process" while maintaining public health and environmental protection.

The transportation secretary, Norman Y. Mineta, said complex permit requirements had increased the time it took to build an airport to an average

of 10 years, a new highway to 13 years.

"Too many transportation projects become mired for too long in the complex web of clearances required by federal and state law," Mr. Mineta said. "This initiative is intended to make our transportation investments more efficient, helping to ease congestion and reduce pollution."

The task force, which would report to the president through the chairman of the Council on Environmental Quality, would include the secretaries of transportation, agriculture, commerce, interior, defense, as well as the administrator of the Environmental Protection Agency and the chairman of the Advisory Council on Historic Preservation.

Environmentalists said the order was part of a sweeping effort by the administration to weaken landmark environmental legislation under the guise of streamlining. They viewed the order in the context of White House initiatives to roll back rules affecting logging in

New York Times, 19 September 2002, p. A32.

national forests and offshore drilling for oil.

"This administration wants to shoot the sheriff protecting our environment so the highway robbers can ride again," said Deron Lovaas, a spokesman for the Natural Resources Defense Council.

The advocates said the administration was seeking to undercut the 32-year-old National Environmental Policy Act, which they consider the Magna Carta of environmental protections. The act sets the terms by which federal agencies must study and disclose the environmental effects of their actions and include the public in decision-making.

A White House spokesman, Scott McClellan, declined to say whether the White House wanted to modify the act. All changes under the president's order "will fully comply with the National Environmental Policy Act and other environmental statutes," Mr. McClellan said.

Mr. McClellan said the new task force would develop several "best practices" to guide decisions on high-priority projects. "Too many projects are being delayed that would actually reduce congestion and emissions," he said.

Representative Don Young, Republican of Alaska, and Senator Max Baucus, Democrat of Montana, are studying ways to alter the act. The Senate Environment and Public Works Committee has scheduled a hearing for Thursday.

Fred Krupp, executive director of Environmental Defense, said the president's order made Congressional action unnecessary. Mr. Krupp disputed claims that environmental impact studies and public comment had needlessly bogged down important projects.

"There are not any projects that have been significantly delayed because of environmental review," he said.

ESSENCE OF THE STORY

- President George W. Bush wants to streamline the environmental-review process for federal projects.
- By executive order (an executive order is not subject to congressional review), Bush created an interagency task force that will identify important federal projects and suggest ways to speed their approval.
- Environmental groups oppose the changes and charge that Bush is undermining Congress's intent when it passed the National Environmental Policy Act.

POLITICAL ANALYSIS

- Executive orders allow the president to create or change policy without having to convince Congress to pass legislation. In this case, Bush believed the environmental-review process was too cumbersome but did not want to be seen as undermining a major piece of environmental legislation.
- The ability of the executive to issue orders is limited by the "intent" of Congress, but "intent" is difficult to define. Often disputes of this kind end up in the Supreme Court.
- Environmental groups see this as the first of many attempts by the administration to weaken environmental protections in favor of business or economic interests.

CHAPTER

7

The Executive Branch: Bureaucracy in a Democracy

Americans depend on government bureaucracies to accomplish the most spectacular achievements as well as the most mundane. Yet they often do not realize that public bureaucracies are essential for providing the services that they use every day and that they rely on in emergencies. On a typical day, a college student might check the weather forecast, drive on an interstate highway, mail the rent check, drink from a public water fountain, check the calories on the side of a yogurt container, attend a class, log on to the Internet, and meet a relative at the airport. Each of these activities is possible because of the work of a government bureaucracy: the U.S. Weather Service, the U.S. Department of Transportation, the U.S. Postal Service, the Environmental Protection Agency, the Food and Drug Administration, the student loan programs of the U.S. Department of Education, the Advanced Research Projects Agency (which developed the Internet in the 1960s), and the Federal Aviation Administration. Without the ongoing work of these agencies, many of these common activities would be impossible, unreliable, or more expensive. Even though bureaucracies provide essential services that all Americans rely on, they are often disparaged by politicians and the general public alike. Criticized as "big government," many federal bureaucracies come into public view only when they are charged with fraud, waste, and abuse.

In emergencies, the national perspective on bureaucracy and, indeed, on "big government" shifts. After the September 11 terrorist attacks, all eyes turned to Washington. The federal government responded by strengthening and reorganizing the bureaucracy to undertake a whole new set of responsibilities designed to keep America safe. The president created the new cabinet-level Department of Homeland Security, charged with coordinating all domestic antiterrorism activities. Law-enforcement agencies gained new powers and resources. Reflecting the shift in priorities from crime investigation to terrorism prevention, the Federal Bureau of Investigation (FBI) received new responsibilities for domestic intelligence. Many other agencies assumed new duties associated with the antiterrorism objectives. The Treasury Department, for example, was assigned to create a financial intelligence-gathering system designed to track terrorists' financial transactions. The Centers for Disease Control (CDC) undertook a new set of activities designed to prevent bioterrorism. Congress created a new Transportation Security Administration within the Department of Transportation. Charged with making all forms of travel safe, the new agency presided over a significant expansion of the federal workforce as it hired thousands of workers to screen passengers at airports.

The war on terrorism has highlighted the extensive range of the tasks shouldered by the federal bureaucracy. Both routine and exceptional tasks require the organization, specialization, and expertise found in bureaucracies. Turn to Table 7.1 on page 274, which identifies the basic characteristics of bureaucracy. To provide services, government bureaucracies employ specialists such as meteorologists, doctors, and scientists. To do their jobs effectively, these specialists require resources and tools (ranging from paper to blood samples); they have to coordinate their work with others (for

CHAPTER OUTLINE

Why Bureaucracy?

- Bureaucratic Organization Enhances Efficiency

- Bureaucracies Allow Governments to Operate

- Bureaucrats Fulfill Important Roles

How Is the Executive Branch Organized?

- Clientele Agencies Serve Particular Interests

- Agencies for Maintenance of the Union Keep the Government Going

- Regulatory Agencies Guide Individual Conduct

- Agencies of Redistribution Implement Fiscal/ Monetary and Welfare Policies

Who Controls the Bureaucracy?

- The President as Chief Executive Can Direct Agencies

- Congress Promotes Responsible Bureaucracy

- Control of the Bureaucracy Is a Principal-Agent Problem

How Can Bureaucracy Be Reduced?

- Termination

- Devolution

- Privatization

TABLE 7.1

The Six Primary Characteristics of Bureaucracy

CHARACTERISTIC	EXPLANATION
Division of labor	Workers are specialized. Each worker develops a skill in a particular job and performs the job routinely and repetitively, thereby increasing productivity.
Allocation of functions	Each task is assigned. No one makes a whole product; each worker depends on the output of other workers.
Allocation of responsibility	Each task becomes a personal responsibility—a contractual obligation. No task can be changed without permission.
Supervision	Some workers are assigned the special task of watching over other workers rather than contributing directly to the creation of the product. Each supervisor watches over a few workers (a situation known as span of control), and communications between workers or between levels move in a prescribed fashion (known as chain of command).
Purchase of full-time employment	The organization controls all the time the worker is on the job, so each worker can be assigned and held to a task. Some part-time and contracted work is tolerated, but it is held to a minimum.
Identification of career within the organization	Workers come to identify with the organization as a way of life. Seniority, pension rights, and promotions are geared to this relationship.

example, the traffic engineers must communicate with construction engineers); and there must be effective outreach to the public (for example, private doctors must be made aware of health warnings). Bureaucracy provides a way to coordinate the many different parts that must work together in order to provide good services.

In this chapter, we will focus on the federal bureaucracy—the administrative structure that on a day-by-day basis *is* the American government. We will first define and describe bureaucracy as a social and political phenomenon. Second, we will look in detail at American bureaucracy in action by examining the government's major administrative agencies, their role in the governmental process, and their political behavior. These details of administration are the very heart and soul of modern government.

We mean for the reader to keep an open mind about bureaucracy. It is often portrayed as "runaway" and "out of control." It is often thought of pejoratively as self-serving, bloated, and highly inefficient. In short, bureaucracy has a very serious public relations problem! But bureaucracy is created by legislation—that is, an agency's existence (both initial and continued) is approved by both houses of Congress and the president. A bureau's authority can be expanded or trimmed by legislative authorization, its budgets increased or decreased via the normal appropriations process, and its actions subjected to scrutiny by legislative oversight committees and executive watchdog agencies. In short, bureaus and agencies of the federal government are the *creatures* of Congress and the president. We should wonder, before castigating bureaus and agencies, whether our elected officials are as much to blame as are appointees and civil servants for the excesses laid at the door of the federal bureaucracy.

WHY BUREAUCRACY?

PREVIEWING THE PRINCIPLES

Bureaucracy is necessary for implementing public policy. Implementing the laws and policies passed by elected officials, bureaucrats can be understood to be agents of Congress and the presidency. As is the case in any principal-agent relationship, the agent (the bureaucracy) is delegated authority and has a certain amount of leeway for independent action. Despite the efforts of elected officials (the principals) to check departments and agencies (the agents), bureaucrats have their own goals and, thus, exercise their own influence on policy. The problem of controlling bureaucracy is a central concern for democracies. Although controlling the growth of bureaucracy is a popular concern, the size of the federal bureaucracy has in fact kept pace with the economy and the needs of society. And since most Americans benefit in some way from programs implemented by government agencies, they are reluctant to cut back on the size and scope of these programs.

Bureaucracies are commonplace because they touch so many aspects of daily life. Government bureaucracies implement the decisions made by the political process. Bureaucracies are full of routine because that assures the regular delivery of the services and ensures that each agency fulfills its mandate. Public bureaucracies are powerful because legislatures and chief executives—and, indeed, the people—delegate to them vast power to make sure a particular job is done, enabling the rest of us to be freer to pursue our private ends. The public sentiments that emerged after September 11 revealed this underlying appreciation of public bureaucracies. When faced with the challenge of making air travel safe again, the public strongly supported giving the federal government responsibility for airport security, even though this meant increasing the size of the federal bureaucracy by making the security screeners federal workers. House majority whip Tom DeLay sought to forestall this growth in the federal government, declaring that "the last thing we can afford to do is erect a new bureaucracy that is unaccountable and unable to protect the American public."[1] But the antibureaucratic language that had been so effective prior to September 11 no longer resonated with a fearful public. Instead, there was a widespread belief that a public bureaucracy would provide more effective protection than the cost-conscious private security companies that had been charged with airport security in the past. Bureaucrats across the federal government felt the new appreciation for their work. As one civil servant at the Pentagon put it, "The whole mood has changed. A couple of months ago we were part of the bloated bureaucracy. Now we're Washington's equivalent of the cops and firemen in New York."[2] How long such sentiments last will depend on the effectiveness of the bureaucracy and on the public's views about whether an expanded bureaucracy is needed when (and if) the immediate threat of terrorism recedes.

Despite the naive tendency to criticize bureaucracy because it is "bureaucratic," most Americans recognize that maintaining order in a large society is impossible without some sort of large governmental apparatus, staffed by professionals with some expertise in public administration. When we approve of what a government agency is doing, we give the phenomenon a positive name, *administration;* when we disapprove, we call the phenomenon *bureaucracy.*

Although the terms *administration* and *bureaucracy* are often used interchangeably, it is useful to distinguish between the two. *Administration* is the more general of the two terms; it refers to all the ways human beings might rationally coordinate their efforts to achieve a common goal. This applies to private as well as public organizations. **Bureaucracy** refers to the actual offices, tasks, and principles of organization that are employed in the most formal and sustained administration. Table 7.1 defines *bureaucracy* by identifying its basic characteristics.

bureaucracy The complex structure of offices, tasks, rules, and principles of organization that are employed by all large-scale institutions to coordinate the work of their personnel.

Bureaucratic Organization Enhances Efficiency

The core of bureaucracy is the *division of labor.* The key to bureaucratic effectiveness is the coordination of experts performing complex tasks. If each job is specialized in order to gain efficiencies, then each worker must depend upon the output of other workers, and that requires careful *allocation* of jobs and resources. Inevitably, bureaucracies become hierarchical, often approximating a pyramid in form. At the base of the organization are workers with the fewest skills and specializations; one supervisor can deal with a relatively large number of these workers. At the next level of the organization, where there are more highly specialized workers, the supervision and coordination of work involves fewer workers per supervisor. Toward the top of the organization, a very small

---

[1]Janet Hook, "U.S. Strikes Back; Political Landscape; GOP Bypasses the Bipartisan Truce," *Los Angeles Times,* 14 October 2001, p. A8.
[2]R. W. Apple, Jr., "White House Letter: Big Government Is Back in Style," *New York Times,* 23 November 2001, p. B2.

number of high-level executives engages in the "management" of the organization, meaning the organization and reorganization of all the tasks and functions, plus the allocation of the appropriate supplies and the distribution of the outputs of the organization to the market (if it is a "private sector" organization) or to the public.

Bureaucracies Allow Governments to Operate

Bureaucracy, when used pejoratively, conjures up endless paperwork, red tape, and lazy, uncaring employees. In fact it represents a rather spectacular human achievement. By dividing up tasks, matching tasks to a labor force that develops appropriately specialized skills, routinizing procedure, and providing the incentive structure and oversight arrangements to get large numbers of people to operate in a coordinated, purposeful fashion, bureaucracies accomplish tasks and missions in a manner that would otherwise be unimaginable. The provision of "government goods" as broad as the defense of people, property, and national borders or as narrow as a subsidy to a wheat farmer, a beef rancher, or a manufacturer of specialty steel requires organization, routines, standards, and, at the end of the day, the authority for someone to cut a check and put it in the mail. Bureaucracies are created to do these things. No large organization would be larger than the sum of its parts, and many would be smaller, without bureaucratizing its activities.

Bureaucracy also consolidates a range of complementary programs and insulates them from the predatory ambitions of out-of-sympathy political forces. Nothing in this world is permanent, but bureaucracies come close. By creating clienteles—in the legislature, the world of interest groups, and public opinion—a bureaucracy establishes a coalition of supporters, some of whom will fight to the end to keep it in place. It is a well-known rule of thumb that everyone in the political world cares deeply and intensely about a subset of policies and the agencies that produce them, and opposes other policies and agencies but not with nearly the same passion. Opponents, to succeed, must clear many hurdles, while proponents, to maintain the status quo, must only marshall their forces at a few veto points. In the final analysis, opponents typically meet obstacle after obstacle and eventually give up their uphill battles and concentrate on protecting and expanding what they care more deeply about. In a complex political system like that in the United States, it is much easier to do the latter. Politicians appreciate this fact of life. Consequently, both opponents and proponents of a particular set of government activities wage the fiercest battles at the time programs are enacted and a bureaucracy is created. Once created, these organizations assume a position of relative permanence.

So, in response to the question of how bureaucracy makes government possible, there is an *efficiency* part to the answer and a *credibility* part. The creation of a bureau is a way to deliver government goods efficiently *and* a device by which to "tie one's hands," thereby providing a credible commitment to the long-term existence of a policy.

Bureaucrats Fulfill Important Roles

"Government by offices and desks" conveys to most people a picture of hundreds of office workers shuffling millions of pieces of paper. There is a lot of truth in that image, but we have to look more closely at what papers are being shuffled and why. More than fifty years ago, an astute observer defined bureaucracy as "continuous routine business."[3] Almost any organization succeeds by reducing its work to routines, with each routine being given to a different specialist. But specialization separates people from each other; one worker's output becomes another worker's input. The timing of such relationships is essential, requiring these workers to stay in communication with each other. In fact, bureaucracy was the first information network. Voluminous routine came as bureaucracies grew and specialized. As bureaucracies have grown, the term *bureaucrat* now connotes sluggishness and inefficiency.

Motivational Considerations   The popular view of bureaucrats as failing to live up to the expectation that they will serve the public interest is judgmental and emotionally laden, not analytical. In a now-classic treatment, the economist William A. Niskanen rejected this misbegotten view entirely.[4] Instead, he proposed that we consider a bureau or department of government as analogous to a division of a private firm and conceive of the bureaucrat just as we would the manager who runs that division. In particular, Niskanen stipulates for the purposes of modeling bureaucratic behavior that a bureau chief or department head be thought of as a maximizer of his or her budget (just as the private-sector counterpart is a maximizer of his or her division's profits).

There are quite a number of different motivational bases on which bureaucratic budget maximizing might be justified. A cynical (though some would say realistic) basis for budget maximizing is that the bureaucrat's own compensation is often tied to the size of his or her budget. Not only might bureaus with large budgets have higher-salaried executives with more elaborate fringe benefits, but also there may be enhanced opportunities for career advancement, travel, a poshly appointed office, possibly even a chauffeur-driven limousine.

A second, related motivation for large budgets is nonmaterial personal gratification. An individual understandably enjoys the prestige and respect that comes from running a major enterprise. You can't take these things to the bank or put them on your family's dinner table, but your sense of esteem and stature are surely buoyed by the conspicuous fact that your bureau or division has a large budget. That you are also boss to a large number of subordinates, made possible by a large bureau budget, is another aspect of this sort of ego gratification.

But personal salary, "on-the-job consumption," and power-tripping are not the only forces driving a bureaucrat toward gaining as large a budget as possible.

Rationality Principle

One view of bureaucratic behavior is that bureaucrats are motivated to maximize their budgets.

---

[3]Arnold Brecht and Comstock Glaser, *The Art and Technique of Administration in German Ministries* (Cambridge, Mass.: Harvard University Press, 1940), p. 6.
[4]William A. Niskanen, Jr., *Bureaucracy and Representative Government* (Chicago: Aldine, 1971).

Some bureaucrats, perhaps most, actually *care* about their missions.[5] They initially choose to go into public safety, or the military, or health care, or social work, or education—as police officers, soldiers, hospital managers, social workers, and teachers, respectively—because they believe in the importance of helping people in their communities. As they rise through the ranks of a public bureaucracy into management responsibilities, they take this mission orientation with them. Thus, as chief of detectives in a big-city police department, as head of procurement in the air force, as director of nursing services in a public hospital, as supervisor of the social work division in a county welfare department, or as assistant superintendent of a town school system, individuals try to secure as large a budget as they can in order to succeed in achieving the missions to which they have devoted their professional lives.

Whether from cynical, self-serving motives or for the noblest of public purposes, it is entirely plausible that individual bureaucrats seek to persuade others (typically legislators or taxpayers) to provide them with as many resources as possible. Indeed, it is sometimes difficult to distinguish the saint from the sinner since each sincerely argues that he or she needs more in order to do more. This is one of the nice features of Niskanen's assumption of budget maximizing: it doesn't really matter *why* a bureaucrat is interested in a big budget; what matters is simply that she wants more resources rather than less.

Critics of the budget-maximizing theory call into question its assumption about the passivity of the legislature. The legislature, the only customer of the bureau's product, in essence tells the bureau how much it is willing to pay for various production levels. The critics suggest that this is akin to a customer walking onto a used-car lot and telling the salesman precisely how much she is willing to spend for each of the vehicles.[6]

In a representative democracy, it may be difficult for the legislature to keep silent about its own willingness to pay. The bureau, at any rate, can do some research in order to judge the preferences of various legislators based on who their constituents are. But legislators can do research, too. Indeed, we suggested in Chapter 5 that the collection, evaluation, and dissemination of information—in this case information about the production costs of bureaucratic supply—are precisely the things in which specialized legislative committees engage. Committees hold hearings, request documentation on production, assign investigatory staff to various research tasks, and query bureau personnel on the veracity of their data and on whether they employ lowest-cost technologies (making it more difficult for the bureau to disguise on-the-job consumption). After the fact, the committees engage in oversight, making sure that what the legislature was told at the time that authorization and appropriations were voted actually holds in practice. In short, the legislature can be much more pro-active than the

---

[5]John Brehm and Scott Gates, *Working, Shirking, and Sabotage: Bureaucratic Response to a Democratic Public* (Ann Arbor: University of Michigan Press, 1997).

[6]This and other related points are drawn from Gary J. Miller and Terry M. Moe, "Bureaucrats, Legislators, and the Size of Government," *American Political Science Review* 77 (1983): 297–323.

Niskanen budget-maximizing theory gives them credit for. And, in the real world, it is, as we shall see later in the chapter.

Before leaving motivational considerations, it should be remarked that budget maximizing is not the only objective that bureaucrats pursue. It needs to be emphasized and re-emphasized that career civil servants and high-level political appointees are *politicians*. They spend their professional lives pursuing political goals, bargaining, forming alliances and coalitions, solving cooperation and collective-action problems, making policy decisions, operating within and interfacing with political institutions—in short, doing what other politicians do. They do not have elections to win, but even elections affect their conditions of employment by determining the composition of the legislature and the partisan and ideological complexion of the chief executive. Bureaucrats are politicians beholden to other politicians for authority and resources. They are servants of many masters.

As politicians subject to the oversight and authority of others, bureaucrats must make contingency plans. They must be strategic and forward thinking. Whichever party wins control of the House or Senate, whichever candidate wins the presidency, whoever becomes chair of the legislative committee with authorization or appropriation responsibility over her agency, life will go on and the bureau chief will have to adjust to the prevailing political winds. To protect and expand authority and resources, bureaucratic politicians seek, in the form of *autonomy* and *discretion*, insurance against political change. They don't always succeed in acquiring this freedom, but they do try to insulate themselves from changes in the broader political world.[7] So bureaucratic motivations include budget-maximizing behavior, to be sure, but bureaucrats also seek the autonomy to weather changes in the political atmosphere and the discretion and flexibility to fine-tune their authority and resources toward the things they most want to achieve.

Collective Action Principle
Coordination among bureaucrats is necessary to carry out the primary task of bureaucracy—implementation.

implementation
The efforts of departments and agencies to translate laws into specific bureaucratic routines.

Bureaucrats Implement Laws   Bureaucrats, whether in public or in private organizations, communicate with each other in order to coordinate all the specializations within their organization. This coordination is necessary to carry out the primary task of bureaucracy, which is ***implementation***—that is, implementing the objectives of the organization as laid down by its board of directors (if a private company) or by law (if a public agency). In government, the "bosses" are ultimately the legislature and the elected chief executive. As we saw in Chapter 1, in a principal-agent relationship, it is the principal who stipulates what he wants done, relying upon the agent's concern for her reputation, appropriate incentives, and other control mechanisms to secure compliance with his wishes. Thus, it may be argued that legislative principals establish bureaucratic agents—in departments, bureaus, agencies, institutes, and commissions of the federal government—to implement the policies promulgated by Congress and the president.

---

[7]For an expanded view of bureaucratic autonomy and insulation, with historical application to the U.S. Department of Agriculture and the U.S. Post Office, see Daniel P. Carpenter, *The Forging of Bureaucratic Autonomy: Reputations, Networks, and Policy Innovation in Executive Agencies, 1862–1928* (Princeton, N.J.: Princeton University Press, 2001).

Bureaucrats Make and Enforce Rules When the bosses—Congress, in particular, when it is making the law—are clear in their instructions to bureaucrats, implementation is a fairly straightforward process. Bureaucrats translate the law into specific routines for each of the employees of an agency. But what happens to routine administrative implementation when there are several bosses who disagree as to what the instructions ought to be? The agent of multiple principals who disagree often finds him- or herself in a real bind. The agent must chart a delicate course, seeking to do the best he or she can and trying not to offend any of the bosses too much. This requires yet another job for bureaucrats: interpretation. Interpretation is a form of implementation in that the bureaucrats still have to carry out what they believe to be the intentions of their superiors. But when bureaucrats have to interpret a law before implementing it, they are in effect engaging in *lawmaking*.[8] Congress often deliberately delegates to an administrative agency the responsibility of lawmaking. Members of Congress often conclude that some area of industry needs regulating or some area of the environment needs protection, but they are unwilling or unable to specify just how that should be done. In such situations, Congress delegates to the appropriate agency a broad authority within which the bureaucrats have to make law, through the procedures of ***rule-making*** and ***administrative adjudication.***

Rule-making is exactly the same as legislation; in fact, it is often referred to as "quasi-legislation." The rules issued by government agencies provide more detailed and specific indications of what the policy actually will mean. For example, the Occupational Health & Safety Administration is charged with ensuring that our workplaces are safe. OSHA has regulated the use of chemicals and other well-known health hazards. In recent years, the widespread use of computers in the workplace has been associated with a growing number of cases of repetitive stress injury, which hurts the hands, arms, and neck. To respond to this new threat to workplace health, OSHA issued a new set of ergonomic rules in November 1999 that tell employers what they must do to prevent and address such injuries among their workers. Such rules only take force after a period of public comment. Reaction from the people or businesses that are subject to the rules may cause an agency to modify the rules they first issue. The rules about ergonomic safety in the workplace, for example, were sure to be contested by many businesses, which viewed them as too costly. The rule-making process is thus a highly political one. Once rules are approved, they are published in the *Federal Register* and have the force of law.

Institution Principle

Legislative principals establish bureaucratic agents to implement policies.

rule-making
A quasi-legislative administrative process that produces regulations by government agencies.

administrative adjudication
Applying rules and precedents to specific cases to settle disputes with regulated parties.

---

[8]When bureaucrats engage in interpretation, the result is what political scientists call bureaucratic drift. Bureaucratic drift occurs because, as we've suggested, the "bosses" (in Congress) and the agents (within the bureaucracy) don't always share the same purposes. Bureaucrats also have their own agendas to fulfill. There exists a vast body of political-science literature on the relationship between Congress and the bureaucracy. For a review, see Kenneth A. Shepsle and Mark S. Bonchek, *Analyzing Politics: Rationality, Behavior, and Institutions* (New York: W. W. Norton, 1997), pp. 355–68. We'll also return to this point at the end of this chapter.

Institution Principle

Congress also delegates authority to bureaucrats to make law through the procedures of rule-making and administrative adjudication.

Bureaucrats Settle Disputes   Administrative adjudication is very similar to what the judiciary ordinarily does: applying rules and precedents to specific cases in order to settle disputes. In administrative adjudication, the agency charges the person or business suspected of violating the law. The ruling in an adjudication dispute applies only to the specific case being considered. Many regulatory agencies use administrative adjudication to make decisions about specific products or practices. For example, in December 1999, the Consumer Product Safety Commission held hearings on the safety of bleachers, sparked by concern over the death of children after falls from bleachers. It issued guidelines about bleacher construction designed to prevent falls. These guidelines have the force of law. Likewise, product recalls are often the result of adjudication.

In sum, government bureaucrats do essentially the same things that bureaucrats in large private organizations do, and neither type deserves the disrespect embodied in the term *bureaucrat*. But because of the authoritative, coercive nature of government, far more constraints are imposed on public bureaucrats than on private bureaucrats, even when their jobs are the same. Public bureaucrats are required to maintain a far more thorough paper trail. Public bureaucrats are also subject to a great deal more access from the public. Newspaper reporters, for example, have access to public bureaucrats. Public access has been vastly facilitated in the past thirty years; the adoption of the Freedom of Information Act (FOIA) in 1966 gave ordinary citizens the right of access to agency files and agency data to determine whether derogatory information exists in the file about citizens themselves and to learn about what the agency is doing in general.

And, finally, citizens are given far more opportunities to participate in the decision-making processes of public agencies. There are limits of time, money, and expertise to this kind of access, but it does exist, and it occupies a great deal of the time of mid-level and senior public bureaucrats. This public exposure and access serves a purpose, but it also cuts down significantly on the efficiency of public bureaucrats. Thus, much of the lower efficiency of public agencies can be attributed to the political, judicial, legal, and publicity restraints put on public bureaucrats.

HOW IS THE EXECUTIVE BRANCH ORGANIZED?

Cabinet departments, agencies, and bureaus are the operating parts of the bureaucratic whole. These parts can be separated into four general types: (1) cabinet departments, (2) independent agencies, (3) government corporations, and (4) independent regulatory commissions.

Although Figure 7.1 is an "organizational chart" of the Department of Agriculture, any other department could have been used as an illustration. At the top is the head of the department, who in the United States is called the "secretary" of the department. Below the department head are several top administrators,

FIGURE 7.1

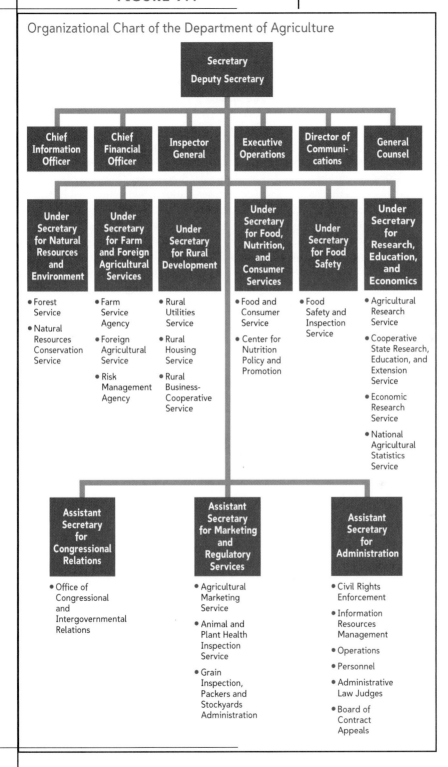

Organizational Chart of the Department of Agriculture

SOURCE: U.S. Department of Agriculture, www.usda.gov/agencies/agchart.htm.

such as the general counsel and the chief financial officer, whose responsibilities cut across the various departmental functions and provide the secretary with the ability to manage the entire organization. Of equal status are the under and assistant secretaries, each of whom has management responsibilities for a group of operating agencies, which are arranged vertically below each of the assistant secretaries.

The next tier, generally called the "bureau level," is the highest level of responsibility for specialized programs. The names of these "bureau-level agencies" are often very well known to the public: the Forest Service and the Food Safety and Inspection Service are two examples. Sometimes they are officially called bureaus, as in the Federal Bureau of Investigation (FBI), which is a bureau in the Department of Justice. Nevertheless, *bureau* is also the generic term for this level of administrative agency. Within the bureaus, there are divisions, offices, services, and units—sometimes designating agencies of the same status, sometimes designating agencies of lesser status.

Not all government agencies are part of cabinet departments. A second type of agency, the independent agency, is set up by Congress outside the departmental structure altogether, even though the president appoints and directs the head of this type of agency. Independent agencies usually have broad powers to provide public services that are either too expensive or too important to be left to private initiatives. Some examples of independent agencies are the National Aeronautics and Space Administration (NASA), the Central Intelligence Agency (CIA), and the Environmental Protection Agency (EPA). Government corporations are a third type of government agency but are more like private businesses performing and charging for a market service, such as delivering the mail (the United States Postal Service) or transporting railroad passengers (Amtrak).

Yet a fourth type of agency is the independent regulatory commission, given broad discretion to make rules. The first regulatory agencies established by Congress, beginning with the Interstate Commerce Commission in 1887, were set up as independent regulatory commissions because Congress recognized that regulatory agencies are "minilegislatures," whose rules are the same as legislation but require the kind of expertise and full-time attention that is beyond the capacity of Congress. Until the 1960s, most of the regulatory agencies that were set up by Congress, such as the Federal Trade Commission (1914) and the Federal Communications Commission (1934), were independent regulatory commissions. But beginning in the late 1960s and the early 1970s, all new regulatory programs, with two or three exceptions (such as the Federal Election Commission), were placed within existing departments and made directly responsible to the president. Since the 1970s, no major new regulatory programs have been established, independent or otherwise.

There are too many agencies in the executive branch to identify, much less to describe, so a simple classification of agencies will be helpful. Instead of dividing the bureaucracy into four general types, as we did above, this classification is organized by the mission of each agency, as defined by its jurisdiction: clientele agencies, agencies for maintenance of the Union, regulatory agencies, and redistributive agencies. We shall examine each of these types of agencies, focusing on both their formal structure and their place in the political process.

Clientele Agencies Serve Particular Interests

The entire Department of Agriculture is an example of a ***clientele agency.*** So are the Departments of the Interior, Labor, and Commerce. Although all administrative agencies have clientele, certain agencies are singled out and called by that name because they are directed by law to foster and promote the interests of their clientele. For example, the Department of Commerce and Labor was founded in 1903 as a single department "to foster, promote, and develop the foreign and domestic commerce, the mining, the manufacturing, the shipping, and fishing industries, and the transportation facilities of the United States."[9] It remained a single department until 1913, when the law created the two separate departments of Commerce and Labor, with each statute providing for the same obligation—to support and foster their respective clienteles.[10] The Department of Agriculture serves the many farming interests that, taken together, are the United States' largest economic sector (agriculture accounts for one-fifth of the U.S. total domestic output).

Most clientele agencies locate a relatively large proportion of their total personnel in field offices dealing directly with the clientele. The Extension Service of the Department of Agriculture is among the most familiar, with its numerous local "extension agents" who consult with farmers on farm productivity. These same agencies also seek to foster the interests of their clientele by providing "functional representation"—that is, they try to learn what their clients' interests and needs are and then operate almost as a lobby in Washington on their behalf. In addition to the Department of Agriculture, other clientele agencies include the Department of the Interior and the five newest cabinet departments: Housing and Urban Development (HUD), created in 1965; Transportation (DOT), created in 1966; Energy (DOE), created in 1977; Education (ED), created in 1979; and Health and Human Services (HHS), created in 1979.[11]

Agencies for Maintenance of the Union Keep the Government Going

These agencies could be called public-order agencies were it not for the fact that the Constitution entrusts so many of the vital functions of public order, such as the police, to the state governments. But some agencies vital to maintaining

clientele agencies Departments or bureaus of government whose mission is to promote, serve, or represent a particular interest.

Policy Principle
The policies of clientele agencies promote the interests of their clientele.

[9]32 Stat. 825; 15 USC 1501.

[10]For a detailed account of the creation of the Department of Commerce and Labor and its split into two separate departments, see Theodore J. Lowi, *The End of Liberalism: The Second Republic of the United States*, 2nd ed. (New York: W. W. Norton, 1979), pp. 78–84.

[11]The Departments of Education and of Health and Human Services until 1979 were joined in a single department, the Department of Health, Education, and Welfare (HEW), which had been established by Congress in 1953.

national bonds do exist in the national government, and they can be grouped for convenience into three categories: (1) agencies for control of the sources of government revenue, (2) agencies for control of conduct defined as a threat to internal national security, and (3) agencies for defending American security from external threats. The departments of greatest power in these three areas are Treasury, Justice, Defense, and State.

Revenue Agencies   The Internal Revenue Service (IRS) is the most important revenue agency. The IRS is also one of the federal government's largest bureaucracies. Over 100,000 employees are spread through 4 regions, 63 districts, 10 service centers, and hundreds of local offices. In 2001, the IRS processed over 200 million tax returns and supplemental documents, with total collections amounting to $2,128,831,182. (It costs the IRS 41 cents to collect every $100 in taxes; this figure has dropped from 60 cents in 1993.) Nearly 17,500 IRS tax auditors and revenue agents are engaged in auditing tax returns, and in 2001 they recommended additional taxes and penalties on 27,703,452 returns, a total of $9.76 billion in additional revenues.[12]

Agencies for Internal Security   As long as the country is not in a state of insurrection, most of the task of maintaining the Union takes the form of legal work, and the main responsibility for that lies with the Department of Justice. It is indeed a luxury, and rare in the world, when national unity can be maintained by routines of civil law instead of imposed by a real army with guns. The largest and most important agency in the Justice Department is the Criminal Division, which is responsible for enforcing all the federal criminal laws, except for a few specifically assigned to other divisions. Criminal litigation is actually done by the U.S. Attorneys. There is a presidentially appointed U.S. Attorney assigned to each federal judicial district, and he or she supervises the work of assistant U.S. Attorneys. The work or jurisdiction of the Antitrust and Civil Rights divisions is described by their official names. Although it looms so very large in American folklore, the Federal Bureau of Investigation (FBI) is simply another bureau of the Department of Justice. The FBI handles no litigation, but instead serves as the information-gathering agency for all the other divisions.

In 2002, Congress created the Department of Homeland Security to coordinate the nation's defense against the threat of terrorism. The new department is responsible for a number of tasks, including protecting commercial airlines from would-be hijackers.

Agencies for External National Security   Two departments occupy center stage here, State and Defense. There are a few key agencies outside State and Defense

[12]These figures are from the *"Time" Almanac 2003 with "Information Please,"* ed. Borgna Brunner (Boston: Information Please, 2002), p. 1020; *Internal Revenue Service Data Book 2001,* Publication 55B (Washington, D.C.: Government Printing Office, 2002), Table 26.

that have external national-security functions. They will be treated in this chapter only as bureaucratic phenomena and as examples of the political problems relevant to administration.

Although diplomacy is generally considered the primary task of the State Department, diplomatic missions are only one of its organizational dimensions. The State Department is also comprised of geographic or regional bureaus concerned with all problems within a defined region of the world; "functional" bureaus, handling such things as economic and business affairs, intelligence and research; and international organizations and bureaus of internal affairs, which handle such areas as security, finance and management, and legal issues.

Despite the importance of the State Department in foreign affairs, fewer than 20 percent of all U.S. government employees working abroad are directly under its authority. By far the largest number of career government professionals working abroad are under the authority of the Defense Department.

The creation of the Department of Defense by legislation from 1947 to 1949 was an effort to unify the two historic military departments, the War Department and the Navy Department, and to integrate with them a new department, the Air Force Department. Real unification, however, did not occur. Instead, the Defense Department adds more pluralism to national security.

America's primary political problem with its military has not been the historic one of how to keep the military out of the politics of governing—a problem that has plagued so many countries in Europe and Latin America. The American military problem is one of the lower politics of the "pork barrel." President Clinton's long list of proposed military base closings, a major part of his budget-cutting drive for 1993, caused a firestorm of opposition even within his own party, including a number of members of Congress who were otherwise prominently in favor of significant reductions in the Pentagon budget. Emphasis on jobs rather than strategy and policy means pork-barrel use of the military for political purposes. This is a classic way for a bureaucracy to defend itself politically in a democracy. It is the distributive tendency, in which the bureaucracy assures political support among elected officials by making sure to distribute things— military bases, contracts, facilities, and jobs—to the states and districts from which the legislators were elected. As is commonly known, it is hard to bite the hand that feeds you! Thus, the best way to understand the military in American politics is to study it within the same bureaucratic framework used to explain the domestic agencies.

Regulatory Agencies Guide Individual Conduct

As we saw in Chapter 3, our national government did not even begin to get involved in the regulation of economic and social affairs until the late nineteenth century. Until then, regulation was strictly a state and local affair. The federal *regulatory agencies* are, as a result, relatively new, most dating from the 1930s. But they have come to be extensive and important. In this section, we will look

Policy Principle
The military pork barrel is an example of the distributive tendency in Congress.

regulatory agencies Departments, bureaus, or independent agencies whose primary mission is to eliminate or restrict certain behaviors defined as being evil in themselves or evil in their consequences.

at these regulatory agencies as an administrative phenomenon, with its attendant politics.

The United States has no Department of Regulation but has many regulatory agencies. Some of these are bureaus within departments, such as the Food and Drug Administration (FDA) in the Department of Health and Human Services, the Occupational Safety & Health Administration (OSHA) in the Department of Labor, and the Animal and Plant Health and Inspection Service (APHIS) in the Department of Agriculture. Other regulatory agencies are independent regulatory commissions. An example is the Federal Trade Commission (FTC). But whether departmental or independent, an agency or commission is regulatory if Congress delegates to it relatively broad powers over a sector of the economy or a type of commercial activity and authorizes it to make rules governing the conduct of people and businesses within that jurisdiction. Rules made by regulatory agencies have the force and effect of legislation; indeed, the rules they make are referred to as *administrative legislation.* And when these agencies make decisions or orders settling disputes between parties or between the government and a party, they are really acting like courts.

administrative legislation Rules made by regulatory agencies and commissions.

Since regulatory agencies exercise a tremendous amount of influence over the economy, and since their rules are a form of legislation, Congress was at first loath to turn them over to the executive branch as ordinary agencies under the control of the president. Consequently, most of the important regulatory programs were delegated to independent commissions with direct responsibility to Congress rather than to the White House. This is the basis of the 1930s reference to them as the "headless fourth branch."[13] With the rise of presidential government, most recent presidents have supported more regulatory programs but have successfully opposed the expansion of regulatory independence. The 1960s and 1970s witnessed adoption of an unprecedented number of new regulatory programs but only four new independent commissions.

Agencies of Redistribution Implement Fiscal/Monetary and Welfare Policies

Welfare agencies and fiscal/monetary agencies are responsible for the transfer of hundreds of billions of dollars annually between the public and the private spheres, and through such transfers these agencies influence how people and corporations spend and invest trillions of dollars annually. We call them agencies of redistribution because they influence the amount of money in the economy and because they directly influence who has money, who has credit, and whether people will want to invest or save their money rather than spend it.

---

[13]*Final Report of the President's Committee on Administrative Management* (Washington, D.C.: Government Printing Office, 1937). The term "headless fourth branch" was invented by a member of the committee staff, Cornell University government professor Robert Cushman.

Fiscal and Monetary Agencies   The best generic term for government activity affecting or relating to money is *fiscal* policy. However, we choose to make a further distinction, reserving *fiscal* for taxing and spending policies and using *monetary* for policies having to do with banks, credit, and currency. And the third, *welfare*, deserves to be treated as an equal member of this redistributive category.

Administration of fiscal policy is primarily performed in the Treasury Department. It is no contradiction to include the Treasury here as well as with the agencies for maintenance of the Union. This indicates (1) that the Treasury is a complex department, performing more than one function of government, and (2) that traditional controls have had to be adapted to modern economic conditions and new technologies.

Today, in addition to administering and policing income tax and other tax collections, the Treasury is also responsible for managing the enormous federal debt.

The Treasury Department is also responsible for printing the currency that we use, but currency represents only a tiny proportion of the entire money economy. Most of the trillions of dollars used in the transactions that comprise the private and public sectors of the U.S. economy exist on printed accounts and computers, not in currency.

Another important fiscal agency (although for technical reasons it is called an agency of monetary policy) is the ***Federal Reserve System,*** headed by the Federal Reserve Board. The Federal Reserve System (the Fed) has authority over the credit rates and lending activities of the nation's most important banks. Established by Congress in 1913, the Fed is responsible for adjusting the supply of money to the needs of banks in the different regions and of the commerce and industry in each. The Fed helps shift money from where there is too much to where it is needed. It also ensures that the banks do not overextend themselves by having lending policies that are too liberal, out of fear that if there is a sudden economic scare, a run on a few banks might be contagious and cause another terrible crash like the one in 1929. The Federal Reserve Board sits at the top of the pyramid of twelve district Federal Reserve Banks, which are "bankers' banks," serving the monetary needs of the hundreds of member banks in the national bank system.

Federal Reserve System (Fed) Consisting of twelve Federal Reserve Banks, the Fed facilitates exchanges of cash, checks, and credit; it regulates member banks; and it uses monetary policies to fight inflation and deflation.

Welfare Agencies   No single government agency is responsible for all the programs comprising the "welfare state." The largest agency in this field is the Social Security Administration (SSA), which manages the social insurance aspects of Social Security and Supplemental Security Income (SSI). Other agencies in the Department of Health and Human Services administer Temporary Assistance to Needy Families (TANF) and Medicaid, and the Department of Agriculture is responsible for the food stamp program. With the exception of Social Security, these are *means-tested* programs, requiring applicants to demonstrate that their total annual cash earnings fall below an officially defined poverty line. These public assistance programs comprise a large administrative burden.

In August 1996, virtually all of the means-tested public assistance programs were legally abolished as national programs and were "devolved" to the states (see also Chapter 3). However, for the five years between fiscal 1996 and 2001, there was still a great deal of national administrative responsibility because federal funding of these programs continued through large, discretionary block grants to each state. Other aspects of state welfare activity were policed by federal agencies, and all of that required about the same size of administrative capacity in welfare as existed before. Those who expected some kind of revolution following adoption of the Personal Responsibility and Work Opportunity Reconciliation Act of 1996 were in for a disappointment.

WHO CONTROLS THE BUREAUCRACY?

Two hundred years, millions of employees, and trillions of dollars after the founding, we must return to James Madison's observation that "you must first enable the government to control the governed; and in the next place oblige it to control itself."[14] Today the problem is the same, but the form has changed. Our problem today is bureaucracy and our inability to keep it accountable to elected political authorities

The President as Chief Executive Can Direct Agencies

In 1937, President Franklin Roosevelt's Committee on Administrative Management gave official sanction to an idea that had been growing increasingly urgent: "The president needs help." The national government had grown rapidly during the preceding twenty-five years, but the structures and procedures necessary to manage the burgeoning executive branch had not yet been established. The response to the call for "help" for the president initially took the form of three management policies: (1) all communications and decisions that related to executive policy decisions must pass through the White House; (2) in order to cope with such a flow, the White House must have adequate staffs of specialists in research, analysis, legislative and legal writing, and public affairs; and (3) the White House must have additional staff to follow through on presidential decisions—to ensure that those decisions are made, communicated to Congress, and carried out by the appropriate agency.

Establishing a management capacity for the presidency began in earnest with FDR, but it did not stop there. The story of the modern presidency can be told largely as a series of responses to the plea for managerial help. Indeed, each expansion of the national government into new policies and programs in the twentieth century was accompanied by a parallel expansion of the president's management authority. This pattern began even before FDR's presidency, with the policy innovations of President Woodrow Wilson between 1913 and 1920. Congress responded to Wilson's policies with the 1921 Budget and Accounting Act, which turned over the prime legislative power of budgeting to the White

---

[14]Clinton Rossiter, ed., *The Federalist Papers* (New York: New American Library, 1961), No. 51.

House. Each successive president has continued this pattern, creating what we now know as the "managerial presidency."

Presidents John Kennedy and Lyndon Johnson were committed both to government expansion and to management expansion, in the spirit of their party's hero, FDR. President Nixon also strengthened and enlarged the managerial presidency but for somewhat different reasons. He sought the strongest possible managerial hand because he had to assume that the overwhelming majority of federal employees had sympathies with the Democratic party, which had controlled the White House and had sponsored governmental growth for twenty-eight of the previous thirty-six years.[15]

President Jimmy Carter was probably more preoccupied with administrative reform and reorganization than any other president in the twentieth century. His reorganization of the civil service will long be recognized as one of the most significant contributions of his presidency. The Civil Service Reform Act of 1978 was the first major revamping of the federal civil service since its creation in 1883. The 1978 act abolished the century-old Civil Service Commission (CSC) and replaced it with three agencies, each designed to handle one of the CSC's functions on the theory that the competing demands of these functions had given the CSC an "identity crisis." The Merit Systems Protection Board (MSPB) was created to defend competitive merit recruitment and promotion from political encroachment. A separate Federal Labor Relations Authority (FLRA) was set up to administer collective bargaining and individual personnel grievances. The third new agency, the Office of Personnel Management (OPM), was created to manage recruiting, testing, training, and the retirement system. The Senior Executive Service was also created at this time to recognize and foster "public management" as a profession and to facilitate the movement of top, "supergrade" career officials across agencies and departments.[16]

Carter also tried to impose a stringent budgetary process on all executive agencies. Called "zero-base budgeting," it was a method of budgeting from the bottom up, wherein each agency was required to rejustify its entire mission rather than merely its next year's increase. Zero-base budgeting did not succeed, but the effort was not lost on President Reagan. Although Reagan gave the impression of being a laid-back president, he actually centralized management to an unprecedented degree. From Carter's "bottom up" approach, Reagan went to a "top down" approach, whereby the initial budgetary decisions would be made in the White House and the agencies would be required to fit within those decisions. This process converted the Office of Management and Budget (OMB) into

---

[15]See Richard P. Nathan, *The Plot That Failed: Nixon and the Administrative Presidency* (New York: Wiley, 1975), pp. 68–76.

[16]For more details and evaluations, see David Rosenbloom, *Public Administration: Understanding Management, Politics, and Law in the Public Sector* (New York: Random House, 1986), pp. 186–221; Charles H. Levine and Rosslyn S. Kleeman, "The Quiet Crisis in the American Public Service" in *Agenda for Excellence: Public Service in America*, ed. Patricia W. Ingraham and Donald F. Kettl (Chatham, N.J.: Chatham House, 1992); and Patricia W. Ingraham and David Rosenbloom, "The State of Merit in the Federal Government," ibid.

an agency of policy determination and presidential management.[17] President George H. W. Bush took Reagan's centralization strategy even further in using the White House staff instead of cabinet secretaries for managing the executive branch.[18]

President Clinton was often criticized for the way he managed his administration. His easygoing approach to administration led critics to liken his management style to college "bull sessions" complete with pizza and "all-nighters." Yet, as we have seen, Clinton also inaugurated one of the most systematic efforts "to change the way government does business" in his National Performance Review. Heavily influenced by the theories of management consultants who prized decentralization, customer responsiveness, and employee initiative, Clinton sought to infuse these new practices into government.[19]

George W. Bush was the first president with a degree in business. His management strategy followed a standard business-school dictum: select skilled subordinates and delegate responsibility to them. Bush followed this model closely in his appointment of highly experienced officials to cabinet positions and in his selection of Dick Cheney for vice president. Indeed, at the outset of his term, Bush often appeared overshadowed by these appointees, (and the vice president in particular). Many observers had the impression that Bush did not lead his own administration. The president's performance during the war in Afghanistan and the war on terrorism dispelled many doubts about his executive capabilities.

The story of the modern presidency can be told largely as a series of responses to the rise of big government. *Each expansion of the national government in the twentieth century was accompanied by a parallel expansion of presidential management authority.*

History Principle

Each expansion of the national government is accompanied by a parallel expansion of presidential management authority.

Congress Promotes Responsible Bureaucracy

Congress is constitutionally essential to responsible bureaucracy because the key to government responsibility is legislation. When a law is passed and its intent is clear, then the president knows what to "faithfully execute" and the responsible agency understands what is expected of it. In our modern age, legislatures rarely make laws directly for citizens; most laws are really instructions to bureaucrats and their agencies. But when Congress enacts vague legislation, agencies are thrown back upon their own interpretations. The president and the federal courts step in to tell them what the legislation intended. And so do the intensely interested groups. But when everybody, from president to courts to interest

---

[17]Lester Salamon and Alan Abramson, "Governance: The Politics of Retrenchment," in *The Reagan Record: An Assessment of America's Changing Domestic Priorities*, ed. John L. Palmer and Isabel V. Sawhill (Cambridge, Mass.: Ballinger, 1984), p. 40.

[18]Colin Campbell, "The White House and the Presidency under the 'Let's Deal' President," in *The Bush Presidency: First Appraisals*, ed. Colin Campbell and Bert A. Rockman (Chatham, N.J.: Chatham House, 1991), pp. 185–222.

[19]See John Micklethwait, "Managing to Look Attractive," *New Statesman* 125, 8 November 1996, p. 24.

FIGURE 7.2

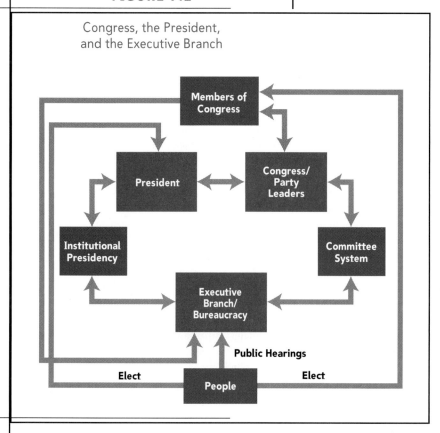

Congress, the President, and the Executive Branch

groups, gets involved in the actual interpretation of legislative intent, to whom is the agency responsible? Even when it has the most sincere desire to behave responsibly, how shall this be accomplished?

The answer is *oversight.* The more legislative power Congress has delegated to the executive, the more it has sought to get back into the game through committee and subcommittee oversight of the agencies. The standing committee system in Congress is well suited for oversight, inasmuch as most of the congressional committees and subcommittees are organized with jurisdictions roughly parallel to one or more executive departments or agencies. Appropriations committees as well as authorization committees have oversight powers—as do their respective subcommittees. In addition to these, there is a committee on government operations both

oversight The effort by Congress, through hearings, investigations, and other techniques, to exercise control over the activities of executive agencies.

in the House and in the Senate, each with oversight powers not limited by departmental jurisdiction.

The best indication of Congress's oversight efforts is the use of public hearings, before which bureaucrats and other witnesses are summoned to discuss and defend agency budgets and past decisions. The data drawn from systematic studies of congressional committee and subcommittee hearings and meetings show dramatically that Congress has tried through oversight to keep pace with the expansion of the executive branch. Between 1950 and 1980, the annual number of committee and subcommittee meetings in the House of Representatives rose steadily from 3,210 to 7,022 and in the Senate from 2,607 to 4,265 (in 1975–1976). Beginning in 1980 in the House and 1978 in the Senate, the number of committee and subcommittee hearings and meetings slowly began to decline, reaching 4,222 in the House and 2,597 in the Senate by the mid-1980s. New questions about the ability of Congress to exercise oversight arose when the Republicans took over Congress in 1995. Reductions in committee staffing and an emphasis on using investigative oversight to uncover scandal meant much less time spent on programmatic oversight. Moreover, congressional Republicans complained that they could not get sufficient information about programs from the White House to conduct effective oversight. Congressional records show that in 1991–1992, when Democrats controlled the House, they issued reports on fifty-five federal programs, while in 1997–1998, the Republican Congress issued only fourteen.[20] On issues of major national importance, multiple committees may initiate oversight hearings simultaneously. No less than a dozen congressional committees (along with the Justice Department and the Securities and Exchange Commission) launched investigations into the collapse of the giant energy company Enron. Enron's close ties to the Bush administration and its campaign contributions to hundreds of politicians from both parties aroused intense public interest in the hearings, many of which were televised live. The investigations covered a broad range of issues, including secret partnerships, public utility laws, 401(k) retirement plans, accounting practices, and Enron's political influence.

Although congressional oversight is potent because of Congress's power to make—and, therefore, to change—the law, often the most effective and influential lever over bureaucratic accountability is "the power of the purse"—the ability of the House and Senate committees and subcommittees on appropriations to look at agency performance through the microscope of the annual appropriations process. This annual process makes bureaucrats attentive to Congress because they know that Congress has a chance each year to reduce their funding.[21] A more recent evaluation of the budget and appropriations process by the NPR expressed one serious concern about oversight through appropriation: pressure to cut appropriations "has put a premium on preserving particular programs,

[20]Richard E. Cohen, "Crackup of the Committees," *National Journal*, 31 July 1999, p. 2214.

[21]See Aaron Wildavsky, *The New Politics of the Budgetary Process*, 2nd ed. (New York: HarperCollins, 1992), pp. 15–16.

projects, and activities from Executive Branch as well as congressional action."[22] This may be another explanation for why there may be some downsizing but almost no terminations of federal agencies.

Oversight can also be carried out by individual members of Congress. Such inquiries addressed to bureaucrats are considered standard congressional "casework" and can turn up significant questions of public responsibility even when the motivation is only to meet the demand of an individual constituent. Oversight also takes place very often through communications between congressional staff and agency staff. Congressional staff has been enlarged tremendously since the Legislative Reorganization Act of 1946, and the legislative staff, especially the staff of the committees, is just as professionalized and specialized as the staff of an executive agency. In addition, Congress has created for itself three quite large agencies whose obligations are to engage in constant research on problems taking place in the executive branch: the General Accounting Office, the Congressional Research Service, and the Congressional Budget Office. Each is designed to give Congress information independent of the information it can get through hearings and other communications directly from the executive branch.[23]

Control of the Bureaucracy Is a Principal-Agent Problem

Two broad categories of control mechanisms enable a principal to guard against opportunistic or incompetent agent behavior. They may be illustrated by a homeowner (the principal) who seeks out a contractor (the agent) to remodel a kitchen. The first category is employed before-the-fact and depends upon the *reputation* an agent possesses. One guards against selecting an incompetent or corrupt agent by relying on various methods for authenticating the promises made by the agent. These include advice from people you trust (your neighbor who just had his kitchen remodeled); certification by various official boards (association of kitchen contractors); letters of recommendation and other testimonials; credentials (specialized training programs); and interviews. Before-the-fact protection relies upon the assumption that an agent's reputation is a valuable asset that he or she does not want to depreciate.

The second class of control mechanisms operates after the fact. Payment may be made contingent on completion of various tasks by specific dates, so that it may be withheld for nonperformance. Alternatively, financial incentives (for

---

[22]National Performance Review, *From Red Tape to Results: Creating a Government That Works Better and Costs Less* (Washington, D.C.: U.S. Government Printing Office, 1993), p. 42.

[23]Until 1983, there was still another official tool of legislative oversight, the legislative veto. Each executive agency was obliged to submit to Congress proposed decisions or rules. These were to lie before both houses for thirty to sixty days; then, if Congress took no action by one-house or two-house resolution explicitly to veto a proposed measure, it became law. The legislative veto was declared unconstitutional by the Supreme Court in 1983 on the grounds that it violated the separation of powers because the resolutions Congress passed to exercise its veto were not subject to presidential veto, as required by the Constitution. See Immigration and Naturalization Service v. Chadha, 462 U.S. 919 (1983).

example, bonuses) for early or on-time completion may be part of the arrangement. The agent may be required to post a bond that is forfeited for lack of performance. An inspection process, after the work is completed, may lead to financial penalties, bonuses, or possibly even legal action. Of course, the principal can always seek legal relief for breach of contract, either in the form of an injunction that the agent comply or an order that the agent pay damages.

How does the principal-agent problem apply to the president's and Congress's control of the bureaucracy?

Suppose the legislation that created the Environmental Protection Agency (EPA) required that after ten years new legislation be passed renewing its existence and mandate. The issue facing the House, the Senate, and the president in their consideration of renewal revolves around how much authority to give this agency and how much money to permit it to spend. The House, conservative on environmental issues, prefers limited authority and a limited budget. The Senate wants the agency to have wide-ranging authority but is prepared to give it only slightly more resources than the House (because of its concern with the budget deficit). The president is happy to split the difference between House and Senate on the matter of authority but feels beholden to environmental types and, thus, is prepared to shower the EPA with resources. Bureaucrats in the EPA want more authority than even the Senate is prepared to condone and more resources than even the president is willing to grant. Eventually, relevant majorities in the House and Senate (including the support of relevant committees) and the president agree on a policy reflecting a compromise among their various points of view.

The bureaucrats are not particularly pleased with this compromise since it gives them considerably less authority and funding than they had hoped for. If they flout the wishes of their principals and implement a policy exactly to their liking, they risk the unified wrath of the House, Senate, and president. Undoubtedly, the politicians would react with new legislation (and also presumably would find other political appointees and career bureaucrats at the EPA to replace the current bureaucratic leadership). If, however, the EPA implemented some policy located between their own preferences and the preferences of their principals, they might be able to get away with it.

Thus, we have a principal-agent relationship in which a political principal formulates policy and creates an implementation agent to execute its details. The agent, however, has policy preferences of its own and, unless subjected to further controls, inevitably will implement a policy that drifts toward its ideal.

A variety of controls might conceivably restrict this **bureaucratic drift.** Indeed, legislative scholars often point to congressional hearings in which bureaucrats may be publicly humiliated; annual appropriations decisions that may be used to punish "out of control" bureaus; and the use of watchdog agents, like the General Accounting Office, to monitor and scrutinize the bureau's performance. But these all come after the fact and aren't really credible threats to the agency.

Before-the-Fact Controls   The most powerful before-the-fact political weapon is the *appointment process*. The adroit control of the political stance of a given bu-

bureaucratic drift The oft-observed phenomenon of bureaucratic implementation that produces policy more to the liking of the bureaucracy than originally legislated, but without triggering a political reaction from elected officials.

Rationality Principle

Bureaucratic drift occurs because bureaucratic agents have different policy preferences from those of members of Congress or the president.

reau by the president and Congress, through their joint powers of nomination and confirmation (especially if they can arrange for appointees who more nearly share the political consensus on policy) is a self-enforcing mechanism for assuring reliable agent performance.

A second powerful before-the-fact weapon is *procedural controls*. The general rules and regulations that direct the manner in which federal agencies conduct their affairs are contained in the Administrative Procedures Act. This act is almost always the boilerplate that enables legislation creating and renewing every federal agency. It is not uncommon, however, for an agency's procedures to be tailored to suit particular circumstances.

Institution Principle

The appointment process and procedural controls allow the president and Congress some before-the-fact control over bureaucratic agents.

Congressional Oversight: Abdication or Strategic Delegation? Congress often grants the executive-branch bureaucracies discretion in determining certain features of a policy during the implementation phase. Although the complexities of governing a modern industrialized democracy make the granting of discretion necessary, there are some who argue that Congress not only gives unelected bureaucrats too much discretion but also delegates too much policy-making authority to them. Congress, they say, has transferred so much power that it has created a "runaway bureaucracy" in which unelected officials accountable neither to the electorate nor to Congress make important policy decisions.[24] By enacting vague statutes that give bureaucrats broad discretion, members of Congress have effectively abdicated their constitutionally designated roles and effectively removed themselves from the policy-making process. The ultimate impact of this extreme delegation has left the legislative branch weak and ineffectual and has dire consequences for the health of our democracy.

Others claim that even though Congress may possess the tools to engage in effective oversight, it fails to do so simply because we do not see Congress actively engaging in much oversight activity.[25] However, Mathew D. McCubbins and Thomas Schwartz argue that these critics have focused on the wrong type of oversight and have missed a type of oversight that benefits members of Congress in their bids for re-election.[26] McCubbins and Schwartz distinguish between two types of oversight: *police patrol* and *fire alarm*. Under the police-patrol variety, Congress systematically initiates investigation into the activity of agencies. Under the fire-alarm variety, members of Congress do not initiate investigations but wait for adversely affected citizens or interest groups to bring bureaucratic perversions of legislative intent to the attention of the relevant congressional committee. To make sure that individuals and groups will bring these violations

[24]Lowi, *The End of Liberalism;* Lawrence C. Dodd and Richard L. Schott, *Congress and the Administrative State* (New York: Wiley, 1979).

[25]Morris S. Ogul, *Congress Oversees the Bureaucracy: Studies in Legislative Supervision* (Pittsburgh: University of Pittsburgh Press, 1976); Peter Woll, *American Bureaucracy*, 2nd ed. (New York: W. W. Norton, 1977).

[26]Mathew D. McCubbins and Thomas Schwartz, "Congressional Oversight Overlooked: Police Patrols versus Fire Alarms," *American Journal of Political Science* 28 (1984): 165–79.

to members' attention, Congress passes laws that help individuals and groups make claims against the bureaucracy, including granting them legal standing before administrative agencies and federal courts.

McCubbins and Schwartz argue that fire-alarm oversight is more efficient than the police-patrol variety, given costs and the electoral incentives of members of Congress. Why should members spend their scarce resources (mainly time) to initiate investigations without having any evidence that they will reap electoral rewards? Police-patrol oversight can waste taxpayer dollars, too, since many investigations will not turn up any evidence on violations of legislative intent. It is much more cost-effective for members to conserve their resources and then claim credit for fixing the problem (and saving the day) after the fire alarms are pulled. McCubbins and Schwartz argue that given the incentives of elected officials, it makes sense that we would see Congress engaging more in fire-alarm oversight than police-patrol oversight.

Collective Action Principle
When Congress and the president are at odds (or coalitions within Congress are at odds), bureaucrats have an opportunity to evade responsibility.

On the other hand, bureaucratic drift might be contained if Congress spent more of its time clarifying its legislative intent and less of its time on oversight activity. If its original intent in the law were clearer, Congress could then afford to defer to presidential management in order to maintain bureaucratic responsibility. Bureaucrats are more responsive to clear legislative guidance than to anything else. But when Congress and the president are at odds (or coalitions within Congress are at odds), bureaucrats have an opportunity to evade responsibility by playing one branch off against the other.

Coalitional Drift as a Collective-Action Problem   Politicians not only want the legislative deals that they strike to be faithfully implemented, they also want those deals to endure. This is especially problematic in American political life with its shifting alignments and absence of permanent political cleavages. Today's coalition transforms itself overnight. Opponents today are partners tomorrow, and vice versa. A victory today, even one implemented in a favorable manner by the bureaucracy, may be undone tomorrow. What is to be done?

To some extent, legislative structure leans against undoing legislation. If such a coalition votes for handsome subsidies to grain farmers, say, it is very hard to reverse this policy without the gatekeeping and agenda-setting resources of members on the House and Senate Agriculture Committees; yet their members undoubtedly participated in the initial deal and are unlikely to turn against it. But even these structural units are unstable, old politicians departing and new ones enlisted.

In short, legislatively formulated and bureaucratically implemented output is subject to ***coalitional drift***.[27] To prevent shifting coalitional patterns among

coalitional drift
The prospect that enacted policy will change because the composition of the enacting coalition is so temporary and provisional.

[27]This idea, offered as a supplement to the analysis of bureaucratic drift, is found in Murray J. Horn and Kenneth A. Shepsle, "Administrative Process and Organizational Form as Legislative Responses to Agency Costs," *Virginia Law Review* 75 (1989): 499–509. It is further elaborated in Kenneth A. Shepsle, "Bureaucratic Drift, Coalitional Drift, and Time Consistency," *Journal of Law, Economics, and Organization* 8 (1992): 111–18.

politicians to endanger carefully fashioned policies, one thing the legislature might do is *insulate* the bureaucracy and its implementation activities from legislative interventions. If an enacting coalition makes it difficult for its *own* members to intervene in implementation, then it also makes it difficult for enemies of the policy to disrupt the flow of bureau output. This political insulation can be provided by giving bureaucratic agencies long lives; their political heads long terms of office and wide-ranging administrative authority; and other political appointees overlapping terms of office and secure sources of revenue. This insulation comes at a price, however. The civil servants and political appointees of bureaus insulated from political overseers are thereby empowered to pursue independent courses of action. Protection from coalitional drift comes at the price of an increased potential for bureaucratic drift. It is one of the great trade-offs in the field of intergovernmental relations.

Collective Action Principle

Coalitional drift makes the long-term implementation of policy more difficult.

Policy Principle

Bureaucratic drift and coalitional drift are contrary tendencies. Fixing them often involves a trade-off.

HOW CAN BUREAUCRACY BE REDUCED?

Americans like to complain about bureaucracy. Americans don't like Big Government because Big Government means Big Bureaucracy, and bureaucracy means *the federal service*—about 2.63 million civilian and 1.46 million military employees.[28] Promises to cut the bureaucracy are popular campaign appeals; "cutting out the fat" with big reductions in the number of federal employees is held out as a sure-fire way of cutting the deficit.

Despite fears of bureaucratic growth getting out of hand, however, the federal service has hardly grown at all during the past thirty years; it reached its peak postwar level in 1968 with 2.9 million civilian employees plus an additional 3.6 million military personnel (a figure swollen by Vietnam). The number of civilian federal executive-branch employees has since remained close to that figure. (In 2002, it was about 2,630,000.)[29] The growth of the federal service is even less imposing when placed in the context of the total workforce and when compared to the size of state and local public employment, which was 18,642,000 in 2002.[30] Figure 7.3 indicates that, since 1950, the ratio of federal service employment to the total workforce has been steady and in fact has declined slightly in the past twenty-five years. Another useful comparison is to be found in Figure 7.4. Although the dollar increase in federal spending shown by the bars looks very impressive, the horizontal line indicates that even here the national government has simply kept pace with the growth of the economy.

[28]This is just under 99 percent of all national government employees. About 1.4 percent work for the legislative branch and for the federal judiciary. See Office of Management and Budget, *Historical Tables, Budget of the United States Government, Fiscal Year 2004* (Washington, D.C.: Government Printing Office, 2003), Table 17.5, p. 306.

[29]Ibid.

[30]Ibid.

FIGURE 7.3

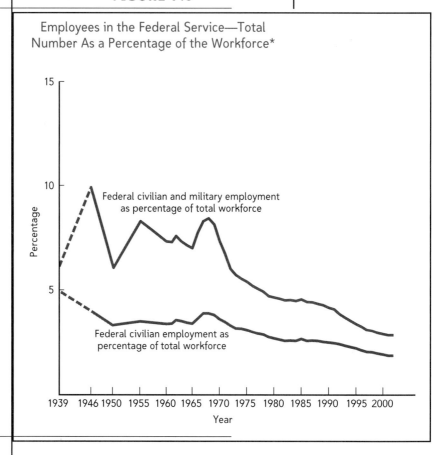

Employees in the Federal Service—Total
Number As a Percentage of the Workforce*

*Workforce includes unemployed persons.

SOURCE: Tax Foundation, *Facts & Figures on Government Finance* (Baltimore: Johns Hopkins University Press, 1990), pp. 22, 44; Office of Management and Budget, *Historical Tables, Budget of the United States Government, Fiscal Year 2002* (Washington, D.C.: Government Printing Office, 2001), p. 304; and U.S. Department of Labor, Bureau of Labor Statistics, Table A-1 at stats.bls.gov/webapps/legacy/cpsatab1.htm. Lines between 1939 and 1946 are broken because they connect the last prewar year with the first postwar year, disregarding the temporary ballooning of federal employees, especially military, during war years.

History Principle

The size of the federal bureaucracy has kept pace with the growth of the economy and the needs of society.

In sum, the national government is indeed "very large," but the federal service has not been growing any faster than the economy or the society. The same is roughly true of the growth pattern of state and local public personnel. Bureaucracy keeps pace with our society, despite our seeming dislike for it, because we

FIGURE 7.4

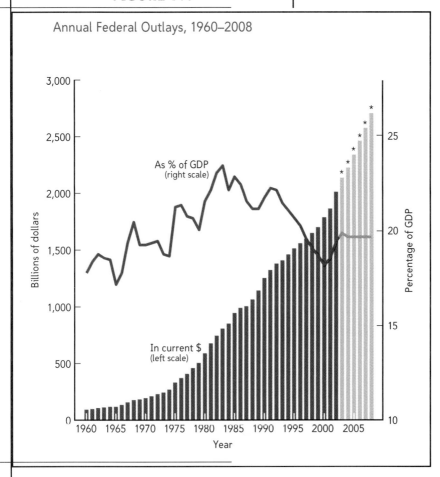

Annual Federal Outlays, 1960–2008

*Data from 2003–2008 are estimated.
SOURCE: Office of Management and Budget, *Historical Tables, Budget of the United States Government, Fiscal Year 2004* (Washington, D.C.: Government Printing Office, 2003), p. 55.

can't operate the control towers, the prisons, the Social Security system, and other essential elements without bureaucracy. And we certainly could not have conducted a successful war in Iraq without a gigantic military bureaucracy.

Nevertheless some Americans continue to argue that bureaucracy is too big and that it should be reduced. In the 1990s Americans seemed particularly enthusiastic about reducing (or to use the popular contemporary word, "downsizing") the federal bureaucracy.

Termination

The only *certain* way to reduce the size of the bureaucracy is to eliminate programs. Variations in the levels of federal personnel and expenditures demonstrate the futility of trying to make permanent cuts in existing agencies. Furthermore, most agencies have a supportive constituency that will fight to reinstate any cuts that are made. Termination is the only way to ensure an agency's reduction, and it is a rare occurrence.

The Republican-led 104th Congress (1995–1996) was committed to the termination of programs. Newt Gingrich, Speaker of the House, took Congress by storm with his promises of a virtual revolution in government. But when the dust had settled at the end of the first session of the first Gingrich-led Congress, no significant progress had been made toward downsizing through termination of agencies and programs.[31] The only two agencies eliminated were the Office of Technology Assessment, which provided research for Congress, and the Advisory Council on Intergovernmental Relations, which studied the relationship between the federal government and the state. Significantly, neither of these agencies had a strong constituency to defend it.

The overall lack of success in terminating bureaucracy is a reflection of Americans' love/hate relationship with the national government. As antagonistic as Americans may be toward bureaucracy in general, they grow attached to the services being rendered and protections being offered by particular bureaucratic agencies—that is, they fiercely defend their favorite agencies while perceiving no inconsistency between that defense and their antagonistic attitude toward the bureaucracy in general. A good case in point was the agonizing problem of closing military bases in the wake of the end of the cold war with the former Soviet Union, when the United States no longer needed so many bases. Since every base is in some congressional member's district, it proved impossible for Congress to decide to close any of them. Consequently, between 1988 and 1990, Congress established a Defense Base Closure and Realignment Commission to decide on base closings, taking the matter out of Congress's hands altogether.[32] And even so, the process has been slow and agonizing.

Elected leaders have come to rely on a more incremental approach to downsizing the bureaucracy. Much has been done by budgetary means, reducing the budgets of all agencies across the board by small percentages, and cutting some

🔲 **History Principle**
Americans have grown attached to the programs implemented by government agencies and, thus, are reluctant to cut back on their size and scope.

---

[31]A thorough review of the first session of the 104th Congress will be found in "Republican's Hopes for 1996 Lie in Unfinished Business," *Congressional Quarterly Weekly Report*, 6 January 1996, pp. 6–18.

[32]Public Law 101-510, Title XXIX, Sections 2,901 and 2,902 of Part A (Defense Base Closure and Realignment Commission).

less-supported agencies by larger amounts. Yet these changes are still incremental, leaving the existence of agencies unaddressed.

An additional approach has been taken to thwart the highly unpopular regulatory agencies, which are so small (relatively) that cutting their budgets contributes virtually nothing to reducing the deficit. This approach is called *deregulation,* simply defined as a reduction in the number of rules promulgated by regulatory agencies. But deregulation by rule reduction is still incremental and has certainly not satisfied the hunger of the American public in general and Washington representatives in particular for a genuine reduction of bureaucracy.

deregulation A policy of reducing or eliminating regulatory restraints on the conduct of individuals or private institutions.

Devolution

The next best approach to genuine reduction of the size of the bureaucracy is *devolution*—downsizing the federal bureaucracy by delegating the implementation of programs to state and local governments. Devolution often alters the pattern of who benefits most from government programs. In the early 1990s, a major devolution of transportation policy sought to open up decisions about transportation to a new set of interests. Since the 1920s, transportation policy had been dominated by road-building interests in the federal and state governments. Many advocates for cities and many environmentalists believed that the emphasis on road building hurt cities and harmed the environment. The 1992 reform, initiated by environmentalists, put more power in the hands of metropolitan planning organizations and lifted many federal restrictions on how the money should be spent. Reformers hoped that these changes would open up the decision-making process so those advocating alternatives to road building, such as mass transit, bike paths, and walking, would have more influence over how federal transportation dollars were spent. Although the pace of change has been slow, devolution has indeed brought new voices into decisions about transportation spending, and alternatives to highways have received increasing attention.

devolution A policy to remove a program from one level of government by deregulating it or passing it down to a lower level of government, such as from the national government to the state and local governments.

Often the central aim of devolution is to provide more efficient and flexible government services. Yet, by its very nature, devolution entails variation across the states. In some states, government services may improve as a consequence of devolution. In other states, services may deteriorate as the states use devolution as an opportunity to cut spending and reduce services. This has been the pattern in the implementation of the welfare reform passed in 1996, the most significant devolution of federal government social programs in many decades. Some states, such as Wisconsin, have used the flexibility of the reform to design innovative programs that respond to clients' needs; other states, such as Idaho, have virtually dismantled their welfare programs. Because the legislation placed a five-year lifetime limit on receiving welfare, the states will take on an even greater role in the future as existing clients lose their eligibility for federal benefits. Welfare reform has been praised by many for reducing welfare rolls and responding to the public desire that welfare be a temporary program. At the same time, it has placed more

The Defense Bureaucracy, from the Cold War to a New World Order

Why do bureaucracies grow? When do they shrink? The rationality principle suggests that Congress and the executive branch will perform a comprehensive assessment of the needs of society, the costs of providing various services, and revenues, and then decide upon the ideal mix of governmental services. In practice, of course, this does not resemble the process in any meaningful way. The five principles teach us that political considerations will pervade this process.

Herbert Simon, in a classic statement of the limitations of human rationality, suggested that we *"satisfice"* rather than "maximize" our utility.[33] The search for the maximum utility, he argued, was too costly, too fraught with uncertainty, and simply beyond the capabilities of most individuals. Politicians and bureaucrats, similarly, are unlikely to search "comprehensively" for the best solution to a problem. Instead, they are more likely to look to what they know best from the preexisting pool of theories, solutions, and bureaucracies. This is the basis of the "incrementalist" model of bureaucratic change.[34]

According to the first principle of politics, all political behavior has a purpose. What about policy makers? The *incrementalist model* of decision making assumes that policy makers have limited information about the problems they must deal with, the effectiveness of proposed solutions, and the effects of policies if enacted. Furthermore, as noted by Principle 4, the eventual policy that they adopt has to consider the preferences of other political actors (such as interest groups and Congress) and the institutional mechanisms at their disposal that may thwart the policy maker's will. A combination of limited insight into the impact of a proposed policy and the pressures of other political actors leads policy makers to prefer a variation of the Hippocratic oath: "Do not create a highly visible policy outcome worse than your predecessor's."

The historical path of policy change, then, is change by small increments rather than through sweeping reform. The creation, destruction, and/or reconstruction of major policies may garner headlines, but it is in the "small steps" of policy evolution where most of the business of government occurs. The incremental nature of policy making creates an inherent conservative stasis in government and in many large and complex organizations.

Incrementalism serves as a protection against harmful programs. However, it can also serve as a barrier to new and innovative ways of doing things, and it can make it difficult to eliminate existing bureaucratic agencies. While bureaucratic change is gradual, historical change is not always so accommodating. For example, the collapse of the Soviet bloc (and eventual dissolution of the Soviet Union itself) in the late 1980s and early 1990s presented the defense bureaucracy with a completely new geo-political environment.

American military policies and infrastructures since World War II had developed in response to one primary historical development: the cold-war struggle with the Soviet Union and its allies. Competition with the Soviets (and the desire to avoid another global conflict) shaped the memories of political actors, provided a ready interpretive framework to understand small regional conflicts, and structured political rivalries both within and between the two political parties.

With the sudden disappearance of that conflict, the U.S. military found itself with a set of policies, organizational structures, and systems no longer suited to the new geostrategic world. Despite the obvious need for reform, many in government resisted proposed changes. This stemmed from a fear of enacting policies that would damage our national security as well as, and perhaps more importantly, a preference on the part of members of Congress to preserve the economic (and electoral) benefits of the existing defense structure.

Unorthodox rules and procedures were crafted for the purpose of overcoming political inertia, an illustration of the fourth principle of politics. For example, a nonpartisan commission was needed to address the issue closing unneeded military bases. In this case, the bureaucracy (the Pentagon) was open to eliminating obsolete bases, but it was the elected leaders, members of Congress, who were loath to see the bases disappear. Similarly, weapons systems such as the B-2 bomber and the now defunct[35] Crusader artillery system continue to have champions in Congress, even with the original purpose of the systems, the arms race with the Soviet Union, no longer in existence.

The changing role of the military in the aftermath of the cold war and the emerging war on terrorism extend this debate over the defense bureaucracy. President George W. Bush's secretary of defense, Donald Rumsfeld, has publicly stated that the military bureaucracy, really unchanged since World War II, must be "transformed" to meet the security and technological challenges of the twenty-first century. Not surprisingly, though, other political actors, such as current members of the armed forces, are wedded to the current structure, while members of Congress still act to preserve existing defense programs that benefit their districts. It is not clear that Rumsfeld will have the political power, or the institutional tools, to implement his vision of the future.

[33]Herbert Simon, *Economics, Bounded Rationality and the Cognitive Revolution*, ed. Massimo Egidi and Robin Marris (Brookfield, Vt.: Elgar, 1995).

[34]John Kingdon, *Agendas, Alternatives, and Public Policies*, 2nd ed. (New York: HarperCollins, 1995); Charles E. Lindblom, *The Intelligence of Democracy: Decision Making through Mutual Adjustment* (New York: Free Press, 1965).

[35]As of June 30, 2003.

low-income women and their children at risk for being left with no form of assistance at all, depending on the state in which they live.

This is the dilemma that devolution poses. To a point, variation can be considered one of the virtues of federalism. But there are dangers inherent in large variations in the provisions of services and benefits in a democracy.

Privatization

Privatization, another downsizing option, seems like a synonym for termination, but that is true only at the extreme. Most of what is called "privatization" is not termination at all but the provision of government goods and services by private contractors under direct government supervision. Except for top-secret strategic materials, virtually all of the production of military hardware, from boats to bullets, is done on a privatized basis by private contractors. Billions of dollars of research services are bought under contract by governments; these private contractors are universities as well as ordinary industrial corporations and private "think tanks." ***Privatization*** simply means that a formerly public activity is picked up under contract by a private company or companies. But such programs are still very much government programs; they are paid for by government and supervised by government. Privatization downsizes the government only in that the workers providing the service are no longer counted as part of the government bureaucracy.

privatization
Removing all or part of a program from the public sector to the private sector.

The central aim of privatization is to reduce the cost of government. When private contractors can perform a task as well as government but for less money, taxpayers win. Often the losers in such situations are the workers. Government workers are generally unionized and, therefore, receive good pay and benefits. Private-sector workers are less likely to be unionized, and private firms often provide lower pay and fewer benefits. For this reason, public-sector unions have been one of the strongest voices arguing against privatization. Other critics of privatization observe that private firms may not be more efficient or less costly than government. This is especially likely when there is little competition among private firms and when public bureaucracies are not granted a fair chance to bid in the contracting competition. When private firms have a monopoly on service provision, they may be less efficient than government and more expensive. This problem raises important questions about how private contractors can be held accountable. As one analyst of Pentagon spending put it, "The Pentagon is supposed to be representing the taxpayer and the public interest—its national security. So it's really important to have transparency, to be able to see these competitions and hold people accountable."[36] As security has become the nation's paramount concern, new worries about privatization have surfaced. Some Pentagon officials fear that too many tasks vital to national security may have already been contracted out and that national security might best be served by limiting privatization.

The new demands of domestic security have altered the thrust of bureaucratic reform. The emphasis on reducing the size of government that was so prominent during the previous two decades is gone. Instead, there is an acceptance that the federal government will grow as needed to ensure the safety on American citizens. The administration's effort to focus the entire federal bureaucracy on a single central mission will require unprecedented levels of coor-

[36]Ellen Nakashima, "Defense Balks at Contract Goals; Essential Services Should Not Be Privatized, Pentagon Tells OMB," *Washington Post*, 30 January 2002, p. A21.

dination among federal agencies. Despite the strong agreement on the goal of fighting terrorism, the effort to streamline the bureaucracy around a single purpose is likely to face considerable obstacles along the way. Reform of public bureaucracies is always complex because strong constituencies may attempt to block changes that they believe will harm them. Initiatives that aim to improve coordination among agencies can easily provoke political disputes if the proposed changes threaten to alter the access of groups to the bureaucracy. And groups that oppose bureaucratic changes can appeal to Congress to intervene on their behalf. As respected reform advocate Donald Kettl said of the effort to reinvent government, "Virtually no reform that really matters can be achieved without at least implicit congressional support."[37] In wartime, many obstacles to bureaucratic reform are lifted. But the war on terrorism is an unusual war that will be fought over an extended period of time. Whether the unique features of this war improve or limit the prospects for bureaucratic reform remains to be seen.

SUMMARY

Most American citizens possess less information and more misinformation about bureaucracy than about any other feature of government. We, therefore, began the chapter with an elementary definition of bureaucracy, identifying its key characteristics and demonstrating the extent to which bureaucracy is not only a phenomenon but an American phenomenon. In the second section of the chapter, we showed how all essential government services and controls are carried out by bureaucracies—or, to be more objective, administrative agencies. Following a very general description of the different types of bureaucratic agencies in the executive branch, we divided up the agencies of the executive branch into four categories according to mission: clientele agencies, agencies for maintaining the Union, regulatory agencies, and redistributive agencies. These illustrate the varieties of administrative experience in American government. Although the bureaucratic phenomenon is universal, not all the bureaucracies are the same in the way they are organized, in the degree of their responsiveness, or in the way they participate in the political process.

Finally, the chapter concluded with a review of all three of the chapters on "representative government" (Chapters 5, 6, and 7) in order to assess how well the two political branches (the legislative and the executive) do the toughest job any government has to do: making the bureaucracy accountable to the people it serves and controls. "Bureaucracy in a Democracy" was the subtitle and theme of the chapter, not because we have succeeded in democratizing bureaucracies but because it is the never-ending challenge of politics in a democracy.

[37]Quoted in Stephen Bar, "Midterm Exam for 'Reinvention': Study Cites 'Impressive Results' but Calls for Strategy to Win Congressional Support," *Washington Post*, 19 August 1994, p. A25.

Rationality Principle	Collective Action Principle	Institution Principle	Policy Principle	History Principle
One view of bureaucratic behavior is that bureaucrats are motivated to maximize their budgets.	Coordination among bureaucrats is necessary to carry out the primary task of bureaucracy—implementation.	Legislative principals establish bureaucratic agents to implement policies.	The policies of clientele agencies promote the interests of their clientele.	Each expansion of the national government is accompanied by a parallel expansion of presidential management authority.
Bureaucratic drift occurs because bureaucratic agents have different policy preferences from those of members of Congress or the president.	When Congress and the president are at odds (or coalitions within Congress are at odds), bureaucrats have an opportunity to evade responsibility.	Congress also delegates authority to bureaucrats to make law through the procedures of rule-making and administrative adjudication.	The military pork barrel is an example of the distributive tendency in Congress.	The size of the federal bureaucracy has kept pace with the growth of the economy and the needs of society.
	Coalition drift makes the long-term implementation of policy more difficult.	The appointment process and procedural controls allow the president and Congress some before-the-fact control over bureaucratic agents.	Bureaucratic drift and coalitional drift are contrary tendencies. Fixing them often involves a trade-off.	Americans have grown attached to the programs implemented by government agencies and, thus, are eluctant to cut back on their size and scope.

FOR FURTHER READING

Arnold, Peri E. *Making the Managerial Presidency: Comprehensive Reorganization Planning, 1905–1980*. Princeton, N.J.: Princeton University Press, 1986.

Downs, Anthony. *Inside Bureaucracy*. Boston: Little, Brown, 1966.

Fesler, James W., and Donald F. Kettl. *The Politics of the Administrative Process*. 2nd ed. Chatham, N.J.: Chatham House, 1996.

Heclo, Hugh. *A Government of Strangers: Executive Politics in Washington*. Washington, D.C.: Brookings Institution, 1977.

Skowronek, Stephen. *Building a New American State: The Expansion of National Administrative Capacities, 1877–1920*. New York: Cambridge University Press, 1982.

Wildavsky, Aaron, and Naomi Caiden. *The New Politics of the Budgetary Process*. 5th ed. New York: Longman, 2003.

Wilson, James Q. *Bureaucracy: What Government Agencies Do and Why They Do It*. New York: Basic Books, 1989.

Wood, Dan B. *Bureaucratic Dynamics: The Role of Bureaucracy in a Democracy*. Boulder, Col.: Westview, 1994.

Congressional Control of the Defense Bureaucracy

Senator Blocks 850 Promotions in the Air Force

By ERIC SCHMITT

Senator Larry E. Craig of Idaho is blocking the promotions of more than 850 Air Force officers . . . in a rare clash between the Pentagon and a senior Republican lawmaker.

Mr. Craig's price to free the frozen promotions now awaiting final Senate approval? Four C-130 cargo planes for the Idaho Air National Guard.

Pentagon officials express outrage that for more than a month Mr. Craig has single-handedly delayed the careers of hundreds of officers and stymied important Air Force business for a handful of parochial planes. They are vowing not to give in to his pressure. Calling the move blackmail, one senior military official said, "If we say yes to this, Katie bar the door." The official, like others contacted for this article, spoke on the condition of anonymity, fearing retribution from the senator.

But Mr. Craig contends that the Air Force has reneged on a promise made seven years ago to station a squadron of eight C-130's at Gowen Field, an Air National Guard base in Boise, his spokesman said. There are now four C-130's and another training aircraft based there. "This is a problem created by the Air Force that can be easily solved by the Air Force," Will Hart, the spokesman, said. . . .

Under a Senate practice intended to encourage consensus, any senator can block action indefinitely and anonymously on a nomination, promotion or legislation. These secret holds are used frequently by senators of both parties to express displeasure not necessarily with a nominee but with an administration's action or policy. . . .

Mr. Craig's action has been felt throughout the Air Force, from young captains and majors to its senior ranks, where the promotions or new-job nominations for more than two dozen generals are in a holding pattern with no end in sight. . . .

A buildup of the guard forces could help shield Gowen Field from a new round of military base closings sched-

New York Times, 9 June 2003, p. A1.

uled to be decided in 2005. Increasing the number of C-130's at the field could make it a less attractive installation to close, defense officials said. Gowen's C-130's returned in January from a tour in Oman, where they supported operations in Afghanistan and the Persian Gulf.

Several states are organizing committees to defend their military bases, which provide jobs and lucrative Pentagon contracts to local communities. "What a lot of people are trying to do is extort such-and-such a service at such-and-such a base to BRAC-proof their base," one senior defense official said, using the acronym for the Base Realignment and Closure Commission, which would recommend such closings.

. . . "We've tried to explain the facts of life to Senator Craig that the Air Force is getting smaller, not bigger," one official said.

Gen. John W. Handy of the Air Force, the head of United States Transportation Command, which controls all transport aircraft, met with Mr. Craig in Washington on May 23 to broker an end to the stalemate, but apparently to no avail. Said one defense official, "Craig is essentially saying, pound sand."

ESSENCE OF THE STORY

- Over time, a tradition called a "hold" has developed that allows individual senators to block a variety of governmental actions.

- Senator Craig is using the "hold" to delay the promotion of military officers, normally an uncontroversial issue. He hopes to force the Air Force to locate transports at an Air National Guard base in Idaho. The Air Force contends that they do not need or want these transports sited in Idaho.

- Because bases provide money, jobs, and prestige, members of Congress fight hard to keep them in their state. This conflict may be related to upcoming announcements on military base closings.

POLITICAL ANALYSIS

- The "hold" is an *institution* that is not a written rule but just an informal norm. But norms can be just as powerful as any rule.

- The Constitution gives individual senators enormous power over presidential appointments, and senators use that power to further their agenda in other areas.

- Good policy dictates a smaller, leaner, more mobile military, but good politics dictates widely dispersed military bases.

8

The Federal Courts: Least Dangerous Branch or Imperial Judiciary?

George W. Bush won the 2000 national presidential election. The final battle in the race, however, was not decided in the electoral arena and did not involve the participation of ordinary Americans. Instead, the battle was fought in the courts, in the Florida state legislature, and in the executive institutions of the Florida state government by small groups of attorneys and political activists. During the course of the dispute, some forty lawsuits were filed in the Florida circuit and supreme courts, the U.S. District Court, the U.S. Court of Appeals, and the U.S. Supreme Court.[1] Together, the two campaigns amassed nearly $10 million in legal fees during the month of litigation. In most of the courtroom battles, the Bush campaign prevailed. Despite two setbacks before the all-Democratic Florida supreme court, Bush attorneys won most of the circuit court cases and the ultimate clash before the U.S. Supreme Court in a narrow 5-to-4 vote.

During the arguments before the Supreme Court, it became clear that the conservative majority was determined to prevent a Gore victory. Conservative

---

[1]"In the Courts," *San Diego Union-Tribune,* 7 December 2000, p. A14.

justices were sharply critical of the arguments presented by Vice President Al Gore's lawyers, while openly sympathetic to the arguments made by Bush's lawyers. Conservative justice Antonin Scalia went so far as to intervene when Bush attorney Theodore Olson responded to a question from Justices Souter and Ginsburg. Scalia evidently sought to ensure that Olson did not concede too much to the Gore argument. "It's part of your submission, I think," Scalia said, "that there is no wrong when a machine does not count those ballots that it's not supposed to count?" Scalia was seeking to remind Olson that when voter error rendered a ballot unreadable by a tabulating machine, it was not appropriate for a court to order them counted by hand. "The voters are instructed to detach the chads entirely," Scalia said, "and if the machine does not count those chads where those instructions are not followed, there isn't any wrong." Olson was happy to accept Scalia's reminder.[2]

Liberal justice John Paul Stevens said the majority opinion smacked of partisan politics. The opinion, he said, "can only lend credence to the most cynical appraisal of the work of judges throughout the land." He concluded, "Although we may never know with complete certainty the identity of the winner of this year's presidential election, the identity of the loser is perfectly clear. It is the nation's confidence in the judge as an impartial guardian of the rule of law." Justice Stevens's eloquent dissent did not change the outcome. Throughout the nation, Democrats saw

[2]Linda Greenhouse, "U.S. Supreme Court Justices Grill Bush, Gore Lawyer in Effort to Close the Book on Presidential Race," *New Orleans Times-Picayune*, 12 December 2000, p. 1.

CHAPTER OUTLINE

the Supreme Court majority's opinion as a blatantly partisan decision. Nevertheless, the contest was over. The next day, Al Gore made a speech conceding the election, and on December 18, 2000, 271 presidential electors—the constitutionally prescribed majority—cast their votes for George W. Bush.

What does the court battle over Florida's twenty-five electoral votes reveal about the power of courts and judges in the American political system? First of all, this battle shows that judges are similar to other politicians in that they have political goals and policy preferences and they act accordingly so that those goals are realized. While thinking of judges as "legislators in robes" is antithetical to the view that judges rule according to a well-thought-out judicial philosophy based on constitutional law, there is evidence that strategic thinking on the part of judges is also a factor in their decision-making process. Second, this battle illustrates the political power that the courts now exercise. Over the past fifty years, the prominence of the courts has been heightened by the sharp increase in the number of major policy issues that have been fought and decided in the judicial realm. But since judges are not elected and accountable to the people, what does this shift in power mean for American democracy?

In this chapter, we will first examine the judicial process, including the types of cases that the federal courts consider and the types of law with which they deal. Second, we will assess the organization and structure of the federal court system as well as explain how judges are appointed to the courts. Third, we will analyze courts as political institutions and consider their roles in the political system. Fourth, we will consider judicial review and how it makes the Supreme Court a "lawmaking body." Fifth, we will examine the flow of cases through the courts and various influences on the Supreme Court's decisions. Finally, we will analyze the power of the federal courts in the American political process, looking in particular at the growth of judicial power in the United States.

The framers of the American Constitution called the Court the "least dangerous branch" of American government. Today, it is not unusual to hear friends and foes of the Court alike refer to it as the "imperial judiciary."[3] However, we must

⊙ **Rationality Principle**

Judges have political goals and policy preferences, and act to achieve them.

⚖ **Policy Principle**

A number of major policy issues have been fought and decided in the courts.

---

[3]See Richard Neely, *How Courts Govern America* (New Haven: Yale University Press, 1981).

look in some detail at America's judicial process before we can understand this transformation and its consequences, and then answer the question: "Is the Supreme Court the 'least dangerous branch' or an 'imperial judiciary'?"

THE JUDICIAL PROCESS

Originally, a "court" was the place where a sovereign ruled—where the king and his entourage governed. Settling disputes between citizens was part of governing. According to the Bible, King Solomon had to settle the dispute between two women over which of them was the mother of the child both claimed. Judging is the settling of disputes, a function that was slowly separated from the king and the king's court and made into a separate institution of government. Courts have taken over from kings the power to settle controversies by hearing the facts on both sides and deciding which side possesses the greater merit. But since judges are not kings, they must have a basis for their authority. That basis in the United States is the Constitution and the law. Courts decide cases by applying the relevant law or principle to the facts.

Court cases in the United States proceed under two broad categories of law: criminal law and civil law. One form of civil law, public law, is so important that we will consider it as a separate category. (See Table 8.1.)

Cases of *criminal law* are those in which the government charges an individual with violating a statute that has been enacted to protect the public health, safety, morals, or welfare. In criminal cases, the government is always the *plaintiff* (the party that brings charges) and alleges that a criminal violation has been committed by a named *defendant.* Most criminal cases arise in state and municipal courts and involve matters ranging from traffic offenses to robbery and murder. While the great bulk of criminal law is still a state matter, a large and growing body of federal criminal law deals with such matters as tax evasion, mail fraud, and the sale of narcotics. Defendants found guilty of criminal violations may be fined or sent to prison.

Cases of *civil law* involve disputes among individuals or between individuals and the government where no criminal violation is charged. Unlike criminal cases, the losers in civil cases cannot be fined or sent to prison, although they may be required to pay monetary damages for their actions. In a civil case, the one who brings a complaint is the plaintiff and the one against whom the complaint is brought is the defendant. The two most common types of civil cases involve contracts and torts. In a typical contract case, an individual or corporation charges that it has suffered because of another's violation of a specific agreement between the two. For example, the Smith Manufacturing Corporation may charge that Jones Distributors failed to honor an agreement to deliver raw materials at a specified time, causing Smith to lose business. Smith asks the court to order Jones to compensate it for the damage allegedly suffered. In a typical tort case, one individual charges that he or she has been injured by another's negligence or malfeasance. Medical malpractice suits are one example of tort cases.

criminal law The branch of law that deals with disputes or actions involving criminal penalties (as opposed to civil law). It regulates the conduct of individuals, defines crimes, and provides punishment for criminal acts.

plaintiff The individual or organization who brings a complaint in court.

defendant The individual or organization charged with a complaint in court.

civil law A system of jurisprudence, including private law and governmental actions, to settle disputes that do not involve criminal penalties.

TABLE 8.1

Types of Laws and Disputes

TYPE OF LAW	TYPE OF CASE OR DISPUTE	FORM OF CASE
Criminal law	Cases arising out of actions that violate laws protecting the health, safety, and morals of the community. The government is always the plaintiff.	*U.S. (or state) v. Jones* *Jones v. U.S. (or state)*, if Jones lost and is appealing
Civil law	Law involving disputes between citizens or between government and citizen where no crime is alleged. Two general types are contract and tort. *Contract cases* are disputes that arise over voluntary actions. *Tort cases* are disputes that arise out of obligations inherent in social life. Negligence and slander are examples of torts.	*Smith v. Jones* *New York v. Jones* *U.S. v. Jones* *Jones v. New York*
Public law	All cases where the powers of government or the rights of citizens are involved. The government is the defendant. *Constitutional law* involves judicial review of the basis of a government's action in relation to specific clauses of the Constitution as interpreted in Supreme Court cases. *Administrative law* involves disputes over the statutory authority, jurisdiction, or procedures of administrative agencies.	*Jones v. U.S. (or state)* *In re Jones* *Smith v. Jones*, if a license or statute is at issue in their private dispute

precedents Prior cases whose principles are used by judges as the bases for their decisions in present cases.

In deciding cases, courts apply statutes (laws) and legal *precedents* (prior decisions). State and federal statutes often govern the conditions under which contracts are and are not legally binding. Jones Distributors might argue that it was not obliged to fulfill its contract with the Smith Corporation because actions by Smith—the failure to make promised payments—constituted fraud under state law. Attorneys for a physician being sued for malpractice, on the other hand, may search for prior instances in which courts ruled that actions similar to those of their client did not constitute negligence. Such precedents are applied under the doctrine of ***stare decisis,*** a Latin phrase meaning "let the decision stand."

A case becomes a matter of the third category, ***public law,*** when a plaintiff or defendant in a civil or criminal case seeks to show that their case involves the powers of government or rights of citizens as defined under the Constitution or by statute. One major form of public law is constitutional law, under which a court will examine the government's actions to see if they conform to the Constitution as it has been interpreted by the judiciary. Thus, what began as an ordinary criminal case may enter the realm of public law if a defendant claims that his or her constitutional rights were violated by the police. Another important arena of public law is administrative law, which involves disputes over the jurisdiction, procedures, or authority of administrative agencies. Under this type of law, civil litigation between an individual and the government may become a matter of public law if the individual asserts that the government is violating a statute or abusing its power under the Constitution. For example, landowners have asserted that federal and state restrictions on land use constitute violations of the Fifth Amendment's restrictions on the government's ability to confiscate private property. Recently, the Supreme Court has been very sympathetic to such claims, which effectively transform an ordinary civil dispute into a major issue of public law.

Most of the Supreme Court cases we will examine in this chapter involve judgments concerning the constitutional or statutory basis of the actions of government agencies. As we shall see, it is in this arena of public law that Court decisions can have significant consequences for American politics and society.

THE ORGANIZATION OF THE COURT SYSTEM

Types of Courts

In the United States, systems of courts have been established both by the federal government and by the governments of the individual states. Both systems have several levels, as shown in Figure 8.1. Nearly 99 percent of all court cases in the United States are heard in state courts. The overwhelming majority of criminal cases, for example, involve violations of state laws prohibiting such actions as murder, robbery, fraud, theft, and assault. If such a case is brought to trial, it will be heard in a state ***trial court*** in front of a judge and sometimes a jury, who will determine whether the defendant violated state law. If the defendant is convicted, he or she may appeal the conviction to a higher court, such as a state ***appellate court,*** and from there to a state's ***supreme court.*** Similarly, in civil cases, most litigation is brought in the courts established by the state in which

stare decisis Literally "let the decision stand." A previous decision by a court applies as a precedent in similar cases until that decision is overruled.

public law Cases involving the action of public agencies or officials.

trial court The first court to hear a criminal or civil case.

appellate court A court that hears the appeals of trial-court decisions.

supreme court The highest court in a particular state or in the United States. This court primarily serves an appellate function.

FIGURE 8.1

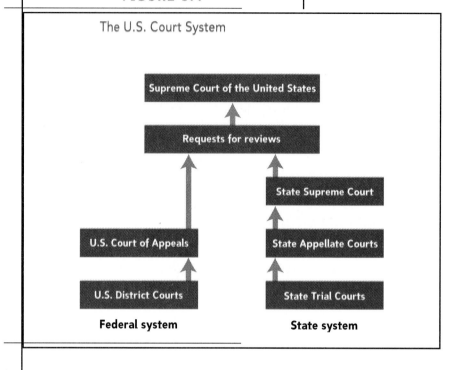

The U.S. Court System

Supreme Court of the United States

Requests for reviews

U.S. Court of Appeals

State Supreme Court

State Appellate Courts

U.S. District Courts

State Trial Courts

Federal system   **State system**

the activity in question took place. For example, a patient bringing suit against a physician for malpractice would file the suit in the appropriate court in the state where the alleged malpractice occurred. The judge hearing the case would apply state law and state precedent to the matter at hand. (It should be noted that in both criminal and civil matters, most cases are settled before trial through negotiated agreements between the parties. In criminal cases, these agreements are called *plea bargains.*)

plea bargains
Negotiated agreements in criminal cases in which a defendant agrees to plead guilty in return for the state's agreement to reduce the severity of the criminal charge the defendant is facing.

In addition, the U.S. military operates its own court system under the Uniform Code of Military Justice, which governs the behavior of men and women in the armed services. On rare occasions, the government has constituted special military tribunals to hear cases deemed inappropriate for the civil courts. Such tribunals tried Nazi saboteurs apprehended in the United States during World War II. More recently, President Bush ordered the creation of military tribunals to try foreigners suspected of acts of terrorism against the United States.

Federal Jurisdiction

Cases are heard in the federal courts if they involve federal laws, treaties with other nations, or the U.S. Constitution; these areas are the official *jurisdiction* of the federal courts. In addition, any case in which the U.S. government is a party is heard in the federal courts. If, for example, an individual is charged with violating a federal criminal statute, such as evading the payment of income taxes, charges would be brought before a federal judge by a federal prosecutor. Civil cases involving the citizens of more than one state and in which more than fifty thousand dollars are at stake may be heard in either the federal or the state courts, usually depending upon the preference of the plaintiff.

Federal courts serve another purpose in addition to trying cases within their jurisdiction: that of hearing appeals from state-level courts. Individuals found guilty of breaking a state criminal law, for example, can appeal their convictions to a federal court by raising a constitutional issue and asking a federal court to determine whether the state's actions were consistent with the requirements of the U.S. Constitution. An appellant might assert, for example, that the state court denied him or her the right to counsel, imposed excessive bail, or otherwise denied the appellant *due process.* Under such circumstances, an appellant can ask the federal court to overturn his or her conviction. Federal courts are not obligated to accept such appeals and will do so only if they feel that the issues raised have considerable merit and if the appellant has exhausted all possible remedies within the state courts. (This procedure is discussed in more detail later in this chapter.) The decisions of state supreme courts may also be appealed to the U.S. Supreme Court if the state court's decision has conflicted with prior U.S. Supreme Court rulings or has raised some important question of federal law. Such appeals are accepted by the U.S. Supreme Court at its discretion.

Of all the cases heard in the United States in 2001, federal district courts (the lowest federal level) received 253,354. Although this number is up substantially from the 87,000 cases heard in 1961, it still constitutes under 1 percent of the judiciary's business. A major reason that the caseload of the federal courts has increased in recent years is that Congress has greatly expanded the number of federal crimes, particularly in the realm of drug possession and sale. Behavior that once was exclusively a state criminal question has, to some extent, come within the reach of federal law. Recently, Chief Justice Rehnquist criticized Congress for federalizing too many offenses and intruding unnecessarily into areas that should be handled by the states.[4] The federal courts of appeal listened to approximately 80,000 cases in 2001, and 5,376 cases were filed with the U.S. Supreme Court during its 2000–2001 term. Most of the cases filed with the Supreme Court are dismissed without a ruling on their merits. The Court has broad latitude to decide what cases it will hear and generally listens only to those cases it deems to raise the most important issues. Only 86 cases were given full-dress Supreme

jurisdiction The sphere of a court's power and authority.

due process The right of every citizen against arbitrary action by national or state governments.

---

[4]Roberto Suro, "Rehnquist: Too Many Offenses Are Becoming Federal Crimes," *Washington Post*, 1 January 1999, p. A2.

Court review (the nine justices actually sitting *en banc*—in full court—and hearing the lawyers argue the case).[5]

Although the federal courts hear only a small fraction of all the civil and criminal cases decided each year in the United States, their decisions are extremely important. It is in the federal courts that the Constitution and federal laws that govern all Americans are interpreted and their meaning and significance established. Moreover, it is in the federal courts that the powers and limitations of the increasingly powerful national government are tested. Finally, through their power to review the decisions of the state courts, it is ultimately the federal courts that dominate the American judicial system.

The Lower Federal Courts

Most of the cases of original federal jurisdiction are handled by the federal district courts. The federal district courts are trial courts of general jurisdiction, and their cases are, in form, indistinguishable from cases in the state trial courts.

There are eighty-nine district courts in the fifty states, plus one in the District of Columbia and one in Puerto Rico, and three territorial courts. In 1978, Congress increased the number of district judgeships from 400 to 517 in an effort to deal with the greatly increased court workload. District judges are assigned to district courts according to the workload; the busiest of these courts may have as many as twenty-eight judges. Only one judge is assigned to each case, except where statutes provide for three-judge courts to deal with special issues. The routines and procedures of the federal district courts are essentially the same as those of the lower state courts except that federal procedural requirements tend to be stricter. States, for example, do not have to provide a grand jury, a twelve-member trial jury, or a unanimous jury verdict. Federal courts must provide all these things. In addition to the district courts, cases are handled by several specialized courts, including the U.S. Tax Court, the Court of Claims, the Customs Court, and the federal regulatory agencies.

The Appellate Courts

Roughly 10 percent of all lower court and agency cases are subsequently reviewed by a federal appeals court. Except for cases filed with the Supreme Court, a properly filed appeal will be heard. The country is divided into twelve judicial circuits, each of which has a U.S. Court of Appeals. Every state and the District of Columbia are assigned to the circuit in the continental United States that is closest to it. A thirteenth appellate court, the U.S. Court of Appeals for the Federal Circuit, is defined by subject matter rather than geographical jurisdiction. This court accepts appeals regarding patents, copyrights, and international trade.

[5]U.S. Bureau of the Census, *Statistical Abstract of the United States, 2002* (Washington, D.C.: Government Printing Office, 2002).

Except for cases selected for review by the Supreme Court, decisions made by the appeals courts are final. Because of this finality, certain safeguards have been built into the system. The most important is the provision of more than one judge for every appeals case. Each court of appeals has from three to fifteen permanent judgeships, depending on the workload of the circuit. Although normally three judges hear appealed cases, in some instances a larger number of judges sit together *en banc*.

Another safeguard is provided by the assignment of a Supreme Court justice as the circuit justice for each of the twelve circuits. Since the creation of the appeals court in 1891, the circuit justice's primary duty has been to review appeals arising in the circuit in order to expedite Supreme Court action. The most frequent and best-known action of circuit justices is that of reviewing requests for stays of execution when the full Court is unable to do so—mainly during the summer, when the Court is in recess.

The Supreme Court

The Supreme Court is America's highest court. Article III of the Constitution vests "the judicial Power of the United States" in the Supreme Court, and this court is supreme in fact as well as form. The Supreme Court is made up of a chief justice and eight associate justices. The **chief justice** presides over the Court's public sessions and conferences. In the Court's actual deliberations and decisions, however, the chief justice has no more authority than his or her colleagues. Each justice casts one vote. To some extent, the influence of the chief justice is a function of his or her own leadership ability. Some chief justices, such as the late Earl Warren, have been able to lead the court in a new direction. In other instances, a forceful associate justice, such as the late Felix Frankfurter, is the dominant figure on the Court.

The Constitution does not specify the number of justices that should sit on the Supreme Court; Congress has the authority to change the Court's size. In the early nineteenth century, there were six Supreme Court justices; later there were seven. Congress set the number of justices at nine in 1869, and the Court has remained that size ever since. In 1937, President Franklin D. Roosevelt, infuriated by several Supreme Court decisions that struck down New Deal programs, asked Congress to enlarge the court so that he could add a few sympathetic justices to the bench. Although Congress balked at Roosevelt's "court packing" plan, the Court gave in to FDR's pressure and began to take a more favorable view of his policy initiatives. The president, in turn, dropped his efforts to enlarge the Court. The Court's surrender to FDR came to be known as "the switch in time that saved nine."

How Judges Are Appointed

Federal judges are appointed by the president and are generally selected from among the more prominent or politically active members of the legal profession. Many federal judges previously served as state court judges or state or local

chief justice
Justice on the Supreme Court who presides over the Court's public sessions.

Collective Action Principle

Appointments to the federal bench involve informal bargaining (senatorial courtesy) as well as formal bargaining (Senate confirmation).

senatorial courtesy The practice whereby the president, before nominating a person formally for a federal judgeship, checks on whether the senators from the candidate's state support the nomination.

prosecutors. Before the president makes a formal nomination, however, the senators from the candidate's own state must indicate that they support the nominee. This is an informal but seldom violated practice called *senatorial courtesy.* Because the Senate will rarely approve a nominee opposed by a senator from his or her own state, the president will usually not bother to present such a nomination to the Senate. Through this arrangement, senators are able to exercise veto power over appointments to the federal bench in their own states. Senators often see such a nomination as a way to reward important allies and contributors in their states. If the state has no senator from the president's party, the governor or members of the state's House delegation may make suggestions. In general, presidents endeavor to appoint judges who possess legal experience and good character and whose partisan and ideological views are similar to the president's own. During the presidencies of Ronald Reagan and George H. W. Bush, most federal judicial appointees were conservative Republicans. Bush established an advisory committee to screen judicial nominees in order to make certain that their legal and political philosophies were sufficiently conservative. Bill Clinton's appointees to the federal bench, on the other hand, tended to be liberal Democrats. Clinton also made a major effort to appoint women and African Americans to the federal courts. Nearly half of his nominees were drawn from these groups.

Once the president has formally nominated an individual, the nominee must be considered by the Senate Judiciary Committee and confirmed by a majority vote in the full Senate. In recent years, the Senate Judiciary Committee has sought to signal the president when it has had qualms about a judicial nomination. After the Republicans won control of the Senate in 1994, for example, Judiciary Committee chair Orrin Hatch of Utah let President Clinton know that he considered two of Clinton's nominees to be too liberal. The president withdrew the nominations.

Federal appeals court nominations follow much the same pattern. Since appeals court judges preside over jurisdictions that include several states, however, senators do not have as strong a role in proposing potential candidates. Instead, potential appeals court candidates are generally suggested to the president by the Justice Department or by important members of the administration. The senators from the nominee's own state are still consulted before the president will formally act.

During President George W. Bush's first two years in office, Democrats controlled the Senate and used their majority on the Judiciary Committee to block eight of the president's first eleven federal court nominations. After the GOP won a narrow Senate majority in the 2002 national elections, Democrats used a filibuster to block action on two Bush federal appeals court nominees, Miguel Estrada and Priscilla Owen. Democratic senators charged that Estrada and Owen were activist conservatives who would use the bench to rewrite federal law. At the same time, though, the Senate voted to confirm several other Bush nominees. Both Democrats and Republicans saw struggles over lower court slots as practice and preparation for all-out partisan warfare over the next Supreme Court vacancy.

If political factors play an important role in the selection of district and appellate court judges, they are decisive when it comes to Supreme Court appointments. Because the high court has so much influence over American law and politics, virtually all presidents have made an effort to select justices who share their own political philosophies. Presidents Ronald Reagan and George H. W. Bush, for example, appointed five justices whom they believed to have conservative perspectives: Justices Sandra Day O'Connor, Antonin Scalia, Anthony M. Kennedy, David Hackett Souter, and Clarence Thomas. Reagan also elevated William Rehnquist to the position of chief justice. Reagan and Bush sought appointees who believed in reducing government intervention in the economy and who supported the moral positions taken by the Republican party in recent years, particularly opposition to abortion. However, not all the Reagan and Bush appointees have fulfilled their sponsors' expectations. Bush appointee David Souter, for example, has been attacked by conservatives as a turncoat for his decisions on school prayer and abortion rights. Nevertheless, through their appointments, Reagan and Bush were able to create a far more conservative Supreme Court. For his part, President Bill Clinton endeavored to appoint liberal justices. Clinton named Ruth Bader Ginsburg and Stephen G. Breyer to the Court, hoping to counteract the influence of the Reagan and Bush appointees. President George W. Bush hopes to appoint conservatives to the Court but must take into account the views of the Democratic-controlled Senate. (Table 8.2 shows information about the current Supreme Court justices.)

In recent years, Supreme Court nominations have come to involve intense partisan struggle. Typically, after the president has named a nominee, interest groups opposed to the nomination have mobilized opposition in the media, the public, and the Senate. When former president Bush proposed conservative judge Clarence Thomas for the Court, for example, liberal groups launched a campaign to discredit Thomas. After extensive research into his background, opponents of the nomination were able to produce evidence suggesting that Thomas had sexually harassed a former subordinate, Anita Hill. Thomas denied the charge. After contentious Senate Judiciary Committee hearings, highlighted by testimony from both Thomas and Hill, Thomas narrowly won confirmation.

Likewise, conservative interest groups carefully scrutinized Bill Clinton's somewhat more liberal nominees, hoping to find information about them that would sabotage their appointments. During his two opportunities to name Supreme Court justices, Clinton was compelled to drop several potential appointees because of information unearthed by political opponents.

These struggles over judicial appointments indicate the growing intensity of partisan struggle in the United States today. They also indicate how much importance competing political forces attach to Supreme Court appointments. Because these contending forces see the outcome as critical, they are willing to engage in a fierce struggle when Supreme Court appointments are at stake.

The matter of judicial appointments became an important issue in the 2000 election. Democrats charged that, if he was elected, George W. Bush would appoint conservative judges who might, among other things, reverse the *Roe v.*

TABLE 8.2

Supreme Court Justices, 2003
(In Order of Seniority)

NAME	YEAR OF BIRTH	PRIOR EXPERIENCE	APPOINTED BY	YEAR OF APPOINTMENT
William H. Rehnquist* *Chief Justice*	1924	Assistant attorney general	Nixon	1972
John Paul Stevens	1920	Federal judge	Ford	1975
Sandra Day O'Connor	1930	State judge	Reagan	1981
Antonin Scalia	1936	Law professor, federal judge	Reagan	1986
Anthony M. Kennedy	1936	Federal judge	Reagan	1988
David Hackett Souter	1939	Federal judge	Bush	1990
Clarence Thomas	1948	Federal judge	Bush	1991
Ruth Bader Ginsburg	1933	Federal judge	Clinton	1993
Stephen G. Breyer	1938	Federal judge	Clinton	1994

*Appointed chief justice by Reagan in 1986.

Wade decision and curb abortion rights. Bush would say only that he would seek judges who would uphold the Constitution without reading their own political biases into the document.

From the liberal perspective, the danger of a conservative judiciary was underlined by the Supreme Court's decision in the Florida election case, *Bush v. Gore*. The Court's conservative bloc, in recent years, has argued that the states deserve considerable deference from the federal courts. In this instance, however, the Supreme Court overturned a decision of the Florida supreme court regarding Florida election law. The Court ruled that its Florida counterpart had ignored the U.S. Constitution's equal protection doctrine when it mandated recounts in some, but not all, Florida counties. By voting to overrule the Florida court, the Supreme Court's conservative justices appeared to disregard the logic of their own decisions—expanding the authority of the states—of the past two decades (see Chapter 3). To be sure, the same liberal justices who voted to uphold the Florida court's decision had frequently argued against deferring to the states in previous decisions. Ideological consistency notwithstanding, defenders of the decision argued that it was doctrinally sound and that it averted the chaos that might have ensued if a recount gave Gore the victory and the Florida legislature carried out its threat to appoint Bush electors. Two competing slates of electors might then have sought congressional certification. Critics of the decision, however, asserted that the Court was merely searching for a rubric under which it could ensure Bush's victory. As a result of the Florida contest, there can be little doubt that the next Supreme Court vacancy will generate sharp fighting in Washington.

HOW DO COURTS WORK AS POLITICAL INSTITUTIONS?

Judges are central players in important political institutions and this makes them politicians. In order to understand what animates judicial behavior, we thus need to place the judge or justice in context by briefly considering the role of the courts in the political system more generally. In doing so, we emphasize the role of courts as *dispute resolvers*, as *coordinators*, and as *interpreters of rules*.

Dispute Resolution

So much of the productive activity that occurs within families, among friends and associates, even between absolute strangers takes place because the participants do not have to devote substantial resources to protecting themselves and their property or monitoring compliance with agreements.[6] For any potential violation of person or property, or defection from an agreement, all parties know in advance that an aggrieved party may take an alleged violator to court. The court, in turn, serves as a venue in which the facts of a case are established, punishment is meted out to violators, and compensation awarded to victims. The court, therefore, is an institution that engages in fact-finding and judgment.

In disputes between private parties, the court serves principally to determine whether claims of violation can be substantiated. An employee, for example, may sue her employer for allegedly violating the terms of a privately negotiated employment contract. Or a consumer may sue a producer for violating the terms of a product warranty. Or a tenant may sue a landlord for violating provisions of a lease. In all of these cases, some issue between private parties is in dispute. The court system provides the service of dispute resolution.

[6]Naturally, some resources are devoted to protection and monitoring. However, if extraordinary resources had to be devoted, then their rising cost would cause the frequency of the productive activities alluded to in the text to decline, according to elementary economic theory. Indeed, since the costs of negotiating, monitoring, and enforcing agreements (what political economists call *transaction costs*) can be very high, they are a serious impediment to social interaction and productive activities of all sorts. Economizing on them—by providing the services of courts and judges, for example—is one of the great contributions of the modern state to social welfare.

The examples in the preceding paragraph involve civil law. An entirely separate category of dispute, one in which the courts also have a role to play, involves criminal law. In these cases "the public" is a party to the dispute because the alleged violation concerns not (only) something involving private parties, but (also) a public law. This brings the public agencies of justice into play as parties to a dispute. When an individual embezzles funds from his partner, he not only violates a privately negotiated agreement between them (namely, a promise of honest dealings), he also violates a public law prohibiting embezzlement generally. A court proceeding, in this case, determines not only whether a violation of a private arrangement has occurred but also whether the alleged perpetrator is innocent or guilty of violating a public law.

In all of these instances, the judge is responsible for managing the fact-finding and judgment phases of dispute resolution (sometimes in collaboration with a jury). Thus, a large part of the daily life of a judge involves making an independent, experienced assessment of the facts, determining whether the dispute involves a violation of a private agreement or a public law (or both), and finally rendering a judgment—a determination of which party (if either) is liable, and what compensation is in order (to the private party victimized and, if judged a criminal activity, to the larger public). Judging is a sophisticated blend of reading a mystery novel, solving a crossword puzzle, and providing wise counsel.

Coordination

Collective Action Principle

The legal system coordinates private behavior by providing incentives and disincentives for specific actions.

Dispute resolution occurs after the fact—that is, after a dispute has already occurred. In a manner of speaking, it represents a failure of the legal system since one function of law and its judicial institutions is to discourage such disputes in the first place. We may also think of courts and judges as before-the-fact *coordination mechanisms* inasmuch as the anticipation of what happens once their services are called upon allows private parties to form rational expectations and thereby coordinate their actions in advance of possible disputes. A prospective embezzler, estimating the odds of getting caught, prosecuted, and subsequently punished, may think twice about cheating his partner. Surely, *some* prospective embezzlers are deterred from their crimes by these prospects. Conversely, the legal system can work as an incentive: two acquaintances, for example, may confidently entertain the possibility of going into business together, knowing that the sword of justice hangs over their collaboration.

In this sense, the court system is as important for what it doesn't do as for what it does. The system of courts and law coordinates private behavior by providing incentives and disincentives for specific actions. To the extent that these work, there are fewer disputes to resolve and thus less after-the-fact dispute resolution for courts and judges to engage in. What makes the incentives and disincentives work is their power (are the rewards and penalties big or small?), their clarity, and the consistency with which judges administer them. Clear incentives, consistently employed, provide powerful motivations for private parties to resolve disputes ahead of time. This sort of advanced coordination, encouraged by a properly functioning legal system, economizes on the transaction costs that would diminish the frequency of, and otherwise discourage, socially desirable activity.

Rule Interpretation

Dispute resolution and coordination affect private behavior and the daily lives of ordinary citizens tremendously. Judges, however, are not entirely free agents (despite the fact that some of them are tyrants in their courtrooms). In matching the facts of a specific case to judicial principles and statutory guidelines, judges must engage in *interpretive* activity. They must determine what particular statutes or judicial principles mean, which of them fit the facts of a particular case, and then, having determined all this, they must ascertain the disposition of the case at hand. Does the statute of 1927 regulating the electronic transmission of radio waves apply to television, cellular phones, ship-to-shore radios, fax machines, and E-mail? Does the law governing the transportation of dangerous substances, passed in 1937, apply to nuclear fuels, infected animals, and artificially created biological hazards? Often, the enacting legislative body has not been crystal clear about the scope of the legislation it passes. Indeed, a legislature acting in 1927 or 1937 could not have anticipated technological developments to come. Nevertheless, cases such as these come up on a regular basis, and judges must make judgment calls, so to speak, on highly complex issues.

Interpreting the rules is probably the single most important activity in which higher courts engage. This is because the court system is *hierarchical* in the sense that judgments by higher courts constrain the discretion of judges in lower courts. If the Supreme Court rules that nuclear fuels are covered by the 1937 law on transporting dangerous substances, then lower courts must render subsequent judgments in a manner consistent with this ruling. The judge in a civil or criminal trial concerning the shipment of nuclear isotopes from a laboratory to a commercial user, for example, must make sure his or her ruling complies with the legal interpretations passed down by the higher courts. Also, because of the federal principle by which the American polity is organized, federal law and interpretations thereof often trump state and local laws.

As we shall see in the following section, courts and judges engage not only in *statutory interpretation* but in *constitutional interpretation* as well. Here they interpret the provisions of the U.S. Constitution, determining their scope and content. In determining, for example, whether the act of Congress regulating the transportation of dangerous substances from one state to another is constitutional, the justices of the Supreme Court might appeal to the commerce clause of the Constitution (allowing the federal government to regulate interstate commerce) to justify the constitutionality of that act. On the other hand, a Supreme Court majority might also rule that a shipment of spent fuel rods from a nuclear reactor in Kansas City to a nuclear waste facility outside of St. Louis is *not* covered by this law since the shipment took place entirely within the boundaries of a single state and, thus, did not constitute interstate commerce.

In short, judges and justices are continually engaged in elaborating, embellishing, even rewriting the rules by which private and public life are organized. In these interpretive acts they are conscious of the fact that their rulings will affect not only the participants in a specific case before them, but also will carry interpretive weight in all similar cases that percolate down to the lower courts. Thus, statutory and constitutional interpretations have authority over subsequent deliberations (and, in turn, are themselves influenced by earlier interpretations according to *stare decisis*).

However, judicial interpretation—elaboration, embellishment, and "redrafting"—of statutes is naturally subject to review. Statutory interpretation, even if it is conducted by the highest court in the land, is exposed to legislative review. If Congress is unhappy with a specific statutory interpretation—for example, suppose the current Congress does not like the idea of federal regulation of E-mail that a federal court claimed to be permissible under the 1927 act on electronic transmission—then it may amend the legislation so as explicitly to reverse the court ruling. Of course, if the court makes a *constitutional* ruling, Congress cannot then abrogate that ruling through new legislation. But Congress can commence the process of constitutional amendment, thereby effectively reversing constitutional interpretations with which it disagrees.

THE POWER OF JUDICIAL REVIEW

judicial review
Power of the courts to declare actions of the legislative and executive branches invalid or unconstitutional. The Supreme Court asserted this power in *Marbury v. Madison*.

Courts have the power of *judicial review*—the authority and the obligation to review any lower-court decision where a substantial issue of public law is involved. The disputes can be over the constitutionality of federal or state laws, over the propriety or constitutionality of the court procedures followed, or over whether public officers are exceeding their authority. The Supreme Court's power of judicial review has come to mean review not only of lower-court decisions but also of state legislation and acts of Congress (see Figure 8.2). For this reason, if for no other, the Supreme Court is more than a judicial agency—it is also a major lawmaking body.

The Supreme Court's power of judicial review over lower-court decisions has never been at issue. Nor has there been any serious quibble over the power of the federal courts to review administrative agencies in order to determine whether their actions and decisions are within the powers delegated to them by Congress. There has, however, been a great deal of controversy occasioned by the Supreme Court's efforts to review acts of Congress and the decisions of state courts and legislatures.

Judicial Review of Acts of Congress

Since the Constitution does not give the Supreme Court the power of judicial review of congressional enactments, the Court's exercise of it is something of a usurpation. Various proposals were debated at the Constitutional Convention.

FIGURE 8.2

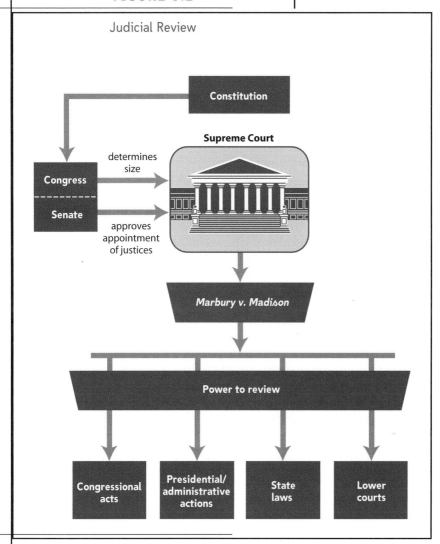

Judicial Review

Constitution

Supreme Court

Congress

Senate

determines
size

approves
appointment
of justices

Marbury v. Madison

Power to review

Congressional
acts

Presidential/
administrative
actions

State
laws

Lower
courts

Among them was the proposal to create a council composed of the president and the judiciary that would share the veto power over legislation. Another proposal would have routed all legislation through the Court as well as through the president; a veto by either one would have required an overruling by a two-thirds vote of the House and Senate. Each proposal was rejected by the delegates, and no further effort was made to give the Supreme Court review power over the other branches.

This does not prove that the framers of the Constitution opposed judicial review, but it does indicate that "if they intended to provide for it in the Constitution, they did so in a most obscure fashion."[7] Disputes over the intentions of the framers were settled in 1803 in the case of *Marbury v. Madison*.[8] Although Congress and the president have often been at odds with the Court, its legal power to review acts of Congress has not been seriously questioned since 1803. One reason is that judicial power has been accepted as natural, if not intended. Another reason is that, over the course of more than two centuries, the Supreme Court has only struck down some 160 acts of Congress. When such acts do come up for review, the Court makes a self-conscious effort to give them an interpretation that will make them constitutional.

Judicial Review of State Actions

supremacy clause
Article VI of the Constitution, which states that all laws passed by the national government and all treaties are the supreme laws of the land and superior to all laws adopted by any state or any subdivision.

The power of the Supreme Court to review state legislation or other state action and to determine its constitutionality is neither granted by the Constitution nor inherent in the federal system. But the logic of the ***supremacy clause*** of Article VI of the Constitution, which declares it and laws made under its authority to be the supreme law of the land, is very strong. Furthermore, in the Judiciary Act of 1789, Congress conferred on the Supreme Court the power to reverse state constitutions and laws whenever they are clearly in conflict with the U.S. Constitution, federal laws, or treaties.[9] This power gives the Supreme Court jurisdiction over all of the millions of cases handled by American courts each year.

The supremacy clause of the Constitution not only established the federal Constitution, statutes, and treaties as the "supreme Law of the Land," but also provided that "the Judges in every State shall be bound thereby, any Thing in the Constitution or Laws of any State to the Contrary notwithstanding." Under this authority, the Supreme Court has frequently overturned state constitutional provisions or statutes and state court decisions it deems to contravene rights or privileges guaranteed under the federal Constitution or federal statutes.

The civil rights area abounds with examples of state laws that were overturned because the statutes violated guarantees of due process and equal protection contained in the Fourteenth Amendment to the Constitution. For example, in the 1954 case of *Brown v. Board of Education*, the Court overturned statutes

---

[7] C. Herman Pritchett, *The American Constitution* (New York: McGraw-Hill, 1959), p. 138.
[8] Marbury v. Madison, 1 Cr. 137 (1803).
[9] This review power was affirmed by the Supreme Court in Martin v. Hunter's Lessee, 1 Wheaton 304 (1816).

from Kansas, South Carolina, Virginia, and Delaware that either required or permitted segregated public schools, on the basis that such statutes denied black schoolchildren equal protection of the law. In 1967, in *Loving v. Virginia*, the Court invalidated a Virginia statute prohibiting interracial marriages.[10]

State statutes in other subject-matter areas are equally subject to challenge. In *Griswold v. Connecticut*, the Court invalidated a Connecticut statute prohibiting the general distribution of contraceptives to married couples on the basis that the statute violated the couples' rights to marital privacy.[11] In *Brandenburg v. Ohio*, the Court overturned an Ohio statute forbidding any person from urging criminal acts as a means of inducing political reform or from joining any association that advocated such activities on the grounds that the statute punished "mere advocacy" and, therefore, violated the free-speech provisions of the Constitution.[12]

Judicial Review of Federal Agency Actions

Though Congress makes the law, as we saw in Chapters 5 and 7, Congress is usually compelled to delegate considerable legislative power to the president and to the agencies of the executive branch to allow the implementation of congressional programs. For example, if Congress wishes to improve air quality, it cannot possibly anticipate all the conditions and circumstances that may arise over the years with respect to its general goal. Inevitably, Congress must delegate to the executive substantial discretionary power to make judgments about the best ways to bring about congressional aims in the face of unforeseen and changing circumstances. Thus, over the years, almost any congressional program will result in thousands and thousands of pages of administrative regulations developed by executive agencies nominally seeking to implement the will of the Congress.

Such delegation is inescapable in the modern era. Congress can hardly administer the thousands of programs it has enacted and must delegate power to the president and to a huge bureaucracy to achieve its purposes. Delegation of power to the executive, however, also poses a number of problems for the Congress and for the federal courts. If Congress delegates broad and discretionary authority to the executive, it risks seeing its goals subordinated to and subverted by those of the executive branch.[13] If, on the other hand, Congress attempts to limit executive discretion by enacting very precise rules and standards to govern the conduct of the president and the executive branch, it risks writing laws that do not conform to real-world conditions and that are too rigid to be adapted to changing circumstances.[14]

---

[10]Brown v. Board of Education, 347 U.S. 483 (1954); Loving v. Virginia, 388 U.S. 1 (1967).

[11]Griswold v. Connecticut, 381 U.S. 479 (1965).

[12]Brandenburg v. Ohio, 395 U.S. 444 (1969).

[13]See Theodore J. Lowi, *The End of Liberalism*, 2nd ed. (New York: W. W. Norton, 1979). See also David Schoenbrod, *Power without Responsibility: How Congress Abuses the People through Delegation* (New Haven: Yale University Press, 1993).

[14]Kenneth Culp Davis, *Discretionary Justice: A Preliminary Inquiry* (Baton Rouge: Louisiana State University Press, 1969), pp. 15–21.

The issue of delegation of power has led to a number of court decisions over the past two centuries generally revolving around the question of the scope of the delegation. Courts have also been called upon to decide whether the rules and regulations adopted by federal agencies are consistent with Congress's express or implied intent.

As presidential power expanded during the New Deal era, one measure of increased congressional subordination to the executive was the enactment of laws that contained few, if any, principles limiting executive discretion. Congress enacted legislation, often at the president's behest, that gave the executive virtually unfettered authority to address a particular concern. For example, the Emergency Price Control Act of 1942 authorized the executive to set "fair and equitable" prices without offering any indication of what these terms might mean.[15] The Court's initial encounters with these new forms of delegation led to three major decisions in which the justices applied the "intelligible principles" standard to strike down delegations of power to the executive. In the 1935 *Panama* case, the Court held that Congress had failed to define the standards governing the authority it had granted the president to exclude oil from interstate commerce. In the *Schechter* case, also decided in 1935, the Court found that the Congress failed to define the "fair competition" that the president was to promote under the National Industrial Recovery Act. In a third case, *Carter v. Carter Coal Company*, decided in 1936, the Court concluded that a delegation to the coal industry, itself, to establish a code of regulations was impermissibly vague.[16]

These decisions were seen, with considerable justification, as a judicial assault on the New Deal and helped spark President Roosevelt's "court packing" plan. The Court retreated from its confrontation with the president and, perhaps as a result, no congressional delegation of power to the president has been struck down as impermissibly broad in the more than six decades since *Carter*. Instead, the Court has effectively rewritten the nondelegation doctrine in the form of the so-called *Chevron* standard. This standard emerged from a 1984 case called *Chevron v. Natural Resources Defense Council.*[17] An environmental group had challenged an Environmental Protection Agency (EPA) regulation as contrary to the intent of the statute it was nominally written to implement. While a federal district court sided with the environmentalists against the agency, the lower court's decision was reversed by the Supreme Court. In its decision, the Supreme Court declared that as long as the executive developed rules and regulations, "based upon a permissible construction" or "reasonable interpretation" of the statute, the judiciary would accept the views of the executive branch. This standard implies that considerable judicial deference should be given to the executive rather than to the Congress. Indeed, the courts now look to the agencies to develop clear standards for statutory implementation rather than to the Con-

---

[15]56 Stat. 23 (30 Jan. 1942).
[16]Carter v. Carter Coal Company, 298 U.S. 238 (1936).
[17]Chevron v. Natural Resources Defense Council, 467 U.S. 837 (1984).

gress to develop standards for the executive branch to follow.[18] In the 2001 case of *United States v. Mead Corp.*, the Court partially qualified the *Chevron* holding by ruling that agencies were entitled to *Chevron* deference only where they were making rules carrying the force of law and not when they were merely issuing opinion letters or undertaking other informal actions.[19] Despite this qualification, *Chevron* still applies to the most important category of administrative activity. This means that the courts give considerable deference to administrative agencies as long as those agencies have engaged in a formal rule-making process and can show that they have carried out the conditions prescribed by the various statutes governing agency rule-making. These include the 1946 Administrative Procedure Act, which requires agencies to give notice to parties affected by proposed rules as well as ample time to comment on such rules before they go into effect.

Judicial Review and Lawmaking

Much of the work of the courts involves the application of statutes to the particular case at hand. Over the centuries, however, judges have developed a body of rules and principles of interpretation that are not grounded in specific statutes. This body of judge-made law is called common law.

Policy Principle

By interpreting existing statutes as well as the Constitution, judges make law.

The appellate courts are in another realm. Their rulings can be considered laws, but they are laws governing the behavior only of the judiciary. They influence citizens' conduct only because, in the words of Justice Oliver Wendell Holmes, who served on the Supreme Court from 1902 to 1932, lawyers make "prophecies of what the courts will do in fact."[20]

The written opinion of an appellate court is about halfway between common law and statutory law. It is judge-made and draws heavily on the precedents of previous cases. But it tries to articulate the rule of law controlling the case in question and future cases like it. In this respect, it is like a statute. But it differs from a statute in that a statute addresses itself to the future conduct of citizens, whereas a written opinion addresses itself mainly to the willingness or ability of courts in the future to take cases and render favorable opinions. Decisions by appellate courts affect citizens by giving them a cause of action or by taking it away from them. That is, they open or close access to the courts.

Institution Principle

Because the court system is hierarchical, decisions by higher courts constrain the discretion of judges in lower courts.

A specific case may help clarify the distinction. Before the Second World War, one of the most insidious forms of racial discrimination was the "restrictive covenant," a clause in a contract whereby the purchasers of a house agreed that if they later decided to sell it, they would sell only to a Caucasian. When a test case finally reached the Supreme Court in 1948, the Court ruled unanimously that citizens had a right to discriminate with restrictive covenants in their sales

---

[18]See Whitman v. American Trucking Associations, 531 U.S. 457 (2001) and AT&T Corp. et al. v. Iowa Utilities Board et al., 525 U.S. 366 (1999).

[19]United States v. Mead Corp., 533 U.S. 218 (2001).

[20]Oliver Wendell Holmes, Jr., "The Path of the Law," *Harvard Law Review* 10 (1897): 457.

contracts but that the courts could not enforce these contracts. Its argument was that enforcement would constitute violation of the Fourteenth Amendment provision that no state shall "deny to any person within its jurisdiction equal protection under the law."[21] The Court was thereby predicting what it would and would not do in future cases of this sort. Most states have now forbidden homeowners to place such covenants in sales contracts.

Gideon v. Wainwright extends the point. When the Supreme Court ordered a new trial for Gideon because he had been denied the right to legal counsel, it said to all trial judges and prosecutors that henceforth they would be wasting their time if they cut corners in trials of indigent defendants.[22] It also invited thousands of prisoners to appeal their convictions.

Many areas of civil law have been constructed in the same way—by judicial messages to other judges, some of which are codified eventually into legislative enactments. An example of great concern to employees and employers is that of liability for injuries sustained at work. Courts have sided with employees so often that it has become virtually useless for employers to fight injury cases. It has become "the law" that employers are liable for such injuries, without regard to negligence. But the law in this instance is simply a series of messages to lawyers that they should advise their corporate clients not to appeal injury decisions.

The appellate courts cannot decide what behavior will henceforth be a crime. They cannot directly prevent the police from forcing confessions or intimidating witnesses. In other words, they cannot directly change the behavior of citizens or eliminate abuses of power. What they can do, however, is make it easier for mistreated persons to gain redress.

In redressing wrongs, the appellate courts—and even the Supreme Court itself—often call for a radical change in legal principle. Changes in race relations, for example, would probably have taken a great deal longer if the Supreme Court had not rendered the 1954 *Brown* decision that redefined the rights of African Americans.

Similarly, the Supreme Court interpreted the separation of church and state doctrine so as to alter significantly the practice of religion in public institutions. For example, in a 1962 case, *Engel v. Vitale*, the Court declared that a once widely observed ritual—the recitation of a prayer by students in a public school—was unconstitutional under the establishment clause of the First Amendment. Almost all the dramatic changes in the treatment of criminals and of persons accused of crimes have been made by the appellate courts, especially the Supreme Court. The Supreme Court brought about a veritable revolution in the criminal process with three cases over less than five years: *Gideon v. Wainwright*, in 1963, was discussed above. *Escobedo v. Illinois*, in 1964, gave suspects the right to remain silent and the right to have counsel present during questioning. But the decision left confusions that allowed differing decisions to be made by lower courts. In *Miranda v. Arizona*, in 1966, the Supreme Court cleared up these confusions by set-

---

[21]Shelley v. Kraemer, 334 U.S. 1 (1948).
[22]Gideon v. Wainwright, 372 U.S. 335 (1963).

ting forth what is known as the ***Miranda rule:*** arrested people have the right to remain silent, the right to be informed that anything they say can be held against them, and the right to counsel before and during police interrogation.[23]

One of the most significant changes brought about by the Supreme Court was the revolution in legislative representation unleashed by the 1962 case of *Baker v. Carr.*[24] In this landmark case, the Supreme Court held that it could no longer avoid reviewing complaints about the apportionment of seats in state legislatures. Following that decision, the federal courts went on to force reapportionment of all state, county, and local legislatures in the country.

Many experts on court history and constitutional law criticize the federal appellate courts for being too willing to introduce radical change, even when these experts agree with the general direction of the changes. Often they are troubled by the courts' (especially the Supreme Court's) willingness to jump into such cases prematurely—before the constitutional issues are fully clarified by many related cases through decisions by district and appeals courts in various parts of the country.[25] But from the perspective of the appellate judiciary, and especially the Supreme Court, the situation is probably one of choosing between the lesser of two evils: They must take the cases as they come and then weigh the risks of opening new options against the risks of embracing the status quo.

Miranda rule
Principles developed by the Supreme Court in the 1966 case of *Miranda v. Arizona* requiring that persons under arrest be informed of their legal rights, including their right to counsel, prior to police interrogation.

THE SUPREME COURT IN ACTION

How Cases Reach the Supreme Court

Given the millions of disputes that arise every year, the job of the Supreme Court would be impossible if it were not able to control the flow of cases and its own caseload. The Supreme Court has original jurisdiction in a limited variety of cases defined by the Constitution. The original jurisdiction includes (1) cases between the United States and one of the fifty states, (2) cases between two or more states, (3) cases involving foreign ambassadors or other ministers, and (4) cases brought by one state against citizens of another state or against a foreign country. The most important of these cases are disputes between states over land, water, or old debts. Generally, the Supreme Court deals with these cases by appointing a "special master," usually a retired judge, to actually hear the case and present a report. The Supreme Court then allows the states involved in the dispute to present arguments for or against the master's opinion.[26]

---

[23]Engel v. Vitale, 370 U.S. 421 (1962); Gideon v. Wainwright, 372 U.S. 335 (1963); Escobedo v. Illinois, 378 U.S. 478 (1964); and Miranda v. Arizona, 384 U.S. 436 (1966).

[24]Baker v. Carr, 369 U.S. 186 (1962).

[25]See Philip B. Kurland, *Politics, the Constitution, and the Warren Court* (Chicago: University of Chicago Press, 1970).

[26]Walter F. Murphy, "The Supreme Court of the United States," in *Encyclopedia of the American Judicial System: Studies of the Principal Institutions and Processes of Law,* ed. Robert J. Janosik (New York: Scribner's, 1987).

Rules of Access Over the years, the courts have developed specific rules that govern which cases within their jurisdiction they will and will not hear. In order to have access to the courts, cases must meet certain criteria that are initially applied by the trial court but may be reconsidered by appellate courts. These rules of access can be broken down into three major categories: case or controversy, standing, and mootness.

Article III of the Constitution and Supreme Court decisions define judicial power as extending only to "cases and controversies." This means that the case before a court must be an actual controversy, not a hypothetical one, with two truly adversarial parties. The courts have interpreted this language to mean that they do not have the power to render advisory opinions to legislatures or agencies about the constitutionality of proposed laws or regulations. Furthermore, even after a law is enacted, the courts will generally refuse to consider its constitutionality until it is actually applied.

Parties to a case must also have *standing*—that is, they must show that they have a substantial stake in the outcome of the case. The traditional requirement for standing has been to show injury to oneself; that injury can be personal, economic, or even aesthetic, for example. In order for a group or class of people to have standing (as in class action suits), each member must show specific injury. This means that a general interest in the environment, for instance, does not provide a group with sufficient basis for standing.

The Supreme Court also uses a third criterion in determining whether it will hear a case: that of *mootness.* In theory, this requirement disqualifies cases that are brought too late—after the relevant facts have changed or the problem has been resolved by other means. The criterion of mootness, however, is subject to the discretion of the courts, which have begun to relax the rules of mootness, particularly in cases where a situation that has been resolved is likely to come up again. In the abortion case *Roe v. Wade*, for example, the Supreme Court rejected the lower court's argument that because the pregnancy had already come to term, the case was moot. The Court agreed to hear the case because no pregnancy was likely to outlast the lengthy appeals process.

Putting aside the formal criteria, the Supreme Court is most likely to accept cases that involve conflicting decisions by the federal circuit courts, cases that present important questions of civil rights or civil liberties, and cases in which the federal government is the appellant.[27] Ultimately, however, the question of which cases to accept can come down to the preferences and priorities of the justices. If a group of justices believes that the Court should intervene in a particular area of policy or politics, these justices are likely to look for a case or cases

that will serve as vehicles for judicial intervention. For many years, for example, the Court was not interested in considering challenges to affirmative action or other programs designed to provide particular benefits to minorities. In recent years, however, several of the Court's more conservative justices have been eager to push back the limits of affirmative action and racial preference, and have,

---

[27]Gregory A. Caldeira and John R. Wright, "Organized Interests and Agenda Setting in the U.S. Supreme Court," *American Political Science Review* 82 (1988): 1109–27.

therefore, accepted a number of cases that would allow them to do so. In 1995, the Court's decisions in *Adarand Constructors, Inc. v. Pena, Missouri v. Jenkins,* and *Miller v. Johnson* placed new restrictions on federal affirmative action programs, school desegregation efforts, and attempts to increase minority representation in Congress through the creation of "minority districts" (see Chapter 10).[28] Similarly, because some justices have felt that the Court had gone too far in the past in restricting public support for religious ideas, the Court accepted the case of *Rosenberger v. University of Virginia.* This case was brought by a Christian student group against the University of Virginia, which had refused to provide student activities fund support for the group's magazine, *Wide Awake.* Other student publications received subsidies from the activities fund, but university policy prohibited grants to religious groups. Lower courts supported the university, finding that support for the magazine would violate the Constitution's prohibition against government support for religion. The Supreme Court, however, ruled in favor of the students' assertion that the university's policies amounted to support for some ideas but not others. The Court said this violated the students' First Amendment right of freedom of expression.[29]

Writs   Decisions handed down by lower courts can reach the Supreme Court in one of two ways: through a ***writ of certiorari*** or, in the case of convicted state prisoners, through a ***writ of habeas corpus.*** A writ is a court document conveying an order of some sort. In recent years, an effort has been made to give the Court more discretion regarding the cases it chooses to hear. Before 1988, the Supreme Court was obligated to review cases on what was called a writ of appeal. This has since been eliminated, and the Court now has virtually complete discretion over what cases it will hear (see Process Box 8.1).

Most cases reach the Supreme Court through the writ of *certiorari,* which is granted whenever four of the nine justices agree to review a case. The Supreme Court was once so inundated with appeals that in 1925 Congress enacted laws giving it some control over its case load with the power to issue writs of *certiorari.* Rule 10 of the Supreme Court's own rules of procedure defines *certiorari* as "not a matter of right, but of sound judicial discretion . . . granted only where there are special and important reasons therefor." The following are the reasons provided for in Rule 10:

1. Where a state has made a decision that conflicts with previous Supreme Court decisions
2. Where a state court has come up with an entirely new federal question
3. Where one court of appeals has rendered a decision in conflict with another
4. Where there are other inconsistent rulings between two or more courts or states
5. Where a single court of appeals has sanctioned too great a departure by a lower court from normal judicial proceedings (a reason rarely given)

writ of *certiorari*
A decision concurred in by at least four of the nine Supreme Court justices to review a decision of a lower court; from the Latin "to make more certain."

writ of *habeas corpus*   A court order demanding that an individual in custody be brought into court and shown the cause for detention. *Habeas corpus* is guaranteed by the Constitution and can be suspended only in cases of rebellion or invasion.

 Collective Action Principle

Four of the nine Supreme Court justices need to agree to review a case.

[28]Adarand Constructors, Inc. v. Pena, 115 S.Ct. 2038 (1995); Missouri v. Jenkins, 115 S.Ct. 2573 (1995); Miller v. Johnson, 115 S.Ct. 2475 (1995).
[29]Rosenberger v. University of Virginia, 115 S.Ct. 2510 (1995).

How Cases Reach the Supreme Court

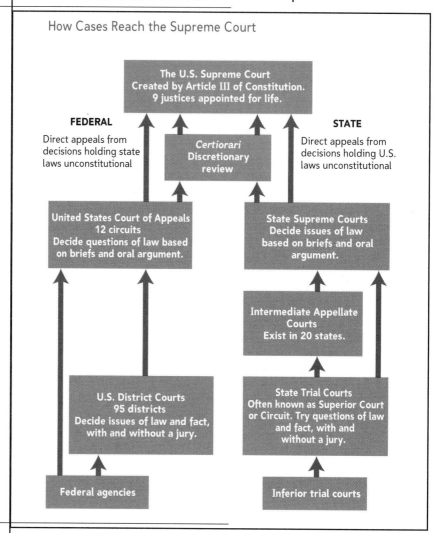

The writ of *habeas corpus* is a fundamental safeguard of individual rights. Its historical purpose is to enable an accused person to challenge arbitrary detention and to force an open trial before a judge. But in 1867, Congress's distrust of Southern courts led it to confer on federal courts the authority to issue writs of *habeas corpus* to prisoners already tried or being tried in state courts of proper jurisdiction, where the constitutional rights of the prisoner were possibly being violated. This writ gives state prisoners a second channel toward Supreme Court review in case their direct appeal from the highest state court fails. The writ of *habeas corpus* is discretionary; that is, the Court can decide which cases to review.

Controlling the Flow of Cases

In addition to the judges themselves, two other actors play an important role in shaping the flow of cases through the federal courts: the solicitor general and federal law clerks.

The Solicitor General If any single person has greater influence than the individual justices over the work of the Supreme Court, it is the solicitor general of the United States. The solicitor general is third in status in the Justice Department (below the attorney general and the deputy attorney general) but is the top government lawyer in virtually all cases before the appellate courts in which the government is a party. Although others can regulate the flow of cases, the solicitor general has the greatest control, with no review of his or her actions by any higher authority in the executive branch. More than half the Supreme Court's total workload consists of cases under the direct charge of the solicitor general.

The solicitor general exercises especially strong influence by screening cases long before they approach the Supreme Court; indeed, the justices rely on the solicitor general to "screen out undeserving litigation and furnish them with an agenda to government cases that deserve serious consideration."[30] Typically, more requests for appeals are rejected than are accepted by the solicitor general. Agency heads may lobby the president or otherwise try to circumvent the solicitor general, and a few of the independent agencies have a statutory right to make direct appeals, but these are almost inevitably doomed to **per curiam** rejection—rejection through a brief, unsigned opinion by the whole Court—if the solicitor general refuses to participate.

The solicitor general, by writing an **amicus curiae** ("friend of the court") brief, can enter a case even when the federal government is not a direct litigant. A "friend of the court" is not a direct party to a case but has a vital interest in its outcome. Thus, when the government has such an interest, the solicitor general can file as *amicus curiae*, or the Court can invite such a brief because it wants an opinion in writing. The solicitor general also has the power to invite others to enter cases as *amici curiae*.

In addition to exercising substantial control over the flow of cases, the solicitor general can shape the arguments used before the Court. Indeed, the Court

per curiam Decision by an appellate court, without a written opinion, that refuses to review the decision of a lower court; amounts to a reaffirmation of the lower court's opinion.

amicus curiae "Friend of the court"; individuals or groups who are not parties to a lawsuit but who seek to assist the court in reaching a decision by presenting additional briefs.

[30]Robert Scigliano, *The Supreme Court and the Presidency* (New York: Free Press, 1971), p. 162. For an interesting critique of the solicitor general's role during the Reagan administration, see Lincoln Caplan, "Annals of the Law," *New Yorker,* 17 August 1987, pp. 30–62.

tends to give special attention to the way the solicitor general characterizes the issues. The solicitor general is the person appearing most frequently before the Court and, theoretically at least, the most disinterested. The credibility of the solicitor general is not hurt when several times each year he or she comes to the Court to withdraw a case with the admission that the government has made an error.

Law Clerks   Every federal judge employs law clerks to research legal issues and assist with the preparation of opinions. Each Supreme Court justice is assigned four clerks. The clerks are almost always honors graduates of the nation's most prestigious law schools. A clerkship with a Supreme Court justice is a great honor and generally indicates that the fortunate individual is likely to reach the very top of the legal profession. One of the most important roles performed by the clerks is to screen the thousands of petitions for writs of *certiorari* that come before the Court.[31] It is also likely that some justices rely heavily upon their clerks for advice in writing opinions and in deciding whether an individual case ought to be heard by the Court. It is often rumored that certain opinions were actually written by a clerk rather than a justice.[32] Although such rumors are difficult to substantiate, it is clear that at the end of long judicial careers, justices such as William O. Douglas and Thurgood Marshall had become so infirm that they were compelled to rely on the judgments of their law clerks.

The Case Pattern

The Supreme Court has discretion over which case will be reviewed. The solicitor general can influence the Court's choice by giving advice and by encouraging particular cases and discouraging or suppressing others. But neither the court nor the solicitor general can suppress altogether the kinds of cases that individuals bring to court. Each new technology, such as computers and communications satellites, produces new disputes and the need for new principles of law. Newly awakened interest groups, such as the black community after World War II or the women's and the environmental movements in the 1970s, produce new legislation, new disputes, and new cases. Lawyers are professionally obligated to appeal their clients' cases to the highest possible court if an issue of law or constitutionality is involved.

The litigation that breaks out with virtually every social change produces a pattern of cases that eventually is recognized by the state and federal appellate courts. Appellate judges may at first resist trying such cases by ordering them remanded (returned) to their court of original jurisdiction for further trial. They may reject some appeals without giving any reason at all (*certiorari* denied *per cu-*

---

[31]H. W. Perry, Jr., *Deciding to Decide: Agenda Setting in the United States Supreme Court* (Cambridge, Mass: Harvard University Press, 1991).

[32]Edward Lazarus, *Closed Chambers: The First Eyewitness Account of the Struggles inside the Supreme Court* (New York: Times Books, 1998).

riam). But eventually, one or more of the cases from the pattern may be reviewed and may indeed make new law.

Although some patterns of cases emerge spontaneously as new problems produce new litigation, many interest groups try to set a pattern as a strategy for expediting their cases through the appeals process. Lawyers representing these groups have to choose the proper client and the proper case, so that the issues in question are most dramatically and appropriately portrayed. They also have to pick the right district or jurisdiction in which to bring the case. Sometimes they even have to wait for an appropriate political climate.

Group litigants have to plan carefully when to use and when to avoid publicity. They must also attempt to develop a proper record at the trial-court level, one that includes some constitutional arguments and even, when possible, errors on the part of the trial court. One of the most effective litigation strategies used in getting cases accepted for review by the appellate courts is bringing the same type of suit in more than one circuit, in the hope that inconsistent treatment by two different courts will improve the chance of a Supreme Court review.

As we shall see more fully in Chapter 12, Congress will sometimes provide interest groups with legislation designed to facilitate their use of litigation. One important recent example is the 1990 Americans with Disabilities Act (ADA), enacted after intense lobbying by public interest and advocacy groups, which, in conjunction with the 1991 Civil Rights Act, opened the way for disabled individuals to make extremely effective use of the courts to press their interests. As the sponsors of ADA had hoped, over time the courts have expanded the rights of the disabled as well as the definition of disability. In 1998, for example, the Supreme Court ruled that individuals with HIV were covered by the act.[33]

The two most notable users of the pattern-of-cases strategy in recent years have been the National Association for the Advancement of Colored People (NAACP) and the American Civil Liberties Union (ACLU). For many years, the NAACP (and its Defense Fund organization—now a separate group) has worked through local chapters and with many individuals to encourage litigation on issues of racial discrimination and segregation. Sometimes it distributes petitions to be signed by parents and filed with local school boards and courts, deliberately sowing the seeds of future litigation. The NAACP and the ACLU often encourage private parties to bring suit, then join the suit as *amici curiae*.

One illustration of an interest group employing a carefully crafted litigation strategy to pursue its goals through the judiciary was the Texas-based effort to establish a right to free public-school education for children of illegal aliens. The issue arose in 1977, when the Texas state legislature, responding to a sudden wave of fear about illegal immigration from Mexico, enacted a law permitting school districts to charge undocumented children a hefty tuition for the privilege of attending public school. A public interest law organization, the Mexican-American Legal Defense Fund, prepared to challenge the law in court after

 Rationality Principle

Groups will often file more than one suit in the hope that this will increase their chances of being heard in Court.

[33]Bragdon v. Abbott, 118 S.Ct. 2186 (1998).

determining that public opposition precluded any chance of persuading the legislature to change its own law.

Part of the defense fund's litigation strategy was to bring a lawsuit in the northern section of Texas, far from the Mexican border, where illegal immigration would be at a minimum. Thus, in Tyler, Texas, where the complaint was initially filed, the trial court found only sixty undocumented alien students in a school district composed of 16,000. This strategy effectively contradicted the state's argument that the Texas law was necessary to reduce the burdens on educational resources created by masses of incoming aliens. Another useful litigation tactic was to select plaintiffs who, although illegal aliens, were nevertheless clearly planning to remain in Texas even without free public education for their children. Thus, all of the plaintiffs came from families that had already lived in Tyler for several years and included at least one child who was an American citizen by virtue of birth in the United States. By emphasizing the stability of such families, the defense fund argued convincingly that the Texas law would not motivate families to return to the poverty in Mexico from which they had fled, but would more likely result in the creation of a subclass of illiterate people who would add to the state's unemployment and crime rates. Five years after the lawsuit on behalf of the Tyler children began, the U.S. Supreme Court, in the case of *Plyler v. Doe*, held that the Texas law was unconstitutional under the equal protection clause of the Fourteenth Amendment.[34]

Thus, regardless of the wishes of the Justice Department or the Supreme Court, many pathbreaking cases are eventually granted *certiorari* because continued refusal to review one or more of them would amount to a rule of law just as much as if the courts had handed down a written opinion. In this sense, the flow of cases, especially the pattern of significant cases, influences the behavior of the appellate judiciary.

The Supreme Court's Procedures

The Preparation   The Supreme Court's decision to accept a case is the beginning of what can be a lengthy and complex process (see Figure 8.3). First, the attorneys on both sides must prepare *briefs*—written documents that may be several hundred pages long in which the attorneys explain why the Court should rule in favor of their client. Briefs are filled with referrals to precedents specifically chosen to show that other courts have frequently ruled in the same way that the Supreme Court is being asked to rule. The attorneys for both sides muster the most compelling precedents they can in support of their arguments.

As the attorneys prepare their briefs, they often ask sympathetic interest groups for their help. Groups are asked to file *amicus curiae* briefs that support the claims of one or the other litigant. In a case involving separation of church and state, for example, liberal groups such as the ACLU and Citizens for the

briefs Written documents in which attorneys explain—using case precedents—why the Court should rule in favor of their client.

Institution Principle

The Supreme Court's procedures allow for various individuals and groups to influence the decision-making process.

[34]Plyler v. Doe, 457 U.S. 202 (1982).

FIGURE 8.3

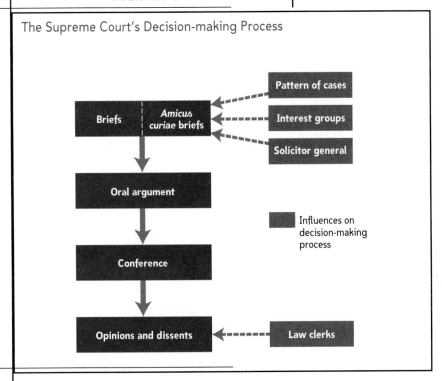

The Supreme Court's Decision-making Process

American Way are likely to be asked to file *amicus* briefs in support of strict separation, whereas conservative religious groups are likely to file *amicus* briefs advocating increased public support for religious ideas. Often, dozens of briefs will be filed on each side of a major case. *Amicus* filings are one of the primary methods used by interest groups to lobby the Court. By filing these briefs, groups indicate to the Court where their group stands and signal to the justices that they believe the case to be an important one.

Oral Argument   The next stage of a case is ***oral argument,*** in which attorneys for both sides appear before the Court to present their positions and answer the justices' questions. Each attorney has only a half hour to present his or her case, and this time includes interruptions for questions. Certain members of the Court, such as Justice Antonin Scalia, are known to interrupt attorneys dozens of

oral argument
Stage in Supreme Court proceedings in which attorneys for both sides appear before the Court to present their positions and answer questions posed by the justices.

times. Others, such as Justice Clarence Thomas, seldom ask questions. For an attorney, the opportunity to argue a case before the Supreme Court is a singular honor and a mark of professional distinction. It can also be a harrowing experience, as justices interrupt a carefully prepared presentation. Nevertheless, oral argument can be very important to the outcome of a case. It allows justices to better understand the heart of the case and to raise questions that might not have been addressed in the opposing side's briefs. It is not uncommon for justices to go beyond the strictly legal issues and ask opposing counsel to discuss the implications of the case for the Court and the nation at large.

The Conference   Following oral argument, the Court discusses the case in its Wednesday or Friday conference. The chief justice presides over the conference and speaks first; the other justices follow in order of seniority. The Court's conference is secret, and no outsiders are permitted to attend. The justices discuss the case and eventually reach a decision on the basis of a majority vote. If the Court is divided, a number of votes may be taken before a final decision is reached. As the case is discussed, justices may try to influence or change one another's opinions. At times, this may result in compromise decisions.

Opinion Writing   After a decision has been reached, one of the members of the majority is assigned to write the **opinion.** This assignment is made by the chief justice, or by the most senior justice in the majority if the chief justice is on the losing side. The assignment of the opinion can make a significant difference to the interpretation of a decision. Every opinion of the Supreme Court sets a major precedent for future cases throughout the judicial system. Lawyers and judges in the lower courts will examine the opinion carefully to ascertain the Supreme Court's meaning. Differences in wording and emphasis can have important implications for future litigation. Once the majority opinion is drafted, it is circulated to the other justices. Some members of the majority may decide that they cannot accept all the language of the opinion and, therefore, write "concurring" opinions that support the decision but offer somewhat different rationales or emphases. In assigning an opinion, serious thought must be given to the impression the case will make on lawyers and on the public, as well as to the probability that one justice's opinion will be more widely accepted than another's.

One of the more dramatic instances of this tactical consideration occurred in 1944, when Chief Justice Harlan F. Stone chose Justice Felix Frankfurter to write the opinion in the "white primary" case *Smith v. Allwright*. The chief justice believed that this sensitive case, which overturned the southern practice of prohibiting black participation in nominating primaries, required the efforts of the most brilliant and scholarly jurist on the Court. But the day after Stone made the assignment, Justice Robert H. Jackson wrote a letter to Stone urging a change of assignment. In his letter, Jackson argued that Frankfurter, a foreign-born Jew from New England, would not win the South with his opinion, regardless of its brilliance. Stone accepted the advice and substituted Justice Stanley F. Reed, an

opinion The written explanation of the Supreme Court's decision in a particular case.

American-born Protestant from Kentucky and a southern Democrat in good standing.[35]

Dissent   Justices who disagree with the majority decision of the Court may choose to publicize the character of their disagreement in the form of a ***dissenting opinion.*** Dissents can be used to express irritation with an outcome or to signal to defeated political forces in the nation that their position is supported by at least some members of the Court. Ironically, the most dependable way an individual justice can exercise a direct and clear influence on the Court is to write a dissent. Because there is no need to please a majority, dissenting opinions can be more eloquent and less guarded than majority opinions. The current Supreme Court often produces 5-to-4 decisions, with dissenters writing long and detailed opinions that, they hope, will help them convince a swing justice to join their side on the next round of cases dealing with a similar topic. Thus, for example, Justice Souter wrote a 34-page dissent in a 2002 case upholding the use of government-funded school vouchers to pay for parochial school tuition. Souter called the decision, "a dramatic departure from basic Establishment Clause principle," which he hoped a "future court will reconsider."[36]

> **dissenting opinion**   Decision written by a justice with the minority opinion in a particular case, in which the justice fully explains the reasoning behind his or her opinion.

Dissent plays a special role in the work and impact of the Court because it amounts to an appeal to lawyers all over the country to keep bringing cases of the sort at issue. Therefore, an effective dissent influences the flow of cases through the Court as well as the arguments that will be used by lawyers in later cases. Even more important, dissent emphasizes the fact that, although the Court speaks with a single opinion, it is the opinion only of the majority.

JUDICIAL DECISION MAKING

The judiciary is conservative in its procedures, but its impact on society can be radical. That impact depends on a variety of influences, two of which stand out above the rest. The first influence is the individual members of the Supreme Court, their attitudes and goals, and their relationships with each other. The second is the other branches of government, particularly Congress.

The Supreme Court Justices

The Supreme Court explains its decisions in terms of law and precedent. But although law and precedent do have an effect on the Court's deliberations and eventual decisions, it is the Supreme Court that decides what laws actually mean and what importance precedents will actually have. Throughout its history, the Court has shaped and reshaped the law. If any individual judges in the country influence the federal judiciary, they are the Supreme Court justices.

[35]Smith v. Allwright, 321 U.S. 649 (1944).
[36]Warren Richey, "Dissenting Opinions as a Window on Future Rulings," *Christian Science Monitor*, 1 July 2002, p. 1.

From the 1950s to the 1980s, the Supreme Court took an activist role in such areas as civil rights, civil liberties, abortion, voting rights, and police procedures. For example, the Supreme Court was more responsible than any other governmental institution for breaking down America's system of racial segregation. The Supreme Court virtually prohibited states from interfering with the right of a woman to seek an abortion and sharply curtailed state restrictions on voting rights. And it was the Supreme Court that placed restrictions on the behavior of local police and prosecutors in criminal cases.

But since the early 1980s, resignations, deaths, and new judicial appointments have led to many shifts in the mix of philosophies and ideologies represented on the Court. In a series of decisions between 1989 and 2001, however, the conservative justices appointed by Reagan and Bush were able to swing the Court to a more conservative position on civil rights, affirmative action, abortion rights, property rights, criminal procedure, voting rights, desegregation, and the power of the national government.

Although they are not the only relevant factor, shifts in judicial philosophy are the prime explanation for these Court tendencies. These shifts, in turn, result from changes in the Court's composition as justices retire and are replaced by new justices who tend to share the philosophical outlook and policy goals of the president who appointed them.

Activism and Restraint   One element of judicial philosophy is the issue of activism versus restraint. Over the years, some justices have believed that courts should interpret the Constitution according to the stated intentions of its framers and defer to the views of Congress when interpreting federal statutes. The late justice Felix Frankfurter, for example, advocated judicial deference to legislative bodies and avoidance of the "political thicket," in which the Court would entangle itself by deciding questions that were essentially political rather than legal in character. Advocates of *judicial restraint* are sometimes called "strict constructionists" because they look strictly to the words of the Constitution in interpreting its meaning.

judicial restraint
Judicial philosophy whose adherents refuse to go beyond the set text of the Constitution in interpreting its meaning.

judicial activism
Judicial philosophy that posits that the Court should see beyond the text of the Constitution or a statute in order to consider broader societal implications for decisions.

The alternative to restraint is *judicial activism.* Activist judges such as former chief justice Earl Warren believed that the Court should go beyond the words of the Constitution or a statute to consider the broader societal implications of its decisions. Activist judges sometimes strike out in new directions, promulgating new interpretations or inventing new legal and constitutional concepts when they believe these to be socially desirable. For example, Justice Harry A. Blackmun's decision in *Roe v. Wade* was based on a constitutional right to privacy that is not found in the words of the Constitution. Blackmun and the other members of the majority in the *Roe* case argued that the right to privacy was implied by other constitutional provisions. In this instance of judicial activism, the Court knew the result it wanted to achieve and was not afraid to make the law conform to the desired outcome.

Activism and restraint are sometimes confused with liberalism and conservatism. For example, conservative politicians often castigate "liberal activist" judges and call for the appointment of conservative jurists who will refrain from reinterpreting the law. To be sure, some liberal jurists are activists and some conservatives have been advocates of restraint, but the relationship is by no means one to one. Indeed, the Rehnquist Court, dominated by conservatives, has been among the most activist Courts in American history, striking out in new directions in such areas as federalism and election law.

Political Ideology   The second component of judicial philosophy is political ideology. The liberal or conservative attitudes of justices play an important role in their decisions.[37] Indeed, the philosophy of activism versus restraint is, to a large extent, a smokescreen for political ideology. For the most part, liberal judges have been activists, willing to use the law to achieve social and political change, whereas conservatives have been associated with judicial restraint. Interestingly, however, in recent years some conservative justices who have long called for restraint have actually become activists in seeking to undo some of the work of liberal jurists over the past three decades.

The importance of ideology was very clear during the Court's 2000–2001 term. In important decisions, the Court's most conservative justices—Scalia, Thomas, and Rehnquist, usually joined by Kennedy—generally voted as a bloc.[38] Indeed, Scalia and Thomas voted together in 99 percent of all cases. At the same time, the Court's most liberal justices—Breyer, Ginsburg, Souter, and Stevens— also generally formed a bloc with Ginsburg and Breyer and Ginsburg and Souter voting together 94 percent of the time.[39] Justice O'Connor, a moderate conservative, was the swing vote in many important cases. This ideological division led to a number of important 5–4 decisions. As we saw, in the main Florida election-law case, *Bush v. Gore*, Justice O'Connor joined with the conservative bloc to give Bush a 5–4 victory.[40] On the other hand, in an important voting-rights case, *Easley v. Cromartie*, Justice O'Connor joined with the four liberals to uphold the creation of a so-called majority–minority congressional district in North Carolina against charges of racial gerrymandering.[41] More than 33 percent of all the cases heard by the court in its 2000–2001 term were decided 5 to 4.

In our discussion of congressional politics in Chapter 5, we described legislators as *policy oriented*. In conceiving of judges as legislators in robes, we are effectively claiming that judges, like other politicians, have policy preferences they seek to implement. For example, in recent years, Justice O'Connor has written a number of decisions that have furthered her goal that Congress return authority back to the states. The most recent of these decisions is the 2001 case of *Board of*

[37]C. Herman Pritchett, *The Roosevelt Court: A Study in Judicial Politics and Values* (New York: Macmillan, 1948); Jeffrey A. Segal and Harold J. Spaeth, *The Supreme Court and the Attitudinal Model* (New York: Cambridge University Press, 1993).

[38]Linda Greenhouse, "In Year of Florida Vote, Supreme Court Also Did Much Other Work," *New York Times*, 2 July 2001, p. A12.

[39]Charles E. Lane, "Laying Down the Law," *Washington Post*, 1 July 2001, p. A6.

[40]*Bush v. Gore*, 531 U.S. 98, 121 S.Ct. 525 (2000).

[41]*Easley v. Cromartie*, 121 S.Ct. 1452 (2001).

What Motivates Judges?

As central players in important political institutions, judges are politicians. Yet, at least for federal court judges, their links to "constituents" are attenuated by the fact that, through lifetime tenure, they don't have to come up for re-election (on the other hand, many state and local judges are elected for fixed terms). Not only is the re-election incentive absent, other "carrots and sticks" commonly found in principal-agent relationships, like performance-based levels of compensation, are absent. What, then, motivates judges? Just as for other ordinary people for whom rationality is a perfectly respectable behavioral hypothesis, is it appropriate to suppose that judges, too, are rational? Can one conceptualize judging as rational responses to the legal and political environment? Richard Posner, a federal court judge and professor of law at the University of Chicago, argues yes and suggests several ways to understand judicial behavior.

Many professionals are motivated by money, but it may be more appropriate to compare judges to managers of nonprofit enterprises. Except for private judges like Judge Judy of television fame, arbitrators, and mediators, judges draw fixed salaries and may not charge fees or user charges. Moreover, their salaries are fixed independent of effort, quality of work, or any other performance-based standard. They are just like salaried managers of a nonprofit system. As a result, should judges be expected on average to not work as hard? The answer is not necessarily. While judges are unable to maximize profits, they often are ambitious individuals for whom popularity among fellow judges, prestige in the larger legal and political community, reputation in the academic world, and track record (especially the desire not to be reversed on appeal by a higher court or the legislature) all may matter. Although the odds of advancement, even for the highest performing judges, are remote, judges' desire for popularity, prestige, and reputation are important in their own right.

One can also think of judges as "swing voters." Judges are like members of a congressional committee in that their participation takes place in a small-group setting in which the chances of being pivotal to an outcome are much more likely. Indeed, some judges are committees of one (federal district court judges), others are members of small panels (federal appeals judges typically sit in panels of three), and still others are members of moderate-sized panels (Supreme Court justices are one of nine). Consistent ideological outliers may rarely be pivotal in a group such as the Supreme Court, but other justices have a substantial probability of being the vote that affects an outcome, at least some of the time. On the current Court, Sandra Day O'Connor is often the "swing voter." It is important to also remember that justices "vote" not only on who should win a case, but, through the opinions they draft, why one side or the other should win. Judges vote not only with ballots but with ideas—ideas about the facts, about judicial principles, about legal reasoning, and about moral values. It is through the opinions they draft, rather than the ballots they cast, that judges may influence a wider collection of interests since these opinions serve to constrain lower-court judges in similar cases in the future.

This leads us to our final analogy, which is to think of judges as "legislators in robes." As noted in the text, judges, like other politicians, have policy preferences they seek to implement. To the degree that higher courts do not merely resolve disputes but, more significantly, shape the legal context in which millions of private citizens interact and in which thousands of public officials exercise power, courts are critical in the formation and implementation of public policy. Higher-court judges, particularly Supreme Court justices, have opportunities to affect the public condition. Given that opportunity, judges with policy preferences treat each case as though it might have a later impact, either directly on national politics or indirectly through its effects on how constitutional or statutory law is subsequently interpreted. It is this recognition that perhaps best explains judicial behavior.

Trustees of the University of Alabama v. Garrett, where the Court held that state employees could not sue the states for alleged violations of the Americans with Disabilities Act.[42]

Other Institutions of Government

Congress   At both the national and state level in the United States, courts and judges are "players" in the policy game because of the separation of powers. Essentially, this means that the legislative branch formulates policy (defined constitutionally and institutionally by a legislative process); that the executive branch implements policy (according to well-defined administrative procedures, and subject to initial approval by the president or the legislative override of his veto); and that the courts, when asked, rule on the faithfulness of the legislated and executed policy either to the substance of the statute or to the Constitution itself. The courts, that is, may strike down an administrative action either because it exceeds the authority granted in the relevant statute (statutory rationale) or because the statute itself exceeds the authority granted the legislature by the Constitution (constitutional rationale).

If the court declares the administrative agent's act as outside the permissible bounds prescribed by the legislation, we suppose the court's majority opinion can declare whatever policy it wishes. If the legislature is unhappy with this judicial action, then it may either recraft the legislation (if the rationale for striking it down were statutory)[43] or initiate a constitutional amendment that would

---

[42]Board of Trustees of the University of Alabama v. Garrett, 531 U.S. 356 (2001).
[43]William N. Eckridge, Jr., "Overriding Supreme Court Statutory Interpretation Decisions," *Yale Law Journal* 101 (1991): 331–55.

Collective Action Principle

In reaching their decisions, Supreme Court judges must anticipate Congress's response.

enable the stricken-down policy to pass constitutional muster (if the rationale for originally striking it down were constitutional).

In reaching their decisions, Supreme Court justices must anticipate Congress's response. As a result, judges will not always vote according to their true preferences because doing so may provoke Congress to enact legislation that moves the policy further away from what the judges prefer. By voting for a lesser preference, the justices can get something they prefer to the status quo without provoking congressional action to overturn their decision. The most famous example of this phenomenon is the "switch in time that saved nine," when several justices voted in favor of New Deal legislation, the constitutionality of which they doubted, in order to diminish congressional support for President Roosevelt's plan to "pack" the Court by increasing the number of justices. In short, the interactions between the Court and Congress are part of a complex strategic "game."[44]

The President   The president's most direct influence on the Court is the power to nominate justices. Presidents typically nominate judges who they believe are close to their policy preferences and close enough to the preferences of a majority of senators, who must confirm the nomination.

Yet the efforts by presidents to reshape the federal judiciary are not always successful. Often in American history, judges have surprised and disappointed the presidents who named them to the bench. Justice Souter, for example, has been far less conservative than President George H. W. Bush and the Republicans who supported Souter's appointment in 1990 thought he would be. Likewise, Justices O'Connor and Kennedy have disappointed conservatives by opposing limitations on abortion.

Nevertheless, with a combined total of twelve years in office, both Reagan and Bush were able to exercise a good deal of influence on the composition of the federal district and appellate courts. By the end of Bush's term, he and Reagan together had appointed nearly half of all federal judges. Thus, whatever impact Reagan and Bush ultimately had on the Supreme Court, their federal appointments have certainly had a continuing influence on the temperament and behavior of the district and circuit courts.

President Clinton promised to appoint more liberal jurists to the district and appellate courts, as well as to increase the number of women and minorities serving on the federal bench. During his first two years in office, Clinton held to this promise (see Figure 8.4). More than 60 percent of his 128 judicial nominees were women or members of minority groups.[45] A large number of judicial va-

[44]A fully strategic analysis of the maneuvering among legislative, executive, and judicial branches in the separation-of-powers arrangement choreographed by the U.S. Constitution may be found in William Eskridge and John Ferejohn, "The Article I, Section 7 Game," *Georgetown Law Review* 80 (1992): 523–65. The entire issue of this journal is devoted to the theme of strategic behavior in American institutional politics.

[45]*Chicago Daily Law Bulletin*, 5 October 1994.

FIGURE 8.4

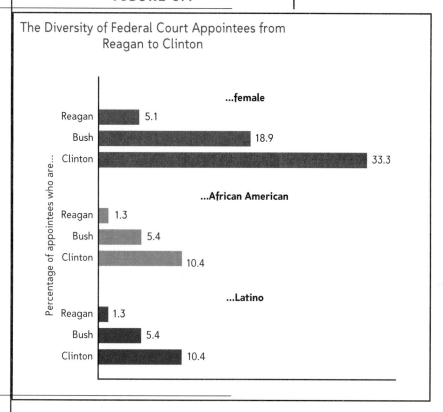

The Diversity of Federal Court Appointees from Reagan to Clinton

...female

Reagan 5.1
Bush 18.9
Clinton 33.3

...African American

Reagan 1.3
Bush 5.4
Clinton 10.4

...Latino

Reagan 1.3
Bush 5.4
Clinton 10.4

Percentage of appointees who are...

SOURCE: Harold W. Stanley and Richard G. Niemi, *Vital Statistics on American Politics, 2001–2002* (Washington, D.C.: Congressional Quarterly Press, 2001), pp. 277–79.

cancies remained unfilled, however, when the Republicans took control of Congress at the end of 1994. Soon after the election, Senator Orrin Hatch of Utah, the new chair of the Senate Judiciary Committee, which confirms judicial nominations, indicated his intention to oppose any nominee whom he deemed to be too liberal. This prompted the Clinton White House to withdraw some nominations and to search for district and appellate nominees who would be more acceptable to the Republicans.[46] It remains to be seen what impact President George W. Bush will have on the Court.

[46]R. W. Apple, Jr., "A Divided Government Remains, and with It the Prospect of Further Combat," *New York Times*, 7 November 1996, p. B6.

JUDICIAL POWER AND POLITICS

One of the most important institutional changes to occur in the United States during the past half-century has been the striking transformation of the role and power of the federal courts, those of the Supreme Court in particular. Understanding how this transformation came about is the key to understanding the contemporary role of the courts in America.

Traditional Limitations on the Federal Courts

For much of American history, the power of the federal courts was subject to five limitations.[47] First, courts were constrained by judicial rules of standing that limited access to the bench. Claimants who simply disagreed with governmental action or inaction could not obtain access. Access to the courts was limited to individuals who could show that they were particularly affected by the government's behavior in some area. This limitation on access to the courts diminished the judiciary's capacity to forge links with important political and social forces. Second, courts were traditionally limited in the character of the relief they could provide. In general, courts acted only to offer relief or assistance to individuals and not to broad social classes, again inhibiting the formation of alliances between the courts and important social forces. Third, courts lacked enforcement powers of their own and were compelled to rely upon executive or state agencies to ensure compliance with their edicts. If the executive or state agencies were unwilling to assist the courts, judicial enactments could go unheeded, as when President Andrew Jackson declined to enforce Chief Justice John Marshall's 1832 order to the state of Georgia to release two missionaries it had arrested on Cherokee lands. Marshall asserted that the state had no right to enter the Cherokee's lands without their assent.[48] Jackson is reputed to have said, "John Marshall has made his decision, now let him enforce it."

Fourth, federal judges are, of course, appointed by the president (with the consent of the Senate). As a result, the president and Congress can shape the composition of the federal courts and ultimately, perhaps, the character of judicial decisions. Finally, Congress has the power to change both the size and jurisdiction of the Supreme Court and other federal courts. For example, Franklin Roosevelt's "court packing" plan encouraged the justices to drop their opposition to New Deal programs. In many areas, federal courts obtain their jurisdiction not from the Constitution but from congressional statutes. On a number of occasions, Congress has threatened to take matters out of the Court's hands when it was unhappy with the Court's policies.[49]

---

[47]For limits on judicial power, see Alexander M. Bickel, *The Least Dangerous Branch: The Supreme Court at the Bar of Politics* (Indianapolis: Bobbs-Merrill, 1962).

[48]Worcester v. Georgia, 6 Peters 515 (1832).

[49]See Walter F. Murphy, *Congress and the Court: A Case Study in the American Political Process* (Chicago: University of Chicago Press, 1962).

In 1996, a Republican Congress succeeded in enacting new limits on the jurisdiction of the federal courts. The Immigration Reform Act limited the ability of the courts to hear class action suits brought on behalf of immigrants seeking to fight deportation proceedings. The Prison Litigation Reform Act limited the ability of federal judges to place state and local prison systems in the hands of special masters. Finally, a provision of the 1996 Budget Act limited the ability of the federal courts to listen to class action suits brought by legal services lawyers.[50] These restrictions were designed to curb what conservatives viewed as the excessive power of the judiciary.

As a result of these five limitations on judicial power, through much of their history the chief function of the federal courts was to provide judicial support for executive agencies and to legitimate acts of Congress by declaring them to be consistent with constitutional principles. Only on rare occasions did the federal courts actually dare to challenge Congress or the executive.[51]

Two Judicial Revolutions

Since the Second World War, however, the role of the federal judiciary has been strengthened and expanded. There have actually been two judicial revolutions in the United States since World War II. The first and most visible of these was the substantive revolution in judicial policy. As we saw in Chapter 4, in policy areas, including school desegregation, legislative apportionment, and criminal procedure, as well as obscenity, abortion, and voting rights, the Supreme Court was at the forefront of a series of sweeping changes in the role of the U.S. government and, ultimately, in the character of American society.[52]

But at the same time that the courts were introducing important policy innovations, they were also bringing about a second, less visible revolution. During the 1960s and 1970s, the Supreme Court and other federal courts instituted a series of institutional changes in judicial procedures that had major consequences by fundamentally expanding the power of the courts in the United States. First, the federal courts liberalized the concept of standing to permit almost any group that seeks to challenge the actions of an administrative agency to bring its case before the federal bench. In 1971, for example, the Supreme Court ruled that public interest groups could use the National Environmental Policy Act to challenge the actions of federal agencies by claiming that the agencies' activities might have adverse environmental consequences.[53] Congress helped to make it even easier for groups dissatisfied with government policies to bring their cases to the courts by adopting Title 42, Section 1988, of the U.S. Code, which permits the practice of

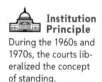

Institution Principle

During the 1960s and 1970s, the courts liberalized the concept of standing.

[50]Linda Greenhouse, "How Congress Curtailed the Courts' Jurisdiction," *New York Times*, 22 October 1996, p. E5.

[51]Robert Dahl, "The Supreme Court and National Policy Making," *Journal of Public Law* 6 (1958): 279.

[52]Martin Shapiro, "The Supreme Court: From Warren to Burger," in *The New American Political System*, ed. Anthony King (Washington, D.C.: American Enterprise Institute, 1978).

[53]Citizens to Preserve Overton Park v. Volpe, 401 U.S. 402 (1971).

"fee shifting." Section 1988 allows citizens who successfully bring a suit against a public official for violating their constitutional rights to collect their attorneys' fees and costs from the government. Thus, Section 1988 encourages individuals and groups to bring their problems to the courts rather than to Congress or the executive branch. These changes have given the courts a far greater role in the administrative process than ever before. Many federal judges are concerned that federal legislation in areas such as health-care reform would create new rights and entitlements that would give rise to a deluge of court cases. "Any time you create a new right, you create a host of disputes and claims," warned Barbara Rothstein, chief judge of the federal district court in Seattle, Washington.[54] Where issues of civil rights are in question, the 1976 Civil Rights Attorney's Fees Awards Act also provides for fee shifting. The act calls for the award of "reasonable attorney's fees" to a prevailing party in a civil rights lawsuit.

Second, the federal courts broadened the scope of relief to permit themselves to act on behalf of broad categories or classes of persons in "class action" cases, rather than just on behalf of individuals.[55] A *class action suit* is a procedural device that permits large numbers of persons with common interests to join together under a representative party to bring or defend a lawsuit. One example is the case of *In re Agent Orange Product Liability Litigation*, in which a federal judge in New York certified Vietnam War veterans as a class with standing to sue a manufacturer of herbicides for damages allegedly incurred from exposure to the defendant's product while in Vietnam.[56] The class potentially numbered in the tens of thousands. In a similar vein, in 1999, a consortium of several dozen law firms prepared to file a class action suit against firearms manufacturers on behalf of victims of gun violence. Claims could amount to billions of dollars. Some of the same law firms were involved earlier in the decade in a massive class action suit against cigarette manufacturers on behalf of the victims of tobacco-related illnesses. This suit eventually led to a settlement in which the tobacco companies agreed to pay out several billion dollars. The beneficiaries of the settlement included the treasuries of all fifty states, which received compensation for costs allegedly borne by the states in treating illnesses due to tobacco. Of course, the attorneys who brought the case also received an enormous settlement, splitting more than $1 billion.

Third, the federal courts began to employ so-called structural remedies, in effect retaining jurisdiction of cases until the court's mandate had actually been implemented to its satisfaction.[57] The best known of these instances was federal judge W. Arthur Garrity's effort to operate the Boston school system from his bench in order to ensure its desegregation. Between 1974 and 1985, Judge Garrity issued fourteen decisions relating to different aspects of the Boston school desegregation plan that had been developed under his authority and put into effect under his supervision.[58] In another recent case, federal judge Leonard B.

class action suit
A lawsuit in which large numbers of persons with common interests join together under a representative party to bring or defend a lawsuit, such as hundreds of workers joining together to sue a company.

[54]Toni Locy, "Bracing for Health Care's Caseload," *Washington Post*, 22 August 1994, p. A15.

[55]See "Developments in the Law—Class Actions," *Harvard Law Review* 89 (1976): 1318.

[56]In re Agent Orange Product Liability Litigation, 100 F.R.D. 718 (D.C.N.Y. 1983).

[57]See Donald L. Horowitz, *The Courts and Social Policy* (Washington, D.C.: Brookings Institution, 1977).

[58]Moran v. McDonough, 540 F. 2nd 527 (1 Cir., 1976; *cert denied* 429 U.S. 1042 [1977]).

Sand imposed fines that would have forced the city of Yonkers, New York, into bankruptcy if it had refused to accept his plan to build public housing in white neighborhoods. After several days of fines, the city gave in to the judge's ruling.

Through these three judicial mechanisms, the federal courts paved the way for an unprecedented expansion of national judicial power. In essence, liberalization of the rules of standing and expansion of the scope of judicial relief drew the federal courts into linkages with important social interests and classes, while the introduction of structural remedies enhanced the courts' ability to serve these constituencies. Thus, during the 1960s and 1970s, the power of the federal courts expanded in the same way the power of the executive expanded during the 1930s—through links with constituencies, such as civil rights, consumer, environmental, and feminist groups, that staunchly defended the Supreme Court in its battles with Congress, the executive, or other interest groups.

> **History Principle**
> In the last fifty years, the power of the judiciary has been strengthened and expanded.

During the 1980s and early 1990s, the Reagan and Bush administrations sought to end the relationship between the Court and liberal political forces. The conservative judges appointed by these Republican presidents modified the Court's position in areas such as abortion, affirmative action, and judicial procedure, though not as completely as some conservatives had hoped. In June, 2003, for example, the Court handed down a series of decisions that pleased many liberals and outraged conservative advocacy groups. Within a period of one week, the Supreme Court affirmed the validity of affirmative action, reaffirmed abortion rights, strengthened gay rights, offered new protection to individuals facing the death penalty, and issued a ruling in favor of a congressional apportionment plan that dispersed minority voters across several districts—a practice that appeared to favor the Democrats.[59] Interestingly, however, the current Court has not been eager to surrender the expanded powers carved out by earlier, liberal Courts. In a number of decisions during the 1980s and 1990s, the Court was willing to make use of its expanded powers on behalf of interests it favored.[60] In the 1992 case of *Lujan v. Defenders of Wildlife*, the Court seemed to retreat to a conception of standing more restrictive than that affirmed by liberal activist jurists.[61] Rather than representing an example of judicial restraint, however, the *Lujan* case was actually a direct judicial challenge to congressional power. The case involved an effort by an environmental group, the Defenders of Wildlife, to make use of the 1973 Endangered Species Act to block the expenditure of federal funds being used by the governments of Egypt and Sri Lanka for public works projects. Environmentalists charged that the projects threatened the habitats of several endangered species of birds and, therefore, that the expenditure of federal funds to support the projects violated the 1973 act. The Interior Department claimed that the act affected only domestic projects.[62]

[59]David Van Drehle, "Court That Liberals Savage Proves to Be Less of a Target," *Washington Post*, 29 June 2003, p. A18.

[60]Mark Silverstein and Benjamin Ginsberg, "The Supreme Court and the New Politics of Judicial Power," *Political Science Quarterly* 102 (Fall 1987): 371–88.

[61]Lujan v. Defenders of Wildlife, 112 S.Ct. 2130 (1992).

[62]Linda Greenhouse, "Court Limits Legal Standing in Suits," *New York Times*, 13 June 1992, p. 12.

The Endangered Species Act, like a number of other pieces of liberal environmental and consumer legislation enacted by Congress, encourages citizen suits—suits by activist groups not directly harmed by the action in question—to challenge government policies that they deem to be inconsistent with the act. Justice Scalia, however, writing for the Court's majority in the *Lujan* decision, reasserted a more traditional conception of standing, requiring those bringing suit against a government policy to show that the policy is likely to cause *them* direct and imminent injury.

Had Scalia stopped at this point, the case might have been seen as an example of judicial restraint. Scalia, however, went on to question the validity of any statutory provision for citizen suits. Such legislative provisions, according to Justice Scalia, violate Article III of the Constitution, which limits the federal courts to consideration of actual "Cases" and "Controversies." This interpretation would strip Congress of its capacity to promote the enforcement of regulatory statutes by encouraging activist groups not directly affected or injured to be on the lookout for violations that could provide the basis for lawsuits. This enforcement mechanism—which conservatives liken to bounty hunting—was an extremely important congressional instrument and played a prominent part in the enforcement of such pieces of legislation as the 1990 Americans with Disabilities Act. Thus, the *Lujan* case offers an example of judicial activism rather than of judicial restraint; even the most conservative justices are reluctant to surrender the powers now wielded by the Court.

There can be little doubt that the contemporary Supreme Court exercises considerably more power than the framers of the Constitution intended. Today, competing interests endeavor to make policy through the courts, and, as we have seen, Congress often enacts regulatory legislation—like the Endangered Species Act—with the presumption that enforcement will be undertaken by the courts rather than the executive branch. Is this an ideal state of affairs? The answer is no. In an ideal world, public policies would be made through the democratically elected branches of our government while the courts would serve to deal with individual problems and injustices. Ours, however, is not always an ideal world. Democratic legislatures sometimes enact programs that violate constitutional rights. Congress and the president sometimes become locked in political struggles that blind them to the interests of certain citizens. On such occasions, we may be grateful that our "least dangerous branch" has some teeth.

SUMMARY

Millions of cases come to trial every year in the United States. The great majority—nearly 99 percent—are tried in state and local courts. The types of law are civil law, criminal law, and public law. There are three types of courts that hear cases: trial court, appellate court, and (state) supreme court.

There are three kinds of federal cases: (1) civil cases involving diversity of citizenship, (2) civil cases where a federal agency is seeking to enforce federal laws that provide for civil penalties, and (3) cases involving federal criminal statutes

Rationality Principle	Collective Action Principle	Institution Principle	Policy Principle	History Principle
Judges have political goals and policy preferences, and act to achieve them.	Appointments to the federal bench involve informal bargaining (senatorial courtesy) as well as formal bargaining (Senate confirmation).	Because the court system is hierarchical, decisions by higher courts constrain the discretion of judges in lower courts.	A number of major policy issues have been fought and decided in the courts.	Since *Marbury v. Madison* (1803), the power of judicial review has not been in question.
The Supreme Court accepts cases based on the preferences and priorities of the justices.	The legal system coordinates private behavior by providing incentives and disincentives for specific actions.	The courts have developed specific rules of access that govern which cases within their jurisdiction they will hear.	By interpreting existing statutes as well as the Constitution, judges make law.	In the last fifty years, the power of the judiciary has been strengthened and expanded.
Groups will often file more than one suit in the hope that this will increase their chances of being heard in Court.	Four of the nine Supreme Court justices need to agree to review a case.	The Supreme Court's procedures allow for various individuals and groups to influence the decision-making process.		
	In reaching their decisions, Supreme Court judges must anticipate Congress's response.	During the 1960s and 1970s the courts liberalized the concept of standing.		

or where state criminal cases have been made issues of public law. Judicial power extends only to cases and controversies. Litigants must have standing to sue, and courts neither hand down opinions on hypothetical issues nor take the initiative. Sometimes appellate courts even return cases to the lower courts for further trial. They may also decline to decide cases by invoking the doctrine of political questions, although this is seldom done today.

The organization of the federal judiciary provides for original jurisdiction in the federal district courts, the U.S. Court of Claims, the U.S. Tax Court, the Customs Court, and federal regulatory agencies.

Each district court is in one of the twelve appellate districts, called circuits, presided over by a court of appeals. Appellate courts admit no new evidence;

their rulings are based solely on the records of the court proceedings or agency hearings that led to the original decision. Appeals court rulings are final unless the Supreme Court chooses to review them.

The Supreme Court has some original jurisdiction, but its major job is to review lower court decisions involving substantial issues of public law. Supreme Court decisions can be reversed by Congress and the state legislatures, but this seldom happens. There is no explicit constitutional authority for the Supreme Court to review acts of Congress. Nonetheless, the 1803 case of *Marbury v. Madison* established the Court's right to review congressional acts. The supremacy clause of Article VI and the Judiciary Act of 1789 give the Court the power to review state constitutions and laws. Cases reach the Court mainly through the writ of *certiorari*. The Supreme Court controls its caseload by issuing few writs and by handing down clear leading opinions that enable lower courts to resolve future cases without further review.

Both appellate and Supreme Court decisions, including the decision not to review a case, make law. The impact of such law usually favors the status quo. Yet, many revolutionary changes in the law have come about through appellate court and Supreme Court rulings—in the criminal process, in apportionment, and in civil rights.

The judiciary as a whole is subject to two major influences: (1) the individual members of the Supreme Court, who have lifetime tenure, and (2) the other branches of government, particularly Congress.

The influence of the individual member of the Supreme Court is limited when the Court is polarized, and close votes in a polarized Court impair the value of the decision rendered. Writing the majority opinion for a case is an opportunity for a justice to influence the judiciary. But the need to frame an opinion in such a way as to develop majority support on the Court may limit such opportunities. Dissenting opinions can have more impact than the majority opinion; they stimulate a continued flow of cases around that issue. The solicitor general is the most important single influence outside the Court itself because he or she controls the flow of cases brought by the Justice Department and also shapes the argument in those cases. But the flow of cases is a force in itself, which the Department of Justice cannot entirely control. Social problems give rise to similar cases that ultimately must be adjudicated and appealed. Some interest groups try to develop such case patterns as a means of gaining power through the courts.

In recent years, the importance of the federal judiciary—the Supreme Court in particular—has increased substantially as the courts have developed new tools of judicial power and forged alliances with important forces in American society.

FOR FURTHER READING

Abraham, Henry J. *The Judicial Process: An Introductory Analysis of the Courts of the United States, England, and France.* 7th ed. New York: Oxford University Press, 1998.

Baum, Lawrence. *The Puzzle of Judicial Behavior.* Ann Arbor: University of Michigan Press, 1997.

Bickel, Alexander M. *The Least Dangerous Branch: The Supreme Court at the Bar of Politics.* Indianapolis: Bobbs-Merrill, 1962.

Epstein, Lee, and Jack Knight. *The Choices Justices Make.* Washington, D.C.: Congressional Quarterly Press, 1998.

Kahn, Ronald. *The Supreme Court and Constitutional Theory, 1953–1993.* Lawrence: University Press of Kansas, 1994.

O'Brien, David M. *Storm Center: The Supreme Court in American Politics.* 6th ed. New York: W. W. Norton, 2003.

Perry, H. W,. Jr. *Deciding to Decide: Agenda Setting in the United States Supreme Court.* Cambridge, Mass: Harvard University Press, 1991.

Segal, Jeffrey A., and Harold J. Spaeth. *The Supreme Court and the Attitudinal Model.* New York: Cambridge University Press, 1993.

Silverstein, Mark. *Judicious Choices: The New Politics of Supreme Court Confirmations.* New York: W. W. Norton, 1994.

Tribe, Laurence H. *Constitutional Choices.* Cambridge, Mass.: Harvard University Press, 1985.

Politics in the News—
Reading between the Lines

Partisanship and the Senate's Approval of Federal Judges

Where the Gloves Are Nearly Always Off

By NEIL A. LEWIS

Such is the level of partisan rancor at Senate Judiciary Committee meetings that some staff aides recently suggested that the Department of Homeland Security screen senators for weapons and sharp objects before they enter the hearing room.

Just a joke, but there is little mistaking either the caustic personal tone of committee debate or the steady deterioration of relations among the committee's members.

. . . In the Judiciary Committee, the bitterness springs partly from an understanding that the federal appeals courts are a principal battlefront in the culture wars. As judges increasingly decide some of the most heated social issues in the nation, the issue of who gets to be a federal judge has increased in importance.

. . . Committee members nowadays are quick to cross the line from professional disagreement into personal criticism, as occurred earlier this month in a debate on the nomination of Judge Charles W. Pickering Sr. to a federal appeals court post.

Senator John Cornyn, a freshman Republican from Texas, took up the lecturing tone that is especially disliked by many Democrats.

"As time goes on," Mr. Cornyn said, "I become more and more troubled by just how bad the process has become and how badly the president's judicial nominees are treated."

Someone must shoulder the blame for this "broken judicial confirmation process," Mr. Cornyn said. He proposed the Democrats. He also accused the Democrats of being biased against Southern nominees.

. . . Democratic Senator Patrick J. Leahy fired off a barrage of statistics demonstrating that Republicans had blocked more of President Bill Clinton's judicial nominees than the Democrats were currently doing in regard to President Bush's.

He took issue with Mr. Cornyn's assertion that Democrats had an anti-Southern bias.

A third of the Clinton nominees rejected by Republicans were from the

New York Times, 28 October 2003, p. A19.

South, Mr. Leahy said, adding, "But being new here, you may have not realized that."

. . . The Democrats are angry because they believe that Republicans blocked Mr. Clinton's judicial nominees to preserve the vacancies for a Republican president, but are now calling the Democrats obstructionists. Over the last year, Democrats have opposed and mounted filibusters to block the confirmations of a handful of Bush appeals court nominees who, the Democrats assert, have such strongly held conservative views that they would shift the courts sharply rightward.

The latest candidate to provoke this debate was Janice Rogers Brown, a justice of the California Supreme Court who has been nominated to a seat on the influential appeals court in Washington.

. . . She insisted at her hearing last week that she was not, as her critics have asserted, "out of the mainstream" of legal philosophy. Ever since the 1987 confirmation hearing of Robert H. Bork to the Supreme Court, the issue of whether a nominee is in the legal mainstream has been a prime debating point.

But Justice Brown has questioned the validity of the so-called incorporation doctrine, under which the essential elements of the Bill of Rights apply to the states. The incorporation doctrine is nowadays as well settled as any judicial principle and is a cornerstone of modern judicial decision making.

Like many Bush nominees before her, Justice Brown asserted that her speeches had little relevance because they were just speeches. She fully accepted that the Supreme Court had upheld the incorporation doctrine, she said.

As an appellate judge, Justice Brown noted, her only role would be to enforce the Supreme Court's doctrines, and her personal philosophy was not relevant.

Her nomination was approved by the committee on a party-line vote. Dem-

ocrats said she was unqualified; she had received a mediocre rating for the job from the American Bar Association, they said. Republicans said she was one of the finest judicial nominees ever to come before the committee.

She will probably soon become the latest of Mr. Bush's candidates to be filibustered in the full Senate.

ESSENCE OF THE STORY

- The Senate Judiciary Committee is assigned the institutional responsibility of reviewing the president's judicial nominees.

- Personal relations among the members of the committee have soured. First, Democrats accused Republicans of treating President Bill Clinton's nominees unfairly. Now, Republicans accuse Democrats of treating President George Bush's nominees similarly badly.

- A recent nominee claims that past speeches that she has given on the incorporation doctrine are not relevant to her judicial philosophy because they were just speeches, not specific cases.

POLITICAL ANALYSIS

- Judicial nominations illustrate the separation-of-powers game. The rules of the game, as enshrined in the Constitution, are clear: the president nominates, and the Senate has the power of advice and consent. The unwritten rules are less clear.

- The party in control of the presidency tends to argue that the Senate needs to defer to the president. The party out of control tends to stress the importance of Senate review.

- This institutional conflict is heightened by a Court that is ideologically split quite evenly and the importance of many social issues (abortion, school prayer, gay rights) that have recently come onto the Court's docket.

three

Politics

CHAPTER

9

Public Opinion

In March 2003, American and British military forces invaded Iraq with the express intent of disarming Iraq's military and driving Iraqi president Saddam Hussein from power. The invasion followed months of diplomatic wrangling and an ultimately unsuccessful effort by President George W. Bush and British Prime Minister Tony Blair to win United Nations support for military action against Iraq. Bush and Blair charged that the Iraqi regime was hiding weapons of mass destruction and had failed to cooperate with weapons inspectors sent by the UN Security Council to investigate Iraq's military programs. In the months prior to the war, many Americans were dubious about the need to attack Iraq and uncertain about President Bush's foreign-policy leadership. For example, according to a CBS News poll taken during the first week in March 2003, only 50 percent of those responding thought removing Saddam Hussein from power was worth the potential costs of war, while 43 percent thought it was not worth it. The same poll reported that only 55 percent of Americans approved of the way President Bush was handling the situation with Iraq. Once the American and British invasion of Iraq began, however, popular support for U.S.

military action rose by 24 points to 77 percent. After the war, popular support for the president declined but rose again when U.S. forces captured Saddam Hussein in December 2003.[1]

Many commentators attributed support for the war to a "rally round the flag" effect that is commonly seen when the president leads Americans into battle. Pundits predicted correctly that support for the war and the president would drop if fighting were prolonged or inconclusive. It also quickly became apparent that support for the president and his war policy varied considerably with demographic and political factors. Men were more supportive than women of the president's policies, indicating a continuation of the "gender gap" that has been a persistent feature of American public opinion. Race was also a factor, with African Americans much more critical than whites of President Bush and his goals. In addition, partisanship was important. Republicans were nearly unanimous in their approval of President Bush's policies, while Democrats were closely divided on the wisdom of going to war. Partisan politics, it seemed, did not stop at the water's edge.

While public opinion on the war shifted from week to week, President Bush's stance was steadfast. For more than a year, Bush had maintained that "regime change" in Iraq was vital to America's security. For months, Bush had moved toward war with Iraq despite lukewarm public support. The president and his aides, to be sure, made a concerted effort to win popular approval but were ready to take action with or without a popular mandate. The White House apparently assumed that a successful military campaign would eventually produce public support. And it did.

Public opinion has become the ultimate standard against which the conduct of contemporary governments is measured. In the democracies, especially in the United States, both the value of government programs and the virtue of public officials are typically judged by the magnitude of their popularity. Most

CHAPTER OUTLINE

What Are the Origins of Public Opinion?

- Common Fundamental Values

- Political Socialization

- Political Ideology

How Are Political Opinions Formed?

- Knowledge and Information

- Government and Political Leaders

- Private Groups

- The Media and Public Opinion

How Is Public Opinion Measured?

- Directly from People

- Surveys

- Limits to Assessing Public Opinion with Polls

- Public Opinion, Political Knowledge, and the Importance of Ignorance

How Does Public Opinion Influence Government Policy?

[1] Data describing opinions on the Iraq war can be found at http://www.pollingreport.com/iraq.htm.

contemporary dictatorships, for their part, are careful at least to give lip service to the idea of popular sovereignty, if only to bolster public support at home and to maintain a favorable image abroad.

Public opinion is the term used to denote the values and attitudes that people have about issues, events, and personalities. Although the terms are sometimes used interchangeably, it is useful to distinguish between values and beliefs on the one hand, and attitudes or opinions on the other. *Values (or beliefs)* are a person's basic orientations to politics. Values represent deep-rooted goals, aspirations, and ideals that shape an individual's perceptions of political issues and events. Liberty, equality, and democracy are basic political values that most Americans hold. Another useful term for understanding public opinion is *ideology*. *Political ideology* refers to a complex and interrelated set of beliefs and values that, as a whole, form a general philosophy about government. As we shall see, liberalism and conservatism are important ideologies in America today. For example, the idea that governmental solutions to problems are inherently inferior to solutions offered by the private sector is a belief also held by many Americans. This general belief, in turn, may lead individuals to have negative views of specific government programs even before they know much about them. An *attitude (or opinion)* is a specific view about a particular issue, personality, or event. An individual may have an opinion about George W. Bush or an attitude toward American policy in Iraq. The attitude or opinion may have emerged from a broad belief about Republicans or military intervention, but an attitude itself is very specific. Some attitudes may be short-lived.

In this chapter, we will examine the role of public opinion in American politics. First, we will examine the political values and beliefs that help Americans form their perceptions of the political process. After reviewing basic American political values, we will analyze how values and beliefs are formed and how certain processes and institutions influence their formation. We conclude this section by considering the ways in which values and beliefs can cumulate to comprise political ideologies. Second, we will see how general values and beliefs help to shape more specific attitudes and opinions. In this discussion we will consider the role of political knowledge and the influence of political leaders, private groups, and the media. We will see why there appear to be so many differences of opinion among Americans. Third, we will assess the science of gathering and measuring public opinion. Finally, we will assess the impact of public opinion on the government and its policies. Is the U.S. government responsive to public opinion? Should it be?

One reason that public policy and public opinion may not always coincide is, of course, that ours is a representative government, not a direct democracy. The framers of the Constitution thought that our nation would be best served by a system of government that allowed the elected representatives of the people an opportunity to reflect and consider their decisions rather than one that bowed immediately to shifts in popular sentiment. A century after the founding, however, the populist movement averred that government was too far removed from the people and introduced procedures for direct popular legislation through the

public opinion
Citizens' attitudes about political issues, leaders, institutions, and events.

values (or beliefs) Basic principles that shape a person's opinions about political issues and events.

political ideology A cohesive set of beliefs that form a general philosophy about the role of government.

attitude (or opinion) A specific preference on a specific issue.

Policy Principle
One reason why policy and opinion may not be consistent is that the United States is a representative government, not a direct democracy.

initiative and referendum. A number of states allow policy issues to be placed on the ballot, where they are resolved by a popular vote. Some modern-day populists believe that initiative and referendum processes should be adopted at the national level as well. Whether this would lead to greater responsiveness, however, is an open question to which we shall return.

WHAT ARE THE ORIGINS OF PUBLIC OPINION?

Opinions are products of an individual's personality, social characteristics, and interests. But opinions are also shaped by institutional, political, and governmental forces that make it more likely that citizens will hold some beliefs and less likely that they will hold others.

Common Fundamental Values

Today most Americans share a common set of political beliefs. First, Americans generally believe in *equality of opportunity:* That is, they assume that all individuals should be allowed to seek personal and material success. Moreover, Americans generally believe that such success should be linked to personal effort and ability rather than family "connections" or other forms of special privilege. Second, Americans strongly believe in individual freedom. They typically support the notion that governmental interference with individuals' lives and property should be kept to the minimum consistent with the general welfare (although in recent years Americans have grown accustomed to greater levels of governmental intervention than would have been deemed appropriate by the founders of liberal theory). Third, most Americans believe in *democracy.* They presume that everyone should have the opportunity to take part in the nation's governmental and policy-making processes and to have some "say" in determining how they are governed (see Figure 9.1).[2]

PREVIEWING THE PRINCIPLES

Underlying political beliefs formed through political socialization often cohere into a political ideology. As a result, ideology can work as an information shortcut by allowing an individual to form an opinion on an issue or candidate while economizing on the costs of becoming informed of the details. Thus, some analysts consider it rational for citizens to be ignorant or partially informed about politics and to form political opinions by following the cues of others, such as government officials, leaders of interest groups, and members of the media. This creates a dilemma, however, since those who have more knowledge of politics also tend to have more influence on political outcomes. This dilemma contributes to a gulf between public opinion and public policy. This gulf is explained, in part, by how institutions shape outcomes. An institutional framework based on representative government limits the extent to which public opinion affects policy outcomes.

equality of opportunity A universally shared American ideal that all have the freedom to use whatever talents and wealth they have to reach their fullest potential.

[2]For a discussion of the political beliefs of Americans, see Everett Carll Ladd, *The American Ideology* (Storrs, Conn.: Roper Center, 1994).

FIGURE 9.1

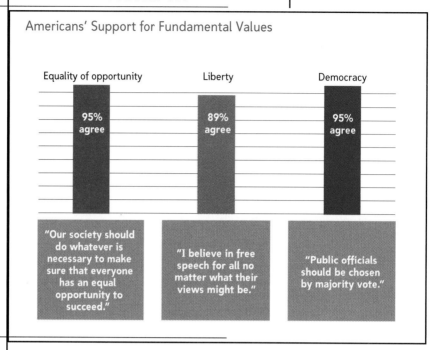

Americans' Support for Fundamental Values

Equality of opportunity	Liberty	Democracy
95% agree	89% agree	95% agree
"Our society should do whatever is necessary to make sure that everyone has an equal opportunity to succeed."	"I believe in free speech for all no matter what their views might be."	"Public officials should be chosen by majority vote."

SOURCE: 1992 American National Election Studies; Herbert McCloskey and John Zaller, *The American Ethos: Public Attitudes toward Capitalism and Democracy* (Cambridge, Mass.: Harvard University Press, 1984), p. 25; and Robert S. Erikson, Norman R. Luttbeg, and Kent L. Tedin, *American Public Opinion: Its Origins, Content, and Impact*, 4th ed. (New York: Macmillan, 1991), p. 108.

One indication that Americans of all political stripes share these fundamental political values is the content of the acceptance speeches delivered by Al Gore and George W. Bush upon receiving their parties' presidential nominations in 2000. Gore and Bush differed on many specific issues and policies. Yet the political visions they presented reveal an underlying similarity. A major emphasis of both candidates was equality of opportunity.

Gore referred frequently to opportunity in his speeches, as in this poignant story about his own parents' efforts to make better lives for themselves and their children:

My father grew up in a small community named Possum Hollow in Middle Tennessee. When he was just eighteen he went to work as a teacher in a one-room school. . . . He entered public service to fight for the people. My mother grew up in a small farming community in northwest Tennessee. She went on to become one of the first women in history to graduate from Vanderbilt Law School. . . . Every hardworking family in America deserves to open the door to their dream.

Bush struck a similar note in his acceptance speech:

We will seize this moment of American promise. . . . And we will extend the promise of prosperity to every forgotten corner of this country. To every man and woman, a chance to succeed. To every child, a chance to learn. To every family, a chance to live with dignity and hope.

Thus, however much the two candidates differed on means and specifics, their understandings of the fundamental goals of government were quite similar.

Agreement on fundamental political values, though certainly not absolute, is probably more widespread in the United States than anywhere else in the Western world. During the course of Western political history, competing economic, social, and political groups put forward a variety of radically divergent views, opinions, and political philosophies. America was never socially or economically homogeneous. But two forces that were extremely powerful and important sources of ideas and beliefs elsewhere in the world were relatively weak or absent in the United States. First, the United States never had the feudal aristocracy that dominated so much of European history. Second, for reasons including America's prosperity and the early availability of political rights, no Socialist movements comparable to those that developed in nineteenth-century Europe were ever able to establish themselves in the United States. As a result, during the course of American history, there existed neither an aristocracy to assert the virtues of inequality, special privilege, and a rigid class structure, nor a powerful American Communist or Socialist party to seriously challenge the desirability of limited government and individualism.[3]

Obviously, the principles that Americans espouse have not always been put into practice. For two hundred years, Americans were able to believe in the principles of equality of opportunity and individual liberty while denying them in practice to generations of African Americans. Yet it is important to note that the strength of the principles ultimately helped to overcome practices that deviated from those principles. Proponents of slavery and, later, of segregation were defeated in the arena of public opinion because their practices differed so sharply from the fundamental principles accepted by most Americans. Ironically, in contemporary politics, Americans' fundamental commitment to equality of opportunity has led to divisions over racial policy. In particular, both proponents and opponents of affirmative action programs cite their belief in equality of opportunity as the justification for their position. Proponents see these programs as necessary to ensure equality of opportunity, while opponents

[3]See Louis Hartz, *The Liberal Tradition in America: An Interpretation of American Political Thought since the Revolution* (New York: Harcourt, Brace, 1955).

believe that affirmative action is a form of preferential treatment that violates basic American values.[4]

Political Socialization

The attitudes that individuals hold about political issues and personalities tend to be shaped by their underlying political beliefs and values. For example, an individual who has basically negative feelings about government intervention into America's economy and society would probably be predisposed to oppose the development of new health care and social programs. Similarly, someone who distrusts the military would likely be suspicious of any call for the use of American troops. The processes through which these underlying political beliefs and values are formed are collectively called *political socialization*.

political socialization
The induction of individuals into the political culture; learning the underlying beliefs and values upon which the political system is based.

The process of political socialization is important. Probably no nation, and certainly no democracy, could survive if its citizens did not share some fundamental beliefs. If Americans had few common values or perspectives, it would be very difficult for them to reach agreement on particular issues. In contemporary America, some elements of the socialization process tend to produce differences in outlook, whereas others promote similarities. Four of the most important *agencies of socialization* that foster differences in political perspectives are the family, membership in social groups, education, and prevailing political conditions.

agencies of socialization
Social institutions, including families and schools, that help to shape individuals' basic political beliefs and values.

No inventory of agencies of socialization can fully explain the development of a given individual's basic political beliefs. In addition to the factors that are important for everyone, forces that are unique to each individual play a role in shaping political orientations. For one person, the character of an early encounter with a member of another racial group can have a lasting impact on that individual's view of the world. For another, a highly salient political event, such as the Vietnam War, can leave an indelible mark on that person's political consciousness. For a third person, some deep-seated personality characteristic, such as paranoia, for example, may strongly influence the formation of political beliefs. Nevertheless, knowing that we cannot fully explain the development of any given individual's political outlook, let us look at some of the most important agencies of socialization that do affect one's beliefs.

The Family   Most people acquire their initial orientation to politics from their families. As might be expected, differences in family background tend to produce divergent political outlooks. Although relatively few parents spend much time teaching their children about politics, political conversations occur in many households and children tend to absorb the political views of parents and other caregivers, perhaps without realizing it. Studies have suggested, for example, that party preferences are initially acquired at home. Children raised in households in

[4]Paul M. Sniderman and Edward G. Carmines, *Reaching beyond Race* (Cambridge, Mass.: Harvard University Press, 1997).

which the primary caregivers are Democrats tend to become Democrats themselves, whereas children raised in homes where their caregivers are Republicans tend to favor the GOP (Grand Old Party, a traditional nickname for the Republican party).[5] Similarly, children reared in politically liberal households are more likely than not to develop a liberal outlook, whereas children raised in politically conservative settings are prone to see the world through conservative lenses. Obviously, not all children absorb their parents' political views. Two of former conservative Republican president Ronald Reagan's three children, for instance, rejected their parents' conservative values. Moreover, even those children whose views are initially shaped by parental values may change their minds as they mature and experience political life for themselves. Nevertheless, the family is an important initial source of political orientation for everyone.

Social Groups   Another important source of divergent political orientations and values are the social groups to which individuals belong. Social groups include those to which individuals belong involuntarily—gender and racial groups, for example—as well as those to which people belong voluntarily—such as political parties, labor unions, and educational and occupational groups. Some social groups have both voluntary and involuntary attributes. For example, individuals are born with a particular social-class background, but as a result of their own efforts people may move up—or down—the class structure.

Membership in social groups can affect political values in a variety of ways. Membership in a particular group can give individuals important experiences and perspectives that shape their view of political and social life. In American society, for example, the experiences of blacks and whites can differ significantly. Blacks are a minority and have been victims of persecution and discrimination throughout American history. Blacks and whites also have different educational and occupational opportunities, often live in separate communities, and may attend separate schools. Such differences tend to produce distinctive political outlooks. For example, in 1995 blacks and whites had very different reactions to the murder trial of former football star O. J. Simpson, who was accused of killing his ex-wife and one of her friends. Seventy percent of the white Americans surveyed believed that Simpson was guilty, based on the evidence presented by the police and prosecutors. But an identical 70 percent of the black Americans surveyed immediately after the trial believed that the police had fabricated evidence and had sought to convict Simpson of a crime he had not committed; these beliefs were presumably based on blacks' experiences with and perceptions of the criminal justice system.[6]

According to other recent surveys, blacks and whites in the United States differ on a number of issues. For example, among middle-income Americans (defined as those earning between $30,000 and $75,000 per year), 65 percent of

---

[5]See Angus Campbell, Philip E. Converse, Warren E. Miller, and Donald E. Stokes, *The American Voter* (New York: Wiley, 1960), p. 147.

[6]Richard Morin, "Poll Reflects Division over Simpson Case," *Washington Post*, 8 October 1995, p. A31.

black respondents and only 35 percent of white respondents thought racism was a major problem in the United States today. Within this same group of respondents, 63 percent of blacks and only 39 percent of whites thought the federal government should provide more services even at the cost of higher taxes.[7] Other issues show a similar pattern of disagreement, reflecting the differences in experience, background, and interests between blacks and whites in America (see Figure 9.2).

Men and women have important differences of opinion as well. Reflecting differences in social roles, political experience, and occupational patterns, women tend to be less militaristic than men on issues of war and peace, more likely than men to favor measures to protect the environment, and more supportive than men of government social and health-care programs (see Table 9.1). Perhaps because of these differences on issues, women are more likely than men to vote for Democratic candidates.[8] This tendency for men's and women's opinions to differ is called the **gender gap.**

gender gap A distinctive pattern of voting behavior reflecting the differences in views between women and men.

Membership in a social group can affect individuals' political orientations in another way: through the efforts of groups themselves to influence their members. Labor unions, for example, often seek to "educate" their members through meetings, rallies, and literature. These activities are designed to shape union members' understanding of politics and to make them more amenable to supporting the political positions favored by union leaders. Similarly, organization can sharpen the impact of membership in an involuntary group. Women's groups, black groups, religious groups, and the like usually endeavor to structure their members' political views through intensive educational programs. The importance of such group efforts can be seen from the impact of group membership on political opinion. Women who belong to women's organizations, for example, are likely to differ more from men in their political views than women without such group affiliation.[9] Other analysts have found that African Americans who belong to black organizations are likely to differ more from whites in their political orientations than blacks who lack such affiliations.[10]

In many cases, no particular efforts are required by groups to affect their members' beliefs and opinions. Often, individuals will consciously or unconsciously adapt their views to those of the groups with which they identify. For example, an African American who is dubious about affirmative action is likely to come under considerable peer pressure and internal pressure to modify his or her views. In this and other cases, dissenters are likely gradually to shift their own

[7]"Middle-Class Views in Black and White," *Washington Post*, 9 October 1995, p. A22.

[8]For data see Rutgers University, Eagleton Institute of Politics, Center for the American Woman in Politics, "Sex Differences in Voter Turnout," August 1994.

[9]Pamela Johnston Conover, "The Role of Social Groups in Political Thinking," *British Journal of Political Science* 18 (1988): 51–78.

[10]See Michael C. Dawson, "Structure and Ideology: The Shaping of Black Opinion," paper presented to the 1995 annual meeting of the Midwest Political Science Association, Chicago, Illinois, 7–9 April 1995. See also Michael C. Dawson, *Behind the Mule: Race and Class in African-American Politics* (Princeton, N.J.: Princeton University Press, 1994).

FIGURE 9.2

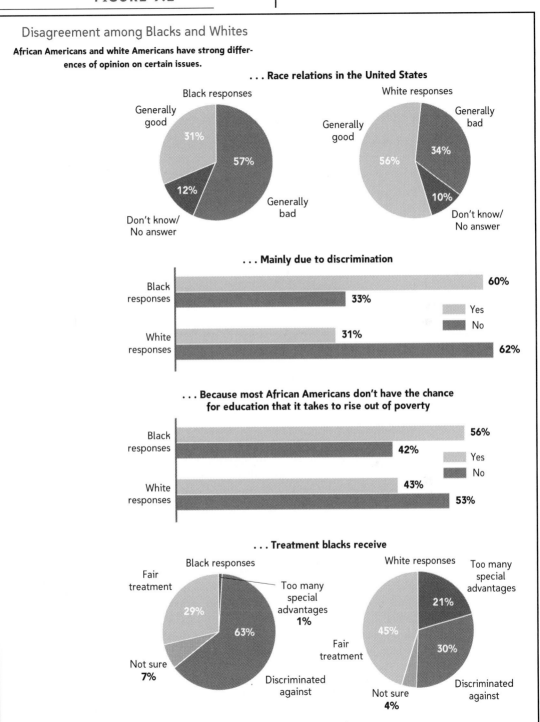

Disagreement among Blacks and Whites

African Americans and white Americans have strong differences of opinion on certain issues.

. . . Race relations in the United States

Black responses

- Generally good 31%
- Generally bad 57%
- Don't know/No answer 12%

White responses

- Generally good 56%
- Generally bad 34%
- Don't know/No answer 10%

. . . Mainly due to discrimination

- Black responses: Yes 60%, No 33%
- White responses: Yes 31%, No 62%

Yes / No

. . . Because most African Americans don't have the chance for education that it takes to rise out of poverty

- Black responses: Yes 56%, No 42%
- White responses: Yes 43%, No 53%

Yes / No

. . . Treatment blacks receive

Black responses

- Fair treatment 29%
- Too many special advantages 1%
- Discriminated against 63%
- Not sure 7%

White responses

- Fair treatment 45%
- Too many special advantages 21%
- Discriminated against 30%
- Not sure 4%

SOURCES: Survey by CBS News, 6–10 February 2000; survey by the National Opinion Research Center—General Social Survey, 1 February–25 June 2000; survey by NBC News/*Wall Street Journal*, 2–5 March 2000.

TABLE 9.1

Disagreements among Men and Women on
Issues of War and Peace

GOVERNMENT ACTION	PERCENTAGE APPROVING OF ACTION	
	MEN	WOMEN
Going to war against Iraq (2003)	66	50
Prefer cease-fire over NATO air strikes on Yugoslavia (1999)	44	51
Ending ban on homosexuals in military (1993)	34	51
Military operation against Somali warlord (1993)	72	60
Going to war against Iraq (1991)	72	53

SOURCE: Gallup Poll, 1991, 1993, 1998, 1999; *Washington Post*, 2003.

views to conform to those of the group. Political psychologist Elisabeth Noelle-Neumann has called this process the "spiral of silence."[11]

A third way that membership in social groups can affect political beliefs is through what might be called objective political interests. On many economic issues, for example, the interests of the rich and poor differ significantly. Inevitably, these differences of interest will produce differences of political outlook. James Madison and other framers of the Constitution thought that the inherent gulf between the rich and the poor would always be the most important source of conflict in political life. Certainly today, struggles over tax policy, welfare policy, health-care policy, and so forth are fueled by differences of interest between wealthier and poorer Americans. In a similar vein, objective differences of interest between "senior citizens" and younger Americans can lead to very different views on such diverse issues as health-care policy, Social Security, and criminal justice. To take another example, in recent decades major differences of opinion and political orientation have developed between American civilians and members of the armed services. Military officers, in particular, are far more conservative in their domestic and foreign-policy views than the public at large and are heavily Republican in their political leanings.[12] Interestingly,

[11]Elisabeth Noelle-Neumann, *The Spiral of Silence: Public Opinion, Our Social Skin* (Chicago: University of Chicago Press, 1984).

[12]Ole R. Holsti, "A Widening Gap between the Military and Society?" in *Some Evidence, 1976–1996*, John M. Olin Institute for Strategic Studies, Harvard University, Working Paper no. 13 (October 1997).

support for the Republicans among military officers climbed sharply during the 1980s and 1990s, decades in which the GOP championed large military budgets. Could this be another case of objective interests swaying ideology?

It is worth pointing out again that, like the other agencies of socialization, group membership can never fully explain a given individual's political views. One's unique personality and life experiences may produce political views very different from those of the group to which one might nominally belong. This is why some African Americans are conservative Republicans, or why an occasional wealthy industrialist is also a socialist. Group membership is conducive to particular outlooks, but it is not determinative.

Differences in Education   A third important source of differences in political perspectives comes from a person's education. In some respects, of course, schooling is a great equalizer. Governments use public education to try to teach all children a common set of civic values. It is mainly in school that Americans acquire their basic belief in liberty, equality, and democracy. In history classes, students are taught that the Founders fought for the principle of liberty. Through participation in class elections and student government, students are taught the virtues of democracy. In the course of studying such topics as the Constitution, the Civil War, and the civil rights movement, students are taught the importance of equality. These lessons are repeated in every grade in a variety of contexts. No wonder they are such an important element in Americans' beliefs.

At the same time, however, differences in educational attainment are strongly associated with differences in political outlook. In particular, those who attend college are often exposed to philosophies and modes of thought that will forever distinguish them from their friends and neighbors who do not pursue college diplomas. Table 9.2 outlines some general differences of opinion that are found between college graduates and other Americans.

In recent years, conservatives have charged that liberal college professors indoctrinate their students with liberal ideas. College does seem to have some "liberalizing" effect upon students, but, more significantly, college seems to convince students of the importance of political participation and of their own capacity to have an impact on politics and policy. Thus, one of the major differences between college graduates and other Americans can be seen in levels of political participation. College graduates vote, write "letters to the editor," join campaigns, take part in protests, and, generally, make their voices heard. Does this mean that college graduates are turned into dangerous radicals by liberal professors? Quite the contrary: college seems to convince individuals that it is important to involve themselves in the nation's politics. What perspective could be more conservative?

Political Conditions   A fourth set of factors that shape political orientations and values are the conditions under which individuals and groups are recruited into and involved in political life. Although political beliefs are influenced by family background and group membership, the precise content and character of these

TABLE 9.2

Education and Public Opinion in 2000

The figures show the percentage of respondents in each category agreeing with the statement.

	EDUCATION			
ISSUES	**DROP-OUT**	**HIGH SCHOOL**	**SOME COLLEGE**	**COLLEGE GRAD.**
1. Women and men should have equal roles.	45%	72%	84%	85%
2. Abortion should never be allowed.	31	16	11	5
3. The government should adopt national health insurance.	50	43	38	37
4. The U.S. should not concern itself with other nations' problems.	27	34	27	12
5. Government should see to fair treatment in jobs for African Americans.	24	33	32	43
6. Government should provide fewer services to reduce government spending.	18	13	19	31

SOURCE: The American National Election Studies, 2000 data, provided by the Inter-University Consortium for Political and Social Research, University of Michigan.

views is, to a large extent, determined by political circumstances. For example, in the nineteenth century, millions of southern Italian peasants left their homes. Some migrated to cities in northern Italy; others came to cities in the United States. Many of those who moved to northern Italy were recruited by socialist and communist parties and became mainstays of the forces of the Italian Left. At the same time, their cousins and neighbors who migrated to American cities were recruited by urban patronage machines and became mainstays of political conservatism. In both instances, group membership influenced political beliefs. Yet the character of those beliefs varied enormously with the political circumstances in which a given group found itself.

In a similar vein, the views held by members of a particular group can shift drastically over time, as political circumstances change. For example, American white southerners were staunch members of the Democratic party from the Civil War through the 1960s. As members of this political group, they became key supporters of liberal New Deal and post–New Deal social programs that greatly expanded the size and power of the American national government. Since the 1960s, however, southern whites have shifted in large numbers to the Republican party. Now they provide a major base of support for efforts to scale back social programs and to sharply reduce the size and power of the national government. The South's move from the Democratic to the Republican camp took place because of white southern opposition to the Democratic party's racial policies and because of determined Republican efforts to win white southern support. It was not a change in the character of white southerners but a change in the political circumstances in which they found themselves that induced this major shift in political allegiances and outlooks in the South.

The moral of this story is that a group's views cannot be inferred simply from the character of the group. College students are not inherently radical or inherently conservative. Jews are not inherently liberal. Southerners are not inherently conservative. Men are not inherently supportive of the military. Any group's political outlooks and orientations are shaped by the political circumstances in which that group finds itself, and those outlooks can change as circumstances change. Quite probably, the generation of American students now coming of political age will have a very different view of the use of American military power than their parents—members of a generation that reached political consciousness during the 1960s, when opposition to the Vietnam War and military conscription were important political phenomena.

Agreement on fundamental values, however, by no means implies that Americans do not differ with one another on a wide variety of issues. As we shall see, American political life is characterized by vigorous debate on economic, foreign policy, and social policy issues; race relations; environmental affairs; and a host of other matters.

Political Ideology

As we have seen, people's beliefs about government can vary widely. But for some individuals, this set of beliefs can fit together into a coherent philosophy about government. This set of underlying orientations, ideas, and beliefs through which we come to understand and interpret politics is called a political ideology.

In America today, people often describe themselves as liberals or conservatives. Liberalism and conservatism are political ideologies that include beliefs about the role of the government, ideas about public policies, and notions about which groups in society should properly exercise power. Historically these terms were defined somewhat differently than they are today. As recently as the nineteenth century, a liberal was an individual who favored freedom from state control, while a conservative was someone who supported the use of governmental power and favored continuation of the influence of church and aristocracy in national life.

Rationality Principle

Ideologies serve as informational shortcuts, allowing individuals to arrive at a view on an issue or a candidate while economizing on the costs of becoming informed of the details.

Today, the term *liberal* has come to imply support for political and social reform; extensive governmental intervention in the economy; the expansion of federal social services; more vigorous efforts on behalf of the poor, minorities, and women; and greater concern for consumers and the environment. In social and cultural areas, liberals generally support abortion rights and oppose state involvement with religious institutions and religious expression. In international affairs, liberal positions are usually seen as including support for arms control, opposition to the development and testing of nuclear weapons, support for aid to poor nations, opposition to the use of American troops to influence the domestic affairs of developing nations, and support for international organizations such as the United Nations. Of course, liberalism is not monolithic. For example, among individuals who view themselves as liberal, many support American military intervention when it is tied to a humanitarian purpose, as in the case of America's military action in Kosovo in 1998–1999. Most liberals supported President George W. Bush's war on terrorism, even when some of the president's actions seemed to curtail civil liberties.

By contrast, the term *conservative* today is used to describe those who generally support the social and economic status quo and are suspicious of efforts to introduce new political formulas and economic arrangements. Conservatives believe strongly that a large and powerful government poses a threat to citizens' freedom. Thus, in the domestic arena, conservatives generally oppose the expansion of governmental activity, asserting that solutions to social and economic problems can be developed in the private sector. Conservatives particularly oppose efforts to impose government regulation on business, pointing out that such regulation is frequently economically inefficient and costly and can ultimately lower the entire nation's standard of living. As to social and cultural positions, many conservatives oppose abortion and support school prayer. In international affairs, conservatism has come to mean support for the maintenance of American military power. Like liberalism, conservatism is far from a monolithic ideology. Some conservatives support many government social programs. Republican George W. Bush calls himself a "compassionate conservative" to indicate that he favors programs that assist the poor and needy. Other conservatives oppose efforts to outlaw abortion, arguing that government intrusion in this area is as misguided as government intervention in the economy. Such a position is sometimes called "libertarian." The real political world is far too complex to be seen in terms of a simple struggle between liberals and conservatives.

Liberal and conservative differences manifest themselves in a variety of contexts. For example, the liberal approach to increasing airline safety in October 2001 was to create a workforce of federal employees that would screen and inspect passenger luggage. The conservative approach was to call for better training of existing employees and supervision of private sector screeners. To some extent, contemporary liberalism and conservatism can be seen as differences of emphasis with regard to the fundamental American political values of liberty and equality. For liberals, equality is the most important of the core values. Liberals are willing to tolerate government intervention in such areas as college admissions and business decisions when these seem to result in high levels of race, class, or gender inequality. For conservatives, on the other hand, liberty is the core value. Conservatives oppose most efforts by the government, however well intentioned, to intrude into private life or the marketplace. This simple formula for distinguishing liberalism and conservatism, however, is not always accurate, because political ideologies seldom lend themselves to neat or logical characterizations.

Often political observers search for logical connections among the various positions identified with liberalism or with conservatism, and they are disappointed or puzzled when they are unable to find a set of coherent philosophical principles that define and unite the several elements of either of these sets of beliefs. On the liberal side, for example, what is the logical connection between opposition to U.S. government intervention in the affairs of foreign nations and calls for greater intervention in America's economy and society? On the conservative side, what is the logical relationship between opposition to governmental regulation of business and support for a ban on abortion? Indeed, the latter would seem to be just the sort of regulation of private conduct that conservatives claim to abhor.

Frequently, the relationships among the various elements of liberalism or the several aspects of conservatism are *political* rather than *logical*. One underlying basis of liberal views is that all or most represent criticisms of or attacks on the foreign and domestic policies and cultural values of the business and commercial strata that have been prominent in the United States for the past century. In some measure, the tenets of contemporary conservatism represent this elite's defense of its positions against its enemies, who include organized labor, minority groups, and some intellectuals and professionals. Thus, liberals attack business and commercial elites by advocating more governmental regulation, including consumer protection and environmental regulation, opposition to military weapons programs, and support for expensive social programs. Conservatives counterattack by asserting that governmental regulation of the economy is ruinous and that military weapons are needed in a changing world.

Of course, it is important to note that many people who call themselves liberals or conservatives accept only part of the liberal or conservative ideology. Although it appears that Americans have adopted more conservative outlooks on some issues, their views in other areas have remained largely unchanged or even have become more liberal in recent years (see Table 9.3). Thus, many individuals who are liberal on social issues are conservative on economic issues. There is certainly nothing illogical about these mixed positions. They simply indicate the relatively open and fluid character of American political debate.

HOW ARE POLITICAL OPINIONS FORMED?

An individual's opinions on particular issues, events, and personalities emerge as he or she evaluates these phenomena through the lenses of the beliefs and orientations that, taken together, comprise his or her political ideology. Thus, if a

TABLE 9.3

Have Americans Become More Conservative?

	1972	1978	1980	1982	1984	1986	1988	1992	1996	1998
Percentage responding "yes" *to the following questions:*										
Should the government help minority groups?	30%	25%	16%	21%	27%	26%	13%	27%	18%	26%
Should the government see to it that everyone has a job and a guaranteed standard of living?	27	17	22	25	28	25	24	30	24	30
Should abortion never be permitted?	9	10	8	13	13	13	12	12	13	12
Should the government provide fewer services and reduce spending?	NA	NA	27	32	28	24	25	33	31	26

NA: Not Asked.
SOURCE: Center for Political Studies of the Institute for Social Research, University of Michigan. Data were made available through the Inter-University Consortium for Political and Social Research.

Rationality Principle

Individuals process new information and new experiences, updating their beliefs about the political world and adjusting their preferences about public policies, issues, and personalities.

conservative is confronted with a plan to expand federal social programs, he or she is likely to express opposition to the endeavor without spending too much time pondering the specific plan. Similarly, if a liberal is asked to comment on former president Ronald Reagan, he or she is not likely to hesitate long before offering a negative view. Underlying beliefs and ideologies tend to automatically color people's perceptions and opinions about politics.

Opinions on particular issues, however, are seldom fully shaped by underlying ideologies. Few individuals possess ideologies so cohesive and intensely held that they will automatically shape all their opinions. Indeed, when we occasionally encounter individuals with rigid worldviews, who see everything through a particular political lens, we tend to dismiss them as "ideologues."

Although ideologies color our political perspectives, they seldom fully determine our views. This is true for a variety of reasons. First, as noted earlier, most individuals' ideologies contain internal contradictions. Take, for example, a conservative view of the issue of abortion. Should conservatives favor outlawing abortion as an appropriate means of preserving public morality, or should they oppose restrictions on abortion because these represent government intrusions into private life? In this instance, as in many others, ideology can point in different directions.

Second, individuals may have difficulty linking particular issues or personalities to their own underlying beliefs. Some issues defy ideological characterizations. Should conservatives support or oppose the formation of the Department of Homeland Security? What should liberals think about America's bombing of Iraq? Each of these policies combines a mix of issues and is too complex to be viewed through simple ideological lenses.

Finally, most people have at least some conflicting underlying attitudes. Most conservatives support *some* federal programs—defense, or tax deductions for businesses, for example—and wish to see them, and hence the government, expanded. Many liberals favor American military intervention in other nations for what they deem to be humanitarian purposes but generally oppose American military intervention in the affairs of other nations.

Thus, most individuals' attitudes on particular issues do not spring automatically from their ideological predispositions. It is true that most people have underlying beliefs that help to shape their opinions on particular issues[13] but other factors are also important: a person's knowledge of political issues and outside influences on that person's views.

Knowledge and Information

As we have seen, general political beliefs can guide the formation of opinions on specific issues, but an individual's beliefs and opinions are not always consistent with one another. Studies of political opinion have shown that most people don't hold specific and clearly defined opinions on every political issue.[14] As a result, they are easily influenced by others. What best explains whether citizens are generally consistent in their political views or inconsistent and open to the influence of others? The key is knowledge and information about political issues. In general, knowledgeable citizens are better able to evaluate new information and determine whether it is relevant to and consistent with their beliefs and opinions.

The average American, however, exhibits little knowledge of political institutions, processes, leaders, and policy debates. For example, in a 1996 poll, only about half of all Americans could correctly identify Newt Gingrich, who was then the Speaker of the House of Representatives.[15] Can the political ignorance of citizens be squared with rationality? It depends. Some analysts have argued that political attentiveness is costly—it means spending time at the very least, but often money as well, to collect, organize, and digest political information.[16] Balanced

---

[13]R. Michael Alvarez and John Brehm, *Hard Choices, Easy Answers: Values, Information, and American Public Opinion* (Princeton, N.J.: Princeton University Press, 2002).

[14]John R. Zaller, *The Nature and Origins of Mass Opinion* (New York: Cambridge University Press, 1992).

[15]Michael X. Delli Carpini and Scott Keeter, *What Americans Know about Politics and Why It Matters* (New Haven: Yale University Press, 1996).

[16]Anthony Downs, *An Economic Theory of Democracy* (New York: Harper, 1957).

against this cost to an individual is the very low probability that he or she will, on the basis of this costly information, take an action that would not otherwise have been taken *and* that this departure in behavior will make a beneficial difference to him or her *and* that difference, if it exists, will exceed the cost of acquiring the information in the first place. That is, since individuals anticipate that informed actions taken by them will rarely make much difference while the costs of informing oneself are often not trivial, it is rational to remain ignorant. A more moderate version of "rational" ignorance recognizes that some kinds of information are inexpensive to acquire, such as soundbites from the evening news, or actually pleasant, such as reading the front page of the newspaper while drinking a cup of coffee. In these cases, an individual may become partially informed, but usually not in detail. Taking cues from trusted others—the local preacher, the TV commentator or newspaper editorialist, an interest-group leader, friends, and relatives—is another "inexpensive" way to become informed.[17] Does this ignorance, no mater how rational, of key political facts matter?

Another important concern is the character of those who possess and act upon the political information that they acquire. Political knowledge, even that which is inexpensive to acquire, is not evenly distributed throughout the population. Those with higher education, income, and occupational status and who are members of social or political organizations are more likely to know about and be active in politics. An interest in politics reinforces an individual's sense of political efficacy and provides more incentive to acquire additional knowledge and information about politics. Those who don't think they can have an effect on government tend not to be interested in learning about or participating in politics. When asked for their views on political issues, they are less able than those with higher levels of education and income to form and articulate coherent and consistent opinions.[18] As a result, individuals with a disproportionate share of income and education also have a disproportionate share of knowledge and influence and are better able to get what they want from government.[19]

When individuals attempt to form opinions about particular political issues, events, and personalities, they seldom do so in isolation. Typically, they are confronted—sometimes bombarded—by the efforts of a host of individuals and groups seeking to persuade them to adopt a particular point of view. Someone trying to decide what to think about Bill Clinton, Al Gore, or George W. Bush could hardly avoid an avalanche of opinions expressed through the media, in meetings, or in conversations with friends. The ***marketplace of ideas*** is the interplay of opinions and views that takes place as competing forces attempt to per-

Policy Principle

Government policies disproportionately reflect the goals and interests of those with higher levels of income and education because these individuals tend to have more knowledge of politics and are more willing to act on it.

marketplace of ideas The public forum in which beliefs and ideas are exchanged and compete.

[17]For a discussion of the role of information in democratic politics in light of the cognitive limitations, restricted interest, and diminished attention span of today's voters, see Arthur Lupia and Mathew D. McCubbins, *The Democratic Dilemma: Can Citizens Learn What They Need to Know?* (New York: Cambridge University Press, 1998).

[18]Adam J. Berinsky, "Silent Voices: Social Welfare Policy Opinions and Political Equality in America," *American Journal of Political Science* 46 (2002): 276–88.

[19]Steven J. Rosenstone and John Mark Hansen, *Mobilization, Participation, and Democracy in America* (New York: Macmillan, 1993).

suade as many people as possible to accept a particular position on a particular event. Given constant exposure to the ideas of others, it is virtually impossible for most individuals to resist some modification of their own beliefs. For example, African Americans and white Americans disagree on a number of matters. Yet, as political scientists Paul M. Sniderman and Edward G. Carmines have shown, considerable cross-racial agreement has evolved on fundamental issues of race and civil rights.[20] Thus, to some extent, public opinion is subject to deliberate shaping and manipulation by **opinion leaders.** For example, in the summer of 1963, the public's attention was riveted to the dramatic struggle of nonviolent protesters attempting to win civil rights in the South. News stories and television film footage repeatedly showed peaceful demonstrators being chased and beaten by police, suffering attacks by dogs, and being sprayed with fire hoses. These scenes filled Americans with shock and outrage. Then, in August 1963, civil rights leaders staged a massive march on Washington (when Martin Luther King, Jr., delivered his famous "I Have a Dream" speech on the steps of the Lincoln Memorial). The impact on public opinion was dramatic: between the spring and summer of that year, the percentage of Americans who considered civil rights to be "the most important issue" facing the country increased from 4 percent to 52 percent—the largest such increase ever recorded.[21] This is also an example of "agenda setting"—the ability of the media to turn the country's focus toward a particular issue (see Chapter 13).

opinion leaders
Those who other citizens turn to for political information and cues.

Few ideas spread spontaneously. Usually, whether they are matters of fashion, science, or politics, ideas must be vigorously promoted to become widely known and accepted. For example, the clothing, sports, and entertainment fads that occasionally seem to appear from nowhere and sweep the country before being replaced by some other new trend are almost always the product of careful marketing campaigns by one or another commercial interest, rather than spontaneous phenomena. Even in the sciences, generally considered *the* bastions of objectivity, new theories, procedures, and findings are not always accepted simply and immediately on their own merit. Often, the proponents of a new scientific principle or practice must campaign within the scientific community on behalf of their views. Like their counterparts in fashion and science, successful—or at least widely held—political ideas are usually the products of carefully orchestrated campaigns by government or by organized groups and interests, rather than the results of spontaneous popular enthusiasm. In general, new ideas are presented in ways that make them seem consistent with, or even logical outgrowths of, Americans' more fundamental beliefs. For example, proponents of affirmative action generally present the policy as a necessary step toward racial equality. Or opponents of a proposed government regulation will vehemently assert that the rule is inconsistent with liberty. Both supporters and

 Collective Action Principle
Widely held political ideas are usually the products of orchestrated campaigns by government, organized groups, or the media.

---

[20]Sniderman and Carmines, *Reaching beyond Race*, Chapter 4.

[21]Michael Robinson, "Television and American Politics 1956–1976," *Public Interest* 48 (Summer 1977): 23.

opponents of campaign finance reform seek to wrap their arguments in the cloak of democracy.[22]

Three forces that play important roles in shaping opinions are the government, private groups, and the news media.

Government and Political Leaders

All governments attempt, to a greater or lesser extent, to influence, manipulate, or manage their citizens' beliefs. In the United States, some efforts have been made by every administration since the nation's founding to influence public sentiment. But efforts to shape opinion did not become a routine and formal official function until World War I, when the Wilson administration created a censorship board, enacted sedition and espionage legislation, and attempted to suppress groups that opposed the war, like the International Workers of the World (IWW) and the Socialist party. Eugene Debs, a prominent Socialist and presidential candidate, was arrested and convicted of having violated the Espionage Law, and he was sentenced to ten years in prison for delivering a speech that defended the IWW.

At the same time, however, World War I was the first modern industrial war requiring a total mobilization of popular effort on the home front for military production. The war effort required the government to persuade the civilian population to bear the costs and make the sacrifices needed to achieve industrial and agricultural, as well as battlefield, success. The chief mechanism for eliciting the support of public opinion was the Committee on Public Information (CPI), chaired by journalist and publicist George Creel. The CPI organized a massive public relations and news management program to promote popular enthusiasm for the war effort. This program included the dissemination of favorable news, the publication of patriotic pamphlets, films, photos, cartoons, bulletins, and periodicals, and the organization of "war expositions" and speakers' tours. Special labor programs were aimed at maintaining the loyalty and productivity of the workforce. Many of the CPI's staff were drawn from the major public relations firms of the time.[23]

The extent to which public opinion is actually affected by governmental public relations efforts is probably limited. The government—despite its size and power—is only one source of information and evaluation in the United States. Very often, governmental claims are disputed by the media, by interest groups, and, at times, by opposing forces within the government itself. Often, too, governmental efforts to manipulate public opinion backfire when the public is made aware of the government's tactics. Thus, in 1971, the United States government's efforts to build popular support for the Vietnam War were hurt when CBS News aired its documentary "The Selling of the Pentagon," which purported to reveal the extent and character of governmental efforts to sway popu-

[22]For an interesting discussion of opinion formation, see Zaller, *The Nature and Origins of Mass Opinion.*
[23]See George Creel, *How We Advertised America* (New York: Harper & Bros., 1920).

lar sentiment. In this documentary, CBS demonstrated the techniques, including planted news stories and faked film footage, that the government had used to misrepresent its activities in Vietnam. These revelations, of course, had the effect of undermining popular trust in all governmental claims. During the 1991 Persian Gulf War, the U.S. military was much more careful about the accuracy of its assertions.

A hallmark of the Clinton administration was the steady use of techniques like those used in election campaigns to bolster popular enthusiasm for White House initiatives. The president established a "political war room" in the Executive Office Building similar to the one that operated in his campaign headquarters. Representatives from all departments met in the war room every day to discuss and coordinate the president's public relations efforts. Many of the same consultants and pollsters who directed the successful Clinton campaign were employed in the selling of the president's programs.[24]

Indeed, the Clinton White House made more sustained and systematic use of public-opinion polling than any previous administration. For example, during his presidency Bill Clinton relied heavily on the polling firm of Penn & Schoen to help him decide which issues to emphasize and what strategies to adopt. During the 1995–1996 budget battle with Congress, the White House commissioned polls almost every night to chart changes in public perceptions about the struggle. Poll data suggested to Clinton that he should present himself as struggling to save Medicare from Republican cuts. Clinton responded by launching a media attack against what he claimed were GOP efforts to hurt the elderly. This proved to be a successful strategy and helped Clinton defeat the Republican budget.[25]

Evidence exists to back up the assertions of the Clinton White House. Political scientists Robert Shapiro and Lawrence Jacobs studied how polls are used by politicians and discovered that the ideology of political leaders, not public opinion, was the decisive influence on the formulation of a policy. They also found that the primary use of polling was to choose the language, rhetoric, and arguments for policy proposals in order to build the public's support.[26] However, according to former Clinton adviser Dick Morris, the president met every week with key aides to examine poll data and devise strategies to bolster his popularity.[27] For example, in April 1996, the administration's polls showed that an initiative to crack down on "deadbeat dads" who failed to pay child support would be popular. Several weeks later, the president announced new regulations requiring states to take more aggressive action to compel payment. Similarly, in July 1996, Clinton signed the Republican-sponsored welfare reform bill, which he

[24]Gerald F. Seib and Michael K. Frisby, "Selling Sacrifice," *Wall Street Journal*, 5 February 1993, p. 1.

[25]Michael K. Frisby, "Clinton Seeks Strategic Edge with Opinion Polls," *Wall Street Journal*, 24 June 1996, p. A16.

[26]Reported in Richard Morin, "Which Comes First, the Politician or the Poll?" *Washington Post National Weekly Edition*, 10 February 1997, p. 31.

[27]John F. Harris, "New Morris Book Portrays How Polls, Clinton, Intersected," *Washington Post*, 22 December 1998, p. A18.

Why Don't Americans Trust Government?

Over forty years ago, President John F. Kennedy challenged the country by telling them "my fellow Americans: ask not what your country can do for you—ask what you can do for your country."[29] Today it seems unlikely that a president could even ask the people to consider what their country could do for them; Americans no longer trust their government.

The question is: Why? Is government seen as one way for people to accomplish their goals (Principle 1) and solve collective-action problems (Principle 2)? If so, then perceived governmental failures, such as the Vietnam War or the War on Poverty, may have caused the declines in trust. If this is the case, we should not worry about declining trust: all we need to do is to reform government. On the other hand, if trust in government is an underlying belief, similar to nationalism, then the quarter-century decline is a cause for great concern. It may indicate that Americans are not supportive of their collective governing institutions. So what is trust in government?

"Moral trust" views trust as a behavioral norm learned in early childhood socialization. Moral trust is as much a characteristic of a community as it is of an individual. If someone is trusting, according to the moral theorist, he or she will behave in a trusting manner nearly all of the time and in nearly any context. Trust is part of our value system, just like religion or party identification.[30]

According to the moral perspective, current levels of trust in government are a product of *history*.

"Rational trust" frames trust in the context of the *rationality principle*. Trust is a product of reciprocal exchanges. Trust depends on individual reputations, past experiences, and the social context. For example, Jill may trust the store clerk Jack to make correct

had previously opposed, when polls indicated that he would gain 8 points in the polls if he signed the bill.[28]

Of course, at the same time that the Clinton administration worked diligently to mobilize popular support, its opponents struggled equally hard to mobilize popular opinion against the White House. A host of public and private interest groups opposed to President Clinton's programs crafted public relations campaigns designed to generate opposition to the president. For example, in 1994, while Clinton campaigned to bolster popular support for his health-care reform proposals, groups representing small business and segments of the insurance industry, among others, developed their own publicity campaigns that ultimately convinced many Americans that Clinton's initiative posed a threat to their own health care. These opposition campaigns played an important role in the eventual

[28]Dick Morris, *Behind the Oval Office: Getting Reelected against All Odds*, 2nd ed. (Los Angeles: Renaissance, 1999).

change, but she probably doesn't trust Jack to file her taxes. Trust is highly malleable and will evolve with changing circumstances.[31]

According to the rational perspective, trust in government has declined because government failed to solve collective-action problems and efficiently provide goods and services.

Both moral-trust and rational-trust scholars agree, however, that trust in government is very different from trusting another individual. The moral scholar does not believe that "trust" is the appropriate way to characterize our relationships with abstract institutions such as "government." He or she believes that we can only favor (or oppose) those currently in power. Unlike the one-on-one exchanges that characterize our everyday lives, the rational-choice scholar finds few reciprocal exchanges that we have with government. While government pervades American life, few of us can point to specific ways that government affects our daily lives.

In the end, neither Hardin or Uslaner worries much about trust in government. If Americans are less likely to sacrifice for their country today, it is probably because we don't have that much faith in the current crop of political leaders. If another charismatic president asked us to sacrifice for our country, we'd probably do so.

[29]President John F. Kennedy, inaugural address, January 20, 1961.

[30]Eric M. Uslaner, *The Moral Foundations of Trust* (New York: Cambridge University Press, 2002).

[31]Russell Hardin, *Trust and Trustworthiness* (New York: Russell Sage, 2002).

---

defeat of the president's proposal. After he assumed office in 2001, President George W. Bush also began making some use of poll data to help shape his own policy agendas. The Bush White House's extensive public relations program was instrumental in coordinating efforts to maintain popular support for the war against terrorism. These efforts included presidential speeches, media appearances by administration officials, numerous press conferences, and thousands of press releases presenting the administration's views.[32] The White House also made a substantial effort to sway opinion in foreign countries, even sending officials to present the administration's views on television networks serving the Arab world.

During the 2003 Iraq war, the administration allowed reporters to accompany combat units into battle and to file real-time photos and reports from the front. The administration hoped that these "embedded" journalists would identify with

[32]Peter Marks, "Adept in Politics and Advertising, 4 Women Shape a Campaign," *New York Times*, 11 November 2001, p. B6.

their military units and provide positive coverage. On the whole, this plan was successful. Many embedded reporters could be heard using the pronoun "we" when referring to the battlefield exploits of the forces they accompanied.

Often, claims and counterclaims by the government and its opponents are aimed chiefly at elites and opinion makers rather than directly at the public. For example, many of the television ads about the health-care debate were aired primarily in and around Washington and New York City, where they were more likely to be seen by persons influential in politics, business, and the media. The presumption behind this strategy is that such individuals are likely to be the key decision makers on most issues. Political, business, and media elites are also seen as "opinion leaders" who have the capacity to sway the views of larger segments of the public.

Private Groups

Collective Action Principle

Part of the "job description" of leaders of well-organized interest groups is to seek out issues around which they can mobilize group members. Organized interests are decidedly at an advantage in this respect, compared to latent, unorganized interests.

Political issues and ideas seldom emerge spontaneously from the grass roots. We have already seen how the government tries to shape public opinion. But the ideas that become prominent in political life are also developed and spread by important economic and political groups searching for issues that will advance their causes. One example is the "right-to-life" issue that has inflamed American politics over the past twenty years.

The notion of right-to-life, whose proponents seek to outlaw abortion and overturn the Supreme Court's *Roe v. Wade* decision, was developed and heavily promoted by conservative politicians who saw the issue of abortion as a means of uniting Catholic and Protestant conservatives and linking both groups to the Republican coalition. These politicians convinced Catholic and evangelical Protestant leaders that they shared similar views on the question of abortion, and they worked with religious leaders to focus public attention on the negative issues in the abortion debate. To advance their cause, leaders of the movement sponsored well-publicized Senate hearings, where testimony, photographs, and other exhibits were presented to illustrate the violent effects of abortion procedures. At the same time, publicists for the movement produced leaflets, articles, books, and films such as *The Silent Scream*, to highlight the agony and pain ostensibly felt by the unborn when they were being aborted. All of this underscored the movement's claim that abortion was nothing more or less than the murder of millions of innocent human beings. Finally, Catholic and evangelical Protestant religious leaders were organized to denounce abortion from their church pulpits and, increasingly, from their electronic pulpits on the Christian Broadcasting Network (CBN) and the various other television forums available for religious programming. Religious leaders also organized demonstrations, pickets, and disruptions at abortion clinics throughout the nation.[33] Abortion rights remains a potent issue; it even influenced the health-care-reform debate.

[33]See Gillian Peele, *Revival and Reaction: The Right in Contemporary America* (Oxford, Eng.: Clarendon Press, 1985). Also see Connie Paige, *The Right to Lifers: Who They Are, How They Operate, Where They Get Their Money* (New York: Summit, 1983).

Typically, ideas are marketed most effectively by groups with access to financial resources, public or private institutional support, and sufficient skill or education to select, develop, and draft ideas that will attract interest and support. Thus, the development and promotion of conservative themes and ideas in recent years has been greatly facilitated by the millions of dollars that conservative corporations and business organizations such as the Chamber of Commerce and the Public Affairs Council spend each year on public information and what is now called in corporate circles "issues management." In addition, conservative businessmen have contributed millions of dollars to such conservative institutions as the Heritage Foundation, the Hoover Institution, and the American Enterprise Institute.[34]

Although they do not usually have access to financial assets that match those available to their conservative opponents, liberal intellectuals and professionals have ample organizational skills, access to the media, and practice in creating, communicating, and using ideas. During the past three decades, the chief vehicle through which liberal intellectuals and professionals have advanced their ideas has been the "public interest group," an institution that relies heavily upon voluntary contributions of time, effort, and interest on the part of its members. Through groups like Common Cause, the National Organization for Women, the Sierra Club, Friends of the Earth, and Physicians for Social Responsibility, intellectuals and professionals have been able to use their organizational skills and educational resources to develop and promote ideas.[35]

Journalist and author Joe Queenan has correctly observed that although political ideas can erupt spontaneously, they almost never do. Instead,

> issues are usually manufactured by tenured professors and obscure employees of think tanks. . . . It is inconceivable that the American people, all by themselves, could independently arrive at the conclusion that the depletion of the ozone layer poses a dire threat to our national well-being, or that an immediate, across-the-board cut in the capital-gains tax is the only thing that stands between us and the economic abyss. The American people do not have that kind of sophistication. *They have to have help.*[36]

The Media and Public Opinion

The communications media are among the most powerful forces operating in the marketplace of ideas. The mass media are not simply neutral messengers for ideas developed by others. Instead, the media have an enormous impact on popular attitudes and opinions. Over time, the ways in which the mass media report

[34]See David Vogel, "The Power of Business in America: A Reappraisal," *British Journal of Political Science* 13 (January 1983): 19–44.

[35]See David Vogel, "The Public Interest Movement and the American Reform Tradition," *Political Science Quarterly* 96 (Winter 1980): 607–27.

[36]Joe Queenan, "Birth of a Notion," *Washington Post*, 20 September 1992, p. C1.

political events help to shape the underlying attitudes and beliefs from which opinions emerge.[37] For example, for the past thirty years, the national news media have relentlessly investigated personal and official wrongdoing on the part of politicians and public officials. This continual media presentation of corruption in government and venality in politics has undoubtedly fostered the general attitude of cynicism and distrust that exists in the general public.

At the same time, the ways in which media coverage interprets or frames specific events can have a major impact on popular responses and opinions about these events.[38] For example, the media presented the 1996 budget battle between President Clinton and then-Speaker of the House Newt Gingrich in a way that served Clinton's interests. By forcing the closing of a number of government agencies, Gingrich hoped that the media would point out how smoothly life could proceed with less government involvement. Instead, the media focused on the hardships the closings inflicted on out-of-work government employees in the months before Christmas. The way in which the media framed the discussion helped turn opinion against Gingrich and handed Clinton an important victory.

HOW IS PUBLIC OPINION MEASURED?

As recently as fifty years ago, American political leaders gauged public opinion by people's applause or cheers and by the presence of crowds in meeting places. This direct exposure to the people's views did not necessarily produce accurate knowledge of public opinion. It did, however, give political leaders confidence in their public support—and, therefore, confidence in their ability to govern by consent.

Abraham Lincoln and Stephen Douglas debated each other seven times in the campaign for the Illinois Senate seat during the summer and autumn of 1858, two years before they became presidential nominees. Their debates took place before audiences in parched cornfields and courthouse squares. A century later, the presidential debates, although seen by millions, take place before a few reporters and technicians in television studios that might as well be on the moon. The public's response cannot be experienced directly. This distance between leaders and followers is one of the agonizing problems of modern democracy. The communication media send information to millions of people, but they are not yet as efficient at getting information back to leaders. Is government by consent possible where the scale of communication is so large and impersonal? In order to compensate for the decline in their ability to experience public opinion for themselves, leaders have turned to science, in particular to the science of opinion polling.

[37]Zaller, *The Nature and Origins of Mass Opinion.*

[38]See Shanto Iyengar, *Is Anyone Responsible? How Television Frames Political Issues* (Chicago: University of Chicago Press, 1991); and Shanto Iyengar, *Do the Media Govern? Politicians, Voters, and Reporters in America* (Thousand Oaks, Calif.: Sage, 1997).

It is no secret that politicians and public officials make extensive use of public opinion polls to help them decide whether to run for office, what policies to support, how to vote on important legislation, and what types of appeals to make in their campaigns. President Lyndon Johnson was famous for carrying the latest Gallup and Roper poll results in his hip pocket, and it is widely believed that he began to withdraw from politics in 1968 because the polls reported losses in public support. All recent presidents and other major political figures have worked closely with polls and pollsters. Yet even the most scientific measurements of public opinion do not necessarily lighten the burden of ignorance.

Directly from People

American politicians want rapport with the people; they want to mingle, to shake hands, to get the feel of the crowd. And where crowds are too large to experience directly, the substitutes also have to be more direct than those described up to this point.

Approaches to the direct measurement of public opinion can be divided conveniently into two types—the impressionistic and the scientific. The impressionistic approach can be subdivided into at least three methods—person-to-person, selective polling, and the use of bellwether districts. The scientific approach may take on several different forms, but they all amount to an effort to use random sampling techniques and established and psychologically validated survey questions.

Person to Person   Politicians traditionally acquire knowledge about opinions through direct exposure to a few people's personal impressions—the person-to-person approach. They attempt to convert these impressions into reliable knowledge by intuition. When they are in doubt about first impressions, they seek further impressions from other people; but the individuals they rely on the most heavily are their friends and acquaintances. Presidents have usually relied on associates for political impressions. These few friends occupy an inner circle, and they give political advice after the experts and special leaders have finished.

The advantage of the person-to-person approach is that it is quick, efficient, and inexpensive. Its major disadvantage is that it can close off unpleasant information or limit the awareness of new issues. Franklin Roosevelt, for example, was one of the best-informed presidents, and yet, when he attempted to influence the Supreme Court by increasing the number of justices on it and when he attempted to punish some of the opposition leaders in Congress by opposing their renomination in local primaries, he was shocked by the degree of negative public reaction. His inner circle had simply lost touch with the post-1936 electorate.

President Nixon's downfall from the Watergate scandal has been attributed in part to the fact that he isolated himself in the White House and relied too heavily on a few close personal advisers. Consequently, it is argued, he was unaware first of the strength of his own position as he approached the 1972 reelection campaign and then to the extent to which his political position had deteriorated because of the scandal.

Selective Polling   When politicians lack confidence in their own intuition or that of their immediate associates, and especially when they distrust the reports they get from group advocates, they turn to rudimentary forms of polling. They may informally interview a few ordinary citizens from each of the major religious faiths or from different occupations in an effort to construct a meaningful distribution of opinions in a constituency. Many politicians have been successful with such impressionistic methods (although skeptics attribute their success to luck). Moreover, these politicians have used more systematic approaches as soon as they could afford to.

Newspapers have followed suit. Not too long ago, the top journalists on major newspapers, such as the *New York Times*, based many of their political articles on selective, impressionistic polling. But in recent years, their newspapers have, at great expense, become clients of Gallup, Roper, and other large scientific polling organizations. Some media organizations have even joined forces to produce their own polls. The *New York Times*/CBS News poll is one example.

Bellwether Districts   The bellwether originally was the lead sheep of a flock, on whose neck a bell was hung. The term now refers generally to something that is used as an indicator of where a group is heading. A ***bellwether district*** or town is assumed to be a good predictor of the attitudes of large segments of the national population. Maine was once an important bellwether state for forecasting national elections (and, therefore, for plotting national campaign strategies). The old saying "As Maine goes, so goes the nation" was based on two facts. First, the distribution of Maine's votes for presidential candidates was often like that of the national popular two-party votes. Second, for many years, the wintry state of Maine held its general election in September rather than November, which provided a meaningful opportunity for forecasting. (Because Maine now holds its election in November like the rest of the states, it is no longer a good bellwether.)

The use of bellwether districts has been brought to greater and greater levels of precision in the past two decades because of advances in methods used by television networks. The three major networks have developed elaborate computerized techniques to predict the outcomes of elections within minutes after the polls close. The networks' news staffs spend months prior to Election Day selecting important districts—especially districts on the East Coast, where the polls close an hour to three hours earlier than in the rest of the country, thereby giving the forecasters a head start. They enter into a large computer the voting history of the selected districts, along with information about the opinions and the economic and social characteristics of the residents. As the voting results flow in from these districts on election night, the computer quickly compares them with prior elections and with other districts in the country in order to make fairly precise predictions about the outcome of the current election.

The commercial and political interests that rely on bellwether-district methods closely guard the exact information they plug into the computer and the exact methods of weighing and comparing results in order to make their forecasts. It is nevertheless possible to evaluate the contributions this approach

bellwether district   A town or district that is a microcosm of the whole population or that has been found to be a good predictor of electoral outcomes.

makes to political knowledge. First, the bellwether method is useful when there is an election involving a limited number of candidates. Second, it tends to work well only when the analysis takes place close to the actual day of the election. Third, the lasting knowledge to be gained from it is limited. No matter how accurately the bellwether-district method forecasts elections, it is not particularly useful for stating what opinions people are holding, how consistently and with what intensity they hold opinions on various issues, why they hold these opinions, and how their opinions might be changing.

Surveys

The population in which pollsters are interested is usually quite large. To conduct their polls they choose a sample from the total population. The selection of this sample is important. Above all, it must be representative; the views of those in the sample must accurately and proportionately reflect the views of the whole. To a large extent, the validity of the poll's results depends on the sampling procedure used, several of which are described below.

Quota sampling is the method used by most commercial polls. In this approach, respondents are selected whose characteristics closely match those of the general population along several significant dimensions, such as geographic region, sex, age, and race.

Probability sampling is the most accurate polling technique. By definition, this method requires that every individual in the population must have a known (usually equal) probability of being chosen as a respondent so that the researcher can give equal weight to all segments of society. A requirement, then, is a complete list of the population or a breakdown of the total population by cities and counties. The simplest methods of obtaining a probability sample are *systematic sampling*, choosing every ninth name from a list, for instance, and *random sampling*, drawing from a container whose contents have been thoroughly mixed. This latter method, of course, can be simulated by computer-generated random numbers. Both quota sampling and probability sampling are best suited for polls of small populations.

For polls of large cities, states, or the whole nation, the method usually employed when a high level of accuracy is desired is *area sampling.* This technique breaks the population down into small, homogeneous units, such as counties. Several of these units are then randomly selected to serve as the sample. These units are, in turn, broken down into even smaller units. The process may extend even to individual dwellings on randomly selected blocks, for example. Area sampling is very costly and generally used only by academic survey researchers.

Some types of sampling do not yield representative samples and so have no scientific value. *Haphazard sampling,* for instance, is an unsystematic choice of respondents. A reporter who stands on a street corner and asks questions of convenient passersby is engaging in haphazard sampling. Systematically biased sampling occurs when an error in technique destroys the representative nature of the sample. A systematic error, for example, may cause a sample to include

quota sampling
A type of sampling of public opinion that is used by most commercial polls. Respondents are selected whose characteristics closely match those of the general population along several significant dimensions, such as geographic region, sex, age, and race.

probability sampling A method used by pollsters to select a sample in which every individual in the population has a known (usually equal) probability of being selected as a respondent so that the correct weight can be given to all segments of the population.

systematic sampling A method used in probability sampling to ensure that every individual in the population has a known probability of being chosen as a respondent—for example, by choosing every ninth name from a list.

random sampling Polls in which respondents are chosen mathematically, at random, with every effort made to avoid bias in the construction of the sample.

area sampling
A polling technique used for large cities, states, or the whole nation, when a high level of accuracy is desired. The population is broken down into small, homogeneous units, such as counties; then several units are randomly selected to serve as the sample.

haphazard sampling A type of sampling of public opinion that is an unsystematic choice of respondents.

too many old people, too many college students, or too few minority group members.

Even with reliable sampling procedures, problems can occur. Validity can be adversely affected by poor question format, faulty ordering of questions, inappropriate vocabulary, ambiguity of questions, or questions with built-in biases. In some instances, bias may be intentional. Polls conducted on behalf of interest groups or political candidates are often designed to allow the sponsors of the poll to claim that they have the support of the American people.[39] Occasionally, respondents and pollsters may have very different conceptions of the meaning of the words used in a question. For example, an early Gallup poll that asked people if they owned any stock found that stock ownership in the Southwest was surprisingly high. It turned out that many of the respondents thought "stock" meant cows and horses rather than securities.[40] Often, apparently minor differences in the wording of a question can convey vastly different meanings to respondents and, thus, produce quite different response patterns. For example, for many years the University of Chicago's National Opinion Research Center has asked respondents whether they think the federal government is spending too much, too little, or about the right amount of money on "assistance for the poor." Answering the question posed this way, about two-thirds of all respondents seem to believe that the government is spending too little. However, the same survey also asks whether the government spends too much, too little, or about the right amount for "welfare." When the word "welfare" is substituted for "assistance for the poor," about half of all respondents indicate that too much is being spent by the government.[41]

In a similar vein, what seemed to be a minor difference in wording in two December 1998 *New York Times* survey questions on presidential impeachment produced vastly different results. The first question asked respondents, "If the full House votes to send impeachment articles to the Senate for a trial, then do you think it would be better for the country if Bill Clinton resigned from office, or not?" The second version of the question asked, "If the full House votes to impeach Bill Clinton, then do you think it would be better for the country if Bill Clinton resigned from office, or not?" Though the two questions seem almost identical, 43 percent of those responding to the first version said the president should resign, while 60 percent of those responding to the second version of the question said Clinton should resign.[42]

In recent years, a new form of bias has been introduced into surveys by the use of a technique called ***push polling.*** This technique involves asking a respondent a loaded question about a political candidate designed to elicit the response

push polling
Polling technique that is designed to shape the respondent's opinion. For example, "If you know that Candidate X was an adulterer, would you support his election?"

[39]August Gribbin, "Two Key Questions in Assessing Polls: 'How?' and 'Why?'" *Washington Times*, 19 October 1998, p. A10.

[40]Charles W. Roll and Albert H. Cantril, *Polls: Their Use and Misuse in Politics* (New York: Basic Books, 1972), p. 106.

[41]Michael Kagay and Janet Elder, "Numbers Are No Problem for Pollsters, Words Are," *New York Times*, 9 August 1992, p. E6.

[42]Richard Morin, "Choice Words," *Washington Post*, 10 January 1999, p. C1.

sought by the pollster and, simultaneously, to shape the respondent's perception of the candidate in question. For example, during the 1996 New Hampshire presidential primary, push pollsters employed by Lamar Alexander's rival campaign called thousands of voters to ask, "If you knew that Lamar Alexander had raised taxes six times in Tennessee, would you be less inclined or more inclined to support him?"[43] More than one hundred consulting firms across the nation now specialize in push polling.[44] Calling push polling the "political equivalent of a drive-by shooting," Representative Joe Barton (R-Tex.) launched a congressional investigation into the practice.[45] Push polls may be one reason that Americans are becoming increasingly skeptical about the practice of polling and increasingly unwilling to answer pollsters' questions.[46]

Sample Size   The degree of precision in polling is a function of sample size, not population size. In American political settings, the typical size of a sample is from 450 to 1,500 respondents. This number, however, reflects a trade-off between cost and degree of precision desired. The degree of accuracy that can be achieved with a small sample can be seen from the polls' success in predicting election outcomes.

Table 9.4 shows how accurate two of the major national polling organizations have been in predicting the outcomes of presidential elections. In only two instances between 1952 and 2000 did the final October poll of a major pollster predict the wrong outcome, and in both instances—Harris in 1968 and Gallup in 1976—the actual election was extremely close and the prediction was off by no more than two percentage points. In 2000, Gallup predicted a Bush victory, and so was technically correct, but Gore received more votes. Even in 1948, when the pollsters were deeply embarrassed by their almost uniform prediction of a Dewey victory over Truman, they were not off by much. For example, Gallup predicted 44.5 percent for Truman, who actually received 49.6 percent. Although Gallup's failure to predict the winner was embarrassing, its actual percentage error would not be considered large by most statisticians.

Since 1948, Gallup has averaged a difference of less than 1 percent between what it predicts and the actual election outcome—and all its predictions have been made on the basis of random samples of not more than 2,500 respondents. In light of a national voting population of more than 100 million, these estimates are impressive.

This ability to predict elections by projecting estimates from small samples to enormous populations validates the methods used in sample survey studies of public opinion: the principles of random sampling, the methods of interviewing,

[43]Donn Tibbetts, "Draft Bill Requires Notice of Push Polling," *Manchester Union Leader,* 3 October 1996, p. A6.

[44]"Dial S for Smear," *Memphis Commercial Appeal,* 22 September 1996, p. 6B.

[45]Amy Keller, "Subcommittee Launches Investigation of Push Polls," *Roll Call,* 3 October 1996, p. 1.

[46]For a discussion of the growing difficulty of persuading people to respond to surveys, see John Brehm, *Phantom Respondents: Opinion Surveys and Political Representation* (Ann Arbor: University of Michigan Press, 1993).

TABLE 9.4

Two Pollsters and Their Records (1948–2000)

		HARRIS	GALLUP	ACTUAL OUTCOME
2000	Bush	47%	48%	48%
	Gore	47	46	49
	Nader	5	4	3
1996	Clinton	51%	52%	49%
	Dole	39	41	41
	Perot	9	7	8
1992	Clinton	44%	44%	43%
	Bush	38	37	38
	Perot	17	14	19
1988	Bush	51%	53%	54%
	Dukakis	47	42	46
1984	Reagan	56%	59%	59%
	Mondale	44	41	41
1980	Reagan	48%	47%	51%
	Carter	43	44	41
	Anderson		8	
1976	Carter	48%	48%	51%
	Ford	45	49	48
1972	Nixon	59%	62%	61%
	McGovern	35	38	38
1968	Nixon	40%	43%	43%
	Humphrey	43	42	43
	G. Wallace	13	15	14
1964	Johnson	62%	64%	61%
	Goldwater	33	36	39
1960	Kennedy	49%	51%	50%
	Nixon	41	49	49
1956	Eisenhower	NA	60%	58%
	Stevenson		41	42
1952	Eisenhower	47%	51%	55%
	Stevenson	42	49	44
1948	Truman	NA	44.5%	49.6%
	Dewey		49.5	45.1

All figures except those for 1948 are rounded. NA = Not asked.

SOURCES: Data from the Gallup Poll and the Harris Survey (New York: Chicago Tribune-New York News Syndicate, various press releases, 1964–2000). Courtesy of the Gallup Organization and Louis Harris Associates.

and the statistical tests and computer programming used in data analysis. It also validates the model of behavior by which social scientists attempt to predict voting behavior on the basis of respondents' characteristics rather than on the basis of only their stated intentions. This model of behavior is built on the respondent's voting intention and includes data on (1) the influence of the respondent's place in the social structure, (2) the influence of habit and previous party loyalty, (3) the influence of particular issues for each election, (4) the direction and strength of the respondent's general ideology, and (5) the respondent's occupational and educational background, income level, and so on. Each of these characteristics is treated as a variable in an equation leading to a choice among the major candidates in the election. The influence of the variables, or correlates, is far greater than most respondents realize.

Polling Errors   The polls are accurate but not infallible. Some analysts believe that poll errors are a subtle form of "liberal bias." Since voters often feel that the media have a liberal and Democratic slant, individuals who support the Republicans are slightly more reluctant to confess their true preferences to interviewers. Indications of this phenomenon have appeared in a number of Western democracies whose major media are deemed to be liberal in their political orientation.[47]

In 1998, Jesse Ventura's victory in the Minnesota gubernatorial election totally confounded the pollsters and revealed another weakness of pre-election polling. A poll conducted by the *Minneapolis Star Tribune* just six weeks before the election showed Ventura running a distant third to Democratic candidate Hubert Humphrey III, who seemed to have the support of 49 percent of the electorate, and the Republican Norm Coleman, whose support stood at 29 percent. Only 10 percent of those polled said they were planning to vote for Ventura. On Election Day, of course, Ventura outpolled both Humphrey and Coleman. Analysis of exit-poll data showed why the pre-election polls had been so wrong. In an effort to be more accurate, pre-election pollsters' predictions often take account of the likelihood that respondents will actually vote. This is accomplished by polling only people who have voted in the past or correcting for past frequency of voting. The *Star Tribune* poll was conducted only among individuals who had voted in the previous election. Ventura, however, brought to the polls not only individuals who had not voted in the last election but many people who had never voted before in their lives. Twelve percent of Minnesota's voters in 1998 said they came to the polls only because Ventura was on the ballot. This surge in turnout was facilitated by the fact that Minnesota permits same-day voter registration. Thus, the pollsters were wrong because Ventura changed the composition of the electorate.[48]

[47]Michael Barone, "Why Opinion Polls Are Worth Less," *U.S. News & World Report*, 9 December 1996, p. 52.

[48]Carl Cannon, "A Pox on Both Our Parties," in David T. Canon, Anne Khademian, and Kenneth R. Mayer, eds., *The Enduring Debate: Classic and Contemporary Readings in American Politics*, 2nd ed. (New York: W. W. Norton, 2000), p. 389.

In 2000, network exit polls also led to a major error on election night. After Florida polls closed, television networks declared Gore the winner in Florida on the basis of exit-poll results. Two hours later, the networks revised their estimates on the basis of actual vote counts and declared Florida too close to call. Furious Republicans asserted that the pollsters' errors might have persuaded GOP supporters that the race was hopeless and discouraged voting on the part of Republicans in western states where polls were still open. At 2 A.M., the networks proclaimed Bush the winner in Florida and, as a result, of the national election. Within one hour, however, they withdrew their projections and announced it was again too close to call. Ultimately, of course, the Florida results were not known until after a lengthy statewide recount and litigation by both presidential hopefuls.

Limits to Assessing Public Opinion with Polls

bandwagon effect A situation wherein reports of voter or delegate opinion can influence the actual outcome of an election or a nominating convention.

The survey, or polling, approach to public opinion has certain inherent problems. The most noted but least serious is the ***bandwagon effect,*** which occurs when polling results influence people to support the candidate marked as the probable victor. Some scholars argue that this bandwagon effect can be offset by an "underdog effect" in favor of the candidate trailing in the polls.[49]

Other problems with polling are more substantial. One, of course, is human error—bad decisions based on poor interpretations of the data. That in itself is a problem of the users of the polls, not of polling itself. But the two most serious problems inherent in polling are the source of most of the human error. They are the illusion of central tendency and the illusion of saliency.

illusion of central tendency The assumption that opinions are "normally distributed"— that responses to opinion questions are heavily distributed toward the center, as in a bell-shaped curve.

The Illusion of Central Tendency   The assumption that attitudes tend toward the average or center is known as the ***illusion of central tendency.*** In any large statistical population, measurements tend to be distributed most heavily toward the middle, or average. Weights, heights, even aptitudes, tend so strongly toward the average that their graphic representation bulges high in the middle and low at each extreme, in the form of a bell-shaped curve. So many characteristics are distributed in the bell shape that it is called a "normal distribution." But are opinions normally distributed also? Some can be. Figure 9.3 shows the distribution for a hypothetical sample of individuals responding to the proposition that business in the United States has too much political influence. Respondents could agree or disagree, could strongly agree or strongly disagree, or could take a moderate to neutral position. The results shown by the figure indicate a bell-shaped curve.

But not all opinions in the United States are normally distributed. On at least a few issues, opinions are likely to be distributed bimodally, as shown in Figure 9.4. On a bimodal distribution of an issue, the population can be said to be po-

---

[49]See Michael Traugott, in "The Impact of Media Polls on the Public," in *Media Polls in American Politics,* ed. Thomas E. Mann and Gary R. Orren (Washington, D.C.: Brookings Institution, 1992), pp. 125–49.

FIGURE 9.3

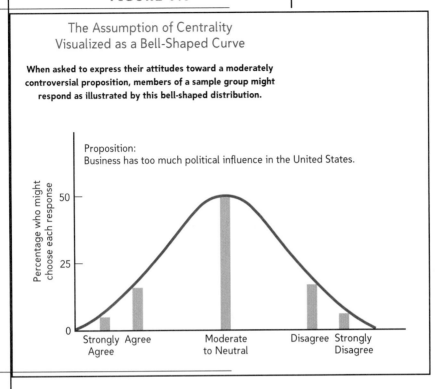

The Assumption of Centrality
Visualized as a Bell-Shaped Curve

When asked to express their attitudes toward a moderately controversial proposition, members of a sample group might respond as illustrated by this bell-shaped distribution.

Proposition:
Business has too much political influence in the United States.

Percentage who might
choose each response

50

25

0

Strongly   Agree   Moderate   Disagree   Strongly
Agree   to Neutral   Disagree

larized. For example, opinions about the right of women to have an abortion are highly polarized. Very few people are neutral; most are either strongly for or strongly against it.

Despite the variation in the actual distribution of opinions, politicians often assume that opinions are distributed more toward neutral and moderate than toward the extremes; and their assumption of (and wish for) a moderate electorate is reinforced by polling. A good poll can counteract this illusion. And, of course, people who come to the wrong conclusions on their own are not the responsibility of the pollsters. But the illusion of central tendency can be produced unintentionally by polls themselves. Respondents are usually required to express opinions in terms of five or six prescribed responses on a questionnaire. But this leaves out many of the issues' complexities. For example, during virtually the entire period of the Watergate affair between 1973 and 1974, the Gallup poll reported that most Americans were opposed when asked, "Should President

FIGURE 9.4

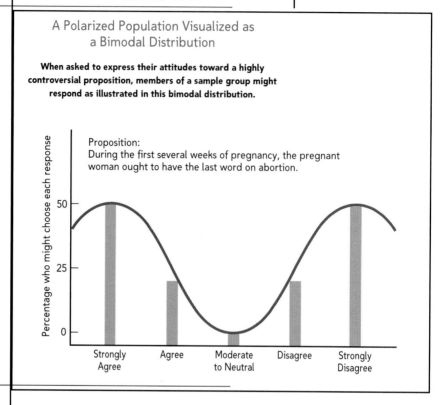

A Polarized Population Visualized as
a Bimodal Distribution

When asked to express their attitudes toward a highly
controversial proposition, members of a sample group might
respond as illustrated in this bimodal distribution.

Proposition:
During the first several weeks of pregnancy, the pregnant
woman ought to have the last word on abortion.

Percentage who might choose each response

50

25

0

Strongly Agree · Agree · Moderate to Neutral · Disagree · Strongly Disagree

Richard Nixon be impeached and compelled to leave the Presidency?" These
findings strengthened the Nixon administration's view that the public supported
the president. However, in mid-1974, the Gallup organization changed the
wording of the question to ask if respondents "think there is enough evidence of
possible wrongdoing in the case of President Nixon to bring him to trial before
the Senate, or not?" With this new wording, as many as two-thirds of those surveyed answered that they favored impeachment. Apparently, most Americans favored impeaching Nixon, as defined by the second question. However, they did
not want to convict him without a trial, as implied by the original question.
Thus, what had been seen by some as Americans' failure to respond to the serious charges made against the president may have actually indicated that respon-

dents' understanding of the impeachment process was more sophisticated than that of the pollsters.[50]

In a similar vein, how does the intelligent person respond to such questions as "Do you think a person has a right to end his or her life?" The more a respondent knows about a given issue, the more subtleties and considerations have to be suppressed in order to report a position to the interviewer. Thus, many moderate and neutral responses are actually the result of a balance among extreme but conflicting views within the individual, called ***ambivalence***.[51] Similarly, the respondent who may have a countervailing concern may end up choosing a moderate "it all depends" response to the question, thus indicating uncertainty. Yet, the moderate attitude is a product of alternatives provided by the interviewer or questionnaire, not a weighing of real opinions.

ambivalence
Public opinion trait in which an individual holds conflicting attitudes about an issue.

Inasmuch as central tendency suggests moderation, and moderation around the center gives the appearance of consensus, then clearly the consensus reported in opinion polls is often artificial. This does not mean that the data or the findings are false. Nor does it mean that they have been deliberately distorted by the pollsters. Rather, an artificial consensus is the result of mixing different opinions through the mechanical limits of questionnaires and multiple-choice responses.

The Illusion of Saliency Salient interests are interests that stand out beyond others, that are of more than ordinary concern to respondents in a survey or to voters in the electorate. Politicians, social scientists, journalists, or pollsters who assume something is important to the public when in fact it is not are creating an ***illusion of saliency.*** This illusion can be created and fostered by polls despite careful controls over sampling, interviewing, and data analysis. In fact, the illusion is strengthened by the credibility that science gives survey results.

illusion of saliency Impression conveyed by polls that something is important to the public when actually it is not.

Thus, if a survey includes questions on twenty subjects—because the pollsters or their clients feel they might be important issues—that survey can actually produce twenty salient issues. Although the responses may be sincere, the cumulative impression is artificial since a high proportion of the respondents may not have concerned themselves with many of the issues until actually confronted with questions by an interviewer. For example, usually not more than 10 percent (rarely more than 20 percent) of the respondents will report that they have no attitude on an issue. Yet, equally seldom will more than 30 percent of a sample spontaneously cite one or more issues as the main reason for their choices. It is nearly impossible to discover how many respondents feel obliged to respond to questions for which they never had any particular concern before the interview.

In a similar vein, an issue may become salient to the public *because* it is receiving a great deal of attention from political leaders and the mass media rather than because of a groundswell of public interest in the issue. For example, the

---

[50]Kagay and Elder, "Numbers Are No Problem."
[51]Alvarez and Brehm, *Hard Choices, Easy Answers.*

issue of health care was frequently cited by poll respondents as one of their major concerns *after* it was introduced by President Clinton in 1993 and after it had been given a great deal of media coverage. Prior to the president's September 1993 speech to the nation on health-care reform, the issue was seldom, if ever, mentioned by members of the public asked to cite what they believed to be important issues. In this instance, as in many others, an issue became salient to the public only after it was introduced by a significant political figure. As the famous Austrian-American economist Joseph Schumpeter once observed, public opinion is usually the product rather than the motivator of the political process. In other words, the public's concerns are often shaped by powerful political forces, rather than the other way around.

Similarly, when asked in the early days of a political campaign which candidates they do, or do not, support, the answers voters give often have little significance because the choice is not yet salient to them. Their preference may change many times before the actual election. This is part of the explanation for the phenomenon of the post-convention "bounce" in the popularity of presidential candidates, which was observed after the 1996 and 2000 Democratic and Republican national conventions. In general, presidential candidates can expect about a five-percentage-point bounce in their poll standings immediately after a national convention, although the effects of the bounce tend to disappear rapidly. In 2000, Bush "bounced" to a solid lead over Gore following the Republican convention, only to see Gore bounce back in front after the Democrats completed their own well-publicized conclave.

The problem of saliency has become especially acute as a result of the proliferation of media polls. The television networks and major national newspapers all make heavy use of opinion polls. Increasingly, polls are being commissioned by local television stations and local and regional newspapers as well.[52] On the positive side, polls allow journalists to make independent assessments of political realities—assessments not influenced by the partisan claims of politicians.

At the same time, however, media polls can allow journalists to make news when none really exists. Polling diminishes journalists' dependence upon news makers. A poll commissioned by a news agency can provide the basis for a good story even when the candidates, politicians, and other news makers refuse to cooperate by engaging in newsworthy activities. Thus, on days when little or nothing is actually taking place in a political campaign, poll results, especially apparent changes in candidate margins, can provide exciting news for voters.

Interestingly, because rapid and dramatic shifts in candidate margins tend to take place when voters' preferences are least fully formed, horse-race news is most likely to make the headlines when it is actually least significant.[53] In other words, media interest in poll results is inversely related to the actual salience of voters' opinions and the significance of the polls' findings.

[52]See Mann and Orren, eds., *Media Polls in American Politics.*
[53]For an excellent and reflective discussion by a journalist, see Richard Morin, "Clinton Slide in Survey Shows Perils of Polling," *Washington Post*, 29 August 1992, p. A6.

However, by influencing perceptions, especially those of major contributors, media polls can influence political realities. A candidate who demonstrates a lead in the polls usually finds it considerably easier to raise campaign funds than a candidate whose poll standing is poor. With additional funds, poll leaders can often afford to pay for television time and other campaign activities that will cement their advantage. For example, Bill Clinton's substantial lead in the polls during much of the summer of 1992 helped the Democrats raise far more money than in any previous campaign, primarily from interests hoping to buy access to a future President Clinton. For once, the Democrats were able to outspend the usually better-heeled Republicans. Thus, the appearance of a lead, according to the polls, helped make Clinton's lead a reality. Much the same effect was seen in 1996, when Clinton's lead in the polls caused many Republicans to write off the contest as hopeless weeks before the election.

The two illusions engendered by polling often put politicians on the horns of a dilemma in which they must choose between a politics of no issues (due to the illusion of central tendency) and a politics of too many trivial issues (due to the illusion of saliency). This has to be at least part of the explanation for why many members of Congress can praise themselves at the end of the year for the hundreds of things they worked on during the past session while not perceiving that they have neglected the one or two overriding issues of the day. Similarly, politicians preparing for major state or national campaigns compose position papers on virtually every conceivable issue—either because they will not make a judgment as to which are the truly salient issues or because they feel that stressing all issues is a way of avoiding a choice among the truly salient ones.

Public Opinion, Political Knowledge, and the Importance of Ignorance

Many people are distressed to find public opinion polls not only unable to discover public opinion, but unable to avoid producing unintentional distortions of their own. No matter how hard pollsters try, no matter how mature the science of opinion polling becomes, politicians forever may remain largely ignorant of public opinion.

Although knowledge is good for its own sake, and knowledge of public opinion may sometimes produce better government, ignorance also has its uses. It can, for example, operate as a restraint on the use of power. Leaders who think they know what the public wants are often autocratic rulers. Leaders who realize that they are always partially in the dark about the public are likely to be more modest in their claims, less intense in their demands, and more uncertain in their uses of power. Their uncertainty may make them more accountable to their constituencies because they will be more likely to continue searching for consent.

One of the most valuable benefits of survey research is actually "negative knowledge"—knowledge that pierces through irresponsible claims about the breadth of opinion or the solidarity of group or mass support. Because this sort of knowledge reveals the complexity and uncertainty of public opinion, it can help make citizens less gullible, group leaders less strident, and politicians less deceitful. This alone gives public opinion research, despite its great limitations, an important place in the future of American politics.[54]

HOW DOES PUBLIC OPINION INFLUENCE GOVERNMENT POLICY?

One of the fundamental notions on which the U.S. government was founded is that "the public" should not be trusted when it comes to governing. The framers designed institutions that, although democratic, somewhat insulated government decision making from popular pressure. For example, the indirect elections of senators and presidents were supposed to prevent the government from being too dependent on the vagaries of public opinion.

Research from the 1950s and 1960s indicates that the framers' concerns were well founded. Individual-level survey analysis reveals that the respondents lacked fundamental political knowledge and had ill-formed opinions about government and public policy.[55] Their answers seemed nothing more than "doorstep opinions"—opinions given off the top of their heads. When an individual was asked the same questions at different times, he or she often gave different answers. The dramatic and unpredictable changes seemed to imply that the public was indeed unreliable as a guide for political decisions.

Benjamin I. Page and Robert Y. Shapiro take issue with the notion that the public should not be trusted when it comes to policy making.[56] They contend that public opinion at the aggregate level is coherent and stable, and that it moves in a predictable fashion in response to changing political, economic, and social circumstances.

How is this possible, given what previous studies have found? Page and Shapiro hypothesize that the individual-level responses are plagued with various types of errors that make the people's opinions seem incoherent and unstable. However, when a large number of individual-level responses to survey questions are added up to produce an aggregate public opinion, the errors or "noise" in the individual responses, if more or less random, will cancel each other out, revealing a collective opinion that is stable, coherent, and meaningful. From their results, Page and Shapiro conclude that the general public can indeed be trusted when it comes to governing. But how closely should elected officials follow public opinion?

[54]For a fuller discussion of the uses of polling and the role of public opinion in American politics, see Benjamin Ginsberg, *The Captive Public: How Mass Opinion Promotes State Power* (New York: Basic Books, 1986).

[55]Campbell, Converse, Miller, and Stokes, *The American Voter*; Philip E. Converse, "The Nature of Belief Systems in Mass Publics," in *Ideology and Discontent*, ed. David E. Apter (New York: Free Press, 1964).

[56]Benjamin I. Page and Robert Y. Shapiro, *The Rational Public: Fifty Years of Trends in Americans' Policy Preferences* (Chicago: University of Chicago Press, 1992).

In democratic nations, leaders should pay heed to public opinion, and most evidence suggests that they do. There are many instances in which public policy and public opinion do not coincide, but in general the government's actions are consistent with citizens' preferences. One study, for example, found that between 1935 and 1979, in about two-thirds of all cases, significant changes in public opinion were followed within one year by changes in government policy consistent with the shift in the popular mood.[57] Other studies have come to similar conclusions about public opinion and government policy at the state level.[58] Do these results imply that elected leaders merely pander to public opinion? The answer is no.

A recent study on the role that public opinion played during the failed attempt to enact health-care reform during 1993–1994 found that public opinion polls had very little influence on individual members of Congress, who used these polls first to justify positions they had already adopted and then to shape public thinking on the issue. However, the study also found that congressional party leaders designed their health-care legislation strategies based on their concerns about the effects of public opinion on the electoral fortunes of individual members. Leaders' concerns about public opinion thus help explain why the congressional policy-making process follows public opinion, even though individual members of Congress do not.[59]

In addition, there are always areas of disagreement between opinion and policy. For example, the majority of Americans favored stricter governmental control of handguns for years before Congress finally adopted the modest restrictions on firearms purchases embodied in the 1994 Brady bill and the Omnibus Crime Control Act. Similarly, most Americans—blacks as well as whites—oppose school busing to achieve racial balance, yet such busing continues to be used in many parts of the nation. Most Americans are far less concerned with the rights of the accused than the federal courts seem to be. Most Americans oppose U.S. military intervention in other nations' affairs, yet such interventions continue to take place and often win public approval after the fact.

Several factors can contribute to a lack of consistency between opinion and governmental policy. First, the nominal majority on a particular issue may not be as intensely committed to its preference as the adherents of the minority viewpoint. An intensely committed minority may often be more willing to commit its time, energy, efforts, and resources to the affirmation of its opinions than an apathetic, even if large, majority. In the case of firearms, for example, although the proponents of gun control are by a wide margin in the majority, most do not regard the issue as one of critical importance to themselves and are not willing to commit much effort to advancing their cause. The opponents of gun control, by

---

[57]Benjamin I. Page and Robert Y. Shapiro, "Effects of Public Opinion on Policy," *American Political Science Review* 77 (March 1983): 175–90.

[58]Robert S. Erikson, Gerald C. Wright, and John P. McIver, *Statehouse Democracy: Public Opinion and Policy in the American States* (New York: Cambridge University Press, 1993).

[59]Lawrence R. Jacobs, Eric D. Lawrence, Robert Y. Shapiro, and Steven S. Smith, "Congressional Leadership of Public Opinion," *Political Science Quarterly* 113 (1998): 21–41.

Institution Principle

Policy and opinion are not always consistent because policy is the product of institutional processes and public opinion is but one of many influences on these.

contrast, are intensely committed, well organized, and well financed, and as a result are usually able to carry the day.

A second important reason that public policy and public opinion may not coincide has to do with the character and structure of the American system of government. The framers of the American Constitution, as we saw in Chapter 2, sought to create a system of government that was based upon popular consent but that did not invariably and automatically translate shifting popular sentiments into public policies. As a result, the American governmental process includes arrangements such as an appointed judiciary that can produce policy decisions that may run contrary to prevailing popular sentiment—at least for a time.

Perhaps the inconsistencies between opinion and policy could be resolved if we made broader use of a mechanism currently employed by a number of states—the ballot initiative. This procedure allows propositions to be placed on the ballot and voted into law by the electorate, bypassing most of the normal machinery of representative government. In recent years, several important propositions sponsored by business and conservative groups have been enacted.[60] For example, California's Proposition 209, approved by the state's voters in 1996, prohibited the state and local government agencies in California from using race or gender preferences in hiring, contracting, or university admissions decisions. Responding to conservatives' success, liberal groups launched a number of ballot initiatives in 2000. For example, in Washington State, voters were asked to consider propositions sponsored by teachers unions that would have required annual cost-of-living raises for teachers and more than $1.8 billion in additional state spending over the next six years.[61]

Initiatives such as these seem to provide the public with an opportunity to express its will. The major problem, however, is that government by initiative offers little opportunity for reflection and compromise. Voters are presented with a proposition, usually sponsored by a special interest group, and are asked to take it or leave it. Perhaps the true will of the people, not to mention their best interest, might lie somewhere between the positions taken by various interest groups. Perhaps, for example, California voters might have wanted affirmative action programs to be modified, but not scrapped altogether as Proposition 209 mandated. In a representative assembly, as opposed to a referendum campaign, a compromise position might have been achieved that was more satisfactory to all the residents of the state. This is one reason the framers of the U.S. Constitution strongly favored representative government rather than direct democracy.[62]

[60]David S. Broder, *Democracy Derailed: Initiative Campaigns and the Power of Money* (New York: Harcourt, 2000).

[61]Robert Tomsho, "Liberals Take a Cue from Conservatives: This Election, the Left Tries to Make Policy with Ballot Initiatives," *Wall Street Journal*, 6 November 2000, p. A12.

[62]For the classic treatment of take-it-or-leave-it referendums and initiatives, see Thomas Romer and Howard Rosenthal, "Political Resource Allocation, Controlled Agendas, and the Status Quo," *Public Choice* 33 (1978): 27–44.

When all is said and done, however, there can be little doubt that in general the actions of the American government do not remain out of line with popular sentiment for very long. A major reason for this is, of course, the electoral process, to which we shall next turn. Lest we become too complacent, however, we should not forget that the close relationship between government and opinion in America may also partly be a result of the government's success in molding opinion.

SUMMARY

All governments claim to obey public opinion, and in the democracies politicians and political leaders actually try to do so.

The American government does not directly regulate opinions and beliefs in the sense that dictatorial regimes often do. Opinion is regulated by an institution that the government constructed and that it maintains—the marketplace of ideas. In this marketplace, opinions and ideas compete for support. In general, opinions supported by upper-class groups have a better chance of succeeding than those views that are mainly advanced by the lower classes.

Americans share a number of values and viewpoints but often classify themselves as liberal or conservative in their basic orientations. The meaning of these terms has changed greatly over the past century. Once liberalism meant opposition to big government. Today, liberals favor an expanded role for the government. Once conservatism meant support for state power and aristocratic rule. Today, conservatives oppose government regulation, at least of business affairs.

Although the United States relies mainly on market mechanisms to regulate opinion, even our government intervenes to some extent, seeking to influence both particular opinions and, more important, the general climate of political opinion. Political leaders' increased distance from the public makes it difficult for them to gauge public opinion. Until recently, public opinion on some issues could be gauged better by studying mass behavior than by studying polls. Population characteristics are also useful in estimating public opinion on some subjects. Another approach is to go directly to the people. Two techniques are used: the impressionistic and the scientific. The impressionistic method relies on person-to-person communication, selective polling, or the use of bellwether districts. A person-to-person approach is quick, efficient, and inexpensive; but because it often depends on an immediate circle of associates, it can also limit awareness of new issues or unpleasant information. Selective polling usually involves interviewing a few people from different walks of life. Although risky, it has been used successfully to gauge public opinion. Bellwether districts are a popular means of predicting election outcomes. They are used by the media as well as by some candidates.

The scientific approach to learning public opinion is random sample polling. One advantage of random sample polling is that elections can be very accurately predicted; using a model of behavior, pollsters are often able to predict

Rationality Principle	**Collective Action Principle**	**Institution Principle**	**Policy Principle**
Individuals process new information and new experiences, updating their beliefs about the political world and adjusting their preferences about public policies, issues, and personalities.	Widely held political ideas are usually the products of orchestrated campaigns by government, organized groups, or the media.	Policy and opinion are not always consistent because policy is the product of institutional processes and public opinion is but one of many influences on these.	One reason why policy and opinion may not be consistent is that the United States is a representative government, not a direct democracy.
Ideologies serve as informational shortcuts, allowing individuals to arrive at a view on an issue or a candidate while economizing on the costs of becoming informed of the details.	Part of the "job description" of leaders of well-organized interest groups is to seek out issues around which they can mobilize group members. Organized interests are decidedly at an advantage in this respect, compared to latent, unorganized interests.		Government policies disproportionately reflect the goals and interests of those with higher levels of income and education because the individuals tend to have more knowledge of politics and are more willing to act on it.

how voters will mark their ballots better than the voters themselves can predict. A second advantage is that polls provide information on the bases and conditions of voting decisions. They make it possible to assess trends in attitudes and the influence of ideology on attitudes.

There are also problems with polling, however. An illusion of central tendency can encourage politicians not to confront issues. The illusion of saliency, on the other hand, can encourage politicians to confront too many trivial issues. Even with scientific polling, politicians cannot be certain that they understand public opinion. Their recognition of this limitation, however, may function as a valuable restraint.

FOR FURTHER READING

Erikson, Robert S., and Kent L. Tedin. *American Public Opinion: Its Origins, Content, and Impact.* 6th ed. New York: Longman, 2001.

Gallup, George, and Saul Forbes Rae. *The Pulse of Democracy: The Public-Opinion Poll and How It Works.* New York: Simon & Schuster, 1940.

Ginsberg, Benjamin. *The Captive Public: How Mass Opinion Promotes State Power.* New York: Basic Books, 1986.

Herbst, Susan. *Numbered Voices: How Opinion Polling Has Shaped American Politics.* Chicago: University of Chicago Press, 1993.

Key, V. O. *Public Opinion and American Democracy.* New York: Knopf, 1961.

Lippmann, Walter. *Public Opinion.* New York: Harcourt, Brace, 1922.

Mueller, John. *Policy and Opinion in the Gulf War.* Chicago: University of Chicago Press, 1994.

Neuman, W. Russell. *The Paradox of Mass Politics: Knowledge and Opinion in the American Electorate.* Cambridge, Mass.: Harvard University Press, 1986.

Page, Benjamin I., and Robert Y. Shapiro. *The Rational Public: Fifty Years of Trends in Americans' Policy Preferences.* Chicago: University of Chicago Press, 1992.

Roll, Charles W., and Albert H. Cantril. *Polls: Their Use and Misuse in Politics.* New York: Basic Books, 1972.

Stimson, James A. *Public Opinion in America: Moods, Cycles, and Swings.* 2nd ed. Boulder, Col.: Westview, 1998.

Sussman, Barry. *What Americans Really Think: And Why Our Politicians Pay No Attention.* New York: Pantheon, 1988.

Zaller, John R. *The Nature and Origins of Mass Opinion.* New York: Cambridge University Press, 1992.

Politics in the News—
Reading between the Lines

Did September 11 Change Americans' Political Opinions?

U.S. Attitudes Altered Little by Sept. 11, Pollsters Say

By ADAM CLYMER

Authorities on public opinion meeting here this weekend expressed doubt that the attacks of Sept. 11 had led to fundamental changes in American attitudes.

Even the nation's willingness to restrict civil liberties after Sept. 11 followed historical patterns, except for resistance to singling out American Muslims, which contrasted with attitudes toward Japanese-Americans in World War II and German-Americans in World War I.

As academic and news media pollsters discussed shifts in public opinion since Sept. 11 at the 57th annual meeting of the American Association for Public Opinion Research, they repeatedly reacted skeptically to the aphorism that "everything has changed."

Tom W. Smith of the National Opinion Research Center said, "Many things changed remarkably, but many things never changed." For example, Dr. Smith said, the crisis did not change attitudes toward capital punishment and gun control.

G. Donald Ferree Jr. of the University of Wisconsin said that while people spoke of religion being increasingly important to the nation after Sept. 11, their patterns of church attendance and reports of the relevance of religion to their own lives had not changed.

Kimberly Downing of the University of Cincinnati reported that after Sept. 11, people polled in the Cincinnati area were able to define what they meant by freedom more specifically. But, Dr. Downing said, only greater definition was overlaying "a relatively stable set of attitudes."

Robert J. Blendon of the Harvard School of Public Health said at one session that research over more than 50 years showed that "during periods of crisis, when security against serious foreign or domestic threats becomes more important, the public will support substantial limits on civil liberties."

"This includes limits on freedom of speech, the press, right to a fair trial and individual privacy, even as they affect

New York Times, 20 May 2002, p. A12.

average citizens," Dr. Blendon said. But support for such curbs is "cyclical" and declines after the threat recedes, he added.

In that context, he said, public support for the use of military tribunals or for eavesdropping on lawyers' conversations with clients was consistent with curbs on liberties the public supported in World War II and at the height of the cold war.

But the country had changed dramatically since then in terms of its attitude toward minorities, he said, and the support for putting Japanese-Americans in concentration camps found no parallel in attitudes toward Muslims today.

Chase Harrison of the University of Connecticut reported that polls showed the public was scarcely readier to restrict the freedom of Muslims than of other Americans. This was demonstrated, Mr. Harrison said, in a survey that identified the targets of possible restrictions, like being jailed without a warrant, as "Muslim or Arab" to half of those polled, but without any specific identification to the other half. The percentages supporting the restrictions were about the same in both groups, he said.

One group that has not supported new government powers is African-Americans.

. . . "Blacks were much more alarmed about the possible loss" of civil liberties than whites were, though none of the Bush administration proposals in the survey focused on them.

George Bishop of the University of Cincinnati argued that several reported changes in public opinion, including trust in government and approval of President Bush's handling of his job, were not changes in attitudes.

The higher numbers expressing trust in government, Dr. Bishop said, reflected only changes in the context in which those polled heard the question.

ESSENCE OF THE STORY

- Americans' trust in government rose substantially after September 11, 2001, leading some to speculate that these events marked a turnaround in a long-run decline in public attitudes.

- People tend to rally around the government in times of crisis, and such support wanes after a while. Public opinion after September 11 displayed this pattern.

- President Bush did remain more popular six months after the tragedy, and the public continued to show support for aggressive government actions meant to combat terrorism.

POLITICAL ANALYSIS

- Even a historic event like September 11 can recede rapidly in the public consciousness. Therefore, political actors try to take advantage of rapidly changing public opinion.

- The burst in public approval was reflected in rapid policy change in Washington D.C. in the year following the tragedy.

- "Approval" and "trust" are amorphous concepts and are not attached to specific policies or individuals. Shorn of a policy context, do we really know what "approval" means?

For Mr. Bush and "government in Washington," he contended, people were concentrated on how he and the government were dealing with terrorism. Contrary to the interpretations of some analysts, he said, there was no sudden affection for big government.

. . . Dr. Bishop said pollsters had an obligation not to make too much of answers to "the vague questions that have become our stock in trade" like "Do you approve or disapprove of the way George Bush is handling his job as president?" He said pollsters had an obligation to follow up and ask people "what they mean when they say they approve or disapprove."

CHAPTER

10

Elections

Over the past two centuries, elections have come to play a significant role in the political processes of most nations. The forms that elections take and the purposes they serve, however, vary greatly from nation to nation. The most important difference among national electoral systems is that some provide the opportunity for opposition while others do not. Democratic electoral systems, such as those that have evolved in the United States and western Europe, allow opposing forces to compete against and even to replace current officeholders. Authoritarian electoral systems, by contrast, do not allow the defeat of those in power. In the authoritarian context, elections are used primarily to mobilize popular enthusiasm for the government, to provide an outlet for popular discontent, and to persuade foreigners that the regime is legitimate—i.e., that it has the support of the people. In the former Soviet Union, for example, citizens were required to vote even though no opposition to Communist party candidates was allowed.

In democracies, elections can also serve as institutions of legitimation and as safety valves for social discontent. But beyond these functions, democratic elections facilitate popular influence, promote leadership accountability, and offer groups in society a measure of protection from the abuse of governmental power. Citizens exercise influence through elections by determining who should control the govern-

Rationality Principle

Elections allow multiple principals—citizens—to choose political agents to act on their behalf. But citizens usually have imperfect information about candidates and don't know how agents will act once in office.

ment. The chance to decide who will govern serves as an opportunity for ordinary citizens to make choices about the policies, programs, and directions of government action. In the United States, for example, recent Democratic and Republican candidates have differed significantly on issues of taxing, social spending, and governmental regulation. As American voters have chosen between the two parties' candidates, they have also made choices about these issues.

Nominally, of course, a democratic election is the collective selection of leaders and representatives. In terms now familiar to the reader, elections are occasions in which multiple *principals*—the citizens—choose political *agents* to act on their behalf. There are two kinds of problems that face even the most rational of citizen-principals in these circumstances. Electoral rules and arrangements may be characterized and ultimately assessed as mechanisms for coming to grips with these.

The first is known as the adverse selection problem. When choosing Candidate A over Candidate B, exactly what are we getting? To some degree, a candidate for office is a "pig in a poke." We may know some things about her and some other things about her opponent, but even in a world of investigative reporters, paparazzi, and Drudge reports on the Internet, we can't always know what we've selected. It may turn out badly, but then again it may not.[1] The

[1] A classic example of adverse selection is presidential selection of Supreme Court justices. Often a president finds that these men and women turn out much differently than expected. It is unlikely, for example, that President Eisenhower would have chosen Earl Warren, the former governor of California and 1948 Republican vice-presidential candidate, to be chief justice of the Supreme Court had he known of Warren's liberal leanings. Nor would he have appointed Justice William J. Brennan, who turned out to be among the most liberal justices on the Court in the twentieth century. President Nixon, to give another example, appointed Harry Blackmun to the Court, the justice who later crafted the famous pro-choice opinion Roe v. Wade. Finally, there was the near-fateful decision of the first President Bush in his elevation of Federal District Court Judge David Souter to the Supreme Court. Souter, in December 2000, joined the minority (only one vote short of a majority) that would have ordered the popular vote in Florida recounted—an action that might well have denied the second President Bush his presidency.

adverse selection
The problem of incomplete information—of choosing alternatives without knowing fully the details of available options.

reason for the possibility of ***adverse selection*** is incomplete information. The candidates themselves affect, in large measure, what we know about them, and it is often in their interest to hide or shroud in ambiguity items about themselves that, though possibly highly relevant to the choices of citizens, might harm their electoral prospects. The solution to this problem is openness and transparency— a wide-open and freewheeling electoral process, a well-heeled political opposition, and an activist press. The latter may at times be perceived as crossing the line between the public and the private—as many felt was the case in the intense scrutiny of former president Clinton's private life—but much better this than a press easily cowed and constrained, since the public depends on an independent press to counter the otherwise self-serving information that is offered up by the candidates themselves.

moral hazard
Not knowing all aspects of the actions taken by an agent (nominally on behalf of the principal but potentially at the principal's expense).

The second problem is known as ***moral hazard.*** If adverse selection is a problem caused by hidden *information*, then moral hazard is a problem produced by hidden *action*. It is the problem of agents who, once selected, cannot easily be monitored in their behavior. A political leader does many things that are public, such as making speeches, attaching their names as sponsors of legislation, and voting on legislative motions. But behind their public records are many private acts that are imperfectly observed at best. These veiled encounters used to take place in the proverbial "smoke-filled rooms" of Washington, but today they take place in the private dining rooms of Capitol Hill, where deals are struck between legislators and special interests, or in the "wink and nod" conversations between presidents and large donors (who may get to spend a night in the Lincoln bedroom of the White House or hitch a ride on *Air Force One*).[2] Political agents can also use their agenda power, their appointment power, and the bully pulpits that public office provides to advance these special interests. Moral hazard, the classic problem of delegation, makes principals vulnerable to abuses of the power just delegated to elected agents. As with the first problem, the solution to moral hazard is found in the way elections are conducted. If agents have strong incentives to want to renew their contracts—to be re-elected or to advance to a higher office—then they will take care not to abuse their delegated power, or at least not to take big risks that, if discovered, could damage their political reputations. Giving incumbents the incentive of possible re-election—indeed, tolerating small advantages that incumbency gives in electoral contests—will encourage them to moderate the inclination to strike private deals.

Thus, elections promote leadership accountability because the threat of defeat at the polls exerts pressure on those in power to conduct themselves in a responsible manner and to take account of popular interests and wishes when they make their decisions. As James Madison observed in *The Federalist Papers*, elected

---

[2]Before his death in an airplane crash, Clinton's secretary of commerce, Ron Brown, a former head of the Democratic National Committee, used the frequent occasions of foreign travel required of his cabinet post to bring along many a Democratic fat cat. Republican officeholders, of course, are no less vigilant in rewarding their fat-cat contributors.

leaders are "compelled to anticipate the moment when their power is to cease, when their exercise of it is to be reviewed, and when they must descend to the level from which they were raised, there forever to remain unless a faithful discharge of their trust shall have established their title to a renewal of it."[3] It is because of this need to anticipate that elected officials constantly monitor public opinion polls as they decide what positions to take on policy issues.

Finally, the right to vote, or *suffrage,* can serve as an important source of protection for groups in American society. The passage of the 1965 Voting Rights Act, for example, enfranchised millions of African Americans in the South, paving the way for the election of thousands of new black public officials at the local, state, and national levels and ensuring that white politicians could no longer ignore the views and needs of African Americans. The Voting Rights Act was one of the chief spurs for the elimination of many overt forms of racial discrimination as well as for the diminution of racist rhetoric in American public life.

suffrage The right to vote.

The 2000 election highlighted a number of problems surrounding our current electoral process. First, despite the expenditure of $3 billion by the candidates and claims by both major parties that they planned major efforts to bring voters to the polls, voter turnout continued to hover at the 50 percent level, as it has in recent decades. Second, the election demonstrated that the ballots used in many parts of the United States, especially those cast using the now-infamous Votomatic machines, were prone to error. Third, the election outcome, as determined by the electoral college, produced a president who won 500,000 fewer popular votes than his opponent. Fourth, a variety of special interests pumped record amounts of money into political campaigns, renewing concerns

PREVIEWING THE PRINCIPLES

Elections can be perceived as institutional opportunities for multiple principals—the citizenry—to select agents—their elected officials—to act on their behalf, even though citizens usually have imperfect information about candidates and don't know how their agents will act once in office. Like any institutional arrangement, the electoral process is subject to rules and regulations that affect outcomes. In addition to the composition of the electorate, the "rules of the game"—what it takes to win and the size and composition of electoral districts—as well as the means of limiting popular involvement in elections—like the electoral college—all play important roles in translating popular sentiment and votes into electoral outcomes. Voters decide, based on multiple criteria including partisan loyalty, issues, and candidate characteristics. When issues dominate a campaign, candidates tend to converge toward the median voter. Voter turnout in the United States is low because candidates and parties often fail to mobilize voters and institutional barriers to participation—such as registration requirements—are too high for many Americans. But on the whole, elections remain important because they socialize and institutionalize political participation to actions within the system.

---

[3]Clinton Rossiter, ed., *The Federalist Papers* (New York: New American Library, 1961), No. 57, p. 352.

that politicians are more accountable to wealthy donors than to mere voters. During the course of this chapter, we will examine these problems and possible solutions.

In this chapter, we will look first at the formal structure and setting of American elections. Second, we will see how—and what—voters decide when they take part in elections. Third, we will focus on recent national elections, including the 2000 presidential race. Fourth, we will discuss the role of money in the election process, particularly in recent elections. Finally, we will assess the place of elections in the American political process, raising the important question, "Do elections matter?"

HOW DOES GOVERNMENT REGULATE THE ELECTORAL PROCESS?

Collective Action Principle

Elections are a mechanism to channel and limit political participation to actions within the system.

In earlier chapters (see Chapter 1) we suggested that the relationship between citizens and elected politicians is an instance of a principal-agent relationship. There are two basic approaches to this relationship—the consent approach and the agency approach. The consent approach and the agency approach are the flip sides of the same conceptual coin, but they place the emphasis differently, and it is worth spelling these differences out. The consent approach emphasizes the historical reality that the right of the citizen to participate in his or her own governance, mainly through the act of voting or other forms of consent, arises from an existing governmental order aimed at making it *easier* for the governors to govern by legitimizing their rule. The governors here are the active ones, and their nominal principals are seen mainly as nuisances that require soothing from time to time. The agency approach, on the other hand, treats *principals* as the active elements in the constitutional order. This approach takes the division and specialization of labor evident in everyday life as a metaphor for political relationships. The typical citizen would much rather devote scarce time and effort to his or her own private affairs instead of spending that time and effort on governance. Therefore, he or she chooses to delegate governance to agents—politicians—controlled through election. Here, the control of agents rather than the soothing of principals is emphasized. Although the emphases differ in these two approaches, they complement each other since, at the end of the day, citizen-principals do control the fate of their political leaders, and politician-agents do try to get away with whatever they can while satisfying their overseers at contract-renewal time.

Institution Principle

The electoral process is governed by a variety of rules and procedures that allow those in power an opportunity to regulate the character and consequences of political participation.

Elections allow citizens to participate in political life on a routine and peaceful basis. Indeed, American voters have the opportunity to select and, if they so desire, depose some of their most important leaders. In this way, Americans have a chance to intervene in and to influence the government's programs and policies. Yet it is important to recall that elections are not spontaneous affairs. Instead, they are formal government institutions. While elections allow citizens a chance to participate in politics, they also allow the government a chance to exert a good deal of control over when, where, how, and which of its citizens will participate. Electoral processes are governed by a variety of rules and procedures that allow those in power a significant opportunity to regulate the character— and perhaps also the consequences—of mass political participation.

Thus, elections provide governments with an excellent opportunity to regulate and control popular involvement. Three general forms of regulation have played especially important roles in the electoral history of the Western democracies. First, governments often attempt to regulate the composition of the electorate in order to diminish the electoral weight of groups they deem to be undesirable. Second, governments frequently seek to manipulate the translation of voters' choices into electoral outcomes. Third, virtually all governments attempt to insulate policy-making processes from electoral intervention through regulation of the relationship between electoral decisions and the composition or organization of the government.

Electoral Composition

Perhaps the oldest and most obvious device used to regulate voting and its consequences is manipulation of the electorate's composition. In the earliest elections in western Europe, for example, the suffrage was generally limited to property owners and others who could be trusted to vote in a manner acceptable to those in power. To cite just one illustration, property qualifications in France prior to 1848 limited the electorate to 240,000 of some 7 million men over the age of twenty-one.[4] Of course, no women were permitted to vote. During the same era, other nations manipulated the electorate's composition by assigning unequal electoral weights to different classes of voters. The 1831 Belgian constitution, for example, assigned individuals anywhere from one to three votes depending upon their property holdings, education, and position.[5] But even in the context of America's ostensibly universal and equal suffrage in the twentieth century, the composition of the electorate is still subject to manipulation. Until recent years, some states manipulated the vote by the discriminatory use of poll taxes and literacy tests or by such practices as the placement of polls and the scheduling of voting hours to depress participation by one or another group. Today the most important example of the regulation of the American electorate's composition is our unique personal registration requirements.

Levels of voter participation in twentieth-century American elections are quite low by comparison to those of the other Western democracies (see Figure 10.1).[6] Indeed, voter participation in presidential elections in the United States

[4]Stein Rokkan, *Citizens, Elections, Parties: Approaches to the Comparative Study of the Processes of Development* (New York: David McKay, 1970), p. 149.
[5]John A. Hawgood, *Modern Constitutions since 1787* (New York: Van Nostrand, 1939), p. 148.
[6]See Walter Dean Burnham, "The Changing Shape of the American Political Universe," *American Political Science Review* 59 (1965): 7–28.

FIGURE 10.1

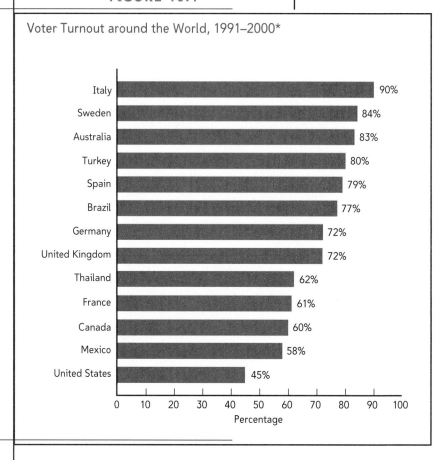

Voter Turnout around the World, 1991–2000*

*NOTE: Average during the 1990s.

SOURCE: Center for Voting Democracy, www.fairvote.org/turnout.

has barely averaged 50 percent recently (see Figure 10.2). Turnout in the 2000 presidential election was 51 percent. During the nineteenth century, by contrast, voter turnout in the United States was extremely high. Records, in fact, indicate that in some counties as many as 105 percent of those eligible voted in presidential elections. Some proportion of this total obviously was artificial—a result of the widespread corruption that characterized American voting practices during that period. Nevertheless, it seems clear that the proportion of eligible voters actually going to the polls was considerably larger in nineteenth-century America than it is today.

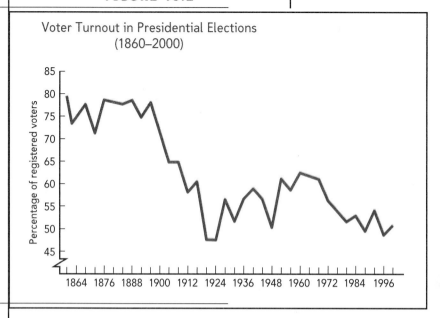

FIGURE 10.2

Voter Turnout in Presidential Elections
(1860–2000)

Percentage of registered voters

85
80
75
70
65
60
55
50
45

1864 1876 1888 1900 1912 1924 1936 1948 1960 1972 1984 1996

SOURCES: For 1860–1928, U.S. Bureau of the Census, *Historical Statistics of the United States, Colonial Times to 1970*, Pt. 2, p. 1071. For 1932–1992, U.S. Bureau of the Census, *Statistical Abstract of the United States, 1993* (Washington, D.C.: Government Printing Office, 1993), p. 284. For 1996 and 2000, author's update.

As Figure 10.2 indicates, the critical years during which voter turnout declined across the United States were between 1890 and 1910. These years coincide with the adoption of laws across much of the nation requiring eligible citizens to appear personally at a registrar's office to register to vote some time prior to the actual date of an election. Personal registration was one of several "Progressive" reforms of political practices initiated at the turn of the century. The ostensible purpose of registration was to discourage fraud and corruption. But to many Progressive reformers, "corruption" was a code word, referring to the type of politics practiced in the large cities, where political parties had organized immigrant and ethnic populations. Reformers not only objected to the corruption that surely was a facet of party politics in this period, but they also opposed the growing political power of urban populations and their leaders.

Personal registration imposed a new burden upon potential voters and altered the format of American elections. Under the registration systems adopted after 1890, it became the duty of individual voters to secure their own eligibility. This duty could prove to be a significant burden for potential voters. During a

History Principle

Between 1890 and 1910, voter turnout declined in the United States as a result of new registration requirements. Since that time, turnout has remained low in comparison with the nineteenth century.

personal appearance before the registrar, individuals seeking to vote were (and are) required to furnish proof of identity, residence, and citizenship. While the inconvenience of registration varied from state to state, usually voters could register only during business hours on weekdays. Many potential voters could not afford to lose a day's pay in order to register. Second, voters were usually required to register well before the next election, in some states up to several months earlier. Third, since most personal registration laws required a periodic purge of the election rolls, ostensibly to keep them up-to-date, voters often had to re-register to maintain their eligibility. Thus, although personal registration requirements helped to diminish the widespread electoral corruption that accompanied a completely open voting process, they also made it much more difficult for citizens to participate in the electoral process.

Registration requirements particularly depress the participation of those with little education and low incomes because registration requires a greater degree of political involvement and interest than does the act of voting itself. To vote, a person need only be concerned with the particular election campaign at hand. Yet, requiring individuals to register before the next election forces them to make a decision to participate on the basis of an abstract interest in the electoral process rather than a simple concern with a specific campaign. Such an abstract interest in electoral politics is largely a product of education. Those with relatively little education may become interested in political events once the stimuli of a particular campaign become salient, but by that time it may be too late to register. As a result, personal registration requirements not only diminish the size of the electorate but also tend to create an electorate that is, in the aggregate, better educated, higher in income and social status, and composed of fewer African Americans and other minorities than the citizenry as a whole. Presumably this is why the elimination of personal registration requirements has not always been viewed favorably by some conservatives.[7]

Over the years, voter registration restrictions have been modified somewhat to make registration easier. In 1993, for example, Congress approved and President Clinton signed the "Motor Voter" bill to ease voter registration by allowing individuals to register when they applied for driver's licenses, as well as in public assistance and military recruitment offices.[8] In Europe, there is typically no registration burden on the individual voter; voter registration is handled automatically by the government. This is one reason that voter turnout rates in Europe are higher than those in the United States.

Another factor explaining low rates of voter turnout in the United States is the weakness of the American party system. During the nineteenth century, American political party machines employed hundreds of thousands of workers to organize and mobilize voters and bring them to the polls. The result was an extremely high rate of turnout, typically more than 90 percent of eligible vot-

---

[7]See Kevin P. Phillips and Paul H. Blackman, *Electoral Reform and Voter Participation: Federal Registration, a False Remedy for Voter Apathy* (Washington, D.C.: American Enterprise Institute, 1975).

[8]Helen Dewar, "'Motor Voter' Agreement Is Reached," *Washington Post*, 28 April 1993, p. A6.

ers.[9] But political party machines began to decline in strength in the early twentieth century and by now have largely disappeared. Without party workers to encourage them to go to the polls and even to bring them there if necessary, many eligible voters will not participate. In the absence of strong parties, participation rates drop the most among poorer and less-educated citizens. Because of the absence of strong political parties, the American electorate is smaller and skewed more toward the middle class than toward the population of all those potentially eligible to vote.

Translating Voters' Choices into Electoral Outcomes

With the exception of America's personal registration requirements, contemporary governments generally do not try to limit the composition of their electorates. Instead, they prefer to allow everyone to vote, and then to manipulate the outcome of the election. This is possible because there is more than one way to decide the relationship between individual votes and electoral outcomes. There are any number of possible rules that can be used to determine how individual votes will be translated. Two types of regulations are especially important: the rules that set the criteria for victory and the rules that define electoral districts.

The Criteria for Winning   In some nations, to win a seat in the parliament or other representative body, a candidate must receive a majority (50 percent plus 1) of all the votes cast in the relevant district. This type of electoral system is called a ***majority system*** and was used in the primary elections of most southern states until recent years. Generally, majority systems have a provision for a second or "runoff" election among the two top candidates if the initial contest drew so many contestants that none received an absolute majority of the votes cast.

In other nations, candidates for office need not receive an absolute majority of the votes cast to win an election. Instead, victory is awarded to the candidate who receives the greatest number of votes in a given election regardless of the actual percentage of votes this represents. Thus, a candidate who received 40 percent or 30 percent of the votes cast may win the contest so long as no rival receives more votes. This type of electoral process is called a ***plurality system,*** and it is the system used in almost all general elections in the United States.[10]

Most European nations employ still a third form of electoral system, called ***proportional representation.*** Under proportional rules, competing political parties

majority system
A type of electoral system in which, to win a seat in the parliament or other representative body, a candidate must receive a majority (50 percent plus 1) of all the votes cast in the relevant district.

plurality system
A type of electoral system in which victory goes to the individual who gets the most votes in an election, not necessarily a majority of votes cast.

proportional representation
A multiple-member district system that allows each political party representation in proportion to its percentage of the vote.

---

[9]Erik W. Austin and Jerome M. Clubb, *Political Facts of the United States since 1789* (New York: Columbia University Press, 1986), pp. 378–79.

[10]There are different types of plurality systems. The one currently utilized in the United States in congressional and presidential elections is single-member districts and first-past-the-post. For an accessible analysis of the different types of plurality systems and a model for analyzing electoral systems, see Kenneth A. Shepsle and Mark S. Bonchek, *Analyzing Politics: Rationality, Behavior, and Institutions* (New York: W.W. Norton, 1997), pp. 178–87.

are awarded legislative seats roughly in proportion to the percentage of the popular vote that they receive. For example, a party that won 30 percent of the votes would receive roughly 30 percent of the seats in the parliament or other representative body. In the United States, proportional representation is used by many states in presidential primary elections. In these primaries, candidates for the Democratic and Republican nominations are awarded convention delegates in rough proportion to the percentage of the popular vote that they received in the primary. Early in the twentieth century, proportional representation systems were employed in many American cities, including New York, to elect city councils. Today these systems have nearly disappeared. Cambridge, Massachusetts, is one of the last cities to use such a system in city-council elections. Elections to the New York City school board are also still conducted using a proportional representation system.

Institution Principle

The rules that set the criteria for winning an election have an effect on the outcome.

Generally, systems of proportional representation work to the electoral advantage of smaller or weaker social groups, while majority and plurality systems tend to help larger and more powerful forces. This is because in legislative elections, proportional representation reduces, while majority and plurality rules increase, the number of votes that political parties must receive to win legislative seats. For instance, in European parliamentary elections, a minor party that wins 10 percent of the national vote will also receive 10 percent of the parliamentary seats. In American congressional elections, by contrast, a party winning only 10 percent of the popular vote would probably receive no congressional seats at all.[11] Obviously, choices among types of electoral systems can have important political consequences. Competing forces often seek to establish an electoral system they believe will serve their political interests while undermining the fortunes of their opponents. For example, in 1937, New York City Council seats were awarded on the basis of proportional representation. This led to the selection of several Communist party council members. During the 1940s, to prevent the election of Communists, the city adopted a plurality system. Under the new rule, the tiny Communist party was unable to muster enough votes to secure a council seat. In a similar vein, the introduction of proportional representation for the selection of delegates to the Democratic party's 1972 national convention was designed in part to maximize the voting strength of minority groups and, not entirely coincidentally, to improve the electoral chances of the candidates they were most likely to favor.[12]

---

[11]For an argument that plurality systems are governance-oriented, whereas proportional systems are representation-oriented, see Shepsle and Bonchek, *Analyzing Politics*, pp. 188–91. This argument derives from the famous Duverger's Law—an argument that plurality systems encourage two-party competition (one party or the other secures a majority of seats in the legislature), whereas proportional systems encourage multiparty competition (many parties hold seats in the legislature, with the very frequent outcome that no party commands a majority on its own, and thus parties must build coalitions). The law was first described systematically by the French political scientist Maurice Duverger in his *Political Parties, Their Organization and Activity in the Modern State*, trans. Barbara North and Robert North (New York: Wiley, 1954).

[12]See Nelson W. Polsby and Aaron Wildavsky, *Presidential Elections: Strategies of American Electoral Politics*, 5th ed. (New York: Scribners, 1980).

Electoral Districts   Despite the occasional use of proportional representation and majority voting systems, most electoral contests in the United States are decided on the basis of plurality rules. Rather than seeking to manipulate the criteria for victory, American politicians have usually sought to influence electoral outcomes by manipulating the organization of electoral districts. Congressional district boundaries in the United States are redrawn by governors and state legislatures every ten years, after the decennial Census determines the number of House seats to which each state is entitled (see Process Box 10.1). The manipulation of electoral districts to increase the likelihood of one or another outcome is called **gerrymandering,** in honor of nineteenth-century Massachusetts governor Elbridge Gerry, who was alleged to have designed a district in the shape of a salamander to promote his party's interests. The principle is a simple one. Different distributions of voters among districts produce different electoral outcomes; those in a position to control the arrangements of districts are also in a position to manipulate the results. For example, until recent years, gerrymandering to dilute the voting strength of racial minorities was employed by many state legislatures. One of the more common strategies involved redrawing congressional boundary lines in such a way as to divide and disperse a black population that would have otherwise constituted a majority within the original district.

This form of racial gerrymandering, sometimes called "cracking," was used in Mississippi during the 1960s and 1970s to prevent the election of a black congressman. Historically, the black population in Mississippi was clustered in the western half of the state, along the Mississippi Delta. From 1882 until 1966, the delta was one congressional district. Although blacks constituted a clear majority within the district (66 percent in 1960), the continuing election of white congressmen was assured simply because blacks were denied the right to register and vote. With Congress's passage of the Voting Rights Act of 1965, however, the Mississippi state legislature moved swiftly to minimize the potential voting power of blacks by redrawing congressional district lines in such a way as to fragment the black population in the delta into four of the state's five congressional districts. Mississippi's gerrymandering scheme was preserved in the state's redistricting plans in 1972 and 1981 and helped to prevent the election of any black representative until 1986, when Mike Espy became the first African American since Reconstruction to represent Mississippi in Congress.

In recent years, the federal government has encouraged what is sometimes called "benign gerrymandering," designed to increase minority representation in Congress. The 1982 amendments to the Voting Rights Act of 1965 encourage the creation of legislative districts with predominantly African American or Hispanic American populations by requiring states, when possible, to draw district lines that take account of concentrations of African American and Hispanic American voters. These amendments were initially supported by Democrats who assumed that minority-controlled districts would guarantee the election of Democratic members of Congress. However, Republicans have championed these efforts, reasoning that if minority voters were concentrated in their own districts, Republican prospects in other districts would be

gerrymandering
Apportionment of voters in districts in such ways as to give unfair advantage to one political party.

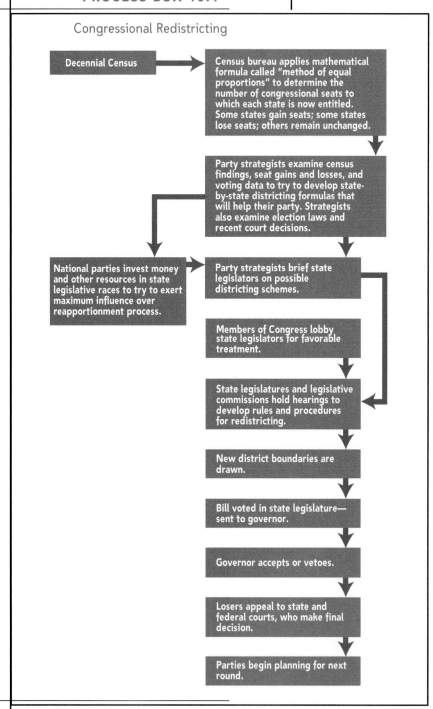

Congressional Redistricting

Decennial Census

Census bureau applies mathematical formula called "method of equal proportions" to determine the number of congressional seats to which each state is now entitled. Some states gain seats; some states lose seats; others remain unchanged.

Party strategists examine census findings, seat gains and losses, and voting data to try to develop state-by-state districting formulas that will help their party. Strategists also examine election laws and recent court decisions.

National parties invest money and other resources in state legislative races to try to exert maximum influence over reapportionment process.

Party strategists brief state legislators on possible districting schemes.

Members of Congress lobby state legislators for favorable treatment.

State legislatures and legislative commissions hold hearings to develop rules and procedures for redistricting.

New district boundaries are drawn.

Bill voted in state legislature—sent to governor.

Governor accepts or vetoes.

Losers appeal to state and federal courts, who make final decision.

Parties begin planning for next round.

enhanced.[13] Moreover, Republicans hoped some Democratic incumbents might be forced from office to make way for minority representatives. In some cases, the Republicans' theory has proved correct. As a result of the creation of a number of new minority districts in 1991, several long-term white Democrats lost their congressional seats. The 1993 Supreme Court decision in *Shaw v. Reno*, however, opened the way for challenges by white voters to the drawing of these districts. In the 5-to-4 majority opinion, Justice O'Connor wrote that if district boundaries were so "bizarre" as to be inexplicable on any grounds other than an effort to ensure the election of minority group members to office, white voters would have reason to assert that they had been the victims of un-constitutional racial gerrymandering.[14] In its 1995 decision in *Miller v. Johnson*, the Court questioned the entire concept of benign racial gerrymandering by as-serting that the use of race as a "predominant factor" in the drawing of district lines was presumptively unconstitutional. However, the Court held open the possibility that race could be *one* of the factors taken into account in legislative redistricting. Similarly, in *Bush v. Vera*, the Court ruled that three Texas con-gressional districts with black or Hispanic majorities were unconstitutional be-cause state officials put too much emphasis on race in drawing boundaries. "Voters," said the Court, "are more than mere racial statistics." In *Shaw v. Hunt*, the Court struck down a North Carolina black-majority voting district for sim-ilar reasons. Most recently, in the 1997 case of *Abrams v. Johnson*, the Court up-held a new Georgia congressional district map that eliminated two of the state's three black-majority districts.[15]

Traditionally, district boundaries have been redrawn only once a decade, fol-lowing the decennial national Census. In recent years, however, the Republican party has adopted an exremely aggressive reapportionment strategy, in some in-stances not waiting for a new Census before launching a redistricting effort that could serve its political interests. In Texas, for example, after the GOP took con-trol of both houses of the state legislature in the 2002 elections, Republican law-makers sought to enact a redistricting plan that promised to shift as many as five congressional seats to the Republican column. This Republican effort was master-minded by U.S. House Majority Leader Tom DeLay, who is himself a Texan. DeLay saw an opportunity to increase the Republican majority in the House and reduce Democratic prospects for regaining control of Congress. In an effort to block DeLay's plan, a group of fifty-one Democratic legislators refused to attend state legislative sessions, leaving the Texas legislature without a quorum and un-able to conduct its business. The legislature's Republican leadership ordered the state police to apprehend the missing Democrats and to return them to the Capi-tol. The Democrats responded by escaping to Oklahoma, beyond the jurisdiction

[13]Roberto Suro, "In Redistricting, New Rules and New Prizes," *New York Times*, 6 May 1990, sec. 4, p. 5.
[14]Shaw v. Reno, 113 S.Ct. 2816 (1993); Linda Greenhouse, "Court Questions Districts Drawn to Aid Minorities," *New York Times*, 29 June 1993, p. 1. See also Joan Biskupic, "Court's Conservatism Un-likely to Be Shifted by a New Justice," *Washington Post*, 30 June 1993, p. 1.
[15]Bush v. Vera, 116 S.Ct. 1941 (1996); Shaw v. Hunt, 64 USLW 4437 (1996); Abrams v. Johnson, 95-1425 (1997).

of the Texas police. Eventually, the Democrats capitulated, and the GOP was able to enact its redistricting plan. The entire matter, however, is now before the courts. A similar GOP redistricting effort in Colorado failed when it was ruled unconstitutional by the state's supreme court. The court declared that the Colorado constitution only permitted the legislature to redistrict the state once every ten years.

Although governments do have the capacity to manipulate electoral outcomes, this capacity is not absolute. Electoral arrangements conceived to be illegitimate may prompt some segments of the electorate to seek other ways of participating in political life. Moreover, no electoral system that provides universal and equal suffrage can, by itself, long prevent an outcome favored by large popular majorities. Yet faced with opposition short of an overwhelming majority, government's ability to manipulate the translation of individual choices into collective decisions can be an important factor in preserving the established distribution of power.

Insulating Decision-Making Processes

Virtually all governments attempt at least partially to insulate decision-making processes from electoral intervention. The most obvious forms of insulation are the confinement of popular election to only some governmental positions, various modes of indirect election, and lengthy tenure in office. In the United States, the framers of the Constitution intended that only members of the House of Representatives would be subject to direct popular selection. The president and members of the Senate were to be indirectly elected for rather long terms to allow them, as *The Federalist Papers* put it, to avoid "an unqualified complaisance to every sudden breeze of passion, or to every transient impulse which the people may receive."[16]

The Electoral College   In the early history of popular voting, nations often made use of indirect elections. In these elections, voters would choose the members of an intermediate body. These members would, in turn, select public officials. The assumption underlying such processes was that ordinary citizens were not really qualified to choose their leaders and could not be trusted to do so directly. The last vestige of this procedure in America is the ***electoral college,*** the group of electors who formally select the president and vice president of the United States.

electoral college
The presidential electors from each state who meet in their respective state capitals after the popular election to cast ballots for president and vice president.

When Americans go to the polls on Election Day, they are technically not voting directly for presidential candidates. Instead, voters within each state are choosing among slates of electors who have either been elected or appointed to their positions some months earlier. The electors who are chosen in the presidential race are pledged to support their own party's presidential candidate. In each state (except for Maine and Nebraska), the slate that wins casts all the state's

[16]Rossiter, ed., *The Federalist Papers*, No. 71, p. 432.

electoral votes for its party's candidate.[17] Each state is entitled to a number of electoral votes equal to the number of the state's senators and representatives combined, for a total of 538 electoral votes for the fifty states and the District of Columbia. Occasionally, an elector breaks his or her pledge and votes for the other party's candidate. For example, in 1976, when the Republicans carried the state of Washington, one Republican elector from that state refused to vote for Gerald Ford, the Republican presidential nominee. Many states have now enacted statutes formally binding electors to their pledges, but some constitutional authorities doubt whether such statutes are enforceable.

In each state, the electors whose slate has won proceed to the state's capital on the Monday following the second Wednesday in December and formally cast their ballots. These are sent to Washington, tallied by the Congress in January, and the name of the winner is formally announced. If no candidate received a majority of all electoral votes, the names of the top three candidates would be submitted to the House, where each state would be able to cast one vote. Whether a state's vote would be decided by a majority, plurality, or some other fraction of the state's delegates would be determined under rules established by the House.

In 1800 and 1824, the electoral college failed to produce a majority for any candidate. In the election of 1800, Thomas Jefferson, the Jeffersonian Republican party's presidential candidate, and Aaron Burr, that party's vice-presidential candidate, received an equal number of votes in the electoral college, throwing the election into the House of Representatives. (The Constitution at that time made no distinction between presidential and vice-presidential candidates, specifying only that the individual receiving a majority of electoral votes would be named president.) Some members of the Federalist party in Congress suggested that they should seize the opportunity to damage the Republican cause by supporting Burr and denying Jefferson the presidency. Federalist leader Alexander Hamilton put a stop to this mischievous notion, however, and made certain that his party supported Jefferson. Hamilton's actions enraged Burr and helped lead to the infamous duel between the two men, in which Hamilton was killed. The Twelfth Amendment, ratified in 1804, was designed to prevent a repetition of such a situation by providing for separate electoral-college votes for president and vice president.

In the 1824 election, four candidates—John Quincy Adams, Andrew Jackson, Henry Clay, and William H. Crawford—divided the electoral vote; no one of them received a majority. The House of Representatives eventually chose Adams over the others, even though Jackson won more electoral and popular votes. This choice resulted from the famous "corrupt bargain" between Adams and Henry Clay. After 1824, the two major political parties had begun to dominate presidential politics to such an extent that by December of each election year, only two candidates remained for the electors to choose between, thus ensuring that one would receive a majority. This freed the parties and the candidates from having to

[17]State legislatures determine the system by which electors are selected, and almost all states use this "winner take all" system. Maine and Nebraska, however, provide that one electoral vote goes to the winner in each congressional district and two electoral votes go to the winner statewide.

plan their campaigns to culminate in Congress, and Congress very quickly ceased to dominate the presidential selection process.

On all but three occasions since 1824, the electoral vote has simply ratified the nationwide popular vote. Since electoral votes are won on a state-by-state basis, it is mathematically possible for a candidate who receives a nationwide popular plurality to fail to carry states whose electoral votes would add up to a majority. Thus, in 1876, Rutherford B. Hayes was the winner in the electoral college despite receiving fewer popular votes than his rival, Samuel Tilden. In 1888, Grover Cleveland received more popular votes than Benjamin Harrison, but received fewer electoral votes. And in 2000, Al Gore outpolled his opponent, George W. Bush, but lost the electoral college by a mere four electoral votes.

Frequency of Elections   Less obvious are the insulating effects of electoral arrangements that permit direct, and even frequent, popular election of public officials but tend to fragment the impact of elections upon the government's composition. In the United States, for example, the constitutional provision of staggered terms of service in the Senate was designed to diminish the impact of shifts in electoral sentiment upon the Senate as an institution. Since only one-third of its members were to be selected at any given point in time, the composition of the institution would be partially protected from changes in electoral preferences. This would prevent what *The Federalist Papers* called "mutability in the public councils arising from a rapid succession of new members."[18]

Size of Electoral Districts   The division of the nation into relatively small, geographically based constituencies for the purpose of selecting members of the House of Representatives was, in part, designed to have a similar effect. Representatives were to be chosen frequently. And although not prescribed by the Constitution, the fact that each was to be selected by a discrete constituency was thought by Madison and others to diminish the government's vulnerability to mass popular movements.

In a sense, the House of Representatives was compartmentalized in the same way that a submarine is divided into watertight sections to confine the impact of any damage to the vessel. First, by dividing the national electorate into small districts, the importance of local issues would increase. Second, the salience of local issues would mean that a representative's electoral fortunes would be more closely tied to factors peculiar to his or her own district than to national responses to issues. Third, given a geographical principle of representation, national groups would be somewhat fragmented while the formation of local forces that might or might not share common underlying attitudes would be encouraged. No matter how well represented individual constituencies might be, the influence of voters on national policy questions would be fragmented. In Madison's terms, the influence of "faction" would thus become "less likely to pervade the whole body than some particular portion of it."[19]

[18]Rossiter, ed., *The Federalist Papers*, No. 62.
[19]Ibid., No. 10.

The Ballot   Another example of an American electoral arrangement that tends to fragment the impact of mass elections upon the government's composition is the Australian ballot (named for its country of origin). Prior to the introduction of this official ballot in the 1890s, voters cast ballots according to political parties. Each party printed its own ballots, listed only its own candidates for each office, and employed party workers to distribute its ballots at the polls. This ballot format had two important consequences. First, the party ballot precluded secrecy in voting. Because each party's ballot was distinctive in size and color, it was not difficult for party workers to determine how individuals intended to vote. This, of course, facilitated the intimidation and bribery of voters. Second, the format of the ballot prevented split-ticket voting. Because only one party's candidates appeared on any ballot, it was difficult for a voter to cast anything other than a straight party vote.

The official ***Australian ballot*** represented a significant change in electoral procedure. The new ballot was prepared and administered by the state rather than the parties. Each ballot was identical and included the names of all candidates for office. This reform, of course, increased the secrecy of voting and reduced the possibility for voter intimidation and bribery. Because all ballots were identical in appearance, even the voter who had been threatened or bribed might still vote as he or she wished, without the knowledge of party workers. But perhaps even more important, the Australian-ballot reform made it possible for voters to make their choices on the basis of the individual rather than the collective merits of a party's candidates. Because all candidates for the same office now appeared on the same ballot, voters were no longer forced to choose a straight party ticket. It was indeed the introduction of the Australian ballot that gave rise to the phenomenon of split-ticket voting in American elections.[20] Ticket splitting is especially prevalent in states that use the "office block" ballot format, which does not group candidates by their partisan affiliations. By contrast, the "party column" format places all the candidates affiliated with a given party in the same row or column. The former facilitates ticket splitting while the latter encourages straight-ticket voting.

Australian ballot
An electoral format that presents the names of all the candidates for any given office on the same ballot. Introduced at the turn of the century, the Australian ballot replaced the partisan ballot and facilitated split-ticket voting.

It is this second consequence of the Australian-ballot reform that tends to fragment the impact of American elections upon the government's composition. Prior to the reform of the ballot, it was not uncommon for an entire incumbent administration to be swept from office and replaced by an entirely new set of officials. In the absence of a real possibility of split-ticket voting, any desire on the part of the electorate for change could be expressed only as a vote against all candidates of the party in power. Because of this, there always existed the possibility, particularly at the state and local levels, that an insurgent slate committed to policy change could be swept into power. The party ballot thus increased the potential impact of elections upon the government's composition. Although this potential may not always have been realized, the party ballot at least increased

[20]Jerold G. Rusk, "The Effect of the Australian Ballot Reform on Split Ticket Voting: 1876–1908," *American Political Science Review* 64 (December 1970): 1220–38.

the chance that electoral decisions could lead to policy changes. By contrast, because it permitted choice on the basis of candidates' individual appeals, the Australian ballot lessened the likelihood that the electorate would sweep an entirely new administration into power. Ticket splitting led to increasingly divided partisan control of government.

The ballots used in the United States are a mix of forms developed as long ago as the 1890s, when the states took over the printing of ballots from the political parties. These were modified during the 1940s and 1950s, when voting machines and punch-card ballots were introduced, and ballots were further updated in some jurisdictions during the 1990s, when more modern and accurate computerized voting methods were introduced. The choice of ballot format is a county decision, and, within any state, various counties may use different formats, depending on local resources and preferences. For example, the Palm Beach County butterfly ballot, which seemed to confuse many voters, was selected by Democratic election officials who thought its larger print would help elderly, predominantly Democratic voters read the names of the candidates. Not infrequently, as turned out to be the case in Florida, neighboring counties used completely different ballot systems. For example, the city of Baltimore, Maryland, introduced voting machines many years ago and continues to use them. Baltimore County, Maryland, uses more modern ballots that are optically scanned by computers. Neighboring Montgomery County, Maryland, employs a cumbersome punch-card system that requires voters to punch several different cards on both sides—a bewildering process that usually results in large numbers of spoiled ballots. In some states, including Florida, different precincts within the same county may use different voting methods, causing still more confusion.

As became only too evident during the struggle over Florida's votes, America's overall balloting process is awkward, confusing, riddled with likely sources of error and bias, and, in cases of close races, incapable of producing a result that will stand up to close scrutiny. Results can take several days to process, and every recount appears to produce a slightly different result. Often, too, the process of counting and recounting is directed by state and county officials with political axes to grind. The Votomatic punch-card machines used in a number of Florida counties are notoriously unreliable. The Votomatics are popular with many county governments because they are inexpensive. About 37 percent of the precincts in America's 3,140 counties use Votomatics or similar machines.[21] However, voters often find it difficult to insert the punch cards properly, frequently punch the wrong hole, or do not sufficiently perforate one or more chads to allow the punch cards to be read by the counting machine. Votomatics and other punch-card voting devices generally yield a much higher rate of spoiled votes than other voting methods. Indeed, a 1988 Florida Senate race was won by Republican Connie Mack in part because of thousands of spoiled Vo-

[21]Chad Terhune and Joni James, "Presidential Race Brings Attention to Business of Voting Machines," *Wall Street Journal*, 16 November 2000, p. A16.

tomatic ballots. To make matters worse, precinct-level election officials—often elderly volunteers—may not understand the rules themselves, and they are, therefore, unable to help voters with questions. These difficulties would not have been subject to public scrutiny as long as they affected only local races. In 2000, however, America's antiquated electoral machinery collapsed under the weight of a presidential election, revealing its flaws for all to see. Despite these problems, electoral officials are often reluctant to change voting methods because changes can affect the outcome of the next election perhaps in ways that run against officials' preferences.

Taken together, regulation of the electorate's composition, regulation of the translation of voters' choices into electoral decisions, and regulation of the impact of those decisions upon the government's composition allow those in power a measure of control over mass participation in political life. These techniques do not necessarily have the effect of diminishing citizens' capacity to influence their rulers' conduct. Rather in the democracies, at least, these techniques are generally used to *influence electoral influence*. They permit governments a measure of control over what citizens will decide that governments should do.

Direct Democracy: The Referendum and Recall

In addition to voting for candidates, some states also provide for referendum voting. The *referendum* process allows citizens to vote directly on proposed laws or other governmental actions. In recent years, voters in several states have voted to set limits on tax rates, to block state and local spending proposals, and to prohibit social services for illegal immigrants. Although it involves voting, a referendum is not an election. The election is an institution of representative government. Through an election, voters choose officials to act for them. The referendum, by contrast, is an institution of direct democracy; it allows voters to govern directly without intervention by government officials. The validity of referenda results, however, are subject to judicial action. If a court finds that a referendum outcome violates the state or national constitution, it can overturn the result. This happened in the case of a 1995 California referendum curtailing social services to illegal aliens.[22]

Eighteen states also have legal provisions for *recall* elections. The recall is an electoral device introduced by turn-of-the-century Populists to allow voters to remove governors and other state officials from office prior to the expiration of their terms. Federal officials such as the president and members of Congress are not subject to recall. Generally speaking, a recall effort begins with a petition campaign. For example, in California, the site of a tumultuous recall battle in 2003, if 12 percent of those who voted in the last general election sign petitions demanding a special recall election, one must be scheduled by the state board of elections. Such petition campaigns are relatively common, but most fail to garner enough signatures to bring the matter to a statewide vote. In the California

---

Institution Principle

The electoral college and the Australian ballot are two instances of how changes in electoral rules can affect the outcomes of elections.

referendum The practice of referring a measure proposed or passed by a legislature to the vote of the electorate for approval or rejection.

recall Removal of a public official by popular vote.

---

[22]League of United Latin American Citizens v. Wilson, CV-94-7569 (C.D. Calif.) (1995).

case, however, a conservative Republican member of Congress, Darrell Issa, led a successful effort to recall Democratic governor Gray Davis. Voters were unhappy about the state's economy, dissatisfied with Davis's performance, and blamed Davis for the state's $38 billion budget deficit. Issa and his followers were able to secure enough signatures to force a vote, and in October 2003 Davis became the second governor in American history to be recalled by his state's electorate (the first was North Dakota governor Lynn Frazier, who was recalled in 1921). Under California law, voters in a special recall election are also asked to choose a replacement for the official whom they dismiss. Californians in 2003 elected movie star Arnold Schwartzenegger to be their governor. While critics charged that the Davis recall had been a "political circus," the campaign had the effect of greatly increasing voter interest and involvement in the political process. More that 400,000 new voters registered in California in 2003, many drawn into the political arena by the opportunity to participate in the recall campaign.

HOW DO VOTERS DECIDE?

Thus far, we have focused on the election as an institution. But the election is also a process in which millions of individuals make decisions and choices that are beyond the government's control. Whatever the capacity of those in power to organize and structure the electoral process, it is these millions of individual decisions that ultimately determine electoral outcomes. Sooner or later the choices of voters weigh more heavily than the schemes of electoral engineers. Three types of factors influence voters' decisions at the polls: partisan loyalty, issue and policy concerns, and candidate characteristics.

Partisan Loyalty

Many studies have shown that most Americans identify more or less strongly with one or the other of the two major political parties. Partisan loyalty was considerably stronger during the 1940s and 1950s than it is today. But even now most voters feel a certain sense of identification or kinship with the Democratic or Republican party. This sense of identification is often handed down from parents to children and is reinforced by social and cultural ties. Partisan identification predisposes voters in favor of their party's candidates and against those of the opposing party. Partisanship is most likely to assert itself in the less-visible races, where issues and the candidates are not very well known. State legislative races, for example, are often decided by voters' party ties. However, even at the level of the presidential contest, in which issues and candidate personalities become very important, many Americans supported George W. Bush or Al Gore only because of partisan loyalty. Once formed, partisan loyalties are resistant to change. But sufficiently strong events and experiences may have the effect of eroding or even reversing them. White males in the South, for example, have, over the latter part of the twentieth century, been transformed from strong partisans of the Democratic party to independents and even supporters of the Republican party. Voters tend to keep their party affiliations unless some crisis causes them to re-examine the bases of their loyalties and to conclude that they have not given their support to the appropriate party. During these relatively infrequent periods of electoral change, millions of voters can change their party ties. For example, at the beginning of the New Deal era between 1932 and 1936, millions of former Republicans transferred their allegiance to Franklin Roosevelt and the Democrats.

Partisan loyalty should be understood as more than a psychological attachment (although it certainly is that as well). It is also an informational shortcut—a way for voters to economize on information collection and processing. In many circumstances, it may be "enough" simply to know what party label a particular candidate wears. Any extra information—issue positions or personal attributes—may not influence the voter's choice once the partisan content has been taken on board. For example, once a particular voter learns that a candidate is a Democrat, he or she knows that this candidate is likely to be the preferred alternative; for another voter, however, that simple fact may be enough to cause him or her to vote for the other guy! In the last several decades, party label has begun to lose its capacity to signal likely candidate characteristics, and more and more voters have found their partisan attachments weakening or disappearing altogether. The phenomenal rise in the proportion of the electorate who now identify only weakly with a party or who declare themselves independents is testimony to this fact.[23]

Issues

Issues and policy preferences are a second factor influencing voters' choices at the polls. Voters may cast their ballots for the candidate whose position on economic issues they believe to be closest to their own. Similarly, they may select the candidate who has what they believe to be the best record on foreign policy. Issues are more important in some races than others. If candidates actually "take issue" with one another—that is, articulate and publicize very different positions on important public questions—then voters are more likely to be able to identify and act upon whatever policy preferences they may have.

The ability of voters to make choices on the basis of issue or policy preferences is diminished, however, if competing candidates do not differ substantially or do not focus their campaigns on policy matters. Very often, candidates deliberately take the safe course and emphasize topics that will not be offensive to

---

[23]For a detailed assessment of the political use of information-economizing devices like party labels, see Arthur Lupia and Mathew D. McCubbins, *The Democratic Dilemma: Can Citizens Learn What They Need to Know?* (New York: Cambridge University Press, 1998). For the classic argument that party loyalty is a *variable*, not a constant, and that the voter updates party loyalty on the basis of his or her experience with the parties and their candidates, see Morris P. Fiorina, *Retrospective Voting in American National Elections* (New Haven: Yale University Press, 1981).

any voters. Thus, candidates often trumpet their opposition to corruption, crime, and inflation. Presumably, few voters favor these things. While it may be perfectly reasonable for candidates to take the safe course and remain as inoffensive as possible, this candidate strategy makes it extremely difficult for voters to make their issue or policy preferences the bases for their choices at the polls.

Similarly, a paucity of information during a campaign can induce the "wrong" decision by "knowledge-challenged" voters. Some analysts claimed that in 2000 Al Gore snatched defeat from the jaws of victory in just this way. In his efforts to distance himself from his scandal-plagued predecessor, he also failed to remind voters of his great successes—eight years of peace and prosperity as Clinton's vice president. Consequently, voters, such as moderate Republicans, who may have been prepared to overlook Gore's party label because of his achievements were not given much opportunity to do so.[24]

prospective voting Voting based on the imagined future performance of a candidate.

Voters' issue choices usually involve a mix of their judgments about the past behavior of competing parties and candidates, and their hopes and fears about candidates' future behavior. Political scientists call choices that focus on future behavior ***prospective voting,*** while those based on past performance are called ***retrospective voting.*** To some extent, whether prospective or retrospective evaluation is more important in a particular election depends on the strategies of competing candidates. Candidates always endeavor to define the issues of an election in terms that will serve their interests. Incumbents running during a period of prosperity will seek to take credit for the economy's happy state and define the election as revolving around their record of success. This strategy encourages voters to make retrospective judgments. By contrast, an insurgent running during a period of economic uncertainty will tell voters it is time for a change and ask them to make prospective judgments. Thus, Bill Clinton focused on change in 1992 and prosperity in 1996, and through well-crafted media campaigns was able to define voters' agenda of choices.

restrospective voting Voting based on the past performance of a candidate.

In 2000, the key issues at the presidential level were taxes, Social Security reform, health care, and education. Bush promised an across-the-board tax cut while Gore asserted that such a move would benefit wealthy Americans at the expense of the middle class. Both candidates proposed plans to strengthen the Social Security system, with Bush advocating partial privatization of the system; Gore, on the other hand, promised to more adequately fund the current system. In the realm of health care, both candidates promised prescription drug plans for seniors. Associated Press exit polls conducted on Election Day indicated that Bush voters saw taxes as the central issue of the campaign, while Gore voters focused on prescription drugs and Social Security.

Rationality Principle

Issue voting motivates candidates to converge toward the median voter.

When voters engage in issue voting, competition between the two candidates has the effect of pushing the candidate issue positions toward the middle of the distribution of voter preferences. This is known as the *median voter theorem,*

[24]This argument is spelled out in Morris Fiorina, Samuel Abrams, and Jeremy Pope, "The 2000 U.S. Presidential Election: Can Retrospective Voting Be Saved?" *British Journal of Political Science* 33 (2003): 163–87.

made famous by Duncan Black and Anthony Downs.[25] To see the logic of this claim, imagine a series of possible stances on a policy issue as points along a line, stretching from zero to one hundred. A voter whose ideal policy lies between, say, zero and twenty-five is said to be a liberal on this policy; one whose ideal lies between seventy-five and one hundred, a conservative; and one whose favorite policy is between twenty-five and seventy-five, a moderate. An issue voter cares only about issue positions, not partisan loyalty or candidate characteristics, and would, therefore, vote for the candidate whose announced policy is closest to his or her own most preferred policy.

Consider now a candidate who announces as his policy the most preferred alternative of the median voter. If his opponent picks any point to the right, then the median voter and all those with ideal policies to the left of the median voter's will support the first candidate. They constitute a majority, by definition of the median, so this candidate will win. Suppose instead that the opponent chose as her policy some point to the left of the median ideal policy. Then the median voter and all those with ideal policies to the right of the median voter's will support the first candidate—and he wins, again. In short, the median voter theorem says that the candidate whose policy position is closest to the ideal policy of the median voter will defeat the other candidate in a majority contest. We can conclude from this brief analysis that issue voting encourages two things—*candidate convergence* (both candidates rush toward the center in order to cozy up to the position of the median voter) and *policy moderation* (candidates adopt policies that are less extreme than they might otherwise prefer in order to sway median voters). Even when voters are not exclusively issue voters, two-candidate competition still encourages a tendency toward convergence and moderation, although it will not fully run its course.

> **Policy Principle**
> The median voter theorem predicts policy moderation on the part of candidates.

Candidate Characteristics

Candidates' personal attributes always influence voters' decisions. Some analysts claim that voters prefer tall candidates to short ones, candidates with shorter names to candidates with longer names, and candidates with lighter hair to candidates with darker hair. Perhaps these rather frivolous criteria do play some role. But the more important candidate characteristics that affect voters' choices are race, ethnicity, religion, gender, geography, and social background. In general, voters prefer candidates who are closer to themselves in terms of these categories. Voters presume that such candidates are likely to have views and perspectives close to their own. Moreover, they may be proud to see someone of their ethnic, religious, or geographic background in a position of leadership. This is why, for many years, politicians sought to "balance the ticket," making certain that their party's ticket included members of as many important groups as possible.

---

[25]See Duncan Black, *The Theory of Committees and Elections*, rev. 2nd ed. (Boston: Kluwer, 1998), and Anthony Downs, *An Economic Theory of Democracy* (New York: Harper, 1957). A general, accessible treatment of this subject is found in Shepsle and Bonchek, *Analyzing Politics*, Chapter 5.

Just as a candidate's personal characteristics may attract some voters, they may repel others. Many voters are prejudiced against candidates of certain ethnic, racial, or religious groups. And for many years voters were reluctant to support the political candidacies of women, although this appears to be changing.

Voters also pay attention to candidates' personality characteristics, such as their "decisiveness," "honesty," and "vigor." In recent years, integrity has become a key election issue. In the 2000 presidential race, Al Gore chose Joe Lieberman as his running mate in part because Lieberman had been sharply critical of Bill Clinton's moral lapses. The senator's presence on the Democratic ticket thus helped to defuse the GOP's efforts to link Gore to Clinton's questionable character. As the race progressed, Gore sought to portray Bush as lacking the intelligence and experience needed for the presidency. This effort met with some success, as a number of talk-show hosts began to caricature Bush as a simpleton who knew little about domestic or foreign policy. Exit polls indicated that many voters also had concerns about Bush's intelligence. For his part, Bush sought to portray Gore as dishonest and duplicitous—a man who would say anything to get elected, such as claiming credit for the development of the Internet. The Bush strategy was to suggest that Gore was morally on a par with his boss, Bill Clinton, an individual whose moral lapses were all too well known to the electorate. Bush's claim that Gore was a liar just like Clinton was designed to thwart Gore's efforts to distance himself from his boss. This effort, too, led to talk-show caricatures and raised concerns among voters. Ultimately, according to Associated Press exit polls, Bush won the votes of those who said they were concerned about "honesty," while Gore received the support of individuals who felt "experience" was an important presidential attribute.

All candidates seek, through polling and other mechanisms, to determine the best image to project to the electorate. At the same time, the communications media—television in particular—exercise a good deal of control over how voters perceive candidates. In recent years, the candidates have developed a number of techniques designed to wrest control of the image-making process away from the media. Among the chief instruments of this "spin control" are candidate talk-show appearances, used quite effectively by both Al Gore and George Bush. During one appearance, Bush gave Oprah Winfrey a big kiss to show that he was friendly and not "stiff" like his opponent, Al Gore. (See Process Box 10.2 to find out how candidates conduct a presidential campaign.)

THE 2000 ELECTIONS

During periods of economic prosperity, Americans generally return the incumbent party to office. The 2000 national elections were held during a period of peace and one of the greatest periods of economic prosperity America has ever known. To further enhance the Democrats' prospects, Democratic partisans continued to outnumber Republican identifiers in the national electorate. Thus, all things considered, it seemed more than likely that Vice President Al Gore and

How a Presidential Campaign Is Conducted

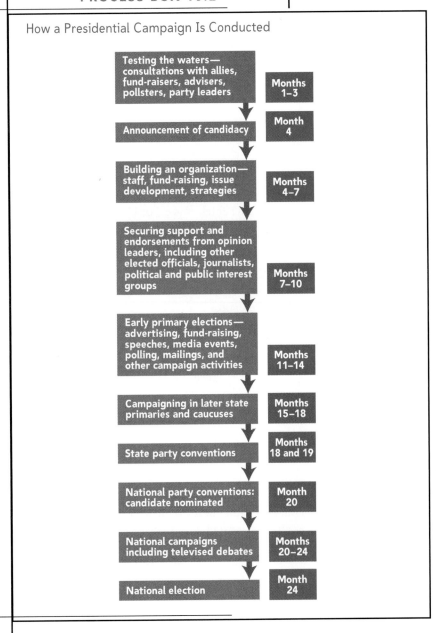

Testing the waters—consultations with allies, fund-raisers, advisers, pollsters, party leaders	Months 1–3
Announcement of candidacy	Month 4
Building an organization—staff, fund-raising, issue development, strategies	Months 4–7
Securing support and endorsements from opinion leaders, including other elected officials, journalists, political and public interest groups	Months 7–10
Early primary elections—advertising, fund-raising, speeches, media events, polling, mailings, and other campaign activities	Months 11–14
Campaigning in later state primaries and caucuses	Months 15–18
State party conventions	Months 18 and 19
National party conventions: candidate nominated	Month 20
National campaigns including televised debates	Months 20–24
National election	Month 24

FIGURE 10.3

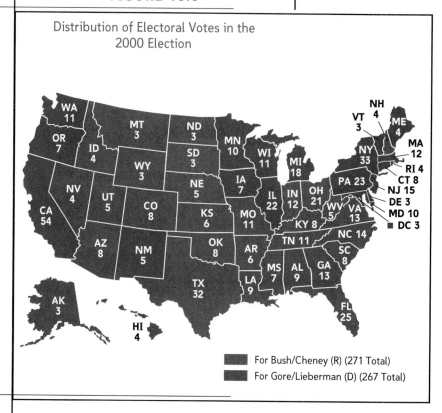

Distribution of Electoral Votes in the 2000 Election

For Bush/Cheney (R) (271 Total)

For Gore/Lieberman (D) (267 Total)

his running mate, Connecticut senator Joe Lieberman, would lead the Democratic party to victory against an inexperienced and little-known Republican presidential nominee—Texas governor George W. Bush. Bush is, of course, the eldest son of former president George H. W. Bush, who was driven from office by Bill Clinton and Al Gore in 1992. Indeed, most academic models of election outcomes predicted an easy Democratic victory, with some even forecasting a Gore landslide.

Nevertheless, when the results of the vote finally became known, George W. Bush and his running mate, former defense secretary Dick Cheney, appeared to have eked out the narrowest of electoral college victories—271 to 267—over Gore and Lieberman (see Figure 10.3). Indeed, in terms of popular vote totals, the Gore/Lieberman ticket actually outpolled the Republicans by slightly more than 500,000 votes, or about one-half of 1 percent of the approximately 103 million votes cast across the nation.

Election night produced unusual drama and confusion when it became clear that the election's outcome would hinge on voting results in Florida, a state with 25 electoral votes. Initially, the television networks declared Gore the winner in Florida on the basis of exit-poll results. This projection seemed to indicate that Gore would likely win the presidency. Later that night, however, as votes were counted, it became clear that the exit polls were incorrect and that the Florida results were much in doubt. In the early hours of the next morning, all of the votes were tallied and Bush seemed to have won by fewer than 2,000 votes, out of nearly 6 million cast across the state. Vice President Gore called Governor Bush and conceded defeat.

Within an hour, however, Gore was on the phone to Bush again—this time to withdraw his concession. Under Florida law, the narrowness of Bush's victory—less than one-tenth of 1 percent—triggered an automatic recount. Moreover, reports of election irregularities had begun to surface. For example, nearly 20,000 votes in Palm Beach County had been invalidated because voters, apparently confused by the ballot, had indicated more than one presidential choice. Given the closeness of the race and the various uncertainties, Democrats decided to await the results of a statewide recount of the vote.

While the recount of the counting of overseas absentee ballots narrowed Bush's margin of victory to a mere 980 votes, it did not change the result. In the meantime, Democrats filed a series of court challenges to the outcome, calling for a hand recount in at least three counties, Miami-Dade, Broward, and Palm Beach. Although Katherine Harris, Florida's top election official, announced that she would not accept the results of these hand recounts, Florida's supreme court ruled that the recounts must be included in the state's official election results. Under disputed circumstances, Miami-Dade County decided not to recount, and Palm Beach County missed the deadline for recounted ballots. Gore gained several hundred votes in Broward County but not enough to change the results. These events led to further lawsuits in the Florida courts, the U.S. Court of Appeals, and the U.S. Supreme Court, as Gore refused to concede defeat until all possible legal appeals had been made. Florida's supreme court gave Gore a last-minute reprieve by ordering the manual recounting of approximately 43,000 ballots statewide. Bush appealed this hand recount to the U.S. Supreme Court. By a narrow 5–4 margin, the Court blocked the further counting of Florida's disputed votes, effectively handing the presidency to Bush after a thirty-five-day struggle.

In Senate and House races, voting was also extremely close. Democrats gained some ground in both congressional chambers but not enough to deprive the GOP of its control of either. Republicans held a narrow six-seat advantage in the House. The Senate was evenly divided 50–50 (although James Jeffords's defection from the GOP in May 2001 later gave the Democrats a slim advantage). Yet on election night, Republicans appeared to have won. Given an extremely buoyant economy, a nation at peace, and an edge in partisan attachments, how could the Democrats have lost? How could the race even have been close?

The 2002 Elections: A Referendum on Presidential Leadership

After his disputed victory in the 2000 presidential election, most pundits predicted that George W. Bush would have enormous difficulty governing the nation. The president's difficulties were quickly exacerbated when the defection of Vermont Senator James Jeffords gave the Democrats control of the U.S. Senate and put them in a position to block Bush's legislative agenda and key appointments. Then came 9/11. In the aftermath of the September 11, 2001, terrorist attacks, President Bush's stature rose dramatically. The president spoke eloquently about the tragedy and, more important, moved decisively to rout terrorists and their backers in Afghanistan. The success of the American military campaign coupled with the sense of determination and decisiveness projected by the White House gave Bush extraordinarily high public-approval ratings. The events in Florida surrounding the 2000 elections faded into the background as arguments about "chads" seemed unimportant compared to concerns about anthrax and nuclear terrorism.

Despite President Bush's popularity, Democrats hoped that they would be able to increase their grip on the Senate and, possibly, even take control of the House of Representatives in the November 2002, elections. Often the party controlling the White House seems to lose congressional seats in the off year, and during this particular off-year election more Republican than Democratic Senate seats were at stake, giving the GOP additional vulnerability. Beyond this, the domestic economy, which had been robust during the Clinton years, had taken a turn for the worse during Bush's first year in office. The long stock-market boom had come to an end, and millions of Americans who had invested their savings and pension funds in the market found themselves forced to borrow money to pay college tuition bills and compelled to postpone retirement. Hundreds of thousands of other Americans lost their jobs as a result of business failures and corporate belt tightening. Some key sectors, including the computer and telecommunications industries, were especially hard hit. Economic hardship usually works against the party in power, and Democrats hoped that voters would blame the GOP for their problems. Generally speaking, too, since the New Deal, voters have tended to view the Democrats as the party best able to deal with the nation's economic problems. In hard times, Americans are apt to return to the party of FDR, and in the winter of 2001 economic times were certainly getting hard.

Unfortunately for Democratic hopes, however, Bush and the Republicans were able to focus public attention on an issue that has traditionally been a source of strength for the GOP—namely, foreign and defense policy. President Bush had already made the war on terrorism and homeland defense the centerpieces of his administration. In summer 2002, though, Bush increased the nation's focus on defense and foreign policy by pointing to Iraq and its dictator, Saddam Hussein, as a major threat to the United States. Bush and his advisers asserted that Saddam was developing weapons of mass destruction that potentially might be used against the United States. The president demanded that Iraq be disarmed and

Saddam ousted. Bush called for United Nations action but, asserting what came to be called the "Bush Doctrine," said that the United States was prepared to employ unilateral military action to preempt threats from Iraq or other sources. After first asserting that it did not need congressional authorization to use force against Iraq, the administration asked for a congressional resolution supporting military action, if the president deemed such action to be necessary.

In the weeks before the election, the president crisscrossed the country, raising $140 million for Republicans and staging rallies in key states and districts. During the last week of the campaign alone, Bush made seventeen campaign appearances in fifteen states. Everywhere, the president reminded loyalists of the importance of homeland defense, the war on terrorism, and Iraq. Democrats sought to counter with the economy, but their message was disjointed and ineffective. Surveys indicated that 55 percent of the electorate trusted President Bush more than the Democrats to deal with the nation's economic problems.

By the morning after the election, it became clear that the GOP had been successful. In House races, Republicans had added four seats to increase their majority. In Senate contests, Republicans won seats in Minnesota, Missouri, and Georgia, which, after subtracting their loss in Arkansas, gave them a Senate majority for the first time in nearly two years. The Democrats took some solace from the fact that they had been successful at the gubernatorial level, including key races in Illinois, Michigan, and Pennsylvania. Voter turnout was estimated at roughly 38 percent of those eligible. Once again, most Americans had stayed home despite the heated campaign.

With their new majorities in both houses of Congress, Republicans pledged to move forward on issues that had been stalled in the Democratic Senate. These included the creation of the new Department of Homeland Security, tax cuts, energy policy, and social security. Republicans also planned to speed the confirmation of a number of Bush federal-court nominees who had been held up in the Senate judiciary committee. Democrats, for their part, pledged not to "play dead" and reminded their Republican colleagues that congressional rules provided numerous opportunities for delay and obstruction by a determined minority. The day after the election, both sides resumed the real political struggle. In 2003, Bush's policy of attacking and disarming Iraq was opposed by a number of Democrats, including several potential Democratic presidential candidates. It seemed that politics might hesitate but never fully stop at the water's edge. Indeed, by the end of 2003, Democrat Howard Dean, a vociferous opponent of the Iraq wars, seemed to be heading toward the 2004 Democratic presidential nomination.

CAMPAIGN FINANCE

Modern national political campaigns are fueled by enormous amounts of money. In a national race, millions of dollars are spent on media time, as well as on public opinion polls and media consultants. In 2000, political candidates and independent groups spent more than $3 billion on election campaigns. The average winning candidate in a campaign for a seat in the House of Representatives spent more than $500,000; the average winner in a senatorial campaign spent $4.5 million.[26] The 2000 Democratic and Republican presidential candidates were eligible to receive a total of $180 million in public funds to run their campaigns.[27] Each presidential candidate was also helped by tens of millions of dollars in so-called independent expenditures on the part of corporate and ideological "political action committees." As long as such political expenditures are not formally coordinated with a candidate's campaign, they are considered to be constitutionally protected free speech and are not subject to legal limitation or even reporting requirements. Likewise, independent soft money spending by political parties is also considered to be an expression of free speech.[28]

Sources of Campaign Funds

Federal Election Commission data suggest that approximately one-fourth of the private funds spent on political campaigns in the United States is raised through small, direct-mail contributions; about one-fourth is provided by large, individual gifts; and another fourth comes from contributions from PACs. The remaining fourth is drawn from the political parties and from candidates' personal or family resources.[29] Another source of campaign funds, which are not required to be reported to the Federal Election Commission, are independent expenditures by interest groups and parties.

Individual Donors   Direct mail serves both as a vehicle for communicating with voters and as a mechanism for raising funds. Direct-mail fund-raising efforts begin with the purchase or rental of computerized mailing lists of voters deemed likely to support the candidate because of their partisan ties, interests, or ideology. Candidates send out pamphlets, letters, and brochures describing their views and appealing for funds. Tens of millions of dollars are raised by national, state, and local candidates through direct mail each year, usually in $25 and $50 contributions, although in 2000, Bush and Gore collected about three-quarters of their donor contributions from individuals giving the then-$1,000 maximum amount.[30]

political action committees (PACs) Private groups that raise and distribute funds for use in election campaigns.

Political Action Committees   *Political action committees (PACs)* are organizations established by corporations, labor unions, or interest groups to channel the contri-

[26]Jonathan Salant, "Million-Dollar Campaigns Proliferate in 105th," *Congressional Quarterly Weekly Report*, 21 December 1996, pp. 3448–51.

[27]U.S. Federal Election Commission, "Financing the 1996 Presidential Campaign," Internet Release, 28 April 1998.

[28]Buckley v. Valeo, 424 U.S. 1 (1976); Colorado Republican Party v. Federal Election Commission, 64 U.S.L.W. 4663 (1996).

[29]FEC reports.

[30]FEC reports.

butions of their members into political campaigns. Under the terms of the 1971 Federal Elections Campaign Act, which governs campaign finance in the United States, PACs are permitted to make larger contributions to any given candidate than individuals are allowed to make. Individuals may donate a maximum of $2,000 to any single candidate, but a PAC may donate as much as $5,000 to each candidate. Moreover, allied or related PACs often coordinate their campaign contributions, greatly increasing the amount of money a candidate actually receives from the same interest group. As a result, PACs have become central to campaign finance in the United States. Many critics assert that PACs corrupt the political process by allowing corporations and other interests to influence politicians with large contributions. It is by no means clear, however, that PACs corrupt the political process any more than large, individual contributions.

More than 4,500 PACs are registered with the Federal Election Commission, which oversees campaign finance practices in the United States. Nearly two-thirds of all PACs represent corporations, trade associations, and other business and professional groups. Alliances of bankers, lawyers, doctors, and merchants all sponsor PACs. One example is the National Beer Wholesaler's Association PAC, which, for many years, was known as "SixPAC." Labor unions also sponsor PACs, as do ideological, public interest, and nonprofit groups. For example, the National Rifle Association sponsors a PAC, as does the Sierra Club. Many congressional and party leaders have also established PACs, known as leadership PACs, to provide funding for their political allies.

In recent years, PACs have raised hundreds of millions of dollars for political campaigns. But, while they have been important fund-raising tools, PAC money has been overshadowed by so-called "soft money" contributed to the political parties and then recycled into campaigns. Soft money was not subject to the limitations of the Federal Election Campaign Act, and, as a result, well-heeled individuals and interests often preferred to make large, anonymous soft-money contributions rather than—or in addition to—relatively small and publicly recorded contributions to PACs. By 2000, as many as three soft-money dollars were spent for every dollar of "hard money" given directly to candidates and PACs, and, thus, subject to FEC regulation. The 2002 campaign finance reform act outlawed many, albeit not all, forms of soft money and, thus, potentially will increase the importance of political action committees in the funding process.

The Candidates   On the basis of the Supreme Court's 1976 decision in *Buckley v. Valeo*, the right of individuals to spend their *own* money to campaign for office is a constitutionally protected matter of free speech and is not subject to limitation. Thus, extremely wealthy candidates often contribute millions of dollars to their own campaigns. Jon Corzine, for example, spent approximately $60 million of his own funds in a successful New Jersey Senate bid in 2000.

Independent Spending   As was noted above, "independent" spending is also free from regulation; private groups, political parties, and wealthy individuals, engaging in what is called **issue advocacy,** may spend as much as they wish to

issue advocacy
Independent spending by individuals or interest groups on a campaign issue but not directly tied to a particular candidate.

help elect one candidate or defeat another, as long as these expenditures are not coordinated with any political campaign. Many business and ideological groups engage in such activities. Some estimates suggest that groups and individuals spent as much as $509 million on issue advocacy—generally through television advertising—during the 2000 elections.[31] The National Rifle Association, for example, spent $3 million to remind voters of the importance of the right to bear arms, while the National Abortion and Reproductive Rights League spent nearly $5 million to express its support for Al Gore.

Some groups are careful not to mention particular candidates in their issue ads to avoid any suggestion that they might merely be fronts for a candidate's campaign committee. Most issue ads, however, are attacks on the opposing candidate's record or character. Organized labor spent more than $35 million in 1996 to attack a number of Republican candidates for the House of Representatives. Business groups launched their own multimillion-dollar issues campaign to defend the GOP House members targeted by labor.[32] In 2000, liberal groups ran ads bashing Bush's record on capital punishment, tax reform, and Social Security. Conservative groups attacked Gore's views on gun ownership, abortion, and environmental regulation.

Parties and Soft Money   Before 2002, most campaign dollars took the form of "soft money" or unregulated contributions to the national parties nominally to assist in party-building or voter-registration efforts rather than for particular campaigns. The amount that the national parties could accept from any individual or PAC for the support of candidates for national office was limited by law. To circumvent the limits, the national parties forwarded much of the money they raised to state and local party organizations—again, nominally, for party-building purposes. At the state and local levels, political-party units used most of these funds in thinly disguised campaign activities such as advertising that stopped just short of urging citizens to vote for or against a particular candidate. For example, in 1996, commercials sponsored by state Democratic party organizations looked just like commercials for Clinton. They praised the president's record while criticizing the GOP. However, because these ads did not specifically ask viewers to vote for Clinton or against his opponent, they were considered issue ads rather than campaign appeals and, thus, did not fall under the authority of the FEC. In 2000, the Democratic and Republican parties together raised nearly $1 billion in soft money mainly from corporate and professional interests.

Federal campaign finance legislation crafted by Senators John McCain and Russell Feingold enacted in 2002 sought to ban soft money by prohibiting the national parties from soliciting, receiving, or directing contributions from corporations, unions, or individuals to their affiliated state parties. The act, known as

---

[31]Kathleen Hall Jamieson, "Issue Advertising in the 1999–2000 Election Cycle," Annenberg Public Policy Center, University of Pennsylvania, February 1, 2001.

[32]David Broder and Ruth Marcus, "Wielding Third Force in Politics," *Washington Post*, 20 September 1997, p. 1.

BCRA or the Bipartisan Campaign Reform Act of 2002, also prohibited issue ads that mentioned candidates by name and used unregulated funds within sixty days of a national election. BCRA may have the effect of weakening political parties, but both parties have moved aggressively to circumvent the new law. Democratic and Republican activists have formed organizations that are nominally unaffiliated with the two parties—and are, thus, not subject to most BCRA provisions—but that plan to participate vigorously in electoral contests. These groups are raising millions of dollars. For example, financier George Soros has donated more than $12 million to groups working for the defeat of George W. Bush. For their part, Republican sympathizers have established groups such as Americans for a Better Country to solicit funds from Republican donors and work on behalf of GOP candidates. As long as these efforts are not coordinated with those of a campaign, they represent constitutionally protected free speech and are not subject to BCRA limitations. Late in 2002, portions of BCRA were invalidated by a federal appeals court. In December 2003, however, the U.S. Supreme Court overturned the lower court decision and upheld BCRA's key provisions.

Public Funding The Federal Elections Campaign Act also provides for public funding of presidential campaigns. As they seek a major party presidential nomination, candidates become eligible for public funds by raising at least $5,000 in individual contributions of $250 or less in each of twenty states. Candidates who reach this threshold may apply for federal funds to match, on a dollar-for-dollar basis, all individual contributions of $250 or less they receive. The funds are drawn from the Presidential Election Campaign Fund. Taxpayers can contribute $1 to this fund, at no additional cost to themselves, by checking a box on the first page of their federal income tax returns. Major party presidential candidates receive a lump sum (currently nearly $90 million) during the summer prior to the general election. They must meet all their general expenses from this money. Third-party candidates are eligible for public funding only if they received at least 5 percent of the vote in the previous presidential race. This stipulation effectively blocks pre-election funding for third-party or independent candidates, although a third party that wins more than 5 percent of the vote can receive public funding after the election. In 1980, John Anderson convinced banks to loan him money for an independent candidacy on the strength of poll data showing that he would receive more than 5 percent of the vote and thus would obtain public funds with which to repay the loans. Under current law, no candidate is required to accept public funding for either the nominating races or general presidential election. Candidates who do not accept public funding are not affected by any expenditure limits. Thus, in 1992 Ross Perot financed his own presidential bid and was not bound by the $55 million limit to which the Democratic and Republican candidates were held that year. Perot accepted public funding in 1996. In 2000, George W. Bush refused public funding and raised enough money to finance his own primary campaign. Eventually, Bush raised and spent nearly $200 million—twice the limit to which matching funds would have subjected him. Al Gore accepted federal funding and was nominally bound by the associated spending limitations. Soft

Campaign Contributions

No individual may contribute more than $2,000 to any one candidate in any single election. Individuals may contribute as much as $25,000 to a national party committee and up to $5,000 to a political action committee. Full disclosure is required by candidates of all contributions over $100. Candidates may not accept cash contributions over $100. Contribution limits are raised for individuals facing "millionaire" opponents.

Political Action Committees

Any corporation, labor union, trade association, or other organization may establish a political action committee (PAC). PACs must contribute to the campaigns of at least five different candidates and may contribute as much as $5,000 per candidate in any given election.

Soft Money

Contributions to state party committees are limited to $10,000 and must be used for get-out-the-vote and registration efforts. National party committees are blocked from most campaign-related expenditures.

Broadcast Advertising

Unions, corporations, and nonprofit agencies may not broadcast "issue ads" mentioning federal candidates within sixty days of a general election and thirty days of a primary election.

Presidential Elections

Candidates in presidential primaries may receive federal matching funds if they raise at least $5,000 in each of twenty states. The money raised must come in contributions of $250 or less. The amount raised by candidates in this way is matched by federal government, dollar for dollar, up to a limit of $5 million. In the general election, major-party candidates' campaigns are fully funded by the federal government. Candidates may spend no money beyond their federal funding. Independent groups may spend money on behalf of a candidate as long as their efforts are not directly tied to the official campaign. Minor-party candidates may get partial federal funding.

Federal Election Commission (FEC)

The six-member FEC supervises federal elections, collects and publicizes campaign finance records, and investigates violations of federal campaign finance law.

money and independent spending, however, not limited by election law at the time, allowed Gore to close the gap with his Republican opponent.

Campaign Finance Reform

The United States is one of the few advanced industrial nations that permit individual candidates to accept large private contributions from individual or corporate donors. Most mandate either public funding of campaigns or, as in the case of Britain, require that large private donations be made to political parties rather than to individual candidates. The logic of such a requirement is that a contribution that might seem very large to an individual candidate would weigh much less heavily if made to a national party. Thus, the chance that a donor could buy influence would be reduced.

After both the 1996 and 2000 national elections, efforts were made to enact reform measures, but these failed. In 2002, however, a scandal involving contributions made by Enron, a giant Texas energy company, gave reformers the ammunition they needed to bring about a set of changes in election law in the form of BCRA. One of the changes brought about by BCRA was a ban on campaign spending by the national party organizations, which had previously used hundreds of millions of dollars in so-called soft money contributions from corporations, unions, and individuals to influence electoral contests. The effects of this reform remain to be seen. Perhaps banning soft money will reduce the influence of wealthy donors; but, at the same time, eliminating soft money is likely to weaken the national parties—now among the few sources of coherence in America's fragmented political process. In the short term, at least, the Democratic party seems to be suffering most from the soft money ban. The Democratic party had come to depend upon a relatively small number of well-heeled contributors who wrote large checks to the national party. Republicans, on the other hand, have developed a broader base of smaller contributors who are accustomed to sending money directly to individual candidates. These "hard money" contributions are not affected by the new law.[33]

Implications for Democracy

The important role played by private funds in American politics affects the balance of power among contending social groups. Politicians need large amounts of money to campaign successfully for major offices. This fact inevitably ties their interests to the interests of the groups and forces that can provide this money. In a nation as large and diverse as the United States, to be sure, campaign contributors represent many different groups and often represent clashing interests. Business groups, labor groups, environmental groups, and pro-choice and right-to-life forces all contribute millions of dollars to political campaigns. Through such

---

[33]Adam Nagourney, "McCain Feingold School Finds Many Bewildered," *New York Times*, 19 February 2003, p. A23.

PACs as EMILY's List, women's groups contribute millions of dollars to women running for political office. One set of trade associations may contribute millions to win politicians' support for telecommunications reform, while another set may contribute just as much to block the same reform efforts. Insurance companies may contribute millions of dollars to Democrats to win their support for changes in the health-care system, while physicians may contribute equal amounts to prevent the same changes from becoming law.

Interests that donate large amounts of money to campaigns expect, and often receive, favorable treatment from the beneficiaries of their largesse. For example, in 2000 a number of major interest groups with specific policy goals made substantial donations to the Bush presidential campaign. These interests included airlines, energy producers, banks, tobacco companies, and a number of others.

After Bush's election, these interests pressed the new president to promote their legislative and regulatory agendas. For example, MBNA America was a major donor to the 2000 Bush campaign. The bank and its executives gave Bush $1.3 million. The bank's president helped raise millions more for Bush and personally gave an additional $100,000 to the president's inaugural committee after the election. All told, MBNA and other banking companies donated $26 million to the GOP in 2000. Within weeks of his election, President Bush signed legislation providing MBNA and the others with something they had sought for years—bankruptcy laws making it more difficult for consumers to escape credit-card debts. Such laws could potentially enhance the earnings of large credit-card issuers like MBNA by tens of millions of dollars every year.

In a similar vein, a coalition of manufacturers led by the U.S. Chamber of Commerce and the National Association of Manufacturers also provided considerable support for Bush's 2000 campaign. This coalition sought, among other things, the repeal of federal rules, promulgated in 2000 by the federal Occupational Safety and Health Administration (OSHA), that were designed to protect workers from repetitive-motion injuries. Again, within weeks of his election, the president approved a resolution rejecting the rules. In March 2001, the House and Senate both voted to kill the ergonomic regulations.

Despite the diversity of contributors, however, not all interests play a role in financing political campaigns. Only those interests that have a good deal of money to spend can make their interests known in this way. These interests are not monolithic, but they do not completely reflect the diversity of American society. The poor, the destitute, and the downtrodden also live in America and have an interest in the outcome of political campaigns. Who speaks for them?

DO ELECTIONS MATTER?

What is the place of elections in the American political process? Unfortunately, recent political trends, such as the increasing importance of money, raise real questions about the continuing ability of ordinary Americans to influence their government through electoral politics.

Why Is There a Decline in Voter Turnout?

Despite the sound and fury of contemporary American politics, one very important fact stands out: participation in the American political process is abysmally low. Politicians in recent years have been locked in intense struggles. As we saw in Chapter 5, partisan division in Congress has reached its highest level of intensity since the nineteenth century. Nevertheless, millions of citizens have remained uninvolved. For every registered voter who voted in the 2000 elections, for example, one stayed home.

Competition and Voter Turnout   Throughout much of American history, the major parties have been the principal agents responsible for giving citizens the motivation and incentive to vote. One of the most interesting pieces of testimony to the lengths to which parties have been willing to go to induce citizens to vote is a list of Chicago precinct captains' activities in the 1920s and 1930s. Among other matters, these party workers helped constituents obtain food, coal, and money for rent; gave advice in dealing with juvenile and domestic problems; helped constituents obtain government and private jobs; adjusted taxes; aided with permits, zoning, and building-code problems; served as liaisons with social, relief, and medical agencies; provided legal assistance and help in dealing with government agencies; handed out Christmas baskets; and attended weddings and funerals.[34] Obviously, all these services were provided in the hope of winning voters' support at election time.

Party competition has long been known to be a key factor in stimulating voting. As political scientists Stanley Kelley, Richard Ayres, and William Bowen note, competition gives citizens an incentive to vote and politicians an incentive to get them to vote.[35] The origins of the American national electorate can be traced to the competitive organizing activities of the Jeffersonian Republicans and the Federalists. According to historian David Fischer,

Rationality Principle

At least until recent years, political parties have been the primary agents for giving citizens the motivation and incentive to vote.

> During the 1790s the Jeffersonians revolutionized electioneering. . . . Their opponents complained bitterly of endless "dinings," "drinkings," and celebrations; of handbills "industriously posted along every road"; of convoys of vehicles which brought voters to the polls by the carload; of candidates "in perpetual motion."[36]

The Federalists, although initially reluctant, soon learned the techniques of mobilizing voters: "mass meetings, barbecues, stump-speaking, festivals of many

[34]Harold F. Gosnell, *Machine Politics, Chicago Model*, rev. ed. (Chicago: University of Chicago Press, 1968), Chapter 4.

[35]Stanley Kelley, Jr., Richard E. Ayres, and William G. Bowen, "Registration and Voting: Putting First Things First," *American Political Science Review* 61 (June 1967): 359–70.

[36]David H. Fischer, *The Revolution of American Conservatism: The Federalist Party in the Era of Jeffersonian Democracy* (New York: Harper & Row, 1965), p. 93. For a full account of parties as agents both of candidate selection and of mass mobilization, see John H. Aldrich, *Why Parties? The Origin and Transformation of Political Parties in America* (Chicago: University of Chicago Press, 1995).

kinds, processions and parades, runners and riders, door-to-door canvassing, the distribution of tickets and ballots, electioneering tours by candidates, free transportation to the polls, outright bribery and corruption of other kinds."[37]

The result of this competition for votes was described by historian Henry Jones Ford in his classic *Rise and Growth of American Politics*.[38] Ford examined the popular clamor against John Adams and Federalist policies in the 1790s that made government a "weak, shakey affair" and appeared to contemporary observers to mark the beginnings of a popular insurrection against the government.[39] Attempts by the Federalists initially to suppress mass discontent, Ford observed, might have "caused an explosion of force which would have blown up the government."[40] What intervened to prevent rebellion was Jefferson's "great unconscious achievement," the creation of an opposition party that served to "open constitutional channels of political agitation."[41] The creation of the Jeffersonian party diverted opposition to the administration into electoral channels. Party competition gave citizens a sense that their votes were valuable and that it was thus not necessary to take to the streets to have an impact upon political affairs. Whether or not Ford was correct in crediting party competition with an ability to curb civil unrest, it is clear that competition between the parties promoted voting.

The parties' competitive efforts to attract citizens to the polls are not their only influence on voting. Individual voters tend to form psychological ties with parties. Although the strength of partisan ties in the United States has declined in recent years, a majority of Americans continue to identify with either the Republican or Democratic party. Party loyalty gives citizens a stake in election outcomes that encourages them to take part with considerably greater regularity than those lacking partisan ties.[42] Even where both legal facilitation and competitiveness are weak, party loyalists vote with great regularity.

In recent decades, as we will see in Chapter 11, the importance of party as a political force in the United States has diminished considerably. The decline of party is undoubtedly one of the factors responsible for the relatively low rates of voter turnout that characterize American national elections. To an extent, the federal and state governments have directly assumed some of the burden of voter mobilization once assigned to the parties.

[37]Ibid., p. 109. With various forms of the secret ballot, it was often difficult to know exactly how a citizen voted—and thus chancy to bribe him if you couldn't know you were getting what you paid for. Because of this, it was often the case that buying votes was transformed into buying *non*participation—paying, that is, for those who opposed your candidates to "go fishing" on Election Day. For evidence of this in rural New York, see Gary Cox and Morgan Kousser, "Turnout and Rural Corruption in New York as a Test Case," *American Journal of Political Science* 25 (Nov. 1981): 646–63.

[38]Henry Jones Ford, *The Rise and Growth of American Politics: A Sketch of Constitutional Development* (New York: Da Capo Press, 1967 reprint of 1898 edition), Chapter 9.

[39]Ibid., p. 125.

[40]Ibid.

[41]Ibid., p. 126.

[42]See Angus Campbell et al., *The American Voter* (New York: Wiley, 1960).

For example, the 1993 Motor Voter bill was a step, though a hesitant one, in the direction of expanded voter participation. This act requires all states to allow voters to register by mail when they renew their driver's licenses (twenty-eight states already had similar mail-in procedures) and provides for the placement of voter registration forms in motor vehicle, public assistance, and military recruitment offices. Motor Voter did result in some increases in voter registration. Thus far, however, few of these newly registered individuals have actually gone to the polls to cast their ballots. After 1996, the percentage of newly registered voters who appeared at the polls actually dropped.[43]

A number of other simple institutional reforms could increase voter turnout. Same-day registration—currently used in several states, including Minnesota—could boost turnout by several percentage points. Weekend voting or, alternatively, making Election Day a federal holiday would make it easier for Americans to go to the polls. Weekend voting in a number of European nations has increased turnout by up to 10 percentage points. One reform that has been suggested but should not be adopted is Internet voting. Computer use and Internet access remain highly correlated with income and education. This method of voting would reinforce the existing class bias in the voting process as well as introduce computer security problems.

Institution Principle

Instituting new election laws, such as same-day voter registration, could increase turnout.

Even with America's current registration rules, higher levels of political participation could be achieved if competing political forces made a serious effort to mobilize voters. Unfortunately, however, contending political forces in the United States have found ways of attacking their opponents that do not require them to engage in voter mobilization, and many prefer to use these methods than to endeavor to bring more voters to the polls. The low levels of popular mobilization that are typical of contemporary American politics are very much a function of the way that politics is conducted in the United States today. The quasi-democratic character of American elections is underscored by the electoral college. This eighteenth-century device may have seemed reasonable to the Constitution's framers as a check on the judgment of a largely illiterate and uneducated electorate. Today, however, this institution undermines both the respect for and the legitimacy of electoral results. Abolition of the electoral college would have consequences for campaigning and for the party system. Candidates would be compelled to campaign throughout the nation rather than in the small number of states they see as the key "battlegrounds" for electoral-college victory. This would be a welcome development. The abolition of the electoral college might also open the way for new parties that could either breathe new life into the political process or add to the confusion of presidential elections, or both. Time would tell.

There is another sense in which low turnout is the "fault" of the way politics is conducted in the United States. The median voter theorem suggests that there

[43]Peter Baker, "Motor Voter Apparently Didn't Drive Up Turnout," *Washington Post*, 6 November 1996, p. B7.

are centripetal forces at work in the first-past-the-post, winner-take-all American electoral system. Candidates—though occasionally they err as Al Gore did in 2000—head for the center and toward one another, much as Bill Clinton succeeded in doing in 1992 and 1996, and George W. Bush in 2000. This sometimes produces disillusionment, even disgust, in voters who find, in the immortal words of former third-party candidate George Wallace, that "there ain't a dime's worth of difference" between the candidates. According to the calculus of voting that we reviewed earlier, not only is the probability of a citizen's vote making a difference low, but with convergence of candidates, the relative benefit of electing one rather than the other has also declined. Many citizens conclude there is not much point to going to the polls. Turnout, according to this view, is a consequence not only of candidates failing to mobilize voters, but also of their failure, via the inexorable pull of the median voter, to differentiate themselves and thus inspire voters.

Is It Rational to Vote?   Compared to other democracies, voter turnout in national elections is extremely low in the United States. It is usually around 50 percent for presidential elections and between 30 percent and 40 percent for midterm elections. In other Western democracies, turnout regularly exceeds 80 percent. In defense of American citizens, it should be pointed out that occasions for voting as a form of civic activity occur more frequently in the United States than in other democracies. There are more offices filled by election in the United States than elsewhere—indeed, more offices per capita, which is somewhat startling given how large a democracy the United States is. Many of these are posts that are filled by appointment in other democracies. Especially unusual in this respect are elected judges in many jurisdictions and elected local "bureaucrats" (like the local sheriff and the proverbial town dog catcher). In addition, there are primaries as well as general elections, and, in many states, there are initiatives and referenda to vote on, too. It is a wonder that American citizens don't suffer from some form of democratic fatigue! Though many scholars have tried to answer the question "Why is turnout so low?" others have argued that the real question should be "Why is turnout so high?" That is, why does anyone turn out to vote at all?

If we think of voter turnout in terms of cost-benefit analysis, then it isn't obvious why people vote.[44] There are many costs to voting. People must take time out of their busy schedules, possibly incurring a loss of wages, in order to show

---

[44]William H. Riker and Peter C. Ordeshook, "A Theory of the Calculus of Voting," *American Political Science Review* 62 (1968): 25–42. Riker and Ordeshook conclude that someone caring only about the relative *benefits* from securing the victory of his or her favorite candidate over the opponent, net of the *costs* of voting, will want to weigh the likelihood that his or her vote is decisive. Since this probability is bound to be low—indeed, infinitesimal in a moderately large electorate (as we discuss in the text shortly)—the benefits will have to be extraordinary, relative to the costs to motivate participation. Hence, Riker and Ordeshook wonder why turnout is "so high" and look to reasons other than the simple (some say, "simplistic") cost-benefit analysis for the explanation.

up at the polls. In many states, voters have to overcome numerous hurdles just to register. If an individual wants to cast an informed vote, he or she must also spend time learning about the candidates and their positions.

Voters must bear these costs no matter what the outcome of the election, yet it is extremely unlikely that an individual's vote will actually affect the outcome, unless the vote makes or breaks a tie. Just making a close election one vote closer by voting for the loser, or the winner one vote more secure by voting for her, doesn't matter much. As the old saw has it, "Closeness only counts in horseshoes and dancing." It is almost certain that if an individual did not incur the costs of voting and stayed home instead, the election results would be the same. The probability of a single vote being decisive in a presidential election is about 1 in 10 million.[45] Given the tiny probability that an individual's vote will determine whether or not the candidate he or she prefers is elected, it seems as if those who turn out to vote are behaving irrationally.[46]

One possible solution to this puzzle is that people are motivated by more than just their preferences for electing a particular candidate—they are, in fact, satisfying their duty as citizens, and this benefit exceeds the costs of voting.[47] Yet this hypothesis still does not provide an adequate answer to the rationality of voting—it only speaks to the fact that people value the *act of voting* itself. That is, people have a "taste" for voting. But rational-choice approach cannot say where tastes come from[48] and, therefore, cannot say much about voter turnout.

John Aldrich offers another possible solution: he looks at the question from the politician's point of view.[49] Candidates calculate how much to invest in campaigns based on their probability of winning. In the unlikely event that an incumbent appears beatable, the challengers often invest heavily in their own campaigns because they believe the investment has a good chance of paying off. In response to these strong challenges, incumbents will not only work harder to raise campaign funds but also spend more of what they raise.[50] Parties seeking to

---

[45]Andrew Gelman, Gary King, and John Boscardin, "Estimating the Probability of Events That Have Never Occurred: When Is Your Vote Decisive?" *Journal of the American Statistical Association* 93, no. 441 (March 1998): 1–9.

[46]A *strategic* cost-benefit analysis plays off the following reasonable argument: "If everyone determines that his or her vote doesn't matter, and no one votes, then *my* vote will determine the outcome!" This kind of strategic conjecturing has been analyzed in Thomas Palfrey and Howard Rosenthal, "Voter Participation and Strategic Uncertainty," *American Political Science Review* 79 (March 1985): 62–79. They conclude that once all the back-and-forth conjecturing is done, the question of why anyone participates remains.

[47]This was Riker and Ordeshook's line of argument. They claim, in effect, that there is an *experiential* as well as an *instrumental* rationale for voting. In more economic terms, this is the view that voting is a form of consumption as much as it is a type of investment. For a brief and user-friendly development of this logic, see Shepsle and Bonchek, *Analyzing Politics*, pp. 251–59.

[48]Brian Barry, *Sociologists, Economists, and Democracy* (London: Collier-Macmillan, 1970).

[49]John H. Aldrich, "Rational Choice and Turnout," *American Journal of Political Science* 37 (February 1993): 246–78.

[50]Gary C. Jacobson and Samuel Kernell, *Strategy and Choice in Congressional Elections*, 2nd ed. (New Haven: Yale University Press, 1983).

Nader Traders and Beyond—
Was It Rational to Vote for Ralph Nader?

In the 2000 election, was it rational to vote for Green party nominee Ralph Nader, or was a vote for a third party a "wasted" vote? The Green party had almost no chance of winning the presidency, yet nearly 3 million people voted for Nader. Most Nader voters were avowed liberals, and those votes might have proved decisive for Democratic nominee Al Gore (for example, Nader received 22,422 votes in Florida, easily enough to provide a winning margin to Gore). Why didn't these voters go with the more likely winner or just save the costs of voting altogether and skip the election?

According to the rationality principle, an individual should choose that candidate who maximizes his utility. This principle has most commonly been expressed in the *spatial model of voting,* in which both voters and candidates are placed in a policy space (for example, liberal to conservative) and voters vote for the candidate who is closest to them in that space.[51]

According to principle 3, however, rules matter. In our case, the rules of the electoral game in the United States are called "plurality voting." Whichever presidential candidate wins the plurality of the votes wins 100 percent of the "seats." This is very different from a proportional representation system, such as that used in most other democracies, where seats in the parliament are allocated according to the proportion of votes in the electorate. This means that voting for a candidate who is unlikely to win, such as Nader, can be a "wasted vote," unlikely to result in the desired outcome.

What does it mean, then, when political goals meet institutions, or when voters who prefer a candidate like Nader (or Perot, or Buchanan, or many other third-party contenders) encounter an electoral system that encourages them to vote for their second-best choice? In addition to voting purely on policy grounds, voters must also consider electability and vote *strategically* for their second choice. And this is precisely what some political scientists have found that voters do.[52]

Some voters, however, simply don't vote on policy grounds or for strategic purposes. If voters have to have a "taste" for voting regardless of who wins or loses, we would expect that other, seemingly irrelevant considerations would enter their decision making. For some of the Nader voters, the goal was to build a stronger third party by capturing 5 percent of the vote or to show the Democratic party that "there is nothing in the middle of the road but yellow stripes and dead armadillos."[53] There was even a national movement, primarily organized via the Internet, called "Nader Traders" that tried to link up Nader voters in states where Gore had a fighting chance, such as Oregon, with Gore voters in states where Gore had no chance, such as Texas. So, the logic goes, the Oregonian would "trade" her Nader vote (and vote for Gore), and the Texan would reciprocate by voting for Nader (rather than Gore). The Nader voter would get what she wants—one vote closer to 5 percent for her preferred candidate—while the Gore voter would get what he wants— one more vote for Gore in a close state.

There is another reason that a policy voter might vote for Nader. What happens when candidates meet institutions? The American electoral system encourages policy moderation and candidate convergence. The result, in the words of George Wallace, governor of Alabama and 1968 presidential candidate, is that there is not a "dime's worth of difference" between the major party contenders.

As the 2000 election made clear, not all voters are moderates. As candidates run to the middle, they may alienate voters whose views are far from the mainstream. These voters "choose" to abstain because they are unhappy with the alternatives. Even though to many liberals it seems like the Green party supporters tipped the election to Bush, it is quite possible that these voters were indifferent between the Republican and Democratic nominees. Nader may have positioned himself in such a way that he captured alienated liberal, pro-union, anti-free-trade, and other Democrats.

[51]See Melvin J. Hinich and Michael C. Munger, *Analytical Politics* (New York: Cambridge University Press, 1997).

[52]See Paul R. Abramsom, John Aldrich, Phil Paolino, and David W. Rohde, "Challenges to the American Two-Party System: Evidence from the 1968, 1980, 1992, and 1996 Presidential Elections," *Political Research Quarterly* 53, no. 3 (2000): 495–522.

[53]To borrow a book title from Jim Hightower (New York: HarperCollins, 1997).

maximize the number of positions in the government they control may also shift resources to help out the candidates in these close races.

More vigorous campaigns will generally lead to increased turnout. The increase is not necessarily due to citizens reacting to the closeness of the race (that is, the perception that their vote may affect the outcome) but to the greater effort and resources that candidates put into close races, which, in turn, reduce the costs of voting. Candidates share some of the costs of voting by helping citizens register and by getting them to the polls on Election Day. Heated advertising campaigns reduce the voters' costs of becoming informed (since candidates flood the public with information about themselves). This decrease in costs to individual voters in what strategic politicians perceive to be a close race at least partially explains why rational individuals would turn out to vote.

Rationality Principle

Given the tiny probability that an individual's vote will determine the winner of an election, candidates need to reduce the cost of voting for citizens in order to mobilize them.

Why Do Elections Matter as Political Institutions?

Voting choices and electoral outcomes can be extremely important in the United States. Yet observing the relationships among voters' choices, leadership composition, and policy output is only the first step toward understanding the significance of democratic elections. Important as they are, voters' choices and electoral results may still be less consequential for government and politics than the simple fact of voting itself. The impact of electoral decisions upon the governmental process is, in some respects, analogous to the impact made upon organized religion by individuals being able to worship at the church of their choice. The fact of worship can be more important than the particular choice. Similarly, the fact of mass electoral participation can be more significant than what or how citizens decide once they participate. Thus, electoral participation has important consequences in that it socializes and institutionalizes political action.

First, democratic elections socialize political activity. Voting is not a natural or spontaneous phenomenon. It is an institutionalized form of mass political involvement. That individuals vote rather than engage in some other form of political behavior is a result of national policies that create the opportunity to vote and discourage other political activities relative to voting. Elections transform what might otherwise consist of sporadic, citizen-initiated acts into a routine public function. This transformation expands and democratizes mass political involvement. At the same time, however, elections help to preserve the government's stability by containing and channeling away potentially more disruptive or dangerous forms of mass political activity. By establishing formal avenues for mass participation and accustoming citizens to their use, government reduces the threat that volatile, unorganized political involvement can pose to the established order.

Second, elections bolster the government's power and authority. Elections help to increase popular support for political leaders and for the regime itself. The formal opportunity to participate in elections serves to convince citizens that the government is responsive to their needs and wishes. Moreover, elections help to persuade citizens to obey. Electoral participation increases popular acceptance of taxes and military service upon which the government depends. Even if popular voting can influence the behavior of those in power, voting serves simultaneously as a form of co-optation. Elections—particularly democratic elections—substitute consent for coercion as the foundation of governmental power.

Institution Principle

Elections matter because they socialize and institutionalize political action.

Finally, elections institutionalize mass influence in politics. Democratic elections permit citizens to select and depose public officials routinely, and elections can serve to promote popular influence over officials' conduct. But however effective this electoral sanction may be, it is hardly the only means through which citizens can reward or punish public officials for their actions. Spontaneous or privately organized forms of political activity, or even the threat of their occurrence, can also induce those in power to heed the public's wishes. The behavior of even the most rigid autocrat, for example, can be influenced by the possibility that his policies may provoke popular disobedience, clandestine movements, or riots and insurrection. The alternative to democratic elections is not clearly and simply the absence of popular influence; it can instead be unregulated and unconstrained popular intervention into governmental processes. It is, indeed, often precisely because spontaneous forms of mass political activity can have too great an impact upon the actions of government that elections are introduced. Walter Lippman, a journalist who helped to pioneer the idea of public opinion voicing itself through the press via the op-ed page, once observed that "new numbers were enfranchised because they had power, and giving them the vote was the least disturbing way of letting them exercise their power."[54] The vote can provide the "least disturbing way" of allowing ordinary people to exercise power. If the people had been powerless to begin with, elections would never have been introduced.

Thus, although citizens can secure enormous benefits from their right to vote, governments secure equally significant benefits from allowing them to do so.

SUMMARY

Allowing citizens to vote represents a calculated risk on the part of power holders. On the one hand, popular participation can generate consent and support for the government. On the other hand, the right to vote may give ordinary citizens more influence in the governmental process than political elites would like.

Voting is only one of many possible types of political participation. The significance of voting is that it is an institutional and formal mode of political activity. Voting is organized and subsidized by the government. This makes voting both more limited and more democratic than other forms of participation.

All governments regulate voting in order to influence its effects. The most important forms of regulation include regulation of the electorate's composition, regulation of the translation of voters' choices into electoral outcomes, and insulation of policy-making processes from electoral intervention.

Voters' choices themselves are based on partisanship, issues, and candidates' personalities. Which of these criteria will be most important varies over time and depends upon the factors that opposing candidates choose to emphasize in their campaigns.

Campaign funds in the United States are provided by small, direct-mail contributions, large gifts, PACs, political parties, candidates' personal resources, and public funding. In 2000, some candidates also benefited from issues advocacy.

Campaign finance is regulated by the Federal Elections Campaign Act of 1971. Following the 1996 elections, the role of soft money was scrutinized. The McCain-Feingold bill, a bipartisan attempt to restrict soft money contributions and issues advocacy, gained passage in Congress in 2002.

Whatever voters decide, elections are important institutions because they socialize political activity, increase governmental authority, and institutionalize popular influence in political life.

[54]Walter Lippman, *The Essential Lippman*, ed. Clinton Rossiter and James Lare (New York: Random House, 1965), p. 12.

Rationality Principle	Collective Action Principle	Institution Principle	Policy Principle	History Principle
Elections allow multiple principals—citizens—to choose political agents to act on their behalf. But citizens usually have imperfect information about candidates and don't know how agents will act once in office.	Elections are a mechanism to channel and limit political participation to actions within the system.	The electoral process is governed by a variety of rules and procedures that allow those in power an opportunity to regulate the character and consequences of political participation.	The median voter theorem predicts policy moderation on the part of candidates.	Between 1890 and 1910, voter turnout declined in the United States as a result of new registration requirements. Since that time, turnout has remained low in comparison with the nineteenth century.
Issue voting motivates candidates to converge toward the median voter.		The rules that set the criteria for winning an election have an effect on the outcome.		
At least until recent years, political parties have been the primary agents for giving citizens the motivation and incentive to vote.		The electoral college and the Australian ballot are two instances of how changes in electoral rules can affect the outcomes of elections.		
Given the tiny probability that an individual's vote will determine the winner of an election, candidates need to reduce the cost of voting for citizens in order to mobilize them.		Instituting new election laws, such as same-day voter registration, could increase turnout.		
		Elections matter because they socialize and institutionalize political action.		

FOR FURTHER READING

Black, Earl, and Merle Black. *The Vital South: How Presidents Are Elected.* Cambridge, Mass.: Harvard University Press, 1992.

Brady, David W. *Critical Elections and Congressional Policy Making.* Stanford, Calif.: Stanford University Press, 1988.

Carmines, Edward G., and James A. Stimson. *Issue Evolution: Race and the Transformation of American Politics.* Princeton, N.J.: Princeton University Press, 1989.

Conway, M. Margaret. *Political Participation in the United States.* 3rd ed. Washington, D.C.: Congressional Quarterly Press, 2000.

Fowler, Linda L. *Candidates, Congress, and the American Democracy.* Ann Arbor: University of Michigan Press, 1994.

Fowler, Linda L., and Robert D. McClure. *Political Ambition: Who Decides to Run for Congress.* New Haven: Yale University Press, 1989.

Ginsberg, Benjamin, and Martin Shefter. *Politics by Other Means: Politicians, Prosecutors, and the Press from Watergate to Whitewater.* 3rd ed. New York: W. W. Norton, 2002.

Jackson, Brooks. *Honest Graft: Big Money and the American Political Process.* Rev. ed. New York: Alfred A. Knopf, 1990.

Piven, Frances Fox, and Richard A. Cloward. *Why Americans Don't Vote.* New York: Pantheon, 1988.

Reed, Adolph L., Jr. *The Jesse Jackson Phenomenon: The Crisis of Purpose in Afro-American Politics.* New Haven: Yale University Press, 1987.

Reichley, A. James, ed. *Elections American Style.* Washington, D.C.: Brookings Institution, 1987.

Sorauf, Frank J. *Inside Campaign Finance: Myths and Realities.* New Haven: Yale University Press, 1992.

Tate, Katherine. *From Protest to Politics: The New Black Voters in American Elections.* Cambridge, Mass.: Harvard University Press, 1994.

Witt, Linda, Karen M. Paget, and Glenna Matthews. *Running as a Woman: Gender and Power in American Politics.* New York: Free Press, 1994.

Voter Mobilization in the 2004 Election

Political Parties Shift Emphasis to Core Voters

By ADAM NAGOURNEY

In a fundamental reassessment of presidential political strategy, White House and Democratic Party officials say that turning out core Republican and Democratic voters will be more critical to next year's election than winning independent voters, long a prime target in national campaigns.

. . . The activity reflects a new view of a political landscape changed because of what each party sees as an increasingly polarized and evenly divided electorate. Americans who move between parties—known as swing voters—are being overshadowed by a growing and very motivated base of Republican and Democratic loyalists.

"There's a realization, having looked at the past few elections, that the party that motivates their base—that makes their base emotional and turn out—has a much higher likelihood of success on Election Day," Matthew Dowd, a senior adviser to Mr. Bush's re-election campaign, said in an interview.

Stanley Greenberg, the Democratic pollster who advised Bill Clinton when he won by appealing to swing voters 11 years ago, said: "Things have changed over the decade since 1992. The partisans are much more polarized. And turnout has actually gone up because the partisans have turned out in much greater numbers and in greater unity."

This shift signals that the 2004 election will have a much greater reliance on identifying supporters and getting them to the polls. That would tip the balance away from the emphasis on developing nuanced messages aimed at swing voters, who make up 10 percent to 20 percent of the electorate, pollsters said.

The change has the potential, several strategists said, of encouraging the presidential candidates to make the kind of unvarnished partisan appeals that they once tried to avoid out of concern of pushing away independent-minded voters. "If both sides are concerned about motivating their base, the agenda difference between the two is much more dramatic," Mr. Dowd said. "I actually think it could make for a much more interesting election."

New York Times, 1 September 2003, p. A1.

Mark Gersh, the Washington director for the National Committee for an Effective Congress, which conducts demographic research for Democrats, said, "I think it does tend to produce more ideological candidates."

. . . This is the latest chapter of a shift that became particularly vivid after the 2000 presidential election, which White House officials believe Mr. Bush nearly lost because the Democrats mounted the kind of highly effective voter turnout effort that had long been identified with the party. Thus, in the 2002 midterm elections, Republicans put in place a plan known as the 72-Hour Task Force to identify Republican voters and get them to the polls. The Republicans beat the Democrats at their own game, winning control of the Senate while widening their margin in the House.

David B. Magleby, the dean of social sciences at Brigham Young University, who conducted a study of spending in the 2002 Congressional election, reported evidence of a sharp change in emphasis away from television advertisements and toward get-out-the-vote efforts.

Republicans are almost certain to enjoy an advantage in their operations because of a huge fund-raising advantage. Officials from each party declined to say how much they were planning to spend on setting up turnout operations, but the parties have already begun registering voters, setting up computer programs and training party officials in ways to identify and turn out supporters.

. . . This is not a case of one strategy entirely supplanting another. The successful campaign strategy combines turning out staunch supporters and competing for swing voters. But the balance is changing, and each side is struggling to keep pace.

There are advantages and disadvantages to each strategy. Getting out the vote tends to be expensive and cumbersome, draining money that might otherwise go to television advertising.

But turning out sure-fire supporters is very attractive to campaigns because it is simpler and less risky than trying to win the battle for swing voters. That requires making a nuanced appeal that, if not done agilely, can alienate base voters and encourage the emergence of a third-party candidacy or a primary challenge. . . .

ESSENCE OF THE STORY

- Both political parties are focusing their general election efforts on turning out their committed partisans, in contrast to past campaigns, where they concentrated on the uncommitted independents.

- Some suggest that this change could result in more distinctive campaigns as candidates work to energize their followers.

- The GOP, with its large fund-raising advantage, could benefit from an election that is based more on get-out-the-vote efforts.

POLITICAL ANALYSIS

- Voting is a two-step decision: first, the citizen must decide to turn out; second, the citizen makes a choice. Candidates and parties may focus on one or both steps.

- Median voter theory implies that the moderate, middle-of-the-road, uncommitted independents are crucial in most elections, especially given American "winner take all" electoral rules. But recent trends indicate that the "middle" may be disappearing in America, and political parties and candidates have to respond to these changes.

- More distinctive campaigns could make electoral decision making easier for the voters, but it also may result in more polarized institutions.

- Recent trends in party polarization in the electorate have been, and will probably continue to be, translated into party polarization among our elected officials.

CHAPTER

11

Political Parties

We often refer to the United States as a nation with a "two-party system." By this we mean that in the United States the Democratic and Republican parties compete for office and power. Most Americans believe that party competition contributes to the health of the democratic process. Certainly, we are more than just a bit suspicious of those nations that claim to be ruled by their people but do not tolerate the existence of opposing parties.

The idea of party competition was not always accepted in the United States. In the early years of the Republic, parties were seen as threats to the social order. In his 1796 "Farewell Address," President George Washington admonished his countrymen to shun partisan politics:

> Let me . . . warn you in the most solemn manner against the baneful effects of the spirit of party, generally. This spirit . . . exists under different shapes in all governments, more or less stifled, controlled, or repressed; but in those of the popular form it is seen in its greatest rankness and is truly their worst enemy.

Often, those in power viewed the formation of political parties by their opponents as acts of treason that merited severe punishment. Thus, in 1798, the Federalist party, which controlled the national government, in effect sought to outlaw its Democratic-Republican opponents through the infamous Alien and Sedition Acts, which, among other things, made it a crime to publish or say anything that might tend to defame or bring into disrepute either the president or the Congress. Under this law, twenty-five individuals—including several Republican newspaper editors—were arrested and convicted.[1]

These efforts to outlaw political parties obviously failed. By the mid-nineteenth century American politics was dominated by powerful "machines" that inspired enormous voter loyalty, controlled electoral politics, and, through elections, exercised immense influence over government and policy in the United States. In recent years, these party machines have all but disappeared. Electoral politics has become a "candidate-centered" affair in which individual candidates for office build their own campaign organizations, while voters make choices based more on their reactions to the candidates than on loyalty to the parties. Party organization, as we saw in Chapter 5, continues to be an important factor in Congress. Even in Congress, however, the influence of party leaders is based more upon ideological affinity than any real power over party members. The

[1]See Richard Hofstadter, *The Idea of a Party System: The Rise of Legitimate Opposition in the United States, 1780–1840* (Berkeley: University of California Press, 1969).

weakness of the party system is an important factor in understanding contemporary American political patterns.[2]

In this chapter, we will examine the realities underlying the changing conceptions of political parties. As long as political parties have existed, they have been criticized for introducing selfish, "partisan" concerns into public debate and national policy. Yet political parties are extremely important to the proper functioning of a democracy. As we shall see, parties expand popular political participation, promote more effective choice in elections, and smooth the flow of public business in the Congress. Our problem in America today is not that political life is too partisan, but that our parties are not strong enough to function effectively. This is one reason that America has such low levels of popular political involvement. Unfortunately, reforms enacted in 2002, such as the elimination of soft money, will likely further erode party strength in America. First, we will look at party organization and its place in the American political process. Second, we will discuss the role of parties in election campaigns and the policy process. Third, we will consider why America has a two-party system, trace the history of each of the major parties, and look at some of the third parties that have come and gone over the past two centuries. Finally, we will address the significance and changing role of parties in American politics today and answer the question "Is the party over?"

PREVIEWING THE PRINCIPLES

Political parties act as solutions to collective-action problems in terms of electoral choice, collective choice in the policy-making process, and problems related to the ambitions of politicians. In elections, parties facilitate collection action by helping candidates attract campaign funds, assemble campaign workers, and mobilize voters. Parties also facilitate a voter's choice by providing cues or brand names to simplify the complex choices voters are given. In terms of policy making, parties work as permanent coalitions of individuals with shared goals and interests and thus facilitate cooperation in Congress. Finally, parties help regulate ambition by resolving competition among party members. Parties represent evolving coalitions of different groups in society, and over time the nature of those coalitions, and thus the nature of party politics, have changed. That is, the collective-action problems that parties seek to overcome are historically determined.

WHY DO POLITICAL PARTIES FORM?

Political parties, like interest groups, are organizations seeking influence over government. Ordinarily, they can be distinguished from interest groups on the basis of their orientation. A party seeks to control the entire government by

---

[2]For an excellent discussion of the fluctuating role of political parties in the United States and the influence of government on that role, see John J. Coleman, *Party Decline in America: Policy, Politics, and the Fiscal State* (Princeton, N.J.: Princeton University Press, 1996).

electing its members to office, thereby controlling the government's personnel. Interest groups, through campaign contributions and other forms of electoral assistance, are also concerned with electing politicians—in particular, those who are inclined in their policy direction. But interest groups ordinarily do not sponsor candidates directly, and, between elections, they usually accept government and its personnel as given and try to influence government policies through them. They are *benefit seekers*, whereas parties are comprised mainly of *office seekers*.[3]

Political parties organize because of three problems with which politicians and other political activists must cope. The first is the problem of collective action. This is chiefly an outgrowth of elections in which a candidate for office must attract campaign funds, assemble a group of activists and workers, and mobilize and persuade prospective voters to vote for him or her. Collective action is also a problem *inside* government, where kindred spirits in a legislature must arrange for, and then engage in, cooperation. The second problem for which parties are sometimes the solution is the problem of collective choice of policy.[4] The give-and-take within a legislature and between the legislature and the executive can make or break policy success and subsequent electoral success. The third problem follows from the fact that fellow politicians, like members of any organization, simultaneously seek success for the organization and success for themselves. This problem of ambition can undermine the collective aspirations of fellow partisans unless astutely managed. We briefly examine each of these three problems below.

To Facilitate Collective Action in the Electoral Process

Political parties as they are known today developed along with the expansion of suffrage and can be understood only in the context of elections. The two are so intertwined that American parties actually take their structure from the electoral process. The shape of party organization in the United States has followed a simple rule: for every district where an election is held, there should be some kind of party unit. These units provide the brand name, the resources—both human and financial—the "buzz," and the link to the larger national organization, which all help the party's candidates to arouse interest in their candidacies, to stimulate

Collective Action Principle
Parties facilitate collective action in the electoral process by helping candidates attract campaign funds, assemble campaign workers, and mobilize voters.

Policy Principle
Parties help resolve collective choice in the policy-making process by acting as permanent coalitions of individuals with similar policy goals.

Rationality Principle
Parties help deal with the threat to cooperation posed by ambitious individuals by regulating career advancement and resolving competition.

---

[3]This distinction is from John H. Aldrich, *Why Parties? The Origin and Transformation of Party Politics in America* (Chicago: University of Chicago Press, 1995).

[4]A slight variation on this theme is emphasized by Gary W. Cox and Mathew D. McCubbins in *Legislative Leviathan: Party Government in the House* (Berkeley: University of California Press, 1993). They suggest that parties in the legislature are electoral machines whose purpose is to preserve and enhance party reputation, thereby giving meaning to the party labels when elections are contested. By keeping order within their ranks, parties make certain that individual actions by members do not discredit the party label. This is an especially challenging task for party leaders when there is diversity within each party, as has often been the case in American political history.

commitment, and ultimately to overcome the free riding that diminishes turnout in general elections.

Party organization is also generally an essential ingredient for effective electoral competition by groups lacking substantial economic or institutional resources. Party building has typically been the strategy pursued by groups that must organize the collective energies of large numbers of individuals to counter their opponents' superior material means or institutional standing. Historically, disciplined and coherent party organizations were generally developed first by groups representing the political aspirations of the working classes. Parties, French political scientist Maurice Duverger notes, "are always more developed on the Left than on the Right because they are always more necessary on the Left than on the Right."[5] Compared to political parties in Europe, parties in the United States have always seemed weak. They have no criteria for party membership—no cards for their members to carry, no dues to pay, no obligatory participation in any activity, no notion of exclusiveness. Today, they seem weaker than ever; they inspire less loyalty and are less able to control nominations. Some people are even talking about a "crisis of political parties," as though party politics were being abandoned. But there continues to be at least some substance to party organizations in the United States.

To Resolve Collective Choice in the Policy-Making Process

Political parties are also essential elements in the process of making policy. Within the government, parties are coalitions of individuals with shared or overlapping interests who, as a rule, will support one another's programs and initiatives. Even though there may be areas of disagreement within each party, a common party label in and of itself gives party members a reason to cooperate. Because they are permanent coalitions, parties greatly facilitate the policy-making process. If alliances had to be formed from scratch for each legislative proposal, the business of government would slow to a crawl or would halt altogether. Parties create a basis for coalition and, thus, sharply reduce the time, energy, and effort needed to advance a legislative proposal. For example, in January 1998, when President Bill Clinton considered a series of new policy initiatives, he met first with the House and Senate leaders of the Democratic party. Although some congressional Democrats disagreed with the president's approach to a number of issues, all felt they had a stake in cooperating with Clinton to burnish the party's image in preparation for the next round of national elections. Without the support of a party, the president would be compelled to undertake the daunting and probably impossible task of forming a completely new coalition for each and every policy proposal—a virtually impossible task.

[5]See Maurice Duverger, *Political Parties: Their Organization and Activity in the Modern State*, trans. Barbara North and Robert North (New York: Wiley, 1954), p. 426.

To Deal with the Problem of Ambition

To the extent that politicians share principles, causes, and constituencies, there is a basis for coordination, common cause, cooperation, and joint enterprise. But individual ambition, sometimes in the background but often in the foreground, constantly threatens to undermine any bases for cooperation. Political parties, by regulating career advancement, by providing for the orderly resolution of ambitious competition, and by attending to the post-career care of elected and appointed party officials, do much to rescue coordination and cooperation and permit fellow partisans to pursue common causes where feasible. Simple devices like primaries, for example, provide a context in which clashing electoral ambitions may be resolved. Representative partisan bodies, like the Democratic Committee on Committees in the House (with comparable bodies in the Senate and for the Republicans), resolve competing claims for power positions. In short, politics does not consist of foot soldiers walking in lockstep, but rather of ambitious and autonomous individuals seeking power. The unchecked and unregulated burnishing of individual careers is a formula for chaos and destructive competition in which the dividends of cooperation are rarely reaped. Political parties constitute organizations of relatively kindred spirits that try to capture some of those dividends by providing a structure in which ambition is not suppressed altogether, but is not so destructive either.

WHAT FUNCTIONS DO PARTIES PERFORM?

Parties perform a wide variety of functions. They are mainly involved in nominations and elections—providing the candidates for office, getting out the vote, and facilitating mass electoral choice. That is, they help solve the problems of collective action and ambition to which we alluded earlier. They also influence the institutions of government—providing the leadership and organization of the various congressional committees. That is, they help solve the problem of collective choice concerning institutional arrangements and policy formulation that we also noted earlier.

Recruiting Candidates

One of the most important but least noticed party activities is the recruitment of candidates for local, state, and national office. Each election year, candidates must be found for thousands of state and local offices as well as for congressional seats. Where they do not have an incumbent running for re-election, party leaders attempt to identify strong candidates and to interest them in entering the campaign.

An ideal candidate will have an unblemished record and the capacity to raise enough money to mount a serious campaign. Party leaders are usually not willing to provide financial backing to candidates who are unable to raise substantial funds on their own. For a House seat this can mean several hundred thousand dollars; for a Senate seat a serious candidate must be able to raise several million dollars. Often, party leaders have difficulty finding attractive candidates and persuading them to run. In 1998, for example, Democratic leaders in Kansas and Washington reported difficulties in recruiting congressional candidates. A number of potential candidates reportedly were reluctant to leave their homes and families for the hectic life of a member of Congress. GOP leaders in Washington and Massachusetts have had similar problems finding candidates to oppose popular Democratic incumbents.[6] Candidate recruitment has become particularly difficult in an era when political campaigns often involve mudslinging and candidates must assume that their personal lives will be intensely scrutinized in the press.[7]

Nominations

Article I, Section 4, of the Constitution makes only a few provisions for elections. It delegates to the states the power to set the "Times, Places and Manner" of holding elections, even for U.S. senators and representatives. It does, however, reserve to Congress the power to make such laws if it chooses to do so. The Constitution has been amended from time to time to expand the right to participate in elections. Congress has also occasionally passed laws about elections, congressional districting, and campaign practices. But the Constitution and the laws are almost completely silent on nominations, setting only citizenship and age requirements for candidates. The president must be at least thirty-five years of age, a natural-born citizen, and a resident of the United States for fourteen years. A senator must be at least thirty, a U.S. citizen for at least nine years, and a resident of the state he or she represents. A member of the House must be at least twenty-five, a U.S. citizen for seven years, and a resident of the state he or she represents.

nomination The process through which political parties select their candidates for election to public office.

Nomination is the process by which a party selects a single candidate to run for each elective office. The nominating process (see Process Box 11.1) can precede the election by many months, as it does when the many candidates for the presidency are eliminated from consideration through a grueling series of debates and state primaries until there is only one survivor in each party—the party's nominee.

Nomination is the parties' most serious and difficult business. When more than one person aspires to an office, the choice can divide friends and associates.

---

[6]Alan Greenblatt, "With Major Issues Fading, Capitol Life Lures Fewer," *Congressional Quarterly Weekly Report*, 25 October 1997, p. 2625.

[7]For an excellent analysis of the parties' role in recruitment, see Paul S. Herrnson, *Congressional Elections: Campaigning at Home and in Washington* (Washington, D.C.: Congressional Quarterly Press, 1995).

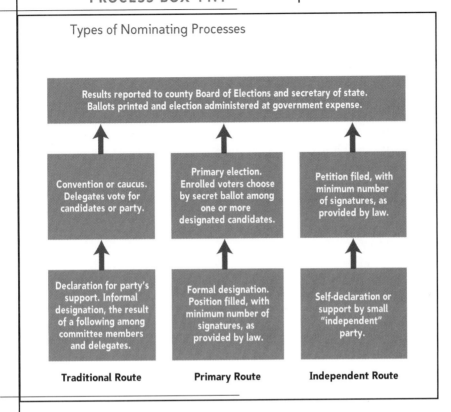

Types of Nominating Processes

Results reported to county Board of Elections and secretary of state. Ballots printed and election administered at government expense.

Convention or caucus. Delegates vote for candidates or party.	Primary election. Enrolled voters choose by secret ballot among one or more designated candidates.	Petition filed, with minimum number of signatures, as provided by law.
Declaration for party's support. Informal designation, the result of a following among committee members and delegates.	Formal designation. Position filled, with minimum number of signatures, as provided by law.	Self-declaration or support by small "independent" party.
Traditional Route	**Primary Route**	**Independent Route**

In comparison to such an internal dispute, the electoral campaign against the opposition is almost fun because there the fight is against the declared adversaries.

Nomination by Convention A nominating convention is a formal caucus bound by a number of rules that govern participation and nominating procedures. Conventions are meetings of delegates elected by party members from the relevant county (county convention) or state (state convention). Delegates to each party's national convention (which nominates the party's presidential candidate) are chosen by party members on a state-by-state basis, for there is no single national delegate selection process.

Nomination by Primary Election In primary elections, party members select the party's nominees directly rather than selecting convention delegates who then select the nominees. Primaries are far from perfect replacements for conventions since it is rare that more than 25 percent of the enrolled voters participate in them. Nevertheless, they are replacing conventions as the dominant method of nomination.[8] At the present time, only a small number of states, including Connecticut, Delaware, and Utah, provide for state conventions to nominate candidates for statewide offices, and even these states also use primaries whenever a substantial minority of delegates vote for one of the defeated aspirants.

closed primary
A primary election in which voters can participate in the nomination of candidates, but only of the party in which they are enrolled for a period of time prior to primary day.

open primary
A primary election in which the voter can wait until the day of the primary to choose which party to enroll in to select candidates for the general election.

Primary elections are mainly of two types—closed and open. In a **_closed primary,_** participation is limited to individuals who have previously declared their affiliation by registering with the party. In an **_open primary,_** individuals declare their party affiliation on the actual day of the primary election. To do so, they simply go to the polling place and ask for the ballot of a particular party. The open primary allows each voter to consider candidates and issues before deciding whether to participate and in which party's contest to participate. Open primaries, therefore, are less conducive to strong political parties. But in either case, primaries are more open than conventions or caucuses to new issues and new types of candidates.

Getting Out the Vote

The actual election period begins immediately after the nominations. Historically, this has been a time of glory for the political parties, whose popular base of support is fully displayed. All the paraphernalia of party committees and all the committee members are activated into local party workforces.

The first step in the electoral process involves voter registration. This aspect of the process takes place all year round. There was a time when party workers were responsible for virtually all of this kind of electoral activity, but they have been supplemented (and in many states virtually displaced) by civic groups such as the League of Women Voters, unions, and chambers of commerce.

Those who have registered have to decide on Election Day whether to go to the polling place, stand in line, and actually vote for the various candidates and referenda on the ballot. Political parties, candidates, and campaigning can make a big difference in convincing the voters to vote. Because it is costly for voters to participate in elections and because many of the benefits that winning parties bestow are public goods (i.e., parties cannot exclude any individual from enjoying them), people will try to free-ride by enjoying the benefits without incurring the costs of electing the party that provided the benefits. This is the _free-rider problem_ (see Chapter 1), and parties are important because they help overcome this by mobilizing the voters to support the candidates.

[8]For a discussion of some of the effects of primary elections, see Peter F. Galderisi and Benjamin Ginsberg, "Primary Elections and the Evanescence of Third Party Activity in the United States," in _Do Elections Matter?_, ed. Benjamin Ginsberg and Alan Stone (Armonk, N.Y.: M. E. Sharpe, 1986), pp. 115–30.

On any general election ballot, there are likely to be only two or three candidacies where the nature of the office and the characteristics and positions of the candidates are well known to voters. But what about the choices for judges, the state comptroller, the state attorney general, and many other elective positions? Without partisan cues, voters are likely to find it extremely difficult to make informed choices about these candidates. And what about referenda? This method of making policy choices is being used more and more as a means of direct democracy. A referendum may ask: Should there be a new bond issue for financing the local schools? Should there be a constitutional amendment to increase the number of county judges? The typical referendum question is one on which few voters have clear and knowledgeable positions. Parties and campaigns help most by giving information when voters must choose among obscure candidates and vote on unclear referenda.

Facilitating Mass Electoral Choice

Parties facilitate mass electoral choice. As the late Harvard political scientist V. O. Key pointed out long ago, the persistence over time of competition between groups possessing a measure of identity and continuity is virtually a necessary condition for electoral control.[9] *Party identification* increases the electorate's capacity to recognize its options. Continuity of party division facilitates organization of the electorate on the long-term basis necessary to sustain any popular influence in the governmental process. In the absence of such identity and continuity of party division, the voter is, in Key's words, confronted constantly by "new faces, new choices."[10] Parties lower information costs of participating by providing a kind of "brand name" recognizability; that is, voters know with a substantial degree of accuracy what positions a candidate will take just by identifying the candidate's party affiliation. In addition, parties give elections a kind of sporting-event atmosphere, with voters treating parties like teams that they can support and cheer on to victory. This enhances the entertainment value of participating in elections. Parties also direct the flow of government benefits, such as patronage jobs, to those who put the party in power. These and other activities encourage individuals to identify with and support one of the two parties.

Although political parties continue to be significant in the United States, the role of party organizations in electoral politics has clearly declined over the past three decades. This decline, and the partial replacement of the party by new forms of electoral technology, is one of the most important developments in twentieth- and twenty-first-century American politics.

Collective Action Principle

Parties can help mobilize voters who are potential free riders.

party identification
An individual voter's psychological ties to one party or another.

Rationality Principle

Parties can lower the cost of voting by facilitating a voter's choice.

---

[9]V. O. Key with Alexander Heard, *Southern Politics in State and Nation* (New York: Knopf, 1949), Chapter 14.
[10]Ibid.

Influencing National Government

The ultimate test of the party system is its relationship to and influence on the institutions of government and the policy-making process. Thus, it is important to examine the party system in relation to Congress and the president.

Parties and Policy   One of the most familiar observations about American politics is that the two major parties try to be all things to all people and are, therefore, indistinguishable from each other. Data and experience give some support to this observation. Parties in the United States are not programmatic or ideological, as they have sometimes been in Britain or other parts of Europe. But this does not mean that there are no differences between them. During the Reagan era, important differences emerged between the positions of Democratic and Republican party leaders on a number of key issues, and these differences are still apparent today. For example, the national leadership of the Republican party supports maintaining high levels of military spending, cuts in social programs, tax relief for middle- and upper-income voters, tax incentives to businesses, and the "social agenda" backed by members of conservative religious denominations. The national Democratic leadership, on the other hand, supports expanded social welfare spending, cuts in military spending, increased regulation of business, and a variety of consumer and environmental programs.

Policy Principle

Policies typically reflect the goals of whichever party is in power.

These positions reflect differences in philosophy as well as in the core constituencies to which the parties seek to appeal. The Democratic party at the national level seeks to unite organized labor, the poor, members of racial minorities, and liberal upper-middle-class professionals. The Republicans, by contrast, appeal to business, upper-middle- and upper-class groups in the private sector, and social conservatives. Often, party leaders will seek to develop issues that they hope will add new groups to their party's constituent base. During the 1980s, for example, under the leadership of Ronald Reagan, the Republicans devised a series of "social issues," including support for school prayer, opposition to abortion, and opposition to affirmative action, designed to cultivate the support of white southerners. This effort was extremely successful in increasing Republican strength in the once solidly Democratic South. In the 1990s, under the leadership of Bill Clinton, who called himself a "new Democrat," the Democratic party sought to develop new social programs designed to solidify the party's base among working-class and poor voters, and new, somewhat more conservative economic programs aimed at attracting the votes of middle- and upper-middle-class voters.

As these examples suggest, parties do not always support policies because they are favored by their constituents. Instead, party leaders can play the role of policy entrepreneurs, seeking ideas and programs that will expand their party's base of support while eroding that of the opposition. It is one of the essential characteristics of party politics in America that a party's programs and policies often lead, rather than follow, public opinion. Like their counterparts in the business world, party leaders seek to identify and develop "products" (programs and policies) that will appeal to the public. The public, of course, has the ultimate voice. With its votes, it decides whether or not to "buy" new policy offerings.

Through members elected to office, both parties have made efforts to translate their general goals into concrete policies. Republicans, for example, implemented tax cuts, increased defense spending, cut social spending, and enacted restrictions on abortion during the 1980s and 1990s. Democrats were able to defend consumer and environmental programs against GOP attacks and sought to expand domestic social programs in the late 1990s. In 2001, President Bush sought large cuts in federal taxes as well as shifts in the administration of federal social programs that would reduce the power of the federal bureaucracy and increase the role of faith-based organizations allied with the Republican party. Both parties, of course, have been hampered by internal divisions and the recurrent pattern of divided control of Congress and the executive branch that has characterized American politics for the past two decades.

The Parties and Congress   Congress, in particular, depends more on the party system than is generally recognized. First, the speakership of the House is essentially a party office. All the members of the House take part in the election of the Speaker. But the actual selection is made by the ***majority party***. When the majority party caucus presents a nominee to the entire House, its choice is then invariably ratified in a straight party-line vote.

The committee system of both houses of Congress is also a product of the two-party system. Although the rules organizing committees and the rules defining the jurisdiction of each are adopted like ordinary legislation by the whole membership, all other features of the committees are shaped by parties. For example, each party is assigned a quota of members for each committee, depending upon the percentage of total seats held by the party. On the rare occasions when an independent or third-party candidate is elected, the leaders of the two parties must agree against whose quota this member's committee assignments will count. Presumably, the member will not be able to serve on any committee until the question of quota is settled.

As we saw in Chapter 5, the assignment of individual members to committees is a party decision. Each party has a "committee on committees" to make such decisions. Permission to transfer to another committee is also a party decision. Moreover, advancement up the committee ladder toward the chair is a party decision. Since the late nineteenth century, most advancements have been automatic—based upon the length of continuous service on the committee. This seniority system has existed only because of the support of the two parties, and each party can depart from it by a simple vote. During the 1970s, both parties reinstituted the practice of reviewing each chairmanship—voting anew every two years on whether each chair would be continued. In 2001, Republicans lived up to their 1995 pledge to limit House committee chairs to three terms. Existing chairmen were forced to step down but were generally replaced by the next most senior Republican member of each committee.

majority party
Party that holds the majority of legislative seats in either the House or the Senate.

Collective Action Principle
Cooperation in Congress is facilitated by the party system.

Why Are the Democrats and Republicans Polarized?

What are political parties? Their institutional form varies almost as much as democracies vary worldwide. Political parties are much more than a cluster of individuals with similar ideological positions. According to the "three images" viewpoint of V. O. Key, a political party includes "party in the electorate" (individuals who affiliate with a particular party); "party in the campaign" (local, grassroots groups; county, state, and national organizations; and individual candidates and their campaign organizations), and "party in government" (party members who hold elected positions).[11]

Regardless of the image, though, political parties are fundamentally organizations used by candidates and party activists who want to gain and hold onto political power.[12] Some interpret this rational-choice account of political parties to imply that politicians have only one goal: seeking and holding onto political power. This is not true. It is just that, in the language of the first principle of politics, holding office is *instrumental* for gaining your other goals, such as passing good legislation or reforming government.

Principle 3 also points to another role for parties: helping to solve the collective-action problem presented by mass democracy. Candidates use parties to help recruit volunteers and mobilize voters during elections. Interestingly, as candidates have been able to build their own financial and personnel organizations over the past few decades, they have found less and less use for parties. Parties, it seems, are no longer so instrumental.[13]

What strategy should parties and their candidates follow to gain that elusive political office? In the classic spatial model of politics, voters and candidates are arrayed across a single policy dimension, typically liberal versus conservative. Political "parties" in this model look like two overlapping bell curves, the Republican party somewhat to the right and the Democratic party somewhat to the left. There is significant overlap because parties in the United States have not been ideologically distinct throughout most of our history. In fact, Principles 3 and 4 help us understand why American parties often seem so similar. Candidates' desires to win office, combined with electoral rules that award 100 percent of the "seats" in a congressional district to the candidate with the most votes, encourage candidates to run to the middle, attempting to "capture" as much ideological space as possible from the opposition.[14]

Some political observers celebrate the "me-too"-ism of American parties because it lends itself to policy stability. In many political systems, a change in governmental control results in dramatic policy changes. In the United States, not a "dime's worth of difference" means that changes in party control seldom result in large changes in social or economic policy. In America, centrist policy dominates.

In recent decades, however, party polarization threatens to undermine the moderating impact of centrism. The U.S. Congress, the president, and, some even suggest, state legislatures throughout the country have become increasingly emptied of moderates. According to the fourth principle of politics, either preferences or institutional procedures must have changed, thus creating this new policy outcome.

Two of the most commonly cited theories are rules-based changes: gerrymandering and the rise of primary elections. Like much of modern life, the computer revolution has radically changed redistricting. With computers, politicians, when redistricting, are allowed a degree of sophistication that did not exist in the past. Party members, both officeholders and party officials, realize that control of the redistricting game can lead to control of the legislature. Map drawers are now fairly confident about the "safety" of an electoral district and have systematically eliminated "swing" districts (which favor moderate candidates) and replaced them with districts that are more homogeneous in both ideology and partisanship.

The use of primary elections to select candidates increased at the same time, after the party reforms of the late 1960s. Primary voters are more ideologically extreme and more committed partisans than their general-election counterparts. As a result, state legislatures and the Congress are becoming increasingly filled with members from the extremes of their party rather than from the center.

The last three decades have seen an increase in the perceived ideological gap between Republicans and Democrats.[15] The lack of issues that cut across party lines has only exacerbated partisan tensions. Thirty years ago policy areas such as gay rights and abortion cut across party lines. Enacting policy in these and other cross-party areas required compromise with members of the opposing party. Since that time, many of these nonpartisan issues have become incorporated into the existing party structure.[16] This has decreased the incentive and opportunity for lawmakers to work with members from across the aisle.

Political deadlock may be a consequence of the increase in political polarization. With increased partisanship, the opportunity for the type of compromises necessary for lawmaking decreases. The decline of moderate members also represents a loss of natural mediators between the two parties. As a result, the legislative process slows, and fights over major policies become more rancorous. The polarization of parties may also be depressing voter turnout. An absence of moderate candidates may be alienating moderate voters, who do not wish to see extremists in either party elected. Presented with only a choice between competing ideologues, moderate voters may simply be opting out of elections altogether.

---

[11]V. O. Key, *Politics, Parties, and Pressure Groups,* 4th ed. (New York: Crowell, 1958). Key was a central figure in political science in the 1950s and 1960s.

[12]"Political parties can be seen as coalitions of elites used to capture and use political office." John Aldrich, *Why Parties? The Origin and Transformation of Party Politics in America* (Chicago: University of Chicago Press, 1995).

[13]Aldrich makes this argument in *Why Parties?*

[14]The underlying logic has been recognized as long as there have been plurality elections (the winner need only gain a plurality) and single-member districts (hence the phrase "100 percent of the 'seats'"). Consider a different set of institutions, where there are multiple seats in a district and they are allocated in proportion to the number of votes. A party could run an ideologically distinct campaign, hold onto a proportion of the electorate, and still win at least some seats in the legislature.

[15]Gary C. Jacobson, "Partisan Polarization in Presidential Support: The Electoral Connection," paper prepared for the 2002 annual meeting of the American Political Science Association, Boston, August 29–September 1, 2002.

[16]Thomas M. Casey and Geoffrey C. Layman, "Party Activists and the Ideological Polarization of American Politics: A Dynamic Model," paper prepared for the annual meeting of the Midwest Political Science Association, Chicago, April 25–28, 2002.

President and Party   As we saw earlier, the party that wins the White House is always led, in title anyway, by the president. The president normally depends upon fellow party members in Congress to support legislative initiatives. At the same time, members of the party in Congress hope that the president's programs and personal prestige will help them raise campaign funds and secure re-election. During his two terms in office, President Bill Clinton had a mixed record as party leader. In the realm of trade policy, Clinton sometimes found more support among Republicans than among Democrats. In addition, although Clinton proved to be an extremely successful fund-raiser, congressional Democrats often complained that he failed to share his largesse with them. At the same time, however, a number of Clinton's policy initiatives seemed calculated to strengthen the Democratic party as a whole. Clinton's early health-care initiative would have linked millions of voters to the Democrats for years to come, much as FDR's Social Security program had done in a previous era. But by the middle of Clinton's second term, the president's acknowledgement of his sexual affair with a White House intern threatened his position as party leader. Initially, Democratic candidates nationwide feared that the scandal would undermine their own chances for election, and many moved to distance themselves from the president. The Democrats' surprisingly good showing in the 1998 elections, however, strengthened Clinton's position and gave him another chance to shape the Democratic agenda.

Between the 1998 and 2000 elections, however, the president's initiatives on Social Security and nuclear disarmament failed to make much headway in a Republican-controlled Congress. The GOP was not prepared to give Clinton anything for which Democrats could claim credit in the 2000 elections. Lacking strong congressional leadership, however, the GOP did agree to many of Clinton's budgetary proposals in 1999 and dropped its own plan for large-scale cuts in federal taxes.

When he assumed office in 2001, President George W. Bush called for a new era of bipartisan cooperation, and the new president did receive the support of some Democratic conservatives. Generally, however, Bush depended on near-unanimous backing from his own party in Congress to implement his plans for cutting taxes as well as other elements of his program. After September 11, both parties united behind Bush's military response. Even then, however, the parties divided on other matters. One example was the airline safety bill, discussed in Chapter 5.

PARTY SYSTEMS

Our understanding of political parties would be incomplete if we only considered what roles the parties perform. America's political parties compete with one another over offices, policies, and power, and, as malleable institutions, have adapted to the demands of the time and age. In short, the history of each party is inextricably linked to that of its major rival. Historians often call the constellation of parties that are important at any given moment a nation's "party system."

The most obvious feature of a party system is the number of major parties competing for power. Usually, the United States has had a two-party system, meaning that only two parties have a serious chance to win national elections. Of course, we have not always had the same two parties, and, as we shall see below, minor parties often put forward candidates.

The term *party system*, however, refers to more than just the number of parties competing for power. It also connotes the organization of the parties, the balance of power between and within party coalitions, the parties' social and institutional bases, and the issues and policies around which party competition is organized. Seen from this broader perspective, the character of a nation's party system can change, even though the number of parties remains the same and even when the same two parties seem to be competing for power. Today's American party system is very different from the party system of fifty years ago, even though the Democrats and Republicans continue to be the major competing forces. The character of a nation's party system can have profound consequences for the relative influence of social forces, the importance of political institutions, and even the types of issues and policies that reach the nation's political agenda. For example, the contemporary American political parties mainly compete for the support of different groups of middle-class Americans. As a result, issues that concern the middle and upper-middle classes, such as the environment, health care, retirement benefits, and taxation, are very much on the political agenda, while issues that concern working-class and poorer Americans, such as welfare and housing, receive short shrift from both parties.[17] Of course, throughout America's history, the creation of new issues did not just *happen*. Rather, it was the fruit of political entrepreneurs looking for opportunities to undermine the prevailing political orthodoxy and its political beneficiaries.[18] (See Process Box 11.2)

Over the course of American history, changes in political forces and alignments have produced six distinctive party systems.

The First Party System: Federalists and Democratic-Republicans

Although George Washington and, in fact, many leaders of the time deplored partisan politics, the two-party system emerged early in the history of the new Republic. Competition in Congress between northeastern mercantile and southern agrarian factions led Alexander Hamilton and the northeasterners to form a

[17]See Matthew A. Crenson and Benjamin Ginsberg, *Downsizing Democracy: How America Sidelined Its Citizens and Privatized Its Public* (Baltimore: Johns Hopkins University Press, 2002).

[18]Such entrepreneurial efforts are not always successful; history tends mainly to remember the successful ones. For an intriguing development of this notion, see William H. Riker, *Liberalism against Populism: A Confrontation between the Theory of Democracy and the Theory of Social Choice* (San Francisco: Freeman, 1982), especially Chapters 8 and 9. See also Andrew J. Polsky, "When Business Speaks: Political Entrepreneurship, Discourse, and Mobilization in American Partisan Regimes," *Journal of Theoretical Politics* 12 (2002): 451–72.

How the Party System Evolved

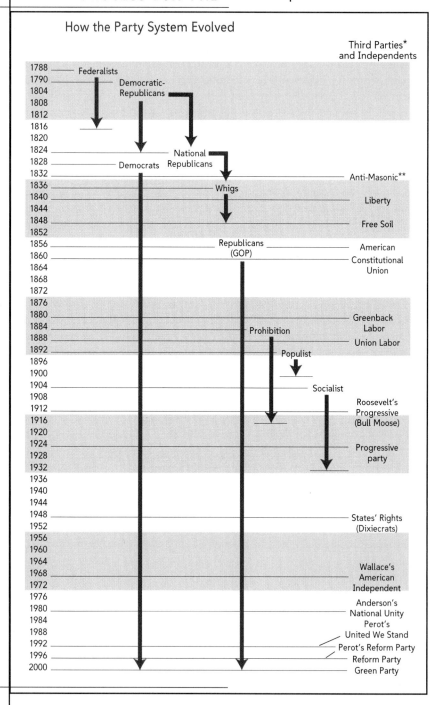

Third Parties*
and Independents

*Or, in some cases, fourth party; most of these are one-term parties.

**The Anti-Masonics not only had the distinction of being the first third party, but they were also the first party to hold a national nominating convention and the first to announce a party platform.

cohesive voting bloc within Congress. The southerners, led by Thomas Jefferson and James Madison, responded by attempting to organize a popular following to change the balance of power within Congress. When the northeasterners replied to this southern strategy, the result was the birth of America's first national parties—the Democratic-Republicans, whose primary base was in the South, and the Federalists, whose strength was greatest in the New England states. The Federalists spoke mainly for New England mercantile groups and supported a program of protective tariffs to encourage manufacturers, assumption of the states' Revolutionary War debts, the creation of a national bank, and resumption of commercial ties with England. The Democratic-Republicans opposed these policies, favoring instead free trade, the promotion of agrarian over commercial interests, and friendship with France.

The rationale behind the formation of both parties was primarily as a means to institutionalize existing voting blocs in Congress around a cohesive policy agenda. While the Federalists and Democratic-Republicans competed in elections, their ties to the electorate were loose. In 1800, the American electorate was small, and deference was an important political factor, with voters generally expected to follow the lead of local political and religious leaders and community notables. Nominations were informal without rules or regulations. Local party leaders would simply gather all the party elites, and they would agree on the person, usually from among themselves, who would be the candidate. The meetings where candidates were nominated were generally called caucuses. In this era before the introduction of the secret ballot, many voters were reluctant to publicly defy the views of influential members of their communities. In this context, the Democratic-Republicans and Federalists organized political clubs and developed newspapers and newsletters designed to mobilize elite opinion and relied upon local elites to bring along their followers. In the election of 1800, Jefferson defeated incumbent Federalist president John Adams and led his party to power. Over the ensuing years, the Federalists gradually weakened. The party disappeared altogether after the pro-British sympathies of some Federalist leaders during the War of 1812 led to charges that the party was guilty of treason.

The Second Party System: Democrats and Whigs

From the collapse of the Federalists until the 1830s, America had only one political party, the Democratic-Republicans. This period of one-party politics is sometimes known as the "era of good feelings," to indicate the absence of party competition. Throughout this period, however, there was intense factional conflict within the Democratic-Republican party, particularly between the supporters and opponents of General Andrew Jackson, America's great military hero of the War of 1812. Jackson was one of five serious party candidates for president in 1824 and won the most popular and electoral votes but a majority of neither, thus throwing the election into the House of Representatives. Jackson's opponents united to deny him the presidency in 1824, but Jackson won election in 1828 and again in 1832.

Jackson was greatly admired by millions of ordinary Americans living in the nation's farms and villages, and the Jacksonians made the most of the general's appeal to the common people by embarking on a program of suffrage expansion that would give Jackson's impecunious but numerous supporters the right to vote. To bring growing numbers of voters to the polls, the Jacksonians built political clubs and held mass rallies and parades, laying the groundwork for a new and more popular politics. Jackson's vice president and eventual successor, Martin Van Buren, was the organizational genius behind the Jacksonian movement, establishing a party central committee, state party organizations, and party newspapers. In response to widespread complaints about cliques of party leaders dominating all the nominations at party caucuses and leaving no place for the other party members who wanted to participate, the Jacksonians also established the state and national party convention as the forums for nominating presidential candidates. The conventions gave control over the presidential nominating process to the new state party organizations that the Jacksonians had created and expected to control. As political scientist John Aldrich has argued, unlike any political leader before him, Van Buren appreciated the possibilities for mass mobilization and the necessity of a well-oiled national organization to overcome free riding and other collective action problems.[19]

The Jacksonians, who came to be known as the Democratic party, were not without opponents, however, especially in the New England states; and during the 1830s, groups opposing Jackson for reasons of personality and politics united to form a new political force—the Whig party—thus giving rise to the second American party system. During the 1830s and 1840s, the Democrats and Whigs built party organizations throughout the nation, and both sought to enlarge their bases of support by expanding the suffrage through the elimination of property restrictions and other barriers to voting—at least voting by white males. This would not be the last time that party competition paved the way for expansion of the electorate. Support for the new Whig party was stronger in the Northeast than in the South and the West and stronger among mercantile groups than among small farmers. Hence, in some measure, the Whigs were the successors of the Federalists. Many, though not all, Whigs favored a national bank, a protective tariff, and federally sponsored internal improvements. The Jacksonians opposed all three policies. Yet conflict between the two parties revolved as much around personalities as policies. The Whigs were a diverse group, united more by opposition to the Democrats than by agreement on programs. In 1840, the Whigs won their first presidential election under the leadership of General William Henry Harrison, a military hero known as "Old Tippecanoe." The 1840 election marked the first time in American history that two parties competed for the presidency in every state in the Union. The Whig campaign carefully avoided issues—since different party factions disagreed on most matters—and emphasized the personal qualities and heroism of the candidate. The Whigs also invested heavily in

---

[19]See Aldrich, *Why Parties?*, Chapter 4.

campaign rallies and entertainment to win the hearts, if not exactly the minds, of the voters. The 1840 campaign came to be called the "hard cider" campaign to denote the then-common practice of using food and, especially, drink to elicit electoral favor.

In the late 1840s and early 1850s, conflicts over slavery produced sharp divisions within both the Whig and Democratic parties, despite the efforts of party leaders like Henry Clay and Stephen Douglas to develop sectional compromises that would bridge the increasing gulf between the North and the South. By 1856, the Whig party had all but disintegrated under the strain. The 1854 Kansas-Nebraska Act overturned the Missouri Compromise of 1820 and the Compromise of 1850, which together had hindered the expansion of slavery in the American territories. The Kansas-Nebraska Act gave each territory the right to decide whether or not to permit slavery. Opposition to this policy led to the formation of a number of antislavery parties, with the Republicans emerging as the strongest of these new forces.[20] It drew its membership from existing political groups—former Whigs, Know-Nothings, Free-Soilers, and antislavery Democrats. In 1856, the party's first presidential candidate, John C. Frémont, won one-third of the popular vote and carried eleven states.

The early Republican platforms appealed to commercial as well as antislavery interests. The Republicans favored homesteading, internal improvements, the construction of a transcontinental railroad, and protective tariffs, as well as the containment of slavery. In 1858, the Republican party won control of the House of Representatives; in 1860, the Republican presidential candidate, Abraham Lincoln, was victorious. Lincoln's victory strengthened Southern calls for secession from the Union and, soon thereafter, to all-out civil war.

The Third Party System, 1860–1896: Republicans and Democrats

During the course of the war, President Lincoln depended heavily upon Republican governors and state legislatures to raise troops, provide funding, and maintain popular support for a long and bloody military conflict. The secession of the South had stripped the Democratic party of many of its leaders and supporters, but, nevertheless, the Democrats remained politically competitive throughout the war and nearly won the 1864 presidential election because of war weariness on the part of the Northern public. With the defeat of the Confederacy in 1865, some congressional Republicans sought to convert the South into a Republican bastion through a program of reconstruction that enfranchised newly freed slaves while disenfranchising many white voters and disqualifying many white politicians from seeking office. This reconstruction program collapsed in the 1870s as a result of divisions within the Republican party in Congress and violent resistance to Reconstruction by Southern whites. With the end of Reconstruction, the former Confederate states regained full

[20]See William E. Gienapp, *The Origins of the Republican Party, 1852–1856* (New York: Oxford University Press, 1994).

membership in the Union and full control of their internal affairs. Throughout the South, African Americans were deprived of political rights, including the right to vote, despite post–Civil War constitutional guarantees to the contrary. The post–Civil War South was solidly Democratic in its political affiliation and, with a firm Southern base, the national Democratic party was able to confront the Republicans on a more or less equal basis. From the end of the Civil War to the 1890s, the Republican party remained the party of the North, with strong business and middle-class support, while the Democratic party was the party of the South, with support from working-class and immigrant groups in the North. Republican candidates campaigned by waving the "bloody shirt" of the Civil War and urging their supporters to "vote the way you shot." Democrats emphasized the issue of the tariff, which they claimed was ruinous to agricultural interests.

Party Machines as a Strategic Innovation   It was during the third party system that party entrepreneurs were most successful in making party organizations well-oiled machines. In the nineteenth and early twentieth centuries, many cities and counties, and even a few states upon occasion, had such well-organized parties that they were called *party machines* and their leaders were bosses. Party machines depended heavily upon the patronage of the spoils system, the party's power to control government jobs. Patronage worked as a selective benefit with anyone the party wished to attract to its side. With thousands of jobs to dispense to the party faithful, party bosses were able to recruit armies of political workers, who, in turn, mobilized millions of voters. During the height of party machines, party and government were virtually interchangeable.

> **party machines**
> In the late nineteenth and early twentieth centuries, local party organizations that controlled local politics through patronage and control of nominations.

Many critics condemned party machines as antidemocratic and corrupt. They argued that machines served the interests of powerful businesses and did not help the working people who voted for them. But one of the most notorious machine leaders in American political history, George Washington Plunkitt of New York City's Tammany Hall, considered machine politics and the spoils system to be "patriotic." Plunkitt grasped a simple, central fact about purposeful behavior and overcoming the collective-action problem. To create and retain political influence and power, "you must study human nature and act accordin'." He argued with some acumen that the country was built by political parties, that the parties needed such patronage to operate and thrive, and that if patronage was withdrawn, the parties would "go to pieces." As we will see next, he was somewhat prescient in making this observation.

Institutional Reforms of the Progressives   Around the turn of the twentieth century, the excessive powers and abuses of party machines and their bosses led to one of the great reform movements in American history, the so-called Progressive era. Many Progressive reformers were undoubtedly motivated by a sincere desire to rid politics of corruption and to improve the quality and efficiency of government in the United States. But, simultaneously, from the perspective of middle- and upper-class Progressives and the financial, commercial, and industrial elites with whom they were often associated, the weakening or elimination of party organization would also mean that power could more readily be acquired and retained by the "best men"—that is, those with wealth, position, and education.

The list of anti-party reforms of the Progressive era is a familiar one. As we saw in Chapter 10, voter registration laws were introduced that required eligible voters to register in person well before the actual election. The Australian-ballot reform took away the parties' privilege of printing and distributing ballots and, thus, introduced the possibility of split-ticket voting (see also Chapter 10). The introduction of nonpartisan local elections eroded grassroots party organization. The extension of "merit systems" for administrative appointments stripped party organizations of their vitally important access to patronage and, thus, reduced party leaders' capacity to control candidate nominations.

These reforms obviously did not destroy political parties as entities, but taken together they did substantially weaken party organizations in the United States. After the turn of the century, the strength of American political parties gradually diminished, and voter turnout declined precipitously. Between the two world wars, organization remained the major tool available to contending electoral forces, but in most areas of the country the "reformed" state and local parties that survived the Progressive era gradually lost their organizational vitality and coherence, and became less effective campaign tools. While most areas of the nation continued to boast Democratic and Republican party groupings, reform did mean the elimination of the permanent mass organizations that had been the parties' principal campaign weapons.

The Fourth Party System, 1896–1932

During the 1890s, profound and rapid social and economic changes led to the emergence of a variety of protest parties, including the Populist party, which won the support of hundreds of thousands of voters in the South and West. The Populists appealed mainly to small farmers but also attracted western mining interests and urban workers as well. In the 1892 presidential election, the Populist party carried four states and elected governors in eight states. In 1896, the Democrats in effect adopted the Populist party platform and nominated William Jennings Bryan, a Democratic senator with pronounced Populist sympathies, for the presidency. The Republicans nominated conservative senator William McKinley. In the ensuing campaign, northern and midwestern business made an all-out effort to defeat what it saw as a radical threat from the Populist-Democratic alliance. When the dust settled, the Republicans had won a resounding victory. In the nation's metropolitan regions, especially in the Northeast and upper Midwest, workers became convinced that the Democratic/Populist alliance threatened the industries that provided their jobs, while immigrants were frightened by the nativist rhetoric employed by some Populist orators and writers. The GOP had carried the northern and midwestern states and confined the Democrats to their bastions in the South and Far West. For the next thirty-six years, the Republicans were the nation's majority party, carrying seven of nine presidential elections and controlling both houses of Congress in fifteen of eighteen contests. The Republican party of this era was very much the party of American business, advocating low taxes, high tariffs, and a minimum of government regulation. The Democrats were far too weak to offer much opposition. Southern Democrats, moreover, were more concerned with maintaining the region's autonomy on issues of race to challenge the Republicans on other fronts.

The Fifth Party System: The New Deal Coalition, 1932–1968

Soon after Republican presidential candidate Herbert Hoover won the 1928 presidential election, the nation's economy collapsed. The Great Depression, which produced unprecedented economic hardship, stemmed from a variety of causes; but from the perspective of millions of Americans, the Republican party had not done enough to promote economic recovery. In 1932, Americans elected Franklin D. Roosevelt and a solidly Democratic Congress. FDR developed a program for economic recovery that he dubbed the "New Deal." Under the auspices of the New Deal, the size and reach of America's national government was substantially increased. The federal government took responsibility for economic management and social welfare to an extent that was unprecedented in American history. Roosevelt designed many of his programs specifically to expand the political base of the Democratic party. He rebuilt the party around a nucleus of unionized workers, upper-middle-class intellectuals and professionals, southern farmers, Jews, Catholics, and northern African Americans (few blacks in the South could vote) that made the Democrats the nation's majority party for the next thirty-six years. Republicans groped for a response to the New Deal and often wound up supporting popular New Deal programs like Social Security in what was sometimes derided as "me too" Republicanism.

The New Deal coalition was severely strained during the 1960s by conflicts over President Lyndon Johnson's Great Society initiative, civil rights, and the Vietnam War. A number of Johnson's Great Society programs, designed to fight poverty and racial discrimination, involved the empowerment of local groups that were often at odds with established city and county governments. These programs touched off battles between local Democratic political machines and the national administration that split the Democratic coalition. For its part, the struggle over civil rights initially divided northern Democrats, who supported the civil rights cause, from white southern Democrats, who defended the system of racial segregation. Subsequently, as the civil rights movement launched a northern campaign aimed at securing access to jobs and education and an end to racial discrimination in such realms as housing, northern Democrats also split, often along class lines, with more blue-collar workers voting Republican. The struggle over the Vietnam War further divided the Democrats, with upper-income liberal Democrats strongly opposing the Johnson administration's decision to send U.S. forces to fight in Southeast Asia. These schisms within the Democratic party provided an opportunity for the GOP to return to power, which it did in 1968 under the leadership of Richard Nixon.

The Sixth Party System?

In the 1960s, conservative Republicans argued that "me-tooism" was a recipe for continual failure and sought to reposition the GOP as a genuine alternative to the Democrats. In 1964, for example, Republican presidential candidate Barry Goldwater, author of a book entitled *The Conscience of a Conservative* (1960), argued in favor of substantially reduced levels of taxation and spending, less government regulation of the economy, and the elimination of many federal social programs. Although Goldwater was defeated by Lyndon Johnson, the ideas he espoused continue to be major themes for the Republican party. The Goldwater message, however, was not enough to lead Republicans to victory. It took Richard Nixon's "southern strategy" to give the GOP the votes it needed to end Democratic dominance of the political process. Nixon appealed strongly to disaffected white southerners and, with the help of independent candidate and former Alabama governor George Wallace, sparked the shift of voters that eventually gave the once-hated "party of Lincoln" a strong position in all the states of the former Confederacy. In the 1980s, under the leadership of Ronald Reagan, Republicans added another important group to their coalition—religious conservatives who were offended by Democratic support for abortion rights as well as alleged Democratic disdain for traditional cultural and religious values.

While Republicans built a political base around economic and social conservatives and white southerners, the Democratic party maintained its support among unionized workers and upper-middle-class intellectuals and professionals. Democrats also appealed strongly to racial minorities. The 1965 Voting Rights Act had greatly increased black voter participation in the South and helped the Democratic party retain some congressional and Senate seats in the South. And, while the GOP appealed to social conservatives, the Democrats appealed strongly to Americans concerned with abortion rights, gay rights, feminism, environmentalism, and other progressive social causes. The result so far has been an even balance between the two parties. As we saw, the 2000 presidential election ended in a virtual tie between George W. Bush and Al Gore, and the two houses of Congress are almost evenly divided between the two parties.

The shift of much of the South from the Democratic to the Republican camp along with the other developments mentioned above also meant that each political party became ideologically more homogeneous after the 1980s. Today, there are few liberal Republicans or conservative Democrats. One consequence of this development is that party loyalty in Congress, which had been weak between the 1950s and 1970s, became a more potent force. Battles over such matters as the Clinton impeachment, for example, resulted in nearly straight party-line voting in the House and Senate. On other matters, including budgetary priorities, judicial appointments, and foreign policy, party-line voting has become far more common than in prior years (see Chapter 5). Party loyalty in Congress has also been enhanced by each party's creation of a national apparatus to recruit candidates and to provide campaign assistance and funding to party stalwarts.

The ideological gap between the two parties has been exacerbated by two other factors: each party's dependence upon ideologically motivated activists, and the changes in the presidential nominating system that were introduced during the 1970s. As to the first of these factors, Democratic political candidates depend heavily upon the support of liberal activists, such as feminists, environmentalists, and civil libertarians, to organize and finance their campaigns, while Republican political candidates depend equally upon the support of conservative activists, including religious fundamentalists. In the nineteenth century, political activists were motivated more by party loyalty and political patronage than by programmatic concerns. Today's issue-oriented activists, by contrast, demand that politicians demonstrate strong commitments to moral principles and political causes in exchange for the activists' support. The demands of party activists have tended to push Democrats further to the political Left and Republicans further to the political Right. Often, efforts by politicians to reach compromises on key issues are attacked by party activists as "sellouts," leading to stalemates on such matters as the budget and judicial appointments.

The parties' ideological split has also been exacerbated by the changes in the presidential nominating system that developed during the 1970s. After the Democratic party's defeat in 1968, liberal forces, through the so-called McGovern-Fraser Commission on party reform, succeeded in changing the rules governing Democratic presidential nominations to reduce the power of party officials and professionals while increasing the role of issue-oriented activists. Among other changes, the new Democratic rules required national convention delegates to be chosen in primaries and caucuses rather than by the state party central committees, as had previously been the practice in many states. Subsequently, Republican activists were able to bring about similar changes in the GOP's rules so that today, in both parties, presidential nominating processes are strongly influenced by precisely the sorts of grassroots activists who are often inclined to oppose centrist or pragmatic politicians in favor of those appearing to manifest ideological purity. As a result, elections have tended to pit liberal Democrats against conservative Republicans. Observers of post–World War II American political parties often dubbed them "Tweedledum and Tweedledee," but the two parties today differ ever more sharply over social, economic, and foreign policy issues.

American Third Parties

third parties
Parties that organize to compete against the two major American political parties.

Although the United States is said to possess a two-party system, we have always had more than two parties. Typically, ***third parties*** in the United States have represented social and economic protests that, for one or another reason, were not given voice by the two major parties.[21] Such parties have had a good deal of influence on ideas and elections in the United States. The Populists, a party centered in the rural areas of the West and Midwest, and the Progressives, spokesmen for the urban middle classes in the late nineteenth and early twentieth centuries, are the most important examples in the past hundred years. More recently, Ross Perot, who ran in 1992 and 1996 as an independent, impressed some voters with his folksy style in the presidential debates and garnered almost 19 percent of the votes cast in the 1992 presidential election.

Table 11.1 shows a listing of all the parties that offered candidates in one or more states in the presidential election of 2000 as well as independent candidates who ran. With the exception of Ralph Nader, the third-party and independent candidates together polled only 1.02 million votes. They gained no electoral votes for president, and most of them disappeared immediately after the presidential election. The significance of Table 11.1 is that it demonstrates the large number of third parties running candidates and appealing to voters. Third-party candidacies also arise at the state and local levels. In New York, the Liberal and Conservative parties have been on the ballot for decades. In 1998, Minnesota elected a third-party governor, former professional wrestler Jesse Ventura.

Although the Republican party was only the third American political party ever to make itself permanent (by replacing the Whigs), other third parties have enjoyed an influence far beyond their electoral size. This was because large parts of their programs were adopted by one or both of the major parties, who sought to appeal to the voters mobilized by the new party and so expand their own electoral strength. The Democratic party, for example, became a great deal more liberal when it adopted most of the Progressive program early in the twentieth century. Many Socialists felt that President Roosevelt's New Deal had adopted most of their party's program, including old-age pensions, unemployment compensation, an agricultural marketing program, and laws guaranteeing workers the right to organize into unions.

This kind of influence explains the short lives of third parties. Their causes are usually eliminated by the ability of the major parties to absorb their programs and to draw their supporters into the mainstream. There are, of course, additional reasons for the short duration of most third parties. One is the usual limitation of their electoral support to one or two regions. Populist support, for example, was primarily midwestern. The 1948 Progressive party, with Henry Wallace as its candidate, drew nearly half its votes from the state of New York. The American Independent party polled nearly 10 million popular votes and 45 electoral votes for George Wallace in 1968—the most electoral votes ever polled by a third-party candidate. But all of Wallace's electoral votes and the majority of his popular vote came from the states of the Deep South.

---

[21]For a discussion of third parties in the United States, see Daniel A. Mazmanian, *Third Parties in Presidential Elections* (Washington, D.C.: Brookings Institution, 1974).

TABLE 11.1

Parties and Candidates in 2000

CANDIDATE	PARTY	VOTE TOTAL	PERCENTAGE OF VOTE*
Al Gore	Democratic	50,996,116	48
George W. Bush	Republican	50,456,169	48
Ralph Nader	Green	2,831,066	3
Pat Buchanan	Reform	447,798	0
Harry Browne	Libertarian	385,515	0
Howard Phillips	Constitution	96,907	0
John Hagelin	Natural Law	83,134	0
James E. Harris	Socialist Workers	7,408	0
L. Neil Smith	Libertarian	5,775	0
Monica Moorehead	Workers World	5,335	0
David McReynolds	Socialist	4,233	0
Cathy Brown	Independent	1,606	0
Denny Lane	Vermont Grassroots	1,044	0
Randall Venson	Independent	535	0
Earl Dodge	Prohibition	208	0
Louie Youngkeit	Independent	161	0
None of the above		3,315	0

*With 99 percent of votes tallied.
SOURCE: www.washingtonpost.com/wp-srv/onpolitics/elections/2000/results/whitehouse.
Updated December 21, 2000.

Americans usually assume that only the candidates nominated by one of the two major parties have any chance of winning an election. Thus, a vote cast for a third-party or independent candidate is often seen as a wasted vote. Voters who would prefer a third-party candidate may feel compelled to vote for the major-party candidate who they regard as the "lesser of two evils" to avoid wasting their vote in a futile gesture. Third-party candidates must struggle—usually without success—to overcome the perception that they cannot win. Thus, in 1996, many voters who favored Ross Perot gave their votes to Bob Dole or Bill Clinton on the presumption that Perot was not really electable.

During the year prior to the 2000 national elections, Perot struggled with Minnesota governor Jesse Ventura for control of the Reform party. Perot backed Pat Buchanan as the party's presidential nominee, while Ventura promoted the candidacy of real-estate tycoon Donald Trump. Buchanan ultimately won the Reform party's nomination, but only after a bitter convention battle that prompted many delegates to storm out of the convention hall. The winner of the nomination was not only guaranteed a spot on the ticket in most states, but also received approximately $12 million in federal campaign funds. Under federal election law, any minor party receiving more than 5 percent of the national presidential vote is entitled to federal funds, though considerably less than the amount that the major parties receive. The Reform party qualified by winning 8.2 percent in 1996. Ralph Nader, the Green party candidate in 2000, hoped to win the 5 percent of the vote that would entitle the Green party to federal funds. Although Nader may have drawn enough liberal votes in New Hampshire and Florida to give those states—and the national election—to the GOP, hopes of achieving the 5 percent threshold were dashed.

As many scholars have pointed out, third-party prospects are also hampered by America's **single-member-district** plurality election system. In many other nations, several individuals can be elected to represent each legislative district. This is called a system of **multiple-member districts.** With this type of system, the candidates of weaker parties have a better chance of winning at least some seats. For their part, voters are less concerned about wasting ballots and usually more willing to support minor-party candidates.

Reinforcing the effects of the single-member district, plurality voting rules (as was noted in Chapter 10) generally have the effect of setting what could be called a high threshold for victory. To win a plurality race, candidates usually must secure many more votes than they would need under most European systems of proportional representation. For example, to win an American plurality election in a single-member district where there are only two candidates, a politician must win more than 50 percent of the votes cast. To win a seat from a European multimember district under proportional rules, a candidate may need to win only 15 or 20 percent of the votes cast. This high American threshold discourages minor parties and encourages the various political factions that might otherwise form minor parties to minimize their differences and remain within the major-party coalitions.[22]

It would nevertheless be incorrect to assert (as some scholars have maintained) that America's single-member plurality election system guarantees that only two parties will compete for power in all regions of the country. All that can be said is that American election law depresses the number of parties likely to survive over long periods of time in the United States. There is nothing magical

[22]See Duverger, *Political Parties.*

single-member district An electorate that is allowed to elect only one representative from each district; the normal method of representation in the United States.

multiple-member district Electorate that selects several candidates at large from the whole district; each voter is given the number of votes equivalent to the number of seats to be filled.

Institution Principle

Third-party prospects for electoral success are hampered by America's single-member-district plurality election system.

about two. Indeed, the single-member plurality system of election can also discourage second parties. After all, if one party consistently receives a large plurality of the vote, people may eventually come to see their vote *even for the second party* as a wasted effort. This happened to the Republican party in the Deep South before World War II.

HOW STRONG ARE POLITICAL PARTIES TODAY?

As a result of Progressive reform, American party organizations entered the twentieth century with rickety substructures. As the use of civil service, primary elections, and the other Progressive innovations spread during the period between the two world wars, the strength of party organizations continued to be eroded. By the end of World War II, political scientists were already bemoaning the absence of party discipline and "party responsibility" in the United States.

High-Tech Politics and the Rise of Candidate-Centered and Capital-Intensive Politics

History Principle
The erosion of the strength of party organizations set the stage for the introduction of new political campaign techniques and the rise of candidate-centered campaigns.

This erosion of the parties' organizational strength set the stage for the introduction of new political techniques. These new methods represented radical departures from the campaign practices perfected during the nineteenth century. In place of manpower and organization, contending forces began to employ intricate electronic communications techniques to attract electoral support. This new political technology includes six basic elements: polling, the broadcast media, phone banks, direct mail, professional public relations, and the Internet.

Polling   Surveys of voter opinion provide the information that candidates and their staffs use to craft campaign strategies. Candidates employ polls to select issues, to assess their own strengths and weaknesses (as well as those of the opposition), to check voter response to the campaign, and to determine the degree to which various constituent groups are susceptible to campaign appeals. Virtually all contemporary campaigns for national and statewide office as well as many local campaigns make extensive use of opinion surveys. As we saw in Chapter 9, President Clinton made extensive use of polling data both during and after the 1996 presidential election to shape his rhetoric and guide his policy initiatives.

The Broadcast Media   Extensive use of the electronic media, television in particular, has become the hallmark of the modern political campaign. One commonly used broadcast technique is the 30- or 60-second television spot advertisement—such as George H. W. Bush's "Willie Horton" ad in 1988 or Lyndon Johnson's famous "daisy girl" ad in 1964—which permits the candidate's message to be delivered to a target audience before uninterested or hostile viewers can psychologically, or physically, tune it out. Television spot ads and other media techniques are designed to establish candidate name recognition, to create a favorable image of the candidate and a negative image of the opponent, to link the candidate with desirable groups in the community, and to communicate the candidate's stands on selected issues. These spot ads can have an important electoral impact. Generally, media campaigns attempt to follow the guidelines indicated by a candidate's polls, emphasizing issues and personal characteristics that appear important in the poll data. The broadcast media are now so central to modern campaigns that most candidates' activities are tied to their media strategies.[23] Candidate activities are designed expressly to stimulate television news coverage. For instance, members of Congress running for re-election or for president almost always sponsor committee or subcommittee hearings to generate publicity.

Phone Banks Through the broadcast media, candidates communicate with voters en masse and impersonally. Phone banks, on the other hand, allow campaign workers to make personal contact with hundreds of thousands of voters. Personal contacts of this sort are thought to be extremely effective. Again, poll data serve to identify the groups that will be targeted for phone calls. Computers select phone numbers from areas in which members of these groups are concentrated. Staffs of paid or volunteer callers, using computer-assisted dialing systems and prepared scripts, then place calls to deliver the candidate's message. The targeted groups are generally those identified by polls as either uncommitted or weakly committed, as well as strong supporters of the candidate who are contacted simply to encourage them to vote.

Direct Mail Direct mail serves both as a vehicle for communicating with voters and as a mechanism for raising funds. The first step in a direct mail campaign is the purchase or rental of a computerized mailing list of voters deemed to have some particular perspective or social characteristic. Often, sets of magazine subscription lists or lists of donors to various causes are employed. For example, a candidate interested in reaching conservative voters might rent subscription lists from the *National Review;* a candidate interested in appealing to liberals might rent subscription lists from the *New York Review of Books* or from the *New Republic.* Considerable fine-tuning is possible. After obtaining the appropriate mailing lists, candidates usually send pamphlets, letters, and brochures describing themselves and their views to voters believed to be sympathetic. Different types of mail appeals are made to different electoral subgroups. Often the letters sent to voters are personalized. The recipient is addressed by name in the text and the letter appears actually to have been signed by the candidate. Of course, these "personal" letters are written and even signed by a computer.

In addition to its use as a political advertising medium, direct mail has also become an important source of campaign funds. Computerized mailing lists permit campaign strategists to pinpoint individuals whose interests, background,

---

[23]Larry Sabato, *The Rise of Political Consultants: New Ways of Winning Elections* (New York: Basic Books, 1981).

and activities suggest that they may be potential donors to the campaign. Letters of solicitation are sent to these potential donors. Some of the money raised is then used to purchase additional mailing lists. Direct-mail solicitation can be enormously effective.[24]

Professional Public Relations   Modern campaigns and the complex technology upon which they rely are typically directed by professional public relations consultants. Virtually all serious contenders for national and statewide office retain the services of professional campaign consultants. Increasingly, candidates for local office, too, have come to rely upon professional campaign managers. Consultants offer candidates the expertise necessary to conduct accurate opinion polls, produce television commercials, organize direct-mail campaigns, and make use of sophisticated computer analyses.

The Internet   A more recent form of new technology has been the Internet. Most candidates for office set up a Web site as an inexpensive means of establishing a public presence. The 1998 election saw increased use of the Internet by political candidates. Virtually all statewide candidates, as well as many candidates for Congress and local offices, developed Web sites providing contact information, press releases, speeches, photos, and information on how to volunteer, contact the candidate, or donate money to the campaign. During his campaign, Florida governor Jeb Bush sold "Jebware," articles of clothing emblazoned with his name, through his Web site. In the 2000 contest, the politician who made the most extensive use of the Internet was John McCain. McCain used his Web site to mobilize volunteers and to raise hundreds of thousands of dollars for his unsuccessful bid for the Republican presidential nomination. In the future, all politicians will use the Web to collect information about potential voters and supporters, which, in turn, will allow them to personalize mailings and calls as well as E-mail advertising. One consultant now refers to politics on the Internet as "netwar," and asserts that "small, smart attackers" can defeat more powerful opponents in the new, information-age "battlespace."[25] Although the Internet has not yet become a dominant force in political campaigns, most politicians and consultants believe that its full potential for customizing political appeals is only now beginning to be realized.

During the 2004 presidential contest, Democratic candidate Howard Dean made extensive use of the Internet as a communication and fund-raising tool. Thousands of bloggers maintained discussion forums that promoted Dean's candidacy and solicited funds. By the end of 2003, Dean had amassed a war chest of more than $15 million, much of it raised on the Internet, for his presidential bid. Dean Internet guru Joe Trippi hoped to persuade 2 million Americans to each give "one hundred dollars online," to match the funds President Bush was expected to accumulate through traditional fund-raising methods.

[24]Ibid., p. 250.
[25]Dana Milbanks, "Virtual Politics," *New Republic*, 5 July 1999, p. 22.

The number of technologically oriented campaigns increased greatly after 1971. The Federal Election Campaign Act of 1971 prompted the creation of large numbers of political action committees (PACs) by a host of corporate and ideological groups. This development increased the availability of funds to political candidates, which meant in turn that the new technology could be used more extensively. Initially, the new techniques were employed mainly by individual candidates who often made little or no effort to coordinate their campaigns with those of other political aspirants sharing the same party label. For this reason, campaigns employing new technology sometimes came to be called "candidate-centered" efforts, as distinguished from the traditional party-coordinated campaign. Nothing about this technology, however, precluded its use by political party leaders seeking to coordinate a number of campaigns. In recent years, party leaders have learned to make good use of modern campaign technology. The difference between the old and new political methods is not that the latter is inherently candidate-centered while the former is strictly a party tool. The difference is, rather, a matter of the types of political resources upon which each method depends.

The displacement of organizational methods by the new political technology is, in essence, a shift from labor-intensive to capital-intensive competitive electoral practices. Campaign tasks were once performed by masses of party workers with some cash. These tasks now require fewer personnel but a great deal more money, for the new political campaign depends on polls, computers, and other electronic paraphernalia. Nevertheless, parties remain important as providers of money, resources, and expertise.

Contemporary Party Organizations

In the United States, party organizations exist at virtually every level of government (see Figure 11.1). These organizations are usually committees made up of a number of active party members. State law and party rules prescribe how such committees are constituted. Usually, committee members are elected at local party meetings—called *caucuses*—or as part of the regular primary election. The best-known examples of these committees are at the national level—the Democratic National Committee and the Republican National Committee.

caucus A normally closed meeting of a political or legislative group to select candidates, plan strategy, or make decisions regarding legislative matters.

National Convention   At the national level, the party's most important institution is the quadrennial national convention. The convention is attended by delegates from each of the states; as a group, they nominate the party's presidential and vice-presidential candidates, draft the party's campaign platform for the presidential race, and approve changes in the rules and regulations governing party procedures. Before World War II, presidential nominations occupied most of the time, energy, and effort expended at the national convention. The nomination process required days of negotiation and compromise among state party leaders and often required many ballots before a nominee was selected. In recent years, however, presidential candidates have essentially nominated themselves by winning enough delegate support in primary elections to win the

FIGURE 11.1

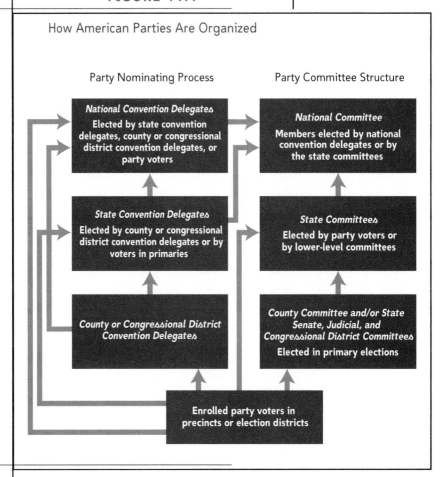

How American Parties Are Organized

Party Nominating Process   **Party Committee Structure**

National Convention Delegates
Elected by state convention delegates, county or congressional district convention delegates, or party voters

National Committee
Members elected by national convention delegates or by the state committees

State Convention Delegates
Elected by county or congressional district convention delegates or by voters in primaries

State Committees
Elected by party voters or by lower-level committees

County or Congressional District Convention Delegates

County Committee and/or State Senate, Judicial, and Congressional District Committees
Elected in primary elections

Enrolled party voters in precincts or election districts

Institution Principle

Party rules can determine the relative influence of competing factions within the party and can also increase or decrease the party's chances for electoral success.

official nomination on the first ballot. The actual convention has played little or no role in selecting the candidates.

The convention's other two tasks, establishing the party's rules and platform, remain important. Party rules can determine the relative influence of competing factions within the party and can also increase or decrease the party's chances for electoral success. In 1972, for example, the Democratic National Convention adopted a new set of rules favored by the party's liberal wing. Under these rules, state delegations to the Democratic convention were required to include women and members of minority groups in rough proportion to those groups' represen-tation among the party's membership in that state. Liberals correctly calculated that women and African Americans would generally support liberal ideas and candidates. The rules also called for the use of proportional representation—a voting system liberals thought would give them an advantage by allowing the election of more women and minority delegates. (Although Republican rules do not require proportional representation for selecting delegates, some state legis-latures have moved to compel both parties to use this system in all their presi-dential primaries.)

The convention also approves the party platform. Platforms are often dis-missed as documents filled with platitudes that are seldom read by voters. To some extent this criticism is well founded. Not one voter in a thousand so much as glances at the party platform, and even the news media pay little attention to the documents. Furthermore, the parties' presidential candidates make little use of the platforms in their campaigns; usually they prefer to develop and promote their own themes. Occasionally, nominees even disavow their party's platform. In 1864, for example, Democratic presidential nominee General George Mc-Clellan repudiated his party's peace platform. Nonetheless, the platform can be an important document. The platform should be understood as a contract in which the various party factions attending the convention state their terms for supporting the ticket. For one faction, welfare reform may be a key issue. For an-other faction, tax reduction may be more important. For a third, the critical issue may be deficit reduction. When one of these "planks" is included in the platform, its promoters are asserting that this is what they want in exchange for their sup-port of the ticket, while other party factions are agreeing that the position seems reasonable and appropriate.

National Committee Between conventions, each national political party is technically headed by its national committee. For the Democrats and Republi-cans, these are called the Democratic National Committee (DNC) and the Re-publican National Committee (RNC), respectively. These national committees raise campaign funds, head off factional disputes within the party, and endeavor to enhance the party's media image. Since 1972, the size of staff and the amount of money raised have increased substantially for both national committees. The actual work of each national committee is overseen by its chairperson. Other committee members are generally major party contributors or fund-raisers and serve in a largely ceremonial capacity.

For the party that controls the White House, the national committee chair is appointed by the president. Typically, this means that that party's national com-mittee becomes little more than an adjunct to the White House staff. For a first-term president, the committee devotes the bulk of its energy to the re-election campaign. The national committee chair of the party not in control of the White House is selected by the committee itself and usually takes a broader view of the party's needs, raising money and performing other activities on behalf of the party's members in Congress and in the state legislatures.

Congressional Campaign Committees Each party forms House and Senate campaign committees to raise funds for House and Senate election campaigns. Their efforts may or may not be coordinated with the activities of the national committees. For the party that controls the White House, the national committee and the congressional campaign committees are often rivals since both groups are seeking donations from the same people but for different candidates: the national committee seeks funds for the presidential race while the congressional campaign committees approach the same contributors for support for the congressional contests. In recent years, the Republican party has attempted to coordinate the fund-raising activities of all its committees. Republicans have sought to give the GOP's national institutions the capacity to invest funds in those close congressional, state, and local races where they can do the most good. The Democrats have been slower to coordinate their various committee activities, and this may have placed them at a disadvantage in recent congressional and local races. The efforts of the parties to centralize and coordinate fund-raising activities have helped bring about greater party unity in Congress. As members have come to rely upon the leadership for campaign funds, they have become more likely to vote with the leadership on major issues. All in all, campaign committees have begun to resemble large-scale campaign consulting firms, hiring full-time political operatives and evolving into professional organizations.

State and Local Party Organizations Each of the two major parties has a central committee in each state. The parties traditionally also have county committees and, in some instances, state senate district committees, judicial district committees, and, in the case of larger cities, city-wide party committees and local assembly district "ward" committees as well. Congressional districts also may have party committees.

Some cities also have precinct committees. Precincts are not districts from which any representative is elected but instead are legally defined subdivisions of wards that are used to register voters and set up ballot boxes or voting machines. A precinct is typically composed of three hundred to six hundred voters. Well-organized political parties—especially the famous old machines of New York, Chicago, and Boston—provide for "precinct captains" and a fairly tight group of party members around them. Precinct captains were usually members of long standing in neighborhood party clubhouses, which were important social centers as well as places for distributing favors to constituents.

Nevertheless, state and local party organizations are very active in recruiting candidates, conducting voter registration drives, and providing financial assistance to candidates. In many respects, federal election law has given state and local party organizations new life. Under current law, state and local party organizations can spend unlimited amounts of money on "party-building" activities such as voter registration and get-out-the-vote drives. As a result, the national party organizations, which have enormous fund-raising abilities but are limited by law in how much they can spend on candidates, each year transfer millions of dollars to the state and local organizations. The state and local parties, in turn, spend these funds, sometimes called soft money, to promote the candidacies of national, as well as state and local, candidates. In this process, as local organizations have become linked financially to the national parties, American political parties have become somewhat more integrated and nationalized than ever before. At the same time, the state and local party organizations have come to control large financial resources and play important roles in elections despite the collapse of the old patronage machines.[26]

The Contemporary Party as Service Provider to Candidates

Party leaders have adapted parties to the modern age. Parties-as-organizations are more professional, better financed, and more organized than ever before.[27] Political scientists argue that parties have evolved into "service organizations," which, though they no longer hold a monopoly over campaigns, still provide services to candidates, without which it would be extremely difficult for candidates to win and hold office. Parties have not declined but have simply adapted to serve the interests of political actors.[28]

Many politicians, however, are able to raise funds, attract volunteers, and win office without much help from local party organizations. Once in office, these politicians often refuse to submit to party discipline; instead they steer independent courses. They are often supported by voters who see independence as a virtue and party discipline as "boss rule." Analysts refer to this pattern as a "candidate-centered" politics to distinguish it from a political process in which parties are the dominant forces. The problem with a candidate-centered politics is that it tends to be associated with low turnout, high levels of special-interest influence, and a lack of effective decision making. In short, many of the problems that have plagued American politics in recent years can be traced directly to the independence of American voters and politicians, and the candidate-centered nature of American national politics.

Parties and Democracy

Political parties make democratic government possible. We often do not appreciate that democratic government is a contradiction in terms. Government implies policies, programs, and decisive action. Democracy, on the other hand, implies an opportunity for all citizens to participate fully in the governmental process. The contradiction is that full participation by everyone is often inconsistent with getting anything done. At what point should participation stop and governance begin? How can we make certain that popular participation will result in a government

[26]For a useful discussion, see John Bibby and Thomas Holbrook, "Parties and Elections," in *Politics in the American States: A Comparative Analysis*, ed. Virginia Gray and Herbert Jacob, 6th ed. (Washington, D.C.: Congressional Quarterly Press, 1996), pp. 78–121.

[27]See Aldrich, *Why Parties?*, Chapter 8.

[28]See Paul S. Herrnson, *Party Campaigning in the 1980s* (Cambridge, Mass.: Harvard University Press, 1988).

capable of making decisions and developing needed policies? The problem of democratic government is especially acute in the United States because of the system of separated powers bequeathed to us by the Constitution's framers. Our system of separated powers means that it is very difficult to link popular participation and effective decision making. Often, after the citizens have spoken and the dust has settled, no single set of political forces has been able to win control of enough of the scattered levers of power to actually do anything. Instead of government, we have a continual political struggle.

Strong political parties are a partial antidote to the inherent contradiction between participation and government. Strong parties can both encourage popular involvement and convert participation into effective government. More than fifty years ago, a committee of the academic American Political Science Association (APSA) called for the development of a more "responsible" party government. By responsible party government, the committee meant political parties that mobilized voters and were sufficiently well organized to develop and implement coherent programs and policies after the election. Strong parties can link democratic participation and government.

Although they are significant factors in politics and government, American political parties today are not as strong as the "responsible parties" advocated by the APSA. Can political parties be strengthened? The answer is, in principle, yes. For example, political parties could be strengthened if the rules governing campaign finance were revised to make candidates more dependent financially upon state and local party organizations rather than on personal resources or private contributors. Such a reform, to be sure, would require stricter regulation of party fund-raising practices to prevent soft money abuses. The potential benefit, however, of a greater party role in political finance could be substantial. If parties controlled the bulk of the campaign funds, they would become more coherent and disciplined, and might come to resemble the responsible parties envisioned by the APSA. In 2002, Congress enacted campaign finance reforms that diminished the role of the national party organizations in financing campaigns but potentially strengthened the parties' state and local organizations. Time will tell what consequences will be brought about by this change. Political parties have been such important features of American democratic politics that we need to think long and hard about how to preserve and strengthen them.

SUMMARY

Political parties seek to control government by controlling its personnel. Elections are one means to this end. Thus, parties take shape from the electoral process. The formal principle of party organization is this: for every district in which an election is held—from the entire nation to the local district, county, or precinct—there should be some kind of party unit.

Nominating and electing are the basic functions of parties. Originally, nominations were made in party caucuses, and individuals who ran as independents

Rationality Principle	Collective Action Principle	Institution Principle	Policy Principle	History Principle
Parties help deal with the threat to cooperation posed by ambitious individuals by regulating career advancement and resolving competition.	Parties facilitate collective action in the electoral process by helping candidates attract campaign funds, assemble campaign workers, and mobilize voters.	Third-party prospects for electoral success are hampered by America's single-member-district plurality election system.	Parties help resolve collective choice in the policy-making process by acting as permanent coalitions of individuals with similar policy goals.	The erosion of the strength of party organizations set the stage for the introduction of new political campaign techniques and the rise of candidate-centered campaigns.
Parties can lower the cost of voting by facilitating a voter's choice.	Parties can help mobilize voters who are potential free riders.	Party rules can determine the relative influence of competing factions within the party and can also increase or decrease the party's chances for electoral success.	Policies typically reflect the goals of whichever party is in power.	
	Cooperation in Congress is facilitated by the party system.			
	The efforts of the parties to centralize and coordinate fund-raising activities have helped bring about greater party unity in Congress.			

had a difficult time getting on the ballot. In the 1830s, dissatisfaction with the cliquish caucuses led to nominating conventions. Although these ended the "King Caucus" that controlled the nomination of presidential candidates and thereby gave the presidency a popular base, they, too, proved unsatisfactory. Primaries now have more or less replaced the conventions. There are both closed and open primaries. The former are more supportive of strong political parties than the latter. Contested primaries sap party strength and financial resources, but they nonetheless serve to resolve important social conflicts and recognize new interest groups. Winning at the top of a party ticket usually depends on the party regulars at the bottom getting out the vote. At all levels, the mass communications media are important. Mass mailings, too, are vital in campaigning. Thus, campaign funds are crucial to success.

Congress is organized around the two-party system. The House speakership is a party office. Parties determine the makeup of congressional committees, including their chairs, which are no longer based entirely on seniority.

The two-party system dominates U.S. politics. While the two parties agree on some major issues, the Democrats generally favor higher levels of social spending funded by higher levels of taxation than the GOP is willing to support. Republicans favor lower levels of domestic activity on the part of the federal government, but also support federal action on a number of social and moral issues such as abortion. Even though party affiliation means less to Americans than it once did, partisanship remains important. What ticket splitting there is occurs mainly at the presidential level.

Third parties are short-lived for several reasons. They have limited electoral support, the tradition of the two-party system is strong, and a major party often adopts their platforms. Single-member districts with two competing parties also discourage third parties.

In recent years, the role of parties in political campaigns has been partially supplanted by the use of new political technologies. These include polling, the broadcast media, phone banks, direct-mail fund-raising and advertising, professional public relations, and the Internet. These techniques are enormously expensive and have led to a shift from labor-intensive to capital-intensive politics. This shift works to the advantage of political forces representing the well-to-do.

FOR FURTHER READING

Aldrich, John H. *Why Parties? The Origin and Transformation of Party Politics in America.* Chicago: University of Chicago Press, 1995.

Beck, Paul Allen, and Marjorie Randon Hershey. *Party Politics in America.* 10th ed. New York: Longman, 2003.

Chambers, William N., and Walter Dean Burnham, eds. *The American Party Systems: Stages of Political Development.* 2nd ed. New York: Oxford University Press, 1975.

Coleman, John J. *Party Decline in America: Policy, Politics, and the Fiscal State.* Princeton, N.J.: Princeton University Press, 1996.

Grimshaw, William J. *Bitter Fruit: Black Politics and the Chicago Machine, 1931–1991.* Chicago: University of Chicago Press, 1992.

Hofstadter, Richard. *The Idea of a Party System: The Rise of Legitimate Opposition in the United States, 1780–1840.* Berkeley: University of California Press, 1969.

Kayden, Xandra, and Eddie Mahe, Jr. *The Party Goes On: The Persistence of the Two-Party System in the United States.* New York: Basic Books, 1985.

Lawson, Kay, and Peter H. Merkl. *When Parties Fail: Emerging Alternative Organizations.* Princeton, N.J.: Princeton University Press, 1988.

Milkis, Sidney M. *The President and the Parties: The Transformation of the American Party System since the New Deal.* New York: Oxford University Press, 1993.

Polsby, Nelson W. *Consequences of Party Reform.* New York: Oxford University Press, 1983.

Shafer, Byron, ed. *Beyond Realignment? Interpreting American Electoral Eras.* Madison: University of Wisconsin Press, 1991.

Smith, Eric R. A. N. *The Unchanging American Voter.* Berkeley: University of California Press, 1989.

Sundquist, James L. *Dynamics of the Party System: Alignment and Realignment of Political Parties in the United States.* Washington, D.C.: Brookings Institution, 1983.

Wattenberg, Martin P. *The Decline of American Political Parties, 1952–1996.* Cambridge, Mass.: Harvard University Press, 1998.

Politics in the News—
Reading between the Lines

Partisan Battles over Redistricting

Across U.S., Redistricting as a Never-Ending Battle

By DAVID M. HABFINGER

For most of the past century, redistricting has been a fairly predictable though often contentious ritual. Every 10 years, state legislators would use the new census data to redraw Congressional district lines, and the party in power would usually manage to draw maps that gave it an advantage.

Now, thanks to a determined effort by United States Representative Tom DeLay, the House majority leader, with the quiet support of the White House, that tradition may be crumbling, as legislatures draw new districts whenever they have a partisan advantage.

Today, the Republican-controlled Texas Legislature opened an extraordinary special session devoted solely to redrawing the state's 32 Congressional districts. If Republicans succeed in doing so, they could remove five or more Democratic congressmen and help their party consolidate its hold on power in Washington.

Republicans did much the same thing last month . . . pushing a new map through the Colorado Legislature specifically to shore up the seat of a freshman congressman who won office with a 121-vote margin. And Democrats are threatening retaliation in New Mexico and Oklahoma, . . . [and] Illinois and California, where far more seats are at stake.

This amped-up partisanship on the state level could soon make redistricting battles a recurring feature of the political landscape . . . reviving the 19th-century practice of redrawing political maps every time a legislature changed hands.

Mr. DeLay, a former Texas legislator himself, has been candid about his reasons for pushing for a new Congressional map, telling reporters at one point, "I'm the majority leader, and we want more seats." . . .

[T]he battle in Texas captured national attention . . . when 51 Democratic members of the state House fled in chartered buses to Ardmore, Okla., holing up in a Holiday Inn for four

The New York Times, 1 July 2003, p. A1.

Political Parties

days until a crucial procedural deadline passed. By denying Republicans a quorum, they killed a redistricting bill for the moment, but the ploy came at a price in scorn from late-night comedians and seemed to alienate many Texans. . . .

Democrats . . . attacked an e-mail notice about the hearings, sent out by Republicans in Houston, with a photo of Representative Sheila Jackson-Lee, a Democrat who is black. "She'll be there to express her views," it said, without identifying her. "Will you be there to express yours?"

The battle over redistricting has rendered the bipartisan comity in Austin made famous by former Gov. George W. Bush a distant memory. But to Republican strategists, that is not necessarily a bad thing.

"Bipartisanship is where both parties gang up against the people," said Grover G. Norquist, president of Americans for Tax Reform, a conservative group, who said that split legislatures were more likely to raise taxes. "I want to take the partisanship in Washington and drive it into the 50 states," added Mr. Norquist.

Some Texas Republicans—including Governor Perry and Tom Craddick, who became speaker of the state House in January when the party took control for the first time in 130 years—argue that the state's Congressional delegation, with 17 Democrats and 15 Republicans, does not reflect Texas voting patterns, in which nearly 60 percent of the votes cast for Congress last year were for Republicans.

They say the current Congressional map is just an old Democratic gerrymander. . . .

Mr. Norquist said the point of the exercise was to help remove centrist Democrats from Congress, leaving only the most liberal behind.

"Sheila Jackson-Lee will be the spokesman for the Democratic Party,

ESSENCE OF THE STORY

- The Texas state legislature has decided to redraw Texas's congressional districts. Traditionally, districts have been redrawn only once, following the decennial Census.

- In the nineteenth century, districts were redrawn much more frequently, often when the control of state legislatures changed party hands.

- National and state Republican leaders do not deny that they want to change the partisan mix of the state delegation but charge that the current delegation is unrepresentative.

- Democratic legislators temporarily stopped the process by hightailing it out of state.

- New redistricting fights have appeared in other states as well, perhaps a portent of the future.

POLITICAL ANALYSIS

- One way that partisan polarization in Congress can increase is if congressional districts are purposely drawn with disparate populations. It is to the political advantage of Texas Republicans, who believe the state is conservative to moderate in its political preferences, to draw a set of districts that help very liberal Democrats (and, simultaneously, conservative Republicans).

- Redistricting as a political institution includes constitutional provisions, state laws, and Supreme Court decisions, but also norms and standard operating procedures. There is no *law* against redistricting more frequently than every ten years. Perhaps a newly polarized party system will encourage state legislators to challenge the norm and transform the institution of redistricting.

- Republicans may win this battle in Texas, but Democrats will retaliate in other states.

and ought to be," he said. "She accurately reflects what the Democratic Party is about."

CHAPTER

12

Groups and Interests

When George W. Bush, a former Texas oilman, won the 2000 presidential election, the nation's energy producers could not have been happier. Many energy companies, including the ill-fated Enron Corporation, had supported Bush's campaign on the expectation that he would be sympathetic to their interests. The president rewarded his supporters by including billions of dollars in energy tax incentives in the energy tax bills he proposed in his next two budgets. Such incentives allow corporations to receive tax credits for particular forms of energy production and are nominally designed to encourage the development of new energy sources that might not initially be profitable. Tax incentives, however, are often merely subsidies to favored groups whose energy technology hardly seems likely to reduce the nation's dependence upon imported oil. For example, the 2003 energy tax bill contained a provision for a tax credit for drawing energy from poultry waste. This credit was the result of a lobbying campaign by an industry group, the "National Broiler Council," and would primarily benefit Perdue Farms, Inc., the operator of a chicken waste-burning plant in eastern Maryland. The aptly named Senator Orin Hatch (R-Utah), champion of the poultry-waste credit said, "Tax credits are needed for the early adoption of new technologies." Critics, however, questioned the merits of a tax credit for "chicken poop."[1]

While the president was willing to provide numerous tax credits to energy interests, the energy producers wanted even more. Three industry groups, in particular, sought benefits beyond those supported by the administration. One group consisted of the owners of small oil refineries organized in the National Petrochemical and Refiners Association. These refiners currently receive a tax credit for the first 50,000 barrels of oil they produce each day. Arguing that they helped the nation achieve a greater level of energy independence, the small refiners sought to raise the daily limit to 75,000 barrels—at a cost of hundreds of millions of dollars to the U.S. Treasury. A second industry group consisted of alternative-fuel producers such as the manufacturers of windmills and ethanol, a fuel derived from corn. The interests of this group are championed by Senator Charles E. Grassley, the powerful chairman of the Senate Finance Committee, who happens to represent Iowa, the nation's largest corn-producing state. A third industry group consisted of the manufacturers of energy-saving technologies such as hybrid gas-electric vehicles and energy-efficient washing machines.

As negotiations over the energy tax bill proceeded, it became clear that the small oil refiners had considerable support in the House of Representatives. This group had managed to organize not only refiners, but independent gasoline distributors and gas-station owners and operators in congressional districts through the country. This gave the refiners enormous leverage in the House, where every member could be approached by distributors and station owners from their own districts. Thus, the House version of the tax bill favored the oil refiners and other traditional energy producers. In the Senate, though, the alternative-fuel producers seemed to

[1]Jill Barshay, "Tax Breaks in House, Senate Energy Bills Differ beyond Dollar Amounts," *Congressional Quarterly Weekly Report* 61, no. 14, 5 April 2003, pp. 820–21.

CHAPTER OUTLINE

What Are the Characteristics of Interest Groups?

- Interest Groups Enhance Democracy . . .

- . . . but Also Represent the Evils of Faction

- Organized Interests Are Predominantly Economic

- All Groups Require Money and Leadership, and Most Need Members

- Group Membership Has an Upper-Class Bias

- Groups Form in Response to Changes in the Political Environment

How and Why Do Interest Groups Form?

- Interest Groups Facilitate Cooperation

- Selective Benefits: A Solution to the Collective Action Problem

- Political Entrepreneurs Organize and Maintain Groups

How Do Interest Groups Influence Policy?

- Direct Lobbying

- Using the Courts

- Mobilizing Public Opinion

- Using Electoral Politics

Groups and Interests: The Dilemma of Reform

have the advantage. Led by such lawmakers as Senator Grassley, champion of ethanol, and Senator Hatch, spokesman for poultry waste, the Senate approved a version of the tax bill that tilted toward alternative fuels. As the two versions of the bill were brought to the House-Senate conference for reconciliation, deals were struck between the oil refiners and alternative-fuel producers that gave each group some of what they wanted. But what of the producers of energy-saving technologies? They were big losers. While it might be argued that hybrid vehicles and energy-saving appliances are more likely than chicken poop to alleviate the nation's energy problems, the energy-saving technology interests were outlobbied and outmaneuvered.

The story of the 2003 energy tax bill suggests the answers to three questions. First, the story suggests why individuals and interests form groups. Second, the story indicates some of the tactics and coalition-building strategies that groups use to get what they want. Third, the story shows that in a democracy, political struggle has its own logic and does not always lead to the most sensible outcomes. High-minded Americans have been complaining about the role of interest groups since the nation's founding. We should remember, however, that vigorous interest-group activity is a consequence and reflection of a free society. As James Madison put it so well in *The Federalist Papers*, No. 10, "Liberty is to faction what air is to fire."[2]

PREVIEWING THE PRINCIPLES

Inasmuch as interest groups are organizations in which a group of individuals work to achieve common policy-related goals, the difficulties associated with collective action are particularly acute. To overcome the obstacles to collective action, groups must provide individuals with incentives to join. Group politics is also organized, in part, through the goal-oriented activities of political entrepreneurs. Despite the obstacles to collective action, the number and types of interest groups in American politics proliferated throughout the twentieth century. Moreover, recognizing the importance of institutions in influencing political outcomes, groups strategically seek out institutional venues they believe will be most hospitable to their goals and interests.

In this chapter, we will examine some of the antecedents and consequences of interest-group politics in the United States. We will analyze the group basis of politics, the problems that result from collective action, and some solutions to these problems. We will seek to understand the character of the interests promoted by interest groups. We will assess the growth of interest-group activity in recent American political history, including the emergence of "public interest" groups. We will review and evaluate the strategies that competing groups use in their struggle for influence. Finally, we will assess the question: Are interest groups too influential in the political process?

[2]Clinton Rossiter, ed., *The Federalist Papers* (New York: New American Library, 1961), No. 10, p.78.

WHAT ARE THE CHARACTERISTICS OF INTEREST GROUPS?

An ***interest group*** is an organized group of people that makes policy-related appeals to government. This definition of interest groups includes membership organizations but also businesses, corporations, universities, and other institutions that do not accept members. Individuals form groups in order to increase the chance that their views will be heard and their interests treated favorably by the government. Interest groups are organized to influence governmental decisions.

Interest groups are sometimes referred to as "lobbies." Interest groups are also sometimes confused with political action committees, which are actually groups that focus on influencing elections rather than trying to influence the elected. One final distinction that we should make is that interest groups are also different from political parties: interest groups tend to concern themselves with the *policies* of government; parties tend to concern themselves with the *personnel* of government.

Interest Groups Enhance Democracy . . .

There are an enormous number of interest groups in the United States, and millions of Americans are members of one or more groups, at least to the extent of paying dues or attending an occasional meeting. By representing the interests of such large numbers of people and encouraging political participation, organized groups can and do enhance American democracy. Organized groups educate their members about issues that affect them. Groups lobby members of Congress and the executive branch, engage in litigation, and generally represent their members' interests in the political arena. Groups mobilize their members for elections and grassroots lobbying efforts, thus encouraging participation. Interest groups also monitor government programs to make certain that their members are not adversely affected. In all these ways, organized interests can be said to promote democratic politics.

. . . but Also Represent the Evils of Faction

The framers of the American Constitution feared the power that could be wielded by organized interests. Madison wrote: "The public good is disregarded in the conflict of rival [factions], . . . citizens . . . who are united and actuated by some common impulse of passion, or of interest, adverse to the rights of other citizens, or to the permanent and aggregate interests of the community."[3] Yet, the Founding Fathers believed that interest groups thrived because of freedom—the freedom that all Americans enjoyed to organize and express their views. To the framers, this problem presented a dilemma. If the government were given

interest group
An organized group of people that makes policy-related appeals to government.

[3]Ibid.

the power to regulate or in any way to forbid efforts by organized interests to interfere in the political process, the government would in effect have the power to suppress freedom. The solution to this dilemma was presented by Madison:

> Take in a greater variety of parties and interest [and] you make it less probable that a majority of the whole will have a common motive to invade the rights of other citizens. . . . [Hence the advantage] enjoyed by a large over a small republic.[4]

According to the Madisonian theory, a good constitution encourages multitudes of interests so that no single interest can ever tyrannize the others. The basic assumption is that competition among interests will produce balance and compromise, with all the interests regulating each other.[5] Today, this Madisonian principle of regulation is called **pluralism.** According to pluralist theory, all interests are and should be free to compete for influence in the United States. Moreover, according to pluralist doctrine, the outcome of this competition is compromise and moderation, since no group is likely to be able to achieve any of its goals without accommodating itself to some of the views of its many competitors.[6]

pluralism The theory that all interests are and should be free to compete for influence in the government. The outcome of this competition is compromise and moderation.

There are tens of thousands of organized groups in the United States, but the huge number of *interest groups* competing for influence in the United States does not mean that all *interests* are fully and equally represented in the American political process. As we shall see, the political deck is heavily stacked in favor of those interests able to organize and to wield substantial economic, social, and institutional resources on behalf of their cause. This means that within the universe of interest-group politics, it is political power—not some abstract conception of the public good—that is likely to prevail. Moreover, this means that interest-group politics, taken as a whole, is a political format that works more to the advantage of some types of interests than others. In general, a politics in which interest groups predominate is a politics with a distinctly upper-class bias.

Organized Interests Are Predominantly Economic

When most people think about interest groups, they immediately think of groups with a direct and private economic interest in governmental actions. These groups are generally supported by groups of producers or manufacturers in a particular economic sector. Examples of this type of group include the National Petroleum Refiners Association, the American Farm Bureau Federation,

[4]Ibid., p. 83.
[5]Ibid.
[6]The best statement of the pluralist view is in David Truman, *The Governmental Process: Political Interests and Public Opinion* (New York: Knopf, 1951), Chapter 2.

and the National Federation of Independent Business, which represents small-business owners. At the same time that broadly representative groups like these are active in Washington, specific companies, like Disney, Shell Oil, IBM, and General Motors, may be active on certain issues that are of particular concern to them.

Labor organizations are equally active lobbyists. The AFL-CIO, the United Mine Workers, and the Teamsters are all groups that lobby on behalf of organized labor. In recent years, lobbies have arisen to further the interests of public employees, the most significant among these being the American Federation of State, County, and Municipal Employees.

Professional lobbies like the American Bar Association and the American Medical Association have been particularly successful in furthering their own interests in state and federal legislatures. Financial institutions, represented by organizations like the American Bankers Association and the National Savings & Loan League, although often less visible than other lobbies, also play an important role in shaping legislative policy.

Recent years have witnessed the growth of a powerful "public interest" lobby purporting to represent interests whose concerns are not addressed by traditional lobbies. These groups have been most visible in the consumer protection and environmental policy areas, although public interest groups cover a broad range of issues. The Natural Resources Defense Council, the Union of Concerned Scientists, and Common Cause are all examples of public interest groups.

The perceived need for representation on Capitol Hill has generated a public-sector lobby in the past several years, including the National League of Cities and the "research" lobby. The latter group comprises think tanks and universities that have an interest in obtaining government funds for research and support, and it includes institutions such as Harvard University, the Brookings Institution, and the American Enterprise Institute. Indeed, universities have expanded their lobbying efforts even as they have reduced faculty positions and course offerings and increased tuition.[7]

All Groups Require Money and Leadership, and Most Need Members

Although there are many interest groups, most share certain key organizational components. First, most groups must attract and keep members. Usually, groups appeal to members not only by promoting political goals or policies that they favor but also by providing them with direct economic or social benefits. Thus, for example, the American Association of Retired Persons (AARP), which promotes the interests of senior citizens, at the same time offers members a variety

[7]Betsy Wagner and David Bowermaster, "B.S. Economics," *Washington Monthly* (November 1992): 19–21.

of insurance benefits and commercial discounts. Similarly, many groups whose goals are chiefly economic or political also seek to attract members through social interaction and good fellowship. Thus, the local chapters of many national groups provide their members with a congenial social environment, while collecting dues that finance the national office's political efforts.

Second, every group must build a financial structure capable of sustaining an organization and funding the group's activities. Most interest groups rely on yearly membership dues and voluntary contributions from sympathizers. Many also sell some ancillary services, such as insurance and vacation tours, to members. Third, every group must have a leadership and decision-making structure. For some groups, this structure is very simple. For others, it can be quite elaborate and involve hundreds of local chapters that are melded into a national apparatus. Finally, most groups include an agency that actually carries out the group's tasks. This may be a research organization, a public relations office, or a lobbying office in Washington or a state capital.

Group Membership Has an Upper-Class Bias

Membership in interest groups is not randomly distributed in the population. People with higher incomes, higher levels of education, and management or professional occupations are much more likely to become members of groups than those who occupy the lower rungs on the socioeconomic ladder.[8] Well-educated, upper-income business and professional people are more likely to have the time and the money, and to have acquired through the educational process the concerns and skills, needed to play a role in a group or association. Moreover, for business and professional people, group membership may provide personal contacts and access to information that can help advance their careers. At the same time, corporate entities—businesses and the like—usually have ample resources to form or participate in groups that seek to advance their causes.

The result is that interest-group politics in the United States tends to have a very pronounced upper-class bias. Certainly, there are many interest groups and political associations that have a working-class or lower-class membership—labor organizations or welfare-rights organizations, for example—but the great majority of interest groups and their members are drawn from the middle and upper-middle classes. In general, the "interests" served by interest groups are the interests of society's "haves." Even when interest groups take opposing positions on issues and policies, the conflicting positions they espouse usually reflect divisions among upper-income strata rather than conflicts between the upper and lower classes.

In general, to obtain adequate political representation, forces from the bottom rungs of the socioeconomic ladder must be organized on the massive scale

---

[8]Kay Lehman Schlozman and John T. Tierney, *Organized Interests and American Democracy* (New York: Harper & Row, 1986), p. 60.

associated with political parties. Parties can organize and mobilize the collective energies of large numbers of people who, as individuals, may have very limited resources. Interest groups, on the other hand, generally organize smaller numbers of the better-to-do. Thus, the relative importance of political parties and interest groups in American politics has far-ranging implications for the distribution of political power in the United States. As we saw in Chapter 11, political parties have declined in influence in recent years. Interest groups, on the other hand, as we shall see shortly, have become much more numerous, more active, and more influential in American politics.

Groups Form in Response to Changes in the Political Environment

If interest groups and our concerns about them were a new phenomenon, we would not have begun this chapter with Madison in the eighteenth century. As long as there is government, as long as government makes policies that add value or impose costs, and as long as there is liberty to organize, interest groups will abound; and if government expands, so will interest groups. There was, for example, a spurt of growth in the national government during the 1880s and 1890s, arising largely from the first governmental efforts at economic intervention to fight large monopolies and to regulate some aspects of interstate commerce. In the latter decade, a parallel spurt of growth occurred in national interest groups, including the imposing National Association of Manufacturers (NAM) and numerous other trade associations. Many groups organized around specific agricultural commodities, as well. This period also marked the beginning of the expansion of trade unions as interest groups. Later, in the 1930s, interest groups with headquarters and representation in Washington began to grow significantly, concurrent with that decade's expansion of the national government.

Over the past thirty-five years, there has been an enormous increase both in the number of interest groups seeking to play a role in the American political process and in the extent of their opportunity to influence that process. A *New York Times* report, for example, noted that during the 1970s, expanded federal regulation of the automobile, oil, gas, education, and health-care industries impelled each of these interests to increase substantially its efforts to influence the government's behavior. These efforts, in turn, had the effect of spurring the organization of other groups to augment or counter the activities of the first.[9] Similarly, federal social programs have occasionally sparked political organization and action on the part of clientele groups seeking to influence the distribution of benefits and, in turn, the organization of groups opposed to the programs or their cost. For example, federal programs and court decisions in such areas as abortion and school prayer were the stimuli for political action and organization by fundamentalist religious groups. The Christian Coalition, for instance, whose

 History Principle

The explosion of interest-group activity has its origins in the expansion of the role of government, especially since the 1960s.

[9]John Herbers, "Special Interests Gaining Power as Voter Disillusionment Grows," *New York Times*, 14 November 1978.

Does the Internet Change the Logic of Collective Action?

On September 12, 2001, Eli Pariser organized three hundred peace activists and garnered media attention from as far away as Romania by simply E-mailing a few friends about his views on war.[10] MoveOn.org, which began in existence in 1998 as a Web page dedicated to fighting the impeachment of President Clinton, has grown by 2003 into a clearinghouse for liberal activists and one of the largest PACs (political action committees) in the Democratic party. Senator John McCain pioneered Internet-based fund-raising during his 2000 campaign for the presidency. Vermont governor Howard Dean transformed himself into a major candidate thanks to Internet donations and electronic recruitment of volunteers.

What all of these examples illustrate is the potential of the Internet for overcoming one of the central problems in politics, the basis of the second principle of politics, and the central lesson of this chapter: Mancur Olson's "logic of collective action." Stripped to its bare essentials, Olson argues that, for most individuals, it is not rational to work toward the provision of a public good. The individual's contribution is unlikely to make a difference, and he or she can enjoy the public good anyway. So why participate?

Olson provides some solutions to the collective-action problem—among them, keep groups small and intimate. So how can we explain the examples shown above? These groups seem to be the opposite: large (national and even international in scope) and anonymous (most individuals know each other only as electronic personae). Has the Internet changed the logic of collective action?

The answer is "no." In fact, the principles of politics help us identify the ways that electronic communications have made it easier to organize as well as show the things that electronic communications are unlikely to change.

Take, for example, the role of political entrepreneurs. These are individuals who have private reasons to organize a group. The Internet is likely to affect the number of entrepreneurs because it lowers costs and thus is likely to increase the possibility that they can organize a group.[11] Cell phones and text messaging make people instantly available, while Web sites and E-mail represent low-cost options for mass communication. The leaders of the American Revolution had to rely on slow-going mail services and pamphlets to coordinate their actions and popularize their views. Modern activists can voice their views through blogs and Web pages, reaching more people and at a lower cost.

This is almost certainly what happened with MoveOn.org. A few vocal activists started a Web site because they were angry about Republican attempts to impeach Clinton. But once the Web site grew so dramatically (and unexpectedly), it became a logical vehicle to organize liberal political interests.[12]

Another way that groups recruit and maintain membership is by providing selective benefits to members. One important benefit is solidarity, friendship, networking, and the sense of belonging that comes with membership in a group. The Internet makes it far easier for groups to provide these solidary benefits. Chat rooms, E-mail lists, and bulletin boards provide cheap and easy venues for interpersonal interaction. E-mailing a newsletter or maintaining a Web site is far less expensive than maintaining local chapters. From the perspective of the individual, these new technologies decrease the costs for membership, further bolstering participation.

An example of this dynamic is the rapid organization that followed the protests against the Seattle meeting of the World Trade Organization (WTO). This movement began as a set of E-mail lists and has since grown to encompass a news and information Web site (Indymedia.org) and an international organization of activists that uses new technologies and techniques to unite ideologically and geographically diverse groups.

While new technologies may be part of the explanation for new social movements, it is not the whole story. The Internet alone does not explain why people continue to turn out in the tens of thousands to protest the meetings of the WTO, World Bank, International Monetary Fund (IMF), or the Group of Seven (G-7). Ideology and group solidarity still matter. Olson's observations about collective action still apply.

What the Internet has changed is some of the costs of creating and maintaining groups.

[10]George Packer, "Smart-Mobbing the War," *New York Times Magazine,* 9 March 2003, p. 46.

[11]Recall that political entrepreneurs gain a benefit only if their private benefits exceed the costs of organizing the group. Thus, if you lower the costs, then you increase the number of entrepreneurs who will find it profitable.

[12]See Michael Falcone, "Dear Campaign Diary: Seizing the Day, Online," *New York Times,* 11 September 2003, p. G1; and Josh Richman, "MoveOn.org Redefines Art of Activism, Fund Raising; Berkeley-based Web Site Claims 850,000 Members, Becomes Virtual Powerhouse," *Alameda Times-Star,* 26 February 2003, p. A1.

major focus is opposition to abortion, has nearly 2 million active members organized in local chapters in every state. Twenty of the state chapters have full-time staff and fifteen have annual budgets over $200,000.[13] The ongoing struggles over abortion and school prayer have helped the Christian Coalition, the Family Research Council, and other organizations comprising the Christian Right to expand the membership rolls of their state and local organizations. Anti-abortion forces, in particular, are organized at the local level throughout the United States and are prepared to participate in political campaigns and legislative battles. The importance of religious conservatives to the Republican party became quite evident in 2001. After his victory in the November 2000 presidential election, George W. Bush announced that his administration would seek to award federal

[13]Rich Lowry, "How the Right Rose," *National Review* 66, 11 December 1995, pp. 64–76.

grants and contracts to religious groups. By using so-called faith-based groups as federal contractors, Bush was seeking to reward religious conservatives for their past loyalty to the GOP and to ensure that these groups would have a continuing stake in Republican success. Thus, the expansion of government in recent decades has also stimulated increased group activity and organization.

Another factor accounting for the explosion of interest-group activity in recent years was the emergence of a new set of forces in American politics that can collectively be called the New Politics movement.

The New Politics movement is made up of upper-middle-class professionals and intellectuals for whom the civil rights and antiwar movements were formative experiences, just as the Great Depression and World War II had been for their parents. The crusade against racial discrimination and the Vietnam War led these young men and women to see themselves as a political force in opposition to the public policies and politicians associated with the nation's postwar regime. In more recent years, the forces of New Politics have focused their attention on such issues as environmental protection, women's rights, and nuclear disarmament.

Members of the New Politics movement constructed or strengthened "public interest" groups such as Common Cause, the Sierra Club, the Environmental Defense Fund, Physicians for Social Responsibility, the National Organization for Women, and the various organizations formed by consumer activist Ralph Nader. Through these groups, New Politics forces were able to influence the media, Congress, and even the judiciary, and enjoyed a remarkable degree of success during the late 1960s and early 1970s in securing the enactment of policies they favored. New Politics activists also played a major role in securing the enactment of environmental, consumer, and occupational health and safety legislation.

Among the factors contributing to the rise and success of New Politics forces was technology. In the 1970s and 1980s, computerized direct-mail campaigns allowed public interest groups to reach hundreds of thousands of potential sympathizers and contributors. Today, the Internet and E-mail serve the same function. Electronic communication allows relatively small groups to efficiently identify and mobilize their adherents throughout the nation. Individuals with perspectives that might be in the minority everywhere can become conscious of one another and mobilize for national political action through the magic of electronic politics.

HOW AND WHY DO INTEREST GROUPS FORM?

Pluralist theory argues that since individuals in the United States are free to join or form groups that reflect their common interests, interest groups should easily form whenever a change in the political environment warrants their formation. If this argument is correct, groups should form roughly in proportion to people's interests. We should find a greater number of organizations around interests shared by a greater number of people. The evidence for this pluralist hypothesis, however, is weak. Kay Schlozman and John Tierney examined interest groups that represent people's occupations and economic roles.[14] Using census data and listings of interest groups, they compared how many people in the United States have particular economic roles and how many organizations represent those roles in Washington. For example, they found that (in the mid-1980s) 4 percent of the population was looking for work, but only a handful of organizations actually represented the unemployed in Washington.[15]

There is a considerable disparity in Washington representation across categories of individuals in the population, as Table 12.1 suggests. Schlozman and Tierney note, for example, that there are at least a dozen groups representing senior citizens, but none for the middle-aged. Ducks Unlimited is an organization dedicated to the preservation of ducks and their habitats; turkeys, on the other hand, have no one working on their behalf. The pluralists' inability to explain why groups form around some interests and not others led some scholars to investigate the dynamics of collective action. Mancur Olson's work, already mentioned in Chapter 1 and discussed later in this chapter, is the most well-known challenge to the pluralists. It is in Olson's insights that we find the basis for interest-group formation.

Interest Groups Facilitate Cooperation

Groups of individuals pursuing some common interest or shared objective—maintenance of a hunting and fishing habitat, creation of a network for sharing computer software, lobbying for favorable legislation, playing a Beethoven symphony, etc.—consist of individuals who bear some cost or make some contribution on behalf of the joint goal. Each member of the Possum Hollow Rod and Gun Club may, for example, pay annual dues and devote one weekend a year to cleaning up the rivers and forests of the club-owned game preserve.

We can think of this in an analytical fashion, somewhat removed from any of these specific examples, as an instance of two-person cooperation writ large. Accordingly, each of a very large number of individuals has, in the simplest situation, two options in his or her behavioral repertoire: "contribute" or "don't contribute" to achieving the jointly shared objective. If the number of contributors to the group enterprise is sufficiently large, then a group goal is achieved. However, just as in the swamp-clearing example in Chapter 1, there is a twist. If the group goal is achieved, then *every member of the group enjoys its benefits, whether he or she contributed to its achievement or not.*

The Prisoners' Dilemma   Researchers often rely on the metaphor of the *prisoners' dilemma* when theorizing about social situations of collective action, like the

Collective Action Principle
The prisoners' dilemma, an example of a collective action problem, explains why cooperation in groups can be difficult to achieve.

---

[14]Schlozman and Tierney, *Organized Interests and American Democracy.*

[15]Of course, the *number* of organizations is at best only a rough measure of the extent to which various categories of citizen are represented in the interest-group world of Washington.

TABLE 12.1

Who Is Represented by Organized Interests

ECONOMIC ROLE OF INDIVIDUAL	% OF U.S. ADULTS	% OF ORGS.	TYPE OF ORG. IN WASHINGTON, D.C.	RATIO OF ORGS./ ADULTS
Managerial/administrative	7	71.0	Business association	10.10
Professional/technical	9	17.0	Professional association	1.90
Student/teacher	4	4.0	Educational organization	1.00
Farm workers	2	1.5	Agricultural organization	0.75
Unable to work	2	0.6	Handicapped organization	0.30
Other non-farm workers	41	4.0	Union	0.10
At home	19	1.8	Women's organizations	0.09
Retired	12	0.8	Senior-citizens organization	0.07
Looking for work	4	0.1	Unemployment organization	0.03

swamp-clearing example of Chapter 1. According to this metaphor, two prisoners (A and B) who are accused of jointly committing a crime are kept in separate interview rooms. The arresting officers do not have enough evidence for a judge to give the prisoners the maximum sentence, so the officers hope that one of the prisoners will provide the additional evidence they require. The prisoners know that the officers have scant evidence against them and that they will probably receive a less severe sentence or escape punishment altogether if they remain silent. Each prisoner is offered the same plea bargain: "Testify against the other prisoner in exchange for freedom, provided that your accomplice does not also testify against you. Remain silent and you will possibly get the maximum sentence if your accomplice testifies against you."

TABLE 12.2

The Prisoners' Dilemma

		PRISONER B	
		Snitch	Don't snitch
PRISONER A	Snitch	A gets three years B gets three years	A gains freedom B gets six years
	Don't snitch	A gets six years B gains freedom	A gets one year B gets one year

If you assume that prisoners A and B are self-interested, rational actors (who, given the choice between two alternatives, will choose the one that offers the best deal) and that they prefer less jail time to more, then they will face an unpleasant choice. Notice that in Table 12.2, prisoner A is better off choosing to "snitch," no matter what prisoner B does. If B chooses to snitch, then A's choice to snitch gets A a three-year jail term, but a "don't snitch" choice by A would have resulted in six years for A—clearly worse. On the other hand, if B chooses not to snitch, then A gets no jail time if he snitches instead of one year if he also chooses not to snitch. In short, A is always better off snitching. But this situation is symmetrical, so it follows that B is better off snitching, too. If both prisoners snitch, the prosecutor is able to convict both of them, and they would each serve three years. If they had both been *irrational* and kept silent, they would only have gotten one year each! In terms of game theory (from which the prisoners' dilemma is drawn), each player has a *dominant strategy*—snitching is best no matter what the other player does—and this leads paradoxically to an outcome in which each player is *worse* off.

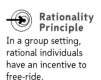 **Rationality Principle**

In a group setting, rational individuals have an incentive to free-ride.

The prisoners' dilemma provides the insight that rational individual behavior does not always lead to rational collective results. The logic of this situation is very compelling—if A appreciates the dilemma and realizes that B appreciates the dilemma, then A will still be drawn to the choice of snitching. The reasons for this are the temptation to get off scot-free (if he testifies and his accomplice doesn't) and the *fear* of being "suckered." The dilemma is brilliant because it applies to a wide range of circumstances.

Consider again the swamp-clearing example in which each person benefits from a drained swamp, even if he or she does not provide the required effort. As long as enough other people do so, any individual can "ride free" on the efforts of the others. This is a multiperson prisoners' dilemma because not providing effort, like snitching, is a dominant strategy, yet it is one that, if everyone avails him- or herself of it, leads to an unwanted outcome—a mosquito-infested swamp. The prospect of free riding, as we shall see next, is the bane of collective action.

The Logic of Collective Action   Mancur Olson, writing in 1965, essentially took on the political-science establishment by noting that the pluralist assumption of the time, that common interests among individuals are automatically transformed into group organization and collective action, was problematic. Individuals are tempted to "free-ride" on the efforts of others, have difficulty coordinating multiple objectives, and may even have differences of opinion about which common interest to pursue (conflicts of interest). In short, the group basis of politics is made of Jell-O: one cannot merely *assume* that groups arise and are maintained. Rather, formation and maintenance are the central problems of group life and politics generally.

Olson is at his most persuasive when talking about large groups and mass collective action, like many of the antiwar demonstrations and civil rights rallies of the 1960s. In these circumstances, the world of politics is a bit like the swamp-clearing example, where each individual has a rational strategy of not contributing. The logic of collective action makes it difficult to induce participation in and contribution to collective goals.

Olson claims that this difficulty is severest in large groups, for three reasons. First, large groups tend to be anonymous. Each household in a city is a taxpaying unit and may share the wish to see property taxes lowered. It is difficult, however, to forge a group identity or induce households to contribute effort or activity for the cause of lower taxes on such a basis. Second, in the anonymity of the large-group context, it is especially plausible to claim that no one individual's contribution makes much difference. Should the head of a household kill the better part of a morning writing a letter to his city council member in support of lower property taxes? Will it make much difference? If hardly anyone else writes, then the council member is unlikely to pay much heed to this one letter; on the other hand, if the council member is inundated with letters, would one more have a significant additional effect? Finally, there is the problem of enforcement. In a large group, are other group members going to punish a slacker? By definition, they cannot prevent the slacker from receiving the benefits of collective action, should those benefits materialize. (Every property owner's taxes will be lowered if anyone's is.) But, more to the point, in a large, anonymous group it is often hard to know who has and who has not contributed, and, because there is only the most limited sort of group identity, it is hard for contributors to identify, much less take action against, slackers. As a consequence, many large groups that share common interests fail to mobilize at all—they remain *latent*.

This same problem plagues small groups, too, as the swamp-clearing problem in Chapter 1 reveals. But Olson argues that small groups manage to overcome the problem of collective action more frequently and to a greater extent than their larger counterparts. Small groups are more personal, and their members are, therefore, more vulnerable to interpersonal persuasion. In small groups, individual contributions may make a more noticeable difference so that individuals feel that their contributions are more essential. Contributors in small groups, moreover, often know who they are and who the slackers are. Thus, punishment, ranging from subtle judgmental pressure to social ostracism, is easier to effect.

In contrast to large groups that often remain latent, Olson calls these small groups *privileged* because of their advantage in overcoming the free-riding, coordination, and conflict-of-interest problems of collective action. It is for these perhaps counterintuitive reasons that small groups often prevail over, or enjoy greater privileges relative to, larger groups. These reasons, therefore, help explain why we so often see producers win out over consumers, owners of capital over owners of labor, and a party's elite over its mass members.

Selective Benefits: A Solution to the Collective Action Problem

Despite the free-rider problem, interest groups offer numerous incentives to join. Most importantly, as Olson shrewdly noted in a most important theoretical insight, they make various "selective benefits" available only to group members (see Chapter 1). These benefits can be informational, material, solidary, or purposive. Table 12.3 gives some examples of the range of benefits in each of these categories.

Informational benefits are the most widespread and important category of selective benefits offered to group members. Information is provided through conferences, training programs, and newsletters and other periodicals sent automatically to those who have paid membership dues.

Material benefits include anything that can be measured monetarily, such as special services, goods, and even money. A broad range of material benefits can be offered by groups to attract members. These benefits often include discount purchasing, shared advertising, and, perhaps most valuable of all, health and retirement insurance.

Another option identified in Table 12.3 is that of *solidary benefits.* The most notable of this class of benefits are the friendship and "networking" opportunities that membership provides. Another benefit that has become extremely important to many of the newer nonprofit and citizen groups is what has come to be called "consciousness-raising." One example of this can be seen in the claims of many women's organizations that active participation conveys to each member of the organization an enhanced sense of her own value and a stronger ability to advance individual as well as collective civil rights. A similar solidary or psychological benefit has been the mainstay of the appeal of group membership to discouraged and disillusioned African Americans since their emergence as a constitutionally free and equal people.

informational benefits Special newsletters, periodicals, training programs, conferences, and other information provided to members of groups to entice others to join.

material benefits Special goods, services, or money provided to members of groups to entice others to join.

solidary benefits Selective benefits of group membership that emphasize friendship, networking, and consciousness-raising.

 Collective Action Principle

Selective benefits are one solution to the collective action problem.

TABLE 12.3

Selective Benefits of Interest-Group Membership

CATEGORY	BENEFITS
Informational benefits	Conferences Professional contacts Training programs Publications Coordination among organizations Research Legal help Professional codes Collective bargaining
Material benefits	Travel packages Insurance Discounts on consumer goods
Solidary benefits	Friendship Networking opportunities
Purposive benefits	Advocacy Representation before government Participation in public affairs

SOURCE: Adapted from Jack L. Walker, Jr., *Mobilizing Interest Groups in America: Patrons, Professions, and Social Movements* (Ann Arbor: University of Michigan Press, 1991), p. 86.

purposive benefits Selective benefits of group membership that emphasize the purpose and accomplishments of the group.

A fourth type of benefit involves the appeal of the purpose of an interest group. The benefits of religious interest groups provide us with the best examples of such ***purposive benefits.*** The Christian Right is a powerful movement made up of a number of interest groups that offer virtually no material benefits to their members. The growth and success of these groups depends upon the religious identifications and affirmations of their members. Many such religiously based interest groups have arisen, especially at state and local levels, throughout American history. For example, both the abolition and the prohibition movements were driven by religious interest groups whose main attractions were nonmaterial benefits.

Ideology itself, or the sharing of a commonly developed ideology, is another important nonmaterial benefit. Many of the most successful interest groups of the past twenty years have been citizen groups or public interest groups, whose members are brought together largely around shared ideological goals, including government reform, election and campaign reform, civil rights, economic equality, "family values," or even opposition to government itself.

Political Entrepreneurs Organize and Maintain Groups

In a review of Olson's book,[16] Richard Wagner noticed that Olson's arguments about groups and politics in general, and his theory of selective incentives in particular, had very little to say about the internal workings of groups. In Wagner's experience, however, groups often came into being and then were maintained in good working order not only because of selective incentives, but also because of the extraordinary efforts of specific individuals—leaders, in ordinary language, or *political entrepreneurs* in Wagner's more colorful expression.

Wagner was motivated to raise the issue of group leaders because, in his view, Olson's theory was too pessimistic. Mass organizations in the real world—labor unions, consumer associations, senior-citizen groups, environmental organizations—all exist, some persisting and prospering over long periods. Contrary to Olson's suggestions, they seem to get jump-started somehow in the real world. Wagner suggests that a special kind of theory of selective incentives is called for. Specifically, he argues that certain selective benefits may accrue to *those who organize and maintain otherwise latent groups.*

Senator Robert Wagner (no relation) in the 1930s and Congressman Claude Pepper in the 1970s each had *private reasons*—electoral incentives—to try to organize laborers and the elderly, respectively. Wagner, a Democrat from New York, had a large constituency of working men and women who would reward him by re-electing him—a private, conditional payment—if he bore the cost of organizing (or at least of facilitating the organization of) workers. And this he did. The law that bears his name, the Wagner Act of 1935, made it much easier for unions to organize in the industrial North.[17] Likewise, Claude Pepper, a Democratic congressman with a large number of elderly constituents in his South Miami district, saw it as serving his own electoral interests to provide the initial investment of effort for the organization of the elderly as a political force.

In general, a political entrepreneur is someone who sees a prospective cooperation dividend that is currently not being enjoyed. This is another way of saying that there is a latent group that, if it were to become manifest, would enjoy

Rationality Principle

Organizing collective action can provide private benefits to a political entrepreneur.

---

[16]Richard Wagner, "Pressure Groups and Political Entrepreneurs," *Papers on Non-Market Decision Making I* (1966): 161–70.

[17]The Wagner Act made it possible for unions to organize by legalizing the so-called *closed shop*. If a worker took a job in a closed shop or plant, he or she was *required* to join the union there. "Do not contribute" was no longer an option, so that workers in closed shops could not free-ride on the efforts made by others to improve wages and working conditions.

the fruits of collective action. For a price, whether in votes (as in the cases of Wagner and Pepper), a percentage of the dividend, nonmaterial glory, or other perks, the entrepreneur bears the costs of organizing, expends effort to monitor individuals for slacker behavior, and sometimes even imposes punishment on slackers (such as expelling them from the group and denying them any of its selective benefits).

To illustrate this phenomenon, there is a story about a British tourist who visited China in the late nineteenth century. She was shocked and appalled to see teams of men pulling barges along the Yangtze River, overseen by whip-wielding masters. She remarked to her guide that such an uncivilized state of affairs would never be tolerated in modern societies like those in the West. The guide, anxious to please but concerned that his employer had come to a wildly erroneous conclusion, hastily responded, "Madam, I think you misunderstand. The man carrying the whip is *employed* by those pulling the barge. He noticed that it is generally difficult, if you are pulling your weight along a tow path, to detect whether any of your team members are pulling theirs or, instead, whether they are 'free-riding' on your labors. He convinced the workers that his entrepreneurial services were required and that they should hire him. For an agreed-upon compensation, he monitors each team member's effort level, whipping those who shirk in their responsibilities. Notice, madam, that he rarely ever uses the whip. His mere presence is sufficient to get the group to accomplish the task."

Thus, political entrepreneurs, such as the whip-wielding driver, may be thought of as complements to Olsonian selective incentives in that both are ways of motivating groups to accomplish collective objectives. Indeed, if selective incentives *resolve* the paradox of collective action, then political entrepreneurs *dissolve* the paradox. Both are helpful, and sometimes both are needed in order to initiate and maintain collective action. Groups that manage, perhaps on their own, to get themselves organized at a low level of activity often take the next step of *creating* leaders and leadership institutions in order to increase the activity level and resulting cooperation dividends. Wagner, in other words, took Olson's theory of selective incentives and suggested an alternative explanation, one that made room for institutional solutions to the problem of collective action.

HOW DO INTEREST GROUPS INFLUENCE POLICY?

Interest groups work to improve the probability that they and their policy interests will be heard and treated favorably by all branches and levels of the government. The quest for political influence or power takes many forms. Insider strategies include access to key decision makers and using the courts. Outsider strategies include going public and using electoral politics. These strategies do not exhaust all the possibilities, but they paint a broad picture of ways that groups utilize their resources in the fierce competition for power (see Process Box 12.1). **Lobbying** is an attempt by a group to influence the policy process

lobbying An attempt by a group to influence the policy process through persuasion of government officials.

How Interest Groups Influence Congress

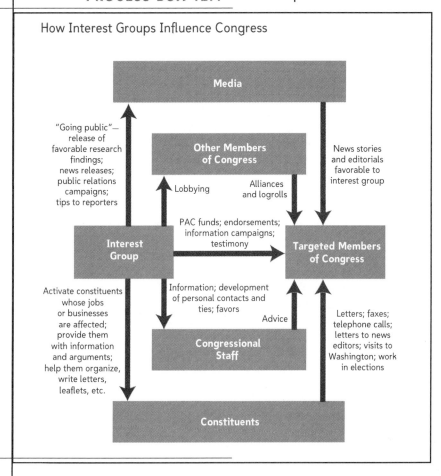

through persuasion of government officials. Most Americans tend to believe that interest groups exert their influence through direct contact with members of Congress, but lobbying encompasses a broad range of activities that groups engage in with all sorts of government officials and the public as a whole.

The 1946 Federal Regulation of Lobbying Act defines a lobbyist as "any person who shall engage himself for pay or any consideration for the purpose of attempting to influence the passage or defeat of any legislation of the Congress of the United States." The 1995 Lobbying Disclosure Act requires all organizations employing lobbyists to register with Congress and to disclose whom they represent, whom they lobby, what they are lobbying for, and how much they are paid. More than 7,000 organizations, collectively employing many thousands of lobbyists, are currently registered.

Many groups employ a mix of insider and outsider strategies. For example, environmental groups like the Sierra Club lobby members of Congress and key congressional staff members, participate in bureaucratic rule-making by offering comments and suggestions to agencies on new environmental rules, and bring lawsuits under various environmental acts like the Endangered Species Act, which authorizes groups and citizens to come to court if they believe the act is being violated. At the same time, the Sierra Club attempts to influence public opinion through media campaigns and to influence electoral politics by supporting candidates who they believe to share their environmental views and opposing candidates who they view as foes of environmentalism.

Direct Lobbying

Lobbying involves a great deal of activity on the part of someone speaking for an interest. Lobbyists badger and buttonhole legislators, administrators, and committee staff members with facts about pertinent issues and facts or claims about public support of them.[18] Lobbyists can serve a useful purpose in the legislative and administrative process by providing this kind of information. In 1978, during debate on a bill to expand the requirement for lobbying disclosures, Democratic senators Edward Kennedy of Massachusetts and Dick Clark of Iowa joined with Republican senator Robert Stafford of Vermont to issue the following statement: "Government without lobbying could not function. The flow of information to Congress and to every federal agency is a vital part of our democratic system."[19]

Lobbying Members of Congress   Interest groups also have substantial influence in setting the legislative agenda and in helping to craft specific language in legislation. Today, sophisticated lobbyists win influence by providing information about policies to busy members of Congress. As one lobbyist noted, "You can't get access without knowledge. . . . I can go in to see [former Energy and Commerce Committee chair] John Dingell, but if I have nothing to offer or nothing to say, he's not going to want to see me."[20] In recent years, interest groups have also begun to build broader coalitions and comprehensive campaigns around particular policy issues.[21] These coalitions do not rise from the grassroots, but in-

---

[18]For discussions of lobbying, see Jeffrey M. Berry, *Lobbying for the People: The Political Behavior of Public Interest Groups* (Princeton, N.J.: Princeton University Press, 1977) and John R. Wright, *Interest Groups and Congress: Lobbying, Contributions, and Influence* (Boston: Allyn & Bacon, 1996).

[19]"The Swarming Lobbyists," *Time*, 7 August 1978, p. 15.

[20]Daniel Franklin, "Tommy Boggs and the Death of Health Care Reform," *Washington Monthly* (April 1995): 36.

[21]Marie Hojnacki, "Interest Groups' Decisions to Join Alliances or Work Alone," *American Journal of Political Science* 41(1997): 61–87; Kevin W. Hula, *Lobbying Together: Interest Group Coalitions in Legislative Politics* (Washington, D.C.: Georgetown University Press, 1999).

stead are put together by Washington lobbyists who launch comprehensive lobbying campaigns that combine stimulated grassroots activity with information
and campaign funding for members of Congress. In recent years, the Republican
leadership worked so closely with lobbyists that critics charged that the boundaries between lobbyists and legislators had been erased, and that lobbyists had
become "adjunct staff to the Republican leadership."[22]

In many instances, the influence of lobbyists is based upon networks of personal relationships and behind-the-scenes services that they are able to perform
for lawmakers. For example, one of Washington's most successful lobbyists is
J. Steven Hart, a senior partner at Williams & Jensen, a well-known Washington,
D.C., lobbying and law firm. Hart's roster of clients includes such firms as Dell Inc.
and Bass Enterprises. What does Hart offer such clients? The most important service Hart provides is direct access to the leadership of Congress. Hart, as it happens, serves as the personal attorney for House majority leader Tom DeLay as well
as a number of other members of the House leadership. Often, this legal work is
performed at a nominal fee, as a "loss leader."[23] As a result of this personal relationship with the majority leader, Hart is able to promise clients that their case will be
heard by the nation's most important officials. Hart, for example, organized a
meeting in DeLay's office in September 2001 in which airline executives were
able to convince congressional leaders of the need for an airline bailout package in
the wake of September 11. On the whole, about 50 percent of Washington lobbyists have prior government experience. Other lobbyists present included Rebecca
Cox, wife of influential congressman Chris Cox of California. Ms. Cox is counsel
for Continental Airlines, one of the firms seeking the bailout. Chris and Rebecca
Cox are one example of a standard Washington phenomenon—a legislator married
to a lobbyist. For instance, Hadassah Lieberman, wife of Connecticut senator and
Democratic presidential candidate Joseph Lieberman, was for many years a lobbyist for the pharmaceutical industry. Lobbyists married to powerful legislators can
certainly promise their clients access to the highest levels of government.

Providing access is only one of the many services lobbyists perform. Lobbyists often testify on behalf of their clients at congressional committee and agency
hearings; lobbyists sometimes help their clients identify potential allies with
whom to construct coalitions; lobbyists provide research and information to government officials; lobbyists often draft proposed legislation or regulations to be
introduced by friendly lawmakers; lobbyists talk to reporters, place ads in newspapers, and organize letter-writing, E-mail, and telegram campaigns. Lobbyists
also play an important role in fund-raising, helping to direct clients' contributions to members of Congress and presidential candidates.

Lobbying the President   All these efforts and more are needed when the target
of a lobbying campaign is the president of the United States. So many individuals

[22]Peter H. Stone, "Follow the Leaders," *National Journal*, 24 June 1995, p. 1641.
[23]Steven Brill, *After: How America Confronted the September 12 Era* (New York: Simon & Shuster, 2003).

and groups clamor for the president's time and attention that only the most skilled and well-connected members of the lobbying community can hope to influence presidential decisions. One Washington lobbyist who fills this bill is Tom Kuhn, president of the Edison Electric Institute, a lobbying organization representing the electric power industry. Kuhn is a friend and former college classmate of President George Bush. In 2000, Kuhn was among the leading "Pioneers"—individuals who raised at least $100,000 for the Bush election campaign. Later, the electric power companies represented by Kuhn gave nearly $20 million to congressional candidates in the 2001–2002 election cycle. Kuhn's close relationship with the president and his efforts on behalf of the president's election have given Kuhn enormous leverage with the White House. During the 2000 transition, candidates for a presidential nomination to head the EPA felt compelled to pay "courtesy calls" to Kuhn. Subsequently, Kuhn led a successful effort to delay and weaken proposed new EPA controls on electric-power-plant emissions of mercury, a toxic substance linked to neurological damage, especially in children.[24] This was a victory for the electric power industry that promised to save the industry hundreds of millions of dollars a year and illustrates the influence that can be brought to bear by a powerful lobbyist.

What happens to interests that do not engage in extensive lobbying? They often find themselves "Microsofted." In 1998, the software giant was facing antitrust action from the Justice Department and had few friends in Congress. One member of the House, Representative Billy Tauzin (R-La.), told Microsoft chairman Bill Gates that without an extensive investment in lobbying, the corporation would continue to be "demonized." Gates responded by quadrupling Microsoft's lobbying expenditures and hiring a group of lobbyists with strong ties to Congress. The result was congressional pressure on the Justice Department resulting in a settlement of the Microsoft suit on terms favorable to the company. Similarly, in 1999, members of Congress advised Wal-Mart that its efforts to win approval to operate savings and loans in its stores were doomed to failure if the retailer did not greatly increase its lobbying efforts. "They don't give money. They don't have congressional representation—so nobody here cares about them," said one influential member. Like Microsoft, Wal-Mart learned its lesson, hired more lobbyists, and got what it wanted.[25]

Lobbying the Executive Branch   Even when an interest group is very successful at getting its bill passed by Congress and signed by the president, the prospect of full and faithful implementation of that law is not guaranteed. Often, a group and its allies do not pack up and go home as soon as the president turns their lobbied-for new law over to the appropriate agency. On average, 40 percent of interest-group representatives regularly contact both legislative and executive

[24]"Edison Electric Institute Lobbying to Weaken Toxic Mercury Standards," http://tristatenews.com, 28 February 2003.

[25]www.commoncause.org, "The Microsoft Playbook: A Report from Common Cause," 25 September 2000.

branch organizations, while 13 percent contact only the legislature and 16 percent only the executive branch.[26]

In some respects, interest-group access to the executive branch is promoted by federal law. The Administrative Procedure Act, first enacted in 1946 and frequently amended in subsequent years, requires most federal agencies to provide notice and an opportunity for comment before implementing proposed new rules and regulations. So-called "notice and comment rule-making" is designed to allow interests an opportunity to make their views known and to participate in the implementation of federal legislation that affects them. In 1990, Congress enacted the Negotiated Rulemaking Act to encourage administrative agencies to engage in direct and open negotiations with affected interests when developing new regulations. These two pieces of legislation—which have been strongly enforced by the federal courts—have played an important role in opening the bureaucratic process to interest-group influence. Today, few federal agencies would consider attempting to implement a new rule without consulting affected interests, who are sometimes known as "stakeholders" in Washington.[27]

Cultivating Access   Exerting influence on Congress or government agencies by providing their members with information about issues, support, and even threats of retaliation requires easy and constant access to decision makers. One interesting example of why groups need to cultivate and maintain access is the dairy farmers. Through the 1960s, dairy farmers were part of the powerful coalition of agricultural interests that had full access to Congress and to the Department of Agriculture. During the 1960s, a series of disputes broke out between the dairy farmers and the producers of corn, grain, and other agricultural commodities over commodities prices. Dairy farmers, whose cows consume grain, prefer low commodities prices, while grain producers obviously prefer to receive high prices. The commodities producers won the battle, and Congress raised commodities prices, in part at the expense of the dairy farmers. In the 1970s, the dairy farmers left the agriculture coalition, set up their own lobby and political action groups, and became heavily involved in public relations campaigns and both congressional and presidential elections. The dairy farmers encountered a number of difficulties in pursuing their new "outsider" strategies. Indeed, the political fortunes of the dairy operations were badly hurt when they were accused of making illegal contributions to President Nixon's re-election campaign in 1972.

Access is usually a result of time and effort spent cultivating a position within the inner councils of government. This method of gaining access often requires the sacrifice of short-run influence. For example, many of the most important organized interests in agriculture devote far more time and resources cultivating

Policy Principle

Public policy can reveal the impact of lobbying and cultivating access by groups affected by it.

Collective Action Principle

Lobbying and cultivating access require coordination across the legislative and executive branches.

[26]John P. Heinz et al., *The Hollow Core: Private Interests in National Policy Making* (Cambridge, Mass.: Harvard University Press, 1993).

[27]For an excellent discussion of the political origins of the Administrative Procedure Act, see Martin Shapiro, "APA: Past, Present, Future," 72 *Virginia Law Review* 377 (March 1986): 447–92.

the staff and trustees of state agriculture schools and county agents back home than buttonholing members of Congress or bureaucrats in Washington.

Regulations on Lobbying   As a result of the constant access to important decision makers that lobbyists seek out and require, stricter guidelines regulating the actions of lobbyists have been adopted in the last decade. For example, as of 1993, businesses may no longer deduct lobbying costs as a business expense. Trade associations must report to members the proportion of their dues that goes to lobbying, and that proportion of the dues may not be reported as a business expense. The most important attempt to limit the influence of lobbyists was the 1995 Lobbying Disclosure Act, which significantly broadened the definition of people and organizations that must register as lobbyists. According to the filings under the Lobbying Disclosure Act of 1995, there were almost 11,500 lobbyists working the halls of Congress.

In 1996, Congress passed legislation limiting the size of gifts to $50 and no more than $100 annually from a single source. It also banned the practice of honoraria, which had been used by special interests to supplement congressional salaries. But Congress did not limit the travel of representatives, senators, their wives, or congressional staff members. Interest groups can pay for congressional travel as long as a trip is related to legislative business and is disclosed on congressional reports within thirty days. On these trips, meals and entertainment expenses are not limited to $50 per event and $100 annually. The rules of Congress allow its members to travel on corporate jets as long as they pay an amount equal to first-class airfare.

Using the Courts

Institution Principle
Groups can turn to the courts if they are not successful in the legislative and executive branches.

Interest groups sometimes turn to the courts to augment other avenues of access. They can use the courts to affect public policy in at least three ways: (1) by bringing suit directly on behalf of the group itself, (2) by financing suits brought by individuals, and (3) by filing a companion brief as *amicus curiae* (literally "friend of the court") to an existing court case.

Among the most significant modern illustrations of the use of the courts as a strategy for political influence are those that accompanied the "sexual revolution" of the 1960s and the emergence of the movement for women's rights. Beginning in the mid-1960s, a series of cases was brought into the federal courts in an effort to force definition of a right to privacy in sexual matters. The effort began with a challenge to state restrictions on obtaining contraceptives for non-medical purposes, a challenge that was effectively made in *Griswold v. Connecticut,* where the Supreme Court held that states could neither prohibit the dissemination of information about nor prohibit the actual use of contraceptives by married couples. That case was soon followed by *Eisenstadt v. Baird*, in which the Court held that the states could not prohibit the use of contraceptives by single persons any more than it could prohibit their use by married couples. One year later, the Court held, in the 1973 case of *Roe v. Wade*, that states could not impose an absolute ban on voluntary abortions. Each of these cases, as well as others, were part of the Court's enunciation of a constitutional doctrine of privacy.[28]

The 1973 abortion case sparked a controversy that brought conservatives to the fore on a national level. These conservative groups made extensive use of the courts to whittle away the scope of the privacy doctrine. They obtained rulings, for example, that prohibit the use of federal funds to pay for voluntary abortions. And in 1989, right-to-life groups were able to use a strategy of litigation that significantly undermined the *Roe v. Wade* decision—namely, in the case of *Webster v. Reproductive Health Services*, which restored the right of states to place restrictions on abortion.[29]

Another extremely significant set of contemporary illustrations of the use of the courts as a strategy for political influence are those found in the history of the NAACP. The most important of these court cases was *Brown v. Board of Education*, in which the U.S. Supreme Court held that legal segregation of the schools was unconstitutional.[30]

Business groups are also frequent users of the courts because of the number of government programs applied to them. Litigation involving large businesses is most mountainous in such areas as taxation, antitrust, interstate transportation, patents, and product quality and standardization. Often a business is brought to litigation against its will by virtue of initiatives taken against it by other businesses or by government agencies. But many individual businesses bring suit themselves in order to influence government policy. Major corporations and their trade associations pay tremendous amounts of money each year in fees to the most prestigious Washington law firms. Some of this money is expended in gaining access. A great proportion of it, however, is used to keep the best and most experienced lawyers prepared to represent the corporations in court or before administrative agencies when necessary.

New Politics forces made significant use of the courts during the 1970s and 1980s, and judicial decisions were instrumental in advancing their goals. Facilitated by rules changes on access to the courts (the rules of standing are discussed in Chapter 8), the New Politics agenda was clearly visible in court decisions handed down in several key policy areas. In the environmental policy area, New Politics groups were able to force federal agencies to pay attention to environmental issues, even when the agency was not directly involved in activities related to environmental quality.

Mobilizing Public Opinion

Going public is a strategy that attempts to mobilize the widest and most favorable climate of opinion. Many groups consider it imperative to maintain this climate at all times, even when they have no issue to fight about. An increased use

---

[28]Griswold v. Connecticut, 381 U.S. 479 (1965); Eisenstadt v. Baird, 405 U.S. 438 (1972); Roe v. Wade, 410 U.S. 113 (1973).
[29]Webster v. Reproductive Health Services, 109 S.Ct. 3049 (1989).
[30]Brown v. Board of Education, 347 U.S. 483 (1954).

of this kind of strategy is usually associated with modern advertising. As early as the 1930s, political analysts were distinguishing between the "old lobby" of direct group representation before Congress and the "new lobby" of public relations professionals addressing the public at large to reach Congress.[31]

One of the best-known ways of going public is the use of institutional advertising. A casual scanning of important mass-circulation magazines and newspapers will provide numerous examples of expensive and well-designed ads by the major oil companies, automobile and steel companies, other large corporations, and trade associations. The ads show how much these organizations are doing for the country, for the protection of the environment, or for the defense of the American way of life. Their purpose is to create and maintain a strongly positive association between the organization and the community at large in the hope that these favorable feelings can be drawn on as needed for specific political campaigns later on.

Collective Action Principle

One means groups use to overcome collective-action problems is to mobilize public opinion in their support.

Many groups resort to protest because they lack the resources, the contacts, or the experience to use other political strategies. The sponsorship of boycotts, sit-ins, mass rallies, and marches by Martin Luther King's Southern Christian Leadership Conference (SCLC) and related organizations in the 1950s and 1960s is one of the most significant and successful cases of going public to create a more favorable climate of opinion by calling attention to abuses. The success of these events inspired similar efforts on the part of women. Organizations such as the National Organization for Women (NOW) used public strategies in their drive for legislation and in their efforts to gain ratification of the Equal Rights Amendment. In 1993, gay rights groups organized a mass rally in their effort to eliminate restrictions on military service and other forms of discrimination against individuals based on their sexual preference.

Another form of going public is the grassroots lobbying campaign. In such a campaign, a lobby group mobilizes ordinary citizens throughout the country to write their representatives in support of the group's position. A grassroots campaign can cost anywhere from $40,000 to sway the votes of one or two crucial members of a committee or subcommittee, to millions of dollars to mount a national effort aimed at the Congress as a whole.

Grassroots lobbying campaigns have been so effective in recent years that a number of Washington consulting firms have begun to specialize in this area. Firms such as Bonner & Associates, for example, will work to generate grassroots telephone campaigns on behalf of or in opposition to important legislative proposals. Such efforts can be very expensive. Reportedly, one trade association recently paid the Bonner firm $3 million to generate and sustain a grassroots effort to defeat a bill on the Senate floor.[32] The annual tab for grassroots lobbying has been estimated at $1 billion.

[31]Pendleton Herring, *Group Representation before Congress* (1928; reissue New York: Russell & Russell, 1967). See also Ken Kollman, *Outside Lobbying: Public Opinion and Interest Group Strategies* (Princeton, N.J.: Princeton University Press, 1998).

[32]Stephen Engelberg, "A New Breed of Hired Hands Cultivates Grass-Roots Anger," *New York Times*, 17 March 1993, p. A1.

Grassroots lobbying has become more prevalent in Washington over the last couple of decades because the adoption of congressional rules limiting gifts to members has made traditional lobbying more difficult. This circumstance makes all the more compelling the question of whether grassroots campaigning has reached an intolerable extreme. One case in particular may have tipped it over: in 1992, ten giant companies in the financial services, manufacturing, and high-tech industries began a grassroots campaign and spent millions of dollars to influence a decision in Congress to limit the ability of investors to sue for fraud. Retaining an expensive consulting firm, these corporations paid for the use of specialized computer software to persuade Congress that there was "an outpouring of popular support for the proposal." Thousands of letters from individuals flooded Capitol Hill. Many of those letters were written and sent by people who sincerely believed that investor lawsuits are often frivolous and should be curtailed. But much of the mail was phony, generated by the Washington-based campaign consultants; the letters came from people who had no strong feelings or even no opinion at all about the issue. More and more people, including leading members of Congress, are becoming quite skeptical of such methods, charging that these are not genuine grassroots campaigns but instead represent "Astroturf lobbying" (a play on the name of an artificial grass used on many sports fields). Such "Astroturf" campaigns have increased in frequency in recent years as members of Congress grow more and more skeptical of Washington lobbyists and far more concerned about demonstrations of support for a particular issue by their constituents. But after the firms mentioned above spent millions of dollars and generated thousands of letters to members of Congress, they came to the somber conclusion that "it's more effective to have 100 letters from your district where constituents took the time to write and understand the issue," because "Congress is sophisticated enough to know the difference."[33]

Using Electoral Politics

In addition to attempting to influence members of Congress and other government officials, interest groups also seek to use the electoral process to elect the right legislators in the first place and to ensure that those who are elected will owe them a debt of gratitude for their support. To put matters into perspective, groups invest far more resources in lobbying than in electoral politics. Nevertheless, financial support and campaign activism can be important tools for organized interests.

Political Action Committees   By far the most common electoral strategy employed by interest groups is that of giving financial support to the parties or to particular candidates. But such support can easily cross the threshold into outright bribery. Therefore, Congress has occasionally made an effort to regulate

[33]Jane Fritsch, "The Grass Roots, Just a Free Phone Call Away," *New York Times*, 23 June 1995, pp. A1 and A22.

this strategy. For example, the Federal Election Campaign Act of 1971 (amended in 1974) limits campaign contributions and requires that each candidate or campaign committee itemize the full name and address, occupation, and principal business of each person who contributes more than $100. These provisions have been effective up to a point, considering the rather large number of embarrassments, indictments, resignations, and criminal convictions in the aftermath of the Watergate scandal.

The Watergate scandal, itself, was triggered by the illegal entry of Republican workers into the office of the Democratic National Committee in the Watergate apartment complex. But an investigation quickly revealed numerous violations of campaign finance laws, involving millions of dollars in unregistered cash from corporate executives to President Nixon's re-election committee. Many of these revelations were made by the famous Ervin Committee, whose official name and jurisdiction was the Senate Select Committee to Investigate the 1972 Presidential Campaign Activities.

Reaction to Watergate produced further legislation on campaign finance in 1974 and 1976, but the effect has been to restrict individual rather than interest-group campaign activity. Individuals may now contribute no more than $2,000 to any candidate for federal office in any primary or general election. A ***political action committee (PAC),*** however, can contribute $5,000, provided it contributes to at least five different federal candidates each year. Beyond this, the laws permit corporations, unions, and other interest groups to form PACs and to pay the costs of soliciting funds from private citizens for the PACs.

Electoral spending by interest groups has been increasing steadily despite the flurry of reform following Watergate. Table 12.4 presents a dramatic picture of the growth of PACs as the source of campaign contributions. The dollar amounts for each year indicate the growth in electoral spending. The number of PACs has also increased significantly—from 608 in 1974 to more than 4,000 in 1999 (see Figure 12.1). Although the reform legislation of the early and mid-1970s attempted to reduce the influence of special interests over elections, the effect has been almost the exact opposite. Opportunities for legally influencing campaigns are now widespread.

Given the enormous costs of television commercials, polls, computers, and other elements of the new political technology (see Chapter 11), most politicians are eager to receive PAC contributions and are at least willing to give a friendly hearing to the needs and interests of contributors. It is probably not the case that most politicians simply sell their votes to the interests that fund their campaigns. But there is considerable evidence to support the contention that interest groups' campaign contributions do influence the overall pattern of political behavior in Congress and in the state legislatures.

Indeed, PACs and campaign contributions provide organized interests with such a useful tool for gaining access to the political process that calls to abolish PACs have been quite frequent among political reformers. Concern about PACs grew through the 1980s and 1990s, creating a constant drumbeat for reform of federal election laws. Proposals were introduced in Congress on many occasions,

political action committee A private group that raises and distributes funds for use in election campaigns.

TABLE 12.4

PAC Spending, 1977–2000

YEARS	CONTRIBUTIONS
1977–1978 (est.)	$77,800,000
1979–1980	131,153,384
1981–1982	190,173,539
1983–1984	266,822,476
1985–1986	339,954,416
1987–1988	364,201,275
1989–1990	357,648,557
1991–1992	394,785,896
1993–1994	388,102,643
1995–1996	429,887,819
1997–1998	470,830,847
1999–2000	579,358,330
2001–2002	685,305,553

SOURCE: Federal Election Commission.

perhaps the most celebrated being the McCain-Feingold bill. When it was originally proposed in 1996, the bill was aimed at reducing or eliminating PACs. But, in a stunning about-face, when campaign finance reform was adopted in 2002, it did not restrict PACs in any significant way. Rather, it eliminated unrestricted "soft money" donations to the national political parties (see Chapter 10). One consequence of this reform was the creation of a host of new organizations, often directed by former party officials but nominally unaffiliated with the two parties. These organizations are free to raise and spend as much money as they are able. Thus, contemporary reforms may have weakened political parties and strengthened interest groups.

Often, the campaign spending of activist groups is carefully kept separate from party and candidate organizations in order to avoid the restrictions of federal campaign finance laws. As long as a group's campaign expenditures are not

FIGURE 12.1

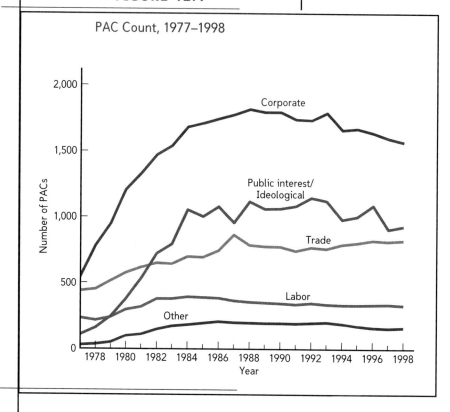

PAC Count, 1977–1998

SOURCE: Federal Election Commission, fecweb1.fec.gov/press/paccnt_grph.html.

coordinated with those of a candidate's own campaign, the group is free to spend as much money as it wishes. Such expenditures are viewed as "issues advocacy" and are protected by the First Amendment and, thus, not subject to statutory limitation.[34]

During the 2000 election campaign, another source of PAC money surfaced—the "stealth PAC," so called because it "flew under the radar" of the Federal Election Commission's requirement that an independent expenditure by an individual or PAC be publicly disclosed. In that year's primaries, stealth PACs engaged in issues advocacy. However, because no reporting requirements were in

---

[34]Ruth Marcus, "Outside Groups Pushing Election Laws into Irrelevance," *Washington Post*, 8 August 1996, p. A9.

place, no one knew exactly how much money they were spending, how many of them existed, where their money came from, or which candidates they supported. Nevertheless, the media and "watchdog" public interest groups were able to bring some details about them to the public's attention. For example, it was discovered that two prominent fund-raisers for George W. Bush's presidential campaign spent $2.5 million on a series of "Republicans for Clean Air" ads that were critical of Senator John McCain, Bush's most formidable opponent in the Republican primaries. Later in 2000, campaign finance reformers in Congress won a small victory when they passed legislation that requires stealth PACs to fully disclose the names of their contributors and to detail where their money is spent. In support of this legislation, Maine senator Olympia Snowe said, "This is a good opportunity to bring sunshine to the political process."

Campaign Activism Financial support is not the only way that organized groups seek influence through electoral politics. Sometimes, activism can be even more important than campaign contributions. Campaign activism on the part of conservative groups played a very important role in bringing about the Republican capture of both houses of Congress in the 1994 congressional elections. For example, Christian Coalition activists played a role in many races, including ones in which Republican candidates were not overly identified with the religious Right. One post-election study suggested that more than 60 percent of the over 600 candidates supported by the Christian Right were successful in state, local, and congressional races in 1994.[35] The efforts of conservative Republican activists to bring voters to the polls is one major reason that turnout among Republicans exceeded Democratic turnout in a midterm election for the first time since 1970. This increased turnout was especially marked in the South, where the Christian Coalition was most active. In many congressional districts, Christian Coalition efforts on behalf of the Republicans were augmented by grassroots campaigns launched by the National Rifle Association (NRA) and the National Federation of Independent Business (NFIB). The NRA had been outraged by Democratic support for gun-control legislation, while NFIB had been energized by its campaign against employer mandates in the failed Clinton health-care reform initiative. Both groups are well organized at the local level and were able to mobilize their members across the country to participate in congressional races.

In 2000, both civil rights groups and organized labor made substantial efforts to mobilize their members for the Democrats. Indeed, it was the NAACP's voter registration drive that brought Al Gore close to victory in Florida, a state that had been considered safely in the Republican column. In Michigan, labor's efforts not only helped Gore carry the state but also brought about the defeat of incumbent Republican senator Spencer Abraham.

[35]Richard L. Burke, "Religious-Right Candidates Gain as GOP Turnout Rises," New York Times, 12 November 1994, p. 10.

initiative The process that allows citizens to propose new laws and submit them for approval by the state's voters.

The Initiative   Another political tactic sometimes used by interest groups is sponsorship of ballot initiatives at the state level. The *initiative,* a device adopted by a number of states around 1900, allows proposed laws to be placed on the general election ballot and submitted directly to the state's voters. This procedure bypasses the state legislature and governor. The initiative was originally promoted by late nineteenth-century Populists as a mechanism that would allow the people to govern directly. Populists saw the initiative as an antidote to interest-group influence in the legislative process.

Ironically, many studies have suggested that most initiative campaigns today are actually sponsored by interest groups seeking to circumvent legislative opposition to their goals. In recent years, for example, initiative campaigns have been sponsored by the insurance industry, trial lawyers' associations, and tobacco companies.[36] The role of interest groups in initiative campaigns should come as no surprise since such campaigns can cost millions of dollars.

GROUPS AND INTERESTS: THE DILEMMA OF REFORM

We would like to think that policies are products of legislators' concepts of the public interest. Yet in reality few programs and policies ever reach the public agenda without the vigorous support of important national interest groups. In the realm of economic policy, social policy, international trade policy, and even such seemingly interest-free areas as criminal justice policy, where, in fact, private prison corporations lobby for longer sentences for lawbreakers, interest-group activity is a central feature of American politics and public policy. But before we throw up our hands in dismay, it is worth remembering that the untidy process and sometimes undesirable outcomes of interest-group politics are virtually inherent aspects of democratic politics. At times, our larger interest in maintaining a vigorous and democratic politics may require us to tolerate such foolish things as tax subsidies for chicken poop.

James Madison wrote that "liberty is to faction what air is to fire."[37] By this he meant that the organization and proliferation of interests was inevitable in a free society. To seek to place limits on the organization of interests, in Madison's view, would be to limit liberty itself. Madison believed that interests should be permitted to regulate themselves by competing with one another. As long as competition among interests was free, open, and vigorous, there would be some balance of power among them, and none would be able to dominate the political or governmental process.

There is considerable competition among organized groups in the United States. Nevertheless, interest-group politics is not as free of bias as Madisonian

---

[36]Elisabeth R. Gerber, *The Populist Paradox: Interest Group Influence and the Promise of Direct Legislation* (Princeton, N.J.: Princeton University Press, 1999), p. 6.
[37]*The Federalist Papers,* No. 10.

theory might suggest. Although the weak and poor do occasionally become organized to assert their rights, interest-group politics is generally a form of political competition in which the wealthy and powerful are best able to engage.

Moreover, although groups sometimes organize to promote broad public concerns, interest groups more often represent relatively narrow, selfish interests. Small, self-interested groups can be organized much more easily than large and more diffuse collectives. For one thing, the members of a relatively small group—say, bankers or hunting enthusiasts—are usually able to recognize their shared interests and the need to pursue them in the political arena. Members of large and more diffuse groups—say, consumers or potential victims of firearms—often find it difficult to recognize their shared interests or the need to engage in collective action to achieve them.[38] This is why causes presented as public interests by their proponents often turn out, upon examination, to be private interests wrapped in a public mantle.

Thus, we have a dilemma to which there is no ideal answer. To regulate interest-group politics is, as Madison warned, to limit freedom and to expand governmental power. Not to regulate interest-group politics, on the other hand, may be to ignore justice. Those who believe that there are simple solutions to the issues of political life would do well to ponder this problem.

SUMMARY

Efforts by organized groups to influence government and policy are becoming an increasingly important part of American politics. Such interest groups use a number of strategies to gain power.

Lobbying is the attempt to influence the policy process through persuasion of government officials. Lobbyists—individuals who receive some form of compensation for lobbying—are required to register with the House and Senate. In spite of an undeserved reputation for corruption, lobbyists serve a useful function, providing members of Congress and other government officials with a vital flow of information.

Access is participation in government. Most groups build up access over time through great effort. They work years to get their members into positions of influence on congressional committees.

Litigation sometimes serves interest groups when other strategies fail. Groups may bring suit on their own behalf, finance suits brought by individuals, or file *amicus curiae* briefs.

Going public is an effort to mobilize the widest and most favorable climate of opinion. Advertising is a common technique in this strategy. Others are boycotts, strikes, rallies, and marches.

---

[38]Mancur Olson, Jr., *The Logic of Collective Action: Public Goods and the Theory of Groups* (Cambridge, Mass.: Harvard University Press, 1971).

Rationality Principle	Collective Action Principle	Institution Principle	Policy Principle	History Principle
In a group setting, rational individuals have an incentive to free-ride.

Organizing collective action can provide private benefits to a political entrepreneur. | The prisoners' dilemma, an example of a collective action problem, explains why cooperation in groups can be difficult to achieve.

Selective benefits are one solution to the collective action problem.

Lobbying and cultivating access require coordination across the legislative and executive branches.

One means groups use to overcome collective-action problems is to mobilize public opinion in their support. | Groups can turn to the courts if they are not successful in the legislative and executive branches. | Public policy can reveal the impact of lobbying and cultivating access by groups affected by it. | The explosion of interest-group activity has its origins in the expansion of the role of government, especially since the 1960s. |

Groups engage in electoral politics either by embracing one of the major parties, usually through financial support, or through a nonpartisan strategy. Interest groups' campaign contributions now seem to be flowing into the coffers of candidates at a faster rate than ever before.

The group basis of politics, present since the founding, is both a curse and a blessing. In overcoming the hurdles of collective action, groups are an important means by which Americans participate in the political process and influence its outcomes. But participation in group life does not draw representatively from the population. So while it increases citizen involvement, influence is not evenly distributed. Collective action thus remains a dilemma.

FOR FURTHER READING

Cigler, Allan J., and Burdett A. Loomis, eds. *Interest Group Politics.* 6th ed. Washington, D.C.: Congressional Quarterly Press, 2002.

Clawson, Dan, Alan Neustadtl, and Denise Scott. *Money Talks: Corporate PACs and Political Influence.* New York: Basic Books, 1992.

Hansen, John Mark. *Gaining Access: Congress and the Farm Lobby, 1919–1981.* Chicago: University of Chicago Press, 1991.

Heinz, John P., et al. *The Hollow Core: Private Interests in National Policy Making.* Cambridge, Mass.: Harvard University Press, 1993.

Lowi, Theodore J. *The End of Liberalism: The Second Republic of the United States.* 2nd ed. New York: W. W. Norton, 1979.

Moe, Terry M. *The Organization of Interests: Incentives and the Internal Dynamics of Political Interest Groups.* Chicago: University of Chicago Press, 1980.

Olson, Mancur, Jr. *The Logic of Collective Action: Public Goods and the Theory of Groups.* Cambridge, Mass.: Harvard University Press, 1965, 1971.

Petracca, Mark P., ed. *The Politics of Interests: Interest Groups Transformed.* Boulder, Col.: Westview, 1992.

Salisbury, Robert H. *Interests and Institutions: Substance and Structure in American Politics.* Pittsburgh: University of Pittsburgh Press, 1992.

Schlozman, Kay Lehman, and John T. Tierney. *Organized Interests and American Democracy.* New York: Harper & Row, 1986.

Truman, David B. *The Governmental Process: Political Interests and Public Opinion.* New York: Knopf, 1951.

Vogel, David. *Fluctuating Fortunes: The Political Power of Business in America.* New York: Basic Books, 1989.

Wright, John R. *Interest Groups and Congress: Lobbying, Contributions, and Influence.* Boston: Allyn & Bacon, 1996.

Politics in the News—
Reading between the Lines

Mobilizing Collective Action

Antiwar Effort Emphasizes Civility Over Confrontation

By KATE ZERNIKE AND DEAN MURPHY

With the war against Iraq in its second week, the most influential antiwar coalitions have shifted away from large-scale disruptive tactics and stepped up efforts to appeal to mainstream Americans.

One of the largest groups, Win Without War, is encouraging the two million people on its e-mail list to send supportive letters to soldiers. Other groups have redoubled their fund-raising for billboards that declare "Peace is Patriotic" and include the giant image of an unfurling American flag. . . .

The week before the war began . . . United for Peace and Justice, declined to join in sponsoring a rally put on by International Answer . . . saying its message was too left-wing and alienating. . . .

"If we're going to be a force that needs to be listened to by our elected officials, by the media, by power, our movement needs to reflect the population," said Leslie Cagan, co-chairwoman of United for Peace and Justice, and a career political organizer.

"The great lesson from Madison Avenue is repetition," Ms. Cagan said. "If you get the same message out in different ways, you begin to break into people's consciousness."

. . . The new antiwar groups take pride in the size of the crowds they have been able to mobilize. They have grown a protest movement the size of which it took Vietnam-era organizers four years to build. . . .

United for Peace and Justice, for example, says it took only six weeks to get 350,000 people to a rally in New York in February, and Win Without War says it took four days to set up 6,800 candlelight vigils the week the war began.

. . . The Internet makes it far easier to organize swiftly and draw out crowds. . . .

When the antiwar protests began to gather steam in the fall, the large-scale rallies were being run by International Answer.

Answer brought together an amalgam of demonstrators, including anti-

New York Times, 29 March 2003, p. B1.

globalization protesters and longtime Socialists. Some of its chief organizers were members of the Workers World Party, a radical Socialist group that has defended Slobodan Milosevic and the North Korean and Iraqi governments.

In the protest community, the group was especially known for good organization: in some cities, Answer would go early in the year and snap up protest permits for the largest public places on the best dates. Last fall, many smaller groups opposed to the war were planning to attend the rally Answer had organized. . . .

But the afternoon before the event, representatives of about 50 groups . . . shar[ed] their concerns that Answer's oratory was too anti-Israel, too angry. They worried that its rallies were not focused enough on the war. . . .

. . . They decided that afternoon to form a new coalition that would operate apart from Answer. They named it United for Peace and Justice. . . .

Later that same October day, eight people from the meeting went out . . . worried . . . that even their new alternative to Answer would not get the support of important mass constituency groups like labor, veterans and churches . . . those eight agreed to create another group, calling this one Win Without War. . . .

. . . As time went on, United for Peace and Justice took on the job of organizing rallies. Win Without War's task focused on the news media. . . .

The Internet would prove crucial to both organizing and media. United for Peace and Justice said 40,000 people signed up for e-mail bulletins about actions against the war. Win Without War says its e-mail list includes more than two million addresses. Earlier this month, Win Without War created a worldwide candlelight vigil online, allowing people to enter their ZIP codes to find the nearest one. . . .

ESSENCE OF THE STORY

- Groups opposed to the war in Iraq differ on strategy—to be more confrontational and possibly alienate mainstream Americans, or to be more mainstream yet dilute the message.

- The new antiwar groups have found that electronic communications make it far easier and faster to recruit participants.

- Opposition to the war in Iraq spans a wider ideological spectrum compared, for example, to that of the Vietnam War era protests.

POLITICAL ANALYSIS

- All collective movements face the tension between keeping a focused appeal, which might attract a smaller but more dedicated audience, or expanding their appeal but potentially alienating their core supporters.

- New information technologies don't change the essential logic of organizing but make some things easier.

- The war in Iraq has allowed a number of disparate groups (antiglobalization, antiwar, and traditional Left) to coalesce around a single issue. This should strengthen the hand of liberals in coming elections.

In January, Mr. Pariser sent out an e-mail message saying that the organization wanted to buy a newspaper advertisement, and could raise $27,000 privately if it could raise the same amount online.

Within two days, Mr. Pariser said, online donors pledged $400,000, and the group bought several newspaper advertisements, a radio commercial, and ultimately, several television spots. One, in which a scene of a small girl plucking daisy petals morphs into military images and a mushroom cloud, borrowed heavily from the "daisy" commercial that Lyndon B. Johnson's campaign used against Barry Goldwater in 1964 to stir fears about nuclear Armageddon.

C H A P T E R

13

The Media

Ⅰn March 2003, American and British forces attacked Iraq in order to oust long-time Iraqi dictator Saddam Hussein. For the first time in history, reporters accompanied the troops into battle and provided real-time photos and accounts from the battlefront twenty-four hours a day, seven days a week. As the U.S. military had hoped, these so-called "embedded" journalists quickly identified with the troops they accompanied and often used the pronoun "we" when discussing military operations.

While the embedded reporters generally provided favorable accounts of U.S. military activities, their colleagues behind the lines reporting from U.S. headquarters in Kuwait or commenting from New York and Washington were not always as kind. Prior to the war, there had been clear divisions within the media regarding the desirability of attacking Iraq. Generally speaking, the more liberal and Democratic press, led by the *New York Times* and several of the networks, had been sharply critical of President Bush's diplomatic efforts and his devious intention to oust Saddam Hussein. For the most part, the more conservative and Republican media, led by such publications as the *Washington Times* and the

Weekly Standard and by *Fox Network News*, staunchly supported the president's policies. Some divisions on the war, to be sure, manifested themselves even within these two camps. For example, the normally liberal and pro-Democratic *Washington Post* and *New Republic* backed the war, while Pat Buchanan's *American Conservative* opposed American intervention in Iraq.

American forces had barely crossed the Iraqi border when journalists—particularly those who had been critical of President Bush's policies—began questioning the conduct of the American campaign. Some journalists and commentators, including several retired military officers employed by the networks, suggested that not enough troops had been committed to the battle, that supplies were inadequate, that Iraqi resistance had been underestimated, and that the war could easily become a Vietnam-style "quagmire." Defense Secretary Donald Rumsfeld and military briefers were subjected to withering questioning from journalists, who clearly doubted the veracity of the answers they were given. Some commentators, again resorting to Vietnam-era imagery, referred to a "credibility gap." And elements of the foreign press were even more critical of U.S. efforts. European and Middle Eastern media focused on Iraqi civilian casualties, the humanitarian problems occasioned by the war, and alleged American military setbacks. Peter Arnett, a veteran freelance reporter employed by NBC, appeared on Baghdad television to assert that Iraqi resistance had thwarted American war plans. After a firestorm of criticism, NBC severed its relationship with Arnett. Some foreign-language media had given so much emphasis to American setbacks and Iraqi resistance that they had a great deal of difficulty explaining the quick American victory and joyful Iraqi popular response. Syrian television solved this problem by ending its coverage of the war. French television claimed that those Iraqis who seemed to welcome U.S. troops were not representative of the majority of the Iraqi people.

Most Americans did not follow foreign press accounts, but critical domestic media coverage had some effect on American public opinion. Prior to the war, more than 60 percent of Americans surveyed thought that the American effort would be quick and successful, and more than 50 percent thought it would last only a few weeks. After a week of news coverage, 50 percent of those surveyed said the war would be long and costly, and 66 percent thought it would last many months.[1]

Of course, when American troops entered Baghdad and were greeted by jubilant crowds after three weeks of fighting, critical coverage temporarily disappeared from print and screen. Within a few months, Iraqi resistance to the American occupation and the difficulties establishing a new democratic government in Iraq became headline news. In October 2003, President Bush accused the media of failing to report American successes in the occupation of Iraq while dwelling only on apparent failures of U.S. policy.

One feature of American journalism highlighted by these events is the tendency of the press to criticize programs, policies, and public officials. This tendency, sometimes called "adversarial journalism," has become commonplace in America. While this form of journalism sometimes irritates many Americans, it should probably be seen as a positive feature of American press coverage. A number of critics, to be sure, have suggested that the media have contributed to popular cynicism and the low levels of citizen participation that characterize American political processes. But before we begin to think about means of compelling the media to adopt a more cheerful view of politicians and political issues, we should consider the possibility that media criticism is one of the major mechanisms of political accountability in the American political process. Without aggressive media coverage, would we have known of Bill Clinton's misdeeds or, for that matter, those of Richard Nixon? Without aggressive media coverage, would important questions be raised about the conduct of American foreign and domestic policy? It is easy to criticize the media for their aggressive tactics, but would our democracy function effectively without the critical role of the press?

We should also evaluate the sometimes adversarial relationship between the media and politicians in terms of the interests each has. Politicians want to sell their policy agenda to citizens and mobilize support for it, but they need the media to help communicate their message. Politicians would prefer to control the content of the news, but since the media have different goals and interests—market share, professional prestige, and, in some cases, political influence—news journalists and elected leaders often come into conflict with another. Finally, we should take into account the interests of citizens—the consumers of the news—and how their demands for certain types and amounts of political news influence the adversarial nature of media politics.[2]

Rationality Principle

Media coverage can be analyzed in terms of the interests of members of the media, politicians, and consumers.

In this chapter, we will examine the role and increasing power of the media in American politics. First, we will look at the media industry and government. Second, we will discuss the factors that help to determine "what's news"—that is, the factors that shape media coverage of events and personalities. Third, we will examine the scope of media power in politics. Finally, we will address the question

[1]Polling data can be found at <u>PollingReport.com</u>. The URL is <u>http://www.pollingreport.com/iraq.htm</u>.
[2]John Zaller, *"A Theory of Media Politics: How the Interests of Politicians, Journalists, and Citizens Shape the News"* (unpublished manuscript).

of responsibility: "In a democracy, to whom are the media accountable for the use of their formidable power?"

THE MEDIA INDUSTRY AND GOVERNMENT

The freedom to speak one's mind is one of the most cherished of American political values—one that is jealously safeguarded by the media. As we mentioned above, a wide variety of newspapers, news magazines, broadcast media, and Web sites regularly present information that is at odds with the government's claims, as well as editorial opinions that are sharply critical of high-ranking officials. Yet even though thousands of media companies exist across the United States, surprisingly little variety appears in what is reported about national events and issues.

PREVIEWING THE PRINCIPLES

Media coverage can be analyzed in terms of the interests of members of the media, politicians, and consumers. The conflicting goals of politicians and members of the media help to explain their adversarial relationship. This relationship can be analyzed as a prisoner's dilemma. Both politicians and members of the media benefit from mutual cooperation but are tempted to defect on occasion to secure even larger gains. The historical relationship between government and media in the United States differs from that in other democracies because of the freedom of the press, guaranteed by the Constitution. This has led the United States away from public ownership and more toward regulation.

Types of Media

Americans obtain their news from three main sources: broadcast media (radio, television), print media (newspapers and magazines), and, increasingly, the Internet. Each of these sources has distinctive characteristics. Television news reaches more Americans than any other single news source. Tens of millions of individuals watch national and local news programs every day. Television news, however, covers relatively few topics and provides little depth of coverage. Television news is more like a series of newspaper headlines connected to pictures. It serves the extremely important function of alerting viewers to issues and events but provides little else.

The twenty-four-hour news stations like Cable News Network (CNN) offer more detail and commentary than the networks' half-hour evening news shows. During the 2003 Iraq war, CNN, Fox, and MSNBC provided twenty-four-hour-a-day coverage of the war, including on-the-scene reports from embedded reporters, expert commentary, and interviews with government officials. In this instance, these networks' depth of coverage rivaled that of the print media. Normally, however, CNN and the others offer more headlines than analysis, especially during their prime-time broadcasts.

Politicians generally view the local broadcast news as a friendlier venue than the national news. National reporters are often inclined to criticize and question, while local reporters often accept the pronouncements of national leaders at face value. For this reason, presidents often introduce new proposals in a series of short visits to a number of cities—indeed, sometimes flying from airport stop to airport stop—in addition to or instead of making a national presentation. For example, in February 2002, President Bush introduced his idea for a new national volunteer corps during his State of the Union message and then made a number of local speeches around the country promoting the same theme. While national reporters questioned the president's plans, local news coverage was overwhelmingly positive.

Radio news is also essentially a headline service but without pictures. In the short time—usually five minutes per hour—that they devote to news, radio stations announce the day's major events without providing much detail. In major cities, all-news stations provide a bit more coverage of major stories, but for the most part these stations fill the day with repetition rather than detail. All-news stations like Washington, D.C.'s WTOP or New York's WCBS assume that most listeners are in their cars and that, as a result, the people in the audience change markedly throughout the day as listeners reach their destinations. Thus, rather than use their time to flesh out a given set of stories, they repeat the same stories each hour to present them to new listeners. In recent years, radio talk shows have become important sources of commentary and opinion. A number of conservative radio hosts such as Rush Limbaugh have huge audiences and have helped to mobilize support for conservative political causes and candidates. Liberals have had less success in the world of talk radio and have complained that biased coverage helped bring about Democratic defeats in 2000 and 2002. In 2003, however, a group of wealthy liberal political activists led by Anita Drobny, a major Democratic party donor, announced plans for the creation of a liberal talk-radio network designed to combat conservative dominance of this important medium. One executive of the nascent network said, "There are so many right-wing talk shows, we think it created a hole in the market you could drive a truck through." Liberals hoped their network would be entertaining as well as informative, specializing in parody and political satire.[3]

The most important source of news is the old-fashioned newspaper. Newspapers remain critically important even though they are not the primary news sources for most Americans. The print media are important for two reasons. First, as we shall see later in this chapter, the broadcast media rely upon leading newspapers such as the *New York Times* and the *Washington Post* to set their news agenda. The broadcast media engage in very little actual reporting; they primarily cover stories that have been "broken," or initially reported, by the print media. For example, sensational charges that President Bill Clinton had an affair with a White House intern were reported first by the *Washington Post* and

[3] CNN.com/Inside Politics, 18 February 2003.

Newsweek before being trumpeted around the world by the broadcast media. It is only a slight exaggeration to observe that if an event is not covered in the *New York Times,* it is not likely to appear on the *CBS Evening News.* Second, the print media provide more detailed and complete information, offering a better context for analysis. Third, the print media are also important because they are the prime source of news for educated and influential individuals. The nation's economic, social, and political elites rely upon the detailed coverage provided by the print media to inform and influence their views about important public matters. The print media may have a smaller audience than their cousins in broadcasting, but they have an audience that matters.

A relatively new source of news is the Internet. Every day, several million Americans, especially younger Americans, scan one of many news sites on the Internet for coverage of current events. For the most part, however, the Internet provides electronic versions of coverage offered by print sources. One great advantage of the Internet is that it allows frequent updating. It potentially can combine the depth of coverage of a newspaper with the timeliness of television and radio, and probably will become a major news source in the next decade. Already, most political candidates and many interest groups have created sites on the World Wide Web. Some of the more sensational aspects of President Clinton's relationship with Monica Lewinsky were first reported on a Web site maintained by Matt Drudge, an individual who specializes in posting sensational charges about public figures. Though many deny it, most reporters scan Drudge's site regularly, hoping to pick up a bit of salacious gossip. In recent years, many Americans have relied on Web sites such as <u>CNN.com</u> for up-to-the-minute election news during the campaign, the dramatic post-election battle in Florida, the terrorist attacks on New York City and Washington, D.C., and the war in Iraq.[4] Acknowledging the growing importance of the Internet as a political communications medium, the U.S. Supreme Court posted its decisions in the Florida election cases as soon as they were issued. Online magazines such as *Slate* have a growing audience and often feature the work of major political writers such as Christopher Hitchens and Ed Finn. In addition, hundreds of thousands of readers turn to more informal sources of Internet news and commentary called Web logs, or "blogs." Blogs are intermittently published online by thousands of individuals and generally feature personal opinion and commentary on national and world events. Some "bloggers," as the authors of blogs are called, occasionally achieve fame or, at least, notoriety among online readers for their political and social views. Many blogs invite readers to post comments and can become online discussion forums. In 2002 and 2003, the Howard Dean presidential campaign relied on hundreds of friendly bloggers to publicize the candidate's views and tout his virtues. Bloggers also helped Dean raise tens of millions of dollars in small contributions to finance his presidential bid. The Dean campaign's own

---

[4]For discussions of the growing role of the Internet, see Leslie Wayne, "On Web, Voters Reinvent Grass-Roots Activism," *New York Times,* 21 May 2000, p. 22. See also James Fallows, "Internet Illusions," *New York Review of Books,* 16 November 2000, p. 28.

blog posted 160,000 comments between June and November, 2003. The Bush campaign also developed a blog but did not post comments from readers.[5] As online access becomes simpler and faster, the Internet could give Americans access to unprecedented quantities of information. If only computers could also give Americans the ability to make good use of that information!

Regulation of the Broadcast and Electronic Media

In some countries, the government controls media content. In other countries, the government owns the broadcast media (for example, the BBC in Britain), but it does not tell the media what to say. In the United States, the government neither owns nor controls the communications networks, but it does regulate the content and ownership of the broadcast media.

American radio and television are regulated by the Federal Communications Commission (FCC), an independent regulatory agency established in 1934. Radio and TV stations must have FCC licenses that have to be renewed every five years. The basic rationale for licensing is that there must be some mechanism to allocate radio and TV frequencies to prevent broadcasts from interfering with and garbling one another. License renewals are almost always granted automatically by the FCC. Indeed, renewal requests are now filed by postcard.

For more than sixty years, the broadcast media were subject to the control of the FCC, but in 1996 Congress passed the Telecommunications Act, a broad effort to do away with regulations in effect since 1934. The act loosened restrictions on media ownership and allowed for telephone companies, cable television providers, and broadcasters to compete with one another for telecommunication services. Following the passage of the act, several mergers occurred between telephone and cable companies and between different segments of the entertainment media, creating an even greater concentration of media ownership.

The Telecommunications Act of 1996 also included an attempt to regulate the content of material transmitted over the Internet. This law, known as the Communications Decency Act, made it illegal to make "indecent" sexual material on the Internet accessible to those under eighteen years of age. The act was immediately denounced by civil libertarians and brought to court as an infringement of free speech. The case reached the Supreme Court in 1997, and the act was ruled an unconstitutional infringement of the First Amendment's right to freedom of speech.

While the government's ability to regulate the content of the electronic media on the Internet has been questioned, the federal government has used its licensing power to impose several regulations that can affect the political content of radio and TV broadcasts. The first of these is the *equal time rule.* Under federal regulations, broadcasters must provide candidates for the same political office equal opportunities to communicate their messages to the public. If, for example, a television station sells commercial time to a state's Republican guber-

History Principle

The historical relationship between government and the media in the United States differs from that of other democracies because of the freedom of the press, guaranteed by the Constitution. This has led the United States away from public ownership and more toward regulation.

equal time rule
A Federal Communications Commission requirement that broadcasters provide candidates for the same political office an equal opportunity to communicate their messages to the public.

[5]Brian Faler, "Add 'Blog' to the Campaign Lexicon," *Washington Post*, 15 November 2003, p. A4.

natorial candidate, it may not refuse to sell time to the Democratic candidate for the same position.

The second FCC regulation affecting the content of broadcasts is the ***right of rebuttal.*** This means that individuals must be given the opportunity to respond to personal attacks. In the 1969 case of *Red Lion Broadcasting Company v. Federal Communications Commission,* for example, the U.S. Supreme Court upheld the FCC's determination that a television station was required to provide a liberal author with an opportunity to respond to an attack from a conservative commentator that the station had aired.[6]

For many years, a third important federal regulation was the ***fairness doctrine.*** Under this doctrine, broadcasters who aired programs on controversial issues were required to provide time for opposing views. In 1985, the FCC stopped enforcing the fairness doctrine on the grounds that there were so many radio and television stations—to say nothing of newspapers and news magazines—that in all likelihood many different viewpoints were already being presented without having to require each station to try to present all sides of an argument. Critics of this FCC decision charge that in many media markets the number of competing viewpoints is small. Nevertheless, a congressional effort to require the FCC to enforce the fairness doctrine was blocked by the Reagan administration in 1987.

Freedom of the Press

Unlike the broadcast media, the print media are not subject to federal regulation. Indeed, the great principle underlying the federal government's relationship with the press is the doctrine against ***prior restraint.*** Beginning with the landmark 1931 case of *Near v. Minnesota,* the U.S. Supreme Court has held that, except under the most extraordinary circumstances, the First Amendment of the U.S. Constitution prohibits government agencies from seeking to prevent newspapers or magazines from publishing whatever they wish.[7] Indeed, in the case of *New York Times v. United States,* the so-called *Pentagon Papers* case, the Supreme Court ruled that the government could not even block publication of secret Defense Department documents furnished to the *New York Times* by a liberal opponent of the Vietnam War who had obtained the documents illegally.[8] In a 1990 case, however, the Supreme Court upheld a lower-court order restraining Cable News Network (CNN) from broadcasting tapes of conversations between former Panamanian leader Manuel Noriega and his lawyer, supposedly recorded by the U.S. government. By a vote of 7 to 2, the Court held that CNN could be restrained from broadcasting the tapes until the trial court in the Noriega case had listened to the tapes and had decided whether their broadcast would violate Noriega's right to a fair trial. This case would seem to weaken the "no prior restraint" doc-

right of rebuttal
A Federal Communications Commission regulation giving individuals the right to have the opportunity to respond to personal attacks made on a radio or TV broadcast.

fairness doctrine
A Federal Communications Commission requirement for broadcasters who air programs on controversial issues to provide time for opposing views.

prior restraint
An effort by a governmental agency to block the publication of material it deems libelous or harmful in some other way; censorship. In the United States, the courts forbid prior restraint except under the most extraordinary circumstances.

---

[6]Red Lion Broadcasting Company v. Federal Communications Commission, 395 U.S. 367 (1969).
[7]Near v. Minnesota, 283 U.S. 697 (1931).
[8]New York Times v. United States, 403 U.S. 731 (1971).

trine. But whether the same standard will apply to the print media has yet to be tested in the courts. In 1994, the Supreme Court ruled that cable television systems were entitled to essentially the same First Amendment protections as the print media.[9]

Even though newspapers may not be restrained from publishing whatever they want, they may be subject to sanctions after the fact. Historically, newspapers were subject to the law of libel, which provided that newspapers that printed false and malicious stories could be compelled to pay damages to those they defamed. In recent years, however, American courts have greatly narrowed the meaning of libel and made it extremely difficult, particularly for politicians or other public figures, to win a libel case against a newspaper. The most important case on this topic is the 1964 U.S. Supreme Court case of *New York Times Co. v. Sullivan*, in which the Court held that to be deemed libelous a story about a public official not only had to be untrue, but had to result from "actual malice" or "reckless disregard" for the truth.[10] In other words, the newspaper had to deliberately print false and malicious material. In practice, it is nearly impossible to prove that a paper deliberately printed false and damaging information, and, as conservatives discovered in the 1980s, it is very difficult for a politician or other public figure to win a libel case. Libel suits against CBS News by General William Westmoreland and against *Time* magazine by General Ariel Sharon of Israel, both financed by conservative legal foundations who hoped to embarrass the media, were both defeated in court because they failed to show "actual malice." In the 1991 case of *Masson v. New Yorker Magazine, Inc.*, this tradition again affirmed the Court's opinion that fabricated quotations attributed to a public figure were libelous only if the fabricated account "materially changed" the meaning of what the person actually said.[11] For all intents and purposes, the print media can publish anything they want about a public figure.

Organization and Ownership of the Media

The United States boasts more than 1,000 television stations, approximately 1,800 daily newspapers, and more than 9,000 radio stations. Even though the number of TV and radio stations and daily newspapers reporting news in the United States is enormous, and local coverage varies greatly from place to place, the number of sources of national news is actually quite small—one wire service, four broadcast networks, public radio and TV, two elite newspapers, three news magazines, and a scattering of other sources such as the national correspondents of a few large local papers, and the small independent radio networks. Most of the national news that is published by local newspapers is provided by the one wire service, the Associated Press. More than five hundred of the nation's TV stations are affiliated with one of the four networks and carry its evening news reports.

[9]Cable News Network v. Noriega, 111 S.Ct. 451 (1990); Turner Broadcasting System, Inc. v. Federal Communications Commission, 93-44 (1994).

[10]New York Times Co. v. Sullivan, 376 U.S. 254 (1964).

[11]Masson v. New Yorker Magazine, Inc., 111 S.Ct. 2419 (1991).

Dozens of others carry PBS (Public Broadcasting System) news. Several hundred local radio stations also carry network news or National Public Radio news broadcasts. At the same time, although there are only three truly national newspapers, the *Wall Street Journal*, the *Christian Science Monitor*, and *USA Today*, two other papers, the *New York Times* and the *Washington Post*, are read by political leaders and other influential Americans throughout the nation. Such is the influence of these two "elite" newspapers that their news coverage sets the standard for virtually all other news outlets. Stories carried in the *New York Times* or the *Washington Post* influence the content of many other papers as well as the network news. Note how often this text, like most others, relies upon *New York Times* and *Washington Post* stories as sources for contemporary events.

National news is also carried to millions of Americans by the three major news magazines—*Time*, *Newsweek*, and *U.S. News & World Report*. Beginning in the late 1980s, Cable News Network (CNN) became another major news source. The importance of CNN increased dramatically after its spectacular coverage of the Persian Gulf War. At one point, CNN was able to provide live coverage of American bombing raids on Baghdad, Iraq, after the major networks' correspondents had been forced to flee to bomb shelters. By 2003, Fox had displaced CNN as the nation's primary cable news source. The rise of Fox had important political implications since its coverage and commentators are considerably more conservative than CNN's. Even the availability of new electronic media on the Internet has failed to expand the number of news sources. Most national news available on the World Wide Web, for example, consists of electronic versions of the conventional print or broadcast media.

The trend toward homogenization of national news has been hastened by dramatic changes in media ownership, which became possible in part due to the relaxation of government regulations since the 1980s. The enactment of the 1996 Telecommunications Act opened the way for further consolidation in the media industry, and a wave of mergers and consolidations has further reduced the field of independent media across the country. Since that time, among the major news networks, ABC was bought by the Walt Disney Company; CBS was bought by Westinghouse Electric and later merged with Viacom, the owner of MTV and Paramount Studios; and CNN was bought by Time Warner. NBC has been owned by General Electric since 1986. Australian press baron Rupert Murdoch owns the Fox network plus a host of radio, television, and newspaper properties around the world. A small number of giant corporations now controls a wide swath of media holdings, including television networks, movie studios, record companies, cable channels and local cable providers, book publishers, magazines, and newspapers. These developments have prompted questions about whether enough competition exists among the media to produce a diverse set of views on political and corporate matters or whether the United States has become the prisoner of media monopolies.[12]

---

[12]For a criticism of the increasing consolidation of the media, see the essays in Patricia Aufderheide et al., *Conglomerates and the Media* (New York: New Press, 1997).

In June 2003, the Federal Communication Commission announced a set of new rules that seemed to pave the way to even more concentration in the media industry. The FCC mandated that the major networks could own TV stations that collectively reached 45 percent of all viewers, up from 35 percent under the old rule. The new FCC rule also permits a single company to own the leading newspaper as well as multiple television and radio outlets in a single market. In the largest cities, this could include a newspaper, three television stations, and as many as eight radio stations.[13] Major media companies, which had long lobbied for the right to expand their activities, welcomed the new FCC rule. Critics, however, expressed grave concern that the decision would result in a narrowing of the range of views and issues presented to the general public. Congressional opponents of the FCC's action sought to overturn the rule but were stymied by opposition from the House Republican leadership as well as a threatened presidential veto. However, a federal appeals court placed the new regulation on hold pending the outcome of several lawsuits filed by groups seeking to compel the FCC to drop its proposal. The suits were expected to be heard in 2004.

Nationalization of the News

In general, the national news media cover more or less the same sets of events, present similar information, and emphasize similar issues and problems. Indeed, the national news services watch one another carefully. It is unlikely that a major story carried by one will not soon find its way into the pages or programming of the others. As a result, we have developed in the United States a centralized national news through which a relatively similar picture of events, issues, and problems is presented to the entire nation.[14] The nationalization of the news was accelerated by the development of radio networks in the 1920s and 1930s, and was brought to a peak by the creation of the television networks after the 1950s. This nationalization of news content has very important consequences for American politics.

Nationalization of the news has contributed greatly to the nationalization of politics and of political perspectives in the United States. Prior to the development of the national media and the nationalization of news coverage, the news traveled very slowly. Every region and city saw national issues and problems mainly through its own local lens. Concerns and perspectives varied greatly from region to region, city to city, and village to village. Today, in large measure as a result of the nationalization of the media, residents of all parts of the country share similar ideas and perspectives.[15] They may not agree on everything, but they at least see the world in similar ways.

---

[13]David Lieberman, "How Will FCC's Action Affect Consumers?" *USA Today*, 4 June 2003, p. 48.

[14]See Leo Bogart, "Newspapers in Transition," *Wilson Quarterly*, special issue (1982); and Richard Harwood, "The Golden Age of Press Diversity," *Washington Post*, 22 July 1994, p. A23.

[15]See Benjamin Ginsberg, *The Captive Public: How Mass Opinion Promotes State Power* (New York: Basic Books, 1986).

WHAT AFFECTS NEWS COVERAGE?

Because of the important role the media can play in national politics, it is essential to understand the factors that affect media coverage.[16] What accounts for the media's agenda of issues and topics? What explains the character of coverage—why does a politician receive good or bad press? What factors determine the interpretation or "spin" that a particular story will receive? Although a host of minor factors play a role, there are three major factors: (1) journalists or producers of the news; (2) politicians, who are usually the sources or topics of the news; and (3) citizens, the audience for the news.

Journalists

First, media content and news coverage are inevitably affected by the views, ideals, and interests of the individuals who seek out, write, and produce news and other stories. At one time, newspaper publishers exercised a great deal of influence over their papers' news content. Publishers such as William Randolph Hearst and Joseph Pulitzer became political powers through their manipulation of news coverage. Hearst, for example, almost single-handedly pushed the United States into war with Spain in 1898 through his newspapers' relentless coverage of the alleged brutality employed by Spain in its efforts to suppress a rebellion in Cuba, then a Spanish colony. The sinking of the American battleship *Maine* in Havana Harbor under mysterious circumstances gave Hearst the ammunition he needed to force a reluctant President McKinley to lead the nation into war. Today, few publishers have that kind of power. Most publishers are more concerned with the business end of the paper than its editorial content, although a few continue to impose their interests and tastes on the news.

More important than publishers, for the most part, are the reporters. The goals and incentives of journalists are varied, but they often include considerations of ratings, career success and professional prestige, and political influence. For all of these reasons, journalists seek not only to *report* the news but also to *interpret* the news. Journalists' goals have a good deal of influence on what is created and reported as news.

Those who cover the news for the national media generally have a lot of discretion or freedom to interpret stories and, as a result, have an opportunity to interject their own views and ideals into news stories. For example, the personal friendship and respect that some reporters felt for Franklin Roosevelt and John F. Kennedy helped to generate more favorable news coverage for these presidents. On the other hand, the dislike and distrust felt by many reporters for Richard Nixon was also communicated to the public. In the case of Ronald Reagan, the

Rationality Principle
The goals and incentives of journalists—such as ratings, career success, and prestige—influence what is created and reported as news.

---

[16]See the discussions in Michael Parenti, *Inventing Reality: The Politics of the Mass Media* (New York: St. Martin's Press, 1986); Herbert Gans, *Deciding What's News: A Study of CBS Evening News, NBC Nightly News, Newsweek, and Time* (New York: Vintage, 1980); and W. Lance Bennett, *News: The Politics of Illusion*, 5th ed. (New York: Longman, 2002).

disdain that many journalists felt for the president was communicated in stories suggesting that he was often asleep or inattentive when important decisions were made.

Conservatives have long charged that the liberal biases of reporters and journalists result in distorted news coverage. A 1996 survey of Washington newspaper bureau chiefs and correspondents seems to support this charge. The study, conducted by the Roper Center and the Freedom Forum, a conservative foundation, found that 61 percent of the bureau chiefs and correspondents polled called themselves "liberal" or "liberal to moderate." Only 9 percent called themselves "conservative" or "conservative to moderate." In a similar vein, 89 percent said that they had voted for Bill Clinton in 1992, while only 7 percent indicated that they had voted for George Bush. Fifty percent said they were Democrats, and only 4 percent claimed to be Republicans.[17] Another survey has indicated that even among the radio talk-show hosts lambasted by President Clinton, Democrats outnumber Republicans by a wide margin: of 112 hosts surveyed, 39 percent had voted for Clinton in 1992, and only 23 percent had supported George Bush.[18] Generally speaking, reporters for major national news outlets tend to be more liberal than their local counterparts who profess moderate or even conservative views.

The linkage between journalists and liberal ideas is by no means absolute. Most reporters, to be sure, attempt to maintain some measure of balance or objectivity, whatever their personal views. Moreover, over the past several years a conservative media complex has emerged in opposition to the liberal media. This complex includes two major newspapers, the *Wall Street Journal* and the *Washington Times*, several magazines such as the *American Spectator* and the *Weekly Standard*, and a host of conservative radio and television talk programs. Also important is media baron Rupert Murdoch, creator of Fox Network News and the financial force behind the *Weekly Standard*. The emergence of this conservative media complex has meant that liberal policies and politicians are virtually certain to come under attack even when the "liberal media" are sympathetic to them.

Probably more important than ideological bias is a selection bias in favor of news that the media view as having a great deal of audience appeal because of its dramatic or entertainment value. In practice, this bias often results in news coverage that focuses on crimes and scandals, especially those involving prominent individuals, despite the fact that the public obviously looks to the media for information about important political debates.[19] For example, even though most journalists may be Democrats, this partisan predisposition did not prevent an enormous media frenzy in January 1998 when reports surfaced that President Clinton may have had an affair with Lewinsky. Once a hint of blood appeared in

[17]Rowan Scarborough, "Leftist Press? Reporters Working in Washington Acknowledge Liberal Leanings in Poll," *Washington Times*, 18 April 1996, p. 1.

[18]Michael Kinsley, "Bias and Baloney," *Washington Post*, 26 November 1992, p. A29; and John H. Fund, "Why Clinton Shouldn't Be Steamed at Talk Radio," *Wall Street Journal*, 7 July 1994, p. A12.

[19]See Joseph N. Cappella and Kathleen Hall Jamieson, *Spiral of Cynicism: The Press and the Public Good* (New York: Oxford University Press, 1997).

the water, partisanship and ideology were swept away by the piranhalike instincts often manifested by journalists.

Politicians

News coverage is also influenced by politicians, who are subjects of the news and whose interests and activities are actual or potential news topics. The president, in particular, has the power to set the news agenda through his speeches and actions. In the almost never-ending battle over public opinion, politicians and journalists vie for control over how images of political leaders are presented to the public. In the last fifty years, the media have, for the most part, won this battle, although political leaders have fought back by developing new strategies. During the 1992 presidential campaign, candidates developed a number of techniques designed to take the manipulation of the image-making process away from journalists and media executives. Among the most important of these techniques were the many town meetings and television talk- and entertainment-show appearances that all the major candidates made. Frequent exposure on such programs as *Larry King Live* and *Today* gave candidates an opportunity to shape and focus their own media images and to overwhelm any negative image that might be projected by the media. Politicians also seek to shape or manipulate their media images by cultivating good relations with reporters as well as through news leaks and staged news events. For example, during the lengthy investigation of President Clinton, which was conducted by Special Counsel Kenneth Starr, both the Office of the Special Counsel and the White House frequently leaked information designed to bolster their respective positions in the struggle. Starr admitted speaking to reporters on a not-for-attribution basis about aspects of his investigation of the president. One journalist, Steven Brill, accused a number of prominent reporters of serving as "lap dogs" for the Special Counsel, recording as fact the information fed to them by Starr.[20]

    More generally, the relationship between a politician and a member of the media may be characterized as a Prisoners' Dilemma (see Chapter 12). The two can cooperate—the politician leaking juicy news to the reporter in exchange for the reporter casting the politician in a favorable light. But each may be tempted to defect. A reporter may decide to turn against his trusted political friend because the opportunity is just "too juicy." The politician may decide to leak a newsworthy tidbit to a competing journalist in exchange for favorable consideration from him or her as a form of insurance. Both the (first) reporter and the politician are worse off as a result of defection, but they fear that if they don't defect, then they will be taken advantage of. So, while "sweetheart" arrangements between the media and the political class certainly do exist, the participants find themselves constantly tempted to defect. The best journalists and the shrewdest politicians resist these temptations and are willing to forgo the immediate windfall resulting from defection in exchange for a long-term relationship

Rationality Principle
News coverage is influenced by the interests of politicians.

Collective Action Principle
The relationship between media members and politicians is a Prisoners' Dilemma. Each participant benefits from mutual cooperation but finds him- or herself tempted to defect on occasion to secure even larger gains.

[20]David Firestone, "Steven Brill Strikes a Nerve in News Media," *New York Times*, 20 June 1998, p. 4.

The Press and Politicians: Caught in a Prisoner's Dilemma?

"You won't have Nixon to kick around anymore, because, gentlemen, this is my last press conference."

—Richard Nixon, Los Angeles, California, November 7, 1962

More than forty years ago, Richard Nixon accused a "biased" media of sabotaging his 1962 gubernatorial campaign. Candidate Nixon returned to the public stage five years later, successfully winning the 1968 presidential contest. Apparently media bias was not sufficient to curtail his political ambitions.

Nixon realized, as do almost all candidates, that the press and politicians are in an uneasy symbiosis, often adversarial, seldom mutually supportive, but always in need of each other.

The press needs politicians and the political institutions that they lead to provide them with their daily dose of newsworthy items. Classic portrayals of the press corps, such as Timothy Crouse's *The Boys on the Bus,* show how reliant reporters are on "official sources." Press spokespersons provide daily quotes; government press offices supply reporters with details; and, of course, anonymous "leaks" and "off the record" interviews help fill the daily byline.[21]

Politicians need the press just as badly. The advent of mass democracy is impossible, some argue, without functioning mass media. Almost all of our political information is "mediated" through one or another source, and the most common source in industrialized nations is the press. At a more strategic level, competing political actors use the press in order to promote their policies to the public, float "trial balloons," attack rival policies, and muster public support. Franklin Roosevelt instituted a series of "fireside chats," covered by the radio networks of the time, initially in an attempt to battle Republican opposition to his New Deal policies. Fast-forward to President George W. Bush flying in a fighter jet, touching down on the USS *Abraham Lincoln,* and announcing that "major combat operations have ended" in Iraq. Within a few days, however, Bush's landing was being criticized as a "stunt" by some of his political opponents, and, of course, this criticism also constituted "news."

In the language of the principles of politics, the press and the politicians are in a prisoner's dilemma. Both benefit from mutual cooperation. The politicians benefit from having their message conveyed to the public. The press benefits from obtaining useful information.

Yet, like a prisoner's dilemma, each party has an incentive to defect. For example, journalists show an overwhelming preference for "conflict," stories that present two sides of an issue.[22] The press may choose to use only part, or none, of what was provided by a politician. Or they may seek out opposing voices in an attempt to provide "balance" to the coverage. After all, the interests of the media, as an institution, and the preferences of reporters as political actors, are more complex than simply parroting official sources.

Politicians also have an incentive to defect—in this case, not provide the full details to the media "players." The politicians are using the media to sell a particular story and to manage public opinion, not necessarily to make sure that the public is fully informed. Media coverage of war illustrates the adversarial symbiosis between the media and the government. Through World War II, the media played the role of "cheerleader" for the war effort, basically repeating, undiluted, military reports supplied by the government.

Everything changed with Vietnam. Daily news reports about U.S. casualties, and the graphic footage that accompanied these reports, were in stark contrast to the positive spin promoted by Presidents Johnson and Nixon, and Pentagon military leaders. Military leaders, and many politicians, accused the press of being anti-military, anti-patriotic, and anti-American. For their part, many in the press accused the government of lying to the American people.[23]

The "game" between the military and the media had broken down. Both sides were mutually defecting. In the first Gulf War in 1991, the press was kept away from the war in Kuwait and had to rely only on press briefings and film provided by the Pentagon.[24]

But just as in an iterated prisoner's dilemma, the military and the media needed each other. Relations began to thaw in Panama and Grenada, as the military began to relax their restrictions on the press. The press, meanwhile, began to view military conflicts in a less critical light.

Fast-forward to the present and the wars in Afghanistan and Iraq. Via a new policy called "embedding," the military assigns journalists with military units engaged in active combat. The coverage is not only positive, but positively celebratory, inviting a few scattered laments at the loss of critical perspective.[25]

Perhaps you think the Pentagon took a risk, putting journalists in direct contact with troops, out of the control of press officers and media-relations specialists. If so, you have forgotten the principles of politics. Placing reporters directly in the combat zone satisfies one of the main preferences of the media: the need for compelling footage and "personal" stories (interviews with the troops).

And placing them in extended contact with a small group of soldiers takes advantage of the logic of collective action: it builds a bond of collective trust and group identity between the reporter and the soldiers. How can you criticize the actions of a soldier who may save your life tomorrow or may have saved your life yesterday?

Journalists are already reexamining the policy of embedding, asking whether this new set of rules has swung the pendulum too far toward pro-government, pro-military coverage.[26]

[21]Timothy Crouse's *Boys on the Bus* (New York: Random House, 1973) portrays press workways during the Nixon White House. See also Herbert J. Gans, *Deciding What's News: A Study of CBS Evening News, NBC Nightly News, Newsweek, and Time* (New York: Vintage, 1980), for a discussion of how the media rely heavily on government officials to help the media decide what is newsworthy.

[22]Cook, Chapters 1 and 5.

[23]See William M. Hammond, *Reporting Vietnam: Media and Military at War* (Lawrence: University Press of Kansas, 1998), and Daniel C. Hallin, *The Uncensored War: The Media and Vietnam* (Berkeley: University of California Press, 1989).

[24]Robert Entman and David Paletz, in *Taken by Storm,* ed. W. Lance Bennett and David L. Paletz (Chicago: University of Chicago Press, 1994), discuss press coverage of the first Gulf War.

[25]See, for instance, the discussion by practicing journalists and media scholars on the PBS "Newshour" of April 1, 2003. Available online at http://www.pbs.org/newshour/bb/media/jan-june03/embeds_04-01.html.

[26]An extensive set of articles has been collected by the Committee of Concerned Journalists, available at their Web site: http://www.journalism.org/resources/briefing/archive/war/embedding.asp.

of cooperation. But some journalists are neither long-run–oriented nor particularly scrupulous. Nor are some politicians.

Some politicians become extremely adept image makers—or at least skilled at hiring publicists who are skillful image makers. Indeed, press releases drafted by skillful publicists often become the basis for reporters' stories. A substantial percentage of the news stories published every day were initially drafted by publicists and later rewritten only slightly, if at all, by busy reporters and editors. Furthermore, political candidates often endeavor to tailor their images for specific audiences. For example, to cultivate a favorable image among younger voters during his 1992 campaign, Bill Clinton made several appearances on MTV, and he continued to grant interviews to MTV after his election. His MTV forays came to an end, however, when he was severely criticized for discussing his preferred type of underwear with members of an MTV audience.

During his presidency, Bill Clinton was able to survive repeated revelations of sexual improprieties, financial irregularities, lying to the public, and illegal campaign fund-raising activities. Clinton and his advisers crafted what the *Washington Post* called a "toolkit" for dealing with potentially damaging media revelations. This toolkit included techniques such as chiding the press, browbeating reporters, referring inquiries quickly to lawyers who would not comment, and acting quickly to change the agenda. These techniques helped Clinton maintain a favorable public image despite the Monica Lewinsky scandal and even the humiliation of a formal impeachment and trial.

President George W. Bush's administration has developed a highly sophisticated communications office initially under the leadership of former presidential aide Karen Hughes. Hughes, who resigned in April 2002, and her staff endeavored to craft a new media message every few days in order to continually shape the nation's press coverage. For example, Bush's reference to nations supporting terrorist groups as an "axis of evil" in February 2002 was designed to give the media a catch phrase that would dominate the headlines and provide ***sound bites***—short, attention-grabbing summaries of a story—for the broadcast media for days. By the time the media tired of the "axis of evil," the White House hoped to have developed a new sound bite for the reporters.

sound bites
Short snippets of information aimed at dramatizing a story, rather than explaining its substantive meaning.

During the Iraq war, the White House sent James Wilkinson, one of the heads of its communications office, to direct communications for military forces in the Persian Gulf region. Wilkinson helped shape a number of communications strategies for American forces. After the dramatic rescue of American POW Jessica Lynch, Wilkinson coined the slogan "America does not leave its heroes behind." This sound bite was repeated by the networks for days.

The Bush team also pays enormous attention to the visual elements of a story. For example, in summer 2002, the president delivered a speech at Mount Rushmore. His media advisers positioned the platform for television crews off to one side so that the cameras would show the president in profile, perfectly aligned with the statues of the four presidents carved into the mountain. In a similar vein, in May 2003 the president spoke in Indiana on his economic plan. Staffers asked people in the audience who might be seen on camera to remove their ties so that they would look like the ordinary individuals the president said would benefit from his tax cuts.[27]

Individual politicians are not the only ones trying to influence news coverage. As we saw in Chapter 9, by using media consultants and "issues managers," many social, economic, and political groups vigorously promote their ideas and interests through speeches, articles, books, news releases, research reports, and other mechanisms designed to attract favorable media coverage. Typically, competing forces seek to present—and to persuade the media to present—their own interests as more general or "public" interests. In recent years, for example, liberals have been very successful in inducing the media to present their environmental, consumer, and political reform proposals as matters of the public interest. Indeed, the advocates of these goals are organized in "public interest" groups. Seldom do the national media ever question a public interest group's equation of its goals with the general interest of all.

The capacity of politicians and groups to influence the news is hardly unlimited. Media consultants and issues managers may shape the news for a time, but it is generally not difficult for the media to penetrate the smoke screens thrown up by the news sources if they have a reason to do so. Thus, for example, despite the administration's media management, by fall 2003 reporters in Iraq were filing numerous accounts of the resistance American occupation forces were encountering. Unfavorable media coverage placed President Bush under enormous pressure to modify his policies in Iraq, and in November 2003 the president intimated that he would speed up efforts to return control of Iraqi affairs to an interim local government. Indeed, media coverage is sometimes shaped by the third and most important factor influencing news content—the audience.

Consumers

The print and broadcast media are businesses that, in general, seek to show a profit. This means that, like any other business, they must cater to the preferences of consumers. This has very important consequences for the content and character of the news media.

 Rationality Principle

Consumer preferences, such as those of the affluent or those of people who watch news for its entertainment value, influence news content.

Catering to the Upscale Audience In general, and especially in the political realm, the print and broadcast media and the publishing industry are not only responsive to the interests of consumers generally, but they are particularly responsive to the interests and views of the better educated and more affluent segments of the audience. The preferences of these audience segments have a profound effect upon the content and orientation of the press, of radio and television programming, and of books, especially in the areas of news and public affairs.[28]

[27]Elisabeth Bumiller, "Keepers of Bush Image Lift Stagecraft to New Heights," *New York Times,* 16 May 2003, p. 1.

[28]See Tom Burnes, "The Organization of Public Opinion," in *Mass Communication and Society,* ed. James Curran et al. (Beverly Hills, Calif: Sage, 1979), pp. 44–230. See also David L. Altheide, *Creating Reality: How TV News Distorts Events* (Beverly Hills, Calif: Sage, 1976).

Although affluent consumers do watch television programs and read periodicals whose contents are designed simply to amuse or entertain, the one area that most directly appeals to the upscale audience is that of news and public affairs. The affluent—who are also typically well educated—are the core audience of news magazines, journals of opinion, books dealing with public affairs, serious newspapers like the *New York Times* and the *Washington Post*, and broadcast news and weekend and evening public-affairs programming. While other segments of the public also read newspapers and watch the television news, their level of interest in world events, national political issues, and the like is closely related to their level of education. As a result, upscale Americans are overrepresented in the news and public-affairs audience. The concentration of these strata in the audience makes news, politics, and public affairs potentially very attractive topics to advertisers, publishers, radio broadcasters, and television executives.

Entire categories of events, issues, and phenomena of interest to lower-middle- and working-class Americans receive scant attention from the national print and broadcast media. For example, trade-union news and events are discussed only in the context of major strikes or revelations of corruption. No network or national periodical routinely covers labor organizations. Religious and church affairs receive little coverage (unless scandal is involved, as was the case in 2002 and 2003 in many dioceses of the Roman Catholic Church). The activities of veterans', fraternal, ethnic, and patriotic organizations are also generally ignored.

The Media and Conflict   While the media respond most to the upscale audience, groups who cannot afford the services of media consultants and issues managers can publicize their views and interests through protest. Frequently, the media are accused of encouraging conflict and even violence as a result of the fact that the audience mostly watches news for the entertainment value that conflict can provide. Clearly, conflict can be an important vehicle for attracting the attention and interest of the media, and thus may provide an opportunity for media attention to groups otherwise lacking the financial or organizational resources to broadcast their views. But while conflict and protest can succeed in drawing media attention, these methods ultimately do not allow groups from the bottom of the social ladder to compete effectively in the media.

The chief problem with protest as a media technique is that, in general, the media upon which the protesters depend have considerable discretion in reporting and interpreting the events they cover. For example, should the media focus on the conflict itself, rather than the issues or concerns created by the conflict? The answer to this question is typically determined by the media, not by the protesters. This means that media interpretation of protest activities is more a reflection of the views of the groups and forces to which the media are responsive—as we have seen, usually segments of the upper-middle class—than it is a function of the wishes of the protesters themselves. It is worth noting that civil rights protesters received their most favorable media coverage when a segment of the white upper-middle class saw blacks as potential political allies in the Democratic party.

Typically, upper-middle-class protesters—student demonstrators and the like—have little difficulty securing favorable publicity for themselves and their causes. Upper-middle-class protesters are often more skilled than their lower-class counterparts in the techniques of media manipulation. That is, they typically have a better sense—often as a result of formal courses on the subject—of how to package messages for media consumption. For example, it is important to know what time of day a protest should occur if it is to be carried on the evening news. Similarly, the setting, definition of the issues, character of the rhetoric used, and so on all help to determine whether a protest will receive favorable media coverage, unfavorable coverage, or no coverage at all. Moreover, upper-middle-class protesters can often produce their own media coverage through "underground" newspapers, college papers, student radio and television stations, and, now, the Internet. The same resources and skills that generally allow upper-middle-class people to publicize their ideas are usually not left behind when segments of this class choose to engage in disruptive forms of political action. Note the media attention given anti-war protesters in 2003 even though polls indicated that such groups were a minor force in American politics.

WHAT ARE THE SOURCES OF MEDIA POWER IN AMERICAN POLITICS?

The content and character of news and public-affairs programming—what the media choose to present and how they present it—can have far-reaching political consequences. Media disclosures can greatly enhance—or fatally damage—the careers of public officials. Media coverage can rally support for—or intensify opposition to—national policies. The media can shape and modify, if not fully form, public perceptions of events, issues, and institutions.

In recent American political history, the media have played a central role in at least three major events. First, the media were critically important factors in the civil rights movement of the 1950s and 1960s. Television photos showing peaceful civil rights marchers attacked by club-swinging police helped to generate sympathy among northern whites for the civil rights struggle and greatly increased the pressure on Congress to bring an end to segregation.[29] Second, the media were instrumental in compelling the government to negotiate an end to the Vietnam War. Beginning in 1967, the national media, reacting in part to a shift in elite opinion, portrayed the war as misguided and unwinnable, and, as a result, helped to turn popular sentiment against continued American involvement.[30] Finally, the media were central actors in the Watergate affair, which ultimately forced

---

[29]David J. Garrow, *Protest at Selma: Martin Luther King, Jr., and the Voting Rights Act of 1965* (New Haven: Yale University Press, 1978).

[30]See Todd Gitlin, *The Whole World Is Watching: Mass Media in the Making and Unmaking of the New Left* (Berkeley: University of California Press, 2003). See also William M. Hammond, *Reporting Vietnam: Media and Military at War* (Lawrence: University Press of Kansas, 1998).

President Richard Nixon, landslide victor in the 1972 presidential election, to resign from office in disgrace. It was the relentless series of investigations launched by the *Washington Post*, the *New York Times*, and the television networks that led to the disclosures of the various abuses of which Nixon was guilty and ultimately forced Nixon to choose between resignation and almost certain impeachment.

Agenda Setting

agenda setting
Activities that help to determine which issues are taken up by political actors and institutions.

The power of the media stems from several sources. The first is *agenda setting,* which means the media help to determine which political issues become part of the public debate. Groups and forces that wish to bring their ideas before the public in order to generate support for policy proposals or political candidacies must somehow secure media coverage. If the media are persuaded that an idea is newsworthy, then they may declare it an "issue" that must be resolved or a "problem" to be solved, thus clearing the first hurdle in the policy-making process. On the other hand, if an idea lacks or loses media appeal, its chance of resulting in new programs or policies is diminished. Some ideas seem to surface, gain media support for a time, lose media appeal, and then resurface.

In most instances, the media serve as conduits for agenda-setting efforts by competing groups and forces. Occasionally, however, journalists themselves play an important role in setting the agenda of political discussion. For example, whereas many of the scandals and investigations surrounding President Clinton were initiated by his political opponents, the Watergate scandal that destroyed Nixon's presidency was in some measure initiated and driven by the *Washington Post* and the national television networks.

Framing

framing The power of the media to influence how events and issues are interpreted.

A second source of the media's power, known as *framing,* is their power to decide how political events and results are interpreted by the American people. For example, during the 1995–1996 struggle between President Clinton and congressional Republicans over the nation's budget—a struggle that led to several partial shutdowns of the federal government—the media's interpretation of events forced the Republicans to back down and agree to a budget on Clinton's terms. At the beginning of the crisis, congressional Republicans, led by then-House Speaker Newt Gingrich, were confident that they could compel Clinton to accept their budget, which called for substantial cuts in domestic social programs. Republicans calculated that Clinton would fear being blamed for lengthy government shutdowns and would quickly accede to their demands, and that once Americans saw that life went on with government agencies closed, they would support the Republicans in asserting that the United States could get along with less government.

For the most part, however, the media did not cooperate with the GOP's plans. Media coverage of the several government shutdowns during this period emphasized the hardships imposed upon federal workers who were being furloughed in the weeks before Christmas. Indeed, Speaker Gingrich, who was generally portrayed as the villain who caused the crisis, came to be called the "Gingrinch" who stole Christmas from the children of hundreds of thousands of federal workers. Rather than suggest that the shutdown demonstrated that America could carry on with less government, media accounts focused on the difficulties encountered by Washington tourists unable to visit the capital's monuments, museums, and galleries. The woes of American travelers whose passports were delayed were given considerable attention. This sort of coverage eventually convinced most Americans that the government shutdown was bad for the country. In the end, Gingrich and the congressional Republicans were forced to surrender and to accept a new budget reflecting many of Clinton's priorities. The Republicans' defeat in the budget showdown contributed to the unraveling of the GOP's legislative program and, ultimately, to the Republicans' poor showing in the 1996 presidential elections. The character of media coverage of an event thus had enormous repercussions of how Americans interpreted it.

In 2001, the Bush White House especially recognized the importance of framing when presidential aides held extensive discussions with television networks and Hollywood filmmakers about the portrayal of America's war on terrorism. The White House asked the media to sound a patriotic note and frame the war as a patriotic duty. By all accounts the media responded favorably, especially after several network news anchors became the targets of anthrax-laden letters that were possibly sent by terrorists.

Priming

A third important media power is **priming**. This occurs when media coverage affects the way the public evaluates political leaders or candidates for office. For example, nearly unanimous media praise for President Bush's speeches to the nation in the wake of the September 11 terrorist attacks prepared, or "primed," the public to view Bush's subsequent response to terrorism in an extremely positive light, even though some aspects of the administration's efforts, most notably those in the realm of bioterrorism, were problematic.

priming A process of preparing the public to take a particular view of an event or a political actor.

In the case of political candidates, the media have considerable influence over whether or not a particular individual will receive public attention, whether or not a particular individual will be taken seriously as a viable contender, and whether the public will evaluate a candidate's performance favorably. Thus, if the media find a candidate interesting, they may treat him or her as a serious contender even though the facts of the matter seem to suggest otherwise. In a similar vein, the media may declare that a candidate has "momentum," a mythical property that the media confer upon candidates, if the candidates happen to exceed the media's expectations. Momentum has no substantive meaning—it is simply a media prediction that a particular candidate will do even better in the future than in the past. Such media prophecies can become self-fulfilling as contributors and supporters jump on the bandwagon of the candidate possessing this "momentum." In 1992, when Bill Clinton's poll standings surged in the wake of the Democratic National Convention, the media determined that Clinton had enormous momentum. In fact, nothing that happened during the remainder of the race led the media to change its collective judgment.

Typically, media coverage of election campaigns focuses on the "horse race" to the detriment of attention to issues and candidate records. During the 2000 presidential contest, Senator John McCain of Arizona was able to use his Senate committee chairmanship to raise enough money to mount a challenge to Bush for the Republican nomination. In reality, McCain had little chance of defeating the front-runner, but seeing the possibility of a "horse race," the media gave McCain a great deal of generally positive coverage and helped him mount a noisy, if brief, challenge. McCain's hopes were dashed, though, when he was trounced by Bush in a series of primaries, including those in South Carolina and other GOP strongholds.

The media's power to influence people's evaluations of public figures is not absolute. Throughout the last decade, politicians implemented new techniques for communicating with the public and shaping their own images. For instance, Bill Clinton pioneered the use of town meetings and television entertainment programs as means of communicating directly with voters in the 1992 election. During the 2000 presidential race between Bush and Gore, both candidates made use of town meetings, as well as talk shows and entertainment programs like *The Oprah Winfrey Show*, *The Tonight Show with Jay Leno*, and *Saturday Night Live*, to reach mass audiences. In 2003, Arnold Schwartzenegger announced his candidacy in California's gubernatorial recall election on *The Tonight Show with Jay Leno* rather than in a more formal setting. During a town meeting, talk show, or entertainment program, politicians are free to craft their own images without interference from journalists.

In 2000, George W. Bush was also able to shape his image by effectively courting the press through informal interaction. Bush's "charm offensive" was successful. Journalists concluded that Bush was a nice fellow, if inexperienced, and refrained from subjecting him to harsh criticism and close scrutiny. Al Gore, on the other hand, seemed to offend journalists by remaining aloof and giving an impression of disdain for the press. Journalists responded by portraying Gore as "stiff." The result was unusually positive coverage for the Republican candidate and unusually negative coverage for the Democratic candidate.

In the fall of 2001, President Bush had little difficulty convincing the media that terrorism and his administration's campaign to combat terrorist attacks merited a dominant place on the agenda. Some stories have such overwhelming significance that political leaders' main concern is not whether the story will receive attention, but whether they will figure prominently and positively in media accounts. The same is true of the 2003 Iraq war.

The Rise of Adversarial Journalism

The political power of the news media has increased greatly in recent years through the growing prominence of "adversarial journalism"—a form of journalism in which the media adopt a hostile posture toward the government and public officials.

During the nineteenth century, American newspapers were completely subordinate to the political parties. Newspapers depended on official patronage—legal notice and party subsidies—for their financial survival and were controlled by party leaders. (A vestige of that era survived into the twentieth century in such newspaper names as the *Springfield Republican* and the *St. Louis Globe-Democrat*.) At the turn of the century, with the development of commercial advertising, newspapers became financially independent. This made possible the emergence of a formally nonpartisan press.

Presidents were the first national officials to see the opportunities in this development. By communicating directly to the electorate through newspapers and magazines, Theodore Roosevelt and Woodrow Wilson established political constituencies independent of party organizations and strengthened their own power relative to Congress. President Franklin Roosevelt used the radio, most notably in his famous fireside chats, to reach out to voters and to make himself the center of American politics. FDR was also adept at developing close personal relationships with reporters, which enabled him to obtain favorable news coverage despite the fact that in his day a majority of newspaper owners and publishers were staunch conservatives. Following Roosevelt's example, subsequent presidents have sought to use the media to enhance their popularity and power. For example, through televised news conferences, President John F. Kennedy mobilized public support for his domestic and foreign policy initiatives.

During the 1950s and early 1960s, a few members of Congress also made successful use of the media—especially television—to mobilize national support for their causes. Senator Estes Kefauver of Tennessee became a major contender for the presidency and won a place on the 1956 Democratic national ticket as a result of his dramatic televised hearings on organized crime. Senator Joseph McCarthy of Wisconsin made himself a powerful national figure through his well-publicized investigations of alleged Communist infiltration of key American institutions. These senators, however, were more exceptional than typical. Through the mid-1960s, the executive branch continued to generate the bulk of news coverage, and the media served as a cornerstone of presidential power.

The Vietnam War shattered this relationship between the press and the presidency. During the early stages of U.S. involvement, American officials in Vietnam who disapproved of the way the war was being conducted leaked information critical of administrative policy to reporters. Publication of this material infuriated the White House, which pressured publishers to block its release; on one occasion, President Kennedy went so far as to ask the *New York Times* to reassign its Saigon correspondent. The national print and broadcast media discovered, however, that there was an audience for critical coverage and investigative reporting among segments of the public skeptical of administration policy. As the Vietnam conflict dragged on, critical media coverage fanned antiwar sentiment. Moreover, growing opposition to the war among liberals encouraged some members of Congress, most notably Senator J. William Fulbright,

History Principle

The Vietnam War shattered the favorable relationship that existed between the news media and elected leaders.

chair of the Senate Foreign Relations Committee, to break with the president. In turn, these shifts in popular and congressional sentiment emboldened journalists and publishers to continue to present critical news reports. Through this process, journalists developed a commitment to adversarial journalism, while a constituency emerged that would rally to the defense of the media when it came under White House attack.

This pattern endured through the 1970s and into the present. Political forces opposed to presidential policies, many members of Congress, and the national news media began to find that their interests often overlapped. Adversarial, or "attack," journalism has become commonplace in America, and some critics have suggested that the media have contributed to popular cynicism and the low levels of citizen participation that characterize contemporary American political processes. But before we begin to think about means of compelling the media to adopt a more positive view of politicians and political issues, we should consider the possibility that media criticism is one of the major mechanisms of political accountability in the American political process. Without aggressive media coverage, would we have known of Bill Clinton's misdeeds or, for that matter, those of Richard Nixon? Without aggressive media coverage, would important questions be raised about the conduct of American foreign and domestic policy? It is easy to criticize the media for their aggressive tactics, but would our democracy function effectively without the critical role of the press? A vigorous and critical media are needed as the "watchdogs" of American politics. Of course, in October 2001, the adversarial relationship between the government and the media was at least temporarily transformed into a much more supportive association as the media helped rally the American people for the fight against terrorism. And, indeed, some commentators have suggested that segments of the media, the more conservative media in particular, have become far less adversarial in their tone during the Bush presidency than in prior years.

The adversarial relationship between the government and segments of the press, however, resumed in the wake of the 2002–2003 Iraq war. Such newspapers as the *Washington Post* and the *New York Times* castigated President Bush for going to war without winning the support of some of America's major allies. When American forces failed to uncover evidence that Iraq possessed weapons of mass destruction—a major reason cited by the administration for launching the war—these newspapers intimated that the war had been based on intelligence failures, if not outright presidential deceptions. The president, as noted earlier, denounced the media for distorting his record. Thus, after a brief interlude of post-9/11 harmony, the customary hostilities between the government and the press seemed to manifest themselves once again.

MEDIA POWER AND RESPONSIBILITY

The free media are absolutely essential to democratic government. We depend upon the media to investigate wrongdoing, to publicize and explain governmental actions, to evaluate programs and politicians, and to bring to light matters that might otherwise be known only to a handful of governmental insiders. In short, without free and active media, popular government would be virtually impossible. Citizens would have few means by which to know or assess the government's actions—other than the claims or pronouncements of the government itself. Moreover, without active—indeed, aggressive—media, citizens would be hard pressed to make informed choices among competing candidates at the polls. Often enough, the media reveal discrepancies between candidates' claims and their actual records, and between the images that candidates seek to project and the underlying realities.

At the same time, the increasing decay of party organizations (see Chapter 11) has made politicians ever more dependent upon favorable media coverage. National political leaders and journalists have had symbiotic relationships, at least since FDR's presidency, but initially politicians were the senior partners. They benefited from media publicity, but they were not totally dependent upon it as long as they could still rely upon party organizations to mobilize votes. Journalists, on the other hand, depended upon their relationships with politicians for access to information and would hesitate to report stories that might antagonize valuable sources. Newsmen and -women feared exclusion from the flow of information in retaliation. Thus, for example, reporters did not publicize potentially embarrassing information, widely known in Washington, about the personal lives of such figures as Franklin Roosevelt and John F. Kennedy.

 History Principle

The increasing decay of party organizations over the past fifty years has made politicians more dependent on the media.

With the decline of party, the balance of power between politicians and journalists has been reversed. Now that politicians have become heavily dependent upon the media to reach their constituents, journalists no longer need fear that their access to information can be restricted in retaliation for negative coverage.

Freedom gives the media enormous power. The media can make or break reputations, help to launch or to destroy political careers, and build support for or rally opposition against programs and institutions.[31] Wherever there is so much power, there exists at least the potential for its abuse or overly zealous use. All things considered, free media are so critically important to the maintenance of a democratic society that we must be prepared to take the risk that the media will occasionally abuse their power. The forms of governmental control that would prevent the media from misusing their power would also certainly destroy our freedom.

SUMMARY

The American news media are among the world's freest. The print and broadcast media regularly present information and opinions critical of the government, political leaders, and policies.

[31]See Martin Linsky, *Impact: How the Press Affects Federal Policy Making* (New York: W. W. Norton, 1991).

Rationality Principle	Collective Action Principle	Institution Principle	Policy Principle	History Principle
Media coverage can be analyzed in terms of the interests of members of the media, politicians, and consumers.

The goals and incentives of journalists—such as ratings, career success, and prestige—influence what is created and reported as news.

News coverage is influenced by the interests of politicians.

Consumer preferences, such as those of the affluent or those of people who watch news for its entertainment value, influence news content. | The relationship between media members and politicians is a Prisoners' Dilemma. Each participant benefits from mutual cooperation but finds him- or herself tempted to defect on occasion to secure even larger gains. | | | The historical relationship between government and the media in the United States differs from that of other democracies because of the freedom of the press, guaranteed by the Constitution. This has led the U.S. away from public ownership and more toward regulation.

The Vietnam War shattered the favorable relationship that existed between the news media and elected leaders.

The increasing decay of party organizations over the past fifty years has made politicians more dependent on the media. |

The media help to determine the agenda or focus of political debate in the United States, to shape popular understanding of political events and results, and to influence popular judgments of politicians and leaders.

Over the past century, the media have helped to nationalize American political perspectives. Media coverage is influenced by the perspectives of journalists, politicians, and upscale audiences. The attention that the media give to protest and conflict is also a function of audience factors.

Free media are an essential ingredient of popular government.

FOR FURTHER READING

Cook, Timothy E. *Making Laws and Making News: Media Strategies in the U.S. House of Representatives.* Washington, D.C.: Brookings Institution, 1989.

Gans, Herbert. *Deciding What's News: A Study of CBS Evening News, NBC Nightly News, Newsweek, and Time.* New York: Vintage, 1980.

Graber, Doris A. *Mass Media and American Politics.* 6th ed. Washington, D.C.: Congressional Quarterly Press, 2002.

Hallin, Daniel C. *The Uncensored War: The Media and Vietnam.* Berkeley: University of California Press, 1986.

Hart, Roderick P. *Seducing America: How Television Charms the Modern Voter.* Rev. ed. Thousand Oaks: Sage, 1999.

Hess, Stephen. *Live From Capitol Hill!: Studies of Congress and the Media.* Washington, D.C.: Brookings Institution, 1991.

Nacos, Brigitte L. *The Press, Presidents, and Crises.* New York: Columbia University Press, 1990.

Owen, Diana. *Media Messages in American Presidential Elections.* New York: Greenwood, 1991.

Spitzer, Robert J., ed. *Media and Public Policy.* Westport, Conn.: Praeger, 1993.

West, Darrell M. *Air Wars: Television Advertising in Election Campaigns, 1952–2000.* 3rd ed. Washington, D.C.: Congressional Quarterly Press, 2001.

Winfield, Betty Houchin. *FDR and the News Media.* Urbana: University of Illinois Press, 1990.

Politics in the News—
Reading between the Lines

The Adversarial Relationship between Politicians and the Media

Press Wars in Baghdad. If the News Turns Bad, the Messenger Takes a Hit

By RAYMOND BONNER

"I HAVE come to hate the media," a senior aide to L. Paul Bremer III, the head of the occupational authority in Iraq, wrote in a recent e-mail message to family and friends. "I have worked in politics for a while and I have always, ALWAYS given them the benefit of the doubt. But, I simply cannot continue to sit here and say, 'Oh well, they will turn around eventually and get the story straight.'"

The "straight story" the journalists are not reporting, she said, is the progress that has been made here in the last six months. "There is LIFE here," she wrote in her message, the latest in a continuing letter to the folks back home, which received wider circulation when one recipient sent it to many others, including officials who continued passing it along. "The streets are full of life," the message said. "There are children playing in the streets with other kids.

". . . The markets are bustling. . . . People are crossing the streets, playing in traffic. Traffic jams are occurring."

While not everyone might see traffic jams as progress, Mr. Bremer's aide is not alone in harboring strong antipathy toward the media. Indeed, the Bush administration has begun what has been described as an anti-media media blitz, to spread news of progress here that it says reporters ignore.

Many journalists dispute that assessment, pointing out that the restoration of electricity, the relative calm of northern and southern Iraq and the reopening of schools have been reported alongside the attacks that have kept the American death toll rising in Baghdad and central Iraq.

Tensions between officials and journalists are nothing new, particularly in war zones; Bosnia is a recent example. But the complaints from officials about the coverage now threaten to politicize

New York Times, 2 November 2003, sec. 4, p. 3.

the subject of what journalists decide is worthy of headlines, much as Presidents Lyndon B. Johnson and Richard M. Nixon did in response to frustrations they faced in Vietnam.

One difference between Vietnam and Iraq is that here, in general, commanders in the field talk to reporters openly, candidly and on the record—a product, presumably, of the practice of embedding reporters with the troops early on.

But today in Baghdad, where the Coalition Provisional Authority can better control access to information, the atmosphere has become very different. It is almost impossible for a journalist to talk to any official from the authority without getting the approval of a public information officer.

Recently, when an army major and the head of operations of an American agency here sought to take a reporter for coffee at the Rashid Hotel, where senior American personnel live and eat, a sentry told them that no reporter could enter the hotel without an escort from the press office.

The American officials were more astonished than the reporter.

If civilian authorities here see reporters as ignoring good news, reporters view the coalition public information officers as determined to withhold information, out of fear that it would become "bad news." The result is gaps in information that make it harder for American readers to assess just how good or bad the news really is.

. . . At a news briefing last week, Brig. Gen. Mark Hertling was asked if he could provide the numbers of those killed and wounded at each police station during a string of attacks on Monday. He declined to do so. "That's too morbid," he said. The total number was provided by other officials. General Hertling suggested to the reporters that their accounts should emphasize not

ESSENCE OF THE STORY

- American officials in Baghdad fault the media for focusing solely on negative news and not covering the positive aspects of the postwar reconstruction.

- Military officials have begun to limit the "bad news" that they release to the press, and information about postwar reconstruction contracts to large American corporations have not been released.

- Reporters hear very different stories from Iraqis in the streets, who are frustrated at the pace of reconstruction.

POLITICAL ANALYSIS

- The "war at home," the battle for public support, can be as important as the war abroad. The media are *the* critical intermediary between events in foreign lands and the American public.

- Almost inevitably, the interests of political and military leaders, who want to focus on good news, and the interests of the media, who want to provide a comprehensive view of a war, will come into conflict.

- The media have become more suspicious of government sources in the post-Vietnam and post-Watergate eras, thus exacerbating these tensions.

- Yet political institutions and the media need each other. Political leaders need the media to communicate information and marshal public support. The media, in turn, rely on government officials for much of their information.

the deaths and injuries, but the heroic efforts of the Iraqi police officer whose actions, he said, had prevented more deaths.

. . . On the reconstruction side, the Bush administration's press officers here urge reporters to write about all the schools built, bridges repaired, and so on. Those numbers and details are made available. But reporters find that no one will answer questions about how much these projects cost and how the money is spent. . . .

CHAPTER

14

Government in Action:
Public Policy and the Economy

Until 1929, most Americans believed that the government had little role to play in managing the economy. The world was guided by Adam Smith's theory that the economy, if left to its own devices, would produce full employment and maximum production. But the government was not entirely uninvolved with the economy. During the nineteenth and early twentieth centuries, it regulated banks, coined and printed money, directed trade through tariffs, and engaged in public works such as building roads, canals, and railroads. Nevertheless, the public philosophy of early twentieth-century America emphasized economic self-reliance and personal effort, with the government playing a secondary role at most. This traditional view of the relationship between government and the economy crumbled with the stark reality of the Great Depression of 1929–1933. Some misfortune befell nearly everyone. Around 20 percent of the workforce became unemployed, and few of these individuals had any monetary resources or the old family farm to fall back on. Banks failed, wiping out the savings of millions who had been prudent enough or fortunate enough to have any. Thousands of businesses failed, throwing middle-class Americans onto the bread lines alongside unemployed laborers and dispossessed farmers. The Great Depression had finally proven to Americans that imperfections in the economic system could exist.

Demands mounted for the federal government to take action. In Congress, some Democrats proposed that the federal government finance public works at an accelerated rate to aid the economy and put people back to work. Other members of Congress introduced legislation to provide federal grants to the states to assist them in their relief efforts.

When President Franklin D. Roosevelt took office in 1933, he energetically threw the federal government into the business of fighting the Depression. He proposed a variety of temporary measures to provide federal relief and work programs. Most of the programs he proposed were financed by the federal government but administered by the states. In addition to these temporary measures, Roosevelt presided over the creation of several important federal programs designed to provide future economic security for Americans. Since that time, the government has been instrumental in ensuring that the economy will never again collapse as it did during the Depression.

For example, just two weeks after the September 11 attacks, Congress enacted a $15-billion financial package designed to prop up the airline industry. Already hurting from a weak economy, the airlines faced a grim future after the terrorist attacks. With the nation's air fleet entirely grounded for three days after the attacks and predictions of sharply reduced business in the weeks and months to come, multiple bankruptcies loomed on the horizon. Congress's swift and nearly unanimous decision to provide assistance underscored the importance of the airline industry to the American economy. It also reflected the widely shared expectation that the federal government would act to address so grave an economic problem.

The airline-industry bailout package and the accompanying air safety measures revealed the many purposes that drive government involvement in the economy. First and foremost is the goal of ensuring a healthy economy. As they debated the legislation, many members of Congress pointed to the strategic importance of the airlines to the entire economy. Government also routinely

CHAPTER OUTLINE

How Does Government Make a Market Economy Possible?

- Establishing Law and Order

- Defining Rules of Property

- Enforcing Contracts

- Governing Rules of Exchange

- Setting Market Standards

- Providing Public Goods

- Creating a Labor Force

- Ameliorating Externalities

- Promoting Competition

- The Bases of Government Involvement

What are the Goals, Tools, and Politics of Economic Policy?

- Public Order and Private Property

- Business Development

- Maintaining a Stable and Strong Economy

intervenes in the economy to protect individual welfare and promote the public good. Air safety measures, which included posting National Guardsmen in airports in the months after the attacks and the subsequent federal takeover of airport security, were the key measures designed to achieve these goals. Such government action is critical because heightened security requires expensive equipment, personnel training, and safety procedures that the airlines had avoided implementing due to cost considerations. After September 11, critics of the air security system charged that industry pressure to reduce costs had created lax security that allowed the attacks to occur in the first place. A final objective of government economic policy is to regulate competition. In 1979, the government deregulated the airline industry, removing federal control over ticket prices and airline routes. The results benefited many consumers as the increased competition produced lower fares. (They also resulted in a less desirable outcome—more cramped seats.) Even in the era of deregulation, however, the federal government continued to subsidize and regulate airline activity in order to provide service to small or remote places. The post–September 11 airline bailout package included special provisions to ensure ongoing service to these less profitable routes.

Government involvement in the economy is now routine and widespread, touching practically every aspect of economic life. Nonetheless, specific decisions about government action in the economy often provoke heated controversy over who benefits (and who doesn't benefit) from government activity. The airline bailout package was no exception. Despite strong support for the measure, there was considerable dissatisfaction among some Democrats, who wanted the package to include specific provisions to help the thousands of laid-off airline workers. The package ensured that airline executives could continue to receive salaries up to $300,000 but did nothing to assist workers. As one frustrated Democrat shouted during the deliberations in the House of Representatives, "Why in this chamber do the big dogs always eat first?"[1] In addition to these divisions within the airline industry, representatives from other industries hard hit by the terrorist attacks, including travel agents, restaurants, hotels, and the insurance industry, descended on Washington to lobby for special assistance.

public policy
A governmental law, rule, statute, or edict that expresses the government's goals and provides for rewards and punishments to promote their attainment.

As Congress considered (and largely rejected) these claimants, it was effectively drawing a line between policies that would serve the larger public interest and policies that would benefit only small segments of the economy.

Rationality Principle
Public policies create incentives for people to alter the direction or intensity of their behavior.

The job of this and the succeeding two chapters is to look at the *purposive* actions of government—the policies. **Public policy** can be defined simply as an officially expressed intention backed by a sanction, which can be a reward or a punishment. Thus, a public policy is a law, a rule, a statute, an edict, a regulation, or an order. Its purpose is to provide incentives, whether carrot-like rewards or stick-like punishments, to induce people either to change what they are currently doing and do something else, or to do more or less of what they are currently doing. In the first section of this chapter, we will discuss the rationale for government's involvement in the economy. In the next section, we will look at the goals of national economic policies. These policies have been organized into three categories:

[1]Frank Swoboda and Martha McNeil Hamilton, "Congress Clears $15 Billion to Aid Airlines," *Washington Post*, 23 September 2001, p. A1.

(1) policies that protect public order and private property; (2) policies that control or influence markets; and (3) policies that are designed to defend or enhance the vitality of our capitalist economy.

As we said in Chapter 1 and emphasized in other chapters, governments do what they do in part because of the concerns, ambitions, and purposes of politicians and other government officials and the institutional contexts in which these concerns, ambitions, and purposes get played out. Since the policy-making process allows many opportunities to change the purposes of government, politicians and officials constantly take advantage of their capacities as *agenda setters*. But policy change requires success at every step of the rather lengthy and intricate policy-making process. The institutional arrangements of a government create hurdles that a proposed change in policy must clear. This often means that change is nearly impossible. Because change is difficult, policies— once put in place—possess a degree of *durability*. This durability, in turn, provides a semblance of order and predictability in an otherwise uncertain world.

PREVIEWING THE PRINCIPLES

Public policies create incentives for people to alter the direction or intensity of their behavior. With regard to economic policy, government can play an important role in establishing the rules and institutions that allow a free market to function. Government has lots of tools to affect the economy, but there is considerable political conflict over which tools to use, how to use them, and when to use them. And because institutional arrangements and historical precedent make change difficult, public policies are durable. Nevertheless, historical events such as the Great Depression or September 11 can motivate government officials to adopt new policies.

This emphasis on analyzing policy as the product of individual preferences and institutional procedures is, however, only part of the story. Historical events, sometimes appearing out of the blue, add another source of motivation for governments to act. This should be more obvious from reflecting on the aftermath of the events of September 11, 2001, a fateful day of terrorist activity in New York City, Washington, D.C., and Pennsylvania. That massive blow to our sense of national security was also an economic blow; policy makers had to begin to cope with the threatened safety of all Americans and an economy pushed into recession. Following that fateful day, national, state, and local agencies crafted responses to and new policy initiatives for the rapidly changing social and economic environment.

Policy Principle

Because institutional arrangements make change difficult, public policies are durable.

History Principle

Historical events can motivate government officials to adopt new policies.

HOW DOES GOVERNMENT MAKE A MARKET ECONOMY POSSIBLE?

Government makes a market economy possible. Government sets the rules that allow markets to function. Government also develops and sustains the institutions necessary to support a market economy. By doing so, government lowers the costs of doing business. In the United States, certain arrangements facilitated the emergence of the modern market economy. These arrangements are institutions that gave participants guarantees or rules of the game that induced them to "enter the market." Our objective here is to examine what these arrangements are and what role government plays in establishing them.

Establishing Law and Order

As we saw in Chapter 1, the first feature is inherent in the very idea of government. There must be a minimal degree of predictability about the basic rules of social interaction. In other words, there must be a system of law and order. Participants in the market must be able to assume not only that they can get to the market safely—that they won't be robbed on the way—but also that, having arrived, the people with whom they are dealing will behave predictably and will be bound by some number of calculable laws.

Defining Rules of Property

The second feature that encourages people to participate in the market focuses on defining and dealing with property. If the market involves exchanges of ownership, there must be clear laws about what constitutes property. Property may be many things—your labor or your ideas or the bed you sleep in—but the very concept of property is inconceivable without laws that define what you can call your own.

Institution Principle

Government can play an important role in establishing the rules and institutions that allow a market economy to function.

Property ownership means that we can exercise dominion over something that we have declared our own, and it is defined by laws that enable us to exercise that dominion. Something is not our own unless we can be reasonably certain that someone else cannot walk away with it. Trespass laws, for example, give concrete meaning to what constitutes property: a trespass law confers upon us a legal right to keep others away from certain kinds of property. It is clear, then, that laws or rules that define property are an essential part of the political economy. Before we can enter a market and participate in an exchange, we must be able to expect not only that we can lay claim to something, but that those around us will respect that claim. In this sense, private property has a public component. The probability of enjoying property would be remote unless there were laws that were widely enforced and accepted.

Enforcing Contracts

A third prerequisite that must be met before a market economy can operate involves rules governing the enforcement of contracts. There are, of course, societies that do not have a recognizable concept of contract, but our Western economy is highly dependent upon contract notions.

Contracts are closely related to property since contracts are only necessary in connection with exchanges of property, broadly construed. A contract refers to a voluntary agreement between two or more private persons that governs future conduct. And while the agreement may be private, it has a distinctively public component: a contract must be enforceable, or it is meaningless.

Governing Rules of Exchange

The fourth prerequisite for the emergence or creation of a market economy is closely tied to the contract requirement. A market exists only when exchanges occur, and there must be rules governing exchange itself. Laws of exchange structure how, when, and under what conditions you can sell your property. You might think that once the laws of property have defined what you own you ought to be able to transfer it, but that transfer is surrounded by rules that govern the transfer itself.

Certain kinds of exchanges are deemed off-limits altogether. For example, you own your own body, but under what conditions can you sell it? Laws about prostitution limit the selling or renting of one's body.

Setting Market Standards

The fifth prerequisite for the emergence of the modern free market is related to the fourth. When people engage in exchanges that are not face-to-face—where they can't point to a good and say "I want that tomato or that fish"—both parties must have some way of understanding what the goods are that they are bargaining over. To do that, terminology must be standardized, and one of the essential acts any government does is to establish standard weights and measures.

With modern products, the standards must go beyond weights and measures; buyers and sellers must be able to specify both quantities and qualities of goods before they enter into their contracts. These buyers and sellers must know, for example, what is meant by long and short staple cotton, and everything in between; they must know what they are getting when they order automobile tires of a particular quality. Many of these standards today are developed by private-sector trade associations, of course, but those standards are often incorporated into government regulations, and so they acquire governmental status—or, more important, they are protected by government action through the courts. If a member of the porcelain enamel association, for example, agrees to produce a certain type of enamel according to the trade association's specifications, the member can be sued if he or she cuts corners and evades those standards.

Providing Public Goods

The sixth prerequisite to the operation of a market economy involves the provision of ***public goods.*** As we saw in Chapter 1, this term refers to facilities that the government may provide because no single participant can afford or is willing to provide those facilities itself. The provision of public goods extends from supplying the physical marketplace itself—like the commons in New England towns—to an interstate highway system to stimulate the trucking industry. The provision of

public goods A good that (1) may be enjoyed by anyone if it is provided and that (2) may not be denied to anyone once it has been provided.

public goods is essential to market operation, and the manner in which the government provides those goods affects the market's character.

Creating a Labor Force

The seventh prerequisite to the emergence of a market economy is the creation of a labor force. Every society has provisions that force people to work. One of the best, albeit most recent, examples of these provisions is the requirement for universal compulsory education in this society: people are educated so that they can learn the skills necessary to function in the market. Long before education laws, however, we had poorhouses, vagrancy laws, and other more police-oriented means of forcing people to work; these rules meant that people could starve or be punished if they failed to earn their own keep. Our welfare system today serves the same purpose: we adjust the welfare system in cycles to be sure that the support we give is uncomfortable enough that people will prefer working to retiring on the low income that they will get from welfare.

Ameliorating Externalities

Another prerequisite is not always obvious, but it is nonetheless critical to creating the conditions for a market economy. To allow the market economy to operate, there must be provisions for allocating responsibility when the social cost of some behavior far exceeds the private cost. For instance, the cost of driving a gas-guzzling car is more than the total of the monthly payments, insurance, and gasoline. The cost also includes the widely distributed impact of smog and the effects of carbon-monoxide emissions. Negative external effects, such as pollution, that can result from market activities are called *externalities.* Such externalities, when individuals or firms engage in private behavior that has broader social consequences, provide government an additional rationale to regulate the economy.

externalities The difference between the private cost and the social cost of economic behavior.

Promoting Competition

Finally, once markets emerge, they must be maintained. This means that it should be reasonably easy for a producer to enter and freely compete in the market. If this is not the case, such as when one company has established a *monopoly,* the efficiency of the market and the equitable distribution of its benefits are threatened. Decreased competition provides government another reason for getting involved in the economy by functioning as a watchdog over potential monopoly control.

monopoly The existence of a single firm in a market that provides all the goods and services of that market; the absence of competition.

The Bases of Government Involvement

It should now be obvious that governments—national, state, and local—are deeply embedded in the operation of a market economy. They provide rules (of property, exchange, liability); they enforce contracts and deliver law and order more generally; they supply public goods; they underwrite market standards and regulate the conditions of work; and they generally oversee the multiple aspects of competition that sustain a market economy. In short, the bases of a market economy are also the *opportunities* for government agents—elected politicians, bureaucrats, judges—to influence economic outcomes.

A benign and not altogether inaccurate perspective on government involvement in the economy begins with the idea of ***market failure.*** Markets sometimes fail to deliver all they promise—the efficient allocation of society's economic resources—because of imperfections of various sorts. A seller, for example, may possess information about his or her product of which a prospective buyer is unaware. (This is known as the *problem of incomplete information.*) This may cause the buyer to buy the product when, if he or she were fully informed, there would have been no purchase. Or this may lead to too many (or too few) transactions compared to what would have transpired under conditions of full and complete information. In this instance the market has misallocated resources, so to speak, because the incomplete information has misled market participants.

<aside>
market failure
Instances when markets fail to produce efficient outcomes.
</aside>

If incomplete information is one way the market may fail, then imperfections in the assignment of property rights is another. Thus, the market may fail to induce appropriate safeguarding of the environment because of a failure to assign property rights in a complete and/or uncontested way. (This is known as the *problem of incomplete property rights.*) Because of the incomplete assignment of rights, no one "owns" the air, and so anyone may use it as dumping ground for pollutants (from their automobile exhaust, from their hairspray aerosol cans, from their chimney). Except to an environmental extremist, *some* air pollution is acceptable (since with none it is impossible to imagine any productive activities at all taking place—no cars, no hairspray, no chimneys); but markets, unaided, do not necessarily encourage "optimal" levels of pollution.

The benign view of government involvement in the economy is one of government as an agent to correct (or at least to ameliorate) these kinds of market failures (and there are others). By providing and enforcing market standards for instance, as mentioned in the previous section, government helps to alleviate information asymmetries between prospective buyers and sellers, thereby correcting an imbalance and a prospective failure to consummate market deals. Imposing a fair-labeling requirement on a manufacturer is an instance of this. So is an obligation of a butcher shop to have a properly working scale. (Aware that the butcher's scale will be inspected from time to time by a government agent, consumers will be more confident about doing business in that shop.) Or, as in the second example above, by establishing (partial and limited) property rights to the air—say, "pollution permits" giving its holders the right to deposit a certain specified amount of particulate matter into the atmosphere—governments in the Los Angeles air basin have controlled pollution levels and improved smog conditions in this locale without abolishing pollution-producing activities altogether (activities like manufacturing, driving autos, barbecuing in the backyard).

Part one, then, of the benign rationale for government involvement in the economy is the reduction of market failures. A second part of the benign view of government involvement involves the production of public goods. As we described earlier, some goods have the property that they may be enjoyed by anyone once they are provided, regardless of whether a person has contributed to their provision or not and regardless of how many other people are enjoying the good. This produces an incentive problem—namely, too few people have an incentive to contribute to the production of this good—and thus it will be undersupplied in the marketplace. (This is known as the *problem of free riding*.) Consequently, it is argued, governments, because they possess the ability to coerce contribution through the imposition of taxes, are the natural provider of goods like defense, transportation infrastructure, or clean air and water. They can provide these public goods by taxing citizens and then, with the revenue that these taxes provide, go out and hire the necessary inputs to make them available.

Some think the benign interpretation is a fairy tale. True, market failures and undersupplied public goods provide an opportunity for a well-intentioned government to step in, take charge, and do good. The same may be said for the provision of property, exchange, and liability rules; for contract enforcement; and for the regulation of work conditions. All these constitute occasions in which markets underperform and, thus, opportunities for social improvement. The portentous and less benign prospect, however, is that it also provides opportunities for self-interested political actors to intervene.

Consider the following example. Senator Robert Byrd of West Virginia, in his previous role as the powerful majority leader of the U.S. Senate in the 1980s and 1990s, was a vigilant defender of the West Virginia coal industry. This industry produces high-sulfur coal, the kind that generates much more serious pollution than low-sulfur coal from the West. Byrd has been very successful in making certain that environmental laws do not adversely affect high-sulfur coal. Specifically, he has made it possible to burn high-sulfur coal while reducing the environmental damage it causes by writing into environmental legislation that coal-fired furnaces must have *scrubbers* installed on their smokestacks (to clean the pollution residue from the smoke after the coal is burned). This is a more expensive environmental "fix" than simply requiring that only low-sulfur (western) coal be burned. The result is that West Virginia coal miners and owners of coal mines are protected at the expense of their fellow miners and owners out West. So, even as the national government uses its powers to provide a public good—clean air—it does so in a manner that nevertheless is advantageous to some and disadvantageous to others.[2]

It should come as no surprise, then, that even when there is consensus over ends, like cleaning up the environment or protecting the nation from terrorism or getting Americans back to work, there is considerable conflict over means. Even when policies produce similar results, they may have different impacts on different parts of the economy or regions of the country. One policy may clean up the environment by requiring scrubbers on all plants using coal-fired furnaces

Rationality Principle
Even if governments seek to "do good," this does not prevent rational politicians from searching for opportunities to take care of their constituents.

---

[2]On the clever manner in which Byrd helped West Virginia coal producers, see Bruce A. Ackerman and William T. Hassler, *Clean Coal/Dirty Air: Or How the Clean Air Act Became a Multi-Billion-Dollar Bail-Out for High-Sulfur Coal Producers and What Should Be Done About It* (New Haven, Conn.: Yale University Press, 1981).

(to eliminate sulfur emissions at the smokestack). Another policy might have precisely the same environmental effect but produce it by requiring that coal-fired furnaces burn only low-sulfur western coal (so that far fewer sulfur particulates are emitted in the first place). The first policy protects the jobs and profits of West Virginians; the second policy threatens them. Consensus on ends, in other words, does not guarantee consensus on means. Agreement on goals is often accompanied by disagreements about tools. Collective action, then, is not only about achieving a shared vision, a common policy, or a joint objective. It is also about "how to get from here to there."

You might wonder how decisions over means get made. This is what politics is all about—and this is why some shadows of doubt accompany the benign rationale for government involvement in the economy. There is no gainsaying the central pieces of the benign rationale—market failures and undersupplied public goods are very real problems for any advanced industrial society. But there is also no gainsaying the existence of clever politicians looking for ways to "take care of their own," even at the expense of others. The benign rationale, that is, requires qualification. Markets create problems for sure. But once we open the door to government, economic and social groups, through their political representatives, will jockey for advantage, looking for ways to get ahead or to hobble their competitors.

To summarize, it is difficult to understand why the modern economy has its present shape without understanding what factors regularly affected its development. The structure of the capitalist economy and every other economic system is highly dependent upon a series of government actions that make it possible for that economy to maintain itself in one form or another.

Governments are neither aloof nor separate from the economy but are inextricably bound up in its activities. Governments provide a structure and a framework—standards, rules, laws—as well as substantive support in the form of subsidies, regulations, and taxes, all of which allow the economy to operate. Through politics, however, governments and their agents create winners and losers. The winners may think of government's policies as benign; the losers do not.

Collective Action Principle

Government has lots of tools that affect the economy, but there is considerable political conflict over which tools to use, how to use them, and when to use them. Government involvement in the economy thus provides opportunities for groups to mobilize in order to become winners or to avoid becoming losers.

WHAT ARE THE GOALS, TOOLS, AND POLITICS OF ECONOMIC POLICY?

The goals of economic policy often shift as a new administration takes power in Washington, but such shifts are usually a matter of emphasis. Political leaders realize that the public expects the government to achieve multiple goals in its economic policy. Public expectations about what government economic policy can and should do have expanded over the course of our nation's history. This growth in public expectations has made economic policy more complex as government strives to achieve multiple goals, some of which may conflict with one another.

Three major goals have guided government involvement in the economy since the early years of our nation's history: promoting a strong and stable economy, encouraging business development, and maintaining public order. Over time, the federal government has taken on greater responsibility for meeting each of these goals. The Great Depression of the 1930s marked a decisive turning point. As Washington created new agencies and new measures to monitor the nation's economic health, it transformed public expectations about the federal role in the economy. The federal government assumed primary responsibility for achieving established goals, and it faced heightened expectations about its ability to reach those goals.

Public Order and Private Property

We begin our discussion with public-order policies for two reasons. First, these policies lay and maintain the foundations of the economy. Second, because so many of these policies are old and established state government policies, most people don't appreciate them as policies and go on believing that the U.S. economy was once "unregulated" by the government.

Federalism and Public Order   Under the American federalist system, there is no national police force, there is no national criminal law, there is no national common law, there are no national property laws. The national government does have a few policies directly concerned with public order, however, most of which are mandated by the Constitution itself. These include laws against counterfeiting, against using the mails to defraud, and against crossing state lines to avoid arrest for a violation of state laws. A few other offenses against public order have simply been presumed to be interstate crimes against which federal statutes have been enacted, mainly in the twentieth century. Important examples include kidnapping, narcotics dealing, and political subversion. But virtually all of the multitudes of other policies dealing with public order and the foundations of the economy are left to the states and their local governments.

In the wake of the terrorist attacks of September 11, 2001, the federal role in public order increased. President George W. Bush, in one of his first acts in response to the attacks, announced the creation of a new cabinet-level agency named the Office of Homeland Defense, which later became the Department of Homeland Security. Its mission is to coordinate the federal government's role in the preservation of public order.

Private Property   Another unique feature of the American approach to public order is the emphasis placed on *private property*. Private property is valued in most of the cultures of the world but not as centrally as in the United States, where it is embodied in the Constitution. Seizing private property for a public use, or *expropriation*, is widely used in the United States, especially in land-use regulation. Almost all public works, from highways to parks to government office buildings, involve the forceful taking of some private property in order to assemble sufficient land and the correct distribution of land for the necessary construction. The vast Interstate Highway Program required expropriation of thousands of narrow strips of private land. Urban redevelopment projects often require city governments to use the powers of seizure in the service of private

expropriation
Confiscation of property with or without compensation.

developers, who actually build the urban projects on the land that would be far too expensive if purchased on the open market. Private utilities that supply electricity and gas to individual subscribers are given powers to take private property whenever a new facility or a right-of-way is needed.

We generally call the power to expropriate **eminent domain,** and the eminent-domain power is recognized as inherent in any government. The Fifth Amendment of the U.S. Constitution surrounds this expropriation power with important safeguards against abuse, so that government agencies in the United States are not permitted to use that power except through a strict due process, and they must offer "fair market value" for the land sought.[3]

Not all the policies toward property are policies that regulate the conduct of people who would take property. Many policies positively encourage property ownership on the theory that property owners are better citizens and, therefore, more respectful of public order. One of the most important national policies in American history was **homesteading,** otherwise called "squatting," which permitted people to gain ownership of property by occupying public or unclaimed lands, living on the land for a specified period of time, and making certain minimal improvements on that land.

Many other policies encourage homeownership today, the most significant being that part of the tax code that permits homeowners to deduct interest paid on mortgage loans from their taxes. In addition, three large federal agencies—the Federal Housing Administration (FHA), the Farmers Home Administration (FMHA), and the Veterans Administration (VA)—encourage homeownership by making mortgage loans available at interest rates below the market rate. The Farm Credit Administration (FCA) operates the extensive Farm Credit System, whose primary function is to make long-term and short-term loans to improve farm and rural real estate, loans available only to bona fide farm operators and farm-related companies who are members of the farm credit system. Many of these agencies make direct loans at below-market rates. Some of them (in particular the FHA and the VA) also insure or guarantee loans so that private commercial banks have less risk and can charge proportionately lower interest rates.

eminent domain
The right of government to take private property for public use, with reasonable compensation awarded for the property.

homesteading
A national policy that permits people to gain ownership of property by occupying public or unclaimed lands, living on the land for a specified period of time, and making certain minimal improvements on that land. Also known as squatting.

Business Development

Promoting Business Development through Promotional Policies During the nineteenth century, the national government was almost exclusively a promoter of markets. National roads and canals were built to tie states and regions together. National tariff policies promoted domestic markets by restricting imported goods; a tax on an import raised its price and weakened its ability to compete with similar domestic products. The national government also heavily subsidized the railroad. Until the 1840s, railroads were thought to be of limited commercial value. But between 1850 and 1872, Congress granted over

[3]For an evaluation of the politics of eminent domain, see Theodore J. Lowi et al., *Poliscide: Big Government, Big Science, Lilliputian Politics* (Lanham, Md.: University Press of America, 1990), p. 235 and *passim*, and especially Chapters 11 and 12, written by Julia and Thomas Vitullo-Martin.

100 million acres of public-domain land to railroad interests, and state and local governments pitched in an estimated $280 million in cash and credit. Before the end of the century, 35,000 miles of track existed—almost half the world's total.

Railroads were not the only clients of federal support aimed at fostering the expansion of private markets. Many sectors of agriculture received federal subsidies during the nineteenth century. Agriculture remains highly subsidized. In 2001, an environmental group caused a stir by putting the exact amounts of subsidies received by individual farmers on a widely publicized Web site (http://www.ewg.org/farm). The top recipient of government aid in Texas, for example, received $1.3 million in 2001. President Bush continued the tradition of generous agricultural subsidies, approving a 2002 law that increased federal payments to farmers by 80 percent.

In the twentieth century, traditional promotional techniques were expanded, and some new ones were invented. For example, a great proportion of the promotional activities of the national government are now done indirectly through *categorical grants-in-aid* (see Chapter 3). The national government offers grants to states on condition that the state (or local) government undertake a particular activity. Thus, in order to use motor transportation to improve national markets, a national highway system of 900,000 miles was built during the 1930s, based on a formula whereby the national government would pay 50 percent of the cost if the state would provide the other 50 percent. And then for over twenty years, beginning in the late 1950s, the federal government constructed over 45,000 miles of interstate highways. This was brought about through a program whereby the national government agreed to pay 90 percent of the construction costs on the condition that each state provide for 10 percent of the costs of any portion of a highway built within its boundaries.[4] There are examples of U.S. government promotional policy in each of the country's major industrial sectors.

categorical grants-in-aid
Funds given by Congress to states and localities, earmarked by law for specific categories such as education or crime prevention.

Tools for Promotional Policy   Subsidies and contracting are the carrots of public policy. Their purpose is to encourage people to do something they might not otherwise do or to get people to do more of what they are already doing. Sometimes the purpose is merely to compensate people for something done in the past.

Subsidies are simply government grants of cash or other valuable commodities, such as land. Although subsidies are often denounced as "giveaways," they have played a fundamental role in the history of government in the United States. Subsidies were the dominant form of public policy of the national government and the state and local governments throughout the nineteenth century. They continue to be an important category of public policy at all levels of government. The first planning document ever written for the national government, Alexander Hamilton's *Report on Manufactures*, was based almost entirely on Hamilton's assumption that American industry could be encouraged by federal subsidies and that these were not only desirable but constitutional.

subsidies
Governmental grants of cash or other valuable commodities such as land to individuals or organizations. Subsidies can be used to promote activities desired by the government, to reward political support, or to buy off political opposition.

[4]The act of 1955 officially designated the interstate highways as the National System of Interstate and Defense Highways. It was indirectly a major part of President Eisenhower's defense program. But it was just as obviously a "pork barrel" policy as any rivers and harbors legislation.

The thrust of Hamilton's plan was not lost on later policy makers. Subsidies in the form of land grants were given to farmers and to railroad companies to encourage western settlement. Substantial cash subsidies have traditionally been given to commercial shipbuilders to help build the commercial fleet and to guarantee the use of the ships as military-personnel carriers in time of war.

Subsidies have always been a technique favored by politicians because subsidies can be treated as "benefits" that can be spread widely in response to many demands that might otherwise produce profound political conflict. Subsidies can, in other words, be used to buy off the opposition.

Contracting   Like any corporation, a government agency must purchase goods and services by contract. The law requires open bidding for a substantial proportion of these contracts because government contracts are extremely valuable to businesses in the private sector and because the opportunities and incentives for abuse are very great. But contracting is more than a method of buying goods and services. Contracting is also an important technique of policy because government agencies are often authorized to use their **contracting power** as a means of encouraging corporations to improve themselves, as a means of helping to build up whole sectors of the economy, and as a means of encouraging certain desirable goals or behavior, such as equal employment opportunity. For example, the infant airline industry of the 1930s was nurtured by the national government's lucrative contracts to carry airmail. A more recent example is the use of government contracting to encourage industries, universities, and other organizations to engage in research and development.

contracting power   The power of government to set conditions on companies seeking to sell goods or services to government agencies.

Military contracting has long been a major element in government spending. So tight was the connection between defense contractors and the federal government during the cold war that, as he was leaving office, President Eisenhower warned the nation to beware of the powerful "military-industrial complex." After the cold war, as military spending and production declined, major defense contractors began to look for alternative business activities to supplement the reduced demand for weapons. For example, Lockheed Martin, the nation's largest defense contractor, began to bid on contracts related to welfare reform. Since September 11, however, the military budget has been awash in new funds, and military contractors are flooded with business. President Bush proposed to increase the Pentagon budget by $48 billion (14.3 percent), requesting so many weapons systems that one observer called the budget a "weapons smorgasbord."[5] Military contractors geared up to produce not only weapons for foreign warfare, but also surveillance systems to enhance domestic security.

Promotional Policy and Logrolling Politics   Promotional policies work largely through encouragement of individuals in the private sector. The government acts like any patron, such as a patron of the arts or a private foundation. A patronage

[5]James Dao, "The Nation; Big Bucks Trip Up the Lean New Army," *New York Times*, 10 February 2002, sec. 4, p. 5.

policy simply authorizes a government agency to take whatever funds are budgeted to it and dispense them to individuals, companies, or groups to encourage new building, to pay for the provision of a particular service, or as an incentive for a private individual to take an initiative that he or she might not otherwise take. Sometimes these funds are distributed according to a contract for work to be done or goods to be bought, as in a contract with a private construction company to build a bridge. At other times, these funds are in the form of a grant to an individual to engage in research or to support an artistic project.

Promotional policy was the dominant type of policy adopted by Congress during the nineteenth century, and it played an important role in our discussion of federalism in Chapter 3. These policies are called "pork barrel" policies because they can be broken up into smaller pieces of resources and distributed to a maximum number of persons (i.e., voters) literally clamoring for a piece of the pork (i.e., government benefits). Just as "pork barrel" best describes these policies, so "logrolling" best describes the *politics* of these policies. ***Logrolling*** is a political relationship between two or more persons who have nothing in common. Their understanding is that "if you will support me on issue A, I will support you on any other issue you want; just tell me when and how you want me to vote. I don't need to know the particulars."[6] These logrolling relationships found a hospitable environment in Congress in the nineteenth century, and congressional committees and political parties flourished through their ability to gain and maintain political support by means of logrolling relationships. Indeed, political scientist Samuel Beer found that most of the nineteenth century was a period of "pork-barrel coalitions," where the members of these coalitions held no common interests but were joined together by the prospect of each member of the coalition being "able to get from the central government the action it needs."[7]

Drawing on these patterns of the past, we can make an informed guess about the power structure of politics in the category of promotional policy today. The following, by the political scientist John Ferejohn, is a brief description of the pattern, written for today but clearly connected to its nineteenth-century ancestry:

> . . . If a bill calling for improvements in a single district is [proposed], it will not pass since all the districts must pay and only one will benefit. Consequently, only an omnibus bill proposing expenditures in at least a majority of the districts has a chance of passage.[8]

logrolling A legislative practice wherein reciprocal agreements are made between legislators, usually in voting for or against a bill. In contrast to bargaining, logrolling unites parties that have nothing in common but their desire to exchange support.

 Policy Principle

In promotional policies, political actors seek to distribute funds and projects to their political supporters.

---

[6]These policy categories and their associated political patterns were first laid out by Theodore J. Lowi in "American Business, Public Policy, Case Studies and Political Theory," *World Politics* 16, no. 4 (July 1964).

[7]Samuel Beer, "The Modernization of American Federalism," *Public Administration Review* 3, no. 2 (Fall 1973): 59, citing Lowi, "American Business, Public Policies, Case Studies and Political Theory."

[8]John A. Ferejohn, *Pork Barrel Politics: Rivers and Harbors Legislation, 1947–1968* (Stanford, Calif.: Stanford University Press, 1974), p. 235. See also Clem Miller, *Member of the House: Letters of a Congressman*, ed. John W. Baker (New York: Scribner, 1962), especially pp. 16–17.

"Omnibus" is the name given a bill or act that is composed of many sections with little substantive or logical connection among them. Each rivers and harbors bill, for example, is a collection of dozens of separate projects. For example, the Water Resources Development Act of 2003 is a true omnibus act with five separate substantive titles, three of which actually provide approvals for specific projects (Title III), authorizations for initial studies and research for future projects (Title IV), and provisions for extensions, repairs, and reports of progress (Title V). All in all, in these three titles, 237 separate sections provide authorization for specific projects. Some of the sections cover reauthorizations and deauthorizations, and some apply to more than one district. But the named projects, each given a section number, amount to exactly 54 percent of the 435 districts of the House of Representatives. This is spectacularly close to the perfect combination in Ferejohn's "law" of pork-barrel policies. Each project is of intense interest to one district and of little interest elsewhere. Supporters of each project agree to support all the other projects in return for the support their own project will receive. Thus, promotional policy has a distinctive pattern of politics.[9]

Institution Principle
American political institutions, particularly the U.S. Congress, allow promotional policies to take the form of pork-barrel legislation through vote trading, logrolling, and omnibus bills.

Promoting Business Development by Regulating Competition   Americans have long been suspicious of concentrations of economic power. Federal economic regulation aims to protect the public against potential abuses by concentrated economic power in two ways. First, the federal government can establish conditions that govern the operation of big businesses to ensure fair competition. For example, it can require business to make information about its activities and account books available to the public. Second, the federal government can force large businesses to break up into smaller companies if it finds that the company has established a monopoly. This is called *antitrust policy.* In addition to economic regulation, the federal government engages in social regulation. Social regulation establishes conditions on businesses in order to protect workers, the environment, and consumers.

antitrust policy
Government regulation of large businesses that have established monopolies.

Federal regulatory policy was a reaction to public demands. As the American economy prospered throughout the nineteenth century, some companies grew so large that they were recognized as possessing "market power." This meant that they were powerful enough to eliminate competitors and to impose conditions on consumers rather than cater to consumer demand. The growth of billion-dollar corporations led to collusion among companies to control prices, much to the dismay of smaller businesses and ordinary consumers. Moreover, the expanding economy was more mechanized, and this involved greater dangers to employees as well as to consumers.

[9]For more on this distinctive pattern of politics that builds upon the notion of distributive politics developed in Lowi, "American Business, Public Policies, Case Studies and Political Theory," see Kenneth A. Shepsle and Barry R. Weingast, "Political Preferences for the Pork Barrel," *American Journal of Political Science* 25 (1981): 96–111; Barry R. Weingast, Kenneth A. Shepsle, and Christopher Johnsen, "The Political Economy of Benefits and Costs: A Neoclassical Approach to Distributive Politics," *Journal of Political Economy* 89 (1981): 642–64; and Robert M. Stein and Kenneth N. Bickers, *Perpetuating the Pork Barrel: Policy Subsystems and American Democracy* (New York: Cambridge University Press, 1995).

Small businesses, laborers, farmers, and consumers all began to clamor for protective regulation. Although the states had been regulating businesses in one way or another all along, interest groups turned toward Washington as economic problems appeared to be beyond the reach of the individual state governments. If markets were national, there would have to be national regulation.[10]

The first national regulatory policy was the Interstate Commerce Act of 1887, which created the first national independent regulatory commission, the Interstate Commerce Commission (ICC), designed to control the monopolistic practices of the railroads. Two years later, the Sherman Antitrust Act extended regulatory power to cover all monopolistic practices, including "trusts" or any other agreement between companies to eliminate competition. These were strengthened in 1914 with the enactment of the Federal Trade Act (creating the Federal Trade Commission, or FTC) and the Clayton Act. The only significant addition of national regulatory policy beyond interstate regulation of trade, however, was the establishment of the Federal Reserve System in 1913, which was given powers to regulate the banking industry along with its general monetary powers.

History Principle

The scope of national regulatory policies expanded during the 1930s, 1960s, and early 1970s, but contracted during the late 1970s to mid 1990s.

The modern epoch of comprehensive national regulation began in the 1930s. Most of the regulatory programs of the 1930s were established to regulate the conduct of companies within specifically designated sectors of American industry. For example, the jurisdiction of one agency was the securities industry; the jurisdiction of another was the radio (and eventually television) industry. Another was banking. Another was coal mining; still another was agriculture. When Congress turned once again toward regulatory policies in the 1970s, it became still more bold, moving beyond the effort to regulate specific sectors of industry toward regulating some aspect of the entire economy. The scope or jurisdiction of agencies such as the Occupational Safety & Health Administration (OSHA), the Consumer Product Safety Commission (CPSC), and the Environmental Protection Agency (EPA) is as broad and as wide as the entire economy, indeed the entire society.

By the late 1970s, a reaction against regulation set in. Businesses complained about the burden of the new regulations they confronted, and many economists began to argue that excessive regulation was hurting the economy. Congress and the president responded with a wave of *deregulation.* President Ford's and President Carter's accomplishments include the Securities Act Amendment of 1975, the Railroad Revitalization Act of 1976, the Airline Deregulation Act of 1978, the Staggers Rail Deregulation Act of 1980, the Depository Institution Deregulation and Monetary Control Act of 1980, and the Motor Carrier Act of 1980. President Reagan went about the task of changing the direction of regulation by way of "presidential oversight." One of his first actions after taking office was Executive Order 12291, issued February 17, 1981, which gave the Office of Management and Budget (OMB) the authority to review all proposals by all executive-branch agencies for new regulations to be applied to companies or people within their jurisdiction. By this means, President Reagan succeeded in

deregulation A policy of reducing or eliminating regulatory restraints on the conduct of individuals or private institutions.

---

[10]For an account of the relationship between mechanization and law, see Lawrence M. Friedman, *A History of American Law* (New York: Simon & Schuster, 1973), pp. 409–29.

reducing the total number of regulations issued by federal agencies to such an extent that the number of pages in the *Federal Register* dropped from 74,000 in 1980 to 49,600 in 1987.[11] During the 1990s, substantial deregulation in the telecommunications industry and in agriculture, and officially supported relaxation of regulatory activity in civil rights, pollution control, protection of endangered species, and natural resources suggest a further retreat from regulation. But by 2000, the *Federal Register* had crept up to a record 74,258 pages.

Regulatory Tools   If promotional tools are the carrots of public policy, regulatory tools can be considered the sticks. ***Regulation*** comes in several forms, but every regulatory technique shares a common trait: direct government control of conduct. When conduct is said to be regulated, the purpose is rarely to eliminate the conduct but rather to influence it toward more appropriate channels, toward more appropriate locations, or toward certain qualified types of persons all for the purpose of minimizing injuries or inconveniences. This type of regulated conduct is sometimes called ***administrative regulation*** because the controls are given over to administrative agencies rather than to the police. Each regulatory agency has extensive powers to keep a sector of the economy under surveillance as well as powers to make rules dealing with the behavior of individual companies and people. But these administrative agencies have fewer powers of punishment than the police and the courts have, and the administrative agencies generally rely on the courts to issue orders enforcing the rules and decisions made by the agencies.

regulation A particular use of government power in which the government adopts rules imposing restrictions on the conduct of private citizens.

administrative regulation Rules made by regulatory agencies and commissions.

Sometimes a government will adopt administrative regulation if an economic activity is considered so important that it is not to be entrusted to competition among several companies in the private sector. This is the rationale for the regulation of local or regional power companies. A single company, traditionally called a "utility," is given an exclusive license (or franchise) to offer these services, but since the one company is made a legal monopoly and is protected from competition by other companies, the government gives an administrative agency the power to regulate the quality of the services rendered, the rates charged for those services, and the margin of profit that the company is permitted to make.

At other times, administrative regulation is the chosen technique because the legislature decides that the economy needs protection from itself—that is, it may set up a regulatory agency to protect companies from destructive or predatory competition on the assumption that economic competition is not always its own solution. This is the rationale behind the Federal Trade Commission, which has the responsibility of watching over such practices as price discrimination or pooling agreements between two or more companies when their purpose is to eliminate competitors.

Regulatory Policy and Pluralist Politics   The key characteristic of regulatory policy is control of individual conduct by directly coercive techniques. Regulatory techniques

[11]The *Federal Register* is the daily publication of all official acts of Congress, the president, and the administrative agencies. A law or executive order is not legally binding until published in the *Federal Register*.

are used to impose obligations, duties, or restrictions on conduct. The *politics* of regulation follows from this directly coercive character of regulatory *policy.*

The best way to define the politics of regulatory policy, thus distinguishing it from the politics of promotional policy, is to compare the politics of nineteenth-century states to the politics of the nineteenth-century national government. Nineteenth-century national government policies were almost exclusively promotional. And the politics of the national government was very stable. It was dominated by political parties, and the individual and sectional conflicts that emerged could be settled peacefully, by logrolling, through the parties in Congress. The national government could expand and could subdivide government resources to meet the demands of individuals and groups. Thus, political conflict could be bought off or tabled until a future time. In contrast, the states in the nineteenth century were doing all of the regulating, and the political patterns of the states were highly unstable, constantly upset by demonstrations, large social movements, and frequent violence. In the less volatile moments, the politics of the states was dominated by interest groups, especially corporate interest groups.[12]

Group politics is the essence of "pluralism," and pluralism is the key to the politics of modern regulatory policy. In the 1930s, when the national government added a significant number of regulatory policies to its repertoire, it also added the *politics* of regulatory policy. And this was the time when "pluralist theory" of American political power became prominent.[13] Because pluralist politics was so public and drew so much attention to itself, a false impression was conveyed that the whole American system of politics was pluralistic. This belief was strengthened by the resemblance of modern pluralist patterns to the theory of James Madison, as set forth particularly in *The Federalist,* No. 10. According to Madison, in popular government, people divide into "factions," with each faction seeking its own satisfaction without any regard for the public interest. As long as there are many groups, with no one group or coalition of groups consistently dominating all the others, power will not become too concentrated, and all groups will be willing to conduct themselves within the constraints of the Constitution. Today these factions are called groups, interests, and power centers, and the competition among them leads to demands so that policies are adopted to

---

[12]Good accounts of the politics of the states in the nineteenth century will be found in V. O. Key, *American State Politics* (Westport, Conn.: Greenwood, 1983; orig. published 1956); V. O. Key, *Southern Politics in State and Nation,* 2nd ed. (Knoxville: University of Tennessee Press, 1984); Bernard L. Hyink and David H. Provost, *Politics and Government in California,* 16th ed. (New York: Longman, 2003); and Frances Fox Piven and Richard A. Cloward, *Poor People's Movements: Why They Succeed, How They Fail* (New York: Pantheon, 1977). For studies of political violence that show the particular affinity of violence to state politics, see Phillip Taft and Phillip Ross, "American Labor Violence: Its Causes, Character, and Outcome," in *The History of Violence in America: Historical and Comparative Perspectives,* ed. Hugh Davis Graham and Ted Robert Gurr (New York: Praeger, 1969); Robert Fogelson, "Violence as Protest," in *Proceedings of the Academy of Political Science* 29, no. 1 (1968); and on vigilantism, see Friedman, *A History of American Law,* pp. 318–22.

[13]For a brief intellectual history of the rise of pluralism as a theory and as an ideology, see Theodore J. Lowi, *The End of Liberalism: The Second Republic of the United States,* 2nd ed. (New York: W. W. Norton, 1979), Chapter 3.

mediate the conflicts. Groups seek to expand their power through lobbying Congress and through forming larger coalitions with other groups, either to dominate the political parties by overpowering electoral support with economic force or by making special arrangements with the parties.[14] Thus, while political parties and local districts have been at the very core of the politics of promotional policy, they have been far less important in the politics of regulatory policy. For example, groups organized around the steel interest, the cotton interest, small business, the trade unions, etc., cross electoral constituencies and, therefore, blur the lines of party politics and elections.

Maintaining a Stable and Strong Economy

A stable and strong economy is the basic goal of all economic policy. What makes reaching this goal so difficult is that the key elements of a strong economy—economic growth, full employment, and low inflation—often appear to conflict with one another. Economic policy must manage the trade-offs among these goals. This is a complicated task because there is much disagreement about whether pursuing one of these economic goals really does mean sacrificing the others. Moreover, the trade-offs among these goals appear to change over time. The expansion of the American economy in the latter half of the 1990s defied all previous expectations about the relationship between growth, employment, and inflation. The fast pace of economic growth, combined with low inflation and very high employment, suggested that it was now possible to combine all three central goals of economic policy.[15] In 2001, an economic downturn reminded policy makers how difficult it is to sustain such high levels of growth. Let us now turn to the actual policies designed to accomplish economic stability and growth.

Monetary Policies **Monetary policies** manipulate the growth of the entire economy by controlling the availability of money to banks. With a very few exceptions cited below, banks in the United States are privately owned and locally operated. Until well into the twentieth century, banks were regulated, if at all, by state legislatures. Each bank was granted a charter, giving it permission to make loans, hold deposits, and make investments. Although more than 25,000 banks continue to be state-chartered banks, they are less important than they used to be in the overall financial picture, as the most important banks now are members of the "federal system."

But banks did not become the core of American capitalism without intense political controversy. The Federalist majority in Congress, led by Alexander Hamilton, did in fact establish a Bank of the United States in 1791, but it was vigorously opposed by agrarian interests led by Thomas Jefferson, based on the fear that the

monetary policies Efforts to regulate the economy through manipulation of the supply of money and credit. America's most powerful institution in the area of monetary policy is the Federal Reserve Board.

---

[14]For the best theoretical statements of pluralism, see Robert A. Dahl, *A Preface to Democratic Theory* (Chicago: University of Chicago Press, 1956); and Robert A. Dahl and Charles E. Lindblom, *Politics, Economics and Welfare: Planning and Politico-economic Systems Resolved into Basic Social Processes* (New York: Harper, 1953).

[15]Louis Uchitelle, "107 Months, and Counting," *New York Times*, 30 January 2000, sec. 3, p. 1.

interests of urban, industrial capitalism would dominate such a bank. The Bank of the United States was terminated during the administration of Andrew Jackson; but the fear of a central, *public* bank still existed eight decades later, when Congress in 1913 established an institution—the **Federal Reserve System**—to integrate private banks into a single system. The Federal Reserve System did not become a central bank in the European tradition, but rather is composed of twelve Federal Reserve banks, each located in a major commercial city. The Federal Reserve banks are not ordinary banks; they are banker's banks, which make loans to other banks, clear checks, and supply the economy with currency and coins. They also play a regulatory role over the member banks. Every national bank must be a member of the Federal Reserve System; each must follow national banking rules and must purchase stock in the Federal Reserve System (which helps make the system self-financing). State banks and savings and loan associations may also join if they accept national rules. At the top of the system is the Federal Reserve Board—"the Fed"—comprising seven members appointed by the president (with Senate confirmation) for fourteen-year terms. The chairman of the Fed is selected by the president from among the seven members of the board for a four-year term. In all other concerns, however, the Fed is an independent agency inasmuch as its members cannot be removed during their terms except "for cause," and the president's executive power does not extend to them or their policies.

The major advantage of belonging to the federal system is that each member bank can borrow money from the Fed, using as collateral the notes on loans already made. This enables them to expand their loan operations continually, as long as there is demand for new loans. This ability of a member bank to borrow money from the Fed is a profoundly important monetary policy. The Fed charges interest, called a ***discount rate,*** on its loans to member banks.

If the Fed significantly decreases the discount rate—i.e., the interest it charges member banks when they come for new credit—that can be a very good shot in the arm of a sagging economy. During 2001, the Fed cut interest rates eleven times to combat the combined effects of recession and the terrorist attacks. If the Fed adopts a policy of higher discount rates, that will serve as a brake on the economy if it is expanding too fast, because the higher rate pushes up the interest rates charged by leading private banks to their customers.

Another monetary policy is one of increasing or decreasing the ***reserve requirement,*** which sets the actual proportion of deposited money that a bank must keep "on demand" as it makes all the rest of the deposits available as new loans.

A third important technique used by the Fed is ***open-market operations***—the buying and selling of Treasury securities to absorb excess dollars or to release more dollars into the economy.

Finally, a fourth power is derived from one of the important services rendered by the Federal Reserve System, which is the opportunity for member banks to borrow from each other. One of the original reasons for creating a Federal Reserve System was to balance regions of the country that might be vigorously expanding with other areas that might be fairly dormant: the national system would enable the banks in a growing region, facing lots of demand for credit, to borrow money from banks in regions of the country where the demand

Federal Reserve System (Fed) Consisting of twelve Federal Reserve Banks, this facilitates exchanges of cash, checks, and credit; it regulates member banks; and it uses monetary policies to fight inflation and deflation.

discount rate The interest rate charged by the Federal Reserve when commercial banks borrow in order to expand their lending operations. An effective tool of monetary policy.

reserve requirement The amount of liquid assets and ready cash that the Federal Reserve requires banks to hold to meet depositors' demands for their money. The ratio revolves above or below 20 percent of all deposits, with the rest being available for new loans.

open-market operations The process whereby the Open Market Committee of the Federal Reserve buys and sells government securities etc. to help finance government operations and to loosen or tighten the total amount of credit circulating in the economy.

for credit is much lower. This exchange is called the "federal funds market," and the interest rate charged by one bank to another, the *federal funds rate,* can be manipulated just like the discount rate, to expand or contract credit.

The federal government also provides insurance to foster credit and encourage private capital investment. The Federal Deposit Insurance Corporation (FDIC) protects bank deposits up to $100,000. Another important promoter of investment is the federal insurance of home mortgages through the Department of Housing and Urban Development (HUD). By federally guaranteeing mortgages, the government reduces the risks that banks run in making such loans, thus allowing banks to lower their interest rates and make such loans more affordable to middle- and lower-income families. These programs have enabled millions of families who could not have otherwise afforded it to finance the purchase of a home.

Fiscal Policies   *Fiscal policies* include the government's taxing and spending powers. Personal and corporate income taxes, which raise most government revenues, are the most prominent examples. While the direct purpose of an income tax is to raise revenue, each tax has a different impact on the economy, and government can plan for the impact (see Process Box 14.1). For example, although the main reason favoring a significant increase in the Social Security tax (which is an income tax) under President Carter was to keep Social Security solvent, a big reason for it in the minds of many legislators was that it would reduce inflation by shrinking the amount of money people had in their hands to buy more goods and services.

Likewise, President Clinton's commitment in his 1992 campaign to a "middle-class tax cut" was motivated by the goal of encouraging economic growth through increased consumption. Soon after the election, upon learning that the deficit would be far larger than had been earlier reported to him, he confessed he would have to break his promise of such a tax cut. Nevertheless, the idea of a middle-class tax cut is an example of a fiscal policy aimed at increased consumption because of the theory that people in middle-income brackets tend to spend a high proportion of unexpected earnings or windfalls, rather than saving or investing them.[16]

Taxation   All   taxes discriminate, leaving to public policy the question of *what kind* of discrimination is called for. The tariff—a tax on imported goods—was the most important tax of the nineteenth century, and the "tax policy" of the tariff put most of the burden of raising revenue on foreigners seeking to export their goods to America. This policy was designed to protect our "infant industries" against the more advanced foreign competitors of the day, the implicit assumption being that the tariff would disappear once our industries were no longer in their infancy.

The most important tax of the twentieth century, and indeed the most important choice Congress ever made about taxation (or about any policy, for that

federal funds rate   The interest rate on loans between banks that the Federal Reserve Board influences by affecting the supply of money available.

 Institution Principle
The autonomy of the Federal Reserve System is a significant design feature of this institution, allowing it either to stimulate or to put a brake on the economy, depending upon economic circumstances, without the explicit concurrence of other branches of government.

fiscal policies The use of taxing, monetary, and spending powers to manipulate the economy.

---

[16]For a fascinating behind-the-scenes look at how and why President Clinton abandoned his campaign commitment to tax cuts and economic stimulus, and instead accepted the fiscal conservatism advocated by the Federal Reserve and its chairman, Alan Greenspan, see Bob Woodward, *The Agenda: Inside the Clinton White House* (New York: Simon and Schuster, 1994).

The Federal Reserve Board as a Political Institution

Alan Greenspan, chairman of the Federal Reserve since 1987, is one of those rare political actors who are praised by both liberals and conservatives. He was appointed by Ronald Reagan, reappointed by Republicans George Bush, Sr. and George Bush, Jr. and Democrat Bill Clinton. Economists from the Right, such as Milton Friedman, and the Left, such as James Tobin, sing his praises.[17] What can Greenspan's long and successful political career teach us about the principles of politics?

The fifth principle of politics teaches us that a series of coincidental events can easily build an irreversible historical path. Part of Greenspan's political success is due to sheer luck. He was chairman of the Fed during the 1990s, a period of unprecedented economic expansion. And he was head of the central bank in the world's largest and most powerful capitalist nation when other competing economic systems seemed to fade away as historical relics.

Economic growth during the 1990s was so impressive that it led the *New York Times* to argue in 2003 for Greenspan's reappointment to a *fifth* term, describing him as the architect of one of the great economic booms in American history.

But is Greenspan really a "political" success? What is "political" about the Federal Reserve? The rules and procedures governing the Federal Reserve are supposed to shield it from politics, but in practice these same rules have made the Fed a powerful political institution.

The authors of the 1913 legislation that set up the Federal Reserve felt that it was vital to insulate monetary policy from undue pressure and influence by partisan politicians obsessed with their own short-range re-election prospects. The Federal Reserve was set up along the lines of an independent regulatory commission, not as just one more agency under the direction of the president and supervised by Congress.

The Federal Reserve System's highest decision-making body is the Board of Governors, consisting of seven members. Members are nominated for their positions by the president of the United States and must be confirmed by the Senate. The members serve long terms (fourteen years) and, once appointed, may not be removed from office except through a cumbersome process of impeachment for personal violations of criminal law. The people selected have nearly always been professional bankers, executives of Wall Street brokerage houses, or occasionally professional economists.[18]

These rules by themselves make the Fed and its chair politically powerful. Economic policy, as you learned in this chapter, is inseparable from politics. The members of the Board of Governors can ignore short-run political pressures; after all, they are in office for fourteen years. The chair is more prone to pressure. Still, his appointment is for four years, purposely designed to be distinct from the presidential and congressional election calendars. Finally, many political institutions struggle with the principal-agent problem, but it is not clear that the Fed is the agent for anyone. In both theory and practice, the Federal

Reserve represents the interests of the "economy." This gives the Fed a great deal of autonomy.

The internal rules of the Fed strengthen its hand vis-à-vis other political institutions. The Federal Reserve Board is a small group of generally like-minded economic experts who benefit from all the advantages of a small, homogeneous group. And, unlike the executive branch and especially the Congress, the deliberations of the Federal Reserve are purposely kept secret. This is done for good economic reasons: if the deliberations of the board were made public too soon, they could roil economic markets. But secrecy is a powerful tool. As we know from the second principle of politics, homogeneity, small size, and confidentiality make it far easier for a group to bargain, negotiate, and reach a collective decision.

Contrast this with the annual debate over the federal budget. Budget politics in recent years have put Congress on display before the American people, and the picture has not been pretty. In the most recent session of Congress (2003), only one defense bill managed to pass both the Senate and the House. It was only the specter of another government shutdown that convinced members in both chambers to pass a reconciliation bill that kept the government running for another year. Who would you trust with your money—Alan Greenspan, with his owlish glasses, confident demeanor, and nonpartisan pose, or 535 argumentative, noisy, and partisan members of Congress?

But don't believe that Alan Greenspan or the Board of Governors of the Federal Reserve are not political actors. Like the Supreme Court, the Federal Reserve Board and its chairman are acutely sensitive to political currents. In 1992, Greenspan, who refused to cut interest rates rapidly enough to encourage an economic recovery, was blamed for George Bush, Sr.'s defeat. But Greenspan, a lifelong Republican, quickly warmed to Bill Clinton and convinced the president to become a deficit hawk in the mid-1990s, even if it meant increasing taxes. In early 2001, however, Greenspan suddenly became an advocate of lowered tax rates, conveniently the same policy promoted by the newly elected George Bush, Jr.

The rules and procedures of the Federal Reserve serve to insulate it from rapid political changes. Combine this with historical events over the past two decades and the adroit political antenna of Chairman Greenspan, and the Federal Reserve has quietly become one of the most powerful institutions in the American government, if not in the world economy.

[17]You can learn more about Greenspan's life and career in Bob Woodward's *Maestro: Greenspan's Fed and the American Boom* (New York: Simon & Schuster, 2000) and Justin Martin's *Greenspan: The Man behind the Money* (Cambridge, Mass.: Perseus, 2001).

[18]Federal Reserve Act of 1913. See also James Livingston, *Origins of the Federal Reserve System: Money, Class, and Corporate Capitalism, 1890–1913* (Ithaca, N.Y.: Cornell University Press, 1986) and William Greider, *Secrets of the Temple: How the Federal Reserve Runs the Country* (New York: Simon & Schuster, 1987).

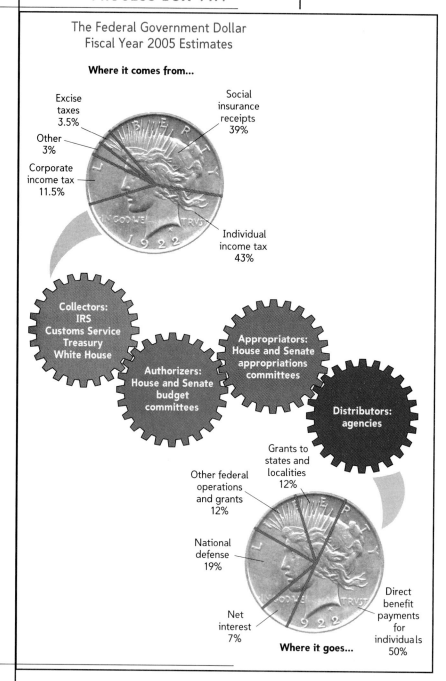

The Federal Government Dollar
Fiscal Year 2005 Estimates

Where it comes from...

Excise taxes 3.5%

Social insurance receipts 39%

Other 3%

Corporate income tax 11.5%

Individual income tax 43%

Collectors:
IRS
Customs Service
Treasury
White House

Authorizers:
House and Senate budget committees

Appropriators:
House and Senate appropriations committees

Distributors:
agencies

Grants to states and localities 12%

Other federal operations and grants 12%

National defense 19%

Direct benefit payments for individuals 50%

Net interest 7%

Where it goes...

SOURCE: Office of Management and Budget, *Budget of the United States Government, Fiscal Year 2005* (Washington, D.C.: Government Printing Office, 2003), pp. 32, 117.

matter), was the decision to raise revenue by taxing personal and corporate incomes—the "income tax."[19] The second most important policy choice Congress made was that the income tax be "progressive" or "graduated," with the heaviest burden carried by those most able to pay. A tax is called ***progressive*** if the rate of taxation goes up with each higher income bracket. A tax is called ***regressive*** if people in lower income brackets pay a higher proportion of their income toward the tax than people in higher income brackets. For example, a sales tax is deemed regressive because everybody pays at the same rate, so that the proportion of total income paid in taxes goes down as the total income goes up (assuming, as is generally the case, that as total income goes up the amount spent on sales-taxable purchases increases at a lower rate). The Social Security tax is another example of a regressive tax. Current law applies a tax of 6.2 percent on the first $87,900 of income for the retirement program and an additional 1.45 percent on all income (without limit) for Medicare benefits, for a total of 7.65 percent in Social Security taxes. This means that a person earning an income of $87,900 pays $6,724.35 in Social Security taxes, a rate of 7.65 percent. But someone earning nearly twice that income, $150,000, pays a total of $7,624.80 in Social Security taxes, the equivalent of a 5.1 percent rate on the entire income. As income continues to rise, the amount of Social Security taxes also rises, but the *rate*, or the percentage of income that goes to taxes, declines.

The graduated income tax is a moderately progressive tax; in other words, as it collects revenue, it pursues a deliberate ***policy of redistribution,*** although moderately redistributive. Table 14.1 demonstrates the success of this policy. Before genuine progressive income taxation was instituted in the 1930s, the disparity between the lowest income bracket and the highest reached its widest stretch, almost 46 percentage points (see Table 14.1). From the 1930s through the 1970s, this gap was reduced. Beginning in the 1980s, however, the gap began to increase again, and it is no coincidence that big across-the-board income tax cuts were adopted in 1981 and 1986. The tax cuts of 2001 and 2003 will accelerate this trend.[20]

Redistribution of wealth is not the only policy being pursued by the American personal and corporate income tax. Another important policy imbedded in that tax is the encouragement of the capitalist economy. When the tax law allows individuals or companies to deduct from their taxable income any money they can justify as an investment or as a "business expense," that is an incentive to individuals and companies to spend money to expand their production, their advertising,

progressive taxation Taxation that hits the upper income brackets more heavily.

regressive taxation Taxation that hits the lower income brackets more heavily.

policy of redistribution An objective of the graduated income tax—to raise revenue in such a way as to reduce the disparities of wealth between the lowest and the highest income brackets.

[19]The U.S. government imposed an income tax during the Civil War that remained in effect until 1872. In 1894, Congress enacted a modest 2 percent tax upon all incomes over $4,000. This $4,000 exemption was in fact fairly high, excluding all working-class people. But in 1895, the Supreme Court declared it unconstitutional, citing the provision of Article I, Section 9, that any direct tax would have to be proportional to the population in each state. See Pollock v. Farmers' Loan and Trust Company, 158 U.S. 601 (1895). In 1913, the Sixteenth Amendment was ratified, effectively reversing the *Pollock* case.

[20]The redistributive effect of the income tax would probably have been even more marked if it had not been neutralized to an extent by other regressive taxes such as Social Security taxes, state sales taxes, many federal excise taxes, and tariffs.

TABLE 14.1

Income Distribution in the United States
(1929–2002): The Proportion of Money Income
Going to Each Fifth of the Population

FAMILY INCOME BRACKET	1929	1934	1944	1950	1960	1970	1980	1990	2002
Lowest fifth	5.4	5.9	4.9	4.5	4.8	4.1	4.3	3.9	3.5
Second fifth	10.1	11.5	10.9	12.0	12.2	10.8	10.3	9.6	8.8
Third fifth	14.4	15.5	16.2	17.4	17.8	17.4	16.9	15.9	14.8
Fourth fifth	18.8	20.4	22.2	23.5	24.0	24.5	24.9	24.0	23.3
Highest fifth	51.3	49.7	45.8	42.6	41.3	43.3	43.7	46.6	49.7
Gap between lowest and highest fifths	45.9	43.8	40.9	38.1	36.5	39.2	39.4	42.7	46.2

Figures are not strictly comparable because of differences in calculating procedures.
SOURCES: Data for the period 1929–50 are from Allan Rosenbaum, "State Government, Political Power, and Public Policy: The Case of Illinois" (Ph.D. diss., University of Chicago, 1974), Chapters 10–11, used by permission. Figures for 1960–2002 are from the U.S. Department of Commerce, Bureau of the Census, *Income in the United States Current Population Reports, 2002* Series P-60 (Washington D.C.: Government Printing Office, 2003).

or their staff, and it reduces the income taxes they pay. These kinds of deductions are called incentives or "equity" by those who support them. For others, they might be called "loopholes." The tax laws of the 1980s actually closed a number of important loopholes. But others still exist—on home mortgages, including second homes, and on business expenses, for example—and others will return, because there is a strong consensus among members of Congress that businesses often need such incentives. They may differ on which incentives are best, but there is almost universal agreement in government that some incentives are justifiable.[21]

The tax reform laws of 1981 and 1986 significantly reduced the progressiveness of the federal income tax. Drastic rate reductions were instituted in 1986; and before Bush's 2001 reform, there were five tax brackets, ranging from a

[21]For a systematic account of the role of government in providing incentives and inducements to business, see Charles E. Lindblom, *Politics and Markets: The World's Political Economic Systems* (New York: Basic Books, 1977), Chapter 13. For a detailed account of the dramatic Reagan tax cuts and reforms, see Jeffrey H. Birnbaum and Alan S. Murray, *Showdown at Gucci Gulch: Lawmakers, Lobbyists, and the Unlikely Triumph of Tax Reform* (New York: Random House, 1987).

15-percent tax on those in the lowest income bracket to 39.6 percent on those in the highest income bracket. Prior to the 1980s, the highest tax brackets sometimes were taxed at a rate of 90 percent on the last $1 million of taxable income earned in a given year. Meanwhile, Social Security taxes—the most regressive taxes of all—remain high and are likely to be increased.

In every presidential election year, both Democrats and Republicans try to woo voters with pledges of tax cuts. In 2001, Bush made good on his promise to introduce major tax cuts. Although congressional Democrats believed that the administration's proposal benefited the wealthy and jeopardized the budget surplus, they eventually agreed on a compromise bill. The bill reduced taxes at all levels of income (although less than Bush had initially proposed), creating a new bottom bracket of 10 percent and reducing the tax rate in each of the other five brackets. In the highest bracket, taxes were cut from 39.6 percent to 35 percent. Most controversial was the provision to repeal the estate tax, a tax that has historically been seen as a way to prevent the emergence of a monied aristocracy in the United States. Reflecting the uneasy compromise that allowed the bill to pass, many of the provisions were slated to phase in over time. The estate tax repeal, for example, does not take effect until 2010. Moreover, all the provisions were subject to a "sunset" provision that automatically repeals the legislation in 2010 unless Congress renews it. Faced with the new budgetary demands of the war on terrorism and a budget deficit, congressional Democrats argued that the Bush tax reform had left the government with insufficient resources. Some urged that the reform be repealed, but Democratic leaders held back, fearing that they would be charged with raising taxes.

Government Spending   The federal government's power to spend is one of the most important tools of economic policy. Decisions about how much to spend affect the overall health of the economy. They also affect every aspect of American life from the distribution of income through the availability of different modes of transportation to the level of education in society. Not surprisingly, the fight for control over spending is one of the most contentious in Washington, as interest groups and politicians strive to create a healthy economy and determine the priorities and appropriate levels of spending. Decisions about spending are made as part of the annual budget process. During the 1990s, when the federal *budget deficit* became a major political issue and when parties were deeply split on spending, the budget process became the focal point of the entire policy-making process. Even though the budget deficit disappeared in the late 1990s, the budget continued to dominate the attention of policy makers. With the deficit on the rise again after September 11, budget politics are sure to remain on the national agenda.

budget deficit
Amount by which government spending exceeds government revenue in a fiscal year.

The president and Congress have each created institutions to assert control over the budget process. The Office of Management and Budget (OMB) in the Executive Office of the President is responsible for preparing the president's budget. This budget contains the president's spending priorities and the estimated costs of the president's policy proposals. It is viewed as the starting point for the annual debate over the budget. When different parties control the presidency and Congress, the president's budget may have little influence on the budget that is ultimately adopted. Members of the president's own party also may have different priorities. In 2002, members of Congress from both parties resisted the president's efforts to cut spending for domestic programs. A key Republican staffer defended congressional prerogatives to shape the budget, declaring, "Our job is not to rubber-stamp what OMB says."[22]

Congress has its own budget institutions. Congress created the Congressional Budget Office (CBO) in 1974 so that it could have reliable information about the costs and economic impact of the policies it considers. At the same time, Congress set up a budget process designed to establish spending priorities and to consider individual expenditures in light of the entire budget. A key element of the process is the annual budget resolution, which designates broad targets for spending. By estimating the costs of policy proposals, Congress hoped to control spending and to reduce deficits. When the congressional budget process proved unable to hold down deficits in the 1980s, Congress instituted stricter measures to control spending, including "spending caps" that limit spending on some types of programs.

A very large and growing proportion of the annual federal budget is **mandatory spending,** expenditures that are, in the words of the OMB, "relatively uncontrollable." Interest payments on the national debt, for example, are determined by the actual size of the national debt. Legislation has mandated payment rates for such programs as retirement under Social Security, retirement for federal employees, unemployment assistance, Medicare, and farm price supports (see Figure 14.1). These payments increase with the cost of living; they increase as the average age of the population goes up; they increase as national and world agricultural surpluses go up. In 1970, 38.6 percent of the total federal budget was made up of these **uncontrollables;** in 1975, 52.5 percent fell into that category; and by 2001, around 64.7 percent was in the uncontrollable category. This means that the national government now has very little **discretionary spending** to increase or decrease spending to counteract fluctuations in the business cycle.

This has a profound political implication. With mandatory, or relatively uncontrollable, spending on the rise, there is less scope for the exercise of discretion. If a budget has to be cut and categories of mandatory spending are taken off the table, then the cuts will disproportionately fall on what remains. With the pain of cutting "available" programs, the prospects for distributing the cuts in a manner acceptable to all interested parties grow dim. Thus, the politics will be more intense and dirty; groups will be more highly mobilized, energized, and at one another's throats; Congress and the president will be eyeball to eyeball as they seek to protect their different constituencies; and political partisans will not be in the mood for compromise.[23]

[22]Karen Masterson, "Bush's Budget Promise Goes Bust," *Houston Chronicle,* 7 May 2002, p. A1.

[23]Of course, it should be underscored that "relatively uncontrollable" is itself a policy decision taken by the president and Congress. It is not carved in granite; it can be undone. To undo some things, like not making a promised payment on the national debt, would have horrible consequences in credit markets. A modest across-the-board reduction in outlays for hospital assistance under Medicare, on the other hand, while painful (literally and figuratively), might nevertheless be accommodated (with hospitals and patients sharing the burden in various ways—e.g., deferral of elective procedures, delaying a salary increase, etc.). That is, things that are alleged to be "off the table" can be put right back on the table.

FIGURE 14.1

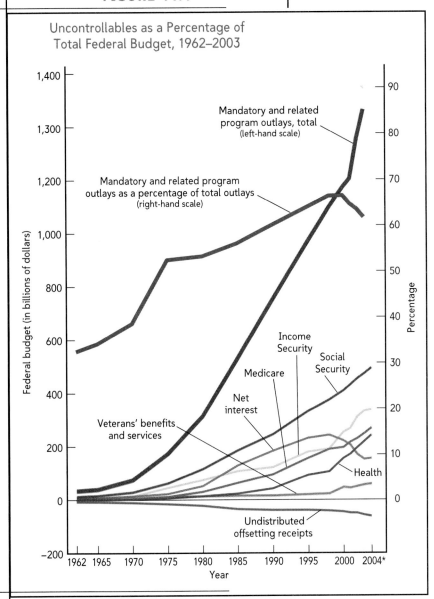

Uncontrollables as a Percentage of Total Federal Budget, 1962–2003

SOURCE: Office of Management and Budget, *Budget of the U.S. Government, Fiscal Year 2005. Historical Tables* (Washington, D.C.: Government Printing Office, 2004), pp. 45, 125, 129.

Government spending as a fiscal policy works fairly well when deliberate deficit spending is used to stop a recession and to speed up the recovery period. But it does not work very well in fighting inflation because elected politicians are politically unable to make the drastic expenditure cuts necessary to balance the budget, much less to produce a budgetary surplus.

The Politics of Redistributive Policy   Redistributive policies seek to control citizens by manipulating their environment rather than by attempting to control their conduct directly. For example, a small percentage change in the interest rate can immediately affect millions of potential homeowners or investors; a change of the top income-tax rate from 39.6 percent to 35.0 percent can be equally effective. Yet in neither of these examples do citizens have to "do" anything to come within the jurisdiction of the law.

This kind of policy illustrates a different kind of political pattern (see Process Box 14.2). One theory describing the politics of redistributive policy is called the "power elite" theory. Offered by many social scientists as a general theory of power in a capitalist nation, it has turned out to be very weak as a general theory but quite strong and accurate as a theory limited to the politics of redistributive policy. According to the power-elite theory, the most important decisions for the society are made by a small political elite, generally composed of individuals and families who enjoy the highest incomes and status of the society. These individuals and families tend to be drawn from (1) corporate leadership, (2) the occupants of the highest political positions, and (3) the highest echelons of the defense establishment. Although these may appear to be distinct sectors of society, power-elite theory holds that they constitute a single elite because these people tend to know each other, go to the same elite schools, and share a general consensus on long-range objectives for the society.[24]

> **Policy Principle**
>
> Redistributive policies reflect the interests of elected leaders in getting re-elected.

The power-elite theory of redistributive politics, however, begs the obvious question: What motivates the power elite? An alternative answer more in line with the rationality principle is that tax policy reflects the interests of elected politicians in being re-elected. If politicians deciding on tax rates are motivated by re-election and the median voter's income is more than the average, the tax system will be less redistributive. Likewise, if the median voter's income is less than the average, the tax system will be more redistributive.[25]

[24]C. Wright Mills, *The Power Elite* (New York: Oxford University Press, 1956); Kenneth Prewitt and Alan Stone, *The Ruling Elites: Elite Theory, Power, and American Democracy* (New York: Harper & Row, 1973); and G. William Domhoff, *Who Rules America Now? A View for the '80s* (Englewood Cliffs, N.J.: Prentice Hall, 1983).

[25]See Allan H. Meltzer and Scott F. Richard, "A Rational Theory of the Size of Government," *Journal of Political Economy* 89 (1981): 914–27.

How Political Patterns Vary among the Three Types of Policy

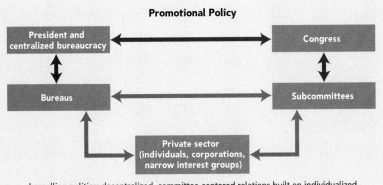

Promotional Policy

Logrolling politics; decentralized, committee-centered relations built on individualized demands; narrow interests

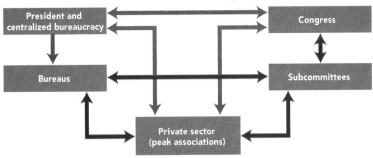

Redistributive Policy

Power-elite politics; few power centers, concentrate on executive branch; ideology strongest here; interests broadest, society-wide

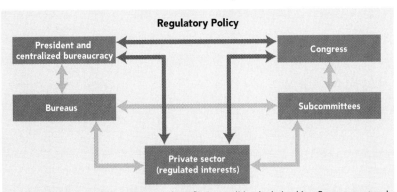

Regulatory Policy

Pluralistic politics; many power centers, with conflictive, coalitional relationships; Congress-centered, less logrolling, more direct compromise; private-sector-level interests overshadow ideology

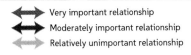

Very important relationship
Moderately important relationship
Relatively unimportant relationship

Rationality Principle	Collective Action Principle	Institution Principle	Policy Principle	History Principle
Public policies create incentives for people to alter the direction or intensity of their behavior.	Government has lots of tools that affect the economy, but there is considerable political conflict over which tools to use, how to use them, and when to use them. Government involvement in the economy thus provides opportunities for groups to mobilize in order to become winners or to avoid becoming losers.	Government can play an important role in establishing the rules and institutions that allow a market economy to function.	Because institutional arrangements make change difficult, public policies are durable.	Historical events can motivate government officials to adopt new policies.
Even if governments seek to "do good," this does not prevent rational politicians from searching for opportunities to take care of their constituents.		American political institutions, particularly the U.S. Congress, allow promotional policies to take the form of pork-barrel legislation through vote trading, logrolling, and omnibus bills.	In promotional policies, political actors seek to distribute funds and projects to their political supporters.	The scope of national regulatory policies expanded during the 1930s, 1960s, and early 1970s, but contracted during the late 1970s to mid-1990s.
		The autonomy of the Federal Reserve System is a significant design feature of this institution, allowing it either to stimulate or to put a brake on the economy, depending upon economic circumstances, without the explicit concurrence of other branches of government.	The politics of regulatory policy tends to be dominated by interest groups, especially those that might be regulated by government. Redistributive policies reflect the interests of elected leaders in getting re-elected.	The budget reflects not only future policy priorities, it mirrors past decisions as well. The historical accumulation of policy promises is ultimately reflected in the cumulative debt that must be "serviced" each year by interest payments.

SUMMARY

To study public policy is to understand government in action, to see how government seeks to control the population by creating incentives for people to alter their behavior. Public policy is a synonym for law, and the use of public policy has become more widespread over the years, probably because it seems more reciprocal, humane, and changeable in response to demands—in a word, democratic.

The first major section of this chapter defined market economy and the conditions needed for creating a modern free market. This was followed by a discussion of the substantive goals of public policies within a market economy—that is, the objectives people seek through government—the tools government utilizes to achieve these goals, and the political patterns typically at work in achieving them. We began with the most fundamental type of policy: public order and private property. Virtually everyone supports these policies, even though people may differ on how much they want and how they want the policies implemented. We went on to another policy also widely and strongly defended in the United States: supporting and maintaining business development. This includes regulating the market, a restrictive approach but one motivated by the goal of making markets more stable and more competitive, not eliminating them. Deregulation is, of course, an aspect of regulation. All of these policies have one major objective—to maintain not only a market economy, but also a sound and fiscally responsible capitalist economy.

FOR FURTHER READING

Birnbaum, Jeffrey H., and Alan S. Murray. *Showdown at Gucci Gulch: Lawmakers, Lobbyists, and the Unlikely Triumph of Tax Reform.* New York: Random House, 1987.

Cochran, Clarke E., Lawrence C. Mayer, T. R. Curr, and N. Joseph Cayer. *American Public Policy: An Introduction,* 7th ed. New York: St. Martin's Press, 2003.

Derthick, Martha, and Paul J. Quirk. *The Politics of Deregulation.* Washington, D.C.: Brookings Institution, 1985.

Greider, William. *Secrets of the Temple: How the Federal Reserve Runs the Country.* New York: Simon & Schuster, 1987.

Heilbroner, Robert L. *The Nature and Logic of Capitalism.* New York: W. W. Norton, 1985.

Holmes, Stephen, and Cass R. Sunstein. *The Cost of Rights: Why Liberty Depends on Taxes.* New York: W. W. Norton, 1999.

Krugman, Paul R. *Peddling Prosperity: Economic Sense and Nonsense in the Age of Diminished Expectations.* New York: W. W. Norton, 1994.

Levy, Frank. *The New Dollars and Dreams: American Incomes and Economic Change.* New York: Russell Sage Foundation, 1998.

Lindblom, Charles. *Politics and Markets: The World's Political Economic Systems.* New York: Basic Books, 1977.

Suskind, Ron. *The Price of Loyalty: George W. Bush, the White House, and the Education of Paul O'Neill.* New York: Simon & Schuster, 2004.

Vogel, David. *Fluctuating Fortunes: The Political Power of Business in America.* New York: Basic Books, 1989.

Politics in the News—
Reading between the Lines

The Partisan Politics of Budget Deficits and Surpluses

Both Sides May Be Wrong About The Budget

By DAVID E. ROSENBAUM

Listening to senators and representatives argue about the budget this month, one might have thought that the future of the United States economy was hanging in the balance. * * *

Senator Don Nickles, the Oklahoma Republican who is chairman of the Budget Committee, declared: "The economy has not been growing. Frankly, we will never balance the budget if the economy is not growing. This budget allows and provides for a growth package."

But no sooner had Mr. Nickles sat down than Senator Kent Conrad of North Dakota, the top Democrat on the committee, took the floor, calling the budget "radical, reckless, dangerous and extreme."

"The best economists in America tell us that this budget proposal hurts long-term economic growth and threatens our economic security," Mr. Conrad said.

So which side is right? The budget plan adopted by lawmakers would allow deep tax cuts, at least $350 billion and up to $550 billion over 10

years, mostly for the well off. It would place no reins on spending for automatic benefits like Social Security and Medicare, which account for two-thirds of federal outlays. But it would strictly limit other domestic programs, from national parks to education, which are less than 15 percent of the total.

Would that lead to an economic boom, as the Republicans have held, or cripple the economy, as the Democrats have argued?

The answer, which could never have been gleaned by listening to the Congressional debate, is probably neither. In a report last month that went largely unnoticed with all the war news, the Congressional Budget Office, which provides Congress with impartial, expert economic counsel, concluded that President Bush's tax and spending plan "would provide a relatively small impetus in an economy the size of the United States's." * * *

The budget was indeed important, but not because of its effect on the economy. All the talk about the wisdom

New York Times, 27 April 2003, sec. 3, p. 4.

of tax cuts and the dangers of deficits was a smoke screen masking the fundamental philosophical divide that has separated Democrats and Republicans since the New Deal.

Republican politicians, by and large, want to shrink the role of the government outside the military. They have never much cared for Social Security and Medicare, the crown jewels of Democratic lawmaking. They dislike most aid to education, environmental regulations and labor laws. They want to cut taxes not so much to buoy the economy as to take money away from the government. Budget deficits, in the Republican view, are better than surpluses. If there is extra money, they believe, the government will waste it.

Democratic politicians generally want to expand the government other than the military. They want universal medical insurance and more generous Medicare benefits. They want more environmental protection and stricter regulation of business. They are comfortable with high income taxes because the poor and the middle class bear little of the burden. And most worry about budget deficits, not because of their economic effect but because deficits prevent the government from offering more services. If the deficits expected over the next decade grew out of a new national insurance program, say, instead of income-tax cuts, few Democrats would complain.

People outside of politics see room for compromise—perhaps a one-year tax cut limited to the middle class, rather than the 10-year plan skewed to the wealthy. Or a prescription drug plan under Medicare that is more generous than what the Republicans envision but less sweeping than the Democrats' version. Or permission for some new oil and gas exploration in Alaska in exchange for tougher auto mileage standards.

ESSENCE OF THE STORY

- Republicans argue that continued tax cuts, as were proposed by President Bush, are critical to the long-term economic health of the nation. Democrats argue that the tax cuts, plus war expenditures, have resulted in a large deficit that threatens the economy.

- A nonpartisan analysis undercuts both sides. The tax and spending cuts are too small, in the context of the U.S. economy, to make much of a difference.

- The argument over tax and spending is a mask for deeper partisan disagreements on the proper role of government.

POLITICAL ANALYSIS

- The return of deficit politics in Washington has changed the political calculus of the new decade. With a growing pie, as in the 1990s, collective action—such as passing tax and spending bills—is easier because you can just cut off a "new slice." But deficits mean that either spending must be decreased, taxes increased, or the deficit raised. It is far harder to broker agreements in this environment.

- The fight we see in the press and on the floor of the House and Senate, such as the first over Bush's tax cuts, often masks deeper fights over ideology and governing philosophy. It is always important to try to understand the deeper divisions that may lurk beneath the surface of many political conflicts.

- Political leaders are often more extreme on partisan and ideological issues than the public that elected them. This means that political actors disagree on points that the mass public seems to believe should be grounds for compromise. Some suggest this leads to long-term public disenchantment with politicians and political institutions.

But senators and representatives tend to be rooted at the edges of the ideological spectrum. That leaves little space for compromise. It leads them to talk past one another, just as they did in the budget debate.

CHAPTER

15

Government and Society

Social policies promote a range of public goals. The first is to protect against the risks and insecurities that most people face over the course of their lives. Theses include illness, disability, temporary unemployment, and the reduced earning capability that comes with old age. Most spending on social welfare in the United States goes to programs such as Social Security and medical insurance for the elderly that serve these purposes. These are widely regarded as successful and popular programs. They are the least controversial areas of social spending, although the debates about funding Social Security reveal that even widely agreed-upon policies can generate conflict. Such conflicts over how to achieve security against risks have prevented the United States from adopting universal health insurance. Despite the fact that most Americans support a public role in guaranteeing health coverage, disputes over how this should be done have blocked repeated efforts at health reform.

More controversial have been the other two goals of social policy: promoting *equality of opportunity* and assisting the poor. While Americans admire the ideal of equal opportunity, there is no general agreement about what government

equality of opportunity
A universally shared American ideal that all have the freedom to use whatever talents and wealth they have to reach their fullest potential.

should do to address inequalities of results: groups that have suffered from past inequality generally support much more extensive government action to promote equality of opportunity than do others. Yet most Americans support some government action, especially in the area of education.

The third goal of social policy—to alleviate poverty—has long generated controversy in the United States. Americans take pride in their strong work ethic and prize the value of self-sufficiency. As a result, the majority of Americans express suspicions that the able-bodied poor will not try hard enough to support themselves if they are offered too much assistance or if they receive the wrong kind of assistance. Yet there is also recognition that poverty may be the product of past inequality of opportunity. Since the 1960s, a variety of educational programs and income assistance policies have sought to end poverty and promote equal opportunity. Much progress has been made toward these goals. However, the disproportionate rates of poverty among minorities suggest that our policies have not solved the problem of unequal opportunity. Likewise, the high rates of child poverty challenge us to find new ways to assist the poor.

There is no way to know precisely when the government ought to be called upon and what the government ought to do to help individuals secure the right to pursue their own happiness. Economic and social transformations pose new challenges and often alter public views about what government should do. In the 1930s, a deep and widespread economic depression created broad public support for new programs such as federal unemployment insurance. Today, the increased numbers of women in the labor force and the growth in single-parent households have prompted calls for more government assistance to help people combine work and family responsibilities more effectively. Yet there is no agreement on what government should do. Likewise, as the economy has changed, inequality among working people has grown. Should the government address such inequality? If so, with what measures? Shifting patterns of risk and opportunity provoke new demands from citizens and, in so doing, place social-policy issues at the center of national politics.

The first section of this chapter will deal with policies concerned with economic insecurity. Most of these come under the conventional label of "social welfare policy" or "the welfare system."

CHAPTER OUTLINE

The History of the Social Welfare System

What Are the Foundations of the Social Welfare System?

• Social Security

• Medicare

• Public Assistance Programs

Analyzing the Welfare System

• Arguments against It

• Arguments for It

How Can Government Create Opportunity?

• Education Policies

• Health Policies

Who Is Poor? What Can Government Do?

We will also look at how the welfare system is financed. Then we will analyze who benefits from social policies and also assess how effectively welfare policies help the poor. Last, we will look at policies aimed at permanently changing the status of America's poorest citizens. Through education, job training, housing assistance, and health care, governments in America help the poor break the cycle of poverty.

THE HISTORY OF THE SOCIAL WELFARE SYSTEM

PREVIEWING THE PRINCIPLES

After the Great Depression and the New Deal, the national government assumed greater responsibility for opening opportunity and addressing poverty. Since that time, the number of Americans receiving direct government benefits has increased with the creation of new social welfare programs such as Medicaid. Critics of the social welfare system have argued that it creates a moral hazard by providing the wrong incentives to its recipients. But reducing the social welfare system may prove to be difficult for two reasons. First, contributory programs like Social Security have the support of millions of active political participants, who can mobilize against any attempt to cut these programs. Second, the Supreme Court has established the concept of entitlement and has created legal obstacles to terminating noncontributory programs.

Americans do not have a long history of taking public responsibility for inequalities of opportunity. First, our faith in individualism was extremely strong. Second, this was fed by the existence of the frontier, which was so enticing that poverty was seen as a temporary condition that could be alleviated by moving westward. Third, Americans conceived of poverty as belonging in two separate classes, the "deserving poor" and the "undeserving poor." The deserving poor were the widows, orphans, and others rendered dependent by some misfortune beyond their control such as national disaster, injury in the course of honest labor, or effects of war. The undeserving poor were able-bodied persons unwilling to work, transients from their communities, or others of whom, for various reasons, the community did not approve. An extensive system of private charity developed during the nineteenth century on the basis of this distinction between the deserving poor and the undeserving poor. Most of this kind of welfare went through churches, related religious groups, and, to an extent, ethnic and fraternal societies. This was called charity, or "Christian love," which was often coupled with a high moral sense of obligation.

Until the end of the nineteenth century, government involvement in charitable activities, or what we today call welfare, was slight, not only because of America's preference for individual endeavors and for private and voluntary approaches to charity, but also because Americans believed that all of the deserving poor would be taken care of by private efforts. Congress did enact pensions for Civil War veterans and their dependents; and for its day, this was considered a generous social policy. But these pension policies were badly undercut by a patronage-ridden administration of the benefits, thus damaging the system and depriving a large segment of American citizens of federal aid.[1] Congress also attempted to reach the lower-income groups with policies that would eliminate child labor, and a number of states joined in with attempts to eliminate the most egregiously dangerous and unsanitary working conditions. But these efforts were soon declared unconstitutional by the Supreme Court. Other efforts, such as the experiment with mothers' pensions and additional protective labor policies, were adopted by a few progressive states. But even as late as 1928, only 11.6 percent of all relief granted in fifteen of the largest cities came from public funds.[2]

The traditional approach, dominated by the private sector with its severe distinction between deserving and undeserving poor, crumbled in 1929 before the stark reality of the Great Depression. During the Depression, misfortune became so widespread and private wealth shrank so drastically that private charity was out of the question and the distinction between deserving and undeserving became impossible to draw. The Great Depression proved to Americans that poverty could be a result of imperfections in the economic system rather than of individual irresponsibility. Americans held to their distinction between the deserving and the undeserving poor but significantly altered their standards regarding who was deserving and who was not.

Once poverty and dependency were accepted as problems inherent in the economy, a large-scale public policy approach became practical. Indeed, there was no longer any real question about whether the national government would assume a major responsibility for poverty; from that time forward, it was a question of how generous or restrictive the government was going to be about the welfare of the poor. The national government's efforts to improve the welfare of the poor can be divided into two responses. First, it instituted policies that attempted to change the economic rules about the condition of work for those who were working and could work. Second, it set in place policies seeking to change the economic rules determining the quality of life of those who could not (and in some cases, would not) work. The first response comes under the heading of policies for labor regulation. We dealt with some of these policies in Chapter 3, showing how the Constitution itself, especially the commerce clause, had to be interpreted in a fundamentally different way in order to reach into local plants and firms to improve the conditions and rewards of work. Since the adoption of the 1935 National Labor Relations (Wagner) Act, there have been revisions (e.g., the Taft-Hartley Act of 1947 and the Landrum-Griffin Labor Management Act of 1959), but no real change of the economic rules established in 1935. These rules were designed to protect laborers so that they could organize and bargain collectively with their employers rather than

History Principle

The Great Depression was a turning point in the national government's decision to be involved in improving the welfare of the poor.

---

[1]See Suzanne Mettler, *Divided Citizens: Gender and Federalism in New Deal Public Policy* (Ithaca, N.Y.: Cornell University Press, 1998), p. 2. See also Theda Skocpol, *Protecting Soldiers and Mothers: The Political Origins of Social Policy in the United States* (Cambridge, Mass.: Harvard University Press, 1992).
[2]Merle Fainsod, Lincoln Gordon, and Joseph C. Palamountain, Jr., *Government and the American Economy*, 3rd ed. (New York: W. W. Norton, 1959), p. 769, based on a WPA study by Ann E. Geddes.

(according to the older economic rules) negotiating as individuals under vastly unequal conditions.

It is possible for public policies to go much further than the rules laid out under the Wagner Act, however. For example, rather than a minimum wage law, there could be a minimum annual income law. President Clinton moved in this direction when he expanded the Earned Income Tax Credit (EITC) by $21 billion in his 1993 five-year budget deal. The purpose of the EITC is to provide relief for employed parents whose earnings are close to or below the poverty line; in 1992 this group comprised 18 percent of all full-time workers. The right to sixty days' notice before closing a plant, once thought radical, was adopted by Congress in 1988. The next step could be worker participation in management decisions about closings or hiring and promotion or even ownership and investment.

The second response to welfare is the one that will most concern us in this section: policies that seek to change the economic rules regarding those who cannot work or who are, for whatever reason, outside the economic system. These policies make up the social welfare system.

WHAT ARE THE FOUNDATIONS OF THE SOCIAL WELFARE SYSTEM?

The foundations of the American welfare system were established by the Social Security Act of 1935. Table 15.1 is an outline of the key programs in the social welfare system.

Social Security

contributory programs
Social programs financed in whole or in part by taxation or other mandatory contributions by their present or future recipients. The most important example is Social Security, which is financed by a payroll tax.

Social Security
A contributory welfare program into which working Americans place a percentage of their wages and from which they receive cash benefits after retirement.

Contributory programs are financed by taxation, which justifiably can be called "forced savings." These contributory programs are what most people have in mind when they refer to *Social Security* or social insurance. Under the original retirement program, old-age insurance, the employer and the employee were each required to pay equal amounts, which in 1937 were set at 1 percent of the first $3,000 of wages, to be deducted from the paycheck of each employee and matched by the same amount from the employer. This percentage has increased over the years; the total contribution is now 7.65 percent, subdivided as follows: 6.2 percent on the first $87,900 of income for Social Security benefits, plus 1.45 percent on all earnings for Medicare.[3]

Social Security is a rather conservative approach to welfare. In effect, the Social Security (FICA) tax, as a forced saving, sends a message that people cannot be trusted to save voluntarily in order to take care of their own retirement needs.

[3]The figures cited are for 2004. Although on paper the employer is taxed, this is all part of "forced savings" because in reality the employer's contribution is nothing more than a mandatory wage supplement that the employee never sees or touches before it goes into the trust funds held exclusively for the contributory programs.

TABLE 15.1

Public Welfare Programs

TYPE OF PROGRAM	YEAR ENACTED	NUMBER OF RECIPIENTS IN 2001 (IN MILLIONS)	FEDERAL OUTLAYS IN 2001 (IN BILLIONS)
Contributory (Insurance) System			
Old Age, Survivors', and Disability Insurance (Social Security)	1935	46.2	406.0
Medicare	1965	39.0	$215.1
Unemployment Compensation	1935	6.9	$21.1
Noncontributory (Public Assistance) System			
Medicaid	1965	33.4	$117.9
Food Stamps	1964	17.2	$18.3
Supplemental Security Income (cash assistance for aged, blind, disabled)	1974	6.3	$29.5
Housing Assistance (to low-income families)	1937	NA	$23.9
School Lunch Program	1946	28.0	$9.2
Temporary Assistance to Needy Families*	1996	NA	$18.3

NA = Not available.

*Replaced Aid to Families with Dependent Children, which was enacted in 1935.

SOURCE: Office of Management and Budget, *Budget of the United States Government, Fiscal Year 2002* (Washington, D.C.: Government Printing Office, 2001), Table 11.3.

But in another sense, it is quite radical. Social Security is not real insurance; workers' contributions do not accumulate in a personal account like an annuity. Consequently, contributors do not receive benefits in proportion to their own contributions, and this means that there is a redistribution of wealth occurring. In brief, contributory Social Security mildly redistributes wealth from higher- to lower-income people, and it quite significantly redistributes wealth from

indexing Periodic process of adjusting social benefits or wages to account for increases in the cost of living.

younger workers to older retirees. Since 1972, Social Security benefits and costs have been adjusted through **indexing**, whereby benefits paid out under contributory programs are modified annually by cost-of-living adjustments (COLAs) based on changes in the Consumer Price Index, so that benefits would increase automatically as the cost of living rose. And to pay for these automatic adjustments, Social Security taxes (contributions) also increased. This made Social Security, in the words of one observer, "a politically ideal program. It bridged partisan conflict by providing liberal benefits under conservative financial auspices."[4] In other words, conservatives could more readily yield to the demands of the well-organized and expanding constituency of elderly voters if benefit increases were guaranteed and automatic; and liberals could cement conservative support by agreeing to finance the expanded benefits through increases in the regressive Social Security tax rather than out of general revenues coming from the more progressive income tax.

Reforming Social Security   Since its creation in 1935, the Social Security system has provided retirement, survivor, and disability benefits to millions of Americans. Up until now, the system has run "in the black"—that is, it has collected more money than it has given out. In 2003, about 47 million Americans received a total of $475 billion in Social Security benefits, given to 32.5 million retirees and dependents, 7 million survivors of deceased workers, and 7.5 million disabled workers and dependents. More than half of all American workers do not have a private pension plan; they will have to rely solely on Social Security for their retirement. If there were no Social Security, half of all senior citizens would be living below the poverty line. Thus, Social Security guarantees a measure of equality.

Nearly all wage earners and self-employed individuals pay into Social Security. Yet many fear that the system cannot sustain itself. When the baby-boomer generation—a large percentage of Americans born between 1946 and 1964—reaches retirement age starting in 2011, their large numbers and longer life expectancies may place too great a demand on the system, forcing today's young people to pay ever more into a system that may be bankrupt by the time they retire.

Those who argue for a major change in Social Security point out that Social Security benefits are not drawn from an interest-bearing account; rather, they are paid for from taxes collected from current workers. Therefore, current workers carry the primary financial burden for the system. When baby boomers retire, their political and economic clout will be so great that they will be able to push aside any effort to limit benefits or relieve the financial burden on a much smaller number of younger wage earners. For Social Security to continue, it may have to borrow, or draw money from the federal Treasury, leaving younger generations with a staggering debt. If no changes are made in the current system, the

---

[4]Edward J. Harpham, "Fiscal Crisis and the Politics of Social Security Reform," in *The Attack on the Welfare State*, ed. Anthony Champagne and Edward J. Harpham (Prospect Heights, Ill.: Waveland Press, 1984), p. 13.

Social Security Trust Fund (the account where surplus monies are held) will, according to projections, go bankrupt by 2044.

Contrary to popular impressions, Social Security benefits are not a simple repayment, plus interest, of money contributed by workers. The average retiree receives back the equivalent of all the money he or she contributed over a lifetime of work, plus interest, in the space of four to eight years. Most retirees receive far more than they put in. Why should today's student-age population provide subsidies to retirees who do not need the extra income? Several reform ideas have been suggested. One proposes an investment shift from the current low-yield, conservative, U.S. government securities to private investment in higher-yield stocks and bonds. Another proposal urges a shift to means testing to reduce or eliminate benefits for those who already have ample income. A third proposal calls for raising the minimum retirement age. The current payroll tax for raising funds could also be altered. As of 2004, income is taxed only up to $87,900, so that a worker making $1 million a year pays the same Social Security taxes as a worker making $88,000.

President Bush came to office supporting Social Security reforms, including the creation of private retirement accounts. Soon after taking office, the president appointed a Social Security Commission, whose final report prominently featured individual accounts as a reform strategy. The commission recommended three reform plans, each of which offered workers the choice of contributing a portion (ranging from 2 to 4 percent) of the payroll tax to an individual account. The worker's traditional benefits would be reduced by the amount diverted to the individual account. According to the commission, individual plans would create a better system because they would allow workers to accumulate assets and build wealth, wealth that could be passed on to their children.[5]

Supporters of the current system are deeply skeptical about the benefits of individual accounts. They charge the president's commission with presenting a rosy scenario that overestimates likely gains through the stock market. When more realistic assumptions are adopted and the costs of the private accounts are considered, they argue, individual accounts do not provide higher benefits than the current system. Moreover, these critics note that the commission also recommended technical reforms that would significantly reduce the traditional Social Security benefit. For all the changes proposed, the reforms would still not solve the budget crisis that Social Security will face.[6]

Finally, supporters of the present system emphasize that Social Security is not just a retirement account; it is a social insurance program that provides "income protection to workers and their families if the wage earner retires, becomes

---

[5]President's Commission to Strengthen Social Security, *Strengthening Social Security and Creating Personal Wealth for All Americans* (Washington, D.C.: President's Commission to Strengthen Social Security, 2001), p. 5.

[6]Christian E. Weller, "Undermining Social Security with Private Accounts," Economic Policy Institute Issue Brief, 21 December 2001 (available at epinet.org); Robert Greenstein, "Social Security Commission Proposals Contain Serious Weaknesses but May Improve the Debate in an Important Respect," Center on Budget and Policy Priorities, 26 December 2001 (www.cbpp.org).

disabled or dies."[7] Because it provides this social insurance protection, supporters argue, Social Security's returns should not be compared to those of a private retirement account.

They contend that advocates of individual accounts have exaggerated the financial problems that the current system faces. Some opponents of individual accounts believe that the funding problems of Social Security can be addressed more simply and safely by eliminating the cap on payroll taxes. In 2002, only the first $84,900 of income was subject to the payroll tax. If this cap were lifted, these critics argue, the resulting revenues would cover more than 75 percent of the expected shortfall in the Social Security Trust Fund.

Medicare

Medicare
National health insurance for the elderly and the disabled.

The biggest single expansion in contributory programs after 1935 was the establishment in 1965 of *Medicare,* which was set up to provide substantial medical services to elderly persons who were already eligible to receive old-age, survivors', and disability insurance under the original Social Security system. Medicare provides hospital insurance but allows beneficiaries to choose whether or not to participate in a government-assisted insurance program to cover doctors' fees. A major role is guaranteed to the private health-care industry by essentially limiting Medicare to a financing system. Program recipients purchase all their health services in the free market. The government's involvement is primarily payment for these services. As a result, there is little government control over the quality of the services provided and the fees that health-care providers charge.

Like Social Security, Medicare is not means-tested. The benefits are available to all former workers and their spouses over the age of sixty-five—over 40 million people today—whether they are poor or not. Spending on Medicare has proved difficult to control in recent years, in part because of the growing numbers of people eligible for the programs but also because of rising health-care costs. Health-care expenditures, especially the cost of prescription drugs, have risen much more sharply than inflation in recent years.

Medicare Reform   Between the 1970s and the 1990s, there was mounting concern among policy makers about the rising costs to Medicare, and cost containment was a constant theme. The start of the Medicare prescription-drug benefit debate in the mid-1990s, stemming from the exorbitant medication costs being borne by people with Medicare, coupled with worries about the impending retirement of the baby-boom generation, led to the birth of a full-fledged movement to "overhaul" Medicare. Proponents of this effort propagated the idea that the Medicare program needed to be "saved," claiming Medicare was out-of-date and on the brink of bankruptcy.

[7]Quoted in Jill Quadragno, "Social Security Policy and the Entitlement Debate," in *Social Policy and the Conservative Agenda*, ed. Clarence Y. H. Lo and Michael Schwartz (Malden, Mass.: Blackwell, 1998), p. 111.

Beginning in the late-1990s, Congress tried and repeatedly failed to agree on legislation overhauling Medicare and adding prescription-drug benefits. During the 2000 campaign, President Bush promised to add drug benefits to Medicare, and in 2002 such a bill passed in the House of Representatives but got held up in the Senate. In November 2002, the Republicans regained control of the Senate, and just two months later, in Bush's State of the Union address, the president proposed adding $400 billion in spending to Medicare, most of it to provide drug coverage. In late 2003, in a narrow vote in both the House and Senate, Congress passed legislation that, starting in 2006, would help older Americans buy prescription drugs by covering about 75 percent of prescription-drug costs up to $2,250 a year. The bill also increased payments to doctors and hospitals as an inducement to get them to provide services through the Medicare program; and it assigned the responsibility of administering the drug benefit plan to the insurance companies, giving them a huge new role in the Medicare program.

Public Assistance Programs

Programs to which beneficiaries do not have to contribute—**noncontributory programs**—are also known as *public assistance programs*, or, derisively, as "welfare." Until 1996, the most important noncontributory program was **Aid to Families with Dependent Children (AFDC,** originally called Aid to Dependent Children, or ADC), which was founded in 1935 by the original Social Security Act. In 1996, Congress abolished AFDC and replaced it with the **Temporary Assistance to Needy Families (TANF)** block grant. Eligibility for public assistance is determined by **means testing,** a procedure that requires applicants to show a financial need for assistance. Between 1935 and 1965, the government created programs to provide housing assistance, school lunches, and food stamps to other needy Americans.

As with contributory programs, the noncontributory public assistance programs also made their most significant advances in the 1960s and 1970s. The largest single category of expansion was the establishment in 1965 of **Medicaid,** a program that provides extended medical services to all low-income persons who have already established eligibility through means testing under AFDC or TANF. Noncontributory programs underwent another major transformation in the 1970s in the level of benefits they provide. Besides being means tested, noncontributory programs are federal rather than national; grants-in-aid are provided by the national government to the states as incentives to establish the programs (see Chapter 3). Thus, from the beginning there were considerable disparities in benefits from state to state. The national government sought to rectify the disparities in levels of old-age benefits in 1974 by creating the **Supplemental Security Income (SSI)** program to augment benefits for the aged, the blind, and the disabled. SSI provides uniform minimum benefits across the entire nation and includes mandatory COLAs. States are allowed to be more generous if they wish, but no state is permitted to provide benefits below the minimum level set by the national government. As a result, twenty-five states increased their own SSI benefits to the mandated level.

noncontributory programs Social programs that assist people based on demonstrated need rather than contributions they have made. Also known as *public assistance programs.*

Aid to Families with Dependent Children (AFDC) Federal funds for children in families that fall below state standards of need. The largest federal cash transfer program. In 1996, Congress abolished AFDC and replaced it with the **Temporary Assistance to Needy Families (TANF)** block grant.

means testing A procedure that determines eligibility for government public assistance programs. A potential beneficiary must show a need and an inability to provide for it.

Medicaid A federally financed, state-operated program for medical services to low-income people.

Supplemental Security Income (SSI) A program providing a minimum monthly income to people who pass a means test and are sixty-five years old or older, blind, or disabled. Financed from general revenues that are not Social Security contributions.

FIGURE 15.1

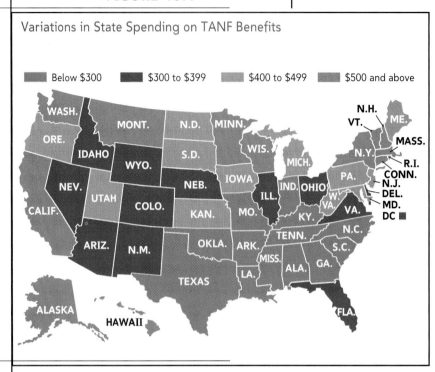

Variations in State Spending on TANF Benefits

Below $300 | $300 to $399 | $400 to $499 | $500 and above

SOURCE: Ways and Means Committee Print. WMCP: 108-6, *2003 Green Book*, at waysandmeans.house.gov/media/pdf/greenbook2003/section7.pdf.

food stamps
The largest in-kind benefits program, administered by the Department of Agriculture, providing coupons to individuals and families who satisfy a means test; the food stamps can be exchanged for food at most grocery stores.

in-kind benefits
Goods and services provided to needy individuals and families by the federal government, as contrasted with cash benefits. The largest in-kind federal welfare program is food stamps.

The new TANF program is also administered by the states, and, like the old-age benefits just discussed, benefit levels vary widely from state to state (see Figure 15.1). For example, the states' monthly TANF benefits varied from $170 in Mississippi to $923 in Alaska.[8] Even the most generous TANF payments are well below the federal poverty line. In 2002, the poverty level for a family of three included those earning less than $14,496, or $1,208 a month.

The number of people receiving AFDC benefits expanded in the 1970s, in part because new welfare programs had been established in the mid-1960s: Medicaid (discussed earlier) and *food stamps,* which are coupons that can be exchanged for food at most grocery stores. These programs provide what are called *in-kind benefits*—noncash goods and services that would otherwise have to be paid for in cash by the beneficiary. In addition to simply adding on the cost of medical services and food to the level of benefits given to AFDC recipients, the

[8]Ways and Means Committee Print, WMCP: 108-6, *2003 Green Book*, at waysandmeans.house.gov/media/pdf/greenbook2003/section7.pdf.

possibility of receiving Medicaid benefits provided an incentive for many poor Americans to establish their eligibility for AFDC, which would also establish their eligibility to receive Medicaid. At the same time, the government significantly expanded its publicity efforts to encourage the dependent unemployed to establish their eligibility for these various programs.

Another, more complex reason for the growth of AFDC in the 1970s was that it became more difficult for the government to terminate people's AFDC benefits for lack of eligibility. In the 1970 case of *Goldberg v. Kelly*, the Supreme Court held that the financial benefits of AFDC could not be revoked without due process— i.e., a hearing at which evidence is presented, etc.[9] This ruling inaugurated the concept of the **entitlement,** a class of government benefits with a status similar to that of property (which, according to the Fourteenth Amendment, cannot be taken from people "without due process of law"). *Goldberg v. Kelly* did not provide that the beneficiary had a "right" to government benefits; it provided that once a person's eligibility for AFDC was established, and as long as the program was still in effect, that person could not be denied benefits without due process. The decision left open the possibility that Congress could terminate the program and its benefits by passing a piece of legislation. If the welfare benefit were truly a property right, Congress would have no authority to deny it by a mere majority vote.

Thus, the establishment of in-kind benefit programs and the legal obstacles involved in terminating benefits contributed to the growth of the welfare state. But it is important to note that real federal spending on AFDC itself did not rise after the mid-1970s. Unlike Social Security, AFDC was not indexed to inflation; without COLAs, the value of AFDC benefits fell by more than one-third. Moreover, the largest noncontributory welfare program, Medicaid (as shown by Table 15.1, p. 615), actually devotes less than one-third of its expenditures to poor families; the rest goes to the disabled and the elderly in nursing homes.[10] Together, these programs have significantly increased the security of the poor and the vulnerable, and must be included in a genuine assessment of the redistributive influence and the cost of the welfare system today.

Welfare Reform   The unpopularity of welfare led to widespread calls for reform as early as the 1960s. Public opinion polls consistently showed that Americans disliked welfare more than any other government program. Although a series of modest reforms were implemented starting in the late 1960s, it took thirty years for Congress to enact a major transformation in the program. Why did welfare become so unpopular, and why was it so hard to reform? How has the 1996 law that replaced AFDC with TANF changed welfare?

From the 1960s to the 1990s, opinion polls consistently showed that the public viewed welfare beneficiaries as "undeserving."[11] Underlying that judgment was

History Principle

The number of people receiving welfare benefits expanded in the 1970s because of the creation of new programs, such as Medicaid and food stamps, in the mid-1960s.

entitlement

Eligibility for benefits by virtue of a category of benefits defined by law. Category can only be changed by legislation. Deprivation of individual benefits can be determined only through due process in court.

History Principle

The Supreme Court's decision in *Goldberg v. Kelly* established the concept of the entitlement and created legal obstacles to terminating welfare benefits.

[9]Goldberg v. Kelly, 397 U.S. 254 (1970).

[10]See U.S. House of Representatives, Committee on Ways and Means, *Where Your Money Goes: The 1994–95 Green Book* (Washington, D.C.: Brassey's, 1994), pp. 325, 802.

[11]See Martin Gilens, *Why Americans Hate Welfare: Race, Media, and the Politics of Antipoverty Policy* (Chicago: University of Chicago Press, 1999), Chapters 3–4.

the belief that welfare recipients did not want to work. The Progressive era reformers who first designed AFDC wanted single mothers to stay at home with their children. Motivated by horror stories of children killed in accidents while their mothers were off working or of children tied up at home all day in order to keep them safe, these reformers believed that it was better for the child if the mother did not work. By the 1960s, as more women entered the labor force and as welfare rolls rose, welfare recipients appeared in a more unfavorable light. Common criticisms charged that welfare recipients were taking advantage of the system; that they were irresponsible people who refused to work. These negative assessments were amplified by racial stereotypes. By 1973, 46 percent of welfare recipients were African American. Although the majority of recipients were white, media portrayals helped to create the widespread perception that the vast majority of welfare recipients were black. A careful study by Martin Gilens has shown how racial stereotypes of blacks as uncommitted to the work ethic reinforced public opposition to welfare.[12]

Despite public opposition, it proved difficult to reform welfare. Congress added modest work requirements in 1967, but little changed in the administration of welfare. A more significant reform in 1988 imposed stricter work requirements but also provided additional support services such as child care and transportation assistance. This compromise legislation reflected a growing consensus that effective reform entailed a combination of sticks (work requirements) and carrots (extra services to make work possible). The 1988 reform also created a new system to identify the absent parent (usually the father) and enforce child-support payments.

These reforms were barely implemented when welfare rolls rose again with the recession of the early 1990s, reaching an all-time high in 1994. Sensing continuing public frustration with welfare, presidential candidate Bill Clinton vowed "to end welfare as we know it," an unusual promise for a Democrat. Once in office, Clinton found it difficult to design a plan that would provide an adequate safety net for recipients who were unable to find work. One possibility—to provide government jobs as a last resort—was rejected as too expensive. Clinton's major achievement in the welfare field was to increase the Earned Income Tax Credit. This credit allows working parents whose annual income falls below approximately $32,000 to file through their income tax return for an income supplement of up to $4,000, depending on their family size. It was a first step toward realizing Clinton's campaign promise to ensure that "if you work, you shouldn't be poor."

Congressional Republicans proposed a much more dramatic reform of welfare, which Clinton, faced with re-election in 1996, signed. The Personal Responsibility and Work Opportunity Reconciliation Act (PRWORA) repealed AFDC. In place of the individual entitlement to assistance, the new law created block grants to the states and allowed states much more discretion in designing

---

[12]*Ibid.*

FIGURE 15.2

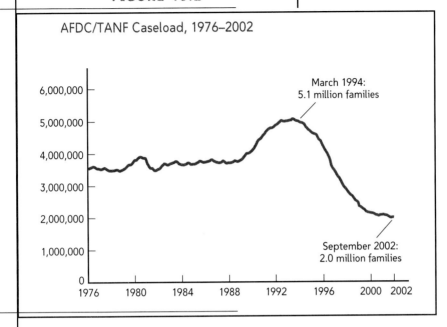

AFDC/TANF Caseload, 1976–2002

March 1994:
5.1 million families

September 2002:
2.0 million families

SOURCE: Figure prepared by the Congressional Research Service on the basis of data from the U.S. Department of Health and Human Services.

their cash-assistance programs to needy families. The new law also established time limits, restricting recipients to two years of assistance and creating a life-time limit of five years. It imposed new work requirements on those receiving welfare, and it restricted most legal immigrants from receiving benefits. The aim of the new law was to reduce welfare caseloads, promote work, and reduce out-of-wedlock births. Notably, reducing poverty was not one of its stated objectives.

After this law was enacted, the number of families receiving assistance dropped by 58 percent nationwide (see Figure 15.2). The sharp decline in the number of recipients was widely hailed as a sign that the welfare reform was working. Indeed, former welfare recipients have been more successful at finding and keeping jobs than many critics of the law predicted. The law has been less successful in other respects: researchers have found no evidence that it has helped reduce out-of-wedlock births. And critics point out that most former welfare recipients are not paid enough to pull their families out of poverty. Moreover, many families eligible for food stamps and Medicaid stopped receiving these benefits when they left the welfare rolls. The law has helped reduce welfare caseloads, but it has done little to reduce poverty.[13]

As Congress prepared to reauthorize the welfare law in 2002, two different perspectives emerged. Democrats proposed changes that would make the welfare law "an antipoverty weapon."[14] They sought to increase spending on child care, allow more education and training, and relax time limits for those working and receiving welfare benefits. Republicans, by contrast, proposed stricter work requirements and advocated programs designed to promote marriage among welfare recipients.[15] Neither party challenged the basic features of the 1996 reform. Nonetheless, as caseloads began to rise again in 2001 due to the combined effects of the recession and the terrorist attacks, both sides were attentive to new problems. Enacted in a period of low unemployment and economic prosperity, welfare reform has yet to confront the consequences of a prolonged economic downturn.

ANALYZING THE WELFARE SYSTEM

Arguments against It

1. The first is the simplest: the welfare system costs too much. Since the 1930s, when the main elements of the welfare system were first created, spending on social policy has grown dramatically. Most striking has been the growth of entitlement programs, the largest of which are Social Security and Medicare. The costs of entitlement programs as a percentage of gross domestic product was around 2 percent in 1960 but could rise to 22 percent by 2050 (see Figure 15.3). But part of the undue cost of the welfare system has to be attributed to political decisions. One of those was to spread coverage too widely and without regard to demographic factors, as outlined earlier. Another unwise decision was to index benefits without taking countervailing factors into account as part of the structure. One of the factors affecting benefits and coverage is lack of attention to the significantly increased life expectancy of Americans and the absence of commitment to a slow but steady stepping up of the retirement age. Another major factor contributing to cost increases is that the whole system became unnecessarily bureaucratic, especially the public assistance system. This is not an inherent feature of the welfare state or of government, but of poor legislative draftsmanship. As referred to earlier in this chapter and in Chapter 7, the Social Security laws lodged far too

---

[13]See the discussion of the law and the data presented in House Ways and Means Committee Print, WMCP: 106-14, *2000 Green Book*, Section 7 from U.S. GPO Online via GPO Access at www. access.gpo.gov/congress/wm001.html.

[14]Robert Pear, "House Democrats Propose Making the '96 Welfare Law an Antipoverty Weapon," *New York Times*, 24 January 2002, p. A22.

[15]Robin Toner, "Welfare Chief Is Hoping to Promote Marriage," *New York Times*, 19 February 2002, p. A1.

FIGURE 15.3

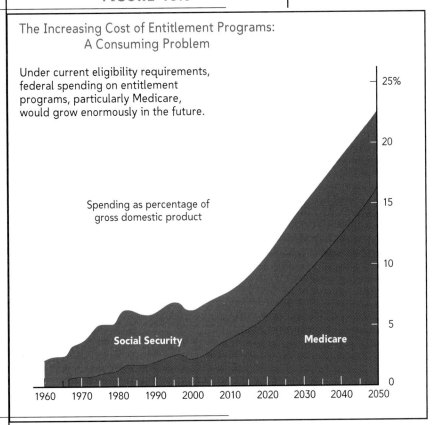

The Increasing Cost of Entitlement Programs:
A Consuming Problem

Under current eligibility requirements,
federal spending on entitlement
programs, particularly Medicare,
would grow enormously in the future.

Spending as percentage of
gross domestic product

Social Security   Medicare

1960 1970 1980 1990 2000 2010 2020 2030 2040 2050

25%

20

15

10

5

0

SOURCE: Congressional Budget Office.

much discretion in the state agencies where public assistance is to be administered, and the more discretion, the more administration, and, of course, the
more staff and red tape. Another factor significantly contributing to unnecessary cost escalation was the "third party" structure of repayment in Medicare
and in Medicaid. Once the systems were set up so that doctors and patients
could establish their relationship without regard to cost, which would be
picked up by the government, this relieved all the parties from any concern
for cost.

2. The welfare system is too paternalistic. The contributory programs are based
on "forced savings," relieving all individuals to some degree of concern for

their future. The noncontributory programs are also paternalistic even though it is true that people in poverty usually don't have the choice to save. There is another aspect of this that will come up under the fourth criticism.

3. The welfare system is an example of *moral hazard.* Although Charles Murray does not use the term in his famous and influential critique of the welfare state, *Losing Ground,* he is probably the best-known exponent of this approach to the evaluation of the welfare system.[16] Moral hazard is the danger or probability that a policy will encourage the behavior or otherwise bring about the problem that it ensures against. For example, many people whose cars are insured will take much less care to prevent their cars from being damaged or stolen. There are four parts to Murray's argument. (a) The safety net would be an example of moral hazard in the welfare state because, as observed above, some, if not all, of the programs weaken self-reliance and individual responsibility to some degree.[17] (b) Entitlement to benefits weakens the work incentive. In fact, even the strongest supporters of noncontributory public assistance agree that care has to be taken to keep the benefits high enough for subsistence but not so high that people will prefer to stay on the benefits rather than take a job. (c) Entitlement to child support "brings more babies" into the world. Even if child support does not "cause" the first birth, the argument goes that it increases the likelihood of a second and perhaps even a third in order to maintain an acceptable level of subsistence. (d) By the same token, aid to the child and to the mother contributes to the breaking up of families by increased divorce and to the choice of the woman not to marry in the first place.[18]

These critiques are not really subject to scientific proof or disproof. They are written like lawyers' briefs, summoning up the best data and logic possible in hopes that "the preponderance of the evidence" will convince the jury—that is, the public and the policy makers. It is undeniably true, for example, that single women on welfare are poor and dependent, and are likely to remain so if they have children. It is also true that many of these single women have additional children while on welfare. But the conclusion that welfare is the cause of the babies and of the delinquency and crime that are attributed to these children does

[16]Charles Murray, *Losing Ground: American Social Policy, 1950–1980,* 2nd paper ed. (New York: Basic Books, 1994).

[17]For a discussion and a defense of subsistence rights, see Frances Fox Piven and Richard A. Cloward, *The New Class War: Reagan's Attack on the Welfare State and Its Consequences* (New York: Pantheon, 1982), esp. pp. 32–48.

[18]These arguments, especially the latter two, have been made most forcefully by Charles Murray and were strengthened during the ten years between the two editions of his book. See Charles Murray, "Does Welfare Bring More Babies?" *Public Interest,* no. 114 (Spring 1994): 17–31. These views were incorporated in the second edition of his book; see note 16, above, esp. Chapter 9, "The Family." A good treatment of "moral hazard" will be found in a book by still another critic of the welfare state, George Gilder, *Wealth and Poverty* (New York: Basic Books, 1981), Chapter 10, "The Moral Hazards of Liberalism."

not logically follow. In fact, many of the most prominent opposers of welfare don't even bother trying to establish proof of this causal relationship. To Charles Murray, what matters is not the birth of babies in poverty, but the *illegitimacy* of those births—in other words, the absence of marriage is the real cause. "Illegitimacy is the single most important social problem of our time—more important than crime, drugs, poverty, illiteracy, welfare or homelessness because it drives everything else."[19]

Arguments for It

1. The welfare system is good fiscal policy. As discussed in the previous chapter, the welfare system is one of the "automatic stabilizers." When the economy is declining, welfare payments go up enough to help maintain consumer demand. In contrast, during inflationary periods, welfare taxes take an extra bite out of consumer dollars, thereby dampening inflation somewhat.

2. The welfare system is paternalistic. A vice to the critics of welfare, paternalism is a virtue to its supporters; paternalism can be good medicine, if not taken in too strong a dose. It is a notorious fact that Americans don't save enough. Welfare taxation has produced a system of universal saving, which is a safety net for employers, just as the benefits aspect of welfare constitutes a safety net for employees. Social Security, unemployment compensation, disability benefits, and other features of the welfare system have cushioned employers, especially those operating on narrow margins, from many of the vicissitudes of the market. For the same reason employers quickly accepted the welfare system, American trade unions were at first ambivalent toward it because union leaders had hoped that the unions would be the channel to provide workers these services as an institutional protection against owners.

3. As a consequence of the first and second arguments, the welfare system is believed by many to be the savior of capitalism. Each and every title in the original Social Security Act creating the welfare system identified a particular imperfection of capitalism and sought to cope with it: age, unemployment, widowhood, disability for injury, illness, birth defects, inadequate education/training, etc. The welfare system is not anti-capitalist. It recognizes that capitalism is neither perfect nor self-perfecting and, therefore, needs various deliberate, public means of dealing with its imperfections.

4. The welfare system lays most of the blame for society's woes on "the system." In other words, it removes the morality (or immorality) from poverty and also relieves employers from a large part of their traditional responsibility to take care of their own employees. This is the brighter side of the "personal responsibility" complaint covered by arguments 2 and 3 made by the critics. Welfare-system proponents have to agree that there are many chiselers and abusers in the contributory as well as the noncontributory parts of the welfare system; but cheating abounds in the private sector as well and

[19]Charles Murray, "The Coming White Underclass," *Wall Street Journal*, 29 October 1993, p. A14.

need not discredit welfare any more than it discredits business. Roughly half the people on welfare at any one time are off it within one year. It should also be noted that a large proportion of recipients of the more respectable Social Security retirement system receive far more in benefits than they contribute in taxes, especially if they live ten or more years beyond their retirement. This gives rise to an interesting question: Which of us isn't taking "welfare"?[20]

5. The welfare system is politically essential. As pro-welfare-system conservative George Will put the case:

Two conservatives (Disraeli and Bismarck) pioneered the welfare state, and did so for impeccably conservative reasons: to reconcile the masses to the vicissitudes and hazards of a dynamic and hierarchical industrial economy. They acted on the principle of "economy of exertion," using government power judiciously to prevent less discriminating, more disruptive uses of power.[21]

In Bismarck's own words, in a speech to the Reichstag in 1899:

I will consider it a great advantage when we have 700,000 small pensioners drawing their annuities from the state, especially if they belong to those classes who otherwise do not have much to lose by an upheaval and erroneously believe they can actually gain much by it.[22]

If this appears to be cynical, so be it. It may be difficult to sympathize in this epoch of relative prosperity and stability, but the likelihood of great social and political disorder, if not revolution, was very much in the minds of the American political leaders in 1933–1935 leading up to the passage of the Social Security Act. In the spring of 1933, for example, Secretary of Labor Frances Perkins was urged by an influential friend to leave Washington for the summer if she possibly could because of expectations of widespread violence in Washington and New York.[23]

There is obviously no simple solution to the welfare system. Most critics and defenders make cogent arguments for their side largely because they emphasize

---

[20]Ruth Rosen, "Which of Us Isn't Taking 'Welfare'?," *Los Angeles Times*, 27 December 1994, p. B5; sources of data: U.S. Department of Commerce; "Who Gets Assistance?" *Current Population Reports*; Household Economic Studies, July 1996.

[21]George F. Will, *Statecraft as Soulcraft: What Government Does* (New York: Simon & Schuster, 1983), p. 126.

[22]Quoted in Gaston V. Rimlinger, *Welfare Policy and Industrialization in Europe, America, and Russia* (New York: Wiley, 1971), p. 121.

[23]Episode reported in Theodore J. Lowi, *The End of Liberalism: Ideology, Policy, and the Crisis of Public Authority* (New York: W. W. Norton, 1969), p. 200. For an entirely different view of the same political phenomenon, see Piven and Cloward, *The New Class War* (note 17, above).

different aspects of the beast.[24] The welfare system was not a solution in the first place. It was a series of improvisations to some intractable problems that every nation faces when it tries, in George Will's words, "to reconcile the masses to the vicissitudes and hazards of a dynamic and hierarchical industrial economy," especially when those come to a head as quickly as they did in the early 1930s.[25] The welfare state is an institution of many parts, and no one approach to the whole will work.

HOW CAN GOVERNMENT CREATE OPPORTUNITY?

The welfare system does not only supply a measure of economic security, it also provides opportunity. The American belief in equality of opportunity makes such programs particularly important. Programs that provide opportunity keep people from falling into poverty, and they offer a hand up to those who are poor. At their best, opportunity policies allow all individuals to rise as high as their talents will take them. Two types of policy stand out as most effective in opening opportunity: education policy and health policy.

Education Policies

Most education of the American people is provided by the public policies of state and local governments. What may be less obvious is that these education policies—especially the policy of universal compulsory public education—are the most important single force in the distribution and redistribution of opportunity in America.

Compared to state and local efforts, the role of *national* education policy pales in comparison. With but three exceptions, the national government did not involve itself at all in education for the first century of its existence as an independent republic (see Table 15.2). The first two of these exceptions were actually prior to the Constitution—the Land Ordinance of 1785 followed by the Northwest Ordinance of 1787. These provided for a survey of all the public lands in the Northwest Territory and required that four sections of the thirty-six sections in each township be reserved for public schools and their maintenance. It was not until 1862, with adoption of the Morrill Act, that Congress took a

---

[24]From the Right, the most serious academic critique is Lawrence M. Mead, *The New Politics of Poverty: The Nonworking Poor in America* (New York: Basic Books, 1992). The best academic defense of the welfare system, in our opinion, is John E. Schwarz and Thomas J. Volgy, *The Forgotten Americans: Thirty Million Working Poor in the Land of Opportunity* (New York: W. W. Norton, 1993); to that must be added an outstanding evaluation of the implications of welfare reform for federalism by Demetrios Caraley, "Dismantling the Federal Safety Net: Fictions versus Realities," *Political Science Quarterly* (Summer 1996): 225–58.

[25]Quote from Will (see note 21, above).

TABLE 15.2

Growth of the Welfare System

	WELFARE	EDUCATION	HEALTH AND HOUSING
State era (1789–1935)	Private and local charity State child labor laws State unemployment and injury compensation State mothers' pensions	Northwest Ordinance of 1787 (federal) Local academies Local public schools State compulsory education laws Federal Morrill Act of 1862 for land-grant colleges	Local public-health ordinances
Federal era (1935–present)	Federal Social Security System Disability Insurance VISTA, OEO* Supplemental Security Income Cost of Living Adjustment (indexing)	GI Bill National Defense Act of 1958 Elementary and Secondary Education Act of 1965 School desegregation Head Start	Public housing Hospital construction School lunch program Food stamps Medicare Medicaid

*VISTA = Volunteers in Service to America; OEO = Office of Economic Opportunity.

third step, establishing the land-grant colleges and universities. Later in the nineteenth century, more federal programs were created for the education of farmers and other rural residents. But the most important national education policies have come only since World War II: the GI Bill of Rights of 1944, the National Defense Education Act (NDEA) of 1958, the Elementary and Secondary Education Act of 1965 (ESEA), and various youth and adult vocational training acts since 1958. Note, however, that since the GI Bill was aimed almost entirely at post-secondary schooling, the national government did not really enter the field of elementary education until after 1957.[26]

[26]There were a couple of minor precedents. One was the Smith-Hughes Act of 1917, which made federal funds available to the states for vocational education at the elementary and secondary levels. Second, the Lanham Act of 1940 made federal funds available to schools in "federally impacted areas"—that is, areas with an unusually large number of government employees and/or where the local tax base was reduced by large amounts of government-owned property.

What finally brought the national government into elementary education was embarrassment over the fact that the Soviets had beaten us into space with the launching of Sputnik. The national policy under NDEA was aimed specifically at improving education in science and mathematics. General federal aid for education did not come until ESEA was passed in 1965, which allocated funds to school districts with substantial numbers of children from families who were unemployed or earning less than $2,000 a year.

Reagan's administration signaled a new focus for federal education policy: the pursuit of higher standards. In 1983, the Department of Education issued *A Nation at Risk*, an influential report that identified low educational standards as the cause of America's declining international economic competitiveness. The report did not suggest any changes in federal policy, but it urged states to make excellence in education their primary goal. This theme was picked up again by President George H. W. Bush. Calling himself the "education president," Bush convened the nation's governors for a highly publicized retreat designed to promote the development of state educational standards. Because Republicans have historically opposed a strong federal role in education, the initiatives of Reagan and Bush remained primarily advisory. But they were very influential in focusing educational reform on standards and testing, now widely practiced across the states.

Both Bill Clinton and George W. Bush further energized the movement for educational achievement. The standards remained voluntary, however; the federal government restricted its role to providing grants to states that developed standards programs.[27] The federal role was substantially increased by President Bush's signature education act, the No Child Left Behind Act of 2001. This act created stronger federal requirements for testing and school accountability. It required that every child in grades 3 through 8 be tested yearly for proficiency in math and reading. Individual schools will be judged on the basis of how well their students perform on these tests. Parents whose child is in a failing school will have the right to transfer the child to a better school. Students in failing schools can also get access to special funds for tutoring and summer programs. Because there was strong congressional opposition to creating a national test, the states will be responsible for setting standards and devising appropriate tests.

The strong bipartisan support for No Child Left Behind reflects the broad consensus supporting higher standards and more accountability in public education. However, the act will not be easy to implement. Many states are unprepared to launch a new system of standards and testing. One of the most serious complaints is that the federal government is demanding big improvements but is not providing sufficient funding to pay for such changes. While federal money aimed at the poorest students did increase by one-third, local educators argue that it hasn't been enough to meet the high standards that the law requires. In

---

[27]See Diane Ravitch, *National Standards in American Education: A Citizen's Guide* (Washington, D.C.: Brookings Institution, 1995).

addition, many education experts contend that yearly test results are too volatile to provide a good measure of school performance. Others worry that failing schools will become even weaker as students transfer out of them.[28] It will be several years before we know if federal imposition of standards and testing will improve public education.

One of the hottest areas of controversy in education is school choice. For over two hundred years, schools have been public institutions in the United States, and many name public schooling as the most important social policy in America. Today, however, there are serious challenges to the public monopoly on education. Some critics of public schools argue that government should simply provide parents with vouchers that they can use to attend the school of their choice, public or private. Supporters of vouchers claim that the public education system is too bureaucratic to provide quality education and does not allow parents enough control over their children's education. Although voucher plans have so far only been implemented on a very small scale in a few places (Cleveland, Milwaukee, and Florida), wealthy supporters of vouchers have funded private voucher plans across the country. In Congress, Republicans sought to use federal influence to spread the use of vouchers. Supporters of public education believe that vouchers will inevitably lead to greater inequalities in education, preventing schools from offering equal opportunity.

Pressures to change the organization of schooling have led to the creation of charter schools across the country. Charter schools are publicly funded schools that are free from the bureaucratic rules and regulations of the school district in which they are located. Charter schools are free to design specialized curricula and to use resources in ways they think most effective. Since the creation of the first charter schools in Minnesota in 1990, states across the country have passed legislation to allow charter schools. The great popularity of such schools suggests that reforms allowing more flexibility and responsiveness to parents may well be possible within the existing public system.

Health Policies

Until recently, no government in the United States—national, state, or local—concerned itself directly with individual health. But public responsibility was always accepted for *public* health. After New York City's newly created Board of Health was credited with holding down a cholera epidemic in 1867, most states followed with the creation of statewide public-health agencies. Within a decade, the results were obvious. Between 1884 and 1894, for example, Massachusetts's rate of infant mortality dropped from 161.3 per 1,000 to 141.4 per 1,000.[29]

---

[28]A summary and overview of the act can be viewed at www.ed.gov/offices/OESE/esea/summary.html; for a critique of the act's provisions, see Thomas Toch, "Bush's Big Test," *Washington Monthly* 33, no. 11 (November 2001): 12–18.

[29]Morton Keller, *Affairs of State: Public Life in Late Nineteenth Century America* (Cambridge: Belknap Press of Harvard University Press, 1977), p. 500.

Reductions in mortality rates produced by local public-health programs during the late nineteenth century may be the most significant contribution ever made by government to human welfare.

The U.S. Public Health Service (USPHS) has been in existence since 1798 but was a small part of public-health policy until after World War II. Created in 1937 but little noticed for twenty years was the National Institutes of Health (NIH), an agency within USPHS created to do biomedical research. Between 1950 and 2002, NIH expenditures by the national government increased from $160 million to $23.3 billion. NIH research on the link between smoking and disease led to one of the most visible public-health campaigns in American history. The NIH's focus turned to cancer and AIDS. As with smoking, its work on AIDS resulted in massive public-health education as well as new products and regulations.

More recent commitments to the improvement of public health are the numerous laws, now housed mainly in the Environmental Protection Agency (1970), addressing hazardous air and water pollutants along with degradation of the natural environment. The Occupational Safety & Health Administration (OSHA) was created in 1970 to make the workplace safer from air pollutants as well as threats from machinery and operations. Laws that attempted to improve the health and safety of consumer products were created in 1972 and housed in the Consumer Product Safety Commission (CPSC).

But by far the most important commitments to public health were made in 1965, with the creation of Medicare and Medicaid. Medicare services are available to all persons already eligible under the Social Security Insurance Program (and it becomes automatic for retired persons when they reach the age of sixty-five). Although there are nutritional programs for the poor, particularly food stamps and the school lunch program, Medicaid is far and away the most important health program for this group.

But public health is only half the health-policy area. The other half is the health-care system—that is, delivery of services between individual doctors and individual patients. Early in his administration, Clinton announced a plan with two key objectives: (1) to limit the rising costs of the American health-care system and (2) to provide universal health-insurance coverage for all Americans (almost 40 million Americans lacked health insurance at that time). Clinton's plan at first garnered enormous public support and seemed likely to win congressional approval in some form. But the plan, which entailed a major expansion of federal administration of the health-care system, gradually lost momentum as resistance to it took root among those who feared changes in a system that worked well for them. Though Clinton had pledged to make health care the centerpiece of his 1994 legislative agenda, no health-care bill even came up for a full congressional vote in 1994. Following the president's failure on health care, Congress passed a much smaller program expanding health-insurance coverage for low-income children not already receiving Medicaid. Called the State Children's Health Insurance Program, the law provides federal funds to states so that they can offer health insurance to more low-income children. The results have been uneven: some states have greatly expanded coverage of uninsured children and

Social Welfare and the Politics of Collective Action

In 1992, presidential candidate Bill Clinton promised to "end welfare as we know it." President Bill Clinton held fast to his promise in 1996, signing the Personal Responsibility and Work Opportunity Act, and basically ended many of the social welfare protections in place since the New Deal.

That a Democratic president ended welfare "as we know it" should come as no surprise. The American welfare system has been under attack for decades, from both the Right and the Left. From both sides of the political aisle, critics, bemoaning "welfare queens," believed that the welfare system had failed and advocated reforms such as time limits, work requirements, and taking advantage of market incentives, all in the name of getting "tough with the poor."

The irony of the American debate over welfare is how misdirected it all was. Non-means-tested social insurance programs (primarily Medicare and Social Security but also unemployment insurance, farm-price supports, and other retirement and disability programs) constitute $910 billion in federal spending as of fiscal year 2002, while means-tested programs, what we typically think of as welfare spending, are less than a third that amount ($286 billion). Thus, more than 75 percent of "welfare" spending is non-means-tested social insurance programs, received by more than 40 million Americans. They constitute the real "welfare state."[30]

The principles of politics provide a ready guide to this debate. Collective action does not just require a shared set of preferences; it also requires organizational and individual resources.

Poor people are not a particularly well-endowed portion of our population. Poor people who are highly concentrated in urban areas can use their voting power to their advantage, possibly to influence politicians to support welfare spending. They have historically organized (or have been organized by political entrepreneurs) via political parties and churches. However, many of our less-well-off are scattered throughout rural America. They are small in numbers relative to large congressional districts. They control few financial or organizational resources. The "intimacy" required to start many collective-action movements seldom exists among the rural poor. As a result, their political influence is minimal.

The elderly, farmers, and veterans groups, in contrast, are very well organized. Retired citizens live in electorally important parts of the country (Florida, Texas, California), and they vote far more regularly than younger and poorer Americans. The largest interest group in the United States—the AARP—spends millions every year lobbying for the interests of older Americans.

Farmers are disadvantaged in some of the same ways as the rural poor are, but because of their business relationships, farmers have regular interactions with other farmers at Grange halls and agricultural commodity-distribution points.

More important, though, is the third principle of politics: the impact of institutions on individual behavior. Members of these groups exist within a web of government rules, regulations, and benefits. The health-care and retirement income of most elderly Americans is partially or fully funded by the government. Agriculture in this country has been heavily subsidized by the government since the 1930s. And veterans receive health benefits and pensions (depending on their length of service) from the government. It is no surprise, then, that these groups are well organized. Governmental institutions *encourage* them to organize.

The result is that the social welfare system in America is heavily skewed toward providing social *insurance* but not much social *welfare.* Over the last decade of reforms, the elderly and veterans continued to receive significant benefits without any means testing. Farm subsidies continued apace even though they have caused serious frictions with our trading partners. Welfare spending to help the most destitute, on the other hand, has been substantially cut.

This may or may not constitute social justice. But it does reflect the realities of the principles of politics. As long as our political system relies on individualized political efforts, self-funded candidates, and well-financed interest groups, and does not have strong political parties (institutions that have incentives to organize as many potential voters as possible), it is likely that the poor will receive the short end of the social welfare stick.

[30]See Theodore R. Marmor, Jerry L. Mashaw, and Philip L. Harvey, *America's Misunderstood Welfare State: Persistent Myths, Enduring Realities* (New York: Basic Books, 1990).

have even sought to insure their parents. Other states have been far less aggressive and have not significantly increased the number of insured children. With the recession of 2002, all states had to cut back on plans for broader coverage as their budgets grew tighter.

WHO IS POOR? WHAT CAN GOVERNMENT DO?

When we study social policies from a group perspective, we see that minorities, women, and children are disproportionately poor. Much of this poverty is the result of disadvantages that stem from the position of these groups in the labor market. African Americans and Latinos tend to be economically less well off than the rest of the American population. Much of this economic inequality stems from the fact that minority workers tend to have low-wage jobs. Minorities are also more likely to become unemployed and to remain unemployed for longer periods of time than are white Americans. African Americans, for example, typically have experienced twice as much unemployment than other Americans have. The combination of low-wage jobs and unemployment often means that minorities are less likely to have jobs that give them access to the shadow welfare state. They are more likely to fall into the precarious categories of the working poor or the nonworking poor.

In the past several decades, policy analysts have begun to talk about the "feminization of poverty," or the fact that women are more likely to be poor than men are. This problem is particularly acute for single mothers, who are more than twice as likely to fall below the poverty line than the average American. When the Social Security Act was passed in 1935, the main programs for poor women were Aid to Dependent Children (ADC) and survivors' insurance for widows. The framers of the act believed that ADC would gradually disappear as more women became eligible for survivors' insurance. The social model behind the Social Security Act was that of a male breadwinner with a wife and children. Women were not expected to work; and if a woman's husband died, ADC or survivors' insurance would help her stay at home and raise her children. The framers of Social Security did not envision today's large number of single women heading families. At the same time, they did not envision that so many women with children would also be working. This combination of changes helped make AFDC (the successor program to ADC) more controversial. Many people ask, Why shouldn't welfare recipients work, if the majority of women who are not on welfare work?

Controversies over the welfare state have led to adaptations in welfare policy in recent years. Similar controversies over affirmative action policies—those that partially determine "who shall be poor"—have led to gradual changes in civil rights policies. But, as we concluded in Chapter 4, although the problems of rights in America are agonizing, they can be looked at optimistically. The United States has a long way to go before it constructs a truly just, "equally protected" society. But it also has come very far in a relatively short time. Groups pressing for equality have been able to use government to change a variety of discriminatory practices. The federal government has become an active partner in ensuring civil rights and political equality. All explicit *de jure* barriers to minorities have been dismantled. Many *de facto* barriers have also been dismantled, and thousands upon thousands of new opportunities have been opened.

Madison set the tone for this chapter in *The Federalist*, No. 51, in prose that has more the character of poetry:

> Justice is the end of government.
>   It is the end of civil society.
>   It ever has been and ever will be pursued
>   Until it be obtained,
>   Or until liberty be lost in the pursuit.

Equality of opportunity has produced unequal results, and the unequal results of one generation can be visited upon later generations. Considerable inequality is acceptable unless the advantages are maintained through laws and rules that favor those already in positions of power and through prejudices that tend to develop against any group that has for a long while been on the lower rungs of society. It is in this context that the more long-standing and extreme inequalities in the United States have been perceived as unjust. Yet efforts to reduce the inequalities or to eliminate the consequences of prejudice can produce their own injustices if government intervention is poorly planned or is too heavy-handed.

SUMMARY

The capitalist system is the most productive type of economy on Earth, but it is not perfect. Poverty amid plenty continues. Many policies have emerged to deal with these imperfections.

The first section of this chapter discussed the welfare system and gave an account of how Americans came to recognize extremes of poverty and dependency and how Congress then attempted to reduce these extremes with policies that moderately redistribute opportunity.

Welfare policies are subdivided into several categories. First there are the contributory programs. Virtually all employed persons are required to contribute a portion of their wages into welfare trust funds, and later on, when workers retire or are disabled, they have a right, or entitlement, to draw upon those contributions. Another category of welfare is composed of noncontributory programs, also called "public assistance." These programs provide benefits and supports for people who can demonstrate need by passing a "means test." Noncontributory programs can involve either cash benefits or in-kind benefits. All of the contributory programs are implemented through cash benefits. Spending on social policies, especially Social Security and Medicare, has increased dramatically in recent decades, raising concerns about how entitlement programs will be paid for in future decades.

The chapter also discussed ways of breaking out of the cycle of poverty. Education and health policies are two ways to break this cycle and redistribute opportunities. The education policies of state and local governments are the most important single force in the distribution and redistribution of opportunity in America. Although states have taken the early lead in the arena of public-health policy, the federal government also adopted policies in the early 1900s to protect citizens from the effects of pollution and other health hazards.

FOR FURTHER READING

Bryner, Gary. *Politics and Public Morality: The Great American Welfare Reform Debate.* New York: W. W. Norton, 1998.

Katz, Michael B. *In the Shadow of the Poorhouse: A Social History of Welfare in America.* Rev. ed. New York: Basic Books, 1996.

Rationality Principle	Collective Action Principle	Institution Principle	Policy Principle	History Principle
Some critics of the welfare state argue that it creates a moral hazard by providing the wrong incentives to welfare recipients.				The Great Depression was a turning point in the national government's decision to be involved in improving the welfare of the poor.
				The number of people receiving welfare benefits expanded in the 1970s because of the creation of new programs, such as Medicaid and food stamps, in the mid-1960s.
				The Supreme Court's decision in *Goldberg v. Kelly* established the concept of the entitlement and created legal obstacles to terminating welfare benefits.

Lemann, Nicholas. *The Promised Land: The Great Black Migration and How It Changed America*. New York: Knopf, 1991.

Levy, Frank. *The New Dollars and Dreams: American Incomes and Economic Change*. New York: Russell Sage Foundation, 1998.

Marmor, Theodore R., Jerry L. Mashaw, and Philip L. Harvey. *America's Misunderstood Welfare State: Persistent Myths, Enduring Realities*. New York: Basic Books, 1990.

Mink, Gwendolyn. *Welfare's End*. Rev. ed. Ithaca, N.Y.: Cornell University Press, 2002.

Murray, Charles. *Losing Ground: American Social Policy, 1950–1980*. 2nd paper ed. New York: Basic Books, 1994.

Piven, Frances Fox, and Richard A. Cloward. *Regulating the Poor: The Functions of Public Welfare*. Updated ed. New York: Vintage, 1993.

Schwarz, John E. *America's Hidden Success: A Reassessment of Public Policy from Kennedy to Reagan.* Rev. ed. New York: W. W. Norton, 1988.

Self, Peter. *Government by the Market? The Politics of Public Choice.* Boulder, Col.: Westview, 1993.

Weir, Margaret, Ann S. Orloff, and Theda Skocpol, eds. *The Politics of Social Policy in the United States.* Princeton: Princeton University Press, 1988.

Politics in the News— Reading between the Lines

Medicare Reform and the Debate over the Role of Government

Hard to Swallow: Medicare, Battleground for a Bigger Struggle

By ROBIN TONER

Congress is supposedly well on the way to passing a historic Medicare law that will, at long last, overhaul the huge government health insurance program and offer new drug benefits to 40 million elderly and disabled Americans. Lawmakers met last week to begin hammering out the differences between the bills already passed by the House and the Senate. All they have to do is split the difference in time-honored legislative style.

Right?

Perhaps. But there is a pessimistic view: that the differences at stake here are not the ordinary stuff of legislative compromise. That the conservatives in the House and the liberals in the Senate have profoundly different visions of Medicare, of social welfare programs and of government in general. And that those divisions will be hard to finesse. . . .

Can you simply split the difference when the two ideological camps are so profoundly at odds on the efficacy of government itself? One side sees middle class entitlements, like Social Security

and Medicare, as enduring achievements . . . the other as promises that cannot be kept unless the programs are modernized and private market involved.

Similarly, liberals increasingly see tax cuts as a calculated attempt to starve the government, and by extension, inexorably trim its services; conservatives see tax cuts as empowering, taking money from a bloated bureaucracy and returning it to the taxpayers.

Medicare is the battleground for this much broader struggle.

Conservatives argue that the program is a relic of the Great Society, a collection of government bureaucrats rigidly administering prices for an oncologist in Des Moines and a hospital in Houston. . . .

Moreover, many conservatives maintain, the program is not affordable, given the huge wave of 76 million baby boom retirees just over the horizon, and the ever growing costs of medical care and new technology. . . .

Given this view, the idea of simply adding a new drug benefit to the basic

New York Times, 20 July 2003, sec. 4, p. 1.

government entitlement program is anathema to conservatives. For them, the political price of a drug benefit must be an overhaul that will vastly increase the role of private health plans in Medicare.

. . . If we lose this, conservatives argue, the traditional vision of a government-run social insurance program will not only endure, but prevail. Moreover, some say, Congress may never get another chance to "reform" Medicare because the closer the powerful baby boomer voting bloc gets to retirement, the harder it will be to do anything that seems to restrict its benefits.

In short, this is the proverbial fork in the road of history. "We have to have an argument," said Stuart M. Butler, a vice president at the conservative Heritage Foundation. "This is not something where you can just say, 'Let's strike a deal.'"

On that, liberals would agree—but little else. They see Medicare as an extraordinarily successful government program that lifted the elderly out of the charity wards and into the mainstream of American medicine, a middle-class entitlement that reminded Americans of the good that government could do. From its start in 1965, Medicare has performed a role that government is uniquely suited to, liberals argue—spreading the risks and the benefits, protecting a vulnerable population.

Moreover, liberals say, the elderly are happy in this last bastion of fee-for-service medicine, with a free choice of doctors and hospitals. * * *

They scoff at the notion that Republicans are simply trying to be good stewards of the program. Many Democrats assert that what Republicans really want to do is move away from a guarantee of defined benefits, spelled out in law, to a far less generous voucher that the elderly use to buy coverage in the private marketplace. * * *

ESSENCE OF THE STORY

- Medicare reform was on the legislative agenda of the president and both political parties in 2003; all want to claim credit for Medicare reform in the 2004 election.

- Medicare reform has become a microcosm of a much deeper divide on the proper role of government. Republicans assert that government programs should be as minimal as possible and that these programs should use market incentives.

- Democrats see Medicare as a shining success story that has lifted many elderly out of poverty, and they are not interested in large-scale tinkering.

- The House, where Republicans can use rules to press their vision, has proposed a far-reaching reform. In the Senate, Democrats have been able to use the process to produce a more moderate bill.

POLITICAL ANALYSIS

- Unlike most European nations, America has long debated the proper role of government in providing a social safety net. This debate is far from ended and reflects one of the unique aspects of American political culture: our strong focus on individualism.

- The looming demographic shift—the retirement of the baby-boomer generation—has pushed many political issues (Social Security, Medicare) onto today's political agenda.

- The House, because of its structured rules and procedures, will continue to produce bills that represent a clear statement of the majority party's principles, which a more individualistic and less organized Senate will allow a minority to change or oppose.

Both camps [think t]hat there are no win-win solutions here. That if Medicare legislation is finally passed, one world view will have won, the other lost. That you cannot split the difference when the two parties are so profoundly at odds on government itself.

16

Foreign Policy and Democracy

Ever since George Washington, in his Farewell Address, warned the American people "to have . . . as little political connection as possible" with foreign nations and to "steer clear of permanent alliances," Americans have been distrustful of foreign policy. Despite this distrust, the United States has been forced to pursue its national interests in the world, even if this has meant fighting a war. As a result of its foreign entanglements, the United States emerged as a world power, but not without maintaining some misgivings about foreign policy. As Alexis de Tocqueville noted in the 1830s, democracies lack the best qualities for the successful pursuit of foreign-policy goals:

> Foreign policies demand scarcely any of those qualities which are peculiar to a democracy; they require, on the contrary, the perfect use of almost all those in which it is deficient. . . . A democracy can only with great difficulty regulate the details of an important undertaking, persevere in a fixed design, and work out its execution in spite of serious obstacles. It cannot combine its measures with secrecy or await their consequences with patience.[1]

[1]Alexis de Tocqueville, *Democracy in America*, trans. Phillips Bradley, 2 vols. (1835; New York: Vintage, 1945), I, p. 243.

Fear and antagonism toward foreign entanglements became a revered American tradition. Only the most extraordinary affront to American sovereignty or American interest could mobilize the American people behind a sustained involvement in foreign affairs, and the mobilization, when it did occur, was usually for war, which required complete demonization of the adversary. Mere conflicts of interest between nations were rarely enough to mobilize Americans.

The cold war, which lasted from 1946 to 1989, seemed to put an end to that tradition. The term itself was coined in 1946 to distinguish America's emerging confrontation with the Soviet Union from "hot war," or "shooting war," to total mobilization for war in order to prevent war.[2] Division of the world into two antagonistic camps, each armed with enough nuclear weapons to annihilate the other, redefined (or "escalated") what had once been considered incidental threats into serious challenges. Investment in total military preparedness became a race to deter the other side from any expansion, with each side attributing to the other an overriding commitment to arms' expansion.

Each of the leading nations in the cold war—the United States and the Soviet Union—developed what we call a "cold war culture." This cold war culture was built on a policy in which (1) the United States must prepare for war in order to prevent war; (2) each day that war did not occur was further confirmation of America's commitment to preparedness and deterrence because American leaders believed that the Soviet Union was aggressive and would expand communist influence wherever weaknesses were detected; and (3) the United States must continually increase its capabilities because whatever prevented Soviet expansion today could be inadequate tomorrow, especially considering that the Soviets, like the United States, were continuing to invest in military power.

[2]William Safire provides a brief and informative account of the history of the term in his *Safire's Political Dictionary* (New York: Random House, 1978), pp. 127–29.

Those were simpler days. The United States' role in the world was clear and its enemy was well known. The cold war ended in 1989, and its culture would pass away in its wake.

Without a clear-cut enemy, the American fear of foreign entanglements seemed to return during the 1990s, as the United States was initially reluctant to get involved with politically troubled countries like Somalia, Bosnia, and Kosovo. But September 11, 2001, changed that. September 11 and its aftermath led to a revision of America's view of its place in the world. America was at war, but not only in Iraq. In the years since September 11, 2001, the United States was engaged in a "war on terror," with American servicemen and women "deployed across the world." This was an international, multicountry conspiracy of evil against good, whose "terrorists continue to plot against America and the civilized world."[3] In his 2004 State of the Union address, President George W. Bush justified this ongoing war as necessary for homeland security, a war that would have to be fought in distant places or else in our own communities.

In this same speech, President Bush went beyond military security to identify still another major goal of foreign policy—a very new and unprecedented goal—of "building a new Iraq" as part of "a mission . . . pursuing a forward strategy of freedom in the greater Middle East." The principal means of achieving this is the military, but with a twist. President Bush envisioned in his message an America leading "a coalition of the willing" of thirty or more nation-states. However, this coalition was not to operate under United Nations auspices: "There is a difference . . . between leading a coalition of many nations, and submitting to the objections of a few. America will never seek a permission slip to defend the security of our people." This alliance of the willing has minimal military value because, except for Great Britain, the members were expected to contribute virtually zero manpower in troops on the ground. They were included to give a form of "moral support," the purpose being to add legitimacy to the worldwide effort. Diplomatic methods were also identified in Bush's message, but they were explicitly limited to keeping the UN informed and working out a role for the UN in humanitarian aspects of nation building. The president's message also included commitment to a significantly increased role to be played by the Voice of America and other broadcast services aimed at the region, in Arabic and Persian languages. Another propaganda channel to be enhanced, by the doubling of its budget, was the National Endowment for Democracy, "to focus its new work on the development of free elections, free markets, free press, and free labor unions in the Middle East." Bush underlined the rebuilding of Middle Eastern countries along American lines with the remark that "it is mistaken and condescending to assume that whole cultures and great religions are incompatible with liberty and self-government." This is part of a general and widely held theory that countries with similar systems of government will not go to war against each other. Consequently, "as long as the Middle East remains a place of tyranny . . . it will continue

---

[3]All quotations are from George W. Bush's 2004 State of the Union address.

to produce men and movements that threaten the safety of America and our friends."

Finally, state building itself is the ultimate means, with Iraq and Afghanistan as only the start. For the Bush administration, state building has less to do with the apparatus of government; it is much more concerned with a new constitution; a new, directly elected assembly; a bill of rights; and the embrace of the values of freedom. After peace and freedom are established, "full sovereignty" would be restored to Iraq; and after that, the Iraq regime will be imitated in other countries. All of this would come to pass without "any desire to dominate" and without any "ambitions of empire." Only time will tell if the Bush administration is successful in its ultimate goal of a democratic Iraq and Afghanistan. But the issues that the Bush team faces, such as overcoming much of the world's antipathy toward the United States'

PREVIEWING THE PRINCIPLES

Foreign-policy interests are pursued through both domestic infighting and strategic interaction with other foreign "players." The one consistent influence on the making of foreign policy is the president as "coordinator in chief," who strategically deploys an array of instruments and coordinates an array of officials and institutions in order to conduct foreign policy. In addition, international institutions such as the United Nations and collective security organizations such as NATO can be utilized by the United States to conduct its foreign policy, but these institutions and organizations can also work as constraints on American foreign policy. Two historical legacies that continue to influence the conduct of American foreign policy are the intermingling of domestic and foreign policy and unilateralism.

power, will certainly outlast the administration, whether it's 2004 or 2008.

The Bush administration's conduct of foreign policy, as expressed by Bush in his 2004 State of the Union address, reveals the many tensions evident in the United States' conduct of its foreign policy in its history. Should the United States fear foreign entanglements, or be engaged in world affairs? What are the United States' foreign-policy goals? Economic self-interest, the spread of democracy around the world, or both? What is the best means for the United States to achieve its goals? The military, diplomacy, or both? Should the United States act unilaterally or multilaterally?

This chapter has no solution to the many foreign-policy issues the United States confronts. Nonetheless, because the conduct of foreign policy is so complex and because there are particular problems facing a democracy such as the United States as it formulates and puts into effect particular foreign policies, a well-balanced analysis of foreign-policy problems is essential. Such an analysis must treat at least four dimensions of foreign policy, which will make up the four main sections of this chapter. We will begin by asking who makes and shapes foreign policy in the United States. From there, we will cover American values: What does the United States want? What are its national interests, if any? What counts as success? In the third section, we will identify and examine the main instruments of foreign policy, such as administrative arrangements, institutions, laws, and programs. Finally, we will discuss how the United States behaves in world politics. Are its roles consistent with its values?

WHO MAKES AND SHAPES FOREIGN POLICY?

As in domestic policy, foreign-policy making is a highly pluralistic arena. First there are the official players, those who comprise the "foreign-policy establishment"; these players and the agencies they head can be called the actual "makers" of foreign policy: the president and his advisers, the bureaucracy, and Congress. But there are other major players, less official but still influential. We call these the "shapers": interest groups and the media.

The President

History Principle

Historically, American presidents have come to office focused primarily on domestic policies and issues.

Most American presidents have been domestic politicians who set out to make their place in history through achievements in domestic policy. This is consistent with the traditional place of foreign policy, which has been treated as virtually an extension of domestic policies. The standard joke during Clinton's 1992 campaign, extending well into his first year, was that he had learned his foreign policy at the International House of Pancakes! Thus, it was not shockingly unusual that President George W. Bush had virtually no foreign-policy preparation. He had traveled very little outside the United States, and he had had virtually no foreign experience as governor of Texas, even though that state has the largest international border of any state in the United States. But, like his immediate predecessor, Bush displayed very soon after his inauguration that he was a quick learner. He stacked his cabinet and subcabinet with foreign- and defense-policy experts of extraordinary training, experience, and knowledge.

His first major foreign-policy action was to bomb Iraq—a safe and inexpensive way to convey the impression that he was determined to be an effective commander in chief. And, whether right or wrong, he was decisive in the initiatives he took to define America's national interest for his administration. Examples include revival of the controversial nuclear missile shield ("Star Wars"); his readiness to abandon the ABM treaty, which meant a serious and ugly confrontation with the Russians; changes in policy priorities away from humanitarian and environmental goals with a far stronger emphasis on goals more directly within the realm of national security; and turning America's concerns (by degree or emphasis) away from Europe and toward an "Asia first" policy. His first real test of leadership—the imbroglio with China over the emergency landing of a U.S. spy plane—was almost universally praised for patience and finesse. His calm and patient approach to the unbelievably intense crisis following the September 11, 2001, terrorist attacks also revealed his leadership abilities. During the weeks following the crisis, general public approval of his job as president remained extremely high, as was public approval of his handling of the war itself.

September 11, 2001, and its aftermath immensely accentuated the president's role and place in foreign policy. By 2002, foreign policy was the centerpiece of the Bush administration's agenda. In a June 1 speech at West Point, the *"Bush Doctrine"* of preemptive war was announced. Bush argued that "our security will require all Americans . . . to be ready for preemptive action when necessary to defend our liberty and to defend our lives." Bush's statement was clearly intended to justify his administration's plans to invade Iraq, but it had much wider implications for international relations (as we shall explore at the end of the chapter), including the central role of the American president in guiding foreign policy.

It should be added that as politicians, presidents' foreign-policy actions are taken, at least partially, with domestic political audiences in mind. For example, a president with sagging public-approval ratings may use foreign policy to rally support (see Chapter 6). And during election years, foreign policy tends to be more politicized.

The Bureaucracy

The major foreign-policy players in the bureaucracy are the secretaries of the Departments of State, Defense, and the Treasury; the Joint Chiefs of Staff (JCOS), especially the chair of the JCOS; and the director of the Central Intelligence Agency (CIA). A separate unit in the bureaucracy comprised of these people and a few others is the National Security Council (NSC), whose main purpose is to iron out the differences among the key players and to integrate their positions in order to confirm or reinforce a decision the president wants to make in foreign policy or military policy. The secretary of commerce has also become an increasingly important foreign-policy maker, with the rise and spread of economic globalization. To this group another has been added: the Department of Homeland Security, headed by former Pennsylvania governor Tom Ridge. The department has four main divisions: Border and Transportation Security; Emergency Preparedness and Response; Chemical, Biological, Radiological, and Nuclear Countermeasures; and Information Analysis and Infrastructure Protection. Although each of the twenty-two agencies within the four main divisions has an expertise in homeland security, their missions are more far-ranging, such as providing relief to victims of natural disasters and stopping counterfeiters.

Coordinating the diverse missions of a single agency is a challenge; coordinating the efforts of multiple agencies is especially problematic. American foreign policy is replete with instances of the CIA heading in one direction while the Department of State or Defense or the Joint Chiefs of Staff head in another. The National Security Council and now the Department of Homeland Security attempt to keep the various players on the same page. But will these agencies—each with its own authority, interests, and priorities—follow the same protocol? It should be understood that this is not merely a matter of coordinating different players on the same team. Each player has his or her own ax to grind. Agencies have different policy priorities and budgetary aspirations.

Bush Doctrine
Foreign policy based on the idea that the United States should take preemptive action against threats to its national security.

 Rationality Principle
Foreign-policy initiatives by the president are taken in light of the domestic political landscape.

Collective Action Principle
Coordinating the efforts of the many agencies of the foreign-policy establishment is especially difficult.

Institution Principle

Institutions such as the National Security Council and Department of Homeland Security attempt to keep the various foreign-policy players on the same page.

In addition to these top cabinet-level officials, key lower-level staff members have policy-making influence as strong as that of the cabinet secretaries—some may occasionally exceed cabinet influence. These include the two or three specialized national security advisers in the White House, the staff of the NSC (headed by the national security adviser), and a few other career bureaucrats in the Departments of State and Defense whose influence varies according to their specialty and to the foreign policy at hand.

Many intelligence agencies have come in for heavy criticism since September 11. Top among these is the Central Intelligence Agency, set up in 1947 to be the supervisor, coordinator, assimilator, and final integrator of all the other agencies in the intelligence community, including the National Security Agency (NSA), which breaks codes and performs electronic eavesdropping; the National Reconnaissance Office (NRO), which coordinates satellite research and development; the Central Imaging Office (CIO), which supervises photographic surveillance; the Defense Intelligence Agency (DIA, in the Defense Department), which performs military intelligence analysis; and the intelligence services of each of the armed-services divisions within the Defense Department. There are also a few civilian intelligence agencies, the most important of which are the Federal Bureau of Investigation (FBI), the U.S. Citizenship and Immigration Services (USCIS, formerly the Immigration and Naturalization Service, or INS), and the Internal Revenue Service (IRS). Although the names of these agencies are familiar to the public, in many respects they are "secret agencies," even down to their actual budgets, not to mention their espionage and sabotage operations.[4] Following World War II, the CIA began to keep strictly to activities outside the United States, and the FBI (in particular) limited itself to the domestic United States. That separation of jurisdiction no longer makes sense in our globalized world. One of the consequences of the creation of the Office (and then Department) of Homeland Security is that central coordination might make these agencies a bit more transparent.

Congress

While the Constitution gives Congress the power to declare war, Congress has exercised this power on only five occasions: the War of 1812, the Mexican War (1846), the Spanish-American War (1898), World War I, and World War II. For the first 150 years of American history, Congress's role was limited because, as we will see, the United States's role in world affairs was limited. During this time, the Senate was the only important congressional foreign-policy player because of its constitutional role in reviewing and approving treaties. The treaty power is still the primary entrée of the Senate into foreign-policy making. But since World War II and the continual involvement of the United States in international security and foreign aid, Congress as a whole has become a major

---

[4]Loch K. Johnson, *Secret Agencies: U.S. Intelligence in a Hostile World* (New Haven: Yale University Press, 1996).

TABLE 16.1

Principal Foreign-Policy Provisions of the Constitution

| | POWER GRANTED TO: | |
	PRESIDENT	CONGRESS
War power	Commander in chief of armed forces	Provide for the common defense; declare war
Treaties	Negotiate treaties	Ratification of treaties, by two-thirds majority (Senate)
Appointments	Nominate high-level government officials	Confirm president's appointments (Senate)
Foreign commerce	No explicit powers, but treaty negotiation and appointment powers pertain	Explicit power "to regulate foreign commerce"
General powers	Executive power; veto	Legislative power; power of the purse; oversight and investigation

foreign-policy maker because most modern foreign policies require financing, which requires both the House of Representatives and the Senate. For example, Congress's first action after September 11 was to authorize the president to use "all necessary and appropriate force," coupled with a $40 billion emergency appropriations bill for homeland defense. And while Bush believed he possessed the constitutional authority to invade Iraq, he still first sought congressional approval, which he received in October 2002. Congress has also become increasingly involved in foreign-policy making because of the increasing use by the president of **executive agreements** to conduct foreign policy. Executive agreements have the force of treaties but do not require prior approval by the Senate. But, according to political scientist Loch K. Johnson, around 95 percent of executive agreements are made prior to or pursuant to congressional authorization. For example, many executive agreements are made to pursue, fulfill, or clear up details of treaties already adopted. Others are carried out under a prior legislative act or are covered by later legislation. This gives both the House and the

executive agreement An agreement between the president and another country that has the force of a treaty but does not require the Senate's "advice and consent."

Senate a genuine institutional role in foreign policy.[5] Another opening for congressional involvement in foreign policy is the fact that, although executive agreements have the force of treaties and do not require prior approval by the Senate, they can in fact be revoked by action of both chambers of Congress. Such action is by "joint resolution," a form of legislative disapproval that the president cannot veto. Yet another aspect of Congress's role in foreign policy is that the Senate has the power to confirm the president's nominations for cabinet members, ambassadors, and other high-ranking officials (such as the director of the CIA, but not the director of the NSC). A final constitutional power for Congress is to "regulate commerce with foreign nations."

Another congressional player is the foreign-policy and military-policy committees: in the Senate these are the Foreign Relations Committee, the Armed Services Committee, and the Intelligence Committee; in the House, these are the International Relations Committee, the Armed Services Committee, and the Intelligence Committee. Usually, a few members of these committees who have spent years specializing in foreign affairs become trusted members of the foreign-policy establishment and are actually makers rather than mere shapers of foreign policy. In fact, several members of Congress have left to become key foreign-affairs cabinet members. After September 11 congressional committees conducted hearings on the failure of the intelligence agencies, but most members of Congress were reluctant to take on these agencies or a popular president.

The shapers of foreign policy are the nonofficial, informal players, but they are typically people or groups that have great influence in the making of foreign policy. Of course, the influence of any given group varies according to the party and the ideology that is dominant at a given moment.

Interest Groups

Far and away the most important category of nonofficial player is the interest group—that is, the interest group to whom one or more foreign-policy issues are of long-standing and vital relevance. The type of interest group with the reputation for the most influence is the economic interest group. Yet the myths about this group's influence far outnumber and outweigh the realities. The actual influence of organized economic interest groups in foreign policy varies enormously from issue to issue and year to year. Most of these groups are "single issue" groups and are, therefore, most active when their particular issue is on the agenda. On many of the broader and more sustained policy issues, such as the North American Free Trade Agreement (NAFTA) or the general question of American involvement in international trade, the larger interest groups, sometimes called "peak associations," find it difficult to maintain tight enough control

---

[5]Loch K. Johnson, *The Making of International Agreements: Congress Confronts the Executive* (New York: New York University Press, 1984).

of their many members to speak with a single voice. The most systematic study of international trade policies and their interest groups concluded that the leaders of these large, economic interest groups spend more time maintaining consensus among their members than they do actually lobbying Congress or pressuring major players in the executive branch.[6] The more successful economic interest groups, in terms of influencing foreign policy, are the narrower, single-issue groups such as the tobacco industry, which over the years has successfully kept American foreign policy from putting heavy restrictions on international trade in and advertising of tobacco products, and the computer hardware and software industries, which have successfully hardened the American attitude toward Chinese piracy of intellectual property rights.

Another type of interest group with a well-founded reputation for influence in foreign policy is made up of people with strong attachments and identifications to their country of national origin. The interest group with the reputation for greatest influence is Jewish Americans, whose family and emotional ties to Israel make them one of the most alert and potentially one of the most active interest groups in the whole field of foreign policy. But note once again how narrowly specialized that interest is—it focuses almost entirely and exclusively on policies toward Israel. Similarly, Americans of Irish heritage, despite having resided in the United States for two, three, or four generations, still maintain a vigilance about American policies toward Ireland and Northern Ireland; many even contribute to the activities of the Irish Republic Army. Many other ethnic and national interest groups wield similar influence over American foreign policy.

A third type of interest group, one with a reputation that has been growing in the past two decades, is the human-rights interest group. Such groups are made up of people who, instead of having self-serving economic or ethnic interests in foreign policy, are genuinely concerned for the welfare and treatment of people throughout the world—particularly those who suffer under harsh political regimes. A relatively small but often quite influential example is Amnesty International, whose exposés of human-rights abuses have altered the practices of many regimes around the world. In recent years, the Christian Right has also been a vocal advocate for the human rights of Christians who are persecuted in other parts of the world, most notably in China, for their religious beliefs. For example, the Christian Coalition joined groups like Amnesty International in lobbying Congress to cut trade with countries that permit attacks against religious believers.

A related type of group with a fast-growing influence is the ecological or environmental group, sometimes called the "greens." Groups of this nature often depend more on demonstrations than on the usual forms and strategies of influence in Washington—lobbying and using electoral politics, for example. Demonstrations in strategically located areas can have significant influence on American foreign policy. The most recent examples are the 1999 protests in Seattle and the

---

[6]Raymond A. Bauer, Ithiel de Sola Pool, and Lewis Anthony Dexter, *American Business and Public Policy: The Politics of Foreign Trade*, 2nd ed. (Chicago: Aldine-Atherton, 1972).

2001 protest in Genoa, Italy, against the World Trade Organization (WTO) and its authority to impose limits and restrictions on sovereign nations (even the United States).

The Media

The most important element of the policy influence of the media is the speed and scale with which the media can spread political communications. In that factor alone, the media's influence is growing—more news reaches more people faster, and people's reaction times are, therefore, shorter. For instance, media coverage of the 2003 Iraq war by about 600 embedded journalists was the most intensive and instantaneous in history. Some scholars have suggested that this type of reporting is a sign of how the government exploits and manipulates the media.[7]

There is another aspect of media influence to consider. Many unhappy politicians complain bitterly of "media bias." The complaint most often heard is that journalists have a liberal (anti-Republican) bias. Although this general complaint has never been adequately documented, one aspect of media bias has been shown. Using survey evidence, Michael Robinson demonstrated that reliance on television as a source of news gave people negative attitudes toward public policies and especially toward government and public officials.[8] Robinson called this attitude "videomalaise." A later study found, in addition, that "television news in particular has an inherent bias toward reporting negative and critical information. In other words, 'videomalaise' [is] as much a product of the medium as of the message."[9] One probable influence of the media on foreign as well as domestic policy has been to make the American people far more cynical and skeptical than they would otherwise have been.

Putting It Together

What can we say about who really makes American foreign policy? First, except for the president, the influence of players and shapers varies from case to case—that is a good reason to look with some care at each example of foreign policy in this chapter. Second, since the one constant influence is the centrality of the president in foreign-policy making, it is best to evaluate other actors and factors as they interact with the president.[10] Third, the reason influence varies from

 Collective Action Principle

The one consistent influence on the making of foreign policy is the president as "coordinator in chief."

[7]W. Lance Bennett and David L. Paletz, eds., *Taken by Storm: The Media, Public Opinion, and U.S. Foreign Policy in the Gulf War* (Chicago: University of Chicago Press, 1994).

[8]Michael J. Robinson, "Public Affairs Television and the Growth of Political Malaise: The Case of 'TV Selling of the Pentagon,'" *American Political Science Review* 70, no. 2 (June 1976): 425.

[9]Seymour Martin Lipset and William Schneider, *The Confidence Gap: Business, Labor, and Government in the Public Mind* (New York: Free Press, 1983), p. 405.

[10]A very good brief outline of the centrality of the president in foreign policy will be found in Paul E. Peterson, "The President's Dominance in Foreign Policy Making," *Political Science Quarterly* 109, no. 2 (Summer 1994): 215, 234.

case to case is that each case arises under different conditions and with vastly different time constraints: for issues that arise and are resolved quickly, the opportunity for influence is limited. Fourth, foreign-policy experts will usually disagree about the level of influence any player or type of player has on policy making.

But just to get started, let's make a few tentative generalizations and then put them to the test with the substance and experience reported in the remainder of this chapter. First, when an important foreign-policy decision has to be made under conditions of crisis—where "time is of the essence"—the influence of the presidency is at its strongest. Second, under those time constraints, access to the decision is limited almost exclusively to the narrowest definition of the "foreign-policy establishment." The arena for participation is tiny; any discussion at all is limited to the officially and constitutionally designated players. To put this another way, in a crisis, the foreign-policy establishment works as it is supposed to.[11] As time becomes less restricted, even when the decision to be made is of great importance, the arena of participation expands to include more government players and more nonofficial, informal players—the most concerned interest groups and the most important journalists. In other words, the arena becomes more pluralistic and, therefore, less distinguishable from the politics of domestic policy making. Third, because there are so many other countries with power and interests on any given issue, there are severe limits on the choices the United States can make. That is, in sharp contrast to domestic politics, U.S. policy makers in the foreign-policy realm are engaged not only in infighting with one another, but also in strategic interaction with those in other nations; their choices are made both in reaction to and anticipation of these strategic interactions. As one author concludes, in foreign affairs, "policy takes precedence over politics."[12] Thus, even though foreign-policy making in noncrisis situations may more closely resemble the pluralistic politics of domestic-policy making, foreign-policy making is still a narrower arena with fewer participants.

 Policy Principle

Because the number of participants in making foreign policy is limited, foreign policy reflects the goals of the president and his circle of advisers.

Rationality Principle

Foreign-policy interests are pursued through both domestic infighting and strategic interaction with foreign "players."

WHAT ARE THE VALUES IN AMERICAN FOREIGN POLICY?

When President Washington was preparing to leave office in 1796, he crafted with great care, and with the help of Alexander Hamilton and James Madison, a farewell address that is one of the most memorable documents in American history. We have already had occasion to look at a portion of Washington's Farewell

[11]One confirmation of this is found in Theodore Lowi, *The End of Liberalism: The Second Republic of the United States*, 2nd ed. (New York: W. W. Norton, 1979), pp. 127–30; another is found in Stephen Krasner, "Are Bureaucracies Important?" *Foreign Policy* 7 (Summer 1972): 159–79. However, it should be added that Krasner was writing his article in disagreement with Graham T. Allison, "Conceptual Models and the Cuban Missile Crisis," *American Political Science Review* 63, no. 3 (September 1969): 689–718.
[12]Peterson, 232.

Address because in it he gave some stern warnings against political parties (see Chapter 11). But Washington's greater concern was to warn the nation against foreign influence:

> History and experience prove that foreign influence is one of the most baneful foes of republican government. . . . The great rule of conduct for us in regard to foreign nations is, in extending our commercial relations to have with them as little *political* connection as possible. So far as we have already formed engagements let them be fulfilled with perfect good faith. Here let us stop. . . . There can be no greater error than to expect or calculate upon real favors from nation to nation. . . . Trust to temporary alliances for extraordinary emergencies, [but in all other instances] steer clear of permanent alliances with any portion of the foreign world. . . . Such an attachment of a small or weak toward a great and powerful nation dooms the former to be the satellite of the latter [emphasis in original].[13]

With the exception of a few leaders such as Thomas Jefferson and Thomas Paine, who were eager to take sides with the French against all others, Washington was probably expressing sentiments shared by most Americans. In fact, during most of the nineteenth century, American foreign policy was to a large extent no foreign policy. But Americans were never isolationist, if isolationism means the refusal to have any associations with the outside world. Americans were eager for trade and for treaties and contracts facilitating trade. Americans were also expansionists, but their vision of expansionism was limited to the North American continent only.

Three familiar historical factors help explain why Washington's sentiments became the tradition and the source of American foreign-policy values. The first was the deep anti-statist ideology shared by most Americans in the nineteenth century and into the twentieth century. Although we witness widespread anti-statism today in the form of calls for tax cuts, deregulation, privatization, and other efforts to "get the government off our backs," such sentiments were far more intense in the past, when many Americans opposed foreign entanglements, a professional military, and secret diplomacy. The second factor was federalism. The third was the position of the United States as a **client state** (a state that has the capacity to carry out its own foreign policy most of the time but that still depends upon the interests of one or more of the major powers). Most nineteenth-century Americans recognized that if the United States became entangled in foreign affairs, national power would naturally grow at the expense of the states, and so would the presidency at the expense of Congress. Why? Because foreign policy meant having a professional diplomatic corps, professional armed forces with a general staff—and secrets. This meant professionalism, elitism, and remoteness from citizens. Being a client state allowed America to keep its foreign policy to a minimum. Moreover, maintaining American sovereignty was in the

client state
A nation-state whose foreign policy is subordinated to that of another nation.

---

[13]A full version of the text of the Farewell Address, along with a discussion of the contribution to it made by Hamilton and Madison, will be found in Daniel J. Boorstin, ed., *An American Primer*, 2 vols. (Chicago: University of Chicago Press, 1966), I, pp. 192–210. This editing is by Richard B. Morris.

interest of the European powers because it prevented any one of them from gaining an advantage over the others in the Western Hemisphere.

Legacies of the Traditional System

Two identifiable legacies flowed from the long tradition based on anti-statism, federalism, and client status. One is the intermingling of domestic- and foreign-policy institutions. The second is unilateralism—America's willingness to go it alone. Each of these reveals a great deal about the values behind today's conduct of foreign policy.

History Principle
The legacies of the United States' traditional system of foreign policy include the intermingling of domestic and foreign policy and unilateralism.

Intermingling of Domestic and Foreign Policy   Because the major European powers once policed the world, American political leaders could treat foreign policy as a mere extension of domestic policy. The tariff is the best example. A tax on one category of imported goods as a favor to interests in one section of the country would directly cause friction elsewhere in the country. But the demands of those adversely affected could be met without directly compromising the original tariff, by adding a tariff to still other goods that would placate those who were complaining about the original tariff. In this manner, Congress was continually adding and adjusting tariffs on more and more classes of commodities.

An important aspect of the treatment of foreign affairs as an extension of domestic policy was amateurism. Unlike many other countries, Americans refused to develop a tradition of a separate foreign service composed of professional people who spent much of their adult lives in foreign countries, learning foreign languages, absorbing foreign cultures, and developing a sympathy for foreign points of view. Instead, Americans have tended to be highly suspicious of any American diplomat or entrepreneur who spoke sympathetically of any foreign viewpoints.[14] No systematic progress was made to create a professional diplomatic corps until after the passage of the Foreign Service Act of 1946.

Unilateralism   Unilateralism, not isolationism, was the American posture toward the world until the middle of the twentieth century. Isolationism means trying to cut off contacts with the outside, to be a self-sufficient fortress. America was never isolationist; it preferred *unilateralism,* or "going it alone." Americans have always been more likely to rally around the president in support of direct action rather than for a sustained, diplomatic involvement.

unilateralism
A foreign policy that seeks to avoid international alliances, entanglements, and permanent commitments in favor of independence, neutrality, and freedom of action.

The Great Leap to World Power

The traditional era of U.S. foreign policy came to an end with World War I for several important reasons. First, the "balance of power" system[15] that had kept

[14]E. E. Schattschneider, *Politics, Pressures and the Tariff* (Englewood Cliffs, N.J.: Prentice-Hall, 1935).

[15]"Balance of power" was the primary foreign-policy role played by the major European powers during the nineteenth century, and it is a role available to the United States in contemporary foreign affairs, a role occasionally adopted but not on a world scale. This is the third of the four roles identified and discussed later in this chapter.

the major European powers from world war for a hundred years had collapsed.[16] In fact, the great powers themselves had collapsed internally. The most devastating of all wars up to that time had ruined their economies, their empires, and, in most cases, their political systems. Second, the United States was no longer a client state but in fact one of the great powers. Third, as we saw in earlier chapters, the United States was soon to shed its traditional domestic system of federalism with its national government of almost pure promotional policy. Thus, virtually all the conditions that contributed to the traditional system of American foreign policy had disappeared. Yet there was no discernible change in America's approach to foreign policy in the period between World War I and World War II. After World War I, as one foreign-policy analyst put it, "the United States withdrew once more into its insularity. Since America was unwilling to use its power, that power, for purposes of foreign policy, did not really exist."[17]

The Great Leap in foreign policy was finally made thirty years after conditions demanded it and only then after another world war. Following World War II, pressure for a new tradition came into direct conflict with the old. The new tradition required foreign entanglements; the old tradition feared them deeply. The new tradition required diplomacy; the old distrusted it. The new tradition required acceptance of antagonistic political systems; the old embraced democracy and was aloof from all else.

The values of the new tradition were all apparent during the cold war. Instead of unilateralism, the United States pursued **multilateralism,** entering into treaties with other nations to achieve its foreign-policy goals. The most notable of these treaties is that which formed the North Atlantic Treaty Organization (NATO) in 1948, which allied the United States, Canada, and most of western Europe. With its NATO allies, the United States practiced a two-pronged policy in dealing with its rival, the Soviet Union: **containment** and **deterrence.** Fearing that the Soviet Union was bent on world domination, the United States fought wars in Korea and Vietnam to "contain" Soviet power. And in order to deter a direct attack against itself or its NATO allies, the United States developed a multibillion-dollar nuclear arsenal capable of destroying the Soviet Union many times over.

An arms race between the United States and the Soviet Union was extremely difficult, if not impossible, to resist because there was no way for either side to know when they had enough deterrent to continue preventing aggression by the other side. As we mentioned in the beginning of this chapter, the cold war ended abruptly in 1989, after the Soviet Union had spent itself into oblivion and allowed its empire to collapse. Many observers called the end of the cold war a victory for democracy. But more important, it was a victory for capitalism over communism,

---

History Principle

Once the United States became a world power following World War II, its foreign policy focused on mutilateralism, containment, and deterrence.

multilateralism A foreign policy that seeks to encourage the involvement of several nation-states in coordinated action, usually in relation to a common adversary, with terms and conditions usually specified in a multicountry treaty, such as NATO.

containment The primary cold war foreign policy of the United States during the 1950s and 1960s, whereby the United States used its political, economic, and military power to prevent the spread of communism to developing or unstable countries.

deterrence The development and maintenance of military strength for the purpose of discouraging attack.

---

[16]The best analysis of what he calls the "100 years' peace" will be found in Karl Polanyi, *The Great Transformation* (orig. 1944; rpt. Boston: Beacon, 1957), pp. 5ff.

[17]John G. Stoessinger, *Crusaders and Pragmatists: Movers of Modern American Foreign Policy,* 2nd ed. (New York: W. W. Norton, 1985), pp. 21, 34.

a vindication of the free market as the best way to produce the greatest wealth of nations. Furthering capitalism has long been one of the values guiding American foreign policy, and this might be more true now than ever before.

WHAT ARE THE INSTRUMENTS OF MODERN AMERICAN FOREIGN POLICY?

Any nation-state has at hand certain instruments, or tools, to use in implementing its foreign policy. An instrument is neutral, capable of serving many goals. There have been many instruments of American foreign policy, and we can deal here only with those instruments we deem to be most important in the modern epoch: diplomacy, the United Nations, the international monetary structure, economic aid, collective security, and military deterrence. Each of these instruments will be evaluated in this section for its utility in the conduct of American foreign policy, and each will be assessed in light of the history and development of American values.

 Rationality Principle

The instruments of foreign policy—economic, diplomatic, institutional, military—are deployed to serve strategic purposes.

Diplomacy

We begin this treatment of instruments with diplomacy because it is the instrument to which all other instruments should be subordinated, although they seldom are. Diplomacy is the representation of a government to other foreign governments. Its purpose is to promote national values or interests by peaceful means. According to Hans Morgenthau, "a diplomacy that ends in war has failed in its primary objective."[18]

The first effort to create a modern diplomatic service in the United States was made through the Rogers Act of 1924, which established the initial framework for a professional foreign-service staff. But it took World War II and the Foreign Service Act of 1946 to forge the foreign service into a fully professional diplomatic corps.

Diplomacy, by its very nature, is overshadowed by spectacular international events, dramatic initiatives, and meetings among heads of state or their direct personal representatives. The traditional American distrust of diplomacy continues today, albeit in weaker form. Impatience with or downright distrust of diplomacy has been built not only into all the other instruments of foreign policy, but also into the modern presidential system itself.[19] So much personal responsibility has been heaped upon the presidency that it is difficult for presidents to entrust any of their authority or responsibility in foreign policy to professional diplomats in the State Department and other bureaucracies.

[18]Hans J. Morgenthau, *Politics among Nations,* 2nd ed. (New York: Knopf, 1956), p. 505.
[19]See Theodore J. Lowi, *The Personal President: Power Invested, Promise Unfulfilled* (Ithaca, N.Y.: Cornell University Press, 1985), pp. 167–69.

Distrust of diplomacy has also produced a tendency among all recent presidents to turn frequently to military and civilian personnel outside the State Department to take on a special diplomatic role as direct personal representatives of the president. As discouraging as it is to those who have dedicated their careers to foreign service to have political hacks appointed over their heads, it is probably even more discouraging when they are displaced from a foreign-policy issue as soon as relations with the country they are posted in begin to heat up. When a special personal representative is sent abroad to represent the president, that envoy holds a status higher than that of the local ambassador, and the embassy becomes the envoy's temporary residence and base of operation. Despite the impressive professionalization of the American foreign service—with advanced training, competitive exams, language requirements, and career commitment—this practice of displacing career ambassadors with political appointees and with special personal presidential representatives continues. For instance, when President Clinton in 1998, sought to boost the peace process in Northern Ireland, he called upon former senator George J. Mitchell. Mitchell received almost unanimous praise for his skill and patience in chairing the Northern Ireland peace talks. The caliber of his work in Northern Ireland led to Senator Mitchell's becoming involved in another of the world's apparently unsolvable conflicts—that between the Israelis and the Palestinians.

Despite the United States' track record of distrust of diplomacy, immediately following the terrorist attacks of September 11, 2001, questions arose about how we could go after terrorist networks without the active cooperation of dozens of governments. Getting access to terrorists in various countries plus putting together and keeping together the worldwide alliance of governments to fight terrorism were diplomatic, not military, chores. In calls to more than eighty nations, Secretary of State Colin Powell helped to extract dozens of pledges that would have been more difficult to get months later, when sympathy for America began to wane. In short, global unity and success in fighting terrorism required constant diplomatic efforts, not only on the part of Powell, but also Secretary of Defense Donald Rumsfeld, National Security Adviser Condoleeza Rice, and even President Bush himself.

The administration's commitment to diplomacy as a tool of foreign policy was less clear by the following summer. The "Bush Doctrine's" basis of preemptive attack is a clear rejection of achieving national interests through diplomacy's peaceful means. It reveals a preference of the Bush administration for achieving its goals through its military superiority, even if the United States has to go it alone, rather than through its diplomatic skills. Regarding Iraq, while hawks such as Rumsfeld and Vice President Dick Cheney favored toppling Saddam Hussein by military force, Powell pushed for a diplomatic approach that used the United Nations inspections program to make sure Iraq wasn't developing weapons of mass destruction. Powell's approach ultimately prevailed, though all through the debate the United States maintained that it would be forced to resort to military measures if diplomatic efforts failed. Many saw the demand for inspections as merely a pretext, assuming that Hussein would reject those demands, for military action.

Rationality Principle

Diplomatic and military instruments may be thought of as complements to be used in tandem. The military option is the "club behind the door," to be used when diplomacy fails.

The significance of diplomacy and its vulnerability to domestic politics may be better appreciated as we proceed to the other instruments. Diplomacy was an instrument more or less imposed on Americans as the prevailing method of dealing among nation-states in the nineteenth century. The other instruments to be identified and assessed below are instruments that Americans self-consciously crafted for themselves to take care of their own chosen place in the world affairs of the second half of the twentieth century. They are, therefore, more reflective of American culture and values than is diplomacy.

The United Nations

The utility of the **United Nations (UN)** to the United States as an instrument of foreign policy can be too easily underestimated because the United Nations is a very large and unwieldly institution with few powers and no armed forces to implement its rules and resolutions. Its supreme body is the UN General Assembly, comprised of one representative of each of the 191 member states, and each member representative has one vote, regardless of the size of the country. Important issues require a two-thirds majority vote, and the annual session of the General Assembly runs only from September to December (although it can call extra sessions). It has little organization that can make it an effective decision-making body, with only six standing committees, few tight rules of procedure, and no political parties to provide priorities and discipline. Its defenders are quick to add that, although it lacks armed forces, it relies on the power of world opinion; and this is not to be taken lightly. The powers of the United Nations devolve mainly to its "executive committee," the UN Security Council, which alone has the real power to make decisions and rulings that member states are obligated by the UN Charter to implement. The Security Council may be called into session at any time, and each member (or a designated alternate) must be present at UN headquarters in New York at all times. It is composed of fifteen members: five are permanent, and ten are elected by the General Assembly for two-year, nonrepeatable terms. The five permanent members are China, France, Russia, the United Kingdom, and the United States. Each of the fifteen members has only one vote, and a nine-vote majority of the fifteen is required on all substantive matters. But each of the five permanent members also has a negative vote, a "veto," and one veto is sufficient to reject any substantive proposal.

During the first decade or more after its founding in 1945, the United Nations was a fairly consistent servant of American interests. The most spectacular example of its use as an instrument of American foreign policy was the official UN authorization and sponsorship of intervention in Korea with an international "peacekeeping force" in 1950. The Soviet Union was boycotting the United Nations at that time, and that deprived it of its ability to use its veto in the Security Council. Consequently, the United States was able to get its legitimizing resolution from the Security Council and to conduct the Korean War under the auspices of the United Nations.

> **United Nations (UN)** An organization of nations founded in 1945 to serve as a channel for negotiation and a means of settling international disputes peaceably. The UN has had frequent successes in providing a forum for negotiation and on some occasions a means of preventing international conflicts from spreading. On a number of occasions, the UN has been a convenient cover for U.S. foreign-policy goals.

The United States provided 40 percent of the UN budget in 1946 (its first full year of operation) and 26 percent of the $1.2 billion UN budget in 1997–1998.[20] Many Americans feel that the United Nations does not give good value for the investment. But any evaluation of the United Nations must take into account the purpose for which the United States sought to create it: to achieve *power without diplomacy*. After World War II, when the United States could no longer remain aloof from foreign policy, the nation's leaders sought to use our power to create an international structure that could be run with a minimum of diplomatic involvement—so that Americans could return to their normal domestic pursuits.

The UN gained a new lease on life in the post–cold war era, especially with its performance in the 1991 Persian Gulf War. Although President George H. W. Bush's immediate reaction to Iraq's invasion of Kuwait was unilateral, he quickly turned to the UN for sponsorship. The UN General Assembly initially adopted resolutions condemning the invasion and approving the full blockade of Iraq. Once the blockade was seen as having failed to achieve the unconditional withdrawal demanded by the UN, the General Assembly adopted further resolutions authorizing the twenty-nine-nation coalition to use force if, by January 15, 1991, the resolutions were not observed. As foreign-policy expert Richard Haass put it, "The UN Security Council's authorization enhanced the undertaking's political and legal appeal, making it easier for the governments [of the twenty-nine-nation alliance] to join the common effort."[21] The Gulf War victory was a UN victory just as much as it was a victory for the United States and the twenty-nine-nation alliance. The cost of the operation was estimated at $61.1 billion. First authorized by the U.S. Congress, actual U.S. outlays were offset by pledges from the other participants—the largest shares coming from Saudi Arabia ($15.6 billion), Kuwait ($16 billion), Japan ($10 billion), and Germany ($6.5 billion). The final U.S. costs were estimated at a maximum of $8 billion.[22]

Of course not all UN-sponsored actions are clear-cut victories. When Yugoslavia's communist regime collapsed in the early 1990s, the country broke apart into war among the ethnically distinct regions. The war concentrated in Bosnia, where fierce fighting broke out among Muslims, Croatians, and Serbians, each fearing they would lose their identity if one of the others dominated Bosnia. The United States and its NATO allies pushed toward peace by creating "safe havens" in several cities and towns. But the United States and its NATO allies turned the maintenance of those "safe havens" over to United Nations troops.

---

[20]In 1997, the next five biggest contributors were Japan (16.0 percent), Germany (9.0 percent), France (6.7 percent), the United Kingdom (5.6 percent), and the Russian federation (4.4 percent). These figures do not include many specific UN operations and organizations or the U.S. contributions to these programs. See the 1998 *Information Please Almanac* (Boston: Houghton Mifflin, 1998), pp. 348–49.

[21]Richard N. Haass, *The Reluctant Sheriff: The United States after the Cold War* (New York: Council on Foreign Relations Press, 1997), p. 94.

[22]There was, in fact, an angry dispute over a "surplus" of at least $2.2 billion, on the basis of which Japan and others demanded a rebate. *Report of the Secretary of Defense to the President and Congress* (Washington, D.C.: Government Printing Office, 1992), p. 26.

President Clinton criticized President Bush for not doing more, but Clinton turned out to be politically unable to muster any more support for the failing UN mission. After this failure of the international community to prevent Serbs from waging a war of aggression, which they themselves called "ethnic cleansing," UN peacekeepers and aid workers were again given the same thankless task in Kosovo immediately following the pullout of hostile Serbian troops in 1999. Despite the difficulty of restoring peace, the United Nations and its peacekeeping troops did an extraordinary job in the former Yugoslavia, dealing both with the intransigence of the warring parties and with the disagreement among the European powers about how to deal with a vicious and destructive civil war.

September 11, 2001, also implicated the UN. Less than three weeks afterward, the UN Security Council unanimously (15 to 0) approved a U.S.-sponsored resolution requiring all countries to deny safe haven to anyone financing or committing a terrorist act. The resolution actually criminalized the financing of terrorist activity and extended its coverage beyond countries to individuals and "entities" within countries. The UN also created a committee of the Security Council members to monitor implementation of the resolution, which included freezing all monetary assets available to terrorists and passing tougher laws to detain suspected terrorists as well as to share intelligence regarding terrorism. Moreover, although this resolution stresses economic rather than military means, it does not prohibit "use of force," which the UN Charter allows, as long as force is used for self-defense and not for "armed reprisals" after the fact.

The UN Security Council was also central in the debate over the United States' potential invasion of Iraq during the fall of 2002. At first, President Bush was reluctant to seek UN approval because he believed that he already had enough UN authority based on past Security Council resolutions that Saddam Hussein had so egregiously disregarded. But growing opposition to unilateral U.S. action against Iraq on the part of several Security Council members produced second thoughts and led Bush to appear at the United Nations and request a renewed and more authoritative, unconditional resolution. In response to this renewed U.S. cooperativeness, the Security Council unanimously adopted a resolution, calling on Iraq's president, Saddam Hussein, to disarm and to allow weapons inspectors into Iraq. Peacekeeping and diplomacy may be the preferred UN modus operandi, but the organization has shown that it is willing even to support war as long as prescribed procedures are followed and appropriate international support is evident. This proved not to be the case in early 2003. Following authorization for weapons inspections, the Bush administration pressured the UN Security Council to support military action in Iraq, but met resistance from France, Russia, and others. Knowing it faced a veto by France and possibly Russia, the Bush administration ultimately decided to go to war without another UN Security Council vote.

This and other recent UN interventions show the promise and the limits of the UN in the post–cold war era. Although the United States can no longer control UN decisions, as it could in the UN's early days, the UN continues to function as a useful instrument of American foreign policy.

 Rationality Principle

The United States typically incorporates the UN into its international engagements (such as the one with Iraq) as long as the collective body does not block or frustrate U.S. purposes.

Does the United States Need the United Nations?

The problems of competition and lack of collective action that underlie the principles of politics are endemic in the international arena. There is no world government—and, thus, few, if any, established rules, procedures, and norms—that may bind nations into cooperative arrangements. According to this "realist" model of international politics, nothing but a nation's self-interest matters in foreign policy.[23]

An alternative viewpoint, called liberalism, argues that, even lacking an international "policeman," international institutions such as the UN do shape the behavior of nations (much in the spirit of the third principle of politics: institutions matter). Some scholars formulate this argument using the same rational-choice language favored by realists. Nations understand that unbridled international competition can result in punishing tariff wars, arms races, and, eventually, wars. Nations realize that they are not, in fact, completely autonomous. Something of an international "society" does exist; therefore, in the long run, it is in a country's self-interest to give up some powers to an international institution.[24]

A new school, termed constructivism, takes the liberal viewpoint one step further, asserting that not just institutions, but norms and values and other ideas can shape international interactions. In the language of our five principles of politics, constructivists focus on the role of preferences. Unlike earlier theories of international relations, constructivists think that nations can have preferences for more than just domination of their opponents in the international sphere and that preferences can end up being enshrined in international institutions such as a World Court and in other aspects of international law.[25]

Each of these three theories conceive of a nation's self-interest in different ways. How has the United States' interests changed in the postwar era, and how does this help us think about U.S. foreign policy today?

One important way to approach this question is to ask: Should the United States act in concert with other nations (multilateralism), or should it go it alone (unilateralism)?

The high point of American multilateralism occurred just after World War II. The United Nations partially evolved out of the World War II alliance against the Axis powers. The principle Allied powers—the United States, the United Kingdom, and the Soviet Union—set aside their considerable ideological and geo-strategic rivalries in the hopes that they could create a new international organization that would be universal in both scope and membership.

Why did we support a United Nations when, just twenty-five years before, we had rejected the League of Nations?[26] Our historical experience in the intervening quarter century (Principle 5) brought us to a point where the United States, along with the other Allied powers, believed that an international arena without international institutions was simply too dangerous. The powers hoped that the new organization would usher in an era of international stability.

Of course, the cold war that followed hamstrung the ability of the UN to fulfill its charter. Nor has the end of the cold war seen a newly empowered United Nations. The UN has found itself unwilling or unable to deal with many emerging international crises, while facing an American "hyperpower" that is increasingly willing to resort to unilateralism. Today, without the threat of emerging powers such as Japan or Germany before World War II or of nuclear competition with the Soviet Union, the United States no longer believes that international competition is in its self-interest.

This has created significant strains with some of our closest allies, who are wedded to the institutional rules and procedures that are embodied within the UN. The war with Iraq has highlighted these strains.

It is a mistake, however, to assume that America's currently rocky relationship with the United Nations is a new phenomenon. U.S. and UN relations have been cyclical since the organization's founding. The diffuse nature of international institutions in the face of national self-interest is always a factor.

In the 1950s, America and its cold war allies dominated the UN through a majority of Security Council votes and a predominance of influence in the General Assembly. As such, American policy makers tended to bolster the United Nations and looked to increase the organization's power in the area of international relations. U.S. influence in the UN greatly waned, starting in the 1960s.

De-colonialization and the nonaligned movement decreased American power in the UN's policy-making organs, while the Vietnam War and support for Israel further alienated America from much of the world. Consequently, U.S. policy makers in the 1960s, 1970s, and 1980s preferred to work outside the United Nations and advocated a diminished role for the organization.

Influenced by the end of the cold war and the Iraqi invasion of Kuwait, President George H. W. Bush placed a new emphasis on the UN as a key to a "new world order." This pro-UN era was short-lived as the Clinton and George W. Bush administrations have been more willing to work and act outside of the United Nations. This new unilateralism has been exemplified by U.S. military actions in Bosnia and Herzegovina, Kosovo, and Iraq. The host of foreign-policy challenges now facing the United States has led some conservative political leaders to advocate America's shying away from working within the context of the United Nations. However, liberals have responded to this criticism by highlighting the limits of American power and the role that the UN could have in making up for these deficiencies.

Today, many neo-conservatives such as Deputy Secretary of Defense Paul Wolfowitz, *Weekly Standard* editor William Kristol, and columnist Charles Krauthammer advocate a diminished role for the United Nations. The UN's role must be marginalized because it has both failed to protect America's security interests (symbolized by the 9/11 attack) and failed to promote collective action between states (symbolized by the UN's unwillingness to support military action against Afghanistan and Iraq). Its concern with low politics obscures state interests, and its treatment of weak and strong states as equal is an obstacle to cooperation among the big powers.

From this perspective the United States should not work within the contexts of the United Nations because the UN can provide a means for other nations to restrict

American power. The American success in replacing the governments of Afghanistan and Iraq points to the validity of the neo-conservative position.

Liberals dispute these conclusions. They point to the limits of American power and the value of the United Nations in solving a growing variety of international problems. For liberals, American victories in the Middle East are irrelevant; these are a function of our overwhelming military power. The ongoing difficulties in establishing stable states in Afghanistan and Iraq and what liberals perceive as a growing terrorist threat demonstrate that American self-interest still lies within a set of healthy international institutions.

[23]For a statement of foreign-policy realism, see Morgenthau, *Politics among Nations*, and Kenneth N. Waltz, *Theory of International Politics* (Boston: McGraw-Hill, 1979).

[24]See Robert O. Keohane and Joseph S. Nye, *Power and Interdependence*, 2nd ed. (Glenview, Ill.: Scott, Foresman, 1989).

[25]A nice explanation of each of the three theories can be found in Stephen Walt, "International Relations: One World, Many Theories," *Foreign Policy* (Spring 1998): 29–46. Also available online at http://www.findarticles.com/cf_0/m1181/n110/20492564/p1/article.jhtml.

[26]Woodrow Wilson attempted to create a League of Nations after World War I, but the treaty was rejected by the United States Senate. The League eventually collapsed.

The International Monetary Structure

Fear of a repeat of the economic devastation that followed World War I brought the United States together with its allies (except the U.S.S.R.) to Bretton Woods, New Hampshire, in 1944 to create a new international economic structure for the postwar world. The result was two institutions: the International Bank for Reconstruction and Development (commonly called the World Bank) and the International Monetary Fund.

The World Bank was set up to finance long-term capital. Leading nations took on the obligation of contributing funds to enable the World Bank to make loans to capital-hungry countries. (The U.S. quota has been about one-third of the total.)

The International Monetary Fund (IMF) was set up to provide for the short-term flow of money. After the war, the dollar, instead of gold, was the chief means by which the currencies of one country would be "changed into" currencies of another country for purposes of making international transactions. To permit debtor countries with no international balances to make purchases and investments, the IMF was set up to lend dollars or other appropriate currencies to needy member countries to help them overcome temporary trade deficits. For many years after World War II, the IMF, along with U.S. foreign aid, in effect constituted the only international medium of exchange.

During the 1990s, the IMF returned to a position of enhanced importance through its efforts to reform some of the largest debtor nations and former communist countries and to bring them more completely into the global capitalist economy. For example, Russia and thirteen other former Soviet republics were invited to join the IMF and the World Bank with the expectation of receiving $10.5 billion from these two agencies, primarily for a ruble-stabilization fund. Each republic was to get a permanent IMF representative, and the IMF increased its staff by at least 10 percent to provide the expertise necessary to cope with the problems of these emerging capitalist economies.[27]

The IMF, with $93 billion, has more money to lend poor countries than the United States, Europe, or Japan (the three leading IMF shareholders) do individually, and it makes its policy decisions in ways that are generally consonant with the interests of the leading shareholders.[28] As an international institution, the IMF plays an important role in inducing cooperation among member countries. Two weeks after September 11, 2001, the IMF had approved a $135 million loan to economically troubled Pakistan, a key player in the war against the Taliban government of Afghanistan because of its strategic location. Turkey, with its strategic location in the Middle East, was also put back in the IMF pipeline.[29]

These activities of the IMF indicate just how effectively it is committed to the extension of capitalist victory. The reforms imposed on poorer countries—imposed as conditions to be met before receiving IMF loans—are reforms that commit a troubled country to joining or maintaining membership in the system of global capital exchange that allows investment to seek the highest profits, without restraint. This goal can ignite a boom—as it did in South Korea, Indonesia, Singapore, and Thailand—but that boom can terminate just as abruptly, leaving the economy in question defenseless.

The future of the IMF, the World Bank, and all other private sources of international investment will depend in part on extension of more credit to the Third World and other developing countries because credit means investment and productivity. But the future may depend even more upon reducing the debt that is already there from previous extensions of credit. "Debt relief" is becoming a more acceptable foreign-policy option. The most spectacular (and some say the most effective) champion and lobbyist for debt relief is Bono, one of the world's most prominent rock stars. In May 2002, in what may turn out to have been a culmination of his efforts, Bono made a two-week tour of Equatorial Africa with Paul O'Neill, the U.S. secretary of treasury, to address investment needs as well as poverty and the AIDS epidemic. Debt relief, however, seemed highest on the

Policy Principle
The lending policies of the IMF reflect the interests of its leading shareholders, most notably the United States.

[27]"IMF: Sleeve-Rolling Time," *Economist*, 2 May 1992, pp. 98–99.

[28]James Dao and Patrick E. Tyler, "U.S. Says Military Strikes Are Just a Part of Big Plan," *The Alliance*, 27 September 2001; and Joseph Kahn, "A Nation Challenged: Global Dollars," *New York Times*, 20 September 2001, p. B1.

[29]Turkey was desperate for help to extricate its economy from its worst recession since 1945. The Afghanistan crisis was going to hurt Turkey all the more; its strategic location helped its case with the IMF. "Official Says Turkey Is Advancing in Drive for I.M.F. Financing," *New York Times*, 6 October 2001, p. A7.

agenda of this "odd couple," who seemed to view it as a kind of prerequisite for the advancement of other social and cultural goals.

Economic Aid

Commitment to rebuilding war-torn countries came as easily as commitment to the basic postwar international monetary structure. This is the way President Franklin Roosevelt put the case in a press conference in November 1942, less than one year after the United States entered World War II:

> Sure, we are going to rehabilitate [other nations after the war]. Why? . . . Not only from the humanitarian point of view . . . but from the viewpoint of our own pocketbooks, and our safety from future war.[30]

History Principle

The United States' commitment to provide economic aid through the Marshall Plan was influenced by Great Britain's inability to provide such aid to other European countries.

The particular form and timing for enacting American foreign aid was heavily influenced by Great Britain's sudden decision in 1947 that it would no longer be able to maintain its commitments to Greece and Turkey (full proof that America would now have to *have* clients rather than *be* one). Within three weeks of that announcement, President Truman recommended a $400 million direct-aid program for Greece and Turkey, and by mid-May of 1947, Congress approved it. Since President Truman had placed the Greece-Turkey action within the larger context of a commitment to help rebuild and defend all countries the world over, wherever the leadership wished to develop democratic systems or to ward off communism, the Greek-Turkish aid was followed quickly by the historically unprecedented program that came to be known as the Marshall Plan, named in honor of Secretary of State (and former five-star general) George C. Marshall.[31]

The Marshall Plan—officially known as the European Recovery Program (ERP)—was essential for the rebuilding of war-ravaged Europe. By 1952, the United States had spent over $34 billion for the relief, reconstruction, and economic recovery of Western Europe. The emphasis was shifted in 1951, with passage of the Mutual Security Act, to building up European military capacity. Of the $48 billion appropriated between 1952 and 1961, over half went for military assistance, the rest for continuing economic aid. Over those years, the geographic emphasis of U.S. aid also shifted, toward South Korea, Taiwan, the Philippines, Vietnam, Iran, Greece, and Turkey—that is, toward the rim of communism. In the 1960s, the emphasis shifted once again, toward what became known as the Third World. From 1962 to 1975, over $100 billion was sent, mainly to Latin America for economic assistance. Other countries of Africa and Asia were also brought in.[32]

---

[30]Quoted in John Lewis Gaddis, *The United States and the Origins of the Cold War, 1941–1947* (New York: Columbia University Press, 1972), p. 21.

[31]The best account of the decision and its purposes will be found in Joseph Jones, *The Fifteen Weeks (February 21–June 4, 1947)* (New York: Viking, 1955).

[32]Robert A. Pastor, *Congress and the Politics of U.S. Foreign Economic Policy, 1929–1976* (Berkeley: University of California Press, 1980), pp. 256–80.

Many critics have argued that foreign aid is really aid for political and economic elites, not for the people. Although this is to a large extent true, it needs to be understood in a broader context. If a country's leaders oppose distributing food or any other form of assistance to its people, there is little that the United States, or any aid organization, can do, short of terminating the assistance. Goods have to be exchanged across national borders before they can reach the people who need them. Needy people would probably be worse off if the United States cut off aid altogether. The lines of international communication must be kept open. That is why diplomacy exists, and foreign aid can facilitate diplomacy, just as diplomacy is necessary to help get foreign aid where it is most needed.

Another important criticism of U.S. foreign-aid policy is that it has not been tied closely enough to U.S. diplomacy. This is precisely the kind of coordination failure we mentioned earlier in this chapter—a case in which one hand did not know or could not control what the other hand was doing. The original Marshall Plan was set up as an independent program outside the State Department and had its own separate missions in each participating country. Essentially, "ERP became a Second State Department."[33] This did not change until the program was reorganized as the Agency for International Development (AID) in the early 1960s. Meanwhile, the Defense Department has always had principal jurisdiction over the substantial proportion of economic aid that goes to military assistance. The Department of Agriculture administers the commodity aid programs, such as Food for Peace. Each department has in effect been able to conduct its own foreign policy, leaving many foreign diplomats to ask, "Who's in charge here?"

That brings us back to the history of U.S. efforts to balance traditional values with the modern needs of world leadership. Economic assistance is an instrument of American foreign policy, but it has been less effective than it might have been because of the inability of American politics to overcome its traditional opposition to foreign entanglements and build a unified foreign policy—something that the older nation-states would call a foreign ministry. The United States has undoubtedly made progress, but other countries still often wonder who is in charge.

Collective Security

In 1947, most Americans hoped that the United States could meet its world obligations through the United Nations and economic structures alone. But most foreign policy makers recognized that it was a vain hope even as they were permitting and encouraging Americans to believe it. They had anticipated the need for military entanglements at the time of drafting the original UN charter by insisting upon language that recognized the right of all nations to provide for their mutual defense independently of the United Nations. And almost immediately after enactment of the Marshall Plan, the White House and a parade of State and

[33]Quoted in Lowi, *The End of Liberalism*, p. 162.

Defense Department officials followed up with an urgent request to the Senate to ratify and to Congress to finance mutual defense alliances.

At first quite reluctant to approve treaties providing for national security alliances, the Senate ultimately agreed with the executive branch. The first collective security agreement was the Rio Treaty (ratified by the Senate in September 1947), which created the Organization of American States (OAS). This was the model treaty, anticipating all succeeding collective security treaties by providing that an armed attack against any of its members "shall be considered as an attack against all the American States," including the United States. A more significant break with U.S. tradition against peacetime entanglements came with the North Atlantic Treaty (signed in April 1949), which created the North Atlantic Treaty Organization (NATO). ANZUS, a treaty tying Australia and New Zealand to the United States, was signed in September 1951. Three years later, the Southeast Asia Treaty created the Southeast Asia Treaty Organization (SEATO).

In addition to these ***multilateral treaties,*** the United States entered into a number of ***bilateral treaties***—treaties between two countries. As one author has observed, the United States has been a *producer* of security while most of its allies have been *consumers* of security.[34] Figure 16.1 demonstrates that the United States has consistently devoted a greater percentage of its gross domestic product (GDP) to defense than have its NATO allies and Japan.

This pattern has continued in the post–cold war era, and its best illustration is in the Persian Gulf War, where the United States provided the initiative, the leadership, and most of the armed forces, even though its allies were obliged to reimburse over 90 percent of the cost.

It is difficult to evaluate collective security and its treaties because the purpose of collective security as an instrument of foreign policy is prevention, and success of this kind has to be measured according to what did *not* happen. The critics have argued that U.S. collective security treaties posed a threat of encirclement to the Soviet Union, forcing it to produce its own collective security, particularly the Warsaw Pact.[35] Nevertheless, no one can deny the counterargument that the planet has enjoyed almost sixty years without world war.

In 1998 the expansion of NATO took its first steps toward former Warsaw Pact members, extending membership to Poland, Hungary, and the Czech Republic. Most of Washington embraced this expansion as the true and fitting end of the cold war, and the U.S. Senate echoed this with a resounding 80-to-19 vote to induct these three former Soviet satellites into NATO. The expansion was also welcomed among European member nations, who quickly approved the move, which was hailed as the final closing of the book on Yalta, the 1945 treaty that divided Europe into Western and Soviet spheres of influence after the defeat of

multilateral treaty A treaty among more than two nations.

bilateral treaty A treaty made between two nations.

 Institution Principle

Mutual security organizations like NATO persist as institutional vehicles for solving collective-action dilemmas involving mutual defense, economic issues, environmental problems, and human rights.

[34]George H. Quester, *The Continuing Problem of International Politics* (Hinsdale, Ill.: Dryden Press, 1974), p. 229.

[35]The Warsaw Pact was signed in 1955 by the Soviet Union, the German Democratic Republic (East Germany), Poland, Hungary, Czechoslovakia, Romania, Bulgaria, and Albania. Albania later dropped out. The Warsaw Pact was terminated in 1991.

FIGURE 16.1

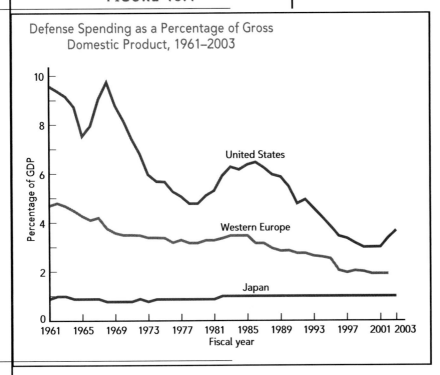

Defense Spending as a Percentage of Gross Domestic Product, 1961–2003

SOURCES: Office of Management and Budget, *Budget of the United States Government, Fiscal Year 2005, Historical Tables* (Washington, D.C.: Government Printing Office, 2004), p. 128; Stockholm International Peace Research Institute, *SIPRI Yearbook 2003* (New York: Oxford University Press, 2003), p. 303.

Germany. Expanded membership seems to have made NATO less threatening and more acceptable to Russia. Russia became a partner when the NATO-Russia Council was formed in 2002. Finally, although the expanded NATO membership (now nineteen countries) reduces the threat to Russia, it also reduces the utility of NATO as a military alliance. The September 11 attack on the United States was the first time in its fifty-plus year history that Article 5 of the North Atlantic Treaty had to be invoked; it provides that an attack on one country is an attack on all the member countries.

In fighting the war on terror, the Bush administration recognized that no matter how preponderant American power was, some aspects of its foreign policy could not be achieved without multilateral cooperation. On the other hand, the United States did not want to be constrained by its alliances. The global coalition initially forged after September 11 numbered over 170 countries. Not all joined the war effort in Afghanistan, but most if not all provided some form of support for some aspect of the war on terrorism, such as economic sanctions and intelligence. The war in Iraq, however, put the "coalition of the willing" to a test. The Bush administration was determined not to make its determination to go to war subject to the UN or NATO or any other international organization. The breadth of the United States' coalition was deemed secondary to its being nonconstraining. As a result, other than Britain, no major power supported the United States' actions.

Military Deterrence

For the first century and a half of its existence as an independent republic, the United States held strongly to a "Minuteman" theory of defense: maintain a small corps of professional officers, a few flagships, and a small contingent of marines; leave the rest of defense to the state militias. In case of war, mobilize as quickly as possible, taking advantage of the country's immense size and its separation from Europe to gain time to mobilize.

The United States applied this policy as recently as the post–World War I years and was beginning to apply it after World War II, until the new policy of preparedness won out. The cycle of demobilization-remobilization was broken, and in its place the United States adopted a new policy of constant mobilization and preparedness: *deterrence*, or the development and maintenance of military strength as a means of discouraging attack. After World War II, military deterrence against the Soviet Union became the fundamental American foreign-policy objective, requiring a vast commitment of national resources. With preparedness as the goal, peacetime defense expenditures grew steadily over the course of the cold war.[36]

The end of the cold war raised public expectations for a "peace divided" at last, after nearly a decade of the largest peacetime defense-budget increases in U.S. history. Many defense experts, liberal and conservative, feared what they called a budget "free fall," not only because deterrence was still needed but also because severe and abrupt cuts could endanger private industry in many friendly foreign countries as well as in the United States.

The Persian Gulf War brought both points dramatically into focus. First, the Iraqi invasion of Kuwait revealed the size, strength, and advanced modern technological base not only of the Iraqi armed forces, but of other countries, Arab and non-Arab, including the capability to make atomic weapons and other weapons of massive destructive power. Moreover, the demand for advanced weaponry was intensifying. The decisive victory of the United States and its allies in the Gulf War, far from discouraging the international arms trade, gave it fresh impetus. Following the Gulf War victory, *Newsweek* reported that "industry reps

---

[36]On the theory of deterrence, the classic arguments are developed in Robert Powell, *Nuclear Deterrence Theory: The Search for Credibility* (New York: Cambridge University Press, 1990).

quickly realized that foreign customers would now be beating a path to their doors, seeking to buy the winning weaponry." The Soviet Union at one time led the list of major world arms sellers, and Russia and several other republics of the former Soviet Union have continued to make international arms sales, particularly since now there are "no ideological limitations" in the competition for customers.[37] The United States now leads the list of military weapons exporters, followed by Russia, France, Great Britain, and China. Thus, some shrinkage of defense expenditure has been desirable, but Democrats and Republicans alike agree that this reduction must be guided by the continuing need to maintain U.S. and allied credibility as a deterrent to post–cold war arms races.

As to the second point, domestic pressures join international demands to fuel post–cold war defense spending. Each cut in military production and each closing of a military base or plant translates into a significant loss of jobs. Moreover, the conversion of defense industries to domestic uses is not a problem faced by the United States alone. Process Box 16.1 conveys a dramatic picture of the "international relations" of the production of one single weapons system: the F-16 fighter airplane.

Support for policies of deterrence was significantly strengthened, and doubts about the applicability of cold war theories of deterrence totally dispelled, by the sudden (because undetected by our intelligence system) entry of two new members into the nuclear club: India and Pakistan successfully tested nuclear devices in May and June of 1998. The profound conflicts between these two countries over religion, ethnic rights, and territories make resort to atomic weapons a distinct possibility. And this possibility moved more toward probability during May and June of 2002, when war threatened to break out between these two traditionally hostile countries over control of Kashmir. But of still greater import is the potential for deliberate or accidental proliferation by lesser powers and organizations. After September 11, there was increased awareness that several countries had at least some capability to develop "weapons of mass destruction," and those same countries were known to be supportive, to varying degrees, of people and organizations that were supportive of or associated with al-Qaeda. This was no longer a threat of a conventional arms race toward some kind of balance—as was the case during the cold war when it was called Mutual Assured Destruction (MAD).[38] One small nuclear, biological, or chemical device delivered in a suitcase, a shipping carton, or a suicide's waistband might be sufficient to bring a powerful nation-state to its knees. Here is deterrence put to its ultimate test.

Indeed, it's this new political reality that served as the impetus for the Bush Doctrine of preemptive use of force. Preemption means striking first, based on credible evidence that the adversary is likely to attack you. Deterrence is based on striking back, on the logic that the threat of second-strike capacity will stop

---

[37]"Arms for Sale," *Newsweek*, 8 April 1991, pp. 22–27.

[38]On Mutual Assured Destruction, see Robert Powell, "Crisis Bargaining Escalation and MAD," *American Political Science Review* 82 (1988): 155–78.

PROCESS BOX 16.1

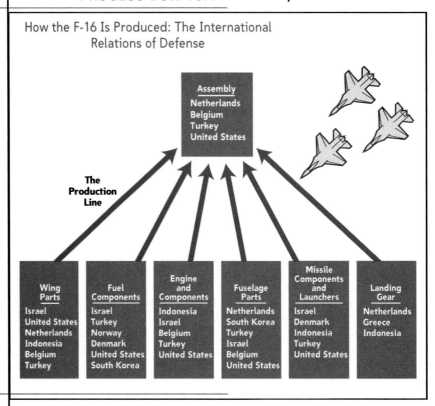

How the F-16 Is Produced: The International Relations of Defense

Assembly
Netherlands
Belgium
Turkey
United States

The Production Line

Wing Parts	Fuel Components	Engine and Components	Fuselage Parts	Missile Components and Launchers	Landing Gear
Israel	Israel	Indonesia	Netherlands	Israel	Netherlands
United States	Turkey	Israel	South Korea	Denmark	Greece
Netherlands	Norway	Belgium	Turkey	Indonesia	Indonesia
Indonesia	Denmark	Turkey	Israel	Turkey	
Belgium	United States	United States	Belgium	United States	
Turkey	South Korea		United States		

SOURCE: U.S. Congress, Office of Technology Assessment, *Arming Our Allies: Cooperation and Competition in Defense Technology*, OTA-ICS-449 (Washington, D.C.: Government Printing Office, May 1990), pp. 42–43, which is an extremely elaborate diagram of at least seventy-five separate parts of the F-16. The information was provided by the primary manufacturer, General Dynamics Corporation.

an adversary from striking first. Although deterrence held up well during the cold war, the nature of the enemy and of the threat has changed in the war on terrorism, requiring, at least according to the Bush Doctrine, a different kind of response. Preemption might not be used often, but proponents argue that it needs to be an option if deterrence fails. Moreover, according to this point of view, credible preemption could strengthen deterrence, letting an adversary know that if it even began to mount a threat, it risked being attacked. As Bush National Security Adviser Condoleeza Rice put it, there are times when "you can't wait to be attacked to respond." The war in Iraq was the first major application of the Bush Doctrine. Some allegations were made of Iraqi connections to al-Qaeda, but the main contention was if Saddam Hussein were not disarmed of his weapons of mass destruction and if he were not removed from power, the threat he posed would escalate from potential to actual. And even if he hadn't consorted and conspired with Osama bin Laden in the past, it was deemed inevitable that whatever their other differences, their anti-Americanism would bring them together. Both before and after the war in Iraq, debate over whether Iraq actually possessed weapons of mass destruction ensued. In the view of Bush's critics, credible and sufficient evidence was never produced by the administration. In addition to questioning the basis of the war, critics of the war also questioned the strategy of the Bush Doctrine. Preemptive force requires careful planning for enemy countermoves and other contingencies including the enemy's own possible decision to act "pre-preemptively" and strike first. These critics further added that if the United States can take preemptive action in the name of its own security, what will stop other countries from doing so? Criticism of Bush also became louder after the war during the rebuilding process of Iraq. Critics argued that the United States cannot win the war unless it also wins the peace, meaning that the United States must work at creating an Iraqi political system that is legitimate in the eyes of the Iraqi people and strong enough to ensure political stability and economic prosperity for its people. These are all legitimate criticisms that will continue to be debated, especially during the 2004 presidential campaign. Does the Bush Doctrine make the world a safer place? It might be too soon to tell, although we think that the point that should guide any foreign-policy decision is "Is there a substitute for war?"

ROLES NATIONS PLAY

Although each president has hundreds of small foreign fires to fight and can choose whichever instruments of policy best fit each particular situation, the primary foreign-policy problem any president faces is choosing an overall role for the country in foreign affairs. Roles help us to define a situation in order to control the element of surprise in international relations. Surprise is in fact the most dangerous aspect of international relations, especially in a world made smaller and more fragile by advances in and the proliferation of military technology.

Choosing a Role

The problem of choosing a role can be understood by identifying a limited number of roles played by nation-states in the past. Four such roles will be drawn from history—the Napoleonic, the Holy Alliance, the balance-of-power, and the economic expansionist roles. Although the definitions given here will be exaggerations of the real world, they do capture in broad outline the basic choices available.

Napoleonic role
A strategy pursued by a powerful nation to prevent aggressive actions against it by improving the internal state of affairs of a particular country, even if this means encouraging revolution in that country. This strategy is based on the assumption that countries with comparable political systems will never go to war against each other.

The Napoleonic Role The *Napoleonic role* takes its name from the role played by postrevolutionary France under Napoleon. The French at that time felt not only that their new democratic system of government was the best on earth but also that France would not be safe until democracy was adopted universally. If this meant intervention into the internal affairs of France's neighbors, and if that meant warlike reactions, then so be it. President Woodrow Wilson expressed a similar viewpoint when he supported the U.S. declaration of war in 1917 with his argument that "the world must be made safe for democracy." Obviously such a position can be adopted by any powerful nation as a rationalization for intervening at its convenience in the internal affairs of another country. But it can also be sincerely espoused, and in the United States it has from time to time enjoyed broad popular consensus. The United States played the Napoleonic role most recently in ousting Philippine dictator Ferdinand Marcos (February 1986), Panamanian leader Manuel Noriega (December 1989), the Sandinista government of Nicaragua (February 1990), and the military rulers of Haiti (September 1994).

Holy Alliance role A strategy pursued by a superpower to prevent any change in the existing distribution of power among nation-states, even if this requires intervention into the internal affairs of the country in order to keep an authoritarian ruler from being overturned.

The Holy Alliance Role The concept of the *Holy Alliance role* emerged out of the defeat of Napoleon and the agreement by the leaders of Great Britain, Russia, Austria, and Prussia to preserve the social order against *all* revolution, including democratic revolution, at whatever cost. (Post-Napoleonic France also joined it.) The Holy Alliance made use of every kind of political instrument available—including political suppression, espionage, sabotage, and outright military intervention—to keep existing governments in power. The Holy Alliance role is comparable to the Napoleonic role in that each operates on the assumption that intervention into the internal affairs of other countries is justified for the maintenance of peace. But Napoleonic intervention is motivated by fear of dictatorship, and it can accept and even encourage revolution. In contrast, Holy Alliance intervention is antagonistic to any form of political change, even when this means supporting an existing dictatorship.[39] Because the Holy Alliance role became more important after the cold war ended, illustrations of this role will be given later in the chapter.

balance-of-power role The strategy whereby many countries form alliances with one country or several other countries in order to counterbalance the behavior of other, usually more powerful, nation-states.

The Balance-of-Power Role The *balance-of-power role* is basically an effort by the major powers to play off against each other so that no great power or combination of great and lesser powers can impose conditions on others. The most relevant example of the use of this strategy is found in the nineteenth century, especially the latter half. The feature of the balance-of-power role that is most distinct from the two previously identified roles is that this role accepts the political system of each country, asking no questions except whether the country

[39]For a thorough and instructive exposition of the original Holy Alliance pattern, see Paul M. Kennedy, *The Rise and Fall of the Great Powers: Economic Change and Military Conflict from 1500 to 2000* (New York: Random House, 1987), pp. 159–60. And for a comparison of the Holy Alliance role with the balance-of-power role, to be discussed next, see Polanyi, pp. 5–11 and 259–62.

will join an alliance and will use its resources to ensure that each country will respect the borders and interests of all the others.[40]

The Economic Expansionist Role   The ***economic expansionist role,*** also called the capitalist role, shares with the balance-of-power role the attitude that the political system or ideology of a country is irrelevant; the only question is whether a country has anything to buy or sell and whether its entrepreneurs, corporations, and government agencies will honor their contracts. Governments and their armies are occasionally drawn into economic expansionist relationships in order to establish, reopen, or expand trade relationships and to keep the lines of commerce open. But the role is political, too. The point can be made that the economic expansionist role was the role consistently played by the United States in Latin and Central America until the cold war (perhaps in the 1960s and beyond) pushed us toward the Holy Alliance role with most of those countries.

Like arms control, however, economic expansion does not happen spontaneously. In the past, economic expansion owed a great deal to military backing because contracts do not enforce themselves, trade deficits are not paid automatically, and new regimes do not always honor the commitments made by regimes they replace. The only way to expand economic relationships is through diplomacy.

economic expansionist role
The strategy often pursued by capitalist countries to adopt foreign policies that will maximize the success of domestic corporations in their dealings with other countries.

Roles for America Today

Although "making the world safe for democracy" was used to justify the United States' entry into World War I, it was taken more seriously after World War II, when at last the United States was willing to play a more sustained part in world affairs. The Napoleonic role was most suited to America's view of the postwar world. To create the world's ruling regimes in the American image would indeed give Americans the opportunity to return to their private pursuits, for if all—or even most—of the world's countries were governed by democratic constitutions, there would be no more war since no democracy would ever attack another democracy—or so it has been assumed.[41]

The Cold War and the Holy Alliance Role   The emergence of the Soviet Union as a superpower was the overwhelming influence on American foreign-policy thinking in the post–World War II era. The distribution of power in the world was "bipolar," and Americans saw the world separated in two, with an "iron curtain" dividing the communist world from the free world. Immediately after the war, America's foreign-policy goal had been "pro-democracy," a Napoleonic role

[40]Felix Gilbert et al., *The Norton History of Modern Europe* (New York: W. W. Norton, 1971), pp. 1222–24.

[41]For a summary of the entire literature about the "democratic peace," see Henry S. Farber and Joanne Gowa, "Politics and Peace," *International Security* 20, no. 2 (Fall 1995): 123–46. See also Jack Levi, "Domestic Politics and War," *Journal of Interdisciplinary History* 18, no. 4 (Spring 1988): 653–73.

dominated by the Marshall Plan and the genuine hope for a democratic world. This quickly shifted toward a Holy Alliance role, with "containment" as the primary foreign-policy criterion.[42] Containment was fundamentally a Holy Alliance concept. According to foreign-policy expert Richard Barnet, during the 1950s and 1960s "the United States used its military or paramilitary power on an average of once every eighteen months either to prevent a government deemed undesirable from coming to power or to overthrow a revolutionary or reformist government considered inimical to America's interests."[43] Although Barnet did not refer to Holy Alliance, his description fits the model perfectly.

During the 1970s, the United States played the Holy Alliance role less frequently, not so much because of the outcome of the Vietnam War as because of the emergence of a multipolar world. In 1972, the United States accepted (and later recognized) the communist government of the People's Republic of China and broke forever its pure bipolar, cold war view of world power distribution. Other powers became politically important as well, including Japan, the European Economic Community (now the European Union), India, and, depending on their own resolve, the countries making up the Organization of Petroleum Exporting Countries (OPEC). The United States experimented with all four of the previously identified roles, depending on which was appropriate to a specific region of the world. In the Middle East, America tended to play an almost classic balance-of-power role, by appearing sometimes cool in its relations with Israel and by playing off one Arab country against another. The United States has been able to do this despite the fact that every country in the Middle East recognizes that for cultural, domestic, and geostrategic reasons, the United States has always considered Israel its most durable and important ally in the region and has unwaveringly committed itself to Israel's survival in a very hostile environment. President Nixon introduced balance-of-power considerations in the Far East by "playing the China card." In other parts of the world, particularly in Latin America, the United States tended to hold to the Holy Alliance and Napoleonic roles.

This multipolar phase ended after 1989, with the collapse of the Soviet Union and the end of the cold war. Soon thereafter the Warsaw Pact collapsed, too, ending armed confrontation in Europe. With almost equal suddenness, the popular demand for "self-determination" produced several new nation-states and the demand for still more. On the one hand, it was indeed good to witness the re-emergence of some twenty-five major nationalities after anywhere from forty-five to seventy-five years of suppression. On the other hand, policy makers with a sense of history are aware that this new world order bears a strong resemblance to the world of 1914. Then, the trend was known as "Balkanization." Balkanization meant nationhood and self-determination, but it also meant war. The Soviet Union after World War I and Yugoslavia after World War II kept more

<hr>

[42]The original theory of containment was articulated by former ambassador and scholar George Kennan in a famous article published under the pseudonym Mr. X, "The Sources of Soviet Conduct," *Foreign Affairs* 25 (1947): 556.

[43]Richard Barnet, "Reflections," *New Yorker*, 9 March 1987, p. 82.

than twenty nationalities from making war against each other for several decades. In 1989 and the years that followed, the world was caught unprepared for the dangers of a new disorder that the re-emergence of these nationalities produced.

The Post–Cold War Era and Global Capitalism   The abrupt end of the cold war unleashed another dynamic factor, the globalization of markets; one could call it the globalization of capitalism. This is good news, but it has its problematic side because the free market can disrupt nationhood. Although the globalization of markets is enormously productive, countries like to enjoy its benefits while attempting at the same time to prevent international economic influences from affecting local jobs, local families, and established class and tribal relationships.

This struggle between capitalism and nationhood produces a new kind of bipolarity in the world. The old world order was shaped by *external bipolarity*—of West versus East. This seems to have been replaced by *internal bipolarity*, wherein each country is struggling to make its own hard policy choices to preserve its cultural uniqueness while competing effectively in the global marketplace.

Approval of the North American Free Trade Agreement (NAFTA) serves as the best example of this struggle within the United States. NAFTA was supported by a majority of Democrats and Republicans on the grounds that a freer global market was in America's national interest. But even as NAFTA was being embraced by large bipartisan majorities in Congress, three important factions were rising to fight it. Former presidential candidate Pat Buchanan led a large segment of conservative Americans to fight NAFTA because, he argued, communities and families would be threatened by job losses and by competition from legal and illegal immigrant workers. Another large faction, led by Ross Perot, opposed NAFTA largely on the theory that American companies would move their operations to Mexico, where labor costs are lower. Organized labor also joined the fight against NAFTA.

Another form of internal bipolarity became evident in 1999 over the World Trade Organization (WTO) and its authority to impose limits and restrictions on sovereign nations, even the United States. The WTO had been around since 1994, when it was set up by the major trading nations to facilitate implementation of treaties made under the General Agreement on Tariffs and Trade (GATT). But protesters in Seattle saw the WTO as a threat to local ways of life and a contributor to job loss, environmental degradation, and violation of human rights.

These battles are examples of the "internal bipolarity" that is coming to the fore around the world. As *New York Times* foreign-affairs columnist Thomas L. Friedman put it, "Now that the free market is triumphing on a global basis, the most interesting conflicts are between the winners and losers within countries. It is these internal battles that will increasingly shape international affairs."[44]

[44]Thomas L. Friedman, "14 Big Macs Later . . . ," *New York Times*, 31 December 1995, sec. 4, p. 9.

The global market is here to stay, and American values have changed enough to incorporate it, despite the toll it may take on community and family tradition. Meanwhile, many of the elements of foreign policy created during the cold war still exist because they turned out to be good adjustments to the modern era. The Marshall Plan and the various forms of international economic aid that succeeded it continue to this day. Although appropriations for foreign aid have been shrinking, only a small minority of members of the Senate and the House favor the outright abolition of foreign-aid programs. NATO and other collective security arrangements continue, as do some aspects of containment, even though there is no longer a Soviet Union, because collective security arrangements have, as we shall see, proven useful in dealing with new democracies and other nations seeking to join the global market. Even though the former Soviet Union is now more often an ally than an adversary, the United States still quite frequently uses unilateral and multilateral means of keeping civil wars contained within their own borders so that conflict does not spread into neighboring states. America is practicing a new form of containment, but one that is based on the values and institutions of cold war containment.

The quest for a global market is more than a search for world prosperity. Economic globalization carries with it the hope that economic competition will displace armed conflict, perhaps even reducing—if not eliminating—the need for traditional diplomacy. But since there are too many instances in world history when economic competition actually led to war rather than avoided it, the United States has added democratization to the recipe of globalization because of the fairly well-supported hypothesis that democracies never go to war against each other. Thus, democratization is a genuine and strongly committed goal of U.S. foreign policy, even if it is secondary to economic expansion. Meanwhile, we play the economic card in hopes that capitalism will contribute not only to world prosperity but also to the expansion of democratization.

The Holy Alliance or the Napoleonic Role in the Post–Cold War Era? During the cold war era, the purpose of the Holy Alliance role was to keep regimes in power as long as they did not espouse Soviet foreign-policy goals. In the post–cold war world, the purpose of the Holy Alliance role is still to keep regimes in power, but only as long as they maintain general stability, keep their nationalities contained within their own borders, and encourage their economies to attain some level of participation in the global market. If countries fail to satisfy these conditions, the United States has shown signs of reverting back to its Napoleonic role. The United States has also continued to confront unfriendly dictators by adopting a Napoleonic strategy of intervention.

One case of the Holy Alliance role in the post–cold war era is Iraq's invasion of Kuwait and our Desert Storm response to it. Desert Storm is in fact a very dramatic case of the Holy Alliance role. Iraq's invasion of Kuwait occurred in July 1990, and Desert Storm was not undertaken until January 1991. In the interim, President Bush was mobilizing Congress and the American people, not only in case the United States had to intervene militarily, but also in hopes that the possibility of such action might convince Saddam Hussein to withdraw voluntarily. President Bush was also putting together a worldwide alliance of twenty-nine nations—he had no intention of leading the United States into Desert Storm without this alliance, even though most of its members did not send troops but instead sent political approval plus what amounted to a monetary subscription. Bush had initially taken a Napoleonic position, urging the people of Iraq to "take matters into their own hands" and to force Hussein to "step aside." But after America withdrew its troops and uprisings inside Iraq began to emerge, President Bush backed away, thus revealing his real intent of leaving the existing dictatorship in power, with or without Hussein. It was enough that the Iraqis stayed within their borders.

Regarding Bosnia, at first, the United States refused to exert leadership, and it deferred to the European nations when civil war erupted after Croatia and Bosnia-Herzegovina declared independence from Yugoslavia. When Europe failed to address the problem adequately, the United States and the United Kingdom stepped in, again to no avail. Although our surprise bombing in 1995 to drive the warring factions to the negotiating table in Dayton, Ohio, was virtually unilateral, what emerged was a new alliance of twenty-five nations acting "in concert" to separate the warring factions from one another. And, although one-third of the 60,000 occupying troops and virtually all the navy and air force units were American, twenty-four other nations established and maintained a physical presence in the field, all in order to maintain the status quo. Almost everything about the Bosnia operation was an acting out of the traditional Holy Alliance role.

Kosovo (part of Yugoslavia) in 1999 is the most recent and the most spectacular case of post–cold war Holy Alliance policy—although history may prove that the United States and virtually the entire Western world stumbled into this war.[45] Throughout 1998 and early 1999, ethnic cleansing was proceeding in Kosovo, but the United States would not go it alone, and the NATO nations (except for Great Britain) were not willing to intervene in Kosovo. As late as January 1999, the CIA reported to President Clinton that "[Yugoslav President Slobodan Milosevic] doesn't believe NATO is going to bomb." It is clear that these delays were due less to American indecision and more to America's or President Clinton's inability to forge a European, multicountry alliance. Prospects of embarrassment at the upcoming fiftieth anniversary of NATO may have forced some European leaders to reconsider an alliance—but only if the United States took the lead and promised to limit the assault to an air war only, which guaranteed a minimum of casualties, especially on the allied side.

So the United States got its alliance—and a precedent-setting one—but without any ground troops. President Clinton deserves some blame for the delays and for the artificial restrictions that allowed Milosevic to make the eventual intervention by the alliance all the more dangerous for the Kosovars, whom the

---

[45]See, for example, the cover story of the *Economist*, "Stumbling into War," 27 March–2 April 1999, pp. 17, 27, 49, 50.

United States wanted to defend and protect. The charge that Clinton's impeachment could not be "compartmentalized" seems to have had some basis to it.[46] But there are inherent limits to multinational coalitions, which President Clinton had to confront no matter what his domestic political distractions were at the time. NATO is simply a more formalized version of any multicountry alliance with the same fundamental problem of any such alliance: *the power of decision tends toward the weakest member.* Opposition within the NATO alliance to intervene in Kosovo came mostly from the weaker and more internally divided Italy and Greece than from Britain, France, or Germany.

The Kosovo campaign validates what we have been observing throughout this chapter: Holy Alliance politics is the prevailing American role in the world today, and the United States draws virtually all its allies and potential allies into that role at one point or another. As the *Washington Post* put it in 1999:

> Whatever the shortcomings, fighting in coalition arrangements appears to be an unavoidable fact of post–Cold War life. . . . "We need partners both for political legitimacy and for risk-sharing," says . . . a senior Pentagon planner earlier in the Clinton administration.[47]

The Economist magazine goes even further:

> The one-superpower world will not last. [China, Russia, and the Muslim world will all become geopolitical competitors.] . . . This is why the alliance of the democracies needs not only new members but also a new purpose. The alliance can no longer be just a protective American arm around Europe's shoulder; it also has to be a way for Europe and America to work together in other parts of the world. . . . This must be done—if it can be done at all—in partnership with America.[48]

The War on Terror: Holy Alliance or Napoleonic Unilateralism?   A new alliance with a new purpose was struck in response to the terrorist attacks of September 11, 2001. Such a great-power alliance for international order has not been seen since the mid-nineteenth century, when the threat came from middle-class revolutionaries rather than religious fanatics. But even though the enemies are different, the goals and strategies are about the same. All countries in the West are vulnerable because al-Qaeda and its associated groups are anti-West. All capitalist and developing countries are susceptible because terrorism is intensely anti-capitalist. And all moderate Arab regimes are vulnerable because they are seen

---

[46]Elaine Sciolino and Ethan Bronner, "How a President, Distracted by Scandal, Entered Balkan War," *New York Times*, 18 April 1999, p. 12. Note the title of this article.

[47]Quoted in Bradley Graham and Dana Priest, "'No Way to Fight a War': The Limits of Coalitions," *Washington Post National Weekly Edition*, 14 June 1999, p. 8.

[48]Editorial, "When the Snarling's Over," *Economist*, 13 March 1999, p. 17.

by al-Qaeda as traitors and collaborators with the West. All of these vulnerable nation-states need each other in order to deprive terrorists of the turf they need for safe havens, headquarters, training, and communication, not to mention financing. Even though the war against the Taliban regime was almost entirely conducted by the United States, there was no hope for a sustained campaign without the substantial cooperation and participation of many other countries. Pakistan was most vital, and its participation came at the risk of undermining its own regime. Russia and several other former Soviet republics on the northern border of Afghanistan were vital as well. The NATO nations were contractually an important part of the alliance, if only because the NATO charter was built on a solemn promise that an attack on any member was tantamount to an attack on all the members.

Yet once the Afghan phase of the war on world terrorism began quieting down, the United States confronted a new challenge: the resurgence of Iraq and the possibility that the weapons of mass destruction Saddam Hussein possessed would be used against the United States or one of its allies. President Bush's response, called the "Bush Doctrine," was a significant departure from the Holy Alliance model and movement toward a Napoleonic role. The tenets of the doctrine allowed the United States (1) to take preemptive action against a hostile state without waiting for an attack on us; (2) to eliminate permanently the threat of weapons of mass destruction; (3) to eliminate the regime itself; and (4) to remain as an occupying power in Iraq long enough to rebuild the country into a modern democratic state.

Although the Holy Alliance role continues to be the principal role among the four historically and conventionally defined roles, it is not the only role America plays, and, more to the point, it is never played exactly the same in all cases. Even in Afghanistan, the alliance to defeat the Taliban and contain terrorism was accompanied by a genuine, albeit secondary, version of the Napoleonic role. The Bush administration seemed determined not to "hit and run" as the United States had done when it fought *with* the Taliban against the Russians in the early 1980s. American policy is strongly committed both to rebuilding the Afghan economy along capitalist lines and to moving the Afghan regime toward some form of democratization. But in the short run at least, the United States quickly settled for an imposed national leader presiding over a domestic coalition of mutually distrustful warlords, with only the barest hint of any kind of democratic process. That is the underlying Holy Alliance at work. Moreover, the Bush administration is just as committed as its predecessors to a balance-of-power role in the perennial Middle East hot spot, the Israel-Palestine conflict. The United States has succeeded in keeping the neighboring Arab countries from forming their own anti-Israel (therefore anti–United States) alliance. (Keeping antagonistic alliances from forming is an essential feature of the balance-of-power role—like spokes on a wheel, keeping each country dependent upon the United States at the hub while keeping each country apart from one another.) But the use of terror by the Palestinians has prevented the United States from playing the balance-of-power role of "honest broker."

No foreign-policy role—however the roles are categorized—can ever relieve the United States of the need for sustained diplomacy. In fact, diplomacy has become all the more important because despotic regimes eventually fail and, in their failure, create instability. Since September 11, it has also become clear that failing regimes can become the breeding grounds for world terrorism. This is not to argue that war is never justifiable or that peace can always be achieved through discussions among professional diplomats. It is only to argue that there are limits to any role a country chooses to play and that failure will come faster and will be more serious if the choice of role is not made with patience, deliberation, rationality, and, most important, a sense of history.

SUMMARY

This chapter began by raising some dilemmas about forming foreign policy in a democracy like the United States. Skepticism about foreign entanglements and the secrecy surrounding many foreign-policy issues form the basis of these dilemmas. Although we cannot provide solutions to the foreign-policy issues that the United States faces, we can provide a well-balanced analysis of the problems of foreign policy. This analysis is based on the four basic dimensions of foreign policy: the players, the values, the instruments, and the roles.

The first section of this chapter looked at the players in foreign policy: the makers and shapers. The influence of institutions and groups varies from case to case, with the important exception of the president. Since the president is central to all foreign policy, it is best to assess how other actors interact with the president. In most instances, this interaction involves only the narrowest element of the foreign-policy establishment. The American people have an opportunity to influence foreign policy, but primarily through Congress or interest groups.

The next section, on values, traced the history of American values that had a particular relevance to American perspectives on the outside world. We found that the American fear of a big government applied to foreign as well as domestic governmental powers. The founders and the active public of the founding period all recognized that foreign policy was special, that the national government had special powers in its dealings with foreigners, and that presidential supremacy was justified in the conduct of foreign affairs. The only way to avoid the big national government and presidential supremacy was to avoid the foreign entanglements that made foreign policy, diplomacy, secrecy, and presidential discretion necessary. Americans held on to their "anti-statist" tradition until World War II, long after world conditions cried out for American involvement. And even as it became involved in world affairs, the United States held on tightly to the legacies of one hundred fifty years of tradition: the intermingling of domestic- and foreign-policy institutions, and unilateralism, the tendency to "go it alone" when confronted with foreign conflicts.

PRINCIPLES OF POLITICS IN REVIEW

Rationality Principle	Collective Action Principle	Institution Principle	Policy Principle	History Principle
Foreign-policy initiatives by the president are taken in light of the domestic political landscape.	Coordinating the efforts of the many agencies of the foreign-policy establishment is especially difficult.	Institutions such as the National Security Council and Department of Homeland Security attempt to keep the various foreign-policy players on the same page.	Because the number of participants in making foreign policy is limited, foreign policy reflects the goals of the president and his circle of advisers.	Historically, American presidents have come to office focused primarily on domestic policies and issues.
Foreign-policy interests are pursued through both domestic infighting and strategic interaction with foreign "players."	The one consistent influence on the making of foreign policy is the president as "coordinator in chief."	Mutual security organizations like NATO persist as institutional vehicles for solving collective-action dilemmas involving mutual defense, economic issues, environmental problems, and	The lending policies of the IMF reflect the interests of its leading shareholders, most notably the United States.	The legacies of the United States' traditional system of foreign policy include the intermingling of domestic and foreign policy and unilateralism.
The instruments of foreign-policy—economic, diplomatic, institutional, military—are deployed to serve strategic purposes.				Once the United States became a world power following World War II, its foreign policy focused on multilateralism, containment, and deterrence.
Diplomatic and military instruments may be thought of as complements to be used in tandem. The military option is the "club behind the door," to be used when diplomacy fails.				The United States' commitment to provide economic aid through the Marshall Plan was influenced by Great Britain's inability to provide such aid to other European countries.
The United States typically incorporates the UN into its international engagements (such as the one with Iraq) as long as the collective body does not block or frustrate U.S. purposes.				

We then looked at the instruments—that is, the tools—of American foreign policy. These are the basic statutes and the institutions by which foreign policy has been conducted since World War II: diplomacy, the United Nations, the international monetary structure, economic aid, collective security, and military deterrence. Although Republicans and Democrats look at the world somewhat differently, and although each president has tried to impose a distinctive flavor on foreign policy, they have all made use of these basic instruments, and that has given foreign policy a certain continuity. When Congress created these instruments after World War II, the old tradition was still so strong that it moved Congress to try to create instruments that would do their international work with a minimum of diplomacy—a minimum of human involvement. This is what we called power without diplomacy.

The next section concentrated on the role or roles the president and Congress have sought to play in the world. To help simplify the tremendous variety of tactics and strategies that foreign-policy leaders can select, we narrowed the field down to four categories of roles nations play, suggesting that there is a certain amount of consistency and stability in the conduct of a nation-state in its dealings with other nation-states. These were labeled according to actual roles that diplomatic historians have identified in the history of major Western nation-states: the Napoleonic, Holy Alliance, balance-of-power, and economic expansionist roles. We also attempted to identify and assess the role of the United States in the post–cold war era, essentially the Holy Alliance role. But whatever its advantages may be, the Holy Alliance approach will never allow the United States to conduct foreign policy without diplomacy. America is tied inextricably to the perils and ambiguities of international relationships, and diplomacy is still the monarch of all available instruments of foreign policy.

FOR FURTHER READING

Crabb, Cecil V., Jr., and Kevin V. Mulcahy. *Presidents and Foreign Policy Making: From FDR to Reagan.* Baton Rouge: Louisiana State University Press, 1986.

Gilpin, Robert. *The Political Economy of International Relations.* Princeton: Princeton University Press, 1987.

Graubard, Stephen, ed. "The Exit from Communism." *Daedalus* 121, no. 2 (Spring 1992).

Graubard, Stephen, ed. "The Quest for World Order." *Daedalus* 124, no. 3 (Summer 1995).

Greenfeld, Liah. *Nationalism: Five Roads to Modernity.* Cambridge, Mass.: Harvard University Press, 1993.

Keller, William W. *Arm in Arm: The Political Economy of the Global Arms Trade.* New York: Basic Books, 1995.

Kennan, George F. *Around the Cragged Hill: A Personal and Political Philosophy.* New York: W. W. Norton, 1993.

Kennedy, Paul M. *The Rise and Fall of the Great Powers: Economic Change and Military Conflict from 1500 to 2000.* New York: Random House, 1987.

LaFeber, Walter. *The American Age: United States Foreign Policy at Home and Abroad since 1750*. 2nd ed. 2 vols. New York: W. W. Norton, 1994.

Smist, Frank J., Jr. *Congress Oversees the United States Intelligence Community, 1947–1994*. 2nd ed. Knoxville: University of Tennessee Press, 1994.

U.S. Congress. *Report of the Congressional Committees Investigating the Iran-Contra Affair.* Washington, D.C.: Government Printing Office, 1987.

Wirls, Daniel. *Buildup: The Politics of Defense in the Reagan Era*. Ithaca, N.Y.: Cornell University Press, 1992.

Is the War in Iraq a Sign of American Hegemony?

Europe Seems to Hear Echoes of Empires Past

By RICHARD BERNSTEIN

As the United States began the task of finding Iraqi leaders to take power after the war is over, there were many in Europe and elsewhere who were reminded of an earlier period in global history—the era of imperialism. * * *

That view . . . is that the war in Iraq confirms the status of the United States as no longer just a superpower, but an unambiguously imperial power. It is seen as a country that uses its might to establish dominion over much of the rest of the world, as Rome once did, or as Britain did in the 18th and 19th centuries.

Many Americans will quarrel with that view, convinced not just of the absence of any American ambition to control foreign territory but persuaded by the Bush administration's assurance that power in Iraq will be turned over to Iraqis as swiftly as possible. It is not generally part of the American self-conception to associate the United States or even the Pax Americana with the great empires of the past.

But elsewhere in the world, the United States is being seen in a new way,

as the latest—and perhaps most powerful—of the imperialist powers that bestrode the globe over the centuries. As evidence, critics cite not just the sudden collapse of Iraqi resistance, but the stunning American military triumphs in recent years, in Afghanistan, Kosovo and in the Persian Gulf war of 1991.

With this observation, that the United States represents what the respected German daily Frankfurter Allgemeine Zeitung this week called a "hegemonic internationalism," comes the question: will it turn out to be a good thing or a bad thing for the rest of the world?

"The key terms of the new imperialism will be the ability of the U.S. to provide security and stability for other nations without imposing an American way of life," Karl-Otto Honrich, a sociologist at Goethe University in Frankfurt, said in a telephone interview. . . . * * *

To some in Europe, the operative word is not so much imperialism as it is unilateralism. The frequently repeated

New York Times, 14 April 2003, p. B13.

American contention that the United States led a broad coalition into Iraq has not been very convincing to those who feel that the war illustrates a new twist on imperial behavior: the use of pre-emption in the face of widespread opposition even from close allies.

. . . The speed of the victory in Iraq is being seen as likely to bolster the prestige and influence of those in Washington who . . . would now like to embark on further military conquests, in Syria, Iran or possibly North Korea.

Outsiders wonder whether the United States will use its power from now on as it has in Iraq, free of the constraints of multilateralism and dismissive of its allies.

Some answer that question with a stark new definition of the American goal, which is . . . to establish unchallenged global dominance. This view, which would seem strange, almost paranoid, to many Americans, is heard in serious and respectable places in Europe.

"The 'war against terrorism' is . . . not in and of itself a primary motive for a strategic new direction in international relations and American world policy," Stefan Frolich, a German scholar . . . wrote. * * *

"In this sense, the war against Iraq can be seen as a logical and necessary defense of American predominance," Mr. Frolich wrote. . . .

No historical period is exactly like another, and few people are arguing that the United States is a new Rome or a new colonialist Britain. In the main view being expressed in Europe, it is not the classic imperialist goal of national wealth and resources that is driving the United States.

In the more radical view of American power . . . the United States is seeking global dominance almost for its own sake. The more moderate view is that Washington has reacted, or perhaps overreacted, to the threat of terrorism. . . . In

ESSENCE OF THE STORY

- International observers wonder whether the American military action in Iraq heralds a new era of American unilateralism, called an "American imperium" by some.

- In the past, the United States has been able to convince countries that joint action was in everyone's self-interest. Now, some argue that the United States does not see the need to convince other nations.

- Never in modern history has there been a single country so dominant militarily as the United States.

POLITICAL ANALYSIS

- As the United States has emerged as the sole superpower, it sees little to be gained by working within broad coalitions.

- At the same time, our traditional allies in Europe are disturbed by the new assertiveness by the United States; it is in their political interest to argue in favor of international institutions, where they have relatively more power.

- Political-science theory develops along with history. The most popular models of international politics in the post–World War II era, especially balance-of-power models, may be less valid in a world with a single hegemonic power.

other words, the motive is good, even if the actions are violent and possibly unjustified.

But there seems to be a strong emerging view that the immensity of American power amounts to something different in the world.

What are the consequences? Some commentators are waiting to see whether new military actions stem from the Iraqi victory, which, they believe, would be final confirmation of the new American imperium.

Appendix

The Declaration of Independence

In Congress, July 4, 1776

When in the course of human events, it becomes necessary for one people to dissolve the political bands which have connected them with another, and to assume among the Powers of the earth, the separate and equal station to which the Laws of Nature and of Nature's God entitle them, a decent respect to the opinions of mankind requires that they should declare the causes which impel them to the separation.

We hold these truths to be self-evident, that all men are created equal, that they are endowed by their Creator with certain unalienable rights, that among these are Life, Liberty, and the pursuit of Happiness. That to secure these rights, Governments are instituted among Men, deriving their just powers from the consent of the governed. That whenever any Form of Government becomes destructive of these ends, it is the Right of the People to alter or to abolish it, and to institute new Government, laying its foundation on such principles and organizing its powers in such form, as to them shall seem most likely to effect their Safety and Happiness. Prudence, indeed, will dictate that Governments long established should not be changed for light and transient causes; and accordingly all experience hath shown, that mankind are more disposed to suffer, while evils are sufferable, than to right themselves by abolishing the forms to which they are accustomed. But when a long train of abuses and usurpations, pursuing invariably the same Object evinces a design to reduce them under absolute Despotism, it is their right, it is their duty, to throw off such Government, and to provide new Guards for their future security.—Such has been the patient sufferance of these Colonies; and such is now the necessity which constrains them to alter their former Systems of Government. The history of the present King of Great Britain is a history of repeated injuries and usurpations, all having in direct object the establishment of an absolute Tyranny over these States. To prove this, let Facts be submitted to a candid world.

He has refused his Assent to Laws, the most wholesome and necessary for the public good.

He has forbidden his Governors to pass Laws of immediate and pressing importance, unless suspended in their operation till his Assent should be obtained; and when so suspended, he has utterly neglected to attend to them.

He has refused to pass other Laws for the accommodation of large districts of people, unless those people would relinquish the right of Representation in the Legislature, a right inestimable to them and formidable to tyrants only.

He has called together legislative bodies at places unusual, uncomfortable, and distant from the depository of their public Records, for the sole purpose of fatiguing them into compliance with his measures.

He has dissolved Representative Houses repeatedly, for opposing with manly firmness his invasions on the rights of the people.

He has refused for a long time, after such dissolutions, to cause others to be elected; whereby the Legislative powers, incapable of Annihilation, have returned to the People at large for their exercise; the State remaining in the mean time exposed to all dangers of invasion from without, and convulsions within.

He has endeavored to prevent the population of these States; for that purpose obstructing the Laws of Naturalization of Foreigners; refusing to pass others to encourage their migrations hither, and raising the conditions of new Appropriations of Lands.

He has obstructed the Administration of Justice, by refusing his Assent to Laws for establishing Judiciary powers.

He has made Judges dependent on his Will alone, for the tenure of their offices, and the amount and payment of their salaries.

He has erected a multitude of New Offices, and sent hither swarms of Officers to harass our People, and eat out their substance.

He has kept among us, in times of peace, Standing Armies without the Consent of our legislature.

He has affected to render the Military independent of and superior to the Civil Power.

He has combined with others to subject us to a jurisdiction foreign to our constitution, and unacknowledged by our laws; giving his Assent to their Acts of pretended Legislation:

For quartering large bodies of armed troops among us:

For protecting them, by a mock Trial, from Punishment for any Murders which they should commit on the Inhabitants of these States:

For cutting off our Trade with all parts of the world:

For imposing taxes on us without our Consent:

For depriving us in many cases, of the benefits of Trial by jury:

For transporting us beyond Seas to be tried for pretended offences:

For abolishing the free System of English Laws in a neighboring Province, establishing therein an Arbitrary government, and enlarging its Boundaries so as to render it at once an example and fit instrument for introducing the same absolute rule into these Colonies:

For taking away our Charters, abolishing our most valuable Laws, and altering fundamentally the Forms of our Governments:

For suspending our own Legislatures, and declaring themselves invested with Power to legislate for us in all cases whatsoever.

He has abdicated Government here, by declaring us out of his Protection and waging War against us.

He has plundered our seas, ravaged our Coasts, burnt our towns, and destroyed the lives of our people.

He is at this time transporting large armies of foreign mercenaries to compleat the works of death, desolation, and tyranny, already begun with circumstances of Cruelty & perfidy scarcely paralleled in the most barbarous ages, and totally unworthy the Head of a civilized nation.

He has constrained our fellow Citizens taken Captive on the high Seas to bear Arms against their Country, to become the executioners of their friends and Brethren, or to fall themselves by their Hands.

He has excited domestic insurrections amongst us, and has endeavored to bring on the inhabitants of our frontiers, the merciless Indian Savages, whose known rule of warfare, is an undistinguished destruction of all ages, sexes, and conditions.

In every stage of these Oppressions We have Petitioned for Redress in the most humble terms: Our repeated Petitions have been answered only by repeated injury. A Prince, whose character is thus marked by every act which may define a Tyrant, is unfit to be the ruler of a free people.

Nor have We been wanting in attention to our British brethren. We have warned them from time to time of attempts by their legislature to extend an unwarrantable jurisdiction over us. We have reminded them of the circumstances of our emigration and settlement here. We have appealed to their native justice and magnanimity, and we have conjured them by the ties of our common kindred to disavow these usurpations, which, would inevitably interrupt our connections and correspondence. They too must have been deaf to the voice of justice and of consanguinity. We must, therefore, acquiesce in the necessity, which denounces our Separation, and hold them, as we hold the rest of mankind, Enemies in War, in Peace Friends.

WE, THEREFORE, the Representatives of the UNITED STATES OF AMERICA, in General Congress, Assembled, appealing to the Supreme Judge of the world for the rectitude of our intentions, do, in the Name, and by Authority of the good People of these Colonies, solemnly publish and declare, That these United Colonies are, and of Right ought to be FREE AND INDEPENDENT STATES; that they are Absolved from all Allegiance to the British Crown, and that all political connection between them and the State of Great Britain, is and ought to be totally dissolved; and that as Free and Independent States, they have full Power to levy War, conclude Peace, contract Alliances, establish Commerce, and to do all other Acts and Things which Independent States may of right do. And for the support of this Declaration, with a firm reliance on the Protection of Divine Providence, we mutually pledge to each other our Lives, our Fortunes, and our sacred Honor.

The foregoing Declaration was, by order of Congress, engrossed, and signed by the following members:

John Hancock

NEW HAMPSHIRE
Josiah Bartlett
William Whipple
Matthew Thornton

MASSACHUSETTS BAY
Samuel Adams
John Adams
Robert Treat Paine
Elbridge Gerry

RHODE ISLAND
Stephen Hopkins
William Ellery

CONNECTICUT
Roger Sherman
Samuel Huntington
William Williams
Oliver Wolcott

NEW YORK
William Floyd
Philip Livingston
Francis Lewis
Lewis Morris

NEW JERSEY
Richard Stockton
John Witherspoon
Francis Hopkinson
John Hart
Abraham Clark

PENNSYLVANIA
Robert Morris
Benjamin Rush
Benjamin Franklin
John Morton
George Clymer
James Smith
George Taylor
James Wilson
George Ross

DELAWARE
Caesar Rodney
George Read
Thomas M'Kean

MARYLAND
Samuel Chase
William Paca
Thomas Stone
Charles Carroll,
  of Carrollton

VIRGINIA
George Wythe
Richard Henry Lee
Thomas Jefferson
Benjamin Harrison
Thomas Nelson, Jr.
Francis Lightfoot Lee
Carter Braxton

NORTH CAROLINA
William Hooper
Joseph Hewes
John Penn

SOUTH CAROLINA
Edward Rutledge
Thomas Heyward, Jr.
Thomas Lynch, Jr.
Arthur Middleton

GEORGIA
Button Gwinnett
Lyman Hall
George Walton

Resolved, That copies of the Declaration be sent to the several assemblies, conventions, and committees, or councils of safety, and to the several commanding officers of the continental troops; that it be proclaimed in each of the United States, at the head of the army.

The Articles of Confederation

Agreed to by Congress November 15, 1777; ratified and in force
March 1, 1781

To all whom these Presents shall come, we the undersigned Delegates of the States affixed to our Names send greeting. Whereas the Delegates of the United States of America in Congress assembled did on the fifteenth day of November in the Year of our Lord One Thousand Seven Hundred and Seventy seven, and in the Second Year of the Independence of America agree to certain articles of Confederation and perpetual Union between the States of Newhampshire, Massachusetts-bay, Rhodeisland and Providence Plantations, Connecticut, New-York, New-Jersey, Pennsylvania, Delaware, Maryland, Virginia, North-Carolina, South-Carolina and Georgia in the Words following, viz. "Articles of Confederation and perpetual Union between the states of Newhampshire, Massachusetts-bay, Rhodeisland and Providence Plantations, Connecticut, New-York, New-Jersey, Pennsylvania, Delaware, Maryland, Virginia, North-Carolina, South-Carolina and Georgia.

Art. I. The Stile of this confederacy shall be "The United States of America."

Art. II. Each state retains its sovereignty, freedom and independence, and every Power, Jurisdiction and right, which is not by this confederation expressly delegated to the United States, in Congress assembled.

Art. III. The said states hereby severally enter into a firm league of friendship with each other, for their common defence, the security of their Liberties, and their mutual and general welfare, binding themselves to assist each other, against all force offered to, or attacks made upon them, or any of them, on account of religion, sovereignty, trade, or any other pretence whatever.

Art. IV. The better to secure and perpetuate mutual friendship and intercourse among the people of the different states in this union, the free inhabitants of each of these states, paupers, vagabonds and fugitives from Justice excepted, shall be entitled to all privileges and immunities of free citizens in the several states; and the people of each state shall have free ingress and regress to and from any other state, and shall enjoy therein all the privileges of trade and commerce, subject to the same duties, impositions and restrictions as the inhabitants thereof respectively, provided that such restriction shall not extend so far as to prevent the removal of property imported into any state, to any other state of which the Owner is an inhabitant; provided also that no imposition, duties or restriction shall be laid by any state, on the property of the united states, or either of them.

If any Person guilty of, or charged with treason, felony, or other high misdemeanor in any state, shall flee from Justice, and be found in any of the united states, he shall upon demand of the Governor or executive power, of the state from which he fled, be delivered up and removed to the state having jurisdiction of his offence.

Full faith and credit shall be given in each of these states to the records, acts and judicial proceedings of the courts and magistrates of every other state.

Art. V. For the more convenient management of the general interests of the united states, delegates shall be annually appointed in such manner as the legislature of each state shall direct, to meet in Congress on the first Monday in November, in every year, with a power reserved to each state, to recall its delegates, or any of them, at any time within the year, and to send others in their stead, for the remainder of the Year.

No state shall be represented in Congress by less than two, nor by more than seven Members; and no person shall be capable of being a delegate for more than three years in any term of six years; nor shall any person, being a delegate, be capable of holding any office under the united states, for which he, or another for his benefit receives any salary, fees or emolument of any kind.

Each state shall maintain its own delegates in a meeting of the states, and while they act as members of the committee of the states.

In determining questions in the united states, in Congress assembled, each state shall have one vote.

Freedom of speech and debate in Congress shall not be impeached or questioned in any Court, or place out of Congress, and the members of congress shall be protected in their persons from arrests and imprisonments, during the time of their going to and from, and attendance on congress, except for treason, felony, or breach of the peace.

Art. VI. No state without the Consent of the united states in congress assembled, shall send any embassy to, or receive any embassy from, or enter into any conference, agreement, or alliance or treaty with any King, prince or state; nor shall any person holding any office or profit or trust under the united states, or any of them, accept of any present, emolument, office or title of any kind whatever from any king, prince or foreign state; nor shall the united states in congress assembled, or any of them, grant any title of nobility.

No two or more states shall enter into any treaty, confederation or alliance whatever between them, without the consent of the united states in congress assembled, specifying accurately the purposes for which the same is to be entered into, and how long it shall continue.

No state shall lay any imposts or duties, which may interfere with any stipulations in treaties, entered into by the united states in congress assembled, with any king, prince or state, in pursuance of any treaties already proposed by congress, to the courts of France and Spain.

No vessels of war shall be kept up in time of peace by any state, except such number only, as shall be deemed necessary by the united states in congress assembled, for the defence of such state, or its trade; nor shall any body of forces be kept up by any state, in time of peace, except such number only, as in the judgment of the united states, in congress assembled, shall be deemed requisite to garrison the forts necessary for the defence of such state; but every state shall always keep up a well regulated and disciplined militia, sufficiently armed and accoutred, and shall provide and constantly have ready for use, in public stores, a due number of field pieces and tents, and a proper quantity of arms, ammunition and camp equipage.

No state shall engage in any war without the consent of the united states in congress assembled, unless such state be actually invaded by enemies, or shall have received certain advice of a resolution being formed by some nation of Indians to invade such state, and the danger is so imminent as not to admit of a delay, till the united states in congress asssembled can be consulted; nor shall any state grant commissions to any ships or vessels of war, nor letters of marque or reprisal, except it be after a declaration of war by the united states in congress assembled, and then only against the kingdom or state and the subjects thereof, against which war has been so declared, and under such regulations as shall be established by the united states in congress assembled, unless such state be infested by pirates; in which case vessels of war may be fitted out for that occasion, and kept so long as the danger shall continue, or until the united states in congress assembled shall determine otherwise.

Art. VII. When land-forces are raised by any state for the common defence, all officers of or under the rank of colonel, shall be appointed by the legislature of each state respectively by whom such forces shall be raised, or in such manner as such state shall direct, and all vacancies shall be filled up by the state which first made the appointment.

Art. VIII. All charges of war, and all other expences that shall be incurred for the common defence or general welfare, and allowed by the united states in congress assembled, shall be defrayed out of a common treasury, which shall be supplied by the several states, in proportion to the value of all land within each state, granted to or surveyed for any Person, as such land and the buildings and improvements thereon shall be estimated according to such mode as the united states in congress assembled, shall from time to time direct and appoint. The taxes for paying that proportion shall be laid and levied by the authority and direction of the legislatures of the several states within the time agreed upon by the united states in congress assembled.

Art. IX. The united states in congress assembled, shall have the sole and exclusive right and power of determining on peace and war, except in the cases mentioned in the sixth article—of sending and receiving ambassadors—entering into treaties and alliances, provided that no treaty of commerce shall be made whereby the legislative power of the respective states shall be restrained from imposing such imposts and duties on foreigners, as their own people are subjected to, or from prohibiting the exportation of any species of goods or commodities whatsoever—of establishing rules for deciding in all cases, what captures on land or water shall be legal, and in what manner prizes taken by land or naval forces in the service of the united states shall be divided or appropriated—of granting letters of marque and reprisal in times of peace—appointing courts for the trial of piracies and felonies committed on the high seas and establishing courts for receiving and determining finally appeals in all cases of captures, provided that no member of congress shall be appointed a judge of any of the said courts.

The united states in congress assembled shall also be the last resort on appeal in all disputes and differences now subsisting or that hereafter may arise between two or more states concerning boundary, jurisdiction or any other cause whatever; which authority shall always be exercised in the manner following. Whenever the legislative or executive authority or lawful agent of any state in controversy with another shall present a petition to congress stating the matter in question and praying for a hearing, notice thereof shall be given by order of congress to the legislative or executive authority of the other state in controversy, and a day assigned for the appearance of the parties by their lawful agents, who shall then be directed to appoint by joint consent, commissioners or judges to constitute a court for hearing and determining the matter in question: but if they cannot agree, congress shall name three persons out of each of the united states, and from the list of such persons each party shall alternately strike out one, the petitioners beginning, until the number shall be reduced to thirteen; and from that number not less than seven, nor more than nine names as congress shall direct, shall in the presence of congress be drawn out by lot, and the persons whose names shall be so drawn or any five of them, shall be commissioners or judges, to hear and finally determine the controversy, so always as a major part of the judges who shall hear the cause shall agree in the determination: and if either party shall neglect to attend at the day appointed, without shewing reasons, which congress shall judge sufficient, or being present shall refuse to strike, the congress shall proceed to nominate three persons out of each state, and the secretary of congress shall strike in behalf of such party absent or refusing; and the judgment and sentence of the court to be appointed, in the manner before prescribed, shall be final and conclusive; and if any of the parties shall refuse to submit to the authority of such court, or to appear to defend their claim or cause, the court shall nevertheless proceed to pronounce sentence, or judgment, which shall in like manner be final and decisive, the judgment or sentence and other proceedings being in either case transmitted to congress, and lodged among the acts of congress for the security of the parties concerned: provided that every commissioner, before he sits in judgment, shall take an oath to be administered by one of the judges of the supreme or superior court of the state, where the cause shall be tried, "well and truly to hear and determine the matter in question, according to the best of his judgment, without favour, affection or hope of reward:" provided also that no state shall be deprived of territory for the benefit of the united states.

All controversies concerning the private right of soil claimed under different grants of two or more states, whose jurisdictions as they may respect such lands, and the states which passed such grants are adjusted, the said grants or either of them being at the same time claimed to have originated antecedent to such settlement of jurisdiction, shall on the petition of either party to the congress of the united states, be finally determined as near as may be in the same manner as is before prescribed for deciding disputes respecting territorial jurisdiction between different states.

The united states in congress assembled shall also have the sole and exclusive right and power of regulating the alloy and value of coin struck by their own authority, or by that of the respective states—fixing the standard of weights and measures throughout the united states—regulating the trade and managing all affairs with the Indians, not members of any of the states, provided that the legislative right of any state within its own limits be not infringed or violated—establishing and regulating post-offices from one state to another, throughout all the united states, and exacting such postage on the papers passing thro' the same as may be requisite to defray the expences of the said office—appointing all officers of the land forces, in the service of the united states, except regimental officers—appointing all the officers of the united states—making rules for the government and regulation of the said land and naval forces, and directing their operations.

The united states in congress assembled shall have the authority to appoint a committee, to sit in the recess of congress, to be denominated "A Committee of the States," and to consist of one delegate from each state; and to appoint such other committees and civil officers as may be necessary for managing the general affairs of the united states under their direction—to appoint one of their number to preside, provided that no person be allowed to serve in the office of president more than one year in any term of three years; to ascertain the necessary sums of Money to be raised for the service of the united states, and to appropriate and apply the same for defraying the public expences—to borrow money, or emit bills on the credit of the united states, transmitting every half year to the respective states an account of the sums of money so borrowed or emitted,—to build and equip a navy—to agree upon the number of land forces, and to make requisitions from each state for its quota, in proportion to the number of white inhabitants in such state; which requisition shall be binding, and thereupon the legislature of each state shall appoint the regimental officers, raise the men and cloath, arm and equip them in a soldier like manner, at the expence of the united states, and the officers and men so cloathed, armed and equipped shall march to the place appointed, and within the time agreed on by the united states in congress assembled: But if the united states in congress assembled shall, on consideration of circumstances judge proper that any state should not raise men, or should raise a smaller number than its quota, and that any other state should raise a greater number of men than the quota thereof, such extra number shall be raised, officered, cloathed, armed and equipped in the same manner as the quota of such state, unless the legislature of such state shall judge that such extra number cannot be safely spared out of the same, in which case they shall raise, officer, cloath, arm and equip as many of such extra number as they judge can be safely spared. And the officers and men so cloathed, armed and equipped, shall march to the place appointed, and within the time agreed on by the united states in congress assembled.

The united states in congress assembled shall never engage in a war, nor grant letters of marque and reprisal in time of peace, nor enter into any treaties or alliances, nor coin money, nor regulate the value thereof, nor ascertain the sums and expences necessary for the defence and welfare of the united states, or any of them, nor emit bills, nor borrow money on the credit of the united states, nor appropriate money, nor agree upon the number of vessels of war, to be built or purchased, or the number of land or sea forces to be raised, nor appoint a commander in chief of the army or navy, unless nine states assent to the same: nor shall a question on any other point, except for adjourning from day to day be determined, unless by the votes of a majority of the united states in congress assembled.

The congress of the united states shall have power to adjourn to any time within the year, and to any place within the united states, so that no period of adjournment be for a longer duration than the space of six Months, and shall publish the Journal of their proceedings monthly, except such parts thereof relating to treaties, alliances or military operations as in their judgment require secresy; and the yeas and nays of the delegates of each state on any question shall be entered on the Journal, when it is desired by any delegate; and the delegates of a state, or any of them, at his or their request shall be furnished with a transcript of the said Journal, except such parts as are above excepted to lay before the legislatures of the several states.

Art. X. The committee of the states, or any nine of them, shall be authorised to execute, in the recess of congress, such of the powers of congress as the united states in congress assembled, by the consent of nine states, shall from time to time think expedient to vest them with; provided that no power be delegated to the said committee, for the exercise of which, by the articles of confederation, the voice of nine states in the congress of the united states assembled is requisite.

Art. XI. Canada acceding to this confederation, and joining in the measures of the united states, shall be admitted into, and entitled to all the advantages of this union: but no other colony shall be admitted into the same, unless such admission be agreed to by nine states.

Art. XII. All bills of credit emitted, monies borrowed and debts contracted by, or under the authority of congress, before the assembling of the united states, in pursuance of the present confederation, shall be deemed and considered as a charge against the united states, for payment and satisfaction whereof the said united states and the public faith are hereby solemnly pledged.

Art. XIII. Every state shall abide by the determinations of the united states in congress assembled, on all questions which by this confederation are submitted to them. And the Articles of this confederation shall be inviolably observed by every state, and the union shall be perpetual; nor shall any alteration at any time hereafter be made in any of them; unless such alteration be agreed to in a congress of the united states, and be afterwards confirmed by the legislatures of every state.

AND WHEREAS it hath pleased the Great Governor of the World to incline the hearts of the legislatures we respectively represent in congress, to approve of, and to authorize us to ratify the said articles of confederation and perpetual union. KNOW YE that we the undersigned delegates, by virtue of the power and authority to us given for that purpose, do by these presents, in the name and in behalf of our respective constituents, fully and entirely ratify and confirm each and every of the said articles of confederation and perpetual union, and all and singular the matters and things therein contained: And we do further solemnly plight and engage the faith of our respective constituents, that they shall abide by the determination of the united states in congress assembled, on all questions, which by the said confederation are submitted to them. And that the articles thereof shall be inviolably observed by the states we respectively represent, and that the union shall be perpetual. In Witness whereof we have hereunto set our hands in Congress. Done at Philadelphia in the state of Pennsylvania the ninth Day of July in the Year of our Lord one Thousand seven Hundred and Seventy-eight and in the third year of the independence of America.

The Constitution of the United States of America

Annotated with references to *The Federalist Papers*

[PREAMBLE]

We the People of the United States, in Order to form a more perfect Union, establish Justice, insure domestic Tranquility, provide for the common defence, promote the general Welfare, and secure the Blessings of Liberty to ourselves and our Posterity, do ordain and establish this Constitution for the United States of America.

84 (Hamilton)

ARTICLE I

Section 1
[LEGISLATIVE POWERS]

All legislative Powers herein granted shall be vested in a Congress of the United States, which shall consist of a Senate and House of Representatives.

10, 45 (Madison)

Section 2
[HOUSE OF REPRESENTATIVES, HOW CONSTITUTED, POWER OF IMPEACHMENT]

The House of Representatives shall be composed of Members chosen every second Year by the People of the several States, and the Electors in each State shall have the Qualifications requisite for Electors of the most numerous Branch of the State Legislature.

39, 45, 52–53, 57 (Madison)

No Person shall be a Representative who shall not have attained to the Age of twenty-five Years, and been seven Years a Citizen of the United States, and who shall not, when elected, be an inhabitant of that State in which he shall be chosen.

52 (Madison)

60 (Hamilton)

Representatives and *direct Taxes*[1] shall be apportioned among the several States which may be included within this Union, according to their respective Numbers, *which shall be determined by adding to the whole Number of free Persons, including those bound to Service for a Term of Years,* and excluding Indians not taxed, *three-fifths of all other Persons.*[2] The actual Enumeration shall be made within three Years after the first Meeting of the Congress of the United States, and within every subsequent Term of ten Years, in such Manner as they shall by Law direct. The Number of Representatives shall not exceed one for every thirty

54, 58 (Madison)

[1]Modified by Sixteenth Amendment.
[2]Modified by Fourteenth Amendment.

55–56 (Madison)

Thousand, but each State shall have at Least one Representative; *and until such enumeration shall be made, the State of New Hampshire shall be entitled to chuse three, Massachusetts eight, Rhode-Island and Providence Plantations one, Connecticut five, New-York six, New Jersey four, Pennsylvania eight, Delaware one, Maryland six, Virginia ten, North Carolina five, South Carolina five, and Georgia three.*[3]

When vacancies happen in the Representation from any State, the Executive Authority thereof shall issue Writs of Election to fill such Vacancies.

79 (Hamilton)

The House of Representatives shall chuse their Speaker and other Officers; and shall have the sole Power of Impeachment.

Section 3
[THE SENATE, HOW CONSTITUTED, IMPEACHMENT TRIALS]

39, 45 (Madison)
60 (Hamilton)

The Senate of the United States shall be composed of two Senators from each State, *chosen by the Legislature thereof,*[4] for six Years; and each Senator shall have one Vote.

62–63 (Madison)
59, 68 (Hamilton)

Immediately after they shall be assembled in Consequence of the first Election, they shall be divided as equally as may be into three Classes. The Seats of the Senators of the first Class shall be vacated at the Expiration of the second Year, of the second Class at the Expiration of the fourth Year, and of the third Class at the Expiration of the sixth Year, so that one third may be chosen every second Year: *and if vacancies happen by Resignation, or otherwise, during the Recess of the Legislature of any State, the Executive thereof may make temporary Appointments until the next Meeting of the Legislature, which shall then fill such Vacancies.*[5]

62 (Madison)
64 (Jay)

No person shall be a Senator who shall not have attained to the Age of thirty Years, and been nine Years a Citizen of the United States, and who shall not, when elected, be an Inhabitant of that State for which he shall be chosen.

The Vice-President of the United States shall be President of the Senate, but shall have no Vote, unless they be equally divided.

The Senate shall chuse their other Officers, and also a President pro tempore, in the Absence of the Vice-President, or when he shall exercise the Office of President of the United States.

39 (Madison)
65–67, 79
(Hamilton)

The Senate shall have the sole Power to try all Impeachments. When sitting for that Purpose, they shall be on Oath or Affirmation. When the President of the United States is tried, the Chief Justice shall preside: And no Person shall be convicted without the Concurrence of two-thirds of the Members present.

84 (Hamilton)

Judgment in Cases of Impeachment shall not extend further than to removal from Office, and disqualification to hold and enjoy any Office of honor, Trust or Profit under the United States: but the Party convicted shall nevertheless be liable and subject to Indictment, Trial, Judgment and Punishment, according to Law.

---

[3]Temporary provision.
[4]Modified by Seventeenth Amendment.
[5]Modified by Seventeenth Amendment.

Section 4
[ELECTION OF SENATORS AND REPRESENTATIVES]

The Times, Places and Manner of holding Elections for Senators and Representatives, shall be prescribed in each State by the Legislature thereof; but the Congress may at any time by Law make or alter such Regulations, except as to the Places of chusing Senators.

The Congress shall assemble at least once in every Year, and such Meeting shall be on the first Monday in December, unless they shall by Law appoint a different Day.[6]

59–61 (Hamilton)

Section 5
[QUORUM, JOURNALS, MEETINGS, ADJOURNMENTS]

Each House shall be the Judge of the Elections, Returns and Qualifications of its own Members, and a Majority of each shall constitute a Quorum to do Business; but a smaller Number may adjourn from day to day, and may be authorized to compel the Attendance of absent Members, in such Manner, and under the Penalties as each House may provide.

Each House may determine the Rules of its Proceedings, punish its Members for disorderly Behavior, and, with the Concurrence of two-thirds, expel a Member.

Each House shall keep a Journal of its Proceedings, and from time to time publish the same, excepting such Parts as may in their Judgment require Secrecy; and the Yeas and Nays of the Members of either House on any questions shall, at the Desire of one-fifth of the present, be entered on the Journal.

Neither House, during the Session of Congress, shall, without the Consent of the other, adjourn for more than three days, nor to any other Place than that in which the two Houses shall be sitting.

Section 6
[COMPENSATION, PRIVILEGES, DISABILITIES]

The Senators and Representatives shall receive a Compensation for their Services, to be ascertained by Law, and paid out of the Treasury of the United States. They shall in all Cases, except Treason, Felony and Breach of the Peace, be privileged from Arrest during their Attendance at the Session of their respective Houses, and in going to and returning from the same; and for any Speech or Debate in either House, they shall not be questioned in any other Place.

No Senator or Representative shall, during the time for which he was elected, be appointed to any civil Office under the authority of the United States, which shall have been created, or the Emoluments whereof shall have been encreased during such time; and no Person holding any Office under the United States, shall be a Member of either House during his Continuance in Office.

55 (Madison)
76 (Hamilton)

[6]Modified by Twentieth Amendment.

Section 7
[PROCEDURE IN PASSING BILLS AND RESOLUTIONS]

66 (Hamilton)

All Bills for raising Revenue shall originate in the House of Representatives; but the Senate may propose or concur with Amendments as on other Bills.

69, 73 (Hamilton)

Every Bill which shall have passed the House of Representatives and the Senate, shall, before it become a Law, be presented to the President of the United States; if he approve he shall sign it, but if not he shall return it, with his Objections to that House in which it shall have originated, who shall enter the Objections at large on their Journal, and proceed to reconsider it. If after such Reconsideration two-thirds of that House shall agree to pass the Bill, it shall be sent, together with the Objections, to the other House, by which it shall likewise be reconsidered, and if approved by two-thirds of that House it shall become a Law. But in all such Cases the Votes of both Houses shall be determined by Yeas and Nays, and the Names of the Persons voting for and against the Bill shall be entered on the Journal of each House respectively. If any Bill shall not be returned by the President within ten Days (Sundays excepted) after it shall have been presented to him, the Same shall be a Law, in like Manner as if he had signed it, unless the Congress by their Adjournment prevent its Return, in which Case it shall not be a Law.

69, 73 (Hamilton)

Every Order, Resolution, or Vote to which the Concurrence of the Senate and House of Representatives may be necessary (except on a question of Adjournment) shall be presented to the President of the United States; and before the Same shall take Effect, shall be approved by him, or being disapproved by him, shall be repassed by two-thirds of the Senate and House of Representatives, according to the Rules and Limitations prescribed in the Case of a Bill.

Section 8
[POWERS OF CONGRESS]

The Congress shall have Power

30–36 (Hamilton)
41 (Madison)

To lay and collect Taxes, Duties, Imposts and Excises, to pay the Debts and provide for the common Defence and general Welfare of the United States; but all Duties, Imposts and excises shall be uniform throughout the United States;

To borrow Money on the Credit of the United States;

56 (Madison)

To regulate Commerce with foreign Nations, and among the several States,

42, 45, 56
(Madison)

and with the Indian Tribes;

32 (Hamilton)

To establish an uniform Rule of Naturalization, and uniform Laws on the subject of Bankruptcies throughout the United States;

42 (Madison)

To coin Money, regulate the Value thereof, and of foreign Coin, and fix the Standard of Weights and Measures;

42 (Madison)

To provide for the Punishment of counterfeiting the Securities and current Coin of the United States;

To establish Post Offices and post Roads;

42 (Madison)

To promote the Progress of Science and useful Arts, by securing for limited

42, 43 (Madison)

Times to Authors and Inventors the exclusive Right to their respective Writings and Discoveries;

81 (Hamilton)

To constitute Tribunals inferior to the supreme Court;

To define and Punish Piracies and Felonies committed on the high Seas, and Offences against the Law of Nations;

42 (Madison)

To declare War, grant Letters of Marque and Reprisal, and make Rules concerning Captures on Land and Water;

41 (Madison)

To raise and support Armies, but no Appropriation of Money to that Use shall be for a longer Term than two Years;

23, 24, 26 (Hamilton)

To provide and maintain a Navy;

41 (Madison)

To make Rules for the Government and Regulation of the land and naval forces;

To provide for calling for the Militia to execute the Laws of the Union, suppress Insurrections and repel Invasions;

29 (Hamilton)

To provide for organizing, arming, and disciplining, the Militia, and for governing such Part of them as may be employed in the Service of the United States, reserving to the States respectively, the Appointment of the Officers, and the Authority of training the Militia according to the discipline prescribed by Congress;

29 (Hamilton)
56 (Madison)

To exercise exclusive Legislation in all Cases whatsoever, over such District (not exceeding ten Miles square) as may, by Cession of particular States, and the Acceptance of Congress, become the Seat of the Government of the United States, and to exercise like Authority over all Places purchased by the Consent of the Legislature of the State in which the Same shall be, for the Erection of Forts, Magazines, Arsenals, dock-Yards, and other needful Buildings;—And

32 (Hamilton)
43 (Madison)

To make all Laws which shall be necessary and proper for carrying into Execution the foregoing Powers, and all other Powers vested by this Constitution in the Government of the United States, or in any Department or Officer thereof.

29, 33 (Hamilton)
44 (Madison)

Section 9
[SOME RESTRICTIONS ON FEDERAL POWER]

The Migration or Importation of such Persons as any of the States now existing shall think proper to admit, shall not be prohibited by the Congress prior to the Year one thousand eight hundred and eight, but a Tax or Duty may be imposed on such Importation, not exceeding ten dollars for each Person.[7]

42 (Madison)

The privilege of the Writ of *Habeas Corpus* shall not be suspended, unless when in Cases of Rebellion or Invasion the public Safety may require it.

83, 84 (Hamilton)

No Bill of Attainder or ex post facto Law shall be passed.

84 (Hamilton)

No Capitation, or other direct, Tax shall be laid, unless in Proportion to the Census or Enumeration herein before directed to be taken.[8]

No Tax or Duty shall be laid on Articles exported from any State.

No Preference shall be given by any Regulation of Commerce or Revenue to the Ports of one State over those of another; nor shall vessels bound to, or from, one State, be obliged to enter, clear, or pay Duties in another.

32 (Hamilton)

No Money shall be drawn from the Treasury, but in Consequence of Appropriations made by Law; and a regular Statement and Account of the Receipts and Expenditures of all public Money shall be published from time to time.

[7]Temporary provision.
[8]Modified by Sixteenth Amendment.

39 (Madison)
84 (Hamilton)

No Title of Nobility shall be granted by the United States: And no Person holding any Office of Profit or Trust under them, shall, without the Consent of the Congress, accept of any present, Emolument, Office or Title, of any kind whatever, from any King, Prince, or foreign State.

Section 10
[RESTRICTIONS UPON POWERS OF STATES]

33 (Hamilton)
44 (Madison)

No State shall enter into any Treaty, Alliance, or Confederation; grant Letters of Marque and Reprisal; coin Money; emit Bills of Credit; make any Thing but gold and silver Coin a Tender in Payment of Debts; pass any Bill of Attainder, ex post facto Law, or Law impairing the Obligation of Contracts, or grant any Title of Nobility.

32 (Hamilton)
44 (Madison)

No State shall, without the Consent of the Congress, lay any Imposts or Duties on Imports or Exports, except what may be absolutely necessary for executing its inspection Laws: and the net Produce of all Duties and Imposts, laid by any State on Imports or Exports, shall be for the Use of the Treasury of the United States; and all such Laws shall be subject to the Revision and Control of the Congress.

No State shall, without the Consent of Congress, lay any Duty of Tonnage, keep Troops, or Ships of War in time of Peace, enter into any Agreement or Compact with another State, or with a foreign Power, or engage in War, unless actually invaded, or in such imminent Danger as will not admit of Delay.

ARTICLE II

Section 1
[EXECUTIVE POWER, ELECTION, QUALIFICATIONS OF THE PRESIDENT]

39 (Madison)
70, 71, 84
(Hamilton)

68, 69, 71, 77
(Hamilton)
39, 45 (Madison)

The executive Power shall be vested in a President of the United States of America. *He shall hold his Office during the Term of four years and, together with the Vice-President, chosen for the same Term, be elected, as follows:*[9]

Each State shall appoint, in such Manner as the Legislature thereof may direct, a Number of Electors, equal to the whole Number of Senators and Representatives to which the State may be entitled in the Congress: but no Senator or Representative, or Person holding an Office of Trust or Profit under the United States, shall be appointed an Elector.

66 (Hamilton)

The electors shall meet in their respective States, and vote by ballot for two Persons, of whom one at least shall not be an Inhabitant of the same State with themselves. And they shall make a List of all the Persons voted for, and of the Number of Votes for each; which List they shall sign and certify, and transmit sealed to the Seat of the Government of the United States, directed to the President of the Senate. The President of the Senate shall, in the Presence of the Senate and House of Representatives, open all the Certificates, and the Votes shall then be counted. The Person having the greatest Number of Votes shall be the

---

[9]Number of terms limited to two by Twenty-second Amendment.

President, if such Number be a Majority of the whole Number of Electors appointed; and if there be more than one who have such Majority and have an equal Number of Votes, then the House of Representatives shall immediately chuse by Ballot one of them for President; and if no person have a Majority, then from the five highest on the List the said House shall in like Manner chuse the President. But in chusing the President, the Votes shall be taken by States, the Representation from each State having one Vote; A quorum for this Purpose shall consist of a Member or Members from two-thirds of the States, and a Majority of all the States shall be necessary to a Choice. In every Case, after the Choice of the President, the person having the greatest Number of Votes of the Electors shall be the Vice-President. But if there should remain two or more who have equal vote, the Senate shall chuse from them by Ballot the Vice-President.[10]

The Congress may determine the Time of chusing the Electors, and the Day on which they shall give their Votes; which Day shall be the same throughout the United States.

No Person except a natural born Citizen, or a Citizen of the United States, at the time of the Adoption of this Constitution, shall be eligible to the Office of President; neither shall any Person be eligible to that Office who shall not have attained to the Age of thirty-five Years, and been fourteen Years a Resident within the United States.　　　64 (Jay)

In Case of the Removal of the President from Office, or his Death, Resignation, or Inability to discharge the Powers and Duties of the said Office, the same shall devolve on the Vice-President, and the Congress may by Law provide for the Case of Removal, Death, Resignation, or Inability, both of the President and Vice-President, declaring what Officer shall then act as President, and such Officer shall act accordingly, until the Disability be removed, or a President shall be elected.

The President shall, at stated Times, receive for his Services, a Compensation, which shall neither be encreased nor diminished during the Period for which he shall have been elected, and he shall not receive within that Period any other Emolument from the United States, or any of them.　　　73, 79 (Hamilton)

Before he enter on the Execution of his Office, he shall take the following Oath or Affirmation:—"I do solemnly swear (or affirm) that I will faithfully execute the Office of President of the United States, and will to the best of my Ability, preserve, protect and defend the Constitution of the United States."

Section 2
[POWERS OF THE PRESIDENT]

The President shall be Commander in Chief of the Army and Navy of the United States, and of the Militia of the several States, when called into the actual Service of the United States; he may require the Opinion, in writing, of the principal Officer in each of the executive Departments, upon any Subject relating to the Duties of their respective Offices, and he shall have Power to grant Reprieves and Pardons for Offences against the United States, except in Cases of Impeachment.　　　69, 74 (Hamilton)

[10]Modified by Twelfth and Twentieth Amendments.

He shall have Power, by and with the Advice and Consent of the Senate, to make Treaties, provided two-thirds of the Senators present concur; and he shall nominate, and by and with the Advice and Consent of the Senate, shall appoint Ambassadors, other public Ministers and Consuls, Judges of the Supreme Court, and all other Officers of the United States, whose Appointments are not herein otherwise provided for, and which shall be established by Law: but the Congress may by Law vest the Appointment of such inferior Officers, as they think proper, in the President alone, in the Courts of Law, or in the Heads of Departments.

The President shall have Power to fill up all Vacancies that may happen during the Recess of the Senate, by granting Commissions which shall expire at the End of their next Session.

Section 3
[POWERS AND DUTIES OF THE PRESIDENT]

He shall from time to time give to the Congress Information of the State of the Union, and recommend to their Consideration such Measures as he shall judge necessary and expedient; he may, on extraordinary Occasions, convene both Houses, or either of them, and in Case of Disagreement between them, with Respect to the Time of Adjournment, he may adjourn them to such Time as he shall think proper; he shall receive Ambassadors and other public Ministers; he shall take Care that the Laws be faithfully executed, and shall Commission all the Officers of the United States.

Section 4
[IMPEACHMENT]

The President, Vice-President and all civil Officers of the United States shall be removed from Office on Impeachment for, and Conviction of, Treason, Bribery, or other high Crimes and Misdemeanors.

ARTICLE III

Section 1
[JUDICIAL POWER, TENURE OF OFFICE]

The judicial Power of the United States, shall be vested in one supreme Court, and in such inferior Courts as the Congress may from time to time ordain and establish. The Judges, both of the supreme and inferior Courts, shall hold their Offices during good Behavior, and shall, at stated Times, receive for their Services, a Compensation, which shall not be diminished during their Continuance in Office.

Section 2
[JURISDICTION]

The judicial Power shall extend to all Cases, in Law and Equity, arising under this Constitution, the Laws of the United States, and Treaties made, or which shall be made, under their Authority;—to all Cases affecting Ambassadors, other public Ministers and Consuls;—to all Cases of admiralty and maritime Jurisdiction;—to Controversies to which the United States shall be a party;—to Controversies between two or more States;—*between a State and Citizens of another State;*—between Citizens of different States,—between Citizens of the same State claiming Lands under Grants of different States, *and between a State*, or the Citizens thereof, *and foreign States, Citizens or Subjects.*[11]

In all Cases affecting Ambassadors, other public Ministers and Consuls, and those in which a State shall be Party, the supreme Court shall have original Jurisdiction. In all the other Cases before mentioned, the supreme Court shall have appellate Jurisdiction, both as to Law and Fact, with such Exceptions, and under such Regulations as Congress shall make.

81 (Hamilton)

The Trial of all Crimes, except in Cases of Impeachment, shall be by Jury; and such Trial shall be held in the State where the said Crimes shall have been committed; but when not committed within any State, the Trial shall be at such Place or Places as the Congress may by Law have directed.

83, 84 (Hamilton)

Section 3
[TREASON, PROOF, AND PUNISHMENT]

Treason against the United States, shall consist only in levying War against them, or in adhering to their Enemies, giving them Aid and Comfort. No Person shall be convicted of Treason unless on the Testimony of two Witnesses to the same overt Act, or on Confession in open Court.

43 (Madison)
84 (Hamilton)

The Congress shall have Power to declare the Punishment of Treason, but no Attainder of Treason shall work Corruption of Blood, or Forfeiture except during the Life of the Person attained.

43 (Madison)
84 (Hamilton)

ARTICLE IV

Section 1
[FAITH AND CREDIT AMONG STATES]

Full Faith and Credit shall be given in each State to the public Acts, Records, and judicial Proceedings of every other State. And the Congress may by general Laws prescribe the Manner in which such Acts, Records and Proceedings shall be proved, and the Effect thereof.

42 (Madison)

Section 2
[PRIVILEGES AND IMMUNITIES, FUGITIVES]

The Citizens of each State shall be entitled to all Privileges and Immunities of Citizens in the several States.

80 (Hamilton)

A person charged in any State with Treason, Felony or other Crime, who shall flee from Justice, and be found in another State, shall on Demand of the executive

[11]Modified by Eleventh Amendment.

Authority of the State from which he fled, be delivered up to be removed to the State having Jurisdiction of the Crime.

No person held to Service or Labour in one State, under the Laws thereof, escaping into another, shall, in Consequence of any Law or Regulation therein, be discharged from such Service or Labour, but shall be delivered up on Claim of the Party to whom such Service or Labour may be due.[12]

Section 3
[ADMISSION OF NEW STATES]

43 (Madison)

New States may be admitted by the Congress into this Union; but no new State shall be formed or erected within the Jurisdiction of any other State; nor any State be formed by the Junction of two or more States, or Parts of States, without the Consent of the Legislatures of the States concerned as well as of the Congress.

43 (Madison)

The Congress shall have Power to dispose of and make all needful Rules and Regulations respecting the Territory or other Property belonging to the United States; and nothing in this Constitution shall be so construed as to Prejudice any Claims of the United States, or of any particular State.

Section 4
[GUARANTEE OF REPUBLICAN GOVERNMENT]

39, 43
(Madison)

The United States shall guarantee to every State in this Union a Republican Form of Government, and shall protect each of them against Invasion; and on Application of the Legislature, or of the Executive (when the Legislature cannot be convened) against domestic Violence.

ARTICLE V

[AMENDMENT OF THE CONSTITUTION]

39, 43 (Madison)
85 (Hamilton)

The Congress, whenever two-thirds of both Houses shall deem it necessary, shall propose Amendments to this Constitution, or, on the Application of the Legislatures of two-thirds of the several States, shall call a Convention for proposing Amendments, which, in either Case, shall be valid to all Intents and Purposes, as Part of this Constitution, when ratified by the Legislatures of three-fourths of the several States, or by Conventions in three-fourths thereof, as the one or the other Mode of Ratification may be proposed by the Congress; *Provided that no Amendment which may be made prior to the Year One thousand eight hundred and eight shall in any Manner affect the first and fourth Clauses in the Ninth Section of the first Article;*[13] and that no State, without its Consent, shall be deprived of its equal Suffrage in the Senate.

[12]Repealed by Thirteenth Amendment.
[13]Temporary provision.

ARTICLE VI

[DEBTS, SUPREMACY, OATH]

All Debts contracted and Engagements entered into, before the Adoption of this Constitution, shall be as valid against the United States under this Constitution, as under the Confederation.

43 (Madison)

This Constitution, and the Laws of the United States which shall be made in Pursuance thereof; and all Treaties made, or which shall be made, under the Authority of the United States, shall be the supreme Law of the Land; and the Judges in every State shall be bound thereby, any Thing in the Constitution or Laws of any State to the Contrary notwithstanding.

27, 33 (Hamilton)
39, 44 (Madison)

The Senators and Representatives before mentioned, and the Members of the several State Legislatures, and all executive and judicial Officers, both of the United States and of the several States, shall be bound by Oath or Affirmation, to support this Constitution; but no religious Test shall be required as a Qualification to any Office or public Trust under the United States.

27 (Hamilton)
44 (Madison)

ARTICLE VII

[RATIFICATION AND ESTABLISHMENT]

The Ratification of the Conventions of nine States, shall be sufficient for the Establishment of this Constitution between the States so ratifying the Same.[14]

39, 40, 43
(Madison)

Done in Convention by the Unanimous Consent of the States present the Seventeenth Day of September in the Year of our Lord one thousand seven hundred and Eighty seven and of the Independence of the United States of America the Twelfth. *In Witness* whereof We have hereunto subscribed our Names,

G:⁰ WASHINGTON—
*Presidt, and Deputy
from Virginia*

New Hampshire	JOHN LANGDON	New York	ALEXANDER HAMILTON
	NICHOLAS GILMAN		
		New Jersey	WIL: LIVINGSTON
Massachusetts	NATHANIEL GORHAM		DAVID BREARLEY
	RUFUS KING		WM PATERSON
			JONA: DAYTON
Connecticut	WM SAML JOHNSON		
	ROGER SHERMAN		

[14]The Constitution was submitted on September 17, 1787, by the Constitutional Convention, was ratified by the conventions of several states at various dates up to May 29, 1790, and became effective on March 4, 1789.

Pennsylvania	B Franklin	Virginia	John Blair—
	Thomas Mifflin		James Madison Jr.
	Robt Morris		
	Geo. Clymer	North	Wm Blount
	Thos. FitzSimons	Carolina	Richd Dobbs Spaight
	Jared Ingersoll		Hu Williamson
	James Wilson		
	Gouv Morris	South	J. Rutledge
		Carolina	Charles Cotesworth Pinckney
Delaware	Geo Read		Charles Pinckney
	Gunning Bedfor Jun		Pierce Butler
	John Dickinson		
	Richard Bassett	Georgia	William Few
	Jaco: Broom		Abr Baldwin
Maryland	James McHenry		
	Dan of St Thos. Jenifer		
	Danl Carroll		

Amendments to the Constitution

Proposed by Congress and Ratified by the Legislatures of the Several States, Pursuant to Article V of the Original Constitution.

Amendments I–X, known as the Bill of Rights, were proposed by Congress on September 25, 1789, and ratified on December 15, 1791. *The Federalist Papers* comments, mainly in opposition to a Bill of Rights, can be found in number 84 (Hamilton).

AMENDMENT I
[FREEDOM OF RELIGION, OF SPEECH, AND OF THE PRESS]

Congress shall make no law respecting an establishment of religion, or prohibiting the free exercise thereof; or abridging the freedom of speech, or of the press; or the right of the people peaceably to assemble, and to petition the Government for a redress of grievances.

AMENDMENT II
[RIGHT TO KEEP AND BEAR ARMS]

A well regulated Militia, being necessary to the security of a free State, the right of the people to keep and bear Arms, shall not be infringed.

AMENDMENT III
[QUARTERING OF SOLDIERS]

No Soldier shall, in time of peace be quartered in any house, without the consent of the Owner, nor in time of war, but in a manner to be prescribed by law.

AMENDMENT IV
[SECURITY FROM UNWARRANTABLE SEARCH AND SEIZURE]

The right of the people to be secure in their persons, houses, papers, and effects, against unreasonable searches and seizures, shall not be violated, and no Warrants shall issue, but upon probable cause, supported by Oath or affirmation, and particularly describing the place to be searched, and the persons or things to be seized.

AMENDMENT V
[RIGHTS OF ACCUSED PERSONS IN CRIMINAL PROCEEDINGS]

No person shall be held to answer for a capital, or otherwise infamous crime, unless on a presentment or indictment of a Grand Jury, except in cases arising in the land or naval forces, or in the Militia, when in actual service in time of War or in public danger; nor shall any person be subject for the same offence to be twice put in jeopardy of life or limb; nor shall be compelled in any Criminal Case to be a witness against himself, nor be deprived of life, liberty, or property, without due process of law; nor shall private property be taken for public use, without just compensation.

AMENDMENT VI
[RIGHT TO SPEEDY TRIAL, WITNESSES, ETC.]

In all criminal prosecutions, the accused shall enjoy the right to a speedy and public trial, by an impartial jury of the State and district wherein the crime shall have been committed, which district shall have been previously ascertained by law, and to be informed of the nature and cause of the accusation; to be confronted with the witnesses against him; to have compulsory process for obtaining Witnesses in his favor, and to have the Assistance of Counsel for his defence.

AMENDMENT VII
[TRIAL BY JURY IN CIVIL CASES]

In suits at common law, where the value in controversy shall exceed twenty dollars, the right of trial by jury shall be preserved, and no fact tried by a jury shall be otherwise re-examined in any Court of the United States, than according to the rules of the common law.

AMENDMENT VIII
[BAILS, FINES, PUNISHMENTS]

Excessive bail shall not be required, nor excessive fines imposed, nor cruel and unusual punishments inflicted.

AMENDMENT IX
[RESERVATION OF RIGHTS OF PEOPLE]

The enumeration in the Constitution, of certain rights, shall not be construed to deny or disparage others retained by the people.

AMENDMENT X
[POWERS RESERVED TO STATES OR PEOPLE]

The powers not delegated to the United States by the Constitution, nor prohibited by it to the States, are reserved to the States respectively, or to the people.

AMENDMENT XI
[Proposed by Congress on March 4, 1794; declared ratified on January 8, 1798.]

The Judicial power of the United States shall not be construed to extend to any suit in law or equity, commenced or prosecuted against one of the United States by Citizens of another State, or by Citizens or Subjects of any Foreign State.

AMENDMENT XII

[Proposed by Congress on December 9, 1803; declared ratified on September 25, 1804.]

[ELECTION OF PRESIDENT AND VICE-PRESIDENT]

The Electors shall meet in their respective states, and vote by ballot for President and Vice-President, one of whom, at least, shall not be an inhabitant of the same state with themselves; they shall name in their ballots the person voted for as President, and in distinct ballots the person voted for as Vice-President, and they shall make distinct lists of all persons voted for as President, and of all persons voted for as Vice-President, and of the number of votes for each, which lists they shall sign and certify, and transmit sealed to the seat of the government of the United States, directed to the President of the Senate;—The President of the Senate shall, in presence of the Senate and House of Representatives, open all the certificates and the votes shall then be counted;—The person having the greatest number of votes for President, shall be the President, if such number be a majority of the whole number of Electors appointed; and if no person have such majority, then from the persons having the highest numbers not exceeding three on the list of those voted for as President, the House of Representatives shall choose immediately, by ballot, the President. But in choosing the President, the votes shall be taken by states, the representation from each state having one vote; a quorum for this purpose shall consist of a member or members from two-thirds of the states, and a majority of all states shall be necessary to a choice. And if the House of Representatives shall not choose a President whenever the right of choice shall devolve upon them, before the fourth day of March next following, then the Vice-President, shall act as President, as in the case of the death or other constitutional disability of the President. The person having the greatest number of votes as Vice-President, shall be the Vice-President, if such a number be a majority of the whole number of Electors appointed, and if no person have a majority, then from the two highest numbers on the list, the Senate shall choose the Vice-President; a quorum for the purpose shall consist of two-thirds of the whole number of Senators, and a majority of the whole number shall be necessary to a choice. But no person constitutionally ineligible to the office of President shall be eligible to that of Vice-President of the United States.

AMENDMENT XIII

[Proposed by Congress on January 31, 1865; declared ratified on December 18, 1865.]

Section 1

[ABOLITION OF SLAVERY]

Neither slavery nor involuntary servitude, except as a punishment for crime whereof the party shall have been duly convicted, shall exist within the United States, or any place subject to their jurisdiction.

Section 2

[POWER TO ENFORCE THIS ARTICLE]

Congress shall have power to enforce this article by appropriate legislation.

AMENDMENT XIV

[Proposed by Congress on June 13, 1866; declared ratified on July 28, 1868.]

Section 1

[CITIZENSHIP RIGHTS NOT TO BE ABRIDGED BY STATES]

All persons born or naturalized in the United States, and subject to the jurisdiction thereof, are citizens of the United States and of the State wherein they reside. No state shall make or enforce any law which shall abridge the privileges or immunities of citizens of the United States; nor shall any State deprive any person of life, liberty, or property, without due process of law; nor deny to any person within its jurisdiction the equal protection of the laws.

Section 2

[APPORTIONMENT OF REPRESENTATIVES IN CONGRESS]

Representatives shall be apportioned among the several States according to their respective numbers, counting the whole number of persons in each State, excluding Indians not taxed. But when the right to vote at any election for the choice of electors for President and Vice-President of the United States, Representatives in Congress, the Executive and Judicial officers of a State, or the members of the Legislature thereof, is denied to any of the male inhabitants of such State, being twenty-one years of age, and citizens of the United States, or in any way abridged, except for participation in rebellion, or other crime, the basis of representation therein shall be reduced in the proportion which the number of such male citizens shall bear to the whole number of male citizens twenty-one years of age in such State.

Section 3

[PERSONS DISQUALIFIED FROM HOLDING OFFICE]

No person shall be a Senator or Representative in Congress, or elector of President and Vice-President, or hold any office, civil or military, under the United States, or under any State, who, having previously taken an oath, as a member of Congress, or as an officer of the United States, or as a member of any State legislature, or as an executive or judicial officer of any State, to support the Constitution of the United States, shall have engaged in insurrection or rebellion against the same, or given aid or comfort to the enemies thereof. But Congress may by a vote of two-thirds of each House, remove such disability.

Section 4
[WHAT PUBLIC DEBTS ARE VALID]

The validity of the public debt of the United States, authorized by law, including debts incurred for payment of pensions and bounties for services in suppressing insurrection or rebellion, shall not be questioned. But neither the United States nor any State shall assume or pay any debt or obligation incurred in aid of insurrection or rebellion against the United States, or any claim for the loss or emancipation of any slave; but all such debts, obligations and claims shall be held illegal and void.

Section 5
[POWER TO ENFORCE THIS ARTICLE]

The Congress shall have power to enforce, by appropriate legislation, the provisions of this article.

AMENDMENT XV

[Proposed by Congress on February 26, 1869; declared ratified on March 30, 1870.]

Section 1
[NEGRO SUFFRAGE]

The right of citizens of the United States to vote shall not be denied or abridged by the United States or by any State on account of race, color, or previous condition of servitude.

Section 2
[POWER TO ENFORCE THIS ARTICLE]

The Congress shall have power to enforce this article by appropriate legislation.

AMENDMENT XVI

[Proposed by Congress on July 12, 1909; declared ratified on February 25, 1913.]
[AUTHORIZING INCOME TAXES]

The Congress shall have power to lay and collect taxes on incomes, from whatever source derived, without apportionment among the several States, and without regard to any census or enumeration.

AMENDMENT XVII

[Proposed by Congress on May 13, 1912; declared ratified on May 31, 1913.]
[POPULAR ELECTION OF SENATORS]

The Senate of the United States shall be composed of two Senators from each State, elected by the people thereof, for six years; and each Senator shall have one vote. The electors in each State shall have the qualifications requisite for electors of the most numerous branch of the State Legislature.

When vacancies happen in the representation of any State in the Senate, the executive authority of such State shall issue writs of election to fill such vacancies:

Provided, That the Legislature of any State may empower the executive thereof to make temporary appointment until the people fill the vacancies by election as the Legislature may direct.

This amendment shall not be so construed as to affect the election or term of any Senator chosen before it becomes valid as part of the Constitution.

AMENDMENT XVIII

[Proposed by Congress December 18, 1917; declared ratified on January 29, 1919.]

Section 1
[NATIONAL LIQUOR PROHIBITION]

After one year from the ratification of this article the manufacture, sale, or transportation of intoxicating liquors within, the importation thereof into, or the exportation thereof from the United States and all territory subject to the jurisdiction thereof for beverage purposes is hereby prohibited.

Section 2
[POWER TO ENFORCE THIS ARTICLE]

The Congress and the several states shall have concurrent power to enforce this article by appropriate legislation.

Section 3
[RATIFICATION WITHIN SEVEN YEARS]

This article shall be inoperative unless it shall have been ratified as an amendment to the Constitution by the legislatures of the several states, as provided in the Constitution, within seven years from the date of the submission hereof to the states by the Congress.[15]

AMENDMENT XIX

[Proposed by Congress on June 4, 1919; declared ratified on August 26, 1920.]
[WOMAN SUFFRAGE]

The right of the citizens of the United States to vote shall not be denied or abridged by the United States or by any state on account of sex.

Congress shall have power to enforce this article by appropriate legislation.

AMENDMENT XX

[Proposed by Congress on March 2, 1932; declared ratified on February 6, 1933.]

Section 1
[TERMS OF OFFICE]

The terms of the President and Vice-President shall end at noon on the 20th day of January, and the terms of the Senators and Representatives at noon on the

[15]Repealed by Twenty-first Amendment.

3rd day of January, of the years in which such terms would have ended if this article had not been ratified; and the terms of their successors shall then begin.

Section 2
[TIME OF CONVENING CONGRESS]

The Congress shall assemble at least once in every year, and such meeting shall begin at noon on the 3rd day of January, unless they shall by law appoint a different day.

Section 3
[DEATH OF PRESIDENT-ELECT]

If, at the time fixed for the beginning of the term of the President, the President-elect shall have died, the Vice-President-elect shall become President. If a President shall not have been chosen before the time fixed for the beginning of his term, or if the President-elect shall have failed to qualify, then the Vice-President-elect shall act as President until a President shall have qualified; and the Congress may by law provide for the case wherein neither a President-elect nor a Vice-President-elect shall have qualified, declaring who shall then act as President, or the manner in which one who is to act shall be selected, and such person shall act accordingly until a President or Vice President shall have qualified.

Section 4
[ELECTION OF THE PRESIDENT]

The Congress may by law provide for the case of the death of any of the persons from whom the House of Representatives may choose a President whenever the right of choice shall have devolved upon them, and for the case of the death of any of the persons from whom the Senate may choose a Vice-President whenever the right of choice shall have devolved upon them.

Section 5
[AMENDMENT TAKES EFFECT]

Sections 1 and 2 shall take effect on the 15th day of October following ratification of this article.

Section 6
[RATIFICATION WITHIN SEVEN YEARS]

This article shall be inoperative unless it shall have been ratified as an amendment to the Constitution by the legislatures of three-fourths of the several States within seven years from the date of its submission.

AMENDMENT XXI

[Proposed by Congress on February 20, 1933; declared ratified on December 5, 1933.]

Section 1
[NATIONAL LIQUOR PROHIBITION REPEALED]

The eighteenth article of amendment to the Constitution of the United States is hereby repealed.

Section 2
[TRANSPORTATION OF LIQUOR INTO "DRY" STATES]

The transportation or importation into any State, Territory, or Possession of the United States for delivery or use therein of intoxicating liquors, in violation of the laws thereof, is hereby prohibited.

Section 3
[RATIFICATION WITHIN SEVEN YEARS]

This article shall be inoperative unless it shall have been ratified as an amendment to the Constitution by conventions in the several States, as provided in the Constitution, within seven years from the date of the submission hereof to the States by the Congress.

AMENDMENT XXII

[Proposed by Congress on March 21, 1947; declared ratified on February 26, 1951.]

Section 1
[TENURE OF PRESIDENT LIMITED]

No person shall be elected to the office of President more than twice, and no person who has held the office of President or acted as President for more than two years of a term to which some other person was elected President shall be elected to the Office of the President more than once. But this Article shall not apply to any person holding the office of President when this Article was proposed by the Congress, and shall not prevent any person who may be holding the office of President, or acting as President, during the term within which this Article becomes operative from holding the office of President or acting as President during the remainder of such term.

Section 2
[RATIFICATION WITHIN SEVEN YEARS]

This Article shall be inoperative unless it shall have been ratified as an amendment to the Constitution by the legislatures of three-fourths of the several states within seven years from the date of its submission to the States by the Congress.

AMENDMENT XXIII

[Proposed by Congress on June 21, 1960; declared ratified on March 29, 1961.]

Section 1
[ELECTORAL COLLEGE VOTES FOR THE DISTRICT OF COLUMBIA]

The District constituting the seat of Government of the United States shall appoint in such manner as the Congress may direct:

A number of electors of President and Vice-President equal to the whole number of Senators and Representatives in Congress to which the District would be entitled if it were a State, but in no event more than the least populous State;

they shall be in addition to those appointed by the States, but they shall be considered, for the purposes of the election of President and Vice-President, to be electors appointed by a State; and they shall meet in the District and perform such duties as provided by the twelfth article of amendment.

Section 2
[POWER TO ENFORCE THIS ARTICLE]

The Congress shall have power to enforce this article by appropriate legislation.

AMENDMENT XXIV

[Proposed by Congress on August 27, 1963; declared ratified on January 23, 1964.]

Section 1
[ANTI-POLL TAX]

The right of citizens of the United States to vote in any primary or other election for President or Vice-President, for electors for President or Vice-President, or for Senator or Representative of Congress, shall not be denied or abridged by the United States or any State by reasons of failure to pay any poll tax or other tax.

Section 2
[POWER TO ENFORCE THIS ARTICLE]

The Congress shall have power to enforce this article by appropriate legislation.

AMENDMENT XXV

[Proposed by Congress on July 7, 1965; declared ratified on February 10, 1967.]

Section 1
[VICE-PRESIDENT TO BECOME PRESIDENT]

In case of the removal of the President from office or his death or resignation, the Vice-President shall become President.

Section 2
[CHOICE OF A NEW VICE-PRESIDENT]

Whenever there is a vacancy in the office of the Vice-President, the President shall nominate a Vice-President who shall take the office upon confirmation by a majority vote of both houses of Congress.

Section 3
[PRESIDENT MAY DECLARE OWN DISABILITY]

Whenever the President transmits to the President pro tempore of the Senate and the Speaker of the House of Representatives his written declaration that he is unable to discharge the powers and duties of his office, and until he transmits to them a written declaration to the contrary, such powers and duties shall be discharged by the Vice-President as Acting President.

Section 4
[ALTERNATE PROCEDURES TO DECLARE AND TO END PRESIDENTIAL DISABILITY]

Whenever the Vice-President and a majority of either the principal officers of the executive departments, or of such other body as Congress may by law provide, transmit to the President pro tempore of the Senate and the Speaker of the House of Representatives their written declaration that the President is unable to discharge the powers and duties of his office, the Vice-President shall immediately assume the powers and duties of the office as Acting President.

Thereafter, when the President transmits to the President pro tempore of the Senate and the Speaker of the House of Representatives his written declaration that no inability exists, he shall resume the powers and duties of his office unless the Vice-President and a majority of either the principal officers of the executive departments, or of such other body as Congress may by law provide, transmit within four days to the President pro tempore of the Senate and the Speaker of the House of Representatives their written declaration that the President is unable to discharge the powers and duties of his office. Thereupon Congress shall decide the issue, assembling within 48 hours for that purpose if not in session. If the Congress, within 21 days after receipt of the latter written declaration, or, if Congress is not in session, within 21 days after Congress is required to assemble, determines by two-thirds vote of both houses that the President is unable to discharge the powers and duties of his office, the Vice-President shall continue to discharge the same as Acting President; otherwise, the President shall resume the powers and duties of his office.

AMENDMENT XXVI

[Proposed by Congress on March 23, 1971; declared ratified on June 30, 1971.]

Section 1
[EIGHTEEN-YEAR-OLD VOTE]

The right of citizens of the United States, who are eighteen years of age or older, to vote shall not be denied or abridged by the United States or by any State on account of age.

Section 2
[POWER TO ENFORCE THIS ARTICLE]

The Congress shall have power to enforce this article by appropriate legislation.

AMENDMENT XXVII

[Proposed by Congress on September 25, 1789; ratified on May 7, 1992.]

No law varying the compensation for the services of the Senators and Representatives shall take effect until an election of Representatives shall have intervened.

Federalist Papers

NO. 10: MADISON

Among the numerous advantages promised by a well-constructed Union, none deserves to be more accurately developed than its tendency to break and control the violence of faction. The friend of popular governments never finds himself so much alarmed for their character and fate as when he contemplates their propensity to this dangerous vice. He will not fail, therefore, to set a due value on any plan which, without violating the principles to which he is attached, provides a proper cure for it. The instability, injustice, and confusion introduced into the public councils have, in truth, been the mortal diseases under which popular governments have everywhere perished, as they continue to be the favorite and fruitful topics from which the adversaries to liberty derive their most specious declamations. The valuable improvements made by the American constitutions on the popular models, both ancient and modern, cannot certainly be too much admired; but it would be an unwarrantable partiality to contend that they have as effectually obviated the danger on this side, as was wished and expected. Complaints are everywhere heard from our most considerate and virtuous citizens, equally the friends of public and private faith and of public and personal liberty, that our governments are too unstable, that the public good is disregarded in the conflicts of rival parties, and that measures are too often decided, not according to the rules of justice and the rights of the minor party, but by the superior force of an interested and overbearing majority. However anxiously we may wish that these complaints had no foundation, the evidence of known facts will not permit us to deny that they are in some degree true. It will be found, indeed, on a candid review of our situation, that some of the distresses under which we labor have been erroneously charged on the operation of our governments; but it will be found, at the same time, that other causes will not alone account for many of our heaviest misfortunes; and, particularly, for that prevailing and increasing distrust of public engagements and alarm for private rights which are echoed from one end of the continent to the other. These must be chiefly, if not wholly, effects of the unsteadiness and injustice with which a factious spirit has tainted our public administration.

By a faction I understand a number of citizens, whether amounting to a majority or minority of the whole, who are united and actuated by some common impulse of passion, or of interest, adverse to the rights of other citizens, or to the permanent and aggregate interests of the community.

There are two methods of curing the mischiefs of faction: the one, by removing its causes; the other, by controlling its effects.

There are again two methods of removing the causes of faction: the one, by destroying the liberty which is essential to its existence; the other, by giving to every citizen the same opinions, the same passions, and the same interests.

It could never be more truly said than of the first remedy that it was worse than the disease. Liberty is to faction what air is to fire, an aliment without which it instantly expires. But it could not be a less folly to abolish liberty, which is essential to political life, because it nourishes faction than it would be to wish the annihilation of air, which is essential to animal life, because it imparts to fire its destructive agency.

The second expedient is as impracticable as the first would be unwise. As long as the reason of man continues fallible, and he is at liberty to exercise it, different opinions will be formed. As long as the connection subsists between his reason and his self-love, his opinions and his passions will have a reciprocal influence on each other; and the former will be objects to which the latter will attach themselves. The diversity in the faculties of men, from which the rights of property originate, is not less an insuperable obstacle to a uniformity of interests. The protection of these faculties is the first object of government. From the protection of different and unequal faculties of acquiring property, the possession of different degrees and kinds of property immediately results; and from the influence of these on the sentiments and views of the respective proprietors ensues a division of the society into different interests and parties.

The latent causes of faction are thus sown in the nature of man; and we see them everywhere brought into different degrees of activity, according to the different circumstances of civil society. A zeal for different opinions concerning religion, concerning government, and many other points, as well of speculation as of practice; an attachment to different leaders ambitiously contending for preeminence and power; or to persons of other descriptions whose fortunes have been interesting to the human passions, have, in turn, divided mankind into parties, inflamed them with mutual animosity, and rendered them much more disposed to vex and oppress each other than to co-operate for their common good. So strong is this propensity of mankind to fall into mutual animosities that where no substantial occasion presents itself the most frivolous and fanciful distinctions have been sufficient to kindle their unfriendly passions and excite their most violent conflicts. But the most common and durable source of factions has been the various and unequal distribution of property. Those who hold and those who are without property have ever formed distinct interests in society. Those who are creditors, and those who are debtors, fall under a like discrimination. A landed interest, a manufacturing interest, a mercantile interest, a moneyed interest, with many lesser interests, grow up of necessity in civilized nations, and divide them into different classes, actuated by different sentiments and views. The regulation of these various and interfering interests forms the principal task of modern legislation and involves the spirit of party and faction in the necessary and ordinary operations of government.

No man is allowed to be judge in his own cause, because his interest would certainly bias his judgment and, not improbably, corrupt his integrity. With equal, nay with greater reason, a body of men are unfit to be both judges and parties at the same time; yet what are many of the most important acts of legislation but so many judicial determinations, not indeed concerning the rights of single persons, but concerning the rights of large bodies of citizens? And what are the different classes of legislators but advocates and parties to the causes which they determine? Is a law proposed concerning private debts? It is a question to which the creditors are parties on one side and the debtors on the other. Justice ought to hold the balance between them. Yet the parties are, and must be, themselves the judges; and the most numerous party, or in other words, the most powerful faction must be expected to prevail. Shall domestic manufacturers be encouraged, and in what degree, by restrictions on foreign manufacturers? are questions which would be differently decided by the landed and the manufacturing classes, and probably by neither with a sole regard to justice and the public good. The apportionment of taxes on the various descriptions of property is an act which seems to require the most exact impartiality; yet there is, perhaps, no legislative act in which greater opportunity and temptation are given to a predominant party to trample on the rules of justice. Every shilling with which they overburden the inferior number is a shilling saved to their own pockets.

It is in vain to say that enlightened statesmen will be able to adjust these clashing interests and render them all subservient to the public good. Enlightened statesmen will not always be at the helm. Nor, in many cases, can such an adjustment be made at all without taking into view indirect and remote considerations, which will rarely prevail over the immediate interest which one party may find in disregarding the rights of another or the good of the whole.

The inference to which we are brought is that the *causes* of faction cannot be removed and that relief is only to be sought in the means of controlling its *effects*.

If a faction consists of less than a majority, relief is supplied by the republican principle, which enables the majority to defeat its sinister views by regular vote. It may clog the administration, it may convulse the society; but it will be unable to execute and mask its violence under the forms of the Constitution. When a majority is included in a faction, the form of popular government, on the other hand, enables it to sacrifice to its ruling passion or interest both the public good and the rights of other citizens. To secure the public good and private rights against the danger of such a faction, and at the same time to preserve the spirit and the form of popular government, is then the great object to which our inquiries are directed. Let me add that it is the great desideratum by which alone this form of government can be rescued from the opprobrium under which it has so long labored and be recommended to the esteem and adoption of mankind.

By what means is this object attainable? Evidently by one of two only. Either the existence of the same passion or interest in a majority at the same time must be prevented, or the majority, having such coexistent passion or interest, must be rendered, by their number and local situation, unable to concert and carry into effect schemes of oppression. If the impulse and the opportunity be suffered to coincide, we well know that neither moral nor religious motives can be relied on as an adequate control. They are not found to be such on the injustice and violence of individuals, and lose their efficacy in proportion to the number combined together, that is, in proportion as their efficacy becomes needful.

From this view of the subject it may be concluded that a pure democracy, by which I mean a society consisting of a small number of citizens, who assemble and administer the government in person, can admit of no cure for the mischiefs of faction. A common passion or interest will, in almost every case, be felt by a majority of the whole; a communication and concert results from the form of government itself; and there is nothing to check the inducements to sacrifice the weaker party or an obnoxious individual. Hence it is that such democracies have ever been spectacles of turbulence and contention; have ever been found incompatible with personal security or the rights of property; and have in general been as short in their lives as they have been violent in their deaths. Theoretic politicians, who have patronized this species of government, have erroneously supposed that by reducing mankind to a perfect equality in their political rights, they would at the same time be perfectly equalized and assimilated in their possessions, their opinions, and their passions.

A republic, by which I mean a government in which the scheme of representation takes place, opens a different prospect and promises the cure for which we are seeking. Let us examine the points in which it varies from pure democracy, and we shall comprehend both the nature of the cure and the efficacy which it must derive from the Union.

The two great points of difference between a democracy and a republic are: first, the delegation of the government, in the latter, to a small number of citizens elected by the rest; secondly, the greater number of citizens and greater sphere of country over which the latter may be extended.

The effect of the first difference is, on the one hand, to refine and enlarge the public views by passing them through the medium of a chosen body of citizens, whose wisdom may best discern the true interest of their country and whose patriotism and love of justice will be least likely to sacrifice it to temporary or partial considerations. Under such a regulation it may well happen that the public voice, pronounced by the representatives of the people, will be more consonant to the public good than if pronounced by the people themselves, convened for the purpose. On the other hand, the effect may be inverted. Men of factious tempers, of local prejudices, or of sinister designs, may, by intrigue, by corruption, or by other means, first obtain the suffrages, and then betray the interests of the people. The question resulting is, whether small or extensive republics are most favorable to the election of proper guardians of the public weal; and it is clearly decided in favor of the latter by two obvious considerations.

In the first place it is to be remarked that however small the republic may be the representatives must be raised to a certain number in order to guard against the cabals of a few; and that however large it may be they must be limited to a certain number in order to guard against the confusion of a multitude. Hence, the number of representatives in the two cases not being in proportion to that of the constituents, and being proportionally greatest in the small republic, it follows that if the proportion of fit characters be not less in the large than in the small republic, the former will present a greater option, and consequently a greater probability of a fit choice.

In the next place, as each representative will be chosen by a greater number of citizens in the large than in the small republic, it will be more difficult for unworthy candidates to practise with success the vicious arts by which elections are too often carried; and the suffrages of the people being more free, will be more likely to center on men who possess the most attractive merit and the most diffusive and established characters.

It must be confessed that in this, as in most other cases, there is a mean, on both sides of which inconveniencies will be found to lie. By enlarging too much the number of electors, you render the representative too little acquainted with all their local circumstances and lesser interests; as by reducing it too much, you render him unduly attached to these, and too little fit to comprehend and pursue great and national objects. The federal Constitution forms a happy combination in this respect; the great and aggregate interests being referred to the national, the local and particular to the State legislatures.

The other point of difference is the greater number of citizens and extent of territory which may be brought within the compass of republican than of democratic government; and it is this circumstance principally which renders factious combinations less to be dreaded in the former than in the latter. The smaller the society, the fewer probably will be the distinct parties and interests composing it; the fewer the distinct parties and interests, the more frequently will a majority be found of the same party; and the smaller the number of individuals composing a majority, and the smaller the compass within which they are placed, the more easily will they concert and execute their plans of oppression. Extend the sphere and you take in a greater variety of parties and interests; you make it less probable that a majority of the whole will have a common motive to invade the rights of other citizens; or if such a common motive exists, it will be more difficult for all who feel it to discover their own strength and to act in unison with each other. Besides other impediments, it may be remarked that, where there is a consciousness of unjust or dishonorable purposes, communication is always checked by distrust in proportion to the number whose concurrence is necessary.

Hence, it clearly appears that the same advantage which a republic has over a democracy in controlling the effects of faction is enjoyed by a large over a small republic—is enjoyed by the Union over the States composing it. Does this advantage consist in the substitution of representatives whose enlightened views and virtuous sentiments render them superior to local prejudices and to schemes of injustice? It will not be denied that the representation of the Union will be most likely to possess these requisite endowments. Does it consist in the greater security afforded by a greater variety of parties, against the event of any one party being able to outnumber and oppress the rest? In an equal degree does the increased variety of parties comprised within the Union increase this security? Does it, in fine, consist in the greater obstacles opposed to the concert and accomplishment of the secret wishes of an unjust and interested majority? Here again the extent of the Union gives it the most palpable advantage.

The influence of factious leaders may kindle a flame within their particular States but will be unable to spread a general conflagration through the other States. A religious sect may degenerate into a political faction in a part of the Confederacy; but the variety of sects dispersed over the entire face of it must secure the national councils against any danger from that source. A rage for paper money, for an abolition of debts, for an equal division of property, or for any other improper or wicked project, will be less apt to pervade the whole body of the Union than a particular member of it, in the same proportion as such a malady is more likely to taint a particular county or district than an entire State.

In the extent and proper structure of the Union, therefore, we behold a republican remedy for the diseases most incident to republican government. And according to the degree of pleasure and pride we feel in being republicans ought to be our zeal in cherishing the spirit and supporting the character of federalist.

PUBLIUS

NO. 51: MADISON

To what expedient, then, shall we finally resort, for maintaining in practice the necessary partition of power among the several departments as laid down in the Constitution? The only answer that can be given is that as all these exterior provisions are found to be inadequate the defect must be supplied, by so contriving the interior structure of the government as that its several constituent parts may, by their mutual relations, be the means of keeping each other in their proper places. Without presuming to undertake a full development of this important idea I will hazard a few general observations which may perhaps place it in a clearer light, and enable us to form a more correct judgment of the principles and structure of the government planned by the convention.

In order to lay a due foundation for that separate and distinct exercise of the different powers of government, which to a certain extent is admitted on all hands to be essential to the preservation of liberty, it is evident that each department should have a will of its own; and consequently should be so constituted that the members of each should have as little agency as possible in the appointment of the members of the others. Were this principle rigorously adhered to, it would require that all the appointments for the supreme executive, legislative, and judiciary magistracies should be drawn from the same fountain of authority, the people, through channels having no communication whatever with one another. Perhaps such a plan of constructing the several departments would be less difficult in practice than it may in contemplation appear. Some difficulties, however, and some additional expense would attend the execution of it. Some deviations, therefore, from the principle must be admitted. In the constitution of the judiciary department in particular, it might be inexpedient to insist rigorously on the principle: first, because peculiar qualifications being essential in the members, the primary consideration ought to be to select that mode of choice which best secures these qualifications; second, because the permanent tenure by which the appointments are held in that department must soon destroy all sense of dependence on the authority conferring them.

It is equally evident that the members of each department should be as little dependent as possible on those of the others for the emoluments annexed to their offices. Were the executive magistrate, or the judges, not independent of the legislature in this particular, their independence in every other would be merely nominal.

But the great security against a gradual concentration of the several powers in the same department consists in giving to those who administer each department the necessary constitutional means and personal motives to resist encroachments of the others. The provision for defense must in this, as in all other cases, be made commensurate to the danger of attack. Ambition must be made to counteract ambition. The interest of the man must be connected with the constitutional rights of the place. It may be a reflection on human nature that such devices should be necessary to control the abuses of government. But what is government itself but the greatest of all reflections on human nature? If men were angels, no government would be necessary. If angels were to govern men, neither external nor internal controls on government would be necessary. In framing a government which is to be administered by men over men, the great difficulty lies in this: you must first enable the government to control the governed; and in the next place oblige it to control itself. A dependence on the people is, no doubt, the primary control on the government; but experience has taught mankind the necessity of auxiliary precautions.

This policy of supplying, by opposite and rival interests, the defect of better motives, might be traced through the whole system of human affairs, private as well as public. We see it particularly displayed in all the subordinate distributions of power, where the constant aim is to divide and arrange the several offices in such a manner as that each may be a check on the other—that the private interest of every individual may be a sentinel over the public rights. These inventions of prudence cannot be less requisite in the distribution of the supreme powers of the State.

But it is not possible to give to each department an equal power of self-defense. In republican government, the legislative authority necessarily predominates. The remedy for this inconveniency is to divide the legislature into different branches; and to render them, by different modes of election and different principles of action, as little connected with each other as the nature of their common functions and their common dependence on the society will admit. It may even be necessary to guard against dangerous encroachments by still further precautions. As the weight of the legislative authority requires that it should be thus divided, the weakness of the executive may require, on the other hand, that it should be fortified. An absolute negative on the legislature appears, at first view, to be the natural defense with which the executive magistrate should be armed. But perhaps it would be neither altogether safe nor alone sufficient. On ordinary occasions it might not be exerted with the requisite firmness, and on extraordinary occasions it might be perfidiously abused. May not this defect of an absolute negative be supplied by some qualified connection between this weaker branch of the stronger department, by which the latter may be led to support the constitutional rights of the former, without being too much detached from the rights of its own department?

If the principles on which these observations are founded be just, as I persuade myself they are, and they be applied as a criterion to the several State constitutions, and to the federal Constitution, it will be found that if the latter does not perfectly correspond with them, the former are infinitely less able to bear such a test.

There are, moreover, two considerations particularly applicable to the federal system of America, which place that system in a very interesting point of view.

First. In a single republic, all the power surrendered by the people is submitted to the administration of a single government; and the usurpations are guarded against by a division of the government into distinct and separate departments. In the compound republic of America, the power surrendered by the people is first divided between two distinct governments, and then the portion allotted to each subdivided among distinct and separate departments. Hence a double security arises to the rights of the people. The different governments will control each other, at the same time that each will be controlled by itself.

Second. It is of great importance in a republic not only to guard the society against the oppression of its rulers, but to guard one part of the society against the injustice of the other part. Different interests necessarily exist in different classes of citizens. If a majority be united by a common interest, the rights of the minority will be insecure. There are but two methods of providing against this evil: the one by creating a will in the community independent of the majority—that is, of the society itself; the other, by comprehending in the society so many separate descriptions of citizens as will render an unjust combination of a majority of the whole very improbable, if not impracticable. The first method prevails in all governments possessing an hereditary or self-appointed authority. This, at best, is but a precarious security; because a power independent of the society may as well espouse the unjust views of the major as the rightful interests of the minor party, and may possibly be turned against both parties. The second method will be exemplified in the federal republic of the United States. Whilst all authority in it will be derived from and dependent on the society, the society itself will be broken into so many parts, interests and classes of citizens, that the rights of individuals, or of the minority, will be in little danger from interested combinations of the majority. In a free government the security for civil rights must be the same as that for religious rights. It consists in the one case in the multiplicity of interests, and in the other in the multiplicity of sects. The degree of security in both cases will depend on the number of interests and sects; and this may be presumed to depend on the extent of country and number of people comprehended under the same government. This view of the subject must particularly recommend a proper federal system to all the sincere and considerate friends of republican government, since it shows that in exact proportion as the territory of the Union may be formed into more circumscribed Confederacies, or States, oppressive combinations of a majority will be facilitated; the best security, under the republican forms, for the rights of every class of citizen, will be diminished; and consequently the stability and independence of some member of the government, the only other security, must be proportionally increased. Justice is the end of government. It is the end of civil society. It ever has been and ever will be pursued until it be obtained, or until liberty be lost in the pursuit. In a society under the forms of which the stronger faction can readily unite and oppress the weaker, anarchy may as truly be said to reign as in a state of nature, where the weaker individual is not secured against the violence of the stronger; and as, in the latter state, even the stronger individuals are prompted, by the uncertainty of their condition, to submit to a government which may protect the weak as well as themselves; so, in the former state, will the more powerful factions or parties be gradually induced, by a like motive, to wish for a government which will protect all parties, the weaker as well as the more powerful. It can be little doubted that if the State of Rhode Island was separated from the Confederacy and left to itself, the insecurity of rights under the popular form of government within such narrow limits would be displayed by such reiterated oppressions of factious majorities that some power altogether independent of the people would soon be called for by the voice of the very factions whose misrule had proved the necessity of it. In the extended republic of the United States, and among the great variety of interests, parties, and sects which it embraces, a coalition of a majority of the whole society could seldom take place on any other principles than those of justice and the general good; whilst there being thus less danger to a minor from the will of a major party, there must be less pretext, also, to provide for the security of the former, by introducing into the government a will not dependent on the latter, or, in other words, a will independent of the society itself. It is no less certain than it is important, notwithstanding the contrary opinions which have been entertained, that the larger the society, provided it lie within a practicable sphere, the more duly capable it will be of self-government. And happily for the *republican cause*, the practicable sphere may be carried to a very great extent by a judicious modification and mixture of the *federal principle*.

PUBLIUS

Glossary of Terms

administrative adjudication   Applying rules and precedents to specific cases to settle disputes with regulated parties.

administrative legislation   Rules made by **regulatory agencies** and commissions.

administrative regulation   Rules made by **regulatory agencies** and commissions.

adverse selection problem   The problem of incomplete information—of choosing alternatives without knowing fully the details of available options.

affirmative action   A policy or program designed to redress historic injustices committed against specific groups by making special efforts to provide members of these groups with access to educational and employment opportunities.

after-the-fact authority   The authority to follow up on the fate of a proposal once it has been approved by the full chamber.

agencies of socialization   Social institutions, including families and schools, that help to shape individuals' basic political **beliefs** and **values.**

agency loss   The difference between what a principal would like an agent to do and the agent's actual performance.

agency representation   The type of representation by which representatives are held accountable to their constituents if they fail to represent them properly; that is, constituents have the power to hire and fire their representatives. This is the incentive for good representation when the personal backgrounds, views, and interests of the representatives differ from their constituents'.

agenda power   Control over what the group will consider for discussion.

agenda setting   Activities that help to determine which issues are taken up by political actors and institutions.

Aid to Families with Dependent Children (AFDC)   Federal funds for children in families that fall below state standards of need. The largest federal cash transfer program. In 1996, Congress abolished AFDC and replaced it with the **Temporary Assistance to Needy Families (TANF) block grant.**

ambivalence   **Public opinion** trait in which an individual holds conflicting attitudes about an issue.

amicus curiae "Friend of the court"; individuals or groups who are not parties to a lawsuit but who seek to assist the court in reaching a decision by presenting additional **briefs.**

antitrust policy **Government** regulation of large businesses that have established **monopolies.**

appellate court A court that hears the appeals of **trial court** decisions.

area sampling A polling technique used for large cities, states, or the whole nation, when a high level of accuracy is desired. The population is broken down into small, homogeneous units, such as counties; then several units are randomly selected to serve as the sample.

Articles of Confederation and Perpetual Union America's first written constitution. Adopted by the Continental Congress in 1777, the Articles of Confederation and Perpetual Union was the formal basis for America's national **government** until 1789, when it was supplanted by the Constitution.

attitude (or opinion) A specific preference on a specific issue.

Australian ballot An electoral format that presents the names of all the candidates for any given office on the same ballot. Introduced at the turn of the twentieth century, the Australian ballot replaced the partisan ballot and facilitated split-ticket voting.

authoritarian government A system of rule in which the **government** recognizes no formal limits but may nevertheless be restrained by the power of other social institutions.

autocracy A form of **government** in which a single individual—a king, queen, or dictator—rules.

balance-of-power role The strategy whereby many countries form alliances with one country or several other countries in order to counterbalance the behavior of other, usually more powerful, nation-states.

bandwagon effect A situation wherein reports of voter or **delegate** opinion can influence the actual outcome of an election or a nominating convention.

bellwether district A town or district that is a microcosm of the whole population or that has been found to be a good predictor of electoral outcomes.

bicameralism Having a legislative assembly composed of two chambers or houses.

bicameral legislature A legislative assembly composed of two chambers or houses.

bilateral treaty A treaty made between two nations.

Bill of Rights The first ten amendments to the U.S. Constitution, ratified in 1791. They ensure certain rights and liberties to the people.

block grants Federal funds given to state **governments** to pay for goods, services, or programs, with relatively few restrictions on how the funds may be spent.

briefs Written documents in which attorneys explain—using case precedents—why the Court should rule in favor of their client.

budget deficit Amount by which **government** spending exceeds government revenue in a fiscal year.

bureaucracy The complex structure of offices, tasks, rules, and principles of organization that are employed by all large-scale institutions to coordinate the work of their personnel.

bureaucratic drift The oft-observed phenomenon of bureaucratic implementation that produces policy more to the liking of the **bureaucracy** than originally legislated, but without triggering a political reaction from elected officials.

Bush Doctrine Foreign policy based on the idea that the United States should take preemptive action against threats to its national security.

by-product theory The idea that groups provide members with private benefits to attract membership; the possibility for group **collective action** emerges as a consequence.

cabinet The secretaries, or chief administrators, of the major departments of the federal **government.** Cabinet secretaries are appointed by the president with the consent of the Senate.

casework An efforts of Congress to gain the trust and support of constituents by providing them with personal service. One important type of casework consists of helping constituents obtain favorable treatment from the federal **bureaucracy.**

categorical grants-in-aid Funds given by Congress to states and localities, earmarked by law for specific categories such as education or crime prevention.

caucus An association of members of Congress based on party, interest, or social group such as gender or race; also, a normally closed meeting of a political or legislative group to select candidates, plan strategy, or make decisions regarding legislative matters.

checks and balances Mechanisms through which each branch of **government** is able to participate in and influence the activities of the other branches. Major examples include the presidential **veto power** over congressional legislation, the power of the Senate to approve presidential appointments, and **judicial review** of congressional enactments.

chief justice Justice on the **Supreme Court** who presides over the Court's public sessions.

civil law A system of jurisprudence, including private law and governmental actions, to settle disputes that do not involve criminal penalties.

civil liberties Protections of citizens from improper **government** action.

civil rights Legal or moral claims that citizens are entitled to make upon the **government.**

class action suit A lawsuit in which large numbers of persons with common interests join together under a representative party to bring or defend a lawsuit, such as hundreds of workers joining together to sue a company.

clientele agencies Departments or bureaus of **government** whose mission is to promote, serve, or represent a particular interest.

client state A nation-state whose foreign policy is subordinated to that of another nation.

closed primary A primary election in which voters can participate in the nomination of candidates, but only of the party in which they are enrolled for a period of time prior to primary day. Contrast with **open primary.**

closed rule Provision by the House Rules Committee prohibiting the introduction of amendments during debate.

cloture A rule allowing a majority of two-thirds or three-fifths of the members in a legislative body to set a time limit on debate over a given bill.

coalitional drift The prospect that enacted policy will change because the composition of the enacting coalition is so temporary and provisional.

collective action The pooling of resources and coordination of effort and activity by a group of people (often a large one) to achieve common goals.

commerce clause Article I, Section 8, of the Constitution, which delegates to Congress the power "to regulate Commerce with foreign Nations, and among the several States, and with the Indian Tribes." This clause was interpreted by the **Supreme Court** in favor of national power over the economy.

concurrent powers Authority possessed by *both* state and national **governments,** such as the power to levy taxes.

conference committee A joint committee created to work out a compromise for House and Senate versions of a piece of legislation.

conscription Compulsory military service, usually for a prescribed period or for the duration of a war; "the draft."

conservative Today this term refers to those who generally support the social and economic status quo and are suspicious of efforts to introduce new political formulas and economic arrangements. Many conservatives also believe that a large and powerful **government** poses a threat to citizens' freedoms.

constituency The district comprising the area from which an official is elected.

constitutionalism A system of rule in which formal and effective limits are placed on the powers of the **government.**

containment The primary cold war foreign policy of the United States during the 1950s and 1960s, whereby the United States used its political, economic, and military power to prevent the spread of communism to developing or unstable countries.

contracting power The power of **government** to set conditions on companies seeking to sell goods or services to government agencies.

contributory programs Social programs financed in whole or in part by taxation or other mandatory contributions by their present or future recipients. The most important example is **Social Security,** which is financed by a payroll tax.

cooperative federalism A type of **federalism** existing since the New Deal era in which **grants-in-aid** have been used strategically to encourage states and localities (without commanding them) to pursue nationally defined goals. Also known as intergovernmental cooperation.

criminal law The branch of law that deals with disputes or actions involving criminal penalties (as opposed to **civil law**). It regulates the conduct of individuals, defines crimes, and provides punishment for criminal acts.

***de facto* segregation** Racial segregation that is not a direct result of law or **government** policy but is, instead, a reflection of residential patterns, income distributions, or other social factors.

defendant The individual or organization charged with a complaint in court.

***de jure* segregation** Racial segregation that is a direct result of law or official policy.

delegate A representative who votes according to the preferences of his or her **constituency.**

delegated powers Constitutional powers assigned to one governmental agency that are exercised by another agency with the express permission of the first.

delegation Transmitting authority to some other official or body for the latter's use (though often with the right of review and revision).

democracy A system of rule that permits citizens to play a significant part in the governmental process, usually through the selection of key public officials.

deregulation A policy of reducing or eliminating regulatory restraints on the conduct of individuals or private institutions.

deterrence The development and maintenance of military strength for the purpose of discouraging attack.

devolution A policy to remove a program from one level of **government** by deregulating it or passing it down to a lower level of government, such as from the national government to the state and local governments.

discount rate The interest rate charged by the **Federal Reserve** when commercial banks borrow in order to expand their lending operations. An effective tool of monetary policy.

discretionary spending Federal spending on programs that are controlled through the regular budget process.

dissenting opinion   Decision written by a justice with the minority opinion in a particular case, in which the justice fully explains the reasoning behind his or her opinion.

distributive tendency   The tendency of Congress to spread the benefits of a policy over a wide range of members' districts.

divided government   The condition in American **government** wherein the presidency is controlled by one party while the opposing party controls one or both houses of Congress.

double jeopardy   Trial more than once for the same crime. The Constitution guarantees that no one shall be subjected to double jeopardy.

dual federalism   The system of **government** that prevailed in the United States from 1789 to 1937 in which most fundamental governmental powers were shared between the federal and state governments. Compare with **cooperative federalism.**

due process   The right of every citizen against arbitrary action by national or state **governments.**

economic expansionist role   The strategy often pursued by capitalist countries to adopt foreign policies that will maximize the success of domestic corporations in their dealings with other countries.

electoral college   The presidential electors from each state who meet in their respective state capitals after the popular election to cast ballots for president and vice president.

eminent domain   The right of **government** to take private property for public use, with reasonable compensation rewarded for the property.

entitlement   Eligibility for benefits by virtue of a category of benefits defined by law. The category can only be changed by legislation. Deprivation of individual benefits can be determined only through **due process** in court.

equality of opportunity   A universally shared American ideal that all have the freedom to use whatever talents and wealth they have to reach their fullest potential.

equal protection clause   Provision of the Fourteenth Amendment guaranteeing citizens "the equal protection of the laws." This clause has served as the basis for the **civil rights** of African Americans, women, and other groups.

equal time rule   A Federal Communications Commission requirement that broadcasters provide candidates for the same political office an equal opportunity to communicate their messages to the public.

executive agreement   An agreement between the president and another country that has the force of a treaty but does not require the Senate's "advice and consent."

executive order   A rule or regulation issued by the president that has the effect and formal status of legislation.

executive privilege The claim that confidential communications between a president and close advisers should not be revealed without the consent of the president.

expressed powers Specific powers granted to Congress under Article I, Section 8, of the Constitution.

expropriation Confiscation of property with or without compensation.

externalities The difference between the private cost and the social cost of economic behavior.

fairness doctrine A Federal Communications Commission requirement for broadcasters who air programs on controversial issues to provide time for opposing views.

federal funds rate The interest rate on loans between banks that the Federal Reserve Board influences by affecting the supply of money available.

federalism System of **government** in which power is divided by a constitution between a central government and regional governments.

Federal Reserve System (Fed) Consisting of twelve Federal Reserve Banks, the Fed facilitates exchanges of cash, checks, and credit; it regulates member banks; and it uses monetary policies to fight inflation and deflation.

filibuster A tactic used by members of the Senate to prevent action on legislation they oppose by continuously holding the floor and speaking until the majority backs down. Once given the floor, senators have unlimited time to speak, and it requires a **cloture** vote of three-fifths of the Senate to end the filibuster.

fiscal policies The use of taxing, monetary, and spending powers to manipulate the economy.

food stamps The largest **in-kind benefits** program, administered by the Department of Agriculture, providing coupons to individuals and families who satisfy a **means test;** the food stamps can be exchanged for food at most grocery stores.

formula grants **Grants-in-aid** in which a formula is used to determine the amount of federal funds a state or local **government** will receive.

framing The power of the media to influence how events and issues are interpreted.

free riding Enjoying the benefits of a good or action and letting others bear the costs. See also **public good.**

full faith and credit clause Provisions from Article IV, Section I, of the Constitution requiring that the states normally honor the public acts and judicial decisions that take place in another state.

gatekeeping authority The right and power to decide if a change in policy will be considered.

gender gap A distinctive pattern of voting behavior reflecting the differences in views between men and women.

gerrymandering   Apportionment of voters in districts in such a way as to give unfair advantage to one political party.

government   Institutions and procedures through which a land and its people are ruled.

grants-in-aid   A general term for funds given by Congress to state and local **governments.** See also **categorical grants-in-aid.**

Great Compromise   Agreement reached at the Constitutional Convention of 1787 that gave each state an equal number of senators regardless of its population, but linked representation in the House of Representatives to population.

haphazard sampling   A type of sampling of **public opinion** that is an unsystematic choice of respondents.

Holy Alliance role   A strategy pursued by a superpower to prevent any change in the existing distribution of power among nation-states, even if this requires intervention into the internal affairs of the country in order to keep an authoritarian ruler from being overturned.

home rule   Power delegated by the state to a local unit of **government** to manage its own affairs.

homesteading   A national policy that permits people to gain ownership of property by occupying public or unclaimed land, living on the land for a specified period of time, and making certain minimal improvements on that land. Also known as squatting.

illusion of central tendency   The assumption that opinions are "normally distributed"—that responses to opinion questions are heavily distributed toward the center, as in a bell-shaped curve.

illusion of saliency   Impression conveyed by polls that something is important to the public when actually it is not.

impeachment   To charge a governmental official (president or otherwise) with "Treason, Bribery, or other high Crimes and Misdemeanors" and bring him or her before Congress to determine guilt.

implementation   The efforts of departments and agencies to translate laws into specific bureaucratic routines.

implied powers   Powers derived from the **necessary and proper clause** of Article I, Section 8, of the Constitution. Such powers are not specifically **expressed** but are **implied** through the expansive interpretation of **delegated powers.**

incumbency   Holding a political office for which one is running.

indexing   Periodic process of adjusting social benefits or wages to account for increases in the cost of living.

informational benefits   Special newsletters, periodicals, training programs, conferences, and other information provided to members of groups to entice others to join.

inherent powers Powers claimed by a president that are not expressed in the Constitution but are inferred from it.

initiative The process that allows citizens to propose new laws and submit them for approval by the state's voters.

in-kind benefits Goods and services provided to needy individuals and families by the federal **government,** as contrasted with cash benefits. The largest in-kind federal welfare program is **food stamps.**

institutions Rules and procedures that provide incentives for political behavior, thereby shaping politics.

instrumental To do something with purpose, sometimes requiring forethought and even calculation.

interest group An organized group of people that makes policy-related appeals to **government.**

issue advocacy Independent spending by individuals or **interest groups** on a campaign issue but not directly tied to a particular candidate.

judicial activism Judicial philosophy that posits that the Court should see beyond the text of the Constitution or a statute to consider broader societal implications for decisions.

judicial restraint Judicial philosophy whose adherents refuse to go beyond the set text of the Constitution in interpreting its meaning.

judicial review Power of the courts to declare actions of the legislative and executive branches invalid or unconstitutional. The **Supreme Court** asserted this power in *Marbury v. Madison.*

jurisdiction The sphere of a court's power and authority.

Kitchen Cabinet An informal group of advisers to whom the president turns for counsel and guidance. Members of the official **cabinet** may or may not also be members of the Kitchen Cabinet.

legislative clearance The power given to the president to require all agencies of the executive branch to submit through the budget director all requests for new legislation along with estimates of their budgetary needs.

legislative supremacy The preeminent position assigned to the Congress by the Constitution.

liberal A liberal today generally supports political and social reform; extensive governmental intervention in the economy; the expansion of federal social services; more vigorous efforts on behalf of the poor, minorities, and women; and greater concern for consumers and the environment.

lobbying An attempt by a group to influence the policy process through persuasion of **government** officials.

logrolling A legislative practice wherein reciprocal agreements are made between legislators, usually in voting for or against a bill. In contrast to bargaining, logrolling unites parties that have nothing in common but their desire to exchange support.

majority leader   The elected leader of the party holding a majority of the seats in the House of Representatives or in the Senate. In the House, the majority leader is subordinate in the party hierarchy to the Speaker.

majority party   The party that holds the majority of legislative seats in either the House or the Senate.

majority system   A type of electoral system in which, to win a seat in the parliament or other representative body, a candidate must receive a majority (50 percent plus 1) of all the votes cast in the relevant district.

mandate (electoral)   A claim by a victorious candidate that the electorate has given him or her special authority to carry out promises made during the campaign.

mandatory spending   Federal spending that is made up of **"uncontrollables,"** budget items that cannot be controlled through the regular budget process.

market failure   Instances when markets fail to produce efficient outcomes.

marketplace of ideas   The public forum in which beliefs and ideas are exchanged and compete.

material benefits   Special goods, services, or money provided to members of groups to entice others to join.

means testing   A procedure that determines eligibility for **government** public assistance programs. A potential beneficiary must show a need and an inability to provide for it.

Medicaid   A federally financed, state-operated program for medical services to low-income people.

Medicare   National health insurance for the elderly and the disabled.

minority leader   The elected leader of the party holding less than a majority of the seats in the House or Senate.

Miranda rule   Principles developed by the **Supreme Court** in the 1966 case of *Miranda v. Arizona* requiring that persons under arrest be informed of their legal rights, including their right to counsel, prior to police interrogation.

monetary policies   Efforts to regulate the economy through manipulation of the supply of money and credit. America's most powerful institution in the area of monetary policy is the Federal Reserve Board.

monopoly   The existence of a single firm in a market that provides all the goods and services of that market; the absence of competition.

mootness   A criterion used by courts to screen cases that no longer require resolution.

moral hazard   Not knowing all aspects of the actions taken by an agent (nominally on behalf of the principal but potentially at the principal's expense).

multilateralism A foreign policy that seeks to encourage the involvement of several nation-states in coordinated action, usually in relation to a common adversary, with terms and conditions usually specified in a multicountry treaty, such as NATO.

multilateral treaty A treaty among more than two nations.

multiple-member district Electorate that selects all candidates at large from the whole district; each voter is given the number of votes equivalent to the number of seats to be filled.

Napoleonic role A strategy pursued by a powerful nation to prevent aggressive actions against it by improving the internal state of affairs of a particular country, even if this means encouraging revolution in that country. This strategy is based on the assumption that countries with comparable political systems will never go to war against each other.

necessary and proper clause Article I, Section 8, of the Constitution, which enumerates the powers of Congress and provides Congress with the authority to make all laws "necessary and proper" to carry them out; also referred to as the "elastic clause."

nomination The process through which political parties select their candidates for election to public office.

noncontributory programs Social programs that assist people based on demonstrated need rather than contributions they have made. Also known as *public assistance programs.*

oligarchy A form of **government** in which a small group of landowners, military officers, or wealthy merchants controls most of the governing decisions.

open-market operations The process whereby the Open Market Committee of the **Federal Reserve** buys and sells **government** securities etc. to help finance government operations and to loosen or tighten the total amount of credit circulating in the economy.

open primary A primary election in which the voter can wait until the day of the primary to choose which party to enroll in to select candidates for the general election. Contrast with **closed primary**.

open rule Provision by the House Rules Committee that permits floor debate and the addition of new amendments to a bill.

opinion The written explanation of the **Supreme Court**'s decision in a particular case.

opinion leaders Those who other citizens turn to for political information and cues.

oral argument Stage in **Supreme Court** procedings in which attorneys for both sides appear before the Court to present their positions and answer questions posed by the justices.

oversight The effort by Congress, through hearings, investigations, and other techniques, to exercise control over the activities of executive agencies.

party caucus A normally closed meeting of a political or legislative group to select candidates, plan strategy, or make decisions regarding legislative matters.

party identification An individual voter's psychological ties to one party or another.

party machines Local party organizations that controlled local politics in the late nineteenth and early twentieth centuries through patronage and control of nominations.

party vote A **roll-call vote** in the House or Senate in which at least 50 percent of the members of one party take a particular position and are opposed by at least 50 percent of the members of the other party. Party votes are rare today, although they were fairly common in the nineteenth century.

path dependency The idea that certain possibilities are made more or less likely because of the historical path taken.

patronage The resources available to higher officials, usually opportunities to make partisan appointments to offices and to confer grants, licenses, or special favors to supporters.

per curiam Decision by an **appellate court,** without a written opinion, that refuses to review the decision of a lower court; amounts to a reaffirmation of the lower court's opinion.

permanent campaign A description of presidential politics in which all presidential actions are taken with re-election in mind.

plaintiff The individual or organization who brings a complaint in court.

plea bargains Negotiated agreements in criminal cases in which a **defendant** agrees to plead guilty in return for the state's agreement to reduce the severity of the criminal charge the defendant is facing.

pluralism The theory that all interests are and should be free to compete for influence in the **government.** The outcome of this competition is compromise and moderation.

plurality system A type of electoral system in which victory goes to the individual who gets the most votes in an election, not necessarily a majority of votes cast.

pocket veto A method by which the president vetoes a bill by taking no action on it when Congress has adjourned. See also **veto.**

police power Power reserved to the **government** to regulate the health, safety, and morals of its citizens.

policy of redistribution An objective of the graduated income tax—to raise revenue in such a way as to reduce the disparities of wealth between the lowest and the highest income brackets.

political action committees (PACs) Private groups that raise and distribute funds for use in election campaigns.

political ideology A cohesive set of beliefs that form a general philosophy about the role of **government.**

political socialization The induction of individuals into the political culture; learning the underlying **beliefs** and **values** upon which the political system is based.

pork-barrel legislation Appropriations made by legislative bodies for local projects that are often not needed but that are created so that local representatives can carry their home district in the next election.

precedents Prior cases whose principles are used by judges as the bases for their decisions in present cases.

priming A process of preparing the public to take a particular view of an event or a political actor.

principal-agent problems The tension that may exist between a principal and his or her agent caused by the fact that each is motivated by self-interest, yet their interests may not be well aligned.

prior restraint An effort by a governmental agency to block the publication of material it deems libelous or harmful in some other way; censorship. In the United States, the courts forbid prior restraint except under the most extraordinary circumstances.

privatization Removing all or part of a program from the public sector to the private sector.

privileges and immunities clause Provision from Article IV, Section 2, of the Constitution that a state cannot discriminate against someone from another state or give its own residents special privileges.

probability sampling A method used by pollsters to select a sample in which every individual in the population has a known (usually equal) probability of being selected as a respondent so that the correct weight can be given to all segments of the population.

professional legislature A legislature with members that serve full time for multiple terms.

progressive taxation Taxation that hits the upper income brackets more heavily.

project grants Grant programs in which state and local **governments** submit proposals to federal agencies and for which funding is provided on a competitive basis.

proportional representation A multiple-member district system that allows each political party representation in proportion to its percentage of the vote.

proposal power The capacity to present a proposal to the full legislature.

prospective voting Voting based on the imagined future performance of a candidate.

public good A good that (1) may be enjoyed by anyone if it is provided, and (2) may not be denied to anyone once it has been provided. See also **free riding.**

public law Cases involving the actions of public agencies or officials.

public opinion Citizens' attitudes about political issues, leaders, institutions, and events.

public policy A governmental law, rule, statute, or edict that expresses the **government's** goals and provides for rewards and punishments to promote their attainment.

purposive benefits **Selective benefits** of group membership that emphasize the purpose and accomplishments of the group.

push polling Polling technique that is designed to shape the respondent's opinion. For example, "If you knew that Candidate X was an adulterer, would you support his election?"

quota sampling A type of sampling of **public opinion** that is used by most commercial polls. Respondents are selected whose characteristics closely match those of the general population along several significant dimensions, such as geographic region, sex, age, and race.

rallying effect The generally favorable reaction of the public to presidential actions taken in foreign policy or, more precisely, to decisions made during international crises.

random sampling Polls in which respondents are chosen mathematically, at random, with every effort made to avoid bias in the construction of the sample.

recall Removal of a public official by popular vote.

referendum The practice of referring a measure proposed or passed by a legislature to the vote of the electorate for approval or rejection.

regressive taxation Taxation that hits the lower income brackets more heavily.

regulation A particular use of **government** power in which the government adopts rules imposing restrictions on the conduct of private citizens.

regulatory agencies Departments, bureaus, or independent agencies whose primary mission is to eliminate or restrict certain behaviors defined as being evil in themselves or evil in their consequences.

reserved powers Powers, derived from the Tenth Amendment to the Constitution, that are not specifically **delegated** to the national government or denied to the states.

reserve requirement The amount of liquid assets and ready cash that the **Federal Reserve** requires banks to hold to meet depositors' demands for their money. The ratio revolves above or below 20 percent of all deposits, with the rest being available for new loans.

retrospective voting Voting based on the past performance of a candidate.

right of rebuttal   A Federal Communications Commission regulation giving individuals the right to have the opportunity to respond to personal attacks made on a radio or TV broadcast.

roll-call vote   A vote in which each legislator's yes or no vote is recorded.

rule-making   A quasi-legislative administrative process that produces regulations by **government** agencies.

selective benefits   Benefits that do not go to everyone, but rather are distributed selectively—only to those who contribute to the group enterprise.

senatorial courtesy   The practice whereby the president, before formally nominating a person for a federal judgeship, checks on whether the senators from the candidate's state support the nomination.

seniority   Priority or status ranking given to an individual on the basis of length of continuous service on a congressional committee.

separate but equal rule   Doctrine that public accommodations could be segregated by race but still be equal.

separation of powers   The division of governmental power among several institutions that must cooperate in decision making.

single-member district   An electorate that is allowed to elect only one representative from each district; the normal method of representation in the United States.

Social Security   A **contributory** welfare **program** into which working Americans place a percentage of their wages and from which they receive cash benefits after retirement.

solidary benefits   Selective benefits of a group membership that emphasize friendship, networking, and consciousness-raising.

sound bites   Short snippets of information aimed at dramatizing a story, rather than explaining its substantive meaning.

sovereignty   Supreme and independent political authority.

Speaker of the House   The chief presiding officer of the House of Representatives. The Speaker is elected at the beginning of every Congress on a straight **party vote.** The Speaker is the most important party and House leader, and can influence the legislative agenda, the fate of individual pieces of legislation, and members' positions within the House.

staff agency   An agency responsible for providing Congress with independent expertise, administration, and **oversight** capability.

standing   The right of an individual or organization to initiate a court case.

standing committee   A permanent legislative committee that considers legislation within its designated subject area; the basic unit of deliberation in the House and Senate.

stare decisis Literally "let the decision stand." A previous decision by a court applies as a precedent in similar cases until that decision is overruled.

state sovereign immunity Legal doctrine that holds that states cannot be sued for violating an act of Congress.

states' rights The principle that states should oppose increasing authority of the national **government;** this was most popular before the Civil War.

subsidies Governmental grants of cash or other valuable commodities such as land to individuals or organizations. Subsidies can be used to promote activities desired by the **government,** to reward political support, or to buy off political opposition.

suffrage The right to vote.

Supplemental Security Income (SSI) A program providing a minimum monthly income to people who pass a **means test** and are sixty-five years old or older, blind, or disabled. Financed from general revenues that are not **Social Security** contributions.

supremacy clause Article VI of the Constitution, which states that all laws passed by the national **government** and all treaties are the supreme laws of the land and superior to all laws adopted by any state or any subdivision.

supreme court The highest court in a particular state or in the United States. This court primarily serves an appellate function.

systematic sampling A method used in **probability sampling** to ensure that every individual in the population has a known probability of being chosen as a respondent—for example, by choosing every ninth name from a list.

Temporary Assistance to Needy Families (TANF) _See_ **Aid to Families with Dependent Children (AFDC).**

third parties Parties that organize to compete against the two major American political parties.

Three-fifths Compromise Agreement reached at the Constitutional Convention of 1787 that stipulated that for purposes of the apportionment of congressional seats, every slave would be counted as three-fifths of a person.

totalitarian government A system of rule in which the **government** recognizes no formal limits on its power and seeks to absorb or eliminate other social institutions that might challenge it.

transaction costs The costs of clarifying each aspect of a principal-agent relationship and monitoring it to make sure arrangements are complied with.

trial court The first court to hear a criminal or civil case.

trustee A representative who votes based on what he or she thinks is best for his or her **constituency.**

tyranny Oppressive and unjust **government** that employs the cruel and unjust use of power and authority.

uncontrollables Budgetary items that are beyond the control of budgetary committees and can be controlled only by substantive legislative action in Congress. Some uncontrollables are beyond the power of Congress because the terms of payments are set in contracts, such as interest on the debt.

unfunded mandates Regulations or conditions for receiving grants that impose costs on state and local **governments** for which they are not reimbursed by the federal government.

unilateralism A foreign policy that seeks to avoid international alliances, entanglements, and permanent commitments in favor of independence, neutrality, and freedom of action.

United Nations (UN) An organization of nations founded in 1945 to serve as a channel for negotiation and a means of settling international disputes peaceably. The UN has had frequent successes in providing a forum for negotiation and on some occasions a means of preventing international conflicts from spreading. On a number of occasions, the UN has been a convenient cover for U.S. foreign-policy goals.

values (or beliefs) Basic principles that shape a person's opinions about political issues and events.

veto The president's constitutional power to turn down acts of Congress. A presidential veto may be overridden by a two-thirds vote of each house of Congress.

veto power The ability to defeat something, even if it has made it onto the agenda of an institution.

whip system Primarily a communications network in each house of Congress, whips take polls of the membership in order to learn their intentions on specific legislative issues and to assist the **majority** and **minority leaders** in various tasks.

writ of *certiorari* A decision concurred in by at least four of the nine **Supreme Court** justices to review a decision of a lower court; from the Latin "to make more certain."

writ of *habeas corpus* A court order demanding that an individual in custody be brought into court and shown the cause for detention. *Habeas corpus* is guaranteed by the Constitution and can be suspended only in cases of rebellion or invasion.

Index

campaign finance reform
and, 447–48
delegation principle and,
21–23, 29, 30
difficulties of, 200–201
direct, 431, 471
"excessive," 28, 49, 50, 51, 72
foreign policy and, 642,
644–45, 682–84
freedom, order and, 29–30
interest groups and, 507
majority rule and, 30
"making world safe for,"
675–78
paradoxes of, 28–30
parliamentary, 264–67
representative, 29, 176–77
Democratic Caucus, 207n
Democratic Forum, 194
Democratic National
Committee, 493, 495
Democratic National
Convention, 422,
493–95
Democratic party, 23n, 36,
213, 477, 608–9
Clinton and, 476
Congress and, 179–84,
213–14, 294, 466, 467,
576
conservative Southerners in,
189
in critical electoral realignment, 377, 484–85
in domestic arena, 59,
640–41
in elections of 2002,
440–41
in elections of 2004,
460–61
history of, 487
Jacksonian, 240, 480
key issues for, 472, 473
liberalizing of, 485–86, 487
money raised by, 444–45,
447–48
National Headquarters of,
532
1992 convention of, 564
political polarization and,
474–75, 485–86
redistricting and, 173–74,
423–26, 502–3
terrorism and, 26, 33
in 2000 election, 436–38,
439
unity of, 476
in U.S. history, 479–86
see also specific elections
Democratic Policy Committee,
181
democratic politics, see democracy

Democratic-Republicans,
477–79
Democratic Study Group, 194
Depository Institution
Deregulation and
Monetary Control Act
(1980), 590
Depression, Great, 5, 96, 242,
246, 484, 574–75, 584,
612, 613
deregulation, 576, 590–93
by administrative means, 591
downsizing and, 303
see also regulatory policy
Derthick, Martha, 84n, 607,
637
Deschler, Lewis, 21n
Deschler's Procedures, 20
desegregation, school, see
school desegregation
deterrence, military, 656, 662,
663, 670–73, 684
Bush Doctrine and, 671–72
defined, 670
military budget and,
670–72
vs. preemption, 671–72
technology and, 670
see also cold war
Detroit, Mich., segregation in,
136
"developed nations," governments of, 9
devolution, 95, 97, 98, 107–8,
289, 303–5
Devroy, Ann, 144n, 262n
Dewar, Helen, 420n
Dewey, Thomas E., 395
Dexter, Lewis Anthony, 651n
DIA (Defense Intelligence
Agency), 648
dictatorships, fear of, 674
Diet, Japanese, 159
DiIulio, John, Jr., 93n
Dingell, John, 524
Dionne, E. J., Jr., 6n
diplomatic corps, see foreign
service officers
diplomatic policy, 287,
657–59, 667, 682–84
postwar foreign policy and,
656
presidency and, 227,
657–58
see also foreign policy, U.S.
direct mail, 442, 457, 491–92,
500, 514
effectiveness of, 491–92
direct popular elections,
50–51, 163, 366–67,
427–28
disabled, discrimination
against, 141

"discount rate," 594
discretionary spending, 602–3
discrimination, 137–49, 637
benign, 142
in employment, 137–38,
140, 142–44, 145–46,
635–36
gender, 138–40, 372
law and, 94
see also affirmative action;
racial discrimination;
racial integration;
school desegregation;
segregation
Disraeli, Benjamin, 628
District Court, U.S., 312
district courts, federal,
319–20, 322, 350–51
District of Columbia, 68n,
130, 133
divided government, 103, 104,
108, 228
division of labor, 276–77
divisions of bureaus, 284
Dixiecrat, 181
Dodd, Lawrence C., 169n,
216, 297n
DOE (Energy Department),
U.S., 285
Doherty, Carroll, 211n
Dole, Robert, 1996 campaign
and, see elections of 1996
don't ask, don't tell policy, 238
DOT (Department of
Transportation), U.S.,
285
double jeopardy, 117, 122–23,
124
Dougherty, Keith L., 43n
Douglas, Stephen, 390, 481
Douglas, William O., 124–25,
340
Downs, Anthony, 31n, 308,
381n, 435
downsizing, 309–7, 609
deregulation and, 303
devolution and, 303–5
privatization and, 306–7
termination and, 302–3
draft, 10
Drake, W. Avon, 152
Dred Scott v. Sandford, 104
Drew, Elizabeth, 269
drift, bureaucratic, 296
Drobny, Anita, 546
Drudge, Matt, 413, 547
Drug Enforcement Agency
(DEA), 5
drug policies, 319, 434
dual citizenship, 118–19, 120,
150
dual federalism, 84, 91, 107
Ducks Unlimited, 515

due process, 117, 120–22, 124*n*, 150, 319, 330–31, 621
Duke Power Company, 138
Duncan v. Louisiana, 124*n*
duties, *see* tariffs
Duverger, Maurice, 422*n*, 466, 489*n*
Dye, Thomas, 84*n*, 100

Earle, E. M., 51*n*
earmarking, 168, 178
Earned Income Tax Credit (EITC), 614, 622
Easley v. Cromwell, 347
East India Company, 39
Eckridge, William N., Jr., 349*n*
economic aid, 664–67, 684
  administration of, 668
  democratic goals as requirement of, 666
  in U.S. foreign policy, 666–67
Economist, 665*n*, 679*n*, 680
economy, U.S.:
  capitalist, *see* capitalism; capitalist economy, U.S.
  collapse of, *see* Great Depression
  Congress and, 242, 575
  control and maintenance of, 593–606
  early national, 70
  federalism and, 87–88
  freedom of, 107
  globalization and, 677–80
  goals, tools and politics in policies of, 583–607
  government and, 575–76
  management of, 574
  market, *see* market economy, U.S.
  as political issue, 440–41, 577–83, 608–9
  taxation and, 595, 599–601
economy, world, *see* international monetary structure
ED (Education Department), U.S., 139, 272, 285, 631
Edison Electric Institute, 526
education, 236, 434
  affirmative action in, 143–49
  college students and, 375, 376
  deficiencies in, 629–32
  government support of, 6, 609, 611, 624, 629–32
  political views and, 375
  poverty fought through, 629–32, 637
  racial separation in, *see* school desegregation

standards in, 95–97
states and, 406
voter participation and, 420, 560
vouchers debate in, 632
Education Act (1972), Title IX of, 139
Education Department (ED), U.S., 139, 272, 285, 631
Edwards, George C., III, 246*n*, 257*n*, 652*n*
Egypt, 355
Eisenhower, Dwight D., 96, 257, 413*n*, 586*n*, 587
  legislative success of, 259
  Little Rock confrontation and, 134, 148, 229–31
Eisenstadt v. Baird, 528–29
EITC (Earned Income Tax Credit), 614, 622
elastic clause, 51
Elazar, Daniel, 110
Elder, Janet, 394*n*, 401*n*
elections, 412–61
  administering of, 426–31, 457
  adverse selection problem in, 413–14
  ballots used in, 429–31
  candidate "momentum" in, 563
  candidates' personalities in, 435–36, 457
  centrist strategies in, 435, 452, 474
  congressional, 50–51, 423–26
  consequences of, *see* critical electoral realignment
  constitutional provisions for, 426–28, 468
  cost of voting in, 452–53, 455
  criteria for winning of, 421–22
  direct popular, 50–51, 163, 366–67, 427–28
  districts in, 335, 423–26, 428, 502–3
  entertainment value of, 471
  forms of, 412
  frequency of, 428
  importance of, 412–16, 448–57
  incumbency and, 166–72
  indirect, 50, 52, 62, 426–28
  as instruments of popular government, 416–17, 426, 455–57
  issues in, 412–13, 433–34, 457
  low turnout at, 417–21, 449–55

media coverage of, 436, 439, 490–91, 563–64
median voter theorem and, 434–35, 451–52, 461
moral hazard problem in, 414–15
multiple-member district system of, 489
participation in, *see* participation, political
participation limited by, 415, 456–57
partisan loyalty in, 432–33, 457
policy moderation and, 435
political parties and, 420–21, 432–33, 449–52, 465–66, 468–76, 496–97
as presidential resource, 254–55
primary, 255, 422, 469–70, 475, 499, 564
principal-agent relationship and, 413, 416
prospective vs. retrospective voting in, 434
rationale for voting in, 452–55
referendum and recall and, 431–32
reform of, 451–52
regulation of, 416–32
representation and, 165–75
requirements for candidacy in, 468
riots vs., 456
runoff, 421
single-member district system of, 489–90, 500
in society, role of, 456–57
split-ticket voting in, 429–30, 500
swing voters in, 460
voter registration for, 419–20, 451, 470
voters' decisions in, bases of, 432–35
voter turnout in, 449–55
see also electorate; suffrage; voting
elections of 1800, 427, 479
elections of 1822, 479
elections of 1824, 427–28, 479
elections of 1832, 479
elections of 1840, 480–81
elections of 1858, 481
elections of 1860, 481
elections of 1864, 220, 481, 495
elections of 1876, 428
elections of 1888, 428
elections of 1892, 483

Hume, David, 11
Humphrey, Hubert, III, 397
Humphrey's Executor v. U.S., 229*n*
Hungary, 668
hung juries, 21
Hurley, Patricia, 204*n*
Hussein, Saddam, 201, 226, 364–65, 440–41, 542, 658, 661, 679, 681
Hyink, Bernard, 592*n*

ICC, *see* Interstate Commerce Commission
Idaho, 97, 303, 310–11
Idelson, Holly, 204*n*
illusion of central tendency, 398–401, 408
illusion of saliency, 401–3, 408
IMF (International Monetary Fund), 664–65
immigration, 431, 483
Immigration and Naturalization Service, 4, 5, 27
Immigration and Naturalization Service v. Chadha, 105*n*, 295*n*
Immigration Reform Act (1996), 353
impeachment:
    Andrew Johnson and, 211, 212
    Clinton and, 105, 165, 211–12, 512, 555, 680
    Congressional power of, 101, 211–12
    grounds for, 211
imperialism, 686–87
implementation, 197–202, 280
implied powers, 81, 86, 87
imposts, *see* tariffs
impoundment, 231*n*
income tax, 37, 68–69, 286
    as progressive and gradu-ated, 599
incumbency, 166–72
    advantages of, 169–72
    franking privilege and, 167–68
    moral hazard and, 414
    patronage and, 168–69
    pork-barrel legislation and, 168–69
    power of, 169–72
    re-election rates and, 169–72
"indecency," 548
independent candidacy, *see* third parties, U.S.
independent counsels, 229*n*
independent regulatory com-missions, 244, 282, 284, 288
    see also regulatory agencies

indexing, 616, 621, 624
India, 671, 676
Indians, *see* Native Americans
indirect election, 50, 52, 62, 426–28
individual freedom, 369, 375
individual rights, 69, 77–78, 81, 98
Indochina, French cause in, *see* Vietnam War
Indonesia, 665
industrial pollution, 581, 582–83, 591, 633
inequality:
    explanations for, 612–13
    legislative and administra-tive changes of, 636–37
infant mortality, 632–33
inflation, 597, 621, 624
    attempted reductions of, 595, 602, 604
influence:
    defined, 12
    interests vs., 178
informal bargaining, 16
informational benefits, 519
Ingraham, Patricia W., 291*n*
inherent powers, 222–23, 224
initiative:
    ballot, 406, 536
    definition of, 536
    legal and constitutional bases of, 255–57
    legislative, 235–38
    as presidential resource, 255–57
initiative and referendum, 367
institutional analysis, 200–201
institutions, 19–24
    decision making by, 20–21
    defined, 19
    delegation and, 21–23
    jurisdiction of, 20
    politics and, 19–24
instrumental behavior, 133
insurance industry, 386, 536
integration, *see* racial integra-tion; school desegregation
intelligence, terrorism and, 273
interest groups, 504
    access gained by, 525, 527–28, 537
    agencies influenced by, 13–14
    antiwar, 540–41
    benefits and incentives of, 519–22
    campaign contributions made by, 203, 526, 531–36, 538
    characteristics of, 506–14
    collective action and, 515–19, 634–35

conservative, 511–14, 535
cooperation in, 515–19
costs of, 530
debate on, 536–37
definition of, 511, 515
economics and, 508–10
elections and, 507
foreign policy and, 650–52
formation of, 514–22
free-rider phenomenon and, 518–19
and free society, 507
going public by, 529–31, 537
government expansion and, 511
growth in number of, 508, 511–185
increasing influence of, 29, 202–3, 209, 511, 536
initiative and, 536
Internet and, 512–13, 541
judiciary used by, 323–24, 342–43, 528–29
leadership of, 509–10
lobbying by, 202–3, 507, 509, 522–28, 529–31, 537
memberships of, 509–11
New Politics and, 514
partisan strategies of, 538
policy and, 522–36
political entrepreneurs and, 521–22
political environment and, 511–18
political parties and, 507, 525
as presidential resource, 259–60
prisoner's dilemma game and, 515–18
public, 340–42, 386–87, 389, 514, 559
regulation of, 508, 536–37
religious, 520, 551–14
strategies of, 508
upper classes favored in, 510–11
Washington-based, 525
Web sites and, 547–48
interest rates, 597, 604
interests, 58–59
    influence vs., 178
    principles vs., 35–36, 70–72, 77
    public, 61, 76–77
    see also interest groups
Interior Department, U.S., 285, 355
internal bipolarity, 677
Internal Revenue Service (IRS), 286, 648

International Bank for
Reconstruction and
Development (World
Bank), 664–65
International Monetary Fund
(IMF), 664–65
international monetary structure, 664–65
debt in, 664–65
international relations, 662–64
international trade, 41
International Workers of the
World (IWW), 384
Internet, 272, 436, 451,
492–93, 512–13, 514,
541, 547–48, 551, 561
interstate commerce, 80, 81,
86–88, 99, 137,
243–44, 332
Interstate Commerce Act
(1887), 88*n*, 242, 243*n*,
590
Interstate Commerce
Commission (ICC), 88*n*,
284, 590
interstate compacts, 83–84
Interstate Highway Program,
89–90, 96, 580, 584, 586
interstate transportation, 529
intervention, foreign, *see* foreign policy, U.S.
intrastate commerce, 88,
243–44
investment activity, 133
Iran, 666, 687
Iran-Contra affair, 228
Iraq, 440–41, 644–46, 664
in Persian Gulf War, 551,
557, 660, 663, 670,
678–79
rebuilding of, 673
in 2003 war, 201, 205, 222,
226, 262, 301, 364–65,
387–88, 441, 540–41,
542–44, 547, 556–57,
558, 564, 566, 570–71,
652, 670, 672, 686–87
weapons inspections in,
658, 661
Ireland, 651
Ireland, Northern, *see*
Northern Ireland
Irish American interest group,
651
Irish Republican Army, 651
IRS (Internal Revenue
Service), 286, 648
isolationism, 654
unilateralism vs., 655
Israel, 651, 658, 663, 676, 681
Issa, Darrell, 432
issues, agreement and disagreement on, 369, 379–81

"issues advocacy," 486, 534
"issues management," 389, 559
Italy, 8, 376, 680
IWW (International Workers
of the World), 384
Iyengar, Shanto, 390*n*

Jackson, Andrew, 222,
240–41, 252, 352, 427,
479–80, 594
Jackson, Brooks, 459
Jackson, Robert H., 344
Jacksonian Democrats, 240,
480
Jacob, Herbert, 497*n*
Jacobs, Lawrence, 239*n*, 385,
405*n*
Jacobson, Gary, 172*n*, 206*n*,
212*n*, 453*n*, 475*n*
James, Joni, 430*n*
Jamieson, Kathleen H., 444*n*,
554*n*
Janosik, Robert J., 335*n*
Japan, 660, 663, 665, 668
Diet of, 159, 264
postwar capitalism in, 676
prewar, 8
Japanese Americans, World
War II confinement of,
221, 410–11
Jay, John, 59–60, 73
JCS (Joint Chiefs of Staff),
250, 647
"Jebware," 492
Jefferson, Thomas, 427, 479,
654
Bill of Rights supported by,
114, 116
Declaration of
Independence written
by, 40
opposition party led by, *see*
Jeffersonian Republicans
presidency of, 222, 240
Senate Manual written by,
21*n*
strong federal government
opposed by, 116,
593–94
Jeffersonian Republicans, 427,
449–50, 463
Jefferson's Manual, 20
Jeffords, James, 439, 440
Jensen, Merrill, 41*n*
Jews:
2000 election and, 250–51
interest group of, 651
Johnson, Andrew, 211, 212,
226
Johnson, J. Bennett, 208–9
Johnson, Loch K., 649, 650*n*
Johnson, Lyndon B., 250, 291,
391

affirmative action and,
142–43, 148
Great Society of, 96, 212,
484
1964 election of, 254, 485,
490
Vietnam policies of,
225–26, 484–85, 557,
571
Joint Chiefs of Staff (JCS),
250, 647
Jones, Charles O., 108*n*, 261
Jones, Joseph, 666*n*
journalists, 653
"embedded," 542, 545, 571
news coverage influenced
by, 553–54
political bias of, 553–55, 652
2003 Iraq war and, 542–43,
570–71
see also magazines, news;
media; newspapers; press
judicial activism, 105, 125–27,
335, 346–49
judicial process, 314, 315–17
judicial relief, expansion of,
353–56
judicial restraint, 346–49
judicial review, 53, 73, 101,
103–7, 125, 314, 321,
328–35
of acts of Congress, 71,
328–30
definition of, 328
of federal agencies, 331–33
lack of constitutional base
of, 328–30
lawmaking and, 333–35
rules of, 103, 336–37
of state actions, 330–31,
358, 431
judiciary, 41, 61, 62, 79, 144,
312–61
in administrative processes,
354
appointment of judges to,
321–25, 350–51, 352
cases in, 315–17, 319–20,
335–39
Congress and, 144, 351
constitutional provision for,
52–53, 73, 315
as coordination mechanism,
326–27
courts, types of, 317–18
dispute resolution and,
325–26
enforcement powers lacked
in, 352
heavy use made of, 319
interest group use of,
323–24, 342–43,
528–29

priming by, 563–64
print, *see* magazines, news; newspapers; press
prisoner's dilemma and, 555–57
public opinion and, 384–85, 387–88, 389–90, 392, 567
regulation of, 548–49, 552
religion and, 560
responsibility and, 544–45, 566–68
sources and, 555
2003 Iraq war and, 542–44, 545, 556–57, 570–71, 652
types of, 545–48
upper class favored by, 559–60, 568
visual elements of, 558–59
median voter theorem, 434–35, 461
Medicaid, 289, 612, 619–21, 625, 633
Medicare, 82, 219, 236, 385, 599, 602, 602n, 608, 609, 610, 618–19, 624, 625, 633, 634
costs of, 618–19
reform of, 634, 640–41
Meltzer, Allan H., 604n
Merida, Kevin, 170n
merit system, for administrative appointments, 483
Merit Systems Protection Board, 291
Merkl, Peter, 500
Mettler, Suzanne, 613n
Mexican-American Legal Defense Fund, 341–42
Mexican War (1846), 648
Mexico, 677
Meyer, Michael J., 118n
Meyerson, Allen R., 209n
Michigan, 83, 535
Michigan, University of, 146–47, 149, 154–55
Micklethwait, John, 292n
Microsoft, 526
Middle East, 676, 680–81
Milbanks, Dana, 492n
military, court system of, 318
military, U.S., 41, 542–44, 570–71, 670–73
changing role of, 304–5
Congress and, 159
credibility and, 543
cuts in, 302, 304–5
growth of, 299
homosexuals in, 141, 237, 530
politics and, 374–75, 377
pork-barrel politics and, 287

president and, 225–26, 227, 229–31
production of hardware for, 306
women in, 139–40
"military-industrial complex," 587
Milkis, Sidney M., 269, 500
Miller, Bill, 3n
Miller, Dan, 170
Miller, Gary J., 279n
Miller, Warren, 163n, 371n, 404n
Miller v. Johnson, 175, 337, 425
Milliken v. Bradley, 136
Milne, Seumas, 686
Milosevic, Slobodan, 679
Mineta, Norman Y., 270
minimum wage, 94, 244n
minimum annual income vs., 614
ministerial portfolios, 264
Mink, Gwendolyn, 638
Minnesota, 127n, 397, 451
Minnesota Star Tribune, 397
minorities:
congressional representation of, 200–201, 337, 423–25
economic inequality of, 611
see also civil rights; *specific minority groups*
minority leaders, 214
in House, 180–81, 207–8
in Senate, 180–81, 204, 207–8
Minow, Martha, 118n, 152
Miranda rule, 124, 334–35
Miranda v. Arizona, 124, 334–35
Mississippi, 145, 423
Missouri, 82, 83, 127n
Missouri Compromise, 481
Missouri ex rel. Gaines v. Canada, 129n
Missouri v. Jenkins, 137, 337
Mitchell, George J., 658
mixed regimes, 55
Moe, Terry M., 246n, 279n, 539
Mondale, Walter, 257–58
monetary policies, 289, 593–95
international, *see* international monetary structure
property ownership encouraged by, 595
see also fiscal policy
monopoly, 580
Monroe, James, 222
Montana, 176
Montesquieu, 54–55, 100

Moore, W. John, 99n
mootness, 336
moral hazard, 414–15
Moran v. McDonough, 354n
Morgan, Dan, 201n
Morgenthau, Hans J., 657, 664n
Morin, Richard, 371n, 385n, 394n, 402n
Morrill Act (1862), 629–30
Morris, Dick, 385, 386n
Morris, Gouverneur, 48
Morris, Richard B., 654n
Morrison, Samuel E., 42n
Morrison v. Olson, 229n
Morrison v. United States, 99–100
mortgage guarantees, 585, 595, 600
Motor Carrier Act (1980), 590
Motor-Voter Act (1993), 420, 451
MSNBC, 545
MTV, 551, 558
Mueller, John, 409
multilateral collective security treaties, 668–69
see also treaties
multilateralism, 662, 669
as U.S. foreign policy, 656
Munger, Michael C., 455n
Murdoch, Rupert, 551, 554
Murphy, Dean, 540
Murphy, Walter F., 335n, 352n
Murray, Alan, 600n, 607
Murray, Charles, 626, 626n, 627n, 638
Mushroom Caucus, 194
Muslims, terrorist attacks of September 11, 2001, and, 410–11
Mutual Assured Destruction (MAD), 671
Mutual Security Act (1951), 666
Myers v. United States, 229n

NAACP, *see* National Association for the Advancement of Colored People
NAACP v. Alabama ex rel. Patterson, 124n
Nacos, Brigitte L., 569
Nader, Ralph, 454–55, 487, 489, 514
NAFTA (North American Free Trade Agreement) (1992), 650, 677
Nagel, Jack H., 234n
Nagourney, Adam, 447n, 460
Nakamura, David, 139n
NAM (National Association of Manufacturers), 511

Napoleon I, Emperor of France, 674
Nathan, Richard, 291*n*
National Abortion and Reproductive Rights League, 444
National Aeronautics and Space Administration (NASA), 284
National Assembly, French, 176
National Association for the Advancement of Colored People (NAACP), 124, 129–30, 148, 341, 529, 535
   Legal Defense Fund of, 129, 341
National Association of Manufacturers (NAM), 448, 511
National Beer Wholesaler's Association, 443
National Broiler Council, 504
National Defense Education Act (NDEA) (1958), 630
National Endowment for Democracy, 644
National Endowment for the Arts, 209
National Environmental Policy Act, 271, 353
National Federation of Independent Business (NFIB), 535
National Guard, 134, 229, 310–11, 576
National Industrial Recovery Act (1933), 105*n*, 245*n*, 332
National Institutes of Health (NIH), 633
nationalism, 60
National Labor Relations Act (Wagner Act) (1935), 243, 613–14
National Labor Relations Board (NLRB), 243
National Labor Relations Board v. Jones & Laughlin Steel Corporation, 123*n*, 243
National League of Cities v. Usery, 244*n*
National Opinion Research Center (NORC), 394
National Organization for Women (NOW), 389, 514, 530
National Performance Review (NPR), 254, 292, 294–95

National Petrochemical and Refiners Association, 502
National Public Radio (NPR), 551
National Reconnaissance Office (NRO), 648
National Review, 491
National Rifle Association (NRA), 443, 444, 535
National Security Agency (NSA), 225, 648
National Security Council (NSC), 225, 247, 248–50, 647–48
national standards, setting of, 90–94
national supremacy, 53, 73, 81, 86–88
National System of Interstate and Defense Highways, 586*n*
nation-states:
   client, 654, 666
   in foreign policy, possible roles for, 673–82
Native Americans, 41, 99, 106
NATO (North Atlantic Treaty Organization), 645, 656, 660, 668–69, 678, 679–80
   expansion of, 668–69
Natural Resources Defense Council, 271
Nava, Michael, 152
Navy Department, U.S., 287
Nazis, 318
NBC News, 543, 551
NDEA (National Defense Education Act) (1958), 630
Neagle, In re, 224, 228
Near v. Minnesota, 122*n*, 549
Nebraska, 426
necessary and proper clause, 51, 73, 81, 86, 160
Neely, Richard, 314*n*
Negotiated Rulemaking Act, 527
Nelson, Michael, 269
Netherlands, 264
Neuman, W. Russell, 409
Neumann, Mark, 180–81
Neustadt, Richard E., 56*n*, 101*n*, 234*n*, 238*n*, 256*n*, 269
Neustadtl, Alan, 539
New Deal, 96, 107, 204, 246, 350, 377, 440, 484, 609, 612
   constitutionality of, 243
   critical electoral realignment in, 433, 484–85, 487

   interest groups in, 259–60
   judiciary and, 321, 332, 352
   legislation of, 105
   presidency and, 212, 242–44, 259–60
   redistributive policies in, 601, 604
   see also Roosevelt, Franklin D.
new federalism, 91, 94–100
New Frontier, 212
New Hampshire, 114–15, 395, 489
New Jersey, 45, 145–46
New Jersey Plan, 45
New Politics:
   interest groups and, 514
   litigation used by, 529
New Republic, 491, 543
newspapers, 545, 546–47, 550–51, 565
   "elite," 551
   underground, 561
   see also media; press
New State Ice Co. v. Liebman, 95*n*
Newsweek, 547, 551, 670–71, 671*n*
New York, N.Y., 422
New York City Board of Health, 632
New York Journal, 60
New York Review of Books, 491
New York State, 45, 60, 115, 487
New York Times, 74*n*, 112*n*, 154, 218*n*, 270*n*, 310*n*, 361*n*, 392, 394, 410*n*, 460*n*, 502*n*, 511, 540*n*, 542, 546, 547, 550, 551, 560, 562, 565, 566, 570, 596
New York Times/CBS polls, 392
New York Times v. Sullivan, 550
New York Times v. U.S., 549*n*
New Zealand, 668
NFIB (National Federation of Independent Business), 535
Nicaragua, Sandinista government in, 674
Nickles, Don, 608
NIH (National Institutes of Health), 633
Niskanen, William, 278–80, 278*n*
Nixon, Richard M., 94, 96, 237, 291, 413*n*, 485
   administration of, 250
   foreign relations of, 676
   media and, 257, 544, 553, 556–57, 566, 571

Polsky, Andrew, 477*n*
Pool, Ithiel de Sola, 651*n*
Poole, Keith T., 205*n*, 206*n*
Pope, Jeremy, 434*n*
popular consent, *see* consent, popular
populist movement, 366–67, 483–84, 536
Populist party, 483, 487
pork barreling, 24, 287, 586*n*, 588
Posner, Paul, 94*n*
Posner, Richard, 348
Postal Service, U.S., 272, 284
poultry waste tax credit, 504–6
poverty, the poor, 484, 611–12, 635–37, 665
    breaking out of, 629–37
    defined, 289, 612, 613
    "deserving" vs. "undeserving," 613
    education policies and, 629–32
    health policies and, 632–35
    race and, 611
    reducing, 623–24
    security for, *see* welfare state
    traditional conceptions of, 613, 635–37
Powell, Colin, 247, 250, 658
Powell, Lewis F., 146, 155
Powell, Robert, 670*n*, 671*n*
power, 12
    abuses of, 58, 63
    agenda, *see* agenda power
    expressed, 223
    freedom and, *see* freedom, power and
    legitimacy and, 77
    powers vs., 238
    representation and, 158–75, 212–14
    veto, *see* veto
power-elite theory, 601, 604
powers:
    concurrent, 81–82
    delegated, 224, 226, 244–46, 293, 331–33
    expressed, 51, 80–81
    implied, 81, 86, 87
    inherent, 222–23, 224
    national, 53
    policy-making, 244
    power vs., 238
    of removal, 227–29
    reserved, 81, 115
    war, 220–22, 225–26
prayer, in schools, 323, 334, 511–13
precedents, 316–17, 333
precinct captains, 496
preemption, 671–72, 681

presidency, 220–71
    administrative transitions and, 252, 253*n*
    bureaucracy and, 296–98
    Congress and, 71, 108, 159–60, 197, 207, 209, 210–11, 212–14, 222, 223–24, 225–26, 227, 228, 231–38, 239–47, 254–57, 271, 287, 288, 290–91, 331–33, 427–28, 650
    constitutional provisions for, 51–52, 71, 73, 223–38, 267
    and delegation of power, 159–60, 220–22, 244–46, 331–33
    democratized, 255
    dual nature of, 222
    early weakness of, 240–41, 267
    enhancement of, 244–45
    executive appointments and, 227–29, 252–53
    executive orders power of, 236–38, 270–71
    in foreign policy, *see* foreign policy, U.S.
    formal resources of, 225–27, 246–54
    immunity and, 228
    independence of, 51–52, 241–42
    informal resources of, 254–62
    institutional, *see* Executive Office of the President
    judicial power of, 225, 226–27
    judiciary and, 105–7, 144–45, 321–25, 350–51
    in legislative process, 213–14, 216, 227–38, 290–91
    lobbying of, 525–26
    managerial, 231–38, 255–57, 290–92
    "mandate" and, 254
    military policy and, 225–26, 227, 229–31, 267
    New Deal and, 242–44, 259–60
    political parties and, 103, 258–59, 267, 426–28, 472, 476
    popular base of, 234–36, 239, 242, 254, 260–62, 267, 499
    press and, 257–58, 565–66
    rise of, 238–45

strength of, 49
    success and failure of, 238–39
    supremacy of, 212
    veto power of, 197, 232–35, 258
    war powers of, 220–22, 225–26
    see also executive branch; Executive Office of the President
president:
    as chief clerk, 222
    as chief executive, 222, 227–29, 290–92
    as commander-in-chief, 225–26
    as head of government, 224, 227–38, 267
    as head of state, 224–27, 267
    indirect election of, 62, 101, 224
    as legislator, *see* legislative process
    see also executive branch
presidential approval ratings, 262, 263
    domestic issues and, 262
    international events and, 262
Presidential Election Campaign Fund, 445
presidential government, 227–38, 245–62
    cabinet in, 247–48, 267
    EOP in, 248–50, 267
    patronage in, 246–47
    rise of, 290–92
    vice presidency in, 250–54
    White House staff in, 248, 249, 267
President's Committee on Administrative Management, 290
press, 545, 546–47
    foreign, 543
    freedom of, 122, 549–50
    libel suits and, 549–50
    presidency and, 565–66
    public opinion in, 457
    see also magazines, news; media; newspapers
pressure groups, *see* interest groups; lobbying
price controls, 332, 589
Priest, Dana, 680*n*
primary elections, 422, 469–70, 475, 499, 564
    see also elections
prime ministers, 264
priming, by media, 563–64
principal-agent problems, 22, 190–91